LATTER-DAY SAINT ART

A CRITICAL READER

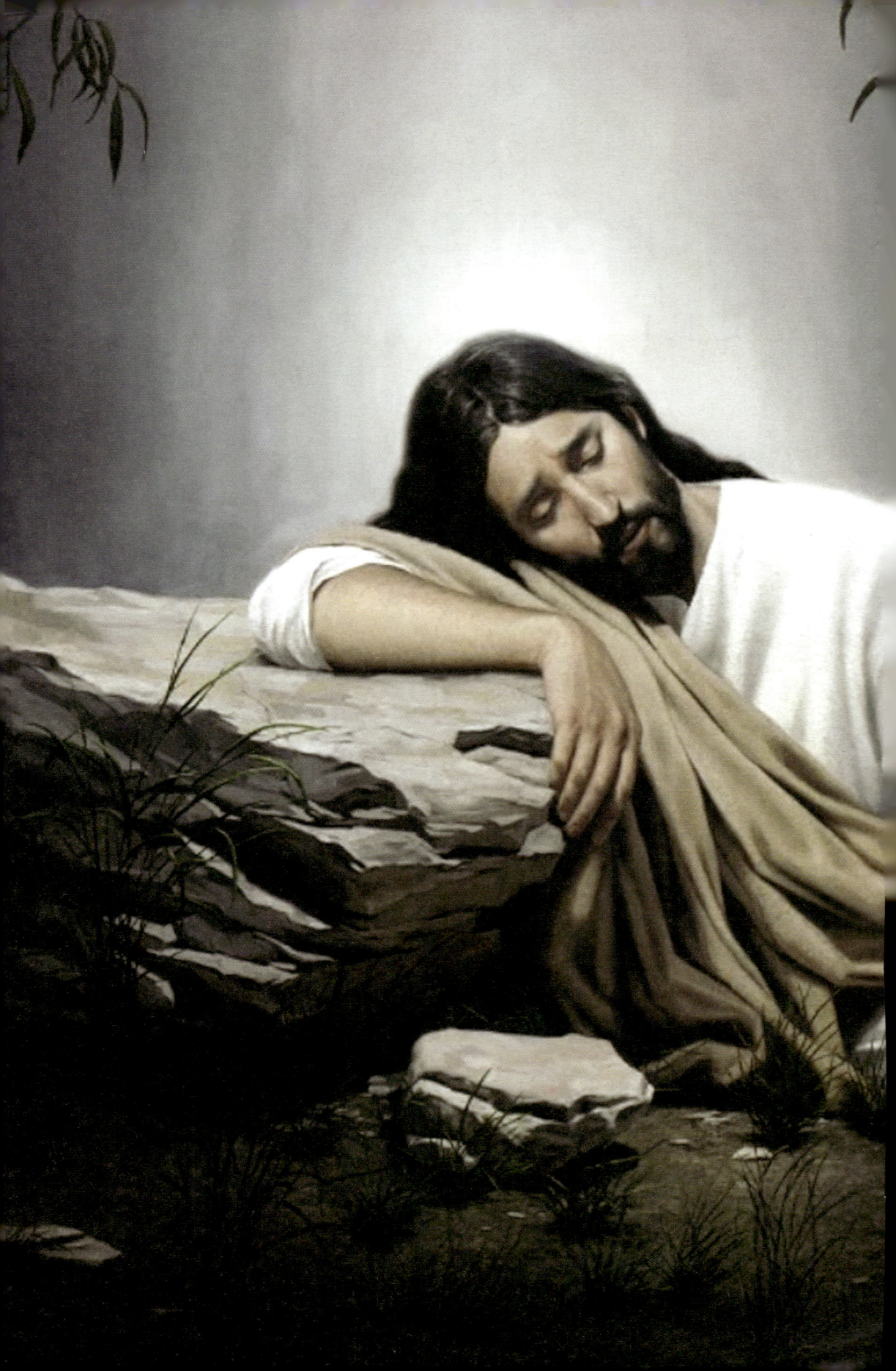

LATTER-DAY SAINT ART

A CRITICAL READER

EDITED BY
AMANDA K. BEARDSLEY AND
MASON KAMANA ALLRED

OXFORD
UNIVERSITY PRESS

OXFORD
UNIVERSITY PRESS

Oxford University Press is a department of the University of Oxford. It furthers
the University's objective of excellence in research, scholarship, and education
by publishing worldwide. Oxford is a registered trade mark of Oxford University
Press in the UK and certain other countries.

Published in the United States of America by Oxford University Press
198 Madison Avenue, New York, NY 10016, United States of America.

Library of Congress Cataloging-in-Publication Data
Names: Beardsley, Amanda K., editor. | Allred, Mason Kamana, editor.
Title: Latter-day Saint Art: A Critical Reader / edited
by Amanda K. Beardsley and Mason Kamana Allred.
Description: New York, NY : Oxford University Press, [2024] |
Includes bibliographical references and index.
Identifiers: LCCN 2024015025 (print) | LCCN 2024015026 (ebook) |
ISBN 9780197632505 (hardback) | ISBN 9780197632529 (epub) |
ISBN 9780197632512 (epdf)| ISBN 9780197632536 (digital-online)
Subjects: LCSH: Latter Day Saint art.
Classification: LCC N8001.L38 G85 2024 (print) | LCC N8001.L38 (ebook) |
DDC 704/.0882893—dc23/eng/20240620
LC record available at https://lccn.loc.gov/2024015025
LC ebook record available at https://lccn.loc.gov/2024015026

DOI: 10.1093/oso/9780197632505.001.0001

Printed by Sheridan Books, Inc., United States of America

TABLE OF CONTENTS

FOREWORD

RICHARD LYMAN BUSHMAN AND GLEN NELSON

A nineteenth-century painting of Mormon pioneers in covered wagons heading west illustrated the cover of the May–June 1970 issue of *Art in America* magazine. The cover story coincided with an exhibition of large paintings then at the Whitney Museum of American Art in New York (*Christensen: A Panorama of Mormon Life,* August 13–September 7, 1970, curated by John I. H. Baur). Inside the magazine, on the table of contents page, appeared the following statement by an unattributed author: "Of the myriad religious sects that have flourished on our soil, only two—the Shakers and the Mormons—have made a serious contribution to American art. Mormon architecture is well known; Mormon painting has been almost totally overlooked."

Now, more than fifty years after that statement was made, the full range of art and objects created by members of the Church of Jesus Christ of Latter-day Saints, as well as art about the faith, remains largely underappreciated by scholars and the general public, even by members themselves. In 2016, the Mormon Arts Center (later the Center for Latter-day Saint Arts) was founded in an effort to close the gap between the existence of these many artists in the church and the public's halting acknowledgment of them. To that end, the center has made an effort to expand awareness by creating databases for our internal use, as well as hosting public events and exhibitions. From the initial database, several thousand artists' names were grouped by discipline. These are artists working throughout the world, and in the case of the production of visual art and objects, they include commercial art illustrators, cartoonists, animators, designers, photographers, artists in the fields of textile art and design, lithographers, and fine artists, who appear regularly in exhibitions and publications, including shows in the leading galleries and museums of the nation. We believe these artists merit attention.

One obstacle to appreciating this body of work is a lack of critical understanding. In 2020, the Center for Latter-day Saint Arts created an online art education program aimed at LDS children, teens, and adults, Art at Home. One of its forty lessons spoke to art history and asked: Is there a canon of Mormon art? To explore possible responses to such a loaded and amorphous question, we asked twenty-one people to compile a list of "ten works you should know"—ten works created by LDS artists that they wished to recommend to readers. This sampling of experts included art museum executive directors, gallery owners, curators, educators, art historians, art collectors, and working artists representing a variety of media and styles. Each of these experts self-identified as LDS, and all of them were deeply involved in the art world. To our surprise, the bottom-line answer to the question of whether there was a canon, at least as represented by this sample group, was a resounding no. Only two works appeared on more than one list. Of the 210 works cited, from nineteenth-century frontier paintings to artworks freshly completed, there was virtually no overlap.

To a large extent, LDS art is uncharted territory and can feel hermetic to those outside the faith, even though artists themselves yearn for larger engagement with a broad public and many have found success individually in the fine art commercial landscape. The veteran art critic Arthur Danto brought the term "art world" into play in a landmark article in the *Journal of Philosophy* in 1964. Danto was struggling with the problem posed by Andy Warhol's famous *Brillo* box. Why was such a seemingly pedestrian object judged art? Danto argued it required a "theoretical revision" of what constituted art: "To see something as art requires something the senses cannot decry—an atmosphere of artistic theory, a knowledge of the history of art: an art world."[1] One reason for the underappreciation of LDS art may be the need for more theory, criticism, and investigation of our place in history.

Beginnings have been made. In the mid-twentieth century, Springville Museum of Art director Vern G. Swanson, art historian Robert S. Olpin, and scholar William S. Seifrit recognized the quality of work by Latter-day Saint artists such as John Hafen, James Harwood, LeConte Stewart, and Minerva Teichert. Artists of Utah were their focus, and to the extent that Utah is a synecdoche for the church, their scholarship sought to contextualize LDS art and validate it. Soon after, the church created a museum of its art and history across the street from Temple Square, Brigham Young University opened an art museum, magazines with LDS readership regularly used contemporary art on their pages as illustrations, and programs of art history and museum studies at BYU created a generation of scholars predisposed to see LDS art approvingly but with a wider perspective on its relationship to other cultures' art and objects.

This book undertakes to build on these foundations in an unprecedented fashion. The Center for Latter-day Saint Arts asked two dozen scholars: What has been accomplished in the field of LDS visual art, and why does it matter? We wanted them to locate LDS art historically and assess its relevance—in short, to deploy scholarship to enrich and nuance the LDS art world.

Our definition of Latter-day Saint art is broad. Latter-day Saint artists produce a flood of "religious art" for home worship, temple decoration, and meetinghouses, but we also include work on whatever subjects move our artists. As Christian art theorist Daniel Blackaby puts it, "While religious art is fittingly understood as being 'Christian,' it does not follow that all 'Christian' art must be 'religious.' Indeed, if 'religious content' is required, then not even God—the Divine Artist—passes the test, as there is nothing religious about a sunset or shooting star."[2] We wish to follow Latter-day Saint artists wherever their sensibilities lead them.

To a large extent even now, LDS art exists in a parallel art world created in relative isolation from the wider art world of global art centers. LDS art developed its own art experts, educators, marketplace, and artists, with the artists often having goals aimed specifically at the betterment of their people.[3] As in the medieval and early modern periods of European history, in Latter-day Saint culture ecclesiastical purchases have constituted a substantial market for devotional Latter-day Saint art. The church decorated its worship spaces and illustrated its official publications with works commissioned by it or sold to it. Increasingly, individual Latter-day Saints acquire art by LDS artists at bookstores, in local galleries, and on the artists' websites. These buyers are largely indifferent to what might be happening in the larger world's art fairs, museums, and national publications, but they are no less committed to bringing art into their lives.

The result today is a plentitude of LDS artists working in numerous styles on every continent. This parallel art market has its significant contemporary luminaries: Brian Kershisnik, Caitlin Connolly, J. Kirk Richards, Walter Rane, and Gary Smith, among many others. There are numerous artists and many works that, though not considered canonical, make frequent appearances in LDS publications, websites, meetinghouse foyers, and museum and gallery exhibitions. Beyond these are less well-known figures who produce high-quality art displayed on their websites, in bookstores, or through distributors.

New circumstances are emerging that are likely to expand the LDS art market even further. First, a new group of highly trained artists has appeared who reach audiences beyond the LDS art world. Wayne Kimball is ranked near the top among lithographers internationally. Some are artists of distinction in the fine art world (including Susan Krueger-Barber, Gregg Deal, Daniel Everett, and Rachel Stallings Thomander), others in the worlds of representational painting (including David Dibble, Kimball Geisler, Corinne Geertsen, and Bryan Mark Taylor), western painting (including Jim C. Norton, Michael Coleman, Albin Veselka, and Kwani Povi Winder), portraiture (including Esther Hi'Ilani Candari, Casey Childs, Jeff Hein, and Mary Sauer), photography (including Chris Burkard, Megan Knobloch Geilman, Mark Hedengren, and Eva Koleva Timothy), and commercial illustration (including David Habben, Brett Helquist, Micah Player, and Brooke Smart), among many other categories of visual art.

The overall structure of the LDS art world is shifting. Many artists, unlike their LDS counterparts a century ago, have few direct connections to Utah. They are born, raised, and educated elsewhere. Their work may or may not read as LDS in a devotional sense, even though they consider themselves to be members of the faith and create work infused with its system of values. Meanwhile, technology has created platforms to share art globally, instantly, and largely without cost, facilitating the entry of a rising generation of artists. The booming market has also attracted artists from outside the faith;

LDS life and worship are being portrayed through their eyes. All these have ignited an explosion in the volume of art that can be identified as Latter-day Saint.

How are we to make sense of this teeming art world? This volume was commissioned as a preliminary response to that question. The book is a testament to the vitality of LDS art and is aimed at a reader who may or may not know anything about the Church of Jesus Christ of Latter-day Saints, its tenets, or its people. It is, we believe, a hopeful launching point. The field of Latter-day Saint art is so large that any number of scholarly approaches might appear with little overlap of materials. This book will have succeeded if it provokes a responding barrage of additional scholarship and art criticism.

NOTES

[1] Arthur Danto, "The Artworld," *Journal of Philosophy* 61, no. 19 (1964): 573, 580.

[2] Daniel Blackaby, "What Makes Christian Art Christian?," The Collision, February 28, 2022, https://thecollision.org/what-makes-christian-art-christian%EF%BF%BC/#:~:text=The%20expected%20content%20of%20Christian,all%20fall%20into%20this%20category.

[3] Richard Bushman, "The Latter-day Saint Art World," *The Season,* January 2023, https://themormonartscenter.squarespace.com/the-season-blog-module/2022/12/31/the-latter-day-saint-art-world.

ACKNOWLEDGMENTS

This ambitious volume was from the outset envisioned to showcase rigorous research and analysis of Latter-day Saint artistic production and culture alongside hundreds of elegant reproductions of Mormon art, including panorama paintings, quilts, architecture, sculpture, and cartoons, to film, gallery installations, indigenous works and more. Pulling it all together was a monumental task that required the labor, energy, and guidance of many.

For the vision of this volume, we thank the Center for Latter-day Saint Arts. For much of its early development, we are indebted to Laura Allred Hurtado. For bringing this publication to life we gratefully acknowledge the creative wrangling of Glen Nelson and sage guidance of Richard Bushman. They, alongside Mykal Urbina, Erin Eastmond, Emily Spung, and Ron Schneider, have been essential in conceiving of the project's potential and scope, and seeing it through to fruition. Generous support from many Center donors provided the funding necessary for the research and writing of this publication. Because the project officially began just as a pandemic shut down most countries and institutions, this volume—as any in its own way does—represents the strong will and collective optimism of the many contributors to overcome all obstacles and persevere. We thank them all for their fantastic work and for their patience.

We want to express a special thanks to the many artists, who shared images of their work and permissions for reproductions. For access and procurement of archival sources and images, we benefited immensely from the expeditious and thorough work of Laura Paulson Howe, Carrie Snow, Kylie Kimball, and many others at various institutions, especially the Church History Museum, Church History Library, the Springville Museum of Art, and Brigham Young University Museum of Art.

Finally, we are grateful to Theodore Calderara, Brent Matheny, Amy Whitmer, and the entire team at Oxford University Press for their professionalism and dedication in bringing the project to print and helping us materialize this ambitious endeavor.

LIST OF CONTRIBUTORS

Richard Lyman Bushman is Gouverneur Morris Professor of History Emeritus at Columbia University and author of *Joseph Smith: Rough Stone Rolling* (2005). He has written on American social and cultural history including *The Refinement of America: Persons, Houses, Cities* (1992) and *From Puritan to Yankee: Character and the Social Order, 1690–1765* (1967), which received the Bancroft Prize in American History.

Glen Nelson is the author of thirty-three books, as well as essays, articles, short fiction, and poetry. As a ghostwriter, three of his books have been nonfiction New York Times bestsellers. He curated the museum exhibition *John Held, Jr.* at the Brigham Young University Museum of Art and co-curated *Joseph Paul Vorst: A Retrospective* at the Church History Museum in Salt Lake City, Utah. His most recent books include the first biography of Joseph Paul Vorst and a volume about the lost fiction of John Held, Jr.

Amanda K. Beardsley is the Cayleff and Sakai Faculty Scholar at San Diego State University and received her PhD in art history from Binghamton University. Her research and publications have ranged from sound studies and feminism in Mormon culture to science and technology studies, gender, and faith.

Mason Kamana Allred is an associate professor of communication, media, and culture at Brigham Young University, Hawaii. He earned his PhD from the University of California, Berkeley, with a designated emphasis in film studies. He is the author of *Weimar Cinema, Embodiment, and Historicity* (2017) and *Seeing Things: Technologies of Vision and the Making of Mormonism* (2023).

Terryl Givens did his graduate work in intellectual history (Cornell) and comparative literature (UNC Chapel Hill). For many years he held the Jabez A. Bostwick Chair of English at the University of Richmond, and he is now the Neal A. Maxwell Research Fellow at Brigham Young University. His work includes a two-volume history of Mormon thought, *Wrestling the Angel* and *Feeding the Flock; People of Paradox: A History of Mormon Culture;* and several studies in LDS scripture, biography, and theology.

Colleen McDannell is a professor of history and the Sterling M. McMurrin Professor of Religious Studies at the University of Utah in Salt Lake City. A recipient of a Guggenheim Fellowship, she is a specialist in American religions. In 2019, her book *Sister Saints: Mormon Women Since the End of Polygamy* won an award given by the Organization of American Historians. Her publications in visual and material culture include the edited volume *Catholics in the Movies* (2007), *Picturing Faith: Photography and the Great Depression* (2004), and the now classic *Material Christianity: Religion and Popular Culture in America* (1995).

Randy Astle is a filmmaker and writer in New York City. His works include *Mormon Cinema: Origins to 1952* (2018) and more than sixty articles and presentations on Mormon art and film. He has also taught Mormon cinema at Brigham Young University, edited special issues of *BYU Studies* and *Mormon Artist,* served as film and photography editor for the Association for Mormon Letters' journal *Irreantum,* programmed film screenings for the Sunstone Summer Symposium, and created the annual academic forum at the first LDS Film Festival in 2001.

Ashlee Whitaker Evans is the head curator and the Roy & Carol Christensen Curator of Religious Art at the Brigham Young University Museum of Art. Prior to coming to BYU, she was associate curator and registrar at the Springville Museum of Art. Whitaker is an alumna of BYU, graduating summa cum laude with degrees in art history and curatorial studies. Her research interests span religious art and visual culture, as well as western regional American art. Ashlee has curated numerous exhibitions, including *Rend the Heavens: Intersections of the Human and Divine, In the Arena: The Art of Mahonri Young, The Interpretation Thereof: Contemporary LDS Art and Scripture, Capturing the Canyons: Artists in the National Parks,* and *Moving Pictures: C. C. A. Christensen's Mormon Panorama.*

Nathan Rees is an associate professor of art history at the University of West Georgia. His research focuses on the intersection of race and religion in American visual culture. He has published and presented on topics ranging from the influence of metaphysical religion on twentieth-century abstractionists' encounters with Native Americans to the representation of race in the visual culture of southeastern shape note hymnody. He is the author of *Mormon Visual Culture and the American West* (2021).

Jennifer Reeder is the nineteenth-century women's history specialist at the LDS Church History Department in Salt Lake City, Utah. She has co-authored three collections of women's writings and written a narrative history of Emma Smith. Reeder grew up playing under the quilts her mother, grandmother, and great-grandmother sewed, and has an innate interest in folk art. At George Mason University, where she earned her PhD in American history, Reeder studied religious history, memory, and material culture.

Heather Belnap is a professor of art history and curatorial studies and a global women's studies affiliate at Brigham Young University. She presents and publishes widely in feminist and cultural history, including the fields of Utah and Mormon studies. Recent publications in these areas include the book *Marianne Meets the Mormons: Representations of Mormonism in Nineteenth-Century France* (2022) and a special issue for the *Utah Historical Quarterly* on Utah women in the arts at midcentury (2023). Belnap is currently working on a biography of Minerva Teichert and a book project on Utah women and the arts.

Josh Edward Probert is an independent historian and historic design consultant who specializes in the material culture of nineteenth-century domestic and religious life. A graduate of the Program in Religion and the Arts at Yale Divinity School and Institute of Sacred Music, he earned a PhD from the University of Delaware in cooperation with the Winterthur Museum.

Mary Campbell is an associate professor of American art history at the University of Tennessee, Knoxville. A lawyer as well as an art historian, she works on the intersections of race, gender, and the law in the arts of the United States. Her first book, *Charles Ellis Johnson and the Erotic Mormon Image* (University of Chicago Press, 2016), received the support of the Stanford Humanities Center and the American Council of Learned Societies. Her current book project, the first art historical monograph on the work of the painter Beauford Delaney (1901–1979), was supported by the UTK Humanities Center and a fellowship from the National Endowment for the Humanities. Campbell received her JD from Yale Law School and her PhD from Stanford University. She clerked for the Honorable Sharon Prost of the U.S. Court of Appeals for the Federal Circuit and is a member of the New York Bar Association.

Rebecca Janzen is a professor of Spanish and comparative literature at the University of South Carolina in Columbia. She is a scholar of gender, disability, and religious studies in Mexican literature and culture whose research focuses on excluded populations in Mexico. She is the author of *The National Body in Mexican Literature: Collective Challenges to Biopolitical Control* (2015), *Liminal Sovereignty: Mennonites and Mormons in Mexican Culture* (2018), and *Unholy Trinity: State, Church and Film in Mexico* (2021). Her most recent book, *Unlawful Violence: Law and Cultural Production in 21st Century Mexico* (2022), is about human rights, law, and literature. The Hagley Library, the Plett Foundation, the Kreider Fellowship at Elizabethtown College, the C. Henry Smith Peace Trust, and the Newberry Library in Chicago have supported her research.

James Swensen is a professor of art history and the history of photography at Brigham Young University. He is the author of *Picturing Migrants: The Grapes of Wrath and New Deal Documentary Photography* (2015) and *In a Rugged Land: Ansel Adams, Dorothea Lange, and the Three Mormon Towns Collaboration, 1953–1954* (2018).

Linda Jones Gibbs, an independent scholar living in New York, has a PhD in art history from the City University of New York with specialties in American and modern art. Jones Gibbs was a former curator at the Museum of Church History in Salt Lake City and the Museum of Art at Brigham Young University. She has written extensively on American artists in France and on the artist Maynard Dixon.

A freelance journalist in Washington, D.C., **Menachem Wecker** holds a master's in art history from George Washington University. He has published frequently on the intersection of faith and the arts, in both general-interest and scholarly publications.

W. Paul Reeve is chair of the History Department and Simmons Chair of Mormon Studies at the University of Utah. He is author of *Religion of a Different Color: Race and the Mormon Struggle for Whiteness* (Oxford, 2015) and *Let's Talk About Race and Priesthood* (Deseret Book, 2023). He is project manager and general editor of an award-winning digital database, *Century of Black Mormons,* designed to name and identify all known Black Latter-day Saints baptized into the faith between 1830 and 1930. The database is live at CenturyofBlackMormons.org.

Carlyle Constantino is a doctoral student in the History Department at the University of California, Santa Barbara. With both a BA and MA in art history and curatorial studies from Brigham Young University, Constantino interrogates race and image in the nineteenth and twentieth centuries. Her current research and dissertation project, titled "Confinable People: The Role of Photography in U.S. Internment Camps," examine several areas of interest: slavery, carceral studies, photography, memory, and citizenship.

Laura Paulsen Howe is the art curator over global acquisitions at the Church History Museum in Salt Lake City, Utah. She curated the *12th International Art Competition: All Are Alike unto God* (2022) and *With This Covenant in My Heart: The Art and Faith of Minerva Teichert* (2023). Her research has focused on places of display, analyzing how the meaning of a work changes when shown in different environments.

Analisa Coats Sato is a doctoral candidate in art history at the Graduate Center of the City University of New York. She has taught twentieth-century art history at colleges throughout the New York City metro area and has worked as a curatorial researcher for the Museo Nacional Centro de Arte Reina Sofía in Madrid and the Dia Art Foundation in New York. Currently she is finishing her dissertation on postwar U.S. fiber art.

Chase Westfall is an artist, musician, and curator. In 2017, he joined VCUarts at Virginia Commonwealth University as curator of student exhibitions and programs, where he serves as director of the Anderson Museum and oversees an evolving program of student and professional exhibitions, including the annual VCUarts MFA thesis exhibition. Recent projects include *Stone's Throw: Arte de Sanación, Arte de Resistencia* (2020), a survey of contemporary Central American artists, curated with Laura August; *Carmen Winant: Fire on World* (2019); *When the Whirlwind Begins* (2019), a student-curated survey of Philadelphia artists; *Ron Rege Jr: From the Word of First Thought* (2019), co-organized with Dem Passwords, Los Angeles; *Daniel Everett and Leah Beeferman: Surface Tension, Surface Tenses* (2019); and *Caitlin Cherry: Etherpaint* (2018). He is the curator of a forthcoming thematic survey of contemporary Latter-day Saint art, *Great Awakening*, organized by the Center for Latter-day Saint Arts, New York.

Laura Allred Hurtado is the executive director of the Utah Museum of Contemporary Art and former global acquisitions art curator at the Church History Museum. Recent curatorial projects include *Guerrilla Girls: A Retrospective* (UMOCA) and *Angels Don't Cry, Demons Don't Cry* (Nox Contemporary). She is the author of several publications, including *A Long Mournful Cry* (Mormon Art Center), *Back of Shadows: Wayne Brungard* (University of Colorado, Denver), *A 15-Year Expanse* (Actual Source), *Immediate Present* (Mormon Arts Center), and *Saints at Devil's Gate* (Church Historian's Press).

INTRODUCTION

AMANDA K. BEARDSLEY

MASON KAMANA ALLRED

A series of blurry portraits captures the struggle to define Mormon art. Each of the 161 canvases, spanning twenty feet, in Latter-day Saint artist J. Kirk Richards's *Untitled* (*Cristo* Series) pictures a slightly different and abstracted version of Christ. Many imagine a Westernized, white-complexioned, bearded face, while others offer variations on skin tone, adornment (crown of thorns, different types of robes), facial expression, size, and even frame type. The largest canvas depicts a blurry abstraction of a bust. A barely discernible hooked nose, represented with a thick, hasty line, centers the composition. Blotches of creamy ivory, taupe, and tan contour the face without much effort to blend or create figurative illusion of surface and depth outside of the hollows of eye sockets or cheeks. With significant portions of canvas showing through, the painting seems unfinished, or even damaged, the way a fresco painting deteriorates under neglect and the passage of time. Exhibited in the center-right quadrant of the collection, the large frame features faux patina on gray wood paneling that contrasts with the white background and draws attention to the piece, creating a visual hierarchy among the constellation of canvases. Smaller, unframed versions with mustard, blue, white, and umber backgrounds create an unwieldy taxonomy of types and kinds, some allowing a beard to demarcate gender, others becoming more ambiguous silhouettes of figures with long hair. Without proper delineation of features, *Cristo* is wonderfully vague.

Cristo was exhibited in 2013 for the Mormon Pavilion at the Utah Museum of Contemporary Art's (UMOCA) first biennial, Mondo Utah. Laura Allred Hurtado, who was the global arts acquisitions specialist at the Church Museum of History and Art at the time (and now is director of UMOCA), curated the pavilion and helped conceive of the work.[1] Even with further development, the series remained untitled. The parenthetical addition, however, invites viewers to question how their knowledge of Christ, as a concept, person, and figure of religious devotion, came to be. Richards seems to agree, as depictions of the religious figure were "something [he'd] thought a lot about." He remarked how "one early work that survives from the 6th century depicts Christ as an attractive white

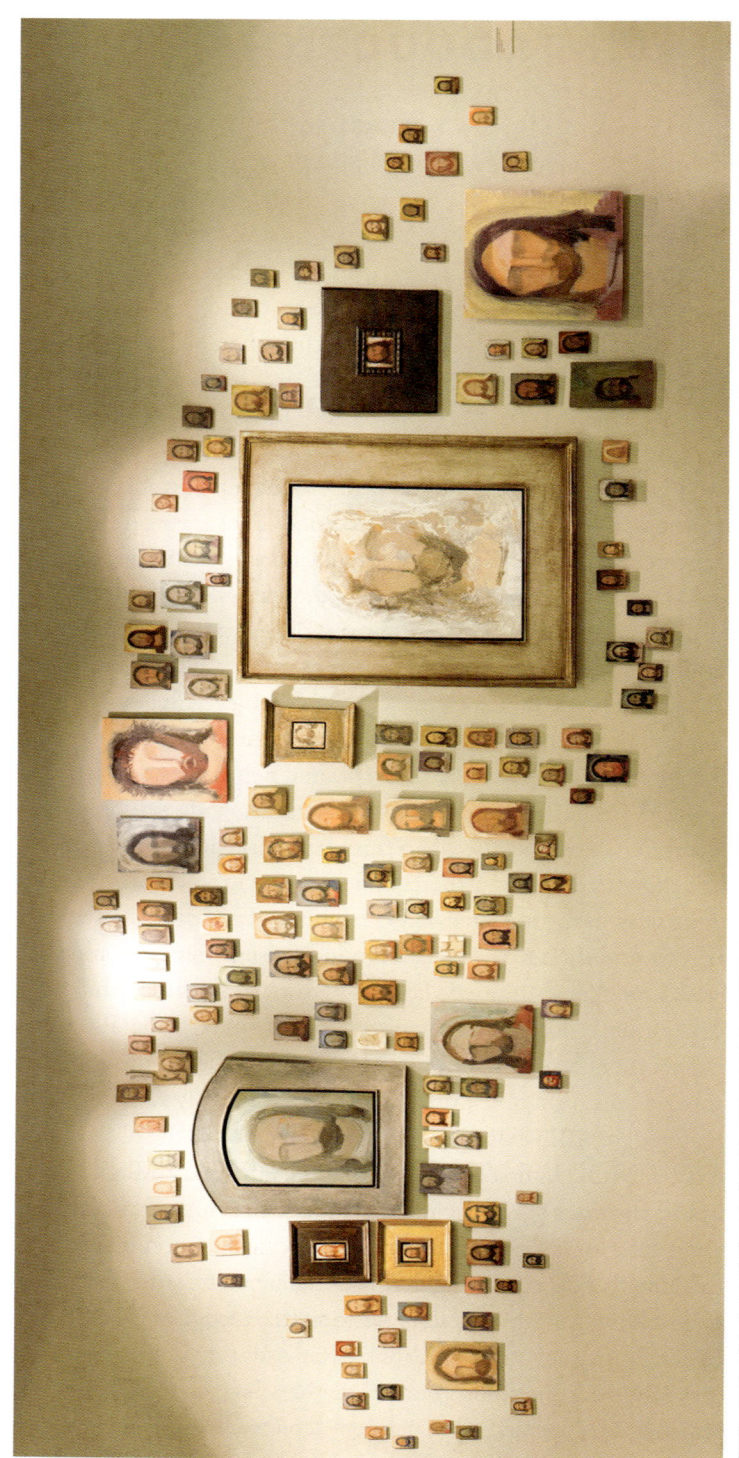

Fig. 0.1 J. Kirk Richard, *Untitled (Cristo Series)*, 2013, oil and acrylic on MDF panels, 17′ × 8′, installation at the Utah Museum of Contemporary Art. Image courtesy of the artist.

man with shoulder-length hair and a beard. And it seems like for 1500 years not much has changed . . . Is there a danger in having such a narrow interpretation of these religious figures?"[2] Richards visualizes the question through abstraction, blank canvas, and hazy contours framed by vague identifiers, foregrounding the recognizability of the iconic elements of traditional Jesus images while calling on the viewer to fill in the gaps. This strategy might challenge viewers to at once recognize the impossibility of a singular image of Christ and acknowledge the importance of variety—to flesh out the image of Christ as a personal engagement. This is art as a relatively open and unfinished encounter.

Richards and Hurtado offer a model of how religious institutions shape identity, and how artists and art historians define art. On the one hand, the *Cristo* series demonstrates the subjectivity inherent in defining art—that is, art as it relates to a person's individual experience of art, as well as faith. On the other, it self-consciously exhibits the institutional power inherent in nevertheless setting the parameters for art and religion. Both religion and art operate through a grid of categorization that creates a logic for power and boundaries for understanding the world. The series asks viewers to reconsider how the history of image-making influences how we collectively mobilize around an image, whether it is art in a museum or a reproduction of Christ at an altar.

Drawing on this initial provocation to identify the ways in which artists and art historians have attempted to define both the boundaries of religion and artistic canons, this volume takes a similar approach, opening with the subjectivity and complexity involved in defining a canon of Mormon art. After all, one of the (many) things that Richards's work does is squarely combat conceptions of Mormonism as either non-Christian or Christian. It focuses on Christ as the center of Latter-day Saint belief and artistic practice, but nonetheless forecloses any simplistic or singular representation. Neither does it provide any sense of finality. Instead, the series approaches Christ in a reductive mode, focusing on the hazy fundamentals that have characterized portraits of him to complicate our understanding of the standardizing power of images. Taken as a whole, our volume is likewise, and inevitably, reductive in its focus on visual art to define a religion. In this self-conscious approach, it generates unprecedented depth, a diversity of voices, and an equal expansion of our vision of what Mormon art was, is, and can be.

DEFINING MORMON ART

Latter-day Saint artists and art historians have used theological concepts particular to the faith as analytical frameworks in their attempts to document and trace Latter-day Saint lineages of art history. Some of these have come in response to wider calls for greatness in Latter-day Saint art from church leaders, art historians, and artists themselves. Many of the authors in this volume address the complexity of these cultural appeals. Hurtado and Menachem Wecker, for instance, write on the institutional and artistic responses to LDS prophet Spencer W. Kimball's notorious 1967 "Gospel Vision of the Arts" address about Mormon arts, which asks for a higher standard for Latter-day Saint art similar to that of the Renaissance.[3]

But Kimball's call was not unprecedented, and though some scholars have assumed, as Karen Lynn Davidson did, that, as "a pioneering society," early Saints saw survival as their primary task and considered the arts "to be principally ornamental," this notion is not entirely true.[4] More recent scholarly attention and archival research, such as that found in this volume, offer a different picture. Latter-day Saints have, since their very beginnings, created and valued art. As Nathan Rees argues, "The paired misconceptions of early Mormon iconoclasm and of 'Mormon art' as a corpus that only emerged in the twentieth century have obscured the critical role that images played for nineteenth-century Latter-day Saints." Rees reveals how Latter-day Saints used images to "facilitate worship, to stage sacred rituals, and to self-fashion Mormon identity."[5] This is evident in Ashlee Whitaker Evans's chapter, which engages with some of the earliest forms of Mormon art. The history of LDS artistic creation and the recent emergence of the Festival of Mormon Arts (now called the Mormon Art Festival) demonstrate that artists have been seminal in crafting the LDS faith, even if they've been largely unacknowledged in their response to calls for great art.[6]

While such calls for artistic creation from church authorities are few, there has been a lasting sense of the importance in Latter-day Saint theology of developing talents, creating, and sharing abilities with the world. Elder Dieter F. Uchtdorf of the Quorum of the Twelve Apostles suggested it was part of humans' shared nature as children of God to want to create, stating that "the desire to create is one of the deepest yearnings of the human soul. No matter our talents, education, backgrounds, or abilities, we each have an inherent wish to create something that did not exist before." Echoing a sentiment from earlier LDS ruminations on art,[7] Uchtdorf insisted that one of the keys to happiness was taking "unorganized matter into our hands" and creating something new.[8] Within this framework, the artistic process was a godly process, one Latter-day Saints could and should participate in to become more like their heavenly parents. Kimball's and Uchtdorf's words suggest a shared, even institutional interest in the development of Latter-day Saint artists and their art.

Rather than call for different futures, one of the more compelling approaches to defining Mormon art has been born in the attempt to delineate its history and current state through methods borrowed from the canons of other religions. Jewish art institutions, specifically, were an inspiration for Hurtado when she wrote about the difficulty of defining and crafting boundaries around a specifically Mormon art for the *Immediate Present* exhibit, hosted at the Riverside Church in Manhattan in 2017. To Hurtado, any definition needed to be expansive, yet as an institutional production sponsored by the Center for Latter-day Saint Arts and the Church History Museum, any curatorial gesture would nevertheless be limiting. The definition she and Glen Nelson settled on was any art or artist that seemed to sit adjacent to Mormonism.[9] This meant that the art of any artist who self-identifies as Mormon (practicing or non-practicing) could be considered within the canon of LDS art. Their definition mentions in passing institutional output—what the LDS Church calls "gospel art"—some of which is made by those who have never identified with the Latter-day Saint faith, such as Bertel Thorvaldsen, Ansel Adams, and Edward Grigware.[10] While a good majority of artists who contribute to gospel art are LDS, some are not, making their adjacent positionality relevant here.

FROM OUTSIDER ART TO MORMON ART

To create their art, Latter-day Saints drew liberally from their environment. It would be misleading to pose a clear pattern or to think that Mormons' interactions with, borrowing of, and translations of the wider art world's styles and sensibilities are uniform or straightforward. However, Mormon visual culture exhibits "discernable outlines both in its subjects and in its aesthetics, [often] rejecting transcendent and symbolic modes of art for an aesthetic of truth-signaling naturalism that better supported Mormonism's understanding of the physicality of spiritual vision."[11] If Mormon visual culture has "discernable outlines," it is not without the influence and adaptation of preexisting movements and styles.

The church's recent adoption of Danish sculptor Bertel Thorvaldsen's iconic *Christus* statue as its official logo speaks to the faith tradition's long history of incorporating outside styles, forms, and images in distinct ways. In the case of *Christus,* members of the Latter-day Saint faith had seen replicas of the statue, but in the 1950s Stephen L. Richards pitched the idea of acquiring and displaying a *Christus* statue somewhere on Temple Square in Salt Lake City, Utah. The deciding factor to move in an unprecedented direction—Christ statues were not a normal feature in Latter-day Saint spaces—was bolstered by the concern over signaling to the world that Mormons were indeed Christians. Some leaders felt visitors to Temple Square saw no visual evidence of Christ during their visit.[12] In this instance, a Lutheran artwork was adopted in a gesture of Mormon self-fashioning and the ornamentation of visitors' centers, but not in worship spaces. Although Mahonri Young's bronze statues of Joseph and Hyrum Smith had been on display since 1907, there were no artistic renderings of Jesus Christ in public or private Mormon spaces. Despite some anxiety around statuary of Deity or the danger of idol worship, the massive eleven-foot-tall statue was installed and surrounded by a rotunda mural by the mid-1960s.

Similar moves to respond to or incorporate art and styles from outside the faith exist in more contemporary efforts to assimilate to a place—such as the Rome, Italy, temple, which was built in 2019 and "features architecture inspired by ancient Rome" (with statues also by Thorvaldsen)[13]—or to utilize earlier forms, such as Gothic and Neoclassical styles, to draw on their rhetorical significance of grandeur or order.[14] These processes of cultural interaction surface in several of the volume's chapters. For instance, Josh Probert's chapter on temple architecture illustrates such influences as he considers Latter-day Saint negotiations between Catholic and Protestant artistic tendencies. Glen Nelson also traces the ways George Dibble's twentieth-century forays into modernism proved polarizing and somewhat incompatible with the wider Mormon culture in Utah. Laura Paulsen Howe shows in her chapter how collecting an increasingly in-ternational array of artwork by Latter-day Saints reveals strategies across cultures to make art forms into Latter-day Saint adaptations. Often adapting forms by inserting scriptural or uniquely Latter-day Saint content, these artists create the conditions for examining the aesthetic forces in action that sit at the intersection of broader faith traditions, artistic movements, and cultural migration.

MORMON ART APPRECIATION

Questions of positionality are also significant when considering the epistemology of Mormon art, especially since much of Latter-day Saint art history has been written by members of the faith. At times this has resulted in a conflict of interest located in the larger field of Mormon studies: separating bias from the more analytical or interpretive approaches that academia generally demands. Indeed, a long-standing concern about LDS scholarship is that its literature is going to be too polemical, with the intent to mo-bilize either pro-Mormon or anti-Mormon rhetoric.[15] Latter-day Saint art history is no different. Though there is little outside of promising journal articles and an upsurge of monographs in the past decade, larger book surveys have been accused of "flattering the Mormon self-image," an accusation that, in the age of institutional critique and postmodernism, is an inevitability in any discipline (any publicity is good publicity).[16] Nevertheless, such volumes have been criticized for being "both oversimplified and nar-rowly prescriptive," with the primary aim of bolstering the LDS agenda.[17]

Perhaps this isn't an entirely unfair critique. Lorin Wheelwright's 1972 *Mormon Arts, Volume I* attempts to "postulate a theological base for an aesthetic reality" by offering an overview of LDS art and its artists. Acknowledging that additional volumes were to come, the book is broad in its reach, covering visual art, poetry, theater, music, ballet, and photography. It even includes the novelty of a vinyl record at the back of the book, a re-cording of the "full-bodied sound [of] the musical and dramatic offerings" of the faith. Wheelwright defines Mormon art not through stylistic similarities but rather through a variety of themes he sees as inherent to the religion. These themes organize the book, with chapters titled "Art as Joy of Man and Instrument of God," "Seeking Aesthetic Experience," and "Divine Creation."

To Wheelwright, the function of Mormon art was to "induce conversion" and "aes-thetic joy."[18] His focus is similar to Uchtdorf's, in that he homes in on the creative potentiality of humans as a parallel to divine creation. This approach underscores one of the more exceptional and controversial LDS beliefs: that humans can eventually be-come deities. But in terms of treatment and representation, it would seem that not every type of human is progressing through art or enjoying its theological benefits. In fact, although Wheelwright's work is a rich primary source for LDS art history, out of the seventy-two works presented only two were by women. And while he did offer a sincere attempt to showcase Mormonism and its art to the art world, Wheelwright's writing is imbued with an earnestness geared toward a readership who are familiar with and/or who share his faith. Notwithstanding critiques of self-flattery, Wheelwright emphatically and sincerely touts the benefits of LDS doctrine through art history.[19]

Several volumes emerged in the wake of Wheelwright's with a similar intent to discuss the power of art to convert while also invoking the divine call to create. Robert Davis and Richard Oman's 1995 *Images of Faith: Art of the Latter-day Saints* is an oversized book survey featuring more than three hundred images of Mormon art and essays written by curators from the Museum of Church History and Art (now known as the Church History Museum). Like Wheelwright's text, *Images of Faith* claims to answer the question "What is Latter-day Saint art?" The authors trace a chronology, offering one of the more global perspectives to date and including a chapter devoted to international art, especially as it related to the church's International Art Competition, which began in 1987. Their scope is expansive, including furniture, ceramics, quilts, wood carvings, sculpture, and painting.

The chronological span is also impressive and allows for a variety of contextualized insights. Unfortunately, there is a missed opportunity to analyze the colonial overtures of claiming land or the critical role art played in legitimating ownership of Utah territories across time. Instead, they cover French-Mormon relations and the sense of place that was crafted alongside the monumental works of Cyrus Dallin and Mahonri M. Young. The section on the early to mid-twentieth century treats some of the more iconic art now associated with gospel art, including that of Minerva Teichert, Arnold Friberg, Richard Burde, and Mabel Frazer. The book ends with "Contemporary Latter-day Saint Art, 1965–1995," which offers a survey of art that represents how "the gospel is for every nation, kindred, tongue, and people," with works by Juan Escobedo, Robert Yellowhair, Victor de la Torre, and Tammy Garcia.[20] Though they veer away somewhat from Wheelwright's proselytizing, Oman and Davis present the narrative of the church as divinely inspired, claiming that "Latter-day Saint art transcends boundaries of culture and time to convey the spirit that drives its creation."[21] *Images of Faith* and *Mormon Arts* serve as precursors to Uchtdorf's more contemporary reflections on Mormon art as matter made through the miracle of creation, and both take members of the church as their target audience.

This trend continues with perhaps more commercially viable approaches. Herman Du Toit's 2016 *Masters of Light: Coming unto Christ Through Inspired Devotional Art* discusses art as a vehicle of transformation to bring viewers closer to the Latter-day Saint faith. Du Toit, who was the head of museum research at BYU's Museum of Art until 2011, also published an anthology of essays titled *Art, Belief, and Meaning* in 2003, which, like Wheelwright's work, defines Mormon art thematically rather than stylistically, based on symposia held at BYU. While both texts integrate art historical methods, including helping the reader understand the value and workings of formal analysis (a central methodology in art history), they are unselfconsciously biased, leaving ample room to think about concepts being discussed and written about in art historical discourse, including the application of affect theory, cultural theory, or religious studies.

Assumptions of divinity in artistic creativity largely shaped the way LDS authors have written and thought about art, where faith-building was more important than other potential functions of art, such as to protest, critique, or bring discomfort.

Outside of specifically art historical undertakings, Terryl Givens and Colleen McDannell offer additional foundational texts that have informed a Latter-day Saint art history. In *People of Paradox* (2007), Givens sets out to "plumb in tentative fashion the range of Mormonism's intellectual and artistic productions" in order "to delineate some key components" and preoccupations emanating from that cultural identity.[22] Due to Givens's deeply resonant characterization of LDS culture as paradoxical, art and cultural historians, including many in this volume, have utilized Givens's work as a means to think about Mormon culture conceptually and recognize trends. McDannell's *Material Christianity* (1995) features several chapters on Latter-day Saint culture that offer a methodological basis for analysis of Mormon materiality. Her work advanced the appreciation of and scholarly engagement with material culture among religious individuals, providing a baseline for unpacking the significance of the everyday objects that might fall outside the purview of "high Art."[23] Though less traditionally art historical in orientation, Givens and McDannell present a fruitful opportunity to build on their work. This volume continues their work insofar as it paves the way for both theoretical and analytical enterprises, and even benefits from fresh contributions from both of them, expanding their initial discourse through a range of scholarly perspectives and artistic objects.

Many other authors in this volume have constructed histories of Mormon art through independent articles, exhibitions, and books. Linda Jones Gibbs, for instance, has long written about and curated LDS art, expanding its exposure beyond Utah to the District of Columbia. Heather Belnap released her book *Marianne Meets the Mormons* in collaboration with Corry Cropper and Daryl Lee in 2022. Both Gibbs and Belnap have been integral in bringing more visibility to women artists and thinking through how gender functions within the faith. Randy Astle has written extensively on Mormon film history. Others have contributed to open-access digital databases of art, such as the *Book of Mormon Art Catalog*, led by art historian Jenny Champoux, which features art inspired by the Book of Mormon.[24] Glen Nelson, Laura Paulsen Howe, and Jenny Reeder have been essential in helping to build collections of Latter-day Saint art and material culture, thereby offering a set of markers around which we define these objects institutionally and commercially. Bringing them together here through their various interests and lenses is an attempt to create a more comprehensive space for imagining a Mormon art history.

APPROACH AND OVERVIEW

As editors, we have been cognizant of the power of tradition to shape and standardize our experience, especially the force of discourse on our understanding of the world and art. Defining style by solidifying certain shared features often means creating categories and manufacturing styles rather than perceiving something already in existence. Without prescribing a single definition of Mormon art, then, we maintain there is something worthwhile about isolating, studying, critiquing, and even appreciating art by Latter-day Saints or about Mormonism in its various and expansive manifestations.

Instead of positing a distinct stylistic exceptionalism or even a stable category, we have gathered together a group of art historians, cultural theorists, artists, and scholars who represent a spectrum of religious devotion from inside the LDS cultural paradigm, outside it, and in between, and whose larger portfolios have sat adjacent to or directly addressed Latter-day Saint culture. Because many of the authors do not come from a background of traditional art historical training, they represent a refreshingly diverse set of approaches and perspectives. Often combining art historical and cultural studies methods with analysis of the artworks themselves, these authors have all brought out new insights. Their approach to Latter-day Saint history and culture through the rigor of art historical methodologies, including formal and contextual analysis, provides a nuanced perspective. It shuffles stale periodization and sheds new light on the ways art can at once reflect and produce religion, ritual, and its embodiment. Taken together, the entries in this volume offer probing questions and potential answers to the search for a Mormon aesthetic. They point to hallmarks and patterns that resonate with shared Latter-day Saint sentiments manifested in visual art. Most importantly, the range of interests and approaches is necessary to underscore the complicated task of defining a unified conglomerate of Latter-day Saint art. Instead of a singular Mormon style, the emergent image of Mormon art consists of many interrelated parts, understood only when viewed in their complexity from multiple vantage points—much like the *Cristo* series does with its multiple versions of Christ.

While all contributors treat intersections of Mormonism and art, each analyzes unique topics and artworks across a long historical range, providing an impressively diverse account of Latter-day Saint art. This volume makes no claims of comprehensive coverage. Nor does it assume that such a lofty undertaking would be possible. The inevitable biases that are evident in any project can be overcome only through additional research, which we welcome and encourage. Many chapters challenge what has been known of Latter-day Saint artistic expressions. Pervasive conceptions of Mormon art still suffer under a provinciality that has not historically coincided with the truly global nature of the modern church. Although many might assume that a predominantly white and American male focus would reflect the majority of Latter-day Saint artists, we have sought to dispel this notion and seek out unfamiliar artists. We strike a precarious balance, covering the more conspicuous and influential practitioners and pieces even as we reach for more. We wanted to highlight hidden or forgotten treasures from the past while also pointing to some bright futures. In both the international artists considered and the visual media analyzed, this volume will have something for even those most knowledgeable in the history of Mormon art and culture.

With all its wonderful insights and its notable length, this volume does have a limited scope. It is focused on visual art, especially painting, sculpture, photography, film, architecture, exhibitions, and various material cultural products. While some of these artworks, such as hair art, buildings, sculptures, and installations, might be tactile and engage more senses, the work herein is predominantly appreciated through the eyes. This means that, as any project must, we have focused on certain artists and media at the inescapable expense of others. A long list of possible additions might include Rose Marie Reid's work in swimsuit design, Ed Roth's Rat Fink illustrations, Michael Allred's comic books, Cécile Pelous's designer fashion, Don Bluth's animation, the gospel art of Simon Dewey, or the far right paintings of Jon McNaughton. One could also imagine entire alternative categories of Mormon art, such as music, film, theater, literature, landscaping, or choreography, that all deserve their own volumes. Nevertheless, the volume's focus on visual art and the Latter-day Saint tradition allows for unprecedented breadth and depth.

Art as Theology

To break up linear narration and its problematic implication of progress and highlight certain shared interests, we have organized this volume's chapters thematically. We begin with investigations of the aesthetics and theology of Mormon art, which in turn craft a foundation for identifying Latter-day Saint material culture. Each chapter engages the fraught prospect of Mormon exceptionalism and how Latter-day Saint cultural and even doctrinal proclivities might shape their artistic expressions, revealing larger preoccupations with capturing truth, creating religious experiences, and shoring up faith. In his far-reaching and intellectually provocative chapter, Terryl Givens brings his theory of paradox to bear on Latter-day Saint aesthetics within a larger context of Western artistic and religious philosophy. He delineates two key tensions in Latter-day Saint art: first, the balance between in-group gathering and assimilation within the larger culture, and second, a penchant for collapsing the sacred and the profane.

While Givens locates these tendencies within the artwork of individuals, such as Del Parson and Rose Datoc Dall, historian Colleen McDannell turns to larger institutional decisions in selecting the artwork displayed in temple interiors. McDannell argues that the Temple Art Committee's concerted effort in the first two decades of the twenty-first century to quietly swap out old paintings for newer, more inclusive, and global ones also supported artists who benefited from the recent development in the wider art world around appreciating contemporary realism. McDannell establishes early on the importance of art as a communicative medium, especially in its vernacular placement within ritualistic spaces.

Lastly, Randy Astle focuses his attention on the cinematic drive by Latter-day Saint directors to document themselves and the world. Analyzing a long list of notable documentary titles, from the inception of the medium to recent YouTube clips, Astle finds a peculiar Mormon insistence on film's potential to testify even as each film must navigate the tension between subjective meaning and objective images. Astle's argument—that some of the greatest Mormon films reveal there is no Mormon aesthetic mode or "subjectivity" but rather a host of individual perspectives that offer truth in their difference—is emblematic of this entire first section of the volume. Mormon thought might shape Mormon art but in a fruitful variety of ways across different media and contexts.

Image-Making

Producing images can create important records and draw a community together through powerful representation of insider knowledge or experience. Approaching the varied ways in which Latter-day Saints found themselves artistically foregrounds the role of gender, mobility, and self-fashioning in the following chapters. Ashlee Whitaker Evans, for instance, considers how art not only documented Mormon community but also served to create that very community. She offers rich visual analysis of portraits, landscapes, and panoramas from the early nineteenth century to trace how early Mormonism carved out various boundaries, from ecclesiastical authority to gender roles, land, and community. Images, in this sense, fostered the creation of collective memory, serving as a useful tool of identity formation.

Nathan Rees further considers Latter-day Saint self-fashioning as a nuanced process of image-making and visuality around the turn of the twentieth century. Rees sees print culture and monuments as a means to distribute social capital. By acknowledging not only the monuments themselves but also the systems and networks surrounding their production, Rees highlights their political clout, capacity to manage bodies, and intent to build community, both spatially and symbolically.

Where Rees and Evans examine works that more forthrightly imagined community at a time when Mormonism was continuing to establish itself as a new religion, Jenny Reeder turns to the often-neglected realm of quilt-making, hair art, and Relief Society halls. By highlighting the work of women who helped settle Utah, Reeder substantiates their monumental efforts to document their community, find expression, and create space for themselves during the second half of the nineteenth century.

Beyond these localized efforts, Heather Belnap knits a rich history of Latter-day Saint women artists who traveled internationally to develop their skills. These women carved out territory in a male-dominated profession to contribute to the shared image of LDS doctrine and scripture during the first half of the twentieth century. Belnap analyzes the nexus of gender, travel, and artistic production to show how Minerva Teichert, Rose Hartwell, Olive Belnap Jenson, Flora Fisher, Mabel Frazer, and Verla Birrell, among others, fashioned individual identities while contributing to the world of Mormon art. Each author provides a distinctive account of foundational efforts to shape Latter-day Saint identity, and consequently gender and class.

Politics of Space

The politics of space, location, and architecture stand out as an especially trenchant topic for a people pushed and pulled between states before settling in self-isolation by colonizing the Intermountain West. As Rosalyn Deutsche has argued, spatial politics are founded on conflict and exclusion.[25] The historical, gendered, and ethnic differences inherent in Latter-day Saint history manifest the politically charged use of both aesthetic space—especially who or what makes it into the photographic frame—and natural and built environments. Josh Probert looks at Latter-day Saint temples to tease out the underlying tension between aesthetic interests of republican frugality and Catholic grandeur. While never quite reveling in opulence, he argues, Latter-day Saint temples are nonetheless material manifestations of a desire to signify salvation in the next life, while performing religiosity, good taste, and social standing in this one.

Mary Campbell then turns to photographs to treat gendered space both within and outside the frame. Using a single photograph of Brigham Young's daughters and a treasure trove of primary sources, she unpacks a complicated family tree, gender and sexuality, and the politics of polygamy in the nineteenth century. Given worries about government meddling, perhaps even incarceration, Latter-day Saint portrayals of polygamous families seem (perhaps deliberately) incomplete by often excluding the many wives. The aesthetic choice to both capture and conceal shaped a Mormon photographic style that spoke to a historical, theological, and cultural context that seems to have inspired and constrained what was done with the camera.

Rebecca Janzen also treats photographs as a space of historical evidence to observe dress, buildings, and art in order to explore the tension between attitudes regarding Indigeneity and modernity as Mormonism took root in Mexico. For some, the conversion to Mormonism might have suggested economic and social opportunities to bolster one's standing. For others, it offered a contested space to work out the integration of different traditions.

Photography provided a contested space but also captured places, especially landscapes, with unprecedented detail. James Swensen addresses the role of photography in constructing and imposing the notion of a "Mormon landscape" from the late nineteenth century throughout the twentieth. Though photography has a history of being associated with truth, Swensen discusses it as a place-making medium with the ability to name and claim a space or to demolish its existence. Early Latter-day Saint photographers and later artists, such as Dorothea Lange, understood the land and architecture in different ways. Their use of photography offers provocative insights into recording, representing, and possessing physical space through aesthetic practices.

Institutions

Though McDannell establishes the importance of material culture in the ritualistic space of LDS temple worship, various other forms of institutional patronage or diverse pedagogy had a profound ripple effect on Mormon art and identity in the late nineteenth century and throughout the twentieth. Linda Jones Gibbs tells the story of dedicated Latter-day Saint artists in Utah who were sent to Paris as missionaries with the unique objective of learning the latest artistic techniques to provide mural paintings for the Salt Lake temple. Gibbs places this LDS art and temple construction within the larger art historical context of patronage, salons, and exhibitions, which played a significant role in both Paris and Utah in shifting dominant paradigms and meeting political needs.

A second ripple effect emanated from the Art Students League of New York. Glen Nelson traces a vivid picture of the league in the early twentieth century as it related to a booming moment of industrialization, attitudes surrounding art and the use of live nude models, and its influence on Latter-day Saint artistic culture. As several of these former students of the league returned to Utah and pursued careers as artists and professors, they helped perpetuate the unorthodox teachings of New York. Like Gibbs and Belnap, Nelson makes a case for the role of outsider art scenes in helping to construct a politics of respectability within the budding LDS colonization of the American West. Where Paris was a strategy to adapt a largely accepted Western canon of art toward crafting an image for a relatively new faith, New York became a means to integrate the modernity of French and German schools into a seemingly more progressive art literacy in the West. Pedagogy and art institutions, in this sense, provided direction in a larger drive toward modernization and image-making on a national and international scale.

Nelson then turns to Mormonism's fraught relationship with midcentury modernism through the lens of Utah artist George Dibble. Nelson's chapter offers a case study in community consciousness, with any monolithic understanding of Mormon art unraveling to show that complicated conversations surrounding artistic identity are in constant tension with institutional authority and social attitudes. The ways modernism could be seen as a pejorative death knell for Latter-day Saint artists shed light on how a seminal work acquired by an institution could end up in a trash can.

Lastly, Menachem Wecker narrates the development of the Art and Belief movement in the second half of the twentieth century. Led by Gary Smith, Dennis Smith, Dale Fletcher, and Trevor Southey, this movement highlights the tensions between believing creators and constraining aesthetic norms within Utah Mormon culture. Although the movement was groundbreaking and exciting, its potential ripple effect was muted and soon disappeared. As Wecker puts it, the movement was too religious for the secular art world to appreciate and too edgy for the Mormon culture or the Latter-day Saint church to appreciate. Revisiting the conflict and drama of this period offers Wecker an opportunity to assess its legacy and potential to provoke passionate, even if contrasting, views on Mormon art. At the same time, Wecker, Nelson, and Gibbs demonstrate the powerful impact of institutions—whether religious or artistic—in delineating the boundaries of art.

Identity

By focusing on various axes of oppression—including gender, race, class, and sexuality—this section highlights the intersectional politics that inevitably cut through artistic production. Identity is itself something fashioned, performed, and solidified through work and expression.[26] While art provides a space where harmful and seemingly banal traditions and normativity can be perpetuated in the form of racist and sexist imagery, it also offers a platform through which such forms can be challenged and exposed.

With keen attention to the way notions of race have inflected Mormon artistic productions, from lithographs to paintings, Paul Reeve shows how whiteness was implied as the default natural order, often associating any other race or ethnicity with deterioration or even a curse. He ends his chapter by highlighting more recent art that seeks to remedy this trend and contribute diverse ethnic and racial perspectives. Carlyle Constantino sketches a similar arc when she turns to representations of Native Americans in art by Latter-day Saints. She highlights the shift in authenticity and power once Latter-day Saint Native Americans move from romanticized or threatening figures in art by others to more fully developed self-representations in their own creations.

In an international turn that diversifies and deepens Western-centric narratives of Mormon cinema, Mason Kamana Allred analyzes lesser-known Mormon feature films produced between 1970 and 2020 to demonstrate the global reach and exclusions of LDS film history. Filmmakers influenced by Latter-day Saint experience employed creative techniques to affect audiences without adopting the more gratuitous depictions of sex, violence, or sentimentality in what Allred calls a "positive theology of embodiment." In turn, Allred underscores a strategy of depicting bodies and media within an aesthetic regime that resonates with Latter-day Saint themes.

Amanda Beardsley continues Reeder and Belnap's historical recognition of women's labor by defining Mormon feminist art through the lens of the genealogical archive. Though archives and oral histories are well-known techniques within feminism to tell histories generally untold, the Latter-day Saint impulse to record, delineate ancestry, and bear record is seen as central to LDS feminist contemporary art. Some of the pieces she treats directly engage with genealogy and gender, while others, as Beardsley reveals, testify to the mundane and material tasks women undertake to express themselves, write themselves into history, and explore their identities as women of faith.

Exhibition and Display

Art is often meant for display, to be shown to others for profit, to spur social change, or even as propaganda. The politics and practices of exhibitions and displays powerfully foreground the relationship between artists, their work, and a constructed audience. Laura Paulsen Howe brings institutional critique to the collecting and exhibition practices of the LDS faith by tracing a history of the triennial International Art Competition. She emphasizes the limitations, even as the competition sought to broaden its horizons with an increasingly international pool of contributors in the twenty-first century.

Analisa Coates Sato looks at art exhibited at a distinct location: the Brigham Young University art department in Provo, Utah. Using a site-specific lens to analyze the work of graduate students Gi Huo and Dalila Sanabria, Coates argues that such art represents an important shift at BYU away from narrative representationalism and toward conceptual work. With the artists' minimalist approach, emphasis on fragility, and deeply personal stories, the exhibitions of works by Huo and Sanabria open up interpretive space to consider latent religious connotations and the artists' specific experiences as women of color at a predominantly white university.

Chase Westfall thinks through art exhibitions as forms of activism, where religious identity might be explored and solidified in generative ways. Westfall surveys past efforts, such as *Fifteen Year Expanse,* to suggest possible futures of Mormon art that might be more vulnerable, caring, and radically open to individuality and the diverse experiences of a shared faith tradition. Howe, Coats, and Westfall characterize contemporary attitudes surrounding exhibition as a politicized act that encompasses a process of selecting, defining, highlighting, and capitalizing on a particular idea, attitude, or theology. To change the parameters of an art competition or publicly reveal the deeply personal narratives embodied in an artistic gesture, environment, or performance, is to recognize the powerful and empowering potential of showcasing art—of recognizing its frames as part of the work itself.

CONCLUSION

Through a variety of approaches and artworks, the chapters in this volume begin to flesh out Mormon art. They give substance and detailed vitality to the beautiful and multidimensional answer to the always inadequate question of singularly defining what Mormon art is. Returning to Richards's *Cristo* series, which invites the viewer to critique the shared expressions and imagine diverse completions, these chapters offer a significant step toward an aggregate whole with the potential to have more additions. By reproducing the image of Jesus more than a hundred times as abstractions, the *Cristo* series exposes foundational iconic features that have shaped and defined past images of Christ, scraping off the aura of any one singular authoritative iteration. Caught in a loop, bouncing between paintings that refuse to fully detail Christ's face, the viewer is invited not only to finish the image mentally but also to expand what that might entail, look like, or even mean. This volume hopes to provoke a similar effect. We are convinced the most productive intensity lies not in any one answer to what Mormon art is but rather in the multidimensional possibilities and approaches to asking new questions. Taken together, the outcome of these exploratory chapters should both shave off the accretion of traditional and confining conceptions of Mormon art and expand our imagination of its power and potential to shape identity, experience, and community with others, as well as the divine.

NOTES

[1] Interview by Katherine Morris, "Episode 10: Laura Allred Hurtado on Curating Contemporary Mormon Art," *Mormon Artist,* March 2015, https://mormonartist.net/podcast/episode-10-laura-allred-hurtado/.

[2] Garrick Infanger, "Big Mac Mormonism," in *Immediate Present,* ed. Laura Allred Hurtado (New York: Mormon Arts Center, 2017), 29.

[3] Laura Allred Hurtado, "The Immediate Present," in *Immediate Present,* ed. Laura Allred Hurtado (New York: Mormon Arts Center, 2017), 2–4; Spencer W. Kimball, "Gospel Vision of the Arts," *Ensign,* July 1967, www.lds.org/ensign/1977/07/the-gospel-vision-of-the-arts?lang=eng; Wecker, in this volume.

[4] Karen Lynn, "The Mormon Sacred and the Mormon Profane: An Aesthetic Dilemma," in *Arts and Inspiration: Mormon Perspectives*, ed. Steve Sondrup (Provo, UT: Brigham Young University Press, 1980), 44.

[5] Nathan Rees, *Mormon Visual Culture and the American West* (New York: Routledge, 2021), 2.

[6] Hurtado, "The Immediate Present," 4–13.

[7] Analisa Coats Sato discusses this in more detail in her chapter in this volume.

[8] Dieter F. Uchtdorf, "Happiness, Your Heritage," *Ensign,* October 2008.

[9] Hurtado, "The Immediate Present," 11–13.

[10] Church of Jesus Christ of Latter-day Saints, "Gospel Art," https://www.churchofjesuschrist.org/media/collection/gospel-art-images?lang=eng; James Swensen, in this volume; Church of Jesus Christ of Latter-day Saints, "Cody Mural Chapel," https://history.churchofjesuschrist.org/subsection/historic-sites/wyoming/cody/cody-chapel?lang=eng.

[11] Nathan Rees, *Mormon Visual Culture and the American West* (New York: Routledge, 2021), 3.

[12] Matthew O. Richardson, *The Christus Legacy* (Sandy, UT: Leatherwood Press, 2007), 27.

[13] Scott Taylor, "Photos Give a First Look Inside the Rome Italy Temple," Church of Jesus Christ of Latter-day Saints, January 15, 2019, https://www.churchofjesuschrist.org/church/news/photos-give-a-first-look-inside-the-rome-italy-temple?lang=eng.

[14] Appropriating styles is not specific to Mormonism. See, for instance, Thomas Jefferson's Rotunda at the University of Virginia, a structure meant to emulate the ancient Roman Pantheon (itself an appropriation of Greek Classicism) to venerate Enlightenment knowledge. Bryan Zygmont, "Thomas Jefferson, Rotunda, University of Virginia," Smarthistory, April 10, 2016, https://smarthistory.org/jefferson-rotunda-uvirginia/.

[15] David J. Whittaker, "Mormon Studies as an Academic Discipline," in *Oxford Handbook of Mormonism*, ed. Terryl Givens and Philip Barlow (New York: Oxford University Press, 2015), 92–108.

[16] Edward Geary, "Review of Theology and Aesthetics, Mormon Arts, Vol. I," *Dialogue* 8, no. 1 (1973): 99–100.

[17] Geary, "Review," 99–100.

[18] Lorin Wheelwright, *Mormon Arts: Volume I* (Provo: Brigham Young University Press, 1972), 12. Statements like "It is the author's judgment that the Church of Jesus Christ of Latter-day Saints, which places its own expression of spiritual values at the apex of all values, is justified in using art instrumentally" is indicative of aggrandizement of the religion.

[19] Wheelwright, *Mormon Arts: Volume I,* 21.

[20] Davis Bitton, "Three Books on Visual Images in the History of the Church," *BYU Studies Quarterly* 36, no. 4 (1996–1997), https://byustudies.byu.edu/article/life-in-zion-an-intimate-look-at-the-latter-day-saints-1820-1995-the-mission-inside-the-church-of-jesus-christ-of-latter-day-saints-images-of-faith-art-of-the-latter-day-saints/.

[21] Richard G. Oman and Robert O. Davis, *Images of Faith: Art of the Latter-Day Saints* (Salt Lake City: Deseret Book, 1995), book cover.

[22] Terryl Givens, *People of Paradox: A History of Mormon Culture* (New York: Oxford University Press, 2007), vii–viii.

[23] See Clement Greenberg, "Avant-Garde and Kitsch," in *Art and Culture* (Boston: Beacon Press, 1961), 3–21.

[24] Book of Mormon Art Catalog, https://bookofmormonartcatalog.org.

[25] Rosalyn Deutsche, *Evictions: Art of Spatial Politics* (Cambridge, MA: MIT Press, 1996), xiii.

[26] Judith Butler, *Gender Trouble: Feminism and the Subversion of Identity* (New York: Routledge, 1990), 25.

1

A THEOLOGY OF MORMON ART

TERRYL GIVENS

Cultural categories should ideally be as inclusive as possible. Yet in culture, as in religion generally, some definition is necessary, if only to substantiate a meaningful correlate to language. As William Temple declared in the case of the church, "There must always be a tension between the right of the individual to freedom and the right of the institution to have a determinate character."[1] Although a solar system may have many diverse bodies—planets and comets and nebular debris—it also has a center of gravity, which gives the system its coherence and its identity. What, then, is the content of a category like "Mormon art"?

Latter-day Saint culture and theology alike are tapestries of many threads. Born in Protestant America, trailing traces of Calvinism in its wake, instituting Catholic-like hierarchy and sacramentalism, rife with charismata that diminished and then disappeared altogether, and progressing from separatism and gathering to staid Americanization and finally an internationalism torn between cultural variety and correlation—can we find any identifying features of a distinct identity?

OF MORMON ART AND CULTURE

"Nothing is more indeterminate," wrote the great German philosopher Johann Gottfried Herder, "than this word [culture]." Frederick Barnard points to Herder's observation that a people "may have the most sublime virtues in some respect and blemishes in others . . . and reveal the most astonishing contradictions and incongruities." Therefore, Barnard writes, "a cultural whole is not necessarily a way of referring to a state of blissful harmony; it may just as conceivably refer to a field of tension."[2]

A field of tension seems a particularly apt way to characterize Mormon culture. It may be that all systems of belief rooted in the notion of a God who dies have, as G. K. Chesterton suggests, "a collision and a contradiction" at their heart.[3] Yet the Latter-day Saint tradition, in which Joseph Smith collapsed sacred distance to bring a whole series

Parts of this essay were delivered at the 2017 Mormon Arts Festival, New York City.

of opposites into radical juxtaposition, seems especially rife with paradox—or tensions that only appear to be logical contradictions. These paradoxes are destabilizing in the best of ways, providing the catalyst, the energy, for perpetual self-examination and healthy discontent. Restoration Christianity is profoundly agonistic—this is its single most important adaptation from the Romantic culture of its origins. The turn from medieval and Neoclassical stasis to Romantic dynamism was most economically captured by William Blake, who said simply, "Without contraries is no progression."[4] So one premise integral to any conceptualizing of Mormon culture, or a Mormon aesthetic, is that it is at its heart an immersion in irresolvable contraries. Like William Wordsworth in his magnificent "Intimations Ode" (which Saints only quote for its nod to preexistence), Mormonism at its best celebrates life's many points of indeterminacy and friction, what the poet called "obstinate questionings / Of sense and outward things, / Fallings from us, vanishings; / Blank misgivings," and "shadowy recollections."[5] Restoration thought does not take refuge in facile resolutions. This is as it should be, as the template laid down in the Garden demonstrated; in the Latter-day Saint interpretation, conflict between competing goods, equally valid imperatives, is inescapable. Emerson wrote of art, "Our music, our poetry, our language itself are not satisfactions, but suggestions. Unluckily, . . . the main attention has been diverted to this object; the old aims have been lost sight of, and *to remove friction has come to be the end*."[6] This discomfort with cognitive dissonance is at the heart of secularism's—and Mormonism's—faith crisis, though it has generated some fruitful patterns in LDS art.

Mormonism is rich in paradoxes. Saints are emphatically individualistic but, like Gregory of Nyssa (c. 335–c. 395), conceive of salvation as ultimately communal. They are wedded to an extensive language of agency ("Know This, That Every Soul Is Free" had pride of place in the church's first hymnbook) but are more authoritarian in church organization and culture than the Catholic Church. Personal revelation is the prerogative and mandate of individual devotion ("Man, being created but little below the angels, only wants to know for himself," proclaimed the first issue of the church newspaper, which Smith oversaw).[7] However, the prophet alone can receive revelations binding on the whole membership, and a 1945 church magazine insisted that "when our leaders speak, the thinking has been done."[8]

The church also proclaims "continuing revelation" and an open canon; at the same time, many members remain entrenched in premodern ways of understanding and engaging scripture (especially the Old Testament), and no new revelation has been added to the corpus of scripture in almost half a century. Finally, no other Christians are so rooted in a language of certainty ("I *know* the church is true"; "I *know* Joseph was a prophet," etc.) while espousing an afterlife as one of endless learning ("It will be a great while after the grave before you learn to understand. . . . It is not all to be comprehended in this world").[9]

Two contraries in Restoration thought stand out as theological distinctives, both of which depart from most varieties of creedal Christianity, and both of which inform a vast array of cultural productions including architecture and the visual arts. The first we may call "the collapse of sacred distance," a conflation of the sacred and the banal. The second takes shape as a perpetual tension between exile and Eden, or between gathering and integration.

PART 1: FROM KOLOB TO KING FOLLETT

The distinction between the sacred and the mundane, between the spiritual and the physical—the duality of a "visible and invisible nature," or what Augustine calls "heaven and earth"[10]—is at the root of most definitions of the religious stance. That is what Samuel Coleridge means when he declares that "the very ground of all miracle is the heterogeneity of spirit and matter."[11] The strict distinction is evident in the very term "supernatural," which is inseparable from religious experience in the West. The ineffable, in other words, must remain forever demarcated from the material. To collapse the two into one would signal the collapse of the sacred itself in most religions.

By the fourth century, church fathers like Gregory of Nyssa were emphasizing the radical transcendence of God: "the divine nature, inasmuch as it transcends all cognitive thought and representation and cannot be likened to anything which is known."[12] An entire mode of theology (apophatic or negative) developed to emphasize what *cannot* be known or spoken about the divine. It reached its zenith with Pseudo-Dionysius the Areopagite (seventh century), who wrote that God "cannot be grasped by Intuition, Language, or Name, and He is not anything in the world nor is he known in anything. He is All Things in all things and Nothing in any, and is known from all things unto all men, and is not known from any unto man."[13]

Centuries later, the emphatic otherness of the divine realm was beyond contestation. As the poet-philosopher Samuel Coleridge put the case, "The very ground of all Miracle is the heterogeneity of Spirit and Matter."[14] From its earliest usage in the English language, the "ineffability" of God has dually denoted that which cannot be expressed in human language and that which must not be uttered among mortal beings. Those boundaries are the parameters of the sacred as sacred, the veil demarcating the divine as beyond approach or comprehension.

Setting limits to what can be spoken is a two-edged sword. It can demarcate this sacred boundary, and thus indicate and preserve a realm of the sacred, the holy, the transcendent and wholly Other. However, demarcating what is expressible or knowable—and what is not—licenses indeterminacy even as it preserves sacred distance. In actual practice, what this has meant is that if one cannot capture in language what God is, then with equal force one cannot say with actual efficacy what God is not (the tradition of negative theology notwithstanding; for instance, history proves that inquisitions and the damnation of billions have not been seen as incompatible with God's nature, exploding any meaningful semantic limits to "God" or his love).

As a consequence of these constructions of the sacred, one strain of Christian devotional art reflects the underlying premise of unbreachable sacred distance by emphatically gesturing *toward*, rather than attempting to *embody or articulate*, the ineffable.

From the spires of Gothic cathedrals, which direct us elsewhere by their aspirational soaring, to the *Ecstasy of St. Teresa* in Santa Maria della Vittoria, which can only depict her reaction to what lies behind the veil, this modality in Christian art places the emphasis on the *mysterium* of the *mysterium tremendum*. In such conceptions, we see the divine only at a remove; the artist, by his very unwillingness to do more than gesture toward the ineffable, affirms its elusive quality.

One would be hard-pressed to find a more consistent pattern in Mormonism's fractious relationship with Christianity than its emphatic repudiation of this reification of sacred distance. Referring to Joseph Smith, the historian William Mulder sympathized that "his was the perennial despair of visionaries striving how to say the unsayable." Mulder goes on to describe Smith and his peers (Jonathan Edwards, Emerson) as "nearly blinded by God's waylaying light, [turning] to analogy and metaphor, finding in nature images and shadows of divine things."[15]

This is to get things precisely as backward as one possibly could when it comes to assessing the singularity of Latter-day Saint cosmology and epistemology alike. Yes, of his encounter with the angel Moroni, Joseph Smith would write that the personage's countenance was "truly like lightning." But such a description is no more than common simile, given the description that precedes it: "His hands were naked and his arms also, a little above the wrist, so, also were his feet naked, as were his legs, a little above the ankles. His head and neck were also bare. I could discover that he had no other clothing on but this robe, as it was open, so that I could see into his bosom."[16]

Neither Joseph's gaze nor his language scrupled to invade celestial space with artless spontaneity. Contrast his description with Rudolf Otto's pronouncement: "A spirit or soul that has been conceived and comprehended no longer prompts to 'shuddering' . . . [and] thereby ceases to be of interest for the psychology of religion."[17] Smith's unrelenting anthropomorphizing; the chronological and geographical specificity of his encounters with the divine; his commitment of heavenly revelation to the process of transcription, publication, and marketing; his enactment of prophetic restoration through the medium of legal incorporation—these and related aspects of his work rendered religious allegorizing of his message impossible.

The stone cut out of the mountain without hands and seen by Daniel might have been figurative, but its fulfillment was not: it occurred "one thousand eight hundred and thirty years since the coming of our Lord and Savior Jesus Christ in the flesh" (to the day) when the kingdom of God was "regularly organized and established agreeable to the laws of our country" (and the state of New York; D&C 1:21). When God commanded Hosea to take a harlot as a wife, the act presumably symbolized something about spiritual apostasy and devotion (Hosea 1:2). But when God commanded Joseph Smith to have Sidney Gilbert "establish a store, that he [might] sell goods" (D&C 57:8), it was fruitless to search for other levels of moral significance. Zion might mean the pure in heart, but it also required—and received—an actual plat with surveyor marks and compass points.

As persecution heated up in Nauvoo, Illinois, in the summer of 1842, the journalist James Gordon Bennett reported with amusement: "Jo goes on prophecying, preaching, and building the temple, and regulating his empire, as if nothing had happened. They are busy all the time establishing factories to make saints and crockery ware, also prophets and white paint."[18] Bennett's blurring of boundaries between the metaphysical and the quotidian was no exaggeration. At every turn, but increasingly toward the end of his life, it seemed Smith was intent on demystifying traditional categories of the sacred, on deconstructing the otherworldly into its this-worldly bases. There seems to be little other motive behind his claim that "there are no angels who minister to this earth but those who do belong or have belonged to it."[19] The fullest implications of this "heresy" were not unfolded until the spring of his last year, at which point he publicly taught that "God himself who sits enthroned in yonder heavens . . . once was a man like one of us . . . is a Man like unto one of yourselves—that is the great secret."[20] The celestial orb nearest his habitation even had a name: Kolob.

These LDS theological currents bleed into cultural practice, finding expression in LDS architecture and visual arts. This is evident in two spaces most directly associated with LDS worship: the temple and the chapel/cultural hall.

Two forces conspire to threaten sacred experience in meetinghouse spaces. On the one hand, chapels are marked by a stark lack of signs of religiosity. With rare exceptions, LDS chapels have no stained glass, religious art, icons, or paraphernalia, and never any crosses or crucifixes. On the other hand, what chapels do have, across the thin barrier of a curtain (which is not even present on overflow occasions), are basketball hoops. In a predominant number of American LDS chapels, the worship space merges seamlessly into (and often encompasses) a basketball court (or "cultural hall"), separated only by a moveable curtain, with both surrounded by banks of classrooms and offices. Such ever-present cultural signifiers are secular, worldly, and boisterous. As one non-Mormon architect complained, "I wouldn't have felt much different in the chapel had I had a basketball in my lap . . . . I had no sense that I had arrived any place. I wasn't in a gymnasium; it was definitely a ward house—I would have felt the same say, for example, if I had had a magazine in my lap. There was no religious connotation to the place."[21] The easy transition from sacramental altar to basketball rims mirrors the "prophets and white paint" alluded to by Bennett—the collapse of sacred distance is in this case literally, spatially realized.

The other sacred space to which the Saints resort for worship is the temple. Here one finds what appears a polar opposite: quietude, restrained activity, and at times unrestrained opulence. There is a stark contrast with the aggressively pedestrian chapel architecture—many chapels are cinderblock construction with burlap wall covering. Chapels have all the sacred aura of an Elks lodge; temples can shock with their architectural sublimity ("Surrender Dorothy," one Washington, D.C., graffiti artist wrote near the temple there).[22] One might interpret the otherworldliness of such temple architecture as the irruption of the indomitable human yearning for the transcendent that

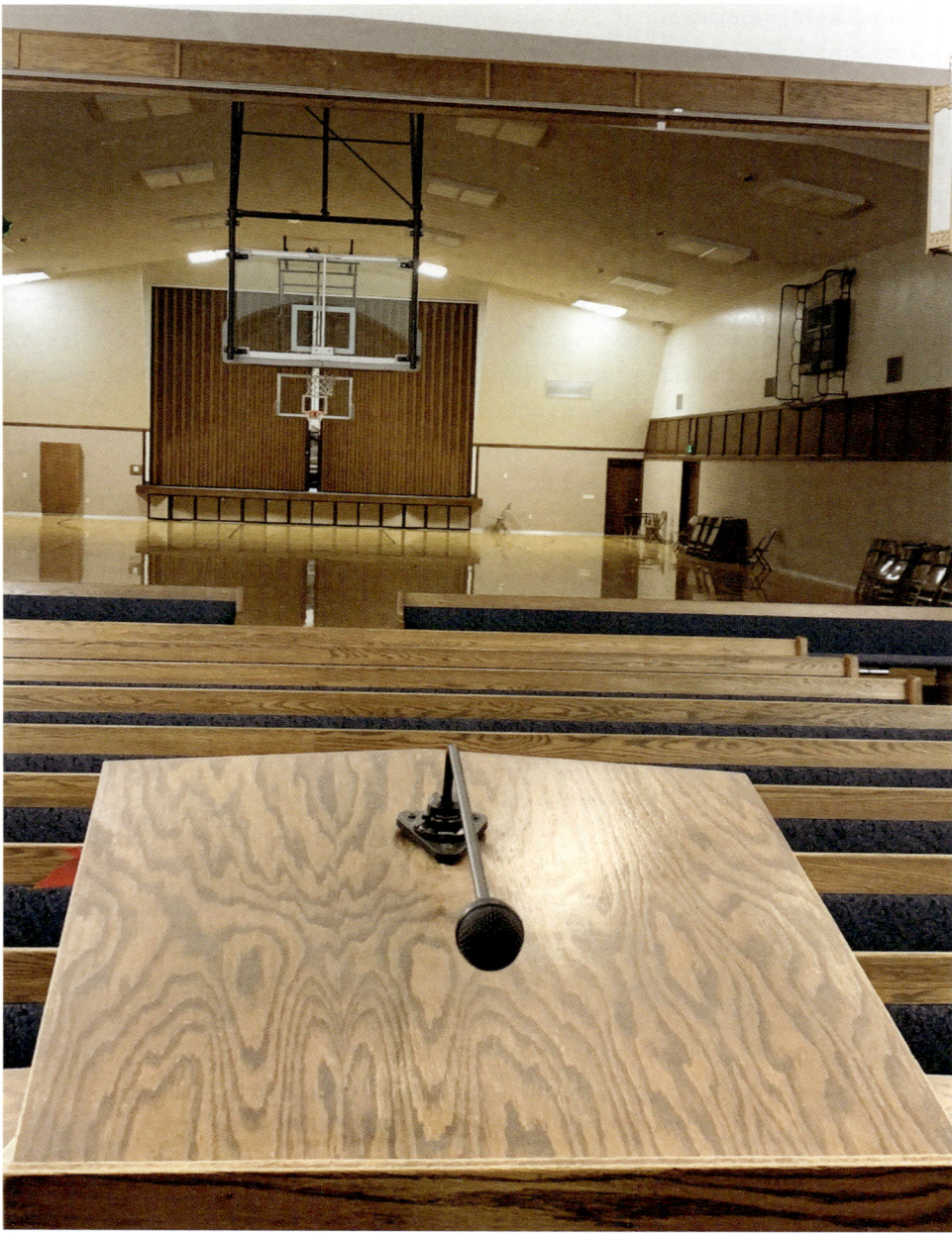

Fig. 1.1 A ward chapel/cultural hall, 2023. Photograph courtesy of the author.

Mormonism so consistently shuns. That sacred distance at the heart of religious experience cannot be entirely suppressed. The psychologist William James wrote of a virtually universal hunger for mystery, for the transcendent, for the ineffable. In his view, "The inner need is [for] something . . . complex, majestic in the hierarchic interrelatedness of its parts, with authority descending from stage to stage, and at every stage objects for adjectives of mystery and splendor."[23]

But in Mormonism such expression exists in blithe harmony with the most quotidian architectural forms. The temple and the meetinghouse are physically distinct locales, yet both are sites for worship, community, and reverence. Both are sacred spaces, where sacred sacraments are performed. Even the altars, however, are at far extremes from one another. In the chapel, unadorned wood or Formica; in the temple, molding and trim, varied colors, cushions, sometimes a chandelier positioned directly above. The otherworldly appearance of temples is a rare expression of LDS longing for transcendence, and a required temple recommend for patrons demarcates it as particularly sacred space. Yet its shared sacramental function with publicly accessible meetinghouses belies any utter divide between the sublime and the quotidian, the heavenly and the earthly.

Of course, not all Christian art retreats from the task of depicting the divine by explicit representation, even if the transcendent cannot be adequately captured in language or in oils. One remembers in this regard the furious reaction of British critics and audiences to John Everett Millais's *Christ in the House of His Parents* (1849–1850), which made of Joseph's house a rustic workshop, of Mary a homely peasant, and of the Savior a rosy-cheeked, redheaded boy with oversized feet. For a Christian sensibility captured by Kierkegaard, who referred to sacred distance as an "infinite qualitative distance" separating the transcendent and the immanent,[24] this earthy rendering was pictorial blasphemy—though the movement toward a more real, accessible Christ gained steam in the era.

Emil Brunner claimed there is "no greater sense of distance than that which lies in the words Creator-Creation . . . Man . . . is separated by an abyss from the Divine manner of being. The greatest dissimilarity between two things which we can express at all . . . is that between the Creator and that which is created."[25] By contrast, Latter-day Saint apostle Parley P. Pratt affirmed that "God, angels, men, [are] all one species."[26] This may be one explanation for the resistance to anything other than rather pedestrian illustration in LDS spaces and publications alike. In a collapsed universe, where the sacred and the quotidian have no hard demarcations, it makes sense to employ direct, realistic representation—and only direct, realistic representation. Hence, those works of sacred persons or themes that have been approved for display in Latter-day Saint chapels and temples are never abstract; nor are they ever blatantly ahistorical appropriations. You will find neither Dali's *Last Supper* nor nativities framed by Tuscan landscapes. You *will* find an omnipresent representation of the Christ that looks more like a Galilean yearbook portrait than a Raphael. This is a consequence of institutional policies that are hypervigilant in requiring art that is strictly illustrative and doctrinally safe. Presently, for instance, chapel art is restricted to work that "depicts the Savior himself or the Savior ministering to others."[27] Such norms are hardly a recipe for artistic exploration.

John Hafen is an early consequence of work that *was* institutionally supported. Hafen, who was sent by church leadership on an ecclesiastically motivated mission to study art

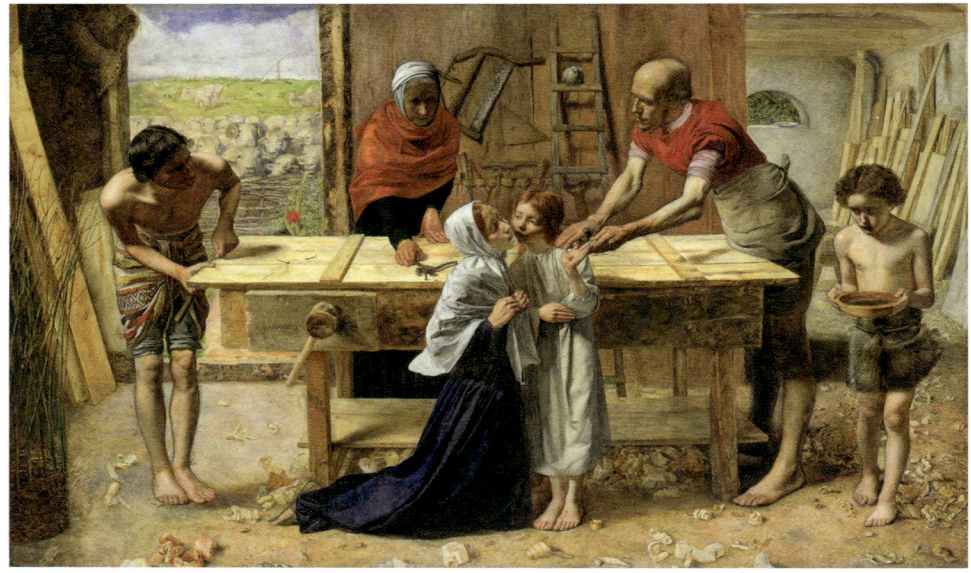

Fig. 1.2 John Everett Millais, *Christ in the House of His Parents,* 1850, oil on canvas, 34″ × 55″.

in Paris academies in the 1890s, took on the task of illustrating a famous poem extolling Mormonism's doctrine of both a Father and Mother in Heaven (Eliza R. Snow's "My Father in Heaven" was set to music and is now sung as "Oh My Father"). In this unprecedented endeavor, an artist's rendering of a literally conceived male and female Christian God, the artist employs realism to depict the Deities in quotidian, non-metaphorical settings. It is an early, disconcerting literalizing of the achievement Brigham Young imputed to Joseph Smith: "He brought heaven down to earth and elevated earth up to heaven." Here we find representations of both God the Father *and* God the Mother rendered with a kind of rev-erential refusal to rationalize the sacred into ineffability. God's corporeality and existence as two distinct divine persons are explicitly affirmed in church teachings.[28]

More recently, the Filipina American artist Rose Datoc Dall and American artist Caitlin Connolly employ less realism, but just as much literalism, in depicting a dual Deity. The fact of a female divine, or Heavenly Mother, is of course conspicuous evidence of an LDS theology unique in Christendom. However, the more general Mormon aes-thetic that is captured in both pieces is in the literalness of heavenly parenthood itself, of divine creation as an emphatic parallel to the human parental creation. We are, a church declaration affirms, "the undeveloped offspring of celestial parentage," in the "similitude of the universal Father and Mother."[29] Hence, in Connolly's language, we find a divine mother and her mortal posterity, who have acquired bodies that are not symbolically or metaphorically but literally "In Her Image."

The collapse of sacred distance achieved in the Restoration was dramatically expressed in two Restoration moments. First was the rootedness of God's renewed covenant in the

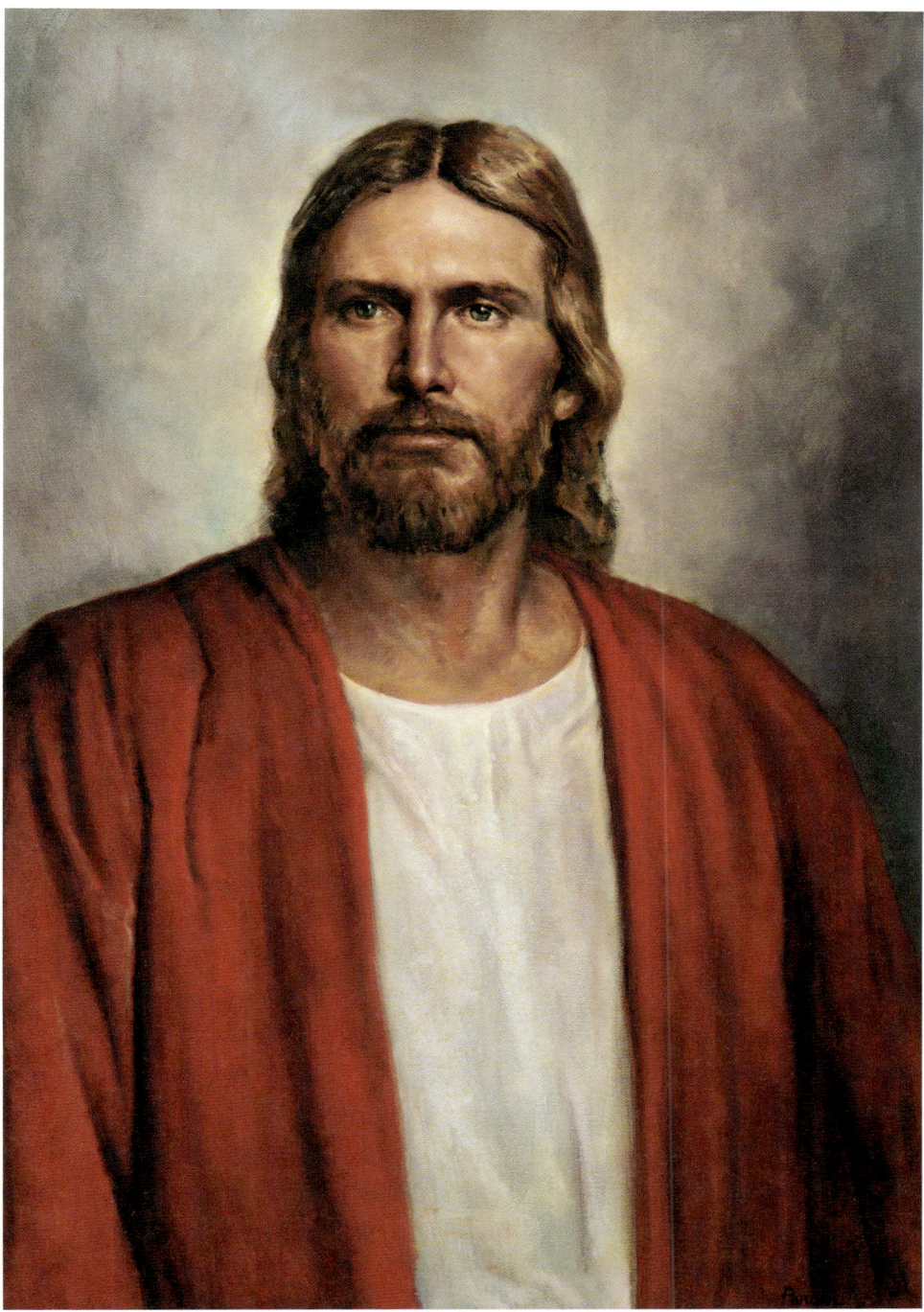

Fig. 1.3 Del Parsons, *Christ in Red Robe*, 1983, oil on canvas. Courtesy of Church of Jesus Christ of Latter-day Saints.

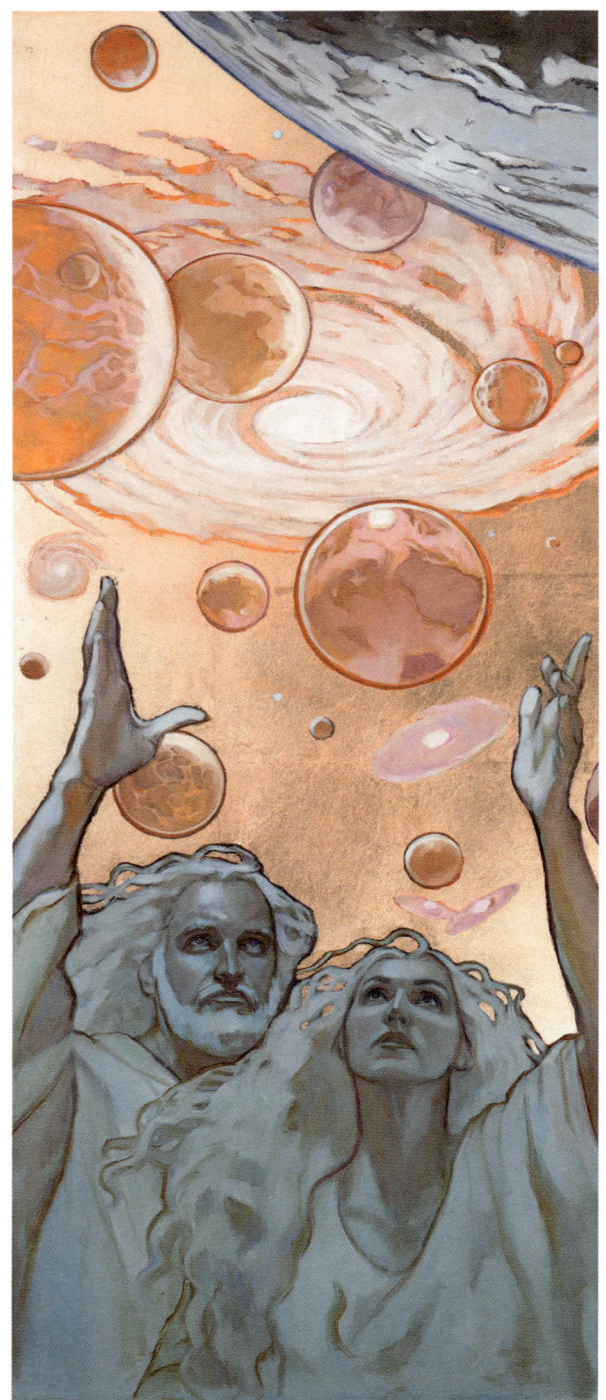

Fig. 1.4 Rose Datoc Dall, *Worlds Without Number*, 2020, oil on canvas. Courtesy of the artist.

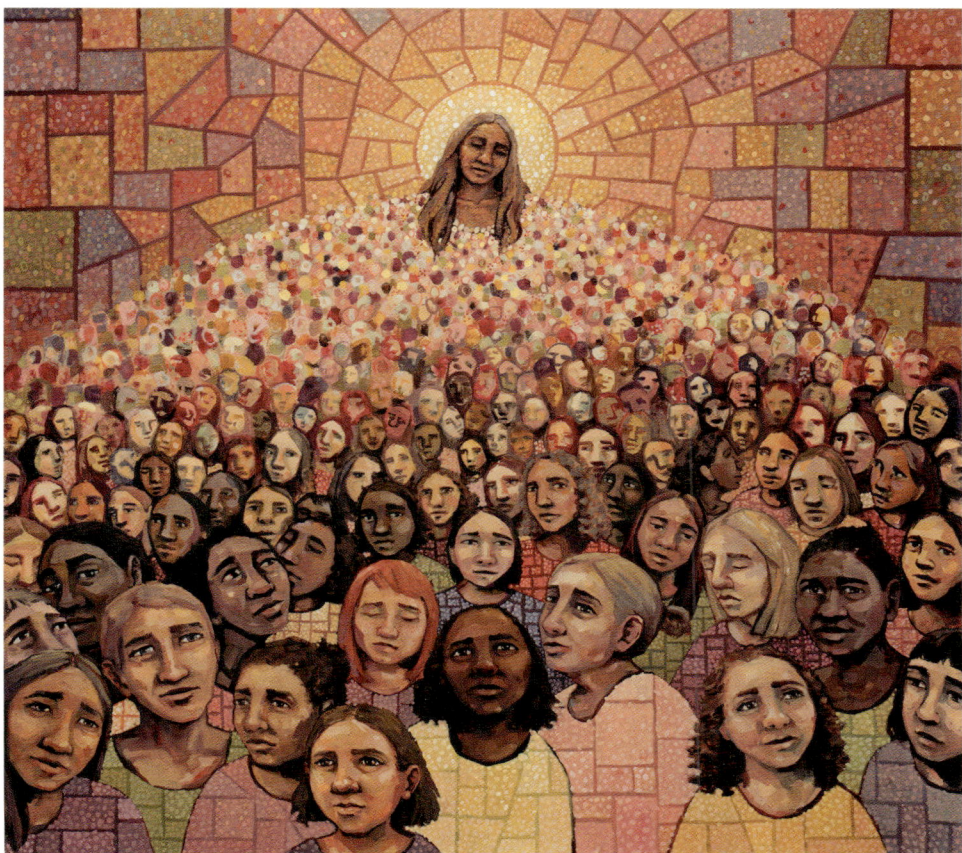

Fig. 1.5 Caitlin Connolly, *In Her Image*, 2021, oil on canvas. Courtesy of the artist.

solid, empirical reality of metal plates, witnessed and handled by witnesses, and fastidiously described by Joseph.

> These records were engraven on plates which had the appearance of gold. Each plate was six inches wide and eight inches long and not quite so thick as common tin. They were filled with engravings in Egyptian characters and bound together in a volume, as the leaves of a book with three rings running through the whole. The volume was something near six inches in thickness, a part of which was sealed. The characters on the unsealed part were small, and beautifully engraved. The whole book exhibited many marks of antiquity in its construction and much skill in the art of engraving.[30]

The passage reads rather like a catalogue description penned by a connoisseur of fine books. It shows not just an eye for detail but also an aesthetic sensibility and an appreciative but restrained regard for the beauty and sheer craftsmanship of what was before

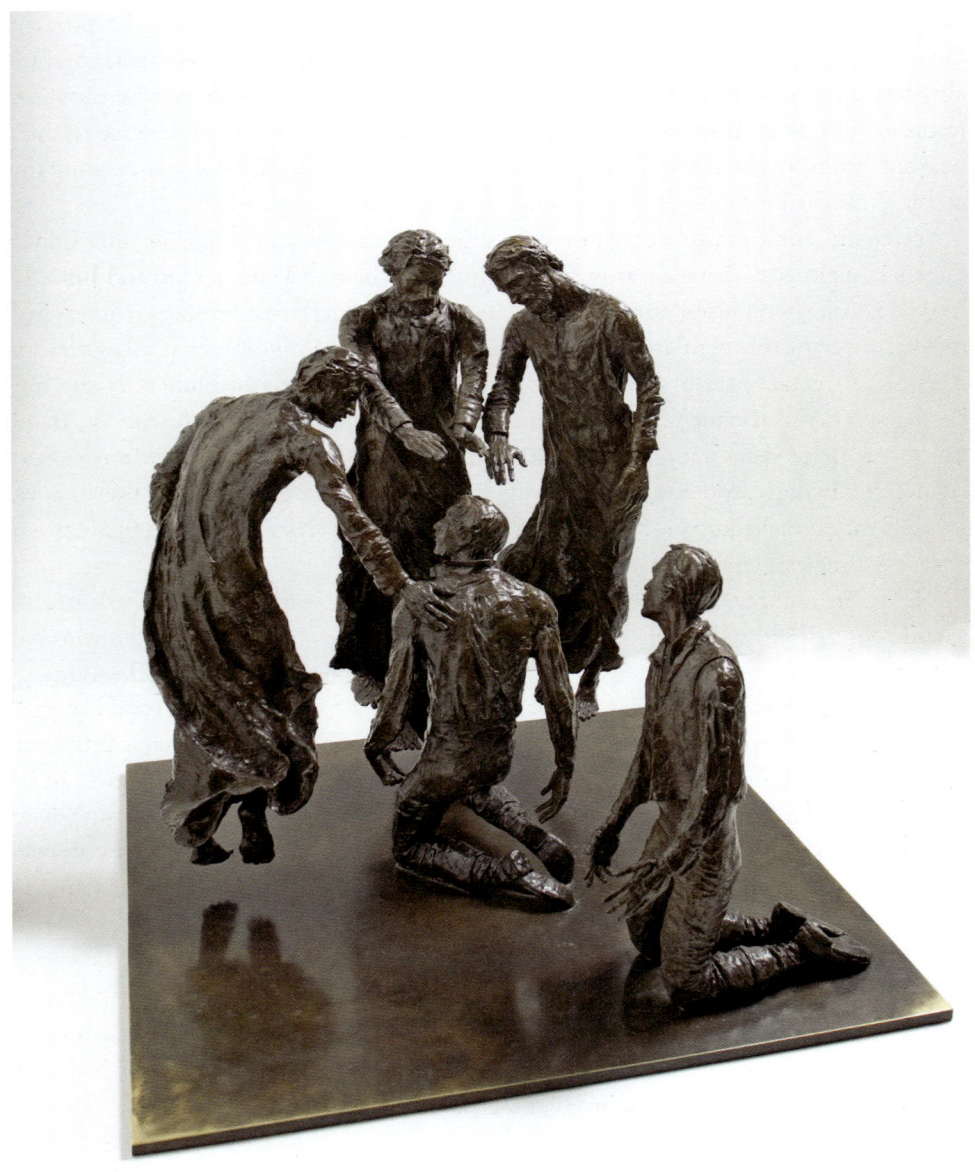

Fig. 1.6 Trevor Southey, *The Moment After*, 1940, bronze, 26¾″ × 27⅓″ × 4″ × 273″ × 27″, Church of Jesus Christ of Latter-day Saints Museum of Church History and Art, Salt Lake City. Courtesy of the Church History Museum.

him. There is something almost uncanny in the dispassion with which the prophet focuses on the pure physicality of the plates—not just insisting on their artifactual reality but also adding physical detail to physical detail in oblivious disregard for the sheer improbability of their reality. Not a hint of supernaturalism, nor any reference to their heavenly transport by celestial beings, finds place or attention. The veil demarcating the realm of the divine and the historical object has vanished completely.

A second such erasure of those distinctions occurred when Joseph and Oliver Cowdery claimed a visitation from three resurrected beings: Peter, James, and John. In Trevor Southey's representation of this event, the medium of cast bronze is summoned to the service of this conflation of spheres. Any attempt to mythologize, allegorize, or interiorize this account of heavenly visitations is emphatically precluded by the imposing solidity of the metal. Monochromatic and undifferentiated by texture or material, the work is a defiant incarnation of the farm boy and his colleague in the form of the resurrected beings. And entirely unlike the monumental statuary of Civil War heroes, iconic figures of antiquity, and multiple renditions of Joseph Smith, this group does not strive for timelessness or transcendence.

Quite the contrary: Southey endows the bronze work with a surprising degree of mobility and fluidity. The work does not point us toward an emblematic, static event but unfolds in real, moving time with real psychological and emotional valence. The moment is not frozen but carries traces of the sacred contact that has just occurred and presages a departure now happening. The whole locates the historical event as a lived reality in an ongoing continuum that connects directly with—and incorporates—the viewer in its temporal domain. This is no monument to a frozen myth that forever lingers outside of human time. It makes apparent the celestial as it bleeds into and suffuses our own world and then casually slips out again. Rather like that startling moment of sacred collapse in the Book of Mormon, when Nephi says with guileless matter-of-factness, "I returned from speaking with the Lord to the tent of my father" (1 Nephi 3:1).

Restoration theology collapses heaven/earth boundaries in yet another way, one that is in high relief when set against Protestant theology. In England, the first—and still Catholic—version of the Book of Common Prayer included this lovely petition over one who had died: "Graunte ... that at the daye of judgement his soule and all the soules of thy electe, departed out of this lyfe, may with us and we with them, fully receive thy promises." Wishing to shun every vestige of Catholic reaching beyond the grave, Thomas Cranmer decided such prayers "smacked of the old religion in which the living could perform religious acts on behalf of the dead," in one scholar's words.[31] Calvin agreed that even "commending [the dead] to his grace" was unscriptural and inappropriate.[32] Three hundred years later, Protestants were still hostile to any gestures that suggested living Christians could influence the disposition of the departed. And all Protestants had been united in rejecting purgatory.

As Calvin's biographer notes, "There is, for Protestants, only heaven and hell," and the disposition to one or the other was final.[33] But if, as Apostle James Talmage pointed out crucially, the LDS faith envisions "the possibility of a universal salvation,"[34] then that

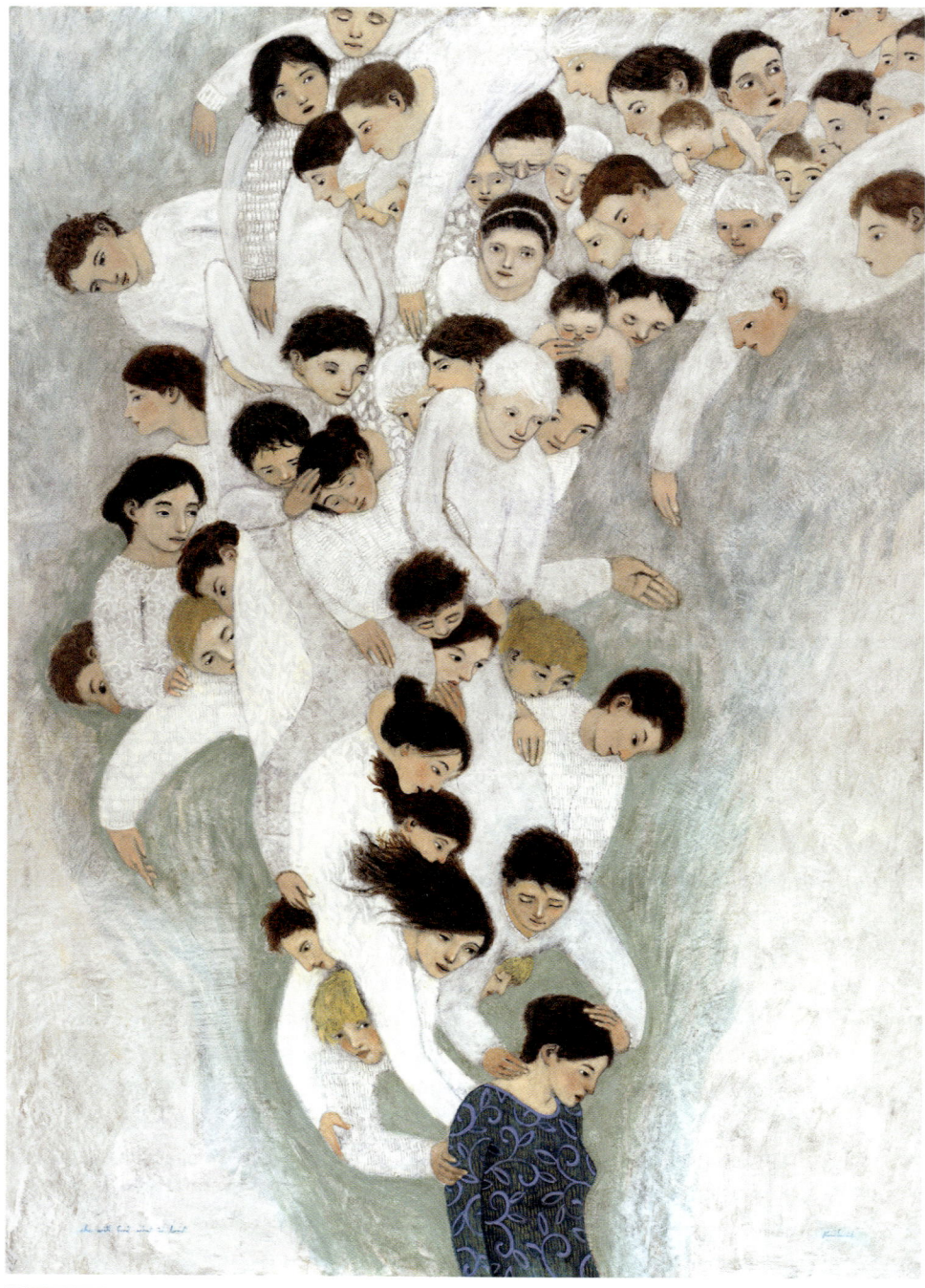

Fig. 1.7 Brian Kershisnik, *She Will Find What Is Lost*, 2012, oil on canvas, 8′ × 11′. Courtesy of the artist.

universalism must find a way to include the vast billions of the uncatechized within its orbit and, in Joseph Smith's language, weld together "a perfect chain from Father Adam to his latest posterity."[35] And so Mormonism developed a theology of the period between mortality and final judgment where evangelizing continues, in a process that encompasses the living and the dead with little regard for boundaries between the two. The permeability of that membrane radically reshapes the nature of human interdependence. And for the Saints, it utterly defines the nature of a celestial sociality, of which all persons are already a part.

Brian Kershishnik's work celebrates the radical interconnections and interdependence of the living and the dead, subsuming both within a vision of an invisible church, a church without walls ("Kirche ohne Mauer," in Jacob Boehme's words).[36] In *She Will Find What Is Lost* (2012), concourses of angels are identifiable as such only by the uniformly white apparel in which they are robed. But neither halos, beatific countenances, nor serene visages imply anything particularly celestial about these beings. In fact, they seem self-evidently of the same species of humanity—and probably of the same bloodline—as the figure they surround in an act of communal blessing. Smith taught that "there are no angels who minister to this earth but those who do belong or have belonged to it" (D&C 130:5). That principle was one more link in his chain that made heaven and earth a seamless continuum rather than dichotomous divide. Virtually all of Kershishnik's works capture moments of sublime contact between the two as utterly routine, ever present, and available to those with seeing eyes and listening ears.

PART 2: EDEN OR EXILE?

A second fertile paradox in LDS theology that informs a strand of LDS art is the ambiguous place of the Saints in the mortal world and among that world's peoples. As Saints and a people restored to their place in covenant Israel—but inhabiting the margins of respectable society—are they in Eden or exile? An early assault on traditional orthodoxy made by the new faith tradition appears in both the Book of Mormon and Smith's emendations to the Bible. In his recounting of the Genesis episode, Eve celebrates rather than laments the events of Eden: "Were it not for our transgression we never should have had seed, and never should have known good and evil, and the joy of our redemption, and the eternal life which God giveth unto all the obedient" (Moses 5:11). A Book of Mormon prophet likewise dismisses any reputed "fall" as a misnomer:

> Behold, all things have been done in the wisdom of him who knoweth all things. Adam fell that men might be; and men are, that they might have joy. (2 Nephi 2:25)

An observer was struck by Joseph Smith's public preaching to this effect: "Joseph said in answer to Mr stout that Adam Did Not Comit sin in [e]ating the fruits for God had Decred that he should Eat & fall—But in complyance with the Decree he should Die."[37]

And yet, Saints recognize, they are all certainly removed from the presence of God and subject to the myriad infirmities of the flesh and the spirit, inevitably making choices

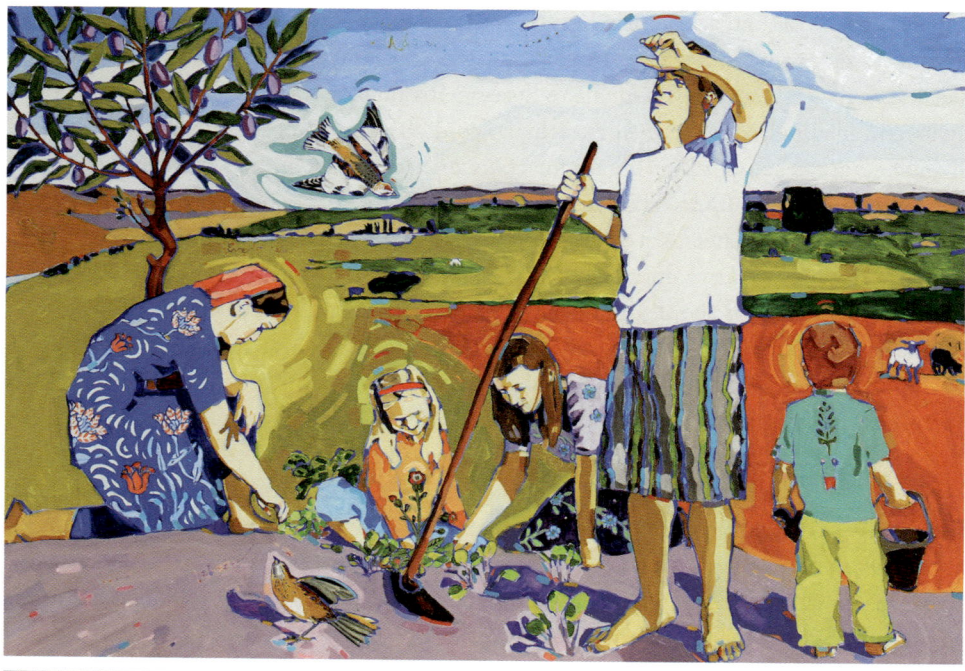

Fig. 1.8 Linda Vance Etherington, *Sweat of His Brow*, 2010, oil on panel, 48″ × 60″. Courtesy of the artist.

that constitute personal fall into sin. So the tension arises: as eternal spirits hailing from celestial realms, we pass through the portal of mortality, tasting the bitter in order to prize the good. Entering into an embodied state, Saints take literally the pronouncement of God that mortals have thereby "become as one of us" (Genesis 1:22). The fall is therefore no fall, but ascent. At the same time, Saints acknowledge their relative "nothingness" before God, as Moses and Benjamin taught (Moses 4:5, 11). And they accept that "all nations, kindreds, tongues and people, must be born again; yea, born of God, changed from their carnal and fallen state, to a state of righteousness, being redeemed of God, becoming his sons and daughters" (Moses 27:25).

In LDS culture, the high anthropology of Moses ("children are whole from the foundation of the world" [Moses 6:54]) generally trumps the low anthropology of Benjamin ("the natural man is an enemy to God" [Mosiah 3:19]). Linda Etherington captures this optimism in her work *Sweat of His Brow* (2010). A vibrantly colored family group is ensconced in a scene redolent with Edenic imagery. Children and others tend young plants; the garden extends into the horizon, with one conspicuous tree in the foreground, and a dove descending earthward. The sweat of this modern-day Adam, who is wearing Bermuda shorts and holding a rake, could be seen as gently ironic, making light of biblical anathemas. However, the family grouping reflects a genuine theological point: the Adamic "curse" was the precondition for an eternal sociality centered on the family. "[Human beings] were *born* into the world by the fall" is how Smith characterizes the fruits of Eve's decision in his first revision of the account in Genesis of the fall.[38] Any "sweat" is part of that educative, productive process by which humans—in family groups—become more fully divine.

LDS culture has expanded that dynamic interplay between Eden and exile from the theological into the sociohistorical realm in response to the LDS experience in their early history. Saints have seen themselves in numerous Old Testament and Restoration scriptures: they are "the chosen," "Israel," "the children of Ephraim," "[the Lord's] church," "[the Lord's] people," members of "the only true and living Church." They have an exclusive stewardship over priesthood keys and the plan of salvation; they will be instrumental in building up Zion and someday rising in clouds of glory to meet Enoch's people and the Lord himself. A legacy of persecution and alienation, proscription and martyrdom, has put the seal to their status as a people apart.

In addition, the enormous institutional demands of religious commitment, personal sacrifice, and distinctive religious practices have welded the adherents of the faith into a people who so powerfully identify with one another that one writer did not hesitate to call them the only instance in American history of a people who became almost an ethnic community.[39] Casting all others as "Gentiles," and fellow Christians rather uncharitably as inheritors of a Great Apostasy, this rhetoric of difference, together with a history of persecution and geographical remoteness, compounded their isolation into a virtue and sign of blessedness.

But that remoteness and isolation have simultaneously been read by the Saints as a burden and a cross. The quest for Zion was for the Saints a search for Eden—but it was always an Eden in exile. Was their hegira to the Salt Lake Valley a journey to the promised land or banishment? Their choir won a silver medal at the 1893 Chicago World's Fair, but the church's public presentation at the contemporaneous Parliament of Religions was relegated to an inconspicuous side street apart from the main venue. They proclaim themselves the Church of Jesus Christ, but in May 2000 the United Methodist Church passed a resolution asserting that the Church of Jesus Christ of Latter-day Saints "does not fit within the bounds of the historic, apostolic tradition of Christian faith." The Presbyterian Church (U.S.A.) and the Southern Baptist Convention passed similar resolutions, followed by the Vatican, which declared Mormon baptisms invalid in 2001.[40] Mormons insist on the need for a gospel restoration, but then feel the sting of being excluded from the fold of Christendom they have just dismissed as irredeemably apostate. "We are Christian! We want the whole world to know it," insisted a General Authority in 1973.[41]

Their awareness of this contested status, claiming chosenness while experiencing exile, appears recurrently in the Mormon psyche as both nostalgia and alienation, and the quest for integration into the larger world they had fled was fueled by both a longing for inclusion and an imperative to redeem the world. In her novelistic treatment of this paradox, Virginia Sorensen makes such alienation a general consequence of LDS history and theology. The irony is that a gospel of universal brotherhood, rooted in a commission to proselytize the world, is so marked on every hand by borders, boundaries, and radical difference. In Sorenson's novel, the character Mercy, a pioneer arrived in Utah, notes this existential isolation, and reacts with a powerful nostalgia for connectedness, in an early passage of remarkable poignancy:

> As it rose higher, it paled, and presently was the moon she knew. There, that was better. After all, the moon had no right to be different anywhere. Even if a woman came west with her family, looking for home, and everything else changed, the land and the people and the talk even, and living grew to be an intense and difficult thing, she should still be able to look up and see the moon the same.[42]

Like the heroine whose life she chronicles, Sorensen's work maintains a fragile dialectic, trying to skirt the perils of complacency toward one's own culture on the one hand and repudiation of a larger social and cultural identity on the other, fully at home in neither realm. Though acclaimed by critics like Clifton Fadiman and Bernard DeVoto, and praised in the *New York Times, The Nation,* and elsewhere, *A Little Lower than the Angels* was condemned by LDS leaders for precisely the same attributes the press lauded. "Poignantly human,"

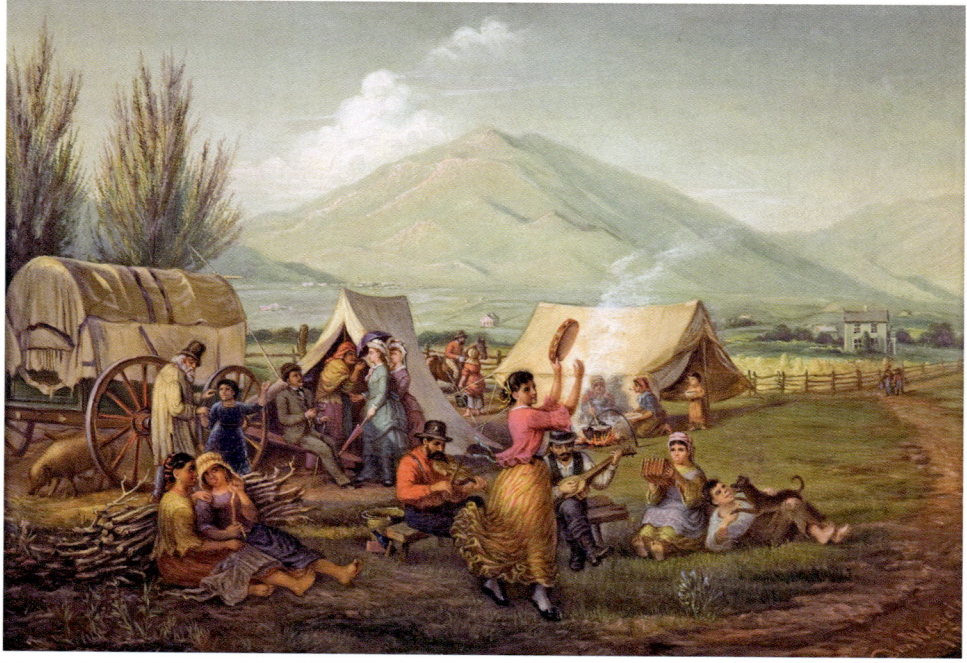

Fig. 1.9 Danquart Anthon Weggeland, *Gypsy Camp (Campsite Along the Mormon Trail),* 1875, oil on panel, 15″ × 23″, Governor's Mansion, Salt Lake City. Courtesy of the Utah Division of Arts & Museums.

opined *Newsweek*'s critic; Joseph and the other characters were portrayed as too "ordinary," complained LDS apostle John A. Widtsoe in a church editorial.[43]

In the visual arts, a poignant illustration of this dilemma might be exemplified in a painting with a remarkable cataloguing history. In this painting, powerfully conflicted feelings of exclusion and of chosen status are manifest—not only in the production of Mormon art but also, and more emphatically, in Mormon response to art.

In 1876, a painting by a Latter-day Saint immigrant from Norway, Danquart Anthon Weggeland, was accepted for the Centennial Exhibition in Philadelphia. After it came into possession of the Utah Museum of Fine Arts, it was catalogued as *Campsite Along the Mormon Trail*,[44] and as recently as 1993, the *Deseret News* referred to it by that title.[45] But the painting involves a profoundly revealing error—in both the title and the patently misidentified subject. The error is a striking indication of how conflicted Latter-day Saint self-identity can be, torn as it is between the opposed feelings of blessed exile and painful marginalization. Utah viewers readily recognized themselves in this scene of westbound travelers, with their wagon and pitched tents, dancing and playing music, with cookfires and a mountain peak in the background, all depicted by a Latter-day Saint artist just a few decades after the forced exodus of his people from Illinois. The scene was readily perceived to be one of innumerable such "campsites along the Mormon trail."

The setting, however, is not deserted prairie or rugged desert; it is fertile farmland with fashionable homes and fields near to hand, but they exist—tellingly—on the other side of sturdy fences. Interfused with the campfires and tents are more subtle elements that poignantly evoke a genteel society, now lost to the Saints. Parasol-carrying ladies mingle with a suited gentleman in front of a crude camp tent, while a mixed-gender band plays music, a boy romps with a puppy, and others prepare food, all in bucolic splendor.

The effect, therefore, is more that of a scene of peasants making merry outside the gates of a rich man's feast than an evocation of the children of Israel fleeing Egypt for a promised land. The overall feeling is one of painfully proximate exile, tenuous gaiety in the face of exclusion. The visitors to the camp may have their finery and bowler hats, smug with their prosperous farms behind their expansive fencing, the artist seems to be saying. But here in exile, we make merry, we sing and dance, and we are happy in our manifest harmony and community.

However, the painting isn't about Mormon pioneers at all. In fact, Weggeland had called it *Gipsy Camp*, and under that title it was hung in that Philadelphia exhibition. Palm readers and pipe-smoking women, tambourines, and gay apparel alongside the wagons of Travelers, not exiled Mormons in pioneer Conestogas or handcarts, mark the scene. The question is, how did viewers make the curious error of reading themselves onto the canvas? One commonly mistakes the identity of a marginalized ethnicity or subculture. But in this case, how did Mormons so readily mistake themselves and forebears for a band of Roma, when so many details should have evidently impeded that reading? Clearly, they saw their own story there—a story of happy exiles, blessedly blissful in the wilderness, even as they yearned for connection to civilization and longed for life on the other side of the fences that barred them from familiar comforts and culture. The Saints' experience of exile and alienation made them all too ready to read themselves into a scene that captured the ambivalence of their own predicament: Was it Eden or Babylon they were leaving behind? Was this the exile of the dispossessed or the triumphal march toward a better, more secure Zion?

A second explanation for the misidentification is the quasi ethnicity with which Mormonism had come to be imbued—and which they so readily accepted. Unlike Native Americans, African Americans, "Mohammedans," Jews, or other minoritized groups of the era, Mormons were not an ethnic group—or, like the Catholics, susceptible to identification *with* an ethnic group (like the Irish). Visible (or imagined) signs of ethnicity in those other cases provided a ready mode of identification. Forewarned is forearmed. And nativist authors and illustrators especially exaggerated ethnic differentiators (of skin color, physiognomy, dress) to provide a sense of distance, insulation, and security from the threat of contamination, or distorted to the point of dehumanization, to ease the guilt of violence against kindred human beings.

Latter-day Saints, however, didn't at first appearance lend themselves to such ready differentiation, because they were disarmingly like the default of white Americans. So popular writers and artists responded with their usual resourcefulness, constructing a distinctive ethnicity where none existed. Relatively few enough had actually seen a Mormon, apparently, that writers could consistently and credibly conjure images of Mormon "orientalism," or just a vaguely limned "Otherness." In novels of the era, Salt Lake was "as Oriental as Damascus" (*Thompson Dunbar*). Jack London's character notes that "they ain't white . . . they're Mormons" (*Star Rover*), Dan Coolidge writes of their "strange, foreign look" (*Fighting Danites*), and illustrators depicted them as caped, Mediterranean-looking cavaliers or as Amish-looking yokels who spoke Elizabethan English.[46]

Science was invoked to sustain the dozens of similar depictions, when two academics argued in an 1861 meeting of the New Orleans Academy of Sciences meeting that Mormons were already developing into a physiologically distinctive "new race."[47] Such seeming absurdities turn out to have foreshadowed—and, no doubt, facilitated—a rather startling state of affairs: in the *Harvard Encyclopedia of Ethnic Groups,* "Mormons" have their own entry.[48] Given their own insistence that they *were* a people apart, the representation of Saints as visually distinct served their own sense of peculiarity, even as it exacerbated stereotyping. Detractors imposed a radical difference on Mormons that achieves a canonical status—one that Mormons came to embrace (spiritual "eugenics," B. H. Roberts called it).[49] Weggeland's canvas and its history are the most concrete embodiment of that paradox.

In a more deliberate way, Lee Greene Richards captures the same mix of nostalgia, loss, and hopefulness provoked by the Mormon experience of dislocation. Himself a descendent of early Mormon stalwarts and honored by the Paris Salon, Richards juxtaposes a long train of exiled Saints, the desolation of the plains, and a remoteness devoid of fixed destination with the portrait of a wistful woman who is not experiencing

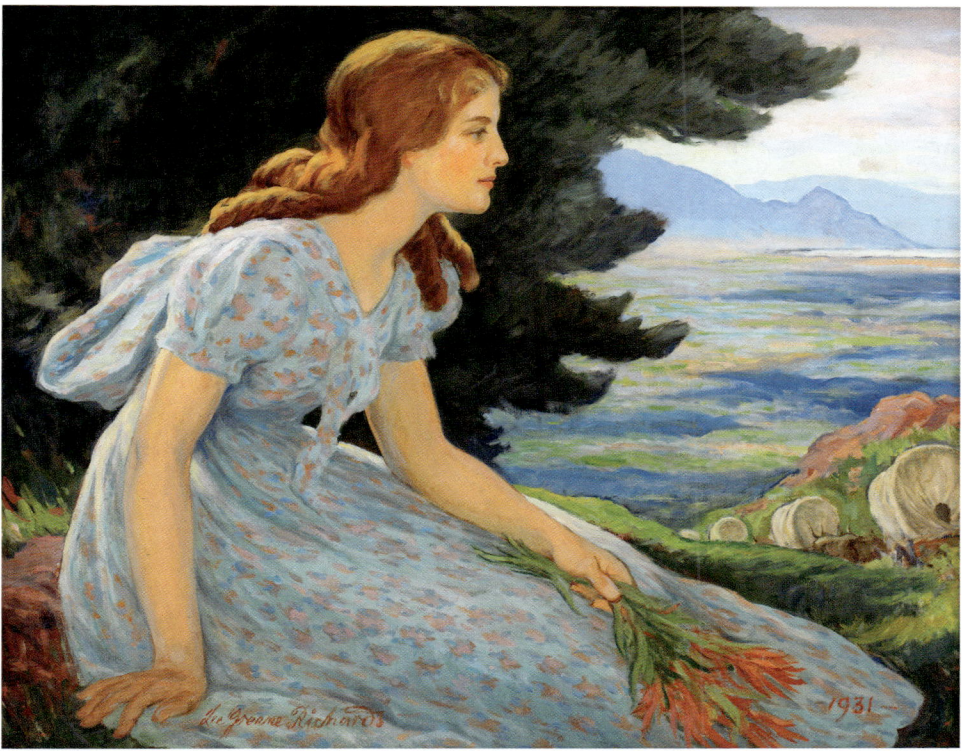

Fig. 1.10 Lee Greene Richards, *Dreaming of Zion,* 1931, oil on canvas, 32″ × 39.5″, Springville Museum of Art, gift from Springville High School, Class of 1935 Trust.

the realities of hardship and isolation, for she is rather "dreaming of Zion," as the title notes. Zion has an emphatically communal denotation in LDS thought, characterized by harmony, sociality, and charitableness; it is noteworthy that in this appropriation of the concept, however, we have only the solitary woman, and a depiction not of society but escape or flight from that society. Eden, in this strange logic, *is* the exile. Her carefully coiffed hair and delicate dress compound the paradox of such displacement as both incongruous (she embodies civilizational and cultural refinements) and aspirational (departure from that hub of community is an idealized "dream").

One of the most famous painters of Mormon pioneer themes is C. C. A. Christensen, whose work has been published in *Art in America* (May–June 1970), was exhibited in the Whitney Museum of American Art (1970), and is omnipresent in LDS chapels, office buildings, and homes. His canvases' hard-edged unsophisticated simplicity accentuates with earnest pathos the rugged theme of pioneer triumph over adversity in its many forms. Similar to *Sweat of His Brow,* his *Handcart Pioneers' First View of Salt Lake Valley* (1890) is entirely typical in its figuring of Mormon religiosity as gritty physical work. Family groupings surround two heavily laden handcarts, both pulled jointly. Proximate

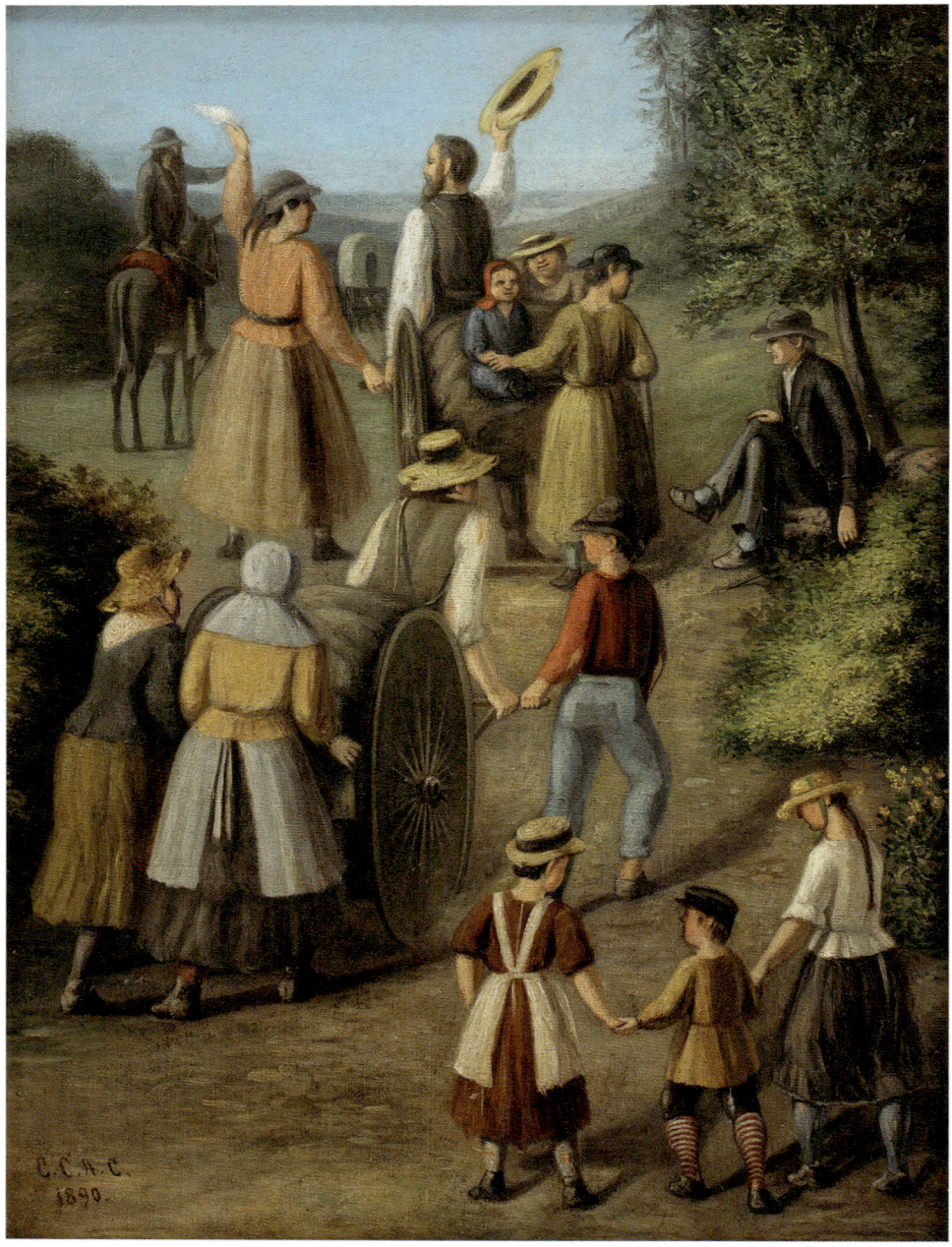

Fig. 1.11 C. C. A. Christensen, *Handcart Pioneers' First View of the Salt Lake Valley*, 1890, oil on canvas, 16″ × 12″, Springville Museum of Art, gift from Neil and Jane Schaerrer.

working hands are echoed by the entwined hands of children. Community—of family, pioneer companies, and the New Zion—is the dominant theme, contrasted with the emptiness of the world they are about to enter.

The small patch of blue at the apogee of the canvas emphasizes by contrast that the path of some fourteen hundred wearily traversed miles has all along been leading heavenward. Attaining the steep mountain summit, a triumphant couple raise hands in a jubilant gesture, worthy of Dante's triumphant pilgrim conquering Mount Purgatory. However, in this case, the azure sky does not betoken a heavenly realm crowning the group's preparations to enter heaven. Both Zion and repose wait upon the group's descent back down into earthly life and labor. It would be hard to more pointedly depict the collapse of the yearning for transcendence into the holiness of the prosaic. Exile, we can see, leads toward rather than away from Eden. But it is an Eden, clearly, that awaits human rather than divine planting. (That the land may already be planted by or sacred to other occupants of the land is not part of these settlers' vision.) In these pilgrims' eyes, the heavenly and earthly cities here blend indissolubly, as do the sacred and the banal.

NEW DIRECTIONS

Recent trends in LDS culture have moved to significantly challenge the harsh contours of a Mormon Zion. The first four Utah temples almost defiantly assert the ideal of the church as "Fortress Zion." Massive walls and towers, stocky shapes, and abundant crenellations convey an unambiguous claim to non-negotiable possession. No more yielding to persecutors or dispossessors, and safety for those who enter these precincts. Indeed, from the nineteenth century on, Zion was often invoked as a place of security and refuge from the world, and was scripturally referred to as such: "And that the gathering together upon the land of Zion, and upon her stakes, may be for a defense, and for a refuge from the storm, and from wrath when it shall be poured out without mixture upon the whole earth" (D&C 115:5–6).

In recent times, the messaging has changed. Increasing calls from the leadership embrace a model of interreligious, multicultural, multiethnic cooperation in the project of building Zion. At the same time, LDS rhetorical shifts and academic work alike have deemphasized past emphasis on peculiarity and "chosenness," and on the "apostasy" of the Christian world.[50] One artistic consequence is that Mormonism's hitherto scrupulous avoidance of symbols and sensibilities common to the ("apostate") Christian world has diminished.

The Restoration, in spite of its traditional characterization of an "apostate" Christendom from which it has clearly differentiated itself, has at times evinced a nostalgia for the sublime achievements of a premodern Christian visual arts tradition. LDS art, in other words, has occasionally appropriated mediums and styles that are resonant with holy ambience, as if in compensation for the collapse of sacred distance in our own depictions.

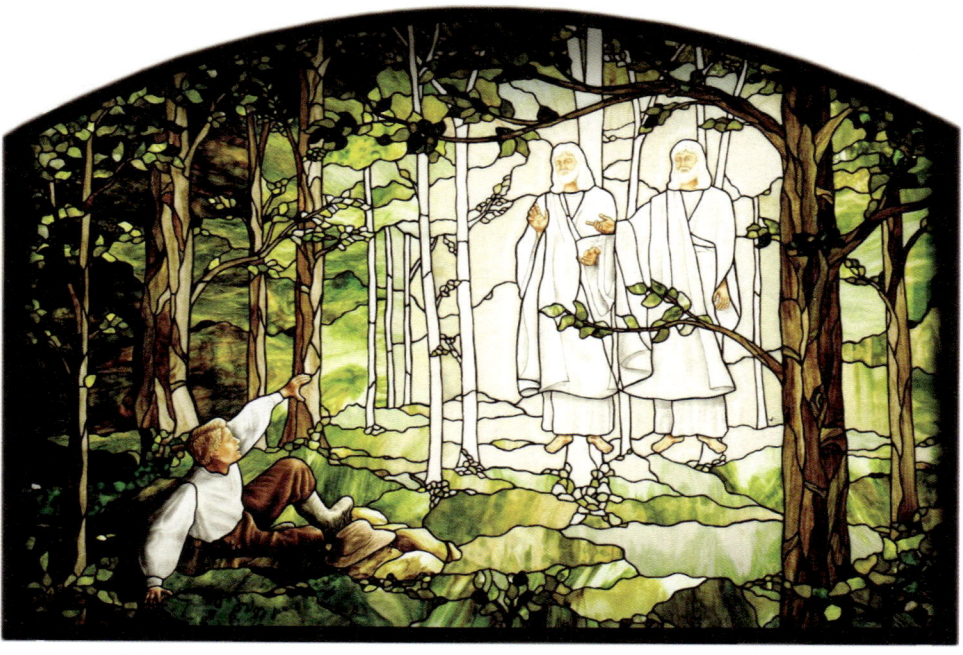

Fig. 1.12 Gayle and Tom Holdman, *Stained Glass of First Vision*, 2000, Palmyra Temple, Palmyra, New York. Courtesy of the Church of Jesus Christ of Latter-day Saints.

Gayle and Tom Holdman's rendering of the First Vision, for instance, offers a striking amalgam that borrows from stained glass and its ancient, reverential associations the aura of sanctity and otherworldliness inherent in the premodern age, in order to dampen the presumption of the modern miraculous. Though far from the norm, numerous instances of stained glass—in temples, meetinghouses, and tabernacles—demonstrate that if Mormonism lacks the mists of history, distance, and ineffability that are markers of the sacred, it can always appropriate a medium that is employed to supply them.[51]

A comparable strategy is evident in Ron Richmond's *Water with Descent* (2016). The artist employs the powerful, suggestive imagery of Restoration sacramentalism, poised against a background of historic Christian crucifixion imagery, to achieve a similar effect: the incorporation of Mormonism's modern eruption on the scene into a long-standing Christian narrative. The distinctive, quotidian simplicity of the church's use of water, portrayed in a simple glass rather than a chalice, against a discontinuous backdrop of an Old Master's rendition of the descent from the cross, is itself a provocative yet reverent gesture. Christ's sacrificial offering links the two images; that the water is spatially distinct from the visual field of the descent acknowledges a rupture even as it makes its claim to continuity. The Restoration is a *new* story, with *new* emblems and a *new* vision of the holy, even as it acknowledges the beauty and power of prior manifestations of sacred worship.

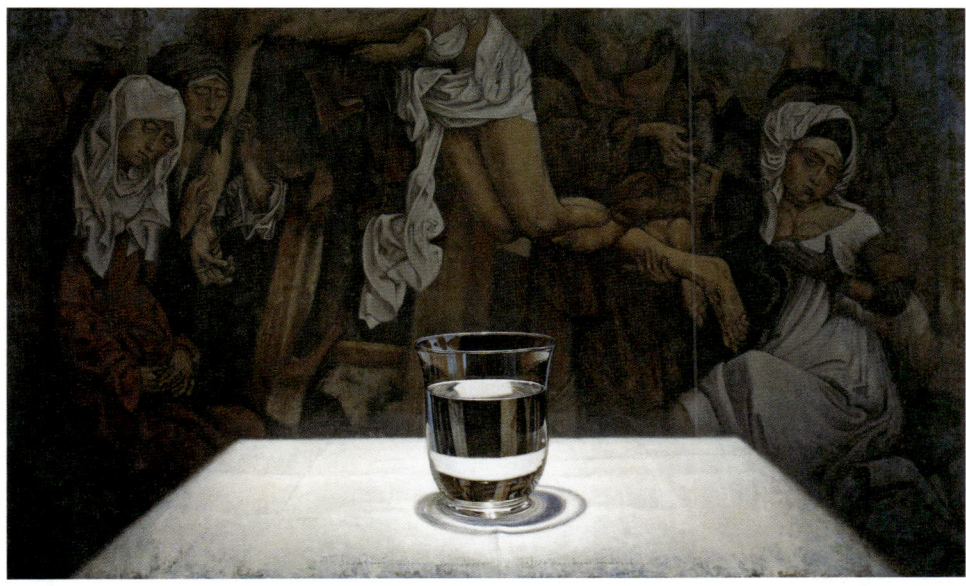

Fig. 1.13 Ron Richmond. *Water with Descent*, 2016, oil on canvas, Church of Jesus Christ of Latter-day Saints Church Museum of History and Art, Salt Lake City. Courtesy of the artist.

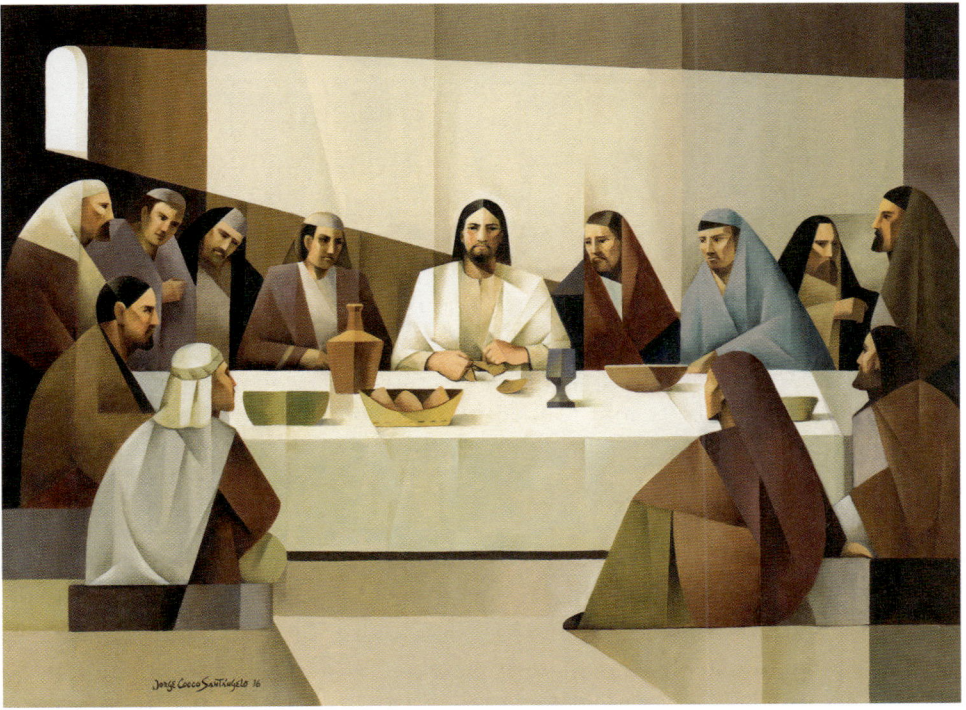

Fig. 1.14 Jorge Cocco, *The Last Supper*, 2016, oil on canvas, 30″ × 40″. Courtesy of the artist.

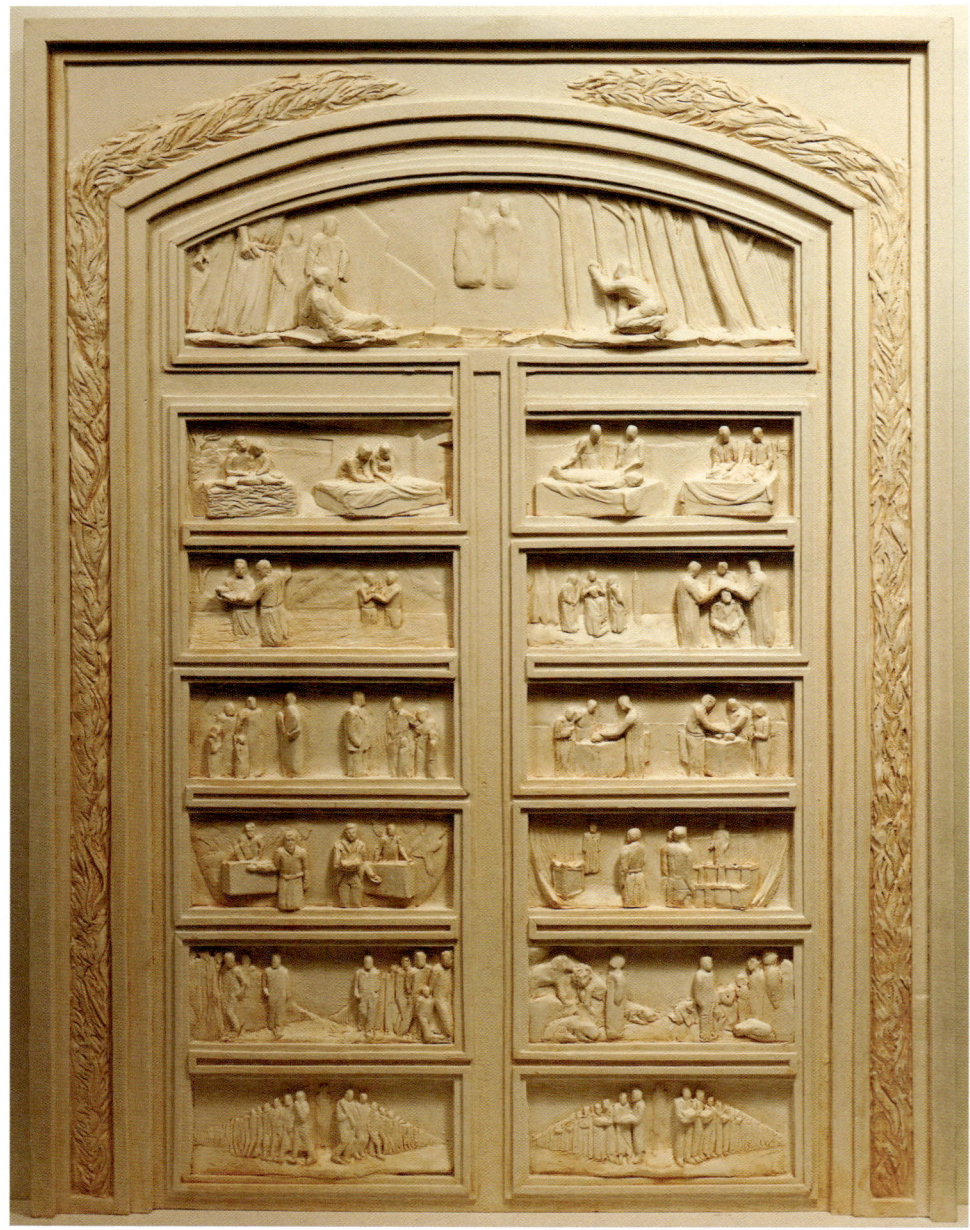

Fig. 1.15 Jacob Dobson, *Articles of Faith Doorway Maquette*, 2018, hydrostone plaster, 35″ × 25″. Courtesy of the artist.

This new landscape of possibilities has more recently been exploited beautifully by Jorge Cocco Santángelo. Born Catholic, Cocco deploys a self-described "sacrocubism" that at times hovers near the borders of Catholic spiritual expression, yet finds a comfortable home in contemporary Mormon spirituality as well.

Jacob Dobson does not so much appropriate Catholic forms to Mormon purposes as he inserts Mormon themes into a famously Catholic form. His *Articles of Faith Doorway* seems a clear homage to Ghiberti's Gates of Paradise doors of the Florence Duomo Baptistry. Ghiberti's focus was on the life of John the Baptist and the Christian virtues. Dobson's work parallels Ghiberti's sequence of panels but juxtaposes Old and New Testament themes with Restoration parallels (including immersive baptism and an LDS version of the Eucharistic service), all surmounted by a relief of Joseph Smith's First Vision.

The twenty-first-century attempt by an artist from a small Utah-based Christian sect to create an artistic and theological complement to one of the Renaissance's greatest achievements in Christian art can be seen as culturally audacious. Intentional or not, the gesture is also a greatly hopeful one. Latter-day Saints have long been accustomed to emphasizing our peculiarity. The sense of distinctness has served the purposes of a people intent on being "distinct and different," in Spencer W. Kimball's words.[52] Difference has also served the ends of a sometimes hostile world anxious to marginalize and quarantine a dangerous "viper on the hearth."[53]

The twenty-first century bodes well to herald a reconfigured relationship. As Saints find more common ground and common purpose with fellow Christians, they might productively find themselves part of a richly diverse choir, rather than a competing quartet. Mormon art seems poised to speak and write and create in a common enterprise, bringing the fruits of a unique history and spiritual sensibility, while not shunning the feast already laid out so marvelously in a larger common past.

"The need for communality [in our] worship is the chief torment of man," Dostoevsky wrote.[54] He was never more wrong. Mormon art may yet play a role in putting that myth to rest.

NOTES

[1] Quoted in G. T. Eddy, *Dr Taylor of Norwich: Wesley's Arch-Heretic* (London: Epworth Press, 2003), 39.

[2] Frederick Barnard, "Culture," in *Dictionary of the History of Ideas*, ed. Philip P. Wiener (New York: Scribner's, 1973), 1:618.

[3] Gilbert K. Chesterton, *Orthodoxy* (New York: John Lane, 1908), 50.

[4] William Blake, "The Marriage of Heaven and Hell," in *Complete Poetry and Selected Prose of John Donne and the Complete Poetry of William Blake,* ed. John Hayward and Geoffrey Keynes (New York: Random House, 1941), 651.

[5] William Wordsworth, "Ode: Intimations of Immortality," in *Poetical Works*, ed. Ernest Selincourt and Helen Darbyshire (Oxford: Oxford University Press, 1989), 499.

[6] Ralph Waldo Emerson, "Nature," in *Essays* (Boston: Houghton Mifflin, 1883), 103. My emphasis added.

[7] *Evening and Morning Star* 1.1 (June 1832): 7.

[8] "Ward Teachers' Message," *Improvement Era*, June 1945, 354.

[9] Stan Larson, "The King Follett Discourse: A Newly Amalgamated Text," *BYU Studies* 18, no. 2 (Winter 1978): 202.

[10] Augustine, *Confessions*, XII.

[11] Samuel T. Coleridge, "Notebooks," in *Samuel Taylor Coleridge*, ed. H. J. Jackson (Oxford: Oxford University Press, 1985), 555.

[12] Gregory of Nyssa, *Gregory of Nyssa: The Life of Moses*, ed. Richard J. Payne, trans. Abraham J. Malherbe and Everett Ferguson, Classics of Western Spirituality (New York: Paulist Press, 1978), 43.

[13] Pseudo-Dionysius, *On the Divine Names and Mystical Theology,* ed. C. E. Rolt (Kila, MT: Kessinger, 1991), 152.

[14] Coleridge, *Samuel Taylor Coleridge,* 555.

[15] William Mulder, "'Essential Gestures': Craft and Calling in Contemporary Mormon Letters," *Weber Studies* 10, no. 3 (Fall 1993): 7.

[16] *Joseph Smith Papers: Histories,* ed. Karen Lynn Davidson, David J. Whittaker, Mark Ashurst-McGee, and Richard L. Jensen (Salt Lake City: Church Historian's Press, 2012), 1:222.

[17] Rudolf Otto, *The Idea of the Holy*, trans. J. W. Harvey (London: Oxford University Press, 1950), 27.

[18] *New York Herald,* August 4, 1842.

[19] D&C 130:5.

[20] Larson, "King Follett," 200–201.

[21] Donald Bergsma et al., "The Lamps of Mormon Architecture," *Dialogue: A Journal of Mormon Thought* 3, no. 1 (Spring 1968): 19.

[22] John Kelly, "'Surrender Dorothy' Painted on a Beltway Overpass—What's the Story?," *Washington Post*, June 24, 2011, https://www.washingtonpost.com/local/surrender-dorothy-painted-on-a-beltway-overp ass—whats-the-story/2011/06/23/AGduf6kH_story.html.

[23] William James, *Varieties of Religious Experience* (Cambridge, MA: Harvard University Press, 1985), 362.

[24] The expression is Soren Kierkegaard's, *Fear and Trembling and the Sickness unto Death* (Princeton, NJ: Princeton University Press, 2013), 459.

[25] Emil Brunner, *Man in Revolt*, trans. Olive Wyon (London: Lutterworth Press, 1953), 90.

[26] Parley P. Pratt, *Key to the Science of Theology* (Liverpool: F. D. Richards, 1855), 33.

[27] Tad Walch, "Art Depicting Jesus Christ to Become the Standard Focus of Foyers in Latter-day Saint Meetinghouses," *Deseret News,* May 11, 2020, https://www.deseret.com/faith/2020/5/11/21254732/art-jesus-christ-church-mormon-lds-meetinghouses.

[28] See D&C 130:22; Church of Jesus Christ of Latter-day Saints, "Mother in Heaven," https://www.chur chofjesuschrist.org/study/manual/gospel-topics-essays/mother-in-heaven?lang=eng.

[29] "The Father and the Son: A Doctrinal Exposition by the First Presidency and the Twelve," in *Messages of the First Presidency,* comp. James R. Clark (Salt Lake City: Bookcraft, 1971), 5:34.

[30] *Times and Seasons,* March 1. 1842.

[31] *The Book of Common Prayer,* 1549 edition, http://justus.anglican.org/resources/BCp/1549/Burial_1549. htm; Mark Chapman, *Anglicanism: A Very Short Introduction* (New York: Oxford University Press, 2006), 26.

[32] Bruce Gordon, *Calvin* (New Haven, CT: Yale University Press, 2009), 255.

[33] Gordon, *Calvin,* 336.

[34] James E. Talmage, *The House of the Lord* (Salt Lake City: Deseret Book, 1971), 54.

[35] Reported in *Complete Discourses of Brigham Young*, ed. Richard S. Van Wagoner (Salt Lake City: Smith-Petit Foundation, 2009), 1:188.

[36] "Die Kirche ohne Mauer," letter 46 in *Jacob Boehme*, ed. Robin Waterfield (Berkeley, CA: North Atlantic Books, 2001), 16.

[37] Andrew F. Ehat and Lyndon W. Cook, eds., *The Words of Joseph Smith* (Orem, UT: Grandin Book, 1991), 63.

[38] Scott H. Faulring, Kent P. Jackson, and Robert J. Matthews, eds., *Joseph Smith's New Translation of the Bible: Original Manuscripts* (Provo, UT: Religious Studies Center, 2004), 102 (Moses 6:59). The 1878 and subsequent editions of the Pearl of Great Price, following OT2, vary slightly: "by reason of transgression cometh the fall, which fall bringeth death."

[39] Thomas O'Dea's claim is paraphrased in Dean L. May, "Mormons," in *Harvard Encyclopedia of American Ethnic Groups*, ed. Stephan Thernstrom (Cambridge, MA: Harvard University Press, 1980), 720.

[40] "United Methodists Claim LDS Not Really Christian," *Idaho Statesman,* May 11, 2000, A2; "Striving for Acceptance," *Washington Post,* February 9, 2002, B9.

[41] Hartman Rector Jr., "The Gospel," BYU devotional, September 29, 1985, https://speeches.byu.edu/talks/hartman-rector-jr/gospel/.

[42] Virginia Sorenson, *A Little Lower than the Angels* (New York: Knopf, 1942; repr., Salt Lake City: Signature, 1997), 4.

43 Mary Lythgoe Bradford, "Preface" to Sorensen, *A Little Lower* (1997), x–xi.

44 The curator of the museum, Leslie Anderson, confirmed that when she assumed her post in 2015, the catalogue designation was *Campsite Along the Mormon Trail*. She corrected the entry, although in deference to modern sensitivities it is identified as *Roma Camp* rather than *Gypsy* (or *Gipsy*) *Camp*. Correspondence from curator to Madilyn Abbe, March 18, 2022.

45 "Pioneer Artists: New Exhibit Features Art by Nine Early Utah Artists," *Deseret News,* September 26, 1993, https://www.deseret.com/1993/9/26/19067714/pioneer-artists-new-exhibit-features-art-by-nine-early-utah-artists.

46 See these and other examples with sources in Terryl Givens, *The Viper on the Hearth: Mormons, Myths, and the Construction of Heresy* (New York: Oxford University Press, 1997), chap. 7, "'They Ain't Whites . . . They're Mormons': Fictive Responses to the Anxiety of Seduction."

47 Surgeon General's Office, *Statistical Report on the Sickness and Mortality in the Army of the United States . . . From January, 1855 to January, 1860* (Washington, DC: George W. Bowman, 1860), 301–302.

48 Dean L. May, "Mormons," in *Harvard Encyclopedia of American Ethnic Groups*, ed. Stephan Thernstrom (Cambridge, MA: Harvard University Press, 1980), 720.

49 B. H. Roberts, *Comprehensive History of the Church of Jesus Christ of Latter-day Saints* (Provo, UT: Brigham Young University Press, 1965), 5:297.

50 "Friends of other faiths" has replaced "investigators." Gordon B. Hinckley warned against the intemperate use of the phrase "only true church" ("They are hard words for those of other faiths. We don't need to exploit them"), *Church News,* June 3, 2000, https://www.thechurchnews.com/2000/6/3/23246390/messages-of-inspiration-from-president-hinckley-87. A recent conference at Brigham Young University replaced the word "apostasy" with the more literal and less offensive rendering of the original Greek as "standing apart." See *Standing Apart*, ed. Miranda Wilcox and John D. Young (New York: Oxford University Press, 2014).

51 See ten such examples in Bridge Talbot, "10 Stunning Examples of Stained Glass Windows in LDS Meeting Houses," *LDS Living,* June 9, 2018, https://www.ldsliving.com/10-stunning-examples-of-stained-glass-windows-in-lds-meeting-houses/s/81007.

52 Spencer W. Kimball, "The Role of Righteous Women," General Conference, October 1979, https://www.churchofjesuschrist.org/study/general-conference/1979/10/the-role-of-righteous-women?lang=eng.

53 The title of a series on the Church by Alfred Henry Lewis published in *Cosmopolitan* magazine in March, April, and May 1911.

54 Fyodor Dostoevsky, *Brothers Karamazov*, trans. Richard Pevear and Larissa Volokhonsky (New York: Knopf, 1992), 254.

2

TEMPLE ART RENEWAL, 2000–2022

COLLEEN MCDANNELL

In the year 2000, cultural critic Tom Wolfe penned a blistering obituary essay commemorating the achievements of a relatively unknown sculptor, Frederick E. Hart (1943–1999). Hart had sculpted three monumental tympana for the west facade of Washington National Cathedral (1974–1982) and the bronze statue *The Three Soldiers* (1984) at the Vietnam memorial. Wolfe marveled at the artist's "God-given genius"— an ability to pull "perfectly formed human figures out of stone and clay at will and rapidly." The essay did not simply acknowledge the passing of a talented artist. It forcefully condemned the art world for having ignored the type of art and artists that Hart represented. From Wolfe's perspective, the New York art establishment ignored Hart because he made realistic, representational art. Perhaps more important, Hart produced art for religious buildings and was personally religious. In a secular world captivated by abstract modernist art, there was no recognition of the brilliance of Frederick Hart.[1]

Toward the end of his essay, Wolfe shifted his perspective. He observed that "with metronomic regularity the dawn of each new century has seen a collapse of one reigning taste and the establishment of another." For Wolfe, what was rising was a new appreciation of figurative and representational painting—a new "avant-garde." Young artists trained in traditional drawing and painting techniques had held a sellout show in an influential New York gallery. Collectors were snapping up their art. Critics gave a fresh look at once disdained French Academic painters such as William-Adolphe Bouguereau and the works of the "fashion painter" James Tissot. Placing Frederic Hart among these once ridiculed, now rediscovered artists, Wolfe concluded that the sculptor "will not have been the first major artist to have died 10 minutes before history absolved him and proved him right."[2]

Always the contrarian, Tom Wolfe cleverly poked fun at the "art worldlings" who celebrated paintings that he asserted took no skill to produce. However, what Wolfe failed to develop in the essay was his own observation of the critical role that religion played in concealing the talent of Frederic Hart. Many of Wolfe's "art worldlings" associated religion with the dreaded opposite of art, kitsch. For Hart, his art was intimately connected to his Christian commitments.[3] Consequently, while Hart's realism separated him from the prevailing modernist paradigm, his frank Catholicism and his work for the Episcopal Church also marginalized him in relation to the art establishment.

Hidden within the folds of the contemporary art world are the efforts of individuals and institutions to produce, support, and display paintings that speak to their deeply held religious convictions. These efforts and the art itself require examination. I argue in this chapter that during the first two decades of the twenty-first century, leaders within the Church of Jesus Christ of Latter-day Saints made a concerted effort to improve the quality of the visual art in their temples. This art renewal was funded and organized by a global, institutional church not known for its artistic sophistication. Indeed, during the previous half century church leaders were satisfied with art produced by non-Mormons and reproduced to the point that it had become stale and hackneyed. At best, this art was "beloved" because the Saints had formed intimate relationships with it through their devotional lives. At worst, it was a type of Mormon wallpaper, which, when inspected closely, revealed problematic racial, regional, and gender stereotypes.

A new consideration of the visual world within the temple has resulted from an intensified focus on temple rituals. In some ways the church was returning to an earlier time in Latter-day Saint history when "art missionaries" studied painting in France and then came home to uplift temple visual culture.[4] Landscapes, a part of nineteenth-century Mormon arts, have again taken on spiritual meaning.[5] In addition, the renewal of temple art reflects twentieth-century trends. A church concerned with correlation and coordination set up committees to oversee the commissioning, purchasing, and donation of paintings as well as to adjudicate their artistic and doctrinal merits. A church committed to making converts in a global religious marketplace wanted art to express racial and ethnic diversity as well as regional identity. Temple art renewal has benefited from the very paradigm shift that Tom Wolfe and others saw within the modern art world. The movement called "contemporary realism" gave figurative and representative painting new legitimacy. Talented Latter-day Saint artists, who had cultivated the skills needed to make such art, could now sell their works in galleries as well as to the church. They could survive as professional artists.

By the start of 2022 more than 160 Latter-day Saint temples had been evaluated and received new murals, original paintings, or improved art reproductions. More than three hundred original easel paintings and forty ordinance room murals have been placed in temples since 2000. For instance, when a new temple was built in Pocatello, Idaho, it contained sixty-six carefully placed images, which included eight original paintings and a restoration of Minerva Teichert's *Not Alone*. The newly renovated Mesa temple, twice the size of the Pocatello temple, houses 213 images, including twenty-three original paintings and four rooms of floor-to-ceiling murals. A giclée of Frederic Church's *Cotopaxi* (1855) secured from the Houston Art Museum is now in the temple in Quito, Ecuador. Church art curators purchase appropriate paintings at art auctions and accept donations from collectors. As new temples are built and older ones renovated, art will no longer be "seen as a decorative element of the temple" but rather considered as something "beautiful to look at" that provides "spiritual renewal."[6]

This chapter explores temple art by first focusing on the religious background that motivated this twenty-first-century renewal. Why did church leaders feel that existing temple art no longer was appropriate? I argue that if temple-going was to become a routine part of Latter-day Saint life, then art had to be supportive of a positive temple experience. Consequently, church leaders sought to oversee which images would be placed in the temple. I next lay out how changes in the wider art world (those changes that Tom Wolfe observed) facilitated the modernization of temple art. The popularity of contemporary realism dovetailed with the church's need for art that clearly communicated spiritual ideas. After presenting the religious and artistic context for renewal, I spend the remainder of the chapter exploring three genres of temple art that I believe may be used to classify the paintings: arts of the scripture, people of the temple, and murals and landscapes. To illustrate how these categories intersect with temple art renewal, I focus on a small handful of talented artists who have placed art in contemporary temples.

A TEMPLE-GOING PEOPLE

To understand the changes in temple art, we must begin with an understanding of the temple. Latter-day Saint temples stand in contrast to Sunday worship space in ward meetinghouses. A ward meetinghouse is not unlike a Protestant church. Architectural historian William Whyte describes churches as "a machine for listening in."[7] In addition to preaching and careful listening, Latter-day Saint churches are expected to provide efficient spaces for meetings and even sports and cultural events. Latter-day Saints and Protestants both assume that weekly worship takes place in a building that comes "alive" only when congregants enter. "The building itself," Whyte explains, "was meant to be meaningless."[8] The Saints intend that the ubiquitous, standardized, modest, and rational modern Mormon meetinghouse be practical.

The temple follows a different trajectory. Calling on the Hebrew Bible, Latter-day Saints see the temple as a way station between heaven and earth. Rather than being an auditory space, it is a performative space more akin to a Catholic cathedral than to an evangelical megachurch. Unlike Latter-day Saint Sunday services, which are accessible and inclusive of all, temple rituals are elaborate, formal, and exclusive. The space provides a heightened access to the divine not open to all. Latter-day Saints understand the temple as "the House of the Lord"—the sacred in a sacred/profane binary.

The temple is not a neutral or inconsequential space. Temple architecture, art, and even furniture and carpets actively participate in the construction of a certain type of experience. In the modern temple, paintings are everywhere. Ordinance rooms (sometimes called "instruction rooms") often have floor-to-ceiling murals. Framed artwork flanks the grand staircase in larger temples. The walls of hallways and waiting rooms are filled with art. There are paintings in the temple basement control rooms, in the copying room, and in staff offices. Only the sealing rooms (where couples and families are bound together for eternity) and the celestial room (the earthly symbol of heaven) typically are devoid of paintings. Sealing rooms have mirrors facing each other to produce "infinite" reflections, and celestial rooms often have magnificent art glass.

Over the past forty years, there has been an increasing number of temples built outside of the United States. Until the 1950s, all eight existing Latter-day Saint temples were in the Intermountain West (with the exception of Hawaii and Canada). At best, most Latter-day Saints "gathered to Zion" to attend those temples once in their lives. By the end of the 1980s, there were temples in places as far away as Frankfurt, Germany, but the regionality of temples still made it difficult for any but Utah Mormons to routinely attend. This orientation changed under the leadership of Gordon B. Hinckley, who in 1997 announced that more and smaller temples were to be built.[9]

President Hinckley wanted temple-going to become a routine religious activity for *all* Latter-day Saints. Delineating a few standardized architectural plans meant that faster temple production could occur. When Hinckley became church president there were forty-seven temples. When he died in 2008 there were 124. In the year 2000 alone, thirty-four temples were dedicated. This focus on temple-building continued with President Russell M. Nelson. By 2022 he had announced the construction of eighty-three temples—six more than Hinckley. Of those, most would be built outside of the United States, especially in the growth area of global Christianity—the Southern Hemisphere.[10] Temple-going thus came to distinguish the Latter-day Saints from other Christians who also sought converts in the global South. During the twentieth century, temple-*building* had become the single most unifying and distinguishing aspect of the church.[11] During the twenty-first century, it was hoped that temple-*going* would become a routine for all members.[12]

Church leaders encouraged members to see the temple as a space for contemplation and renewal as well as for performing rituals for themselves and the dead. In 2018, a directive was sent by temple executive director Larry Y. Wilson to temple presidents regarding how the Saints should be treated within the temple. Patrons should be made to feel welcome and comfortable so that they might decide to linger in the temple after performing their ordinances. While Latter-day Saints have always been encouraged to reflect or meditate in the celestial room following their participation in temple rituals, the directive urged temple presidents to be more flexible in permitting patrons to visit other areas of the temple such as the baptistry and sealing rooms. Patrons should feel free to walk down hallways as part of their worship experience, to sit and reflect, to view and ponder the temple artwork without disruption.[13]

Behind the statements in the directive was the problem of balancing temple efficiency with the frequently messy spiritual needs of people. Art was not essential for ordinances, but if creating a spiritual experience was to be a temple goal, then art had merit. Church leaders sought to cultivate the long-standing idea of the temple as a place of refuge. So it made no sense to tell patrons to "move along" when they paused to look at a piece of art.[14] Art would be a critical element in expanding the temple's role as a sacred space of solace, comfort, and rest. Patrons should be able to finish their ordinances and then spend the rest of their day experiencing the full temple.

ENSURING BETTER ART

What had church leaders found problematic about the art previously placed in temples? One problem may be summarized as a "lack of cohesiveness."[15] Since the 1980s, temples had been built with little care taken to how the visual arts might heighten the temple experience. There was little relationship between the images on the walls and the values or covenants conveyed within the temple ordinances. A related problem was that the art placed in the temples was the same art that appeared in numerous Latter-day Saint publications, in visitor centers, and on the walls of Mormon homes. Some of this art had originally been prepared for the Mormon Pavilion at the 1964 World's Fair. Other images came from the 1973 Gospel in Art program that encouraged the Saints to fill their homes with scriptural imagery. While past artists were talented illustrators, years of reproducing the works of Harry Anderson, Arnold Friberg, Tom Lovell, and John Scott rendered their work unremarkable. For lack of a better term, some temple art expressed a technically unsophisticated "Deseret Book style." Other prints were faded, drained of their original color. Even newspaper reporters who covered the openings of new temples asked why there was no original art in spaces filled with exquisitely crafted furniture and handmade carpets.[16]

There also was the problem of geocentrism. Although temples were being built all over the United States and even the world, many paintings within the temples echoed the landscapes of Utah. If church leaders counseled members to build up Zion where they lived, why would the Atlanta temple have two prints of Utah mountains? How could the Saints feel a sense of being in their spiritual home when the temple looked like an alien territory? Would it be possible to balance the feel of otherworldliness with familiarity? Church leaders decided that members would be more inclined to attend their local temple if it reflected and celebrated indigenous landscapes.

Around the year 2000, church leaders began to commission original art.[17] Given the centrality of the temple, institutional control over art selection was imperative. In 2001 an Art Evaluation Committee (AEC) was formed by the First Presidency to recommend works of art for temples, meetinghouses, and special projects that supported the mission of the church.[18] If at the end of that review process the piece was acceptable, the First Presidency then judged whether or not it would "help all patrons feel God's divine love."[19] The First Presidency had the last word. At no level were reasons given for any decision—although rumors and speculation circulated.

Art renewal was also coordinated by an influential director of the Temple Department. In 2011 Larry Y. Wilson became a General Authority Seventy and soon after assumed oversight over the global construction of the church's temples along with the Presiding Bishopric. Shortly after becoming director, he toured the temple in Provo, Utah. Built in 1972, the massive structure had a modernist circular design but conventional art. Wilson was dismayed to find that three prints of Harry Anderson's *The Second Coming* (1969) were placed at different spots in the temple.[20] Unlike other Latter-day Saints who may have had little exposure to the arts, Wilson was a part of the Mormon elite: undergraduate degree from Harvard, MBA from Stanford, years working as an executive in California healthcare, and a high-level church authority in Hong Kong. Since the nineteenth century, Latter-day Saints understood their art as proof of their respectability, gentility, refinement, and sophistication.[21] Increasingly highly educated and well traveled, Latter-day Saints like Wilson had high expectations for their church. The holy space of the temple should display better art.

By the time Larry Wilson was released from his calling in 2019, art renewal was secured. Wilson had found institutional support in Bill Williams, director of temple architecture and design. Williams, who had been a church architect since 2003, had long been a supporter of design elements tailored to local themes as well as sustainable architecture. Wilson had secured a commitment from the First Presidency to increase the budget for art. That enabled hiring Arch Williams, who was appointed manager of temple art in 2016. Larry Wilson had participated in a seminar on temple art, telling artists about the directive encouraging temple patrons to "view and ponder artwork without disruption."[22] In addition, Wilson determined that any new art commissioned for the temples would appear only in temples. Artists would have to give over copyright to the church, and the church would make high-quality reproductions (giclées) for exclusive use in temples. Latter-day Saints would no longer see temple images in church publications or visitor centers. Temple art would be "special."

CONTEMPORARY CLASSICAL REALISM AND CHURCH ARTISTS

Parallel to this institutional commitment to upgrading temple art was the shift occurring in contemporary art that Tom Wolfe noted in his 2000 obituary essay on Fredrick Hart. During the 1960s, church leaders did not have many places to turn to in the art world to secure the type of art that they felt was appropriate for church use. It made sense that they would seek out magazine illustrators like Harry Anderson because prevailing trends in the fine arts leaned toward the abstract. Modernist art followed the lead of Wassily Kandinsky, who urged artists in *On the Spiritual in Art* (1912) to reject the "religious" as shallow, descriptive, and decorative and instead to embrace the "spiritual" as the essence of color and form. True art did not simply represent an object but should seek deeper dimensions and elicit multiple meanings. The human figure should be portrayed by implication, not imitation. Other modernist artists insisted that art should make political statements, innovate with design materials, and deconstruct the commonplace. Modernism valued breaking with conventions, rather than clearly communicating eternal truths.

While realism (like that of Frederick Hart's sculptures) did have a long history in American art, by the mid-twentieth century it frequently was disparaged as domestic, regional, sentimental, and/or didactic. But realism was about to go through an artistic revival. In 1969, the same year that Harry Anderson painted *The Second Coming,* Richard F. Lack (1929–2009) established Atelier Lack in Minneapolis. There, in a very quiet Minnesotan way, he pushed back against midcentury modernism. At a time when modernism dominated art colleges and universities, Lack returned to the atelier model of the nineteenth-century French academies, where intensive training in drawing and painting produced highly realistic landscapes, still lifes, and portraiture. Lack sought mastery of color and light rather than innovation. His goal was to train his eye to see shapes, not to create political or personal statements. Rather than reject the artistic traditions of the past, he sought to continue the old ways of teaching in which students learned from masters. Lack termed this style of art "classical realism."[23]

Realism was not isolated to Minnesota. Utah had its own notable realist artists: Alvin Gittins (1922–1981), Le Conte Stewart (1891–1990), and William "Bill" Whitaker (1943–2018). Classical realism was also not the only kind of realism. Students trained at Atelier Lack established teaching studios in Florence, Italy, and New York City. In 1981, the Pennsylvania Academy of Fine Arts hosted the exhibition *Contemporary American Realism Since 1960,* and a year later the art critic at *Newsweek* published "Art Imitates Life: The Revival of Realism."[24] A lively and incredibly diverse set of artists was making realist paintings and sculptures all along the East Coast. "Art should be about life and not about art," became their anti-modernist rallying cry.[25] Although the artists chronicled by *Newsweek* preferred their postmodern realism to be ironic and edgy, other painters echoed Jacob Collins (1964–), who affirmed, "I am motivated by beauty."[26] While modernism and postmodernism certainly did not retreat from the art world, by the new millennium contemporary realism was now a commercially viable and pluralistically rich third stream within modern art.

The popularity of contemporary realism in its various forms ensured that there were more serious, professional artists painting in this style. There was a market for art that was beautiful, orderly, deliberate, and disciplined. Realism no longer was laughable in fine art circles. The aesthetic of classical realism resonated with the aesthetic and religious sensibilities of Latter-day Saint church leaders. By the year 2000, those leaders no longer needed to commission paintings from commercial artists for temples. Latter-day Saint artists who worked in this style could sell their art in galleries as well as to the church. A confluence had formed between a modern art movement and Latter-day Saint temple aesthetics.

THE ARTS OF SCRIPTURE

One of the earliest artists who painted in classical realist style to catch the eye of the church was Jeffrey Hein (1974–). Hein studied painting and drawing at various schools in Idaho and Utah, went on a Latter-day Saint mission, and began a full-time painting career in 2002. Initially, Hein was not interested in painting religious subjects because his experience growing up in a Latter-day Saint community had convinced him that church art was not particularly "artistic." He described this point of view in an interview: "When I started painting twenty years ago, the standard church painting was so illustrative and kind of *frou frou*. It's much more classical now. Classical realist artists are setting the standard."[27] Hein moves easily between preparing his carefully crafted portraits, teaching artists in his atelier, and painting religious pieces.

Jeffrey Hein is a master of what I will call the "arts of scripture." By this I mean art depicting narratives of the Old and New Testaments, the Book of Mormon, or the Doctrine and Covenants. Both his biblical narrative, *Doubting Thomas* (2002), and his historical narrative, *First Vision* (2002), were purchased by the Church History Museum. His best-known painting, *Christ in America*, illustrates a popular passage from the Book of Mormon (with a parallel in the New Testament). After addressing the assembled multitude in the New World, Jesus blessed their children and said, "Behold your little ones" (3 Nephi 17). In 2011, Hein's original painting was placed behind the recommend desk in the newly built temple in San Salvador, El Salvador. Giclée copies were then displayed in multiple temples, including those in Concepción, Chile (2018), Arequipa, Peru (2019), and Mesa, Arizona (2021). Hein believes that every temple in Utah (except the Salt Lake temple, currently being renovated) has a copy of *Christ in America*.[28] It is one of the most popular and sophisticated examples of classical realism in the church's temples.

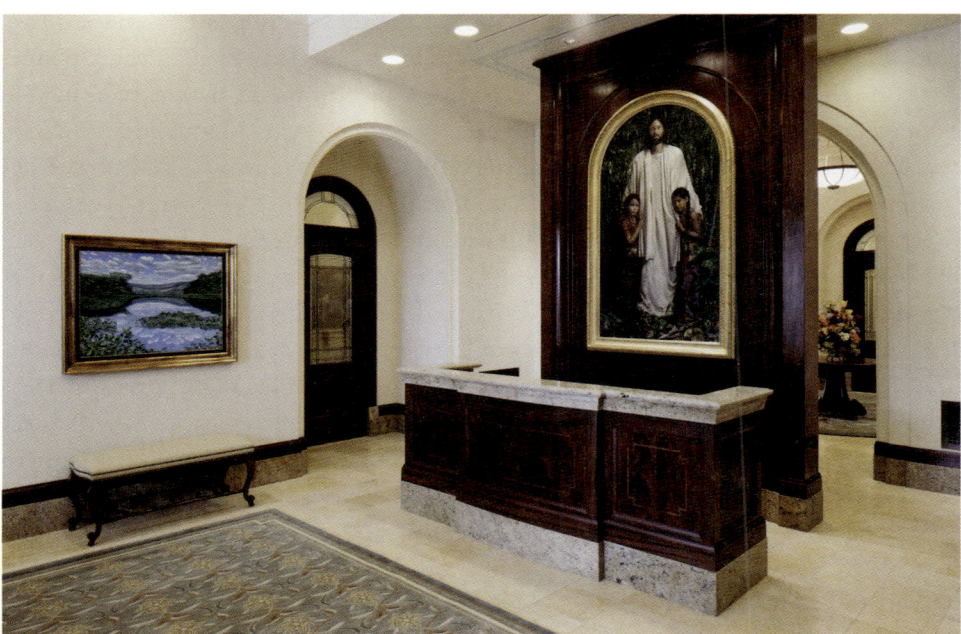

Fig. 2.1 Placement of the original oil painting *Christ in America*, by Jeffrey Hein, behind the recommend desk in the San Salvador, El Salvador, temple in 2011. © Intellectual Reserve, Inc.

Christ in America is a large, frontal, full-length portrait set against dense tropical greenery. Two children snuggle next to a draped figure who commands the exact center of the canvas. In contrast to the classical robes of Christ, the stunning array of green hues of the jungle, the children's jewelry, and their leather and fur purses all serve to create an ancient "native" feel. While the tableau is exotic, the faces of the children and the Savior are profoundly familiar. The children look apprehensive, as if a stranger had approached, but they are calmed by his steady, supporting arms. These are not generic children nor a universal Christ but individual and specific people. All three of the faces look directly outward, welcoming the viewer to also enter into that secure space.

Christ in America is intimate and quiet. Hein follows the Latter-day Saint pictorial convention of eliminating halos, underscoring the humanity of Christ. Unlike other artists who paint from photographs, Hein followed the Old Master tradition of using live models.[29] Art was to be a representation of something that was "really" there. *Christ in America* took seven months to prepare and involved working with a pair of seven-year-old models, one of whom was Hein's daughter.[30] Like a father's, the Savior's arms gently tuck around the children. The children themselves are painted such that they symmetrically balance each other, and their expressions are of subtle concern rather than of pious devotion. The figures in *Christ in America* also have darker hair and facial tones than do earlier Latter-day Saint biblical narratives. *Christ in America* aptly sets the mood for what church leaders hope will be the temple experience: that through the ordinances each specific and individual member will experience the gentle warmth of the Savior.

As often noted, the Church of Jesus Christ of Latter-day Saints has in the past fifty years placed images of Christ "essentially everywhere."[31] Indeed, in 2020 church president Russell M. Nelson announced that a representation of Bertel Thorvaldsen's marble statue *Christus* (1833) would be the church's "symbol" or logo.[32] In addition to Hein, many Latter-day Saint artists (e.g., Michael Malm, Elspeth Young, Al R. Young, Albin Veselka, and Dan Wilson) have painted standing or full-figure representations of Christ for temples. These images do not set Jesus in a biblical narrative (although many others do) but rather present him either alone or with a child or single individual. Christ is represented as the authoritative, ever-present companion. Church leaders seek to offer temple patrons many possible depictions of Jesus so that no one single image becomes, in effect, canonized. The Art Evaluation Committee also encouraged artists to paint what the committee calls the "historical" Jesus, meaning a man who is "Semitic" and not a blond, blue-eyed Jesus.[33] Given that many temples are opening in the Southern Hemisphere, the hope is to "broaden the image of Jesus more culturally."[34]

Artist Jeffrey Hein insists that the church does not determine how he paints. The temple art he produces comes from his own artistic sensibilities and his commitment to Christ. "Painting people is really rather magical," he explained to me. "You paint and paint and paint. Then there is a short window of time when the face comes into focus. And it is just, like, whoa! It's almost like you've created life."[35] Unlike earlier artists, who, following the standards of commercial art, altered their works to fit the needs of the

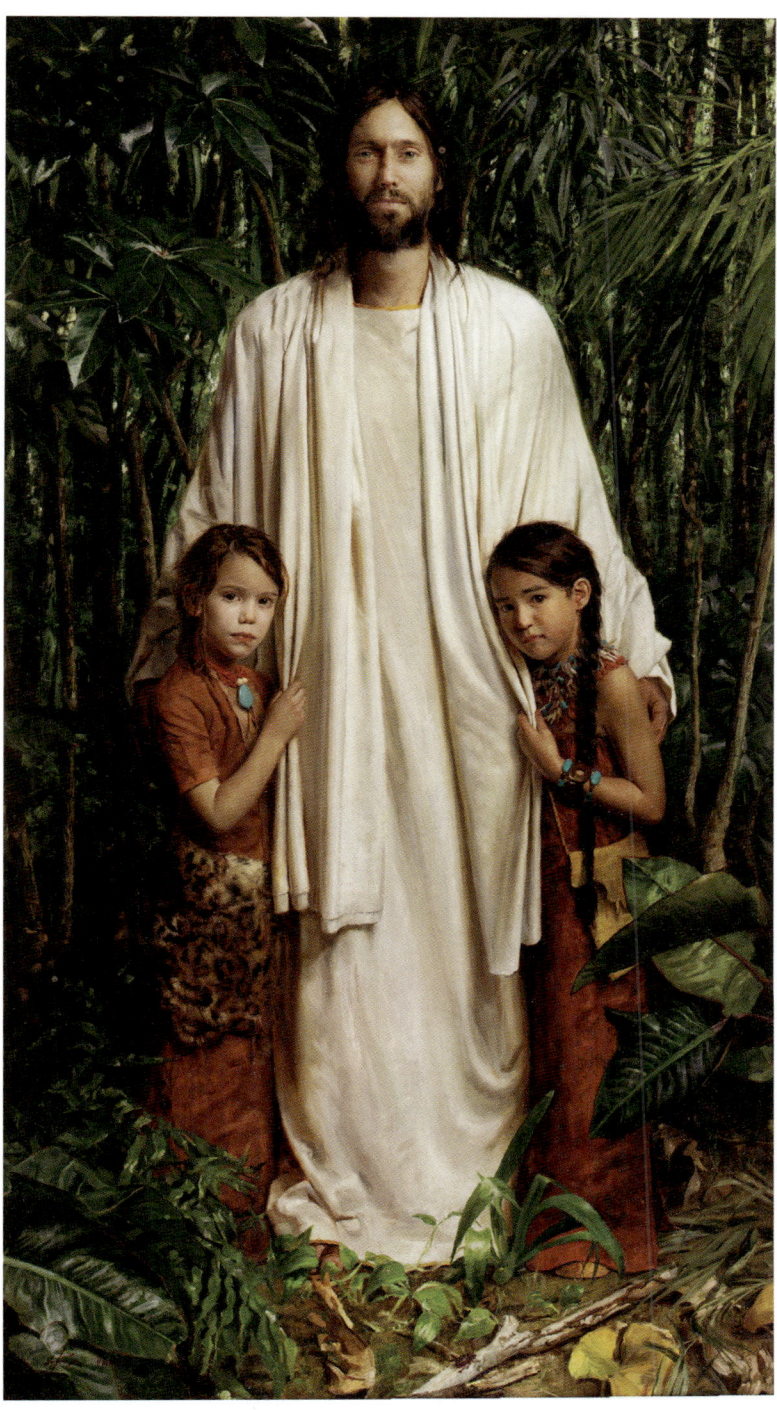

Fig. 2.2 Jeffrey Hein, *Christ in America*, 2010, oil on canvas, 72″ × 40″. © Intellectual Reserves, Inc.

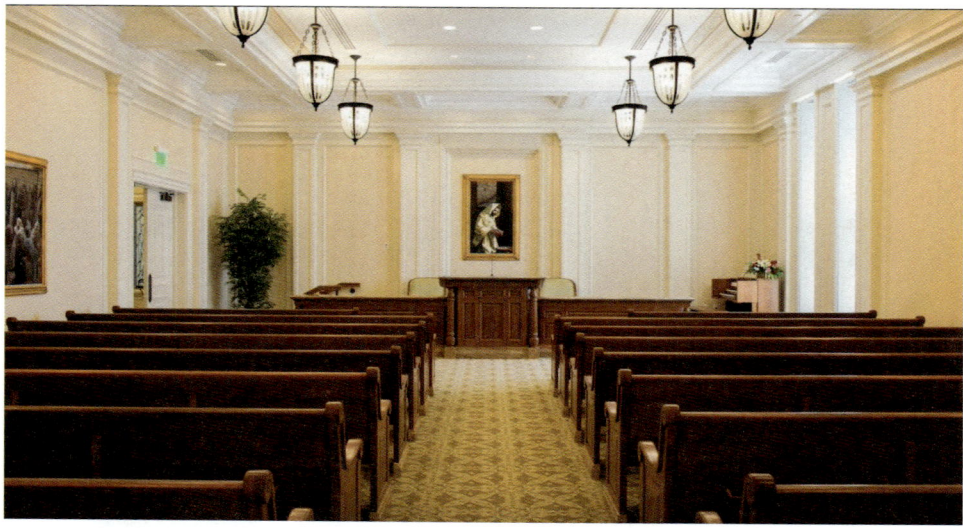

Fig. 2.3 Original of Al Young's *He Hath Anointed Me* displayed in the Payson, Utah, temple.

customer, Hein follows the codes of the fine arts. He understands his painting as a cohesive, creative expression of his own vision. The customer—whether someone strolling in a gallery or a person employed by the LDS Church—accepts the painting as it is and either buys it or not. Hein is honored that his artwork is hung in temples and in church museums and conference centers. But he knows that if for whatever reason the church altered its aesthetics, he would continue to paint in the same way.

To have a profound commitment to one's artistic vision does not mean that artists have an easy time with the church. Jeffrey Hein was given a commission (with an agreed-upon fee) for a painting to be placed in a temple. The piece he completed, *As a Hen Gathereth*, was based on scriptural passages where the protective character of God is compared to a hen who gathers her chicks around her (Luke 13:34 and 3 Nephi 10:6). *As a Hen Gathereth* went on to win the Director's Award at the 2012 Springville Museum's *Spiritual and Religious* exhibition. While the Art Evaluation Committee approved of the painting, it was eventually rejected at a higher level—in spite of it having been commissioned. Was it because it was too expensive? Did someone feel that chickens did not belong in temple art? Whatever the reason, the sense was that the painting was "tainted." Hein then could only sell it to a dealer for half its worth. The dealer sold it for even less to a collector. Poignantly, the collector eventually donated the painting to the church, and it was subsequently placed in the Jordan River temple in South Jordan, Utah.

For Hein, the experience was hurtful. He retained the copyright on *As a Hen Gathereth*, but normally the church retains copyright on art it purchases, and so artists cannot oversee (or financially benefit from) the work's reproduction. While currently artists are paid market value for their art and may reproduce a limited number of prints, this was not the case in the early years of the artistic renewal. Initially, artists could

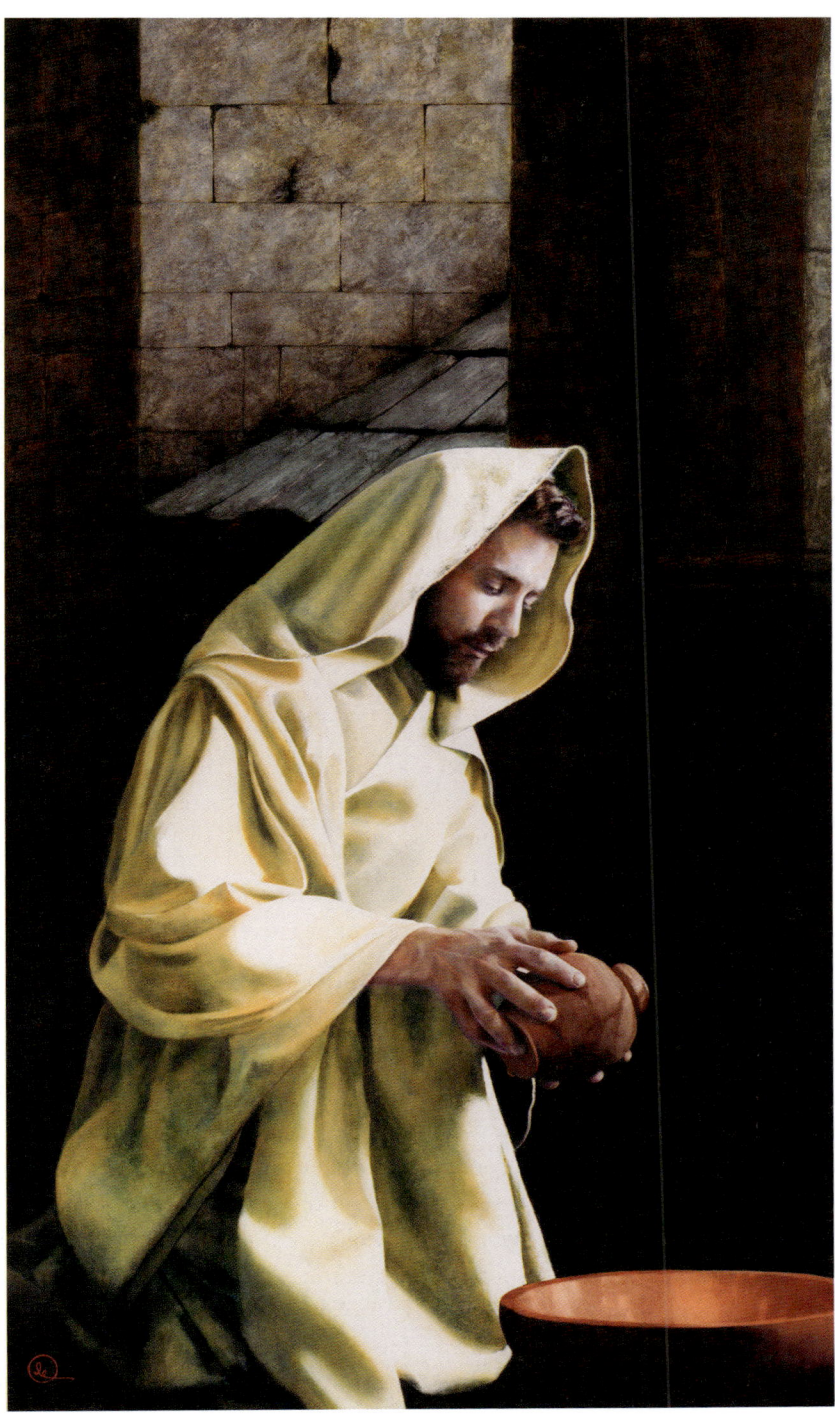

Fig. 2.4   Al Young, *He Hath Anointed Me*, 2015, oil on canvas, 51″ × 30″. © Intellectual Reserves, Inc.

not even sign their temple art or include it in their portfolio, but this too has changed. Many temples display *Christ in America,* but church leaders do not want to devalue the image by mass-producing it. In spite of his difficulties with the church, Hein insists that his commitment to the gospel is strong, and he acknowledges the efforts that church leaders have made to be more professional in their dealings with artists.

Negotiating with living artists is only one way that the church secures art. In 2014, real estate investor Jack R. Wheatley bought at auction Edmund Blair Leighton's (1852–1922) painting *The Blind Man at the Pool of Siloam* (1879) for $65,000 and donated it to Brigham Young University.[36] For a short time, the painting was placed in the Manhattan temple and a giclée was made for the Mesa temple. While the biblical story is about Jesus healing a blind man (John 9:6–41), the painting depicts neither Jesus nor the healed man. Instead, it illustrates people lingering around the pool just as a blind man is about to enter the water as commanded by Jesus. The palette is muted. What draws the viewer's eye is not the healing but the various positions of the people and the multiple planes of architectural structures. While the biblical narrative is there, it is not obvious.

Likewise, in Albin Veselka's (1979–) *The Work of the Sabbath* the figures are realistically painted but the painting is modern in its intimation of, rather than imitation of, the biblical story. Veselka, who received his BFA at Brigham Young University–Idaho, has more than thirty original paintings in the church's temples and many more giclées.[37] *The Work of the Sabbath* is drawn from John 5:1–16, where Jesus heals an invalid man who had been sitting at the pool of Bethesda. When the healed man takes up his mat and walks, the Jewish leaders tell him it is not lawful for him to move his bed on the Sabbath. As with *The Blind Man at the Pool of Siloam,* the healing Savior is not the central focus of the painting but rather the person made whole. The divine healer stands at a distance from the healed man, who is carrying his mat and conversing with the Jews. Following a long-standing Christian convention of negatively portraying the Jews, they walk in a shadow while Jesus is bathed in light in the background. The dark folds of the priestly robes, the men's headdresses, and their jewelry present them as regal and prosperous (and perhaps even pretentious). The details ensnare the viewer in the scene. The decentered Jesus, however, makes the viewer "work" somewhat to recall this particular gospel narrative of supernatural healing. It is not a simple representation of a Bible story.

Veselka's paintings are highly saturated with color and filled with architectural and landscape detail. In previous years, because the church owns the copyright of the art it purchases, temple designers felt free to make altered giclées of Veselka's expansive paintings. Now, however, designers may not crop out the broad horizon of *Cast Your Nets on the Right Side* to make the figure of Christ larger, as they did in the Pocatello temple. The Savior must remain in the distance, with the action focused on the fishermen who are following his directive. Designers no longer may take precedence over the cohesiveness of the art as conceived by the artist.[38]

Keeping designers from altering a painting is one way of maintaining the "truth" or what contemporary church curators call the "accuracy" of art placed in a temple. Beginning in

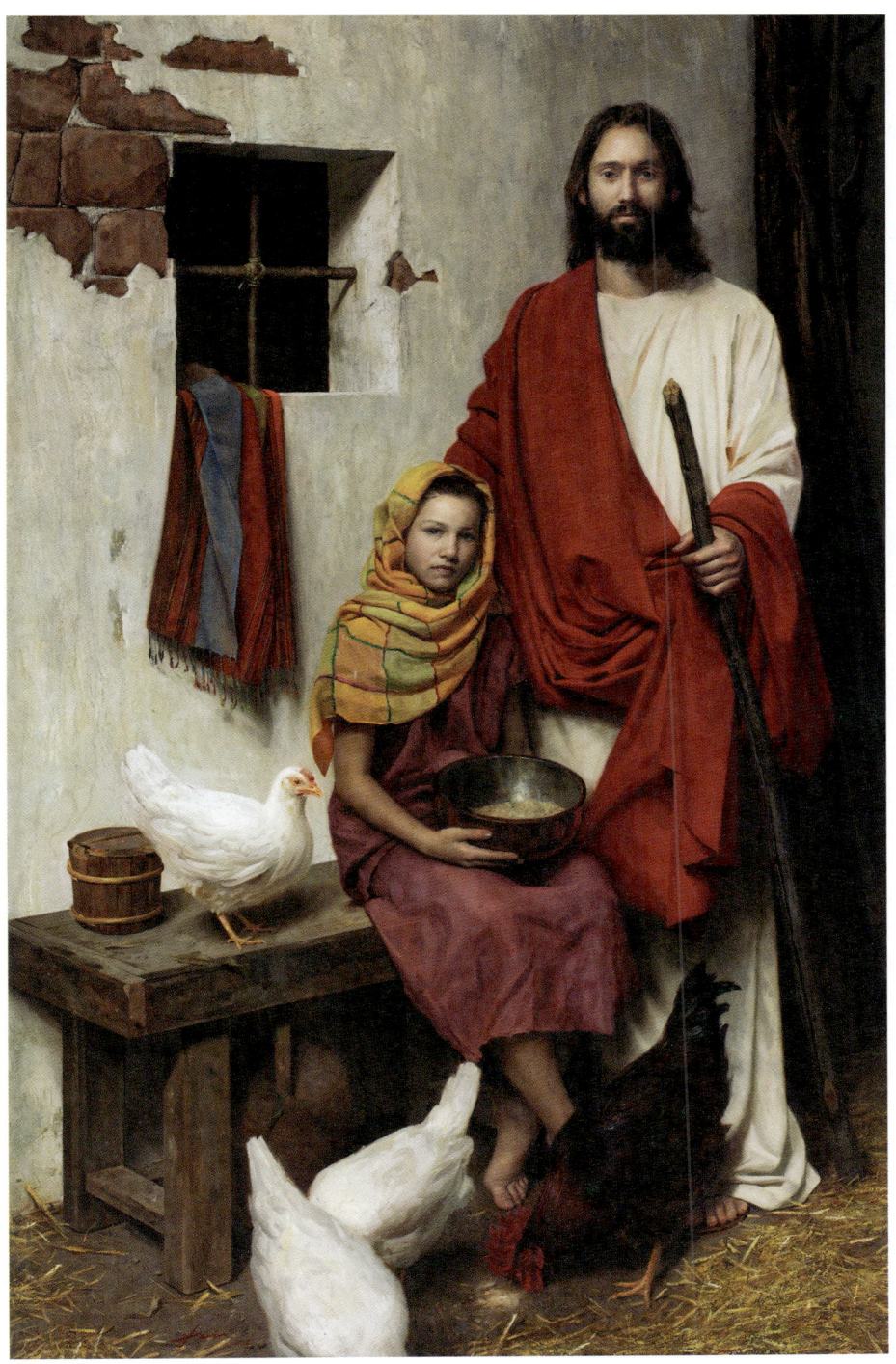

Fig. 2.5 Jeffery Hein, *As a Hen Gathereth*, 2012, oil on canvas, 74″ × 47″.

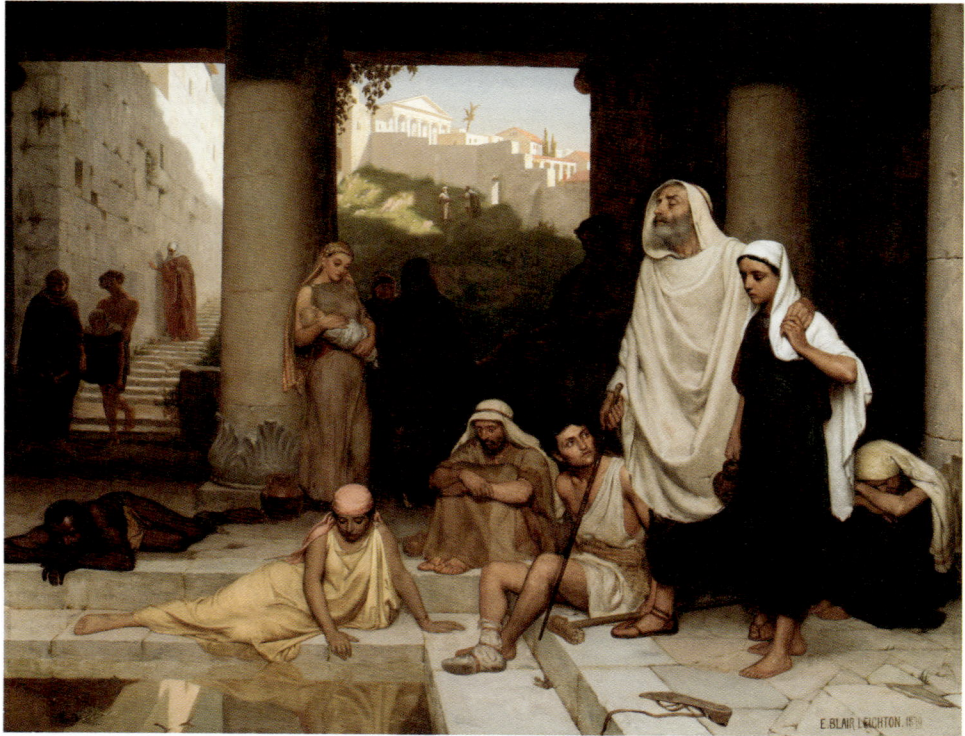

Fig. 2.6 Edmund Blair Leighton, *The Blind Man at the Pool of Siloam*, 1879, oil on canvas, 40 1/4″ × 50 5/16″, Brigham Young University Museum of Art, purchased with funds provided by Jack R. Wheatley, 2014. Image courtesy of Brigham Young University.

the nineteenth century with the visions of Joseph Smith, the church privileged sight as the most direct access to truth. A visual substitute, art too could pass on saving knowledge.[39] "Truthfulness," notes art historian Nathan Rees, was the "primary means of judging art."[40] Defining precisely what "truthfulness" was, especially regarding events occurring in ancient time (as believers hold) or mythological time (as others might hold), was no easy task. At times it could simply be upholding Latter-day Saint doctrine, such as that angels—because they were formerly mortal human beings—had no wings.[41] At other times it was the more complicated task of researching historical material culture and assembling specific details to capture the physical appearance of a particular time and place.

Artists like Elspeth Young assert the truthfulness of her paintings by associating specific artistic details with historical "facts." Young graduated with a fine arts degree from Brigham Young University in 2003 and found her studies provided an important foundation for her art. She thinks of herself as taking a "scholarly approach," as she spends much time researching her subjects before she begins to paint.[42] Young is unique among temple artists in that she offers explanations of her paintings on her studio's website. She has found that people read her reflections not only because they are interested in the subject of the painting but also because they are curious to learn how an artist makes and thinks about art.

In her discussion of *She Had Compassion* (2017), Young tells how she assembled fragments from Egyptian material culture in order to construct her painting of Pharoah's daughter pulling baby Moses from the Nile (Exodus 2:5–10). The colors of the robe "are based on wall paintings from Queen Nefertari," and the gold crown follows one "belonging to the Nubian princess, Khnumet." The woman's "tightly wound spiral curls are also characteristic of the intricate wigs common at the time." The riverside reeds and even the dragonfly are of the types "native to Egypt."[43] While Young associates most of the elements of her painting with Egypt, she does note that the weave of the baby's basket "was inspired by the ancient boat baskets of Vietnam."

In the case of Elspeth Young's paintings, accuracy is less about a historically consistent reality (much of which scholars would argue is speculation anyway) than about a pastiche of possibilities. It is in *narrating* possibilities that Young suggests the painting is truthful enough to belong in a temple. On a general and most basic level, accuracy is about geography. Crowns and dragonflies can be found in Egypt, where the event took place. Slightly more significant in accuracy are the historical associations—Young paints the crown after one worn by a specific Egyptian woman. However, geography and history may be overruled by function. Vietnam, not Egypt, has "boat baskets" that provide inspiration for what Moses's mother might have woven to save her child. The basket is "true" ("true" enough) because it was not dreamed up by Young but was actually something that has been used in the real world. Young points out in her description that "the identity of this daughter of Pharaoh is unknown," but she constructs the truthfulness of the whole painting through pointing out the accuracy of its various parts.

What is most striking about *She Had Compassion* is not commented on in the online description. Young represents Pharoah's daughter as a Black woman. While Young mentions that she modeled the crown after one belonging to a Nubian princess, she does not state that the Pharaoh of Exodus had a daughter with dark skin. Doing so would have engaged her in a highly politicized argument about race and ancient Egypt. Far better to simply mention "Nubia," with its traditional association with Black Africa. Although there is no historical evidence that Khnumet had any connection to Nubia, it was a civilization that traded with Egypt. Both Young and church leaders seek to create a temple environment where Black patrons can see artistic representations of people who resemble them. Since making Pharaoh's daughter Black does not contravene Latter-day Saint doctrine (and the artist could point to the "fact" that she lived in Africa), such a possibility is added to the "accuracy narrative" of crowns and dragonflies. Through assembling such a pastiche of possibilities, a narrative of truthfulness parallels the artistic inspiration of the artist.

Scriptural narratives depicted in the temple are the most successful when they depict images of the miraculous and the hopeful—such as Jesus's healing and baby Moses being saved by an influential Egyptian. Much of the theology, religious practices, and artistic representations within Mormonism offer a positive orientation toward life, encouraging members to concentrate on the resurrection. Yes, individuals will have tribulations, but through Christ they can obtain happiness and cheer. From church talks

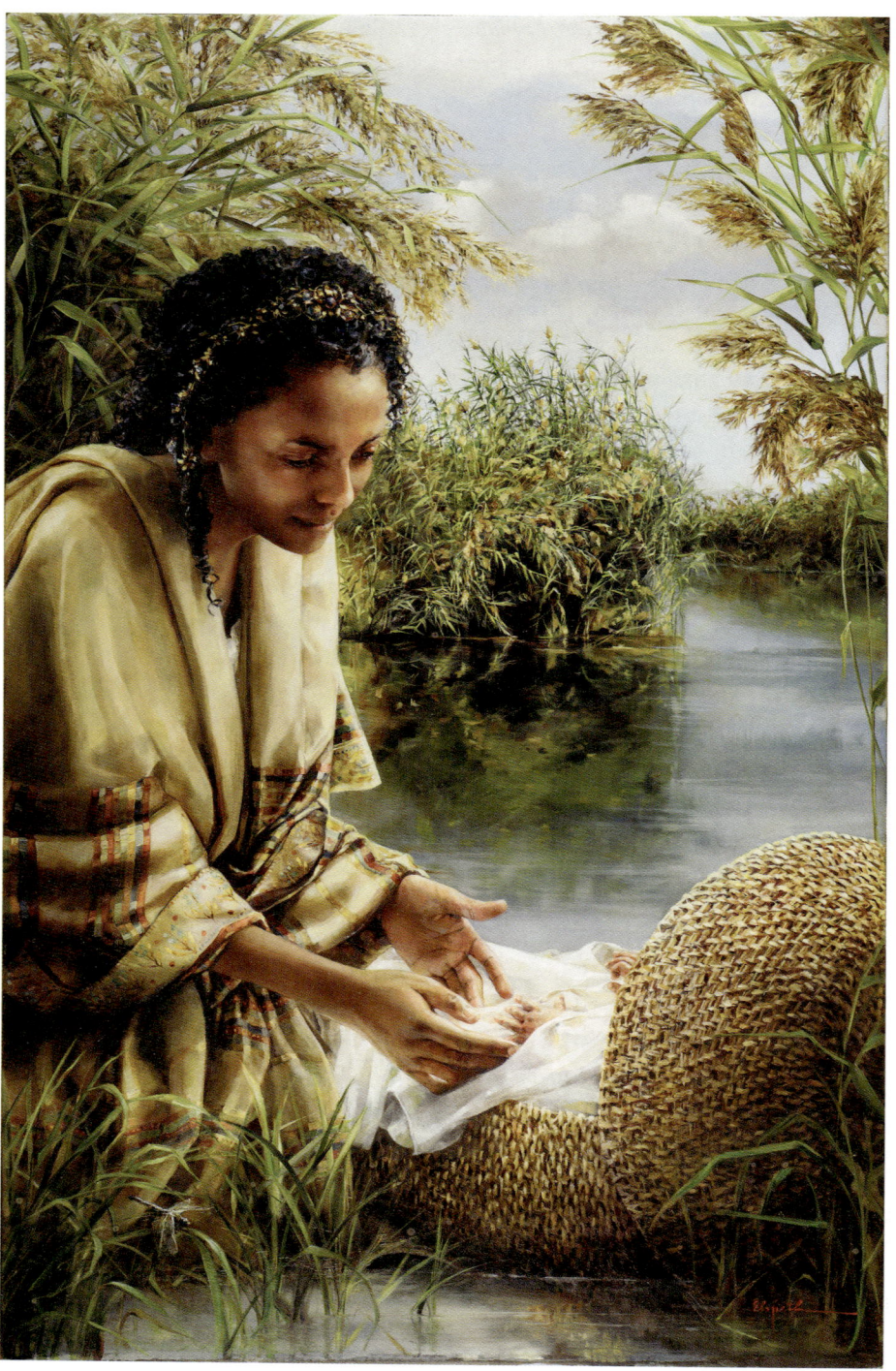

Fig. 2.7 Elspeth Young, *She Had Compassion*, 2017, oil on canvas, 50″ × 34″. © Intellectual Reserves, Inc.

to "mommy blogs," the Saints are told that God intends for them to "have joy" (2 Nephi 2:25). In this, Latter-day Saints participate in a general American therapeutic culture that asserts that positive thinking enables individuals to achieve happiness as well as a satisfying and worthwhile life.

While scriptural art in temples usually depicts uplifting and hopeful scenes, a rare representation of the Garden of Gethsemane (Matthew 26:36) is a painting by Dan Wilson. *Thy Will Be Done* fails to engage the dramatic force of this New Testament text or the "literally unlimited" suffering of Christ that enables salvation.[44] In Wilson's painting, Jesus only slightly furrows his brow and his hands are relaxed. Rather than being consumed by taking on the sins of the world or contemplating the terror that awaits, he seems to be having an unsettling dream. Indeed, Jesus—as well as the apostles—all appear to be napping after their evening meal. Dan Wilson has neither captured the power of divine atonement nor the turmoil of human pain. He has not conveyed the sense of pious acquiescence to the will of God. Instead, the painting skirts the problem of suffering and returns to the sentimental representations of Gethsemane by artists Harry Anderson and Henrich Hofmann. *Thy Will Be Done* does little to connect the atonement to the temple experience, leaving the notion of divine sacrifice exclusively within the ordinance itself.

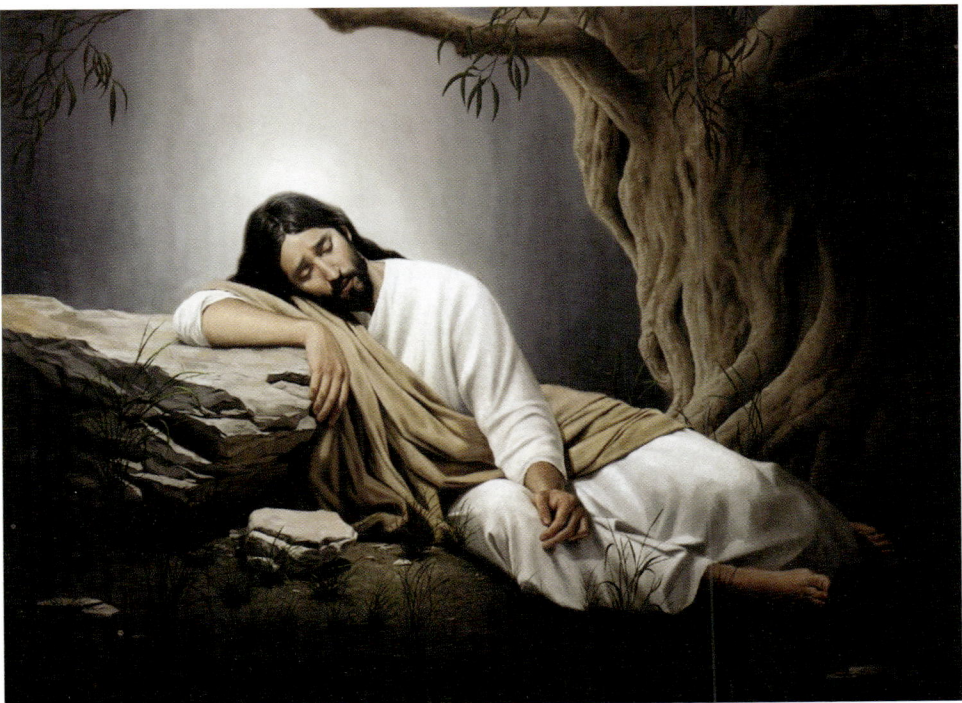

Fig. 2.8 Dan Wilson, *Thy Will Be Done*, date unknown, oil on canvas, 60″ × 80″. © Intellectual Reserves, Inc.

The artists who paint scriptural art for temples are confined by the sensibilities of church authorities, the specific text they seek to narrate visually, and the conventions of Christian art familiar to temple-goers. Temple art must be "truthful," so as to both re-inforce scriptural messages and uphold doctrinal positions. One method of persuading the viewer of truthfulness is to realistically depict architecture, landscape, and natural flora. It also must be "truthful" in reflecting wider Mormon cultural assumptions, such as the rejection of a "gloomy" Christianity of divine suffering. Still, paintings purchased from contemporary artists as well as nineteenth-century artworks bought at auction at times come at scriptural narratives from uncommon angles. Dan Wilson represents Christ's agony not as he prays but as he sleeps, much the way his followers sleep. Both the Leighton and the Veselka decenter Jesus, placing human characters at the center of the narrative. Elspeth Young depicts Pharaoh's daughter as Black, breaking with artistic conventions that represent her as fair-skinned. While Jesus is rarely depicted as Black (as he has recently been by British realist artist Lorna May Wadsworth), he should be "Semitic."[45] These are subtle but significant deviations from the art of the past.

PEOPLE OF THE TEMPLE

Elspeth's Young's portrayal of the biblical Pharaoh's daughter was neither the first nor the most well-known of her paintings in Latter-day Saint temples. Young is more fa-mous for her depictions of the second genre of temple paintings: depictions of faithful Latter-day Saints, ones not associated with the scriptures. In 2011, Elspeth Young re-ceived a letter inviting her to submit a painting to be considered for placement in a temple.[46] Although she does not know specifically why she was contacted, she, like Jeffrey Hein, had sold other paintings to the church.

Elspeth Young recalls that it was her mother who suggested that she submit a painting not of a biblical character but of a Black woman. During her time as a student, Young had taken a course on Latter-day Saint church history and learned about an African American pioneer: Jane Manning James. A free Black born in Connecticut, James had converted in 1842 and then traveled to Nauvoo, where she became a servant in the household of Joseph Smith. Arriving in 1847 with the first pioneer company, James was active in Salt Lake City community life. As a person of African descent, Jane Manning James was excluded from most temple rituals—although she consistently petitioned for an exception based on her close associations with the prophet. Eventually she was sealed by proxy as a servant to Joseph Smith—an act that did not satisfy her desire for full membership in the church she clearly loved. Jane Manning James died in 1908, during a period of peak racism in the United States. Shortly after the policy on admitting Blacks to the priesthood and temples was altered in 1978, a brief article outlining her life and faithfulness was published in the church magazine *Ensign*.[47] From that point onward, her story has been often told.

While Elspeth Young was painting biblical figures for Camille Fronk Olson's *Women of the Old Testament* (2009), she was on the lookout for a Black woman who might model for a "portrait" of Jane Manning James. Young had become more aware of the lack of images of people of color within the church and the need for paintings where people could "see" themselves in art. In the summer of 2012, Young's brother pointed out a picture of a Black woman who was engaged to one of his friends. Young contacted Josephine Bills and eventually made 230 photographs of her in several poses. It turned out that Bills's family had come from Ghana, and her grandfather had played an important role in establishing the church there. Elspeth Young would paint three portraits of Josephine Bills: *And Thou Didst Hear Me* (2012) and *Behold Your Little Ones* (2016) hang in temples, while *'Til We Meet Again* (2013) is displayed at the Latter-day Saint Conference Center in Salt Lake City.[48]

Young's temple painting *And Thou Didst Hear Me* is a stylistic departure from Young's portraits of biblical women, where dark backgrounds contrast with facial expressions bathed in light. The biblical portraits often include bits of architecture: a stone arched window, the footing of a colonnade, a Gothic staircase. In *And Thou Didst Hear Me* the praying figure rests in an indeterminate place, where the floor and the sky blend into each other with a yellow glow. Young uses a sfumato technique, painting a smoky haze that imparts a dreamy quality to the background. The coloration accentuates the praying figure. Although the woman is realistically portrayed, her placement in space lends an ethereal, otherworldly feel to the painting. The whole painting is in light, with shadows occurring only on the folds of her white dress. It is the model's dark face and hands that serve as contrast to the background and the clothing. Only a small portion of her bowed head is painted with lighter tones, which draw the viewer's attention to her serene face. Nothing in the painting firmly roots her in a historical time, although the woman's shawl gives the painting a traditional feel. While Young's biblical women are dressed in rich reds and ochers, *And Thou Didst Hear Me* references the white clothing worn by women in the temple.

The woman's white clothes set against the sfumato background underscore the importance of light within the temple. Unlike walking into a Gothic cathedral, where daylight is filtered through panes of stained glass—lending a dim and mysterious feel to the space—Latter-day Saint temples are filled with artificial light. In Mormon culture, there is a strong association between light, the color white, and the celestial realm. While lights are dimmed during the ordinance rituals in the instruction rooms, the hallways and waiting areas are brightly lit. The celestial room, where patrons often meditate and pray (and which typically has no paintings), is flooded with light, which reflects off mirrors and sparkles in crystal chandeliers. Latter-day Saints see the soul as progressing from the darkness of woes, heartaches, and doubt into the light of peace, security, and knowledge. "I feel that I bring myself and all my worries, heartaches, and woes (great or small)" to the temple, explains Elspeth Young, "and that God hears." For Young, "I gain a confidence and peace knowing that all will be taken care of in His own time and way." Such reassurance is what Young hopes to capture in *And Thou Didst Hear Me*.[49]

In 2012, the original of *And Thou Didst Hear Me* was placed in the temple in Johannesburg, South Africa. It was the first painting in modern times to depict a faithful Saint who was not either a church hero or a biblical figure. Giclées of *And Thou Didst Hear Me* are in many temples, including one in Winnipeg, Canada. The following year, the church purchased another of Young's paintings in a similar style, *Prepare Your*

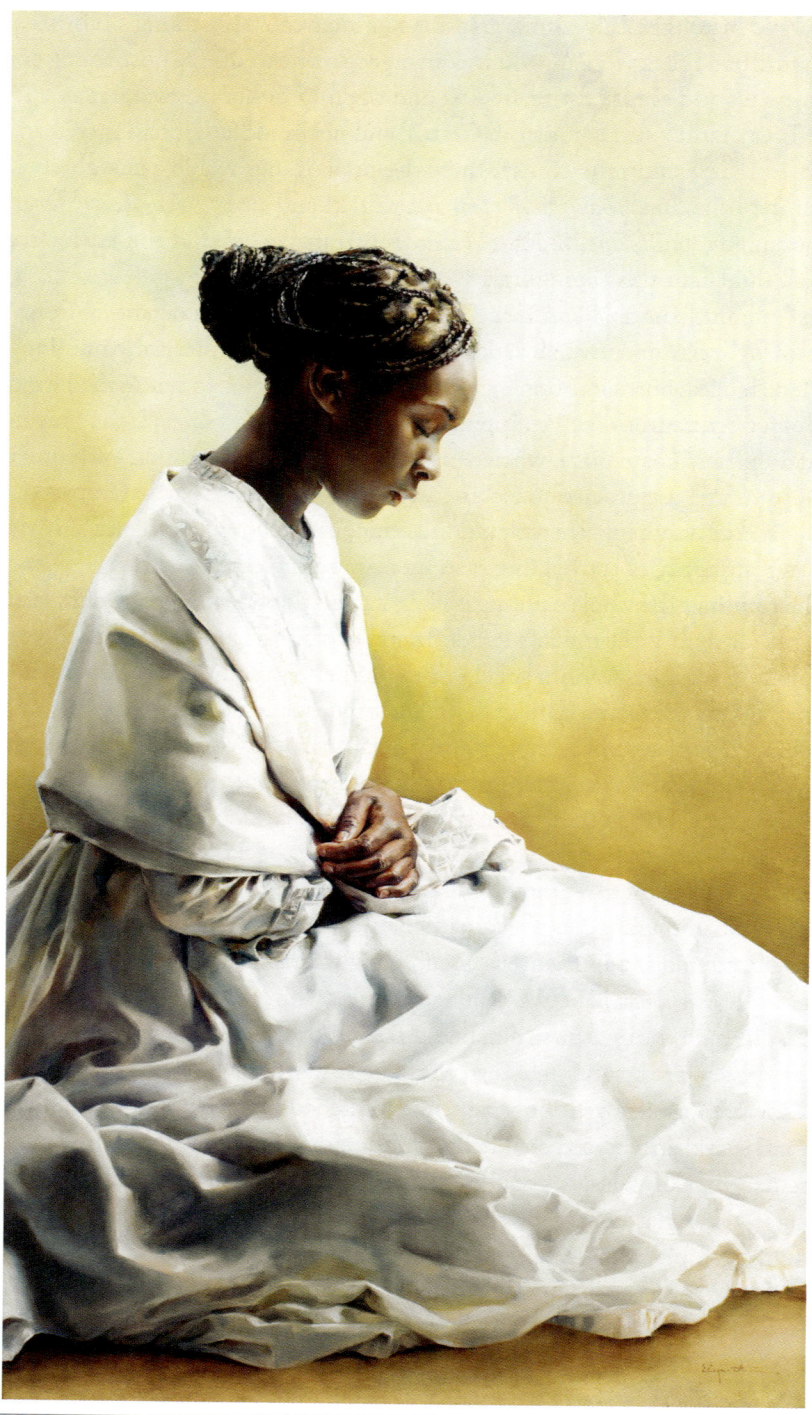

Fig. 2.9 Elspeth Young, *And Thou Didst Hear Me*, 2012, oil on canvas, 48″ × 27″. © Intellectual Reserves, Inc.

Minds for the Morrow (2014). It too illustrated a woman of color, dressed in white (only this time with a light green shawl), in a contemplative position. A bouquet of flowers rests on the woman's lap. Young explains that she understands this painting as "a study of worship—that attitude and orientation of soul sufficiently pure and powerful to keep God close."[50] The original was placed in the temple in Tijuana, Mexico, and giclées often appear in rooms where brides prepare for their marriage. *With a Sincere Heart* (2015), *He Restoreth My Soul* (2015), *The Pure of Heart* (2016), and *The Covenant of Peace* (2017) all duplicate this "contemplative woman" style.[51] Young's descriptions of the paintings reference culturally inflected costuming: the *baro't saya* of the Philippines, the traditional wedding dress of Mexico. In her later paintings, the women's flowers also "symbolize" their countries of origin: white anemones from Japan, dahlias from Mexico, jasmine sampuguita from the Philippines.

Elspeth Young has paintings of pioneer women and female characters from the Book of Mormon hanging in temples, but these "contemplative women" are distinct. Their costuming might have a cultural inflection, but more recognizable is that they are wearing appropriate dresses for the temple: modest, simple, and white. Each of the women assumes an attitude that stresses her intimate communication with the divine: head bowed in humility or lifted upward as if to answer a heavenly call. The women are intensely feminine, with soft curls framing their faces or long hair pulled back in a humble bun. Their handheld flowers recall a bride awaiting her groom. The passivity of the women contrasts with *The Blessings of the Fathers* (2018), a temple painting of a Black man who actively expresses his priesthood power by giving his son a blessing.

As with her other paintings, Young seeks to convey the diversity of the church—indeed, of the world—which is made up of people of many ethnicities. Yet there is a homogeneity among these "contemplative women," who are uniformly young and beautiful. The shapes of their bodies are concealed under the folds of their dresses and shawls, which drape around them in a desexualized manner. The women are both idealized and intensely individual. Cultural and racial differences may be celebrated, but only to the extent that they do not contravene church standards or the wider aesthetic traditions constructed by Euro-American Latter-day Saints. Temple patrons should see themselves in these images so that they can relate to the stories of the past and the virtues of the present. Racial and ethnic markers must not remind patrons of the fraught territory of difference but rather serve to celebrate the universal character of the church.

LANDSCAPES OF THE DIVINE

The third genre of art included in temples is that of landscapes, which are expressed in two forms: in murals and in framed paintings. Latter-day Saints are unique among Christians in placing landscapes so extensively in their worship spaces. The inclusion of scenes of nature began in the late nineteenth century, when, in order to facilitate the drama being performed during the endowment ceremony, floor-to-ceiling murals were painted on the rooms' walls. The murals served as a theatrical backdrop to the ritual drama. In 1890, the church sent John Hafen, Lorus Pratt, and John B. Fairbanks to Paris to study art in the hopes of making better murals for the Salt Lake temple, which was completed in 1893.[52] That temple also held two framed landscape paintings by Alfred Lambourne (1850–1926): *Adam-ondi-Ahman* and *Hill Cumorah*. In addition to temples in several cities in the continental United States, murals were painted for temples in Hawaii, Canada, and New Zealand. The last temple to have a full set of murals in its ordinance rooms was the Los Angeles temple, which was dedicated in 1956.

Landscapes were not simply theatrical backdrops. During the first third of the nineteenth century—at the period of Mormonism's birth—representations of nature were seen to be imbued with symbolic power. At the very time that Americans were settling and commercializing natural resources, they imagined an untouched nature as possessing "universal truths of beauty, independence, and freedom." Following the European Romantic tradition, nature came to symbolize the divine presence. The universe was God's handiwork, and those who sought God should look for him in the beauty of nature. Americans as diverse as Henry David Thoreau and John Muir "venerated nature in its untouched state, suggesting that encountering the wilderness could enable individuals to reclaim their own lost innocence and wonder."[53] Such nature was perceived to be a harmonious Edenic wilderness uncorrupted by sin. "The landscape," wrote historian Barbara Novak, is "a holy text which reveals truth."[54] In providing renditions of nature, artists participated in a spiritual endeavor.

For the painters of the Hudson River School, such as Thomas Cole, Albert Bierstadt, Frederic Edwin Church, and Thomas Moran, nature was God's temple captured in their art. Carrying on the Hudson River School into the Rocky Mountains, early Latter-day Saint painters were influenced by the prevailing fashion for associating "virgin" nature with Eden and God's creation. More than other Christians, Latter-day Saints understood specific places as being designated by God for their use. Coming to the Utah Territory was coming to Zion, to the promised land. The mountains, waterfalls, sunsets, and valleys of Utah "symbolized purity, the majesty of God as seen through the vastness of his creations."[55] Such wildness protected Zion from the destructive forces of Babylon, thus fulfilling Isaiah's prophecy that in the last days "the mountain of the Lord's house shall be established in the top of the mountains . . . and all nations shall flow unto it" (Isaiah 2:2). Temples would be built on high points of land, and landscapes would remind patrons of God's world before sin.

Landscape murals returned to the visual culture of Latter-day Saints after a hiatus of almost fifty years. In 2002, the rebuilt Nauvoo temple was dedicated with extensive murals. The original temple had been constructed in 1841, and by 1850 it was a pile of ruins. In 1999, church president Gordon B. Hinckley announced its rebuilding. From the outside the structure would follow the original plans, but the interior would be fully modernized. Six artists, Douglas Fryer, James C. Christensen, Robert Marshall, Christopher Young, Ernest Smith, and Frank Magleby, were called to paint murals for the creation room, the garden room, and the world room. Fifty-four original paintings were also placed in the newly reconstructed historic temple.[56]

Twenty-first-century murals do not narrate the plan of salvation as played out in the endowment ceremony but depict a natural environment "untouched by human hands." This landscape should be recognizable by patrons as "local" rather than a newly formed cosmos or an ancient Eden. The temple in Newport Beach, California (2005), for instance, is a highly detailed, finely crafted exposition of the California coastline. Painted by one of the Nauvoo muralists, Christopher Young (1963–), it is a masterpiece of trompe l'oeil. Rather than causing the viewer to notice the corner of the room, the coastline draws the eye away from the defining architecture. The scene is calm and contemplative. The light suggests the "golden hour" at dawn and dusk when the sun is low in the sky and its light is soft and diffuse. Rays of pale orange and blue illuminate the clouds (or perhaps fog) that drift just off the coastline. Verdant greenery punctuates the rocky hillside and tempers the arid landscape. Hidden in the shadows, blending into a niche in the rock, is a resting mountain lion.

While the mural exemplifies contemporary realism, it is a perfected scene. The mountain lion does not menace but rather is incorporated into a balanced natural order. "I try to enhance reality," Young explains of his art, "to enhance the tactile illusion without pushing it to the point where it is not believable. If I paint a rose, I want to paint the ultimate, symbolic rose of all roses."[57] The coastal landscape refers to the area around the temple, but in a form of Edenic splendor. As with the figurative art, the landscape is both idealized and familiar.

Landscape artist Brad Aldridge (1965–) has painted six temple murals. Two are in Peru, with the others in Sapporo, Japan; Hartford, Connecticut; Fort Lauderdale, Florida; and Raleigh, North Carolina. His framed landscapes hang in many temples. When he reflects on his art, Aldridge sees the influence of the Hudson River School as well as the American Romantic writers Emerson and Thoreau. "I am sort of looking for the idyllic; looking for home," he explains. Aldridge, who was a well-traveled "Army brat," has fine arts degrees from BYU and the University of Arkansas. Like Jeffrey Hein and Elspeth Young, Aldridge's Latter-day Saint beliefs stress the intimate connection between people and Deity. "It's a matter of being a creator," Aldridge reflects. "I relate to that religiously, being the child of a Creator. It's in our DNA that we want to make things, to create things—to organize unorganized matter."[58] Aldridge sees his efforts as tapping into the creative spirit that humans carry over from their pre-mortal existence. Art itself, be it explicitly religious or not, has a deeper dimension when it seeks to make sense of a chaotic world. Artists such as Aldridge, Young, and Hein share with Latter-day Saint leaders such as Larry Wilson and Arch Williams the commitment that art functions best when it reflects the God-given order and harmony of creation. Art should help us make sense of what is, at first glance, meaningless. When meaning is successfully communicated, truth, emotion, and spiritual experience result.

The "matter of being a creator" is no easy task for those artists who paint temple murals. Once commissioned, the artist travels to where the temple is being built and photographs the locale, staying only a short period. During the trip, the artist learns about indigenous plants and animals as well as the regional geography. After returning

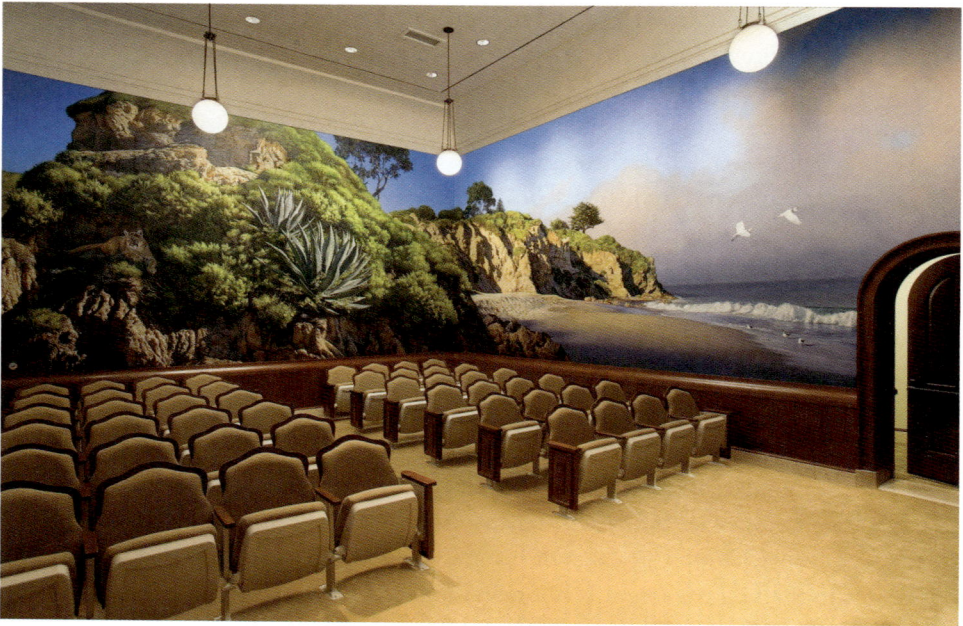

Fig. 2.10 Christopher Young, 2005, oil on canvas, mural in Newport Beach, California, temple. © Intellectual Reserves, Inc.

home, the artists prepares a fuller design from the assembled photographs. The point is to create "an intricate, beautiful, varied surface that also tells a story. It's a beautiful landscape," which temple patrons should recognize as their own.[59] Mural panels are typically ten feet high and twenty-five feet long, and it may take several of them to cover one room. The temple in Raleigh, North Carolina, for instance, required three panels. Panels are painted near the artist's studio, usually in a large rented building that can accommodate sizable scaffolding and lighting. Brad Aldridge enjoys this artistic challenge because there are so "many things you can learn from painting large."[60] He uses paint rollers and four-inch house-painting brushes as well as ones with fine tips. When the painting is finished, the canvas is rolled up and shipped. Then it is glued onto the ordinance room's walls. The artist usually travels again to the site to supervise the mural's installation and to touch up any remaining problems. In recent years, however, the church has slowed down the commissioning of murals for ordinance rooms.[61]

Landscape murals do not raise the same issues of gender, ethnicity, and race as does figurative art. Their production, however, can provide a lens into the difficult negotiations that take place between foreign cultures and a Utah-run church. Within any given culture, nature has its own symbolism that may not be obvious to well-intentioned outsiders. In order to have his or her mural proposal accepted for a commission, the artist must convince a variety of art professionals and church leaders that the mural will be sensitive to the unique location of the temple. Patrons must recognize that the landscape is their space, even if it is devoid of buildings. At the same time, the various

Utah-based church committees must recognize the images as in fact "local" and indicative of a place they probably have never visited. When Brad Aldridge made his proposal painting for the Sapporo temple, he included bonsai-like trees. Aldridge, as well as the other Americans looking at the proposal, thought, "Yes, that looks Japanese." But when the proposal painting was shown to a Japanese temple site manager, he did not like the trees. He told the painter, "No, that's Shinto." What Aldridge and others read as culturally Japanese, the Japanese Latter-day Saint read as religious. Something Shinto was not appropriate for an LDS temple. Aldridge altered the image.[62]

In general, landscape paintings do not have human figures in them. One exception to this is when a landscape is placed in the temple baptistry. Those paintings typically show foliage, a body of water, and a small group of people being baptized. When Brad Aldridge was commissioned to paint a baptism scene for the temple in Kinshasa, Democratic Republic of the Congo (2019), he did not travel to Kinshasa. Instead, he was sent a series of historical photographs of baptisms in the area. In the photographs, white missionaries baptized Black people.[63] These photographs might have been of a white senior couple from Utah who had arrived in 1986 as the first Latter-day Saint missionaries to come to what was then Zaire.[64] Aldridge felt that duplicating that arrangement was "a little insulting" because it erased the activities of Black missionaries and members. Instead, he proposed to paint a white missionary, a Black missionary, a Black missionary witnessing, and a Black person being baptized. Temple designers, however, rejected this arrangement and insisted that all of the figures be Black. Precisely why they preferred this is unclear, but by 2019 there were over 62,000 Congolese members. While white missionaries still came to Africa, the local church was made up of Black members, and increasingly it was Black missionaries who served in Africa.

Brad Aldridge complied with the wishes of the temple designers. However, the small coterie being baptized can barely be seen in the framed painting. The group is dwarfed by the natural landscape—dramatic clouds, a lush green riverbank, and a meandering river. While the temple does sit near the Congo River, early church baptisms were performed in swimming pools and in an abandoned copper mine pit that had filled with water.[65] Contemporary baptisms probably occur in one of the 178 Congolese wards, not in the river. The romantic landscape, however, continues the goal of situating the rebirthed and newly baptized in an Edenic atmosphere devoid of the realities of colonialism, environmental decay, or urbanization. The scene is local, but it also is idealized.

Framed landscape paintings are as frequent in temples as are biblical narratives or the portraits of faithful Latter-day Saints. The temple in Mesa, Arizona, which was dedicated in 1921 but fully renovated in 2021, contains two original landscapes by Ken Stockton (1955–) and many giclées by other artists. Both of Stockton's paintings are of desert scenes with cacti and barren mountains. Yet the arid Arizona landscape is balanced by orange poppies and blue lupines. The flowers' foliage is a lush green. The paintings recall the promise made in the biblical book of Isaiah of a hopeful future where "the wilderness and the solitary place shall be glad for them; and the desert shall rejoice, and blossom as the rose" (Isaiah 35:1). For the Latter-day Saint pioneers who settled in the dry Intermountain West, they believed this prophecy was literally coming to fruition as they diverted streams from the mountains to make a verdant land of Zion. As with the art of Christopher Young, the Stockton paintings enhance reality through highly saturated colors and bright backlighting.

While Latter-day Saint artists such as Ken Stockton reflect the contemporary realist style that prefers bright and vibrant tones, other landscape paintings hark back to the darker palette of the Hudson Valley School. This particularly is the case with paintings bought at auction. As with the Victorian painter Edmund Blair Leighton, artist Wilson Hurley (1924–2008) had no connection to the church. His painting of the desert Southwest bought "some years ago" dramatically portrays the power of the sky as a thunderstorm moved across a valley.[66] A noted artist of the western landscape, Hurley painted in the tradition of Thomas Moran and Albert Bierstadt, men who accentuated the intensity of nature through heightened contrasts of light and dark. After purchasing the original, the church secured the copyright from the wife of the painter so that giclées could be prepared and displayed in other temples. Before the Mesa temple was dedicated, Hurley's family was invited to see the installed painting and was given a private tour of the temple.

Landscape art contributes to the creation within the temple of a non-historical time, in the context of which Saints can imagine (in the fullest sense of that term) a time before the advent of humanity. In the same way that figurative art underscores the miraculous and the hopeful (and fails at integrating divine sacrifice), temple landscapes echo the beauty

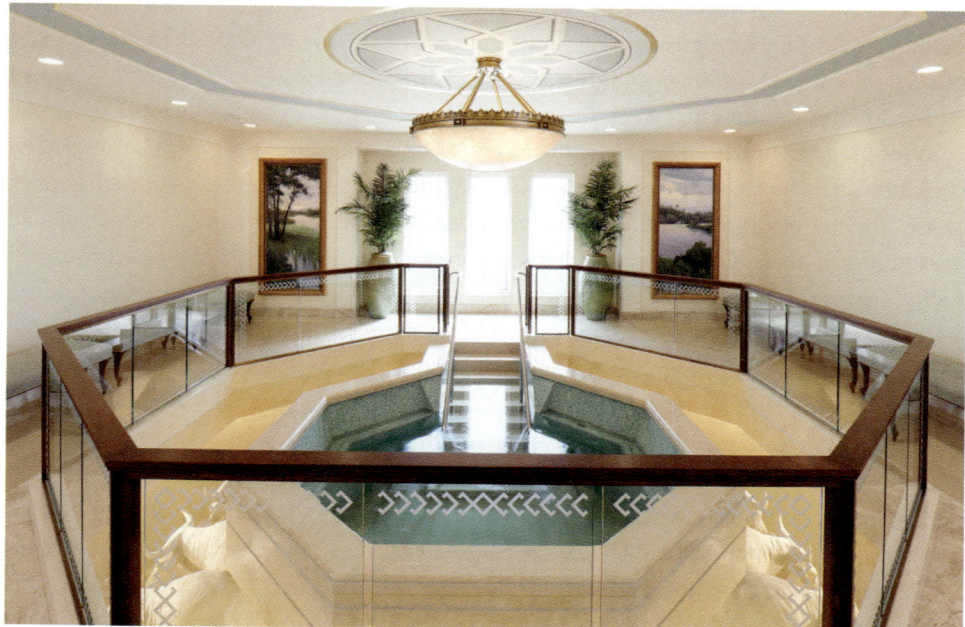

Fig. 2.11 Brad Aldridge, 2019, oil on canvas, mural in Kinshasha, Democratic Republic of the Congo, temple. © Intellectual Reserves, Inc.

of the prelapsarian world before Adam and Eve sinned. While the actual production of the landscapes might entail challenges and strife, the resulting art itself reflects an Edenic world devoid of problems. When human beings do enter into this perfected space, they too are in balance and in harmony with the beauty of a divinely created order. Especially in mural art, this differs from an earlier period in which images of people were included in art in the celestial room (as in the Idaho Falls temple [1945]), Adam and Eve experienced a dreary world (Los Angeles [1956]), and animals devour each other (Cardston, Alberta [1923]). Once a film came to narrate the plan of salvation depicted in the ordinance liturgy, landscape art came to depict God's perfected handiwork.

CONCLUSION

Temple art renewal during the first two decades of the twenty-first century was a concerted effort by church leaders and Latter-day Saint artists to make sophisticated art that would serve as foundation for a specific set of religious beliefs and values. While the architecture remained the same, renewing the artworks and installing classical realist paintings provided a way to update temples to make them contemplative, authentic, and spiritual for current patrons. At this point in the church's history, leaders want art that uplifts, comforts, and inspires. Art must be accessible, familiar, and non-threatening. Scriptural narratives (from the Old Testament, the New Testament, or the Book of Mormon) should connect theologically with the ordinances performed in the temple, especially baptism and ordination. Paintings should represent God fulfilling promises, the triumphal elements of the gospel, and the magnificence of the natural environment.

Temple art may have elements of modernism, as it gently decenters Jesus from some biblical stories, asking viewers to come at the New Testament from different angles. Although church leaders and artists might deny this, the inclusion of racially diverse "contemplative women" and a "Semitic" Christ are responses to current movements in American society and culture as much as they are celebrations of a multiethnic global church and the recognition of a historical Jesus. Jesus, in effect, is subtly placed in time and into specific, perhaps more authentic, contexts. While the temple has always been perceived as a refuge and a home, the elimination of any elements of strife (or minimizing it by poorly representing it) functions to heighten the binary between the sacred space of the temple and the profane space of the world. Figures might have modern-looking faces that resemble temple patrons, but everything else about them serves to transport the viewers to an ideal, perfected world.

A centralized, hierarchical church with concerns for the bottom line and only a basic understanding of the art world has faced a steep learning curve regarding how to treat its artists. Over a period of twenty years, however, it has moved not only to purchase more sophisticated art but also to recognize the ability of that art to convey current church values. The popularity of contemporary realism has meant that Latter-day Saint artists can paint both for the secular marketplace and for the church. Most of the artists discussed have deep personal commitments both to the gospel of Jesus Christ and to its expression within the Church of Jesus Christ of Latter-day Saints. They are patient with the foibles of an institutional church because their art generates its own spiritual intensity and evidence of the truth of their faith.

The temple provides a glimpse of both a past Eden and a future heaven. It is presented not only as "the House of the Lord" but also as the comforting home to the faithful Saints. All those spaces are defined in opposition to what currently is taking place on earth. If the earth is a place of spiritual progress through the assertion of one's agency to choose good over evil, then the art in the temple is constructed to illustrate the end of that journey. This preference for art that expresses order, harmony, innocence, balance, light, and the miraculous obviously limits what kind of art can be placed in the temple. Temple art renewal seeks to accomplish the difficult task of providing diverse members of a global church familiar images of landscapes and scriptural stories geared to transporting the Saints to a sacred world.

NOTES

[1] Tom Wolfe, "The Lives They Lived: Frederick Hart, b. 1943; The Artist the Art World Couldn't See," *New York Times Magazine*, January 2, 2000, https://www.nytimes.com/2000/01/02/magazine/the-lives-they-lived-frederick-hart-b-1943-the-artist-the-art-world.html.

[2] Wolfe, "The Lives They Lived."

[3] Henry Allen, "Appreciation: An Artist with Heart," *Washington Post*, August 17, 1999, https://www.washingtonpost.com/wp-srv/style/daily/aug99/hart17.htm.

[4] See Linda Gibbs's chapter in this volume.

[5] See Ashlee Whitaker Evans's chapter in this volume.

[6] All the statistics and observations in the above paragraph come from Arch Williams, interviewed by Colleen McDannell, August 27, 2021.

[7] William Whyte, *Unlocking the Church* (New York: Oxford University Press, 2017), 43.

[8] Whyte, *Unlocking the Church*, 44.

[9] Steve Fidel, "Small New LDS Temples to Dot the Globe," *Deseret News*, October 5, 1997, https://www.deseret.com/1997/10/5/19337905/small-new-lds-temples-to-dot-globe.

[10] Tad Walch, "A Brief History of Latter-day Saint Temple Announcements," *Deseret News*, October 7, 2021, https://www.deseret.com/2021/10/7/22712932/churchbeat-newsletter-president-nelson-has-announced-a-record-83-temples.

[11] Samuel Ross Palfreyman, "The Landscape of Modern Mormonism: Understanding the Church of Jsues Christ of Lattter-day Saints Through Its Twentieth-Century Architecture" (PhD diss., Boston University, 2020), 19, 94.

[12] For instance, see Thomas S. Monson, "Blessings of the Temple," 185th Annual General Conference, May 2015, https://www.churchofjesuschrist.org/study/ensign/2015/05/sunday-morning-session/blessings-of-the-temple?lang=eng.

[13] I have not been permitted to read this letter or to ascertain its exact date. Arch Williams has summarized the letter for me and dates it to the later part of 2018. At a temple art seminar given in mid-June 2019, Larry Wilson also stressed that temple administration should enhance the experience for temple patrons by eliminating curt remarks or actions (e.g., the "move along" attitude) and instead treating patrons as the Lord would. Patrons should be helped to feel God's divine love and welcomed to view the artwork without disruption. Latter-day Saints, however, who regularly visit temples have varying opinions on both the feasibility of this reorientation and whether or not it has been adopted on any level.

[14] Arch Williams recalled, "I am in the Salt Lake Temple, and I am standing in front of and looking at one of the Tiffany windows. The one where Adam and Eve are being driven out of the garden. There is not a more beautiful piece of art in the church. . . . And this beautiful sister walks up and says, 'Brother, where are you supposed to be?' And I said, 'I am supposed to be right here.' I blew her poor mind. She didn't know

what to do with that. That's not in the program." He explains that the new goal is for people "to come to the temple and rest and think about their lives, we want them to come and perform an ordinance." Patrons should "go to the chapel and read your scriptures. Nobody is going to tell you to 'move along.'" Arch Williams, interviewed by Colleen McDannell, Mesa temple tour, December 1, 2021.

15 Williams interview, August 27, 2021.

16 Peggy Fletcher Stack (*Salt Lake Tribune* religion reporter), interviewed by Colleen McDannell, March 12, 2022.

17 Peggy Fletcher Stack recalls that after her question about the lack of original art in the Boston temple (2000), she was told shortly after that new original art was being commissioned. Stack interview.

18 In February 2022 the committee was changed and renamed the Temple Art Committee to indicate its more exclusive role. However, in the remainder of the chapter I will use its original title.

19 Temple art seminar, mid-June 2019. Notes taken by Ashlee Whitaker Evans, in author's possession.

20 Williams interview, December 1, 2021. On Harry Anderson with examples of *The Second Coming,* see R. Scott Lloyd, "Harry Anderson's Paint Studies on Exhibit at Church History Museum," Church of Jesus Christ of Latter-day Saints, October 6, 2015, https://www.churchofjesuschrist.org/church/news/harry-andersons-paint-studies-on-exhibit-at-church-history-museum?lang=eng.

21 Nathan Rees, *Mormon Visual Culture and the American West* (New York: Routledge, 2021), 30.

22 Temple Art Seminar, mid-June 2019. Notes taken by Ashlee Whitaker Evans, in author's possession.

23 Lack and his students exhibited at the Springville Art Museum, and the term was coined for use at the exhibition and in the catalogue, *Classical Realism: The Other Twentieth Century* (n.p.: Springville Museum of Art, Amarillo Art Center, and Maryhill Museum of Art, 1982).

24 Mark Stevens, "Art Imitates Life: The Revival of Realism," *Newsweek,* June 7, 1982.

25 Statement made by Frank H. Goodyear, curator of the Pennsylvania Academy of the Fine Arts, regarding realist artists in the catalogue for their exhibition *Contemporary American Realism Since 1960* (New York: Little, Brown, 1981), 30.

26 As quoted by James F. Cooper, "Realism: A Path to Beauty," in *Slow Painting: A Deliberate Renaissance* (exhibition catalogue) (Brookhaven, GA: Oglethorpe University Museum of Art, 2006), 8.

27 Jeffrey Hein, interviewed by Colleen McDannell, October 4, 2021.

28 Hein interview, October 4, 2021.

29 In recent years, Hein has decided to abandon this practice.

30 "The Unveiling of Jeff Hein's Painting," *Jeff Hein: Art and Process* (blog), May 7, 2011, https://jeffreyhein.wordpress.com/2011/05/07/the-unveiling-of-jeff-heins-painting/

31 Peggy Fletcher Stack, "The Mormon Jesus: Just How Different Is He than the Traditional Christ?," *Salt Lake Tribune,* June 9, 2016 referencing John G. Turner, *The Mormon Jesus: A Biography* (Cambridge, MA: Harvard University Press, 2016).

32 "The Church's New Symbol Emphasizes the Centrality of the Savior," Church of Jesus Christ of Latter-day Saints, April 4, 2020, https://newsroom.churchofjesuschrist.org/article/new-symbol-church-of-jesus-christ.

33 Temple Art Seminar notes.

34 Williams interview, December 1, 2021.

35 Hein interview, October 4, 2021.

36 Personal correspondence, Ashlee Whitaker Evans, February 28, 2022.

37 Williams interview, December 1, 2021. A glimpse of "The Work of the Sabbath" may be seen at: https://www.albinveselkareligiousart.com/ And in an interior photograph of the lobby of the Winnepeg Canada Temple, https://churchofjesuschristtemples.org/winnipeg-manitoba-temple/photographs/#Official-14

38 Williams interview, December 1, 2021. A glimpse of "Cast Your Nets on the Right Side" may be seen at: https://www.albinveselkareligiousart.com/

39 Rees, *Mormon Visual Culture,* 13.

40 Rees, *Mormon Visual Culture,* 25.

41 Joseph Smith stated that "an angel of God never has wings" in Joseph Smith, *History of the Church* (Salt Lake City: Deseret Book, 1939), 3:392, https://byustudies.byu.edu/further-study-lesson/volume-3-chapter-26/. For an LDS explanation of how to interpret Christian art where angels *do* have wings, see David A.

Edwards, "Angels We Have Heard," *Ensign,* December 2014, https://www.churchofjesuschrist.org/study/ensign/2014/12/angels-we-have-heard?lang=eng.

[42] Elspeth Young, interviewed by Colleen McDannell, March 7, 2022.

[43] Elspeth Young, "She Had Compassion," https://www.alyoung.com/art/work-daughter_of_pharaoh.html.

[44] Blake T. Ostler, "The Compassion Theory of Atonement," in *Exploring Mormon Thought: The Problems of Theism and the Love of God* (Salt Lake City: Kofford Books, 2006), 236–237. I would like to thank Brian Birch for giving me this reference.

[45] See Lorna May Wadsworth's painting *A Last Supper* (2009), exhibited in various cathedrals in the United Kingdom, http://lornamaywadsworth.com/exhibitions#onshow-now.

[46] Young interview; letter dated September 20, 2011, from the Temple and Special Projects Department, in possession of Elspeth Young.

[47] Linda King Newell and Valeen Tippetts Avery, "Jane Manning James," *Ensign*, August 1979, 26–29, https://www.churchofjesuschrist.org/study/ensign/1979/08/jane-manning-james-black-saint-1847-pioneer?lang=eng

[48] Elspeth Young, "Chronology" and correspondence with author, March 11, 2022, in author's possession. See *'Til We Meet Again* at https://www.alyoung.com/art/work-jane_elizabeth_manning.html.

[49] Elspeth C. Young, personal journal, December 16, 2012, as cited in "Chronology."

[50] Elspeth Young, "Symbolism in *Prepare Your Minds for Tomorrow*," https://www.alyoung.com/art/work-prepare_your_minds_for_the_morrow.html

[51] However, when *The Covenant of Peace* was prepared for the temple in Paris, France, it had a blond white woman sitting in front of a body of water and a field of sunflowers. See https://www.alyoung.com/art/work-covenant_of_peace.html.

[52] See Linda Gibbs's chapter in this volume.

[53] Elissa Yukiko Weichbrodt, "Found or Recovered? Competing Views of Paradise in Late Nineteenth-Century Hawaiian Landscape Painting," *Religion and the Arts* 22 (2018): 119.

[54] Barbara Novak, *Nature and Culture: American Landscape and Painting, 1825–1875* (New York: Oxford University Press, 2007), 52.

[55] Richard G. Oman and Robert O. Davis, *Images of Faith: Art of the Latter-day Saints* (Salt Lake City: Deseret Book, 1995), 20.

[56] Sarah Jane Weaver, "Murals Grace Temple Walls," *Church News*, May 3, 2002 https://www.thechurchnews.com/archives/2002-05-04/murals-grace-temple-walls-108484.

[57] Chris Young biography, CODA Gallery, https://codagallery.com/artist/1228-chris-young/cv?ppage=24.

[58] Brad Aldridge, interviewed by Colleen McDannell, November 3, 2021.

[59] Aldridge interview.

[60] Aldridge interview.

[61] If one looks at https://churchofjesuschristtemples.org/, a count can be made of the temples where murals appear in the official photographs. This does not take into account temples that might have murals but no photographs posted of them. Given that caveat, of the temples dedicated from 2000 through 2002, there were ten with at least one mural (out of forty-four total); from 2003 through 2005 it was six of eight; from 2006 through 2008 it was six of six; from 2009 through 2011 it was eight of eight; from 2012 through 2014 it was seven of eight; from 2015 through 2017 it was eight of ten; from 2018 through 2021 it was seven of eleven.

[62] Aldridge interview. For the final mural, see https://churchofjesuschristtemples.org/sapporo-japan-temple/photographs/#Official-11.

[63] Aldridge interview.

[64] Scott Taylor, "How Three Members Helped the Church Be Officially Recognized in DR Congo," *Church News,* April 18, 2019, https://www.thechurchnews.com/members/2019-04-18/how-3-members-church-helped-mormon-lds-congo-3060 See also "History of the Church of Jesus Christ of Latter-day Saints in the Democratic Republic of Congo," Southeast Africa Area, Church of Jesus Christ of Latter-day Saints, Johannesburg, South Africa, 2019, https://content-preview.churchofjesuschrist.org/acp/bc/Africa%20Southeast%20Area/Downloads/history-of-the-kinshasa-temple-and-of-the-church-of-jesus-christ-of-latter-day-saints-in-the-democratic-republic-of-the-congo_eng_0205.pdf.

[65] Taylor, "How Three Members."

[66] All the information in this paragraph is from Williams interview, December 1, 2021.

3

MOVING PICTURES

Subjectivity and Mormon Identity in Documentary Film

RANDY ASTLE

In his final film, *Moving Pictures* (2000), the celebrated Canadian documentarian Colin Low reflects upon his life as a filmmaker and artist. Made, like all his movies, for the National Film Board of Canada, the film is a cinematic memoir—part essay, part autobiography—as Low gently meanders through his thoughts about drawing, engraving, photography, horses, guns, war, and his own life as the progeny of Mormon pioneers to, first, the Salt Lake Valley and, later, the polygamist colony of Cardston near the Alberta-Montana border. Throughout, he examines how meaning is constructed from imagery—the title is a pun about motion pictures and the ways in which all pictures can be emotionally moving—and how something as personal as individual perception and memory, or something as societal as political forces intent on creating a new propagandistic narrative, can alter the meaning of an image, including movies, to fit their own agenda.

In the final moments he films himself walking over the debris of his childhood home, "leveled now by the west wind," and gazes out over his father's old wheat fields turned to grass, the buffalo herds replaced by cattle. Low made this ranch internationally famous in his breakthrough film, *Corral,* in 1954, but in many ways what he sees now doesn't match the memory in his mind. The land itself, however, is the same: there in the distance stands Chief Mountain, a sacred Blackfoot Indian site where for generations young warriors would ascend on vision quests to see their futures. The mountain was always constant, of course, but the visions varied for every man. So it is with artists, Low seems to say. A few moments earlier, over photographs of himself as a young man making his celebrated scientific documentary *Universe* (1960), he speaks in voice-over narration: "Artists and filmmakers often escape from the world through the instruments of their art, and, in doing so, they reinterpret reality. . . . I have also escaped in my drawings and films, from as far back as I can remember." Despite the disillusioning, propagandistic purposes to which film is often put, Low's filmmaking has been his own vision quest, undertaken behind a camera eyepiece—the figurative mountain where he went to escape—that has given us his reinterpretation of reality through his hundreds of films. But in this final moment of his final picture, he wants us to remember that though we may share briefly in his, or any filmmaker's, vision, it remains a vision—an artist's attempt to present their personal interpretation of reality. It always remains up to the viewer to identify that vision and evaluate it according to their own perception of what is real, true, and even moral.[1]

This may seem like an odd position to take relative to documentary films in particular, as they draw their raw material so directly from the world around us, perhaps making it easy to accept them as objectively true. The issue of subjectivity and objectivity in documentary, however, is essentially as old as the medium itself: moving pictures began with nonfiction scientific projects, leading to the brothers Auguste and Louis Lumière inaugurating cinema proper in 1895 with subjects like workers leaving their factory or a train pulling into a railroad station. Many commentators saw these films as objectively revealing physical reality in a way that no other art form—including

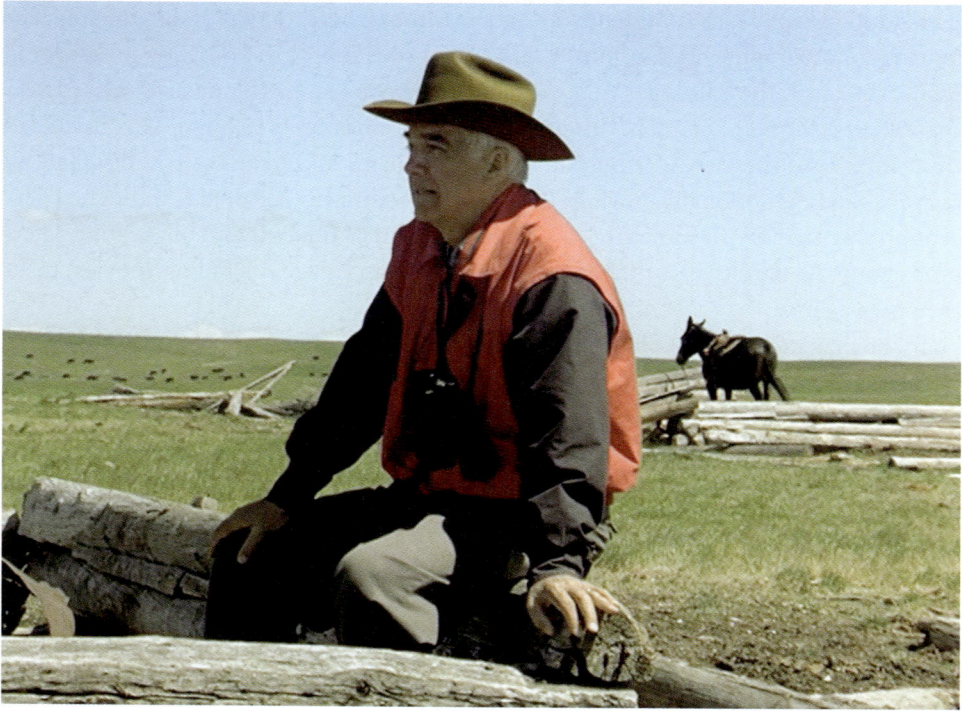

Fig. 3.1 The late Canadian filmmaker Colin Low, arguably the most accomplished filmmaker that Mormonism has ever produced, muses on his life and legacy at the end of his final film, *Moving Pictures* (2000).

photography—could, at times even surpassing the naked eye by emphasizing aspects of reality that normally pass unnoticed, such as "the ripple of the leaves stirred by the wind."[2] Others, however, soon challenged this view. Documentaries as we know them today emerged in the 1920s with the work of men like Robert Flaherty and Dziga Vertov, both of whom famously manipulated and reinterpreted their subjects rather than attempt to observe dispassionately. And when portable camera and sound equipment allowed for increased location shooting in the 1960s, it sparked a decades-long ethical debate about how documentary filmmakers' very presence influences the subjects they're filming: proponents of observational or direct cinema attempted to eliminate the filmmaker's presence as much as possible, like "a fly on the wall," while supporters of cinema verité claimed that the filmmaker's presence will always influence events and should therefore be acknowledged and even foregrounded in the film itself. Meanwhile, critics working in fields such as semiotics and psychology pointed out that all films are mediated through their creators' individuality or even the mechanical process of filmmaking, such as framing a shot or selecting and editing the footage together. All of this has shown how documentaries are anything but objective: they may begin in the real world, but they are the result of their creators' visions just as much as paintings, sculptures, and novels.

We can see this from the earliest days of cinema, even in the Lumières' ostensibly objective short films. In *Feeding the Baby* (1895), Auguste Lumière filmed himself and his wife feeding their child in the family garden—essentially the world's first home movie. This single shot may initially appear like a slice of life surreptitiously caught on the fly, but there is a world of presuppositions inherent in the camera placement, the staging of the scene, French middle-class society at the turn of the century, and political, sociological, and feminist layers of meaning, making it a bourgeois construct of the Lumière family, rather than whatever "reality" the family actually existed in outside of these sixty seconds on film. By setting up the scene, recording it precisely, and releasing it to the world, Lumière showed how he wanted to be seen by others and probably even how he saw himself—a perfect example of Low's "reinterpretation of reality" that all artists perform but with the extra resonance that, as an autobiographical film, carries all the importance that presenting oneself to the world brings with it.

The stakes can be similarly high for Mormon documentarians who take their faith and culture as their subjects. From the medium's beginning, Mormons have used non-fiction film to assert their subjectivity and self-perception of who they are and what they value. In the words of film scholar Michael Renov, they present a "multilayered construction of selfhood imagined, performed, and assigned," provoking questions about the resulting films' techniques and ethics as they present their cultural and autobiographical claims. "These questions are intellectually compelling but also of substantial political import. The assertion of 'who we are,' particularly for a citizenry massively separated from the engines of representation . . . is a vital expression of agency. We are not only what we do in a world of images; we are also what we show ourselves to be."[3]

In other words, asserting a subjective self-portrait is an act of agency—a central tenet of Mormon thought—and political will as representatives of Mormonism's subculture make their subjective voices heard, often in contrast with the dominant perspective of their larger host culture.

For decades critics have noted the uneasy relationship between Mormons and the United States or other national cultures. By and large, Mormons see themselves as God's chosen people, set apart from the world, while simultaneously longing to be accepted by the world around them.[4] Because the national perception of the church has often not matched how Mormons see themselves, LDS documentarians are keenly aware that any work they produce will potentially contrast their own self-perception—their subjectivity and view of who they are as individuals and a people—with the dominant national perspective. These pressures have resulted in two main strains of nonfiction LDS films. The first could be described as facing outward to a general audience, often attempting to put the best possible veneer on the faith. This derives largely from the beliefs that the church is God's institution on earth and that its members should therefore preach the gospel to all the world. This desire to convert can tend to minimize flaws and emphasize homogeneity within the Mormon population, as well as to slip into the realms of overt proselytizing and outright propaganda. The second mode could be characterized as facing inward—Mormon filmmakers speaking by and large with a Mormon audience—and possibly stems from another Mormon dogma, to create accurate records for personal, family, and institutional history. These films tend to emphasize their subjects' individuality, examining them in all their complexity and idiosyncrasy.

In both modes, the filmmakers embrace their own subjectivity and try to tell the truth as they see it, whether they focus on Mormons as an idealized *chosen* people or as a flawed but engrossing chosen *people*. In the end, these filmmaking styles blend into each other, as there is no universal Mormon subjectivity, just a myriad of individual subjectivities of people whose lives have intersected with the faith—and of documentarians who have attempted to show these lives as they perceive them, including the full range of believing, disaffected, and former church members. The remainder of this chapter will look at each of these modes and examine how Mormon documentarians have expressed this subjectivity in their work. While there are hundreds or even thousands of Mormon documentaries in the historical, reportorial, lyrical, and experimental veins, I will focus particularly on those that seek to convey a portrait of an individual person or group, putting us primarily in the realm of direct cinema, cinema verité, and personal essay films; these frequently feature as a subject the filmmakers themselves, or someone close to them.

FACING OUTWARD

We can see Mormons asserting their vision of themselves in film from the very beginning. The faith's first recorded encounter with motion pictures came in 1898 when a largely Mormon cavalry company of Rough Riders was filmed during the

Spanish-American War. Eight years after the nominal cessation of polygamy and just two after Utah gained statehood, church president Wilford Woodruff saw the war as a means to rehabilitate his people's public image from an isolated polygamous enclave to patriotic U.S. citizens. That April his First Presidency announced that church members should support the war, and Mormons such as these Rough Riders responded enthusiastically to what was essentially a public relations campaign. The company was delayed by a train derailment while en route from Utah, causing them to still be in Florida when a film crew from the American Mutoscope Company arrived that July to film the popular troops; the Mormons drilled their horses for several short films that were released throughout the nation with titles like *Salt Lake City Company of Rocky Mountain Riders* and *Rocky Mountain Riders Rough Riding*. Though the Mormons were not involved in the films' production or release, the movies perfectly matched how church leadership hoped to present themselves to the nation.[5]

In the following decades, as Mormon filmmakers took up the camera themselves, they were continuously conscious of how their work depicted the faith to the outside

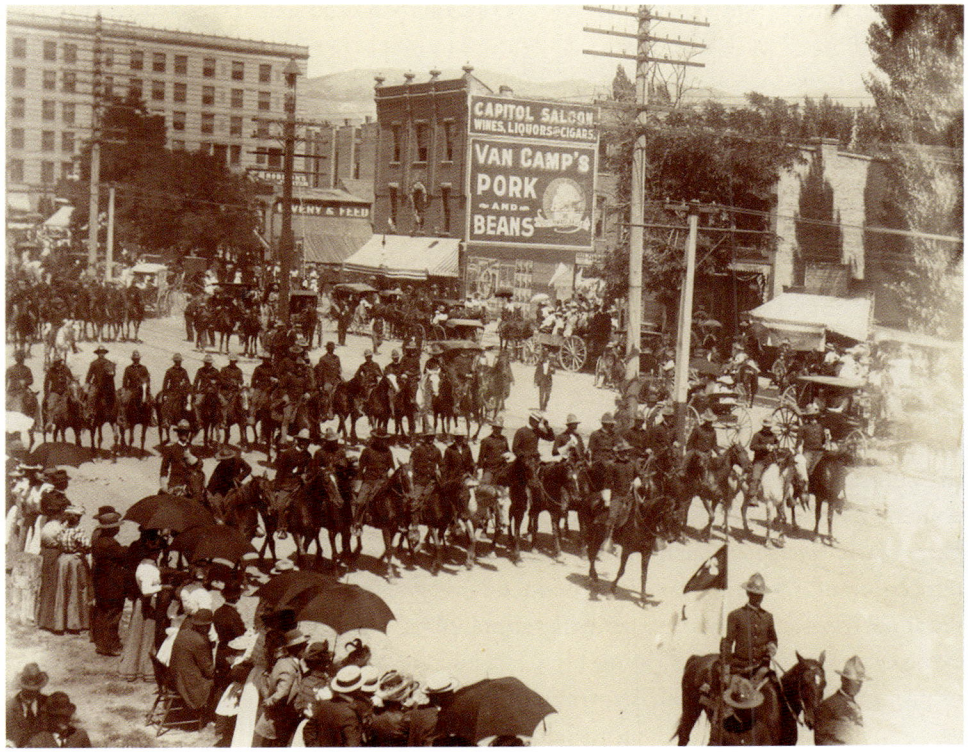

Fig. 3.2 Though the Utah Rough Riders' films have been lost, this photograph shows their triumphal return to Salt Lake City in late 1898, after they became, a few months earlier, the first Mormons—or Utahns—to ever be filmed in a motion picture.

world, from newsreel footage of church activities shot by brothers Shirl and Chet Clawson in the 1910s up to the latest video posted by a Mormon online this morning. In fact, online video indicates the scale of Mormon voices at play in documentaries today, as it's currently one of the largest Mormon art forms by volume, perhaps rivaled only by the singing of hymns. In 2009 a Google search for "Mormon videos" returned 1.9 million hits; in 2022 the number is 44.3 million, with more using other terms like "LDS"—and the vast majority of these are nonfiction.[6] It's simply impossible to maintain a unified image amid such a sea of content. Mormonism was born out of media— it literally began with the publication of a book, and could not have spread as it did without the printing press—and since the 1830s church leadership has used media to portray their desired doctrines, history, and values to the world and their own membership. The rise of the internet, however, has broken the institution's near monopoly on its public image; now its voice is merely one of thousands contesting what the faith stands for, and many believe this online democratization of information—both written and in podcasts and videos—has been pivotal in the recent decline of conversions and retention of new converts and longtime members. What this means for subjectivity in film is that space has opened up for countless perspectives to take the place of the monolithic image the church previously controlled. As scholar Jan Shipps said in 2000, early in this process:

> What [the Mormon] image will become in the new millennium is by no means clear. Moreover, as studies in perception go forward, things are changing so rapidly that I suspect soon it will not be legitimate (or even possible) to delineate the Mormon image. Despite the "cookie-cutter effect" of a carefully elaborated program the church has instituted in recent years to set standards of LDS belief and behavior, never again is there likely to be a single Mormon image. It is much more probable that along with nuance will come multiple images of the Latter-day Saints.[7]

Let's examine, then, the image that some LDS filmmakers want to convey, beginning with those who have assumed the idyllic, outward-facing, proselytizing focus.

In 1913 the church invested a great deal of resources into the fiction film *One Hundred Years of Mormonism*, which presented the faith's history from its origins through the establishment of their Utah civilization. Church Seventy Levi Edgar Young, who advised on the picture, wrote a glowing appraisal of the film's potential, which he then extrapolated outward, describing how various recent inventions "added to the means of promulgating the gospel," continuing, "So the moving picture, another modern invention, is to do much to inculcate a knowledge of the world and art . . . [This] picture will help the world at large to an understanding of our history. It will serve as a means to an end. . . . The moving picture together with all the other modern inventions is to help us carry the Mission of Christ to all the world, and to bring humanity home to the true principles of salvation."[8] Such an activist mentality places Mormons in league with filmmakers like Pare Lorentz, Michael Moore, and Alex Gibney, except that the Mormons' focus is to promote the church rather than effect social change. This is still social propaganda, in other words, but one that finds solutions in a religious society rather than a secular one.

The first documentarians to exemplify this were Shirl and Chet Clawson, mentioned above, whose first church-sponsored film came in 1916 with *The Eighty-Sixth Annual Conference of the Church of Jesus Christ of Latter-day Saints*, although they had been filming church events since as early as 1910. As grandchildren of Brigham Young and sons of the prominent Salt Lake City businessman Hiram Clawson, Shirl and Chet had incredible access to the church hierarchy, which they used to produce a steady stream of footage taken in both formal and candid settings. Much of their surviving work depicts church leaders walking around the temple grounds, saluting each other, and shaking hands in actions that were obviously directed—subjects can be seen pausing when they believe they're out of frame, or even backtracking to perform a second take. At other times the brothers were on hand to capture events like Joseph F. Smith being driven away in an automobile—the chauffeur so anxious to perform his role that he tears away before Smith can even fully sit and close the door—and they were even allowed to accompany Heber J. Grant on a private vacation to Southern California to film him playing golf. Throughout their silent film footage, the portraits that emerge are of kindly, wise, but practical men wearing modern suits and surrounded by the trappings of contemporary corporate America. They also recorded the common Mormon people, such as at community events like conferences, celebrations, and BYU track meets. These films don't share the individual touch of the portraits created of the General Authorities, but they do present the Mormon populace as creatures of the twentieth century—monogamous nuclear families enjoying a day out, young men participating in the national Boy Scouts of America organization, and even liberated female athletes running in university track and field events.

Why they would choose such subject matter becomes obvious when we realize the political component of their work. As Michael Renov noted, when minority groups assert their autobiographical subjectivity in their films, it is a political act of self-determination. Throughout the history of this mode of LDS documentary film, religiously faithful filmmakers like the Clawsons saw themselves as positioning their view of Mormonism in contrast to the outside world's perspective, which at that time still lingered in nineteenth-century beliefs about a remote desert kingdom led by bearded polygamous patriarchs, as exemplified by a slew of recent derogatory fiction films such as *A Victim of the Mormons* (1911), *The Mountain Meadows Massacre, Marriage or Death* (both 1912), and others. As far as we know, the Clawsons saw the church hierarchy as called of God and inspired to lead, and they were proud of the industry, culture, and physical beauty of Utah and its people that they recorded. Thus they took it upon themselves to show their insider's perspective of what the church was to them: a

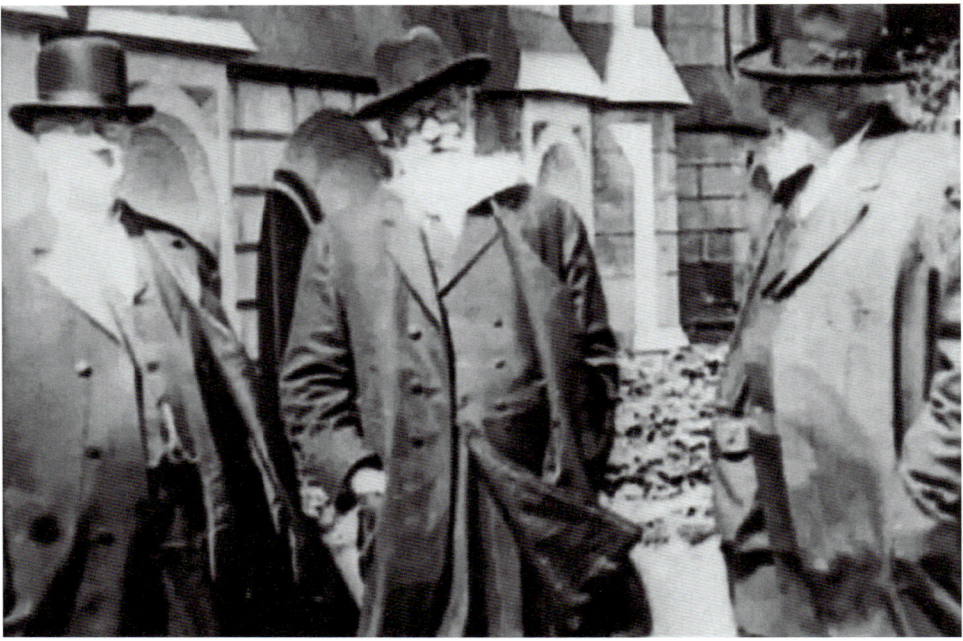

Fig. 3.3 LDS Church president Joseph F. Smith and his counselors Anthon H. Lund and John
Henry Smith all follow Shirl Clawson's direction to hold a pose on a bright and blustery day at the
Salt Lake temple grounds during the April 1910 General Conference, in some of the first footage
ever shot by Shirl and Chet Clawson.

well-run bureaucracy, emblematic of the Progressive Era and led by canny businessmen
like President Grant. By asserting their subjectivity in this manner, they were making
a statement that was both religious and political, staking their claim on the debated
Mormon image and doing a great deal to push their perspective into the rest of the
country during this period of Mormon rapprochement with the mainstream American
majority in the 1910s and 1920s.

Their work ended tragically on October 23, 1929, when a fire in their studio killed
Shirl, injured Chet, and destroyed nearly all of their footage, making it difficult to
gauge the full range of their work today. They also left no writing about how they intended their films to influence public opinion. But noting the date when they first
began filming news coverage fills in some of the gaps regarding their films' intended use.
While recordkeeping for future generations certainly played a major role, there was always an intent to show their films outside Utah to help sway the public. When they first
filmed the crowds at the General Conference in 1916, the *Salt Lake Tribune* wondered
"whether it was to be sent broadcast as a sort of educational topic on the Mormon
church or whether it was to be placed in the archives of the church, to be kept for the
private view of future generations,"[9] but the *Salt Lake Telegram,* with perhaps better

reporting, claimed simply: "The film was taken for the purpose of being sent broadcast throughout the United States."[10] The world was fully intended to see the Clawsons' modern, robust, and familial Mormon subjects, with their motorcars and their picnic lunches, bathing in the Great Salt Lake. This was Shirl and Chet Clawson's subjective take on the Mormon experience, meant for outsiders.

Though they are generally considered conservative or even reactionary filmmakers due to their uncritical praise of the institution and their antiquated 1890s style of a two-person filmmaking crew, the Clawsons in this respect can be seen as quite radical. They worked alone against the hegemony of the filmmaking centers in New York and Los Angeles, and in doing so bear a surprising resemblance to their contemporary Dziga Vertov. An ardent Bolshevik, he spent the 1920s creating newsreels and feature-length documentaries lauding the achievements of the new USSR for both his fellow Soviets and the outside world. While the Clawsons did not share Vertov's politics or imitate his stylistic innovations, their motivation to bear witness to truth as they believed it was identical, as was their love for their people and homeland.

As with the Clawsons, Vertov's "subject matter was seldom spectacular. This was part of its essential quality: drama was revealed in 'the prose of life.' It caught the moment when a Moscow trolley line, long out of operation in torn-up streets, was finally put in repair and began running again. Army tanks, used as tractors, were leveling an area for an airport. A children's hospital was trying to salvage war-starved children."[11] The Clawsons' conference attendees, Boy Scouts, and children's parades were the Mormon equivalent of these scenes, and represent the same use of their subjective viewpoint to accentuate the greatness of their people. Had more of their footage survived, today it would have proved as much a celebration of the Mormon way of life as Vertov's films are a celebration of the Soviet one.

If the first Mormon documentarians echoed Vertov's fervor, for subsequent genera-tions the model would become John Grierson. Grierson, a Scottish documentarian who created government-funded filmmaking units in Britain, Canada, and elsewhere from the 1920s through the 1950s—and who coined the term "documentary" in 1926—is often invoked as an inspiration for Mormon filmmakers up to the present. In 1933, near the beginning of his career, he wrote: "I look on cinema as a pulpit, and use it as a propa-gandist. . . . Cinema is to be conceived as a medium, like writing, capable of many forms and many functions. A professional propagandist may well be especially interested in it."[12] Elsewhere, in one of his most famous pronouncements, he asserted that "it is as a hammer, not a mirror, that I have sought to use the medium that came to my somewhat restive hand."[13] In Grierson's view, film had work to do; for Mormon filmmakers facing outward to the world, this work remained Levi Edgar Young's call to "carry the Mission of Christ to all the world."

After the Clawsons' fire, church filmmaking entered a hiatus that lasted through the Depression and World War II. Wartime documentary films—largely a result of Grierson's work in the 1930s—convinced church leaders of the instructional power of cinema, and sporadic filmmaking efforts led to the creation of a motion picture department at Brigham Young University in 1953, the precursor of today's LDS Motion Picture Studio and the church's Audiovisual Department. Its first director was "Judge" Wetzel Whitaker, and though he's better remembered for fiction films like *The Windows of Heaven* (1963) and *Johnny Lingo* (1969), he directed just as many nonfiction productions, from *Church Welfare in Action* (1948) to the reportorial-style *Church in Action* series in the 1970s.

Whitaker drew his nonfiction style directly from Griersonian techniques, building his films around a script, often by his brother Scott, with an authoritative male narrator speaking in voice-over—later sometimes criticized as the "voice of God" for its implied patriarchal omniscience. This narration developed an argument orally, along with relevant footage and the occasional on-camera interview. We can see this technique in the original *Meet the Mormons* (1973), for instance, which begins with shots of pedestrians on a crowded street and the narrator intoning, "This is the story of a way of life and of a people, a people very much like your next-door neighbors." The film thus begins by normalizing Mormons, reflecting Whitaker's subjective view at this moment of the church's peak assimilation into American society in the twentieth century. For twenty-four minutes the narrator asserts Mormons' similarities to the viewer, while also introducing some beliefs and practices that make them distinct. There is no deep doctrine or beliefs that differ extremely from mainstream Protestantism, but instead cultural practices like church attendance, family home evenings, volunteer missionary service, and home and visiting teaching programs, all presented as admirable practices that all viewers could emulate. There is some direct address to the camera, as when a missionary briefly pauses in the street to explain his calling; this type of interview—which originated in Grierson's earlier films, such as *Housing Problems* (1935)—makes the missionary approachable. As with most of Whitaker's work, this is a stylistically conservative film, which spoke to its audience of middle-class white Christian Americans who had probably already let a pair of missionaries into their home.

Whitaker's nonfiction work, like the Clawsons', may initially appear conservative or out of touch, but again the truth is that it was quite effective. In this case, by asserting his subjective view of Mormonism as a legitimate component of American and other national cultures (*Meet the Mormons* was shot in several countries), Whitaker is making an effective political argument that Mormons deserve to be treated as part of the collective, and not as a dangerous Other. In *The Search for Truth* (1962) he shows that Mormons accept science; in *Latter-day Saint Temples* (1956) he demystifies LDS temple worship by showing the history of biblical temples; in *Time Pulls the Trigger* (1960) he emphasizes the dangers of smoking; and in *The Fruitful Years* (1957) he depicts the beauty of Utah Valley's fruit orchards and the community centered around BYU. His purpose with all of these, of course, was to build internal pride within Mormon culture, strengthen relationships with outsiders, and even create converts to the church.

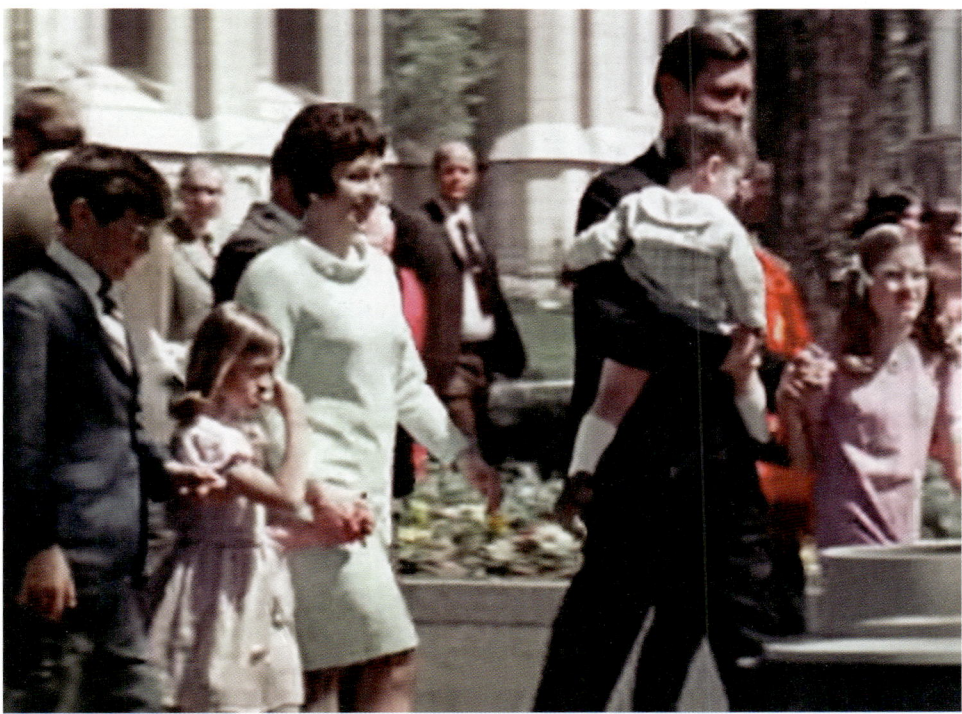

Fig. 3.4 A modern family—in 1973—enjoys a break between General Conference sessions on Temple Square in Judge Whitaker's documentary *Meet the Mormons*.

All of BYU's nonfiction films of the midcentury period thus represent a shared pride in the church's beliefs and social admirability. This is a subjective perspective, but one that's sublimated into institutional goals of growth and self-promotion, and it's fair to say that the image presented is more idealized than introspective. It is, however, also effective, and church-employed filmmakers have used it up to the present. One example is Blair Treu's short film *Called to Serve* (1991), which is essentially an instructional video teaching missionaries how to be missionaries. It depicts the process of receiving a mission call, entering the Missionary Training Center (MTC), and serving away from home before finally returning to an awaiting family. There are some stylistic changes from Whitaker's midcentury films, however. By this point the "voice of God" was falling out of favor, and Treu eliminates it in favor of a chorus of voice-over statements and sit-down interviews with missionaries describing their work. This moved the "narration" away from the voice of an adult man and put it into that of its intended audience. For more than twenty years *Called to Serve* was used as a recruitment film to excite Mormon teens to serve missions; it even showed multiple times each week at the MTC as families said goodbye to their departing missionaries—an event actually depicted in the film![14]

Church films from this period were also affected by Mormonism's shifting place within broader society. Where the Clawsons had reacted against nineteenth-century stereotypes to depict the church as modern and bureaucratic, Mormonism had now largely assimilated into the mainstream of conservative American culture, with an image focused on middle-class white prosperity and nuclear-family values. However, this remarkable transformation occurred, ironically, at the same time that much of American culture was shifting away from this: the counterculture of the 1960s and 1970s, including the sexual revolution, feminism, civil rights, and gay rights, now positioned Mormonism's new respectability as outdated and even dangerous, something made clear when the church took steps to support the Vietnam War or oppose the Equal Rights Amendment and, a generation later, oppose Proposition 8 legalizing same-sex marriage in California.

For many years the church hierarchy embraced this position as a bastion of old-fashioned family values: Judge Whitaker made many fiction films villainizing drugs and alcohol, premarital sex, and even hippies, and in the 1980s the church-owned Bonneville Communications broadcast television public service announcements with slogans like "Family . . . isn't it about time?" But soon the church's public relations professionals,

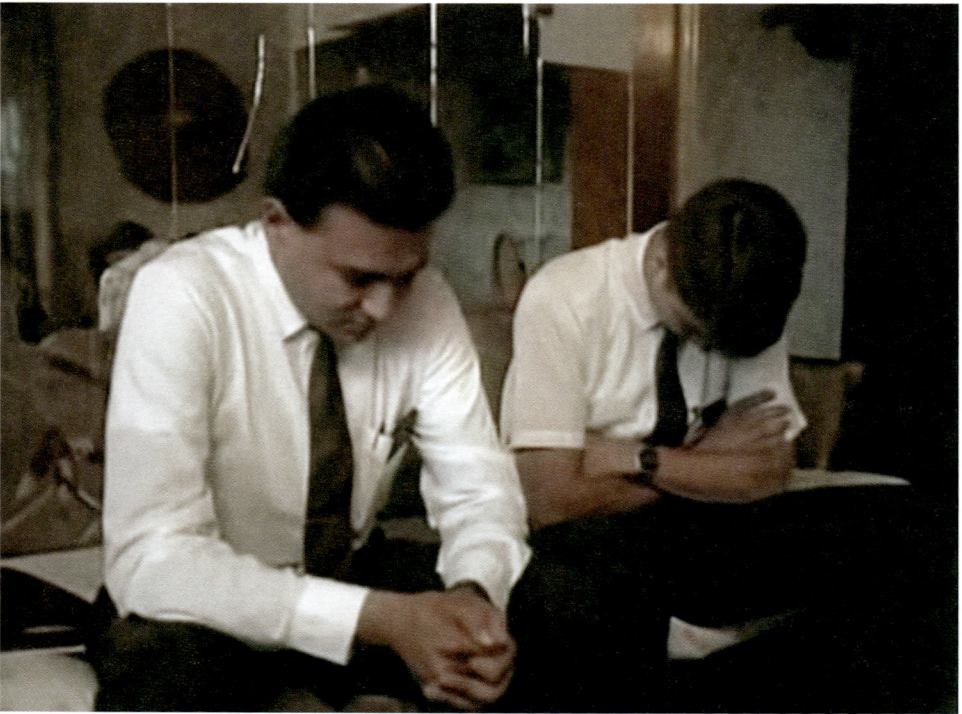

Fig. 3.5 In *Called to Serve* (1991), Blair Treu captured LDS missionaries in all moments of their service, including this companionship holding a prayer with an investigating family.

under the canny guidance of church president Gordon B. Hinckley, saw a need to update the church's image, resulting in twin advertising and online video campaigns known as "Mormon Messages" and "I'm a Mormon." While these didn't change standards on things such as premarital sex, they did actively seek to present a Mormonism divorced from the staid images of conservative white homogeneity, centering as many unmarried people, people of color, people outside the Mormon heartland, and people with unique or surprising stories, careers, and interests as possible.

Thus, two decades after *Called to Serve*, Blair Treu directed a much different movie with a remake of *Meet the Mormons* (2014)—and the differences are even more pronounced from Judge Whitaker's original. The seventy-eight-minute running time meant that Treu had to employ a narrator in order to navigate the structure and connect different subjects, but rather than use a disembodied voice he selected the attractive young comedian Jenna Kim Jones and brought her onscreen, updating the narrator from what would now be seen as out of touch and untrustworthy to a very specific human being, one who's nearly dancing through Times Square—not Salt Lake City— and laughing about how corny or straitlaced her faith can be, while interpolating clips from popular TV shows and films that openly mock the faith.

Opening in this way says that Mormons today are hip and can take a joke, and they're diverse too: rather than exploring the church's religious practices, as the 1973 film does, this *Meet the Mormons* takes its lessons from the "I'm a Mormon" campaign and instead profiles individuals: a Black convert and bishop from Atlanta, a Polynesian American football coach, a Costa Rican woman who fights in mixed martial arts, a Nepali humanitarian, a white pilot from the Berlin Airlift, and a white mother who struggled as a single parent. This is not by any means how a typical Utah congregation looks, but for Treu it represents the modern global church.

Still, the diversity has its limits: these Mormons are progressive, hip, and worldly, but still devout and successful. They are, in other words, ideal twenty-first-century Mormons, unique but orthodox. From the believing church member's perspective, these people demonstrate how deeply normal Mormons are; it can be deflating, then, when the outside world still sees only the weirdness and Otherness in Mormonism, as reviews for the film indicated.[15] To overcome that kind of barrier, filmmakers might shift away from the idealization of their faith that they hope will impress friends or win converts, and instead focus on individual Mormons' lives with no agenda beyond making a human record.

FACING INWARD

Recordkeeping is an intrinsic component of Mormon culture, stemming from scriptural commands and practices like genealogical work and maintaining church histories. Over the years Mormons have used a variety of technologies to create personal and institutional records, including photography, microfilm, audiotape, and of course film. But while Mormonism has given rise to hundreds of historical and reportorial

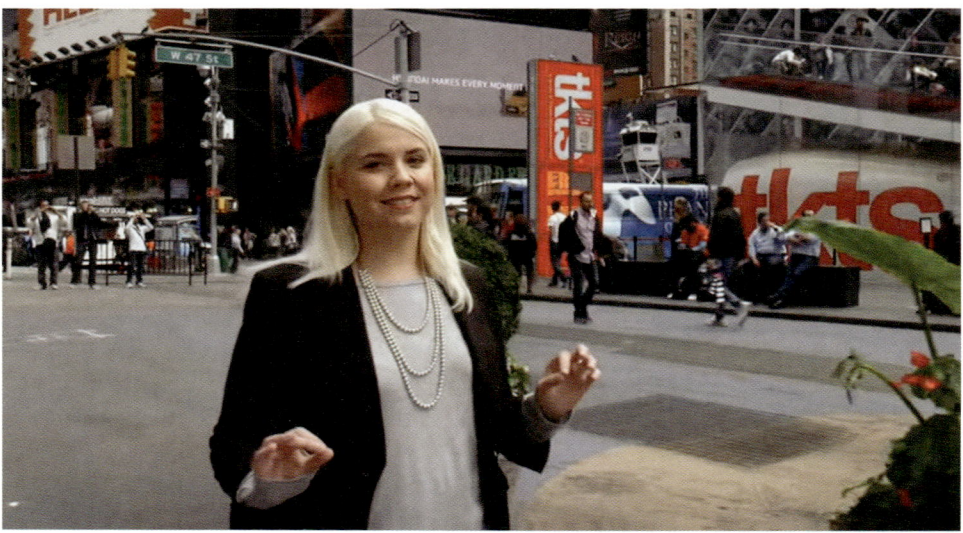

Fig. 3.6 Writer and stand-up comedian Jenna Kim Jones walks through the Times Square area while introducing Blair Treu's *Meet the Mormons* (2014), a dramatically hip updating from Judge Whitaker's original.

documentaries, our interest here lies primarily with those that resemble an essay, a portrait, or an autobiography. These are films based in the present rather than looking back to the past; like a personal diary, they will accrue historical significance only in the future. At their best, they have a limited scope, focusing on one person or perhaps one family, who are not meant to stand in as synecdoches for the entire church, and they accept the limited perspective that comes with this territory. Indeed, autobiography and the personal essay are by definition subjective: there is no other way to work in these forms. They embrace their subjectivity and don't pretend to omniscience. Rather than driving toward a predetermined outcome, such as proving that Mormons are admirable people, they feel content to meander, to pause and contemplate, or merely to appreciate the beauty of their subjects' lives.

Mormon culture is fertile soil for cinematic portraits like these. Over 190 years of recording and sharing personal stories has primed Mormons to be uniquely attuned to such works' possibilities and qualities, and a church with a democratic lay leadership where every member is called a "Saint" means that a moving story can come from anywhere and be about anyone. Thus Mormonism's most compelling cinematic portraits are not of public figures like Mitt Romney in *Mitt* (2014), Jon Huntsman in *All Eyes and Ears* (2015), or even Mark Hofmann in *Murder Among the Mormons* (2021) but of rank-and-file church members going about their daily lives. Folklorist William A. Wilson has claimed that it's "the quiet lives of committed service that . . . lay at the heart of the Mormon experience,"[16] adding elsewhere that "because these stories are cut from the marrow of everyday experience and reflect the hopes, fears, joys, and anxieties of common church members, they bring us about as close as we are likely to get to Mormon hearts and minds and to an understanding, from the lay membership's point of view, of what it really means to be Mormon."[17]

Take Elaine Dart. Born with cerebral palsy that caused her to live in a high-care facility and denied her the use of her hands, she nevertheless persevered in using her feet to develop several remarkable talents. In the 1975 film *Elaine Dart: Not Like Other People*, she says, "I like to sew, I like to do needlepoint, I like to do embroidery. I like to do anything I can get my feet on"—said with a grin at her turn of phrase. And director T. C. Christensen lets us see her do all of these, his camera lingering in steady extreme close-up, the narrator silent, as Elaine's toes open a padlock, write in cursive, load paper into a typewriter, work on a bead lace necklace, and painstakingly thread a needle. "Her head sways spasmodically back and forth," the narrator says, "she has had a cataract removed from each eye, and still, in less than eighteen seconds, the needle is threaded." Her achievements are remarkable—we see a painting and an embroidery that she created of the Last Supper, and hear how she presented a sweater to Jacqueline Kennedy—but it's also in the more mundane moments that we see what her life must really be like, as her boyfriend, a fellow resident, patiently feeds her, and as they dance together—an opportunity, the narrator says, "where her feet can move to music instead of moving mountains." A thirteen-minute film cannot fully convey what Elaine's life is like in all its complexity, but it's still sufficient to paint a portrait of the determination and optimism that are her driving personality traits.

Reflections (1978) is a forty-minute autobiographical group portrait of Mormon women in Southern California, produced by a ward Relief Society president, Irene Bates, and directed by her daughter Lynda Taylor. Shot during the national debate over the ERA, in which Mormon women took high-profile positions on both sides, *Reflections* shows a plethora of subjective positions, from an elderly widow who feels lost without her husband to a working single mother who fled her husband after his PTSD from the Vietnam War made him abusive. The film operates primarily through interviews, and the women discuss their views on family, marriage, and careers, each one unique. Taylor's own subjective perspective, then, revels in the diversity of opinions and life experiences that make up her Mormon sisterhood and doesn't attempt to persuade the viewer in any direction. The film ends on a stay-at-home mother, who has previously complained about sacrificing her career, asking, "Always at night I think, you know, what is it that I really want to do? What is it that I want to be?" The screen cuts to black, leaving such an intensely subjective question lingering for the viewer to ponder herself.[18]

Other portraits, of individuals and groups, abound. Steve Olpin's *The Potter's Meal* (1992) depicts the ceramic artist Joseph Bennion as he forms, fires, and sells his pots in his central Utah home studio. Bennion is incredibly articulate about his own subjective outlook on life—why he chose this lifestyle and how working with clay helps

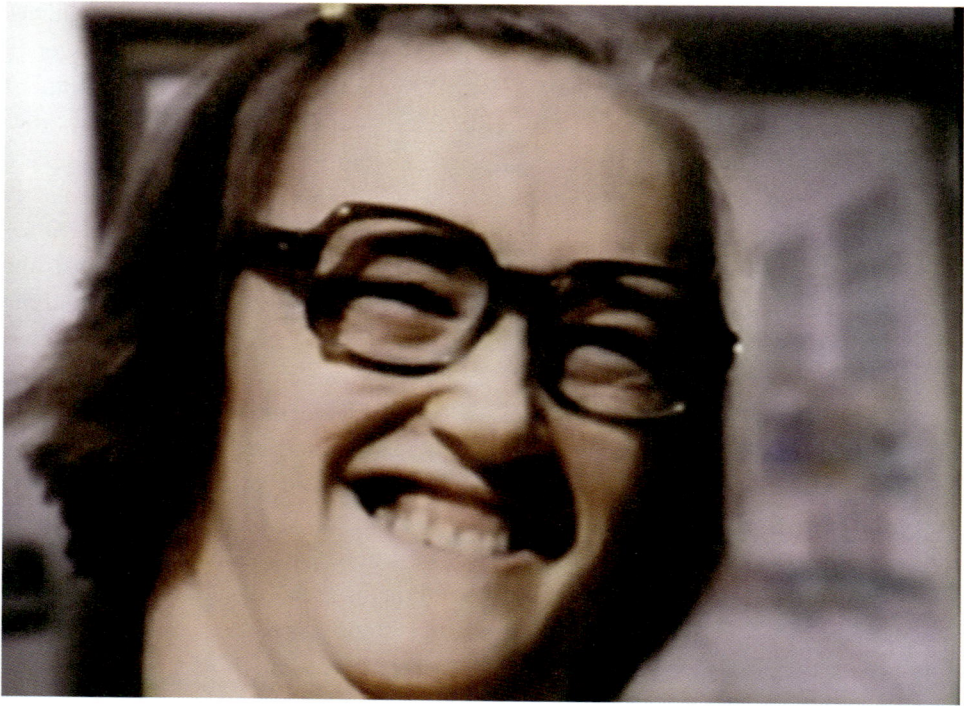

Fig. 3.7 Elaine can't help but smile for the camera, her personality shining through her disability, in *Elaine Dart: Not Like Other People* (1975).

him feel close to the earth and to God. *The Plan* (1980) uses a cinema verité approach to follow Michele Meservy, named Utah's Young Mother of the Year for 1978, as she struggles with her demanding young children and caring but absent husband; the film ends with the couple watching and commenting on the footage at an editing table, thus allowing them to express their perspectives on the film itself.[19] In *Sisterz in Zion* (2006) director Melissa Puente uses a similar style to follow a group of economically under-privileged teen girls from Manhattan as they journey to BYU for a week of religious activities at an Especially for Youth camp; the initial culture shock and distrust between these young women of color and their wealthy white counterparts eventually soften into understanding and friendship. And in the fourteen-minute *Polygamy and Me* (2003) Lareena Smith recounts her own journey from the mainstream LDS Church into fundamentalism and three failed polygamous marriages and finally to leaving religion and pursuing her dream of writing and filmmaking. Smith's autobiographical subjectivity filters through layers of postmodern self-referential irony and humor, such as using actors to reenact a hammed-up version of her life story and even read her first-person narration, resulting in a film with a quirky and optimistic flair despite the darkness of the underlying reality; this is definitely one person's exaggerated memory of their lived experience with polygamy rather than a polemic about its morality.

One of Mormonism's greatest films is Greg Whiteley's debut documentary *New York Doll* (2005), about Arthur "Killer" Kane, the former bassist of the defunct glam rock band the New York Dolls and now a Mormon convert and part-time assistant at the church's Family History Center near the Los Angeles temple. Kane had soared high as a 1980s celebrity, then hit rock bottom after the band, decimated by drugs and alcohol, broke up. His conversion to Mormonism started a second chapter in his life, and when the musician Morrissey undertook to engineer a Dolls reunion at an upcoming music festival in London, Whiteley began filming Arthur as they went to get his bass out of the pawn shop. Thus the movie, through interviews, archival film, and Whiteley's footage, chronicles Arthur's journey from rock star to family history worker and back to rock star again. It's a gripping portrait of a man struggling with his past demons and his present doubts, as he wonders if he'll be able to play his music again or, more importantly, make up with his old bandmates, with whom he fell out years before. He stands at the crux of two seemingly incompatible worlds, and he knows it, but he does his best to fit in with the rock musicians without losing his new identity as a disciple of Jesus, while his "gentle voice and tranquil speech betoken a steady calm at a swirling vortex of contradictions."[20]

For scholar Terryl Givens this is the heart of the film, and he centers his critique around one moment when Sir Bob Geldorf laments that Arthur will have to go back to his mundane Mormon life instead of remaining a star. Sitting next to him, "Chrissie Hynde, lead singer of the Pretenders, softly mutters, 'There is room for both.'"[21] The film seems to bear this out by taking on added typological weight at the Royal Festival Hall performance when Arthur dons a costume that reminds him of Joseph Smith—though others think he's a pirate—out of sheer respect for the man and the faith that literally saved his life. The concert is a success, and now his friends such as Geldorf worry if he'll be all right going back to his Family History Center job. Arthur isn't worried, though—he's anxious to return. Upon arriving back in L.A., however, he feels unwell, visits the hospital, and within two hours is dead from leukemia. As Arthur's reunited friend David Johansen sings the hymn "A Poor Wayfaring Man of Grief" over the closing credits, it's not clear if he's singing about Arthur or Jesus or both. By including this song after the film's narrative conclusion, Whiteley, without any heavy-handed hagiography, provides his view on his friend and film subject: a man of sorrows, acquainted with grief, Arthur Kane nevertheless was a Saint.[22]

Perhaps the best example of a quiet biographical group portrait of Mormonism comes in the collection of short documentaries at BYU known as the Fit for the Kingdom project. Begun by film professor Dean Duncan with a coalition of students and faculty members in 2002, Fit for the Kingdom seeks to "portray and appreciate ordinary people in their ordinary circumstances, to the end that we do not mistake fantasy for reality, celebrity for substance, escapism for anxious engagement" and to "provide means through

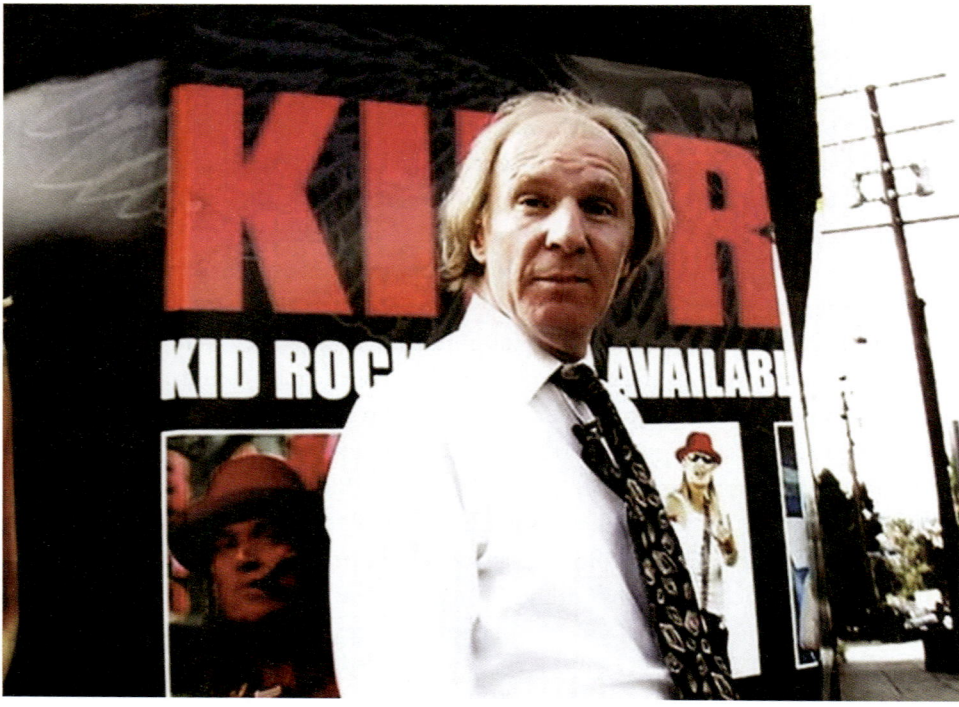

Fig. 3.8 Former New York Dolls bassist and glam rock icon Arthur "Killer" Kane pauses to talk to his close friend and director Greg Whiteley, behind the camera, in front of a poster for a newer musical act in the phenomenal feature-length film *New York Doll* (2005).

which the silent can speak and the obscure be acknowledged."[23] The idealism and urgency here echo the manifestos of men like Vertov and Grierson, although there's also a distinct Mormon flavor present, as Duncan holds that people can best "work out their salvation" in the quiet quotidian moments of their lives. The name of the project, Fit for the Kingdom, is from the hymn "More Holiness Give Me," which is essentially a prayer for sanctity—and salvation—to work its way through the singer's heart and spirit. The films, then, are designed as sacred moments clothed in the robes of family meetings, preparing dinner, camping, gardening, driving, and lifting weights. As short films, they are fleeting moments rather than feature-length biopics like *New York Doll,* and they evoke Impressionist paintings—a glance at a scene that is entirely subject to where the viewer is looking right then; one second later and the light will have changed and the scene shifted. This makes these entirely subjective films: there is no authoritative perspective here, just a friend or a father filming their loved one at that particular place and in that particular moment in time.

Duncan himself admits that his aims may sound "lofty and even abstract,"[24] but in practice the films are quite simple. One of the first, *Leroy Pratt: Crossings* (2001; later restyled as *Leroy* to match the other films' titles), directed by Ben Unguren, is about a retired man who now volunteers as a crossing guard in Provo, Utah. He jokes with the children and chats with Unguren behind the camera. As these are true cinema verité films, which acknowledge the filmmakers' presence, Leroy even answers the children's questions about why a man is filming him: "Because I'm so pretty he wants my picture," he quips. After all the children have gone, Leroy walks away, heading home to plant a tree. "I'll never live to get any shade out of it," he says in voice-over, "but I'll go home and plant it." He then turns the interrogation back on Unguren, and by extension every viewer, asking, "What are you going to do when you leave here?" The unanswered question ends the seven-minute film, like in *Reflections,* leaving viewers to ponder how they will live their lives having shared this moment from his.

Other Fit for the Kingdom films have waded into seemingly deeper territory—subjects including the death of a pet, substance abuse, and child abuse—but never in a sensational way. This is true even in *Angie* (2006), an unusually long film, running fifty-three minutes, in which BYU film professor Tom Russell chronicles his wife's battle with terminal cancer. We see an adoring portrait of a resolute wife and mother, a mourning

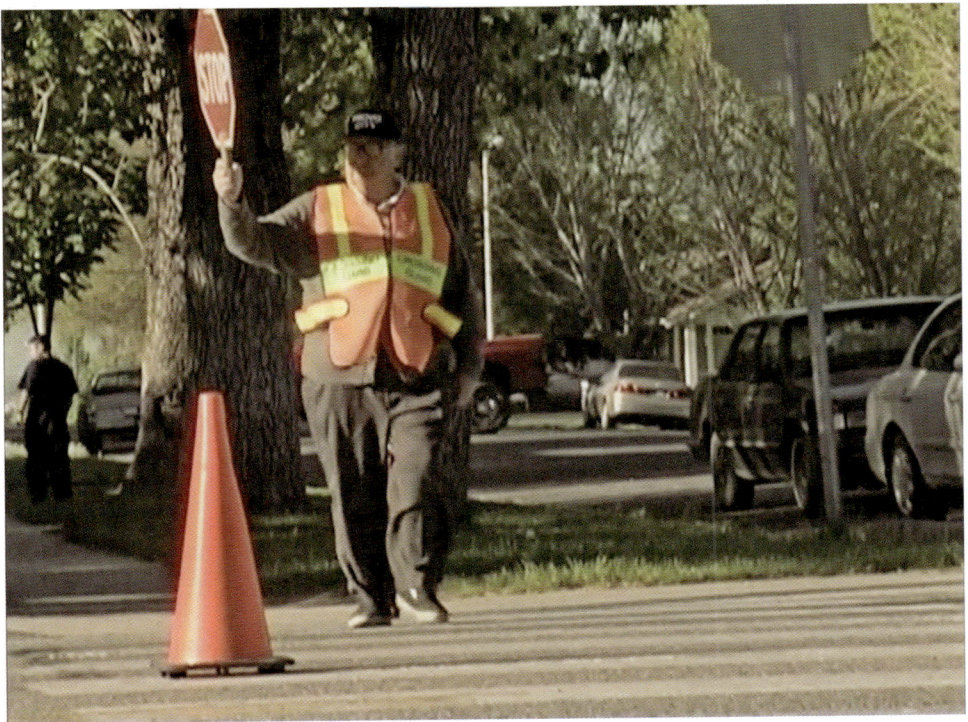

Fig. 3.9 Eighty-two-year-old volunteer crossing guard Leroy Pratt stops traffic for some Provo, Utah, neighborhood children in the first Fit for the Kingdom film, *Leroy* (2001), a film of quiet discipleship that provided the blueprint for all subsequent Fit for the Kingdom profiles.

family, and an entire community rallying around their friend and neighbor. The aesthetic is of a home movie, meaning things like shaky camera work and sarcastic teenage shenanigans, but it is deceptively skillfully assembled. The most important thing about it is all the time that the camera is off, elisions in the narrative when the family was living through their lives and their grief. As a group self-portrait—they all take turns behind the camera—the family's subjectivity is foregrounded throughout. This is partly true precisely because the Russells were filming themselves, creating a home movie for their family, not for public release, so they could let their guard down and truly be themselves. And when the moments were too overwhelming, such as the entirety of Angie's final months, they didn't need to put on pretenses but could simply put the camera away. The result is more raw, real, and unmediated than Auguste Lumière feeding his baby or the uncannily upbeat subjects of *Meet the Mormons*. There's no idealized image projected outward to the world, but the completely personal record of what it was like for this family to lose their mom.[25]

At present the most recent film on the Fit for the Kingdom website is *Afrikaans 101* (2009), by Mark Lewis, which simply shows an elderly South African instructor,

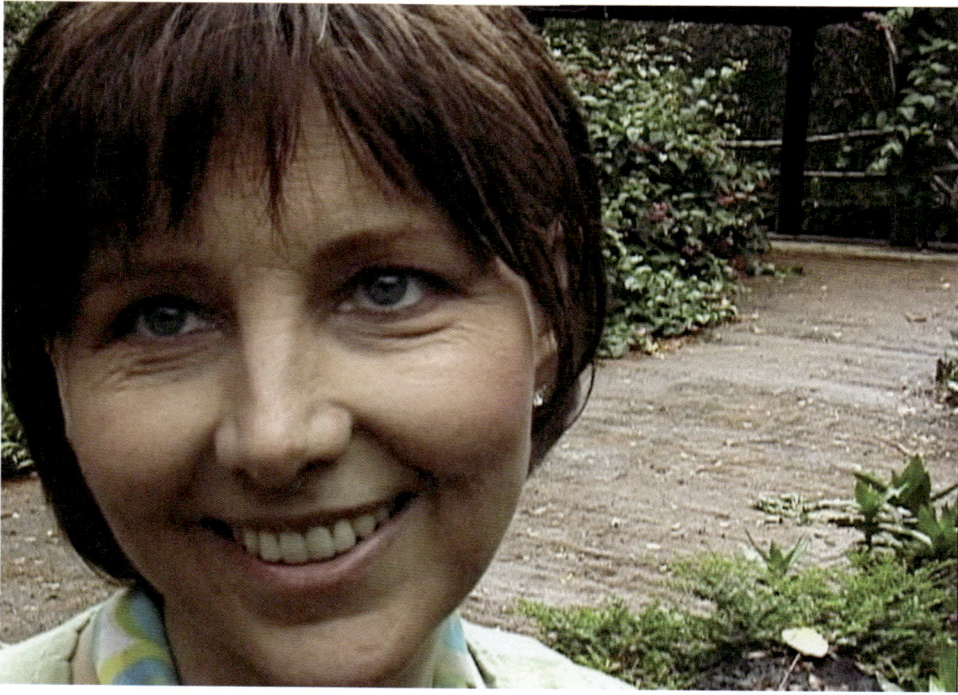

Fig. 3.10 The final frame from *Angie* (2006), as filmmaker Tom Russell tells his ailing wife how beautiful she is. This image is frozen over several seconds, as voice-over audio lets the audience realize that Angie Russell has died and mourn her loss after coming to know and love her over the previous hour.

Barry Hornabrook, teaching a night class in Afrikaans in a basement classroom some-where on the BYU campus. The class itself is mundane and even boring, as Barry and his students, seated around a conference table, go over vocabulary, verb conjugations, and even grading procedures. As class ends and the students shuffle out Barry bids them goodbye—"See you on Thursday"—then finally engages with Lewis, who is filming. It becomes clear they know each other, and their casual banter even makes it seem like Barry allowed him to come film his class as a personal favor, though, as with Leroy Pratt, he doesn't see why this would make an interesting film. In the best tradition of cinema verité, the men shake hands, jiggling the camera, and Barry asks if Lewis will turn off the light and close the door when he leaves. He walks down the hallway, sending his regards to Amanda, and disappears around the corner. As he does, text at the bottom of the screen states that he died of a heart attack early the next morning. The revelation of this moment retroactively gives meaning to everything that came before: even without knowing anything about him beyond a few banal moments of language instruction, we can feel the weight of a life ended, prompting the same introspection into our own lives that so many of these films induce. Such a powerful moment can come only in a docu-mentary film, of course, and it's aided by Lewis's restraint from providing any more con-text into Barry's life; subjectively we're seeing through his eyes, and Barry's death hits us, in a small way, close to how it must have hit him.

FACING UPWARD

Finally, the state of the church today has given rise to a new breed of filmmaker, those who are making their subjective voices heard in opposition against either the church directly or at least the homogeneous culture that it dominates in the Great Basin. When the Clawson brothers began their work, Mormons were an ostracized and misunderstood minority, but a century later the church is a multibillion-dollar entity with powerful political and cultural influence. Those who are marginalized or feel un-represented in this culture—such as people who identify as female, LGBTQ+, and BIPOC—or those who have left the church or have a heterodox relationship with it can now create films that assert their own autobiography and subjective experience against the church's hegemony in this political arena. As many young Mormons no longer iden-tify with traditional LDS norms, this tension is set to be a primary locus of conflict and disaffection over the next several years, and one that will play out in film and video, as the activists and filmmakers among them create documentaries that highlight their own subjective experience within the larger Mormon and American cultures.

For some groups this obviously began years ago, as with the women who made *Reflections* in the 1970s. Others have less precedent. Very few films had been made about the Black Mormon experience, for instance, before *Nobody Knows: The Untold Story of Black Mormons*—which primarily uses a historical film format—in 2008. People have left the church since its beginning, often at a rate as high as two for every one who joins, but before the internet it was difficult for them to find a community to help them process the trauma that church membership might have caused. With social media, however, there is a vibrant global post-Mormon community, and after the success of the "I'm a Mormon" campaign many former church members began making their own videos, called "I'm an Ex-Mormon," not to attack the church but to help others like them who were dealing with a faith transition. These short online videos certainly represent a new perspective within Mormon film that didn't exist before 2010.

Queer Mormons and their allies have been among the most active in telling their stories on camera. Among dozens of titles, the short film *Families Are Forever* (2013) takes the perspective of Tom and Wendy Montgomery, the devout heterosexual parents of a young teenage son who shook their worldview when he came out as gay. The film, directed by Vivian Kleiman, explores their love for their son and pain that their church, which they also love, will not accept his orientation as anything but deviant. Another short, Torben Bernhard's *Transmormon* (2014), centers around Eri Hayward, a transgender woman who was raised as a devout Mormon boy in Orem, Utah. Hayward is now a young adult well into her transition, and the film shows how she has found peace with her gender identity and her faith but still struggles in the face of her frequently transphobic Mormon community.

One of the most recent Mormon films on LGBTQ+ issues is the feature-length *Same-Sex Attracted* (2020), which deals with the status of queer students at BYU. The film is unabashedly propagandistic, advocating for an end to policies that punish queer students, such as ejecting them from student-approved housing, and for other policies that would help include them as fully accepted members of the student body, such as approval for a student-run LGBTQ organization. While this is obviously a piece of advocacy, directors Maddy Purves and Zoie Young make their case by profiling a small group of individual students and their struggles and successes negotiating their various sexual orientations and gender identities. There's not enough time to come to know any one of them on the level of an Arthur Kane or Angie Russell, but when the scenes are taken together as a group portrait, it is a remarkable entrée into the unique community of queer students at the conservative school.

Other Gen Z students at BYU have chosen to bypass the feature-length documentary and employ more immediate technology to tell their stories. In early 2022 five students of color organized as the Black Menaces and launched a TikTok channel to post short videos. Thus far their videos, filmed on cellphones in a vertical aspect ratio, consist entirely of approaching people on campus and asking them questions relating to marginalized communities, such as "What did you learn during Black History Month?," "Should same-sex students be able to date?," and "Are you a feminist?" Their question-and-answer format differs somewhat from the other films discussed in this section, but it hearkens back to the groundbreaking 1961 film *Chronicle of a Summer,* in which the directors approached people on the streets of Paris and simply asked them if they were happy. Like this, the Black Menaces' videos are cinema verité at its most direct, and the responses from white students, while often either funny or embarrassing,

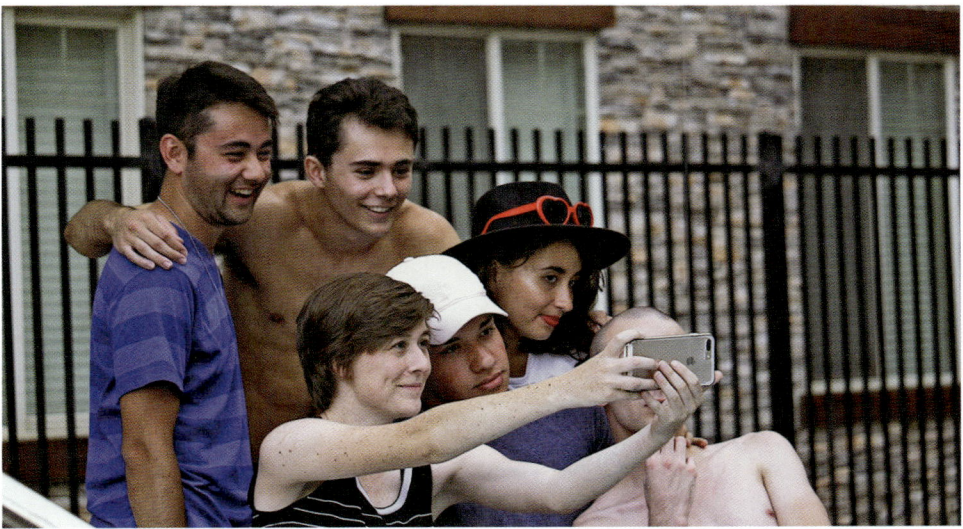

Fig. 3.11 *Same-Sex Attracted* (2020) appropriates the dismissive language of the LDS Church hierarchy to show how gay, lesbian, nonbinary, transgender, and other gender non-conforming Gen Z BYU students are claiming their space within Mormon society in a manner that previous generations could never achieve.

reveal the extent to which they haven't considered the Black or queer experience. "We're highlighting the reality here for people like us," Rachel Weaver told the *Salt Lake Tribune.* "It might seem provocative to some, but it's just that most people don't know what it's like being Black at a church-owned institution or even a majority white institution."[26]

In other words, these five activists are using nonfiction video to share their subjectivity with their peers who had not previously considered it. In doing so, they are exercising political power to stake out their place within the university community, reportedly drawing the ire of some students and university officials. Many others, though, are receptive to their message; not only does their TikTok account currently have over 725,000 followers, but the encounters in the videos themselves are always upbeat and friendly, with many respondees expressing a desire to learn new perspectives and accept people who don't fit into the school's heterosexual white norm.[27] With *Same-Sex Attracted,* the Black Menaces, and other BYU students using their phones' video functions to protest injustice, we're seeing a new generation of nonfiction filmmakers emerging to once again alter and complicate the Mormon image. The monolithic image from the eras of the Clawsons and Judge Whitaker must now make way for a strand of Mormon subjectivity that was previously silenced.

In fact, what we see today is Mormonism itself becoming increasingly subjective. If there are as many ways to be Mormon or ex-Mormon as there are people who have

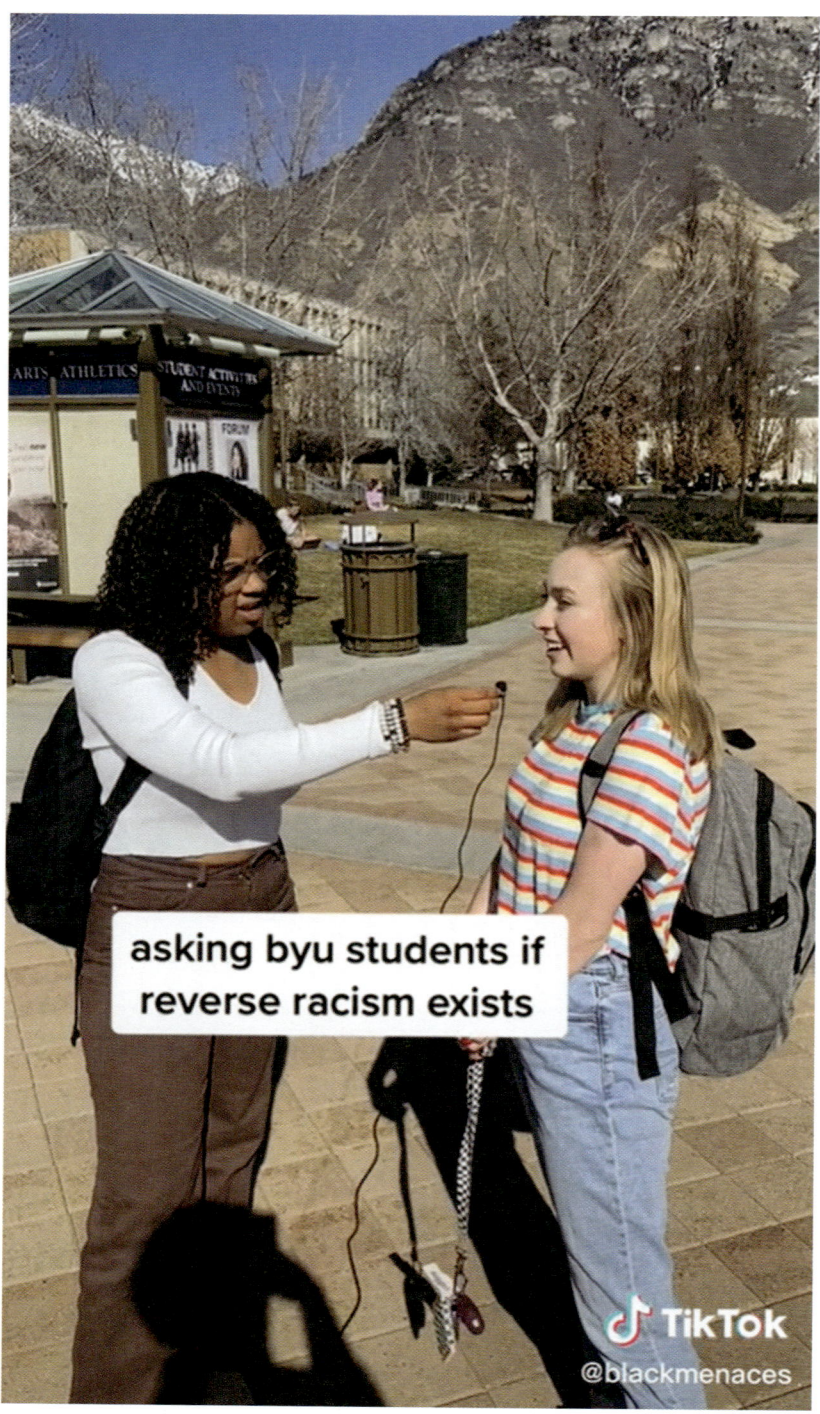

asking byu students if reverse racism exists

TikTok
@blackmenaces

Fig. 3.12 A member of the Black Menaces interviews a sympathetic white BYU student in spring 2022. Since beginning within the conservative Mormon society at BYU, the Black Menaces have spread their movement to multiple college campuses—with no Mormon connection—across the United States, showing how, in the 2020s, Mormon racial and social issues are actually national issues.

passed through the faith, then what does it mean to be Mormon at all? There is, of course, no definitive answer to this, but it is the question that future filmmakers will continue to probe. And the very nuance, the lack of institutional hegemony, is what will bring their documentaries to life. The limited subjective humanity of the filmmakers and their subjects will be enough.

In this brave new world of multivalent twenty-first-century (post-)Mormonism, many orthodox or longtime church members may find themselves standing on the debris of their childhood home, looking back at what it has meant to be Mormon over the past 130 years, since Mormon cavalrymen were filmed as part of a war effort and church leaders fraternized in front of the temple for the camera. Since that time Mormons have shifted in both public perception and personal subjectivity, from progressive corporate Americans to middle-class nuclear families to a multitude of possibilities—like Costa Rican kickboxers, former rock stars, and Black social activists—and now even the devotional component of Mormon life is no longer certain, as members consume and assume Mormonism in whatever way works best for their subjective experience, even if that means heterodox or previously "forbidden" ways like drinking coffee or embracing a queer identity. The church hierarchy, which in recent years has even disavowed the term "Mormon," no longer controls what it means to be one, and documentary films are there to record those myriad limited subjectivities and reflect them back in a mosaic of films. In the church's religious terms, this signifies people exercising their agency. In Jan Shipp's academic terms, it means that "never again is there likely to be a single Mormon image." In Colin Low's poetic terms, it means that past Mormon experiences, like his father's ranch, now exist only in memory—and on celluloid in films like *Corral, Reflections, The Potter's Meal, The Plan, Afrikaans 101, Angie, New York Doll,* and *Moving Pictures*. The mountain is still there, but every film—and every person—can now have their own vision.

NOTES

[1] Though little-known among Latter-day Saints today, Low, who died in 2016, was arguably the most accomplished filmmaker to ever come out of Mormonism. See, for instance, D. B. Jones, "The Canadian Film Board Unit B," in *New Challenges for Documentary*, ed. Alan Rosenthal (Berkeley: University of California Press, 1988), 133–147.

[2] The full relevant statement, by theorist Sigfried Kracauer, states: "Films come into their own when they record and reveal physical reality. Now this reality includes many phenomena which would hardly be perceived were it not for the motion picture camera's ability to catch them on the wing. And since any medium is partial to the things it is uniquely equipped to render, the cinema is conceivably animated by a desire to picture transient material life, life at its most ephemeral. Street crowds, involuntary gestures, and other fleeting impressions are its very meat. Significantly, the contemporaries of Lumière praised his films—the first ever to be made—for showing 'the ripple of the leaves stirred by the wind." Siegfried Kracauer, *Theory of Film: The Redemption of Physical Reality* (Oxford: Oxford University Press, 1960), ix.

[3] Michael Renov, *The Subject of Documentary* (Minneapolis: University of Minnesota Press, 2004), xvi.

[4] For two book-length studies, see Armand L. Mauss, *The Angel and the Beehive: The Mormon Struggle with Assimilation* (Urbana: University of Illinois Press, 1994) and Terryl L. Givens, *People of Paradox: A History of Mormon Culture* (Oxford: Oxford University Press, 2007).

[5] D. Michael Quinn, *The Mormon Hierarchy: Extensions of Power* (Salt Lake City: Signature Books/Smith Research Associates, 1997), 800; A. Prentiss, *The History of the Utah Volunteers in the Spanish-American War and in the Philippine Islands* (Salt Lake City: W. F. Ford, 1900), 51; Richard I. Reeves II, "Utah and the Spanish-American War" (master's thesis, Brigham Young University, 1998), 105; Elias Savada, comp., *The*

American Film Institute Catalog of Motion Pictures Produced in the United States: Film Beginnings, 1893–1910 (Metuchen, NJ: Scarecrow Press, 1995), 938.

6 Randy Astle, "Mormon Cinema on the Web," *BYU Studies* 48, no. 1 (Spring 2009): 179; "Mormon videos," Google search page, https://www.google.com/search?q=mormon+videos, accessed March 5, 2022.

7 Jan Shipps, *Sojourner in the Promised Land: Forty Years Among the Mormons* (Urbana: University of Illinois Press, 2000), 115.

8 Levi Edgar Young, "Mormonism in Picture," *Young Woman's Journal* 24, no. 2 (February 1913): 80.

9 "Church President as Picture Actor," *Salt Lake Tribune*, April 9, 1916, https://dcms.lds.org/delivery/Delivery-ManagerServlet?_pid=IE386420, image 103.

10 "Church Officials See Themselves on Movie Screen," *Salt Lake Telegram*, April 15, 1916, Richard Alan Nelson Collection, L. Tom Perry Special Collections, Harold B. Lee Library, Brigham Young University, box 2, folder 10.

11 Eric Barnouw, *Documentary: A History of the Non-Fiction Film*, 2nd ed. (New York: Oxford University Press, 1993), 57.

12 John Grierson, *Grierson on Documentary*, ed. Forsyth Hardy (New York: Praeger, 1966), 16.

13 Grierson, *Grierson on Documentary,* 29.

14 For a book-length analysis of propaganda techniques in *Called to Serve,* see Susan Clayton Rather, "Film, Propaganda, and the Christian Way of Knowing Truth: A Look at LDS Documentary Filmmaking" (master's thesis, Brigham Young University, 1997).

15 The *Hollywood Reporter,* for instance, began its review with the satirical comment "Mormons are people, too, and really nice ones at that," and later adds that it's "strictly for the converted." "'Meet the Mormons': Film Review," *Hollywood Reporter,* October 9, 2014, https://www.hollywoodreporter.com/movies/movie-reviews/meet-mormons-film-review-739497.

16 William A. Wilson, "The Study of Mormon Folklore: An Uncertain Mirror for Truth," *Dialogue: A Journal of Mormon Thought* 22, no. 4 (Winter 1989): 108–109.

17 William A. Wilson, "Mormon Folklore," in *Mormon Americana: A Guide to Sources and Collections in the United States*, ed. David J. Whittaker (Provo, UT: BYU Studies Monographs, 1995), 437.

18 See Irene M. Bates, "*Reflections*: A Film About Women," *Sunstone* 4, no. 3 (May–June 1979): 38–42.

19 The device of allowing subjects to view and comment on a film originated in Jean Rouch and Edgar Morin's cinema verité film *Chronicle of a Summer* (1961) and has been used in many films since, including Colin Low's *Challenge for Change* films.

20 Terryl L. Givens, "'There Is Room for Both': Mormon Cinema and the Paradoxes of Mormon Culture," *BYU Studies* 46, no. 2 (Summer 2007): 205.

21 Givens, "'There Is Room for Both,'" 206.

22 See also Nathan Richardson, "*New York Doll*: Directed by Greg Whiteley," *BYU Studies* 46, no. 2 (Summer 2007): 321–323, and my own review at Randy Astle, "The Ascension of a Saint: *New York Doll*," *Irreantum: A Review of Mormon Literature and Film* 7, no. 3 (2005): 57–60.

23 Dean Duncan, "Mission Statement," Fit for the Kingdom website, https://fitforthekingdom.prod.brigham-young.psdops.com/our-manifesto, accessed April 27, 2022. The films are also available to view on this site. While this is the mission statement currently posted on the Fit for the Kingdom website, the original proposal, submitted to the university's Media Projects Committee on February 12, 2002, can be found at "A Manifesto for 'Fit for the Kingdom': Dean Duncan's Proposal for a Mormon Documentary Series," *BYU Studies* 46, no. 2 (Summer 2007): 267–273. This article was printed under the name of Gideon Burton, who wrote a brief introduction to the proposal, but properly should have been attributed to Duncan.

24 Duncan, "Mission Statement."

25 See my review at Randy Astle, "A Glimpse Inside the Last Wagon," *Irreantum: A Review of Mormon Literature and Film* 8, no. 1 (2006): 163–169.

26 Courtney Tanner, "These Black Students at BYU Are Using TikTok to Document Attitudes in the LDS Church," *Salt Lake Tribune*, May 2, 2022, https://www.sltrib.com/news/education/2022/05/02/how-black-menaces-are.

27 "Blackmenaces," TikTok, https://www.tiktok.com/@blackmenaces, accessed December 27, 2022.

ESTABLISHING ZION

Identity and *Communitas* in Early Latter-day Saint Art

ASHLEE WHITAKER EVANS

In late 1845, facing increasing harassment and threats of violence, members of the Church of Jesus Christ of Latter-day Saints prepared to abandon their beloved city of Nauvoo, Illinois, to travel west—but not before performing ritual ordinances in their newly dedicated temple.[1] This stately edifice represented the culmination of Latter-day Saint covenant theology and was considered sacred. It may seem surprising, then, that the Saints decorated the temple's Celestial Room, a space symbolic of heaven's highest reward, not with exalted religious imagery but with genteel portraits. Although the Saints' imminent departure from Nauvoo afforded neither time nor justification for a permanent aesthetic scheme, these portraits tell more than a story of haste and decorative expediency.[2] They embodied a significant ideological message pointing to covenant and community—cultural priorities of the fledgling faith.

During the Church's earliest years, evidence suggests that popular art genres prevailed over extensive religious imagery. Some leaders had portraits painted while living in Kirtland, Ohio.[3] In Nauvoo, with numerous Latter-day Saints hailing from the Old World and with the church's growing community situated along the bustling Mississippi thoroughfare, individuals would have been exposed to popular art images in prints, cards, and publications.[4] Artists such as British-born painters William Major and Sutcliffe Maudsley and American converts Selah van Sickle, Robert Campbell, and Bathsheba Smith produced portrait "likenesses" in line with popular trends in Victorian-era art.[5] Some Latter-day Saints likely experienced painted panoramas in nearby St. Louis.[6] Just two weeks prior to his death, Joseph Smith noted that a reproduction of American artist Benjamin West's *Death on a Pale Horse* was displayed in his sitting room for a few days.[7]

The lack of extensive religious imagery among the Saints may be in part due to the relative transience of the Latter-day Saints community between 1831 and 1839 or to the limited pool of artists among its membership prior to Nauvoo, but it also could be reflective of the faith's theology.[8] With the cultural kinship between the Latter-day Saints and Protestant movements, one might anticipate a wariness in depicting the divine; however, many denominations with cautions regarding such imagery still embraced images of scriptural narratives. For Latter-day Saints, a religious order based on continuing revelation through a charismatic oracle who dwelled among his followers, not much stereotypical religious imagery predominated. Early Latter-day Saint culture rested heavily on belief in actual visions and visitations and in a dynamic living scriptural text through real-time revelation. Furthermore, the early church had few formal worship structures necessitating such decor.

The martyrdom of the prophet Joseph Smith and his brother-counselor Hyrum in June 1844 and the Latter-day Saints' subsequent exodus to the American West in 1846 began a new chapter in the faith's history and identity formation, as well as Latter-day Saints visual art production—elements of which are visible in the Nauvoo temple interior. With its founding prophet dead, the church faced a pivotal moment that prompted new imagery that instead spoke to the unique theology and administrative ideology of the church in this era. A significant body of work emerged across genres that reflected and reinforced notions of authority and covenant duty and perpetuated dialogues of collective identity.

These concepts were vital in galvanizing community and kinship bonds among Latter-day Saints to enable the institution's growth and fulfillment of their divine mandate: to form a heavenly society on earth, called Zion. Furthermore, as artists established a visual memory of the faith, imagery also enabled followers to experience a form of reenactment and initiation that could assimilate subsequent converts, including immigrant members and succeeding generations, into Zion's distinctive *communitas*. The anthropological concept of *communitas* provides a useful framework for understanding Latter-day Saint identity formation at this time and the role of visual imagery in reinforcing and reflecting its covenant community.[9] Anthropologists discuss this type of community-shaping and tribal initiation by analyzing three phases, each of which echoes the faith's early experience. First, a separation occurs, where constituents within the group are removed from the existing social order. This is followed by a liminal experience, which divorces individuals or groups from society's normative social rites and expectations, resulting in a transformation and initiation that binds them to their chosen tribe in new ways. After this liminal phase, individuals then step into a new social order in which they must reintegrate or assimilate to the expectations and needs of the new collective.[10] This communal order, or *communitas,* is forged together beyond normative transactional social structures because of shared experience and mutually accepted ideologies that fuel a singular identity and purpose.

For early Latter-day Saints, this process began in 1830. Individuals gravitated to the Church of Jesus Christ of Latter-day Saints from various walks of life, a conceptual and (for most) physical removal from prior social and religious affiliations, in response to Joseph Smith's declaration of restored truth and mandate to form a Zion society. Asserting itself as a restoration of Christ's own church with divinely sanctioned priesthood authority and additional scripture, the church's unique doctrine distanced it from Christian contemporaries. Members' repeated persecution and exile from their settlements heightened the sense of separateness, even from national identities. The liminality reached a climax through the establishment of temple ordinances—rituals of covenant initiation that functioned outside of time or space and solidified adherence to the group—the practice of plural marriage and the Saints' exodus to western territory, beyond the boundaries of the United States, after the martyrdom of their prophet-leader.

The Latter-day Saint gathering continued after the main body of Saints relocated to the Great Basin. This ongoing process of integrating converts from the United States and Europe into a new social order—a demanding experiment of desert cultivation, settlement-building, and theocracy—required a structured vision and delimiting of expectations and duties. This early faith community manifested and strove to maintain characteristics of *communitas*: shared identity and values, obedience to divinely ordained leaders, sacred instruction, maximization of religious attitudes, and a unifying homogeneity.[11]

Between the martyrdom of Joseph Smith in 1844 and 1890, Mormon art often reflected these goals of aggregation within the *communitas* of the Church of Jesus Christ. This chapter focuses on how artists used portraiture, landscape, and commemorative scenes to visually delineate "customary norms and ethical standards appropriate to the new settled state," including affirming priesthood authority and leadership, the necessity of building temporal Zion, and perpetuating covenant kinship through sacrifice.[12] This unique period of theocratic separatism and community-building shifted in 1890 when the church called for an end to its peculiar practice of polygamy and began reintegrating with the broader culture in a more pointed way, including sponsoring visual artists to leave Zion and study in Europe's artistic center.

PORTRAITURE: REINFORCING AUTHORITY AND OBEDIENCE

While the parlor-like decor in the Nauvoo temple's celestial room reflected prominent American portrait styles, within its sacred context it also reflected the Saints' important theological beliefs and aspects of covenant identity. As Jill Major points out, most of the likenesses—many of which were loaned to the temple—featured prominent church leaders, a handful of whom also had companion portraits of their wives. This may have had a precedent in the earlier Kirtland, Ohio, temple; yet, displayed in this setting, they pragmatically assert the newly revealed Latter-day Saint theology of celestial life as family life and the doctrine of eternal marriage as experienced in the present.[13] For faithful church members who accepted temple ordinances and covenants, heaven's reward was a continuation of spousal relations and posterity.[14]

More importantly, after Joseph and Hyrum Smith's martyrdom, portraiture began to be utilized to counter the looming succession crisis and assert the primacy of obedience to divinely appointed leadership. Following Joseph Smith's death, church members found themselves in an unprecedented situation. Smith had not publicly codified the process of leadership succession, and an intense debate ensued. Brigham Young, designated as the president of the church's Quorum of the Twelve Apostles, and the other eleven apostles filled the role vacated by the prophet's death, though other individuals— including Smith's son—claimed a right to succeed.[15] As Young and the Twelve asserted, they had received the priesthood authority from Joseph Smith prior to his martyrdom and thus were his rightful successors. Young was eventually selected to be the new prophet, which caused a schism among some members.

The most prominent image in the celestial room, both in size and position, was Selah van Sickle's portrait of Brigham Young, *Delivering the Law of the Lord,* a depiction that clearly indicated that authority to preside, as well as exalt or condemn, lay in his jurisdiction as president of the Twelve Apostles. Young had van Sickle paint the portrait in the summer of 1845. The full-length standing pose shows the leader with his hand resting on *The Book of the Law of the Lord*—a volume instigated by Joseph Smith that recorded individuals' contributions to the temple and also contained some of the prophet's writings and revelations.[16] This image underscored Brigham Young as Smith's successor and the one who would continue to administer the Law. A Bible and Book of Mormon lay on the table beside the *Book of the Law,* implying that members' acts of covenant commitment, as recorded by priesthood leaders, were parallel with holy scripture and another record from which they would be judged.[17] Though other portraits of Young already existed, he selected the theme of this commission, nearly seven feet tall, for the temple space.[18] For a church reliant on real-time revelation and prophetic instruction, Young's assertion of legitimacy was vital.[19] His authority remained equally vital and complex after the Saints left Nauvoo in 1846 and settled in the West, where Young served as both ecclesiastical and political leader—a blurring of roles that at times was tense.

Many of the portraits in the temple's celestial room were of current members of the Quorum of the Twelve Apostles, among them Heber C. Kimball, Willard Richards, and Orson Hyde, a pointed message directed at Saints regarding the rightful heirs of prophetic authority. The other couples featured were among those who supported Young and the Apostles—such as Patriarch John Young and his wife, Clarissa, and Bishop George Miller and his wife, Mary Catherine—reinforcing obedience as a requirement of celestial blessings.[20]

Two additional portraits honor the Smith family and imply support of the prophet's successors. Hyrum Smith's widow, Mary Fielding Smith, loaned a likeness of her

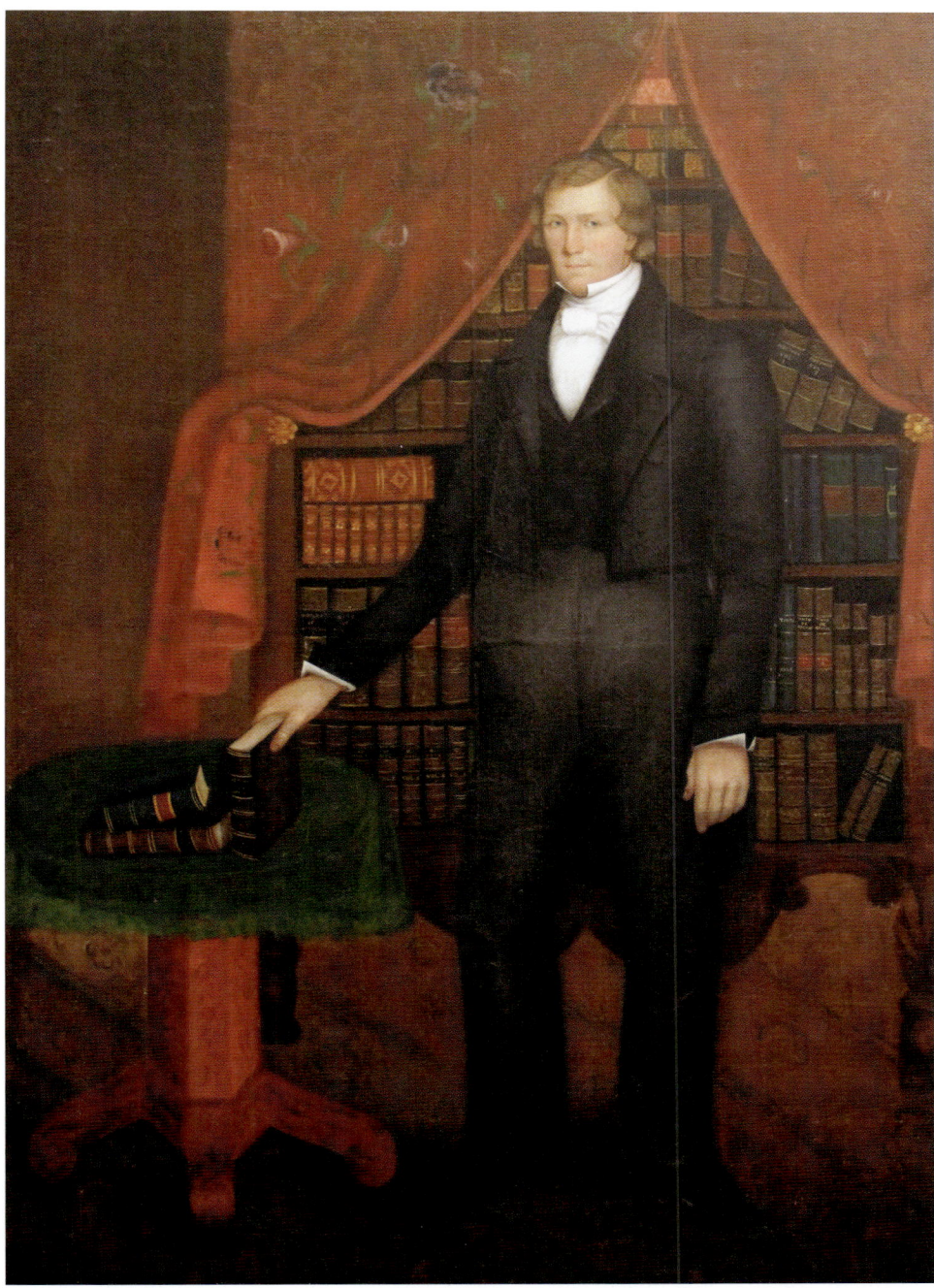

Fig. 4.1   Selah van Sickle, *Brigham Young Delivering the Law of the Lord,* 1845, oil, 84″ × 59 1/2″,
International Society of Daughters of the Utah Pioneers.

martyred husband; a prominent picture of Lucy Mack Smith, Joseph and Hyrum's mother, was also displayed.[21] The presence of her image may have been a tribute to this revered matriarch, for whom Brigham Young had a special fondness and who also helped paint the decorative trim of the temple.[22] It also effectively associated "Mother" Smith with those who supported Brigham Young and the Twelve following her sons' deaths. Interestingly, the only reference to Joseph Smith was a small profile figure by Sutcliffe Maudsley included on a printed map of Nauvoo, the "City of Joseph," hung on the west wall.[23] This may reflect strained relations between Emma Hale Smith, the prophet's widow, and Young, but ultimately it heightens the forward-looking message of leadership.[24] The "City of God" ideal established by Joseph Smith in his city-planning also would be a guiding principle of church leadership as the Saints settled in the West.

As new members gathered to the U.S. West from Scandinavia, Continental Europe, Australia, and the Pacific Islands, adherence to leadership and the duties of Zion-building remained important assertions among the Saints.[25] By the 1870s almost 35 percent of the region's population was foreign-born, many of whom spoke languages other than English and had not been personally acquainted with prominent church leaders. As they faced the rigors of settling barren lands, to obey and unify was to survive both spiritually and temporally in their new social order, and reminders of communal expectations were vital.[26]

Though Brigham Young and other leaders traveled throughout the Mormon corridor imparting such messages, imagery could play an important role in conveying their authority to congregations, and it reflected the ideology of leadership. Many bust-length portraits of Young and other leaders such as Heber C. Kimball and John Taylor existed, and photographs of the earliest meetinghouses show that portraits of leaders were the most common imagery in worship spaces.[27] A unique example of this motif is Sarah Ann Burbage Long's *Brigham Young and His Friends*. Long—one of the few women painters known in the early church—painted the group prior to 1866, though the circumstances of its commission and display are unclear.[28] The image presents the prophet and his inner circle, influential men who served in both ecclesiastic and civic leadership, including John Varah Long (the artist's husband and Young's clerk), John Young (Brigham's brother and patriarch), George A. Smith (church historian), Lorenzo Snow and Heber C. Kimball (apostles), and Daniel H. Wells (superintendent of public works). Books and documents placed near the sitters reference their roles, acting as hagiographic emblems.[29] Interestingly, the composition includes portraits of deceased church leaders Jedediah M. Grant of the Quorum of the Twelve, Joseph and Hyrum Smith, and a bust of Willard Richards—who was an apostle and witness to the Smiths' martyrdom. The red curtain and cords serve as an honorific compositional device visually linking the deceased leaders to the living and represent the divine authority passed down from Joseph Smith, now dead almost twenty years, to Young and his fellow leaders. Brigham points toward George A. Smith, who holds a document, "History of Joseph Smith," that underscores this idea.

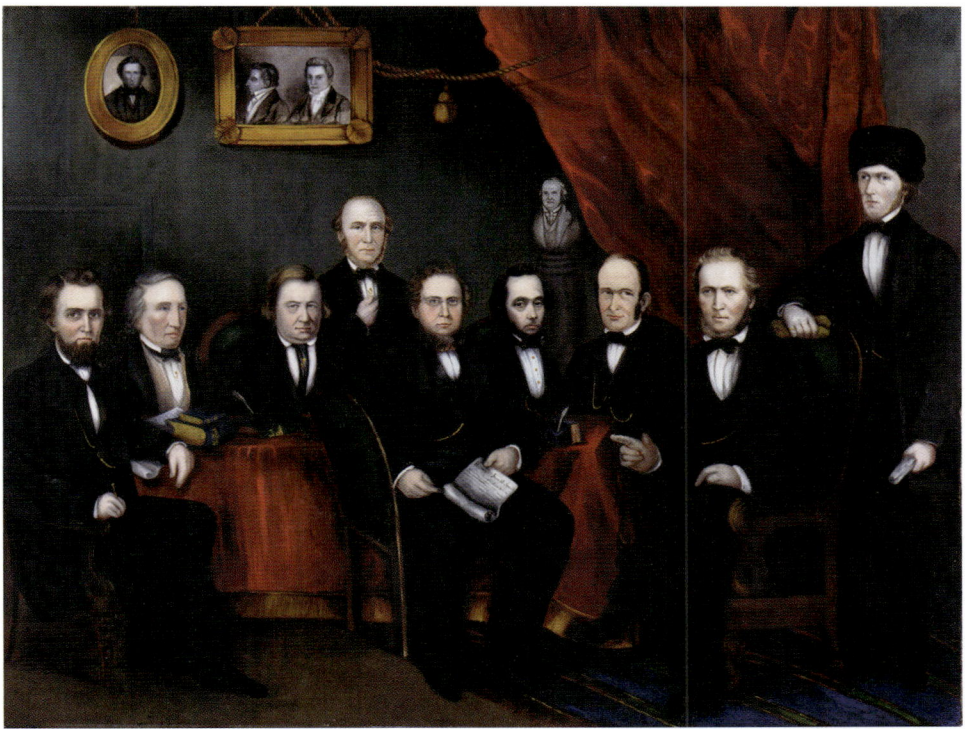

Fig. 4.2 Sarah Ann Burbage Long, *Brigham Young and His Friends*, c. 1864, oil on canvas, 34″ × 44″, Church of Jesus Christ of Latter-day Saints Church History Museum. © Intellectual Reserve Inc.

Long's composition conveys a sense of boundary between viewer and subject. The gentlemen—each part of Zion's theocratic governance—are seated in a line close to the foreground, evoking an authoritative barrier that leaves little visual space for admittance. The obscure hand gestures and glances between figures imply an elite group, excluding those outside the Latter-day Saint church's privileged leadership, including women; perhaps this was perceived by Long herself. In contrast to Long's portrayal, William Warner Major's portrait *Joseph Smith and His Friends* (c. 1845) presents a more open composition. Joseph Smith stands in the middle as a teacher, his hands pointing down both axes of men, suggesting the transmission of his knowledge and authority. As Burbage Long's painting demonstrates, the present-day authority held by Young and the other church leaders was reliant upon their connection to Smith, as were many members' conversions.

Thus, perpetuating the Prophet Joseph's memory continued to run parallel with notions of authority. The creation and dissemination of memorial portraits of Joseph and Hyrum Smith also served a role in bringing together the *communitas* of the early church and preserving their instructive legacy. For example, following the martyrdom of Joseph and Hyrum Smith, death masks were created and reproduced. John

Taylor had portrait busts created from the mask reproductions and made available to Saints in honor of their fallen leaders.[30] Honorific images included Danquart Weggeland's mural of Joseph Smith for the Bountiful tabernacle, commissioned by Brigham Young in 1863. Weggeland's mural assimilates Joseph's popular death mask

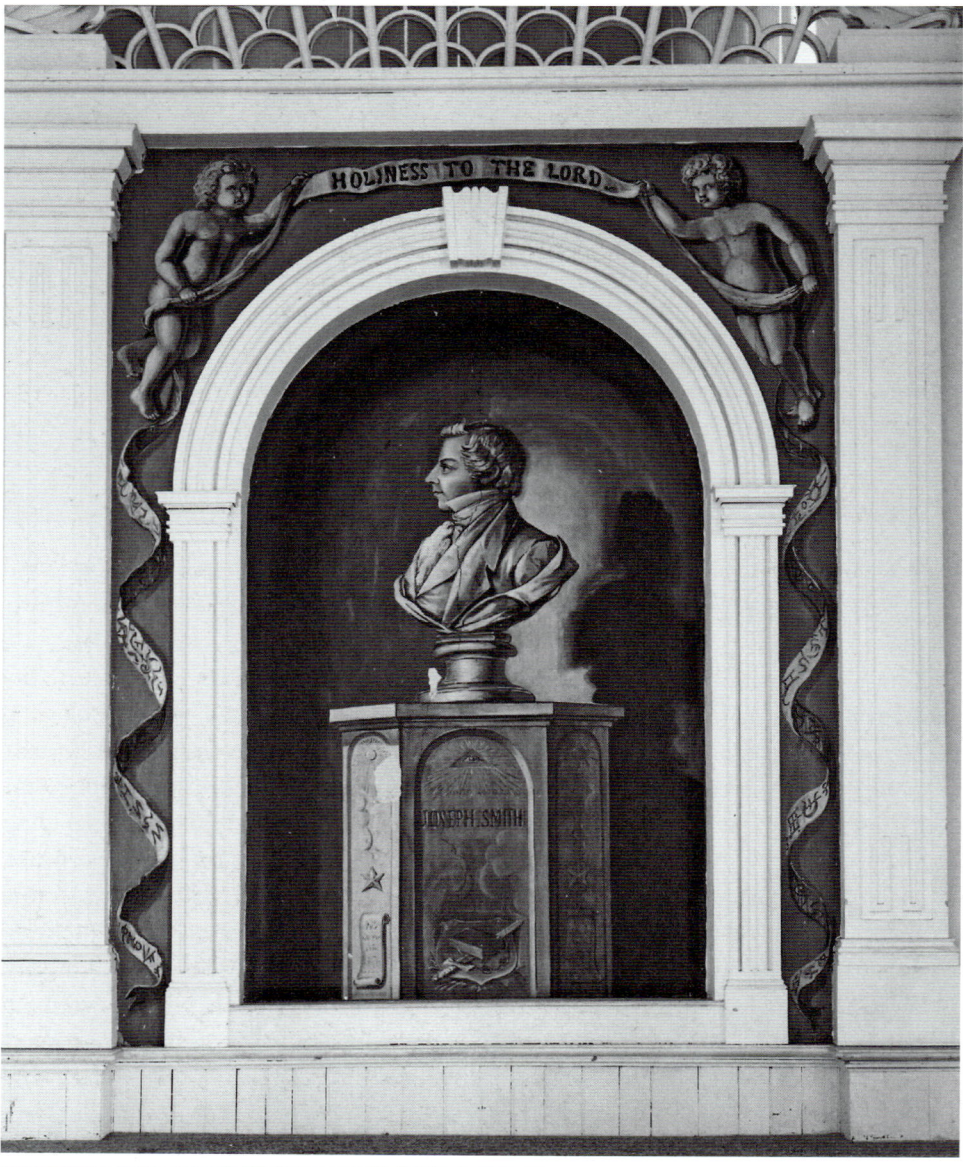

Fig. 4.3 Danquart Weggeland, *Mural of Joseph Smith for the Bountiful Tabernacle*, 1863, oil tempera on plaster, 141″ × 128″, Church of Jesus Christ of Latter-day Saints Church History Museum. © Intellectual Reserve Inc.

into the motif of a Roman victor's bust under a triumphal arch.[31] The prophet faces symbolically west, anticipating the Saints' settlement of Zion, and is surrounded by symbols including the *Book of Mormon,* signifiers of his divine work. Through such iconography, Joseph's legacy lived on through the perpetuation of the church's priesthood lines, doctrine, and the Latter-day Saint community. His sacrifice legitimized and promoted faith and a shared identity and would endure as an important genre of Latter-day Saint imagery.

PRACTICAL RELIGION: LANDSCAPE AND GENRE IMAGES IN ASSIMILATING ZION

In the West, the Saints settled into a region whose terrain seemed a metaphor for God's providence and their identity as a chosen people.[32] Images of the territory's distinctive landscape abounded in paintings, photographs, and prints in the early decades after settlement. British converts such as the artists Alfred Lambourne and Reuben Kirkham drew upon the nineteenth-century Romantic vision of a divinely infused landscape to reflect members' rhetoric of their "mountain sanctuary" as God-given.[33] At the same time, images of the Saints' human-made landscape, communities, and homesteads became common subjects for a number of artists, exemplified in works created by Scandinavian converts whose training attuned them to depict everyday life.[34]

In the case of both landscape genres, the pioneer settlers' perception of Zion's land as a God-given inheritance largely erased the Indigenous tribes whose environment and ways of life were transformed by Mormon settlement. Those artworks that do include Indigenous peoples veil the complexity and frequent tensions of associations with native tribes and reflect colonial rhetoric.[35] A pair of images painted by Danish immigrant artist C. C. A. Christensen demonstrate the Latter-day Saint belief in the divine purpose of their settlement and the assertion of their Kingdom's civilizing influence on Indigenous inhabitants. Though the two paintings were not necessarily created as a set, they were hung together in the temple in Manti, Utah, and depict the temple site, known as "Temple Hill," at two different times.

Christensen's *Temple Hill in Manti, November 1849* (see Figure 17.1, page 462) envisioned the area at the time of the pioneers' first arrival, prior to its development as a sacred site.[36] The settlement party arrived on November 19 and reportedly made camp near the hillside following the declaration of the group's leader, Isaac Morley.[37] According to pioneer accounts, the hill was actually a rocky area with sparse vegetation. However, Christensen presents it as a verdant incline bordered with trees and unseasonably green terrain stretching into the horizon. Indigenous inhabitants, presumably the Sanpitch tribe of the Ute nation, occupy the foreground space amid the trees. The Sanpitch are depicted with tepees, engaging in everyday activities—some conversing, while others move toward the woods to gather. The caravan of pioneer wagons is circled for protection in the distance as a pair of riders approaches the community. Christensen's composition aligns the Indigenous inhabitants with wilderness as represented by the trees, fallen wood, and rocks—perpetuating a common American mindset, extant among many Latter-day Saints, of "Native Americans as 'wild'" and "regress[ed] from civilized settlement."[38] In the minds of nineteenth-century settlers, such forested land was unproductive for farming or settlement, whereas the pioneer wagons are shown occupying the visibly unclaimed and fertile valley expanse. This image reinforces a motif visible in other contemporaneous imagery that portrays Indigenous occupants as inhabiting mountain and wilderness areas rather than the open valleys by choice. As Nathan Rees asserts, such staging affirms a colonialist justification for the Saints' settlement of the land and their transformation of seemingly untamed wilderness into a palatial House of God, a fulfillment of the Latter-day Saint call to literally build Zion. Rees writes, "Imagining Native Americans as inhabitants of the mountains allowed Mormon farmers to believe that their agricultural operations merely 'reclaimed' empty desert. In fact . . . colonists' farms and livestock disrupted Indigenous food resources."[39] While the settlement of the Manti area was an instance where tribal leaders invited the Saints to settle and eventually deeded the land to the church, the Sanpitch Utes' story ultimately followed that of other Indigenous groups in the Utah Territory. Increasingly limited resources and cultural misunderstandings led to tensions and ultimately the Black Hawk War, and the Sanpitch people were relocated to the Uintah Reservation.[40]

In Christensen's *Manti Temple* both the wilderness and the Native peoples are absent; the image celebrates the Saints' fulfillment of their covenant to create Zion and develop the desert. The towering edifice was the third temple constructed in Utah, requiring over ten years of labor, and was dedicated as a sacred space for ordinances and instruction.[41] Records indicate that Christensen first painted the temple in 1889 as a commission from the local Relief Society, the women's organization of the church, which they intended as a submission for the 1893 Chicago World's Fair.[42] Christensen renders the structure with precision, the strong vertical buttressing and crenellated walls and towers accentuating its heavenward reach. Its orderliness is echoed in the horizontal planes of the terraces, a structural solution developed in order to construct the building on the hill. The Saints' intervention converted its rocky site from a wilderness to a harnessed, cultivated, and acculturated landscape garden. Christensen's vista echoes the terraced gardens of Old World palaces and estates, with figures promenading the site. Such images typified Latter-day Saint dialogues that celebrated settlers' ability to tame the land and appropriate it for the purposes of *communitas*, erecting a fortress-like temple amid the arid western deserts. Furthermore, given that the work was intended for the World's Fair audience, Christensen displays the sophistication and cultivation of the Latter-day Saints built environment, as its temple represented the community's finest efforts in architecture and craftsmanship.

During the early decades of settlement, images that showcased the cultivation of the land reflected an industrious, upright society, asserting Latter-day Saint propriety at a time when they were subject to fascination and speculation in the popular press.

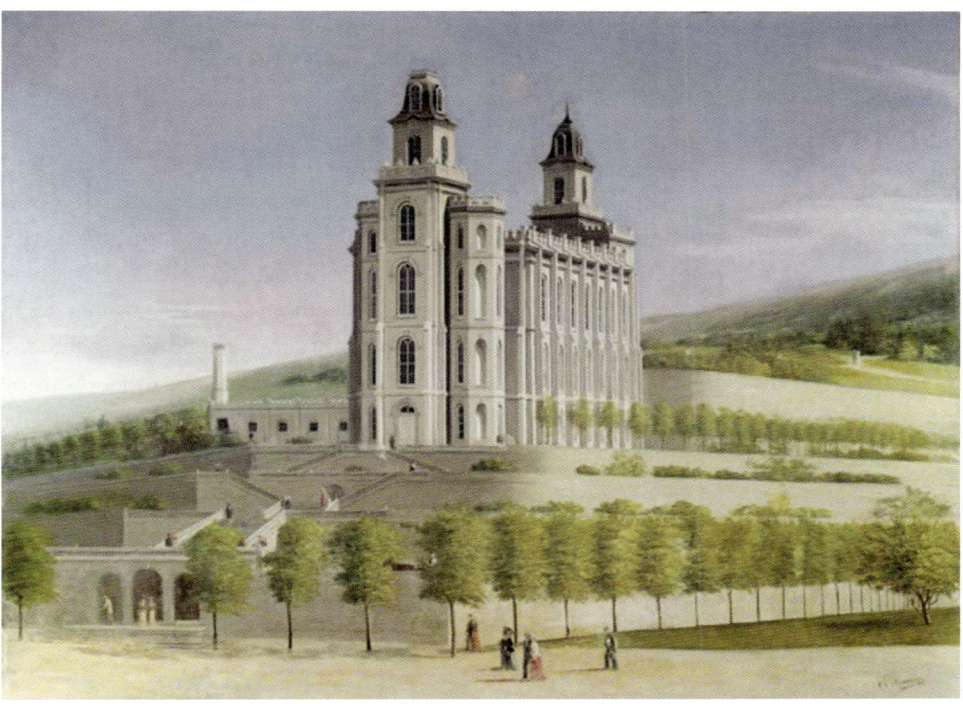

Fig. 4.4 C. C. A. Christensen, *Manti Temple*, 1889, oil on canvas, 54 1/4″ × 72 3/8″, Church of Jesus Christ of Latter-day Saints Church History Museum. © Intellectual Reserve Inc.

However, most of these images seem to have remained destined for an insular audience. Within Zion's visual field, such displays of developing land and property documented covenant-keeping practices. They evidenced a practical religion, as leaders at the time repeatedly preached that the building up and beautification of temporal Zion was the duty of the Latter-day Saint people. Brigham Young taught:

> There is a great work for the Saints to do; progress and improve upon and make beautiful everything around you. . . . Build cities, adorn your habitations, make gardens, orchards and vineyards, and render the earth so pleasant that when you look upon your labors you may do so with pleasure, and that angels may delight to come and visit your beautiful locations.[43]

For those who shirked this oft-repeated responsibility, Brigham Young warned, "Such neglect of duty is the very way to bring the power of the Devil upon us."[44] Apostle John Taylor, likewise taught:

> Look to it that you are found in the line of your duty. You have a beautiful location, and I would like to see you make the most of it. I would like to see at least a hundred

times more apple, pear, and cherry trees planted out; and all of your streets lined with shade trees. And improve your dwelling houses. If you cannot find the style of a house to suit you, go off to other places until you do find one, and then come back and build a better one.[45]

The development of land and settlements within Zion was a central task for those who professed to be modern-day Israel. Not only were their labors part of practical survival and communal prosperity, but also they could expedite the assimilation of various cultures and languages into a more cohesive community, an effort that church leaders encouraged in various ways. Brigham Young reportedly emphasized this when he addressed a group of newly arrived immigrants:

Look about this valley into which you have been called. Your first duty is to learn how to grow a cabbage, and along with this cabbage an onion, a tomato, a sweet potato; then how to feed a pig, to build a house, to plant a garden, to rear cattle, and to bake bread; in one word, your first duty is to live. The next duty—for those who, being Danes, French, and Swiss, cannot speak it now—is to learn English; the language of God, the language of the Book of Mormon, the language of the Latter Days. These things you must do first; the rest will be added to you in proper seasons.[46]

To these freshly arrived immigrants, assimilation through obedience, labor, and even language was preached as a key component of integrating into Zion. Interestingly, not only were foreign-born converts encouraged to learn English, but in addition Young and other leaders pursued the introduction of a unique alphabet system, known as the Deseret Alphabet, based on phonetic sounds, in order to strengthen *communitas*.[47] While preached extensively from the pulpit, the encouragement and celebration of the Saints' Zion-building endeavors also became evident in imagery.

Norwegian-born Danquart Weggeland was perhaps the most prominent early Latter-day Saint artist to regularly portray members' properties and farms. He painted multiple views of Brigham Young's estate from the north. In a version created in 1868, a small crew of workers continues improvements to Young's land, including irrigation and fencing. Young's Beehive House and orderly barn evidence industry, propriety, and a sense of establishment. Sitting adjacent is the steepled Eighteenth Ward schoolhouse, commonly referred to as the "Young family school," highlighting the value of proper education for his large family.[48] Weggeland painted six known versions of this view, three of which are dated prior to 1889.[49] Records indicate that Brigham Young had this image hanging over a fireplace in his home and delighted in showing it to visitors.[50] The uses of the other pictures are currently unsubstantiated; however, the artist's replication of this scene is telling. Productivity, order, and education were expectations of the Saints, as preached by the prophet and, according to Weggeland's images, practiced on his own properties.

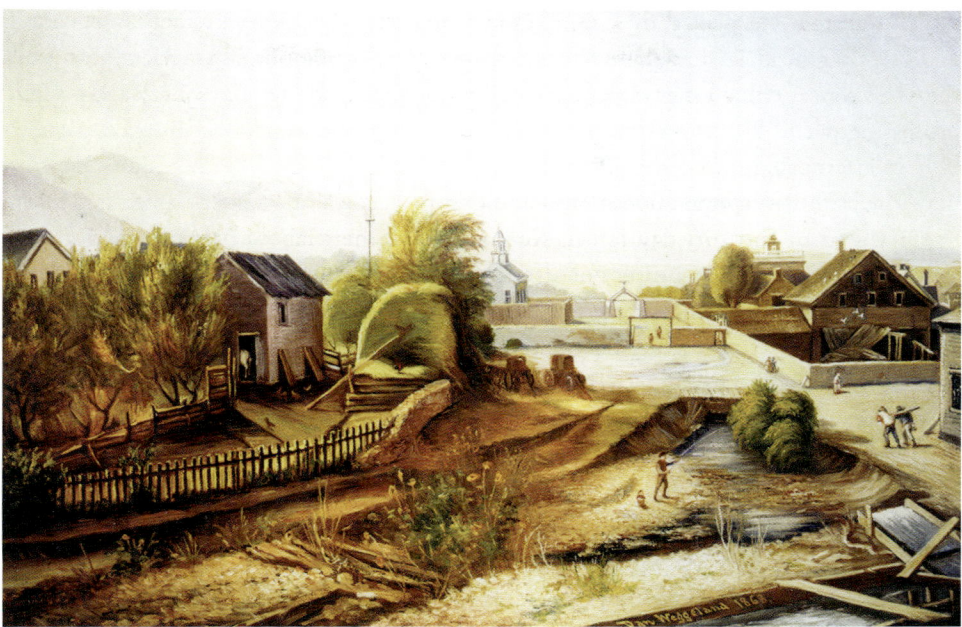

Fig. 4.5   Danquart Weggeland, *Eagle Gate of Brigham Young's Backyard,* 1868, oil on canvas.

This model of pioneer improvements is echoed in other homestead images, like Weggeland's depiction of Bishop Samuel Bennion's farm.[51] The painting was likely commissioned by Bennion, a prosperous businessman who also served in civic positions and as the first Latter-day Saint congregational leader in his settlement.[52] Bennion's farm is shown from an advantageous bird's-eye perspective on the nearby bluffs, highlighting its abundant orchards, pastures, and bar amid the arid surroundings. A little boy opening the gate as a dog runs out lends a sense of everyday realism to a scene that also largely plays into the visual rhetoric of proper Mormon duties of the time: to improve and beautify the land.

Imagery of prosperous properties expressed industry, bounty, and privilege, yet may have existed only as aspirational scenes for many of the settlers who arrived destitute or, though hearing reports of the desert blossoming as the rose, found working the barren land to be a protracted struggle.[53] However, even Weggeland's paintings of more humble settings, such as *Homestead Family, Utah Lake,* evince Latter-day Saint community-building behaviors and their ideal of stewarding one's resources with dignity. Despite the poverty implied in their earthen dugout—reflecting the reality many pioneer settlers faced—the family is shown neatly groomed, multiple generations cooperating at fishing, hunting, and tending, exploiting the abundant fish and fowl for which Utah Lake was known at the time.[54] The small United States flag flying above their boat may signify the family as immigrants, eager to claim a new identity through affiliation with the church that compelled their emigration and integration into an English-speaking and largely American-based culture. The paradoxical assertion of Americanness amid the *communitas* reflects a prevalent tension among early Latter-day Saints: that while professing peculiarity and even isolation, they also sought broader acceptance, particularly in attempting to receive statehood in the Utah Territory. Their lakeshore location may reflect the overpopulation many immigrants faced as newcomers continued to arrive in the Utah Territory, prompting them to find new spaces to settle.[55]

While Weggeland's examples of settlements highlight individual industry, in Zion's *communitas* all efforts contributed to the temporal and spiritual whole of the group, and each settlement was physically linked to the larger community through ecclesiastical oversight and discourse. This physical and spiritual gathering was an important emphasis among church leaders, who strategically organized townships throughout the Utah Territory—often settled by assignment and infused with ideological rhetoric and economic benefit. Young's counsel for united efforts was echoed by other church leaders, emphasizing the spiritual and practical necessity of gathering.[56] With a constant infusion of new immigrants, successful communities relied on communicating

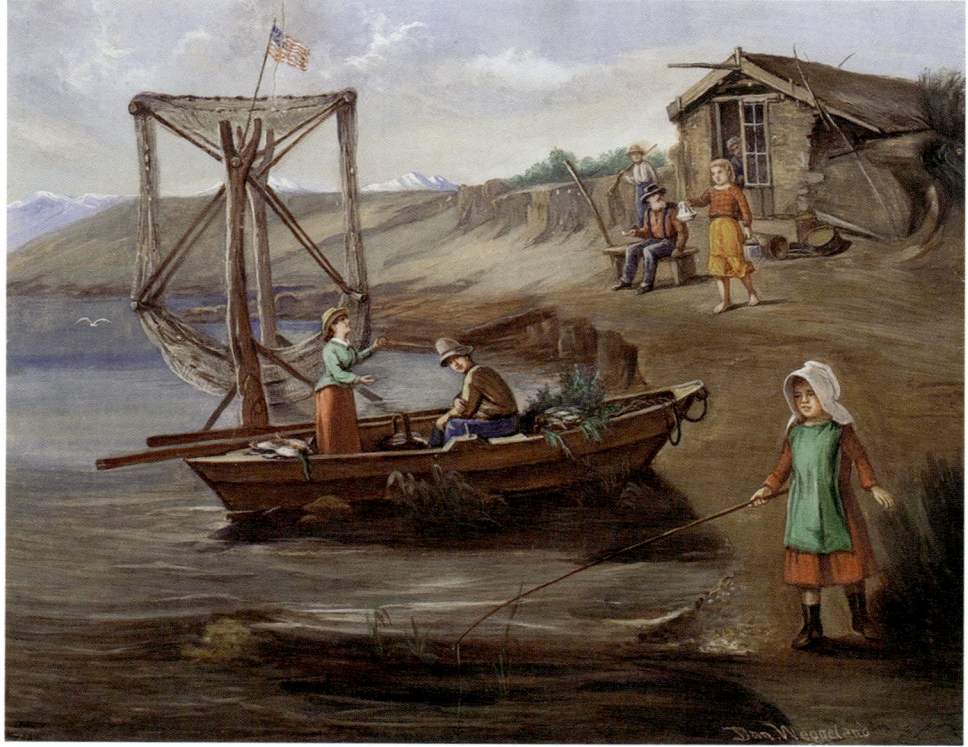

Fig. 4.6 Danquart Weggeland, *Homestead Family, Utah Lake,* n.d., gouache on cardboard-type panel, 21″ × 26″, State of Utah Alice Merrill Horne Art Collection.

the expectations and systems of Zion. Additionally, it was important that all Saints considered each other truly as kin, not just in the titular designations of "Brother" and "Sister." As Brigham Young taught:

> Let every individual in this city feel the same interest for the public good as he does for his own, and you will at once see this community still more prosperous and still more rapidly increasing in wealth, influence, and power. . . . Let every man and woman be industrious, prudent, and economical in their acts and feelings, and while gathering to themselves, let each one strive to identify his or her interests with the interests of this community, with those of their neighbor and neighborhood, let them seek their happiness and welfare in that of all, and we will be blessed and prospered.[57]

Thus, Young's idea of the sociality within the Latter-day Saints *communitas* allowed for the development of one's own interest in alignment with the contribution of individuals to the group, a goal more easily attained and maintained in compact and cohesive settlements.

The communal order of early Mormonism is visually demonstrated in C. C. A. Christensen's painting of new immigrants arriving in (presumably) the Eighth Ward square in Salt Lake City, *Reunion of the Saints*.[58] Amid well-cultivated streets and shops, a young family greets an older couple warmly, receiving them into their care. The older woman's more traditional dress contrasts with the young woman and daughter's apparel, perhaps an indication of Old World conventions in comparison to the fresh beliefs and outlook found within the church and as a result of the prosperity of the territory, represented by their fashionable clothing.[59] Their reunion is echoed by the dogs and birds that seem to greet each other in pairs, and an air of enthusiasm can be inferred from the nearby bandwagon and people engaged in conversation. Other groups walk toward the square, prepared to receive the newcomers—those initiates for whom messages of unity and Latter-day Saint identity became instructive reminders.

Just as with their property, households were also encouraged to follow the mandates of covenant community in family relationships, including the practice of plural marriage—a system that encouraged men to marry multiple wives. The church's commitment to this order of family life had theological underpinnings based on Latter-day Saint belief in the heavenly order as a familial order, the divinity of Joseph Smith's revelations, and Brigham Young's continued authority. The system promoted *communitas* as it allowed for the growth of large families and facilitated the temporal support of many single and widowed women joining the burgeoning faith.[60] Polygamy further provided a vital method for integrating Saints in close kinship networks aiding the community's cohesion and, in cases of intermarriage between Saints of different nationalities, an additional way of assimilating into a common cultural group.[61] However, the Saints' espousal of this institution was the subject of widespread social opposition to and criticism of the faith, particularly in the context of nineteenth-century Victorian morals, and was

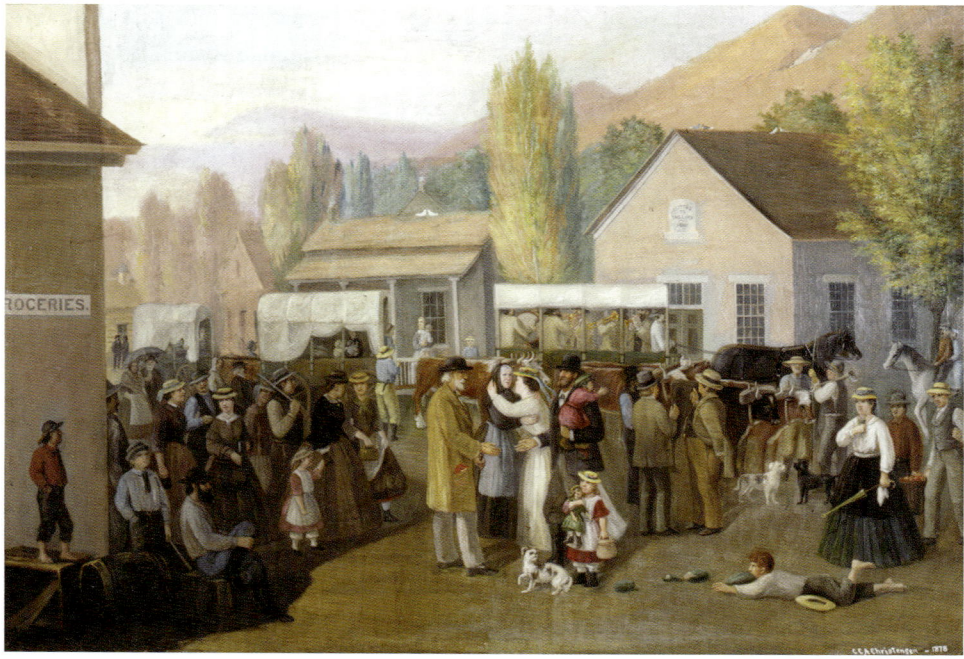

Fig. 4.7 C. C. A. Christensen, *Reunion of the Saints*, 1878, oil on canvas, 34″ × 49 1/2″, International Society of Daughters of the Utah Pioneers.

decried along with slavery as one of the "twin barbarisms" in the United States.[62] The federal government's punitive efforts toward men who lived in polygamous relationships brought increased hardships for the early Latter-day Saints, galvanizing some in their beliefs while raising doubts in others.

Christensen himself married a second wife and is one of the few artists known to have imaged the *communitas* of polygamous life.[63] His *Weighing the Baby* (1872) portrays the polygamist family of a fellow Scandinavian, Frederick Ferdinand Dorius, following the birth of a new child, though it is a somewhat veiled depiction of this unique family system. As the mother lies in bed, another wife aids the midwife in taking the baby's weight, but their identities are not specified.[64] Many immigrants from Scandinavia were among those who entered polygamous relationships; in fact, the broader American press spoke of immigrants as "fueling the insidious practice."[65] However, Christensen's image highlights the mutual support possible between wives in polygamous households, offering displays of self-sufficiency and concord that mirrored the goals of Zion.

THE KINSHIP OF THE SAINTS: SACRIFICE

A willingness to sacrifice is considered a fundamental aspect of *communitas*—vital to an individual's motivation to undergo separation, liminality, and aggregation into the new social and ideological order, efface self and embrace the collective.[66] Much of the visual production in the decades following the church's western settlement honored acts of devotion. These images functioned as reminders of covenant expectations within the faith, preserving memory and initiating new generations into a shared identity and history.

Latter-day Saint adherence to the revealed principle of plural marriage not only constituted a gesture of communal unity but also was a lifestyle deeply connected to ideals of covenant consecration. Plural marriages were believed to merit the highest degree of heavenly reward and were performed as part of an orderly system, as the unions were authorized by both church leadership and a man's existing wife.[67] Although the majority of Latter-day Saint households remained monogamous, all were expected to uphold the practice as a fundamental aspect of the church's doctrine and an exalting ideal to be sought after.[68] The federal government began efforts to end polygamy in 1862, with legal pressure and economic penalties mounting throughout the 1870s. In 1882, Congress passed the Edmunds Act (followed by the 1887 Edmunds-Tucker Act), which allowed for prosecution of Latter-day Saint men living in plural households. Men convicted at trial were often sentenced to serve prison time, typically six months, and pay a fine of $300. Many accounts evidence the honor and brotherhood felt by those who were willing to suffer for "doing the works of Abraham," citing the experience of the biblical patriarch who had multiple wives.[69] After completing their sentences, these men were frequently honored by their church communities and families for adhering to their covenants, as "Prisoners for Conscience Sake."[70]

Paintings of the territorial penitentiaries that housed polygamist prisoners became a unique commemorative genre in the 1880s. The prevalence of these jail images speaks to the kinship experienced by these Latter-day Saint men and their families, their imprisonment heralded as a mark of distinction. Francis "Frank" Treseder, a member of the church who was repeatedly jailed for unlawful activities, took to painting during his final term in the territorial prison and had a studio space in the prison basement.[71] Treseder produced numerous images of the penitentiary in Salt Lake as souvenir paintings, many of which contain only slight variations in their composition. Rudger Clawson, a later apostle of the church who served three years in prison for practicing plural marriage, wrote of Treseder in his journal and noted his natural talent: "His efforts with the brush were directed largely to landscape painting. I was pleased with his two pictures of the penitentiary, interior and exterior, and purchased them."[72] A set of exterior and interior views by Treseder also belonged to Apostle Marriner Wood Merrill and were reportedly gifted to his son Marriner W. Merrill.[73] Though the apostle avoided incarceration for his plural marriages, his son Marriner Jr. served a five-month sentence in 1888.[74] These penitentiary scenes were typically modest in size, easily collected by incarcerated men as tokens celebrating their choice of faith over governmental prescription. The absence of these men from their families also implicitly honors the women who would have maintained the families in their husbands' absence, their contribution to upholding the *communitas*.

The ordeals of the earliest generation of Latter-day Saints became the ritual passages and liminal events that forged the Mormon identity, establishing a legacy of covenant duty. Following Latter-day Saint settlement in the Utah Territory, the pioneer experience was celebrated through performative reenactments and commemorative days focused on key groups such as Zion's Camp, the Pioneers of 1847, and the Mormon Battalion. These celebrations constituted a rehearsal of the church's history, casting the sacrificing Saints as exemplary icons, helping to standardize the historical narrative and move the community to an emotional investment in the faith's founding chronicle.[75]

A commemorative banner designed by Thomas Bullock for the Pioneer Day celebration of 1861, *The Names of the Pioneers of 1847*, honors the individuals in the vanguard company, the first of thousands of pioneers to cross the American frontier.[76] The banner, which Bullock carried in the parade, categorizes the men, women, and children, as well as the three African American servants in the advance company—Green Flake, Hark Lay (Wales), and Oscar Crosby (Smith)—who helped create the pioneer path into the valley.[77] Bullock likely hired an artist to create the banner; the artist's identity is not confirmed, but it may have been Dan Weggeland.[78] At the top, Joseph Smith is portrayed as an angel heralding their sacrifices. Notably, the deceased prophet-emissary wears the sacred, symbolic robe and hat piece worn by Latter-day Saints in their temple rituals.[79] Thus, the banner signifies their pioneer journey as an act of consecration, confirming their initiation into the covenant belonging of the

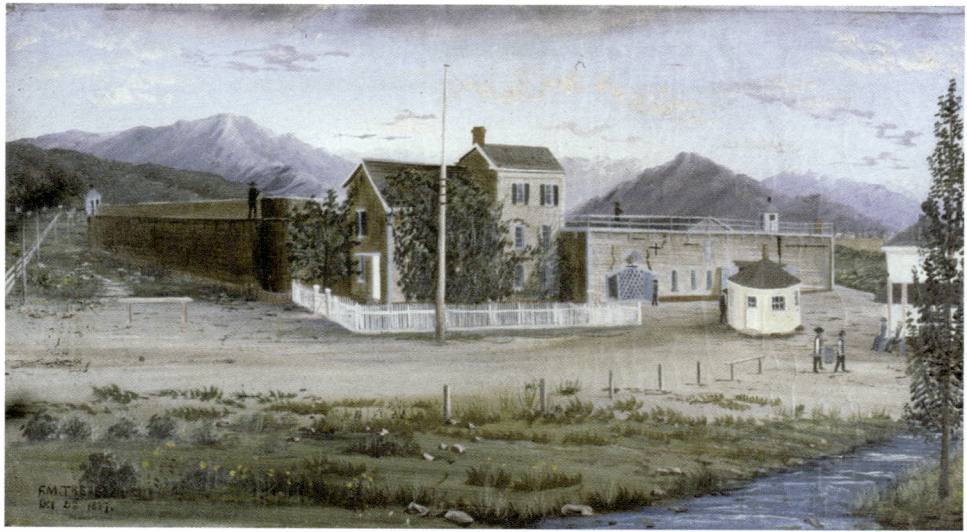

Fig. 4.8 Frank Treseder, *Territorial Penitentiary, Salt Lake County, Utah*, c. 1888, oil on canvas, 9″ × 22″, Church of Jesus Christ of Latter-day Saints Church History Museum. © Intellectual Reserve Inc.

faith; though, for the African American pioneers among the group, those ordinances would not be available until generations later.[80] Placing Joseph Smith—whose own works and martyrdom presumed his salvific glory—as the herald implies the imminent glory of those named on the banner, the import of such sacrifices not being limited to earthly memory.

This idea is also evident in Danquart Weggeland's *The Pioneers of 1847, Crossing the Platte*. A painted banner at the top of the canvas reads "Blessings Follow Sacrifice" and is accompanied by two hands clasped—a symbol of friendship, unity, and covenant—as well as the all-seeing eye of God, motifs frequently found on pioneer-era art and decorative items and later included on the Salt Lake temple exterior.[81] The men of the vanguard party are shown laboring, constructing and operating the wooden ferries that became known as the "Mormon Ferry" and which significantly expedited crossings. The image closely aligns with the description of a commemorative banner featured at the first festival celebrating the Mormon Battalion in 1855, and its design and origins may have been connected with that event.[82]

George Ottinger, an American-born convert who immigrated to Utah in 1861 and became one of the region's most prolific painters, likewise honored the sacrifices of early pioneers, some images even inspired by his own experience.[83] Ottinger traveled west in the Milo Andrus company, which left Florence, Nebraska, on July 2, 1861. According to the company's journal, Ottinger served as clerk for the company. The company record, which he presumably kept, notes that the group departed energized by the communal vision of Zion: "[Stepped] out to the tune of 'The Girl I left behind me' but 'Oh Babylon Oh Babylon we bid thee Adieu' living in the heart of every Saint in the Company."[84]

Ottinger's painting *Wolf Creek July 25th 1861 Burial of John Morse* memorializes the loss of company member John Moss (whose name Ottinger misspells on the canvas) a few weeks following their departure. The camp journal notes, "Burried this Evening John Moss a native of England age about 50 years[.] he was burried about 1½ miles East of the Creek on a little Bluff 20 or 25 yards North of the road[.]"[85] Ottinger presents it as a hallowed moment. The burial party stands atop the bluff in the moonlight; light emanates from the group, perhaps from an unspecified lantern, forming a radiant halo around the figures. Moss's roughly rendered form is shrouded in white. The company's wagons are circled below for protection from the prowling wolves in the opposite corner; yet the cluster of white wagon tops in the dark landscape seems to underscore the sense of sanctity and communal dependence amid their liminal wilderness experience. A circular opening in the clouds echoes the wagon formation, allowing the moonlight to shine onto the company and implying divine awareness and favor. Ottinger created another version of this painting, which appears slightly more finished and heightens the sense of the holy light around the burial party and the moonlight shining down on the pioneers' circled wagons.[86]

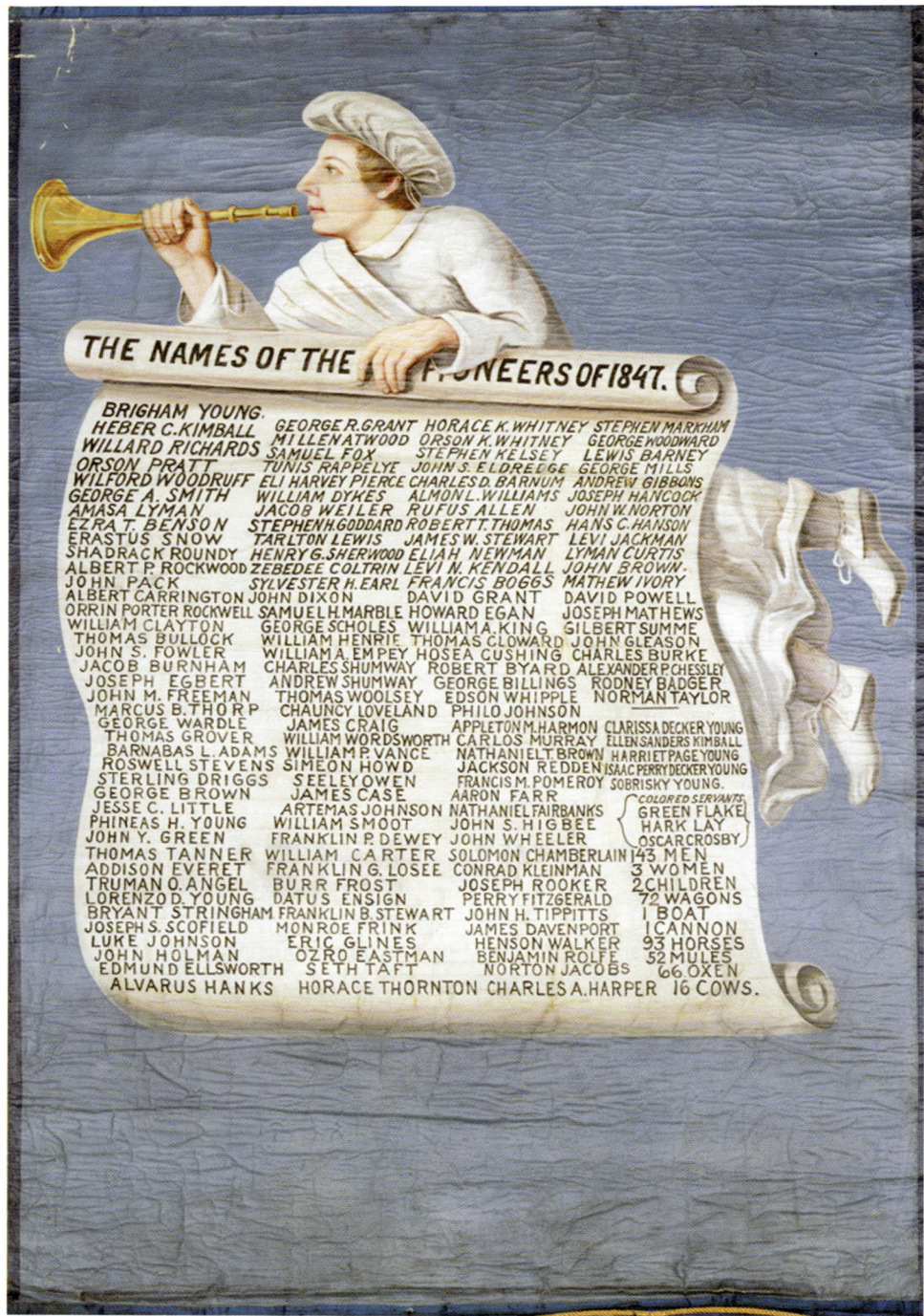

Fig. 4.9 Unknown, *The Names of the Pioneers of 1847*, c. 1861, 46″ × 68″, Church of Jesus Christ of Latter-day Saints Church History Museum. © Intellectual Reserve Inc.

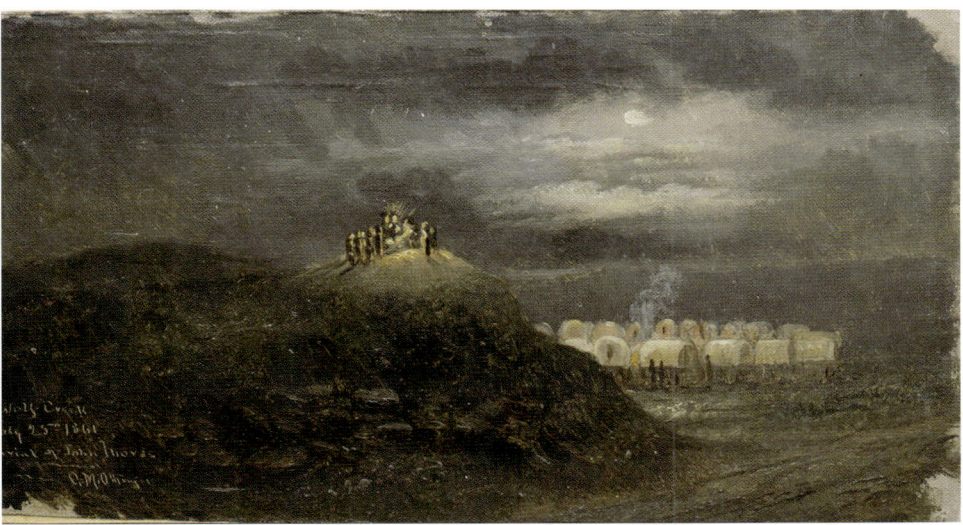

Fig. 4.10 George Ottinger, *Wolf Creek July 25th, 1961, Burial of John Morse,* 1861, oil on canvas, 7″ × 13″, Church of Jesus Christ of Latter-day Saints Church History Museum. © Intellectual Reserve Inc.

Scenes such as these became a visual record of the faith's history, documenting and purveying instances of *communitas*-shaping. However, certain Latter-day Saint artists would draw upon the popular medium of the panorama to portray similar events in a way that could enact a transportive experience and visceral witness that would strengthen *communitas*.

GALVANIZING FAITH: PANORAMAS AND SURROGATE PILGRIMAGE

Latter-day Saint creatives Philo Dibble and C. C. A. Christensen employed panorama paintings to reinforce *communitas*, bringing scenes of the church's early history to life in order to memorably convey its founding narratives, bolster group identity, and revitalize a shared faith. Panoramas were a popular form of entertainment between the 1830s and the early 1900s. Typically consisting of oversized horizontal images or a series of paintings stitched together to form a large, continuous canvas, these elaborate displays brought real and fictional events and places to life. As one scholar writes, "In an age before illustrated journalism and mass travel, panoramas acted as newsreels and magazines, serving the public's passionate curiosity about foreign lands, historic events, and patriotic exploits."[87] Panoramas could be wound on frames like a large scroll and reeled either horizontally or vertically, encompassing the viewer's visual field and creating the illusion of passing scenery and events. Showmen added rousing narration, music, weather effects, and smells to mimic sensations felt in real life. Moving panoramas became convincing multisensory experiences that enthralled millions of Americans until the advent of cinematic motion pictures.

Though a handful of other Latter-day Saint artists created panoramas, Dibble and Christensen's history-focused projects remain the most notable.[88] Both artists felt divinely called to create their works, though economic considerations certainly encouraged their endeavors. Their creative works most pointedly and purposefully asserted an authentic framing of their people's past experiences to sustain both personal and community interest.

Philo Dibble began his panorama with a team of artists following Joseph and Hyrum Smith's death. Dibble, who like many early church members enjoyed personal associations with the prophet, had a series of dreams that he interpreted as a mandate to create a panorama of the martyrdom, perhaps inspired by similar displays in nearby St. Louis, Missouri.[89] He commissioned Robert Campbell and William Warner Major to paint the 128-foot-long scenes.[90] Although Dibble envisioned illustrating several major events of early church history, only a few were completed.[91] The first, *The Massacre of Joseph & Hyrum Smith,* was advertised as being displayed August 6, 1845, in Nauvoo's Masonic Hall, though newspaper listings imply that the painting was at least far enough along to be shown during the church's April conference earlier that year, an advantageous time to garner an audience.[92]

Dibble intended to utilize the immersive panoramic images to uphold the founding prophet's legacy and maintain collective commitment to the church. In at least one instance, Dibble was willing to concede historical accuracy in order to achieve a more compelling "didactic, idealized image."[93] He also paired his presentation with copies of Joseph and Hyrum's death masks, arguably the most accurate likenesses of the brothers, furthering participants' sense of an authentic witnessing experience and personal connection with the prophet. Dibble described the effectiveness of his early presentations:

> Every Exhibition increases the interest, inasmuch as they display [a]t one glance the most striking likenesses of the great actors of these scenes; the familiarity they associated with times, places, buildings &c., even the persons who are the spectators have frequently to exclaim, "I was there"; so that all, while they feel anxious to hand down to posterity our illustrious martyrs, and record these visions of the past events, at once embrace subjects connecting their own salvation interest with these sceneries.[94]

The panoramic medium offered viewers—both individually and communally—a transportive experience that physically, imaginatively, and emotively allowed for their own visualization of past events. As Mason Allred has asserted, of paramount importance was the ability of the visually stimulating scale of the images to "energize [an] embodied experience" of the deceased prophet and thereby solidify members' adherence to church leadership in the post-martyrdom succession crisis—a vital reinforcement of *communitas*.[95] Dibble received the endorsement of the Quorum of the Twelve Apostles for his enterprise. Brigham Young offered early support for the project, gifting Dibble funds to aid in purchasing the canvas. By 1848, the entire Presidency and Quorum officially "sanctioned" and "signed their names to it," likely aware of its potential to create a shared understanding of Smith's prophetic mission, now passed to them.[96]

Following settlement in Utah, Dibble continued traveling with his panorama, though there is an indication he switched to showing lantern slides of his images in later years rather than the originals.[97] Unfortunately, his canvases have yet to be located, perhaps having deteriorated from use, though one of Robert Campbell's sketches for the project survives.[98] However, Dibble's enterprise—and sense of *communitas*—was threatened when C. C. A. Christensen began his panoramic presentation in 1878. Dibble wrote a letter to John Taylor, Brigham Young's successor as church president, distressed by the actions of Christensen and his brother, who had created a panorama of church history and established themselves as competitors to Dibble.[99] Taylor's response to Dibble's petition remains unknown; however, one of Christensen's advertisements lists Taylor among the prominent figures who endorsed the project.[100] Christensen's panorama emerged at the time Dibble's own travels seemed to be waning and was eventually developed into a larger visual concept—a presentation involving twenty-three scenes, regarded as one of the most significant works of early Latter-day Saint art.[101]

C. C. A. Christensen created his *Mormon Panorama* as a pointed interpretation of early Latter-day Saint history that functioned as entertainment, testimonial, and visual pilgrimage intended to influence viewers' identification with the events and the covenant community. Christensen and his brother Frederik began touring the panorama throughout Utah, Idaho, Wyoming, and Arizona in 1879, with approximately seven scenes complete. He eventually added sixteen more images to the presentation, traveling with it until the early twentieth century. In contrast to Dibble's wide-scale panorama, Christensen's individual paintings measured approximately six and a half feet by ten feet, and all twenty-three canvases were stitched together to form a vertical scroll 175 feet long. Christensen enhanced the theatrical and multisensory nature of the presentation by draping curtains around the supporting poles and using kerosene lamps as footlights, making a stage-like setting beside which Christensen narrated each event based on eyewitness accounts.[102] Music too was incorporated, and the audience was invited to sing familiar hymns at appropriate points. One viewer who saw the presentation, despite critiquing Christensen's artistic deficiencies, described its effect as "beyond compare of words."[103]

Christensen cited objectives similar to Dibble's: to allow the founding experiences of the faith—those liminal passages that had forged the group of disparate converts into a kingdom of Saints—to come to life again for viewers, particularly those of the rising generation who had not endured those events themselves. As he stated, "History will preserve much, but art alone can make the narrative of the suffering of the Saints comprehensible for posterity."[104] The handbill advertising the panorama emphasized, "These artistically executed pictures will impress indelibly upon [young Latter-day Saints'] minds the trying ordeals through which the church had passed before it found a resting place in the valleys of the mountains." This attempt to simulate reality was enhanced by Christensen's straightforward realist style, his citations of historical sources within the narrative, and his script's repeated assertion of his images as "true representations."[105]

Christensen's panorama received notable attention from local press as it toured. Yet, as Nathan Rees demonstrates, published responses reflect a variety of opinions as to content, artistic quality, and even the delivery of the narrative in Christensen's heavily accented English—demonstrating a "polyglot" audience informed by varied cultural ideals.[106] Regardless, such assessments evidence the presence of these images in the cultural mind of the time and the need for ongoing efforts to encourage *communitas*. Many found the artist's endeavor effective. William C. Staines described: "There is not a person who sees and hears, no matter how young, but becomes immediately acquainted with a very important part of the history of the Latter-day Saints. . . . I have heard a number of children, who have seen the pictures and heard the lecture . . . when asked to give an explanation of the picture of the 'Haun's Mill Massacre,' they gave it as correctly as I could myself."[107] The *Ogden Daily Herald* wrote, "We know of no better way of impressing those things upon the minds of the young than by a pictorial representation such as that which is now being exhibited through the country by Brother Christensen."[108]

The *Mormon Panorama* began with Joseph Smith's First Vision and ended with the pioneers' arrival in the Salt Lake Valley. Many of the images focused on the unjust treatment of the early Latter-day Saints and Smith in particular, and included scenes of persecution and forced exodus. *Jackson County, Missouri* illustrates the grievous mob violence against the early Saints after they settled in Missouri in the early 1830s. Christensen places the viewers at the center of the stage-like scene, allowing them to become eyewitnesses to the harsh events. A woman spotlighted in white is frozen at center holding an infant in her arms as she flees before the aggressors, who hold a gun to the baby's head. An elderly man on the right defends himself in hand-to-hand combat, his spouse aiding in his protection. On the left, "Brother Bennett is in the hands of villains who beat him until his head was almost a jelly," Christensen vividly describes; a woman, presumably Bennett's wife, pleads for mercy.[109] Women and children flee into the darkening woods as the Missouri mobbers tear down the hearth of a cabin, a summative symbol of the aggressors' disregard for proper values and the virtue of the Saints.

Though the panorama's stirring scenes of opposition and endurance occurred decades before its display, Christensen's project was purposeful and timely, its intended to strengthen *communitas* in a time of increasing pressure. Its evocative depictions projected the same liminal struggle onto the trials faced by church audiences in their contemporary moment. Governmental attempts at territorial oversight, conflicts with Native peoples, new influxes of "Gentile" influences after the railroad's arrival in 1869, and especially legislative actions against polygamy were persistent difficulties facing the Latter-day Saints settlers during the years in which Christensen created and displayed the panorama.[110] It echoed the plea of church leaders for faithful perseverance and allegiance. As President George Q. Cannon taught:

> We need not, therefore, be discouraged at what we see and what we are passing through. But if we are united, brethren, and stand together, this power can not prevail against us. Our opponents may secure temporary victories in places . . . but if we are united, I tell you that God our eternal Father will overrule these events for our good, and He will bring us great *deliverance*.[111]

Throughout the presentation, Christensen interspersed moments of injustice with miraculous events where the beleaguered Saints received divine aid, including violent storms protecting them from mob attack, a providential icy river crossing, and an account of quail descending on a camp of weak and sickly Saints forced out of

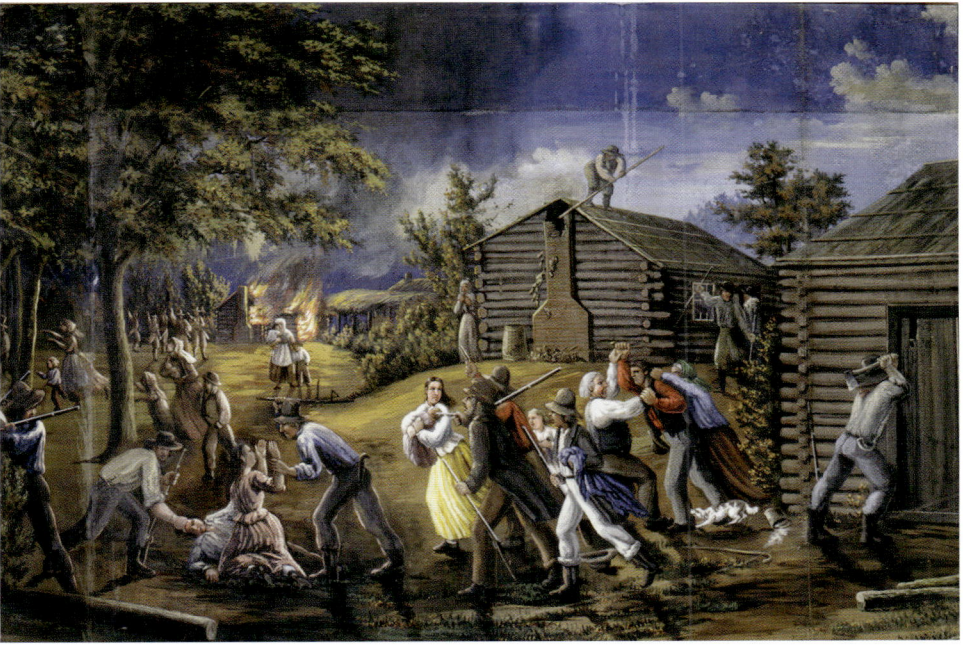

Fig. 4.11 C. C. A. Christensen, *Saints Driven from Jackson County, Missouri,* c. 1878, tempera on muslin, 77 1/4″ × 113″, Brigham Young University Museum of Art, gift of the grandchildren of C. C. A. Christensen.

Nauvoo—underscoring the Saints' identification with biblical Israel under Moses.[112] This emphasis on narratives of injustice and deliverance, paralleling scriptural types, aligned with what Steven Harper describes as a "sense of exceptional, chosen, persecuted status" prevalent among church members, and "transmitted it to converts and especially to the next generation."[113]

The *Mormon Panorama*'s ability to simulate travel across time and space made these locales and events more accessible to audiences—an important element that helped it inspire adherence within the *communitas*. Essentially, its unique format and content facilitated a surrogate pilgrimage experience, a devotional act of journeying that could tie the faithful more firmly into their covenantal identity and commitment to sustain the Kingdom of God.[114] While individuals who undergo religious pilgrimage typically do so intentionally and such a "journey" may not have been anticipated by Christensen's audience, as Rees asserts, Christensen's willingness to "[blur] the boundaries between entertainment and religious practice" offered viewers a "presentation that was richly redolent of contemporaneous Latter-day Saint worship experience."[115] Over its short duration, the experience invited a religious journey befitting the circumstances of frontier Saints as evidenced in certain principal aspects of the panorama.

The *Mormon Panorama* focused on key sites associated with miraculous divine experiences and hallowed sacrifice, considered holy places of the faith—a fundamental aspect of pilgrimage.[116] More importantly, Christensen's presentation brought viewers to these locations as witnesses to these foundational moments. Beginning with an illustration of Joseph Smith's First Vision (now lost), Christensen dramatically presented the scene and surroundings of Smith's theophany—a pivotal moment that revealed new understanding about the nature of God and commenced his calling to restore Jesus Christ's church. This event was followed by another divine manifestation at the Hill Cumorah, also in upstate New York, the location where Joseph Smith found the ancient metal plates that he translated as *The Book of Mormon*. These spaces could evoke seminal truths for viewers—in this case, the communication of restored truth directly from Deity and restored scripture.

For George Manwaring, a British convert who journeyed west in 1871, the experience of viewing Christensen's *Vision* painting, even as an isolated image, proved so vivid that it inspired the young composer to write a musical narrative of the scene. Manwaring's hymn "Joseph Smith's First Prayer," beloved among Latter-day Saints to the present time, re-creates the moment, beginning with the phrase: "Oh, how lovely was the morning; radiant beamed the sun above . . ." For a people who did not yet have formal monuments and largely did not possess the means to revisit many of these faraway locales, the panorama brought those moments to the faithful where they were. Interestingly, the Hill Cumorah and the Sacred Grove were the first locations on which church leaders established formal monuments in the early twentieth century.[117]

Through the *Mormon Panorama* experience, viewers, like pilgrims, became increasingly circumscribed by "sacralized features of the topography" as well as "symbolic structures" iconized within the faith's chronicles.[118] Along with the Sacred Grove and Hill Cumorah, Christensen features sites such as Liberty Jail and the Nauvoo temple. Rather than depicting those places as interior narrative scenes, Christensen focuses on their familiar exteriors. In fact, Christensen specifies in his script that his depiction of Liberty Jail derived from "an actual photograph" previously published, in order to claim it as a "true representation."[119] The audience is given a front-row seat to the incarceration of Joseph Smith and other leaders. The panorama image of the Nauvoo temple is devoid of narrative, yet also offers audiences a traveler's view of the sacred site—a memorial to the structure, destroyed by arson. Both buildings indexically reference consecrated offerings and sacred occurrences, including the receipt of significant revelation at the "temple-prison" of Liberty Jail and bestowal of sacred ordinances in Nauvoo's temple—associating key tenets of the faith's doctrines.[120]

Pilgrimage revivified participants' faith by immersing them in "root paradigms" of the religious order—the core values that constitute "the deposit of faith," often centered in the founding leaders' experience and teachings.[121] Christensen's work weighted heavily toward portraying experiences of the prophet Joseph Smith, an individual the artist never personally knew, as missionaries did not arrive in Denmark until 1849, five years after Smith's death. As Jenny Champoux notes, despite the death of Brigham Young the year prior to Christensen's panorama, Christensen never depicts Young, even when the leader is mentioned in narrative.[122] The artist recognized that a witness of Joseph Smith's authority created a necessary scaffolding for faith in the contemporary church. He illustrates Smith's persecution, being tarred and feathered, betrayed to the Missouri mob's authorities, and martyred. Throughout these scenes, the mobs are presented as unruly ruffians, even enshrouded in darkness, while Smith is shown as genteel in clothing and demeanor. These episodes are briefly intermixed with depictions of Joseph's uprightness in action, such as his proselyting efforts to Indigenous tribes and his establishment of a well-ordered militia in Nauvoo. Christensen's collective presentation allowed for a personal witness of the prophet's character and role.

Moreover, Smith's suffering and eventual martyrdom epitomized the whole-hearted requirement of discipleship and validated his testimony. Thus, Christensen placed the scene of Joseph Smith's martyrdom in the middle of the panorama, further paralleling a prominent theme of pilgrimage. The event, which occurred in a small jailhouse room in Carthage, Illinois, is the only interior within the series. Christensen presents it as a theatrical stage with Joseph Smith positioned at center background, allowing the audience to occupy the foreground. Christensen depicts Smith in white clothing, his brother Hyrum already shot and lying on the ground, while fellow leaders attempt to fend off the mob. The prophet appears frozen in the moment, perhaps allowing the audience to consider the event and their associations of the leader. Moments later, Smith would run to the window, drawing mob gunfire that ended his life—the next scene illustrated by Christensen. A caption at the bottom of this image, the only text in the series, reads "The Blood of the Martyrs is the Seed of the Church." This phrase echoed the teachings of church leader Joseph F. Smith, delivered in 1877, just prior to Christensen's work on the panorama, in which Joseph F. Smith (the son of Hyrum Smith and nephew of Joseph) spoke about the trials besetting the current church and invoked those words of the early Christian writer Tertullian:

> When the Prophet Joseph Smith was assassinated the press and pulpit
> universally joined in predicting the end of "Mormonism." But instead of
> there being any truth in their predictions, "The blood of the martyrs
> was the seed of the church"; for the church grew as fast as it had ever
> done before, and it took deeper and firmer root.[123]

This powerful directive underscored for audiences the fundamentals of the faith's root paradigm—sacrifice, devotion, and witness.

Furthermore, it asserted that the tribulations endured by Joseph Smith and early church members served to strengthen the faith's collective resolve rather than diminish or destroy it. Christensen conveyed this in subsequent images in the panorama where the Saints are shown undertaking their exodus to the West, working together and receiving divine aid during their transformative rite of passage. The final scene of the

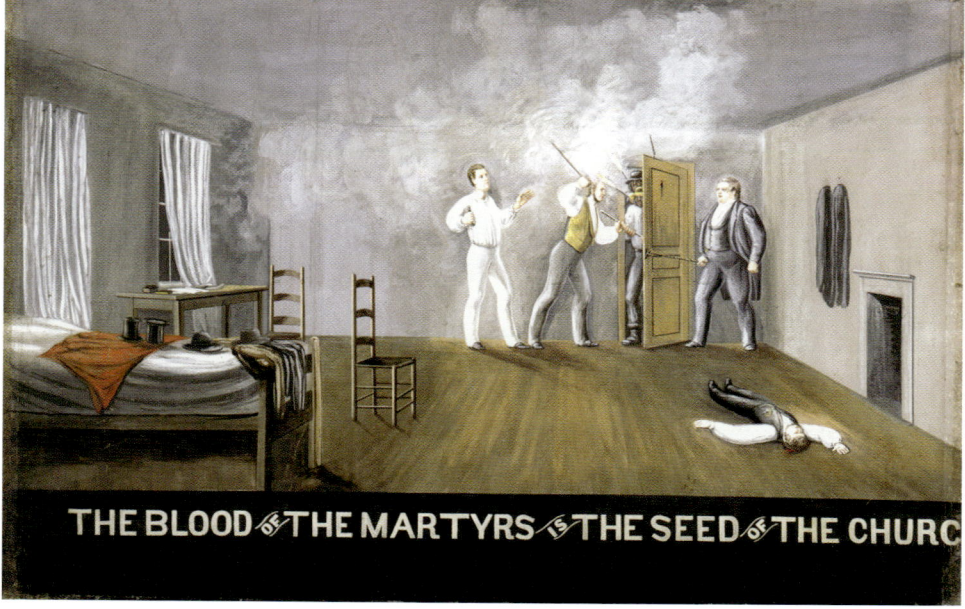

Fig. 4.12 C. C. A. Christensen, *Interior of Carthage Jail*, c. 1878, tempera on muslin, 78″ × 120″, Brigham Young University Museum of Art, gift of the grandchildren of C. C. A. Christensen.

panorama shows the wagon trains entering the Salt Lake Valley, placing viewers behind the pioneers as they crest the canyon and view the semi-arid valley below. Christensen's narrative ends with the work of establishing the new Zion, stating: "They at once began plowing the ground and planting seed."[124] Indeed, the labor of establishing *communitas* in their new promised land would be the focus of subsequent decades, a vision that was fueled by shared identity and belief in the sacredness of their cause.

CONCLUSION

The martyrdom of Joseph Smith marked an important evolution in Latter-day Saint collective identity and in its visual culture. The Saints' departure west—camps of Israel leaving Babylon—signaled an opportunity to truly engage in *communitas*. Portraits, landscapes, and commemorative historical imagery created by a growing number of convert-artists reflected and reinforced the ideals and discourse of Latter-day Saints' temporal and spiritual community building. However, the distinctive ideology and social order of nineteenth-century Latter-day Saints in the Great Basin had to concede that Zion's cause could be advanced by being perceived as genteel, sophisticated, and moral to broader society, especially as they sought statehood to ensure their civic and religious privileges. By 1890, church president Wilford Woodruff called for an end to polygamous unions in order for the church to retain its properties, particularly its sacred temples, and for its people to enjoy continued rights and freedoms. With construction of the Salt Lake temple finally nearing completion, church leaders recognized the need for artists with more advanced training and mastery—a new generation to advance the cause of Zion by immersing themselves in the art centers of Europe and America.

Even with these later developments of artistic talent, the power of Latter-day Saint art to bolster authority, assimilate disparate members, and create meaningful bonds through the depiction of collective sacrifice would persist. Examining this latter half of the nineteenth century highlights how integral these early artistic projects were in fashioning a Latter-day tribe—passionate, faithful, and resilient—indeed, a *communitas* of fellow Saints.

NOTES

[1] Because of the protracted construction timeline, the desire to utilize the temple space, and the increasing likelihood of leaving Nauvoo due to outside threats, leaders dedicated portions of the Nauvoo temple as they were completed. After the exterior was finished, Brigham Young dedicated the structure "thus far completed" in October 1845. The attic area where sacred ordinances were performed was ready for use and dedicated on November 30, 1845. See Don F. Colvin, *Nauvoo Temple: A Story of Faith* (American Fork, UT: Covenant Communications, 2002), 246.

[2] Jill C. Major, "Artworks in the Celestial Room of the First Nauvoo Temple," *BYU Studies* 41, no. 2 (2002): 47.

[3] Ron Romig, "Presidents Portrait Series Unveiled," *Saints' Herald,* April 1998. Lachlan Mackay, former director of the Kirtland Temple Historic Site for the Church of Christ, confirmed this information in conversation with author, April 20, 2023.

[4] Bathsheba Smith notes that she copied famous artworks from prints brought from England by her teacher, William Warner Major; see Major, "Artworks in the Celestial Room," 54. Nathan Rees discusses how access to works of art through missionary travel, periodicals, and print publications continued after Latter-day Saint settlement in the West, complicating the long-held narrative of Mormonism's artistic insularity in the Great Basin. See Nathan Rees, *Mormon Visual Culture and the American West,* Routledge Research in Art and Religion (New York: Routledge, 2021), 4.

[5] William Major and Selah van Sickle seem to have been regarded as the most accomplished of the Nauvoo portraitists. The two occupied a joint studio that received significant business and commissions based on 1845 records. Bathsheba Smith studied with William Warner Major, and many of her impressive portraits survive.

[6] Noel Carmack, "'One of the Most Interesting Seeneries [*sic*] That Can Be Found in Zion': Philo Dibble's Museum and Panorama," *Nauvoo Journal* 9, no. 2 (Fall 1997): 25.

[7] Noel Carmack, "Of Prophets and Pale Horses: Joseph Smith, Benjamin West, and the American Millenarian Tradition," *Dialogue* 29, no. 3 (Autumn 1996): 165.

[8] During the years 1831–1839, church membership gathered in the Ohio and Missouri areas. Particularly in Missouri, the growing body of Latter-day Saints experienced a series of persecutions that prompted multiple instances of resettlement. Anthony Sweat further suggests that the most qualified convert-artists did not arrive until Nauvoo, thus enabling the beginnings of a visual art tradition. See Anthony Sweat, "Visualizing the Vision: The History and Future of First Vision Art," *BYU Studies Quarterly* 59, no. 2 (2020): 227.

[9] Victor Turner, *The Ritual Process: Structure and Anti-structure* (Chicago: Aldine, 1969), 96–97, 106–107. Turner draws on the work of Arnold van Gennep to consider how tribal identities and kinship networks are forged, speaking of transformative, liminal events experienced by individuals and collective groups, passages, which reshape and define a new collective identity.

[10] Victor Turner, *Image and Pilgrimage in Christian Culture: Anthropological Perspectives* (New York: Columbia University Press, 1978), 43.

[11] Turner, *Image and Pilgrimage,* 111.

[12] Turner, *Image and Pilgrimage,* 111.

[13] Romig, "Presidents Portrait Series Unveiled"; author conversation with Lachlan Mackay, Church of Christ Historic Sites, April 20, 2023.

[14] One Latter-day Saint leader, George Q. Cannon, later proposed that this very doctrine of eternal relationships heightened the significance of portraiture for Latter-day Saints, as "our religion creates within us an interest in our kindred greater than that felt by other people for theirs." see Rees, *Mormon Visual Culture,* 31.

[15] Church of Jesus Christ of Latter-day Saints, "Succession in the Presidency of the Church of Jesus Christ of Latter-day Saints," https://newsroom.churchofjesuschrist.org/additional-resource/succession-in-the-presidency-of-the-church-of-jesus-christ-of-latter-day-saints, accessed December 31, 2022; Ronald W. Walker, "Six Days in August: Brigham Young and the Succession Crisis of 1844," in *A Firm Foundation: Church Organization and Administration,* ed. David J. Whittaker and Arnold K. Garr (Provo, UT: Religious Studies Center, Brigham Young University, 2011), 161–196.

[16] Alex D. Smith, "The Book of the Law of the Lord," *Journal of Mormon History* 38, no. 4 (Fall 2012): 131–141.

[17] Revelations 20:12 and 3 Nephi 27:23–26 (in the Book of Mormon) speak of human actions recorded in a book of judgments.

[18] Major, "Artworks in the Celestial Room," 48.

[19] Earlier in 1845, the Quorum of the Twelve seemed to be aware of the importance of asserting their cohesive identity as the new church leadership. John Taylor wrote in his journal of assisting artist William Major in designing a seal for the Twelve Apostles—an effort to brand their collective identity. After the vanguard company left Nauvoo and camped at Winter Quarters, apostle Wilford Woodruff wrote that Major also took likenesses of himself and "others of the Twelve [Apostles]" to create a group portrait. See Carmack, "'One of the Most Interesting Seeneries,'" 31.

[20] Major, "Artworks in the Celestial Room," 50.

21 The Church of Christ collection has a portrait of Lucy Mack Smith that follows the half-length format similar to the other portraits in the room and which historian Lachlan Mackay believes was the image in the Nauvoo celestial room. Author conversation with Lachlan Mackay, April 21, 2023.

22 Major, "Artworks in the Celestial Room," 54, 56.

23 The *Plat Map of Nauvoo* was drawn by Gustavas Hills and printed by J. Childs in 1842. Considering his revelation of temple doctrines and indelible legacy on the church, the absence of a formal image, whether loaned or commissioned, is striking. The aspect of Smith's legacy that seems to be emphasized through the Nauvoo map's display is his vision of a City of God, based on his Plat of Zion. Nauvoo's layout, with its even blocks and initial plot divisions, cardinally oriented streets, and temple focus, reflected the ideal community the Saints envisioned for Zion—a space centered on God and radiating outward in orderly, inspired form. See Marjorie E. Eddy, "The Precepts of Zion and Joseph Smith's City of Zion Plan: Major Influences for the Planning of Nauvoo" (master's thesis, Brigham Young University, 1999), 41–45, https://scholarsarchive.byu.edu/etd/4661. Beyond reflecting the church's earthly communal aspirations, it served as an *imago mundi,* a temporal pattern of the heavenly ideal and the relationships anticipated in a celestial state. See Steven L. Olsen, "Joseph Smith's Concept of the City of Zion," in *Joseph Smith: The Prophet, the Man*, ed. Susan Easton Black and Charles D. Tate Jr. (Provo, UT: Religious Studies Center, Brigham Young University, 1993), 203–211, https://rsc.byu.edu/joseph-smith-prophet-man/joseph-smiths-concept-city-zion.

24 Emma Smith owned at least one portrait of Joseph Smith. Major suggests the Smith family portrait of Joseph would not have been lent to the purpose due to Emma Smith's animosity toward Brigham Young. See Major, "Artworks in the Celestial Room," 58.

25 Beginning in the 1850s, much of the church's growth came from Scandinavia, which opened to the preaching of the gospel in 1849. From 1850 to 1905, more than 22,000 Scandinavian converts immigrated to the territory, though populations of German, Dutch, Swiss, Italian, Australian, and Pacific Island converts were also among those who gathered to Utah. Rachel Gianni Abbott, *The Scandinavian Immigrant Experience in Utah, 1850–1920: Using Material Culture to Assess Cultural Adaption* (PhD diss., University of Alaska, Fairbanks, 2013), 89. See also Richard L. Jensen, "Immigration to Utah," *Utah History Encyclopedia* online, https://www.uen.org/utah_history_encyclopedia/i/IMMIGRATION.shtml, accessed December 30, 2022.

26 Leonard J. Arrington, *Great Basin Kingdom: An Economic History of the Latter-day Saints, 1830–1900,* new ed. (Urbana: University of Illinois Press, 2005), 96–97. Arrington notes the frequent praise of the Mormon cooperative work ethic from visitors to the area, as well as the economic advantages of the gathering to support Zion's temporal welfare.

27 Bridger Talbot, "Artwork in the Sacred Space: A History of Art in LDS Chapels," manuscript shared with the author, and email correspondence, December 29, 2022.

28 A convert from England, Sarah Ann made a living teaching and giving art lessons. She eventually married John Varah Long as a plural wife. Her husband, who sits in this portrait, was excommunicated in 1866 for "conduct unbecoming a saint," including his reported participation in Gentile social clubs, and would no longer have been working as Young's scribe.

29 Richard G. Oman, "The Foundation of Latter-day Saint Art, 1835–1890," in Museum of Church History and Art, *Images of Faith: Art of the Latter-day Saints* (Salt Lake City: Deseret Book, 1995), 9. This information was substantiated by curator Laura Paulsen Howe, with additional notes: Between John V. Long and John Lyon are two blue books, one of which says "NoteBook," possibly referencing Lyon's work as a poet and librarian. The green book near Patriarch John Young is titled "Records of Blessings." George A. Smith's scroll reads "History of Joseph Smith," indicating his work as editor for *The History of the Church,* originally published as *History of Joseph Smith* in 1858. Daniel H. Wells's rolled scroll refers to his role overseeing construction of the Salt Lake temple and tabernacle. Email correspondence with Laura Paulsen Howe, February 28, 2022.

30 Carmack, "'One of the Most Interesting Seeneries,'" 30.

31 Oman, "Foundation," 25.

32 Jared Farmer, *On Zion's Mount: Mormons, Indians, and the American Landscape* (Cambridge, MA: Harvard University Press, 2008), 149–155.

[33] Oman, "Foundation," 20.

[34] Oman, "Foundation," 25.

[35] Rees, *Mormon Visual Culture,* 41–43.

[36] Richard L. Jensen and Robert Oman, *C. C. A. Christensen, 1831–1912, Mormon Immigrant Artist: An Exhibition at the Museum of Church History and Art* (Salt Lake City: Church of Jesus Christ of Latter-day Saints, 1984), 54. Jensen dates this painting as 1893. Due to the close proximity of its creation to the dates delimited in this chapter's discussion and its continuity of dialogue and form, I have decided to include it here.

[37] Glen R. Stubbs, "A History of the Manti Temple" (master's thesis, Brigham Young University, 1960), 1, 3, https://scholarsarchive.byu.edu/etd/5150.

[38] Rees, *Mormon Visual Culture,* 81.

[39] Rees, *Mormon Visual Culture,* 79.

[40] W. Paul Reeve, *Religion of a Different Color: Race and the Mormon Struggle for Whiteness* (New York: Oxford University Press, 2015), 77–79. See also Rees, *Mormon Visual Culture,* 49–53. Despite Mormons' unique belief in Native Americans as the descendants of Book of Mormon peoples, relations eventually deteriorated.

[41] Christensen was deeply invested in the construction of a temple in Manti, Utah, a town close to Christensen's own home. Not only was it a source of spiritual anticipation, but Christensen assisted by painting murals inside the temple as well as painting the exterior roof. See Jensen and Oman, *C. C. A. Christensen,* 20.

[42] Jensen and Oman, *C. C. A. Christensen,* 53.

[43] Brigham Young, quoted in Richard Francaviglia, *The Mormon Landscape: Existence, Creation, and Perception of a Unique Image in the American West* (New York: AMS Press, 1974), 86.

[44] "Government of the Tongue—Impartiality in Judgment—Sealing," remarks by President Brigham Young, made in the Tabernacle, Great Salt Lake City, April 6, 1862, reported by G. D. Watt, *Journal of Discourses* 9 (1862): 269.

[45] Francaviglia, *The Mormon Landscape,* 85.

[46] Lynne E. Henrichsen and George Bailey, "No More Strangers and Foreigners: The Dual Focus of the LDS Language Program for Scandinavian Immigrants, 1850–1935," *Mormon Historical Studies* 11, no. 2 (Fall 2010): 29.

[47] Church of Jesus Christ of Latter-day Saints, "Deseret Alphabet," https://www.churchofjesuschrist.org/study/history/topics/deseret-alphabet?lang=eng, accessed January 4, 2023.

[48] Oman, "Foundation," 30.

[49] Weggeland created copies of this painting that are now housed in the Pioneer Memorial Museum (Daughters of the Utah Pioneers), three versions at the Church History Museum, the State of Utah's Alice Collection, and the Brigham Young University Museum of Art.

[50] Robert L. Olpin, *Signs and Symbols in Early and Sometimes Much Later Utah Art: A Slide Collage* (Salt Lake City: Frederick William Reynolds Association, 1988).

[51] *Bishop Sam Bennion Farm, Taylorsville,* c. 1879, oil on canvas, mounted, Springville Museum of Art collection, 1986.002.

[52] Robert S. Olpin and Roger Roper, "Painting and Reality: Did Utah's Early Painters Show Things the Way They Really Were?," *Utah Preservation* 5 (2001): 59.

[53] William Mulder, *Homeward to Zion: The Mormon Migration from Scandinavia* (Minneapolis: University of Minnesota Press, 1999), 189–225. Mulder's research into the experience of Scandinavian settlers offers an insightful lens into the experience of immigrant settlers.

[54] For a rich history of the natural water resources of Utah Valley and use of its fisheries by Indigenous communities and pioneer settlers, see the chapter "Liquid Antecedents" in Farmer, *On Zion's Mount.*

[55] Leonard J. Arrington, "Colonization of Utah," *Utah History Encyclopedia* (1994),, accessed online at https://historytogo.utah.gov/colonization-utah/.

56 The compact focus and interdependence of these townships reflected Joseph Smith's Plat of Zion. As John Taylor taught, "By [gathering] the people can retain their ecclesiastical organizations. . . . They can also cooperate for the good of all in financial and secular matters, in making ditches, fencing fields, building bridges, and other necessary improvements. Further than this they are a mutual protection and source of strength against horse and cattle thieves, land jumpers, etc., and against hostile Indians, should there be any; while their compact organization gives them many advantages . . . which might be lost . . . by spreading out so thinly that inter-communication is difficult, dangerous, inconvenient and expensive." Quoted in Craig D. Galli, "Building Zion: The Latter-day Saint Legacy of Urban Planning," *BYU Studies Quarterly* 44, no. 1 (2005): 114. Images of these orderly settlements can be found and serve as documents of the fort-like gathering of early townships.

57 Brigham Young, in *Journal of Discourses* 3 (1856): 330.

58 Christensen's piece of 1878 doesn't specify, though the Eighth Ward square was the typical meeting and greeting spot for newly arrived immigrants to the Salt Lake Valley and was often termed Emigration or Washington Square. The developed architecture, streets, and trees seem to reflect this; see Mulder, *Homeward to Zion*, 199.

59 I am grateful to Melanie Allred for this suggestion. Given that modesty in dress and expenditures was perpetually preached by leaders over the pulpit (see Rees, *Mormon Visual Culture*, 111–115), such an emphasis on fashion here may be a ideological symbol.

60 Kathryn Daynes, *More Wives than One: Transformation of the Mormon Marriage System, 1840–1910* (Urbana: University of Illinois Press, 2001), 76. Examples of the practical benefit of plural marriage are also discussed in Mulder, *Homeward to Zion*, 243–245.

61 Kathryn M. Daynes, "Celestial Marriage (Eternal and Plural)," in *The Oxford Handbook of Mormonism*, ed. Terryl L. Givens and Philip L. Barlow (New York: Oxford University Press, 2015).

62 John Taylor, sermon, February 10, 1884, *Journal of Discourses* 15 (1884): 92, cited in Mulder, *Homeward to Zion*, 349.

63 Rees, *Mormon Visual Culture*, 91. Rees cites polygamist families' concerns about popular misuse of such imagery because of widespread national antagonism toward the practice, as well as Mary Campbell's assertion of the fear of such images being used as evidence to prosecute those in plural families. See Mary Campbell, *Charles Ellis Johnson and the Erotic Mormon Image* (Chicago: University of Chicago Press, 2016), 125–128.

64 Laurel Thatcher Ulrich, *A House Full of Females: Plural Marriage and Women's Rights in Early Mormonism, 1835–1870* (New York: Vintage Books, 2017), xix

65 Mulder, *Homeward to Zion*, 274.

66 Turner, *The Ritual Process*, 111. Turner offers a useful summation of attributes of *communitas*, including "'all are equal in the sight of God' . . . abolition of rank, humility, disregard for personal appearance, unselfishness, total obedience to the prophet or leader, sacred instruction, the maximization of religious, as opposed to secular, attitudes and behavior, suspension of kinship rights and obligations (all are siblings or comrades to one another regardless of previous secular ties)."

67 Daynes, "Celestial Marriage," 338.

68 Daynes, "Celestial Marriage," 339.

69 Mulder, *Homeward to Zion*, 242.

70 Daynes, "Celestial Marriage," 343. Mulder recounts the experience of several Scandinavian members who were imprisoned for practicing plural marriage, including Andrew Jenson, who compiled a book, *Prisoners for Conscience Sake*, listing those incarcerated in three prisons for polygamy; see Mulder, *Homeward to Zion*, 241.

71 Roselyn Slade, "Francis McKay Treseder—An Early Utah Artist," Family Search, https://www.familysearch.org/photos/artifacts/33757779/francis-frank-mckay-treseder-an-early-utah-artist.

72 Vern G. Swanson, Jessica Weiss, Ashlee Whitaker, and Nicole C. Romney, *Springville Museum of Art: History and Collection* (Springville, UT: CFI, 2013), 88. Additionally, a note on the file of a similar painting by Treseder at the Heritage Museum of Layton, Utah, comments that Abraham Cannon purchased similar paintings from Treseder for $4 and $6, respectively. For information about Rudger Clawson, see Lawrence

R. Flake, *Prophets and Apostles of the Last Dispensation* (Provo, UT: Religious Studies Center, Brigham Young University, 2001), 259–263.

[73] Provenance information provided by Laura Paulsen Howe, curator, Church Museum, email correspondence with the author, January 17, 2023.

[74] Marriner Wood Merrill, *Utah Pioneer and Apostle Marriner Wood Merrill: And His Family* (Salt Lake City: n.p., 1937), 100.

[75] Davis Bitton, "The Ritualization of Mormon History," *Utah Historical Quarterly* 43, no. 1 (1975): 73.

[76] "Thomas Bullock," in *Our Pioneer Heritage* (Salt Lake City: Daughters of the Utah Pioneers, 1958–1977), 8:260. I am indebted to Laura Paulsen Howe for sharing this source and its information, which had been transcribed into the Church Museum database. Bullock was a member of the vanguard pioneer wagon train and likely commissioned an artist to create the banner based on his concept. A second version of this banner, created by Dan Weggeland and dated 1897, resides in the Daughters of the Utah Pioneers' Pioneer Memorial Museum in Salt Lake City. According to this same record, the church commissioned Weggeland to create "an exact copy" of it that could be given to Thomas Bullock's family in exchange for the original "relic." The donation of this Weggeland copy to the Pioneer Memorial Museum is corroborated by an October 7, 1965, *Deseret News* article, "DUP Receives Historic Gift."

[77] Select contemporary sources indicate the three men were enslaved servants, baptized in the Mississippi area prior to being sent by their owners on the vanguard trek west. Once in the Salt Lake Valley, they would have prepared land and lodgings for their enslavers. After being released from slavery, two of them changed their names to Hark Wales and Oscar Smith. See individual biographies at https://exhibits.lib.utah.edu/s/century-of-black-mormons. See also Ronald G. Coleman, "A History of Blacks in Utah, 1825–1910" (PhD diss., University of Utah, 1980).

[78] *Our Pioneer Heritage,* 260.

[79] Church of Jesus Christ of Latter-day Saints, "Sacred Temple Clothing," https://www.churchofjesuschrist.org/temples/sacred-temple-clothing?lang=eng, accessed December 28, 2022.

[80] Church of Jesus Christ of Latter-day Saints, "Race and the Priesthood," https://www.churchofjesuschrist.org/study/manual/gospel-topics-essays/race-and-the-priesthood?lang=eng, accessed December 28, 2022. Though during the early years of the church Joseph Smith offered African Americans full participation in church worship and ordinances, after the Utah settlement Brigham Young announced that individuals of African descent would be unable to be ordained to priesthood offices or receive temple ordinances. This policy ended in 1978.

[81] Richard A. Cowan, "The Design, Construction, and Role of the Salt Lake Temple," in *Salt Lake City: The Place Which God Prepared,* ed. Scott C. Esplin and Kenneth L. Alford (Provo, UT: Brigham Young University, Religious Studies Center, 2011), 58. Oman cites the symbol of clasped hands as prolific among the Saints in both public and domestic objects; Oman, "Foundation," 14.

[82] J. V. Long. *Report of the First General Festival of the Renowned Mormon Battalion, Which Came Off on Tuesday and Wednesday, Feb. 6 and 7, 1855, in the Social Hall, G.S.L. City* (Salt Lake City: T. S. Williams, 1855), 4.

[83] Ottinger became an influential artist and teacher in the early Utah Territory. His oeuvre represents a compelling array of historical subjects, including scenes from American history and literature, Aztec narratives, Latter-day Saint stories, and genre scenes.

[84] Church of Jesus Christ of Latter-day Saints, "Transcript for Milo Andrus Emigrating Company Journal, 1861 April–May and July–August," https://history.churchofjesuschrist.org/chd/transcript?lang=eng&name=transcript-for-milo-andrus-emigrating-company-journal-1861-april-may-and-july, accessed April 5, 2023.

[85] Church of Jesus Christ of Latter-day Saints, "Transcript for Milo Andrus Emigrating Company Journal, 1861 April–May and July–August," https://history.churchofjesuschrist.org/chd/transcript?lang=eng&name=transcript-for-milo-andrus-emigrating-company-journal-1861-april-may-and-july, accessed April 5, 2023.

[86] In the presumably later and more finished composition, also in the Church Museum collection, the artist includes Chimney Rock, a notable landmark along the Mormon Trail, even though Moss's death and internment took place approximately nine days' time and over a hundred miles from the landmark. The rock

formation could serve as a signifier of the distance traveled as well as a poignant natural monument to the deceased and nearly two thousand like him who died along the the trail after leaving Nebraska, heightening the sacred tribute of the scene. See Melvin Bashore, Dennis Tolley, and the BYU Pioneer Mortality Team, "Mortality on the Mormon Trail, 1847–1868," *BYU Studies Quarterly* 53, no. 4 (2014): 117.

[87] Robert Thorne, "Panoramania," *History Today* 38 (November 1988): 51.

[88] Latter-day Saint artists such as Reuben Kirkham and Alfred Lambourne, both of whom painted backdrops for the Salt Lake Theater, also created and exhibited panoramas. Reuben Kirkham's "Book of Mormon" panorama (1880–1889) and a collaborative panorama with Lambourne, "Across the Continent, or From Ocean to Ocean" (1875), were among those entertainments featured. See "To-night Kirkham's great panorama of the Book of Mormon," advertisement, 1880–1889, Church History library catalog M222.084 T665a 188-?, and "Salt Lake Theatre!: One night only: Tuesday evening, Dec. 14th, 1875: will be presented for the first time, the new beautiful panorama . . . ," advertisement, 1875, Church History Museum catalog M284.3 S176a 1875.

[89] Mason Kamana Allred, "Panoramic Vision: Consolidating the Early Mormon Gaze," *Material Religion: The Journal of Objects, Art, and Belief* 16, no. 5 (2020): 3.

[90] Carmack, "'One of the Most Interesting Seeneries,'" 29. Carmack also implies that Sutcliffe Maudsley may have helped create studies as well, but Dibble does not mention that artist. "Fine Arts," *Nauvoo Neighbor,* April 16, 1845, 2–3.

[91] Dibble filed a copyright in March 1845 for eight large paintings (Allred, "Panoramic Vision," 3). He hoped to re-create events such as the Battle of Crooked River, the tragedy at Haun's Mill, the surrender of Far West, the martyrdom, the exodus from Nauvoo, and the Mormon Battalion. Contemporary accounts provide evidence that he completed the scene of the martyrdom of Joseph and Hyrum, Joseph addressing the Nauvoo Legion, and the Mormon Battalion marching to Mexico, and the exodus from Nauvoo. One account refers to Dibble's panoramic display as including a canvas that showed "the early mobbings of the Saints," implying one of the earlier scenes of persecution may have been completed; see Carmack, "'One of the Most Interesting Seeneries,'" 32.

[92] "Will Be Exhibited," *Nauvoo Neighbor,* July 30, 1845, http://boap.org/LDS/Nauvoo-Neighbor/1845/7-30-1845.pdf.

[93] Dibble subsequently undertook another large, horizontal depiction of Joseph Smith addressing the Nauvoo Legion, an event that took place on June 18, 1844, days prior to his martyrdom. See Carmack, "'One of the Most Interesting Seeneries,'" 27. According to sources, members of the Nauvoo Legion took issue with Campbell for including certain personalities in the scene who were no longer affiliated with the church, as well as the various positions of individuals within the Legion's hierarchy, (Hosea Stout Journal, September 8, 1845). After some debate, Dibble concurred and justified the project as "a more didactic, idealized image than historically accurate depiction of the event."

[94] Carmack, "'One of the Most Interesting Seeneries,'" 29.

[95] Allred, "Panoramic Vision," 4–5.

[96] Carmack, "'One of the Most Interesting Seeneries,'" 28.

[97] Carmack, "'One of the Most Interesting Seeneries,'" 30, 32. Dibble's large panoramas remained in Kanesville until family members could bring them out to the Utah Territory in 1854, after which he began presentations.

[98] Dibble's letters mention Robert Campbell making sketches of individuals and creating studies for the intended panorama scenes; see Carmack, "'One of the Most Interesting Seeneries,'" 27, 29. A small painting by Campbell, *General Joseph Smith Addressing the Nauvoo Legion,* in the Church Museum collection, is believed to a be a study for the larger panorama.

[99] Philo Dibble letter, Springville, Utah, to John Taylor, March 16, 1879, Church History Library CR 1 180. According to Dibble, Christensen even tried to steal away Dibble's artist, a Scandinavian convert living in Provo. One possible candidate for Dibble's Provo artist is Danish artist Samuel Hans Jepperson.

[100] "It Is Coming! The Grand Historical Exhibition," handbill image, BYU Museum of Art curatorial file, "C.C.A. Christensen Mormon Panorama," accessed October 10, 2022.

[101] The *Mormon Panorama* is the work of art most often discussed in terms of early Latter-day Saint Art, because twenty-two of its large-scale scenes survive in remarkable condition and mark one of the first

documentations of Latter-day Saint history. Its "discovery" by the broader art historical world and its exhibition at the Whitney Museum of American Art in 1970 celebrated it as a visual manifestation of pioneer folk art, based on Christensen's less developed academic style.

102 Jensen and Oman, *C. C. A. Christensen,* 18. They generally traveled during the winter months, when farm chores were minimal, transporting the large scroll on a wagon. After setting up in a church or schoolhouse, they enlisted local children to distribute handbills advertising the "historical" presentation. Although the presenters preferred cash, the townspeople often paid for admission in produce or other commodities. As a handcart immigrant in 1857, Christensen himself did not personally witness the events; however, he drew on interviews and eyewitness accounts in shaping his images, some of which he revised throughout his travels.

103 Rees, *Mormon Visual Culture,* 1, 5.

104 Jensen and Oman, *C. C. A. Christensen,* 18.

105 Jennifer Champoux, "'In Their Promised Canaan Stand': Outlawry, Landscape, and Memory in C. C. A. Christensen's Mormon Panorama," *BYU Studies Quarterly* 60, no. 2 (2021): 9.

106 Rees, *Mormon Visual Culture,* 4–6.

107 Rees, *Mormon Visual Culture,* 95.

108 "Mormon Panorama," *Ogden Daily Herald,* April 18, 1885, https://newspapers.lib.utah.edu/ark:/87278/s6t44ttj/7388870.

109 Charles J. Christensen, "Mormon Panorama Lectures of C. C. A. Christensen," Scene III, typescript manuscript in Brigham Young University Museum of Art curatorial files, donated by the Christensen family.

110 Rees, *Mormon Visual Culture,* 90–92. Rees discusses how Christensen himself felt these challenges keenly. Because the artist had married two wives, he left Utah and his family to serve missions in Scandinavia and avoid incarceration. The artist also was keenly attuned to Utah settlers' tensions with the Indigenous peoples in the area, as the Black Hawk War touched Christensen's community in Sanpete County. According to Rees, Christensen demonstrates a less idealized perspective of Native Americans in his subsequent panorama projects.

111 George Q. Cannon, sermon, 1889, https://www.lds-general-conference.org/.

112 Jensen and Oman, *C. C. A. Christensen,* 110.

113 Steven Harper, *First Vision: Memory and Mormon Origins* (New York: Oxford University Press, 2019), 112.

114 Turner, *Image and Pilgrimage,* 43–68. Turner's exploration of pilgrimage as liminal experience in Christian tradition offers rich perspectives on the transformative nature of pilgrimage as a liminal rite of passage.

115 Rees, *Mormon Visual Culture,* 101. The expectation of both bodily and spiritual participation and the idea of a simulated journey through the experience of forebears align with the presentation format of Latter-day Saint temple rituals.

116 Turner, *Image and Pilgrimage,* 47.

117 Kathleen Flake, "Re-placing Memory: LDS Use of Historical Monuments and Narrative in the Early 20th Century," *Religion and American Culture: A Journal of Interpretation* 13, no. 1 (2003): 76–77, 80–81.

118 Turner, *Image and Pilgrimage,* 49.

119 Champoux, "'In Their Promised Canaan Stand,'" 29.

120 During this incarceration, Joseph Smith received revelations now recorded in the Doctrine and Covenants 121–123. Smith's consecration amid the deprivation of this trial prompted one present-day church leader to describe Liberty Jail as a "prison-temple." See Jeffrey R. Holland, "Lessons from Liberty Jail," Church Educational System Fireside for Young Adults, September 7, 2008. As a dedicated temple, the Nauvoo temple was the site of sacred instruction and covenant rituals that would have been considered inappropriate to depict for a public audience but understood as a sacred site by viewers.

121 Turner, *Image and Pilgrimage,* 49. As Turner writes of the pilgrimage journey, "Through [the] very vividness [of scene and site], [the pilgrim] become increasingly capable of entering in imagination and with sympathy into the . . . experiences of the founder and of those persons depicted as standing in some close relationship to him."

122 Champoux, "'In Their Promised Canaan Stand,'" 45–46.

123 Rees, *Mormon Visual Culture,* 88–89. Rees points out that this phrase, "The blood of the martyrs . . . ," was prevalent in nineteenth-century America and had been invoked by church members following the martyrdom in the 1840s, reiterated here by Joseph F. Smith and Christensen.

124 "Mormon Panorama Lectures of C.C.A. Christensen," Scene XXI.

5

THE PUBLIC IMAGE

How the World Learned to See Mormonism, from Cartoons to World's Fairs

NATHAN REES

Since the Church of Jesus Christ of Latter-day Saints' founding in the early nineteenth century, its public image has been fervently contested through representations from both within and without. Much of this discourse played out in written form as pro- and anti-Mormon authors voiced their competing perspectives in printed texts. Yet Mormonism was also defined through visual culture—the wide range of images including works of fine art, engravings, photographs, public displays, and mass-market printed images of all sorts.[1] This survey explores just a small sample of the extensive visual culture that represented Mormonism to nineteenth- and early twentieth-century audiences, revealing how Latter-day Saints and their opponents fashioned competing representations of Mormon beliefs and social practices, and how Latter-day Saints struggled to command this contested visual terrain with increasingly monumental self-representations. I explore how visual culture shaped the Mormon image through a tumultuous period spanning roughly the century after the church's founding.

Images promoted the opposing ideologies held by Latter-day Saints and their detractors, representing, on the one hand, Mormons as theocratic polygamists threatening American values and, on the other, Mormons as honorable, nation-building pioneers. Careful scrutiny, however, reveals that the Mormon image was fashioned with far more complexity than a simple binary between pro- and anti-Mormon representations might suggest. Latter-day Saints were astute consumers and producers of images, whose nuanced representations targeted specific audiences or furthered the aims of particular subsets of the Mormon populace. In other cases, Latter-day Saints worked *with* external constituencies to create mutually beneficial representations. Despite this complexity, one trait unites the visual culture of Mormonism across this era: no matter how anodyne, illustrational, or objective they might appear, images of

Mormonism made for public consumption participated in the contested discourse defining the place of Latter-day Saints within contemporaneous America.

I focus on two forms of visual representation that might initially seem complete opposites: print media and monumental works (including public statuary and exhibitions at world's fairs). While the first is characterized by ephemerality and intimate scale and the second emphasizes permanence and grandness, the crucial connection between these disparate realms of visual culture is their broad public audience. Unlike many of the paintings, sculptures, and works of fine art discussed in other chapters in this volume, printed images and public monuments, despite their differences in scale, were created for mass audiences with the intent of persuading the public of their creators' interpretation of Mormonism. Following Harold Innis's theory of time versus space biases of media, printed images and monuments project power across both axes—print media allowed for the widest possible dissemination, while monuments asserted the permanence of their messages through their emphatic, massive fixity.[2] Despite the different audiences that each form reached and the different discursive modalities each employed, considering both in conversation is essential in order to understand how visual culture shaped the Mormon public image. Space constrains this essay from addressing expressions of Mormonism other than the Utah-based Church of Jesus Christ of Latter-day Saints (LDS) or representations from outside the United States. In offering a broad overview, this essay is necessarily limited to just a few examples drawn from the vast range of representations of Mormonism from this period.

I begin by investigating the rhetorical strategies employed in early anti-Mormon periodical print culture, and then continue by tracing the history of Mormon visual self-representations in print. Next, I explore the LDS Church's strategy of enhancing its public image through monumental artworks and visual displays as the church developed new approaches to self-representation following the end of polygamy, continuing through early twentieth-century world's fairs. I conclude by considering the contested legacies of these representations in the present. Visual culture in the public sphere—whether ephemeral or monumental—has played a critical role in representing Mormonism to the world. The competing images that argued for and against Mormon morality, civility, and respectability in the religious movement's first century gave visual form to discourses surrounding gender, sexuality, race, and colonialism that continue to shape perceptions both inside and outside the church. From the beginning, images have been crucial in defining not only what Mormonism looks like but also what Mormonism means.

ANTI-MORMON PERIODICAL PRINT CULTURE

Many of the earliest surviving representations of Mormonism were created not by Latter-day Saints but by their opponents.[3] Gary L. Bunker and Davis Bitton have documented how texts opposing Mormonism began featuring illustrations mocking Joseph Smith and his followers shortly after the church's organization in 1830.[4] In the

mid-nineteenth century, Mormons' political and social struggles brought increasing national attention and elicited a surge of visual representations. By far the most popular
trope within this body of imagery represented the Latter-day Saint practice of polygamy,
which had been rumored for over a decade before being publicly announced in 1852.[5]
The genre's high point coincided with the apex of the struggle over polygamy in the
1870s and 1880s, when major national publications frequently caricatured Mormonism
as a stark departure from American social standards and a menace to public morality.
The Elders' Happy Home, by Charles Kendrick, published in the New York magazine
Chic in 1881, for example, mocked Latter-day Saint leaders as hapless and feminized.
Rather than exhibiting the virile prowess that his "harem" of ten or more wives might
suggest, the elder in the cartoon is emasculated by his lack of control over his undisci-
plined female household.[6] The caricature makes a more sophisticated argument than
it might appear at first glance, critiquing Mormonism's violation of gender and sexual
norms, but also alleging Latter-day Saint racial aberrance. As Paul Reeve has discussed,
the image asserts a sense of "racial deterioration inherent in Mormon polygamy" by including a stereotyped African American baby among the wailing infants in the crib in
the foreground.[7]

Beyond the periodicals where they were first published, these images sometimes
had long, polysemous lives. Australian tourist James Francis Hogan, for example,
encountered a print of *The Elders' Happy Home* for sale at a bookstore in Ogden in 1887.

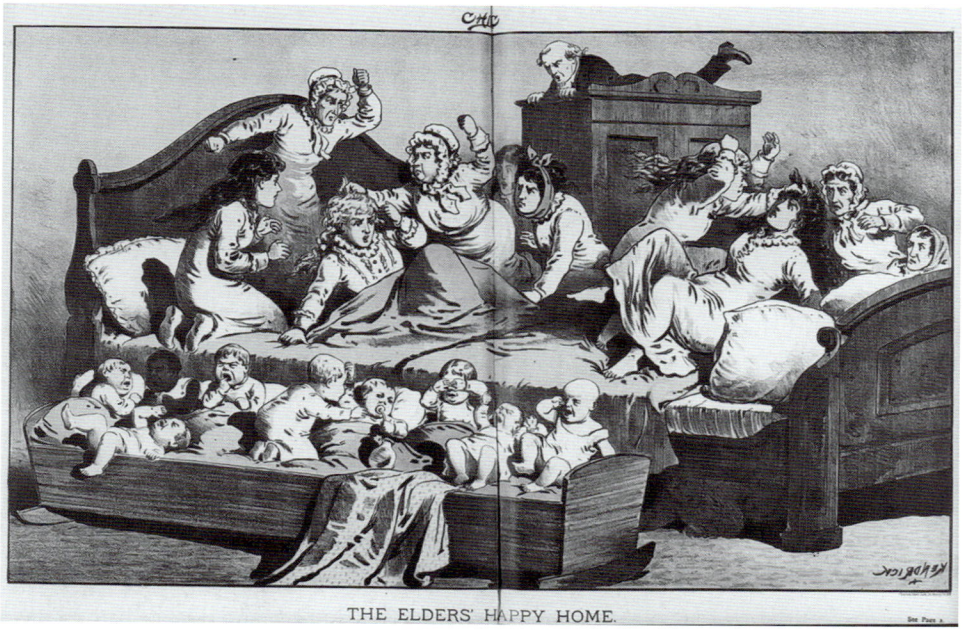

THE ELDERS' HAPPY HOME.

Fig. 5.1 Charles Kendrick, *The Elders' Happy Home,* 1881, chromolithograph. Courtesy Library of
Congress.

For the bookseller, it was an opportunity to appeal to tourists' desire for a salacious peek inside the allegedly degenerate households they encountered in Utah. For Hogan, it was less an image of the reality of Mormonism than an "intensely comical" example of the "pictorial reflections on the reigning religious powers." For Hogan's guide, it was an opportunity to critique Mormonism from a very different perspective, demonstrating Latter-day Saints' diminishing power even within Utah—as the guide told Hogan, displaying such an image in prior decades would have elicited extreme punishment, but "the Mormons are no longer in supreme power in the territory of their choice, and they have to bear with a good many annoyances at the hands of the Gentiles."[8] Despite their often humorous tone, nineteenth-century caricatures of Mormonism were more than superficial satire—they addressed multiple political concerns related to Mormon social and religious practices, and were read by diverse audiences from a variety of nuanced perspectives.

While scholarship on anti-Mormon imagery from this era has focused mostly on periodicals, illustrations in books also helped construct the image of Mormonism for the outside world. A few early anti-Mormon texts included engravings, but cheaper and more accessible printing technologies along with escalating national interest in Mormonism spurred a slew of illustrated volumes later in the nineteenth century. Perhaps because these images tended more toward biting realism than the humorous caricature of many periodical illustrations, modern scholars have been less interested in book illustrations. But in their cold, realist portrayals of Mormons violating Victorian social conventions, book illustrations offered a different but equally powerful critique.

Exposés of polygamy by women who had left plural marriages featured many of the most forcefully critical images. These illustrations created a powerful sense of unease by representing realistic, ordinary households similar to those that their viewers would have been intimately familiar with—but twisted through the lens of polygamy to upend Victorian social conventions. In her damning critique of Mormon plural marriage, *Wife No. 19* (1876), Ann Eliza Young (who had divorced Brigham Young in 1873) published numerous disturbing images of polygamous households.[9] *A Scene in Polygamy— "Greeting the Favorite,"* by Stanley Fox, for example, shows a Mormon man embracing a woman, while five others look on.[10]

Rather than caricaturing Mormon difference, Fox represented the family in ordinary clothes of the era, standing in a typical contemporary parlor. The narrative context, however, encourages viewers to react with horror at the scandalous glimpse of moral degeneracy the image affords. The man is singling out his favorite wife for affection upon arriving home, treating his five other wives with callous indifference. Her clothing, more fashionable and ornate than the other wives', also hints at her favored status. The setting's ordinariness makes its upended vision of domestic norms all the more effective—that this could be any quotidian middle-class household makes the social violation it represents seem all the more real and thus more terrifying.

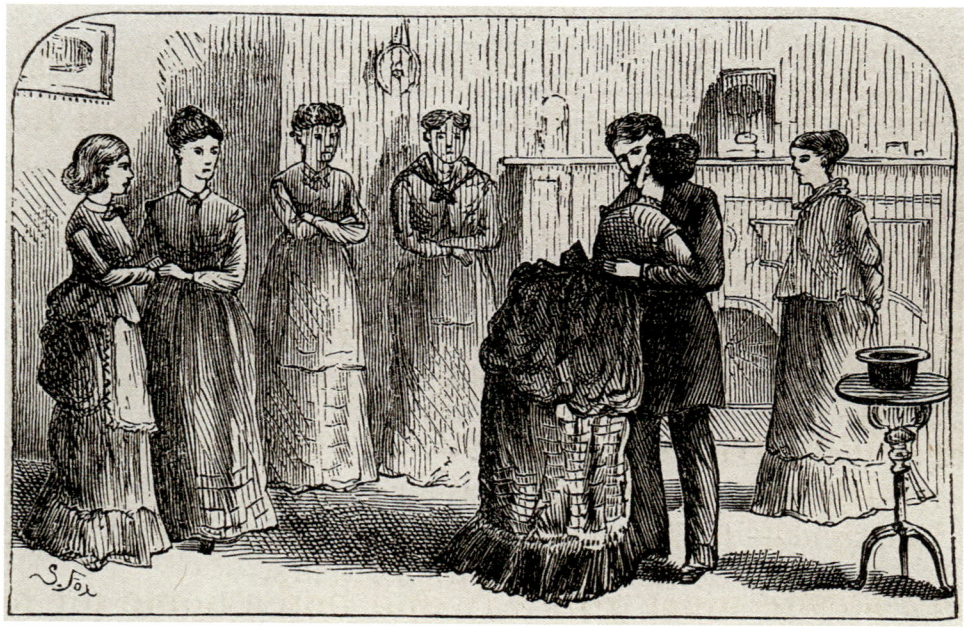

Fig. 5.2 Stanley Fox, *Greeting the Favorite*, 1876, engraving.

Far from the conception of plural marriage as the key to familial happiness then promoted by the Church of Jesus Christ of Latter-day Saints, Young and Fox frame polygamy as an institution that destroyed the domestic bliss that Victorian culture elevated as a woman's most important source of pleasure and fulfillment. Fox's illustrations reinforce Young's claim that polygamy fostered unchecked male sexuality, such that a man "lost all the respect and chivalrous regard he once had for the sex," and that "women died of broken hearts."[11] *A Scene in Polygamy—"Greeting the Favorite"* hints at the prospect of licentiousness—the man draws his favorite wife's body toward him with his hand at her waist, the couple's mouths align so closely as to suggest that their embrace will become even more intimate, and the urgency of the man's desire is intimated by the hat left hastily on a table. Nor has he stopped to remove his topcoat. The image sought to discomfit its viewers with a clear suggestion of the base sexuality it asserted as the basis of Mormon polygamy. Viewers were meant to identify not with the central couple but with the five brokenhearted women on the periphery standing stern-faced with arms folded in disappointment or locking hands like the pair on the left in an attempt to reinforce each other's resolve, standing literally in the shadow of the "favorite." We as viewing subjects are asked to share their looks of horror, incredulity, or disgust as we join the onlookers in judging the gross violation of contemporary social standards.

MORMON SELF-REPRESENTATIONS IN PRINT CULTURE

Whether in caricatures like *The Elder's Happy Home* or in realist illustrations like *Greeting the Favorite,* most visual representations of Mormonism in nineteenth-century print culture were created by, circulated among, and marketed to the church's opponents rather than its supporters. Yet, recognizing the power that images could muster in achieving their social and political aims, Latter-day Saints created their own positive self-representations beginning not long after the church's founding. These included well-known portraits of Mormon leaders and paintings of the church's history that are discussed elsewhere in this volume, but Latter-day Saints also produced illustrations in print media that offered a counternarrative to anti-Mormon caricatures. Indeed, although modern audiences are more familiar with Mormon art through works of painting and sculpture, nineteenth-century Americans were far likelier to encounter it in printed form.

The limited printing technology available in Mormon settlements in the Midwest and in early Utah meant that most images had to be produced in urban centers in the eastern United States or in Europe, frequently by artists and printers who were not themselves Latter-day Saints. Nonetheless, Mormons commissioned numerous printed images that advanced their own perspective during this era. An early example is a lithograph issued in 1847 by William Hart Miles, a church leader in the New York City area, titled *The Two Martyrs.*[12] Created by an unattributed artist at the firm of Sarony & Major in New York, it represents Hyrum Smith (left) and Joseph Smith (right) in facing profile portraits based on earlier works by Sutcliffe Maudsley, an English artist who immigrated to Nauvoo in 1842, where he painted a number of small profile portraits of Latter-day Saint leaders.[13]

The Two Martyrs offers a self-representation countering the negative imagery then pervasive in the popular press. Rather than celebrating the Smiths for their deeds or showcasing their accomplishments, the print emphasizes Mormon respectability. Arguing against the visual rhetoric of Mormons as repugnant and degraded, Miles's engraving amplifies the markers of gentility from Maudsley's originals, proclaiming Joseph and Hyrum Smith's status as gentlemen. Their elegant tailcoats, stocks, waistcoats, and trousers, in a variety of contrasting hues, mark them as fashionably refined, as do their polished shoes and carefully coiffed hair. Posed with hands resting on canes—and, for Joseph, his left arm jauntily akimbo—they could easily be mistaken for intellectuals or leaders in business or politics, or perhaps even fashion plates in contemporaneous publications. That was surely Miles's aim, at a time when the Mormon converts he welcomed at America's largest port of immigration were derided as desperate, ignorant, and impoverished, and when Joseph Smith was routinely caricatured as exhibiting the worst of perceived Mormon depravity. Subsequent derivative prints demonstrate that the image maintained its resonance over ensuing decades, when, as Richard Bushman has described, Latter-day Saints in Utah strove continually to project an image of "refinement

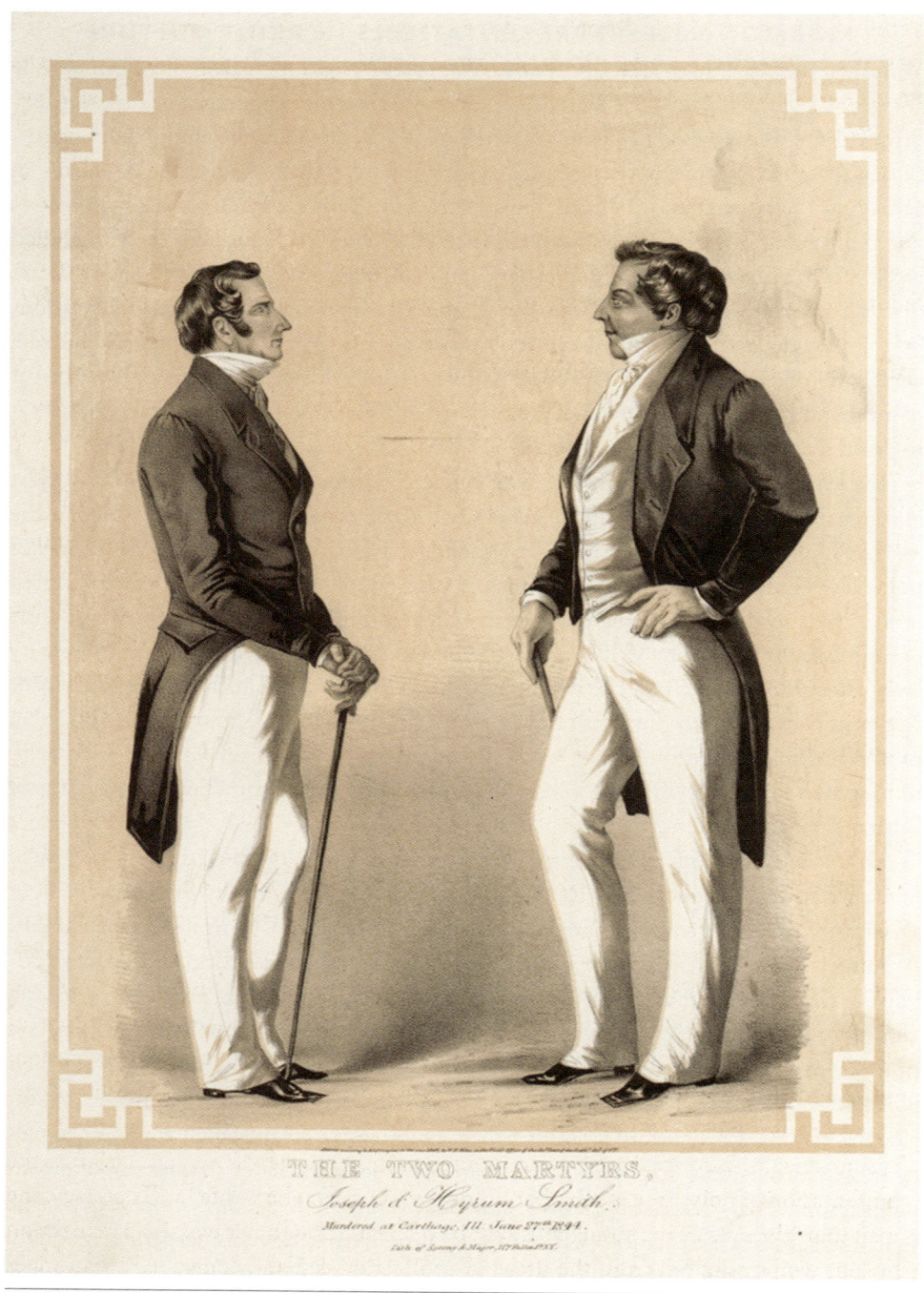

Fig. 5.3 Sarony and Major, *The Two Martyrs*, 1847, lithograph. Courtesy Library of Congress.

in the wilderness."[14] While the main body of Latter-day Saints were navigating the flight from Nauvoo, suffering calamitous deprivation in Winter Quarters, Miles leveraged his access to commercial lithographers in New York to create an image that argued for Mormon refinement and respectability, based on the work of a Latter-day Saint artist.

REPRESENTING MORMON WOMEN

Some nineteenth-century representations challenge a simplistic "us versus them" binary between external and self-representations. Even within the Utah Territory, Latter-day Saints were not a monolithic bloc—and Mormon visual culture represented the wide spectrum of cultural, ethnic, class, linguistic, and other distinctions that characterized individuals and communities within Mormonism. Gender was the subject of especially intense visual scrutiny, as Mormon women rebutted degrading representations from without while asserting their own empowerment within Mormonism. Augusta Joyce Crocheron, a poet, artist, and church leader who served as secretary of the Young Ladies' Mutual Improvement Association for the Salt Lake Stake, designed and published a lithograph in 1883 titled *Representative Women of Deseret* that simultaneously refuted anti-polygamist slanders while advancing the cause of women within Mormon society. Crocheron engaged the Graphic Company of New York to reproduce her drawing celebrating twenty female Mormon leaders as a large-scale, two-color lithograph. To achieve the highest-quality representations (and presumably avoid engraving expenses), Crocheron left blank ovals in the lithograph and then pasted in actual albumen silver photographic portraits.[15] Crocheron chose to include leaders of the Relief Society, Young Ladies' Mutual Improvement Association, and Primary Association, as well as other influential women in professions and the arts.[16] The lithograph was accompanied by a small book with biographical sketches of each of its subjects.

Representative Women of Deseret follows earlier Mormon self-representations in emphasizing the gentility and refinement of its subjects. Along with the photographs of well-dressed, seriously comported, sophisticated women, Crocheron included emblems representing their achievements, ranging from books bearing the titles of well-known works to musical instruments, a painting palette, and a hospital bed. As Jennifer Reeder has argued, the lithograph boldly rebutted the representation of Mormon women that proliferated in the popular press as "ignorant, uneducated, and uncivilized."[17] In the accompanying book, Crocheron frankly acknowledged the women's participation in plural marriages, ensuring that viewers would see these women as evidence against the representation of polygamy as a barbarous degradation. As she wrote in the preface, she hoped that "the eyes of the stranger" might be opened through her work to a realization that "our women are not from the dregs of civilization, led and controlled by stronger minds without a knowledge within themselves for their course."[18] In Crocheron's design, the multiplicity of portraits in a crowded visual field argues for the abundant work being done by polygamous Mormon women—while the lithograph's grand scale and high-end printing help reinforce the sense of their power and sophistication. The

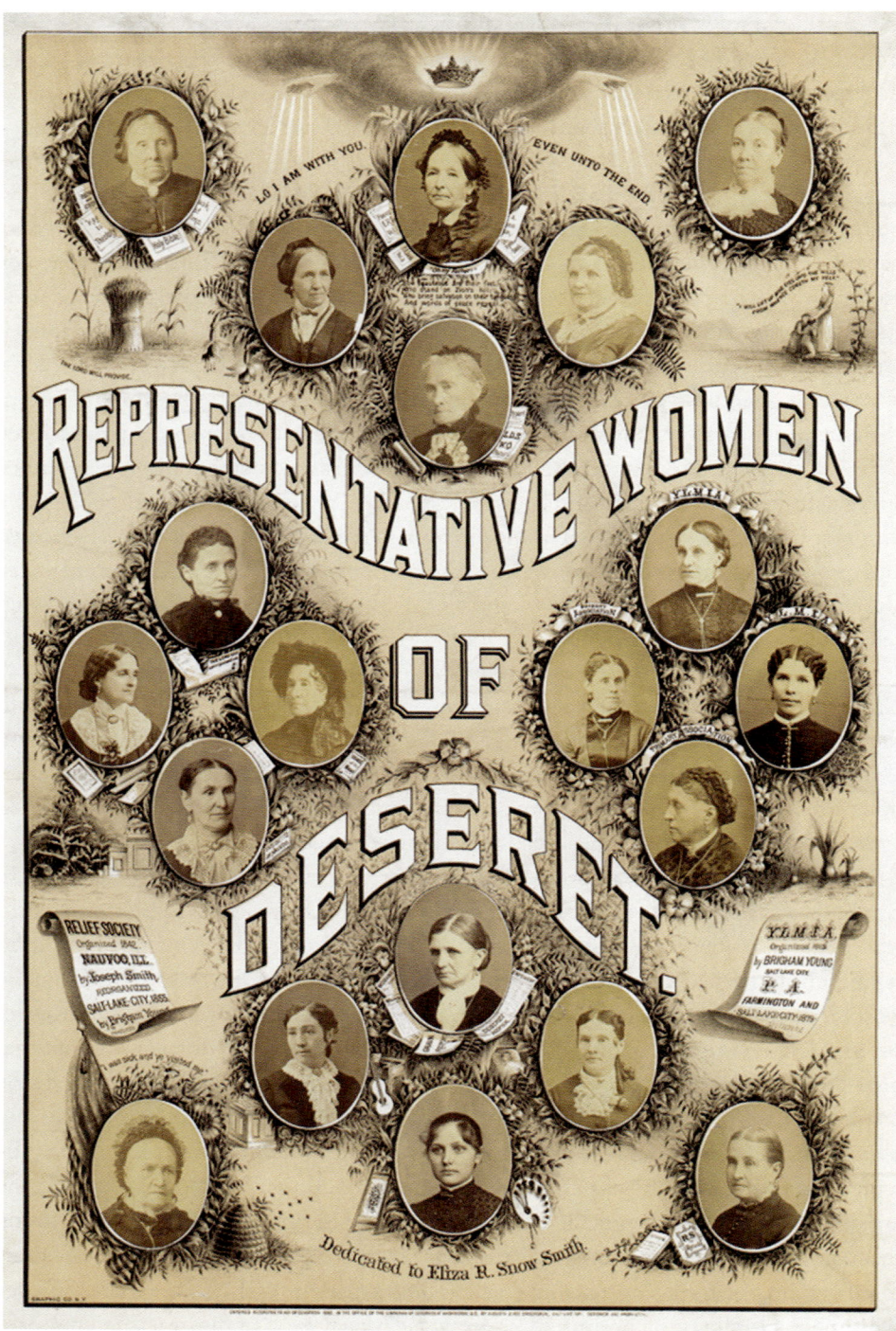

Fig. 5.4 Augusta Joyce Crocheron, *Representative Women of Deseret*, 1883, lithograph with applied photograph. Courtesy National Portrait Gallery.

complete reversal of Charles Kendrick's nearly contemporaneous illustration in *Chic*, Crocheron's lithograph uses a mass of polygamous wives to amplify rather than diminish Mormon women's social power.

Crocheron's work also argued for the power of women *within* Mormonism. While her preface addresses the image to an imagined non-Mormon viewer, the lithograph was finished and sold from Salt Lake City rather than New York, and there is little evidence of its circulation outside the Utah Territory.[19] The artwork's message served an equally important rhetorical aim among Mormon audiences, showcasing what women had achieved within a highly patriarchal society whose institutional leadership had been visually represented primarily through images of men. *Representative Women of Deseret* argues for the hard-fought autonomy and self-determination of the Church of Jesus Christ of Latter-day Saints' women's organizations by reminding Mormon viewers of their female leaders' eminent qualifications and monumental accomplishments. Even the artwork itself furthers this argument; unlike other art projects that Crocheron completed with the help of male art professionals, this project was entirely her own, a fact noted in several contemporary publications.[20] *Representative Women of Deseret* was both a representation and a physical manifestation of female accomplishment in the contemporary Mormon world.

REPRESENTING MORMONISM FOR CHILDREN

Crocheron appealed to another specific sub-audience in framing her work. Along with the non-Mormons whose eyes she hoped it would open, she addressed the lithograph to "the young of our people," hoping that "this work shall cause them to appreciate their honored parents more by the nobility they have proven."[21] Numerous late nineteenth-century Mormon leaders were concerned that the church's youth who had not experienced the faith-hardening trials of the early church would lack the resolve to stay committed to Mormonism. As they worked to appeal to their youth, Latter-day Saints recognized the powerful impact that images could have. Perhaps the most important proponent of visual culture for Mormon youth was George Q. Cannon, editor of the *Juvenile Instructor,* a quasi-official church publication for young people. Beginning with the journal's first issue in 1866, he worked diligently to find woodcuts and other printing plates with engraved images to include in the magazine. Relying on images produced outside a Mormon context, however, meant that uniquely Latter-day Saint themes— the core of the publication's content—had to go unillustrated or were accompanied by images that were only tangentially related to the text. Cannon worked to help Mormon artists develop skills in engraving, but with limited success.[22] Once halftone printing technology was introduced in the 1880s, allowing for the publication of photographic reproductions of artworks, children's books and periodicals produced by Latter-day Saint publishers became an increasingly important avenue for disseminating positive visual self-representations. Among the first major publications to commission Mormon artists for children's illustrations was George Reynolds's *Story of the Book of Mormon* (1888), which featured fourteen images by four Latter-day Saint artists.[23]

Reynolds worked with Cannon to bring original artwork into the *Juvenile Instructor* as well, organizing a competition in 1890 for artists to illustrate specific scenes from the Book of Mormon.[24] Spaced throughout its 1891 issues, the *Juvenile Instructor* published the winning entries as *Lessons from the Life of Nephi*, twelve paintings by C. C. A. Christensen and one by George M. Ottinger reproduced as halftones. These were later reworked by artists at the Forbes Lithograph Manufacturing Company in Boston and distributed by the Deseret Sunday School Union.[25] Christensen's *The Building of the Ship*, from the July 15, 1891, issue, depicts Nephi directing his family as they constructed the vessel that would carry them to the Americas in the Book of Mormon narrative.

Christensen's copious details, though somewhat obscured in the halftone, address numerous salient points in the scriptural account, from his brothers' disputatious reception of Nephi's plan in the foreground to the figures in the background hewing planks and smelting ore to make tools following Nephi's revealed instructions. But beyond illustrating the Book of Mormon, these images asserted the legitimacy of Mormonism as a form of Christianity. Christensen's and Ottinger's Book of Mormon images not only drew on the language of contemporaneous children's Bible illustration but also were featured in the *Juvenile Instructor* along with biblical engravings by non-Mormon artists, and they were distributed as lithographs alongside "Bible picture charts" produced by Protestant organizations.[26] These artworks adapted recognizable forms of broader Christian visual culture to assert the Book of Mormon as a work of scripture on par with the Bible, while encouraging young Mormons to see their church as a sophisticated organization capable of competing visually with the nation's prominent Protestant denominations. In subsequent decades, Mormon artists would create numerous illustrations for youthful audiences that reinforced this perspective, especially in church-sponsored publications including the *Children's Friend*, the *Young Woman's Journal*, and the *Juvenile Instructor*'s successor, the *Instructor*. The artworks with the broadest impact to emerge from this context are likely the series of Book of Mormon paintings commissioned from Arnold Friberg for the *Children's Friend*, which were published in church-authorized printings of the Book of Mormon beginning in 1963.[27] Mormon youth have always been just as important as an audience for Mormon self-representations as any other group inside or outside the church. Latter-day Saints have continually striven to secure the loyalty of emerging generations through images that not only teach Latter-day Saint principles but also fashion Mormonism as a legitimate, respectable religion deserving their continued support.

MONUMENTAL REPRESENTATIONS OF MORMONISM

While print media was an important vehicle for shaping the Mormon image, the public also learned about the Latter-day Saints from artworks on the opposite end of the size spectrum—monumental public representations. Although these two realms of visual

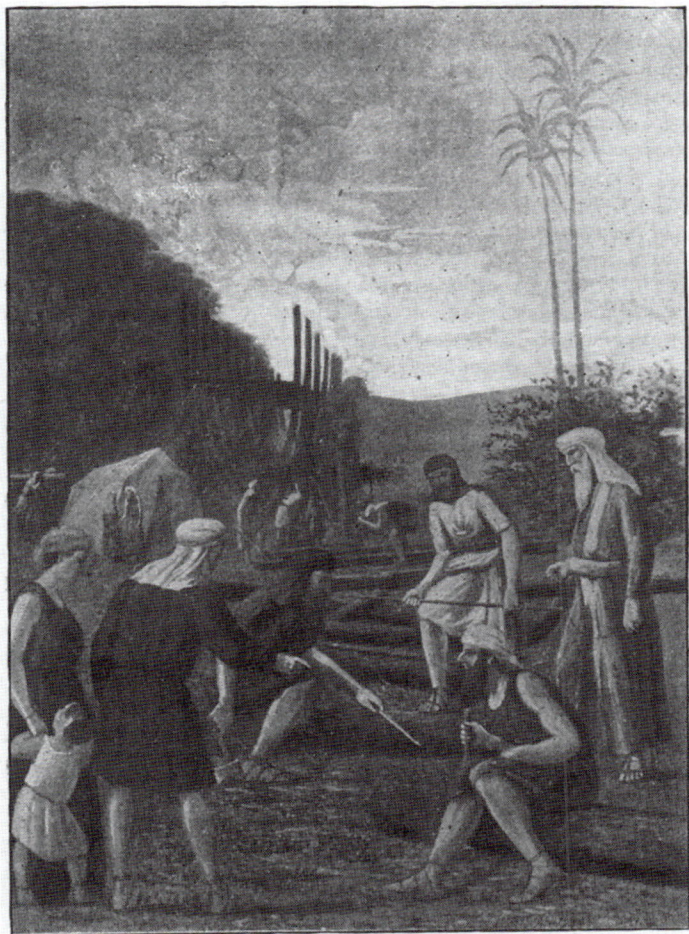

THE BUILDING OF THE SHIP.

Fig. 5.5 C. C. A. Christensen, *Lessons from the Life of Nephi: The Building of the Ship,* 1891, halftone reproduction of painting.

culture might seem radically different, both were effective means of broad dissemination, whether through the mass distribution of printed imagery or the inescapable public presence of monuments. Exhibitions at world's fairs and other ephemeral large-scale works leveraged the communicative capacities of both modalities, operating as mass-media spectacle for the sizeable audiences that encountered their temporally limited displays, while bringing a sense of lasting gravity through their monumental scale and their representation of the LDS Church as an entrenched, historical, and permanent institution.

The Church of Jesus Christ of Latter-day Saints began investing in large-scale monuments near the end of the nineteenth century, partly in response to the increasing interest in major public art projects in the Salt Lake Valley as its population swelled, but also in order to control the visual narrative in a tumultuous time when the church's relationship with the nation as a whole was rapidly transforming. As Kathleen Flake has argued, the church's burgeoning interest during this era in preserving historical sites and memorializing its own history was about forgetting as much as remembering—refocusing the historical narrative away from the struggle over polygamy in order to "forget a past they could not carry with them into the future."[28] Forced to abandon polygamy, communitarian economics, and overt political control, the LDS Church pursued a reconciliatory and assimilationist course, seeking the benefits of better relations with political and religious institutions that had formerly been foes.[29] Artists played a major role in fostering the church's effort to reframe Mormonism as a reputable American religion. Even before Wilford Woodruff's 1890 "Manifesto" initiating the LDS Church's withdrawal from polygamy, Utahns came together across religious lines to create works of art that promoted their mutual interests—especially in achieving national enfranchisement through statehood.

Beyond merely depicting the strengthening relationships between Latter-day Saints and others, some works helped build these relationships through collaborative art endeavors. In 1888, the Salt Lake City Chamber of Commerce sponsored an Exposition Car, a railcar provided by the Union Pacific Railroad, filled with Utah agricultural, mineral, and industrial products, and decorated with paintings of Utah landscapes and produce by local artists.[30] While the car was sponsored by a religiously unaffiliated organization, it had broad support from both Mormon and non-Mormon Utahns.[31] Latter-day Saints saw it as an opportunity to promote Mormon sophistication and success, while non-Mormons were eager to showcase Utah's industrial and agricultural potential—and its waning theocratic character—in order to amplify investment in the territory.

Artist Henry L. A. Culmer was the project's art director. He enlisted Alfred Lambourne, John Tullidge, and Dan Weggeland (three of Utah's best-known painters at the time) in fitting the car's exterior with rugged mountain landscapes, pastoral scenes, and still lifes of more than a dozen varieties of fruits and vegetables raised in the territory.[32] Both Mormon and non-Mormon supporters hoped that the Exposition Car's celebration of Utah's wild landscapes would promote tourism, and that by showcasing Utah's agricultural and mineral products, it would spur outside investment in the territory. The Exposition Car's backers claimed enormous success in changing public attitudes in eastern cities, but the project was also an important step in solidifying interreligious ties within the territory. Fred Simon, a Jewish businessman who would become president of the Salt Lake City Chamber of Commerce in 1890, applauded the Exposition Car as evidence that "while religious and political differences exist, they are being obviated as quickly as circumstances could possibly permit."[33] Reframing the

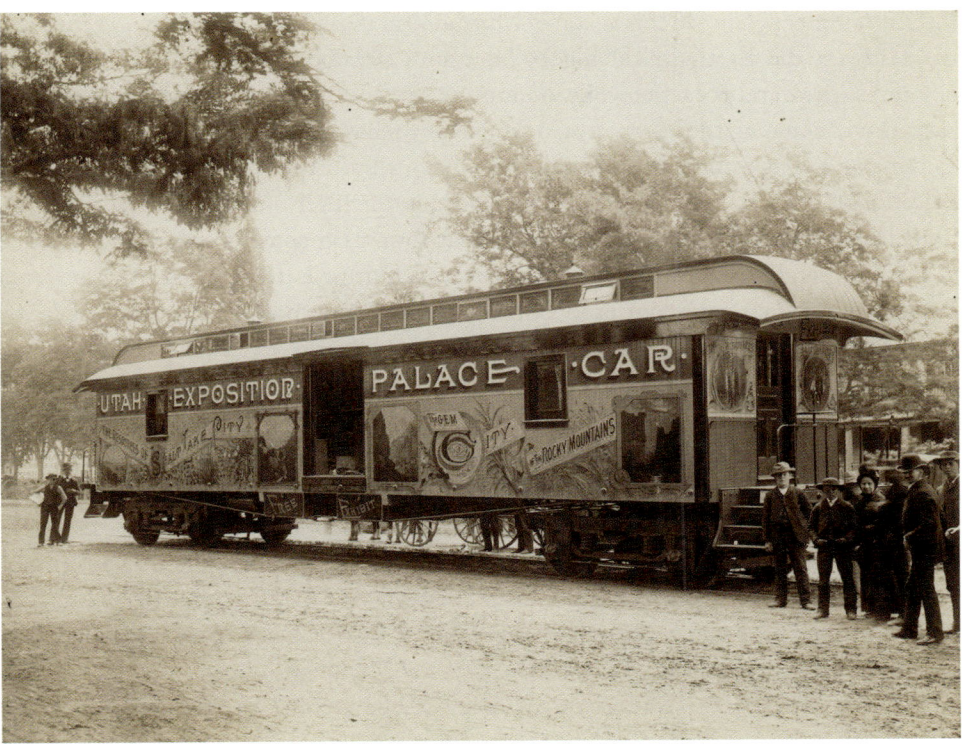

Fig. 5.6 Newcombe Photography Studio, Utah Exposition palace car, 1888, photograph, 25 cm × 30 cm, Church History Library, The Church of Jesus Christ of Latter-day Saints.

public image of Utah by representing scenes of agricultural bounty and natural beauty instead of the images of Mormon landmarks and caricatures of Latter-day Saints that prevailed in contemporaneous American visual culture helped to obviate these differences. Indeed, Weggeland's fruits and produce give no hint of the mostly Mormon farming communities that produced them, while the landscapes by Culmer, Tullidge, and Lambourne are devoid of human subjects and shown completely excised from the Mormon settlements surrounding them. The Exposition Car defied viewers' expectations, separating the image of Utah from the image of Mormonism in order to represent the soon-to-be state as a potential site of investment not defined by its association with the Church of Jesus Christ of Latter-day Saints.

Latter-day Saints in Utah were willing to embrace this apparent erasure because they understood the potential for positive self-representation that this new image of Utah could bring, even without representing Mormonism directly. For Latter-day Saints, the combination of wilderness and pastoral landscapes took on additional valences, as they claimed that their agricultural success in the semi-arid region was evidence of divine favor, proof of having fulfilled Isaiah's prophecy that the desert would "blossom as the rose."[34] Culmer promoted this vision of Mormonism as he traveled with the car through the Midwest and East, introducing, by his count, 190,000 visitors to Utah's commercial and agricultural potential while attempting to clear the "dense ignorance [that] has prevailed concerning the Mormons," downplaying polygamy and instead characterizing Latter-day Saints as industrious, enlightened contributors to the national economy.[35] Additionally, the car's promoters emphasized that the high-quality artworks were entirely the work of Utah artists. All of the territory's constituencies sought recognition of the level of refinement that Utahns had achieved, but for Latter-day Saints, the status brought by the patronage and production of fine art was a powerful argument against the caricature of degraded, ignorant Mormons still pervasive in the national press, just as the crisis over polygamy was reaching its apex.

THE BRIGHAM YOUNG MONUMENT AND THE WORLD'S COLUMBIAN EXPOSITION

The Exposition Car's promoters hoped that it would help steer Utah toward statehood. That process took more than a public relations effort, however, and became a possibility only once church president Wilford Woodruff issued the 1890 "Manifesto" announcing that the Church of Jesus Christ of Latter-day Saints would begin complying with federal anti-polygamy statutes.[36] Following the "Manifesto," Latter-day Saints and non-Mormons collaborated on another major public artwork as they worked toward statehood: Cyrus Dallin's monumental statue of Brigham Young exhibited at the World's Columbian Exposition in Chicago in 1893, then brought to Salt Lake City and eventually expanded as the Brigham Young Monument, completed in 1900.

While the Salt Lake City Chamber of Commerce sponsored the Utah Exposition Car, the Church of Jesus Christ of Latter-day Saints took the leading role in creating the Brigham Young Monument. Dallin was raised in Utah but left for Boston at the age of nineteen and was never a Latter-day Saint.[37] Church leaders recognized that despite his religious difference, Dallin's success in the East Coast art world and his association with Utah would help promote their narrative of the territory as fostering a cosmopolitan, refined populace. Although the church's endorsement and fundraising efforts were critical to the project's success, leaders worked to gather broad civic support from non-Mormon constituents. While organizers had little trouble convincing Mormon Utahns of their subject's worthiness, they enjoined readers in a letter published in several regional newspapers (including the adamantly non-Mormon *Salt Lake Tribune*) that "it is not necessary to dwell upon the character of Brigham Young. . . . Whether we think of him as a religious leader, or a statesman, or a pioneer, or a city builder—in whatsoever capacity he is regarded, he is the same grand personality."[38]

Church leaders' decision to build the monument may have been spurred by the first major post-"Manifesto" opportunity to showcase their faith publicly: the World's Columbian Exposition in Chicago in 1893. The church was largely sidelined at the World's Parliament of Religions, but Latter-day Saints employed the Utah Territory

Building to promote positive self-representations.[39] Much as they had for the Utah Exposition Car, the territory's Mormon and non-Mormon constituencies recognized their mutual interest in collaborating to frame Utah as a place that, though built on pioneering efforts, had matured into a modern, cosmopolitan society. Exhibits in the Utah Building demonstrated the territory's agricultural, industrial, and mineral wealth, while promoting the intellectual and cultural achievements of its citizens.[40] George M. Ottinger headed the territory's Fine Arts Department for the exposition, assembling a selection of exceptional work by the territory's best artists that, at least from a Utah fair-goer's perspective, equaled any work in the exposition and gave Utah "every reason to be proud."[41]

As a monumental, elite work of fine art, Dallin's statue of Brigham Young asserted the cultural refinement the territory had achieved. Noting that he modeled his design after the Gambetta Monument, unveiled in Paris just five years earlier, Dallin gave Utah an artwork attuned to the latest currents in contemporary transatlantic cultural centers, dramatically countering the stereotype of the territory as an uncultured wilderness out-post.[42] In a similar vein, the Mormon Tabernacle Choir found a surprisingly warm reception at the exposition, and the choir's impressive showing in a rarefied cultural arena similarly countered stereotypes of Mormon degeneracy.[43] While fair organizers objected to the direct representation of Mormon belief that church leaders had hoped to present at the World's Parliament of Religions, expressions of Mormon achievement in the fine arts elicited comparatively moderate criticism, even arousing occasional public appreciation—a rare experience for Latter-day Saints at the time.

Long after the Columbian Exposition, Dallin's sculpture continued projecting an image of Mormonism not just as Utah's founding religion but also as a faith integral to the American republic. Once the fair closed, the statue was transported to Salt Lake City, where it was placed on a plinth near the tabernacle until funds could be raised to complete the entire monument. Although the bronze figures and bas-relief on the granite shaft were not completed until 1900, church leaders staged an initial unveiling of the still-incomplete monument to launch the 1897 Pioneer Day celebrations commemorating the fiftieth anniversary of Mormon settlement.[44] Latter-day Saints leveraged the jubilee as an opportunity to move past the acrimonious conflict over po-lygamy. At the monument's unveiling, which the press claimed was attended by twenty thousand spectators, church leaders focused instead on the Latter-day Saints' accom-plishment in building a flourishing settlement that had finally reached the goal of state-hood just a year prior. In his invocation, church president Wilford Woodruff expressed gratitude for Young's role in leading his people "out of bondage to liberty," but he also rejoiced that "those who once regarded us as enemies" were now friends, and that "the bitternesses of the past are gone."[45]

Just as the monument's staging sought to reframe Mormons as good neighbors, the artwork itself worked to redefine Latter-day Saints as pioneers integral to building America, rather than radicals who had existed outside the nation's republican

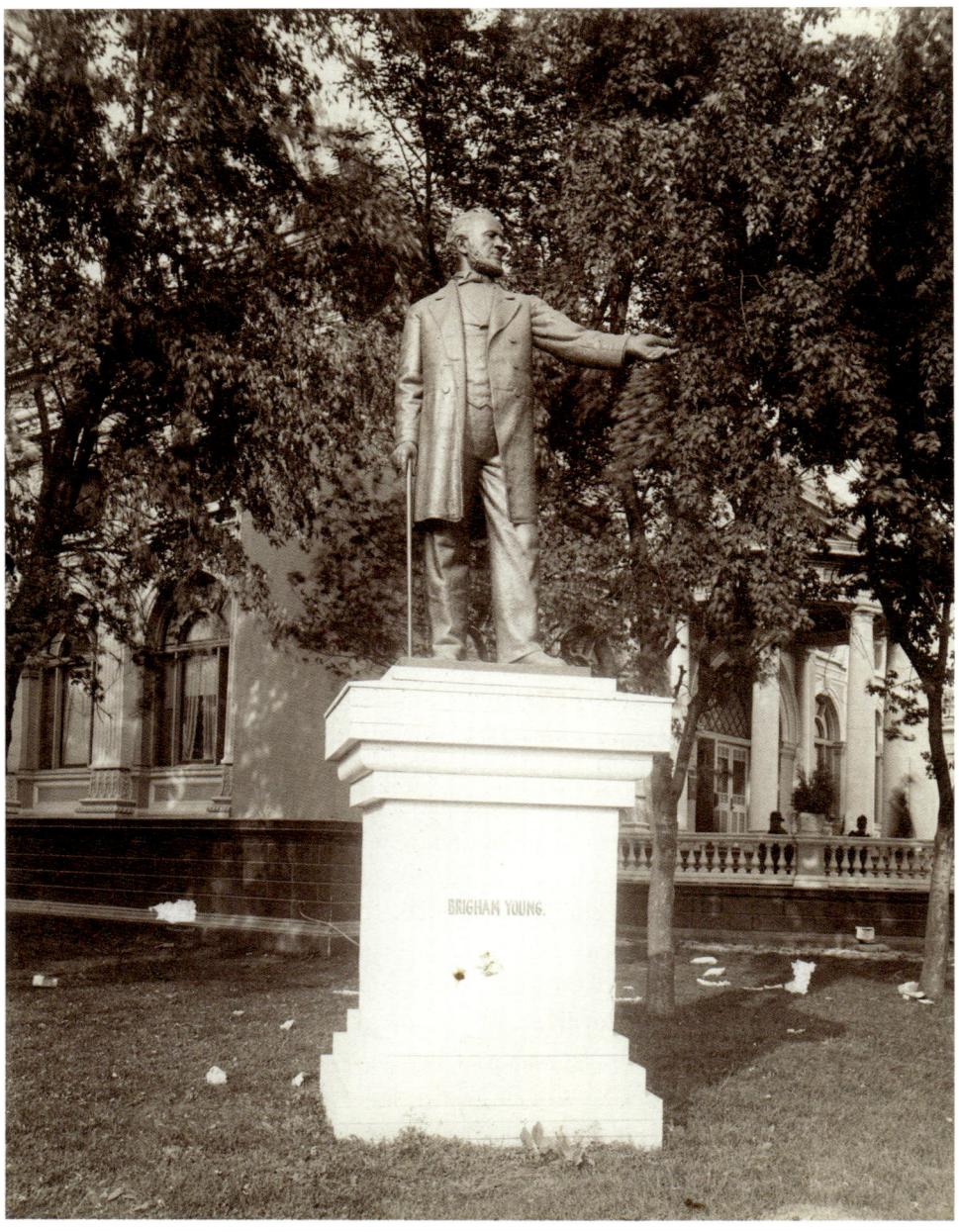

Fig. 5.7 Unknown, Brigham Young statue at the Chicago World's Fair, 1893, photograph, 30 cm × 20 cm, Church History Library, The Church of Jesus Christ of Latter-day Saints.

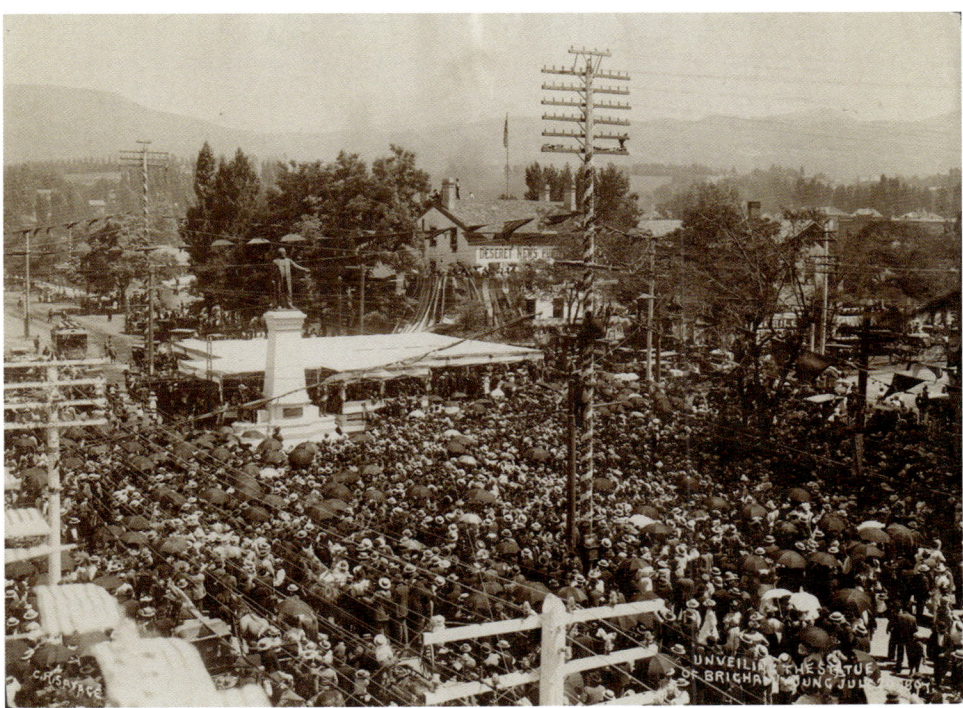

Fig. 5.8 Charles R. Savage, *Unveiling the Statue of Brigham Young*, 1897, photograph, Church History Library, The Church of Jesus Christ of Latter-day Saints.

framework. The monument works through a clear visual hierarchy to assert the civilizing role of Mormon pioneers under the leadership of Brigham Young. On the base's lowest level are two life-size bronzes; to Young's left is a Native American man, representing the region prior to settlement. On the opposite side is a "trapper," representing early incursions by white Americans. Both are sitting obeisantly, looking outward and away from the viewer's anticipated sightline, surrendering their claim on the region in deference to the figures placed on the monument's next vertical register—the Mormon pioneers that the monument asserts as having "civilized" the region. Unlike the figures seated on his side, the pioneer man stands erect in an active stance, gazing directly out over the viewer.

As Cynthia Culver Prescott has argued, the bas-relief "emphasizes the centrality of the patriarchal family to turn-of-the-century Mormon culture," minimizing the contributions of female settlers.[46] The pioneer family also reads as a *monogamous* family, a point that might seem unremarkable in nearly any other nineteenth-century American monument but which bears consideration in a work celebrating the most famous polygamist in the nation's history. Dallin made Young a palatable subject for a civic monument by redefining his legacy, promoting him as a visionary colonizer rather than a radical who upended domestic and social norms—the revised perspective that has continued to inform the image of Brigham Young throughout the twentieth century and up to the present. More broadly, the Brigham Young Monument worked to position Mormons within the discourse of American pioneering, arguing that Latter-day Saints had played a vital role in national expansion by settling the Intermountain West.

Latter-day Saints of the era capitalized on the concept of the "pioneer" as a rehabilitated vision of the Mormon past. Pioneer mythology asked turn-of-the-century Americans to forget the earlier image of Mormons as radical outliers whose polygamous theocracy seemed a dangerous affront to the nation's republican values, claiming instead that Latter-day Saints had worked alongside other settlers to civilize the West and bring it into the American republic.[47] Recasting Mormons as pioneers helped Latter-day Saints in their project of building better relations with non-Mormons in Utah and in the nation as a whole, beginning the dramatic shift in perspective as the national press went from casting Mormons as fundamentally unamerican in the mid-nineteenth century, to characterizing them as *quintessential* Americans by the second half of the twentieth.[48] The LDS Church's interest in encouraging this new outlook was already on display at both the monument's 1897 and 1900 dedications; each time, the banners concealing the statuary prior to its unveiling consisted of American flags, and on both occasions "America" ("My Country 'Tis of Thee") was performed following the unveiling.[49]

In the twentieth century, this perspective was reinforced by a series of monuments to Mormon pioneers erected with the church's support, beginning with Mahonri Young's Seagull Monument on Temple Square, completed in 1913, and continuing through his massive This Is the Place Monument overlooking Salt Lake City, dedicated for the centennial of the Latter-day Saints' arrival in 1847.[50] As the twentieth century progressed, the Church of Jesus Christ of Latter-day Saints sponsored, promoted, or encouraged a wide range of representations that framed Mormon settlers as heroic American pioneers, ranging from public memorials (like the Mormon Pioneer Cemetery in Omaha, Nebraska), to mass media imagery (like the mostly positive portrayal of the title character in Darryl F. Zanuck's 1940 film *Brigham Young*).[51]

MANAGING THE MORMON IMAGE IN EARLY TWENTIETH-CENTURY WORLD'S FAIRS

In subsequent decades, the Church of Jesus Christ of Latter-day Saints continued to invest in self-representations at world's fairs. Initially, church leaders employed lessons from their experience at the Chicago exposition as they crafted self-representations for twentieth-century world's fairs, choosing to focus on Mormonism's contribution to Western settlement while downplaying controversial issues in Mormon history and potentially divisive religious beliefs. Yet over the course of the twentieth century, as public perceptions of Mormonism steadily warmed, Latter-day Saints began introducing Mormon theology more directly in public representations.

Apostle Orson F. Whitney followed the earlier, pioneering-focused approach as he developed an exhibition for the 1909 Alaska-Yukon-Pacific Exposition in Seattle. Unlike previous fairs, where the church had participated through the state of Utah's exhibits, the Smithsonian Institution invited the Church of Jesus Christ of Latter-day Saints (among other religious organizations) to create its own exhibition documenting its impact on the West.[52] Whitney's display featured artifacts representing Mormon contributions to settlement, including a pioneer odometer, the first printing press used by the *Deseret News,* and early Utah coins.[53] The centerpieces of the exhibition were scale models of the Salt Lake temple by sculptor J. Jepperson and the Salt Lake tabernacle by architect and builder Abraham Reister Wright Jr., who had helped construct the original building. The model tabernacle featured a miniature version of the famous organ by woodcarver S. Masuda.[54] The exhibit framed Latter-day Saints as enterprising colonists worthy of recognition for their collective industrial and cultural advancement, while avoiding controversial aspects of Mormon belief. The two model buildings supported this reading; the tabernacle featured a detailed cutaway view of the interior, inviting visitors to marvel at the brilliant engineering of its pioneer builders. The temple, whose carefully guarded interior spaces manifest distinctive Mormon beliefs, had no such cutaway view. Although viewers could not see inside, its windows were illuminated from within, quietly arguing for Mormonism as enlightening the world without confronting viewers with details of the church's controversial theology.

The church's next major exhibit was at the 1933 A Century of Progress International Exposition in Chicago. Three members of the Fairbanks family created a multimedia art exhibit with mural paintings by John B. Fairbanks, stained glass by his oldest son, J. Leo, and sculptural works by his youngest son, Avard. Many elements of the exhibit represented Latter-day Saint theology more directly than the church's earlier world's fair exhibits. The stained glass panels by J. Leo Fairbanks represented Joseph Smith's First Vision and Elijah the prophet holding the keys of temple work and standing in front of the Salt Lake temple. The centerpiece of the exhibition was Avard Fairbanks's sculptural frieze representing the theme "Eternal Progress," a pointed expansion of the fair's theme.[55] A pamphlet published by the Northern States Mission expounded its symbolism in detail, explaining that the figure in the center represented the Mormon conception of eternal progress. The figure, depicted as a generic human spirit to suggest the universality of the message, is surrounded by "rays which represent radiating energy that is constant in time and space," the artist's attempt to capture the Latter-day Saint theology of the "subtle and refined substance" of a spirit body. Flanking the figure are representations of the earthly pathway to eternal progress through the work of "social groups" (on the left) and individual activity (on the right). Fairbanks conceived of the path toward divinity as encompassing the efforts of science, health, education, and priesthood organizations, as well as the pursuit of familial fulfillment and character development through learning and "creative recreation" in the arts. Underlying this narrative on the column supporting the central figure are images of the sun, moon, and stars,

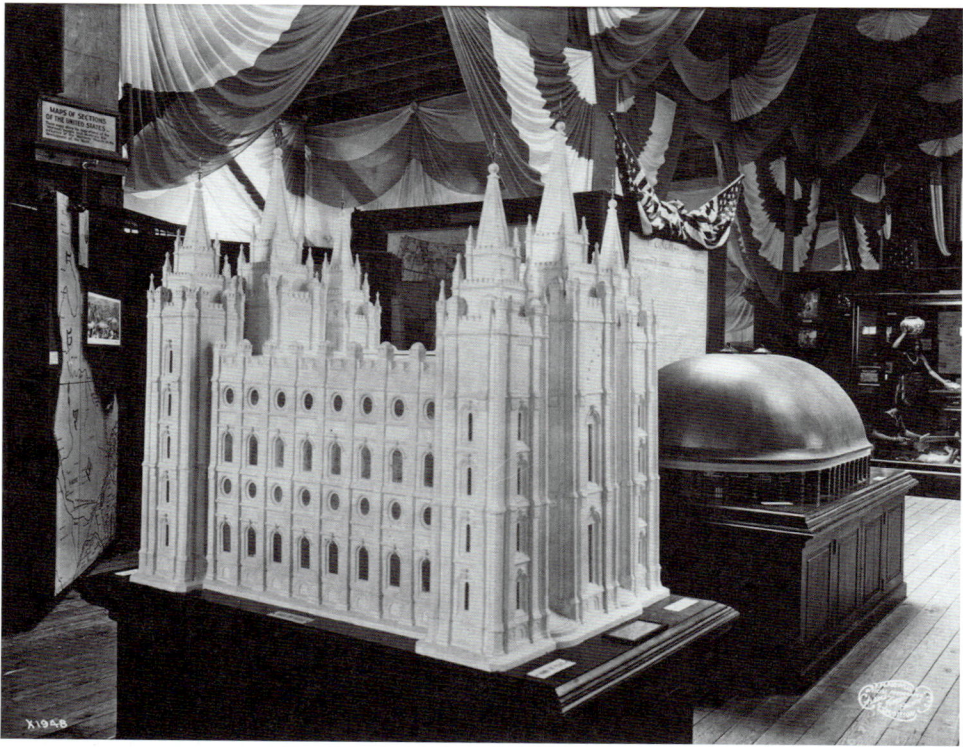

Fig. 5.9 Model of Salt Lake City's Mormon Temple, Alaska Yukon Pacific Exposition, 1909, photograph (unspecifed format), University of Washington Library Special Collections. The photographer is Frank H. Nowell.

representing the "'Degrees of Glory' to which we may obtain," the ultimate goals of eternal progress.[56]

Casual viewers could quickly glean a sense of the Latter-day Saints' theology of eternal progress, while those who were interested in learning more could read the printed pamphlet or speak with the missionaries who staffed the display. *The Improvement Era* touted the exhibit's proselytizing success, claiming that three to five thousand people visited the display on a daily basis, and that hundreds of thousands of pamphlets were distributed by the missionary guides.[57] By the 1930s, Latter-day Saint belief and social practice no longer provoked widespread animus in the United States. The self-consciously modern style Fairbanks employed for the *Eternal Progress* frieze reinforced the perception of Mormonism as having emerged from its contentious past as a modern religion with contemporary relevance. Although traditional compared with advanced modernism of the era, its bold, simplified geometrical forms nodded to the Art Deco style prevalent at the exposition, a stylistically adventurous move for a typically conservative artist. Fairbanks worked to ensure that viewers interpreted Mormonism as a vital force in the present rather than a relic of the past.

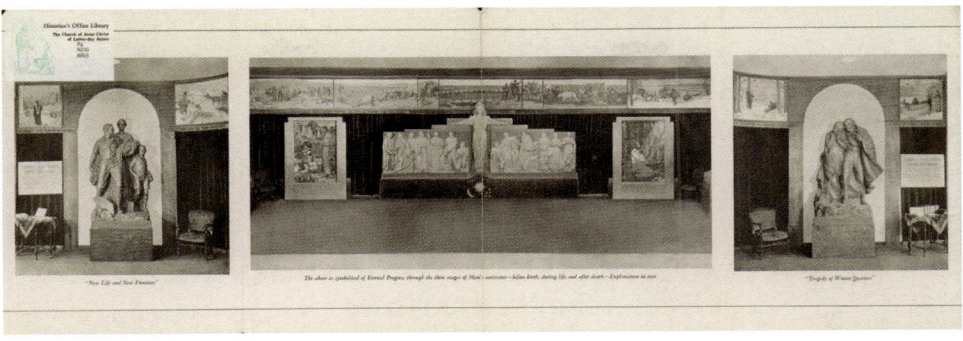

Fig. 5.10 Mormon exhibit, *Century of Progress*, Chicago, 1934, halftone, Church History Library, The Church of Jesus Christ of Latter-day Saints.

Yet church leaders still understood that the image of Mormonism that other Americans were most likely to embrace was the "pioneer" mythology that they had developed in earlier public representations. The *Eternal Progress* frieze was surrounded by images of early Mormon history narrating the Latter-day Saints' flight to the Great Basin. The two images of contemporary Latter-day Saints (John B. Fairbanks's painting of the modern Salt Lake Valley and Avard Fairbanks's sculpture *New Life and New Frontiers*) positioned modern Mormonism as the culmination of the pioneer experience, asserting Latter-day Saints' contemporary success as the endpoint of the pioneers' struggle. As Apostle David O. McKay observed, it was not the missionaries or the artworks that first lured would-be visitors into the exhibit—it was the model Wright and Masuda created of the Salt Lake tabernacle for the 1909 exposition in Seattle (borrowed back from the Smithsonian) that "seemed to be the magnet that first attracted the crowds." As McKay described, the history of the famous pioneer-era building focused visitors' attention so that "missionaries found willing listeners to the story of the Pioneers and to the explanation of principles and ideals of the church as depicted in the artistic paintings and bas-reliefs on the walls of the booth."[58] The image of pioneering Mormons still worked as the most compelling public face of Mormonism. This approach was so successful, in fact, that the church sponsored a nearly identical exhibition as a stand-alone pavilion at the California Pacific International Exposition in 1935, reusing most of the artworks from the Century of Progress International Exhibition as well as the models of the tabernacle and temple.[59] At the 1939 Golden Gate International Exhibition, the church not only displayed the model tabernacle by Wright and Masuda but also engaged the architectural firm of Fetzer and Fetzer to create a larger "miniature Tabernacle," complete with a working organ, that could seat up to fifty visitors.[60] The church's display for the Texas Centennial Exposition in 1936 strove for a similar balance in emphasis between Mormonism's pioneering past, its doctrinal uniqueness, and its place in the modern world, but with an even stronger emphasis on the power of fine art to communicate this message. Paintings, photographs, and projected images addressed each of these perspectives, including, for example, a photograph of the "first log cabin in Utah," original paintings by Minerva Teichert depicting the "miracle of the gulls" and the arrival of handcart pioneers, a slide projection of Lewis A. Ramsey's painting of Joseph Smith receiving the gold plates from the angel Moroni, and contemporary images of Temple Square.[61]

A CONTESTED LEGACY OF MONUMENTAL REPRESENTATIONS

By the time the Church of Jesus Christ of Latter-day Saints next mounted a significant exhibition for a world's fair, in New York in 1964–1965, the church had made great strides in shaping the public perception of Mormonism as a non-threatening religion espousing "traditional" American values.[62] Concurrently, the LDS Church sponsored or supported monuments that reinforced the conception of Mormon pioneers as quintessential American settlers rather than radical outliers. Mid-twentieth-century monuments honoring Brigham Young, including Mahonri Young's This Is the Place Monument in Salt Lake City and Brigham Young statue for the United States Capitol, followed Dallin in marshaling the rhetoric of the heroic "pioneer," eliding any reference to Brigham Young's controversial promotion of polygamy and conflict with federal authority.[63] As other chapters in this volume addressing later twentieth- and twenty-first-century artworks demonstrate, Latter-day Saints continued to produce monumental representations to steer the public image of Mormonism. And, as those authors demonstrate, these representations were not merely illustrative but convey a diversity of theological and social perspectives. Studying representations of Mormonism created during the church's first century—both by adherents and by antagonists—is a useful reminder that artists never simply recorded the events and figures that shaped their history but argued for their own interpretations of that history using sophisticated visual rhetoric.

The public discourse surrounding Mormonism has shifted so dramatically that nineteenth-century anti-Mormon imagery has lost most of its bite; contemporary Latter-day Saints seem increasingly inclined to find humor rather than offense in its vilifying exaggerations. Images produced to celebrate Latter-day Saints from this period, however, have largely gone unquestioned, even when those images reproduce aspects of nineteenth-century culture that perpetuate outdated or harmful ideas, including some that the LDS Church has abandoned. The Brigham Young Monument, for example, engages stereotypes of Native American subservience and female servility, reflecting racist and patriarchal nineteenth-century viewpoints in excluding women and non-whites from its vision of the region's rightful ownership.[64] Furthermore, the monument's plaque listing the names of each of the members of the first Mormon company to reach Salt Lake City is segregated by race; three enslaved men brought to the valley are listed separately as "colored servants." In the 1970s, the Salt Lake City Council debated changing the wording on the plaque, although they deferred to a descendant of one of the enslaved people who argued that the monument, as one of the few public acknowledgments of the existence of slavery in early Mormon Utah, played an important role in reminding viewers of that history despite its original racist intent.[65] The monument's perpetuation of inequitable representations of women and Native Americans awaits further consideration. As this one example suggests, communities housing monuments to Mormonism have only just begun to address their engagement with race, gender, colonialism, and other contentious issues.[66]

These emerging discussions of the legacy of Mormon history as represented in monuments highlight the power of images to promulgate ideologically charged representations. The world did not learn to see Mormonism through a simple binary of pro- and anti-Mormon imagery. Instead, the visual culture of Mormonism developed as a complicated network of intertwining and competing agendas, expressed by numerous agents with varied levels of investment in Mormonism as a religion and as a set of cultural practices. As a result, Mormonism's image has been multivalent, mutable, and contested from the beginning.

NOTES

[1] On the definition and methodologies of visual culture as a discipline, see Nicholas Mirzoeff, "What Is Visual Culture?," in *The Visual Culture Reader*, ed. Nicholas Mirzoeff (London: Routledge, 1998), 3–13.

[2] See Harold A. Innis, *The Bias of Communication* (Toronto: University of Toronto Press, 1964), 33–35.

[3] Spencer Fluhman has argued for the importance of studying anti-Mormonism in order to understand not just the church's historical reception but also its own history, as Latter-day Saint belief, practice, and self-representation each developed in dialogue with external criticism. See *A Peculiar People: Anti-Mormonism and the Making of Religion in Nineteenth-Century America* (Chapel Hill: University of North Carolina Press, 2012).

[4] Gary L. Bunker and Davis Bitton, "Illustrated Periodical Images of Mormons, 1850–1860," *Dialogue* 10, no. 3 (Spring 1977): 82–94; Gary L. Bunker and Davis Bitton, *The Mormon Graphic Image, 1834–1914: Cartoons, Caricatures, and Illustrations* (Salt Lake City: University of Utah Press, 1983).

[5] David J. Whittaker, "The Bone in the Throat: Orson Pratt and the Public Announcement of Plural Marriage," *Western Historical Quarterly* 18, no. 3 (1987): 293–314.

[6] Bunker and Bitton, *The Mormon Graphic Image*, 87; on Kendrick's work for *Chic*, see Patricia Marks, "'Sal' Bernhardt and the Men About Town: Theater Resources in 'Chic,'" *American Periodicals* 1, no. 1 (Fall 1991): 86–104.

[7] W. Paul Reeve, *Religion of a Different Color: Race and the Mormon Struggle for Whiteness* (New York: Oxford University Press, 2015), 179.

[8] James Francis Hogan, *The Australian in London and America* (London: Ward & Downey, 1889), 54.

[9] For a biography of Ann Eliza Young, see Kathryn Zabelle Derounian-Stodola, "Ann Eliza Webb Young (Denning)," *Legacy* 26, no. 1 (2009): 150–159.

[10] Fox was a moderately recognized wood engraver who contributed to *Harper's Weekly* and the *Daily Graphic*, among other publications. See *The Art Journal for 1876* (New York: D. Appleton, 1876), 2:31.

[11] Ann Eliza Young, *Wife No. 19* (Hartford, CT: Dustin, Gilman, 1876), 292.

[12] For a biography of Miles, see Hyrum L. Andrus, John Bluth, and Ray Bingham, "Register of the William Hart Miles Collection, 1841–1936," http://files.lib.byu.edu/ead/XML/MSS1459.xml, accessed June 25, 2021.

[13] Steven Bule, *From Calico Printer to Portrait Painter: Sutcliffe Maudsley, Nauvoo Profilist* (Orem, UT: A Better Place, 2002), 40–41.

[14] Richard Lyman Bushman, "Was Joseph Smith a Gentleman? The Standard for Refinement in Utah," in *Nearly Everything Imaginable: The Everyday Life of Utah's Mormon Pioneers*, ed. Doris R. Dant and Ronald W. Walker (Provo, UT: Brigham Young University Press, 1999), 29.

[15] "Women of Deseret," *Deseret News*, January 30, 1884, 9.

[16] Maureen Ursenbach Beecher, "The 'Leading Sisters': A Female Hierarchy in Nineteenth Century Mormon Society," *Journal of Mormon History* 9 (1982): 27.

[17] Jennifer Reeder, "Turning the Key: Understanding Mormon Women's Material Culture," in *Women and Mormonism: Historical and Contemporary Perspectives*, ed. Matthew Bowman and Kate Holbrook (Salt Lake City: University of Utah Press, 2016), 74.

[18] Augusta Joyce Crocheron, *Representative Women of Deseret: A Book of Biographical Sketches to Accompany the Picture Bearing the Same Title* (Salt Lake City: J. C. Graham, 1884), ii.

[19] The book seems to have reached a wider audience. Emeline B. Wells promoted it in an address at the World's Columbian Exposition in 1893, and several Mormon publications printed a favorable letter from a non-Mormon reader. See "Woman's Relief Society," *Woman's Exponent*, June 15, 1893, 178; A. C. Reeves, "A Methodist on the 'Marriage Relation,'" *Deseret News*, December 17, 1884, 14.

[20] For example, Crocheron's drawing *Joseph Smith Rebuking the Guards* was reworked and painted by Dan Weggeland prior to publication. See "Some of Our Poets," *The Juvenile Instructor* 38, no. 5 (March 1, 1903): 130. Newspaper articles noting her sole work on *Representative Women of Deseret* include "Editorial Notes," *Woman's Exponent*, September 15, 1883, 64; "Women of Deseret," 9.

[21] Crocheron, *Representative Women of Deseret*, ii.

[22] Nathan Rees, *Mormon Visual Culture and the American West* (New York: Routledge, 2021), 96–98.

[23] See Noel A. Carmack, "'A Picturesque and Dramatic History': George Reynolds's *Story of the Book of Mormon*," *BYU Studies* 47, no. 2 (2008): 115–141.

[24] George Q. Cannon, "To the Artists of Utah: Premiums for Which They May Compete," *The Juvenile Instructor* 25, no. 5 (March 1, 1890): 146.

[25] Richard L. Jensen and Richard G. Oman, *CCA Christensen, 1831-1912: Mormon Immigrant Artist: An Exhibition at the Museum of Church History and Art: Essay and Catalog* (Salt Lake City: Church of Jesus Christ of Latter-day Saints, 1984), 22.

[26] Cannon, "To the Artists of Utah," 146.

[27] Adele Cannon Howells, general president of the Primary, personally commissioned the artwork when the church declined to fund the project. See Vern Swanson, "The Book of Mormon Art of Arnold Friberg: Painter of Scripture," *Journal of Book of Mormon Studies* 10, no. 1 (2001): 29–31.

[28] Kathleen Flake, "Re-Placing Memory: Latter-Day Saint Use of Historical Monuments and Narrative in the Early Twentieth Century," *Religion and American Culture: A Journal of Interpretation* 13, no. 1 (2003): 80–81.

[29] Key works on this period include Gustive O. Larson, *The "Americanization" of Utah for Statehood* (San Marino, CA: Huntington Library, 1971); Thomas G. Alexander, *Mormonism in Transition: A History of the Latter-Day Saints, 1890–1930* (Urbana: University of Illinois Press, 1986); Armand L. Mauss, *The Angel and the Beehive: The Mormon Struggle with Assimilation* (Urbana: University of Illinois Press, 1994).

[30] Rees, *Mormon Visual Culture*, 76–79.

[31] David Walker, *Railroading Religion: Mormons, Tourists, and the Corporate Spirit of the West* (Chapel Hill: University of North Carolina Press, 2019), 215.

[32] "The Exposition Car," *Salt Lake Herald*, June 2, 1888, 8.

[33] Fred Simon, "The Exposition Car," *Salt Lake Herald-Republican*, August 21, 1888, 8.

[34] On the ubiquity of this phrasing in the Mormon settlement region, see Bernard DeVoto, *The Western Paradox: A Conservation Reader*, ed. Douglas Brinkley and Patricia Nelson Limerick (New Haven, CT: Yale University Press, 2000), 272.

[35] "The Car Returns," *Salt Lake Herald-Republican*, September 4, 1888, 5; W.H.H., "The Exposition Car," *Salt Lake Herald*, August 18, 1888, 5.

[36] Thomas G. Alexander, *Things in Heaven and Earth: The Life and Times of Wilford Woodruff, a Mormon Prophet* (Salt Lake City: Signature Books, 1991), 266–269.

37 Rell G. Francis, *Cyrus E. Dallin: Let Justice Be Done* (Springville, UT: Springville Museum of Art, 1976), 3–10.

38 James Sharp and Heber M. Wells, "The Brigham Young Memorial," *Salt Lake Tribune*, December 19, 1891, 5.

39 Konden Rich Smith, "Appropriating the Secular: Mormonism and the World's Columbian Exposition of 1893," *Journal of Mormon History* 34, no. 4 (2008): 168.

40 Reid Neilson, *Exhibiting Mormonism: The Latter-day Saints and the 1893 Chicago World's Fair* (New York: Oxford University Press, 2011), 63–74.

41 "Utah at the World's Fair," *Salt Lake Herald-Republican*, July 16, 1893, 10.

42 "The Young Statue," *Salt Lake Herald-Republican*, February 21, 1892, 5. The comparison to Jean-Paul Aubé and Louis-Charles Boileau's Gambetta Monument is clearer in the monument's final state, with seated figures on either side of the plinth.

43 Neilson, *Exhibiting Mormonism*, 131–140.

44 J. Michael Hunter, "The Monument to Brigham Young and the Pioneers: One Hundred Years of Controversy," *Utah Historical Quarterly* 68, no. 4 (Fall 2000): 337–339.

45 Woodruff was present but asked Orson F. Whitney to read the prayer, as he was "not feeling well enough to undergo the exertion." "The Opening Exercises in Honor of Pioneers," *Salt Lake Herald-Republican*, July 21, 1897, 2.

46 Cynthia Culver Prescott, *Pioneer Mother Monuments: Constructing Cultural Memory* (Norman: University of Oklahoma Press, 2019), 141–142.

47 Cristine Hutchinson-Jones, "Reviling and Revering the Mormons: Defining American Values, 1890–2008" (Ph.D. dissertation, Boston University, 2011), 102–115.

48 Jan Shipps traces this trajectory in American periodical publications in *Sojourner in the Promised Land: Forty Years Among the Mormons* (Urbana: University of Illinois Press, 2000), 51–97. On the contemporary significance of pioneer mythology in Mormonism, see Sara M. Patterson, *Pioneers in the Attic* (New York: Oxford University Press, 2020).

49 "The Opening Exercises in Honor of Pioneers," 2; "Ceremonies at Monument," *Salt Lake Tribune*, July 25, 1900, 5.

50 On the Seagull Monument, see Rees, *Mormon Visual Culture*, 133–142; on the This Is the Place Monument, see Sara M. Patterson, "The Plymouth Rock of the American West: Remembering, Forgetting, and Becoming American in Utah," *Material Religion* 11, no. 3 (2015): 329–353.

51 On the Omaha memorial and many others, see Patterson, *Pioneers in the Attic;* James V. D'Arc, "Darryl F. Zanuck's 'Brigham Young': A Film in Context," *BYU Studies* 29, no. 1 (Winter 1989): 5–33.

52 Gerald Joseph Peterson, "History of Mormon Exhibits in World Expositions" (M.A. thesis, Brigham Young University, 1974), 30.

53 *The Exhibits of the Smithsonian Institution and United States National Museum at the Alaska-Yukon-Pacific Exposition* (Washington, DC: Judd & Detweiler, 1909), 38–41.

54 "Great Exhibit for Mormonism," *Inter-Mountain Republican*, May 14, 1909, 9. Jepperson was likely Jeppe Jepperson (1837–1924), who had done construction work for the Salt Lake Temple and for the Chicago World's Columbian Exposition. See "Jeppe Jepperson Will Be Buried Friday," *Deseret News*, November 14, 1924, 12. The *Intermountain Republican* described Masuda as "an expert wood carver who arrived in Salt Lake recently from Kobe, Japan." He may have been Santaro Masuda, who died in Salt Lake the following year.

55 On the proselytizing function of Fairbanks's work in conjunction with the Mormon Tabernacle Choir's performances at the fair, see Michael Hicks, *The Mormon Tabernacle Choir: A Biography* (Urbana: University of Illinois Press, 2015), 81–82.

56 *Century of Progress Exposition, Chicago, 1933* (Chicago: Northern States Mission of the Church of Jesus Christ of Latter-day Saints, 1933).

57 "The Century of Progress Display," *The Improvement Era* 36, no. 14 (December 1, 1933): 864.

58 "The Century of Progress Display," 865. Although not mentioned by McKay, the display also featured a newly commissioned wooden model of the Salt Lake temple by Christian Schreiner. See "Temple Model Dispatched," *Salt Lake Telegram,* August 31, 1933, 5.

59 Peterson, "History of Mormon Exhibits in World Expositions," 49–50.

60 "Church Contacts over Million Persons Through Golden Gate Exposition Exhibit," *Deseret News,* December 2, 1939, 5.

61 "L.D.S. Booth Near Ready at Exposition," *Deseret News,* June 30, 1936, 18.

62 For a bibliography of Mormon media studies, see Sherry Baker and Daniel Stout, "Mormons and the Media, 1898–2003: A Selected, Annotated, and Indexed Bibliography," *BYU Studies* 42, no. 3 (July 2003): 124–181; on later twentieth-century public relations of the LDS Church, see J. B. Haws, *The Mormon Image in the American Mind: Fifty Years of Public Perception* (New York: Oxford University Press, 2013).

63 Patterson, "The Plymouth Rock of the American West," 344–345. The only significant controversy elicited by the Brigham Young statue in the Capitol rotunda was an argument about where it should be placed. See Norma S. Davis, *A Song of Joys: The Biography of Mahonri Mackintosh Young* (Provo, UT: Brigham Young University Press, 1999), 266–267.

64 Prescott, *Pioneer Mother Monuments,* 136–143.

65 Hunter, "The Monument to Brigham Young," 344.

66 The most prominent recent example is an incident in which anonymous actors painted the word "racist" and poured red paint on a statue at Brigham Young University. See Courtney Tanner, "Statue of Brigham Young Covered in Paint at BYU with the Word 'Racist' Sprayed at the Base," *Salt Lake Tribune,* June 2020, https://www.sltrib.com/news/education/2020/06/19/statue-brigham-young/. Recent scholarship on the This Is the Place Monument's representation of race and gender includes Elise Boxer, "'This Is the Place!': Disrupting Mormon Settler Colonialism," in *Decolonizing Mormonism: Approaching a Postcolonial Zion,* ed. Joanna Brooks and Gina Colvin (Salt Lake City: University of Utah Press, 2018), 77–99; Cynthia Culver Prescott, Nathan Rees, and Rebecca Weaver-Hightower, "This Is the Place Salt Lake City, Utah and the Voortrekker Monument Pretoria: Monuments to Settler Constructions of History, Race, and Religion," *Safundi* 22 (2021); Cynthia Culver Prescott, Rebecca Weaver-Hightower, and Nathan Rees, "Enshrining Gender in Monuments to Settler Whiteness: South Africa's Voortrekker Monument and the United States' This Is the Place Monument," *Humanities* 10 (2021): 41.

CREATING SOMETHING EXTRAORDINARY

Nineteenth-Century Latter-day Saint Women and Their Folk Art

JENNIFER REEDER

Latter-day Saint midwife Patty Sessions, who assisted in countless births and deaths along the pioneer trail and in early Utah, left a bookmark pressed between the pages of an 1842 medical book.[1] The strip of manufactured webbing had embroidered on it the phrase "Remember Me" in vibrant turkey red decorative font, with contrast light and dark green flourishes.[2] The textile message was much more than a simple marker in a well-used textbook; the stitches expressed her fervent appeal to not be forgotten. Its placement in a book denoting her profession and its elegance stood separate from what must have been a messy trade. Such is the satisfaction of folk art.

Lucy Mack Smith painted homemade oilcloth coverings to decorate floors, tables, and walls in upstate New York.[3] Mary Musselman Whitmer embroidered a sampler to demonstrate both her sewing skills and her German heritage.[4] Emma Hale Smith manufactured raw material to sew suits for early missionaries of the church.[5] Each produced early Latter-day Saint material culture, whether to support the family economy or the needs of the church, or to follow a female-centric domestic activity, using skills gained in their local areas. Twelve years after Emma Smith made missionary suits, she stood at the head of the Nauvoo Relief Society and told the women, "We are going to do something extraordinary."[6] Neither of the Smith women's work survived and none of these women traveled west to settle with the Saints, but their artisan skills—which indeed were extraordinary—influenced generations of Latter-day Saint heritage. This chapter will examine three specific types of nineteenth-century Latter-day Saint folk art created by women: quilts, hair art, and buildings—Relief Society halls, cooperative stores, and granaries. These compelling pieces attest to their living memory.

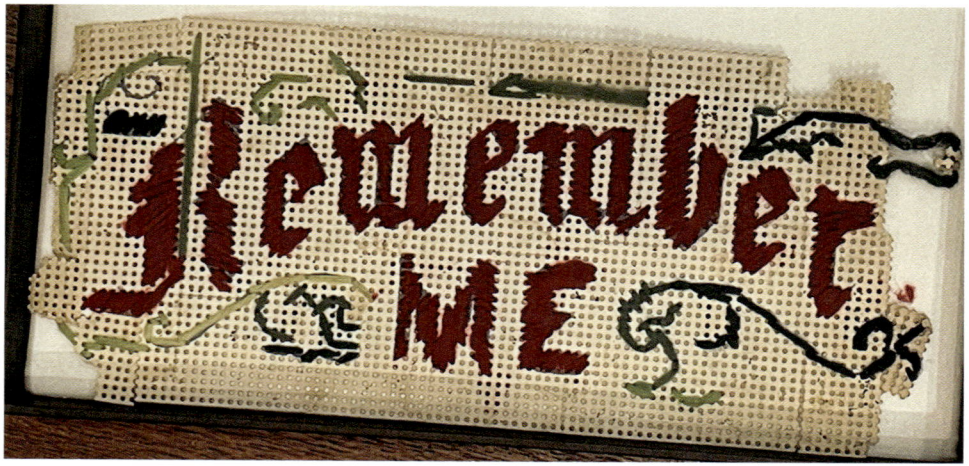

Fig. 6.1 *Remember Me*, cross-stitched book plate, date unknown, found in Patty Sessions's medical book (W. Beach, *The Family Physician*), owned by Norma A. Earl. Courtesy of Syracuse Syracuse Regional Museum.

A DISCLAIMER ABOUT FOLK ART

These early artifacts created by these women demonstrate the development of a distinctive Latter-day Saint folk art. Rarely placed on pedestals or classified as high art, such vernacular artifacts assert three things. First, they illustrate a specific community as a collection of shared values.[7] Second, they reveal work of everyday people who seek to embellish the used material of their lives in ways to show refinement, class, and status.[8] Active efforts at refinement confirmed valuable social prestige.[9] And lastly, each piece indicates a snapshot of history, revealing lived religion, culture, economy, and politics, both local and democratic.[10] Folk art is the material manifestation of culture of a specific time and place, something ordinary made extraordinary.[11]

LATTER-DAY SAINT FOLK ART

Sidney Rigdon described the building of Zion in 1836 Missouri: "It will be by her becoming more wise, more learned, more refined, more noble" through proper cultivation, enriching literature, magnificent buildings, and fine dress. "Let the Saints," he wrote in the *Messenger and Advocate*, "seek learning and wisdom, refinement and elegance. Let industry and enterprise be encouraged, not merely as appendages of our religion; but as an identity with it, as part of it."[12] In 1842, Joseph Smith wrote to Chicago newspaper editor John Wentworth, proclaiming the church's decree to seek anything "virtuous, lovely, or of good report or praiseworthy."[13] Built into the lived religion of Mormonism was an inherent desire for beauty and art with an inherent sense of agency and action that could bolster a public image.

Rigdon, Smith, and other early members of the new church developed its theology and practice over time. The transient nature of the Saints—moving from New York to Ohio to Missouri to Illinois, hoping in each location to build their Zion, only to be run out of town—prevented deep roots until they arrived in Utah. There, in relative isolation for a few decades, members of the Church of Jesus Christ of Latter-day Saints laid a permanent foundation.

Latter-day Saint folk art in nineteenth-century territorial Utah reflected an attempt to tame what they saw as a wilderness and make a garden—a form of religious worship.[14] Like other Americans, once they colonized an area they sought refinement as evidence of their ability to conquer the land, using local resources.[15] Early homes were made of precious and sometimes rare timber, until they learned to produce adobe. Early vernacular architectural styles were simple and humble due to practical adaptations to a frontier environment.[16]

The Saints gathered a provincial Israel with converts from around the United States, Great Britain, Scandinavia, and the Pacific Islands. Many brought with them a diversity of tools, skills, and aesthetic traditions, and they taught each other. They shared a belief in provident living with religious and temporal cooperation.[17] Architecture, craft, furniture, household items, textiles, gravestones, and sericulture constitute vernacular Latter-day Saint folk art. These items often displayed significant symbols such as beehives, clasped hands, an all-seeing eye, or the phrase "Holiness to the Lord."[18] These symbols were taken from several outside traditional sources and blended secular context with a specific Latter-day Saint theology, making them a distinct people.[19]

In Utah, Latter-day Saint communities demarcated a new religious culture. Craftspeople found an open canvas in the undeveloped land, and new creativity worked with tradition.[20] Building Zion shifted to refining Zion. Missives from top leadership encouraged the Saints to embellish or adorn their surroundings. Brigham Young preached in May 1874 to "beautify every place with the workmanship of our own hands."[21] The third Latter-day Saint president, John Taylor, taught in 1886: "It is our duty to adorn and beautify [the earth]—to make it so lovely and attractive that angels may condescend to visit it."[22] Refined folk art made the Saints citizens of their land with their own culture.

Young, a trained carpenter, worked tirelessly to encourage Saints to become self-sufficient through home manufacture and cooperative efforts. He sought manufacturers of all kinds: carpenters, coopers, potters, blacksmiths, tinsmiths, millwrights, weavers, tanners, and shoemakers.[23] He did not want his people to become dependent on "Gentile" merchandise, especially with the coming of the transcontinental railroad in 1869.[24] He designated a county in southern Utah to manufacture iron, a much-needed commodity for the entire territory. Another county was designed to produce cotton. Each far-flung settlement required carpenters and blacksmiths.[25] Young delegated the production of sugar and silk. In line with their early identification of the Utah Territory as "Deseret," meaning "honeybee," Latter-day Saints worked like bees, in synchronicity, with tenacity, and with great industry.

Religion permeated daily activity, government, social and cultural efforts, and of course folk art. For example, Latter-day Saint regional furniture was defined not necessarily by style but rather by principles, beliefs, and lived religion. Household and church property made of local softwood was painted and stylized as grained hardwood (unavailable in the Great Basin), and often carvings of beehives or sego lilies demonstrated thrift and fortitude. Furniture also expressed the social dynamic or hierarchy of refinement: fine pieces in homes of church leaders were emulated and imitated in homes of church members.[26] In addition to making utilitarian furniture, they demonstrated their faith, building profound spiritual meaning, creating religious consecration, gathering Israel, expanding Zion, and practicing both the secular and the sacred.[27]

WOMEN'S FOLK ART

Women's material culture from this time demonstrates extraordinary efforts at refinement with a particular concern for ancestry and kinship, often within the domestic realm.[28] Latter-day Saint women were not one whit behind their global female counterparts. Eliza R. Snow, for example, grew up on the Ohio frontier in the early 1800s. Her mother trained her in "the magnificent structure of womanly accomplishments," including needlework and braiding straw.[29] Snow preserved a woolen blanket she wove as a young girl; it now exists in the Salt Lake City Daughters of Utah Pioneers collection, attesting to her impeccable handiwork at such an early age.[30]

Not much has survived from the early years. The Nauvoo Relief Society minute book lists an exchange of services—millinery, weaving, dressmaking, needlework, rugs, quilts, candlemaking, and supplies for such articles—indicating the diversity of craft skills among women at the time.[31] That which does survive reveals snapshots in time: Mary Whitmer's sampler, illustrating her German heritage, and one by her granddaughter Maria Louise Cowdery reside in the Museum of Church History and Art. This same museum also houses work by Mary Ann Broomhead, who at the age of thirteen embroidered a sampler commemorating the martyrdom of Joseph and Hyrum Smith, and Ann Eckford, a young English girl, whose sampler marks the construction and dedication of the Nauvoo temple.

Latter-day Saint women had many reasons to be self-sufficient. Husbands were often assigned to foreign or domestic missions for indefinite periods of time, leaving wives to farm and build settlements in their stead.[32] The practice of plural marriage required independence, as women either shared domestic responsibilities or lived entirely on their own, raising children, livestock, and crops. Resourcefulness in frontier settlements, efforts to seek female authority and to demarcate their environment, and expressions of individualism within a strong community reveal Latter-day Saint women in their context, reflecting their religious and cultural beliefs.

Quilts

Women's folk art demonstrates extraordinary efforts at refinement with a particular concern for ancestry and kinship, often within the home.[33] Quilts covering beds—providing warmth, comfort, and beauty—are a very common type of female-aligned folk art; they were also methods of building relationships and lineages.[34] They became symbols of neighborly exchange as exhibited in Nauvoo and crossing the plains.[35] Each quilt serves as a textile text, speaking its maker's desires and beliefs, hopes and fears.[36]

Relief Society women gathered often to make quilts. The women worked together to care for the poor among their congregations and neighbors. Beyond making utilitarian quilts for the needy, women came together to sharpen their skills, to exhibit refinement, and to express their identity, both collectively and individually. Some local ward organizations created album or friendship quilts to commemorate their sisterhood—a collection of blocks like an autograph album, with each block made by a specific woman. Each album quilt illustrates that tenuous link between individual and group.[37] The Salt Lake City Fourteenth Ward Relief Society created an intricately stitched album quilt in 1857.[38] In 1872, the Eighth Ward Relief Society sewed an album quilt for their bishop.[39] Every ward in the Bear Lake Stake contributed to a commemorative quilt given to their stake Primary president, Annie Bryson Laker.[40] In a different cultural tradition, the women of the Iosepa Relief Society in Skull Valley, Utah, all originally from the Pacific Islands, presented a Hawaiian quilt to Wilford Woodruff to commemorate the 1897 pioneer jubilee. The plumeria leaf design in light green symbolized a Hawaiian lei flower—a material message of love, friendship, celebration, and honor—with the beige background showcasing their island heritage for a beloved prophet.[41]

The Salt Lake City Twentieth Ward Relief Society members pieced an album quilt in 1870.[42] The women presented the quilt to their president, Margaret T. Smoot, when she relocated in 1872.[43] Fifty-six individual blocks demonstrate a variety of cultural and national backgrounds, political and theological beliefs, and a shared Relief Society history, most of them attributed to their maker.[44] The quilt contains gleanings of feminist impulses at a time when Utah women arguably expressed one of the strongest national political voices through their newly gained suffrage. Stitched together, these pieces create a community map of the ward, collecting different skill levels and designs into one whole.

The women prominently featured religious motifs, typical of many American quilts of the time, including scripture verses from the Bible, the Book of Mormon, and Doctrine and Covenants. For example, quilter Emily Dye's verse came from the New Testament: "Consider the lilies."[45] Sarah Cushion stitched "Though I speak with the tongue of men and angels and have not charity"—from a popular New Testament epistle, but also within the context of a significant Nauvoo Relief Society teaching.[46] Ann Paul's block combined Bible and restorationist scripture with an anchor and the phrase "faith, hope, and charity."[47] The doctrine may have held personal significance

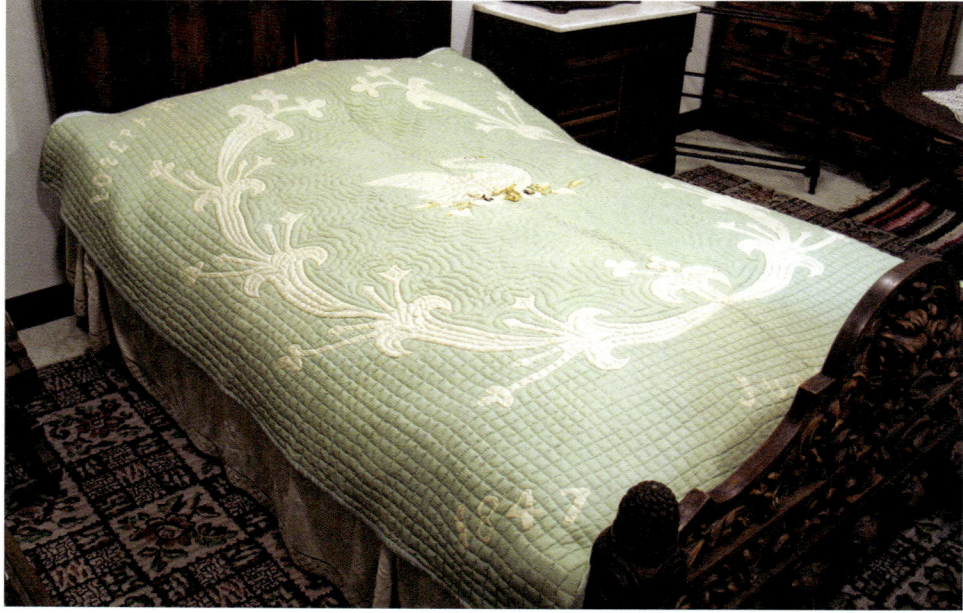

Fig. 6.2 Iosepa/Skull Valley Relief Society, Relief Society medallion whole piece quilt, for Wilford Woodruff, 1897. Courtesy of International Daughters of Utah Pioneers Museum, Salt Lake City.

for her, as she had experienced the deaths of three babies and was pregnant with another as she stitched this block.[48] Mary Luff adorned her block with honeysuckle and the verse "God is love."[49] Sarah M. Napper's block included the psalm "I muse on the work of thy hands."[50] Other blocks included biblical phrases from Proverbs, Isaiah, and Revelation.[51] A block by Maggie Smoot referenced a nineteenth-century Latter-day Saint interpretation of Eve: "Temptation: Eve at the apple." On May 7, 1868, Bishop Sharp had admonished the Twentieth Ward Relief Society to consider Mother Eve as "one of the Elect Ladies who stepped from the Courts of Heaven to perform her duty here."[52] These women were women of the Word.[53]

Another religious theme shown in the Twentieth Ward quilt was home and family, an appropriate medium for Latter-day Saints.[54] Mary Ann Sansom's block depicted flowers with the phrase "Love at home," a refrain from a well-known hymn sung by Latter-day Saints.[55] Her toddler daughter Louise had died of "teething and bowel complaint," and so her home was most likely a grief-stricken environment in the wake of the death.[56] Martha Zina Paul commemorated her two-year-old daughter, who had died the previous year, when she sewed "Christ died that all might live" into her block.[57] The quilt also presented close family relationships among quilters. Sisters, mothers, daughters, mothers-in-law, daughters-in-law, and sisters-in-law all participated.[58] Eliza R. Snow and Zina D. H. Young, both honorary members of the Twentieth Ward Relief Society who contributed blocks, had nieces living in the Twentieth Ward who also

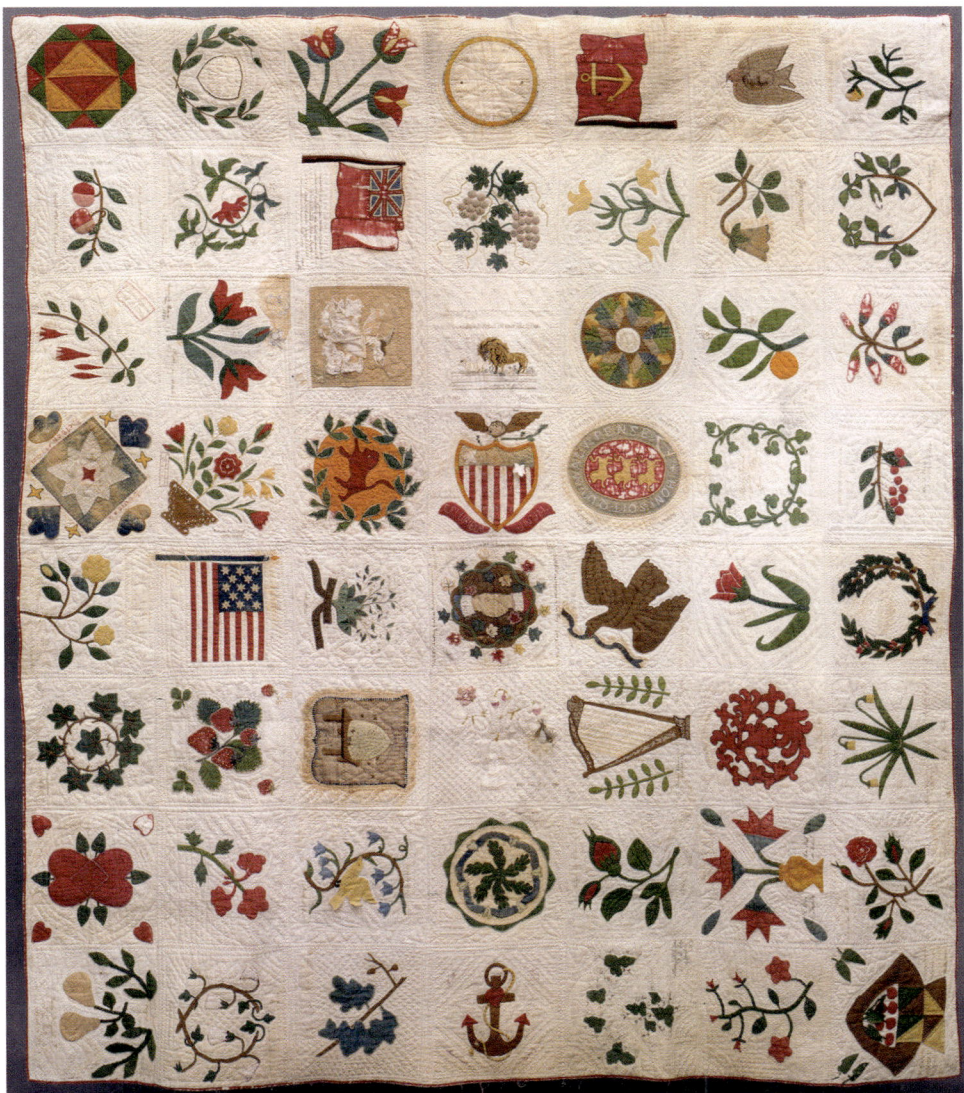

Fig. 6.3 Salt Lake City 20th Ward Relief Society, album quilt. Courtesy of International Daughters of Utah Pioneers Museum, Salt Lake City.

submitted blocks—Eliza Snow Dunford and Martha Zina Paul, both named after their aunts.[59]

While family and home were portrayed in traditional American quilts, Latter-day Saint women worked from a distinct family theology. Their doctrine identified women as elect ladies, mothers in Israel, and daughters in Zion. In January 1870, Latter-day Saint women gathered en masse to protest proposed federal anti-polygamy legislation

and to defend their religious freedoms.[60] Although there is no recorded public proclamation by any member of the Twentieth Ward at the mass meeting, it is likely some
were among the five thousand in attendance. The album quilt was created over the next
few months as women expressed their sentiments through formats other than words.
The textile medium was a safe place for traditionally non-vocal women, some of whom
spoke English as a second language. Within this historical context, quilted quotations
such as "Let sisterly love continue," "Chastity," "Celestial marriage," "Wives honor your
husbands," and "Love at home" took on a more nuanced meaning. At least twenty-
one of the fifty-three women who made quilt blocks were plural wives, twelve of them
within the same six families. The blocks connected makers from the same bloodlines
and across marriages, linking generations and celebrating distinct religious roles in a
way that marked their autonomy.

President Margaret Smoot and her plural wives formed an extraordinary sisterhood. She warmly welcomed one sister-wife, Anna Kristine Mauritzen Smoot, from
Norway, into the country and the family.[61] Anna's block read, "The gospel power is
strong it gathers from every land." Another sister-wife, Diana Eldredge Smoot, stitched
a garland of flowers, demonstrating the budding relationship between the women. A
block was made by Margaret Smoot Jr., or Mattie, daughter of sister-wife Emily Hill
Smoot. Mattie lived with "Ma" Margaret Smoot when her mother and family moved to
Provo with their father.[62] As the women cut fabric to make their own appliqués, they
deconstructed their marriages and female roles to claim a sense of interdependence as
well as individuality.

Other sister-wives participated. Elizabeth S. Ramsay's block showcased a vine
of leaves and flowers with the inscription "Our mountain home." Born in England,
Ramsey immigrated to Utah in 1858, married Ralph Ramsay as his second wife, and
joined the family in northeast Salt Lake City. Twentieth Ward bishop John Sharp and
counselor William L. N. Allen had plural wives or daughters who contributed blocks,
including Jane S. P. Sharp, Margaret Sharp, Hannah Allen, and Mary Jane Snowball
Allen. The quilt was a family tree of sorts, crossing lines and connecting lineages not
captured on a traditional genealogical chart.

As Relief Society women defended plural marriage, other groups worked in a similar fashion to discount Latter-day Saint women and polygamy. The Woman's Home
Mission Society, a female auxiliary of the Methodist Episcopal Church in Ogden, Utah,
created an anti-polygamy quilt in 1882. Like the Twentieth Ward quilt, the Methodist
quilt included signatures of prominent women, both nationally and locally, including
Lucy Webb Hayes, wife of United States president Rutherford B. Hayes. This quilt
was presented to Vermont senator George F. Edmunds, whose name was featured in
the center of the quilt.[63] Edmunds had sponsored a bill in Congress earlier that year
declaring polygamy a felony.[64] The quilt medium presented an appropriate political
tribute for women both protesting and protecting marriage laws and practices.

The Twentieth Ward quilt revealed a resourcefulness that marked frontier life with the effort to domesticate a harsh environment—both politically and physically. In his address to the Relief Society at their organization meeting on April 22, 1868, Bishop Sharp counseled, "One great and important item of your duty as a society will be to invent your own fashions of dress and to take the lead therein, also the manufacture of straw hats, as there are many in the ward who are good braiders of straw and others who are equally as good at making the braid into hats and bonnets."[65] Martha Artwell repurposed the idea on her block with her phrase, "Let the daughters of Zion adorn themselves with the workmanship of their own hands."[66] President Smoot was known for her home manufacture, including spinning and weaving. Her biographer Olive Smoot Bean, a daughter of a sister-wife, wrote that Ma Smoot "was considered a good judge of homemade cloth." Margaret won awards for needlework at the Deseret Agricultural and Manufacturing Society and often served as a member of the awards committee at local fairs.[67] The Twentieth Ward women were familiar with home industry and resourcefulness.

The coupled efforts of home industry (as instructed by Young) and refinement come to a juncture in this quilt including Utah silk in its fabrics. Mattie T. Smoot stitched "Long life to Brigham Young" on her block. At the April 1868 general conference, Young exhorted the Saints to cultivate silk as part of the home industry movement—to produce their own silk rather than importing it.[68] Utah silk production expanded a

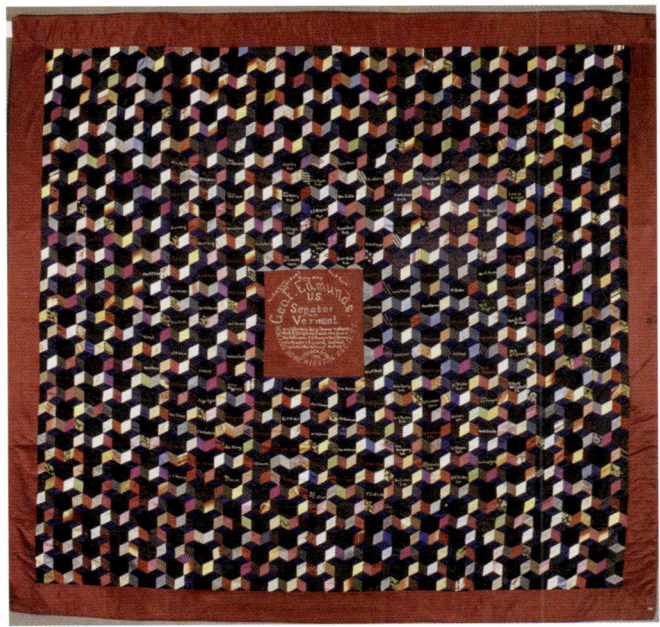

Fig. 6.4 Woman's Home Mission Society of the Methodist Episcopal Church, anti-polygamy quilt, 1882, Church History Museum, Church of Jesus Christ of Latter-day Saints, Salt Lake City.

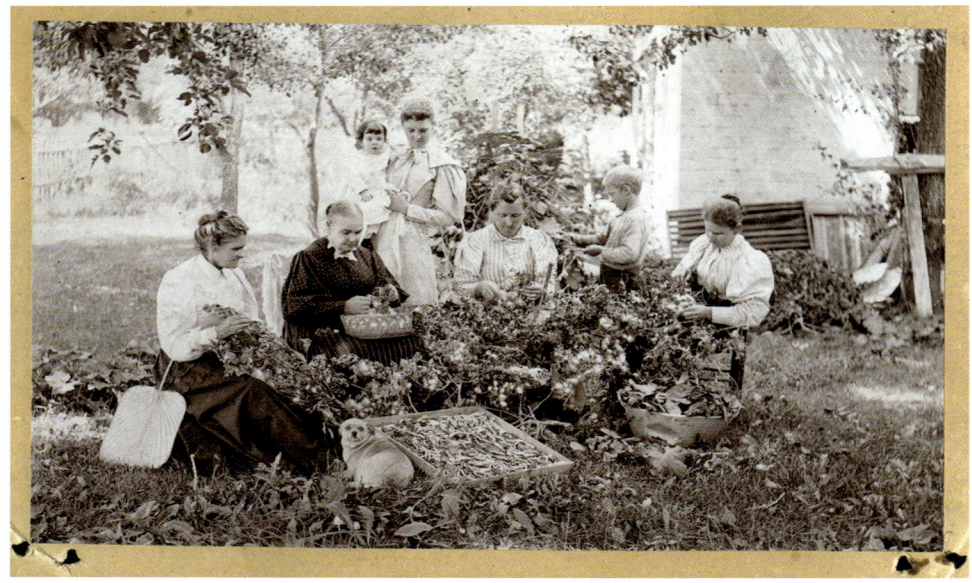

Fig. 6.5 George Edward Anderson, *Women Manufacturing Silk Worms*, c. 1895, Church History Library, The Church of Jesus Christ of Latter-day Saints Salt Lake City.

cottage industry that had largely disappeared during the Industrial Revolution.[69] The trend of cultivating Utah silk set Latter-day Saint women apart from their American counterparts and illustrated their imitation of current fashion trends using local resources.

From fabric to depicted images, the Twentieth Ward women emulated the refined needlework typical of their time. Embroidered, appliquéd, and pieced, blocks included flora, fauna, and wildlife, presenting quilters' efforts to transform and refine their environment.[70] Fruits provide insight into the Utah diet from 1857 to 1870. Many berry varieties grew wild in Utah, including strawberries, serviceberries, choke cherries, currants, raspberries, and elderberries.[71] Augusta T. Lewis sewed a sprig of strawberries and the word "delicious."[72] Two blocks depicted cherries: one of cherries on a stem, another of harvested cherries in a basket. The reproduction of grapes and berries symbolized abundance, the textile equivalent to still-life oil paintings; Mary Brain and Harriet Bunting's blocks depicted grapes.[73] Several apple varieties thrived in Utah; Mattie Smoot included them on her block.[74] Jane T. Lynch displayed golden pears on her block. Citrus fruits were a popular luxury item in nineteenth-century Utah, transported from tropical climes; Mary Ann Lewis appliquéd an orange branch.[75] These blocks documented Latter-day Saint efforts to make the desert blossom as a rose, an important illustration of what was seen as religious refinement.[76]

In addition to fruit imagery, flowers appeared in the Twentieth Ward quilt. Not unlike their Victorian counterparts, Latter-day Saint women utilized plants for herbal medicines and foods, gardens, and indoor decor, endowed with deliberate symbolism.[77] Emily Dye's block featured slender yellow lilies with the phrase "Consider the lilies," connecting the idea of spiritual care and attention to things of beauty.[78] Mary Davies's block showed roses with the adage "Every rose has its thorn." A block made to commemorate Susan Schettler, who died in December 1869, included forget-me-nots, a popular Victorian symbol. Emma P. Toone stitched a pot filled with numerous colorful flowers and the word "unity," combining different varieties for a proper garden. Popular flowers found on the Twentieth Ward quilt included tulips, lilies, roses, lilies of the valley, thistles, shamrocks, olive branches, and honeysuckle—some flowers native to Utah and others imported across the plains. Their choice of specific flowers communicated devoted affection and bonds of love according to trends of floriology, infusing common flowers and fruits with meaning specific to the Latter-day Saint experience in Utah.[79]

Fruits and flowers revealed an effort to both harness and embellish the natural environment. Beyond flowers, blocks represented pine and oak trees. Some blocks included birds and animals: doves, eagles, bees, unicorns, and Eliza R. Snow's lamb and lion.[80] Other blocks displayed non-organic pieces; baskets, pots, and vases captured and domesticated nature's offerings.[81] Lisadore Williams depicted a harp with a verse from the New Testament book of Revelation: "I heard the voice of harpers harping with their harps."[82] An anchor and a clock in two blocks illustrated efforts to remain steadfast and mindful of time. The maker of the clock block inscribed, "Time is the cradle of hope, but the grave of ambition." These blocks revealed both a respect for nature and an effort to control or manipulate the natural environment. Some of these women and their families moved to other settlements in the Utah Territory, taking with them the spirit of refinement and community.

The Twentieth Ward quilt contained symbols memorializing their Nauvoo Relief Society and Utah heritage. The center block showcased a vine wreath surrounding clasped hands of fellowship with dates of the society's founding in 1842 in Nauvoo by Joseph Smith, and its reorganization in 1867 in Salt Lake City by Brigham Young. In Latter-day Saint folk art, vines represented ancient Israel and Jesus Christ.[83] Clasped hands, a Masonic ritual appropriated by the Saints, were also found in architectural elements.[84] Zina Young's block included a beehive.[85]

A significant hierarchy occurs in the placement of quilt blocks. Prominent in the center, surrounding the commemorative Nauvoo block, are blocks by Eliza R. Snow and Zina Young, original Nauvoo Relief Society members and honorary members of the Twentieth Ward Relief Society. On either side of ward president Smoot's block were those of her two counselors, Jane S. P. Sharp and Annie A. Savage.

The Twentieth Ward quilt additionally furnished a textile map, identifying members of a specific Salt Lake City neighborhood. An 1888 ward map laid out the neighborhood much like the blocks of the quilt. The map and the quilt provided clues about the proximity and relationship of women. Property, location, and families and neighbors reveal shared fabrics and values.[86] The majority of families on these blocks joined the church following the Nauvoo period (1849–1846) and arrived in the Salt Lake Valley after 1856, when the ward split from the adjoining Eighteenth Ward.[87] For example, both the George Luff family and the Harry Luff family resided on the same block, putting mother-in-law Mary Luff and daughter-in-law Lovina Luff's blocks into perspective. The leaves on their blocks were cut from the same material, demonstrating both resourcefulness and family economy. The Lewis and Sansom families also lived on the same block. Mary Ann Squires Lewis married the brother of Mary Ann Lewis Sansom, and their adjoining lots illustrated their family relationships.

Women in the Twentieth Ward Relief Society came from several different countries but shared a neighborhood and a pride in Utah and the United States. Hannah Lewis embroidered the American flag, and Margaret Smoot displayed the seal of the American government with an eagle holding an olive branch in its talons. While the eagle was a very popular symbol, appearing on furniture, silver, and ceramics during the Federal period, at the time of this quilt's construction the people of the Utah Territory expressed dissatisfaction with the country due to popular anti-Mormon sentiment and legislation.[88] Three blocks celebrated Utah as a location of women's rights. Both Elizabeth B. Ramsay and Martha Moore came from England to settle in Salt Lake City. Ramsay's block included an eagle with a ribbon and the phrase "Peace be to Utah." She came to the territory uneducated, but once there, she learned and practiced nursing and midwifery.[89] Moore's block included flowers and buds with the phrase "Women's rights in Utah."

While the Twentieth Ward quilt celebrated unity, it also commemorated Western European diversity. Jane S. P. Sharp designed a block with the Scottish emblem, a red lion on an orange background surrounded by Scottish thistles.[90] Both Jane and her husband, John Sharp, a bishop, were born in Scotland. British woman Annie Adkins Savage's block displayed the emblem of England with three running lions and the French phrase "Honi soit qui mal y pense" (Shame to who thinks evil). Mary Jane Snowball Allen, a native of Newcastle, England, included the British naval flag on her block with the phrase "English hearts of oak will defend the standard of Zion with as much zeal as they ever did their flag. Don't give up the ship."[91] Mary Lynch, a founding member of the Twentieth Ward Relief Society, appliquéd shamrocks and the phrase "Shamrock of Ireland, lightheartedness" on her block. She proudly commemorated her homeland: Cork, Ireland. Ellen Toronto embroidered the name of her country of origin, Wales, onto her block, along with a vase of flowers and the proclamation "In God we trust." Perhaps there are so many United Kingdom connections because Abraham O. Smoot, husband of three of the quilt makers, served a mission there from 1851 to 1856.[92]

Scandinavian heritage also ran strong in this neighborhood. On May 22, 1868, William Allen, a counselor in the Twentieth Ward bishopric, suggested that a Danish woman be appointed to minister to other Danish women who did not understand English.[93] A month later, President Smoot expressed concern for these immigrants:

"Let our influence be for good for the Spirit, which we have, our stranger sisters will partake of when they arrive from the old countries." One Dane stitched her nationality into her block with a white star and blue hearts. Norwegian Annie K. Smoot notated on her block, "The gospel power is strong it gathers from every land." The representation of immigrant status in quilt form is a powerful testimony to the spirit of inclusion in the early church, on the one hand, and the longing and loss perhaps felt by various cultural identities, on the other.

Contemporary gendered identities are also stitched into the blocks of the Twentieth Ward Quilt, blending current trends with Latter-day Saint doctrine and practice. Ann Erskin's block commented on Victorian gendered roles: "Man is the lofty rugged pine— Woman is the slender clasping vine," lines from a Samuel Woodworth poem in a popular women's newspaper.[94]

The Twentieth Ward Relief Society quilt presents layers of multiple identities, including neighborhood, religion, nationality, gender, and politics. The quilt also demonstrates the skill of these women and their efforts at refinement, including a coat of arms and to brand a particular identity. But the presence of the quilt, as outlined by Olive Smoot Bean, became a "memento of their energy and industry."[95] And for Margaret, the quilt held memories of relationships and work with her Relief Society sisters.

Hair Art

Quilts commemorated relationships and ideology. Around the same time, the invention and continued technological development of photographs captured community. Both photography—daguerreotype, ambrotype, tintype, and albumen prints—and quilts embodied windows into the past and materialized memory into relics or icons.[96] It took some time for photography to become standard in nineteenth-century Utah, other than those pictures carried with pioneers to remember family not with them.[97] Yet the desire to protect memory across distances proved important.

A popular Victorian type of folk art literally came from heads: art made from hair. A form of commemoration of a specific time, each work provides distinct historical and decorative context made from the most immediate resource: the human body. The practice of making wreaths, decor, and jewelry out of hair was not limited to the Latter-day Saint community; this work originated in late eighteenth-century Scandinavia, France, Germany, and England, then spread to the United States.[98] Hair was a very workable material due to its texture, pliability, and tensile strength—it could easily be molded into intricate designs.[99] Popular motifs included flowers, plants, trees, birds, butterflies, and bees. Other formats wove hair in the same way as bobbin lace: braided and twisted, set in a particular formation.[100] Artisans formed the hair into jewelry, placed it in lockets, and collected it like signatures in friendship albums.[101] Hair wreaths for wall display ranged from one to four feet in diameter and were often framed in shadow boxes to hold their three-dimensional forms.

Hair could depict a family tree with a trunk woven of hair from progenitors and branches made of descendants. Sometimes hair from the paternal side would constitute half the scene, while hair from the maternal side filled the other half, accompanied by a genealogical key delineating each contributor.[102] It becomes even more complicated on paper with plural marriage, but in the medium of hair, strands blend together, mixing color and texture into one.

Hair art honored different relationships, including engagements and friendships.[103] People often exchanged locks of hair in the nineteenth century as they would later exchange wallet-size photographs.[104] Hair artifacts embodied relationships altered by physical separation and acted as a synecdoche, or a tangible memorial symbol of a loved one.[105] While hair on a living person changes color and texture over time, cut locks preserved a specific moment in time.[106]

The use of hair in territorial Utah demonstrated a sense of pioneer resourcefulness—a readily available medium. Jane Blood created a hair wreath to demonstrate love for a dear friend in Kaysville in 1880.[107] Margaret T. Smoot requested a lock of hair from her missionary husband to place in a locket with his picture.[108] Others were created either to hang in temples or to raise funds for temple construction. The Logan Primary children made a hair wreath for the Logan temple in December 1885.[109] Young ladies in Fillmore held a bazaar to raise money for the Manti temple in 1886, selling homemade articles such as wax flowers, album quilts, and a hair wreath.[110]

Hair art also demonstrated Latter-day Saint efforts at refinement. Because of their Victorian ornate quality, hair wreaths were often displayed in fashionable parlors.[111] The Saints placed hair wreaths in temples, either in the celestial room—the church's finest Victorian parlor (see Josh Probert's chapter in this volume)—or the temple's grand entrance.[112] Women's hair art—in the Manti temple, the Salt Lake temple, and general Relief Society headquarters—illustrates the decoration and refinement of sacred spaces. The collection of physical evidence, both individually and intertwined, reveals much about the nineteenth-century Latter-day Saint ideology: that women were integral to religious practice and lived experience, often guiding it—or making it, in the case of the hair art. There was no temple ordinance or worship without women.

Women in Manti, Utah, anxiously prepared for the completion of the temple in their area in 1887.[113] Perhaps influenced by the preponderant European population in Sanpete County—immigrants from Denmark, Sweden, Switzerland, England, Wales, and Scotland—Mary W. Wintch created a decorative hair wreath for the new temple in 1888.[114] The hair in the arrangement reflected this global membership and included a tight collection of flowers woven from the hair of different individuals. While a handwritten attribution of the creator appeared at the bottom of the piece, no indication reveals what hair belonged to whom. The fact that different colors of hair are woven together without identity or individuality demonstrated a new sisterhood of consecration, without rank or hierarchy.

In the piece, Wintch designed a grandiose floral display in a vertical arrangement, placed in a wooden-chip font on the backs of oxen, on a fashionable parquet floor, surrounded by an open wreath. She framed her composition in a large octagonal shadowbox, 35 inches in height, 29 inches in width, and 6½ inches thick. The wooden font or urn was created by Janne Mattson Sjödhal, a Swedish immigrant who edited the local newspaper.[115] Sjödhal was the first person endowed in the Manti temple and the first

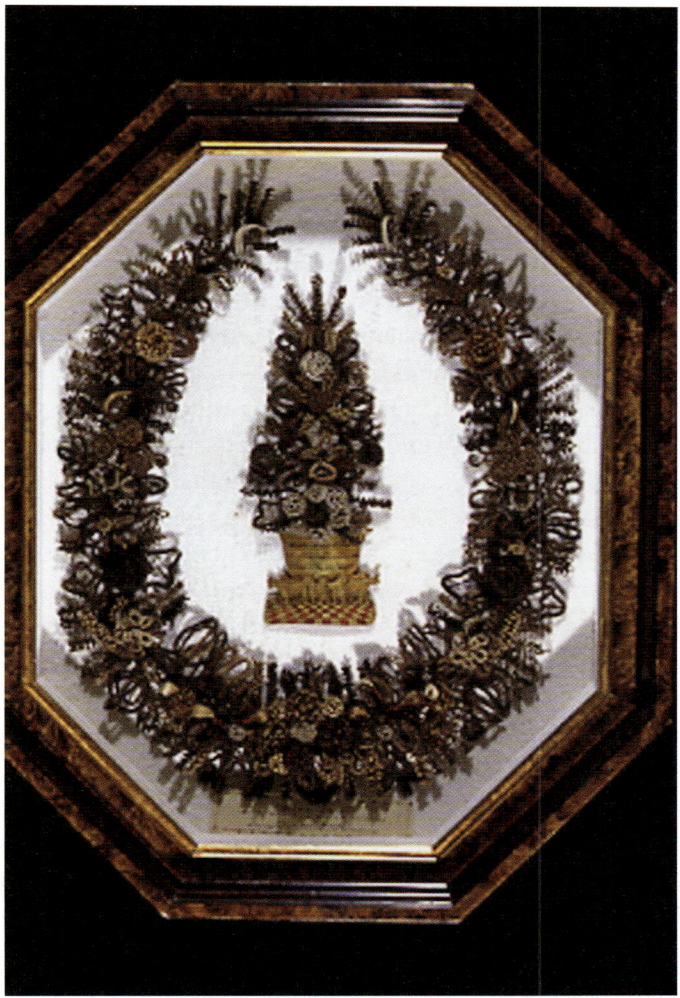

Fig. 6.6 Mary W. Wintch, Manti North Relief Society, hair art, shadow box, Church History Museum, Church of Jesus Christ of Latter-day Saints, Salt Lake City.

to be sealed as a couple with his wife, Christiana Wilhelmina Christofferson, a Relief Society sister with Wintch.

In a typical refined fashion for the time, the Manti temple hair art featured a Victorian floral mourning wreath open at the top, symbolizing an ascent into heaven.[116] The message inscribed on the piece articulated this belief: "These locks of hair, O Lord, thou hast seen us wear, so now we commit them to Thy Holy Temple's care." These women linked their physical bodies with a promised resurrection where not one hair of their heads would be lost. They also wanted to share that eternal hope and religious ritual of sealing with their deceased ancestors and descendants. The Manti temple hair wreath encircled a baptismal font where ordinances were performed by proxy for the dead, representing a distinct Latter-day Saint practice.[117]

Another equally significant piece of hair art hung in the Salt Lake temple, completed in 1893. Made from the hair of eight female leaders and twenty-nine male leaders, this piece is attributed to Harriet Critchlow Jensen.[118] The hair of these individuals forms a willow tree, a common mourning symbol in the early modern period.[119] A slender trunk bears branches bending back toward the stem. A ring of offshoots surrounds the trunk like a fountain of youth. Unlike the Manti temple hair wreath, with indistinguishable hair, this one carefully divides the donors: each branch constitutes a separate color and type of hair. A key lists the names of each contributor. This artifact hung in the temple's main entrance until 1967, when updates were made to feature modern decor.[120] The use of nature imagery was popular in mourning folk art, often appearing on headstones. Nature represented heaven, and the combination of death, heaven, and remembrance, especially in temple hair art, seemed appropriate to Latter-day Saints, who blended the mortal with the immortal.[121] The Saints transformed the universal symbol in an entirely new way singular to their theological beliefs when placed in a temple sacred space, connecting the living and the dead.

This artifact presents a significant "family" history of Latter-day Saints with expanded definitions of family, both in bloodlines and in congregations full of brothers and sisters. Sixteen of the thirty-nine people included were related to each other, through either blood or marriage. Maria Young Dougall, for example, was the daughter of Brigham Young, both of whom have hair displayed in this piece. Zina D. H. Young, whose hair is included, was married to Young; when Dougall's mother, Clarissa, died, Zina raised the young girl, an important family connection. Another one appeared nearby: Zina's sister, Presendia H. Kimball. Two sets of spouses appeared: Bathsheba W. and George A. Smith, and Jane S. and Franklin D. Richards. Three of the women were sealed to Joseph Smith and two were married plurally to Heber C. Kimball. And there are sets of cousins: Joseph Smith and George A. Smith, and Brigham Young and Willard Richards.

A traditional family tree includes both patrilineal and matrilineal lines. This institutional family tree blends together hair from significant male and female leaders of church hierarchy and collective history. Each of the four presidents of the church to this point

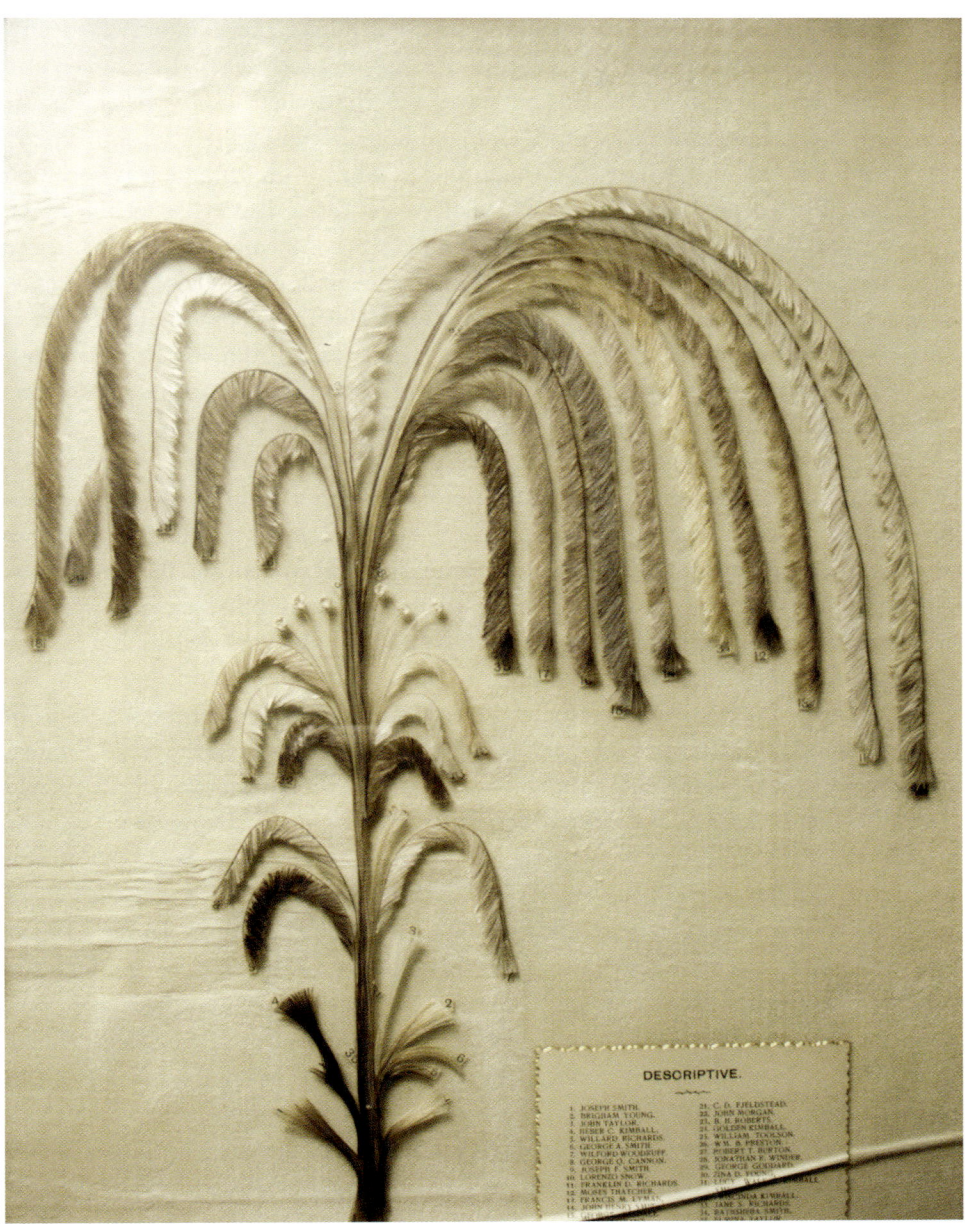

Fig. 6.7 Harriet Critchlow Jensen, Salt Lake City temple hair art, 1893. Courtesy of International Daughters of Utah Pioneers Museum, Salt Lake City.

was represented (Joseph Smith, Brigham Young, John Taylor, and Wilford Woodruff), as well as all members of the Quorum of Twelve Apostles in 1893.[122] The women also played important leadership roles. Zina Young was the Relief Society general president with counselors Bathsheba Smith and Jane Richards and secretary Emmeline B. Wells; each has hair in the piece. The Young Ladies' Mutual Improvement Association presidency was included, too: Elmina S. Taylor, Maria Young Dougall, and Martha H. Tingey. Lillie T. Freeze represented the children's Primary general presidency. George Q. Cannon and George Stoddard represented the general Sunday school superintendency; John Smith was the presiding patriarch, and William B. Preston and Robert T. Burton were in the presiding bishopric. The inclusion of hair from both Joseph Smith and Brigham H. Roberts, a member of the Quorum of the Seventy born thirteen years after Smith's death, demonstrated this flattening of time.[123]

The Relief Society Building hair wreath appears to have been created as a mourning piece: a black grosgrain ribbon adorns the stems of hair flowers.[124] Elizabeth Ann Whitney passed on February 15, 1882, and the bow is situated prominently over her penned name at the bottom of the wreath. Latter-day Saint women had distinct interest in living human hair: they had been authorized by Joseph Smith in Nauvoo to heal the sick by the laying on of hands on the head.[125] Whitney had been specially assigned by Smith to provide such ministrations.[126]

The hair wreath also includes some important plural marriage connections. Three of the twelve women included were sister-wives, intermarrying within the same families. Nine participated in plural marriages, six as the first wife. This, as well as others, depicted Latter-day Saint family charts in a different structure in a visually aesthetic fashion. In addition to the family-kin networks among the women in this piece is a matrilineal pedigree or lineage among these female leaders. Each woman portrayed had belonged to the Nauvoo Relief Society except for two who joined the church later.[127] Phebe Woodruff and Elizabeth Ann Whitney left their parents and families of origin to join the Latter-day Saints.[128]

The hair wreath illustrated a distinct Relief Society hierarchy. With Eliza R. Snow at the head, Elizabeth Ann Whitney at the root, and other women branching out of each side, this collectivity of Relief Society women became an intermediary family—a sisterhood. The hierarchy is clear: Snow, who served as the secretary in Illinois and in Utah, stood as the head of the Relief Society. Whitney was second counselor in Nauvoo and first counselor in Utah. Jane S. Richards was the first stake Relief Society president in 1877. Margaret T. Smoot resigned from her post as president of the Salt Lake City Twentieth Ward Relief Society to move to Provo with her husband in 1872, where she later became stake Relief Society president in Utah County. Wilmirth East moved to southeastern Arizona with her family on a colonizing mission in 1877, where she served as president of the Gila Valley Stake Relief Society and the St. Joseph Stake Relief Society. Many of these women served as officiators in the temple, both in Nauvoo and in the Salt Lake City Endowment House before the temple there was completed. While

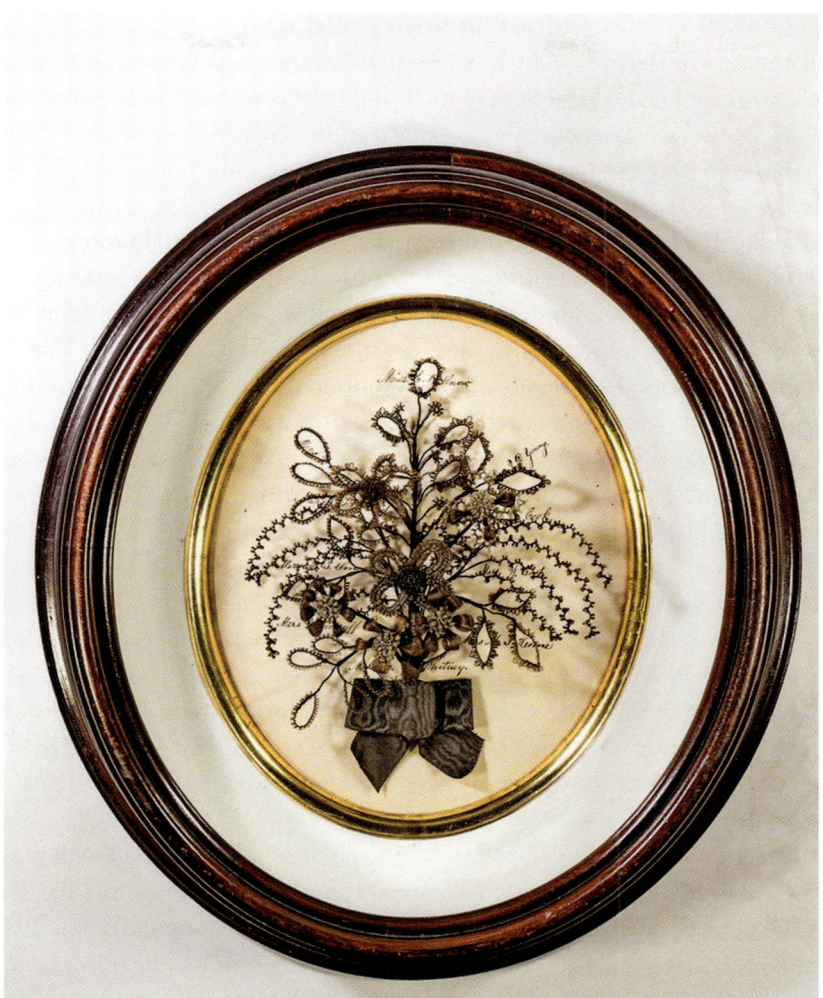

Fig. 6.8 Relief Society building hair wreath, ca. 1882. Church History Museum, Church of Jesus Christ of Latter-day Saints, Salt Lake City.

the women were geographically spread across the map, they were united in one place with their hair wreath, a literal representation of their sisterhood.

Although no longer displayed prominently, these hair wreaths illustrated a collectivity as individuals contributed their hair. The arrangement and original placement revealed a distinct Latter-day Saint identity, providing insight into social hierarchy and doctrine.

Relief Society Buildings

The construction of Relief Society halls, cooperative stores, and granaries instituted re-finement, albeit etched into the wilderness. This type of vernacular architecture designed specifically for women occurred throughout settlements in nineteenth-century Utah, Idaho, Wyoming, and Arizona. The brick, adobe, log, and stone buildings reflected their local environment as much as they insinuated general locations of permanence, legiti-macy, and sacred space coded for women. These buildings also allowed women to ex-press their gendered authority and business acumen within their communities.

Sarah M. Kimball, president of the Salt Lake City Fifteenth Ward Relief Society, came up with the idea to construct a separate building for the purposes of her women's organization in 1868. "The wheels of progress have been permitted to run until they have brought us to a more extended field of useful labor for female minds and hands," she proclaimed. Such a building would enable woman to "exercise all her God-given powers and faculties in the manner best calculated to strengthen, and develop, and per-fect her."[129] The design, funding, construction, and use of the hall were administered entirely by women.

An elaborate cornerstone ceremony was laid on November 13, 1868, endowing the women with a sense of legitimacy as a proper, socially accepted organization. They formed a procession and marched to the location, then gathered in precision around the foundation while Kimball ceremoniously laid the cornerstone.[130] She remarked: "A silver trowel and mallet were furnished me by a master mason, and surrounded by an as-semblage of people I had the honor of laying the corner stone of the first Relief Society building in this dispensation."[131]

The Fifteenth Ward's hall dedication in August 1869 was also filled with pomp and ceremony, adhering to classical tradition. A dedicatory hymn, penned by Eliza R. Snow, defined the performance and ritual associated with the hall as a petition for divine ap-proval and consecrating the edifice in the manner of a temple for the purpose of union, wisdom, welfare, instruction, and love:

> We dedicate this House to Thee,
>   As love and labor's bower;
> May Zion's welfare ever be
>   Its ruling motive power.
>
> And here may thought and speech be free
>   Instruction to impart,
> Commercially and financially—
>   In science and in art.[132]

The divine appeal covered intellectual, social, economic, and spiritual endowments for women's work and displayed a genteel society. Their female autonomy, supported by

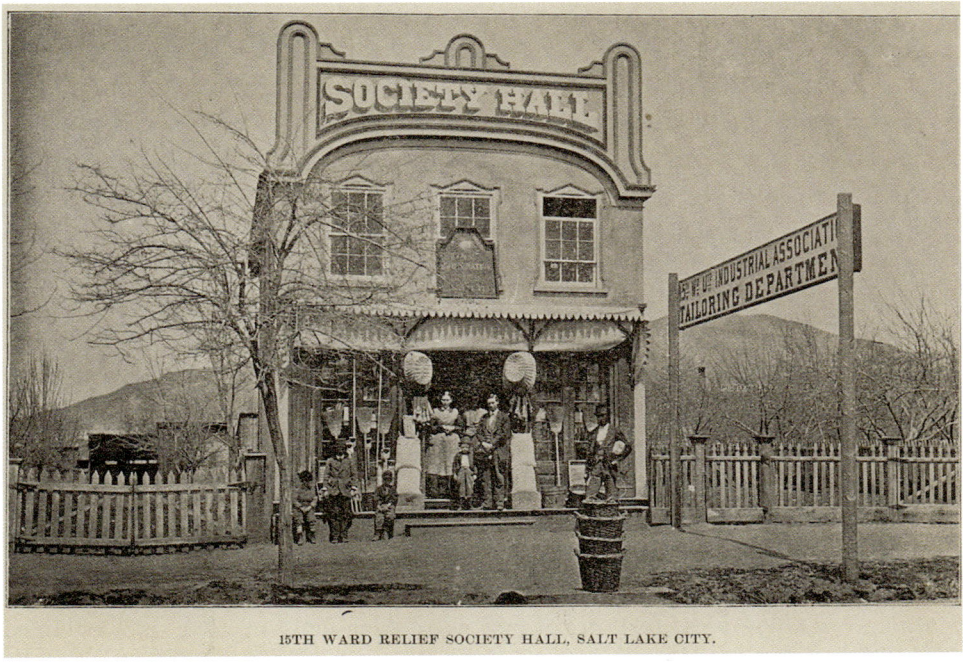

15TH WARD RELIEF SOCIETY HALL, SALT LAKE CITY.

Fig. 6.9 Salt Lake City 15th Ward Relief Society Hall, 1869. Church History Library, The Church of Jesus Christ of Latter-day Saints. Printed in Emmeline B. Wells, *Charities and Philanthropies: Women's Work in Utah*, p. 11.

priesthood leadership, allowed women to expand the breadth and depth of their organization through architecture.

Kimball designed the first Relief Society hall, utilizing the ground floor as the women's cooperative store, a close imitation of Joseph Smith's dry goods store in Nauvoo. Blueprints included plans for shelving, counters, doors, display cases, and proper ventilation.[133] Many other halls soon followed. The women acted in accordance with Brigham Young's promotion of home manufacture sold in cooperative retail stores. He encouraged women to work as bookkeepers, accountants, and storekeepers, and these stores gave them that opportunity.[134]

Soon, women's cooperative stores opened in Relief Society halls throughout the territory.[135] The Salt Lake City Fourteenth Ward Relief Society built their two-story brick building under the direction of president Mary Isabella Horne. She, like Kimball, had been a member of the original Nauvoo Relief Society.[136] Her hall also held a cooperative store on the first level and meeting rooms above. The Manti Relief Society constructed a two-story oolite building; the two rooms on the main level were used for a store and a millinery shop.[137] The Kaysville Relief Society constructed a hall that was unfortunately destroyed by wind.[138] When a second hall was built and dedicated in 1876, Daniel H. Wells, a member of the First Presidency, remarked, "The kingdom of God, like any other kingdom, requires space, territory, and people to be subjects of it." He added, "The accomplishment of these purposes requires determination, skill, application and perseverance. In carrying out some of these purposes women are indispensable."[139]

The success of local women's cooperative stores prompted the opening of a centralized Woman's Commission House in the Old Constitution Building in Salt Lake City in 1876, under the direction of the Relief Society.[140] Banners proudly proclaimed popular Latter-day Saint mottos, such as "Knowledge Is Power," "In Union Is Strength," and "Success to Industry." The banners, sewed in white lettering on a blue background, hung prominently next to an American flag, placing religion alongside national symbols.[141] The store's stock included local woven fabrics, shawls, socks, cuffs, clothing, hats, and domestic items.[142] These cooperative stores allowed women to utilize domestic folk art in a new entrepreneurial manner and to publicly display their work.

Relief Society buildings provided locations for work—handwork for charitable donations, storing grain, and producing silk. Women met for work meetings where quilts, rugs, and other homemade articles were made. Kimball hoped women would "encourage home manufacture, with habits of economy."[143] Young's 1876 assignment to Emmeline B. Wells to lead a grain storage program led women to other economic ventures, including research strategies and negotiating grain markets. They obtained wheat through donations, purchase, gleaning fields, and raising lots, and bought, sold, traded, and loaned their grain. Some groups constructed their own granaries, while others rented space.[144]

Again, Kimball's Fifteenth Ward Relief Society pioneered the movement. Shortly after Wells began her assignment, Kimball and her team met with their bishop to plan the construction of a granary, hoping to build a state-of-the-art facility. Kimball oversaw the completion of a "fireproof granary, built of rock with tin roof, brick floor underlaid with concrete, double door, inside nicely finished bin, that may be subdivided as circumstances require."[145] The Seventeenth Ward Relief Society built a more rustic structure, constructed on a solid rock foundation, capable of holding twelve hundred bushels of wheat.[146] Local Relief Society organizations also purchased lots for mulberry orchards to contribute to the sericulture mission. The Santa Clara Relief Society in southern Utah erected a two-story adobe structure with the upper room reserved for silkworms. The ground level included grain storage bins.[147]

A careful analysis of Relief Society halls demonstrates the way they changed over time. Initially, pioneer Utah architectural trends favored utilitarian design, drawing upon natural resources and community donations. In Thurber (now Bicknell), Wayne County, Utah, the women led the construction of their hall, but they found the finished product unappealing. They sent their husbands forty miles away to collect red mud to recast their red adobe bricks in imitation of the Nauvoo red brick store.[148] The Beaver Relief Society hall was made of local pink stone or tuff found in a quarry about four miles east of town. The soft rock allowed masons to display tooling on the facade. It was a fine juxtaposition to other buildings built of local black lava rock, elevating the settlement to a full-fledged town.[149]

After their tenuous arrival in the Utah Territory and the effort to build up functioning settlements, attention turned to fine detail. Building design shifted from utilitarian to more popular patterns of Greek Revival—with additions to the typically symmetrical, low-gabled rectangular buildings, adding such characteristics as molded cornices—and High Victorian styles. The Relief Society hall in Washington, southern Utah, completed in 1875, was built on a black lava rock foundation laid in clay sand mortar, standard materials in the southern Utah desert, then constructed of adobe with added architectural elements such as molded cornices.[150] The Torrey Relief Society hall-meetinghouse-school was constructed of logs in the Greek Revival style, utilizing local material to present popular classical architecture. Over each of the symmetric windows is a hybrid lintel-pedimented head. A square bell tower covered with planks and a truncated hip roof with flared eaves on the tall, steeply pitched hip roof, crowns the rustic building.[151] Such classical architectural elements insinuated permanence and an aura of authority in a polite society.[152]

Later Relief Society halls incorporated contemporary High Victorian architectural details. The inclusion of medieval elements followed national trends during the second half of the nineteenth century, embracing Romantic, Gothic, and Romanesque revival components.[153] The Weber Stake Relief Society hall presents an excellent example of Victorian Gothic architecture with its prominent steeply pitched gable roof and three point-arched windows in the principal facade, highlighted with low-relief brick arches.[154] The Relief Society hall built in Deseret, Millard County, included a gabled roof, cornice returns, Queen Anne detailing, lathe-turned columns with spindled brackets, and a transom over the door.[155] The Santa Clara Relief Society hall in Washington County included a unique masonry false front with a rounded top to conceal the gable.[156] Such rich details were certainly not a part of Sarah Kimball's initial vision of a utilitarian building, though she did name her 1869 Fifteenth Ward Relief Society hall not just a "temple" (a place of salvific work: charity, service, blessings of healing) but also a place of work (sewing, collecting donations, learning obstetrics).[157] Rather, these elaborate architectural details could turn a small, newly settled town on the edge of the frontier into an upscale mini urban center simply by using contemporary architectural style.

Additionally, the construction of serviceable Relief Society halls and granaries instilled a sense of pride. Emmeline B. Wells described the Brigham City Relief Society granary as the best in the territory, "and is such a large and substantial structure that it is a source of laudable pride to the women of the society everywhere."[158] Wells described the hall as a "creditable building," indicating community value and prestige.[159] She also characterized the Gunnison Relief Society hall as "a good illustration of the executive ability women have shown who have managed the various practical enterprizes that ha[ve] made this great organization such a success financially."[160] These women were revolutionary in their business acumen, community building, and artistry.

Relief Society buildings exhibited the expansion of settlements with Old Country skills. When the Beaver East Ward constructed their building, they called upon the Beeson family, who had been British brick masons. The Beesons added architectural details including a gable facing the street in the main facade, point-arched windows and door, stained white mortar joints with Flemish bond, and raised bead, all common British techniques.[161]

The construction of Relief Society halls continued throughout and beyond the Wasatch Front into the early twentieth century. By then, however, buildings and granaries had fallen into disrepair, and the church encouraged combining all organizations under one roof. Some of these Relief Society buildings became schools, post offices, cultural centers, or storehouses. When their original uses were no longer needed, women lost an opportunity to realize the larger goals of combining utility with refinement and ingenuity with agency.

CONCLUSION

While Patty Sessions's stitched bookmark sits in a small historical museum, none of Lucy Mack Smith's oilcloth coverings exist. Many Relief Society halls have been reduced, repurposed, or built over. Hair art has certainly lost its popularity in the twenty-first century and now sits on museum walls or in storage. Quilts are folded up in family trunks or in museum exhibit cases. However, nineteenth-century samplers, quilts, hair art, and Relief Society buildings all played a significant part in the development of Latter-day Saint art. They created community and celebrated individualism, displayed refinement, and utilized resourcefulness. For some, they are material relics when no texts remain. For others, they illustrate a global effort to build a Zion in the Intermountain West. These extraordinary material artifacts tell a story of time, effort, culture, and theology, of family shapes and sizes, and of life on the rugged frontier in the development of Mormonism. Each piece helps us to *remember*.

NOTES

[1] Wooster Beach, *The Family Physician: Being the Scientific System of Medicine* (New York: James McAlister, 1847).

[2] The artifact is owned by the Syracuse Regional Museum in Syracuse, Utah. Thanks to Patty Sessions Hartley, a descendant, who helped me locate it.

[3] Lucy Mack Smith, *History, 1944–1845,* book 3, 7, Church History Library.

[4] Kimberly Reid, "Mary Whitmer and Maria Louise Cowdery Samplers," September 7, 2018, https://history.churchofjesuschrist.org/content/museum/mary-whitmer-and-maria-louise-cowdery-samplers?lang=eng.

[5] See Jennifer Reeder, *First: The Life and Faith of Emma Smith* (Salt Lake City: Deseret Book, 2021), 105.

[6] Nauvoo Relief Society Minutes (1842–1844), March 17, 1842, 12, Church History Library.

7 See Henry Glassie, *The Spirit of Folk Art*, (New York: Harry N. Abrams, 1989), 7, 36, 197. Curator Richard Miller maintains that folk art "strengthens our awareness of the connections that bind us." Richard Miller, "A Distinction with a Difference: The Art of American Folk Art," in Barbara L. Gordon et al., *A Shared Legacy: Folk Art in America* (New York: Skira Rizzoli, 2014), 29.

8 Miller, "A Distinction with a Difference"; Glassie, *The Spirit of Folk Art*, 81, 53; Cynthia G. Falk and Lisa Minardy, "Pennsylvania, German, and Beyond," in Barbara L. Gordon et al., *A Shared Legacy: Folk Art in America* (New York: Skira Rizzoli, 2014).

9 Richard L. Bushman, *The Refinement of America: Persons, Houses, Cities* (New York: Vintage Books, 1993). See also Richard Lyman Bushman, "Was Joseph Smith a Gentleman? The Standards for Refinement in Utah," in *Nearly Everything Imaginable: The Everyday Life of Utah's Mormon Pioneers*, ed. Ronald W. Walker and Doris R. Dant (Provo, UT: Brigham Young University, BYU Studies and Joseph Fielding Smith Institute for Latter-day Saint History, 1999), 28–29;.

10 Glassie, *The Spirit of Folk Art*, 36, 192, 197; Laurel Thatcher Ulrich, Ivan Gaskell, Sara J. Schechner, and Sarah Anne Carter, *Tangible Things: Making History Through Objects* (New York: Oxford University Press, 2015), 3, 14, 163

11 Lynn K. Rogerson, "Acknowledgments," in Barbara L. Gordon et al., *A Shared Legacy: Folk Art in America* (New York: Skira Rizzoli, 2014), 6; Larkin, *Where We Lived*, 5; Falk and Minardy, "Pennsylvania, German, and Beyond."

12 Sidney Rigdon, "The Saints and the World," *Latter Day Saints' Messenger and Advocate* 3, no. 21 (December 1836): 421–422.

13 Joseph Smith, "Church History," *Times and Seasons* 3, no. 9 (March 1, 1842): 709.

14 See Isaiah 35:1; Leonard J. Arrington, "The Economic Role of Pioneer Mormon Women," *Western Humanities Review* 9 (Spring 1955): 152.

15 Bushman, "Was Joseph Smith a Gentleman," 29, 34.

16 Tom Carter, "Folk Design in Utah Architecture," in *Utah Folk Art: A Catalog of Material Culture*, ed. Hal Cannon (Provo, UT: Brigham Young University Press, 1980).

17 See Falk and Minardy, "Pennsylvania, German, and Beyond"; Larkin, *Where We Lived*, 226; Richard G. Oman, "The Homemade Kingdom: Mormon Regional Furniture," in *Nearly Everything Imaginable: The Everyday Life of Utah's Mormon Pioneers*, ed. Ronald W. Walker and Doris R. Dant (Provo, UT: Brigham Young University, BYU Studies and Joseph Fielding Smith Institute for Latter-day Saint History, 1999), 159–160.

18 See Richard Oman and Susan Oman, "Mormon Iconography," in *Utah Folk Art: A Catalog of Material Culture*, ed. Hal Cannon (Provo, UT: Brigham Young University Press, 1980); Richard H. Jackson, "Mormon Cemeteries in Stone," in *Nearly Everything Imaginable: The Everyday Life of Utah's Mormon Pioneers*, ed. Ronald W. Walker and Doris R. Dant (Provo, UT: Brigham Young University, BYU Studies and Joseph Fielding Smith Institute for Latter-day Saint History, 1999), 405.

19 Richard C. Poulsen, *The Pure Experience of Order: Essays on the Symbolic in the Folk Material Culture of Western America* (Albuquerque: University of New Mexico Press, 1982), 47; see Glassie, *The Spirit of Folk Art*, 128–129.

20 Hal Cannon, ed., *Utah Folk Art: A Catalog of Material Culture* (Provo, UT: Brigham Young University Press, 1980).

21 "Discourse by President Brigham Young," May 3, 1874, reprinted in *Deseret Evening News*, May 5, 1874.

22 "The Epistle of the First Presidency to the Church of Jesus Christ of Latter-day Saints in General Conference Assembled," *Millennial Star* 48, no. 21 (May 24, 1886): 321.

23 See Nancy Richards, "Craft," in *Utah Folk Art: A Catalog of Material Culture*, ed. Hal Cannon (Provo, UT: Brigham Young University Press, 1980).

24 See Leonard J. Arrington, Feramorz Y. Fox, and Dean L. May, *Building the City of God: Community and Cooperation Among the Mormons* (Salt Lake City: Deseret Book, 1976).

25 Oman, "The Homemade Kingdom," 163.

26 Marilyn Conover Barker, *The Legacy of Mormon Furniture: The Mormon Material Culture, Undergirded by Faith, Commitment, and Craftsmanship* (Salt Lake City: Gibbs-Smith, 1995), 11–12.

27 Oman, "The Homemade Kingdom," 157, 159.

28 Avis Berman, "Uncommon Women and the Art of the Common Man: The Role of Women in the Discovery, Promotion, and Collection of American Folk Art," in Barbara L. Gordon et al., *A Shared Legacy: Folk Art in America* (New York: Skira Rizzoli, 2014).

29 Eliza R. Snow, "Sketch of My Life," *Relief Society Magazine* 31, no. 3 (March 1944): 132.

30 Snow's wool blanket is now in the International Daughters of Utah Pioneers Memorial Museum in Salt Lake City. See "A Relic Tells Its Story: Eliza Roxcy Snow," in *Our Pioneer Heritage,* ed. Kate B. Carter (Salt Lake City: Daughters of Utah Pioneers, 1958–1977), 8:133. See also Jennifer Reeder, "'A Woman of Property': Eliza R. Snow and Her Handiwork," presentation, Mormon History Association, Provo, Utah, 2006.

31 See, for example, Nauvoo Relief Society, March 17, 1842, 12; April 19, 1842, 33; July 7, 1843, 94, Church History Library.

32 Andrew H. Hedges, "Battle on the Homefront: The Early Pioneer Act of Homemaking," in *Nearly Everything Imaginable: The Everyday Life of Utah's Mormon Pioneers,* ed. Ronald W. Walker and Doris R. Dant (Provo, UT: Brigham Young University, BYU Studies and Joseph Fielding Smith Institute for Latter-day Saint History, 1999), 120.

33 Avis Berman, "Uncommon Women and the Art of the Common Man: The Role of Women in the Discovery, Promotion, and Collecting of American Folk Art," in Barbara L. Gordon et al., *A Shared Legacy: Folk Art in America* (New York: Skira Rizzoli, 2014).

34 Laurel Thatcher Ulrich, *The Age of Homespun: Objects and Stories in the Creation of an American Myth* (New York: Random House, 2001), 111.

35 Patty Sessions recorded making a comforter as she visited sick women. *Mormon Midwife: The 1846–1888 Diaries of Patty Bartlett Sessions,* ed. Donna Toland Smart (Logan: Utah State University, 1997), March 22–24, 1847, 76. See also Eliza R. Snow, trail diary, in *The Personal Writings of Eliza Roxcy Snow,* ed. Maureen Ursenbach Beecher (Salt Lake City: University of Utah Press, 1995), April 22, 1847, 166; June 1, 1847, 176; September 24, 1847, 202; October 7–16, 1847, 206–207; October 28, 1847, 210; November 1, 1847, 211; November 13, 1847, 212.

36 See Judy Elsley, *Quilts as Text(iles): The Semiotics of Quilting* (New York: Peter Lang, 1996), 1.

37 The album quilt pattern originated in Baltimore, Maryland, in 1820. Its popularity spread throughout the United States, culminating in the 1870s. See John Rice Irwin, *A People and Their Quilts* (West Chester, PA: Schiffer, 1984), 52; Pat Ferrero, Elaine Hedges, and Julie Silber, *Hearts and Hands: The Influence of Women and Quilts on American Society* (San Francisco: Quilt Digest Press, 1987), 64; Linda Otto Lipsett, *Remember Me: Women and Their Friendship Quilts* (San Francisco: Quilt Digest Press, 1985), 19.

38 The quilt was raffled to raise money. The winner then cut the quilt apart diagonally to give to two descendants. Laurel Thatcher Ulrich, "An American Album, 1857," *American Historical Review* 115, no. 1 (Feb. 2010): 1–25; Carol Holindrake Nielson, *The Salt Lake City 14th Ward Album Quilt, 1857: Stories of the Relief Society Women and Their Quilt* (Salt Lake City: University of Utah Press, 2004).

39 See Richard G. Oman, "Quilting Sisters," *BYU Studies* 33, no. 1 (1993): 146–147.

40 The white cashmere with blue cashmere lining highlighted in embroidery the name of the apostle who organized the stake and the name of the stake presidency in the center of the quilt. Names of the original officers and dates of stake Relief Society organizations were embroidered in smaller ovals around the edge. "Pioneer Quilts," in *Our Pioneer Heritage* (Salt Lake City: Daughters of Utah Pioneers, 1958–1977), 18:78.

41 "Pioneer Quilts," 64. In the 1820s, American missionary wives taught Hawaiian women how to make patchwork quilts. Tradition states that Louisa Barnes Pratt, a Latter-day Saint missionary serving with her family in Tubuai, French Polynesia, taught women there to quilt. Hawaiian women later adapted the practice to highlight their native culture, using two solid colors—a background and an appliquéd symmetrical design representing Hawaiian nature motifs. See also Poakalani Serrraro, John Serraro, Radene Correia, and Cissy Serraro, *The Hawaiian Quilt: The Tradition Continues* (Honolulu: Mutual Publishing, 2007); Richard Romney, "Polynesian Pearls," *Liahona,* October 2005.

42 This quilt is owned by the International Daughters of Utah Pioneers Museum in Salt Lake City, Utah, donated by Polly Jones Smith, wife of Smoot's son William Cochran Adkinson Smoot, in 1924. "Pioneer Quilts," 71.

[43] This was a common practice to memorialize friendships. Patricia Cox Crews, *A Flowering of Quilts* (Lincoln: University of Nebraska Press, 2001), 36.

[44] A description of the quilt and who made each block is found in a contemporary biography of Smoot. Olive Smoot Bean, "Biographical Sketch of Margaret T. Smoot," Abraham O. Smoot papers, L. Tom Perry Special Collections, Harold B. Lee Library, Brigham Young University, Provo, UT.

[45] Matthew 6:28; Luke 12:27.

[46] 1 Corinthians 13:1. At the opening meeting of the Nauvoo Relief Society, Joseph Smith encouraged the women in "searching after objects of charity, and in administering to their wants." Nauvoo Relief Society minutes, March 17, 1842, 7. Smith taught specifically about this verse on April 28, 1842, 29, Church History Library.

[47] 1 Corinthians 13:13; Ether 12:28; Alma 7:24; Moroni 7:1; D&C 4:5; 6:19.

[48] According to familysearch.org, Priscilla Paul was born January 6, 1868, and died January 23, 1868; twins Edmund Young Paul and Sarah Irvin Paul were born March 22, 1869, and Edmund died on March 24 and Sarah on May 25 of that year. Her son Frank Orson Paul was born on September 16, 1870, just after this quilt was completed.

[49] 1 John 4:16–18.

[50] Psalms 143:5.

[51] Eliza R. Snow quoted Isaiah 11:9, "Thou shalt not hurt nor destroy in all my holy mountain." Lisadore Williams quilted from Revelation 14:2, "I heard the voice of harpers harping with their harps," while her sister Eliza M. Williams included Proverbs 20:15, "There is gold, and a multitude of rubies."

[52] Twentieth Ward, Relief Society Minutes, May 7, 1868, Church History Library. See Susanna Morrill, "The Mother in Heaven and Eve: Models of Femaleness in Early Mormonism," presented at the Marty Center Religion and Culture Web Forum, University of Chicago Divinity School, 2004, 14–18.

[53] See Ricky Clark, *Quilts of the Ohio Western Reserve* (Athens: Ohio University Press, 2005), 14.

[54] "Quilts have become the romanticized embodiment of domestic comfort and warmth, a symbol of familial security." Jack R. Lindsey, "Nineteenth-Century Applique Quilts," *Bulletin: Philadelphia Museum of Art* 85, no. 363–364 (Fall 1989): 38–39; see also Pat Ferrero, Linda Reuther, and Julie Silber, "A Legacy of Hearts and Hands," in *American Quilts: A Handmade Legacy*, ed. L. Thomas Frye (Oakland, CA: Oakland Museum, 1981), 27.

[55] John Hugh McNaughton wrote "Love at Home" in 1866, with the message that home makes life more beautiful and satisfying. Karen Lynn Davidson, *Our Latter-day Hymns: The Stories and the Messages* (Salt Lake City: Deseret Book, 1988), 279.

[56] Dorothy P. Blanpied, "The Necklace of Elizabeth Sansom Barnes," in *An Enduring Legacy* 12 (1989): 291–292.

[57] The child was Zina Prescendia Paul.

[58] Eliza M. Williams and Lisadore Williams were sisters. Matilda Brain was the daughter of Mary A. Brain. Jane T. Lynch was the daughter of Mary Lynch. Margaret Sharp was the daughter of Jane S. P. Sharp. Harriet Lewis was the daughter of Mary Ann Squire Lewis. Lovina Luff was the daughter-in-law of Mary Luff. Mary Ann Lewis's sister-in-law was Mary Ann Lewis Sansom. Ann Paul and Martha Paul married brothers.

[59] Dunford was the daughter of Snow's brother Lorenzo Snow and Sarah Ann Pritchard; Paul was the daughter of Young's brother Dimick Huntington and Fannie Maria Allen.

[60] "Great Indignation Meeting of the Ladies of Salt Lake City, to Protest Against the Passage of Cullom's Bill," *Deseret Evening News*, Jan. 14 and 15, 1870.

[61] Olive Smoot Bean, "Biographical Sketch of Margaret T. Smoot," Abraham O. Smoot papers, L. Tom Perry Special Collections, Harold B. Lee Library, Brigham Young University, Provo, UT.

[62] Bean, "Biographical Sketch."

[63] Mary Bywater Cross, "The Anti-Polygamy Quilt by the Ogden Methodist Quilting Bee," *Uncoverings* 24 (2003): 17–48.

[64] The anti-polygamy Edmunds Act of 1882 prevented polygamists from serving on juries to protect each other and removed the burden of proof. Punishment by imprisonment was promised to all men guilty of

unlawful cohabitation. Sarah B. Gordon, *The Mormon Question: Polygamy and Constitutional Conflict in Nineteenth-Century America* (Chapel Hill: University of North Carolina Press, 2002), 151–153.

[65] Twentieth Ward, Relief Society Minutes, April 22, 1868, Church History Library.

[66] See D&C 42:40. Wilford Woodruff quoted Brigham Young with this phrase on October 8, 1875; *Journal of Discourses*, 18:129. See also D&C 42:40.

[67] Bean, "Biographical Sketch."

[68] Leonard J. Arrington, *Great Basin Kingdom: An Economic History of the Latter-day Saints, 1830–1900* (Urbana: University of Illinois Press, 2005), 254.

[69] As early as 1855, when cotton and flax proved difficult to produce in the arid western climate, Brigham Young assigned Latter-day Saint missionaries in France to return to Utah with mulberry trees and silkworms. By 1866, the settlers grew trees throughout the territory. Chris Rigby Arrington, "The Finest Fabrics: Mormon Women and the Silk Industry in Early Utah," *Utah Historical Quarterly* 46, no. 4 (Fall 1978): 377–378.

[70] Bushman, *The Refinement of America*, xii.

[71] Jill Mulvay Derr, "'I Have Eaten Nearly Everything Imaginable': Pioneer Diet," in *Nearly Everything Imaginable: The Everyday Life of Utah's Mormon Pioneers*, ed. Ronald W. Walker and Doris R. Dant (Provo, UT: Brigham Young University, BYU Studies and Joseph Fielding Smith Institute for Latter-day Saint History, 1999), 228–230. Ellen Parker embroidered a similar design of leaves and red strawberries studded with tiny yellow seeds in the 1857 Fourteenth Ward quilt. Carol Holindrake Nielson, *The Salt Lake City 14th Ward Album Quilt, 1857* (Salt Lake City: University of Utah Press, 2004), 134.

[72] According to Olive Smoot, Margaret Smoot's niece and biographer, the "bright red strawberries and green leaves look[ed] natural enough to almost tempt one to taste." Bean, "Biographical Sketch."

[73] Crews, *A Flowering of Quilts*, 58. The Bunting family helped settle Kanab in southern Utah, colonized in part to produce grapes. Harriet Dye Bunting, "Charity Never Faileth," in *Heart Throbs of the West*, ed. Kate B. Carter (Salt Lake City: Daughters of Utah Pioneers, 1939), 3:157.

[74] Derr, "I Have Eaten Nearly Everything Imaginable,'" 235.

[75] Crews, *A Flowering of Quilts*, 48.

[76] On July 24, 1867, Eliza R. Snow dedicated a poem to Margaret T. Smoot, "Twenty Years Ago," describing Utah's desert landscape and the efforts of the early pioneers to create a fertile atmosphere. *Eliza R. Snow: The Complete Poetry*, ed. Jill Mulvay Derr and Karen Lynn Davidson (Provo, UT: Brigham Young University Press, 2009), 756–758.

[77] Susan Curtis, "Blessed Be God for Flowers: Nineteenth-Century Quilt Design," in Crews, *A Flowering of Quilts*, 11.

[78] Matthew 6:28 and Luke 12:27.

[79] Flowers were used as symbols in the Bible, art, and Shakespeare but became a trend among women in the nineteenth century. Sarah Josepha Hale, editor of the *Ladies' Magazine* and co-editor of *Godey's Lady's Book*, ran articles about flower symbolism in the United States from 1832 through the 1860s. See also Jessica Roux, *Floriography: An Illustrated Guide to the Victorian Language of Flowers* (Kansas City, MO: Andrew McMeel, 2020)

[80] Snow stitched "And there shall be nothing to hurt or destroy in all my holy mountain, saith the Lord" (Isaiah 11:19).

[81] Baskets were often featured in nineteenth-century quilts, reflecting a popular garden trend in the 1830s and 1840s. Crews, *A Flowering of Quilts*, 106–107.

[82] Revelation 14:2.

[83] Oman, "Quilting Sisters," 146.

[84] See Laurel B. Andrew, *The Early Temples of the Mormons: The Architecture of the Millennial Kingdom in the American West* (Albany: State University of New York Press, 1978), 121.

[85] The beehive originated as an Egyptian symbol of obedient people and later was adopted by the Freemasons. E. Cecil McGavin, *Mormonism and Masonry* (Salt Lake City: Stevens and Wallis, 1947), 61. A. Hoagland, Mary C. Taylor, and Elizabeth C. Taylor also embroidered small versions of beehives in

their quilt blocks. Phebe Woodruff included a beehive in her block in the 1857 Fourteenth Ward quilt. See Nielson, *The Salt Lake City 14th Ward Album Quilt*, 39, 108–116.

[86] For example, Susan Price Miller examined the blocks of the 1867 Circuit Rider's Quilt. Through genealogical research and examination of land ownership maps in Miami County, Ohio, she determined the interlinking of family members and neighbors for each name on each quilt block. The concentration of names and fabrics suggests that "the women in a family coordinated their design and construction activities, whether intentionally or by default." Susan Price Miller, "The Circuit Rider's Quilt: Reality and Romance," *Uncoverings* 29 (2008): 19.

[87] The first eighteen wards in Salt Lake City were divided geographically upon arrival. When later arrivals expanded neighborhoods and wards, the Nineteenth and Twentieth Wards were created with more recent converts and immigrants. Orson F. Whitney, *History of Utah, Comprising Preliminary Chapters on the Previous History of Her Founders, Accounts of Early Spanish and American Explorations in the Rocky Mountain Region, the Advent of the Mormon Pioneers, the Establishment and Dissolution of the Provisional Government of the State of Deseret, and the Subsequent Creation of the Territory of Utah* (Salt Lake City: George Q. Cannon, 1892), 4:205; Andrew Jenson, *Encyclopedic History of the Church of Jesus Christ of Latter-day Saints* (Salt Lake City: Deseret News, 1941), 753–754; Andrew Jensen, "Church Encyclopedia," *The Historical Record: A Monthly Periodical* 6, nos. 9–12 (December 1887): 329.

[88] See Gloria Seaman Allen and Nancy Gibson Tuckhorn, *A Maryland Album: Quiltmaking Traditions, 1634–1934* (Nashville, TN: Rutledge Hill Press, 1995); Gordon, *The Mormon Question*.

[89] One biographer described her: "With faith, confidence, and the will to do, she successfully operated, amputated, set broken bones, and cured the common ailments of that period. She delivered over three hundred fifty babies without losing a case." Melissa Ramsay Cluff, "Set Apart," in *Our Pioneer Heritage* (Salt Lake City: Daughters of Utah Pioneers, 1958–1977), 2:103.

[90] Laura P. Angell King, "Pioneer Quilts," in *Heart Throbs of the West,* ed. Kate B. Carter (Salt Lake City: Daughters of Utah Pioneers, 1939), 2:485.

[91] The reference to a British naval ditty expressed a deep British loyalty to the oak tree used to build ships. Tim Richardson, "Hearts of Oak Forever," *The Telegraph*, February 28, 2009, telegraph.co.uk/earth/countryside/4863957/Hearts-of-oak-for-ever.html.

[92] Andrew Jensen, *Latter-day Saint Biographical Encyclopedia* (Salt Lake City: Andrew Jensen, 1901), 1:485.

[93] Twentieth Ward Relief Society Minutes, May 22, 1868, Church History Library.

[94] Samuel Woodward, "Man and Woman," *Ladies' Literary Cabinet* 1, no. 17 (September 4, 1819): 136. The poem was reprinted several times in various publications throughout the first half of the nineteenth century.

[95] Bean, "Biographical Sketch."

[96] See Rachel McBride Lindsey, *A Communion of Shadows: Religion* and *Photography in Nineteenth-Century America* (Chapel Hill: University of North Carolina Press, 2017), 1–8.

[97] See Martha A. Sandweiss, *Print the Legend: Photography and the American West* (New Haven, CT: Yale University Press, 2002), 3–4.

[98] Ruth Gordon, "Victorian Hairwork," *Piecework* 4, no. 2 (April 1996): 36; Mlle. Defour, "Hair Work, No. 1," *Peterson's Magazine,* November 1850.

[99] Frances Lichten, *Decorative Art of Victoria's Era* (New York: Charles Scribner, 1950), 192.

[100] Irene Guggenheim Navarro, "Hairwork of the Nineteenth Century," *Antiques* 159, no. 3 (March 2001): 489; Stuart Blersch, "Victorian Jewelry Made of Hair," *Nineteenth Century* 6, no. 1 (Spring 1980): 43.

[101] Lichten, *Decorative Art*, 192; Helen Sheumaker, *Love Entwined: The Curious History of Hairwork in America* (Philadelphia: University of Pennsylvania Press, 2007), 1–15.

[102] These types of hair wreaths tended to be more popular in America than in Europe. Navarro, "Hairwork of the Nineteenth Century," 490. See also Allison Kyle Leopold, "The Lost Art of Victorian Hair Work: What It Meant to Nineteenth-Century Americans Then . . . What We Think of It Today," *Victorian Homes* 7, no. 1 (Winter 1988): 86.

[103] Leopold, "The Lost Art of Victorian Hair Work," 69; Navarro, "Hairwork of the Nineteenth Century," 485.

[104] Gordon, "Victorian Hairwork," 38.

[105] Deborah Lutz, *Relics in Victorian Literature and Culture* (Cambridge: Cambridge University Press, 2015), 1, 9; Geoffrey Batchen, *Forget Me Not: Photography and Remembrance* (New York: Princeton Architectural Press, 2004), 65.

[106] Sheumaker, *Love Entwined*, 27.

[107] Jane Wilkie Hooper Blood, *Jane Wilkie Hooper Blood Autobiography and Abridged Diary*, ed. Ivy Hooper Blood Hill (Logan, UT: J. P. Smith, 1965), 35.

[108] Bean, "Biographical Sketch," 26.

[109] Alice Pearson, "R.S., Y.L.M.I.A., and P.A. Reports: Logan Primary Conference," *Woman's Exponent* 14, no. 14 (December 15, 1885): 110.

[110] M. A. Greenhalgh, "Y.L.M.I.A. Fair," *Woman's Exponent* 15, no. 7 (September 1, 1886): 54.

[111] Scheumaker, *Love Entwined*, 77.

[112] Josh E. Probert, "Mormon Hair Art as Relic," Mormon History Association, 2008, in author's possession, 3.

[113] On October 20, 1887, Wilford Woodruff requested contributions to complete the temple. Wilford Woodruff, "An Address from President Wilford Woodruff," *Woman's Exponent* 16, no. 11 (November 1, 1887): 84.

[114] This hair wreath is held by the Church History Museum.

[115] Mark Staker, "'By Their Works Ye Shall Know Them': The World View Expressed in Mormon Folk Art," *BYU Studies* 35, no. 3 (1995–1996): 84.

[116] Gordon, "Victorian Hairwork," 38.

[117] Bernt G. Lundgren, "Janne Mattson Sjödhal—Baptist Minister, Convert to Mormonism, Editor, Author and Missionary" (MA thesis, Brigham Young University, 1971), 19.

[118] "Museum Artifacts," in *An Enduring Legacy* 3 (1980): 338.

[119] Marcia Pointon, "These Fragments I Have Shored Against My Ruins," in *The Story of Time*, ed. Kristen Lippincott (London: Merrell Holberton and National Maritime Museum, 1999), 200.

[120] Staker, "By Their Works," 83. The piece is now owned by the International Daughters of Utah Pioneers Memorial Museum in Salt Lake City.

[121] See Lawrence Taylor, "Symbolic Death: An Anthropological View of Mourning Ritual in the Nineteenth Century," in *A Time to Mourn: Expressions of Grief in Nineteenth Century America*, ed. Martha V. Pike and Janice Gray Armstrong (Stony Brook, NY: Museums at Stony Brook, 1980), 43.

[122] Lorenzo Snow, Franklin D. Richards, George Q. Cannon, Joseph F. Smith, George A. Smith, Moses Thatcher, Francis M. Lyman, John Henry Smith, George Teasdale, Heber J. Grant, Marriner W. Merrill, and Abraham H. Cannon. Snow, Joseph F. Smith, and Grant would later serve as presidents.

[123] See Alison Landsberg, *Prosthetic Memory: The Transformation of American Remembrance in the Age of Mass Culture* (New York: Columbia University Press, 2004), 2–8.

[124] This piece belongs to the general Relief Society in Salt Lake City. This piece also poses some interesting questions. Because there is no provenance attached to the piece, the reason for and date of its creation are speculative, but it was likely sometime between the late 1860s and 1877.

[125] Nauvoo Relief Society Minutes, April 28, 1842, Church History Library.

[126] Elizabeth Ann Whitney, "A Leaf from an Autobiography," *Woman's Exponent* 7, no. 12 (November 15, 1878): 91.

[127] Mary E. Cook came to Utah in the late 1860s and became the Salt Lake County superintendent of schools, then served as the secretary of the general Young Ladies' Mutual Improvement Association from 1889 to 1891. Susa Young Gates, *History of the Young Ladies' Mutual Improvement Association of the Church of Jesus Christ of Latter-day Saints from November 1869 to June 1910* (Salt Lake City: Deseret News, 1911), 128. Wilmirth East moved to Utah in 1855 from Texas. The East family moved to Arizona in 1877. Maureen Beecher considered East as a member of the second echelon of leading women based on her relationship with women in the "inner core." Maureen Ursenbach Beecher, "The 'Leading Sisters': A Female Hierarchy in Nineteenth-Century Mormon Society," *Journal of Mormon History* 9 (1982): 19–41.

[128] Emmeline B. Wells, "In Memoriam," *Woman's Exponent* 14, no. 12 (November 15, 1885): 92; Emmeline B. Wells, "In Memoriam: Elizabeth Ann Whitney," *Woman's Exponent* 10, no. 18 (15 Feb. 1882): 140.

[129] Sarah M. Kimball, "Salt Lake City, 13th November 1868," *Woman's Exponent* 14, no. 2 (June 15, 1885): 14.

[130] Fifteenth Ward Relief Society, November 12, 1868, Church History Library.

[131] The Nauvoo Relief Society also met in a location considered a Masonic hall. Emmeline B. Wells, "A Grand and Noble Woman," *Deseret News*, December 10, 1893, 13; Sarah M. Kimball, Relief Society Record (1880–1882), 30, 82, Church History Library. See also Kimball, "Salt Lake City," 14–15.

[132] Eliza R. Snow, "The Relief Society," Eliza R. Snow papers, Special Collections, Western Americana, J. Willard Marriott Library, Salt Lake City, August 5, 1869. See also Snow, *The Complete Poetry*, 795–796.

[133] Salt Lake City Fifteenth Ward, Salt Lake Stake, Relief Society Minutes, vol. 2 (1869–1875), Church History Library.

[134] Brigham Young preached, "The ladies can learn to keep books as well as the men; we have some few, already, who are just as good accountants as any of our brethren. Why not teach more to keep books and sell goods, and let them do this business, . . . and do something or other to beautify the earth and help to make it like the Garden of Eden?" Brigham Young, "Remarks," *Deseret News,* May 26, 1869, 7.

[135] Ronald S. Hanson, *The Relief Society: Its Meeting Halls, Granaries, Cooperative Stores and Its Impact on Nineteenth Century Utah* (North Salt Lake City, UT: DMT, 2007), 46.

[136] Mary Isabella Horne joined the Nauvoo Relief Society on June 9, 1842. Nauvoo Relief Society Minutes, June 9, 1842, 64, Church History Library.

[137] "Miscellaneous News Items," in *An Enduring Legacy* 3 (1980): 5; "Ladies Co-op Stores," in *Our Pioneer Heritage* (Salt Lake City: Daughters of Utah Pioneers, 1958–1977), 12:154.

[138] *Kaysville Historic Tour* (Kaysville, UT: Kaysville City, n.d.), 2.

[139] "Report of the Dedication of the Kaysville Relief Society House, Nov. 12, 1876," *Woman's Exponent* 5, no. 19 (March 1, 1877): 149.

[140] "Woman's Commission House," *Woman's Exponent* 5, no. 12 (November 15, 1876): 92.

[141] Mrs. Frank Leslie, *California: A Pleasure Trip from Gotham to the Golden Gate (April, May, June, 1877)* (New York: Carlton Press, 1877), 78–79.

[142] "Woman's Commission House."

[143] "Relief Society Annual Message," 1873, 2–3, Fifteenth Ward, Salt Lake Stake, Relief Society, Church History Library.

[144] See Jessie L. Embry, "Relief Society Grain Storage Program 1876–1940" (master's thesis, Brigham Young University, 1974), 13.

[145] Fifteenth Ward Relief Society Minutes and Records, November 23, 1876, Church History Library.

[146] "Home Affairs," *Woman's Exponent* 6, no. 9 (October 1, 1877): 69.

[147] "Santa Clara Relief Society Hall," Heritage Conservation and Recreation Service, United States Department of the Interior, December 27, 1993, 5.

[148] Kate B. Carter, ed., *Heart Throbs of the West* (Salt Lake City: Daughters of Utah Pioneers, 1939), 6:143–144.

[149] "Historic Resources of Beaver," National Register of Historic Places, National Park Service, United States Department of the Interior, August 4, 1982, 6; Beaver Relief Society Meetinghouse, Utah State Historical Society, Historic Preservation Office, October 18, 1983, 2.

[150] "Washington Relief Society Hall," National Register of Historic Places Inventory, nomination form, Heritage Conservation and Recreation Service, United States Department of the Interior, August 27, 1980, 2.

[151] "Torrey Log Church/Schoolhouse," National Register of Historic Places, National Park Service, United States Department of the Interior, May 14, 1993, 2.

[152] Bushman, *The Refinement of America*, xii.

[153] Robin Fleming, "Picturesque History and the Medieval in Nineteenth-Century America," *American Historical Review* 100, no. 4 (October 1995): 1061.

[154] "Weber Stake Relief Society Hall," Heritage Conservation and Recreation Service, United States Department of the Interior, December 20, 1988, 2.

155 "Deseret Relief Society Hall," Heritage Conservation and Recreation Service, United States Department of the Interior, November 6, 1995, 3.

156 "Santa Clara Relief Society Hall," Heritage Conservation and Recreation Service, United States Department of the Interior, December 27, 1993, 3.

157 Kimball, "Salt Lake City," 14.

158 Emmeline B. Wells, *Charities and Philanthropies: Woman's Work in Utah* (Salt Lake City: George Q. Cannon, 1893), 23.

159 The building included a large hall and stage, accommodating 150 people in the audience, "furnished with nice chairs and seats, the stage and aisles carpeted; and it also contained a very good library and organ for the use of the Relief and other similar Societies." Wells, *Charities and Philanthropies,* 72.

160 Wells, *Charities and Philanthropies,* 19.

161 Utah State Historical Society, "Beaver Relief Society Meetinghouse," 2.

GLOBETROTTING MORMON WOMEN ARTISTS AND THE ART OF TRAVEL, 1900–1950

HEATHER BELNAP

In 1901, LDS artist Mary Teasdel made a triumphal return home after her nearly three-year study of art in Europe. The local press had followed her experiences abroad with much enthusiasm, with headlines such as "Utah Artist's Success: Miss Mary Teasdel Has Work Accepted in Paris" broadcasting her accomplishments.[1] When she arrived in Salt Lake City, Teasdel was inundated with speaking invitations and requests to join various arts organizations—in fact, she was soon appointed president of the newly formed Utah Art Institute. In a matter of a few short years, Teasdel went from an able local painter to one of the leaders of the state's nascent art scene. As a contemporary reviewer noted: "Teasdel came back from Paris brimming with the new artistic vigor. . . . She came back here prepared to translate the western scene into this vigorous, even if experimental and formative art that she felt even before her studies in Paris, and to which she was [now?] prepared to give her full conception."[2]

Indeed, Mary Teasdel's post-European oeuvre reflected a mapping of her artistic training in turn-of-the-century Paris onto scenes that would have resonated with viewers in Mormon Utah—women caring for infants, charming home gardens, and picturesque sites in the Wasatch Mountains and Salt Lake Valley. Her painting *Mother and Child* (1901), executed during her Paris period, is typical of her work. Its subject is a woman, sitting indoors, who holds a sleeping infant in her arms and gazes out the adjacent window. Arrayed in the ubiquitous blue dress of working-class Frenchwomen and the Holy Mother herself, she cradles a baby neatly swaddled in white. The serene faces of both mother and child are gently bathed in sunlight, which streams inside by means of the slight opening in the window's diaphanous curtain. This gap, perhaps created by a gentle breeze blowing through, enables the woman to cast an unobtrusive eye on the bucolic scene beyond. The window frames a cottage, painted white and roofed in slate and terra cotta, its angular lines softened by the surrounding verdant foliage. Executed

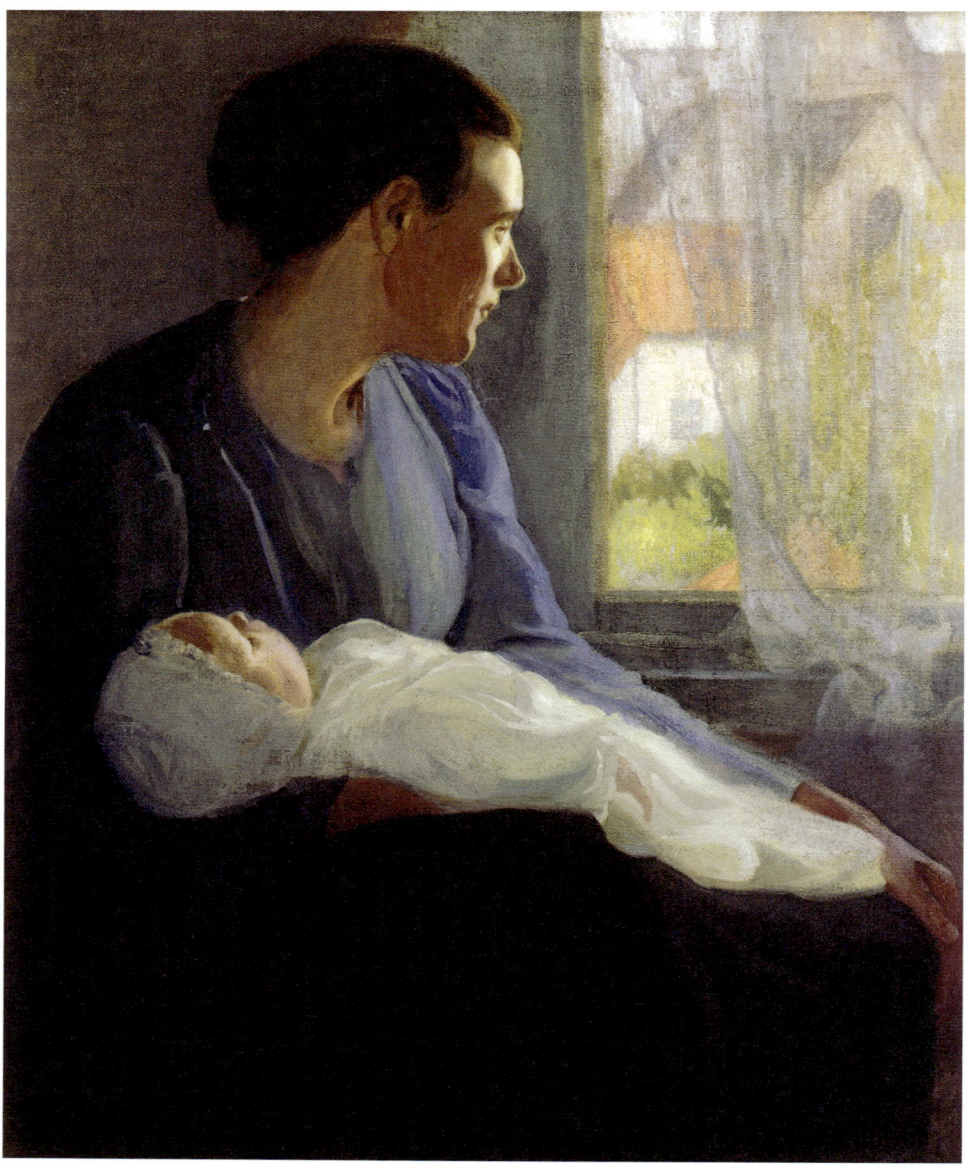

Fig. 7.1 Mary Teasdel, *Mother and Child*, 1901, oil on canvas, 31″ × 25″, State of Utah Alice Merrill Horne Collection. Courtesy Utah Arts & Museums.

in a naturalistic vein, an approach that sought to capture contemporary quotidian life through stylistic means combining academic and impressionistic sensibilities, Teasdel's *Mother and Child* struck a chord with its turn-of-the-century Utah Mormon audience. It possessed an appropriate amount of artistic sophistication (educated viewers would have recognized the artist's nod to the Madonna and Child iconographic tradition) as well as foreignness (elements of the painting, such as the woman's physical features and architectural details, point to a certain degree of "Frenchness") to indicate the artist's European education. At the same time, the genre scene evinces a strong sense of the familiar, with its emphasis on the LDS activities and values associated with home, family, and community. It is no surprise that Teasdel's painting garnered the Best of Show award at the 1902 Utah Art Institute's exhibition and was featured on the cover of the November issue of the church's *Young Woman's Journal* that year.

Mary Teasdel took the lessons learned while studying and traveling abroad and translated these in such a way as to produce artworks that spoke to and of her Latter-day Saint community and attested to her position as a professional artist. For those who followed in her footsteps, obtaining an expansive education that included foreign travel and then ably translating this into a vernacular accessible to those back home was a critical component of their vocation. While much of the training, artistic choices in subject and style, exhibition practices, and career development of these women artists were undergirded by their shared commitment to spread what Alice Merrill Horne termed "the Gospel of Beauty," these individuals were also intent upon establishing careers as artists.[3] One could produce art to glorify God and build his Kingdom and also produce in ways that could be personally meaningful and professionally profitable. Travel and study abroad played no small part in the professionalization of early twentieth-century Latter-day Saint women artists. Their globetrotting roughly occurred in two waves: the first included professional pilgrimages to Europe for formal training to establish their credentials as artists, and the second revolved around scripturally inflected travel to Latin America and the Middle East in search of authenticity in visual representation. This chapter will demonstrate the ways in which travel and study abroad were critical to LDS women artists between 1900 and 1950 and the enterprise of expanding the definitions of Mormon womanhood.

Coming of age during the Progressive Era (c. 1890–1930) and post-polygamist age meant that Mormon women of that period were in many ways different from those of the early church.[4] The LDS Church was working assiduously to "de-peculiarize" the Saints of the west and better integrate into American society. This meant not only eschewing the controversial practice of polygamy and adoption of the two-party political system but also an emphasis on the values Mormons shared with middle-class Protestants, such as the importance of education, civic engagement, industry, and religious piety.[5] Such progressivism espoused the belief that the cultivation of morally edifying arts was critical to the health of a society, and saw women as central to this mission.[6] Mormon women of this era were also influenced by the ubiquitous figure of the New Woman, who emerged in the final decades of the nineteenth century in the United States and Europe, and who was generally characterized as an independent, educated, active, and public figure.[7] Many of the LDS women of the Progressive Era and beyond who were leaders in the church, civic, and professional communities would have identified with the general contours of this persona but would have wanted to put a finer point on it, specifying the ways faith and culture inflected womanhood.[8]

Freedom of movement became a critical marker of modern womanhood, and LDS women appeared eager to demonstrate that, contrary to popular notions of their status as prisoners of the patriarchy, they too possessed such autonomy. The last decades of the nineteenth century witnessed a veritable explosion in American women's foreign travel—a phenomenon Mary Suzanne Schriber describes as a "seizing for themselves the freedom of movement that had been the historical prerogative of men"—and intrepid Mormon women were joining these ranks.[9] While there were notable examples of prominent LDS matriarchs going abroad, with Eliza Snow's participation in the 1871–1872 trip through Europe and pilgrimage to the Holy Land with President George A. Smith and other church leaders as perhaps the most noteworthy, it wasn't until the turn of the century that this became more widespread.[10]

The introduction in 1898 of a missionary program for single LDS sisters, known as the Lady Missionary program, was also a significant marker in signaling Mormon women's freedom of movement. Worth noting is that the sister missionary program appears to have been established not only to expand the ranks of Mormon evangelists but also to demonstrate that women in the church were not the caricatures of oppressed sister-wives that were much promoted in Anglo-American media.[11] Women traveling and living abroad on church business meant that trips to far-flung areas of the world taken by Mormon women in general became more normalized.

THE FIRST WAVE: LATTER-DAY SAINT WOMEN ARTISTS IN EUROPE

For those women with artistic ambitions, study abroad in Europe was viewed as a necessity. While there was solid art training to be had in major U.S. cities, it was only with an extended stint in the studios of Europe (and particularly the ateliers of Paris) that one could avail oneself of an art education comparable to that given to men and a highly developed professional network.[12] As Dianne Sachko Macleod outlines in her introductory essay to the edited volume *Intrepid Women: Victorian Artists Travel,* there were several key motives for women artists to travel abroad in this era, including professional recognition, greater freedoms from restrictive social conventions and gender expectations, and increased opportunities for self-definition.[13]

Between 1880 and 1950, dozens of Mormon women traveled to the major art centers of Europe, with Paris as the ultimate destination.[14] An early motivating force behind this was Alice Merrill Horne, the undisputed leader of the Utah art scene, who urged artists to go abroad to gain the best art education possible. This is a leitmotif of her magnum opus, *Devotees and Their Shrines: A Handbook of Utah Art* (1914), in which she repeatedly references European art and its institutions and even includes a section titled "Winners of Honors Abroad."[15] She lavishes praise on Mary Teasdel (1863–1937) in particular, boasting: "Often even men are not given credit for excellence in the field of art. Women painters are apt to be considered as only 'females.' It has been a great shock to this simple class of the dear public to see a woman given so many honors as Miss Teasdel has won both at home and abroad."[16] The Latter-day Saint artist, who had previously studied art at the University of Utah, the National Academy of Design, and the Art Students League in New York City, arrived in Paris in 1898 determined to learn the principles of "true art," as she called it.[17] Like so many aspiring American artists in the City of Light, she enrolled at the Académie Julian, a studio system that had pioneered an art education for women on par with that given to men, and even took classes at James McNeill Whistler's Parisian studio for a time.[18] In a letter penned during Teasdel's student years and published in the *Young Woman's Journal,* she provided a window into life as an art student in Paris.[19] While she neither understated its rigors nor glossed over its hardships, her missive was on the whole quite encouraging to those young women with artistic ambitions. Emphasizing the parity of instruction for men and women in the Académie Julian system, along with the meritocracy in the studio, wherein the only thing that mattered was one's artistic skill, Teasdel described a professional pathway for determined and hardworking young women.[20]

Once home, Teasdel applied the lessons she had learned in French Impressionism and Whistler's Aestheticism to the Utah landscape, thereby encouraging Utah Mormon audiences to view local sites in a new light. Her watercolor *Garfield Pier, Great Salt Lake* (c. 1904) is less a representation of a favorite recreational haunt and more a study in blues, greens, grays, and white and evocation of a contemplative, even melancholic mood. The briny water serves as the primary visual interest, the suggestion of movement conveyed through short, almost calligraphic horizontal brushstrokes of the limited color palette. While the waters of the Great Salt Lake might not compare to those of the Atlantic Ocean immortalized by Claude Monet, she ably translates his style in this modest painting. Teasdel also channels her teacher Whistler in this painting; by veiling the pavilion in a misty fog and emptying the waters of bathers, her *Garfield Pier, Great Salt Lake* accomplishes the Romantic aim of defamiliarizing the familiar.

Studying in Paris at roughly the same time as Teasdel was fellow Utah artist Nina Rosabel "Rose" Hartwell (Whiteley) (1861–1917), who, according to Merrill Horne, "pioneered the way for women to study art abroad."[21] In 1895, Hartwell left Salt Lake City for Paris to spend three years studying in the City of Light, studying at the Académie Vitti and spending time at the American Girls' Club, an organization the artist credited with providing much-needed professional and social support. In addition to studying art in Paris, she spent a summer painting in Monet's Giverny, where she "lived in daily view of the artist's picturesque home."[22]

Perhaps it was during this extended stay outside the capital that Hartwell executed *French Village* (c. 1900), a painting foregrounding her art education abroad. Featured prominently in the middle ground are several haystacks, an object frequently used by American artists who had studied in France to indicate their intimate acquaintance with Impressionism and its leader Monet's iconic renderings of these. The

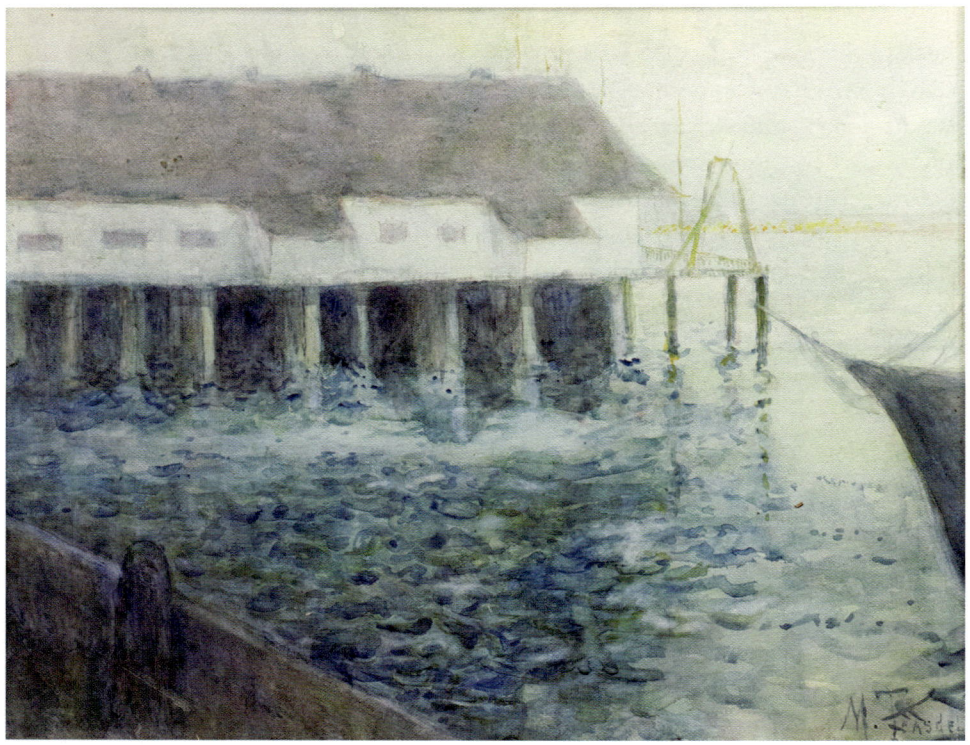

Fig. 7.2 Mary Teasdel, *Garfield Pier, Great Salt Lake,* 1904, watercolor, 14.75″ × 18″, Springville Museum of Art.

composition of Hartwell's *French Village* also mimics the organizational structure and tonalities of Camille Pissarro's famous canvases of rural French life such as *Hoarfrost at Ennery* (1873) and *Red Roofs, Corner of a Village, Winter* (1877). While displaying Hartwell's conversance with the modern French art world, it also exposes the artist's Utah Mormon roots. Such a homely landscape scene, with its sense of order, emphasis on communal living and rural labor, accent on humankind's harmony with (even mastery over) nature, and celebration of rural life, would have appealed to her supporters back home.

Rose Hartwell was an ambitious artist whose experience traveling and studying abroad was much reported in the local press and lauded in LDS Church auxiliary magazines.[23] In a series of letters to Merrill Horne, she shared her experiences training in Europe and journeying to other foreign lands; this correspondence was later reproduced in the *Young Woman's Journal* and in Merrill Horne's *Devotees and Their Shrines.*[24] In addition to speaking to living conditions and the rigors of a French art education, the peripatetic artist confided that "in Paris and Florence I am more at home than in Salt Lake City. To me, travel seems as necessary to one's education as books, and

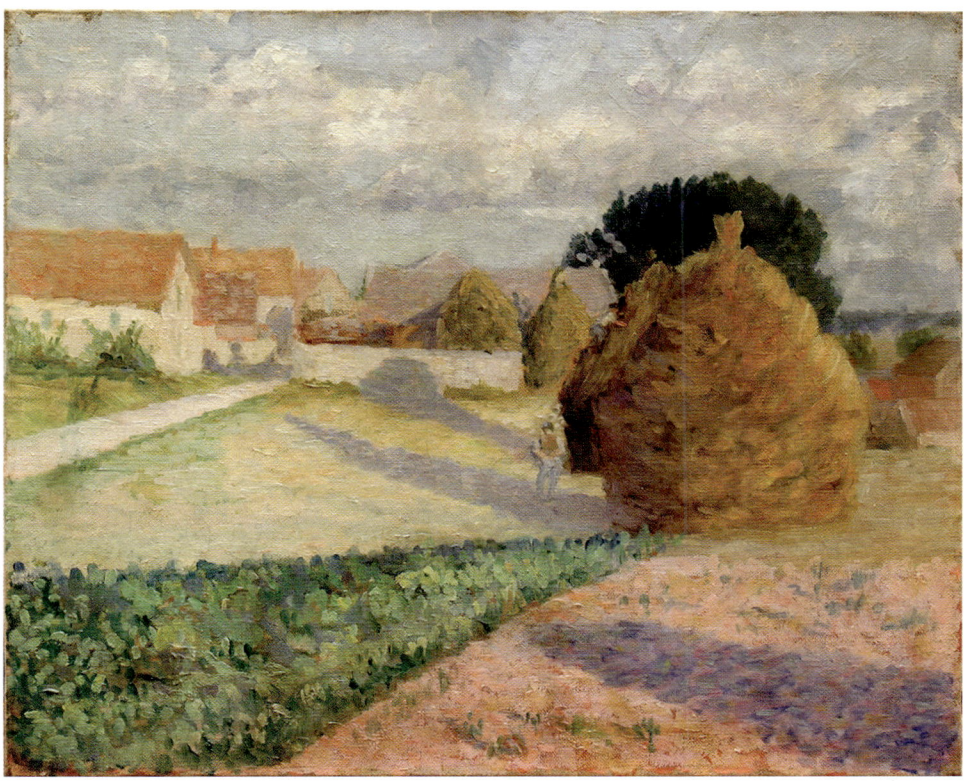

Fig. 7.3 Rose Hartwell, *French Village*, c. 1900, oil on canvas, Brigham Young University Museum of Art.

it is through travel only that one gets clear and concise, yes, and independent, ideas of a country."[25]

Of all the early Mormon women artists who studied outside the country, Rose Hartwell was certainly the most itinerant. She spent the better part of two decades studying art abroad and traveling not just in the Old World but into Africa and the Middle East as well, and was proud of her experience as a world traveler, stating:

> You wish to know what countries I have visited. It would almost be easier to tell you what countries I have not visited. England, Ireland, Scotland, Wales, three times over; France, Holland, Belgium, Switzerland, Italy, Norway, Germany, Austria, Egypt, Greece and Turkey. To visit many of these I have returned a third or fourth time and to some I intend to go again.[26]

Her small watercolor *Street Scene in Egypt* (c. 1900) records her impressions of quotidian life in a community halfway around the world from her own desert home. In the

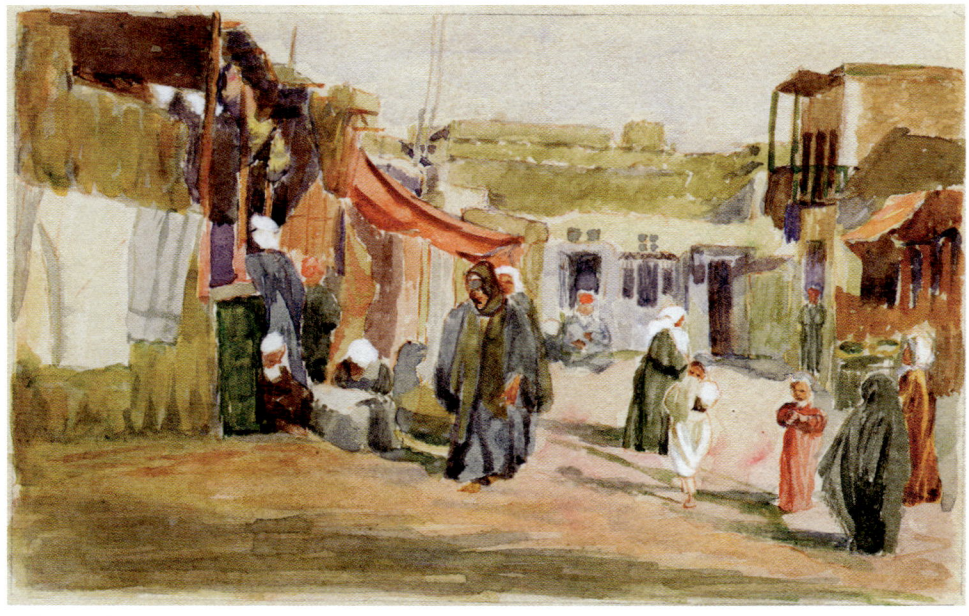

Fig. 7.4 Rose Hartwell, *Street in Egypt*, c. 1900, watercolor, 4 1/4″ × 6 1/4″, Brigham Young University Museum of Art.

spirit of the watercolor sketches in Eugène Delacroix's *Moroccan Notebooks,* Hartwell's painting attempts to convey the much commented-upon uniqueness of the quality of light and color palette in Egypt. Here her adeptness as a colorist is especially evident. The overall sandy tonality of the painting is punctuated by strokes of vivid red, green, blue, and purple to indicate brightly attired Egyptians or entryways to shops and homes. Although it is an unassuming picture of men, women, and children going about their daily tasks, there is something almost reverential in Hartwell's representation. Rather than render romanticized or fantastical images of regions of the world considered exotic, as so many Western artists were wont to do, Hartwell gravitated to scenes of humble, everyday life. The choice of subject and the direct, accessible way it was portrayed were certainly influenced by the artist's upbringing in Mormon Utah.

THE SECOND WAVE: LATTER-DAY SAINT WOMEN ARTISTS IN EUROPE

Rose Hartwell's ventures beyond Europe and commitment to traveling as much as possible foreshadowed new directions in Latter-day Saint women's globetrotting. Travel became both more affordable and more accessible for women after World War I. Budget travel options emerged that enabled middle- and working-class women to go abroad. Inexpensive tours proliferated, and college-age women flocked to Europe and other locales en masse during their summer holidays.[27] University study programs also began forming during the interwar years, and by 1940 travel programs at BYU provided opportunities for Mormon coeds in a variety of disciplines to broaden and deepen their education.[28]

Furthermore, church publications paid increasing attention to the topic of travel, thus suggesting that this was a matter of some importance to the community. One LDS youth organization hosted a Traveling Mutual event that involved a lecture series on places beyond the Intermountain West.[29] A series in the *Young Woman's Journal* published in 1917 and 1918, "Susanne Goes A-Travelling," traced the visits of a fictional LDS woman visiting areas such as India, Java, and the Philippines.[30] Travelogues with titles such as "Venetian Memories" or "Impressions of Egypt" or "Playground of Europe" (i.e., Switzerland) rehearsed details of women's time abroad and waxed nostalgic about their adventures.[31] Those travel tales that focused on destinations known for their rich artistic tradition, such as "Fascinating Italy," were copiously illustrated with photographs taken by the authors or others.[32]

During the interwar era, Mormon women artists began to go off the beaten path to Europe and extend their travel to Latin America, the Middle East, Asia, the Pacific Islands, and elsewhere. One region that drew several LDS women artists to it was Central America. Given that this was an era in which scholarly studies of the Book of Mormon began developing in earnest, it was not a surprising development.[33] Intent upon adding as much archaeological veracity and authentic local color to their illustrations of ancient scripture as possible, artists traveled to immerse themselves in the foreign landscapes and artistic and archaeological traditions of these regions.[34] Perusal of their journals, correspondence, and artworks reveals how critical their art education abroad, which included sketching at museums, archaeological sites, and points of local interest, and even short-term training in foreign art schools, was to their professional development.

Interestingly, the beloved and best-known LDS woman artist, Minerva Teichert (1888–1976), did not take the European tour nor travel extensively outside the United States—a deficiency that may have contributed to her position as a bit of an outsider in the midcentury Utah art scene. In her formative years, she did go east for training—first to Chicago's Art Institute from 1909 to 1912 and then to New York City's Art Students League in 1915–1916. In New York, she studied under perhaps the most influential American modernist artist of the day, Robert Henri. In one of Teichert's most oft-quoted experiences, Henri asked his young pupil if any artists had painted the Mormon story, to which she boldly replied, "Not to suit me." His exhortation that she do so kindled an interest that would develop into a deep-seated testimony: that it was Teichert's sacred calling to chronicle the history of the LDS Church and its people, from ancient scripture to the Restoration of the Church of Jesus Christ and emigration of the Saints to Zion.

In a move that would astonish many, Teichert declined two opportunities to study art in Europe. The first was in 1917, when she was offered a scholarship by the Art Students League to study at the Royal Academy in London but turned it down, choosing to return home to Idaho and marry.[35] Her daughter, Laurie Teichert Eastwood, wrote that "inwardly, Minerva may have had some regrets about not being able to study in Europe, but she said America had it all."[36] Seven years later, she was invited to travel to Europe with her mentor Henri and his wife. Such a trip would have afforded her the opportunity to study the great European art tradition firsthand, which could both improve one's artmaking and also bolster one's credentials. But Teichert reports having a dream about a future daughter that made such a strong impression that she immediately sent her regrets. Teichert's dream, which she had some days before their scheduled departure, vividly illustrated her walking down a long gallery where there were "grand things" on the walls, but as she approached them, the beautiful "things turned brown and curled up in its frame." The same thing occurred with each new hall explored, until she spotted a portrait of a teenage girl in a pink dress. She recounts:

> As we were pushed on out by the crowd I said, "Oh my heavens if I could only paint like that!" The registrar answered very calmly, "You can. That was your daughter." She was suddenly gone. I felt the night air on my face. Then I woke up with a thrill. I wrote the Henris not to wait for me that I would not be going abroad. *I had seen my daughter.*[37]

However, years later, Teichert did travel with her family to Mexico in 1941 and then to accompany this same "beautiful, blue-eyed daughter" to Mexico City when she was a student there in 1944. Teichert always had an interest in the art and architecture of the region, and in her earlier works devoted to themes from the LDS scripture she had drawn from photographs of ancient American ruins in Guatemala and Mexico found in *National Geographic,* a publication to which her family regularly subscribed.[38] Intent upon supporting their children's interest in the Spanish language (son Robert Henri Teichert served a Spanish-speaking mission in Colorado and California in 1940), the Teichert family traveled to Mexico City, and then south a hundred miles to Tasco.

On this trip, Teichert sketched genre and landscape scenes.[39] Although most of these are loose pencil drawings, there is a more finished watercolor sketch of a group of musicians titled *Tasco* (1941) in the notebook she used on this trip.[40] While the subject is a stereotypical one that conformed to preconceived ideas of traditional Mexico—the three musicians are shown leaning against a white stucco wall, wearing sombreros and holding traditional instruments—the individual figures are rendered sensitively, there is a sense of intimacy to the grouping, and the touches of teal, orange, and smoky gray paint create a visual liveliness.

When daughter Laurie was awarded a scholarship as a BYU student to spend the summer term of 1944 studying at the University of Mexico, Teichert was keen to accompany her. Letters between the two in the months leading up to the trip are full of references to her preparations, which included purchasing "a good dictionary, medical book, *Will Rogers, Conquest of Mexico,* also *Old Civilizations of Mexico and South America* and *Audubon Bird Life.*"[41] Her correspondence also indicates that she hoped to train

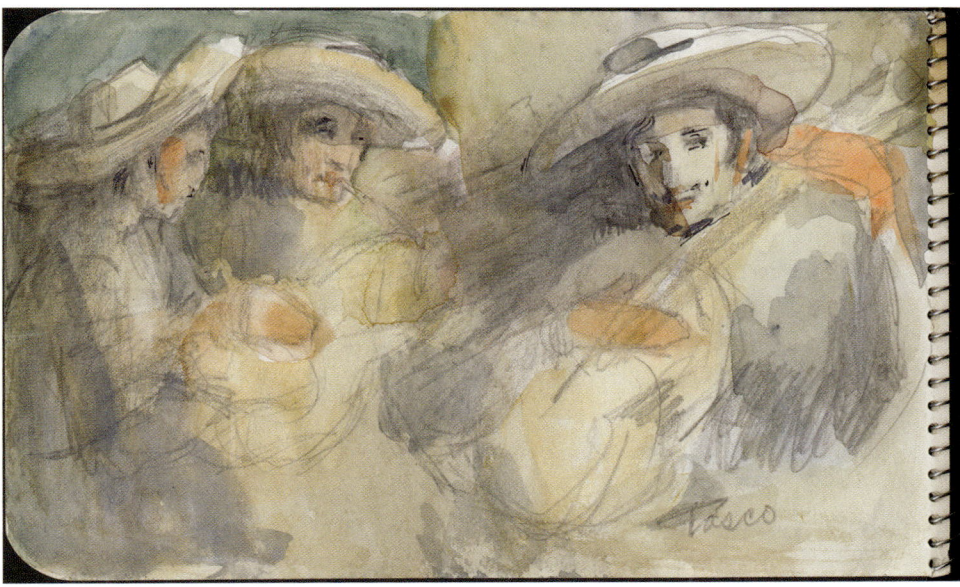

Fig. 7.5 Minerva Kohlhepp Teichert, *Tasco*, 1941, pencil sketch and watercolor, L. Tom Perry Special Collections, Brigham Young University.

with the artist Luis Mora while in Mexico—an artist "of Spanish descent" whose work Alice Merrill Horne had admired at a 1932 exhibition in California—but couldn't locate him.[42] Subsequently, Teichert applied to the Art Students League to "get credits or record as they call it"—a sign that she wanted her study of art abroad to receive institutional recognition and thus add to her official credentials.[43] In the only published letter written during their study abroad, Teichert mentions that she met several artists at a place called Sanborn's—including a woman she had studied with in Chicago some thirty-five years prior. Of their time there, daughter Laurie records that while she attended classes in the morning, her mother "painted in their room and sketched in the streets. They visited galleries, fiestas, markets, palaces, ruins, and the opera in the Palacio de Bellas Artes."[44]

Although Teichert's study abroad in Mexico inspired several paintings, most remain unlocated. The economic disparity that she found so troubling and commented upon in an unpublished letter to Alice Merrill Horne was the impetus to produce two paintings, *The Rich in Mexico* and *The Poor in Mexico*.[45] Some twenty years after this trip, the *Salt Lake Tribune* reproduced one of her paintings, described as "a Mohammedan mosque near University of Mexico and street scene" and on display in ZCMI's Tiffin Room.[46] We know that a genre scene she produced was hung in her dining room, perhaps as a testament to Teichert's desire to display a souvenir of her trip with Laurie, but also possibly to remind visitors that she had studied her craft in a foreign land.

During the 1930s and 1940s, the art and archaeology of Mexico and Central America, as well as their modern mural traditions, were garnering attention from the artists in the United States and Europe, and this was especially true for midcentury Mormons, as they believed this was where the events narrated in the Book of Mormon took place.[47] In fact, it could be argued that when Teichert visited these regions, she saw them through the eyes of a reader of this Latter-day scripture. For example, she titled a drawing *Land of Desolation North of Chihuahua*, the first three words being the same descriptor used in the Book of Mormon for a dreary wilderness.[48] Marian Wardle, the artist's granddaughter and the leading expert on Teichert, surmises that these trips south of the border were inspirational for her celebrated 1949–1951 painting series on the Book of Mormon:

> The palm trees in *The Promised Land;* the vegetation, quetzal birds and architecture in *Mosiah Discovers Zarahemla;* the decorative architectural motifs in *Trial of Abinadi;* and the landscape settings for *Alma Baptizes in the Waters of Mormon, Escape of King Limhi and His People,* and *An Angel Appears to Alma and the Sons of Mosiah* probably derive from sketches Teichert made in Mexico.[49]

Teichert's *Mosiah Discovers Zarahemla* abounds with Aztec and Mayan architectural elements and iconography, as well as some modern Mexican motifs. (Some of the artifacts and sites the artist saw in person; others could be found in a photo book of famous sites in Mexico that was in her possession.)[50] The pyramid in the background seems to be an amalgam of ruins at Chichén Itzá and Palenque in the Yucatan, as well as the temple of Quetzalcoatl and pyramids of San Juan at the Teotihuacán site, with the adjacent tower more derivative of the Spanish colonial architecture Teichert would have seen in Mexico City. The Mayan headdress she sketched on her 1944 trip may have served as the basis for the helmets on Mosiah and his men in the foreground.[51] Furthermore, the painting's elaborate border—a signature stylistic element of Teichert's—and quetzal birds were key elements of the Aztec artistic tradition. Lastly, Teichert took pains to include vegetation native to this land; witness the two agave plants that spill out onto the bottom border.

Not only was the trip productive in that it provided material for her Book of Mormon series, but it also inspired her to renew her advocacy for a Latter-day Saints arts center. In April 1940 she had penned a letter to J. Reuben Clark, who was then at the helm of the church administration, proposing "a Latter Day Saint Art Gallery near the temple block for all the world to see."[52] When Teichert was asked to join the centennial celebration committee in 1947, she then wrote to the new president of the church, George Albert Smith, about creating "a building much like the Bellas Artes [in Mexico City], music and art etc. in one."[53] She even drew up a plan for such a facility.[54] Hence her travel not only influenced her painting but also enabled her to envision how her local cultural institutions could be modeled after international ones.[55]

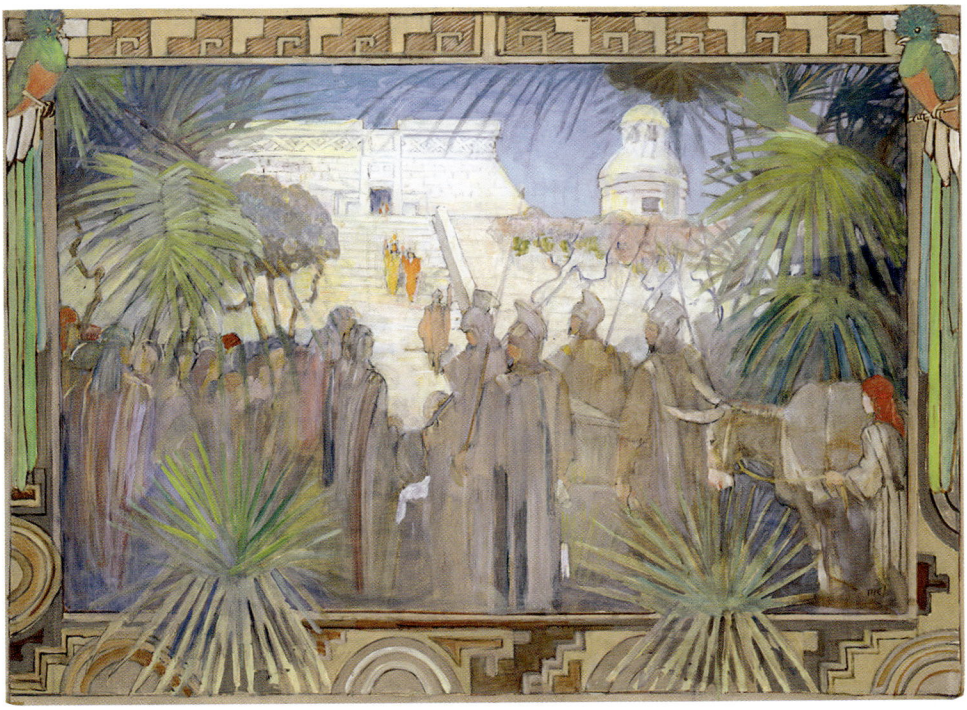

Fig. 7.6 Minerva Kolhepp Teichert, *Mosiah Discovers Zarahemla*, c. 1949–1951, oil on masonite, Brigham Young University Museum of Art.

In 1958, Teichert made one more international trip, and it was a grand one—a month-long business trip with her husband, Herman, to South America. Accounts of this trip suggest that this was related to their cattle-ranching enterprises; however, in a letter to her daughter, Laurie, Teichert emphasized that this was for her professional development as an artist. In fact, the month-long adventure, which included stays in Argentina, Peru, Chile, Ecuador, Uruguay, Brazil, and Panama, was funded by a Mr. Stark, a man in the oil business who advanced Teichert $3,000 on paintings.[56] The artist talked of being inspired by the "wild conglomeration" of Brazil she had witnessed to commence a mural of what she termed the "Sambo" [sic], and which was later titled *Samba in Rio*.[57] Given that this Afro-Brazilian ballroom dance was enjoying great popularity across the globe at midcentury, it isn't surprising that Teichert wanted to paint such a scene; the Teichert family's often tenuous financial circumstances necessitated selecting subjects for her paintings that she believed were marketable. Ever mindful of the need to make good on her promise to make the trip profitable, Teichert also purchased art while abroad. In a letter posted from Buenos Aires, she gleefully reported that she had acquired several paintings during their travels and that these "should be excuse enough to pay for our trip. Two of them very

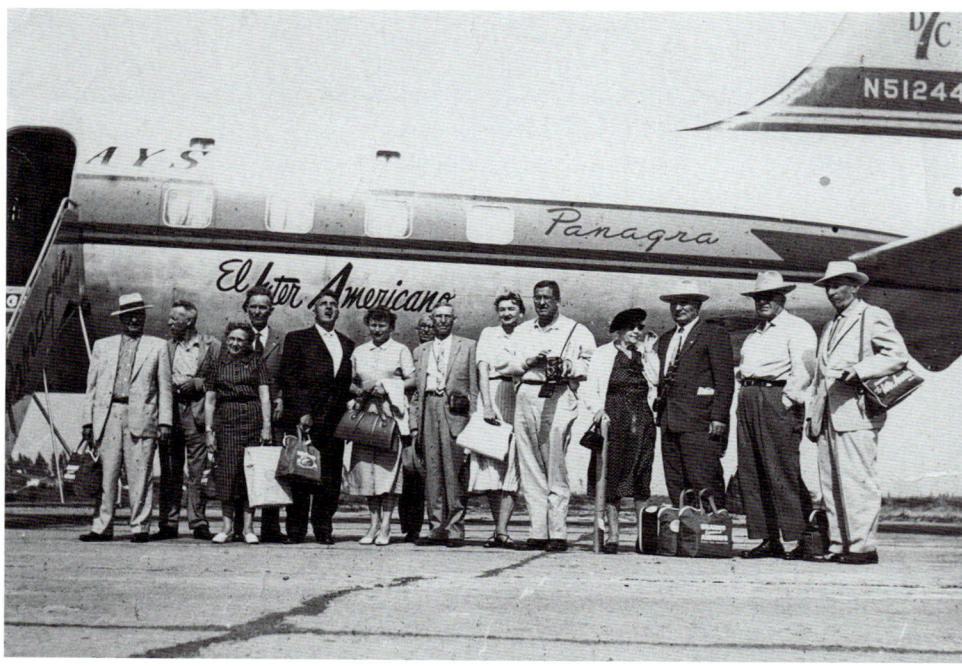

Fig. 7.7 Photograph of Minerva and Herman Teichert by plane on South American trip, 1956, L. Tom Perry Special Collections, Brigham Young University. Herman and Minerva are third and fourth from right.

pre[c]ious by a Flemish painter."[58] These still lifes, which she had to cut out of their frames to smuggle back to the United States, were so beautifully executed that "if the students in America could see them every day it would soon put an end to 'modern' art," she declared.[59]

Another artist of this generation, Mabel Pearl Frazer (1887–1981), also ventured to Central America, as well as to the British Isles, the Continent, and even North Africa. Hailing from small-town Beaver, Utah, Frazer spent her youth dreaming of becoming an artist and became one of the first to earn a degree from the University of Utah's newly formed art department. After graduating, she taught in Salt Lake Valley secondary schools to finance art training back east at the New York Evening School of Industrial Art, Beaux-Arts Institute, and Art Students League. She returned to her alma mater as a professor, teaching courses in studio, design, and art history for over thirty years.[60] While Frazer was a popular professor and active participant in campus, church, and civic art scenes—among her many leadership roles, she was vice president of the Utah Art Institute, chair of the Utah Chapter of the American Artists' Congress, and chair of the art section for the Utah Educational Association—she experienced significant challenges as a single professional Mormon woman.[61] Refusing to comply with the expectations of Mormon spinsterhood, which meant possessing an unassuming demeanor, being dependent upon others, and showing deference to patriarchal authority, Frazer lived on her own terms.

Her 1930–1931 trip to the Old World with student Helen Homer, which included six months touring Europe and the Mediterranean region and seventeen months in Florence learning the time-honored techniques of Italian Renaissance fresco painting, was formative to her art practice. Not only was Frazer able to view the art of the Old Masters and the European modernists and gain new skills, but this sojourn also cemented her professional bona fides. To that point, she was invited to exhibit two large oil paintings—a study of a yucca tree in the American desert and the magisterial *Sunrise, North Rim Grand Canyon*—at the 1930 Sindicato Nazionale Fascista Belle Arte exhibition at the Mostra Regional d'Arte Toscana, where she met the crown prince and princess of Italy.[62]

The effects of Mabel's firsthand education in both Italian art and European modernism are readily apparent in her *Venice Canal,* an oil painting dating to her residency in Italy. Given the itinerant nature of study abroad, she was forced to move from her preferred mode of large-scale works to smaller ones. But although modest in size, it is positively immoderate in its palette of strident reds, blues, and oranges, as well as its radical compression of space and aggressive brushwork. The rigorous architectonic structuring of the painting and studied building of form through color seen in *Venice Canal* is a tour-de-force demonstration of lessons she was learning from the masters of the European art world. It is certainly informed by twentieth-century Expressionism (French Fauvism, Italian Futurism) and late Cubism, but it is also the product of her study of Italian art and its tradition of complex perspectival schemata. Experimentation regarding the relationships between object and space, as found in both Florentine Quattrocento and contemporary *scuola metafisica* painting, is evident in Frazer's canvas. *Venice Canal* is a sophisticated work that bears witness to the value to be had from immersing oneself in artistic traditions beyond one's borders and from experiencing and producing art in situ.

It could be argued that Frazer's European trip was a turning point in her career in that it appeared to increase her visibility on the Utah art scene. Newspapers along the Wasatch Front charted her travel abroad, with articles bearing headlines such as "Utah Artist Honored in Italy."[63] In a feature article in the *Salt Lake Tribune* regarding her training in Italy, she emphasized her focus on quality and working at her own pace, writing:

In a way I have grown very disgusted with our mad American jury and the precipitate way we rush at things. I have acquired a great respect for the more deliberate and thorough way the ancients went about their creations; and, while I know I am preparing a nice big disappointment for expectant friends at home, I shall make no apology whatever when I come back with only a little handful of half-baked studies at the end of two years. Someone some day must have the cool crust to do that—to reverse our growing habit of quantity. I am striving—not to master two new processes, but to learn enough

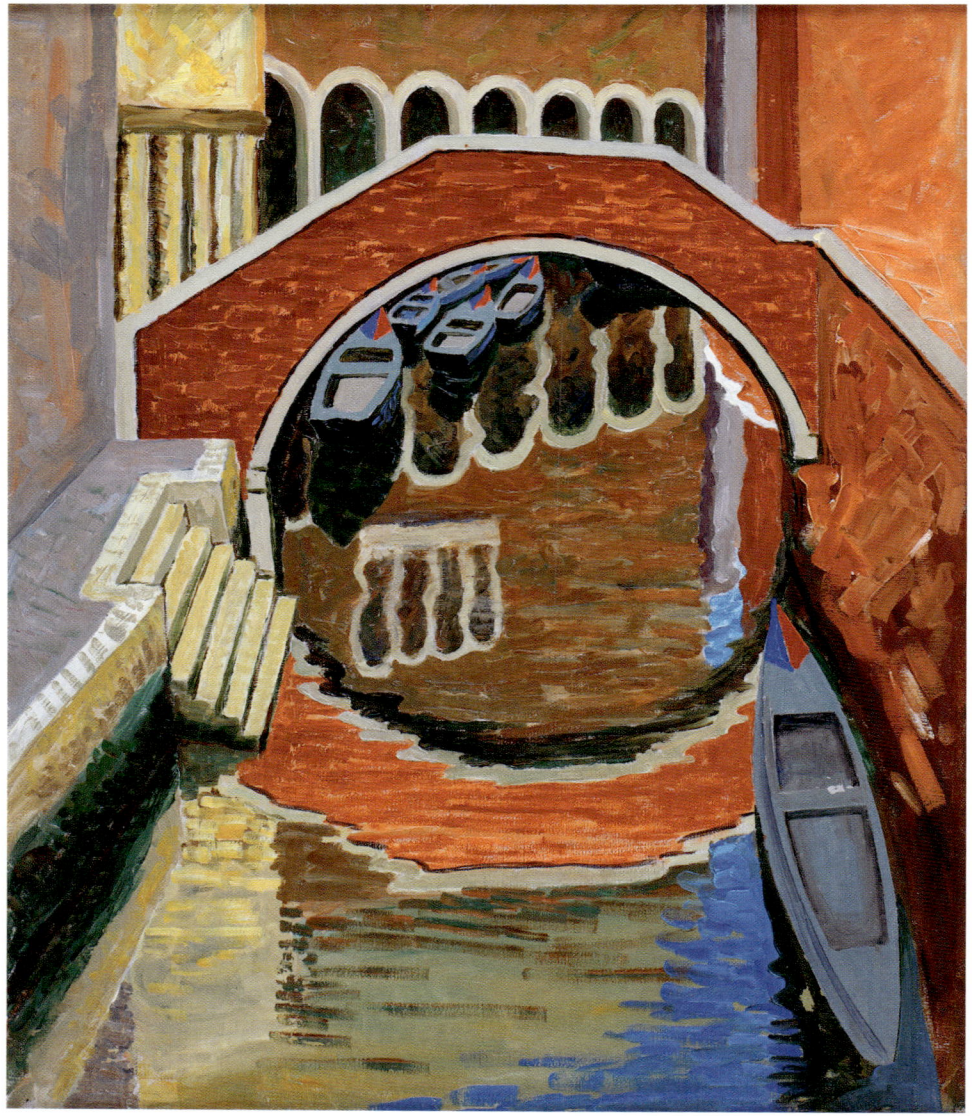

Fig. 7.8 Mabel Pearl Frazer, *Venice Canal,* 1930, oil on canvas, Springville Museum of Art, gift from A. Merlin and Alice Steed Trust.

about them that I can develop them through the future years, and to acquire a certain creative independence that I have never quite felt I had before.[64]

When Frazer returned, she was invited to lecture on her newly gained expertise, and her study in Europe was frequently mentioned in subsequent reviews of her work.[65]

In 1947, Mabel Frazer was commissioned to create a mural for the Salt Lake City Thirty-Third Ward building, and subsequently took two trips to Latin America in preparation for executing the large-scale *Christ Among the Nephites* (1954). The painting's blanched color palette, matte paint, and processional disposition of figures draw from the Italian fresco tradition that Mabel had studied while in Italy some twenty years earlier, while the Mesoamerican pyramid and the artifacts littered at its base and at the feet of Christ and his followers point to her time in the Yucatan. In a 1977 interview with Richard Oman, Mabel Frazer explained that her travel was catalyzed by her desire to achieve historical exactitude in this mural—and that these visits served to confirm the widely held LDS belief that she was in the lands of the Nephites, Lamanites, and other ancient peoples mentioned in the Book of Mormon:

> I took off for Mexico to go down and see the old buildings. I've been to [Palenque] three times. The first time I had heard of [Palenque], I knew there was supposed to be a chapel there, I didn't know what it was for but I got down there and that first time I was only there two days, there sure enough was a temple of Jesus Christ that today we could go through and perform exactly the same ceremonies that we do in the temple here and in all the sixteen temples over the world. The second time I went back I went clear down to the end, way down into South America, clear down through Central America, and I saw the architecture down there, and then I went to [Palenque] and I spent either five or six weeks and I measured every holograph ever done.[66]

Frazer invested a great deal of time, money, and effort into the mural, estimating that she "spent seven solid years every minute that I could get, and $2000 of my own money to paint it," and she clearly considered it her masterpiece.[67] Congregants from her ward

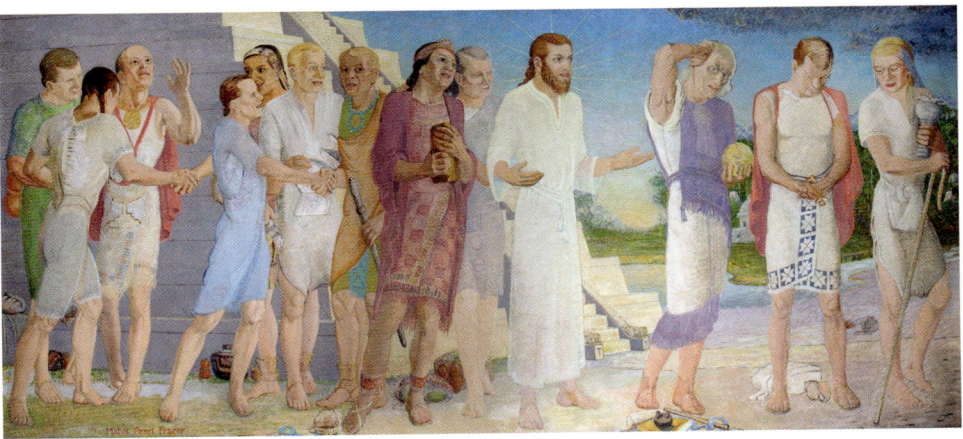

Fig. 7.9 Mabel Pearl Frazer, *Christ Among the Nephites*, 1954, oil on canvas, Springville Museum of Art, gift from the Pioneer Craft House, Salt Lake City.

report that she would stand next to it each Sunday and explain its narrative and symbolism to anyone willing to listen. Few would dispute that it's not nearly as accomplished as she believed: the awkwardly posed bodies of Christ and the disciples uneasily occupy the shallow foreground space, their figures almost as large as the ancient temple pictured behind them. Generally speaking, the mural does bear some resemblance to Minerva Teichert's work of the same period, and one wonders if Frazer harbored similar aspirations of doing a series of large-scale paintings of the Book of Mormon. If she did, this interest seems to have passed quickly, as she never did return to religious subject matter.

Hailed by Alice Merrill Horne as a "globe-trotter,"[68] artist Verla Birrell (1903–2001) certainly merited this moniker. In 1935, she made her first foray into Europe to visit her sister and brother-in-law and ultimately spent three and a half months visiting seventeen countries. Her time abroad generated works such as *Market Place, Lucerne; Austrian Silhouette;* and *Azores Coastal Vista,* which were shown the following year in the Art Barn, Salt Lake City's premier venue for contemporary art.[69] Beginning in the late 1930s and continuing well into the 1950s, Birrell began traveling extensively throughout Latin America. In 1946, she reported taking more than fifty flights and visiting nineteen countries in four months.[70] In an article titled "Extensive Travel Has Given Verla Birrell Broad Outlook," the author justly claimed that "no artist in this vicinity has traveled more extensively" than Birrell.[71]

The accomplishments of Verla Birrell were legion. Possessed of a seemingly insatiable appetite for knowledge, she earned multiple university degrees and was a prolific artist and writer. Her training included the Chicago Art Institute, the University of Utah (BS), the Art Students League and Columbia University (EdD) in New York, Claremont College in California (MFA), and the Escuela de Belles Artes at San Miguel Allende, Mexico. Birrell taught in BYU's Department of Art (1937–1948) and in the University of Utah's Department of Home Economics (1948–1972). Furthermore, she was an active participant in the midcentury Utah art scene and assumed many leadership roles, including that of president of the Associated Utah Artists organization.[72] Birrell self-published two books—*Portfolio of Historic Design* (1947) and *The Book of Mormon Guide Book* (1948)—and published the textbook *Textile Arts: A Handbook of Weaving, Braiding, Printing, and Other Textile Techniques* with Harper Brothers of New York in 1959.[73] Verla was also a devout member of the Church of Jesus Christ of Latter-day Saints and credited the Holy Ghost for its role in her development as an artist, testifying: "It has provided me with a means of contacting my Maker and Master. It has provided me with special insight and given me the ability to carry out inspiration and creative projects."[74]

Birrell's work associated with her time abroad in Latin America deserves special attention. In 1942 and then again in 1945, she held two exhibits in Salt Lake City that featured numerous works devoted to her time in Mexico and Central America. Without a doubt, the painting that garnered the most attention in the first show is *Anita*

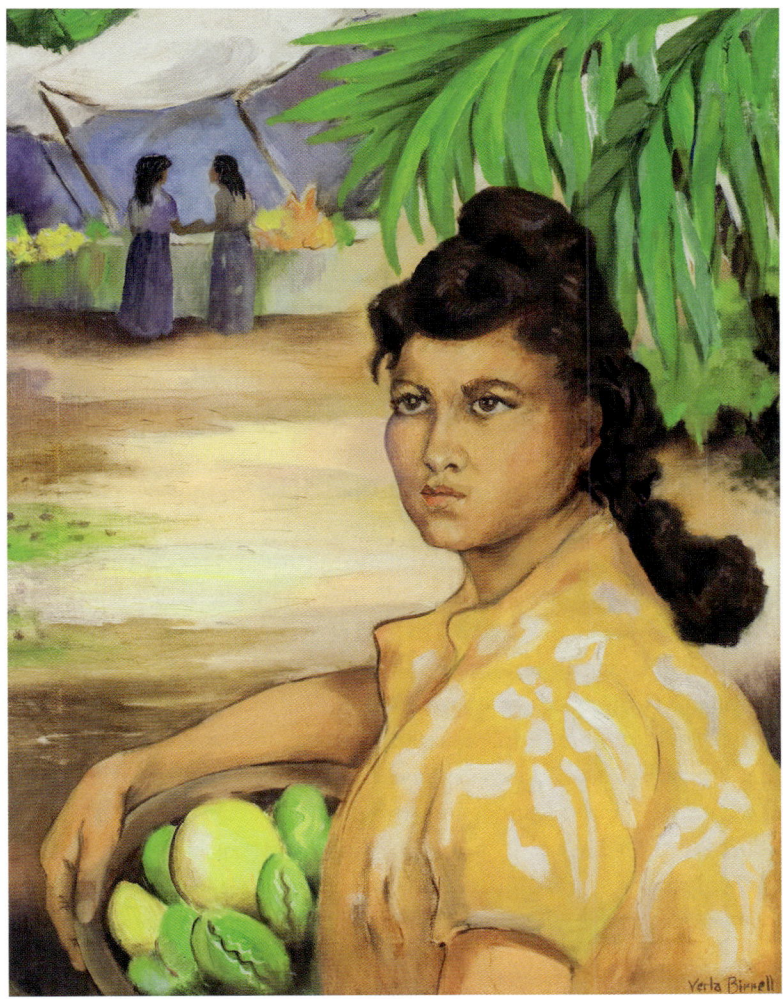

Fig. 7.10 Verla Leone Birrell, *Anita*, 1942, oil on canvas, 29″ × 22.50″, State of Utah Alice Merrill Horne Collection. Courtesy Utah Arts & Museums.

(c. 1942).[75] A review of the painting indicates that this was not a generalized genre painting, noting: "A portrait of a Mexican student, *Anita*, will be of special interest because the subject is now attending the university [BYU]."[76] That said, the sitter is placed in surroundings that were an amalgam of the landscapes, village scenes, costumes, and objects captured in Verla's sketches and studies of Anita's native country, as well as contemporary representational schemata of Mexican women. Anita bears a striking resemblance to images of María Bibiana Uribe, who was named as the winner of the Mexican newspaper *El Universal*'s "India Bonita" contest of 1921.[77] She is also positioned somewhat awkwardly in the front right corner of the picture plane so that a good portion of the painting can be filled with "local color" (i.e., women at the market, tropical flora). Her arms encircle a basket of fruit, which could be viewed as a tired motif popularized by turn-of-the-century French artist Paul Gauguin to signify Indigenous women's connection to nature and to symbolize their fertility, but also in keeping with motifs used by contemporary Mexican women artists such as María Izquierdo and Frida Kahlo.[78]

Birrell's other influential exhibition of her early forays into Central America was a 1945 exhibition of watercolors promoted as including "market groups, landscape vistas, sets of flower studies from gardens of San Angel Inn near Mexico City and from subtropical Guatemala."[79] Contrary to Orientalist depictions of countries characterized as "unspoiled" or "developing," Birrell's *Untitled #5* (1944) renders daily life in one of the villages she visited with a sense of vitality, purposefulness, and even ordinariness. The sunlit scene and its vibrant coloration of terra cotta, teal, red, and lavender immediately draw in the viewer. Filled with women going about everyday tasks of selling, shopping, talking with neighbors, rearing children, and so on—much as one would see on the streets of small-town Utah—the watercolor refuses the traditional modes of representing women from so-called exotic locales, which often veered toward objectifying, sexualizing, or demeaning their subjects. The one man included in this painting is endowed with visual parity and relational reciprocity to his companion. Moreover, Birrell's rendering of a Latin American village scene refuses a stereotypical trope of picturing such spaces as dilapidated and chaotic. Rather, in her *Untitled #5* order pervades: buildings are simple in construction, but freshly painted and in good repair, and the streets are clean and evenly paved. She draws upon her extensive knowledge of Indigenous textiles and costumes to provide variety and veracity to the Indigenous clothing worn by the villagers. In all, while the watercolor is undoubtedly somewhat idealized, its emphasis on the similarities between Latin American village life and everyday life on the Wasatch Front works to build connections between viewers and those represented.

One could also argue that her wanderlust fueled a greater awareness of and empathy for individuals and cultures well beyond the bounds of mid-twentieth-century Mormon Utah, and that this is reflected in the choice of subject matter in her art. Upon returning from a one-year sabbatical trip to Central America in 1944, Birrell used the press's interest in her trip as an opening to critique the U.S. military personnel stationed in those areas for encouraging profiteering for goods and services and thereby creating "a distinct hardship of native workers whose salaries have not kept pace with the rise of prices." The article concludes with a quote by the artist, who said her time abroad "gave her a better appreciation, understanding, sympathy and admiration for our neighbors to the south."[80]

Clearly, one of the roles Birrell seems to have embraced was that of cultural emissary. While teaching at BYU, she spoke with several civic groups in Utah County about her study abroad.[81] These were later developed into a series of illustrated lectures

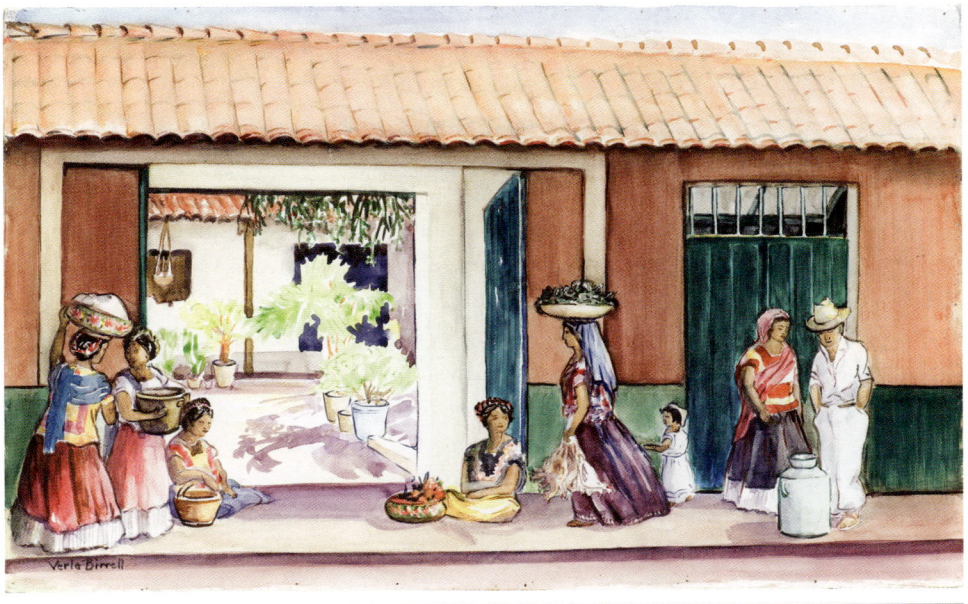

Fig. 7.11 Verla Leone Birrell, *Untitled #5*, c. 1952, watercolor, 14″ × 23″, State of Utah Alice Merrill Horne Collection. Courtesy Utah Arts & Museums.

titled "Art and Archaeology of the Latin American Countries."[82] These were frequently accompanied by displays of the costumes of Indigenous peoples, of which she was an avid collector and explicator.[83] In fact, there are several photographs of Birrell wearing native dress, suggesting a self-fashioning as an exotic traveler.[84] In 1950, she advertised a group tour she was conducting to Old Mexico and Guatemala, promising that they would visit "romantic, cultural, and historic points of our good neighbors to the south" (it is unclear whether or not this tour occurred).[85] Furthermore, Birrell held leadership positions in the Inter-American Council of Utah, a civic group devoted to promoting understanding of and cooperation between many nations in the Americas.

Verla Birrell's professional life was integral to her identity. In reading over her curriculum vitae, work-related papers, and massive collection of press clippings, correspondence, and the like, one is struck by both how driven she appears—there seemed to have been no end to her quest for knowledge and mastery of myriad fields—and how much she seemed to be consumed by recognition in the professional sphere. In some ways, she was the most modern of these modern Mormon women artists. While Birrell was clearly a woman of faith and this imbued her perspectives and positions in significant ways, she neither felt compelled to rationalize her artistic pursuits as part of Alice Merrill Horne's Gospel of Beauty initiative nor to produce artworks of LDS subjects. She found education, professional associations, and study abroad meaningful and even congruent with discipleship, and was unapologetic in the course she pursued.

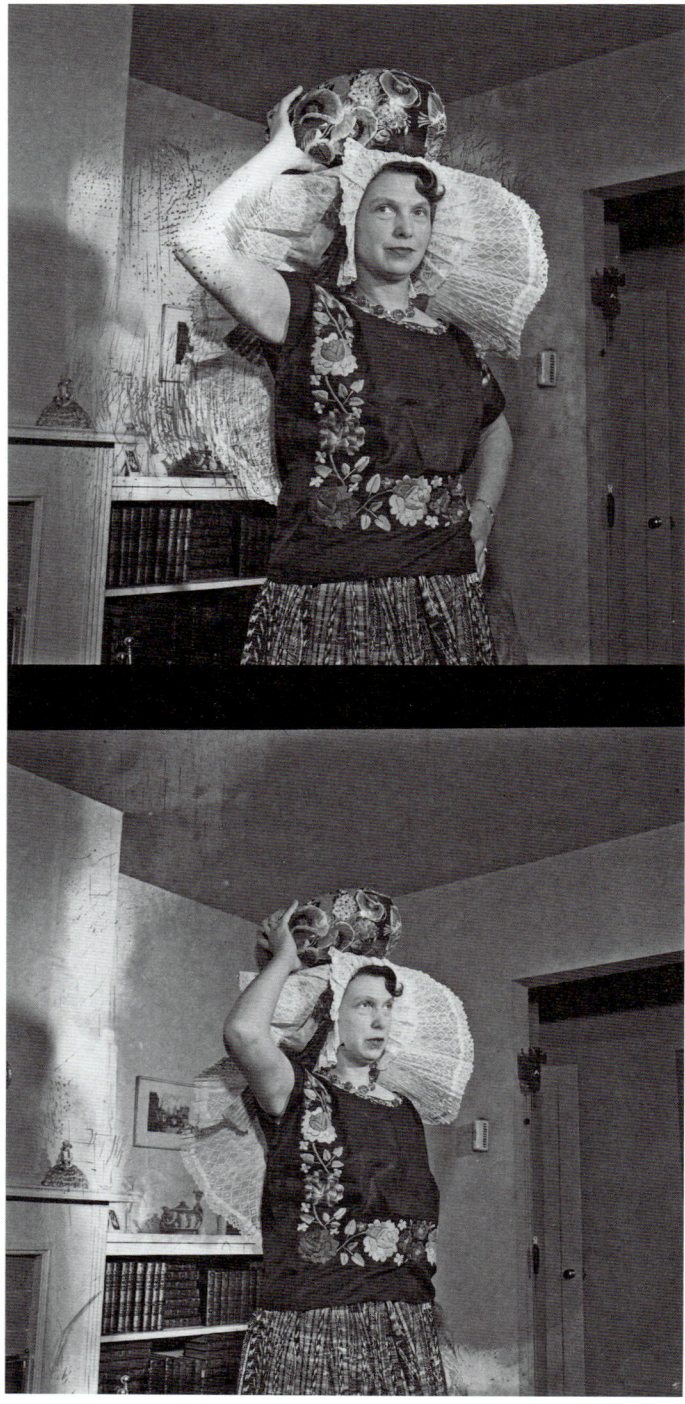

Fig. 7.12   Photograph of Verla Birrell in Central American traditional dress, *Salt Lake Tribune*, November 5, 1951, *Salt Lake Tribune* Negative Collection, published by Utah State History, digitized by Backstage Library Works, hosted by J. Willard Marriott Library, University of Utah.

CONCLUSION: EXPANDING THE FRONTIERS OF LDS IDEALS OF WOMANHOOD

Mormon women's travel had an impact on the development of their identity as members of the Church of Jesus Christ of Latter-day Saints, for the foreign lands, peoples, and cultures encouraged—and sometimes even forced—a grappling with religious beliefs and practices and exploration of self-definition.[86] William Stowe's characterization of the uses of travel by nineteenth-century Americans remains apt for those going abroad in the twentieth century: "For traveler after traveler . . . Europe served as a stage for in-dependent self-definition, for establishing personal relations with culture and society that did not necessarily fit the standard patterns prescribed by hometown and family standards."[87] In her 1944–1945 serialized essay "A Few Gifted Utah Women Artists," Merrill Horne characterized the value of Verla Birrell's travel as follows:

> Every summer this ambitious artist travels and paints. Verla has visited Europe, Africa, and South America, the East, and West, for subjects. She is not only intellectually endowed, not only possessed of a lofty attitude of mind and heart, but she goes forth with a certain openness to inspirations which come with new contacts, new themes, new environments, which she makes her own in her pictures.[88]

Hence, when these Latter-day Saint women artists went abroad, they "succeeded in expanding the frontiers of their identities" on several fronts.[89] Whereas one prominent scholar of the art of the American West contends that the departure of Mary Teasdel and Rose Hartwell from Salt Lake to Paris was their way of "resisting the power of Mormon theology" and its definitions of ideal womanhood, I would argue that it was their way of *expanding* these definitions.[90] Early and mid-twentieth-century Mormon women did not view their ambitions as artists as antithetical to their religious and cultural iden-tity or to definitions of Mormon womanhood. Rather, by all accounts—journals, letters, artworks, and so on—these women viewed their work as professional artists as being wholly consonant with their discipleship and the covenants they had made to build up the Kingdom of God. These women artists built upon their foundations of religiosity and worked within the church's institutional frameworks to forge successful careers. In sum, attention to how these globetrotting Mormon women artists grafted the perspectives and professional skills they gained while traveling and studying abroad onto their spir-itual convictions and cultural values illuminates the formation of the identity of a modern Mormon woman.

NOTES

1 *Salt Lake Tribune,* March 3, 1900. Teasdel had a (now lost) painting titled *The Pensioner of Chelsea* ac-cepted at the World's Fair of 1900, as well as several miniatures accepted in subsequent salons.

2 "Mary Teasdel: Western Art," *Deseret News,* March 12, 1934.

3 See Heather Belnap, "Aesthetic Evangelism, Artistic Sisterhood, and the Gospel of Beauty: Mormon Women Artists at Home and Abroad, c. 1890–1920," in *Beyond Biography: Sources and Contexts for Mormon Women's History*, ed. Rachel Cope, Amy Easton-Flake, Keith Erekson, and Lisa Olsen Tait (Madison, NJ: Fairleigh Dickinson University Press, 2017), 141–166.

4 See Colleen McDannell, "Uplifting Humanity," in *Sister Saints: Mormon Women Since the End of Polygamy* (New York: Oxford University Press, 2019), 35–52; Thomas G. Alexander, "Church and Community: Latter-day Saint Women in the Progressive Era, 1890–1930," in *New Scholarship on Latter-day Saint Women in the Twentieth Century: Selections from the Women's History Initiative Seminars, 2003–2004*, ed. Carol Cornwall Madsen and Cherry B. Silver (Provo, UT: Joseph Fielding Smith Institute for Latter-day Saint History, 2005), 9–18.

5 See Thomas G. Alexander, *Mormonism in Transition: A History of the Latter-day Saints, 1890–1930* (Champaign: University of Illinois Press, 1986; repr., Salt Lake City: Greg Kofford Books, 2012) and Lawrence Foster, *Women, Family, and Utopia: Communal Experiments of the Shakers, the Oneida Community, and the Mormons* (Syracuse, NY: Syracuse University Press, 1991).

6 See Bailey van Hook, *Angels of Art: Women and Art in American Society, 1876–1914* (University Park: Pennsylvania State University Press, 1996)

7 Sally Ledger, *The New Woman: Fiction and Feminism at the Fin de Siècle* (Manchester: Manchester University Press, 1997); Martha Banta, *Imaging American Women: Idea and Ideals in Cultural History* (New York: Columbia University Press, 1987); and Mary Louise Roberts, *Disruptive Acts: The New Woman in Fin de Siècle France* (Chicago: University of Chicago Press, 2005).

8 A detailed history of LDS women of either the Progressive or wartime era has yet to be written. See the relevant chapters in Colleen McDannell's *Sister Saints* and Thomas Alexander's "Church and Community" for surveys of these period.

9 Mary Suzanne Schriber, *Telling Travels: Selected Writings by Nineteenth-Century Women Abroad* (DeKalb: Northern Illinois University Press, 1995), xvi.

10 For a discussion of Eliza's time in France, see Heather Belnap, Corry Cropper, and Daryl Lee, *Marianne Meets the Mormons: Representations of Mormonism in Nineteenth-Century France* (Champaign: University of Illinois Press, 2022), 20–22; and George Albert Smith, Eliza R. Snow, Lorenzo Snow, and Paul A. Schettler, *Correspondence of Palestine Tourists, Comprising a Series of Letters by George A. Smith, Lorenzo Snow, Paul A. Schettler and Eliza R. Snow, of Utah* (1875; New York: Arno Press, 1977).

11 This is discussed in Joseph W. McMurrin, "Lady Missionaries," *Young Woman's Journal* 15, no. 12 (December 1904): 539–541. See Kelly Lelegren, "'Real, Live Mormon Women': Understanding the Role of Early Twentieth-Century LDS Lady Missionaries" (master's thesis, Utah State University, 2009); Matthew McBride, "'Female Brethren': Gender Dynamics in a Newly Integrated Missionary Force, 1898–1915," *Journal of Mormon History* 44, no. 4 (October 2018): 40–67; and Tally S. Payne, "'Our Wise and Prudent Women': Twentieth-Century Trends in Female Missionary Service," in *New Scholarship on Latter-day Saint Women in the Twentieth Century: Selections from the Women's History Initiative Seminars, 2003–2004*, ed. Carol Cornwall Madsen and Cherry B. Silver (Provo, UT: Joseph Fielding Smith Institute for Latter-day Saint History, 2005), 125–140.

12 Laurence Madeline et al., *Women Artists in Paris, 1850–1900* (New Haven, CT: Yale University Press, 2017); and Kirsten Swinth, "Illustrious Men and True Companionship: Parisian Study," in *Painting Professionals: Women Artists and the Development of Modern American Art, 1870–1930* (Chapel Hill: University of North Carolina Press, 2001), 37–62.

13 Dianne Sachko Macleod, "Introduction: Women's Artistic Passages," in *Intrepid Women: Victorian Artists Travel* (Burlington, VT: Ashgate, 2005), 1–9.

14 See my "Pioneering Women: Lessons from Paris and the Making of an Art Scene in the American West, 1890–1940," presented at the colloquium *Faire oeuvre: La formation et la professionalisation des artistes femmes aux XIX et XXe siècles*, Paris, 2023.

15 Alice Merrill Horne, *Devotees and Their Shrines: A Handbook of Utah Art* (Salt Lake City: Deseret, 1914).

16 Horne, *Devotees and Their Shrines,* 63.

17 Martha S. Bradley, "Mary Teasdel: Yet Another American in Paris," *Utah Historical Quarterly* 58, no. 3 (Summer 1990): 244–260.

18 Gabriel P. Weisberg and Jane R. Becker, eds., *Overcoming All Obstacles: The Women of the Académie Julian* (New Brunswick, NJ: Rutgers University Press, 1999).

19 Alice Merrill Horne, "Mary Teasdel: The Utah Impressionistic Painter," *Young Woman's Journal* 21, no. 3 (March 1910): 130–137.

20 Horne, "Mary Teasdel," 61–62.

21 Alice Merrill Horne, "Letters from Miss Hartwell," excerpts published in the *Young Woman's Journal* 22 (1911): 127.

22 Horne, "Letters from Miss Hartwell," 100.

23 For example, "Utah Girl Honored," *Salt Lake Herald,* April 15, 1900, 9, and "Utah Girl Artist Receives Honors in the Paris Salon," *Salt Lake Telegram,* April 24, 1902, 8.

24 Alice Merrill Horne, "Rose Hartwell—The Utah Colorist," *Young Woman's Journal* 22, no. 3 (1911): 127–132, reproduced and elaborated upon in Horne, *Devotees,* 65–71.

25 Quoted in Horne, *Devotees,* 71.

26 Quoted in Horne, *Devotees,* 71.

27 Bess Beatty, *Traveling Beyond Her Sphere: American Women on the Grand Tour, 1814–1914* (Washington, DC: New Academia, 2016), 239.

28 See Susie Butler, "My Trip to Europe: June–August 1953," MSS SC 1015, L. Tom Perry Special Collections, Harold B. Lee Library, Brigham Young University, Provo, Utah.

29 "Our Traveling Mutual," *Young Woman's Journal* 10, no. 2 (February 1899): 2.

30 "Susanne Goes A-Travelling: Sailing the South Seas," *Young Woman's Journal* 28, no. 8 (August 1917): 438–443; "Susanne Goes A-Travelling: In New Zealand and Australia," *Young Woman's Journal* 28, no. 9 (September 1917): 488–492; "Susanne Goes A-Travelling: In Java," *Young Woman's Journal* 28, no. 10 (October 2017): 537–541; "Susanne Goes A-Travelling: In India," *Young Woman's Journal* 28, no. 11 (November 2017): 605–609; "Susanne Goes A-Travelling: In China," *Young Woman's Journal* 28, no. 12 (December 2017): 665–669; "Susanne Goes A-Travelling: In Japan," *Young Woman's Journal* 29, no. 1 (January 2018): 14–18; "Susanne Goes A-Travelling: In a Floating Palace," *Young Woman's Journal* 29, no. 3 (March 1918): 139–143; "Susanne Goes A-Travelling: In Manila," *Young Woman's Journal* 29, no. 4 (April 2018): 196–201.

31 Lucy M. Blanchard, "Venetian Memories," *Young Woman's Journal* 28, no. 8 (August 1917): 435–436; Eulalia Stuart Stauffer, "Impressions of Egypt," *Young Woman's Journal* 36, no. 3 (March 1925): 139–146; Elsie Hoffmann Buchanan, "The Playground of Europe," *Young Woman's Journal* 40, no. 6 (June 1929): 374–379.

32 Elsie Hoffmann Buchanan, "Fascinating Italy," *Young Woman's Journal* 39, no. 9 (September 1928): 543–547 and vol. 39, no. 10 (October 1929): 631–635.

33 See Noel B. Reynolds, "The Coming Forth of the Book of Mormon in the Twentieth Century," *BYU Studies Quarterly* 38, no. 2 (1993), 6–47.

34 From the beginning of their artistic tradition, Latter-day Saint artists had adopted Orientalist and primitivist modes (henceforth referred to as exoticist) of representing peoples and cultures outside their European and American contexts. Representations of the so-called Other by artists of this generation contain racist, sexist, and classist elements, and this remains one of the least discussed issues in Latter-day Saint art and visual culture. Work on race and representation in Mormon art is beginning to gain traction. See Breanne Robertson, "Poster Children of the Sun: George M. Ottinger's Mesoamerican History Paintings and Latter-day Saint Identity in the U.S.-Mexico Borderlands," *American Art* 36, no. 1 (Spring 2022): 1–29; and Nathan Rees, "Envisioning 'Lamanites,'" in *Mormon Visual Culture and the American West* (New York: Routledge, 2021), 40–65.

35 Letter from Minerva Teichert to Ella Hickman Kohlhepp, October 2, 1915, Teichert Papers, cited in Emily Kelly Hinchey, "Chronology," in Marian Wardle, *Minerva Teichert: Pageants in Paint* (Provo, UT: Brigham Young University Museum of Art, 2007), 184n39.

36 Laurie Teichert Eastwood, "Introduction," in *Letters of Minerva Kohlhepp Teichert,* ed. Laurie Teichert Eastwood (Provo, UT: BYU Studies, 1998), 8.

37 Minerva Teichert quoted in Tiffany Alvey Dennison, "Autobiography of Minerva Kohlhepp Teichert (1937)," in Marian Wardle, *Minerva Teichert: Pageants in Paint* (Provo, UT: Brigham Young University Museum of Art, 2007), 212.

38 Wardle, *Minerva Teichert: Pageants in Paint,* 86.

39 Marian Eastwood Wardle, "That He Who Runs May Read," in *The Book of Mormon Paintings of Minerva Teichert,* ed. John Welch and Doris D. Dant (Provo, UT: BYU Studies, 1997), 38.

40 "Sketches—Sketchpad," Laurie Teichert Eastwood collection on Minerva Kohlhepp and Herman A. Teichert, MSS 2243, Box 7, Folder 13, L. Tom Perry Special Collections, Harold B. Lee Library, Brigham Young University, Provo, Utah.

41 Letter from Minerva Teichert to Laurie Teichert, February 2, 1944, in *Letters of Minerva Teichert,* 61.

42 Letter from Alice Merrill Horne to Minerva Teichert, February 29, 1932, Laurie Teichert Eastwood collection on Minerva Kohlhepp and Herman A. Teichert, MSS 2243, Folder 4, Incoming Letters of Alice Merrill Horne, 1931–36, L. Tom Perry Special Collections, Harold B. Lee Library, Brigham Young University, Provo, Utah.

43 Letter from Minerva Teichert to Laurie Teichert, May 21, 1944, in *Letters of Minerva Teichert,* 65.

44 Letter from Minerva and Laurie to Herman and Johnny Teichert, July 2, 1944, in *Letters of Minerva Teichert,* 66n85.

45 These two works are referenced in a letter from Alice Merrill Horne to Minerva Teichert, April 10, 1945, Laurie Teichert Eastwood collection on Minerva Kohlhepp and Herman A. Teichert, MS2243, Box 4, Folder 11, Incoming Letters: Horne, Alice Merrill (1937–1947), Tom Perry Special Collections, Harold B. Lee Library, Brigham Young University, Provo, Utah. Teichert would again echo this sentiment in a letter sent from her sojourn in South America, where she lamented that "the poverty of the poor and the affluence of the bold rich is sickening." Letter from Minerva Teichert to Laurie Teichert and family, March 10, 1958, in *Letters of Minerva Teichert,* 177.

46 "Minerva Teichert Is Wife, Artist," *Salt Lake Tribune,* April 28, 1946, 44.

47 Turn-of-the-century scholars B. H. Roberts and Benjamin Cluff were among the first to advocate geographical and archaeological studies of the Book of Mormon, and the search for such evidence of the scripture's veracity escalated after World War II. For an overview of this phenomenon, see Terryl L. Givens, "'I, Nephi, Wrote This Record': *The Book of Mormon* as Ancient History, Part I—the Search for a Mesoamerican Troy," in *By the Hand of Mormon: The American Scripture That Launched a New World Religion* (New York: Oxford University Press, 2022), 89–116.

48 Reproduced in Welch and Dant, eds., *The Book of Mormon Paintings of Minerva Teichert,* plate 5, 20.

49 Wardle, "That He Who Runs May Read," 39.

50 "Research—Mexico (Undated)," Laurie Teichert Eastwood collection on Minerva Kohlhepp and Herman A. Teichert, MSS 2243, Box 6, Folder 1, L. Tom Perry Special Collections, Harold B. Lee Library, Brigham Young University, Provo, Utah.

51 Wardle, *Minerva Teichert: Pageants in Paint,* 104.

52 Letter from Minerva Teichert to President J. Reuben Clark, April 9, 1940, in *Letters of Minerva Teichert,* 34. As Laurie comments in note 30, it is possible that this letter was never sent, for "Minerva probably would have sent the letter typewritten but perhaps not." A reproduction of the handwritten letter, which offers a sustained and compelling argument for such a center, is on 35–38.

53 Letter from Minerva Teichert to Laurie Teichert, December 15, 1945, in *Letters of Minerva Teichert,* 77.

54 "Sketches—Sketchpads (Undated)," Laurie Teichert Eastwood collection on Minerva Kohlhepp and Herman A. Teichert, MSS 2243, Box 7, Folder 14, L. Tom Perry Special Collections, Harold B. Lee Library, Brigham Young University, Provo, Utah. This vision of an LDS art center was one that her agent and friend, Alice Merrill Horne, had also been promoting for many years. See letter from Alice Merrill Horne to President Joseph F. Smith et al., March 10, 1903, First Presidency administrative files, 1878–1918; Alice Merrill Horne, 1903, Church History Library.

55 Mexico came to hold a special place in the Teichert family. Laurie returned to Mexico to serve an LDS mission in the spring of 1946, and her daughter, Elisa Eastwood Pulido, is the author of *The Spiritual Evolution of Margarito Bautista: Mexican Mormon Evangelizer, Polygamist Dissident, and Utopian Founder, 1878–1961* (New York: Oxford University Press, 2020).

56 Letter from Minerva Teichert to Laurie Teichert and family, January 4, 1958, in *Letters of Minerva Teichert,* 174.

57 Letters from Minerva Teichert to Laurie Teichert and family, March 10, 1958, and March 22, 1958, in *Letters of Minerva Teichert,* 176–177.

58 Letter from Minerva Teichert to Laurie y Carlos, February 19–20, 1958, in *Letters of Minerva Teichert,* 176.

59 Letters from Minerva Teichert to Laurie Teichert and family, March 10, 1958, and March 22, 1958, in *Letters of Minerva Teichert,* 176–177.

60 Madeleine F. Wallis, "A Biographical Sketch of Professor Mabel Pearl Frazer" (Salt Lake City: M.F. Waldis, 1984).

61 See Emily Larsen and Heather Belnap, "'Sure a Strong Devil': Mabel Frazer, A. B. Wright, and the University of Utah Art Department's 1937 Sexual Misconduct Case," *Utah Historical Quarterly,* Summer 2022, 196–214.

62 Carma Rose Anderson de Jong, "Mabel Pearl Frazer: Professor of Art," exhibition brochure, B. F. Larsen Gallery, Brigham Young University, October 1–29, 1980, Springville Museum of Art curatorial file.

63 "University Teacher and Pupil Leave for Year Abroad," *Salt Lake Tribune,* September 21, 1930, and "Utah Artist Honored in Italy," *Salt Lake Tribune,* June 28, 1931.

64 "To Cotine [*sic*] Study in Italy," *Salt Lake Tribune,* October 11, 1931.

65 "Italian Art Lecture Scheduled for Sunday," *Deseret News,* September 9, 1933.

66 Richard Oman and Arlene Wilson, "Interview with Mabel Frasier [*sic*], February 1977," CR 100–899, Church History Library, Salt Lake City, Utah.

67 Oman and Wilson, "Interview."

68 Alice Merrill Horne, "A Few of Our Gifted Women Artists," *Relief Society Magazine,* 1944, 683.

69 "Item Found in Art Barn," *Salt Lake Tribune,* May 24, 1936.

70 "Miss Verla Birrell," *Daily Herald,* May 16, 1946, and "BYU Art Professor Ends South American Trip," *Salt Lake Tribune,* October 11, 1946.

71 *Daily Herald,* December 28, 1947.

72 Emily Larsen, "Negotiating Postwar Mormon Femininity: Verla Birrell, the 'Globe-Trotter' of Utah Art," paper presented at the 2021 Mormon History Association conference.

73 Verla Birrell and students, *Portfolio of Historic Design: Practice Plates for Reference or for Design Application Useful in Courses of: Art History, Costume Design, Historic Costume, Design, Textile Design, Architectural Design, Applied Art Work (Ceramics, Jewelry, Metal, Block Print, Stencil, Etc.)* (Provo, UT: Verla Birrell, 1947); Verla Birrell, *The Book of Mormon Guide Book: An Internal Reconstruction of the Archaeology, History, and Religious Teachings of the Ancient Peoples of the* Book of Mormon (Salt Lake City: Verla Birrell, 1948); and Verla Birrell, *The Textile Arts: A Handbook of Fabric Structure and Design Processes: Ancient and Modern Weaving, Braiding, Printing, and Other Textile Techniques* (New York: Harper & Brothers, 1959).

74 Quoted in Emily Larsen, "Art, Mortality, and Religion Among Utah's Historic Women Artists," *15 Bytes: Utah's Art Magazine,* April 6, 2020, http://artistsofutah.org/15Bytes/index.php/art-mortality-and-religion-amongst-utahs-historic-women-artists/.

75 Although undated in the Utah Art Collection database, the painting was almost certainly executed in 1942. It was referenced in exhibition reviews of a December 1942 show at BYU: "Salt Lake Faculty Member Now Exhibiting at Provo 'U,'" *Salt Lake Tribune,* December 6, 1942, and "Birrell Art Exhibit Being Shown at 'Y,'" *Provo Daily Herald,* December 7, 1942. A reproduction of this painting accompanied the article "Representative Show Assembled for State Fair," *Salt Lake Tribune,* September 5, 1943, as marked in the Association of Utah Artists (UAU) Scrapbook pages, Box 1, Book 3, Utah State Archives.

76 "'Y' Art Exhibit Opens Monday," *Salt Lake Tribune,* December 6, 1947.

[77] Adriana Zavala, *Becoming Modern, Becoming Tradition: Women, Gender, and Representation in Mexican Art* (University Park: Pennsylvania State University Press, 2010), 161–167.

[78] See Dina Comisarenco Mirkin, "To Paint the Unspeakable: Mexican Female Artists' Iconography of the 1930s and Early 1940s," *Woman's Art Journal* 29, no. 1 (Spring–Summer 2008): 21–32. There is little doubt that Birrell had visited the 1937 *Mexican Collection* exhibition held at the Art Barn, which featured works by Kahlo and other contemporary artists and was hailed by exhibition chair Helen Sheets as "the most important group of pictures ever exhibited in Salt Lake." Will South, *Making and Breaking Tradition: A History of the Salt Lake Art Center* (Salt Lake City: Salt Lake Art Center, 1991), 10.

[79] "Marine and Mexican Scenes Are Shown," *Salt Lake Tribune,* September 30, 1945.

[80] "Utah Criticizes Americans for Extravagant Buying from Merchants in Neighbor Lands," *Salt Lake Tribune,* January 28, 1945.

[81] "P.H.S. Women [Miss Verla Birrell will give a lecture on 'Mexican Art']," *Daily Herald,* March 13, 1945; "Orem Women's Club [Verla Birrell, assistant professor at the BYU will address the group on 'South of the Border in Search of Art']," *Daily Herald,* October 11, 1945; "Talk on Mexico; Art Exhibit at Readers' Guild Open Meet," *Daily Herald,* November 18, 1945; and "Mexico, South America Trip Told," *Daily Herald,* November 18, 1946.

[82] "BYU Art Professor Leaves Here for U. of U. Position," *Daily Herald,* September 19, 1948; "Literary Club Tells of Program," *Deseret News,* February 11, 1951; "Illustrated Lecture, Miss Verla Birrell," *Ephraim Enterprise,* January 12, 1951; "Archaeology Section," *Salt Lake Tribune,* January 8, 1955.

[83] "Verla Birrell Takes Up Art South of the Border," *Salt Lake Telegram,* November 8, 1951.

[84] "On the Scene of Leadership Week [LDS Church]," *Deseret News,* February 4, 1946; "She Has a Wardrobe Full of Costumes," *Salt Lake Telegram,* November 8, 1951. See also University of Utah Historical Faculty Files, Verla Birrell, ACC 0526, Box 5, Folder 84, University Archives and Records Management, J. Willard Marriott Library, University of Utah.

[85] *Ogden Standard Examiner,* July 17, 1950; *Salt Lake Telegram,* July 24, 1950.

[86] On the relationship between religious identity and travel during this era, see Melissa R. Klapper, "The Great Adventure of 1929: The Impact of Travel Abroad on American Jewish Women's Identity," *American Jewish History* 102, no. 1 (2018): 85–107.

[87] William W. Stowe, *Going Abroad: European Travel in Nineteenth-Century American Culture* (Princeton, NJ: Princeton University Press, 1994), 5.

[88] Horne, "A Few of Our Gifted Women Artists," 683.

[89] Macleod, "Introduction," 3.

[90] Erika Doss, "I *Must* Paint: Women Artists of the Rocky Mountain Region," in *Independent Spirits: Women Painters of the American West, 1890–1945*, ed. Patricia Trenton (Los Angeles: University of California Press, 1995), 216.

8

LATTER-DAY SAINT TEMPLE DESIGN: ASPIRATIONS OF GRANDEUR AND TEMPERING RESTRAINTS

JOSH EDWARD PROBERT

While the earliest Latter-day Saints, those of the 1830s and 1840s, were a biblical preaching people, they radically parted ways with their evangelical Protestant cousins by embracing a priestly sacramental theology that blended Old and New Testament worlds with nineteenth-century religious innovations to create a new religious tradition. As Jan Shipps has written, "Mormonism is Christianity *plus*."[1] Temple theology and temple rituals account for much of the "plus" that Shipps identifies.[2] The longer that church founder Joseph Smith lived, the more elaborate the Mormon system of salvation became, and the complex system of sacramental rites he introduced necessitated a new building type, the Mormon temple. This architecture is the result of church leaders and architects drawing on existing forms and reassembling them into new ones in an interpenetrative process of borrowing, adopting, and repurposing.

While LDS meetinghouses are simple utilitarian buildings used for Sunday meetings and are more of a twentieth-century form than a nineteenth-century one, temples are finer buildings that are imbued with a higher level of sacerdotalism and are used for the esoteric rites of salvation and exaltation unique to Mormonism.[3] These rites include proxy baptisms for the dead, metaphorical washings and priestly anointings, a series of teachings and covenant-makings called "the endowment," and eternal sealings. To accommodate these rituals, the interiors are divided into many compartmentalized spaces specifically designated for each ritual instead of a large meeting hall with pews facing a pulpit, which one normally expects of Christian buildings.

The meaning, form, and function of the phrase "temple" evolved and changed over the nineteenth century. At the outset in the 1830s, temple designs were like those of Protestant churches but with some unique interior configurations. By the end of the century, they were entirely unique, a novel amalgam of religious, hospitality, theater, and Masonic architecture. This chapter seeks to provide a brief historical overview of this evolution and to situate Mormon temples within nineteenth-century debates regarding sacramentalism, sacred space, and the ritual efficacy of ornament and iconography.

It further discusses the tensions between Joseph Smith's revelatory calls to grandiose sumptuousness and the heritage of Protestant restraint and republican frugality that have tempered those calls; the sacralization of Victorian refinement and parlor culture and the ways that the church enlisted temples in its campaign for social acceptability; and the complicated ways that race and gender played out in these buildings. The chapter will then highlight some of the ways that nineteenth-century discourses shaped temple design in the twentieth and twenty-first centuries and the negotiations that church leaders and architects made with modernity and technological efficiency that have changed the patron experience from an immersive, participatory type of liturgical theater to a passively rote one of rational efficiency. The global expansion of the church and the hundreds of temples that have been built outside of the United States merit volumes of study, but they are beyond the scope of this chapter. Yet the chapter will provide a few thoughts on the exportation of temple aesthetics and the challenges of global enculturation.

CONSTRUCTING SACRED SPACE ON THE AMERICAN FRONTIER

Shortly after publishing the Book of Mormon and founding the church in 1830, Joseph Smith shifted his attention to an ambitious millennialist project of building an American city of Zion with a temple at its center. In doing so, he innovated on existing traditions of the New Jerusalem being established in America and of Protestant city planning with religious buildings at their center.[4] In Smith's cosmology, the temple—and the rites performed therein—formed a theological foundation upon which all the other work of the church was built. In an 1844 meeting with church leaders about building priorities at the time, he instructed them, "We need the temple more than anything else."[5] Smith's use of the phrase "temple" was not altogether novel. Anglicans had referred to their churches as temples as early as the seventeenth century.[6] Congregationalists referred to their churches as temples in dedicatory sermons in the early nineteenth century.[7] And one of the definitions of "temple" in Noah Webster's 1828 dictionary was "A church; an edifice erected among Christians as a place of public worship."[8] Yet, as with other religious concepts of the early nineteenth century, Smith reinterpreted and expanded upon what "temple" meant. In the wake of these theological innovations, Mormon temples became something quite different from the "Houses of the Lord" Webster was familiar with.

The earliest evidence of LDS temple design is a drawing from 1833 for a temple intended to be built in Independence, Missouri. Never brought to fruition, this plan was used a few years later in a modified way for the temple in Kirtland, Ohio. With its

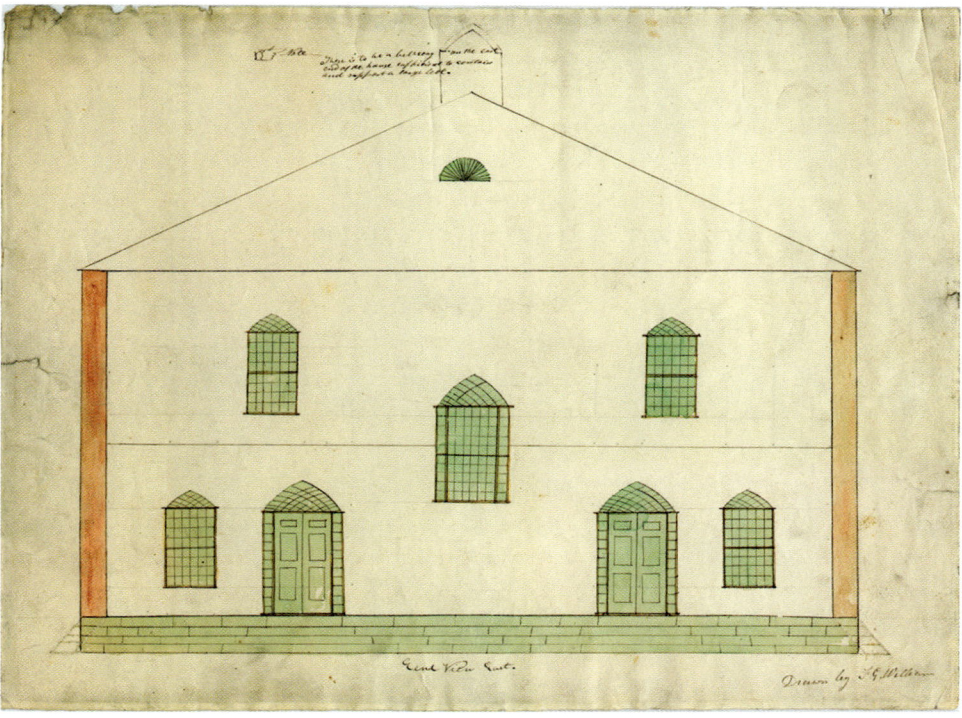

Fig. 8.1 Proposal drawing for east elevation of temple in Independence, Missouri, 1833, Church History Library, The Church of Jesus Christ of Latter-day Saints.

pedimented massing and vernacular Gothic fenestration, the design closely resembled a Protestant church. Yet the interior plan departed from popular convention in that it had a second assembly room constructed on a second floor and elevated tiered pulpits on the ends of each hall, representing the Mormon priesthoods. By and large, the Kirtland temple functioned similarly to a traditional meetinghouse, accommodating both religious and secular assemblies, as Smith had not yet introduced many of the rites that brought together the material significance of a temple and the ritual embodiments meant to be enacted inside it. Yet there were adumbrations of that future when priesthood leaders used the upper rooms of the temple for ritual foot washings and priestly washings and anointings.[9]

Soon after the Saints were exiled from Ohio and Missouri and gathered in Nauvoo, Illinois, Smith became preoccupied with fashioning not just a temple-centered city but a refined and genteel one. His revelations began to lay out dreams of architectural grandeur. In January 1841, he dictated a revelation that, drawing upon Psalm 144:12, instructed the Saints that Nauvoo was to "be polished with that refinement which is after the similitude of a palace" (D&C 124:2). The revelation's injunction presaged several more that directed the Saints to pursue palatial refinement as part of their religious

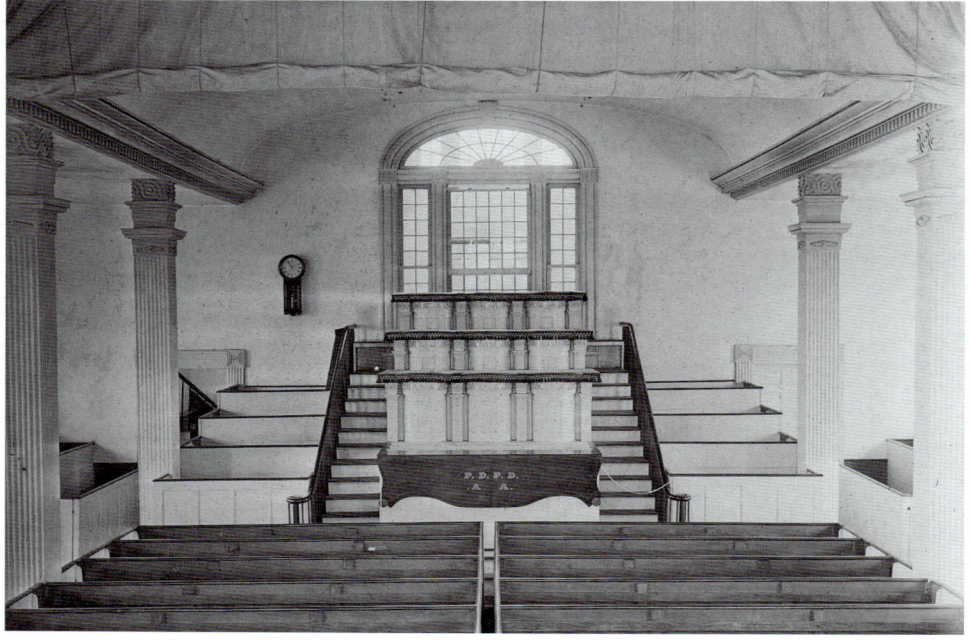

Fig. 8.2 George Edward Anderson, interior of Kirtland Temple, 1880–1920, photograph, L. Tom Perry Special Collections, Brigham Young University.

enterprise. In 1843, Smith taught that the temple would be the foundation of "aggrandizement" for God's kingdom on earth. In 1843, a revelation was even more explicit about the public relations role the Nauvoo temple should play and the type of people God wanted it to attract: "Build a Temple to my great name, and call the attention of the great, the rich, and the noble."[10]

Because of the eternal significance of temple rituals in the LDS work of salvation and exaltation—what the Book of Mormon prophet Alma calls the "great plan of happiness" (Alma 42:8)—the building needed to match the message. A meetinghouse would not do. Thus, Smith's vision for temples went beyond the restrained refinement that many Protestant churches possessed and called for an exuberant architecture that would rival the most splendid buildings in the world. In January 1841, Smith received a revelation that directed, "Come ye, with all your gold, and your silver, and your precious stones, and with all your antiquities . . . together with all the precious trees of the earth . . . and build a house to my name" (D&C 124:26–27). Another revelation from the same year reiterated the call for a splendid temple: "Hasten then to Zion and contribute to the erection of temples, sanctuaries, and palaces, such as the world never saw, with their walls finished with th[e] pencil of Raphael, decorated with gold and pearls, and precious stones, beautified by the finger of God."[11]

The Latter-day Saints' consideration of what and how luxuriant the House of the Lord should be took place at the same time many Protestants were renegotiating ideas of holiness, ornament, and iconography in the worship space. During the colonial period, Anglicans had preferred ecclesiastical churches with arched windows, barrel-vaulted ceilings, and carvings of angels and cherubim, while Puritans preferred plain-style congregational meetinghouses that doubled as spaces for civic business.[12] During the late eighteenth and early nineteenth centuries, Puritans began changing course and built churches that looked more like Anglican ones.[13] And during the early to mid-nineteenth century, Anglicans and Episcopalians in the United States under the influence of the Oxford movement embraced an even more sacramental theology with an accompanying revival of medieval Catholic design and ornament that made their churches more and more ornate.[14] Puritan descendants along with the burgeoning Methodists started to reject the austerity of their building traditions and began to construct, instead of "meetinghouses," buildings called "churches" in Gothic and Romanesque styles with crosses, stained glass windows, and organs in heavily carved wooden cases.[15]

THE ENDOWMENT AND THE PROGRESS OF WESTERN CIVILIZATION

Smith's introduction of a rite that came to be called "the endowment" changed the direction of temple design and temple use, leading to a full integration of the material with the sacramental in temple worship. The endowment consisted of a series of teachings, hymns, and Masonic-like oaths associated with covenants of virtue, morality, and consecration. Smith administered the rite in a series of makeshift rooms that acted as metaphorical backdrops for each stage of earthly and godly progression in the plan of salvation, beginning in the primordial history of creation with Adam and Eve's placement in the Garden of Eden and ending in the afterlife and the Celestial Kingdom (the highest kingdom one can inhabit in the afterlife). These rooms, which eventually became permanent features of the temples in Utah, are known as the creation room, garden room, world room, terrestrial room, and celestial room.[16]

At the culmination of the endowment's novel account of the Adam and Eve story, participants passed from the terrestrial room to the celestial room through a highly sacred portiere called the "veil of the temple," the transition doubling as a symbol of both death and the ancient Hebrew veil of the temple. Upon passing through the veil, participants entered a space like a Victorian parlor that symbolized the arrival of Adam and Eve in the presence of God and on their own path to godhood. These spaces imagined a domesticated heaven at a time when Latter-day Saint theology viewed the (Celestial Kingdom as being populated by family kingdoms. Celestial rooms literalized Jesus's statement "In my Father's house are many mansions. . . . I go to prepare a place for you."[17]

Contemporary accounts describe the makeshift celestial room in the attic of the Nauvoo temple as "a very large and spacious room, perfectly lit, all nicely furnished" with "two splendid tables and four splendid sofa[s]." The walls were lined with mirrors, portraits, and maps.[18] Church member William Clayton recorded in his journal that the space had "a very splendid and comfortable appearance."[19] Clayton's account captures the overarching framework of Victorian parlor making—the deployment of a fashionable interior to demonstrate a family's good taste that was at the same time a reposeful retreat of hearth and home. Historian Katherine C. Grier calls this framing construct "culture and comfort."[20] Whether or not the temple interior possessed a type of vernacular splendor, nowhere did the touch of a Raphael appear, and nowhere were there precious woods, precious stones, or other "precious things of the earth." While the building's Neoclassical detailing did conform to "a knowledge of antiquities" that the revelation prescribed, the building's Classicism did not match the more robust revivals of antiquity at the time, to say nothing of the Renaissance-era buildings of the Vatican.

The irony of the Nauvoo temple was that despite all of Joseph Smith's bold calls for a dazzling architecture the world had never seen, the Nauvoo Temple was a very familiar Protestant-looking building. Although a handsome stone structure that rivaled the finest East Coast churches, it was a far cry from the soaring standards set forth in the revelations. The interior was like that of the earlier Kirtland temple—two assembly rooms, one on top of the other. The woodwork was restrained and dignified, having much in common with Neoclassical buildings of the time. Yet the interior was a step back from the interior of the Kirtland temple. Records for purchasing gold leaf survive, indicating that something on the Nauvoo interior was gilded, but the architectural woodwork was overall simpler, and there was less of it. Drawings of the interior show the intent was always to be something far more modest than the exterior.[21]

Nauvoo is not the only temple to fall short of the soaring expectations set by Smith's revelations. Perhaps a reason for this is that the resources of the church in the mid-nineteenth century were limited, and had Smith lived longer, his vision might have been realized. But numerous poor immigrant communities built resplendent buildings as monuments to their faith during the nineteenth century. As a newspaper writer observed during the construction of St. Patrick's Cathedral in New York, the building was a result "not of the superfluity of wealth, but for the most part out of offerings of poverty."[22] Even today, when the LDS church is wealthy beyond what the nineteenth-century members could have ever imagined, temples generally share the same characteristics of the Nauvoo temple—handsome buildings with stone exteriors that make a public statement on the landscape, a spire or spires on most that identify them as religious buildings, and conservatively tasteful interiors that are comfortably appointed, pristinely clean, and designed to facilitate functionality.[23] Even the most impressive temples fail to rival the likes of St. Peter's Basilica, St. Paul's Cathedral, or the great European palaces such as Versailles, the Hermitage, and the Dolmabahçe. These early temples, and the hundreds that have followed since—evidence two dyads: first, the degree to which Latter-day Saints have adhered to revelations calling for Old

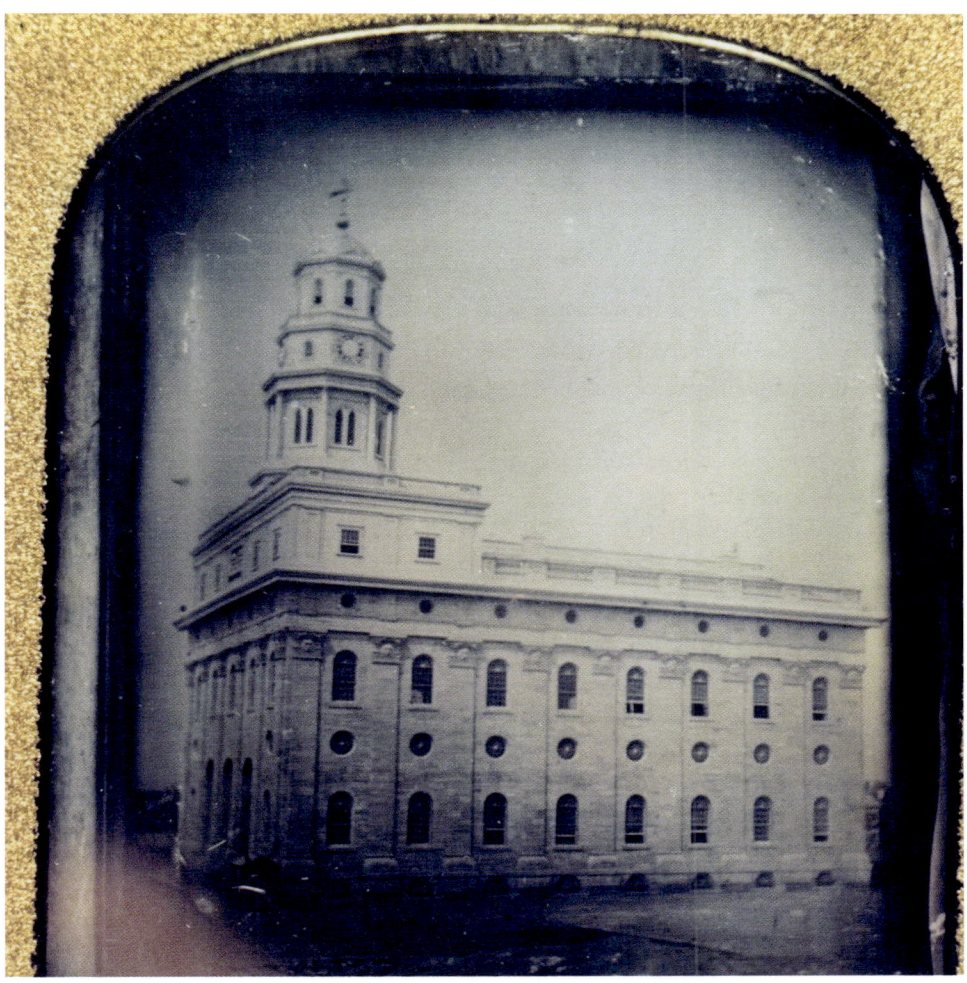

Fig. 8.3 Attributed to Louis B. Chaffin, Nauvoo Temple, c. 1847, daguerreotype, Cedar City Camp, International Society Daughters of the Utah Pioneers.

Testament grandeur versus the early nineteenth-century Protestant restraint from which Mormonism sprang; and second, the employment of gentility and good taste as indices of godliness versus a republican frugality that viewed luxuriousness as ostentatious, wasteful, and potentially prideful. In a sense, temples are Catholic but not too Catholic—the same balance that nineteenth-century Protestants who rejected Reformation-era aesthetics were trying to strike.

THE SALT LAKE AND MANTI TEMPLES AS GRAND EXPRESSIONS OF MORMON ASPIRATIONS

In the Utah Territory, the exteriors of the St. George (1877), Logan (1884), Manti (1888), and Salt Lake Temples drew upon medieval Romanticism to create grand fortress-like monuments. These buildings towered over the houses, shops, and farms, presiding both literally and symbolically over the vernacular landscapes of Mormon settlement. The interiors varied widely in their styles and levels of sophistication. While St. George and Logan were characterized by a type of simple vernacular elegance on a grand scale, the interiors of Manti (1888) and Salt Lake City were more in keeping with the visually intricate design trends of the time.

Although the Salt Lake Temple is the most recognizable of the nineteenth-century temples, the Manti Temple is of a similar caliber of work and has even been lauded by one architectural historian as "the finest of LDS buildings, past and present."[24] Both temples signal Gothic Revival with their vertical massing, engaged buttresses, and castellated walls. While the gray granite Salt Lake Temple has French Renaissance spires with acanthus buds at the east and west ends, the cream-colored limestone Manti temple has mansard roofs set on Italianate cupolas. As architectural historian Thomas Carter has noted, the cupolas on the Manti Temple are more characteristic of domestic architecture, particularly the church's Gardo House (1883) in Salt Lake City, and architect

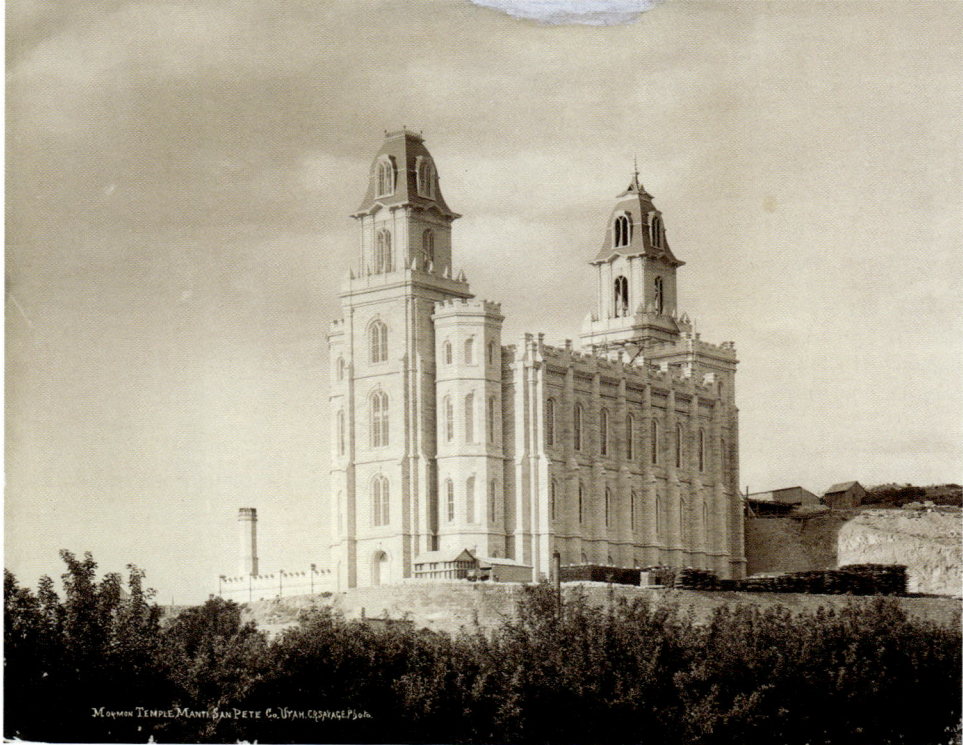

Fig. 8.4 Charles Roscoe Savage, Manti Temple, c. 1887, photograph, Church History Library, The Church of Jesus Christ of Latter-day Saints.

William Folsom's incorporation of them made the appellation "House of the Lord" even more literal.[25]

The Salt Lake Temple, with its highly articulated exterior, is perhaps the most Catholic cathedral-like building in the history of LDS architecture. Its exterior walls feature an elaborate program of esoteric symbolism carved into the granite walls, typifying a comfort with symbolism that disappeared during the twentieth century.[26] Building on the precedents set by the Nauvoo Temple, the bas-relief sculpture included star, moon, and sun stones but added cloud stones with hands holding trumpets, the constellation Ursa Major, and clasped hands popular on gravestones. Each symbol carries particular theological meanings about the priesthood, the heavens, and covenant-making. Both the building and the symbolic program represent gestures of confidence in communal uniqueness and self-expression.

THE ANGEL MORONI

Although Latter-day Saints have expended great effort striving for inclusion in the family of Christian faiths, they have generally abstained from using the cross as a symbol of their faith, including on or in temples. This absence is a continuation of the Reformed Protestant tradition of not using the cross, a general predilection that early Mormons possessed.[27] Yet while most Protestants had embraced the cross by the end of the nineteenth century, Latter-day Saints never did. Instead of a cross, the gilded statue of the Book of Mormon figure Moroni on top of the temple's center spires is an iconic feature of Mormon temples. The statue has its origins in the Protestant practice of placing weathervanes on top of meetinghouses and churches, the most popular being made in the shape of a rooster, a dove, or the angel Gabriel.[28] An angel weathervane with a Masonic compass and square added above it was placed on the Nauvoo Temple's tower.[29] For the Salt Lake Temple, the church drew upon the Nauvoo precedent, but instead of a weathervane, the spire on the finial was to be a monumental statue. The church commissioned Cyrus Edwin Dallin, a celebrated American sculptor who grew up in Utah, to create the now-iconic figure for the center-east spire. Instead of Gabriel, this figure became Moroni, the last of the Book of Mormon writers who appeared to Joseph Smith and delivered the golden plates from which Smith translated the record.[30]

Dallin worked during the golden age of American Neoclassical sculpture, and his angelic figure shared characteristics with the public sculpture of his contemporaries. For instance, Saint-Gaudens's *Diana* was placed on Madison Square Garden in 1893, the same year the Salt Lake temple was dedicated, and a statue of William Penn was placed on the top spire of Philadelphia's City Hall the next year. Dallin's angel was almost identical to contemporary depictions of Gabriel, which appeared on everything from Tiffany windows to Arts and Crafts textiles to socialist propaganda posters.[31] Similar to Calder's statue of Penn, Dallin posed his monumental Moroni in contrapposto, with the weight placed on the front right foot, the hips being moved out of plane, adding a sense of dimensionality and movement to the work. Moroni's head is tilted upward to blow a

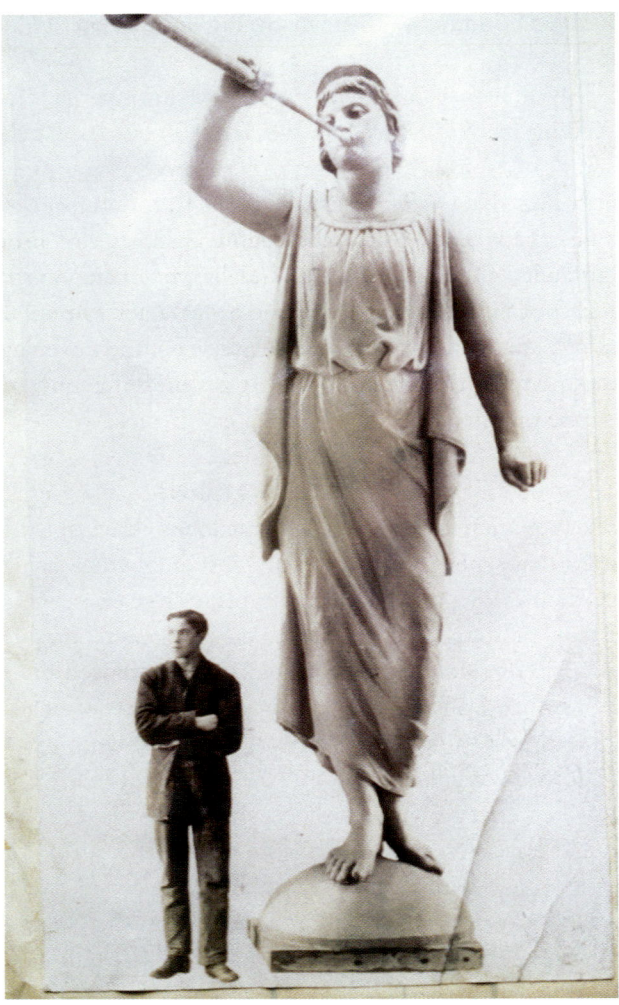

Fig. 8.5 Angel Moroni statue at the W. H. Mullins Company in Salem, Ohio, with man who is assumed to be Cyrus Dallin, c. 1892, Church History Library, The Church of Jesus Christ of Latter-day Saints.

long slender trumpet aimed toward the east. The left arm is extended, bent at the elbow, balancing the upheld right arm. The left hand is positioned as if it were holding something to retain balance. Like Saint-Gaudens's *Diana,* Dallin's Moroni stands atop a sphere, a device that visually separates and elevates the piece and augments the graceful poise that the figure exudes. The statue continues to function as a symbol of the church. It and later interpretations of the same basic composition top the towers of more than half of all temples today. However, in recent years, the church has dramatically reduced its use on new temples in a move away from cultural uniqueness toward further cultural integration.[32]

GOD'S PARLOR: THE VISUAL RHETORIC OF HEAVENLY GENTILITY

Seeing the celestial room as a parlor further demonstrates the pull between the opulence of Smith's vision for temples and the counterdiscourses of Protestant austerity and republican frugality. Whereas the parlor-as-heaven metaphor was gestural and makeshift in the attic of the Nauvoo Temple and in the Endowment House on Temple Square in Salt Lake City, the metaphor was fully expressed in the Salt Lake and Manti Temples. Celestial rooms in these buildings were grand salons approximating the opulence of Gilded Age mansions and hotels. Both had Beaux Arts Neoclassical interior architecture with elaborate details, damask draperies, detailed plasterwork, and wall-to-wall Axminster carpets. The walls of the Manti celestial room were painted with sophisticated trompe l'oeil murals of drapery that made the real drapery covering the veil appear to continue around the rest of the room.[33]

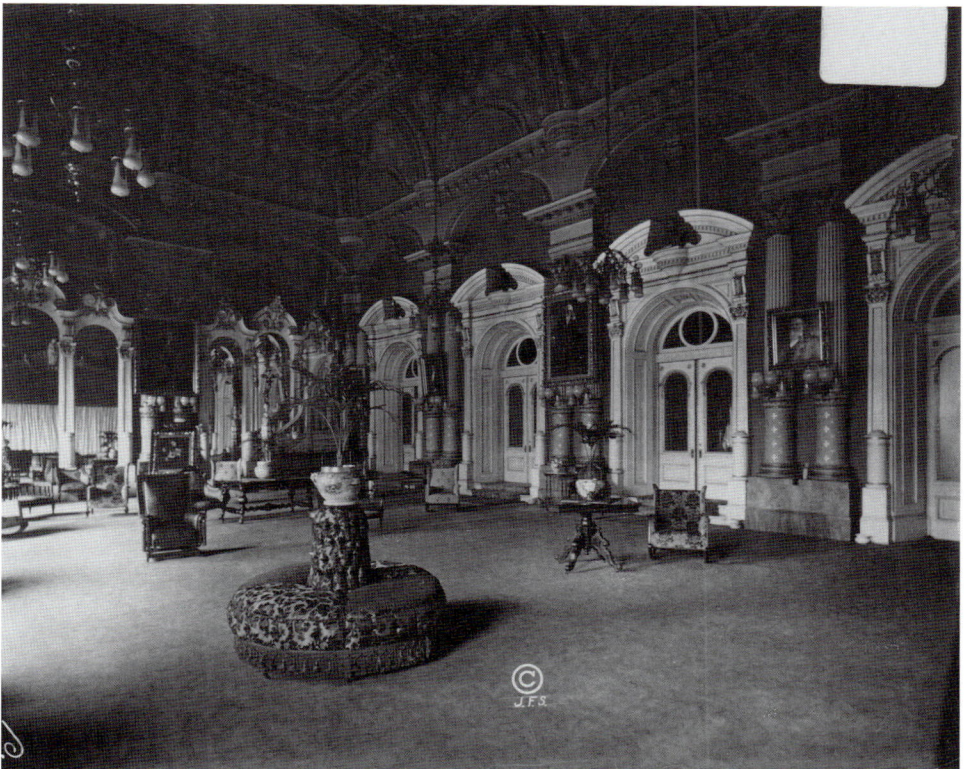

Fig. 8.6 Ralph Savage, Salt Lake Temple celestial room, 1911, photograph, Church History Library, The Church of Jesus Christ of Latter-day Saints.

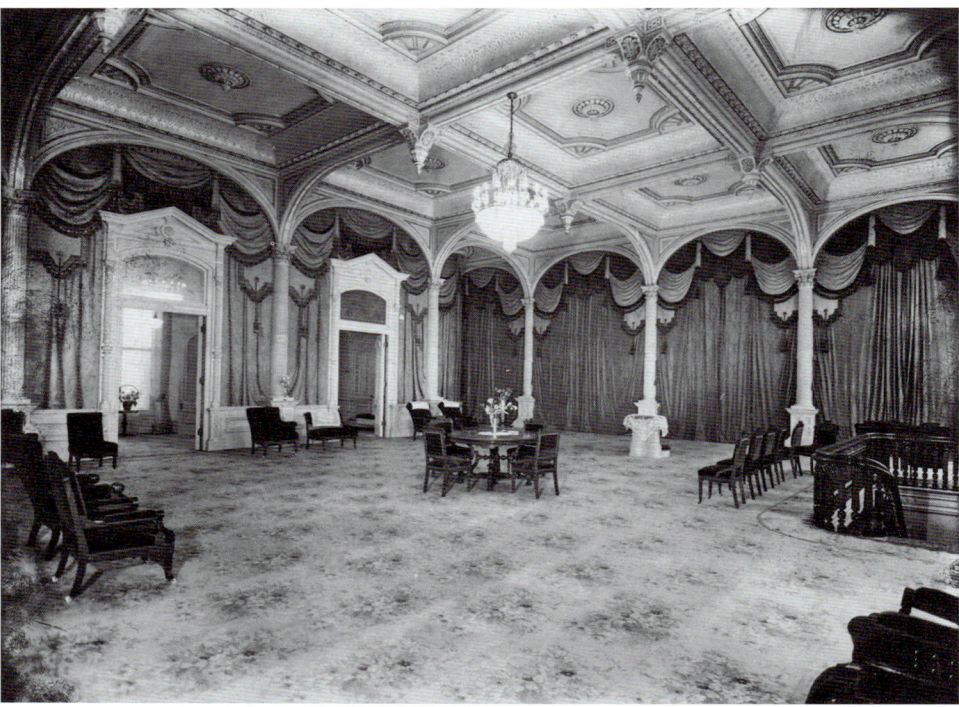

Fig. 8.7 Manti Temple celestial room, undated photograph, Church History Library, The Church of Jesus Christ of Latter-day Saints.

While much of the interior architecture of both the Manti and Salt Lake Temples was elegantly designed and built, many of the rooms and almost all the furnishings did not possess the same level of sophistication. The pews in the assembly rooms, for example, were simple and vernacular in their design. Hallways and meeting rooms had similarly nondescript benches and run-of-the-mill seating. In Manti, although the architecture and murals were elaborate, the furniture in the celestial room was factory-produced middle-class parlor furniture. The contrast of such furniture sitting on a twenty-four-color Axminster carpet amid elaborate architecture and muraled walls in Manti represents an ever-present tension in temple design: that the temples should be nice but not too nice.

The earliest photos of the Salt Lake Temple celestial room evidence the use the languages of art and gentility to create a semiotics of priesthood power (see Figure 8.6). In the photos of the celestial room, images of priesthood leaders saturate the space. Portraits of Brigham Young, George A. Smith, Lorenzo Snow, and Wilford Woodruff hung on the walls and sat on easels. Sculptural portrait busts of Joseph Smith, Brigham Young, Wilford Woodruff, George Q. Cannon, and Joseph F. Smith were placed in the broken pediments above each of the monumental doorways. The portraits acted similarly to their counterparts that lined the walls of countless churches, civic buildings, and

Masonic temples. They added a sense of historic nostalgia and reverence for beloved leaders, most of whom had passed away, and lent a patina of masculinity to the room. As priesthood holders, these men possessed "sealing power"—an authority to perform the most exalting ordinances of the temple—acting as gatekeepers to the mansion of God that the celestial room represented.

Though images of men generally dominated the walls of the temple, images of women were not entirely absent from the Salt Lake Temple. A plaster sculpture of a female angel was located over the veil. In a nod to the corporeality of heavenly beings in Mormon thought, the architect omitted the angel's wings that one would have seen in contemporary Abbott Thayer paintings or Augustus Saint-Gaudens sculptures. Standing in a *Birth of Venus*–like half shell and flanked by cherubs, the figure was more a piece of Neoclassical ornament that complemented the Renaissance Revival interior than a theological statement of female authority. Nevertheless, the piece added a touch of feminine spirituality to the space.

The explicit statements of female authority were portraits of temple matrons, including Eliza R. Snow—the "priestess of Zion"—that were hanging in the hallway outside the celestial room by 1911.[34] The women in these portraits were the leaders of the church's women's organization and largely oversaw women's ordinance work, including temple rituals, throughout the church.[35] Joseph Smith had expanded their involvement in the priesthood, as he designated them co-officiators in many of the temple rituals he introduced in Nauvoo. By making marriage a prerequisite to godhood, women were essential to the exaltation of humanity altogether.[36] The positioning of portraits signified the complex way that women were involved in the work of salvation: any explicit sign of that role was liminal, as their images were relegated to the tertiary corridors of the building and not in the most important room.[37]

The theological foundations of Mormon thought further complicate the way that celestial rooms and temples altogether can be thought of as gendered. Latter-day Saint thought posits God the Father and Jesus Christ as separate embodied male beings. Whereas the traditional Christian creeds strictly demarcate the divine from the corporeal, Joseph Smith collapsed this sacred distance and imbued the material with the divine. God is "an exalted man," Smith taught on one occasion. And on another: "That which is without body, parts, and passions is nothing."[38] This radical anthropomorphizing of godhood has led to the logical conclusion that for God to have children, a heavenly mother must also exist. Intimations of this belief emerged during the 1840s, but they were fully articulated by the completion of the Utah Temples.[39] As George Q. Cannon—whose bust portrait was one of those in the Salt Lake Temple's celestial room in 1911—taught, "God is a married Being, has a wife . . . [and] we are the offspring of Him and His wife."[40] Was the House of the Lord then the house of both a father and a mother? And if plural marriage was an exalting practice, was the temple the house of multiple mothers? These ambiguities have never been resolved, but the discourse surrounding temples has been overwhelmingly masculine. The positioning of the portraits of male and female church leaders in the Salt Lake Temple echoed the teachings about God, as they reasserted the primacy of those who hold the priesthood as gatekeepers to God's parlor. The appellation "House of the Lord" and the gendering of the temple interior as largely male was not dissimilar to the way newspapers referred to Gilded Age mansions by men's names—"Mr. Carnegie's house" or "Mr. Rockefeller's mansion"—even though prominent men were married and had socially prominent wives who also wielded social power.

THE TIGHTROPE OF WEALTH AND RIGHTEOUSNESS

When Joseph Smith fashioned the series of teachings, covenants, and blessings into the ritual that came to be known as "the endowment," he theologically overlaid the Victorian ideology of the progress of Western civilization onto that of Adam and Eve. As participants in the liturgy metaphorically reenacted the journey from the Garden of Eden, moved through mortality, and ended in the celestial room, they equated godhood with the genteel heights of western progress. To both the Saints and broader American attitudes, "civilization" denoted technological progress, scientific advancement, industrialized production, capitalist financial systems, and refined places and persons in domestic and public life. To be civilized was to distance oneself from nature and Indigenous thought and action—ways of life that existed in many of the regions being colonized by Western powers.[41]

At the same time that temple-goers participated in the endowment and absorbed its explicit and implicit messaging, church leaders urged members to prepare for the construction of the New Jerusalem by becoming experts in architecture and interior furnishing. Leah Dunford Widtsoe urged the women of the church in particular to study architecture and design to prepare for the construction of the New Jerusalem, where the buildings, including "magnificent temples," would produce "splendor and grandeur of which has never been conceived on this earth."[42] Joseph Smith's dream for spectacular buildings—"such as the world never saw"—was alive and well among his followers half a century after his death. And Widtsoe's goal was to ensure that the women of the church would be involved in placing the members of the church not only as part of civilization but also as leaders of it.[43]

Latter-day Saint theology is preoccupied with the social ordering of the heavens through priesthood authority, and the art and architecture of temples have facilitated this ordering. The material trappings of the endowment and sealings, in particular, have framed the rituals that order participants in a type of anticipated heavenly class ranking. In doing so, temple art and architecture—celestial rooms, in particular—carried the potential to suggest material wealth as a characteristic of righteousness. Money was already a prerequisite if the nineteenth-century Saints were going to attract the respect and even the awe of Victorian elites. But for late-nineteenth-century church members, the expensive architecture and interiors were material manifestations of a prosperity that evidenced God's favor among them.

At the time the Salt Lake Temple was dedicated, many people in rural Utah still lived in simple cramped log homes, eking out a subsistence living at best. For these struggling Saints, the interior architecture, artwork, and furnishings of the temple were perhaps like those of a medieval cathedral—completely beyond their daily experience. This chasm undoubtedly strengthened the metaphorical power of the temple's interior to represent the glories of godhood. Soaring ceilings, elaborate plasterwork, fine carpet, damask fabrics, and French furniture created a metaphorical promise that these religious strivers would one day inhabit celestial worlds that were beyond the realities of day-to-day living.

The relationship between wealth and righteousness in temple design reinforced a Calvinistic-Old Testament strain in LDS theology that if God's people are righteous, they will prosper financially. The Book of Mormon repeatedly promises that if the descendants of Lehi keep the commandments, they will "prosper in the land."[44] Joseph Smith's revelations similarly promised that if the Saints were obedient, "Zion would prosper." But, the Book of Mormon also taught, prosperity was a precarious position to be in. Pride and vanity soon followed, setting up entire civilizations for collapse.[45] Brigham Young had similarly warned, "The worst fear I have about this people is that they will get rich in this country, forget God and his people, wax fat, and kick themselves out of the Church and go to hell. This people will stand mobbing, robbing, poverty, and all manner of persecution, and be true. But my greater fear for them is that they cannot stand wealth."[46] This double-edged attraction to and fear of wealth is one of the dyads of Mormon culture that has framed temple design.

Latter-day Saints have not been alone in navigating this tension between material splendor and prudent restraint, as debates about the dyad, including ones about church architecture and interior decor, have been endemic to American life since the colonial period. As Richard Bushman has written, nineteenth-century Protestants were faced with the popularity of two worldviews that, in their origins, had different goals. The first was the culture of genteel refinement, which originated in European courts and enforced cultural hierarchies; the other was Christian tradition with its concern for Christlike humility, self-sacrifice, and concern for the poor.[47] The marriage of the two ideologies came to characterize religious architecture by the second half of the nineteenth century. Episcopalians led the way in refined taste-making, and other religionists followed their lead to varying degrees and updated their buildings to more ornamented churchly styles to meet the changing tastes of their flocks. Latter-day Saints were among these.[48]

While LDS temples adapted the conventions of Victorian domestic and public architecture to religious purposes, they also upended some of the ideologies that undergirded those conventions. At a time when many churches continued to have pew rentals, thus restricting access to some of the nation's most beautiful spaces largely to elites, access to the Mormon temple was based upon confessional orthodoxy and moral worthiness, not upon financial income, schools attended, or family pedigree. As Apostle James E. Talmage wrote, "The blessings of the House of the Lord are restricted to no privileged class."[49] Similar to the way that the Book of Revelation promised godhood to those martyred by Roman persecution, members of the church who had been forced to eke out a living in the mountain deserts of the West would attain godhood in celestial splendor in the next life, something the Gentiles would never experience.

At the same time, access to God's parlor was not unrestricted, and it shared characteristics of Victorian gatekeeping. Non-LDS people were not allowed in. And being a member of the church alone did not guarantee one access to the inner precincts of the temple, particularly the endowment and sealing rooms. Only adults who were recommended as worthy by their local priesthood leaders were allowed to participate in temple rites. Local leaders presented these individuals with a signed letter, now a small card known as a "temple recommend," that patrons presented to the doorkeeper of a temple.[50] These recommends can be thought of as a blend between communion tokens and Victorian calling cards, the latter being especially popular among elite women during the late nineteenth century.[51] Temple recommends were different, though, in that they were not based on class and status but instead demonstrated adherence to confessional and behavioral orthodoxy. In 1856, for example, First Presidency member Heber C. Kimball went so far as to explicitly urge local leaders to include "the old and infirm, the lame halt and blind and the righteous poor" among those recommended to participate in the blessings bestowed in the Endowment House, a proto-temple structure used to administer temple ordinances at the time.[52]

Racial barriers were another way that church leaders restricted access to the temple. In 1852 Brigham Young unilaterally banned people of African descent from holding the Mormon priesthood; since temples functioned under the auspices of that priesthood, he consequently banned African Americans from entering them with the exception of some baptisms for the dead.[53] Even in 1894, when Black Latter-day Saint Jane Manning James was ritually "attached" by proxy to the long-deceased Joseph Smith in the Salt Lake temple, it was only as a servant.[54] Meanwhile, other members were sealed as husbands, wives, and children in family kingdoms. While some, like James, were able to perform proxy baptisms in the temple, they were not allowed in the more ornate rooms reserved for the endowment and for sealings.[55] It was not until 1978 that the policy was reversed and race was eliminated as a factor in temple access.[56]

The Eurocentric design vocabularies of the nineteenth-century temples performed a supporting role in the racial boundary. Historian Paul Reeve has documented the ways in which the American Protestant establishment increasingly viewed Mormons as non-white over the course of the nineteenth century—so much so that by the end of the century, some viewed Mormons as constituting an altogether new and unique race. To counter this exclusion, white Mormons sought to demonstrate their whiteness bona fides, and this included theologically positioning themselves as superior to Black communities.[57] Demonstrating refinement and gentility in architecture and interior decor was another way that Latter-day Saints could exhibit their whiteness. While the stone monuments of Neoclassical and Gothic Revival temple design facilitated spiritual renewal and approximated the grandeur of God, they also demonstrated a shared visual rhetoric with the Protestant establishment that spurned them. This yearning to be part of the family of Christianity whose creeds Mormon revelation deemed "an abomination" characterizes one of the paradoxes Terryl Givens has identified that frame Mormon culture—a sense of being the elect of God while also being an exile yearning for acceptance.[58] Temple design during the nineteenth century and since has embodied this dualism, as Latter-day Saints have never created a unique style, but the massing and configuration of existing styles into unique forms have created a uniquely Mormon type of architecture.

TEMPLE DESIGN IN THE WAKE OF THE NINETEENTH CENTURY

As soon as the Latter-day Saints seemed to settle on a Neo-Gothic crenellated style with rectangular massing and two towers for their temples during the late nineteenth century, for their temples, they abruptly shifted course at the outset of the twentieth century. The temples in Laie, Hawaii (1919), and Cardston, Alberta (1923), were highly successful adaptations of Frank Lloyd Wright's Prairie Style. Instead of soaring spires that reached to the heavens, these temples hugged the earth, and their interiors exchanged Victorian design idioms for modern rectilinear forms in rich woods, muraled walls, and custom furniture to match. Ensuing temples likewise followed stylistic trends with the Colonial Revival Mesa temple in 1927 and the modernist Art Deco style of the Idaho Falls temple in 1945.

An overarching difference between these buildings and their late nineteenth-century precedents is the later buildings' negotiation with modernism in both style and ideology.[59] Like their Protestant neighbors, Latter-day Saints selectively borrowed from the styles and concepts that revolutionized architecture during the twentieth century. An aesthetic concerned with a rationalist simplicity and a hostility toward ornament and symbolism, modernism was on its surface ill-suited to religious purposes, but religionists of all types adopted its design vocabularies to construct new places of worship throughout the world.[60] The LDS temples in Bern, Switzerland (1955), Los Angeles, California (1956), and London, England (1958), were among these. Each was a rectangular box made of smooth white surfaces, stripped-down versions of nineteenth-century Protestant steeples, and spare voluminous interiors.

While church leaders and architects changed the appearance of temples to be au courant in modern modes, modernism's affection for technological efficiencies influenced the way the rites themselves were administered and continues to do so. While some religionists have shunned the technological trappings of modernity, Latter-day Saints have enthusiastically embraced them, adapted them, and geared them to their purposes. The efficiencies introduced by technology were an attractive addition to temple work and temple design. Mormons have always conceived of the performance of temple rituals as work and still use the phrase "temple work."[61] The Saints share in some of the anxiety that Max Weber argued fueled the Protestant work ethic, but they were also driven by a belief similar to that of Catholics in regard to requiem masses—that if their ancestors did not have their temple work performed for them, those ancestors would be stuck in a type of purgatory, not able to attain the degrees of glory that temple rituals made accessible. The technological gadgets of the twentieth century have expedited this work. Computers, printers, barcodes, digital databases, movie projectors, speakers, audio recordings, and timing systems have all expedited temple work.

The transition from having individuals act out the parts and orally recite the rituals of the endowment to using video projection and recorded voices has been the most consequential of these adaptations. The Swiss Temple was the first to adopt the video presentation of the endowment. The church filmed the video on stage sets constructed in the assembly room of the Salt Lake temple in multiple European languages so that the rituals could be presented in language-specific sessions to members from across Europe.[62] Church architect Edward O. Anderson enlisted MGM Studios to produce the movie screen, remote control, and other electronic devices to transform what had been a Victorian endowment room into a modern movie theater.[63] The adoption of the technologies in the Swiss temple and the accompanying elimination of multiple endowment rooms set in motion a series of changes that revolutionized the way temple patrons would experience the endowment. These changes accelerated the transition of the ritual from the immersive, highly participatory experience of the nineteenth and early twentieth centuries to the streamlined, largely passive one of today.

The design of the Ogden and Provo Temples in the late 1960s marked the apogee of applying modern, even Taylorist models of manufacturing efficiency to temple rituals. In an echo of Le Corbusier's 1927 declaration that a home was "a machine for living," these temples were designed to be machines for salvation.[64] The *Church News* reported that the Ogden Temple "represents a new functional approach in temple building, emphasizing convenience and efficiency for patrons."[65] Instead of patrons progressing through a series of rooms, they spent the entire time in only one of the several endowment rooms that ringed a central celestial room, for maximum throughput. Escalators moved patrons up and down the floors, and lockers in dressing rooms were creatively designed to accommodate more patrons in less space.[66] Dedicated within months of each other in early 1972, the Provo and Ogden Temples demonstrated the church's strident embrace businesslike efficiency.

While temples of the early twentieth century received high praise of the kind Joseph Smith had sought and that the Nauvoo temple had received, the reaction to later twentieth-century temples was more mixed. The unique designs of the Provo and Ogden temples with their round bank-like massing and central spires made them ripe for criticism.[67] One architectural critic summed up his lengthy analysis of them: "A wealthy church . . . owes its faithful more than they have been offered in these designs."[68]

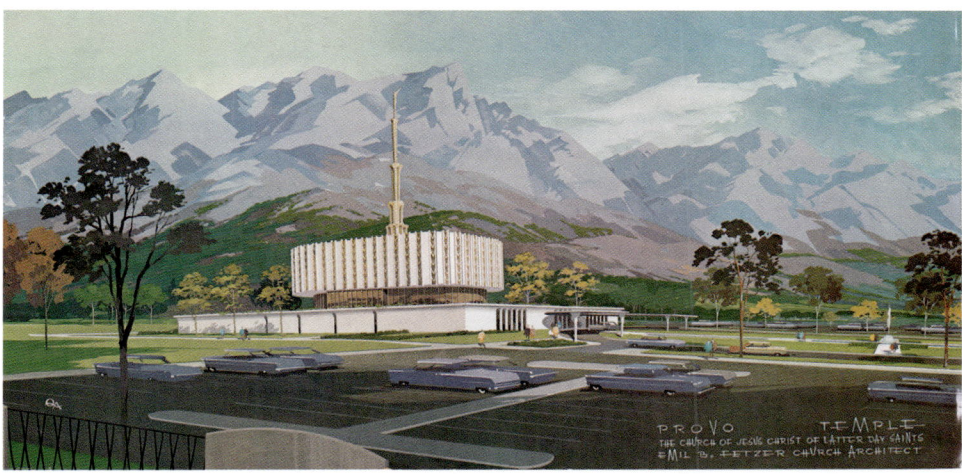

Fig. 8.8 Emil B. Fetzer, architectural rendering of the Provo Temple, c. 1968, drawing, L. Tom Perry Special Collections, Brigham Young University.

The Washington D.C. Temple returned to the monumental scale and massing of the late nineteenth-century temples with its sleek postmodern reinterpretation of the Salt Lake Temple. Its interior was designed for "speeding up sessions, similar to . . . the Ogden and Provo Temples."[69] At the dedication in 1974, the church's *Ensign* magazine reported one local visitor finding the interior "rich, plain, simple, and all done in such good taste."[70] At the same time, Paul Goldberger, the nation's foremost architectural critic of the time, was not so impressed. He wrote in the *New York Times*, "The futuristic aura disappears inside, replaced by what tries desperately to be 'good taste.' . . . If good taste consists of ringing a crystal chandelier with fluorescent lighting, then it succeeds." He went on to say that "none of the rooms are particularly interesting" and marveled that "so much money could yield such dullness."[71]

In recent decades, the LDS church has dramatically increased the number of temples throughout the world. These new buildings are, on the whole, handsome stone-clad structures that, brightly lit at night, stake out a prominent international presence. They act as an architectural public face for an American religion gone global and demonstrate a type of collective class consciousness of the church. In building hundreds of temples outside of the United States, the church has largely exported the Western aesthetic of its American ones, although the church makes efforts to indigenize the designs by incorporating local design motifs—for example, lilacs carved in the art glass windows and tatami mat patterns carved in the marble flooring in Sapporo, Japan, and hand-painted earthenware tiles and hacienda-style profiles in Tijuana, Mexico.

From the late twentieth century up to the present, the church has taken extensive measures to reduce the distance patrons have to travel to reach a temple. As early as the 1970s, church president Gordon B. Hinckley had been concerned about the

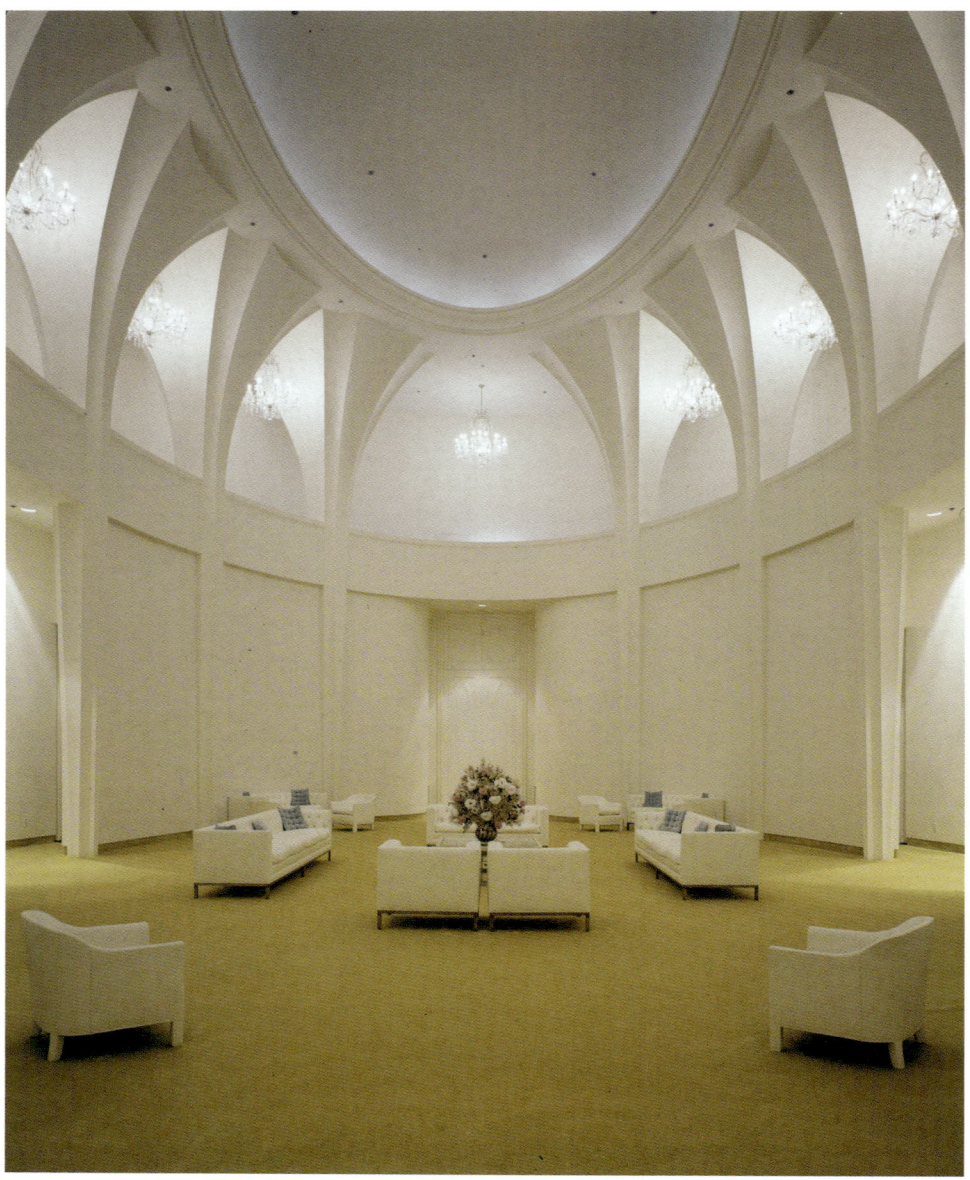

Fig. 8.9 Photograph of Washington D.C. Temple celestial room, 1972, Church History Library, The Church of Jesus Christ of Latter-day Saints.

prohibitive distances many members of the church worldwide had to go in order to get to a temple. During the construction of the Washington D.C. Temple, he wrote in his journal that the church could build many small temples for the same cost as this large new temple.[72] Years later, as president of the church, he sketched a proposed layout for

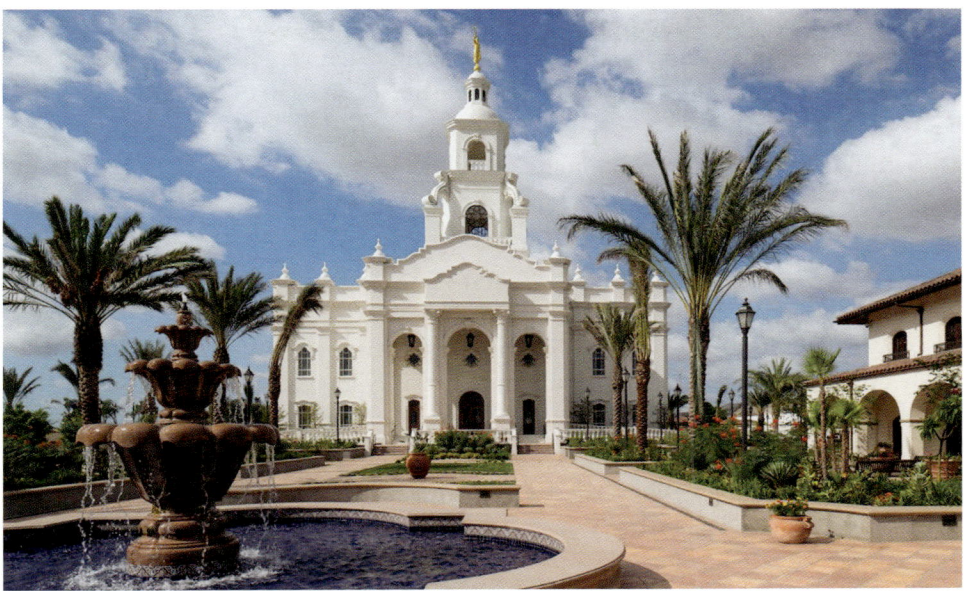

Fig. 8.10 Tijuana Mexico Temple, 2015. © Intellectual Reserve, Inc.

what a small temple could look like and directed the beginnings of two experimental ones in Monticello, Utah, and Colonia Juarez, Mexico. In April 1998, he launched an ambitious initiative to construct thirty "small, beautiful, and serviceable" temples.[73] In recent years, church president Russell M. Nelson has continued the effort to construct small, accessible temples by enlisting the technologies of modular construction in which temples are prefabricated and assembled on-site, the first one being completed in Helena, Montana.[74] These temples are compact versions of the larger temples—stone-clad exteriors in eclectic, historically informed styles with handsome interiors—that, although not monumental on their landscapes, provide similar material environments as the large ones.

In using the visual discourses of material refinement and stylish design as a metaphor for godhood, Latter-day Saints have tethered the metaphorical effectiveness of the temple to changing notions of taste. But taste is a moving target, so new temples can soon fall out of fashion in an age of ever-accelerating style cycles. Because of this—and because of the inevitable obsolescence of mechanical systems—renovation of temples has become a constant undertaking. In recent years, some temples have been remodeled, some partially remodeled, and several entirely rebuilt. Church leaders recently decided, for example, to tear down the Ogden and Provo Temples and replace them with new designs. The more spartan temple interiors—especially those from the 1980s—have been upgraded in their level of architectural sophistication and interior decor, and, overall, the collective mood of temple design has swung in favor of higher-quality, more-ornate work. The same is true for new temples. The Hartford, Connecticut, temple (2016) is among these. *Architectural Digest* named the temple, a Colonial Revival jewel, the most beautiful religious building in the state of Connecticut.[75]

As discussed by Colleen McDannell in her chapter in this volume, the church has recently adopted a largely uniform program of visual imagery for its temples. Most of the images are landscapes and vignettes from Book of Mormon and Bible narratives. The commissioning and deploying of these images demonstrate another way that the church continues to negotiate its identity in terms of its Protestant heritage and aspirations to high-style design. To begin with, populating a building with giclée reproductions—the descendants of nineteenth-century chromolithographs—is in and of itself not a particularly upscale way of furnishing a building, especially a multimillion-dollar one. Then there are the images themselves. Some are copies of works by highly skilled painters, including nineteenth-century masterworks such as those by Carl Heinrich Bloch, while many of the figural and genre works lean toward the illustrative and the saccharine. The prints are, by and large, hung in ancillary spaces and hallways, not in ritual spaces. The hallways of temples act as picture galleries, similar to the way nineteenth-century Protestants introduced biblically based images into their worship spaces.[76] Only a small handful of temples have any imagery in their celestial rooms. The portraits of prominent leaders seen in the earliest photos of the Salt Lake temple celestial room have long since been removed. In an inversion of Catholic aesthetics, the most holy places of Mormonism are largely void of visual imagery.

The iconography, like other loci of temple design, demonstrates the presence of the Victorian past in the temple-building present. Striking an aesthetic balance between being Catholic but not too Catholic and creating spaces of beauty in good taste without being pretentious or prideful continues to frame the field of cultural production that is LDS temple-building. The twentieth century has added new tensions: providing patrons with an immersive, abundant ritual experience versus a liturgically abbreviated and expedited one, incorporating Indigenous architectural and artistic traditions as opposed to Western ones, and constructing monumental buildings as visual statements versus building smaller buildings designed for areas with fewer patrons.

Part of the success of The Church of Jesus Christ of Latter-day Saints has been its ability to adapt to changing cultural conditions while retaining fidelity to the founding narratives and theologies of the 1830s and 1840s. The great diversity in the catalogue of temple architecture—which, like the church, has had one foot in the present and one foot in the Victorian past—demonstrates this adaptability. Each temple is the result of the negotiations of power in relation to the dyads discussed by a continually changing constellation of church leaders and design professionals. In this way, temple architecture is culture made material, and as such, each temple has been a solution to a particular set of cultural problems, and each renovation demonstrates adaptation to new sets of cultural problems. These have included how to create sacred space on the American frontier, how to architecturally frame an entirely new set of Christian rituals, how to accommodate patrons of diverse geographies, how to make temple rituals available to those who live far from a temple, and how to adapt temple work to new technologies. No doubt the future will bring more.

NOTES

[1] Quoted in Jennifer Dobner, "President Hinckley: 'A Man for His Time,'" *Salt Lake Tribune,* April 2, 2005, https://archive.sltrib.com/story.php?ref=/faith/ci_2636954; Jan Shipps, *Mormonism: The Story of a New Religious Tradition* (Urbana: University of Illinois Press, 1985).

[2] Philip Barlow, "Jan Shipps and the Mainstreaming of Mormon Studies," *Church History* 73, no. 2 (June 2004): 412–426. Emphasis mine.

[3] For a survey of LDS meetinghouses, see Richard Jackson, *Places of Worship: 150 Years of Latter-day Saint Architecture* (Provo, UT: Religious Studies Center, Brigham Young University, 2003).

[4] Craig S. Campbell, *Images of the New Jerusalem: Latter Day Saint Faction Interpretations of Independence, Missouri* (Knoxville: University of Tennessee Press, 2004), 1–22.

[5] On the changes in Protestant architecture, see Gretchen Buggeln, *Temples of Grace: The Material Transformation of Connecticut's Churches, 1890–1840* (Lebanon, NH: University Press of New England, 2003), and Ryan K. Smith, *Gothic Arches, Latin Crosses: Anti-Catholicism and American Church Designs in the Nineteenth Century* (Chapel Hill: University of North Carolina Press, 2006).

[6] Louis P. Nelson, *The Beauty of Holiness: Anglicanism and Architecture in Colonial South Carolina* (Chapel Hill: University of North Carolina Press, 2008), 149.

[7] Buggeln, *Temples of Grace,* 140, 158.

[8] Noah Webster, *An American Dictionary of the English Language,* vol. 1 (New York: S. Converse, 1828), n.p.

[9] Richard Lyman Bushman, *Joseph Smith: Rough Stone Rolling* (New York: Knopf, 2005), 311–315.

[10] "History, 1838–1856, volume D-1 [1 August 1842–1 July 1843]," p. 1474, Joseph Smith Papers, https://www.josephsmithpapers.org/paper-summary/history-1838-1856-volume-d-1-1-august-1842-1-july-1843/117. The revelations frame the temple as a type of cultural capital, a concept explored in Pierre Bourdieu, *Distinction* (Cambridge, MA: MIT Press, 1984). On Joseph Smith's genteel aspirations, see Richard Lyman Bushman, "Was Joseph Smith a Gentleman? The Standard for Refinement in Utah," in *Nearly Everything Imaginable: The Everyday Life of Utah's Mormon Pioneers,* ed. Ronald W. Walker and Doris R. Dant (Provo, UT: Brigham Young University Press, 1999), 27–46.

[11] "Proclamation, Between 19 January and 27 August 1841," p. 2, Joseph Smith Papers, https://www.joseph smithpapers.org/paper-summary/proclamation-between-19january-and-27august-1841/2.

[12] Nelson, *The Beauty of Holiness,* 141–174; Dell Upton, *Holy Things and Profane: Anglican Parish Churches in Colonial Virginia* (New Haven, CT: Yale University Press, 1986), 47–98. On congregational meetinghouses, see Kevin M. Sweeney, "Meetinghouses, Town Houses, and Churches: Changing Perceptions of Sacred and Secular Space in Southern New England, 1720–185," *Winterthur Portfolio* 28 (Spring 1993): 59–93.

[13] Buggeln, *Temples of Grace*; Peter W. Williams, *Houses of God: Region, Religion, and Architecture in the United States* (Urbana: University of Illinois Press, 1997), 8–12.

[14] Peter B. Nockles, "The Oxford Movement and the United States," in *The Oxford Movement: Europe and the Wider World, 1830–1930,* ed. Stewart J. Brown and Peter B. Nockles (Cambridge: Cambridge University Press, 2014), 133–150; Peter Doll, "The Architectural Impact of the Oxford Movement," in *The Oxford Handbook of the Oxford Movement,* ed. Stewart J. Brown, Peter Nockles, and James Pereiro (New York: Oxford University Press, 2017), 362–375.

[15] Smith, *Gothic Arches, Latin Crosses.* The later nineteenth century is explored in Jeanne Halgren Kilde, *When Church Became Theater: The Transformation of Evangelical Architecture and Worship in Nineteenth-Century America* (New York: Oxford University Press, 2002).

[16] Glen M. Leonard, *Nauvoo: A Place of Peace, a People of Promise* (Salt Lake City: Deseret Book, 2002), 257–265; David J. Buerger, *The Mysteries of Godliness: A History of Mormon Temple Worship* (Salt Lake City: Signature Books, 2016); Devry S. Anderson, *The Development of LDS Temple Worship, 1846–2000* (Salt Lake City: Signature Books, 2013).

[17] On the theologies of sealing, see Jonathan A. Stapley, *The Power of Godliness: Mormon Liturgy and Cosmology* (New York: Oxford University Press, 2018), 34–56.

[18] Lisle G. Brown, "The Sacred Departments for Temple Work in Nauvoo: The Assembly Room and the Council Chamber," *BYU Studies* 19, no. 3 (1979): 1–13; Jill C. Major, "Artworks in the Celestial Room of the First Nauvoo Temple," *BYU Studies* 41, no. 2 (2002): 47–69.

[19] Quoted in Major, "Artworks in the Celestial Room," 47.

[20] Katherine C. Grier, *Culture and Comfort: People, Parlors, and Upholstery, 1850–1930* (Rochester, NY: Margaret Woodbury Strong Museum, 1988), 1.

[21] Matthew S. McBride, *A House for the Most High: The Story of the Original Nauvoo Temple* (Salt Lake City: Greg Kofford Books, 2007); Leonard, *Nauvoo,* 235–254.

[22] Robert A. M. Stern, Thomas Mellins, and David Fisherman, *New York 1880: Architecture and Urbanism in the Gilded Age* (New York: Monacelli Press, 1999), 317.

[23] On the church's wealth, see D. Michael Quinn, *The Mormon Hierarchy: Wealth and Corporate Power* (Salt Lake City: Signature Books, 2017).

[24] Thomas Carter, *Building Zion: The Material World of Mormon Settlement* (Minneapolis: University of Minnesota Press, 2015), 240.

[25] Carter, *Building Zion,* 257, 271–273. See also Paul L. Anderson, "William Harrison Folsom: Pioneer Architect," *Utah Historical Quarterly* 43, no. 3 (Summer 1975): 259.

[26] Allen D. Roberts, "Where Are the All-Seeing Eyes? The Origin, Use, and Decline of Early Mormon Symbolism," *Sunstone,* May 1985, 36–48.

[27] Michael Reed, *Banishing the Cross: The Emergence of a Mormon Taboo* (Independence, MO: John Whitmer Books, 2012.

[28] Glenn A. Knoblock and David W. Wemmer, *Weathervanes of New England* (Jefferson, NC: McFarland, 2018), 87–92.

[29] A proposal drawing for the weathervane survives in the Church History Library: William Weeks, "Scaled Drawing of Proposed Angel Weathervane."

[30] When the identity of the angel solidified into Moroni and who did the identifying is unclear. Helen Mar Whitney identified the statue as Moroni and called it "grand & impressive" at the capstone-laying ceremony in April 1892. *A Widow's Tale: The 1884–1896 Diary of Helen Mar Whitney,* ed. Charles M. Hatch and Todd Compton (Logan: Utah State University Press, 2003), 497. But at the same time, the church's newspaper called it Moroni. John Nicholson, "The Statue of Moroni," *Deseret Weekly,* April 9, 1892, 1. The statue is called Gabriel in *Temple Souvenir Album,* April 1892.

[31] See, for example, Walter Crane, *Socialist Allegory,* pen-and-ink drawing, 1885, and Angel Gabriel textile designed by Herbert Percy Horne for the Century Guild in 1884, the latter being in the collections of the Victoria and Albert Museum.

[32] Peggy Fletcher Stack, "Statue of Limitations: Under Russell Nelson, Fewer and Fewer Temples Have an Angel Moroni," *Salt Lake Tribune,* October 2, 2020, https://www.sltrib.com/religion/2020/10/02/statue-limitations-under/accessed; Peggy Fletcher Stack, "'Mormon' Vanquished; Moroni Missing; Pageants Pulled: Is the LDS Church Losing Its Identity?," *Salt Lake Tribune,* September 26, 2021, https://www.sltrib.com/religion/2021/09/26/mormon-vanquished-moroni/.

[33] Carter, *Building Zion*, 271–273. The trompe l'oeil murals were painted over sometime in the mid-twentieth century.

[34] A view of the hall and portraits is available in James E. Talmage, *The House of the Lord: A Study of Holy Sanctuaries Ancient and Modern* (Salt Lake City: Deseret News, 1912), 268. The portraits are now in the Museum of Church History.

[35] Jonathan Stapley, *The Power of Godliness: Mormon Liturgy and Cosmology* (New York: Oxford University Press, 2018), 26

[36] On the role of women in temple priesthood, see Stapley, 26.

[37] On the history of women's relationship to the LDS priesthood more broadly, see Lisa Olsen Tait, "What Is Women's Relationship to Priesthood?," *BYU Studies Quarterly* 60, no. 3 (2021): 241–272.

[38] Joseph Smith, *Teachings of the Prophet Joseph Smith,* comp. Joseph Fielding Smith (Salt Lake City: Deseret Book, 1938), 181.

[39] David Paulsen and Martin Pulido, "'A Mother There': A Survey of Historical Teachings About Mother in Heaven," *BYU Studies* 50, no. 1 (2011): 70–97.

[40] "Mr. Canon's [*sic*] Lecture," *Salt Lake Daily Herald*, April 14, 1884, 8.

[41] William DeHertburn Washington, *Progress and Prosperity* (New York: National Educational Publishing, 1911), frontispiece. The image is illustrated and analyzed in Grier, *Culture and Comfort*, 14–142.

[42] Leah E. Widtsoe, "Studies in Household Art I. A Glance at the History of Architecture," *Young Woman's Journal* 10, no. 2 (February 1899): 87.

[43] Josh E. Probert, "Leah Dunford Widtsoe, Alice Merrill Horne, and the Sacralization of Artistic Taste in Mormon Homes, Circa 1900," in *Mormon Women's History: Beyond Biography*, ed. Rachel Cope, Amy Easton-Flake, Keith A. Erekson, and Lisa Olsen Tait (Madison, NJ: Fairleigh Dickinson University Press, 2020), 167–183.

[44] Passages include 2 Nephi 1:20, 2 Nephi 4:4, Alma 48:15, and Alma 50:20.

[45] See, for example, Helaman 4:11–17; Grant Hardy, *Understanding the Book of Mormon: A Reader's Guide* (New York: Oxford University Press, 2010), 114.

[46] Quoted in Preston Nibley, *Brigham Young, the Man and His Work* (Salt Lake City: Zion's Print & Publishing, 1944), 128.

[47] Richard Lyman Bushman, *The Refinement of America: People, Cities, Houses* (New York: Alfred A. Knopf, 1992), 350–352.

[48] Bushman, *The Refinement of America*, 313–352; Buggeln, *Temples of Grace*, 142.

[49] Talmage, *The House of the Lord*, 100–101.

[50] Edward L. Kimball, "The History of LDS Temple Admission Standards," *Journal of Mormon History* 24, no. 1 (Spring 1988): 135–179.

[51] Mary E. Norton, "Pewter Communion Tokens at Winterthur," *Winterthur Portfolio* 1 (1964): 182–187; Kenneth W. Ames, *Death in the Dining Room and other Tales of Victorian Culture* (Philadelphia: Temple University Press, 1992), 35–41.

[52] Quoted in Kimball, "The History of LDS Temple Admission Standards," 140.

[53] "Speech in Joint Legislature," February 5, 1852, published in Matthew L. Harris and Newell G. Bringhurst, eds., *The Mormon Church and Blacks: A Documentary History* (Urbana: University of Illinois Press, 2015), 37–40; Tonya Reiter, "Black Saviors on Mount Zion: Proxy Baptisms and Latter-day Saints of African Descent," *Journal of Mormon History* 43, no. 4 (October 2017): 100–123.

[54] Quincy D. Newell, *"Your Sister in the Gospel": The Life of Jane Manning James, a Nineteenth-Century Black Mormon* (New York: Oxford University Press, 2019), 112–114.

[55] Newell, *"Your Sister in the Gospel,"* 106–108, 119–120.

[56] Edward L. Kimball, "Spencer W. Kimball and the Revelation on Priesthood," *BYU Studies* 47, no. 2 (2008): 5–78; W. Paul Reeve, *Religion of a Different Color: Race and the Mormon Struggle for Whiteness* (New York: Oxford University Press, 2015).

[57] Reeve, *Religion of a Different Color*.

[58] Terryl C. Givens, *People of Paradox: A History of Mormon Culture* (New York: Oxford University Press, 2007), 53–62.

[59] Paul L. Anderson, "Mormon Moderne: Latter-day Saint Architecture, 1925–1945," *Journal of Mormon History* 9 (1982): 71–84.

[60] Gretchen Buggeln, *The Suburban Church: Modernism and Community in Postwar America* (Minneapolis: University of Minnesota Press, 2015); Anat Geva, *Modernism and Mid-20th Century Sacred Architecture* (London: Routledge, 2019).

[61] In a general conference talk, for example, Elder Neal A. Maxwell said, "Though joyful, temple work is work." Neal A. Maxwell, "Put Your Shoulder to the Wheel," *Ensign* 29, no. 5 (May 1998): 38.

[62] Sheri L. Dew, *Go Forward with Faith: The Biography of Gordon B. Hinckley* (Salt Lake City: Deseret Book, 1996), 176–182.

[63] Dale Z. Kirby, *The History of the Swiss Temple* (n.p.: n.p., 1969), 16–17.

[64] Le Corbusier, *Toward an Architecture*, trans. John Goodman (Los Angeles: Getty Research Institute, 2007).

[65] "New Ogden Temple Dedicated," *Church News* 42, no. 4 (January 22, 1972): 3.

[66] Doyle L. Green, "Two Temples to Be Dedicated," *Ensign* 2, no. 1 (January 1972): 6–15; "Inside a House of the Lord," *The New Era* 2, no. 4 (April 1972): 25–28.

[67] "Provo Temple Open for Public Viewing," *Church News* 42, no. 3 (Jan. 15, 1972): 5; "New Ogden Temple Dedicated."

[68] Donald J. Bergsma, "The Temple as Symbol," *Dialogue: A Journal of Mormon Thought* 3, no. 1 (Spring 1968): 28.

[69] "Washington Temple Construction Progressing Rapidly on Schedule," *Church News* 42, no. 4 (January 22, 1972): 15.

[70] "Washington Temple: Missionary Tool," *Ensign* 4, no. 12 (December 1974): 72–74.

[71] Paul Goldberger, "New Mormon Temple $15 Million Conversation Piece," *New York Times,* November 12, 1974, 30.

[72] Dew, *Go Forward with Faith*, 325.

[73] Gordon B. Hinckley, "New Temples to Provide 'Crowning Blessings' of the Gospel," *Ensign,* May 1998, 87–88; Gordon B. Hinckley, preliminary sketch of small temple floor plan, 1997, located in the Church History Library, Church of Jesus Christ of Latter-day Saints.

[74] Church of Jesus Christ of Latter-day Saints, "Helena Montana Temple Latest News," https://churchofjesuschristtemples.org/helena-montana-temple/news/, accessed February 5, 2023.

[75] Kristine Hansen, "The Most Beautiful Place of Worship in Every State," *Architectural Digest,* January 17, 2018, https://www.architecturaldigest.com/story/most-beautiful-place-of-worship-every-state.

[76] Josh Edward Probert, "Gilded Religion in the Age of Tiffany, 1877–1932" (PhD diss., University of Delaware, 2014), 269–280.

SUCCESS IN CIRCUIT

Brigham Young's Big Ten

MARY CAMPBELL

celestial marriage, plural marriage, spiritual wifery, the Principle: synonyms for polygamy, and specifically polygyny, as practiced by members of the Church of Jesus
Christ of Latter-day Saints during the nineteenth and early twentieth centuries

ONE

I imagine the photograph counting. Quietly, persistently, maybe only to itself. Ten
young women arranged for the picture in two rows of five, each girl hovering somewhere between fourteen and eighteen years old. Ten oval faces arranged for the camera
in two lines of five, all but one set of eyes gazing directly at the lens. Ten female figures sorted into two tiers of five, each girl wearing a dress that, with its scooped neck,
dropped armscyes, and high waist, might have been cut from the same pattern. Ten variations on one theme, dresses and flesh; a dozen pale hands linking with arms and resting
on shoulders as if to emphasize the group's existence as one body.

Judging from the writing at the bottom left of the photograph, someone claimed
this body. The first word is almost illegible, but the other two pull the caption into focus:
"Brigham Youngs Daughters." At some point, someone wrote this on the negative itself, ensuring that all subsequent prints would be tagged with the name of the second
president, prophet, seer, and revelator of the Church of Jesus Christ of Latter-day Saints
(LDS Church).[1] Admittedly, the caption is misleading: it leaves too many people un-
counted. Brigham Young (1801–1877) married fifty-six women over the course of
forty-eight years, and he fathered fifty-five children by sixteen of them.[2] Here we see
a fraction of the thirty-one daughters his polygamous wives bore him, specifically the
group known as the Big Ten. "All very large, fine-looking girls, and nearly all the same
age," the Big Ten lived with many of their other siblings, half-siblings, mothers, and polygamous "aunts" in the Lion House, the adobe mansion Young built for his enormous

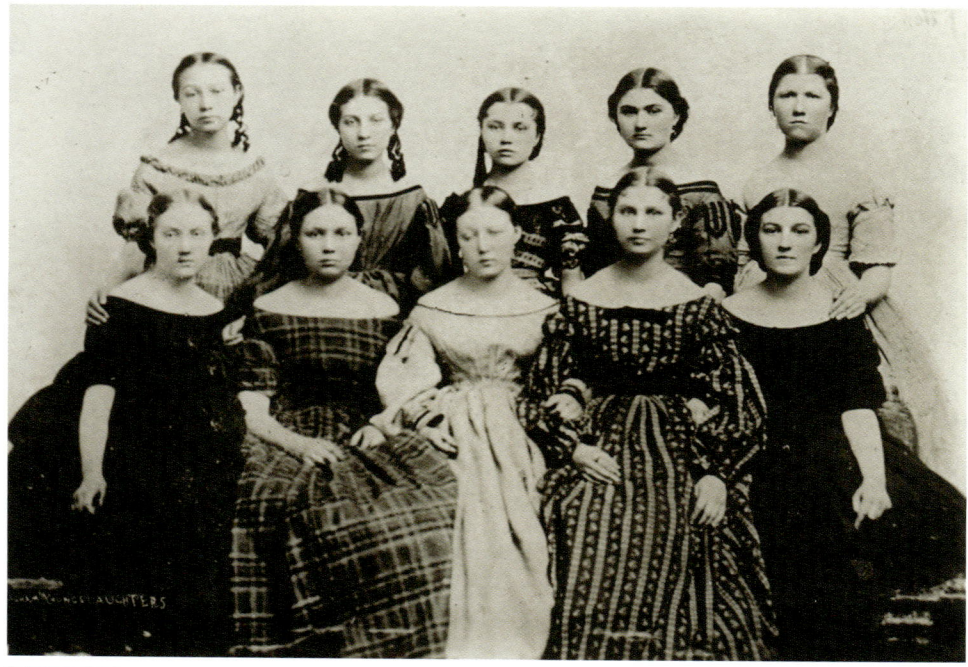

Fig. 9.1 Anonymous, portrait of ten of Brigham Young's daughters, c. 1865, photograph, 12 cm ×
17 cm, Church History Library, The Church of Jesus Christ of Latter-day Saints.

family in downtown Salt Lake City.[3] "These 'Young' maidens were among the prettiest
and most popular of Salt Lake's girls. They were called the Big Ten, not that they were
very large, but simply to contrast them with the next eight, for [Young's] family was
numerous."[4]

   Numerous, but not often photographed. At least not in its entirety. As we will see,
this undated picture of the Big Ten is the closest thing Young left to a polygamous
family portrait. Effectively using his daughters as a proxy for his multiple wives and,
behind them, the male relationships plural marriage sought to divinize, the second
prophet established a photographic tradition that would erase countless LDS women's
investment in spiritual marriage even as it protected their husbands from indictment
under the country's anti-cohabitation laws.

TWO

Copies of *The Big Ten* appear in a handful of twentieth-century publications, including
M. R. Werner's 1925 biography of Brigham Young. Werner mistakenly identified the
image as a picture of "Brigham Young's Ten Tallest Daughters," adding to the confusion about the source of the girls' collective moniker, not to mention their size.[5]
Questions of height notwithstanding, Werner was on to something when he described

"the labyrinthine enchantments of Mormon family trees," their polygamous "intricacies affor[ding] all the fascinations of an ingenious puzzle."[6] *The Big Ten* exists as just such a puzzle, a visual maze of domestic relationships that exceed traditional Western categories of familial connection. To begin, then, an accounting of whom the photograph does—and does not—show.

Just as the Big Ten were presumably not the tallest of Young's daughters, they were not his oldest, either. Although their father would eventually go down in history as "the much-married prophet," Young's first five daughters were born into monogamous homes.[7] Young married his first wife, Miriam Works (1806–1832), in 1824, six years before Joseph Smith Jr. (1805–1844) founded the LDS Church and nearly two decades before Smith recorded his revelation directing devout Mormon men to emulate the Old Testament patriarchs by taking multiple wives.[8] The couple had two children, Elizabeth (1825–1903) and Vilate (1830–1902), before Works died of tuberculosis in 1832. Eighteen months later, Young remarried. His second wife was an early convert to the faith named Mary Ann Angell (1803–1882), and together they had six children, including Mary Ann (1836–1843), Alice (1839–1874), and Luna (1832–1922). None of Works's or Angell's daughters appears in *The Big Ten*.

Shortly after Angell became pregnant with Luna, Smith instructed Young to "go & get another wife."[9] Young later remembered being appalled at the command. "I felt as if the grave was better for me [than polygamy]," he recalled. Nonetheless, he "quickly moved from apprehension to exhilaration," so "filled with the Holy Ghost" that he soon proposed to a seventeen-year-old English girl named Martha Brotherton.[10] When Brotherton declined, Young, now in his forties, turned to a twenty-year-old Saint named Lucy Ann Decker (1822–1891). Decker wed Young roughly two months before Angell gave birth to Luna, becoming the future prophet's third wife and first polygynous spouse. Before Smith's assassination in June 1844, Young would marry three more women, including Decker's older sister Clarissa (1828–1889). By the time he formally assumed the title of Smith's successor prophet in December 1847, Young had evacuated almost fifteen thousand Latter-day Saints from increasingly hostile conditions in Nauvoo, Illinois, and led them on a thousand-mile journey across the plains to their mountain refuge in the Salt Lake Valley. He had also married another thirty-seven women, including nine of Smith's polygamous widows.

THREE

As Laurel Thatcher Ulrich has observed, it was rare for LDS men to have children with their plural wives before Smith's death. "Scholars have long puzzled over the absence of documented births to women sealed to Joseph Smith," she writes. "Almost as startling is the scarcity of babies born to other plural wives in this period. Either sexual intercourse was a less essential part of these marriages, or couples were practicing some form of contraception."[11] Young conformed to this pattern. "No one would marry more women in Nauvoo than Brigham Young," but he fathered only three children, all boys, by his polygamous spouses before heading west.[12] His eighth wife, Louisa Beaman (1815–1850), gave birth to yet another son during the winter of 1847, but the infant died seven months later. Although in Smith's theology "reproduction was the great work of heaven," it remained slow going during the Saints' early days.[13]

This began to change around the time Young and his first party of pioneers reached the Rocky Mountains. In June 1847, Clarissa Chase Ross (1814–1857) gave birth to the prophet's thirteenth child, a daughter named Mary Eliza, or "Mamie," as she was called. Three months later, Emmeline Free (1826–1875) had another Young girl, this one named Ella. Sadly, 1848 saw nothing but infant mortality for the prophet's family, with Louisa Beaman bearing and then losing her first set of twin boys. That said, "1849 was one of Brigham Young's most prolific years."[14] Between January 25 and December 14, five of his plural wives gave birth to a daughter apiece. The following year, Beaman lost yet another pair of twin sons, but Young's tenth and twenty-fourth wives each bore a girl, both of whom survived well into adulthood. In 1851, the prophet welcomed another daughter, as well as two boys.[15]

FOUR

The Big Ten seems to celebrate this sudden abundance of daughters. Here we see all the Young girls born during that first flush of polygamous fertility. Mamie stands in the back, second from the right, while Ella sits in the center front, eyes cast to the side. The five 1849 girls all find a place in the photograph too. The eldest, Lucy Decker's daughter Fanny (January), sits at the far right, directly in front of another Cross child, Clarissa Maria (December), and next to Emily Augusta (March), daughter of Brigham Young's ninth wife, Emily Dow Partridge (1824–1899). At the far right of the front row, we find Emmeline Free's second daughter, Marinda (July). Jeanette (December), daughter of Clarissa Decker, stands in the middle of the back row, to the right of Evelyn, born to Maria Alley (1825–1852) in July 1850. Evelyn's half-sister Zina Presendia, only three months older and the daughter of Zina Diantha (1821–1901), stands to her right. Rounding out the ten, Emily Partridge's second daughter, Caroline, born in early 1851, sits second from the left, between Marinda and Ella.

It is a complicated sororal situation, to say the least: ten half-siblings, three sets of full sisters (Ella and Marinda; Emily Augusta and Caroline; Mamie and Clarissa Maria), and two cousins (Fanny and Jeanette). Adding to the complexity, Emily Partridge and Zina Diantha were stepsisters, rendering Zina Presendia a stepcousin as well as half-sister to Emily Augusta and Caroline. (Because Partridge and Diantha were also Joseph Smith's widows as well as Young's wives, their daughters were destined to join the first prophet's family as theological full sisters in the afterlife.) Moreover, when Clarissa Ross died in 1857, Diantha stepped in as a second mother to her four children, including Mamie and Clarissa Maria. Thus Zina Presendia grew up thinking of them as full siblings. Similarly, when Evelyn's mother died in 1852, Clarissa Decker took responsibility for the child, effectively making Evelyn an adoptive full sister to Jeanette and cousin to Fanny. Finally, more than half of the Big Ten would become plural wives themselves, further entangling their genealogies. Between 1865 and 1868, Mamie and Caroline married the same man, adding "sister-wife" to their list of family connections. And although neither of Mary Ann Angell's two surviving daughters appears in the picture, Alice would eventually share a husband with Emily Augusta, as Luna would with Fanny.

FIVE

As innocuous as *The Big Ten* initially appears, it splits into a vision of polygamous abundance for those in the know. The "in the know" part is key. Without the reference to Brigham Young inscribed at the bottom of the frame, the photograph could be a picture of any ten young women posed in party dresses around the middle of the 1860s. In terms of a date for the photo, that number remains uncertain. The prophet's daughters appear roughly sixteen years old in the image, as half of the Big Ten would have been in 1865. The picture clearly predates the winter of 1869, when many of the girls assumed leadership positions in the Retrenchment Association their father founded to encourage young LDS women "to be simple and sensible in their dress."[16] "We do not want to look like Quakers but we want to look neat and respectable," the association avowed.[17] Exposed shoulders did not fit this sartorial bill by 1869.[18] At a moment when young American women of any means (or faith) generally arrived at the photographer's studio in a dress or shirtwaist that buttoned to the neck, *The Big Ten* resembles nothing so much as a pioneer riff on Franz Xaver Winterhalter's iconic 1855 painting of Empress Eugénie encircled by eight of her ladies-in-waiting.[19] Trading the French court's lustrous silks for sturdy cotton, the prophet's daughters retained an unexpectedly Napoleonic devotion to deep necklines and ringlets.

SIX

It is possible the Big Ten were in costume, similar to the subjects in Winterhalter's work, when they posed for this photograph. According to Brigham Young, his strict Methodist upbringing had denied him the joy of music and dancing as a child. "I had not a chance to dance when I was young and never heard the enchanting tones of the violin until I was eleven years of age," he recalled.[20] Determined not to repeat such artistic privations at the Lion House, he made sure "a private music teacher was always a part of the family life" and "welcomed dancing parties hosted by his children."[21] He also arranged for many of his daughters to take lessons in interpretative dance, or "fairy dancing," as it was called.[22] This training proved useful during the fall of 1863, when a pair of traveling performers suggested "there should be a perfectly gorgeous and superb fairy play in which [Young's] own 'Ten Big Girls' should appear as the charming illusive sprites, dancing and smiling themselves into the good graces of the audience to be assembled in the Salt Lake Theater."[23] As one of the Ten's younger sisters remembered,

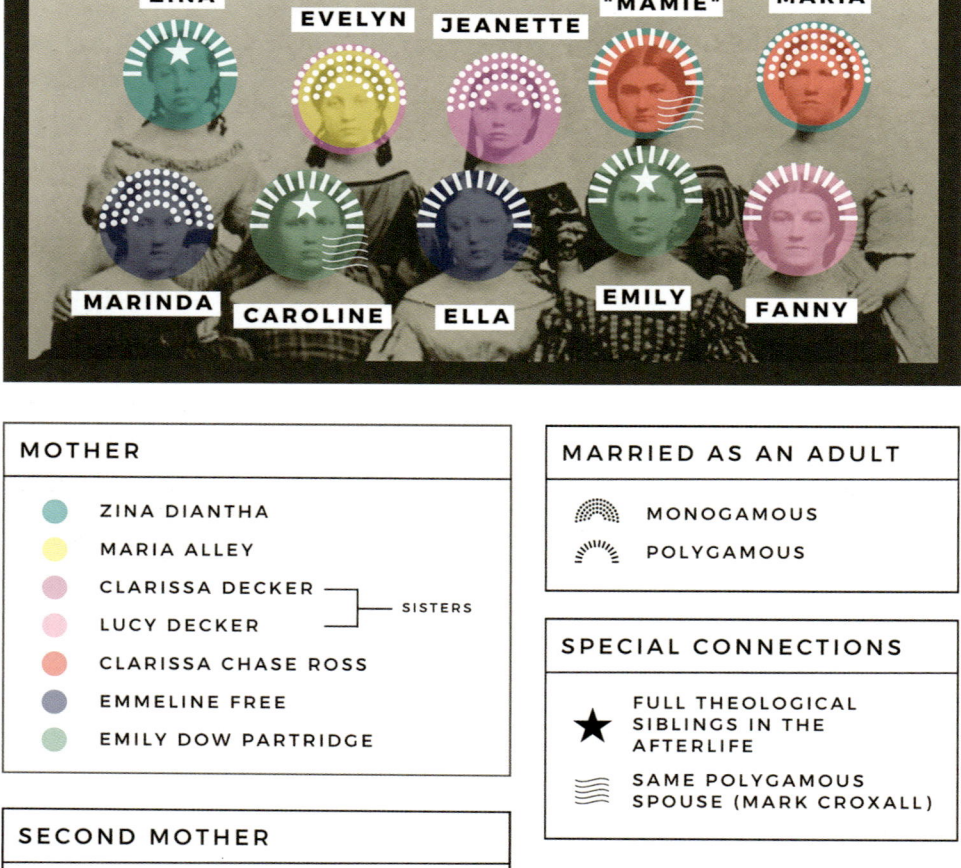

Fig. 9.2 Graphic based on the Big Ten image by Aimee Chico, 2022. Courtesy of the artist.

a "delightful confusion and bustle" overtook the Lion House "when it was announced that the Ten Big Girls were to be clothed in apparel that would rival Solomon in all his vain glory when they appeared as fairies in this thrilling piece."[24]

It is not clear whether *The Big Ten* commemorates this performance, but the dates line up. Alternatively, the photo might be a memento of a different play from the same period. The girls danced for the Salt Lake Theater somewhat regularly and might even have earned their collective nickname through their repeat appearances on its stage. "'The 'Big Ten,' [was] a chorus of the elder daughters of Brigham Young, [and] was

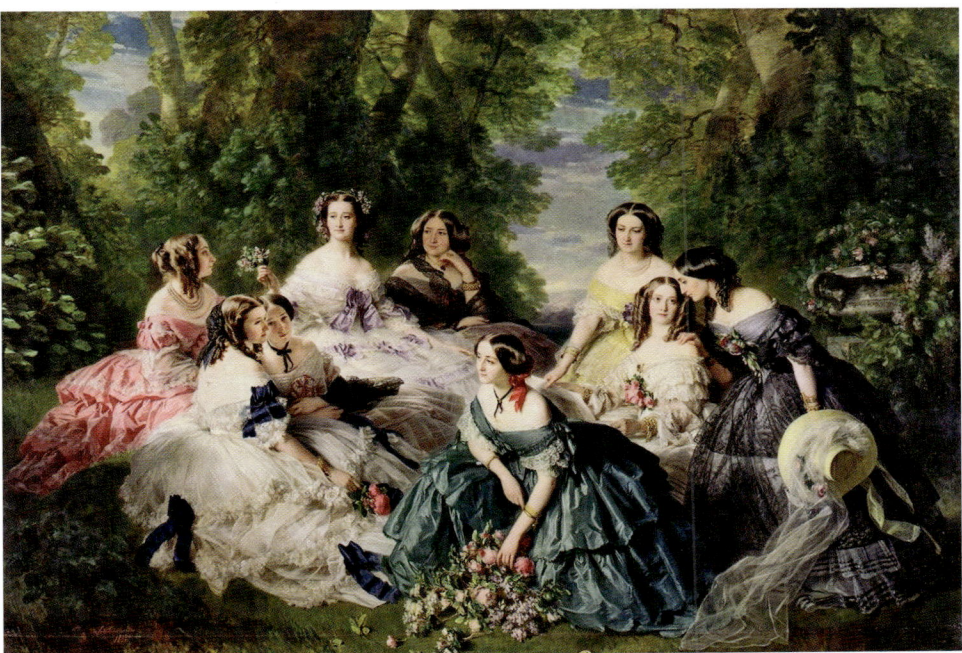

Fig. 9.3 Franz Xaver Winterhalter, *Empress Eugénie Surrounded by Her Ladies in Waiting*, 1855, 300 cm × 420 cm, Château de Compiègne, Compiègne.

a popular feature on early programs at the theater," a local newspaper reported.[25] The girls were certainly popular with the theater's staff. In 1868, Emily Augusta became the fourth wife of the manager, Hiram Clawson. (Her elder half-sister Alice was his third.) Similarly, the Big Ten's performance in the 1863–1864 fairy play seems to have exerted a narcotic effect on certain members of the orchestra pit. "When the Big Ten were in the midst of their gayest evolutions," their sister wrote, "the most thrilling notes pleaded out from the shining brass cornet held in the hands of the handsome and dashing young cornetist, Mark Croxall, straight into the willing ear of lovely sister Mamie."[26] Soon after the fairy play ended, Croxall married Mamie. Three years later, he married her sister-dancer Caroline too.

SEVEN

At some point between 1863 and 1869, the Big Ten posed for this photograph—a puzzle of a picture that requires another picture to decode. As the need for explanatory imagery reveals, *The Big Ten* is quiet, recalcitrant even. Even with the reference to Young's daughters, it refuses to speak fully to the uninitiated. Instead, it withholds a full sense of the polygamous family it points to for those already capable of running its convoluted maternal math.

A certain defiance inheres in this pictorial quietude. Superficially a photograph of ten young women in dancing gowns, the image shows all the daughters born to Brigham Young's plural wives before 1852, the year he publicly announced celestial marriage as an official part of LDS theology.[27] (Having been tarred, feathered, and nearly castrated for mere rumors of Mormon sexual misconduct, Joseph Smith went to his grave with thirty-eight spouses and an unflagging commitment to declaring himself a monogamist.)[28] "Anyone with eyes to see knew that polygamy was being practiced" among the Saints between 1847 and 1852. Nonetheless, spiritual wifery "was not to be acknowledged in any document going to Washington."[29] *The Big Ten* simultaneously celebrates and conceals the daughters born to Brigham Young's plural wives during this liminal period of quasi secrecy, sequestering them behind a veil of middle-class photographic conventions and incomplete information.[30]

The fact that Young either commissioned this picture or simply allowed the girls to pose for it around 1864 adds an extra layer of possible rebellion to *The Big Ten*, muted as that rebellion might be. In 1859, the Supreme Court ruled that photographs could be admitted as evidence in criminal cases.[31] Three years later, Congress passed the Morrill Act, the first of numerous statutes to criminalize LDS polygamy.[32] The law ultimately proved useless because it required prosecutors to prove a defendant had married twice. The Territory of Utah had no laws governing secular marriages at the time, and it kept no records of non-ecclesiastical unions. Moreover, Latter-day Saints faithful enough to practice the Principle married in LDS temples, where they were explicitly sworn to secrecy. Faced with such evidentiary hurdles, prosecutors did not indict a single polygamist under the statute. "When the federal government finally did indict its first [LDS] polygamist in 1871, it ignored the Morrill Act, choosing instead to indict the defendant for having adulterous relations with his plural wife."[33] For all this statutory impotence, it was still the bold Saint who would pose for a family portrait with a multitude of spouses or sister-wives after the passage of the Morrill Act. Introduced as proof of polygamous relations, such a picture could lead to a felony conviction, the equivalent of a $14,000 fine, and a five-year prison sentence.[34]

Perhaps we see Brigham Young hedging his legal bets with *The Big Ten*. Like so many Latter-day Saints, the second LDS prophet embraced "the beautiful art of photography" from the technology's early days.[35] More than that, he seems to have enjoyed having his picture taken, sitting for more than fifty daguerreotypes, ambrotypes, photographs, and other such images over the course of his life. As a result, the visual record overflows with pictures of Young posing with everything from top hats and canes to all four of his brothers to other members of the church's all-male leadership. Despite this photographic enthusiasm, Young appears to have actively avoided being pictured with his numerous wives and children. Sifting through thousands of family photos and albums, one finds no images of the prophet with his offspring and only two pictures of him accompanied by a recognizable spouse.[36] Sometime around 1853, he sat for a daguerreotype with his twentieth wife, Margaret Pierce (1823–1907). Roughly a decade

later, he posed for a photograph with his fifty-first, Amelia Folsom (1838–1910). The
LDS Church History Library holds a third image of him seated next to an unidentified
woman during the late 1840s or early 1850s. "Daguerreotype portrait of Young and a
woman presumed to be one of his wives. Facial image of wife has been obliterated," the
archive notes read.[37] From the looks of it, someone rubbed the silver off a portion of the
image, effectively decapitating the prophet's female companion. Like *The Big Ten* and
Young's family photos in general, this vandalized picture hides as much as it reveals.

"Tell all the truth but tell it slant— / Success in Circuit lies."[38] As if heeding Emily
Dickinson's poetic directive, Young and his family took the oblique route when it came
to memorializing their domestic world in photographs. During a period when not only
prosecutors but Gentile tourists clamored for a view of polygamous excess in Utah, the
prophet and his wives collectively declined.[39] While Young abstained from all but the
rarest of spousal photos and never posed with his sons or daughters en masse, his plural
wives tended to arrive at the photographer's studio alone or with their own children.
Examining a photograph of Zina Diantha with a young Zina Presendia, one would have
no idea Diantha was her husband's tenth wife, nor that she lived in Room 43 of the Lion
House, next to Martha Bowker (Mrs. Young no. 28) and across the hall from Harriet
Cook (Mrs. Young no. 5).[40] Similarly, nothing about a midcentury daguerreotype of

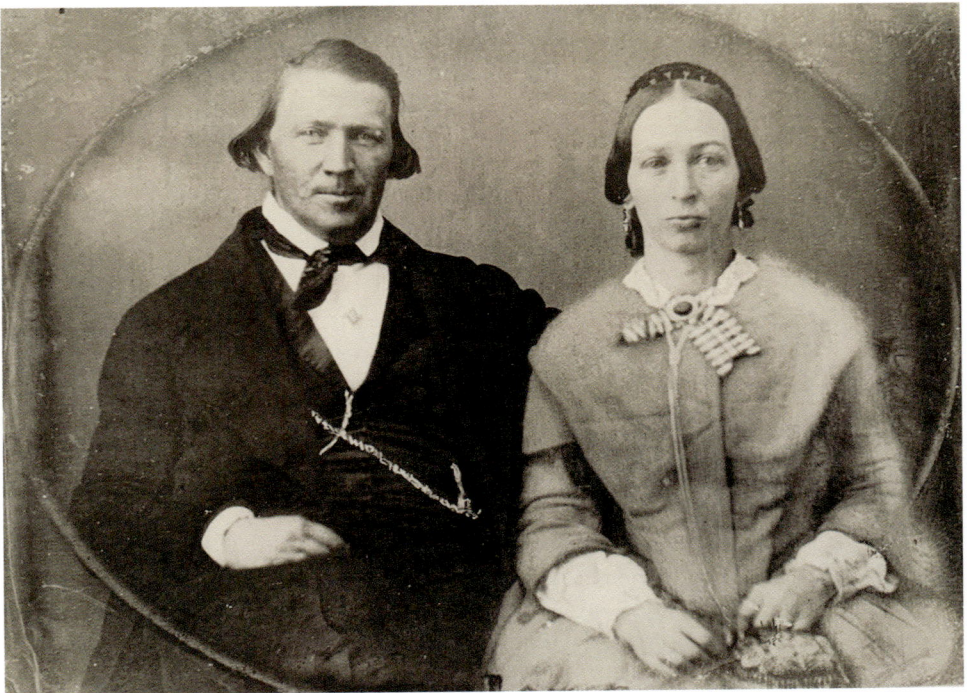

Fig. 9.4 Marsena Cannon (attrib.), Brigham Young and unidentified woman, c. early 1850s,
daguerreotype, 9.5 cm × 8 cm, Church History Library, The Church of Jesus Christ of
Latter-day Saints.

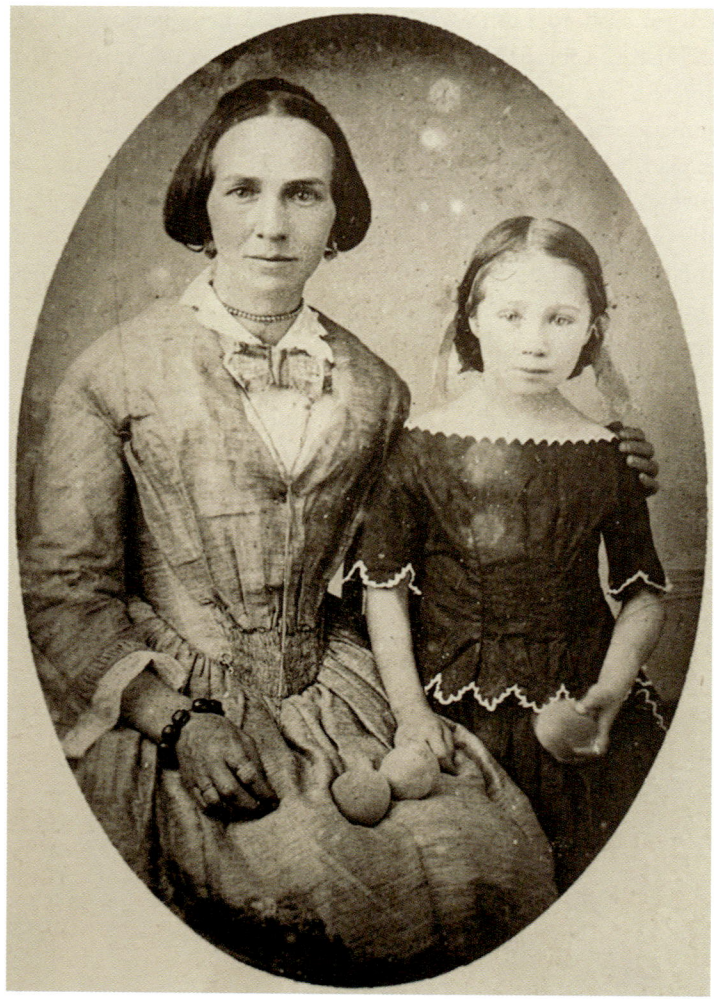

Fig. 9.5 Anonymous, portrait of Zina Huntington Young and her daughter, Zina Presendia Young, c. 1856, postcard. Church History Library, The Church of Jesus Christ of Latter-day Saints.

Emily Dow Partridge seated between her eldest son and a two-year-old Emily Augusta speaks to Partridge's position as Joseph Smith's twentieth wife and Young's ninth. Already pregnant with Young's twenty-seventh child, Partridge gazes serenely at the camera, a model of refined nineteenth-century domesticity.

Eventually the tourist industry would generate pictures of Young surrounded by individual portraits of his most noteworthy wives or, less frequently, his wives and daughters. Around the turn of the century, Salt Lake City photographer and man-about-town Charles Ellis Johnson (1857–1926) tried his hand at a montage of Young encircled by vignettes of seventeen of his sons. These were collage jobs: fabricated memorabilia

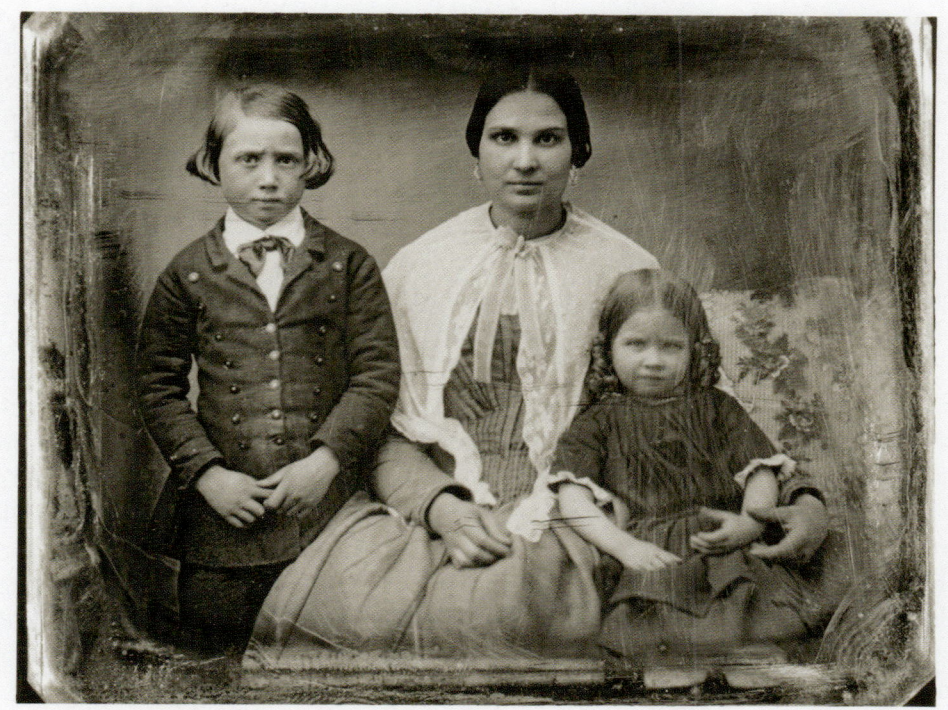

Fig. 9.6 Anonymous, Emily Dow Partridge Young and children, 1851, daguerreotype, 8.5 cm × 9.5 cm (half case), Church History Library, The Church of Jesus Christ of Latter-day Saints.

that local businessmen created to cater to Gentile America's prurient interest in what it imagined went on behind closed Mormon doors. Nonetheless, certain members of the prophet's household collected these souvenir pictures, likely in lieu of more traditional family photos. Susa Young Gates (1856–1933), daughter of Brigham Young's forty-second wife, Lucy Bigelow (1830–1905), and committed family historian, saved a copy of Johnson's best-selling card *Brigham Young and His Wives* (1906) among her personal effects.[41] A slightly different version of the card appears in a collection of family photographs kept by a great-grandson of Luna Young, Mary Ann Angell's daughter and sister-wife to *The Big Ten*'s Fanny.[42] The pictures do something unexpected in this context, morphing from a mass-produced peek at what most Americans viewed as martial freakery to a cherished family artifact. One wonders how many of Young's descendants repurposed the pop cultural byproducts of the country's lurid interest in the Saints this way.

EIGHT

Deeply distrustful of lawyers, Brigham Young did not pose for pictures that could lead to his conviction as a polygamist.[43] All too aware of the hordes of tourists who gathered outside the Lion House for a view of his family, he did not sit for photos that could sate such Gentile appetites.[44] Finally, as the leader of a faith that promised that polygamy would make pious LDS men gods in the afterlife, Young showed little interest in being photographed with the women he required to guarantee his deification. "For Young and many mid- to late nineteenth-century church leaders, achieving godhood meant participation in [the] work of creation, the creation of spirit children and the creation of worlds on which those children would assume bodies and themselves progress toward divinity," John Turner writes.[45] Such godly creation remained the purview of male Saints in the polygamous church, scattered references to divine mothers in heaven notwithstanding.[46] Celestial marriage might have demanded that a man attach himself to numerous women, but it did so to bind him to other men. "At its heart, Joseph Smith's religion taught men how to suture themselves into the divine line that, Smith vowed, would tie polygamous LDS husbands to the Old Testament patriarchs, God, and the shadowy anterior deities who stood behind him."[47] In the words of the LDS apostle Bruce R. McConkie, "Those who shall hereafter rule and reign in eternity as exalted beings will form a patriarchal chain which will begin with Father Adam and spread out until every exalted person is linked in."[48] Women remain an afterthought in this cosmology, necessary yet unseen. As I have written elsewhere, we find echoes of this theological invisibility in Young's failure to memorialize his plural wives *as* plural wives by posing with them as a group.[49] When it comes to the church's polygamous aspirations— all those righteous men hoping to solder themselves into their faith's great homosocial chain—the religion repeatedly obscures female desires and sacrifices. Success in such patriarchal circuits necessarily conceals. Sometimes it outright lies.

NINE

Regardless of Young's reasons for avoiding plural family portraits, he seems to have set a precedent that other polygamous households followed. In general, LDS polygamists did not sit for pictures with more than one wife at a time. Images of sister-wives posed together without their husband are even rarer. A thorough search of the archives yields exceptions. A photograph of one Latter-day polygamist flanked by two wives, a daguerreotype of another posed with three—with enough time and effort, one finds a handful of images like these. Interestingly, the sixth LDS prophet, Joseph F. Smith (1838–1918), appears to have been particularly enthusiastic—some might say reckless— when it came to picturing his expansive family. The nephew of the first LDS prophet, Joseph F. celebrated both his sixtieth and sixty-sixth birthdays by posing for formal portraits with his five wives, numerous children, and plethora of grandchildren.[50] Here we find the visual tribute to celestial marriage one might have expected from Brigham

Young. Joseph F. sits at the center of a constellation of family in both pictures, a budding god enshrined in polygamous majesty. "A hundred years will not pass away before I will become millions myself," the LDS apostle (and husband to forty-four women) Heber C. Kimball declared of the extensive progeny celestial marriage promised to grant him.[51] Examining these two photographs of Joseph F., we see something of these polygamous ambitions.

Even Joseph F. limited the number of times he posed with his full family, however. In general, he sat for pictures with individual wives or commissioned group portraits of his numerous children. "8 daughters of Jos. F. Smith, all under 9 years of age," someone wrote on the cardboard mount of a sepia-toned photograph taken by Salt Lake City's Fox & Symons studio on December 12, 1896. Like *The Big Ten,* this picture presents a pretty grouping of girls, all outfitted in coordinating dresses, lace collars, and hair bows. Anyone unfamiliar with the history of LDS polygamy might wonder at the caption, searching for several sets of twins or even triplets among the prophet's daughters and puzzling at the gestational situation capable of producing so many children in such a short period of time. The picture's companion photograph, shot a week later, would do little to relieve the mystery. "8 Sons of Jos. F. Smith Taken Dec. 19th, 1896," this second image announces, presenting the viewer with an equally formal tableau of a passel of boys arranged on a gilded settee.[52] The eldest of the group appears no older than twelve, while the smallest wears the loose dress reserved for boys too young to have yet been breeched. Clearly, no single woman could have birthed all sixteen of these

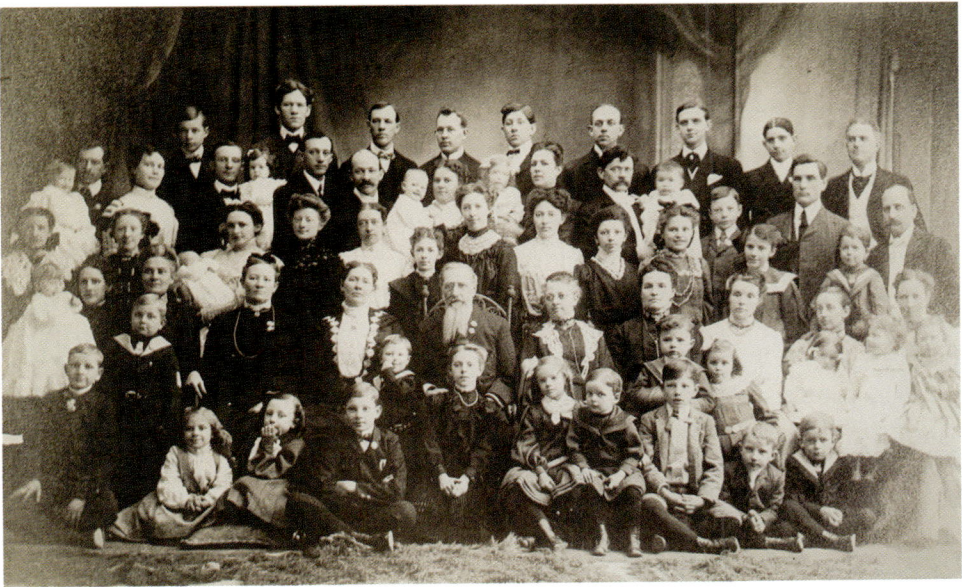

Fig. 9.7 Fox and Symons Studio, portrait of Joseph F. Smith and his family, November 13, 1904, Church History Library, The Church of Jesus Christ of Latter-day Saints.

children, leaving the average viewer to speculate about the prophet's apparent penchant for adoption. Without the identifying information written beneath each picture, it is unlikely this viewer would even recognize the children as siblings, much less the off-spring of Joseph F. Like *The Big Ten*, these two pictures camouflage the very family they commemorate.

"I have married many wives and am the father of fifty one children. I say may God bless the heir to my Photograph fifty years from now," the LDS apostle Charles C. Rich (1809–1883) wrote on the back of his cabinet card portrait in 1881.[53] Some five decades later, his son Ezra and granddaughter Gladys undertook the substantial task of assembling four generations of Rich family photographs into a single album. It is the most extensive pictorial record of a polygamous LDS family I have ever seen. More than seventy pages long, it begins with individual portraits of each of Rich's six wives, as well as photographs of certain wives posed with their own children and in front of their own homes. Turning the album's heavy pages, I found hundreds of pictures of well-dressed Saints assembled for the camera, all but a few labeled with neatly typed captions. Moving past the family's polygamous period and into their monogamous years, I discovered an article from a 1947 issue of *Life* magazine pasted into the album's pages. "A Mormon Family Has a Reunion: Four Hundred and One of His 2,000 Living Descendants Gather to Honor Apostle Charles C. Rich and His Six Wives," the head-line proclaims. "Rich's first wife chose the others," a side panel declares above a com-posite picture of the apostle and his spouses.[54] It is the only image of Rich with more than one wife to be found in the entire album. Like Susa Young Gates and Luna Young's great-grandson, Rich's photographic heirs had to rely on America's ongoing fascination with LDS polygamy to get a picture of their progenitor with all the women he married. Rich might have depended on these women to make him a god, but he never paid direct tribute to that arrangement in photographs.

So it goes with polygamous family pictures. Anyone searching for a trove of photos of LDS men posed with their plural wives will be disappointed. Instead, images such as *The Big Ten* and *Eight Daughters of Jos. F. Smith* are the closest thing to plural family portraits that regularly surface in the archives.[55] Rich's sons sat for one of these—or at least seventeen of the twenty-six did. So did all ten of the seventh LDS prophet's daughters. Sometime around 1890, seventeen of John Taylor's sons posed for such a photograph. The third LDS prophet, Taylor (1808–1887) had recently recorded a rev-elation on spiritual wifery, reaffirming the necessity of celestial marriage for LDS men seeking deification after death despite increasing legal pressure to abandon the practice. "All those who would enter into my glory must and shall obey my law [plural marriage]," God commands in this revelation. "And have I not commanded men that if they were Abraham's seed and would enter into my glory, they must do the works of Abraham."[56] Taylor himself did this Old Testament work, marrying eighteen women and fathering thirty-five children by seven of them. When federal authorities moved to prosecute him for criminal cohabitation under the 1882 Edmunds Act, the seventy-nine-year-old

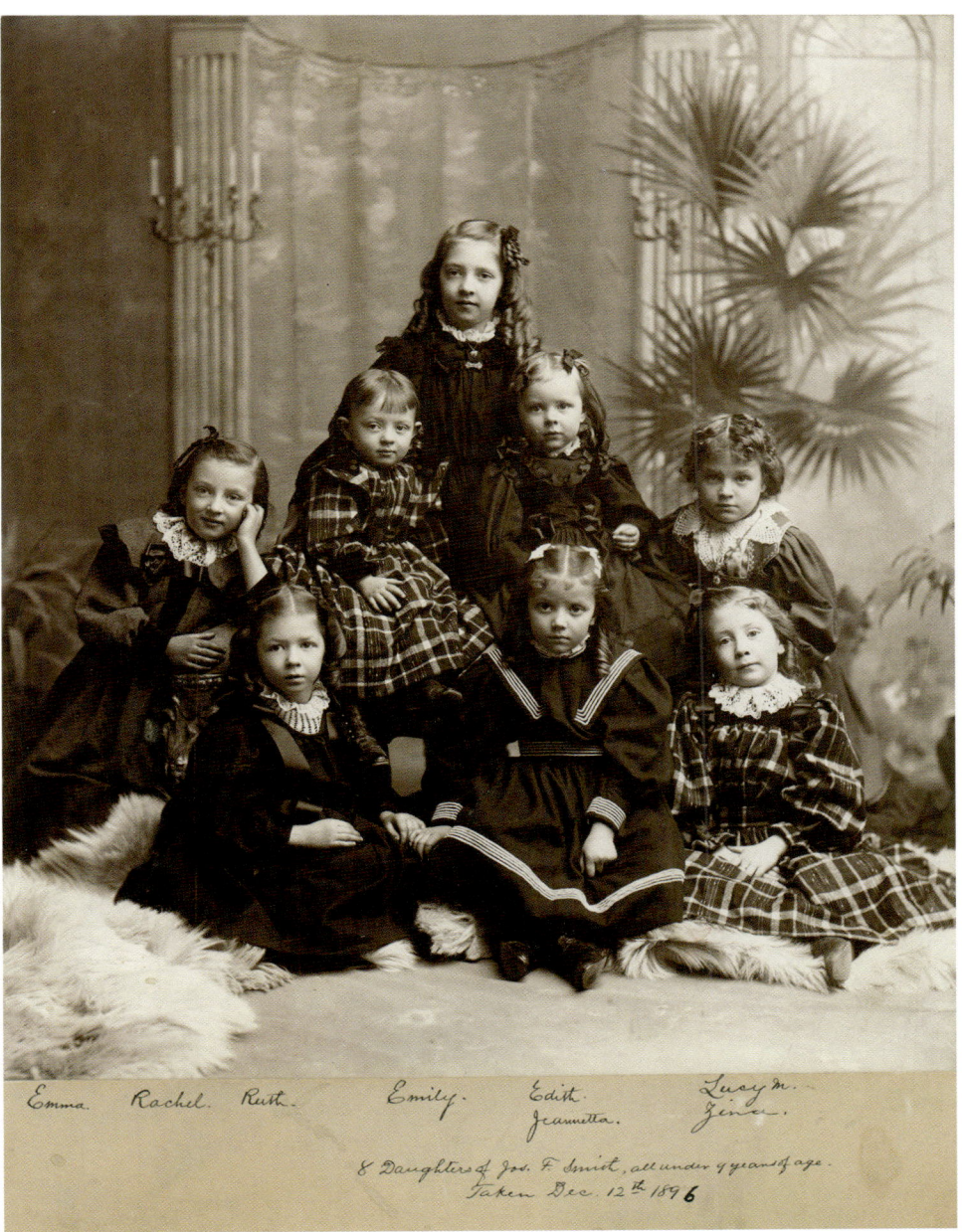

Fig. 9.8 C. R. Savage, children Jesus Joseph F. Smith, 1896, 38 cm × 33 cm, photograph, Church History Library, The Church of Jesus Christ of Latter-day Saints.

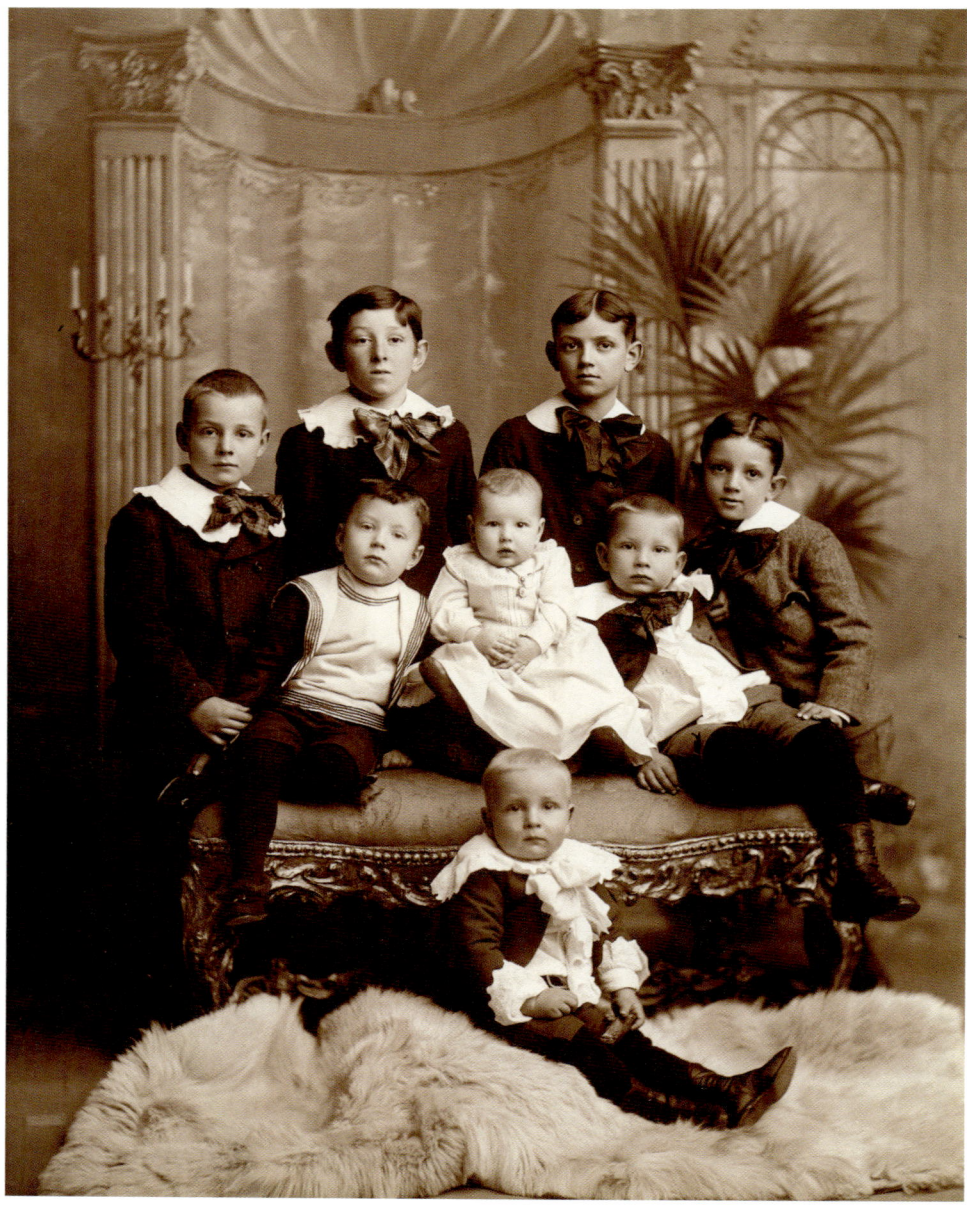

Fig. 9.9 C. R. Savage, sons of Joseph F. Smith, December 1896, photograph, 41 cm × 32 cm, Church History Library, The Church of Jesus Christ of Latter-day Saints.

prophet went into hiding. He never made it home. Maybe Taylor's sons posed for this picture to commemorate their father's death. Strung across the photographer's studio in their matching suits and ties, they present a living celebration of polygamy's promise to bless devout LDS men with progeny "as innumerable as the stars; or . . . the sand upon the sea-shore." Slinging elbows and knees around each other until they seem to form a single, shifting mass, they incarnate Joseph Smith's original revelation that the Principle would enable righteous men to live and multiply forever: "Then shall they be gods, because they have no end."[57]

Taylor was not the only LDS polygamist to go into hiding, nor did he go alone. Instead, he took with him his first counselor, George Q. Cannon (1827–1901). Cannon advised every LDS prophet from Brigham Young (number two) through Lorenzo Snow (number five)—a position that prompted the *New York Times* to christen him the "Richelieu of Mormonism."[58] Husband to six and father to twenty-four, Cannon was more than willing to suffer for polygamy. Although he did not die in hiding like Taylor, he did forfeit the equivalent of nearly $1.5 million in bail; jump from a moving

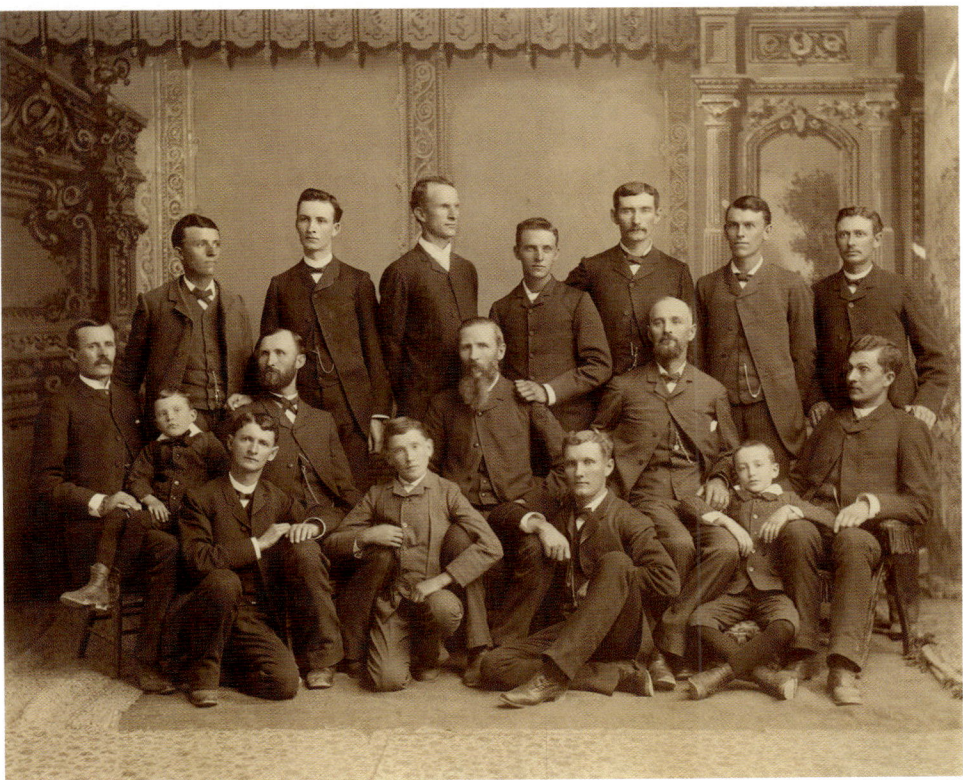

Fig. 9.10 Anonymous, sons of John Taylor, c. 1890, photograph, 42 cm × 51 cm, Church History Library, The Church of Jesus Christ of Latter-day Saints.

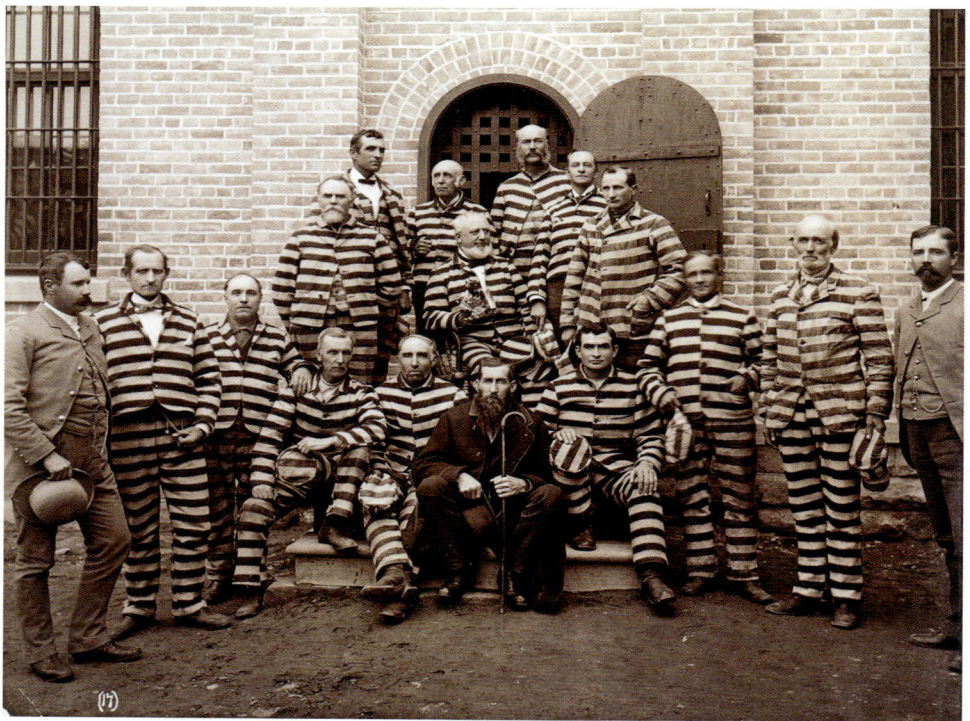

Fig. 9.11 C. R. Savage, polygamists in prison, 1889, photograph, 23.2 cm × 21.2 cm, Church History Library, The Church of Jesus Christ of Latter-day Saints.

train to escape federal marshals (he was sixty years old at the time); and, having been escorted back to Utah under armed guard, spend six months in the Utah Territorial Penitentiary. As if proclaiming his continued allegiance to celestial marriage, Cannon posed for several photographs during his prison sentence. The most famous of these shows him seated at the helm of a long stretch of LDS inmates, his prison stripes neatly accessorized with a bow tie. Cannon looks strikingly dignified in this picture, his regal bearing nearly identical to the posture he assumed in a portrait he posed for with seventeen of his sons around the time of his conviction. The formal similarities between the two images reveal the extent to which polygamy exists as *men's* work in Cannon's pictorial world, as it does in most of the images we have seen in this chapter. "Brigham Youngs Daughters," "8 Sons of Jos. F. Smith," the profusion of male bodies that radiate from Cannon's at every photographic turn—repeatedly these pictures exile plural wives and mothers from both caption and image to cast the Principle as "a patriarchal chain."

TEN

"A great glory is bestowed on woman, for she is permitted to bring forth the souls of men," Cannon proclaimed in 1867.[59] We find a visual analogue to this declaration in

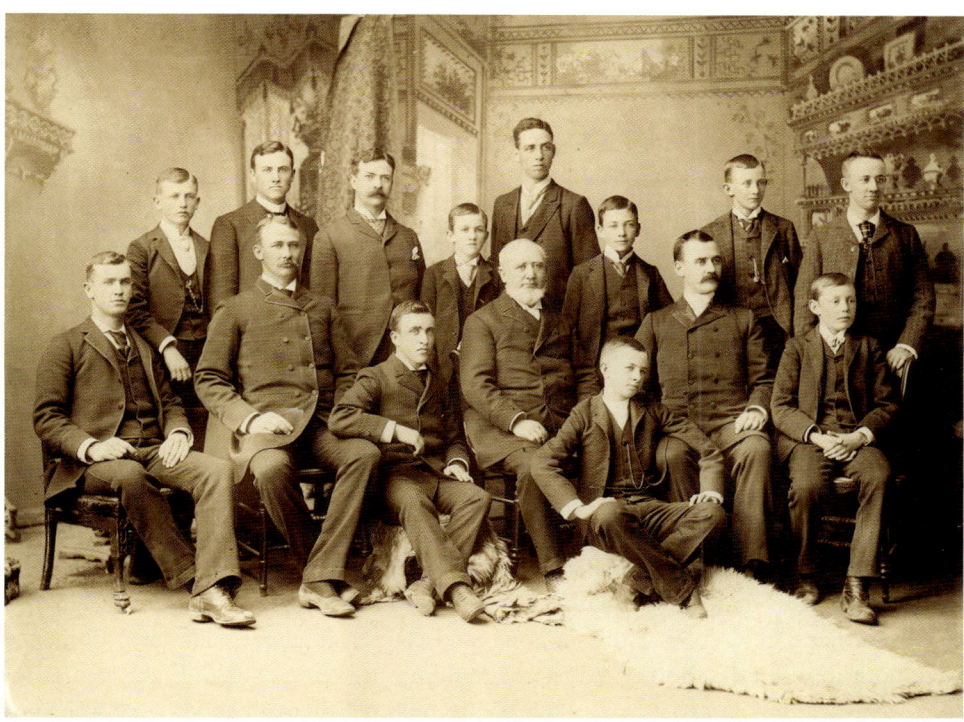

Fig. 9.12 C. R. Savage, George Q. Cannon and his sons, c. 1885–1890, photograph, size unmarked, Church History Library, The Church of Jesus Christ of Latter-day Saints.

the Latter-day Saints' collective reluctance to memorialize plural wives as such. "A practice rooted in the belief that a man could sail to godhood on a vessel rigged with female bodies," LDS polygamy repeatedly valued women "for what they produced rather than for what they were or could ever be."[60] Casting the Principle's female participants as the anonymous base material for their husbands' eventual exaltation—Cannon's generic "woman" ushering in the particularized souls of so many men—the faith did not give rise to a photographic culture that honored the dedication and sacrifices of its sister-wives. This is not to say there were not ongoing practical reasons for the Saints to keep polygamy out of the photographer's studio.[61] Technically, the Fifth Amendment's prohibition against double jeopardy should have freed convicted polygamists to pose for pictures *en pleine famille* without fear of legal repercussions. Cannon and Joseph F. both fell into this category, as did the fifth LDS prophet, Lorenzo Snow (1814–1901); the seventh, Heber J. Grant (1856–1945); and some 1,300 other LDS men, including my own grandmother's great-grandfather, William Jordan Flake (1839–1932). To the extent that the LDS Church's continued existence—not to mention Utah's dreams of statehood—hung on the Saints abandoning the practice, however, perhaps we should not be surprised at the scarcity of plural family portraits.

My own family has exactly two photographs of our polygamous ancestor: a picture of William J. Flake on a horse and another of him in his prison uniform. I have also found individual portraits of Flake's two wives, Lucy Hannah (1842–1900) and Prudence Jane (1859–1896), as well as a photo of Flake posed with ten of the twenty children they collectively bore him. I have never seen a photo of Lucy and Prudence together, with or without the husband they shared. Whether the lack of such pictures stems from the country's legal regime, the disabling depression Flake's marriage to Prudence inflicted on Lucy, or the polygamous church's patriarchal dreams, I do not know. I do know the only stories I ever heard about the family as I was growing up cast Flake as an exemplary husband to Lucy and Prudence, both of whom were always described as loving sister-wives, happily bound to each other in the Principle. It was only when I read Paula Kelly Harline's book *The Polygamous Wives Writing Club* that I learned about the toll Flake's marriage to Prudence took on Lucy and the way the new couple neglected my great-grandmother's grandmother, leaving Lucy with chronic headaches and an inability to get out of bed for months on end.[62]

According to family lore, Flake took his first and only airplane ride shortly before he died. A pilot had come to town with a biplane, and Flake decided to pay for the chance to climb in and get a look at the Arizona landscape from above. Lucy and Prudence were both dead by that point, and as my grandmother remembered, Flake wanted to see the world from an aerial perspective so he could tell them all about it when he got to heaven. I imagine my great-great-great-grandfather soaring above the tiny town he had founded, taking in the sights for two women who likely hated each other but who had bound themselves to be his divine queens in the afterlife nonetheless. I imagine him looping through the sky, ventriloquizing the desires of two dead women, at least one of whom had suffered terribly for their shared faith. Success in such circuits—slanted circuits, their circuits, *my* circuits—lies.

NOTES

[1] The Church of Jesus Christ of Latter-day Saints currently asks that one "avoid using the abbreviation 'LDS' or the nickname 'Mormon' as substitutes for the name of the Church." See "Style Guide—The Name of the Church," https://newsroom.churchofjesuschrist.org/style-guide, accessed March 7, 2022. Although I have no desire to disrespect the church by disregarding its desires, such strictures leave little in the way of adjectives or synonyms. Moreover, the church's preferred nomenclature ("members of the Church of Jesus Christ of Latter-day Saints," "members of the restored Church of Jesus Christ") is not particularly conducive to fluid writing. As such, I use the adjective "LDS" where necessary and, less frequently, the noun "Mormon."
[2] See George D. Smith, *Nauvoo Polygamy* (Salt Lake City: Signature Books, 2011), appendix B, 622. I rely on George D. Smith's count of the original Mormon leadership's plural wives throughout this article.
[3] James Thomas Jakeman, *Album "Daughters of the Utah Pioneers and Their Mothers"* (n.p.: Western, 1915), unpaginated.
[4] George D. Pyper, *The Romance of an Old Playhouse*, 2nd ed. (Salt Lake City: Deseret News Press, 1937), 120.
[5] M. R. Werner, *Brigham Young* (New York: Harcourt, Brace and Company, 1925), 338–339.
[6] Werner, Brigham Young, 325.

[7] "Brigham Young's Heirs," *New York Times*, March 10, 1879.

[8] D&C 132:32. Smith recorded this revelation on July 12, 1843.

[9] Quoted in John G. Turner, *Brigham Young, Pioneer Prophet* (Cambridge, MA: Belknap Press of Harvard University Press, 2014), 91.

[10] Turner, Brigham Young, 91.

[11] Laurel Thatcher Ulrich, *A House Full of Females: Plural Marriage and Women's Rights in Early Mormonism, 1835–1870* (New York: Alfred A. Knopf, 2017), 95.

[12] Turner, *Brigham Young,* 91.

[13] Ulrich, *A House Full of Females,* 92.

[14] Werner, *Brigham Young,* 338.

[15] Between 1852 and 1858, an average of three Young babies were born each year, with no children arriving in 1859 and three making their entrance in 1860. The prophet settled into a pattern of two babies a year during the period between 1861 and 1863, sired one daughter in 1864, and then took a five-year pause before fathering one last girl in 1870.

[16] Martha Sontag Bradley and Mary Brown Firmage Woodward, *4 Zinas: A Story of Mothers and Daughters on the Mormon Frontier* (Salt Lake City: Signature Books, 2000), 297. As Bradley and Firmage write, "The transcontinental railroad had been completed just six months earlier, and Brigham was also concerned about gentile influences, worldly distractions, and public opinion that was steadily solidifying against polygamy."

[17] Quoted in Bradley and Woodward, *4 Zinas,* 297.

[18] See Linda Setnick, *Victorian Fashions for Women and Children: Society's Impact on Dess* (Atglen, PA: Schifer, 2012), 63: "While no longer enjoying the popularity it had achived during the sixties, the short-sleeve, off-the-shoulder look still lingered in day wear for children [between 1869 and 1875]. Though allowed to youngsters under ten, normally by the age of seven, shoulders were hidden and arms fully encased in long coat sleeves, or, mor rarely, the fuller pagoda [sleeve]."

[19] For 1860s fashion in the photographer's studio, see Joan L. Severa, *Dressed for the Photographer: Ordinary Americans and Fashion, 1840–1900* (Kent, OH: Kent State University Press, 1999), 213–291.

[20] Turner, *Brigham Young,* 12.

[21] Susa Young Gates, *History of the Young Ladies' Mutual Improvement Association of the Church of Jesus Christ of Latter-day Saints from November 1869 to June 1910* (Salt Lake City: Deseret News, 1911), 98 (music teacher); Bradley and Firmage, *4 Zinas,* 293 (dancing parties at the Lion House).

[22] Bradley and Firmage, *4 Zinas,* 294.

[23] Susan Young Gates, quoted in Pyper, *Romance of an Old Playhouse,* 120–121.

[24] Pyper, *Romance of an Old Playhouse,* 121.

[25] "Old Salt Lake Theater Widely Known Among Old Time Stars of Footlights," *Salt Lake Telegram,* June 5, 1934.

[26] Susa Young Gates, quoted in Pyper, *Romance of an Old Playhouse,* 123. The Salt Lake Theater's first manager, Hiram Clawson (1826–1912), also found love among the Big Ten, marrying dancer Emily Augusta Young in 1868, sixteen years after he wed her half-sister Alice. Alice and Emily Augusta were his third and fourth wives, respectively.

[27] Technically, the LDS apostle Orson Pratt made the announcement. On August 29, 1852, Pratt took the podium at the Latter-day Saints' biannual meeting to confirm what most of the faithful seemed to already know. Judging by the text of Pratt's declaration, his audience's familiarity with the topic did not make the news any easier to share. "It is rather new ground for me," he explained, "that is I have not been in the habit of publicly speaking upon this subject and it is rather new ground to all of the inhabitants of the United States not only them but to all of inhabitants of Europe the greater portion of them not been in habit of preaching a doctrine of this description consequently we shall have to break up new ground." As it turned out, breaking up this new ground nearly destroyed the church. Orson Pratt, discourse delivered August 29, 1852, reprinted in Brigham Young, George D. Watt, and J. V. Long, eds., *Journal of Discourses* (Liverpool: F. D. Richards, 1854–1886), 1:54–66.

28 For an account of Smith's brush with castration, see Richard Lyman Bushman, *Joseph Smith: Rough Stone Rolling* (New York: Knopf, 2005), 178–179. Bushman rejects the idea that Smith's attackers "meant to punish Joseph for an intimacy with [one of the group's] sister," concluding that the "hypothesis fails for lack of evidence." On the other hand, the mob's interest in Smith's genitals provides relatively solid evidence that the prophet's alleged crime was sexual in nature.

29 Ulrich, *A House Full of Females*, 215.

30 Two Young girls were born in 1852: Clarissa Decker's second daughter, Nabbie (1852–1894), and Lucy Bigelow's first, Dora (1852–1921). Although both arrived before Pratt's August announcement, neither appears in *The Big Ten*.

31 *Luco v. United States*, 64 U.S. 515 (1859).

32 Morrill Act, ch. 125, § 1, 12 Stat. 501 (1862) (codified at Rev. Stat. § 5352).

33 Mary K. Campbell, "Mr. Peay's Horses: The Federal Response to Mormon Polygamy, 1854–1887," *Yale Journal of Law and Feminism* 13 (2001): 39. "It is doubtful that this legal distinction made much difference to one Mr. Thomas Hawkins, adulterer. The court still saw fit to sentence him to a five hundred dollar fine and three years of hard labor" (39n85).

34 The Morrill Act states that "every person having a husband or wife living, who shall marry any other person, whether married or single, in a Territory of the United States, or other place over which the United States have exclusive jurisdiction, shall, except in the cases specified in the proviso to this section, be adjudged guilty of bigamy, and, upon conviction thereof, shall be punished by a fine not exceeding five hundred dollars, and by imprisonment for a term not exceeding five years."

35 *Luco v. United States*, 530.

36 Richard Neitzel Holzapfel and R. Q. Shupe have collected every image of the second prophet in *Brigham Young: Images of a Mormon Prophet* (Salt Lake City: Eagle Gate, 2000).

37 See LDS Church History Library, PH 7848, "Brigham Young and Unidentified Woman, Circa Early 1850s."

38 Emily Dickinson (1914), "Tell All the Truth but Tell It Slant—1263," in *The Poems of Emily Dickinson: Reading Edition* (Cambridge, MA: Belknap Press of Harvard University Press, 1998).

39 For a discussion of Gentile tourists in Salt Lake City, see Mary Campbell, *Charles Ellis Johnson and the Erotic Mormon Image* (Chicago: University of Chicago Press, 2016), 18–32, 82–97; Thomas K. Hafen, "City of Saints, City of Sinners: The Development of Salt Lake City as a Tourist Attraction, 1869–1900," *Western Historical Quarterly* 28 (Autumn 1997): 344–349.

40 I rely here on "Plans of the Lion House" in Catherine Van Valkenberg Waite, *The Mormon Prophet and His Harem; or, An Authentic History of Brigham Young, and His Numerous Wives and Children*, 2nd ed. (Chicago: J. S. Goodman, 1868).

41 I found this card among Gates's papers at the Utah Division of State History in Salt Lake City, Utah. Because the Division of State History is currently undergoing renovations, I have no call number for the item.

42 LDS Church History Library, George W. Thatcher Blair family photographs, circa 1850–1910, PH 5269.

43 See "A Discourse by President Brigham Young, Delivered in the Tabernacle, Great Salt Lake City, February 24, 1856: Lawyers, and Those Who Practice Attending Law Courts, Rebuked—a Curse Pronounced Upon All Who Love Litigation and Do Not Repent," *Journal of Discourses* 3:240: "To sit among them is like sitting in the depths of hell . . . they are a stink in the nostrils of God and angels."

44 Werner, *Brigham Young*, 322: "One lady visitor asked Brigham Young if she might see his wives, to which he replied, 'They are not on exhibition, madam.'"

45 John G. Turner, *The Mormon Jesus: A Biography* (Cambridge, MA: Belknap Press of Harvard University Press, 2016), 171.

46 See Campbell, *Charles Ellis Johnson and the Erotic Mormon Image*, 129–130.

47 Campbell, *Charles Ellis Johnson and the Erotic Mormon Image*, 128–129.

48 Bruce R. McConkie, *Mormon Doctrine*, 2nd ed. (Salt Lake City: Bookcraft, 1979), 558 (emphasis in original).

49 See Campbell, *Charles Ellis Johnson and the Erotic Mormon Image*, 115–144.

50 The sixth prophet's family posed for the first photograph in 1898 and the second in 1904.

51 Quoted in *Deseret News,* February 8, 1857, cited in B. Carmon Hardy, *Doing the Works of Abraham: Mormon Polygamy—Its Origin, Practice, and Demise* (Norman, OK: Arthur H. Clark, 2007), 122.

52 As I discuss below, Joseph F. Smith's family was not the only one to separate children by gender when posing for photographs. Whether this was an actual photographic trend among the early Saints remains a topic for further exploration.

53 LDS Church History Library, Charles C. Rich Family Photograph Album, undated, MS 9162.

54 It remains unclear whether this was a preexisting composite photograph or whether *Life* produced the collage of Rich and his family itself.

55 Even these pictures are far from ubiquitous, if only because the majority of LDS polygamists had only two wives. As Ulrich writes, "[Husbands] who had four or more [wives] were often members of high church councils or bishops of local congregations," Ulrich, *A House Full of Females,* xix.

56 Fred C. Collier, ed., *Unpublished Revelations of the Prophets and Presidents of the Church of Jesus Christ of Latter-day Saints,* 3rd ed. (New York: Collier's, 2011), 1:146.

57 D&C 132:20.

58 "George Q. Cannon Is Dead," *New York Times,* April 13, 1901.

59 George Q. Cannon, discouse delivered on March 3, 1867, reprinted in *Journal of Discourses,* 11:338.

60 Campbell, *Charles Ellis Johnson and the Erotic Mormon Image,* 134.

61 For a fuller discussion of LDS women as a visual absence in the photographic record, see my treatment of the issue in Campbell, *Charles Ellis Johnson and the Erotic Mormon Image,* 115–144.

62 Paula Kelly Harline, *The Polygamous Wives Writing Club, from the Diaries of Mormon Pioneer Women* (New York: Oxford University Press, 2014), 93–104.

MORMON ART AND ARCHITECTURE IN MEXICO

Between Mexico and the United States

REBECCA JANZEN

Mormonism is a deeply Mexican religion. After all, in 1846, when Brigham Young opted to build a Mormon settlement near the Great Salt Lake, Utah was still Mexican territory.[1] In the 1870s, Daniel Webster Jones and Melitón Trejo translated the Book of Mormon into Spanish. Shortly thereafter, in 1876, Jones, together with Anthony W. Ivins, Helaman Pratt, Robert H. Smith, James Z. Stewart, and Amon Jenney, entered Mexico and distributed Books of Mormon in the state of Chihuahua.[2] The LDS faith was attractive to elite and Indigenous people in various parts of the country. Mormon missionary work was suspended from 1889 to 1901, and Mormons established colonies in the Mexican states of Chihuahua and Sonora during that time. When missionary work resumed in 1907, many from the Mormon colonies (who were bilingual) traveled to other parts of Mexico on behalf of their church, until revolutionary violence forced it to stop again.

Since the late nineteenth century, Mormons in Mexico have lived out the tension between their lived experiences and professing a faith U.S. and U.S.-descendant missionaries introduced to them.[3] This chapter studies images of Mormon people and Mormon worship spaces alongside examples of Mormon religious art to show that Mormonism in Mexico is in constant negotiation with Mexican culture and U.S. norms fostered by the LDS Church and a broader desire to modernize. It focuses on three time periods: the early twentieth century (1910s–1920s), the mid-twentieth century (1940s–1960s), and the late twentieth and early twenty-first centuries (late 1970s–2010s).

EARLY TWENTIETH CENTURY: PORTRAITS OF INDIVIDUALS IN THE EMERGING MORMON COMMUNITY IN SAN MARCOS, HIDALGO

As Mormonism took root in Mexico, members experienced tension between Mexican and American identity. In joining the church, people accepted something akin to American identity and modernization even as other parts of their lives remained profoundly Mexican. Photographs of the Monroy family, who were members of the San Marcos, Hidalgo, branch, provide a case study for examining these tensions. The Monroy family sent family portraits, images of mourning, and portraits of leaders from Mexico and the United States to Mormon missionaries who had left Mexico during the revolution. Such images reflect cultural exchange, the ongoing importance of Catholic and Indigenous beliefs, and connections around ongoing plural marriage or polygamy.

The Monroy family and the San Marcos branch are important because San Marcos is one of the first locations where a community of Mormons arose in central Mexico and was home to Rafael Monroy and Vicente Morales, two men sometimes considered to be Mormon martyrs.[4] In addition to this, the Monroys had long-standing relationships with the United States, through business and marriage, prior to joining the Mormon tradition. When Rafael Monroy joined the church in 1913, he already had commercial connections to the United States as the owner of a small store and through his brother-in-law.[5] Shortly after, his mother, Jesusita (Jesús Mera de Monroy), and his daughters, Jovita Monroy and Guadalupe Monroy, joined the church as well.[6] This family continued to subscribe to Mormonism throughout the Mexican Revolution, even when the mission president, Rey L. Pratt, and his wife, Mary (May) Stark Pratt, left the country in 1912, and even after the family patriarch, Rafael Monroy, was killed in 1915.

In 1917, Jesús Mera de Monroy sent three photographs likely taken in 1911 to May Pratt.[7] They are of her son Rafael, of herself, and of her family. Jesusita may have given these to Pratt when he stayed with the family when he traveled to visit many Mormons in Mexico in 1917, or it may have been as part of the two families' correspondence.[8] The act of sending photographs and the photographs themselves convey Jesús Mera de Monroy's regard for May, the wife of the mission president. Short notes on the back of the portraits of Jesús and Rafael confirm this: Jesusita shared a precious memory of her now deceased son Rafael. The note on the back of the photograph of Rafael states: "Hermana Pratt: las hermanas Monroy le dedican el presente retrato de nuestro querido e inolvidable hermano Rafael Monroy" [Sister Pratt: The Monroy sisters dedicate this portrait of our beloved and unforgettable brother Rafael Monroy to you].[9] The inscription on the back of the photograph of Jesús Mera de Monroy continues in the same vein. It also addresses Sister Pratt and states, "Siempre que vea usted el presente retrato, no olvide a una hermana en fe" [Whenever you look at this portrait do not forget a sister in faith].[10] A series of lines in pencil appear on the back of the portraits, too. Mera's daughters, Natalia, Jovita, and María Guadalupe, were teachers.[11] Perhaps one of these women traced these lines. Whatever the case, two different people wrote notes in impeccable handwriting. Jesusita and her daughters attended to these inscriptions with great care and clearly wanted May Pratt to know that they had not forgotten her and that she was still important to them.

While the photographs emphasize the regard she had for Pratt, Jesusita's reply also documented a visual testimony of the Monroy family's economic standing and the desire to modernize—that is, to mimic the styles and gestures of the United States—and other family members' desire to remain connected to their roots. There are two formal portraits and one posed family photograph. The portraits, like many nineteenth-century century cartes de visite, are sepia-toned and printed on cardstock.[12] The portrait of Rafael has a studio name (Napoleón Fotógrafo) and location (Profesa no. 7, Mexico) imprinted at the bottom. The figures in each portrait, Jesús Mera de Monroy and Rafael Monroy, compose the lower two-thirds of the image. Each individual portrait displays its subject's head and chest, Rafael wearing a suit and Jesusita a European-style dress. Both Jesusita and Rafael look slightly to the right, in the way of studio photographs at the time and perhaps to avoid any focus on the ways their noses might deviate from the European ideal. The style of both portraits is so similar that both were likely taken in the same location. The family would have made a trip to Mexico's capital city, some forty-five miles away from their home in San Marcos, to sit for them. Mexican families, like most others in the early twentieth century, did not have many photographs of their loved ones, and so sending it to May Pratt was an exceptional act of kindness. This also means that after Rafael's death, this photograph of Rafael would have been even more precious for the family because it is one of the few they would have had.

The hairstyle and dress in the images further illustrate U.S. influence on ideas of modernity. This aligns with the United States' own struggle for modernization and becoming distinctly American rather than derivative of European ideals. For this family, Mormonism was one way to align themselves with what they perceived to be economic progress. The first portrait in sepia, that of Rafael Monroy, is of the head and upper body of a relatively young man.[13] Monroy sports a well-groomed mustache and short hair parted slightly on the left. He wears a plaid blazer and matching vest over a white shirt and tie. His clothing shows that he was part of the vanguard of progress and change in his country. The edges of his head, in the top third of the image, and his shoulders, toward the middle, fade into the background in accordance with portrait norms of the early twentieth century. His head faces slightly to the right. A photograph in profile would have highlighted what historian Lamond Tullis calls the Monroy family's Otomí features.[14] As a member of the commercial class, Monroy would not have wanted to highlight those ties because Indigenous people like the Otomí were understood to be regressive, preventing Mexico from reaching its potential as a nation.[15] The photographic carte de visite style draws on trends in the United States and Europe, further aligning him with modern ideas in Mexico.

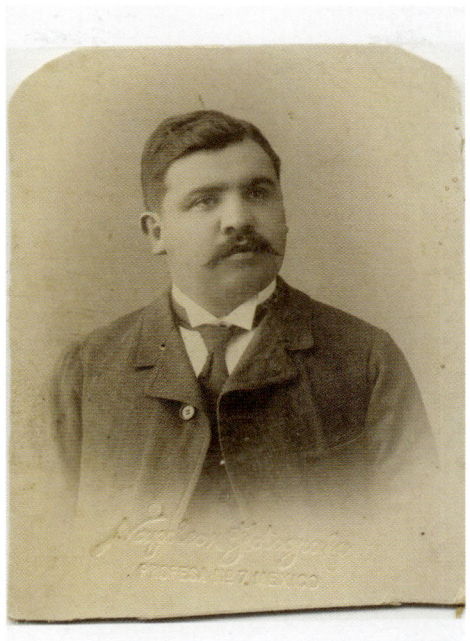

Fig. 10.1 Photograph of Rafael Monroy, 1915, Church History Library, The Church of Jesus Christ of Latter-day Saints.

The second portrait, of Jesús Mera de Monroy, is equally striking and shows a woman committed to modernization even as she retained her Catholic background.[16] In the image, she looks relatively young. Her head is placed a bit lower on the page than her son's in his portrait, centered instead in the middle third of the image, while her shoulders and the upper part of her torso occupy the bottom third of the image. Like Rafael's portrait, the lower half fades slightly into the background, matching the fashions of turn-of-the-century portraiture. Jesusita looks slightly to the right to similarly highlight the European aspects of her appearance. Her long hair is parted in the middle and tied back. She does not smile. She is dressed modestly, like most women in Mexico and the United States at that time. She wears a long-sleeved dark-colored dress with sleeves that puff slightly at the shoulders. This color is likely in recognition of her status as a widow. Jesús Mera de Monroy was part of a group of Mexicans invested in modernizing their country and had joined a U.S.-based church that aligned with those goals.

Jesús Mera de Monroy's dress and jewelry also display gleanings of Mexican culture, Indigenous dress, and Catholic tradition. In the photograph, she wears small hoop earrings with a design on the bottom. This would have been nearly universal for Mexican women. Two lines of ribbon adorn the collar around her neck, and another two lines of

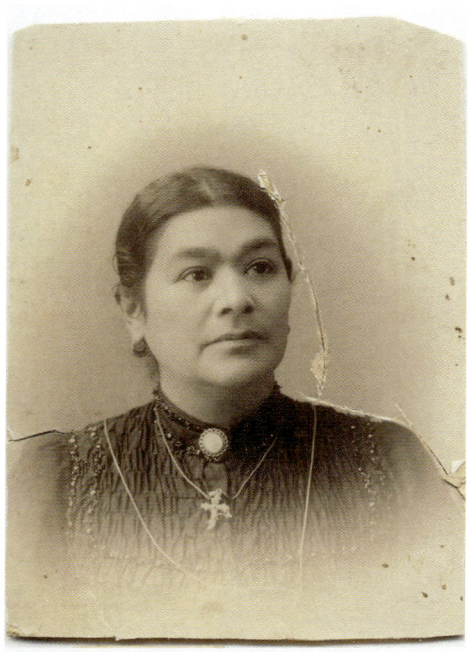

Fig. 10.2 Photograph of Jesús Mera de Monroy, 1915, Church History Library, The Church of Jesus Christ of Latter-day Saints.

ribbon decorate the edges of the smocking from her shoulders to the top of her bustline. This ribbon evokes the Otomí tradition of embroidery and broader trends in Indigenous dress in Mexico,[17] as well as U.S. womenswear from the 1900–1910 period.[18] An ivory brooch set in carved ivory or metal sits at the center of her collar and is engraved with a figure that appears to be an image of a saint or the Virgin (these would have been the likely motifs of the time). A double string with a cross on it falls slightly below and to the left of her brooch. The fact that the cross is on string suggests that it may have been a scapular, or two small pieces of cloth, typically bearing an image of a saint or other religious figure, positioned in the middle of one's chest and back, connected by a string, and blessed by a priest. Wearing a crucifix was common for Mormon women at the turn of the twentieth century, though it receded in importance by the middle of the twentieth century.[19] The beautiful portrait Jesús Mera de Monroy shared with May Pratt thus included aspects of her appearance that would have been outside of the norm for Mormon women in the United States and, consequently, ideas of modernity from that country. This ability to blend cultures was an expression of her devotion to her new faith and her family's investment in modernization.

The third photograph Jesús Mera de Monroy sent May Pratt (at least, it is archived together with the other two) was a family portrait taken before Rafael Monroy's death.[20]

The photograph pictures Rafael Monroy on the left, holding his daughter, María Concepción. At the right of the composition are his wife, Guadalupe Hernández de Monroy; his sister Natalia Monroy; his mother, Jesusita; and his sisters Jovita Monroy and Guadalupe Monroy.[21] The seven people stand in front of a brick building with large windows. A plant in the front of the group obscures the bottom of three of the women's skirts. A passport-size photograph of an older woman has been pasted in the upper right-hand corner, perhaps another Monroy family member who would have been familiar to May Pratt.[22]

The family wears their best clothing, which in some cases follows U.S./European norms and in other cases Mexican and/or Indigenous norms. Rafael, for instance, wears a suit similar to the one in his portrait, and a wide-brimmed hat. His daughter wears a dress with impeccable collar and cuffs, stockings, and shoes. The U.S. and European style of the outfit along with the more refined fabric used in the dress and trimmings (as opposed to homespun style of traditional Mexican garments) point to the family's economic standing. Guadalupe, Natalia, and Jovita wear long dresses and corsets or girdles to create an hourglass shape fashionable at the time. Ruffles decorate Guadalupe's skirt, which has a smocked design on the bodice. Natalia's dress includes what looks like embroidered clasps along the middle of the front and fresh lace cuffs near her wrists.

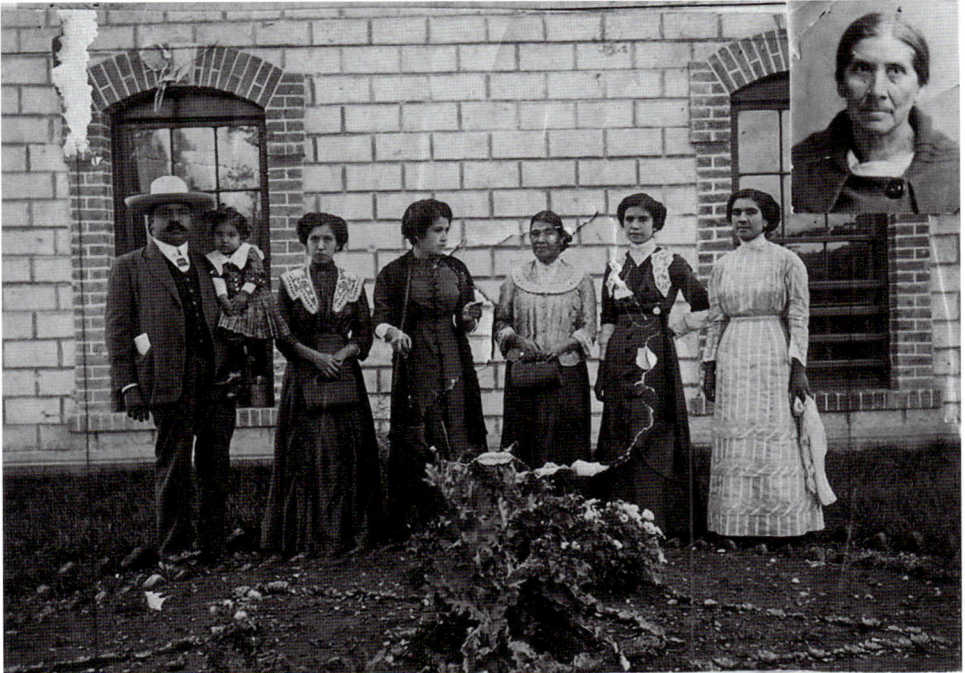

Fig. 10.3 Photograph of the Monroy family members, 1915, Church History Library, The Church of Jesus Christ of Latter-day Saints.

A dark shawl encircles her frame. A long overdress adorned with lace at her shoulders, buttons down the front, and a sash with tassels at the waist covers Jovita's black skirt and high-necked white shirt. In contrast, María's light shirtwaist and skirt, made from the same striped fabric with contrasting bands toward her ankles, are not quite as stylish as her older sisters' dresses. Her styling suggests that she was not quite old enough to wear a corset and that her dress may be so new to her that she does not require a special collar or cuffs. The younger women sport "Gibson girl" puffs and curls of hair around their faces, evocative of modern styles. In contrast, Jesusita wears clothes that more pointedly evoke Mexican culture. She wears a shirtwaist over a long skirt and carries a small purse. Her parted hair is gathered in a bun, much like in the portrait she sent May Pratt. The variations in women's clothing and hair illustrate that the family was negotiating a tension with Mexican norms along generational lines.

Another photograph taken by Elmer P. Bright and sent to the Pratts in the 1920s, this one of the Monroy family at Rafael's grave, demonstrates that even if the younger family members had more "modern" tendencies, they remained very connected to their heritage. In the photograph, Jesusita and her daughters circle Rafael's gravesite.[23] At the leftmost side of the photograph there is an unadorned grave with an empty basket on top. A cross sits at the head of the grave and a second basket at its feet. To the right stands a young woman, likely María Concepción, and to her right is Rafael's grave covered in flowers.[24] A second unidentified person stands at the head of the grave. Jesús Mera de Monroy stands to the right. A broad-brimmed hat and a sarape rest on a fence to the far right of the composition.

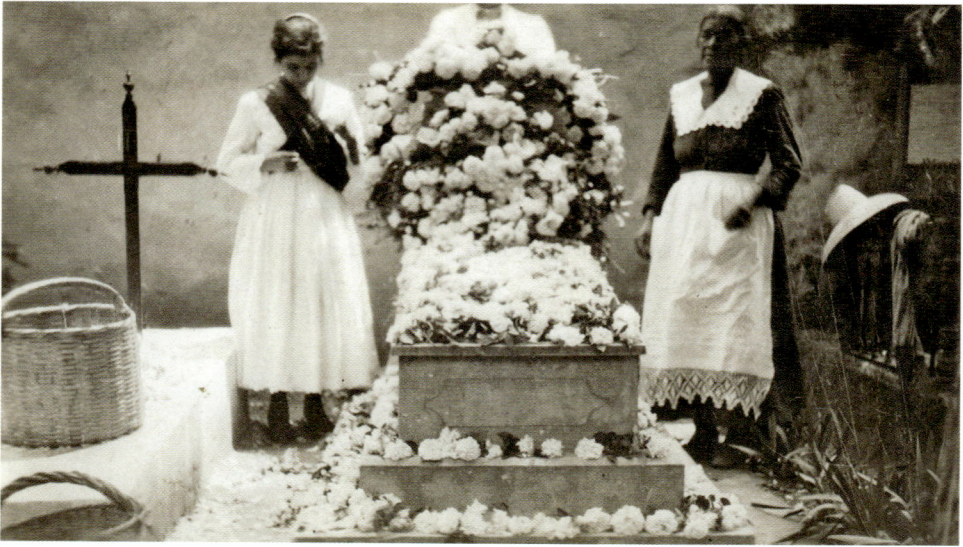

Fig. 10.4 Photograph of Rafael Monroy's mother and sister, 1920–1923, Church History Library, The Church of Jesus Christ of Latter-day Saints.

The cultural symbols around Rafael Monroy's grave evoke Indigenous traditions. Rafael's tomb is a three-tiered rectangular concrete structure, like other tombs in Mexico. It is also covered in cempasúchil (Mexican marigold) flowers, with a large wreath at the head. This would be common for the anniversary of his death or the Day of the Dead. The flowers along with a cross placed nearby place the deceased and his family in Mexico. Like the other images sent to the Pratts, the clothing worn by the sitters further connects the Monroy family to Mexico. The young woman on the left wears a traditional white dress with black sash in an X shape across her torso, evoking the bands of bullets *soldaderas* wore during the revolution. Her hair is pulled back and unadorned. Jesusita wears a black dress with a large square collar trimmed with lace that extends to her shoulders and the top of her bustline. Her white, lace-trimmed apron extends almost to the hem of her dress. The women shared an intimate familial moment of profound grief with a Mormon missionary. Their clothing and way of adorning the gravesite suggest that, despite the adoption of new and modern ways, there was a return to tradition during an important life ritual.

Dress and hairstyle in a photograph of the Monroys and U.S. Mormon leaders in front of the San Marcos chapel illustrate further connections between modern and traditional. In the 1925 image, ten people stand in front of San Marcos's first chapel, rooting the Mormon community in Mexico. While the LDS Church had abandoned polygamy by that time, several figures in the photograph are connected to ongoing practices of polygamy in the United States or emerging practices of polygamy in other expressions of Mormonism in Mexico.[25] Guadalupe Monroy, Jesús Mera de Monroy, Guadalupe Hernández de Monroy, and Jovita Monroy de Parra sit on chairs in front, while María Concepción Monroy and Amalia Monroy Flores stand behind them. In the back row stand Bernabé Parra, an unidentified man, LDS apostle Richard R. Lyman, and mission president Rey L. Pratt. The group stands slightly to the left in a well-swept courtyard. The whitewashed chapel dominates the background behind them. A short white picket fence encircles the chapel, while tall stalks of corn appear against a clear sky. The contrast between the American ideal of a picket fence and the Mexican-style courtyard in front of corn, which is a staple of the Mexican diet, mirrors the contrasts within the people's dress and hair. Visiting leaders Pratt and Lyman, from northern Mexico and the United States, respectively, wear gray suits with vests and ties. The members of the San Marcos branch may have adapted their dress in honor of the distinguished visitors. Jesusita wears a long black dress over a high-necked white blouse, her hair still in a traditional style. Her daughters and daughter-in-law sitting next to her wear flapper-style dresses with drop waists that do not require girdles or corsets. All the women have conceded to certain changes in style, but Jesusita continues to have elements of lace in her attire, signifying more traditional styles of the region. Bernabé Parra and the man on his right wear black suits, but Parra is without a visible vest. Their ties are slightly higher at their necks. Bernabé's tie has a smaller knot, and the other man wears a winged collar, so his tie is visible around his neck. The members of the San Marcos branch dressed formally in a modern style to welcome their distinguished guests, but Jesús Mera de Monroy's lace trim and Bernabé Parra's lack of vest remind us of Mexican adaptations of clothing from outside of their region.

This photograph and another from around the same time include three men who practiced polygamy or used the historical practice to justify present behavior: Apostle Richard R. Lyman, Margarito Bautista, and Bernabé Parra.[26] Lyman was publicly excommunicated from the church in 1943 for breaking the Law of Chastity, an LDS edict that restricts premarital sex. He had married Amy Brown in 1896, and then began a relationship with Anna Jacobsen Hegsted in the 1930s.[27] Lyman's justification of his own behavior may have given implicit permission to the local leader Bernabé Parra, who was doing much the same thing.

Margarito Bautista, a prominent Mexican Mormon leader, also would have influenced the Mormons in San Marcos. He visited San Marcos around the same time as Lyman. For instance, he may have been present when the Monroys bid farewell to Lyman at the local train station in La Tolteca, Hidalgo.[28] Even if Bautista was not present at the train station, Guadalupe Monroy's memoir states that Parra and the Monroys were familiar with Bautista and his ideas.[29] Tullis adds that Bautista visited the San Marcos, Hidalgo, branch in 1925.[30] Bautista integrated advocacy for Indigenous rights with Mormon beliefs. One of his strategies for integration was polygamy. He

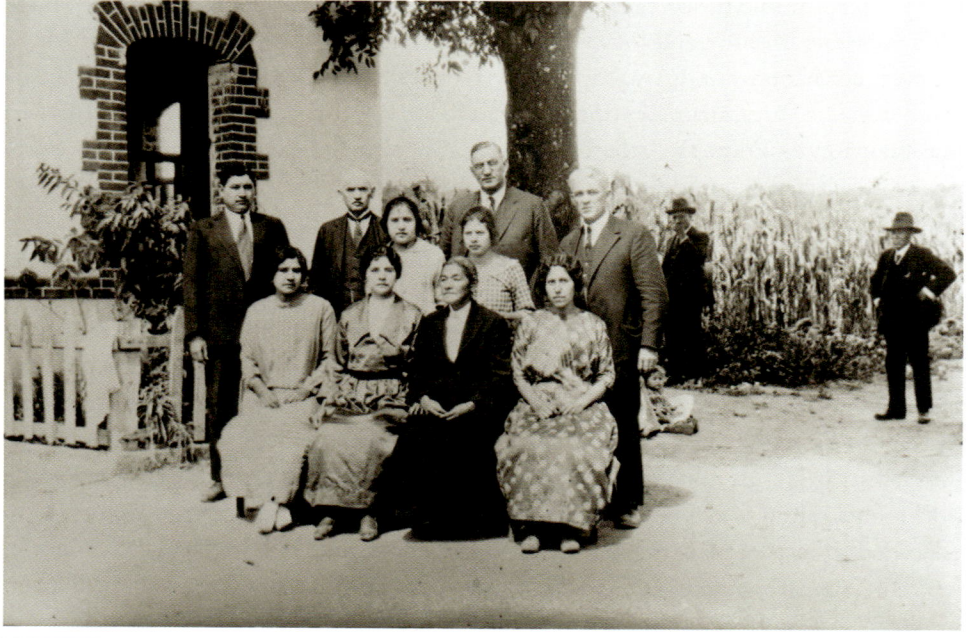

Fig. 10.5 Group of Mexican members with Richard R. Lyman in front of San Marcos chapel, 1924–1925, Church History Library, The Church of Jesus Christ of Latter-day Saints.

noticed how frequently Mormon missionaries criticized some Mexican men's sexual practices because they broke the Law of Chastity. In other words, missionaries would criticize men who had a wife and a mistress, or two families at the same time. Rather than seeking to change this practice, Bautista considered this a form of polygamy, which he understood as part of the Mormon tradition, thanks to his own study of Mormon history and doctrine.[31] While many people who become Mormon study this same history and doctrine without practicing it, starting in 1922 Bautista advocated for spiritual polygamy, and by 1935 he practiced it.[32]

Bautista and Lyman may have influenced local leader Bernabé Parra's life and practice of polygamy. Parra joined the church in 1913, as an employee of Rafael Monroy's hacienda, and Pratt ordained him as branch president in 1917.[33] He and Jovita Mera were engaged in 1917 and married in 1920. Six months after their wedding, Eulalia Mera—Jesús Mera de Monroy's niece—gave birth to his daughter, Elena.[34] Parra was removed from his leadership position and readmitted a year later, in 1921. Then, in 1936 and 1939, he fathered two children with Jovita Monroy's niece Amalia Monroy Flores, daughter of Rafael Monroy and Monclovia Flores Pérez, an employee on his hacienda.[35] The church excommunicated him by 1938, and he was rebaptized in 1946.[36] Historians like Tullis excuse his behavior: "Parra's scorching desire for more children of his own that Jovita could not give him, coupled with the powerful temptations that had taken him down once before, undid him anew."[37] He adds, "Bernabé and Amalia fell into a pattern that was entrenched in traditional Mexican culture and, although Parra was anxious to have heirs that his wife, Jovita, could not give him, having these heirs with Amalia was nevertheless a profound departure from the long trek that adopting a gospel culture entails, especially for a leader of his stature."[38] In other words, Parra had behaved in a way that was unacceptable to the church, but for scholars like Tullis, this behavior was minor in comparison to the gifts that Parra gave the church. Tullis also acknowledges the coincidence of Parra photographed with Lyman. Parra married Amalia Monroy in 1960, after Jovita died, and may have simply been engaging in a tradition of wealthier men having more than one family. The fact that he was excommunicated twice, readmitted, and promoted to leadership in the LDS Church, however, implies that LDS leaders on a global level at least tacitly accepted Parra's behavior even though it went against then-acceptable practices. This could be because of the church's history of polygamy, or because of Parra's influence on a local level, pointing to another way that Mexican Mormons aligned with church edicts in some ways but in other ways did not.

Photographs of the Monroy family in Hidalgo in the early part of the twentieth century, then, show that people who became Mormon embraced local missionary presence. Jesús Mera de Monroy and her daughters missed the Pratts after they left because of the revolution. In several photographs, younger women's hairstyle and clothing suggest a desire to be modern and American, even as Jesús Mera de Monroy's dress, jewelry, and hairstyle maintain Mexican culture and tradition. The photograph of Rafael Monroy's gravesite emphasizes that rituals associated with transition remain firmly Mexican. A photograph of the family outside of the San Marcos chapel shows a similar negotiation between Mexican, modern, and Mormon ideals and alludes to the ways that Mexican Mormon men may have adapted Mormon polygamy to their own context. The Monroys, like other Mexican Mormons, did not abandon their background, as they became modern and Mormon.[39]

MID-TWENTIETH CENTURY: CHURCH BUILDINGS

Photographs of church buildings also point out how Mexican Mormons adapted to their new faith and how it adapted to them. In particular, Mormons from the United States designed buildings for Mexico that included colonial architecture. And as meetinghouses became standardized in the 1960s, Mormons adapted existing structures for their own purposes, renovating or rethinking how to use older hacienda-style homes as meetinghouses by adding a raised platform, a pulpit, and rows of chairs.

New Mormon church buildings in Mexico from the 1930s to the 1960s integrate architecture of colonial Spain. These buildings reflect growing standardization within Mormonism alongside a projection of U.S. views onto Mormons in Mexico, and they align with the rising use of Spanish colonial style in the southwestern United States.[40] Single-story buildings with two-story bell towers or steeples, Spanish tile roofs, and whitewashed exteriors in Mexico City, Ciudad Juárez, and San Marcos exemplify this trend.[41] The fact that Mormonism, a U.S.-based religion, imitated an American style that copied Spanish colonizers further reminds us that mission work has colonial and neocolonial tendencies. People's clothing and hair in photographs show that the Mormons in Mexico did not accept either colonizer completely. The American Mormon idea of Mexico as "Spanish" coexisted with the Mexican emphasis on shedding Indigeneity to become modern and mestizo, or "mixed race," identifying with a mixed-race ancestry rather than Indigeneity.[42]

American architects designed the buildings in a colonial Spanish style because, to them, it seemed "Mexican," while ironically, Mexicans had joined the Mormon church thinking it would be another way for them to align with ideas from the United States. Spanish colonial architecture was prevalent in the United States in the early twentieth century and was not part of architectural styles in Mexico at that time. Albert Fu, for instance, explains that this style was popular in California among "Anglos despite its historic/mythic vocabulary and Hispanic roots."[43] For 1920s architects, the Spanish Colonial Revival style was a way of expressing modernity. In 1926, for instance, architect Henry Allen explained that new construction in Santa Barbara was "coming closer and closer to the achievement of that Spanish atmosphere which was the glory of early California."[44] In other words, Spanish Colonial Revival architecture was a modern style that hearkened back to California's roots.

During the same time period, architectural preoccupations in Mexico were different. While architects there sought to imagine buildings that would be appropriate for modernity, in Mexico this modernity meant building a post-revolutionary nation. Susan Antebi discussed these tendencies in *Embodied Archive*. José Vasconcelos, a prominent Mexican philosopher who was secretary of education from 1920 to 1925, for instance, decried buildings with utilitarian tendencies. He promoted beautiful buildings that would combine the contributions of various cultures and facilitate racial and spiritual transformation.[45] For other Mexican architects such as Juan O'Gorman, architecture would be didactic and directly related to revolutionary goals.[46] Neither of these tendencies sought inspiration in the colonial period.

Several examples of churches built in this period illustrate these tensions between colonizer/colonized and modern/traditional, including San Pedro Mártir in Mexico City, a church in San Marcos, Hidalgo, and (several decades later) a church in Ciudad Juárez, Chihuahua.[47] The San Pedro Mártir chapel in Mexico City, built in 1938, for instance, is a single-story building with Spanish tile roof. Made of stone or plaster, the building is painted off-white, resembling a hacienda building. In a photograph from 1958, windows decorate the side of the chapel, in the center and right-hand two-thirds of the image. Larger windows flank an ornate design in the front of the chapel, which we see in the left third of the photograph. A small tower or belfry sits to the left in the background.[48]

Nearly two thousand miles away at the Mexico-U.S. border, the La Caseta branch in Ciudad Juárez met in a building in a similar small compound. The fenced-off plot

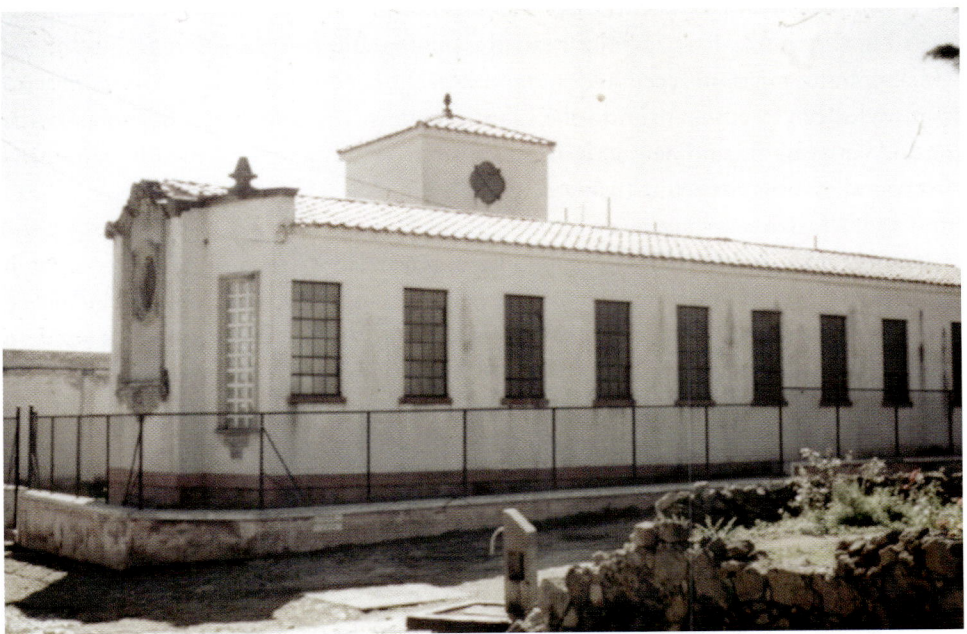

Fig. 10.6 Photograph of the San Pedro Mártir chapel by Gerald S. Millward, ca. 1958, private collection. Courtesy of photographer.

of land included two buildings. One was a long single-story building with a tower and a second single-story building, likely for church meetings. Both are whitewashed and have a Spanish tile roof.[49] The chapel in San Marcos, for its part, is relatively large, and is also part of a two-building complex. The larger building, likely for sacrament meetings, is a long building with windows on the sides and a tower at the center. A circular window sits above the door, and both the window and the door have ornately carved frames. The second building was used for meetings and Sunday school classes. Both buildings reflect U.S. architects' imaginings of Mexico and conform to architectural tendencies from the United States in this time period.

Several decades later, the members' clothing and hairstyles in photographs from the La Caseta and San Marcos branches exhibit a similar tension between existing as modern Mexican people who would adapt to global norms and ideas of how they are supposed to be "Mexican" as imagined by people from the United States. In a Mexican context, this represents the consolidation of power after the revolution; in other words, this period (1940–1968) is one of economic growth and industrialization within the country, elements that further align Mexicans with ideals from outside of their country. A photograph taken of twenty-one people in La Caseta in 1950 shows that the community was of modest means and had only begun to modernize during this period of rapid industrialization throughout Mexico. Though many in the image have adapted to some elements of modernization, their styles are markedly distinct from those of the white men in the photograph. Likely a local missionary and a man in a leadership position, these two men wear pants, shirts, ties, and blazers uncharacteristic of clothing responsive to northern Mexico's sun and heat. The photograph reflects different dress styles, which point to a certain acceptance of modernization; nevertheless, the community remains Mexican in comparison to the visiting leaders. The way that people dress—the tension between old and new seen in the diversity of clothing—mirrors the same tension found in the architecture (using outmoded colonial styles to represent an American fantasy of Mexico onto an already modern people).

Similar tensions are evident in a photograph of a large group of members in front of a chapel.[50] The photograph shows the congregation. A few older women, including one at the front on the center-right, wear the traditional rural and Indigenous *rebozo*, a shawl that covers their necks and shoulders, and which would have, in earlier decades, been worn over their heads as well. These women's hair is parted in the middle and tied back, a further affiliation with tradition. The majority of the women in the photograph have short hair and wear modern dresses. This variation—also evident in the women photographed in front of the La Caseta branch—shows different levels of acceptance of modernization, and potential differences in the economic ability to afford the newest styles. At least one man in the front, on the far right, holds a Panama hat in his hands, which points to their rural and Indigenous roots; others wear three-piece suits or sweaters and jackets. The visiting leader wears pants, a shirt and tie, and a sports coat considerably less formal than Parra's suit. The variation in clothing and dress mirrors the

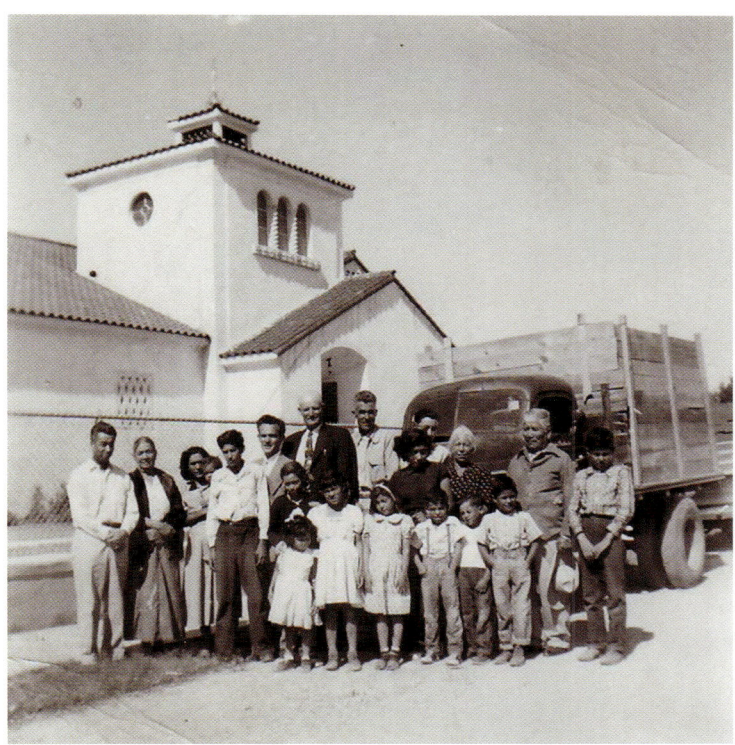

Fig. 10.7 Photograph of Latter-day Saint members in front of La Caseta branch, October 1950, Church History Library, The Church of Jesus Christ of Latter-day Saints.

variation and tension between their religious tradition and their background. After all, they were members of a U.S.-based church who worshiped in a colonial-style building in a modernizing Mexico.

Mormons in Mexico also renovated or reappropriated existing buildings, which in turn demonstrated a Mormonism that adapted to the Mexican context. Photographs taken during a special visit of Mormon leaders to Tapachula, Chiapas, in 1961 illustrate this adaptation strategy.[51] The photographs show Mormons in Tapachula gathered to hear Marion G. Romney, a General Authority who had just been appointed general area supervisor for the LDS Church in Mexico; Apostle Howard W. Hunter, first counselor; Joseph T. Bentley; an unnamed missionary (known to the congregation); and Mexico mission president in a "house of prayer."[52]

Photographs of this special event show a large worship space with a main room and side alcoves that are part of a larger structure constructed around a courtyard. Each photograph of the space (such as Figure 10.9) is taken from a standing position from the back of the room or from a middle aisle, likely in an attempt to capture the leaders at the front of the room. Three sets of pews and two aisles fill the main room. Stone

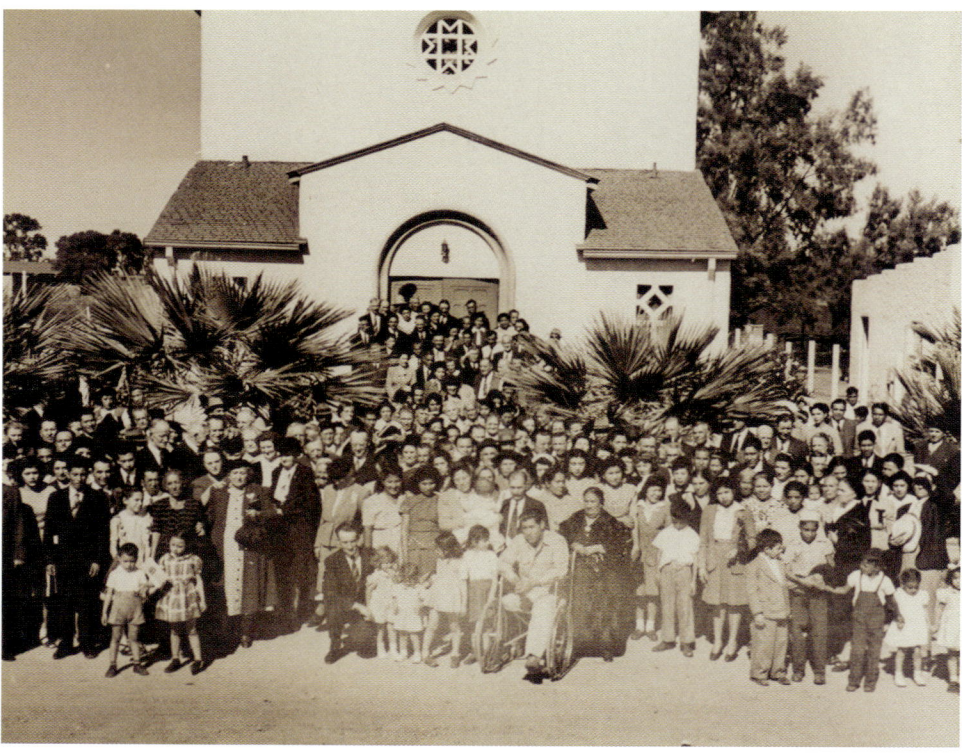

Fig. 10.8 Photograph of a large group of members spilling out of a white chapel, undated, Fernando R. and Enriqueta Gomez Mormon Mexican History Collection, Claremont Colleges Digital Library.

archways create three informal divisions within the space: first, between congregation and speakers; second, between the main room and temporary seating areas in the alcoves; and third, between the main room and the interior courtyard. There is no raised stage, so a pulpit and several chairs to its right serve as a visual divide between speakers/authorities and congregants. Four vases full of flowers decorate the leaders' seating area, further demarcating their space. While having a raised platform is more characteristic of LDS spaces, the photographs suggest that the Mormons were adaptable—they used a property that was available to them and which was relatively unadorned (that is, there were no stained glass windows, there were no religious images on the walls, and there were flowers in solid-colored vases in the front of the room). This would have been in accordance with their religious needs, even though certain elements were not ideal (such as a religious service based on public speaking without a raised platform for the speakers).

The men's clothing in several photographs illustrates strong cultural differences between the Mexican Mormon leaders and their visiting dignitaries.[53] Visiting leaders

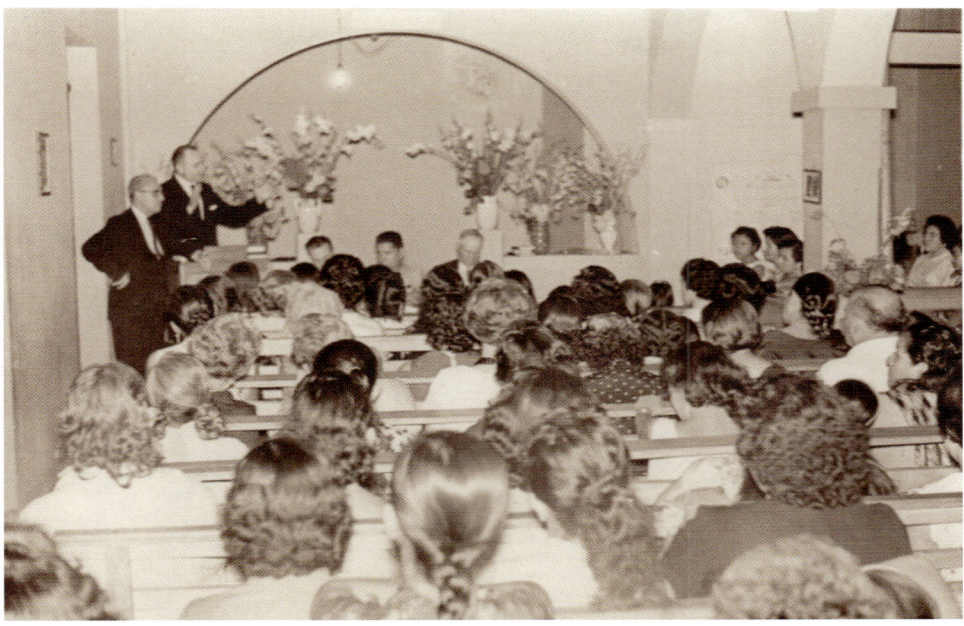

Fig. 10.9 Photograph of the Tapachula branch conference held on May 9–10, 1961, Church History Library, The Church of Jesus Christ of Latter-day Saints.

Romney, Hunter, and a mission president wear black suits, starched white collared dress shirts, and ties. The Mexico mission president has a pen in his blazer pocket, and Hunter has paper in his. They look every bit the clean-cut American men of the time. They appear to stand or sit with ease, suggesting that they are comfortable being photographed. The missionary is dressed almost identically. He acts as a go-between the Mexican and American leaders. In one photograph, for instance, a young boy sits with his arm around the young missionary, exhibiting a familiarity with the local congregants not present with the LDS authorities.[54] One of the Mexican leaders, Tapachulan branch president Salustio Arrevillaga, sports formal wear that deviates from regional norms: khaki pants, a visible belt, a polo shirt, reading glasses in his pocket, and slicked-back hair. Other church members don similar modern dress, a sign that they wanted to be part of their country's progress, and that, for them, Mormonism aligned with these existing desires. The branch president and these members may also have worn these more American or modern clothes to honor visiting leaders. At the same time, other Tapachulan men in the photograph wear guayaberas, the dress shirt more common for men in this region. Some of the women wear shirts with what appear to be embroidered flowers on them, in a nod toward their Indigenous heritage. So, there is a variety of types of dress; everyone is dressing to appeal to the authorities, and for some that means modern dress, while for others it means nods to Mexican Indigenous traditions.

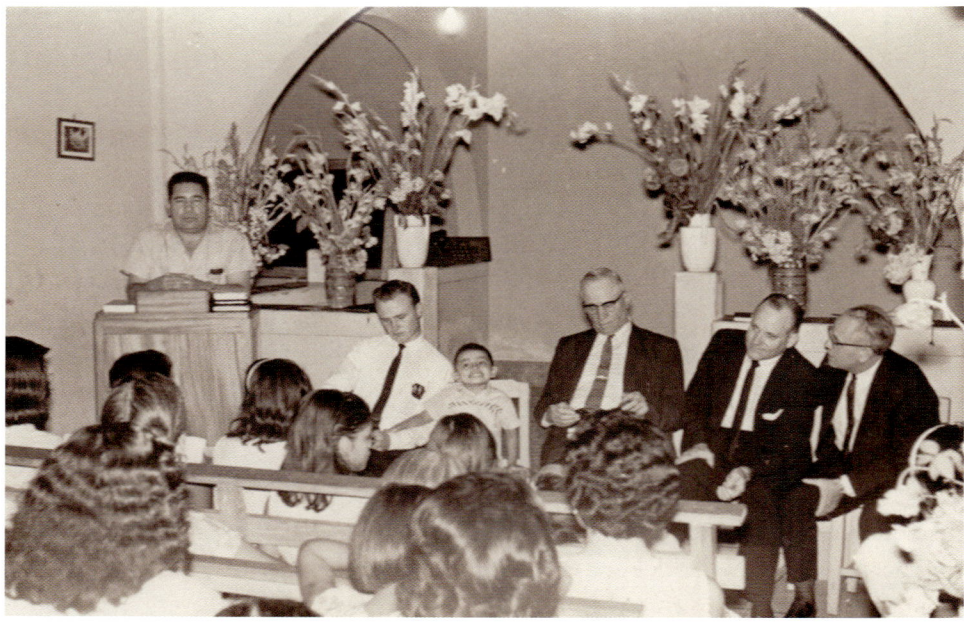

Fig. 10.10 Photograph of the Tapachula branch conference held on May 9–10, 1961, Church History Library, The Church of Jesus Christ of Latter-day Saints.

The photographs of church buildings and congregations point to competing influences in the lives of Mexican Mormons in a rapidly modernizing country and a U.S.-based church. The buildings reflect the colonial period, either by adapting buildings from this period to modern use, as in the case of Tapachula, or by constructing new buildings designed in this style, as in San Pedro Mártir, La Caseta, and San Marcos. Some Mexican Mormons, as seen in photographs of the congregations, and particularly those in older generations, continued to dress in traditional ways or incorporate traditional elements of shawls, hats, and hairstyle even into the middle of the twentieth century. Other Mexican Mormons acceded to progress, modernity, or U.S. norms in their dress and hairstyle, at least on occasions in which they were offering hospitality to leaders from the United States or leaders with roots in the Mormon colonies Juárez and Dublán, near Casas Grandes, Chihuahua, Mexico. The American leaders' clothing remains distinct from that of modern Mexican Mormons. This, and the ways that communities used their worship spaces, demonstrates that Mormons in Mexico engaged with competing influences from economic and social change, US influence, and their religious tradition, on their own terms.

RELIGIOUS ART AND ARCHITECTURE IN THE LATE TWENTIETH AND EARLY TWENTY-FIRST CENTURIES

Mexican Mormons continue to negotiate the role of Indigeneity in their faith, country, and a place for their religion in a predominantly Catholic country in the late twentieth and early twenty-first centuries. According to the 2010 Mexican census and church records, there were 1.3 million (active and inactive) Mormons in Mexico, the third-largest non-Catholic religious group in the country.[55] This final section further analyzes cultural artifacts from the 1990s to the 2010s, including gifts from Mexican Mormons to the church president, women's clothing, hair, home decorations, the architecture of the Mexico City temple, and visual art representing said temple. This analysis will demonstrate Mexican Mormons' ongoing cultural negotiation between their Mexican background and their new tradition.

In 1997, church members in Mexico gave the church president a ceramic plate in honor of the LDS pioneer sesquicentennial of colonizing the western United States, in a unique combination of Mormon roots and Mexican ideals. This flat plate has a deep blue border with intricate blue and white floral design between two circles of lighter blue around its edges. In the center, the words "Fe en cada paso [Faith in every step], 1847–1997" surround a blue circle with a white stylized image of a man leading a woman and a wagon. The words "Puebla, Mexico" are painted underneath the years, in the white space between the border and the center. The plate mirrors the position of Mexican Mormons: it includes pioneer imagery and slogans that pertain to the Mormon trek across the United States even as it is made in a style common to the Mexican state of Puebla and proudly proclaims this origin.

Clothing, hair, and homes offer further examples of cultural negotiation. A photograph of Elisa Escobar Moreno de Campbell taken the day she shared her life and testimony with Mario and Lavonnie Ortiz from the LDS Church History Library portrays a lively older woman in her kitchen in December 2016, when she was eighty-seven years old. Elisa talked about how she came to know the church through the Sepúlveda family, and her service in the Spanish American mission in Texas and Ciudad Juárez.[56] In the image, she appears in the foreground wearing a white zip-up knit sweater with fake fur at the collar, a tan trench coat, and a knotted scarf with flowers around her neck. A turquoise shirt peeks out between the sweater and scarf. Her hair is short and curled. She wears large pink-tinted glasses with a line indicating bifocals. She presents herself in the best way possible, as she is meeting a person important to her religious community, and she is every bit an older Mexican woman in the early twenty-first century.

The objects in the background of the photograph give a tantalizing glimpse into her life on the borders between Mexico and the United States, Spanish and English, and her Catholic upbringing and devout Mormon faith. A calendar in the right-hand side of the frame, with a single image and tear-off months, is for a meat market. The English-language calendar for a business in Mexico suggests that she lives on the border between

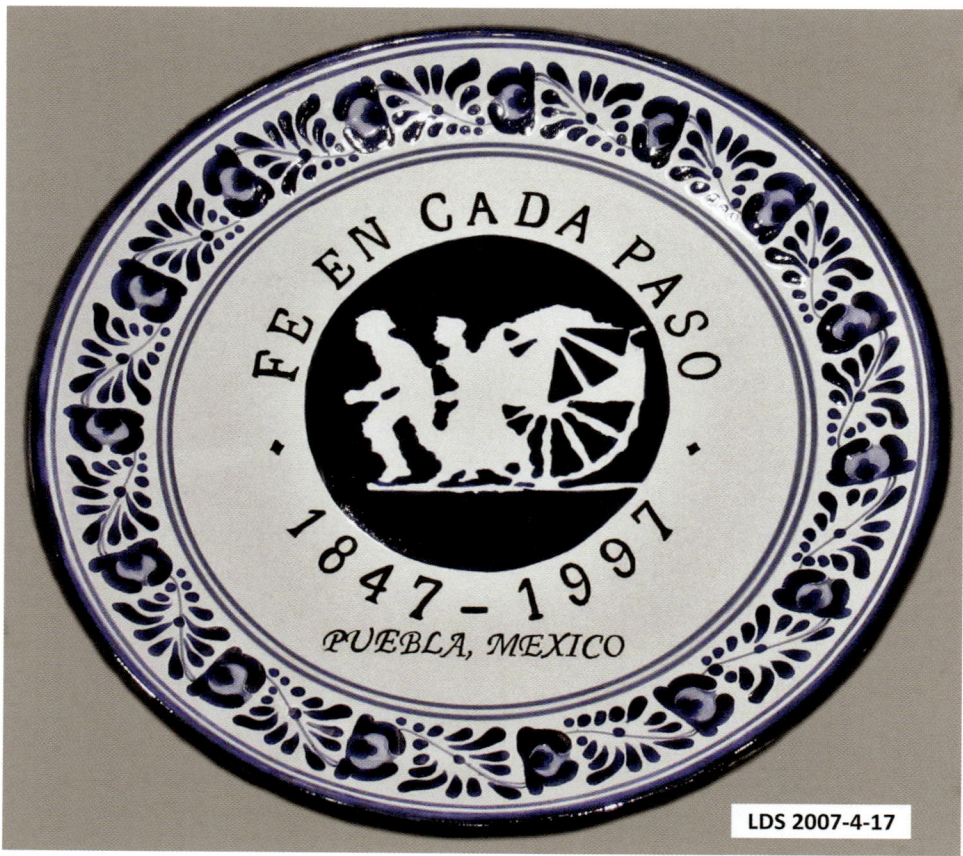

Fig. 10.11 Talavera Arte, *Plate*, 1997, ceramic plate, Church History Museum The Church of Jesus Christ of Latter-day Saints.

Mexican Spanish and U.S. English. An unidentifiable image of a saint appears in the upper right of the photograph, above the calendar, in a sturdy wooden frame, implying that she also lives on a religious border with a hint of Catholic presence. The photograph of this Mexican Mormon woman at home calls to mind tension between modernity and Mormonism and shows that Mexican Mormons will be Mexican and Mormon in their own ways.

The Mexico City temple is a further example of tensions between American ideas of Mexico and Mexican Mormons claiming religious legitimacy by referring to Mexico's pre-conquest history. This temple was designed by architect Emil Fetzer and built between 1979 and 1983. Its Mayan Revival style evokes architecture popular in California and Mexico in the period following World War II.[57] According to Samuel Ross Palfreyman, "The temple's ornate main volume sits atop a raised base. This effect reinforces the monolithic strivings of the architecture as well as serves a practical

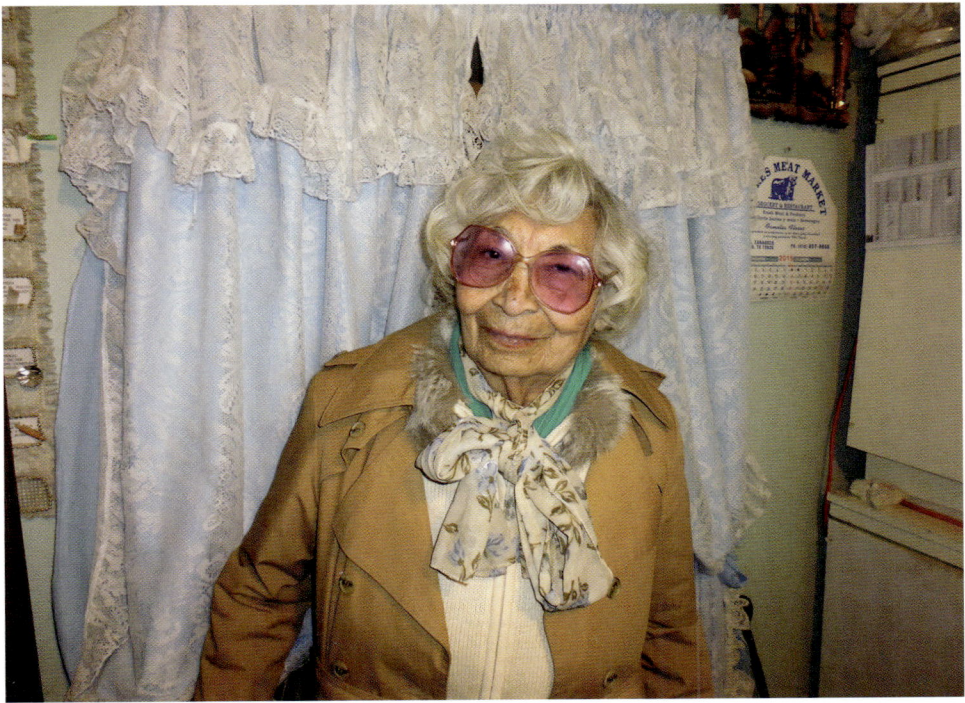

Fig. 10.12 Photograph of Elisa Escobar Moreno de Campbell, 2010, Church History Library,
The Church of Jesus Christ of Latter-day Saints.

programmatic function: it minimizes visual access into the building from the outside
concealing the sacred, guarded rites performed within."[58] The temple's windows, doors,
and other inlays were purportedly meant to "appear as authentic as possible" in their
reproduction of Mayan patterns.[59] According to Palfreyman, "The tower and spire continue in Mayan patterns and culminate in a golden statue" of the angel Moroni, who
holds the golden plates in addition to the trumpet.[60] This is one of only a few artistic
representations of the angel Moroni with this addition, and as the golden plates were
said to come from Mesoamerica, it emphasizes the connection between Mormonism
and the region.[61]

A painting of the Mexico City temple held in the church history archives further
highlights the intent to employ Mayan design and inlay.[62] This part of the rendering
has the greatest amount of depth, and it is in a slightly diagonal line just the right of
center, so the eye is drawn toward the inlay. The inlay looks like the statues and designs
on the edge of a pre-conquest temple, and the inlay, which is just below the center line
on a horizontal axis, strengthens this impression. The temple design, then, illustrates
that some reference to Indigenous tradition was important for the LDS Church. The
U.S.-based architect and church employed this imagery because they no longer thought

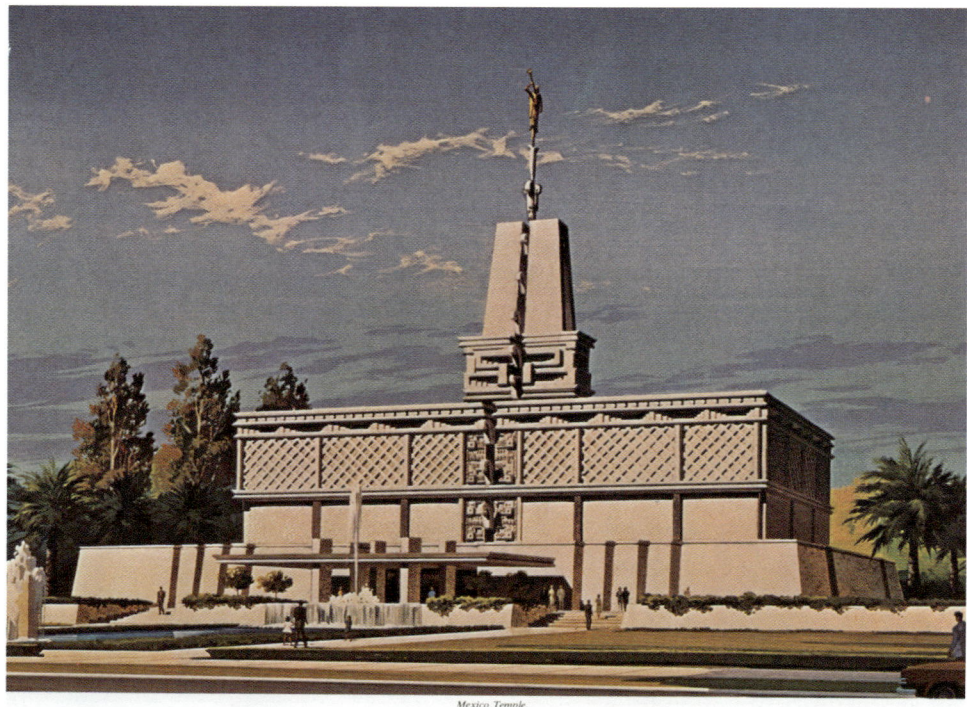

Fig. 10.13 Mexico City temple rendering from the inside cover of the 1979 *Ensign*, Church History Library, The Church of Jesus Christ of Latter-day Saints.

Mexico was Spanish (as it had been considered in the middle of the twentieth century) but rather considered Mexico to be a country with strong Indigenous roots. This came out of the early incarnations of Mayan Revival architecture, which "includes a broad sampling of loosely referenced Toltec, Zapotec, Aztec, Maya, Amerindian, and other non-Western iconography, decoration, and structural forms during a time period when many 'exotic' styles were used somewhat interchangeably and inconsistently."[63] This would have become important again in the United States when the Mexico City temple was being built, as the Chicano liberation movement of the 1960s and 1970s similarly based its claims on an Aztlán, or mythic Aztec homeland, that would span Mexico and the southwestern United States.[64] This temple, like much of Mayan Revival architecture, mixed multiple Indigenous references rather than faithfully reproducing those belonging to a single culture, and in this way created a distinctly Mexican Mormonism.[65] It was reductive in a different—but no less problematic—way than architectural references to Spanish colonization.

The Mormon temple also parallels the most popular religious site in Mexico. It would make sense that the temple would want to be connected to the Basilica of Our Lady of Guadalupe in Mexico City and its surrounding 100-acre site, because the basilica is considered the most significant Catholic religious site in Mexico. The basilica commemorates where the Virgin Mary purportedly first appeared in Mexico in the sixteenth century to an Indigenous man called Juan Diego, and a papal decree elevated it to a basilica in honor of its importance to Catholics in Mexico. The LDS temple is in the northern part of Mexico City, the same general area as the basilica. Temple construction began in 1979, three years after the newest church building was consecrated on the basilica grounds. Today, visitors can see the mountains and volcanoes that surround Mexico City on a clear day, and there are large outdoor masses on feast days and papal visits. There are also multiple examples of Indigenous elements at the site, and for Mexican Mormons the temple's outdoor and Mayan elements may call to mind the basilica. The temple deliberately or inadvertently parallels this existing important structure.

Mexican artistic interpretations of the temple highlight its Indigenous and modern elements. Blanca Estela Pavón Martínez's *Earthly Symbol of a Spiritual Reality* (2002) is a mixed-media representation of a group of five people in front of the Mexico City temple, with a smaller image of the Nauvoo Temple in the upper left-hand corner.[66] *Earthly Symbol* was created for an international art competition and designed to be legible to Mormon judges in the United States. This appeal to an international audience may have influenced the subject of representation as well as the media used, which call to mind Indigenous tradition, Mexican artistic tradition, and Mormon ideals.[67] It includes intricate beadwork and materials that are not generally associated with "high art." Instead, this work embraces the everyday materials that make up Indigenous visual and material culture throughout the Americas, including thread and abstract patterning. The figures in the image are not realistic representations but instead veer toward abstraction, flattened out and pixilated. The work also depicts the intricate inlays in the upper levels of the Mexico City temple and its cross-hatch second level. Pavón Martínez opted to highlight pan-Indigenous elements to represent Mexico to the U.S. judges as a Mexican idea of what the United States would consider "Mexican"—an inverse to the temple in Mexico City, which was designed by Mormon architects in the United States and which employed a U.S. idea of "Mexican architecture" for an important religious site for Mexican Mormons.

This artist, however, does not identify roots in any Mayan group or the Indigenous community more broadly.[68] As a non-Indigenous artist employing these traditions, Pavón Martínez adopts the approach Mexican artists such as Dr. Atl, Tina Modotti, and others have taken to represent their country in the United States since the 1920s.[69] The image of the family and of the Nauvoo Temple are paper cutouts pasted on the beadwork. The collage style evokes artists such as Pablo Picasso and Henri Matisse, positioning Pavón Martínez's work in a global conversation. The family's clothing displays some traditional elements and some modern ones, like the women in photographs of Mexican Mormons earlier in the twentieth century. The three women in the front of the group wear brightly colored modern dresses, and the maternal figure on the right wears a shawl

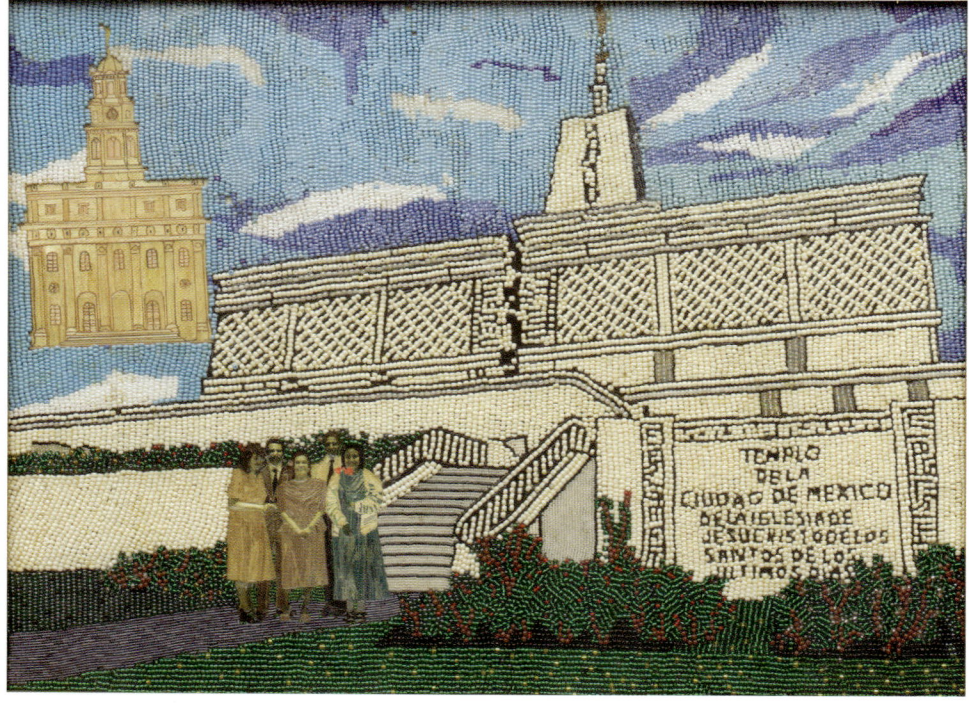

Fig. 10.14 Blanca Estela Pavón de Martínez, *Earthly Symbol of a Spiritual Reality*, 2002, beads and mixed media, Church of Jesus Christ of Latter-day Saints Church History Museum.

over her shoulders, evoking Indigenous tradition. The paternal figure wears an impeccable suit and the other man a shirt and tie, in the style of Mormon missionaries. This faithful family represents Mormon ideals in the tradition's most sacred space, about to participate in sacred temple rituals, such as a wedding. Pavón Martínez's *Earthly Symbol* shows the ways that Mormons in Mexico are connected to Indigeneity, and that they deploy it to make themselves understandable to people in the United States. They also understand themselves as modern and Mexican, which includes elements of modern dress, and connections to a global artistic tradition. All these elements are present in her creative interpretation of the temple.

CONCLUSION

This chapter has examined changes in Mormonism in Mexico from the early twentieth century to the early twenty-first by analyzing photographs of faithful Mormons and their worship spaces, as well as other examples of art. Mormons in Mexico, from the Monroys to Mrs. Campbell, understood that joining the LDS Church would bring them closer to modernity and alignment with U.S. ideas, which is evident in changes in clothing and hair, just as the rest of the country changed and adapted to these same outside influences. Many photographs and artwork were gifts to leaders, or taken with visiting leaders, so while these visual memorabilia offer insight into the practices of the time, it is important to note that they represent a bias in terms of showing a great interest in U.S. ideas or even a genuine adoption of some American ways. At the same time, as Mexican Mormons became part of an industrialized country, Mormon leaders in Utah projected a stereotypical "Spanish" and later "Mayan" stylization onto chapels and later temples. These ideas have been interpreted and reinterpreted over the past century, and I anticipate that such reinterpretation will continue in the next.

NOTES

[1] Jason Dormady, "Introduction," in *Just South of Zion: The Mormons in Mexico and Its Borderlands*, ed. Jason Dormady and Jared Tamez (Albuquerque: University of New Mexico Press, 2015), 2.

[2] Elisa Eastwood Pulido, *The Spiritual Evolution of Margarito Bautista: Mexican Mormon Evangelizer, Polygamous Dissident, and Utopian Founder, 1878–1961* (Oxford: Oxford University Press, 2020), 31.

[3] Matthew Butler's "Porfirian Saints or Latter-Day Revolutionaries: Mormons in Modern Mexico," in *Just South of Zion: The Mormons in Mexico and Its Borderlands,* ed. Jason Dormady and Jared Tamez (Albuquerque: University of New Mexico Press, 2015), 181–201, summarizes contributions in the collection that employ sources such as interviews and demographic documents. This chapter and others deal with Mexican mormonism from the mid-nineteenth to the early twentieth century. Butler discusses the ways that Mexicans made Mormonism their own, reinterpreting the church's hierarchy, adapting religious rituals, and bringing ideas about the Mexican nation to their practice of Mormonism. I begin where these contributions end (in the early twentieth century) and continue into the twenty-first, employing various types of sources, and as I focus on photography, clothing, jewelry, and architecture, I draw on the contributions in that volume. In the same way, while much attention has been paid to Mormon architecture (especially of the early years of Mormonism) in the United States, very little focus has been given to Mexican Mormon architecture, outside of a discussion of the temple in Samuel Palfreyman's dissertation. When Mormons design buildings in Mexico they turn to ideas of what they thought Mexico would be—as a Spanish colony or a pan-Indigenous identity, through the Spanish Colonial Revival and Mayan Revival styles.

[4] Walter Ernest Young, "A Brief Biography of Rafael Monroy and Companion Vicente Morales, Both Martyrs for Their Testimonies," n.d., Church History Library, MS 3976, 1.

[5] Mark L. Grover, "Execution in Mexico: The Deaths of Rafael Monroy and Vicente Morales," *BYU Studies* 35, no. 3–4 (1996): 12.

[6] Young, "A Brief Biography," 1.

[7] F. Lamond Tullis, *Martyrs in Mexico: A Mormon Story of Revolution and Redemption* (Provo, UT: Brigham Young University Press, 2018), 3, 5.

[8] Monroy, "Como llegó el evangelio restaurado," 8–9, Rey L. Pratt papers, 1901–1959, Church History Library, MS 2730.

[9] "Monroy Family Members, Circa 1915," Church History Library, PH 6110.

[10] "Monroy Family Members, Circa 1915," Church History Library, PH 6110.

[11] Guadalupe Monroy, "Como llegó el evangelio restaurado al pueblo de San Marcos, Tula de Allende, Estado de Hidalgo. He aquí la historia escrita por la hermana María Guadalupe Monroy de la Rama de San Marcos, Hidalgo," typescript, Church History Library, 1.

[12] For more information about cartes de visite, see, for example, Cheryl Finley, "Photography and the Archive," *Critical Arts* 33, no. 6 (2019): 8–23; Stephen Burstow, "The Carte de Visite and Domestic Digital Photography," *Photographies* 9, no. 3 (2016): 290. John Tagg states that "*Cartes-de-visite* photographs [of the popular classes] were made to a formula. Posing was standardised and quick, and the figures in the resultant pictures were so small that the figures could not be studied." He contrasts this with portraits wealthier people would distribute to their friends and family, or that the public would collect of celebrities. John Tagg,

The Burden of Representation: Essays on Photographies and Histories (Amherst: University of Massachusetts Press, 1988), 50.

[13] "Monroy Family Members, Circa 1915," Church History Library, PH 6110.

[14] Tullis, *Martyrs in Mexico,* 11.

[15] Claudio Lomnitz, *Deep Mexico, Silent Mexico: An Anthropology of Nationalism* (Minneapolis: University of Minnesota Press, 2001), 53; Aníbal Quijano, "Coloniality of Power, Eurocentrism and Latin America," trans. Michael Ennis, *Nepantla: Views from the South* 1, no. 3 (2000): 555–556.

[16] "Monroy Family Members, Circa 1915," Church History Library, PH 6110.

[17] Tanya Meléndez Escalante, "El Arte de la Indumentaria y la Moda en México, 1940–2015, Palacio de Cultura Banamex-Palacio de Iturbide, Mexico City, May 4–September 25, 2016," *Fashion Theory* 24, no. 2 (2020): 266; Margot Blum Schevill, "America, Central, and Mexico: History of Dress," in *Encyclopedia of Clothing and Fashion*, vol. 1, ed. Valerie Steele (Detroit: Gale, 2005), 37–38.

[18] Karina Reddy, "1900–1909," Fashion History Timeline, Fashion Institute of New York, accessed May 26, 2021, https://fashionhistory.fitnyc.edu/1900-1909/.

[19] Michael Reed, *Banishing the Cross: The Emergence of a Mormon Taboo* (Independence, MO: John Whitmer Books, 2012), 79; Michael De Groote, "Sunstone Speaker Attempts to Explain LDS 'Aversion' to Cross," *Deseret News,* September 10, 2009, https://www.deseret.com/2009/9/10/20376797/sunstone-speaker-attempts-to-explain-lds-aversion-to-cross. This is sharply different from reports from the October 2022 General Conference ("Elder Jeffrey R. Holland: 'Lifted Up UPON the Cross,'" *Church News,* October 2, 2022, https://www.thechurchnews.com/general-conference/2022/10/2/23381222/elder-holland-october-2022-general-conference-cross-crucifixion).

[20] "Monroy Family Members, Circa 1915," Church History Library, PH 6110.

[21] Tullis, *Martyrs in Mexico,* 31.

[22] There is a similar version of the photograph without this passport-size addition in the Amalia C. Monroy Collection, Church History Library. Tullis's *Martyrs in Mexico,* 31, analyzes the photographs as they appear in the Amalia C. Monroy Collection and does not mention this other version; thus, the woman remains anonymous.

[23] "Rafael Monroy's Mother and Sister," Elmer P. Bright Papers, 1920 November–1923 March, Church History Library, MS 10129; Grover, "Execution in Mexico," 25, dates this to 1922.

[24] The back of the phtoograph states that the women in the photograph are "Right: Sister Monroy, mother of Rafael (who was killed in 1915). Left: Sister Monroy's daughter" ("Rafael Monroy's Mother and Sister," Elmer P. Bright Papers, 1920 November–1923 March, Church History Library, MS 10129); Grover's "Execution in Mexico," 25, states that the women are Jesús Mera de Monroy and María Concepción Monroy.

[25] "María C. Monroy Hernández de Villalobos Photographs, Circa 1924–1930," Church History Library, PH 43.

[26] Gary James Bergera, "Transgression in the Latter-day Saint Community: The Cases of Albert Carrington, Richard R. Lyman, and Joseph F. Smith. Part 2: Richard R. Lyman," *Journal of Mormon History* 37 (Fall 2011): 175–80; Pulido, *Spiritual Evolution,* 142–143; Tullis, *Martyrs in Mexico,* 6.

[27] There is some debate regarding the nature of their relationship. Historian Lavina Fielding Anderson ("A Ministry of Blessing: Nicholas Groesbeck Smith," *Dialogue* 31, no. 3 [Fall 1998[: 75–76, posits that they were married, and Michael Quinn states that they had a covenant (*Mormon Hierarchy: Extensions of Power* [Salt Lake City: Signature Books, 1994], 819). Bergera's discussion of the events is based on documentary evidence. He and Dave Hall's *A Faded Legacy: Amy Brown Lyman and Mormon Women's Activism, 1872–1959* (Salt Lake City: University of Utah Press, 2015), 161–166, analyze Lyman's letters and propose that Lyman used the doctrine of polygamy to justify his own behavior, and there is not clear evidence a wedding between Lyman and Jacobsen Hegsted ever took place.

[28] "María C. Monroy Hernández de Villalobos Photographs, Circa 1924–1930," Church History Library, PH 43.

[29] Guadalupe Monroy, "Como llegó el evangelio restaurado," 88.

[30] Tullis, *Martyrs in Mexico,* 104.

[31] Pulido, *The Spiritual Evolution of Margarito Bautista,* 14.

[32] Pulido, *The Spiritual Evolution of Margarito Bautista,* 93, 142–153.

[33] Tullis, *Martyrs in Mexico,* 28, 94.

[34] Tullis, *Martyrs in Mexico,* 97.

[35] Tullis, *Martyrs in Mexico,* 6.

[36] Tullis, *Martyrs in Mexico,* 114.

[37] Tullis, *Martyrs in Mexico,* 114.

[38] Tullis, *Martyrs in Mexico,* 119.

[39] Butler, "Porfirian Saints," 185–187.

[40] Phoebe S. K. Young, "The Spanish Colonial Solution: The Politics of Style in Southern California, 1890s–1930s," in *Found in Translation: Design in California and Mexico, 1915–1985,* ed. Wendy Kaplan (Los Angeles: Los Angeles County Museum of Art, 2017), 58.

[41] This building is like the buildings of the Berkeley Ward in Berkeley, California, and the Sunset Ward in San Francisco, California, both designed by architect Theodor Ruegg, and the Phoenix Third Ward, in Phoenix, Arizona, designed by architect Douglas W. Burton (based on observing images in Joseph H. Weston, ed. *Mormon Architecture* [Salt Lake City: Weston, 1949], 28, 47, 62).

[42] Lomnitz, *Deep Mexico,* 51–54.

[43] Albert Fu, "Materializing Spanish-Colonial Revival Architecture: History and Cultural Production in Southern California," *Home Cultures: The Journal of Architecture, Design and Domestic Space* 9, no. 2 (2012): 152;

[44] Henry Allen, "Spanish Atmosphere," *Pacific Coast Architect* 29, no. 5 (1926): 5–6.

[45] Susan Antebi, *Embodied Archive: Disability in Post-Revolutionary Mexican Cultural Production* (Ann Arbor: University of Michigan Press, 2021), 132; José Vasconcelos, "Estética," in *Obras completas* (Mexico City: Libreros Mexicanos Unidos, 1957), 5:1611. This racial transformation aligned with Vasconcelos's idea of *mestizaje.*

[46] Antebi explains that O'Gorman was committed to designing new public schools in Mexico and that for him, the commitment to technique was more important than visual style. Although, as Antebi observes, form and function are inextricably linked (*Embodied Archive,* 128–130).

[47] The photographs of buildings come from the middle of the twentieth century as the LDS Church expanded in Mexico. This expansion coincided with the fact that ordinary people in the United States could access cameras, and so missionaries were able to take photographs more easily to share with the archives, or send email to the author of this chapter.

[48] Humberto Mesa Méndez, comp., *Breve historia de la Iglesia en México* (Tepic: Nayarit, 2010), manuscript in the Church History Library, 38.

[49] Weston, ed., *Mormon Architecture,* 27.

[50] Fernando R. and Enriqueta Gomez Mormon Mexican History Collection, Claremont Colleges Library, Special Collections and Archives.

[51] "Efraín Chang Mendoza Photo Collection, Circa 1961–1965, 2015," Church History Library, MS 29502, index 1–2. The photograph is dated 1963 in this index.

[52] "Efraín Chang Mendoza Photo Collection, Circa 1961–1965, 2015," Church History Library, MS 29502, index 1–2. Later photographs in the same collection are of chapel construction, so we must assume this was before then. Tapachula branch files from 1964 report a branch conference with President E. Seville Hatch, so he may have been the president in the photographs.

[53] "Efraín Chang Mendoza Photo Collection, Circa 1961–1965, 2015," Church History Library, MS 29502.

[54] "Efraín Chang Mendoza Photo Collection, Circa 1961–1965, 2015," Church History Library, MS 29502.

[55] Dormady, "Introduction," 13–15.

[56] "Elisa Escobar Moreno Interview: Doctor Porfirio Parra, Chihuahua, México, 2016 December 18," Church History Library, OH 10642.

[57] James Oles, "Reviving the Pre-Hispanic Past, from Mexico to California," in *Found in Translation: Design in California and Mexico, 1915-1985*, ed. Wendy Kaplan (Los Angeles: Los Angeles County Museum of Art, 2017), 128–129.

[58] Samuel Ross Palfreyman, "The Landscape of Modern Mormonism: Understanding the Church of Jesus Christ of Latter-Day Saints Through Its Twentieth-Century Architecture" (PhD diss., Boston University, 2020), 78.

[59] Palfreyman, "The Landscape of Mormonism," 78.

[60] Palfreyman, "The Landscape of Mormonism," 78.

[61] Playfreyman, "The Landscape of Mormonism," 78–79.

[62] Palfreyman, "The Landscape of Mormonism," fig. 1.48.

[63] Elizabeth Dean Miller, "The U.S. Imagination of Maya Ruins: Criticial Reflections on Art and Architecture, 1839–1972" (Ph.D. diss., University of California, San Diego, 2018). 69.

[64] Renée de la Torre and Cristina Gutiérrez Zúñiga, in "Chicano Spirituality and the Construction of an Imagined Nation: Aztlán," *Social Compass* 60, no. 2 (2013): 218–225, discuss how this desire for a "pan-Indigenous ancestry" affected popular expressions of religion.

[65] Oles, "Reviving the Pre-Hispanic Past," 129.

[66] Blanca Estela Pavón Martínez, *Earthly Symbol of Spiritual Reality,* 2002, beads attached to a wax sub-strate, photographs, palm leaf, 21.75" × 26.5", Church History Museum, Provo, Utah.

[67] Schevill, "America, Central, and Mexico," 40.

[68] "Victor Valdez Hernández and Blanca Pavón Martínez de Valdez Interview: Netzahualcoyotl [*sic*] City, Mexico, 2013 February 10," Church History Library, OH 6932.

[69] Staci Steinberger, "Journeys to the Land of 'Colorful Handcraft,'" in *Found in Translation: Design in California and Mexico, 1915–1985,* ed. Wendy Kaplan (Los Angeles: Los Angeles County Museum of Art, 2017), 214.

11

DEFINING THE MORMON LANDSCAPE

Photography and the Representation and Evolution of a Distinctive American Space

JAMES SWENSEN

In 1940 the photographer Russell Lee documented a wide and lonely expanse in northern Utah. Prior to making this photograph he spent time in Salt Lake City, where he toured Temple Square and other sites, gaining what he called a good "Mormon background" and learning, as others before him, that when it comes to the Church of Jesus Christ of Latter-day Saints, "everything begins and ends there."[1] From the capital he traveled to Box Elder County to document farming for the federal government. At some point during his assignment, he turned his lens westward to photograph a landscape of sagebrush and juniper that looks no different from other swaths of the western United States and the Great Basin. For Lee, however, this was no typical landscape, as suggested by his caption: "Over land similar to this Brigham Young looked when he said, 'This is the place.'"[2] Despite the fact that the background is relatively nondescript outside of fauna specific to a geographic region, the title of the work sets apart this seemingly desolate landscape by marking it as a distinctive Mormon place.

Lee's photograph provides an example of how the simple act of naming and representing landscape can overlay an identity. Indeed, as cultural geographer J. B. Jackson and others have observed, landscapes are more than depictions of the natural world—they are social and cultural constructs. They are not, Jackson stated, "a natural feature of the environment but a synthetic space, a human-made system functioning and evolving not according to natural laws but to serve a community."[3] This is particularly true in the Mormon West, where the meaning of the landscape is "contingent and time-bound" and where, as historian Jared Farmer pointed out, "a perceptual landscape

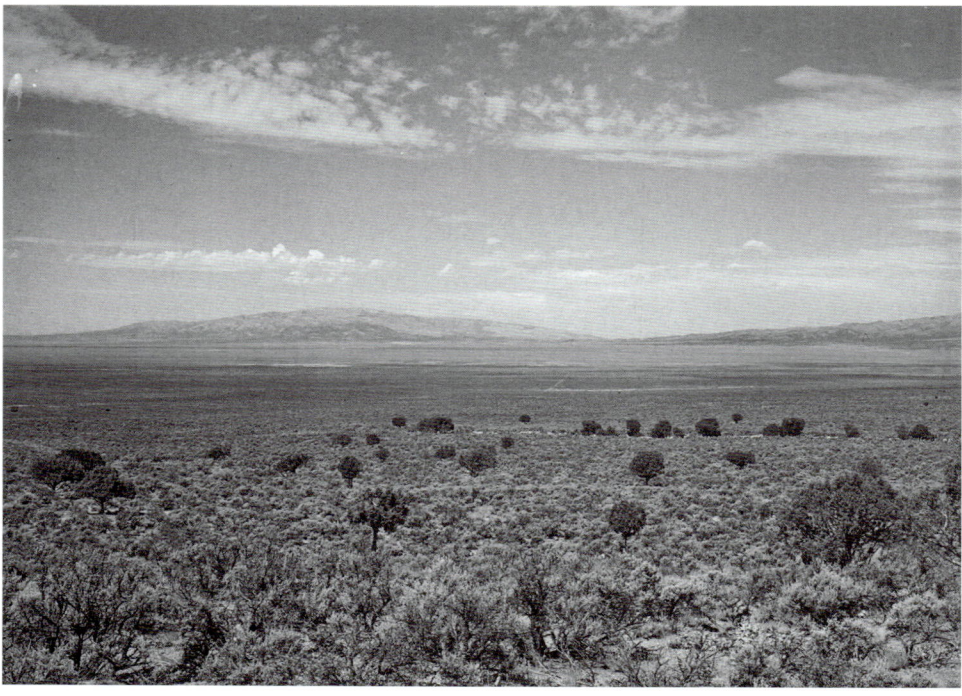

Fig. 11.1 Russell Lee, *Upon Land Similar to This Brigham Young Looked When He Said, "This Is the Place,"* Box Elder County, Utah, 1940, LC-USF34- 037280-D, Library of Congress, Washington, D.C.

overlaps the physical one."[4] Lee's depiction of northern Utah also demonstrates the ways in which a photograph, like a landscape, is dependent on outside information for the construction of its understanding. Full of details and visual information, photographic images "can describe, but they rarely explain."[5] Grounding information—like titles and captions—further contributes to what a photograph means to a given group. Indeed, both photographs and landscapes are ultimately reliant on outside agents to define meaning and to set interpretations to work.[6]

The camera has and continues to describe and define what has come to be called the "Mormon landscape," or, more specifically, the region in the American West that was colonized by people who historically self-identified as Mormon.[7] This essay explores photography's active role in the visual representation and, in turn, construction of the Mormon landscape. While not the only visual format defining this cultural landscape, photography significantly contributes to sculpting a visual identity for Latter-day Saints in the three distinct centuries they have occupied the Intermountain West.[8] It will, moreover, examine the work of key photographers inside, outside, and on the borders of the faith who, for various reasons and through changing styles, have invested time and energy in documenting a distinctive and evolving Mormon landscape, and discuss what that reveals about the experience of the Latter-day Saints in the West.

I

Mormons predated the Mormon landscape. Despite a legacy of inhabitation and building wherever the Latter-day Saints gathered, whether in New York, Ohio, Missouri, or Illinois, the formation of a distinct landscape was not possible until after 1847, when they began colonization of the Intermountain West. For the Shoshone and Goshute, the region was defined by its most prominent feature, the Great Salt Lake, which they referred to as Pi'a-pa or "Big Water" and Ti'ta-pa or "Bad Water."[9] Not long after the Mormons arrived in 1847, the Shoshone called the Salt Lake Valley Soonte-Kahni, "Many Houses."[10] For the newcomers, this was their Zion that they called Deseret. Federal officials called the territory Utah.[11] With greater interaction with the outside world, it also became known as Mormondom, Mormon Country, and "the genius of Mormonism."[12] Over time these names became nearly synonymous and collectively designated a specific region with distinctive traits that differed from other areas in the United States.

The places where Mormons settled in the West became visibly distinct from other examples of homesteading. Once they arrived in the valleys of Utah and the surrounding regions—places that had been inhabited for centuries by Native American tribes, including the Ute, Shoshone, Goshute, and Paiute, among others—they implemented a plan to settle the space. Not only would Mormons control how the landscape was perceived, but they were active in shaping and manipulating the physical environment.[13] By design, they left a "visible imprint on the land," which became central to how this space was seen and recorded.[14] Key among the physical changes they brought to the West was the implementation of the "Plat of Zion," which was based on an earlier revelation given to the church's founder, Joseph Smith, and which established the pattern of city planning that Brigham Young implemented once the Mormons arrived in the Great Basin.[15] In addition to an orderly grid layout, the plat had other visible features, including the centrality of religious buildings, wide streets, and modest homes clustered in town and away from farmland. This form of civil engineering created a built environment designed to keep the Saints together and circled around their religion.

In the romance projected onto this emblematic American space, the Mormon West was often eclipsed by "other Wests," which featured cowboys and other inhabitants.[16] "Of all the regions of the United States the Mormon Country is the least known outside," Wallace Stegner argued in 1947. "Utah is a blank. . . . The Mormon Country has never caught the national imagination, has never acquired glamour."[17] This may have been generally true, but by the mid-twentieth century the region became the focus of historians, social scientists, and others who recognized and recorded the distinct elements of the "Mormon culture region."[18] Key among these scholars was geographer Richard Francaviglia, who, beginning in the 1970s, identified a distinctive region with several visible markers, which he called the "Mormon landscape."[19] Well before Francaviglia and others studied this landscape, however, photographers had already traversed and worked in this space and had noted and recorded many of its features. Indeed, for those actually in the American West, it was difficult to bypass the Mormon landscape.

II

Unlike other American religious communities, the LDS Church embraced technology from its inception.[20] This included photography, which, like the church, was a product of the 1830s. Like Americans in general, church members and leadership sought out photographers and participated in the marketplace of photography. This was particularly true of Brigham Young, who, judging from the numerous extant photographs of the church's second prophet, seems to have relished having his picture made.[21] By 1850 Marsena Cannon, a daguerreotypist, had established an active studio in Salt Lake City. Charles Roscoe (C. R.) Savage, an English convert, began working in Cannon's studio within two days of his arrival in the Salt Lake Valley in 1860. When Cannon left the capital and his practice, Savage established himself as the primary photographer in Utah. Over the next five decades, and despite two studio fires that destroyed thousands of his glass plate negatives (the first in 1883 and a second that occurred two years after his death, which was in 1909), Savage played a central role in photography and the arts of the territory.

Savage was born in 1832 near Southampton, England, the son of an impoverished gardener. He was baptized into the LDS Church in 1848, immigrated to the United States in 1856, and trekked west to Salt Lake City four years later.[22] His religion and his turn to photography were what, he believed, pulled him out of poverty and obscurity to become a prominent member of the community. Through his practice and trade, he became close to church leadership, especially Young, whom he photographed on several occasions. He also traveled with the church leader and held him in the highest esteem.[23] In a period of profound change and challenge in the church, Savage remained steadfast in his faith and dedication to its principles.[24] He also played a central role in a nascent art community. He was patron and friend to many of the leading artists of the territory, including his longtime business partner, George Ottinger. As the most prominent photographer in Salt Lake City and a key supplier of photographic materials, he also befriended many of the leading photographers working in the West, including William Henry Jackson, Timothy O'Sullivan, A. J. Russell, and Carleton Watkins. Not only did he supply his peers, but he often ventured out of the studio with them to create his own "views of the Great West."[25]

Shortly after opening his own studio, Savage created a panorama of the Salt Lake Valley by piecing together three photographs that, when united, revealed the valley's full breadth from east to west. The view, looking down East Temple Street (today's State Street) from Arsenal Hill, highlighted the emerging city cradled by mountains.

More than creating a picturesque scene, Savage encouraged a deeper reading of this landscape, even encouraging viewers to use field glasses or a telescope to see additional details.[26] Upon closer inspection, it is possible to see abundant trees and foliage that fill the gaps between homes and buildings. The town appears tidy, organized, and prosperous. Images like this were clearly constructed to combat the notion that the Saints were a peculiar people living in a peculiar part of the world. Rather, Savage's view effectively expands beyond the "spatial quarantine" of Deseret to present a vision of a verdant American town within a spectacular setting to an outside audience that was eager to know more about the Latter-day Saints in the distant West.[27] Yet closer inspection would reveal visual indications that this was not a typical American town. Many of the features that mark Mormon settlement are already visible, including the immensely wide streets flanked by irrigation ditches. The stone foundation of the Salt Lake temple is visible, and upon its completion nearly thirty-three years later the temple would become the symbol of the church's presence.

Not long after its creation, Savage's view of Great Salt Lake City was faithfully converted into a woodblock print suitable for mass production.[28] In 1866, *Harper's Weekly* reproduced Savage's panorama along with some of his other images, including vignettes of the construction of the Salt Lake tabernacle, the tithing house, and an early rendering of the Salt Lake temple. Amid these architectural markers were photographic portraits, also by Savage, of church leaders orbiting the bust of President Young. The constellation of images illustrated the hierarchy of the church with remarkable clarity. The caption for the full-page spread read: "We cannot close this notice without adding that with whatever differences of opinion may be entertained of the Mormon faith, the great virtue of labor cannot be denied to the Mormon population; and high admiration is universally expressed of the executive ability of Brigham Young, who allegedly redeemed the wilderness, made it a fruitful field, and 'made the desert to blossom as a rose.'"[29]

The inclusion in *Harper's* of Savage's panorama was the terra firma for the oft-repeated claim that Young and his followers had made the "desert bloom."[30] Although the potential of the valley was not as dire as reported, its redemption became a central theme in the narrative that early settlers and outside observers propagated.[31] It was a narrative of a "wilderness," an empty expanse, converted into a "land teeming with abundance," filled with prosperous homes, gardens, and farms.[32] Indeed, there was no indication of the vast populations of Shoshone, Paiute, Goshute, and Ute tribes who had cultivated this land for centuries.[33] Their concealment created the sense of a place awaiting conversion.[34] For Young, the Salt Lake Valley was "as arid a sand and sage barren as can be found anywhere" in the West.[35] Mormons "were the first," he proclaimed, "to plant out orchards and to improve the desert country, making it like the Garden of Eden.[36] Savage viewed himself as a participant in this great endeavor, claiming to have "pulled the sage brush and planted the vine."[37] Zion's alleged success was difficult to dismiss, and even critics begrudgingly gave the Saints credit for the transformation, including

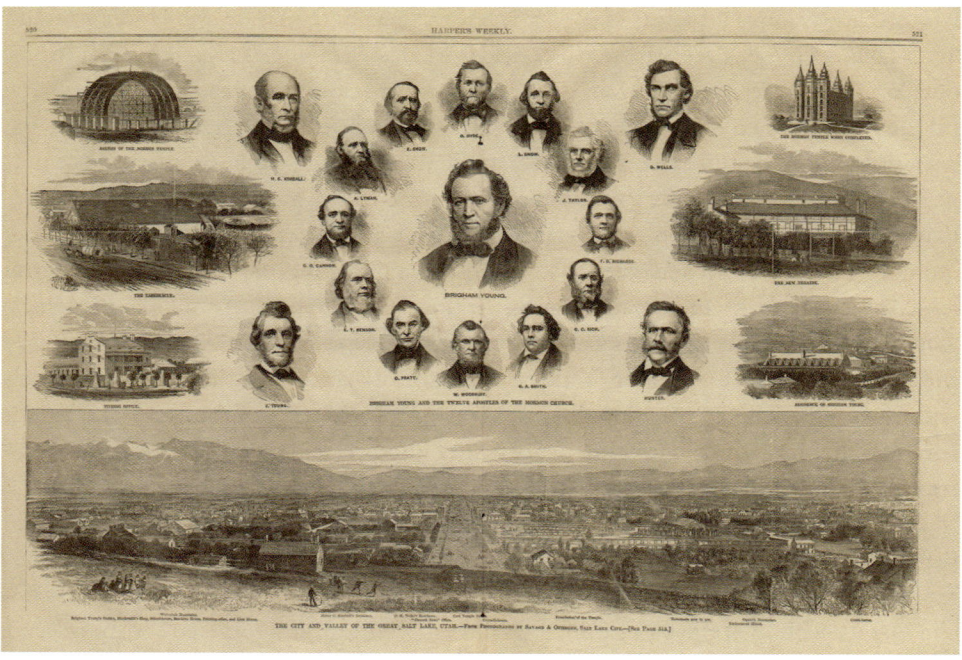

Fig. 11.2   After C. R. Savage, *Great Salt Lake City Panorama,* c. 1863, woodblock print from *Harper's Weekly,* August 18, 1866, pp. 520–521. Courtesy L. Tom Perry Special Collections, Harold B. Lee Library, Brigham Young University, Provo Utah.

Mark Twain, who discovered in Salt Lake a "general air of neatness, repair, thrift, and comfort, around and over the whole."[38]

Through the translation of Savage's panorama to a woodblock print, *Harper's* artists continued to play off this central theme. Adding to the notion of growth, a row of trees was placed along the busy central thoroughfare in the woodblock image, and foliage was carefully embellished and delineated by thicker lines. The engravers added well-dressed figures (absent in Savage's photographs), who engage in recreation and take in the bucolic scenery. Captions mark the homes of well-known Mormon leaders, including Brigham Young and Heber C. Kimball, as well as the site of the temple, the "old" Salt Lake tabernacle (built in 1852, twelve years before its more famous predecessor at Temple Square), and the Endowment House. The captions also marked the Wasatch Front to the left and the Oquirrh Mountains on the right. At an "air-distance" of twenty miles to these ranges, Savage's image reveals vast tracts in the distant background that could be opened for the budding "metropolis of the mountains."[39] Moreover, the overall orientation offers a sense of further expansion running longitudinally along the Wasatch Front, where many of its largest settlements were to be located. Yet it was the capital that represented Utah; it was "the cosmos, the center place of the Mormon World, evidence of what was possible."[40]

In 1869 Savage's friend and fellow explorer A. J. Russell created a similar photograph of Salt Lake City. As the official photographer for the Union Pacific Railroad, Russell traveled from Omaha to Salt Lake during the construction of the transcontinental line. An artist by training, the New York native documented the rugged landscapes along the line, including sights like Green River, Wyoming, and Echo Canyon, Utah.

If Savage's view was longitudinal, looking straight down the axis of the Salt Lake Valley, Russell's photograph provides a perpendicular cross section of the city. Working from the roof of the tabernacle on an early spring evening, he captured the central buildings of Salt Lake and the foundations of the temple in the foreground in the raking light of the setting sun. The eastern orientation of the image is significant in that this work was created for East Coast audiences who were anxious to see the "New Jerusalem." He also included this photograph in his popular album *The Great West Illustrated*, which was created to provide "positive and substantial knowledge" of a subject that had hitherto been "vague and insignificant."[41]

In Russell's image the angular order of the white buildings and walls provided an elegant contrast to the organic lines of the mountains and canyons in the distance. Seemingly more prosaic than Savage's grand panorama, it shows an inhabited space filled with ordinary activities.[42] While the theme of a budding prosperity may be seen, it also emphasized polygamy through a sampling of compounds that housed various relationship configurations. As Russell knew, polygamy was a topic of particular intrigue.[43] In his caption, the photographer directed viewers to the home of the "Mormon Prophet," known as Lion House, with its "many windows" looking out from its pointed gables.[44] With a reported twenty-seven wives and fifty-six children, Young's fecundity was well known to audiences in the United States and abroad.[45] For Twain, the Lion House was both "hennery" and "harem."[46] Others found the practice of polygamy morally reprehensible but endlessly fascinating. As the "model for polygamous architecture," the Lion House became a symbol of this distinctive Mormon practice, which was of particular interest to those coming to Utah or those visiting vicariously through photographs.[47]

One item absent from Savage's view but clearly visible in Russell's photograph is the presence of Camp Douglas in the distance, which he noted in his captions. Established in 1862, the camp, later named Fort Douglas, began quartering federal troops in 1863 to monitor and control the Saints and their leader. Young mounted a telescope on the square cupola of the Beehive House, his official residence, whose gleaming white tower can be seen above the roof of the Lion House, almost as if it were a countersurveillance measure.[48] Thus, Young's scope created a direct line of sight along the orientation of Russell's photograph between east and west, Mormon and Gentile, the federal government and the "Lion" of Deseret.

Absent from both Savage's and Russell's views is the presence of Native Americans. By the 1860s Ute and Shoshone tribes had already been pushed out of the Salt Lake and Utah Valleys by Mormon arrivals, though violent conflicts between Mormons

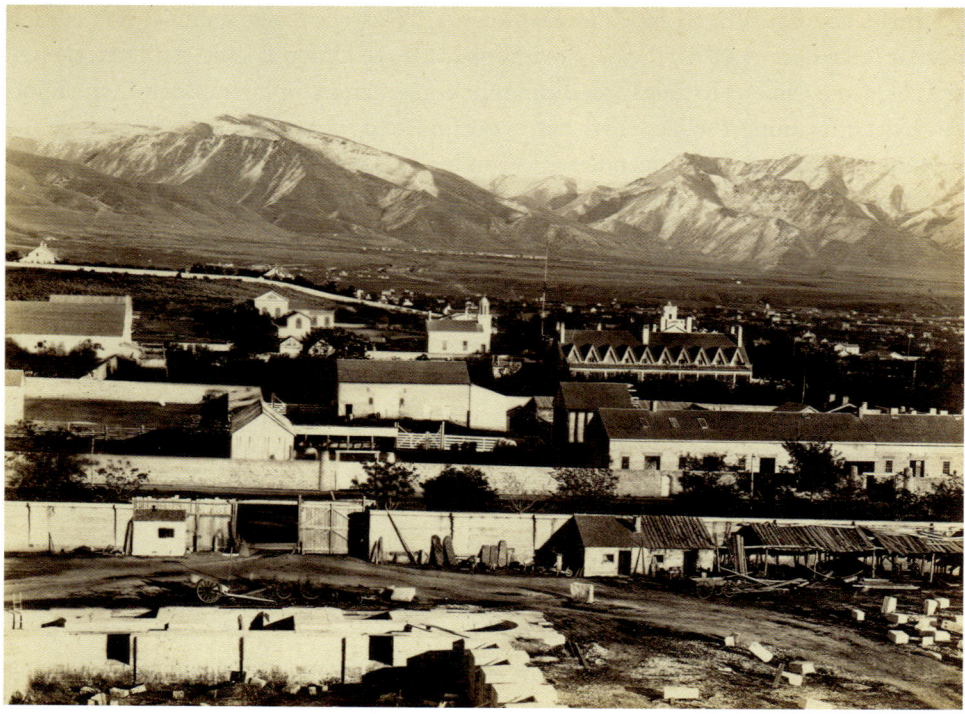

Fig. 11.3 A. J. Russell, *Salt Lake City, from the Top of the Tabernacle,* from *The Great West Illustrated,* 1869, Miriam and Ira D. Wallach Division of Art, Prints and Photographs: Photography Collection, New York Public Library.

and Native tribes continued in southern Utah.[49] Throughout his career, Savage frequently invited local tribe members into his studio to sit for portraits, and he sold their photographs to clients around the United States who were eager to collect images of western types.[50] Yet he saw them as "motley" neighbors and the "swarthy and fierce denizens of the mountains."[51] Their absence in these photographs of cultivated Mormon landscapes suggests their erasure in the face of colonization. According to Rees, "every image of Utah's landscape was already a representation of the divine mandate that Mormons claimed to justify their colonial project."[52] Paintings, photographs, and other visual imagery all seemed to confirm that Salt Lake was already an area marking "Mormon conquests."[53]

George Edward Anderson began an apprenticeship with Savage in 1874 at age fourteen and three years later opened his own business. While Savage found most of his clientele in the state capital, Anderson canvassed the state, gaining the title "village photographer," "running the largest and most complete art studio in the state of Utah."[54] In addition to portable tent and wagon studios, he established permanent studios in Manti in 1886 and later in Springville, where he and his wife, Olive, raised their family. A fixture of many small communities throughout the state, he made thousands of portraits as well as documented people's homes, farms, churches, and anything else he believed would be of benefit to his community and that he could sell.

During his travels across the state, Anderson photographed numerous sights that implied the budding prosperity of the Latter-day Saints, including winsome towns and farms, temples, and tidy churches. By the turn of the century, Anderson's work helped define the "outlands," or the rural areas beyond the larger cities.[55] The Mormon landscape was no longer synonymous with the urban environments documented by Savage and Russell. If at one point Salt Lake City had been emblematic of Utah and its success, Anderson's work implied that the broader place once called Deseret was reaping the rewards of hard work and divine aid. As a devout Mormon who was committed to using his craft to advance his church—even, at times, at the expense of his family's well-being—Anderson was personally and religiously vested in creating and reflecting a positive view of Zion by highlighting what he saw as the industriousness of its people.[56]

An example of the intersection of faith and trade is his photograph of a family standing among dozens of shocks of freshly cut wheat and in front of a sturdy home, highlighted by the distant mountain range. The scene presents prosperity punctuated by the visible fecundity of land and family. The photograph shows Gladys Boyer and her three young children (Keith, Lamar, and Phyllis, the baby) on their property outside of Springville, Utah. By the time he made this photograph, Anderson had known the Boyers for more than two decades. He had been their bishop and baptized Gladys's husband, Selvoy, who was serving a mission at the time of the photograph. The man behind the young mother was her father-in-law, John Boyer, who helped harvest the wheat and sugar beets in his son's absence. "We had little spare time in those years," Selvoy Boyer remembered, "we worked all the time."[57] Despite sacrifice and hardship, or rather because of them, Anderson suggests, this family has become prosperous and blessed.

One of the most important subjects Anderson photographed throughout his career was the Manti temple in central Utah. Temples made up a fraction of the religious structures built by the church, but they became (and continue to be) prominent and visible symbols of the faith, even though access is limited to a carefully vetted membership. This was especially evident in the nineteenth century, when these "unique theological statements in stone" were found only in Utah.[58] Whereas the Salt Lake temple, completed in 1896, would become a defining symbol of the faith, temples like the one in Manti, built in the hinterlands rather than in the capital, became another key marker of Mormon country.[59] With its dramatic placement on the edge of town, the Manti temple became a crowning feature of the Mormon landscape.

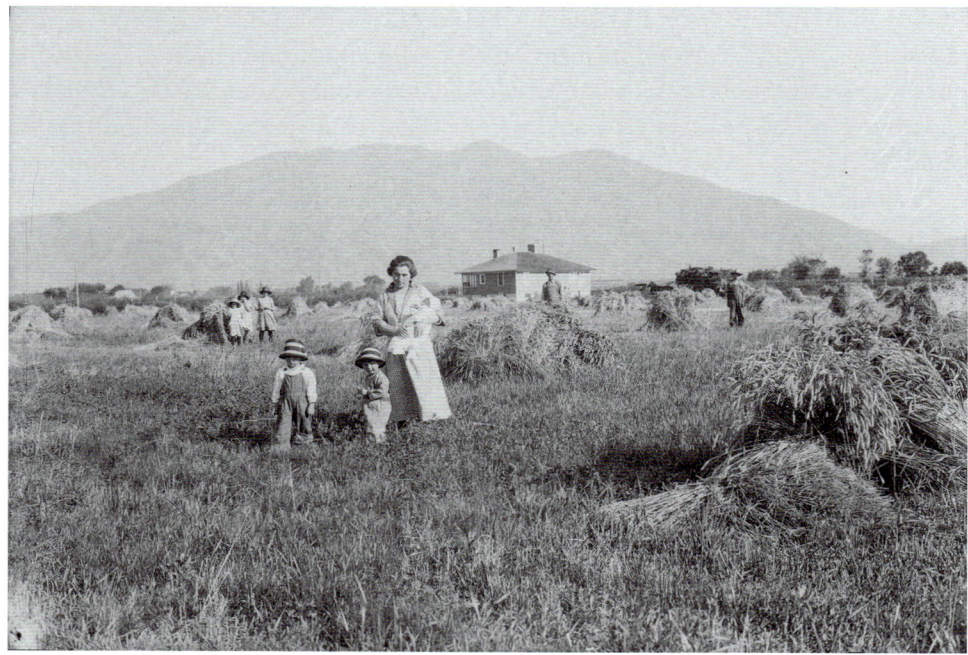

Fig. 11.4 George E. Anderson, *Boyer Family*, Springville, c. 1923. Courtesy L. Tom Perry Special Collections, Harold B. Lee Library, Brigham Young University.

Built by architect William Folsom from cream-colored oölitic limestone quarried on-site, the Manti temple is considered one of the best examples of "Mormonesque" architecture.[60] Furthermore, its placement on Temple Hill, at the northeastern corner of town, represented an important shift away from building temples within cities, as was done in Salt Lake and St. George.[61] This shift placed the temple out in the landscape, where it would be frequently represented by artists and photographers. While its inside access was exclusive, its public face became a visible symbol frequently captured by the camera.

Anderson had a professional, personal, and spiritual tie to this structure. Living nearby, he documented its construction as the massive blocks came together to form its delicate features, including its twin mansard cupolas built in the French Empire style. Upon its completion, he was married there—the second marriage performed inside—and over his career he continued to record the ways in which it majestically loomed over the rural settlement, out of place anywhere else in the United States except for the Mormon West. Savage may have recorded the laying of the temple's foundation, but Anderson made its photography a central part of his work, recording it more than fifty times. In one of these many photographs, Anderson recorded the temple from a distance, directly along its axis. The photographer centered the structure

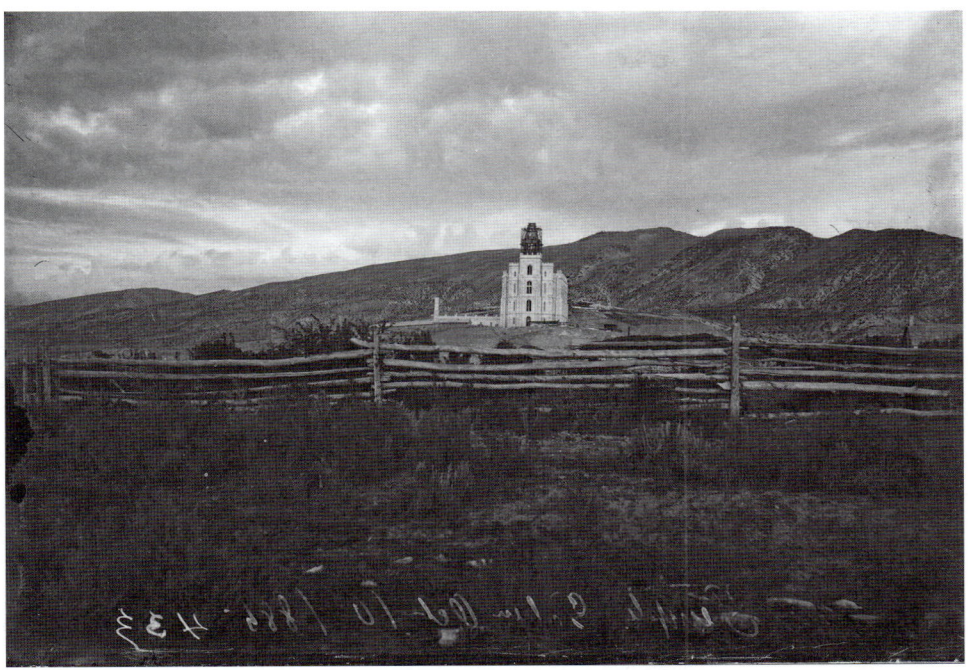

Fig. 11.5 George E. Anderson, *Manti Temple*, c. 1888. Courtesy L. Tom Perry Special Collections, Harold B. Lee Library, Brigham Young University.

behind a rough, unpainted fence—another hallmark of Mormon Country—and framed it against the mountains and swirling sky.[62] With its western tower nearing completion and standing on its own, the white temple seems to be literally emerging from humble beginnings and a vast wilderness; it is a symbol of an ascendant faith emerging de novo.[63]

III

Anderson continued to contribute to the Mormon landscape until his death in 1928. Three years later, photographer Dorothea Lange, who was not a Latter-day Saint, made her first trip to southern Utah with her husband, the painter Maynard Dixon. Over several months, the two explored Zion National Park and the surrounding scenery, becoming acquainted with the Mormon villages of southern Utah and their hardy inhabitants. One of her early works from her time in this area included a portrait of Mary Anne Savage (no relation to C. R. Savage), who as a young girl immigrated from England and made an arduous migration across the plains with the ill-fated Willie Handcart Company (who nearly starved, endured several deaths, and required rescue). She became a polygamous wife to Levi Savage and helped found the southern Utah hamlet of Toquerville. In her profile, Lange accentuated the older woman's wrinkles and the waves of her hair. Lange's photograph of the pioneer woman's features presented a stark and important counter to portrayals of the West as an idealized, allegorical female representation, such as in John Gast's well-known *Westward Ho! [American Progress]* (1872). While hers is not a direct image of the Mormon landscape, Lange succeeded in creating a metaphorical topography of trial, a landscape of endurance and accomplishment in colonizing the West.[64]

By the time Lange returned to Utah in 1936, much had changed. The Great Depression took its toll on her marriage, which ended in divorce in 1935. It also forced her to reevaluate her work and take her camera to the streets and the byways of the West in search of the downtrodden and forgotten. Poverty and dislocation became her focus, and soon she was working for the Resettlement Administration (RA), part of President Franklin Roosevelt's New Deal. Under the direction of Roy Stryker, Lange and Russell Lee were tasked with documenting the plight of rural America and the ways in which the RA was helping farm families across the nation. "North, south, east, and west, the lens follows the destitute man," Stryker insisted.[65] Working for the RA honed Lange's skills at recording hardship and gaining access to the lives and trials of her subjects. For her, everything, including landscape, reflected the human condition. "I don't know," Lange admitted, "where the human leaves off and the inhuman begins."[66]

When Lange returned to Utah in the spring of 1936, she did not come unprepared. As she would do throughout her career, she consulted a rich network of friends in the Bay Area that included historians, writers, and sociologists such as Lowry Nelson, who knew and studied the unique features of the Utah Territory. Over the next two decades, her most important assignments for the RA in Utah were the documentation of Widtsoe and Escalante, two small farming towns located in the south-central part of the state. The first was already slated for resettlement by the federal government due to a history of insufficient yields; the second was in danger of a similar fate.

Settled in 1876, Escalante grew as a farming and ranching community even as its inhabitants struggled to secure an existence in the beautiful but rugged landscape that surrounds the town. Though resettlement was on the horizon, Escalante had certain advantages that would help it avoid mandated abandonment. It had a history of survival and visible reminders of its pioneer roots. For Nelson, Escalante's "extreme geographic isolation" made it a perfect case study to explore the unique elements of the Mormon village.[67] It was laid out on the typical grid pattern, featuring extra-wide streets, which Lange noted were "according to patterns laid down by the Mormon Church," and irrigation ditches running through town.[68] Lange would also photograph distinctive village homes clustered in the center of the community, crude fences, and the "typical" barn. She documented the tithing house and the white ward house rising from a bluff in the center of town. Forty years later, as part of his larger investigation of the West, Francaviglia proposed ten distinct visual markers that defined the Mormon landscape.[69] In Escalante, Lange recorded nine of the ten markers identified by the geographer.[70]

Through her photographs she created one of the most important documentations of the Mormon village.[71]

However, Lange suggests that it was these distinctive elements, this visible heritage, that provided the depth and strength that would save Escalante from ruin. Although Widtsoe was younger than Escalante, by 1930 it was already in sharp decline. After nearly a decade of inadequate rainfall, early frosts, drought, and poor harvests, the town, located in a high, windswept valley north of Bryce Canyon, was barely surviving. The town was named in honor of John A. Widtsoe, an LDS apostle and internationally recognized expert on farming, who wrote that "the destiny of man is to possess the whole earth; and the destiny of the earth is to be subject to man. There can be no full conquest of the earth, and no real satisfaction to humanity, if large portions of the earth remain beyond his highest control."[72] In 1935, the population of Widtsoe was slated for resettlement, with the town to be "wiped off the map" by the federal government.[73] Years earlier, however, the village had prospered. The town was established in 1910 in remote Johns Valley, decades after the initial push to settle the Mormon West was over but when the zeal to build up "the waste places of Zion" was still intact.[74] Within ten years, the farming community had a population of 1,100 and boasted two hotels and four stores. For a while Widtsoe seemed to reflect its namesake's optimism for new lands and new opportunities, especially when tied to divine favor. In 1924 another apostle, Melvin J. Ballard, promised that the valley would be a Garden of Eden if its inhabitants kept God's commandments and stayed out of debt.[75]

Despite an apostolic promise and the efforts of its inhabitants, Widtsoe continued to deteriorate, and by the time Lange arrived most of the town's residents had left a landscape already dotted by abandoned buildings and farms. Those who remained awaited the assistance of the RA. Lange noted in her field book that Widtsoe was predominantly Mormon, "as are all the settlements in the Great Basin," and, having seen many similar towns, she knew that this community was in peril. The general anxiety was evident in the words of one resident, who told the photographer, "People jist been settin' here waitin' and hopin'."[76] Lange's sharply focused photographs captured the reasons for distress. In one example taken from the general store, once prosperous fields appear as a desolate and barren waste. One house is boarded up and another, in the distance, is already abandoned. It would not be long, viewers are to assume, until the store, sign, and gas pump would disappear.

In many ways, Lange's coverage fulfilled the mandate of the RA, which hoped to use Widtsoe as a "showcase project." Her photographs made the case that there was no future for Widtsoe. The images were proof, according to one national outlet, "that a community can be closed if it fails to justify its existence."[77] This was a damning accusation for Mormon communities, which typically did not have to justify their existence beyond Manifest Destiny. Moreover, Lange's work refutes the notion that every valley in the Great Basin could be cultivated to blossom as the rose. Wilderness, in this case, had won; the Mormons had seemingly reached the end of their land supply.[78] Lange's work

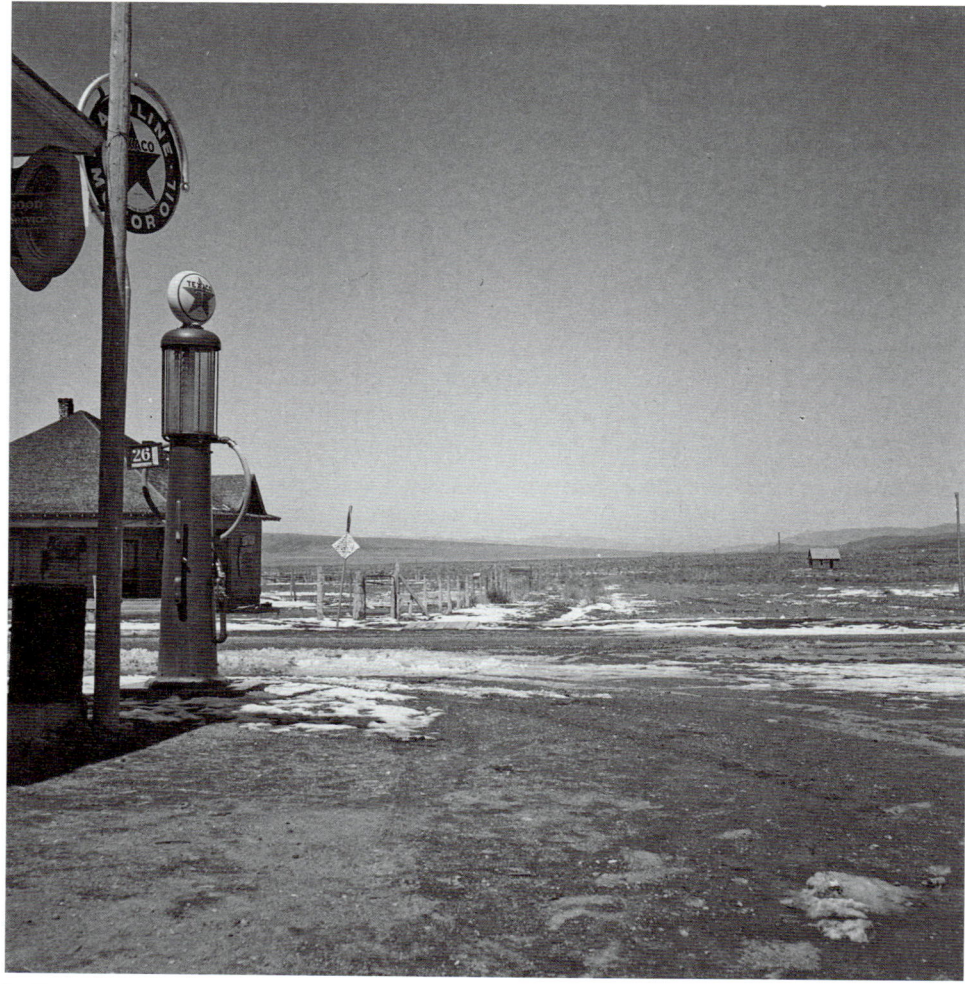

Fig. 11.6 Dorothea Lange, *View of Widtsoe Area from General Store. The Farmlands Purchase Lies on the Floor of the Valley*, Utah, April 1940, Library of Congress.

suggests that there was a limit to the proverbial transformative power of the Latter-day Saints and pragmatic checks to what could become a Mormon landscape. As a result, the U.S. government moved many of those who lived in Johns Valley to other locations throughout the state, including Utah County.

The perception of the Mormon landscape, however, would endure through its representation by the camera. George Midgley, son-in-law and business partner of Heber J. Grant, an apostle and the seventh president of the LDS Church, began as a painter but switched to photography when he learned, as one friend noted, that "it was just a question of being a mediocre painter or the best photographer in Utah."[79] In 1910 he taught himself the basics of photography by reading British instructional texts and contemporary periodicals, and within four years he was exhibiting his work. At the time, the leading photographic style was known as Pictorialism, which sought to elevate photography to a fine art by making photographs look like something else. Through physical manipulation and technique, a photograph could resemble another artistic format, such as watercolor or etching, overcoming some of the stigmas characterizing it as a mere mechanical process. To create his visual effects, Midgley mastered the difficult bromoil transfer process, which allowed him to create gauzy and richly textured images in different hues. His work was nationally recognized for its artistry and painterly effect, which he continued to produce over the course of a long and successful amateur career, and well after the movement had waned.[80]

A resident of Salt Lake City, Midgley was drawn to rural subject matter. Increasingly for urban artists, farm life and the countryside represented a better, more natural way to live.[81] Rural areas were seen as a more beautiful past and a nostalgic escape. Working mostly in the rural corners of northern Utah, Midgley was drawn to details such as Lombardy poplars, which he photographed on numerous occasions. Poplars had been brought to the Great Basin by European LDS converts to remind them of the more verdant world they left behind, to beautify their homes, farms, and gardens, and to act as breaks against the hard winds of the West. They became so ubiquitous and so attached to definitions of the Mormon landscape that Stegner labeled them "Mormon trees."[82] Like other artists, Midgley was evidently drawn to the rhythmic patterns of the poplars against the sky, but, like those native to the space, or observant visitors, he must have also been aware of their special designation and symbolic value representing strength and order.

Midgley also traveled farther afield in search of picturesque sites. Decades after Anderson made his photograph of the Manti temple, Midgley created his own. By this point, the temple was more than a half century old and its potency as a symbol of Mormon Country had only grown. His soft-focus image taken on the northern edge of Manti shows a shepherd on horseback leading a flock of sheep down the road toward the dramatic silhouette of the temple, which seems to emerge from land, cloud, and sky. Midgley's photograph offered, as Thomas Carter proposed, a view of heaven apart from the world (or town).[83] It is an expression that must have resonated with the artist on several levels. Created late in his career, it speaks to mortality and salvation with allusions to a good shepherd with the temple representing a higher, holier sphere.[84] On the other hand, this is a nostalgic image that yearns for simpler times, a slower world, and a romanticized past. It looks back at and even re-creates a connection to the rural Mormon landscape that many believed was already slipping away.

At almost the same time that Midgley created his artistic rendition of the Manti temple, Ansel Adams photographed the same structure, but with a very different purpose and outcome. Adams frequently worked in Utah. He was drawn to its scenery and recognized its distinctive characteristics. In 1948, on his way to drop off his son at

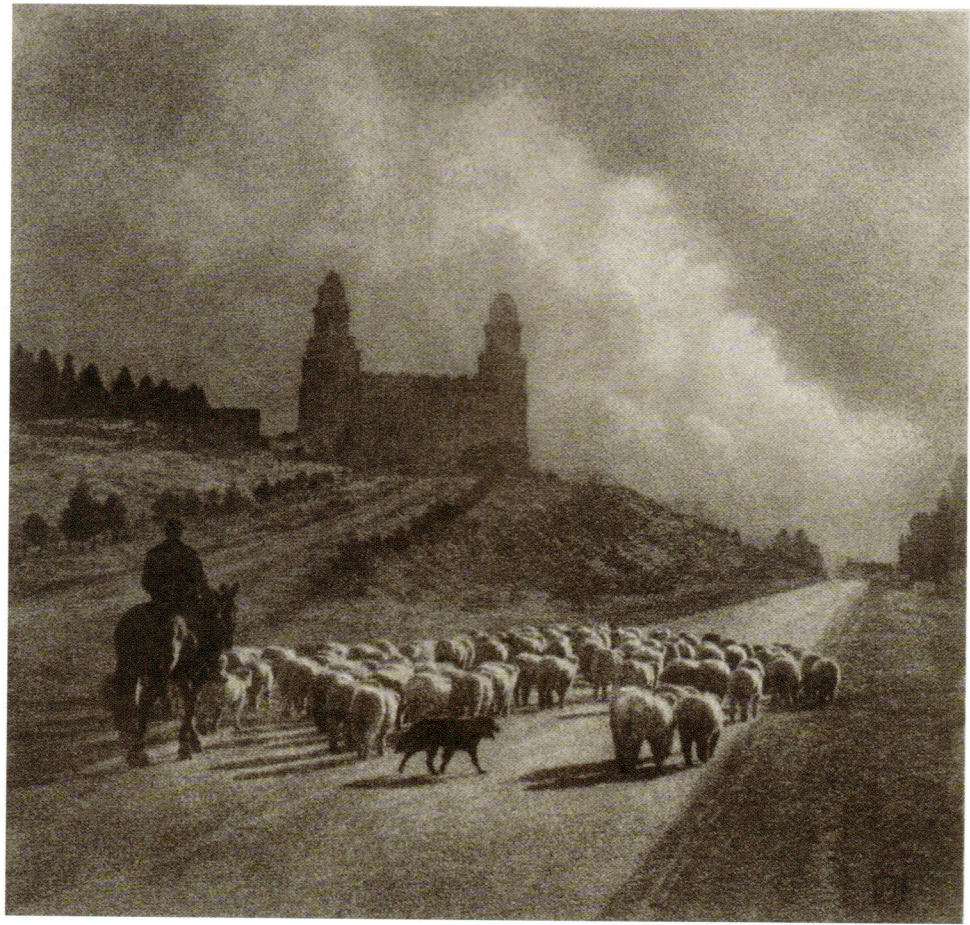

Fig. 11.7 J. George Midgley, *Homeward*, 1950, photograph (bromoil transfer print), 10″ × 10″.
Courtesy Church History Museum.

Wasatch Academy, a prep school in Mt. Pleasant, Utah, he photographed the Mormon
temple in Manti. Like Anderson, Adams recorded the building from straight on, but
he moved in closer to the decorative iron gates at the base of Temple Hill. With its
sharp detail and cool, calculated formality, Adams's photograph provides a striking
contrast to Midgley's atmospheric creation. Adams loathed Pictorialism and all outward manipulations of the camera, negative, or print. Rather, he was a modernist who
espoused what he called "purely photographic methods."[85]

Throughout his career Adams photographed churches and other religious structures,
not as a believer but as a pilgrim in search of visual harmonies. He tended to favor
his eye over his heart. "I am not a churchgoer," Adams freely professed, "but I admire

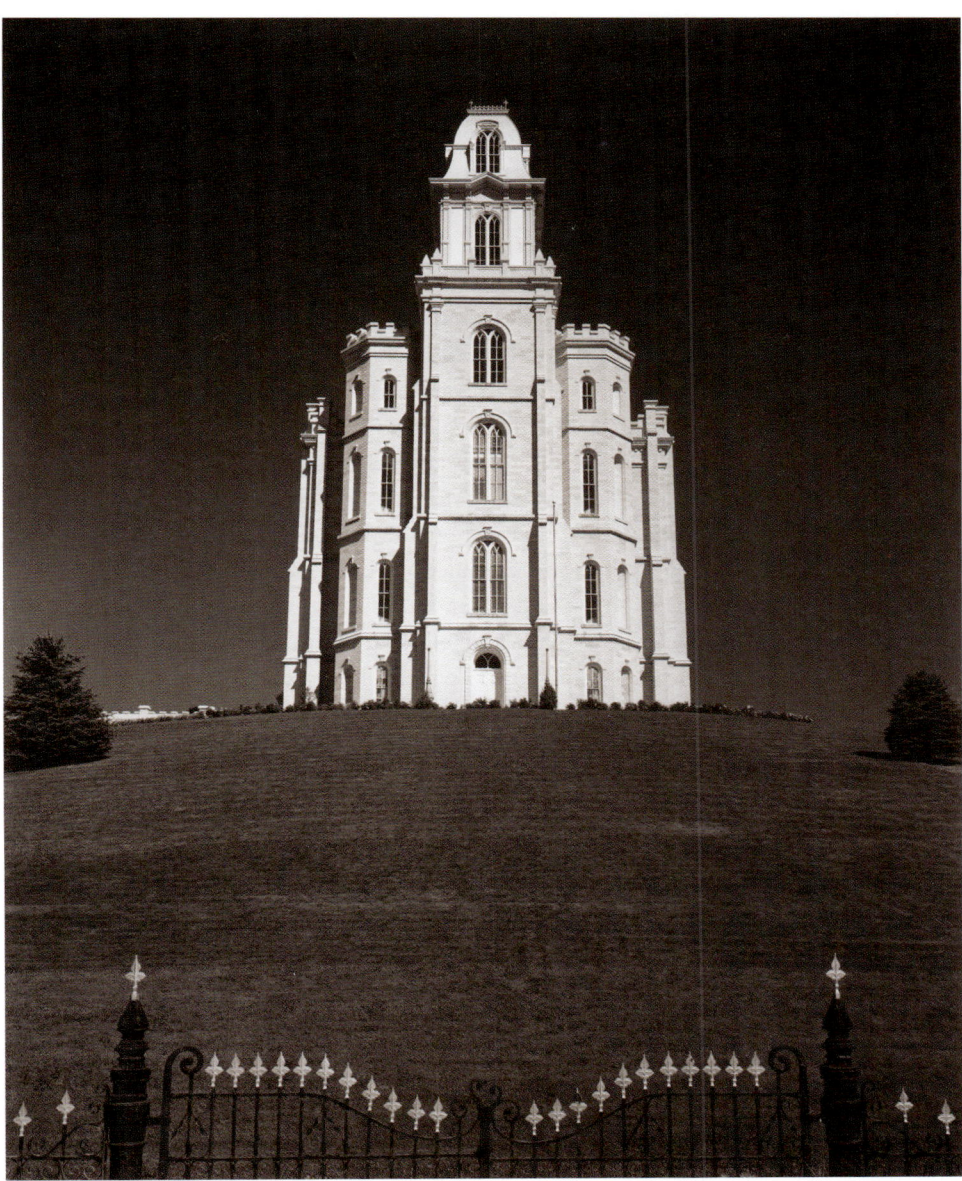

Fig. 11.8 Ansel Adams, *Mormon Temple, Manti*, 1948. © 2023 The Ansel Adams Publishing Trust.

the temples of belief when it is obvious, they represent depth of devotion and integrity of style."[86] Photographed in the brilliant midday sun and without a distracting cloud, the structure and its immediate surroundings exhibit "integrity of style."[87] This was achieved through the balance of form, the cropped symmetry of the scene, and the crisply delineated and integrated patterns found in the fence, the hillside, and the temple's geometric features. Adams also played up the striking contrasts between the gleaming white facade, the uniformly dark sky, and the changing tones of the hillside. Adams included this work in his first portfolio in 1948, where it was featured alongside photographs of snow-covered Denali, rocky beaches, towering oaks, and his mentor Alfred Stieglitz, all of which were included to show his breadth as a photographer.[88] For Adams these photographs were "expressions without doctrine . . . ends in themselves, images of the endless moments of the world."[89]

Despite Adams's modernist belief in the universal self-contained image, his photographs were not ineffable expressions but timebound and contingent. In reality, there are no expressions without some form of doctrine. While his photograph of the Manti temple may have celebrated the patterns, form, and the "plain, stark beauty" he often found in vernacular architecture, the structure and grounds were based on out-side forms of expression and pattern that became associated with Mormonism.[90] In 1867 the humorist Charles Browne noted that "neatness is a great characteristic of the Mormons."[91] Indeed, neatness and order were features broadcast by Latter-day Saints, as evinced by Savage's panorama, and commonly observed by outsiders visiting the Mormon West. It was this neatness and order, found in the temple's facade, matching bushes, and precisely mowed lawn, that attracted Adams's attention. Adams was drawn to its form, Midgley to its symbolism, but while their photographs differed in style, both emphasized the importance of the Manti temple as a key landmark in the Mormon landscape.

Five years later, Adams returned to Utah with Lange, his lifelong friend. *Life* maga-zine commissioned the celebrated photographers to explore and document small-town life in southern Utah.[92] Back home in the Bay Area, they witnessed the ways in which urbanization, consumerism, and other factors eroded the notion of a white middle-class "hometown."[93] Not only did the pair desire to show their work in the popular maga-zine, but, like Midgley, they also were drawn to the region by a nostalgic desire to doc-ument small Mormon communities before they faded away. They returned to Utah to see whether they would survive. In her field book Lange recorded: "The People are *still* fighting to stay in this country" and "Pioneering never stops."[94] From their previous experience, Adams and Lange knew and understood the Mormon landscape and its salient features. For assistance they also consulted their friends Juanita Brooks, a noted LDS historian and local expert, and Edwin Banfield, a sociologist who had completed a lengthy field study of the small hamlet of Gunlock, which became one of the towns on which the photographers focused their energies.

From a black-rock ridge above Gunlock, Lange and Adams photographed a bowing slice of green juxtaposed against a jagged landscape. The contrast between the fertility of the land and the seemingly inhospitable nature of the surroundings is a classic example of what Francaviglia called the "desert-garden complex."[95] Remarkably, the small strip of land nestled along the Santa Clara River supported twenty-two families. In town, Lange and Adams documented the typical characteristics of a Mormon settlement and a closely knit community full of youth and energy. Yet they acknowledged that physical limitations would radically affect Gunlock and many other towns in Mormon Country. They understood that "the fertility of the land [had] been outstripped by the fertility of the people."[96] Pioneering had to slow, and the children needed to look elsewhere to live and work. The children of Utah, Nels Anderson wrote, "have gone to the cities of Babylon, from whence their fathers escaped to build an isolated civilization in the valleys of the mountains."[97]

Lange and Adams feared that Mormon communities were already losing their distinct character. To them and others, it seemed as if there were already fewer "Mormon portions" of Utah.[98] The visible signs of the Mormon landscape were still visible and unmistakable, but the communities were losing local color and becoming more Americanized. They witnessed this in places such as St. George, with its busy, tourist-filled streets and a J. C. Penney store. "St. George becomes a highway town," Lange lamented, "raucous, paved, treeless, harsh competitor, garish imitator of all the others. Its history buried. Its tradition silenced."[99] Even the most remote regions of the Mormon landscape were changing and evolving. As scholar Thomas O'Dea observed, Utah was a "foreign-land-gone-American."[100] In 1953 the *Saturday Evening Post* announced that

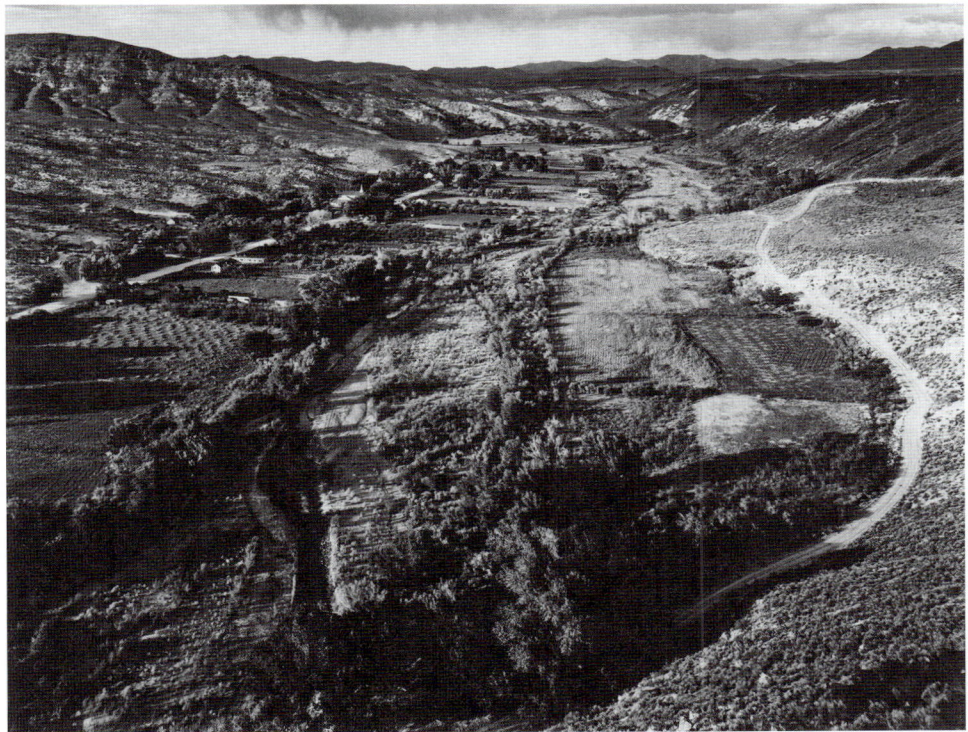

Fig. 11.9   Dorothea Lange [and Ansel Adams], *Gunlock*, 1953. © The Dorothea Lange Collection, the Oakland Museum of California.

Utah's "roads, schools, per capita ownership of Fords, patriotism, sewer system and modernity of office appliances are, in fact, well above average."[101] Mormons were becoming fully enveloped in American culture and were no longer seen as outsiders but increasingly touted as model citizens.

IV

Even as the Mormon landscape became a topic of interest among historians, geographers, and sociologists, it failed to remain a subject for the camera lens. For the rest of the twentieth century, photographers largely came to the state for other reasons than to depict what was considered just another subculture of the United States. They were attracted to the national parks and not the exoticism of a distinctly Mormon landscape. Even prominent LDS photographers such as John Telford and Craig Law were more apt to follow Adams into wilder locations than Mormon Country.[102]

It was not until the twenty-first century that the places in between Utah's scenic parks became a subject of renewed interest among a new generation of younger photographers. As a photo student at Brigham Young University in Provo, Christine Armbruster began making frequent trips into rural Utah to photograph small towns.[103] Her project, which became known as *Population 800* (2010–2016), was influenced by Lange's work in Utah in 1953. Like Lange, Armbruster nurtured a talent for accessing and depicting the lives of people during her travels. In her project, she photographed the citizens of these smaller communities and the surrounding landscapes, which, she believed, revealed the immensity of the space and the hardscrabble beauty of isolation.[104] A Texas native, Armbruster was originally disappointed by the vast desert landscape and "endless sagebrush," but through her travels she began to see how landscape shapes the culture and the people who inhabit it. Working in and around small Utah towns taught her "to actually be able to see and learn the differences."[105]

Throughout her travels, which she likened to an escape and therapy, Armbruster learned, like others before her, that each town "has a different feeling."[106] Yet, for her, that feeling was less and less tied to a Mormon past, and she admitted that she was not interested in perpetuating the "big religious stereotype" of Utah.[107] Her work brings into focus the fact that rural Utah is not as visibly distinct as it once was. This is evident in her photograph of Snowville, Utah, a small town of roughly two hundred inhabitants located on the Utah-Idaho border. According to the photographer, "It was a quiet town, late in the day, mostly a town with a large truck stop and a few farms."[108] Working in color, Armbruster brings out the dominant hue of rust. She photographed a plastic water tank and an old "Mormon" fence, but the juxtaposition of the tightly bound hay bales and the decaying farm structure with several generations of ruined roofs also catch her attention. In many ways old and new are indicative of the realities of mechanized farming in Snowville, which have similarities to farming in other areas across the United States. In addition to struggling farms, Armbruster photographed other signs of a changing landscape, including cowboys drinking Mountain Dew and workers from

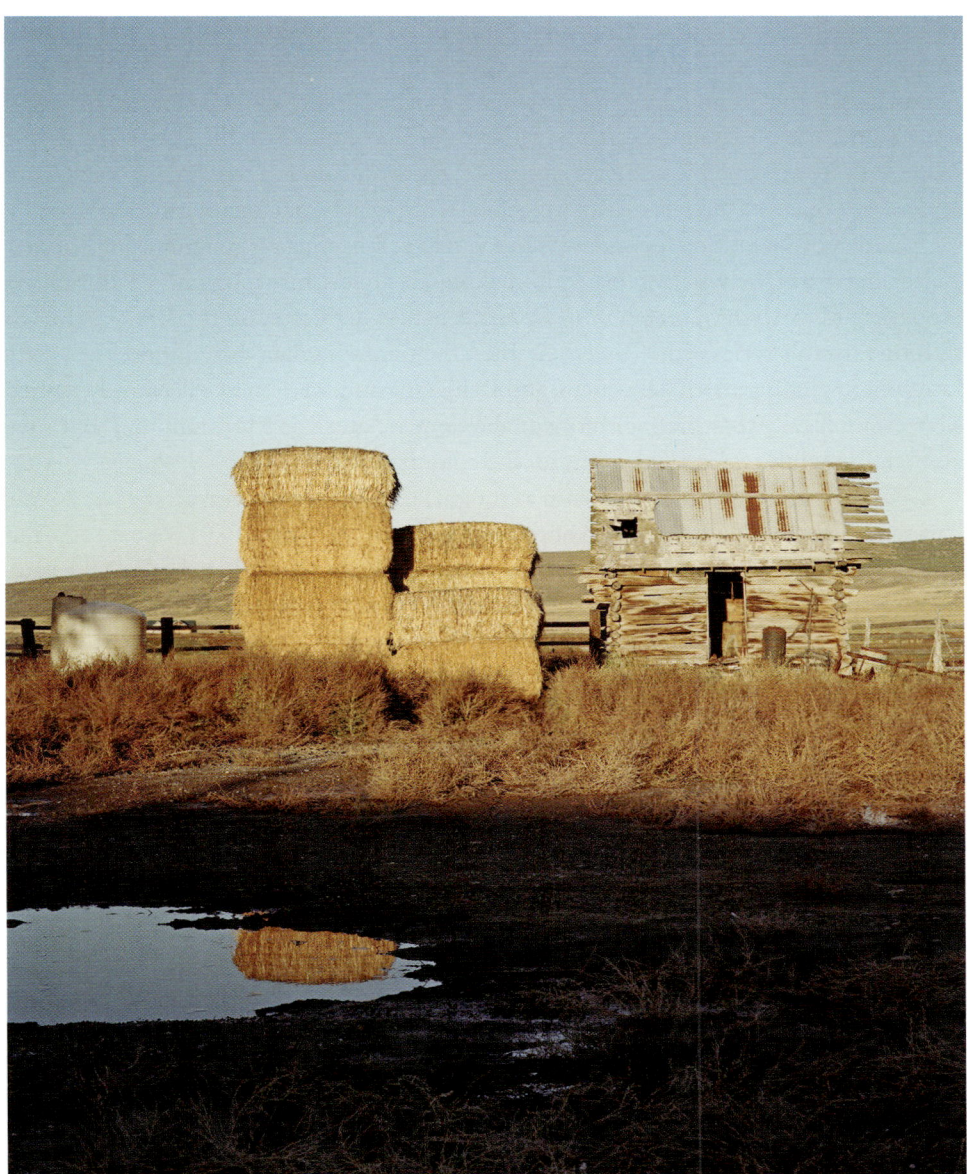

Fig. 11.10 Christine Armbruster, *Snowville the Northern Most Small Town on I-84. Population 170,* c. 2015. Used courtesy of the artist.

Central Asia in the local "greasy spoon" restaurant. In all, her work emphasizes not a Mormon past but an American present.

Even as the Mormon West was appearing more and more like other American places, the presence of the Mormon landscape did not disappear, and its visible reminders were still apparent in a new century. It is still difficult to miss the large streets in small communities like Escalante, as it is to overlook the presence of the Mani temple. Around 2017 the photographer Daniel George visited Manti early in the morning and documented the proud temple standing above the preparations for the Latter-day Saints Miracle Pageant, which would overtake this scene by the end of the day. George's work represents a renewed interest in exploring and recording a Latter-day Saints landscape.[109]

A native of Nebraska, George was not interested in making religious art, but as a Latter-day Saint, he was "interested in making art about [his] religion."[110] This desire brought him to Utah in search of places with names derived from the Bible and LDS scripture. In this series, titled *God to Go West,* the photographer visited more than sixty locations, including Eden, Jerusalem, and Lehi. Not only were these evocatively named sites examples of what Stegner termed "the nomenclature of Mormondom," but they also reaffirmed the aspirations of those who colonized the space.[111]

George documented these places in a straightforward style now associated with New Topographics, an influential group of photographers who in the 1970s were recognized for creating a more realistic portrayal of a "new" American West.[112] Instead of the pristine and sublime, which Ansel Adams favored, they sought contradictions, incongruities, and ironies. Those associated with the New Topographics style documented a more complex western landscape, with its varied assortments of strip malls, suburbs, vacant lots, and gas stations. George was profoundly influenced by this style and pursued "ironic relationships" and "the incongruity of idealism and reality" while employing a "pointed, if humorous, lens."[113]

George photographed the Manti temple from an angle that reveals his intentions. His view differed from Anderson's image of the temple emerging from the landscape and Adams's investigation of order and form. His viewpoint was also the opposite of Midgley's approach, yet in a similar fashion the temple seems to be hovering, disconnected and ethereal, in the distance. Unlike the other photographs, his work brings the emblematic structure into a new century by presenting it in its surroundings as a product of a distinctive culture in the twenty-first century. It is not an image of beauty, emergence, or redemption but a tongue-in-cheek investigation of the peculiarities of Mormondom.

Presented on the slope of Temple Hill, the Latter-day Saints Miracle Pageant was put on by local congregations and an army of volunteers from 1967 until 2019. Billed as a faith-promoting experience, it took its theme from LDS scripture and featured music, elaborate staging, and a large cast. Taken before the arrival of crews and crowds, George's photograph captures the infrastructure of and preparations for the large undertaking. It reveals six dark towers needed for sound and spotlights as well as large platforms disguised as artificial boulders awkwardly perched on the hillside. In the background the temple provides an elaborate backdrop to the festivities, which seem in George's image to be more stagecraft than structure. The army of empty chairs awaiting visitors, however, might be the most interesting element of this photograph. Not a part

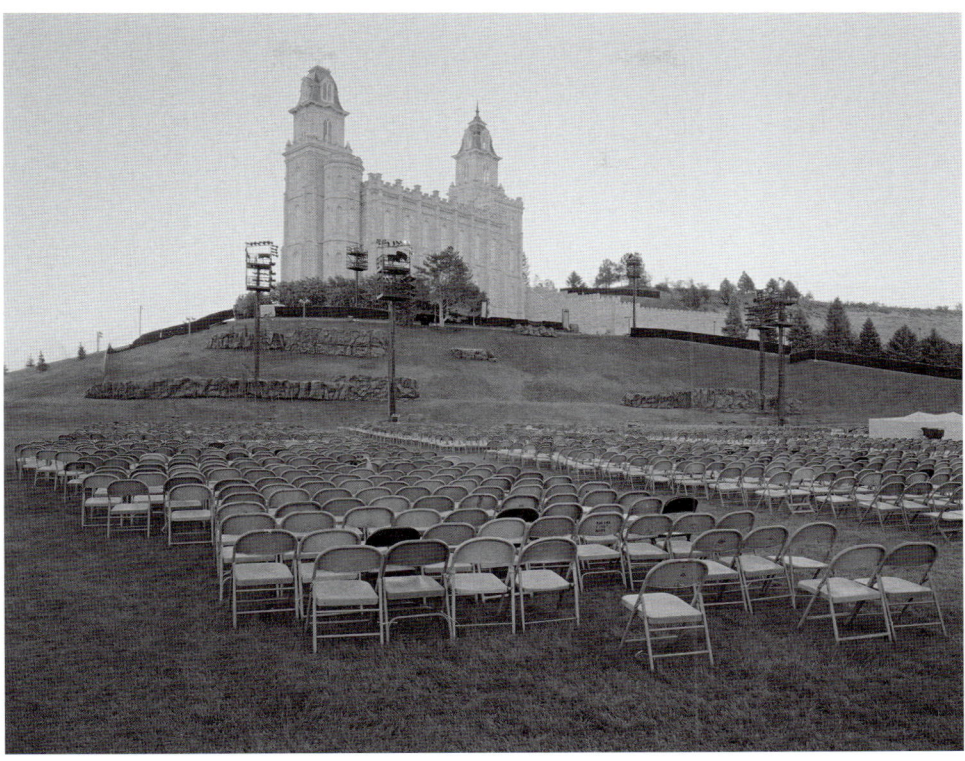

Fig. 11.11 Daniel George, *Manti, UT*, c. 2017–2019. Used courtesy of the artist.

of the Mormon landscape as much as the Mormon experience, folding metal chairs, like those in the photograph, are a common feature in LDS meeting houses and gatherings, providing "a winsome homogeneity and a reassuring sense of familiar simplicity" for those who use them.[114] Here, outside in quiet rows, they stand proxy for those who will later attend, and as symbol for the order and attention of the Saints.

V

In 2007 the New York–based photographer Vicky Sambunaris recorded the Salt Lake Valley from its eastern benches, basing herself on a street named Mohawk Way. In many ways this work brings this discussion full circle. For the Yale-trained photographer, who came out west for the first time later in her life, Utah is a place of diverse scenery and distinctive colors.[115] This photograph was not made as a statement on the Mormon landscape, but it certainly updates the conversation. Any photograph of Salt Lake City still connotes a Mormon past and presence. Sambunaris's image seems to be the fulfillment of Savage's view and aspiration, as it presents a seemingly prosperous and well-connected valley bisected by Interstate 80 and dotted by a golf course, tennis bubble, and grocery stores. Indeed, the desert seems to have blossomed as the modern rose.

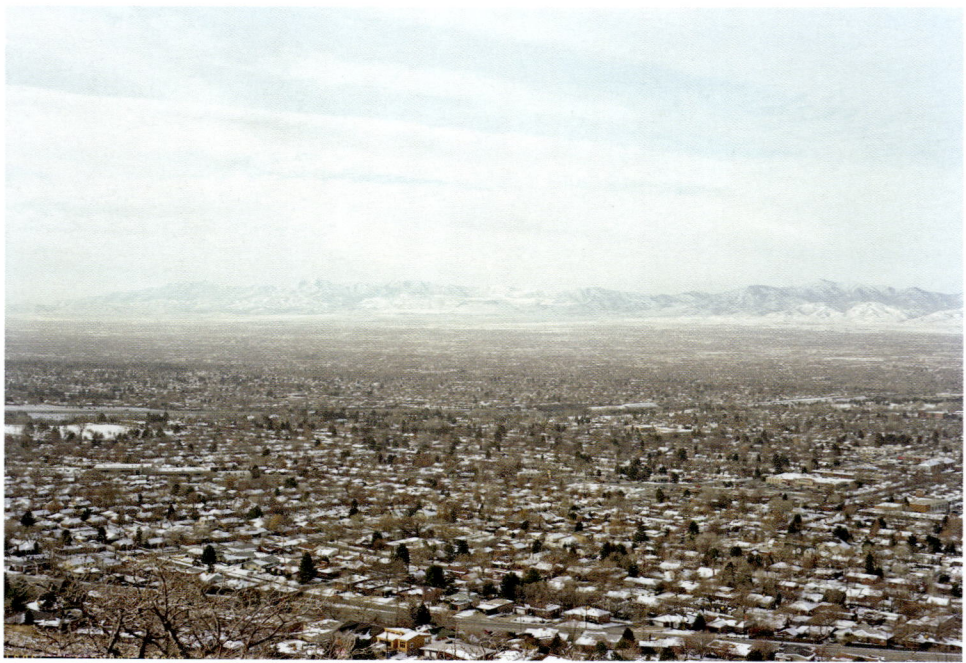

Fig. 11.12 Victoria Sambunaris, *Untitled [Salt Lake Looking at Oquirrh Mountains]*, Salt Lake City, Utah, 2007. Used courtesy of the artist.

However, unlike Savage's view, Sambunaris's image is not aligned with the city's grid. Instead, the photographer angled her camera to the southwest, away from the high-rise buildings that surround the Salt Lake temple and toward the Oquirrh Mountains and the massive physical disruption of the Kennecott Copper Mine. This is no longer a place that is insular.[116] More than eighty years earlier, Lange photographed the limitations of this landscape. While not as drastic as those seen in Widtsoe, there are consequences of overextension seen in the ever-present winter smog, created by the legion of automobiles needed to keep this city alive. The empty spaces in the valley in Savage's panorama have become a wide tract of snow-covered homes that have displaced rural populations across the Intermountain West. Springville, where Anderson worked and photographed families in the fields, will eventually be part of a continuous metropolitan area, a "strip city" stretching along the Wasatch Front that, as evinced by this photograph, increasingly looks like any other location in the West.[117] Yet farther afield, in places such as Manti and other small communities across Utah, perhaps a Mormon landscape is still present and visible, and will continue to have potential for the camera even as changes shape this distinctive space in the American West.

NOTES

1 Russell Lee to Roy Stryker, August 16, 1940, Roy Stryker Papers, University of Louisville Photographic Archives, Louisville, Kentucky; Sam Taylor, "Tourist Holiday," in *Among the Mormons: Historic Accounts by Contemporary Observers*, ed. William Mulder and A. Russell Mortensen (Lincoln: University of Nebraska Press, 1973), 460.

2 Russell Lee, caption to photograph, LC-USF34-037363-D, Library of Congress, Washington, D.C.

3 J. B. Jackson, "The Vernacular Landscape," in *Landscape Meanings and Values*, ed. Edmund C. Penning-Rowsell and David Lowenthal (Boston: Allen and Unwin, 1986), 68.

4 Jared Farmer, *On Zion's Mount: Mormons, Indians, and the American Landscape* (Cambridge, MA: Harvard University Press, 2008), 6, 9.

5 Martha A. Sandweiss, *Print the Legend: Photography and the American West* (New Haven, CT: Yale University Press, 2002), 160.

6 John Tagg, *Burden of Representation: Essays on Photographies and Histories* (Amherst: University of Massachusetts Press, 1988), 118. See also Roland Barthes, "Rhetoric of the Image," in *Classic Essays on Photography*, ed. Alan Trachtenberg (New Haven, CT: Leete's Island Books, 1980), 272.

7 Thomas Carter, *Building Zion: The Material World of Mormon Settlement* (Minneapolis: University of Minnesota Press, 2015), 284.

8 Nathan Rees, *Mormon Visual Culture and the American West* (New York: Routledge, 2021), 5–6. See also Richard V. Francaviglia, *The Mormon Landscape: Existence, Creation, and Perception of a Unique Image in the American West* (New York: AMS Press, 1978), 127–133.

9 Ralph V. Chamberlin, "Place and Personal Names of the Gosuite Indians of Utah," *Proceedings of the American Philosophical Society* 52, no. 208 (January–April 1913): 9, 12.

10 See map from Native Places at https://mlibgisservices.maps.arcgis.com/apps/webappviewer/index.html?id=82b345020c4248a9a0a27cb1febf3072.

11 Nels Anderson, *Desert Saints: The Mormon Frontier in Utah* (1942; Chicago: University of Chicago Press, 1966), 287.

12 Wallace Stegner, *Mormon Country* (New York: Bonanza Books, 1942); Fitz Hugh Ludlow, "Among the Mormons," *The Atlantic*, April 1864, 479.

13 Richard V. Francaviglia, *Go East, Young Man: Imagining the American West as Orient* (Logan: Utah State University Press, 2011), 13.

14 D. W. Meinig, "Mormon Culture Region: Strategies and Patterns in the Geography of the American West, 1847–1964," *Annals of the Association of American Geographers* 55, no. 2 (June 1965): 193.

15 For more on the Plat of Zion and its implementation, see C. Mark Hamilton, *Nineteenth-Century Mormon Architecture and City Planning* (New York: Oxford University Press, 1995), 24–31.

16 Thomas R. Vale and Geraldine R. Vale, *Western Images, Western Landscapes: Travels Along U.S. 89* (Tucson: University of Arizona Press, 1989), 88.

17 Stegner, *Mormon Country*, 345.

18 Meinig, "Mormon Culture Region." See also Wilbur Zelinsky, *The Cultural Geography of the United States* (Englewood Cliffs, NJ: Prentice-Hall, 1992), 47, 99.

19 Francaviglia, *The Mormon Landscape*, xv.

20 Rell G. Francis, *The Utah Photographs of George Edward Anderson* (Lincoln: University of Nebraska Press, 1979), 3; Paul F. Starrs, "Meetinghouses in the Mormon Mind: Ideology, Architecture, and Turbulent Streams of an Expanding Church," *Geographical Review* 99, no. 3 (July 2009): 335.

21 See Richard Neitzel Holzapfel and R. Q. Shupe, *Brigham Young: Images of a Mormon Prophet* (Salt Lake City: Eagle Gate, 2000). For more on the varied uses of photography by the LDS Church and its members, see Douglas F. Tobler and Nelson B. Wadsworth, *The History of the Mormons in Photographs and Text: 1830 to the Present* (New York: St. Martin's Press, 1987); Mary Campbell, *Charles Ellis Johnson and the Erotic Mormon Image* (Chicago: University of Chicago Press, 2016).

22 For more on the life and career of Savage, see Bradley W. Richards, *The Savage View: Charles Savage, Pioneer Mormon Photographer* (Nevada City, CA: Carl Mautz, 1995).

23 See C. R. Savage, "A Trip South with President Young in 1870," *Improvement Era* 3, no. 6 (April 1900): 293–299, 363–369, 431–436.

24 See Thomas Alexander, *Mormonism in Transition: A History of The Latter-Day Saints, 1890–1930* (Urbana: University of Illinois Press, 1986).

25 See Robert Taft, *Photography and the American Scene: A Social History, 1839–1889* (New York: Dover, 1964), 272.

26 C. R. Savage, *Views of Utah and Tourist's Guide* (Salt Lake City: Deseret News, 1887), 4–5; J. Philip Gruen, *Manifest Destinations: Cities and Tourists in the Nineteenth-Century American West* (Norman: University of Oklahoma Press, 2014), 62.

27 Patricia Nelson Limerick, *The Legacy of Conquest* (New York: W. W. Norton, 1987), 282.

28 Technical challenges prohibited photographs from being reproduced in printed media until the turn of the nineteenth century. The name "Great Salt Lake City" was adopted on August 22, 1847, and the "Great" was dropped twenty-one years later. John W. Van Cott, *Utah Place Names* (Salt Lake City: University of Utah Press, 1990), 327.

29 *Harper's Weekly,* August 18, 1866, 520–521.

30 Federal Writers' Program (WPA), *Utah: A Guide to the State* (New York: Hastings House, 1941), 98–99. See also Francaviglia, *Go East,* 93–94; Campbell, *Charles Ellis Johnson and the Erotic Mormon Image,* 1.

31 Rees, *Mormon Visual Culture,* 73; Leonard J. Arrington, *Great Basin Kingdom: An History of the Latter-day Saints, 1830–1900* (1958; Urbana: University of Illinois Press, 2005), 44.

32 *Salt Lake City: A Sketch of the Route of the Union and Central Pacific Railroads, from Omaha to Salt Lake City, and from Ogden to San Francisco with 12 Illustrations from Photographs by C. R. Savage* (New York: T. Nelson and Sons, 1870), 31.

33 See Marlin Jensen, "The Rest of the Story: Latter-day Saint Relations with Utah's Native Americans," *Mormon Historical Studies* 12 (September 1, 2011): 16–25.

34 "St. George Items," *Latter-day Saints Millennial Star* 37, no. 16 (April 19, 1875): 247.

35 Fitz Hugh Ludlow, *The Heart of the Continent: A Record of Travel Across the Plains and in Oregon* (New York: Hurd and Houghton, 1870), 325.

36 John A. Widtsoe, ed., *Discourses of Brigham Young: Second President of the Church of Jesus Christ of Latter-Day Saints* (Salt Lake City: Deseret Book, 1978), 474.

37 Savage quoted in Madeleine B. Stern, "A Rocky Mountain Book Store, Savage and Ottinger of Utah," *BYU Studies Quarterly* 9, no. 2 (1969): 152.

38 Ludlow, *The Heart of the Continent,* 302–303; Mark Twain, *Roughing It,* in *The Works of Mark Twain* (Berkeley: University of California Press, 1972), 2:115.

39 See Savage, *Views of Utah,* 18; C. R. Savage, "A Photographic Tour of Nearly 9000 Miles," *Philadelphia Photographer* 4 (1867): 288.

40 Federal Writers' Program, *Utah: A Guide,* 231; Martha Bradley Evans, "Constructing Zion: Faith, Grit, and the Realm of Possibility," *Utah Historical Quarterly* 89, no. 1 (Winter 2021): 68.

41 A. J. Russell, *The Great West Illustrated in a Series of Photographic Views Across the Continent; Taken Along the Line of the Union Pacific Railroad, West of Omaha, Nebraska* (New York: Union Pacific Railroad, 1869), n.p.

42 Evans, "Constructing Zion," 67.

43 See Russell, *The Great West Illustrated.*

44 Russell, *The Great West Illustrated.*

45 Gruen, *Manifest Destinations,* 172–175.

46 Twain, *Roughing It,* 122.

47 Carter, *Building Zion,* 135.

48 Federal Writers' Project, *Utah: A Guide,* 231.

49 For more on the complicated relationship between Mormons and the original residents of Utah, see Howard Christy, "Open Hand and Mailed Fist: Mormon Indian Relations in Utah, 1847–1852," *Utah Historical Quarterly* 46 no. 3 (Summer 1978); Paul Reeve, *Religion of a Different Color: Race and the Mormon Struggle for Whiteness* (New York: Oxford University Press, 2015).

[50] See Paula Richardson Fleming, *Native American Photography at the Smithsonian: The Schindler Catalogue* (Washington, DC: Smithsonian Books, 2003), 276–298.

[51] Charles R. Savage, "Correspondence: Dixie in and out of the Camera," *Deseret News,* April 17, 1875, 1.

[52] Rees, *Mormon Visual Culture,* 8.

[53] Ludlow, *The Heart of the Continent,* 302.

[54] Francis, *Utah Photographs,* 3.

[55] Federal Writers' Project, *Utah: A Guide*, 4.

[56] For more on Anderson and his work, including his five-year mission in which he photographed many sites of historical significance and which nearly ruined his family and his marriage, see Nelson B. Wadsworth, *Set in Stone, Fixed in Glass: The Mormons, The West, and Their Photographers* (Salt Lake City: Signature, 1996);

[57] Selvoy Boyer, *My Life's Story* (Springville, UT: Selvoy Boyer, 1984), 19.

[58] Chad F. Emmett, "The Evolving Landscape of the 21st Century," in *Geography, Culture and Change in the Mormon West, 1847–2003,* ed. Richard H. Jackson and Mark W. Jackson (Jacksonville, AL: National Council for Geographic Education, 2003), 59.

[59] Starrs, "Meetinghouses in the Mormon Mind," 331.

[60] Paul L. Anderson, "William Harrison Folsom: Pioneer Architect," *Utah Historical Quarterly* 43, no. 3 (Fall 1975): 253–254; Evans, *An Architectural Guide,* 334; Hamilton, *Nineteenth-Century Mormon Architecture,* 50–51; Federal Writers' Project, *Utah: A Guide*, 184.

[61] Carter, *Building Zion,* 183.

[62] See Francaviglia, *The Mormon Landscape,* 104.

[63] See Carter, *Building Zion,* 183, 241–242.

[64] See Fazal Shiekh and Terry Tempest Williams, *The Moon Is Behind Us: 30 Letters in Response to 30 Moons* (Göttingen: Stiedl, 2021), 31.

[65] Roy Stryker quoted in Rosa Reilly, "Photographing the America of Today," Popular *Photography* 3 (November 1938): 76.

[66] Dorothea Lange, quoted in Anne Whiston Spirn, *Daring to Look: Dorothea Lange's Photographs and Reports from the Field* (Chicago: University of Chicago Press, 2008), 56.

[67] Lowry Nelson, *The Mormon Village: A Pattern and Technique of Land Settlement* (Salt Lake City: University of Utah Press, 1952), 83.

[68] Dorothea Lange, caption, LC-USF-34-001357-C, Library of Congress.

[69] Francaviglia, *The Mormon Landscape,* 67–68.

[70] See James Swensen, "Dorothea Lange's Portrait of Utah's Great Depression," *Utah Historical Quarterly* 70, no. 1 (Winter 2002): 57–58.

[71] For more on the study of the Mormon village, consult Howard M. Bahr, *Saints Observed: Studies of Mormon Village Life, 1850–2005* (Salt Lake City: University of Utah Press, 2014).

[72] John A. Widtsoe, *Success on Irrigation Projects* (New York: John Wiley and Sons, 1928), 138.

[73] Khyber Forrester, "Mercy Death for Towns: Widtsoe Utah Taken off the Map," *Nation's Business* 25 (April 1, 1937): 64.

[74] Stegner, *Mormon Country,* 51.

[75] Brian Q. Cannon, "Struggle Against the Odds: Challenges in Utah's Marginal Agricultural Areas, 1925–39," *Utah Historical Quarterly* 54 (Fall 1986): 320; Karl C. Sandberg, "Telling the Tales and Telling the Truth: Writing the History of Widtsoe," *Dialogue: A Journal of Mormon Thought* 26 (Winter 1993), 103–104.

[76] Dorothea Lange, Field Notes, 27A, Dorothea Lange Archive, Oakland Museum of California, Oakland, California.

[77] Forrester, "Mercy Death for Towns," 64.

[78] Anderson, *Desert Saints,* 443.

[79] Church of Jesus Christ of Latter-day Saints, "Landscape and Life," https://history.churchofjesuschrist.org/exhibit/landscape-and-life-the-rural-setting-of-the-latter-day-saints?lang=eng#room-1, acessed December 2020.

[80] Clarence White, John Paul Edwards, et al., eds., *Pictorial* Photography in *America* (New York: Tennant and Ward, 1920), 72.

[81] See Grant Wood, "Revolt Against the City (1935)," in *John Steuart Currey and Grant Wood: A Portrait of Rural America*, ed. Joseph S. Czestochowski (Columbia: University of Missouri Press, 1981); Charles Morrow Wilson, *Roots of America: A Travelogue of American Personalities* (New York: Funk and Wagnalls, 1936), 4.

[82] Stegner, *Mormon Country,* 21–24. See also Marguerite Johnson [Maya Angelou], "Route U.S. 89: America's Rainbow Road," *Chrysler Events,* May 1956, 7.

[83] Carter, *Building Zion,* 177.

[84] See Richard G. Oman and Robert O. Davis, *Images of Faith: Art of the Latter-Day Saints* (Salt Lake City: Deseret Book, 1995), 104–105.

[85] Ansel Adams, "An Exposition of My Photographic Technique," *Camera Craft,* January 1934, 19.

[86] Ansel Adams, *Examples: The Making of 40 Photographs* (Boston: Little, Brown, 1983), 137.

[87] Adams, *Examples,* 137.

[88] See Ansel Adams, *The Portfolios of Ansel Adams* (Boston: Little, Brown, 1981), n.p.

[89] Adams, *The Portfolios of Ansel Adams.*

[90] Adams, *Examples,* 137.

[91] Charles Farrar Browne, "Artemus Ward's Panorama," in *The Complete Words of Artemus Ward* (New York: A.L. Burt Company, 1898), 362.

[92] For more on Adams and Lange's collaboration, see James Swensen, *In a Rugged Land: Ansel Adams, Dorothea Lange, and the Three Mormon Towns Collaboration, 1953–1954* (Salt Lake City: University of Utah Press, 2018).

[93] Charles Wollenberg, *Photographing the Second Gold Rush: Dorothea Lange and the Bay Area at War, 1941–1945* (Berkeley: Heyday Books, 1995), 16, 19.

[94] Emphasis in original. Dorothea Lange, Field Books, n.p., Lange Archive.

[95] Francaviglia, *The Mormon Landscape,* 125.

[96] Federal Writers' Project, *Utah: A Guide,* 9.

[97] Anderson, *Desert Saints,* 444.

[98] Joseph Earle Spencer, "Agricultural Villages in Southern Utah," *Agricultural History* 14, no. 4 (October 1940): 188–189.

[99] Dorothea Lange, Field Notes, n.p., Lange Archive.

[100] Thomas F. O'Dea, *The Mormons* (Chicago: University of Chicago Press, 1957), 238.

[101] Harold H. Martin, "Elder Benson Is Going to Catch It," *Saturday Evening Post* 225, no. 39 (March 28, 1953). See also Zelinsky, *Cultural Geography,* 86.

[102] An important exception to this lacunae may be Law's documentary project on Garland, Utah, which he completed in the 1970s. Unfortunately, this series has not been shown in public for decades.

[103] For more on Armbruster's series, see James Swensen, "Utah: 800: Christine Armbruster's Photo-essay and the Continuing Documentation of Small-Town Utah, 2010–2016," *Utah Historical Quarterly* 86, no. 4 (Fall 2018): 350–365.

[104] Christine Armbruster, email conversation with the author, May 2022.

[105] Armbruster, email conversation with the author, May 2022.

[106] Armbruster, email conversation with the author, May 2022.

[107] Christine Armbruster, interview with the author, February 17, 2017.

[108] Armbruster, email conversation with the author, May 2022.

[109] For more, see James Swensen, "The Old Toponymy and New Topography of Zion: Utah, Photography, and Daniel George's Series *God to Go West,*" *Utah Historical Quarterly* 90, no. 3 (Summer 2022): 228–244.

[110] Daniel George, "A Pointed Lens," interview with Glen Nelson, in *God to Go West* (New York: Center for Latter-day Saint Arts, 2019), n.p.

[111] Wallace Stegner, *Beyond the Hundredth Meridian: John Wesley Powell and the Second Opening of the West* (New York: Penguin Books, 1954), 192.

112 For more on New Topographics, see William Jenkins, *New Topographics: Photographs of Man-Altered Landscape* (Rochester, NY: George Eastman House, 1975); Britt Salvesen, *New Topographics: Robert Adams, Lewis Baltz, Bernd and Hilla Becher, Joe Deal, Frank Gohlke, Nicolas Nixon, John Schott, Stephen Shore, Henry Wessel, Jr.* (Göttingen: Steidl, 2009).

113 George, "A Pointed Lens."

114 Greg Allen, "Building Mormonism: History and Controversy in the Architecture of the Latter-day Saints," *Art in America*, December 22, 2022.

115 See Vicky Sambunaris, *Taxonomy of a Landscape* (Santa Fe, NM: Radius Books, 2013).

116 See Anderson, *Desert Saints*, 443.

117 Ron Molen, "The Mormon Village: Model for Sustainability," in *New Genesis: A Mormon Reader on Land and Community,* ed. Terry Tempest Williams, William B. Smart, Gibbs M. Smith (Salt Lake City: Gibbs Smith, 1998), 43.

12

THE PARIS ART MISSION

LINDA JONES GIBBS

In the spring of 1890, after nearly forty years of construction, the massive Mormon temple in the heart of Salt Lake City was nearing completion.[1] The importance of the presence of this towering Neo-Gothic structure cannot be overstated; it provided a symbol of endurance and permanence for a religious body that had been persecuted and repeatedly forced to relocate in search of peace and autonomy. Like the few Utah temples that were completed before it, the edifice would surely be decorated with interior large-scale murals.[2] Yet no plans had been made to adorn the interior walls with paintings and no artists had been commissioned.

Anticipating that such a need would eventually arise, Utah artist John Hafen (1856–1910) met with George Q. Cannon, first counselor in the Presidency, to broach the subject of church subsidy for art training in France for himself and fellow LDS artists Lorus Pratt (1855–1923) and John B. Fairbanks (1855–1940). Upon completion of their studies, they would use their enhanced skills to paint murals in the Salt Lake temple. At Cannon's request, Hafen researched the cost of such a venture, conferring with James T. Harwood (1860–1940), the first artist from Utah to study in Paris, who had gone in 1888. Based on Harwood's information, Hafen asked the church for $1,800 for one year in Paris for all three men and an extra $30 a month to help his financially struggling family.

Hafen followed up the meeting with a letter and an impassioned query. "What are we going to do, Brother Cannon," Hafen asked, "when one beautiful temple in Salt Lake City is ready to receive inside decorations? . . . Who is there amongst all people capable to do . . . justice to artwork that should be executed therein? If it should ever fall to my lot to receive assistance in this way," he continued, "I would esteem it the highest honor and the crowning point of my ambition."[3] As the ecclesiastical leaders were deliberating the artists' proposal, Hafen, Fairbanks, and Pratt hiked up to Ensign Peak in the foothills just north of the temple site, where they prayed for a positive response. There is no question as to Hafen and the other artists' religious devotion. However, they also must have realized that the art mission would provide them with an opportunity to enhance their skills and advance their careers in a way they could not otherwise afford. Within a few weeks, they received word that their request was approved, and they immediately made plans to leave by summer to give themselves time to study French before school started. The three artists, along with Edwin Evans (1860–1946), who would come in the fall, and Herman Haag (1871–1895), who arrived the following year, became known as "art missionaries."[4]

Before their journey to Paris, these Utah artists had been applying their craft with limited success. Hafen and Fairbanks both worked as portrait painters and supplemented their income with photography.[5] Pratt too was a painter but also worked as an English teacher at the University of Deseret (later the University of Utah).[6] Opportunities for exposure to the fine arts were limited in the Utah Territory. Before the Paris Art Mission, the talents of Hafen, Fairbanks, and Pratt were nurtured at the University of Deseret, where they took drawing and painting lessons from the first generation of Utah artists, George Ottinger (1833–1917), Danquart Anthon Weggeland (1827–1918), and Alfred Lambourne (1850–1926). Lambourne was self-taught, the Norwegian-born Weggeland had had a year of formal training at the Danish Royal Academy in Copenhagen, and the Pennsylvania-born Ottinger had studied briefly with J. Alden Weir in New York and later at the Pennsylvania Academy of Fine Arts. Their paintings, although charming at times, are generally unsophisticated, their figures primitive in their modeling and the backgrounds often formulaic. Likewise, the known paintings produced by Hafen, Fairbanks, and Pratt before going to France are rudimentary and sometimes nothing more than copies of second-rate European paintings. But Ottinger and Weggeland were clearly aware of their own artistic limitations in Utah and encouraged their aspiring students to seek further education abroad.

With the completion of the temple looming, the time seemed right to seek that education with a devotional intent for its application. On June 3, 1890, Hafen, Fairbanks, and Pratt were officially set apart as art missionaries by Apostles Anthon H. Lund and Heber J. Grant and by Seymour B. Young of the First Council of the Seventy. The missionaries were not to proselytize but rather were charged with a singular focus to enhance their artistic skills and, in so doing, benefit the building of the Kingdom of God on earth.[7] On June 23, the men boarded the Denver and Rio Grande Railroad en route to New York.

Separation from their families was difficult for all involved—Hafen left a wife and five children, Pratt a pregnant wife and four children, and Fairbanks a wife and seven children. The same rail system that propelled them on their journey east had also brought homesteaders west in such large numbers that the superintendent of the census that same year declared the "frontier" was no more.[8] Nevertheless, the artists were heading for a cosmopolitan milieu unlike any they had previously experienced. Soon Hafen would acknowledge from his new home in Paris: "There is much to see and learn for a young man who has been raised in a pioneer life thousands of miles from the confines of civilizations and culture."[9]

IN FRANCE

After an eleven-day ocean voyage, the art missionaries landed in Liverpool and traveled to London, where they bought art supplies and visited museums. They arrived in Paris on July 24, the much-celebrated annual Pioneer Day in Utah. As their fellow Utahns back home were commemorating the forty-third anniversary of the Mormon pioneers' arrival in the Salt Lake Valley, these "pioneers in reverse" secured housing in the Latin Quarter. They were assisted by Utah artists currently living in the French capital, Cyrus Dallin (1861–1944) and John Willard Clawson (1858–1936).

Paris in 1890 was an exhilarating city of modernity. The Eiffel Tower had opened the previous year in time for the Universal Exposition of 1899, and the Beaux Arts–style Pont Alexandre III, a marvel of nineteenth-century bridge engineering spanning the Seine, was under construction. The art missionaries were among the approximately fifteen hundred Americans who were studying in this uncontested art center of the Western world. While they may not have quite shared American artist William Merritt Chase's exclamation that he would rather go to Europe than to heaven, the art missionaries were thrilled to be there. Hafen declared that "the very air seems pregnant with art and refinement."[10]

The Utah artists attended the Académie Julian, a private school founded in 1868 by painter Rodolphe Julian.[11] It was open to any aspiring artist and was originally intended to serve as a training ground to prepare students for the rigorous entrance requirements to the prestigious government-sponsored École des Beaux-Arts. As the popularity of Julian's school grew among international students, largely Americans, it came to rival the government school in attendance. In twenty-five years it had grown from twenty pupils to over one thousand and from a single studio to five branches throughout the city.

Hafen recalled walking the three miles from his apartment to the atelier and his shock at the unglamorous appearance of the school's exterior and interior:

> Leaving those grand boulevards, we entered Rue St. Denis, a narrow street. With quick steps we pass grocery shops, drug, dry goods, vegetable, and every other kind of shop . . . expecting every moment to behold the magnificent Academy building my fancy had pictured when all at once here we are! Yes we were here in a narrow court or yard of a feather cleaning and pillow factory among packing boxes, and rickety patched up old buildings. Ascending an old stairway, we landed in the skylit atelier of the renowned school of painting. Part of the walls were covered with prize studies from models and part with daubs and smears of waste paint flipped on the wall with the palette knife.[12]

Unlike the École des Beaux-Arts, the curriculum at the Académie Julian offered neither theory nor art history. Technical facility was paramount. At both academies students were first taught the fundamentals of draftsmanship, which they were required to master by copying engravings and plaster casts, before moving on to drawing and finally painting the human figure. Although any sketching was seen as an integral part of the creative process, it was ultimately to be refined by careful reworking in order to appear "finished." The artists were up early, often by 5:00 or 5:30 a.m., to study French or anatomy before breakfast. They arrived at the Julian by 8:00 a.m., where on Mondays professional models were lined up waiting for a job. The students voted on both the models and the poses, which would last for one week. Hafen described the daily routine:

> The model poses 45 minutes and rests fifteen repeating this from eight to twelve a.m. and from one to five p.m. every day of the week. When the school is full which is generally the case during the winter months there is a model posing in each room.... [T]he professors, all of whom are eminent French painters, visit the ateliers Wednesday and Saturday morning and give each student a short but telling criticism. It is truly wonderful how these master minds understand the needs or failings of each student and how readily they grasp the individuality of each artist.[13]

By September, the three art missionaries had been joined by a fourth, Edwin Evans, who also enrolled in the Académie Julian. In a letter to his former teacher Weggeland, Evans described his reaction to the art on view in the Luxembourg Palace and the Louvre: "These paintings are so far beyond expectation that I could only stand viewing them in blank amazement." He extolled the virtues of Paris. "Everybody takes a great interest in art," he wrote. "The air is full of it, and the show windows are lined with it."[14]

Academy students would often spend three to four weeks on a single drawing. One prime example of a life study is Edwin Evans's *Female Nude* (1892). This carefully delineated standing nude woman leaning against the end of a table epitomizes academic drawing with its carefully developed halftones, solid grasp of anatomy, and superb draftsmanship. The model's head, slightly turned away and drawn from a low vantage point, is expertly rendered, especially given the foreshortening. Her profile is drawn with precise, delicate lines and modeled with an adept handling of shadow and light.

The Académie Julien ateliers were overseen by some of the most prestigious academic painters of the day, primarily portrait and historical painters who had exhibited regularly at the salon of the Société des Artistes Français and were often recipients of prestigious awards. The instructors frequently taught in teams of two and often varied significantly from one to another in both methods and personality. This allowed the students more chances to find a sympathetic teacher in line with their own proclivities.[15] Hafen recalled: "The conduct of the school partakes more of the idea of a workshop than a school no one presides . . . everyone is left to choose his own 'course.'"[16] Jules Joseph Lefebvre (1836–1911), one of Hafen's teachers, was liberal in his approach, never insisting that a student adopt his style even though he personally emphasized finesse of line over energetic expression. One team with whom the Utah artists studied, Jean-Paul Laurens (1838–1921) and Benjamin Constant (1845–1902), had harsh disagreements with each other. Laurens offered training akin to Beaux-Arts methods—rigid drawing

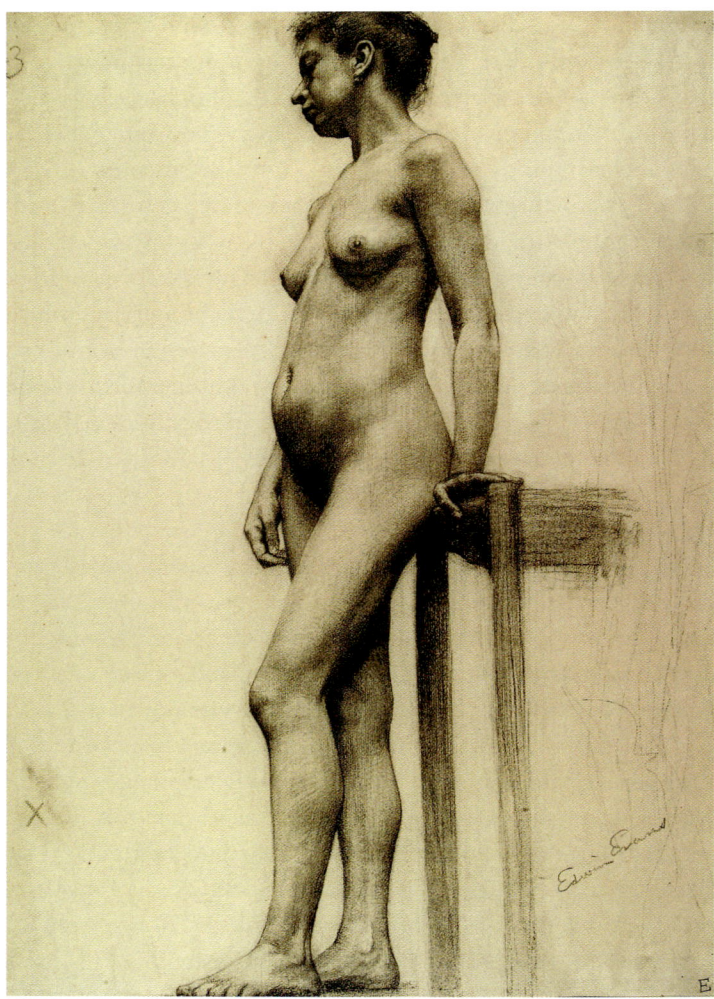

Fig. 12.1 Edwin Evans, *Female Nude*, 1892, charcoal, 24 3/4″ × 18″, Brigham Young University Museum of Art.

and painting with precise tone and color—while Constant embraced the value of observation from nature.

After initial frustrations due to lack of proper preparation for the rigors of academic study, the Utahns found that their work at the Julian eventually held up well. Hafen had two drawings accepted into the weekly competitions, the *concours,* in which the best student works were voted on and hung on the academy walls. Edwin Evans would join Hafen and Pratt in having a drawing accepted in the weekly *concours.* The fifth art missionary to study at the academy, Herman Haag, joined the group sometime in 1891. The youngest, at only nineteen years of age, he had shown great promise as a student under

James T. Harwood in Utah. Haag too would distinguish himself at the Académie Julian, competing with forty other students to win a prize in composition a year after his arrival for a drawing, *John the Baptist Presenting Christ Before the People*.[17]

The artist missionaries joined the newly formed American Art Association of Paris, a gathering place near their living quarters for American art students, complete with a library and reading room that featured exhibits, lectures, and various forms of entertainment. The Utahns would have felt comfortable not only associating with fellow countrymen but also in an atmosphere that did not allow gambling or liquor. The city's liberal environment, however, was at times a challenge. Fairbanks informed his wife that he would never let an unmarried son of his go to Paris without the best of companions. Although, ironically, the art missionaries expressed no discomfort drawing the female nude (see Figure 12.1), Fairbanks was appalled that even unmarried women could walk into a room when a nude man was posing.

The letters that the art missionaries wrote home contain no mention of what specific art they saw outside their studios, but they had ample opportunity to view a multiplicity of styles in 1890 Paris—Academicism, Realism, Tonalism, Impressionism, Pointillism, and the Symbolist movement. Three major exhibitions at the time attracted hundreds of thousands of visitors—the popular salons of the Société des Artistes Français, the Salon des Indépendants, and the salons of the Société Nationale des Beaux-Arts.[18] In addition, artists increasingly chose to show their works to better advantage in smaller galleries and clubs. Hafen wrote of the benefits of free entrance to the galleries of the Luxembourg and the Louvre.

Of all the styles the art missionaries were exposed to, the naturalism of Impressionism and its precursor, the Barbizon School, both with the attendant replications of the sensorial experience of the out-of-doors, left a lasting impression.[19] Adherents of both movements rejected historical, biblical, and mythological themes that were prized by the official salons and academies in favor of direct observation of nature as subject. In Impressionism, figures and forms in nature became most important as surfaces that reflect light and appeared different in different atmospheres. There was a shift from permanence to the fleeting moment and immediate sensation, achieved through the use of loose brushstrokes and brilliant color.

Upon their arrival in Paris, Impressionism was no longer the controversial movement it had been in previous decades, when its tenets first challenged the ideals of the official salon of the Société des Artistes Français. Even though the novelty of Impressionism had worn off among the artistic elite, one could still see Monet's now famous haystack series, fifteen of which were exhibited in May 1891 at the popular Galeries Durand-Ruel in Paris. It is not known if the Utah artists saw Monet's works, but the fact remains that there is a proliferation of Impressionist haystack scenes painted by the Utah artists, produced both in France and after their return home. Edwin Evans's *Hayfield* (1904) is particularly Monet-like in its focus on a single haystack looming large and slightly off-center in the landscape. As was typical with Impressionist painting, brushstrokes are loosely applied, capturing the flickering nature of sunlight; their vigor adds to the sense of immediacy. The oblique shadow of the haystack, indicative of an afternoon sun, evokes Monet's interest in the nuances of various times of day and seasons. The shadow itself is filled with subtle color, consistent with the absence in Impressionism of dark colors. A dirt path curves from the foreground to a trio of grain stacks in the middle ground, beyond which are atmospheric lavender hues of a distant landscape.

Edwin Evans's *Grain Fields*, painted in France in 1890, also shows the influence of Impressionism with its sunlit atmosphere, loose brushstrokes, and pastel hues. However, the composition is more structured than that of many French Impressionist paintings. The haystacks and field of uncut hay are arranged in diagonal lines that lead the viewer to the small figure, farmhouse, and distant tree-dotted horizon. The inclusion of a peasant working in the fields thematically ties the painting to the Barbizon School, but here the worker serves no social/political purpose, as field laborers often did in the paintings of Jules Breton or Jean-François Millet, in which they often loom larger against the land-scape, their hard work heroized. In Evans's work the figure is small and relegated to the background, dwarfed by the large stacks of grain.

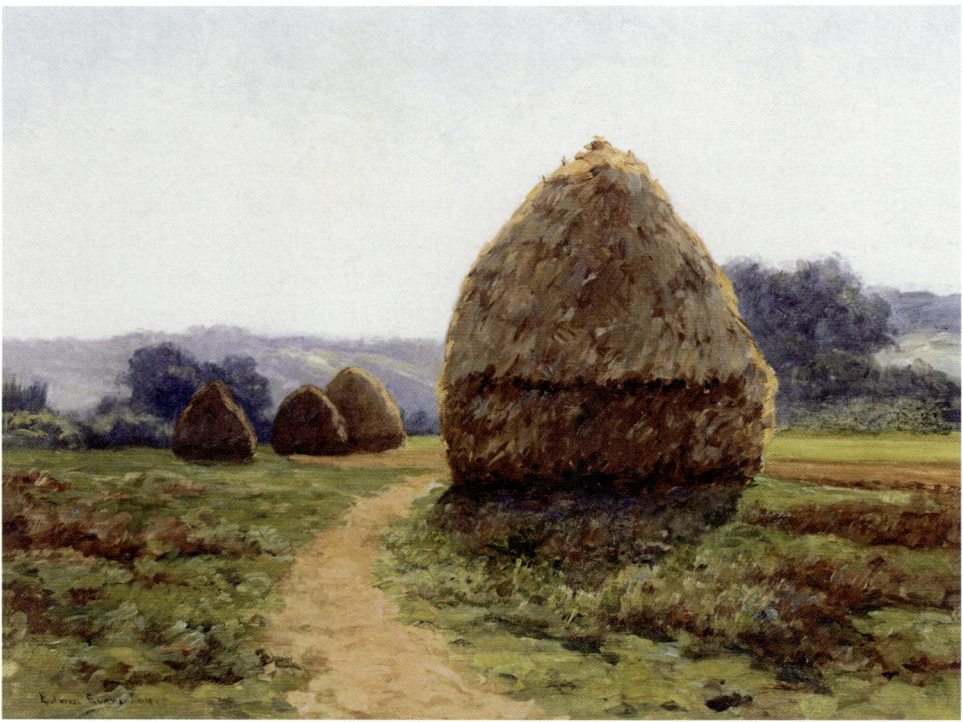

Fig. 12.2 Edwin Evans, *Hayfield,* 1904, oil on canvas, 26" × 33 3/4", State of Utah Alice Merrill Horne Art Collection. Courtesy Utah Arts & Museums.

This underlying compositional armature and coherent organization of pictorial elements are reflective of academic principles and typical of many paintings done by American Impressionists, who couldn't quite give themselves over entirely to the Impressionist notion of capturing a fleeting moment.[20] It is highly possible that the art missionaries saw the works of their expat contemporaries. In June 1891, Galeries Durand-Ruel showed a large exhibition of leading American artists, including Childe Hassam, John Twachtman, and William Merritt Chase, all of whom would become leading proponents of American Impressionism in the early twentieth century.[21]

Early into his studies Hafen seemed to have become disenchanted with the painstaking exactitude of academic draftsmanship. "I still love carefull [*sic*] fine work with an absence of brush daubs in it," he wrote after only three months in Paris, "only I am trying to get more power, life, and spirit into my work."[22] This was achieved not only through exposure to Impressionist and Tonalist painting but also through his own excursions into the countryside to paint in the out-of-doors. As early as their first month at the Académie Julian, Hafen, Fairbanks, and Pratt traveled to Auvers-sur-Oise, just north of Paris, for a week of *plein air* painting. Auvers had long attracted painters, including Paul Cezanne (1839–1906), Camille Pissarro (1830–1903), and Charles-François Daubigny (1817–1878). That very summer, on July 29, a then unknown artist by the name of Vincent Van Gogh (1853–890) had taken his own life on the outskirts of the village.

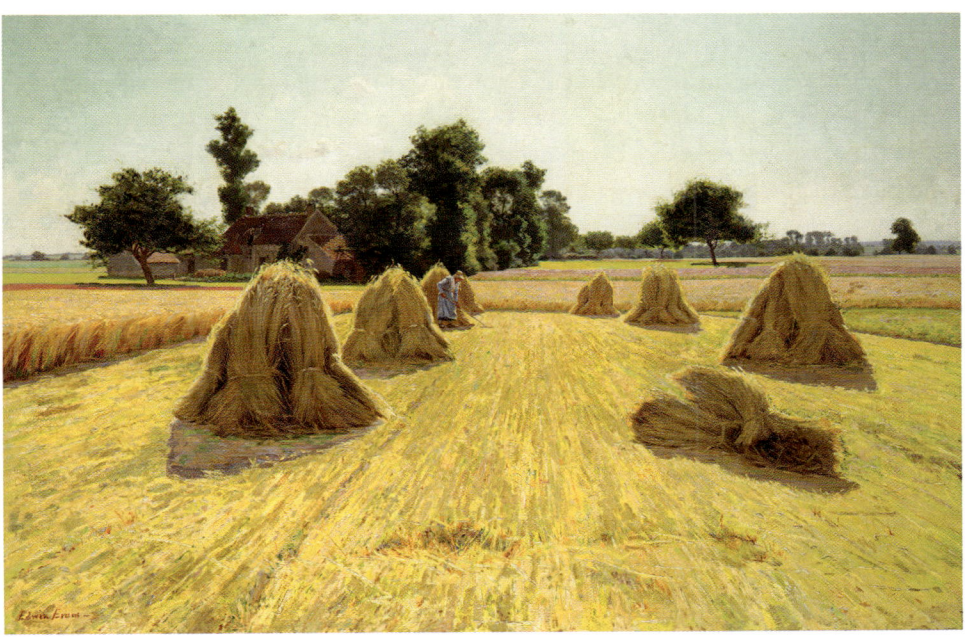

Fig. 12.3 Edwin Evans, *Grain Fields*, c. 1890, oil on canvas, 38 3/4″ × 57 7/8″, Brigham Young University Museum of Art.

Like most art students in Paris, the art missionaries also spent the summer months away from the crowded, cigarette-smoke-filled, noisy, and unventilated atmosphere of the atelier to paint in the countryside. In a letter to George Q. Cannon, Hafen explained, "We all quit school in the summer and study from nature outdoors."[23] In an undated letter home he wrote, "I have now about 15 or 18 sketches from nature: nearly all represent a change or turning point in my art career. . . . [T]hey are all studies . . . striving after truthful drawing and blocking in the pure lights and shades of nature without any regard for detail."[24] Hafen returned to Auvers in April 1891, and the following summer he and Fairbanks painted and sketched in the village of Chilleurs-au-Bois, about sixty miles south of Paris. En route, Hafen wrote of "passing quaint French villages through forests and fields. Peasants are working on their acres and farming vineyards, plowing and generly [sic] preparing for seed time."[25] The experience of painting out-of-doors greatly influenced Hafen, who would later declare: "The painter should disabuse his mind of all traditional theories . . . and must look to nature for inspiration."[26]

In March 1891, Hafen received a letter from George Q. Cannon, who assured him that the artists would become useful upon returning home by imparting the knowledge and skill they were gaining and "in giving pleasure to those who have a taste for art."[27] Cannon also promised to send an additional $500 to be shared among them and that more would soon follow. He expressed the First Presidency's support should they need to stay longer to complete their education despite the fact that "money is exceedingly close with us now." He continued: "We have had the most stringent time for three months past that has ever been seen in the territory," and he went on to reference "heavy taxes, mismanagement, squandering of funds."[28]

It is unclear what mismanagement Cannon was referring to, but temple construction costs were over budget. Furthermore, church resources were severely threatened with the passage by the U.S. government in 1887 of the Edmunds-Tucker Act, which prohibited the practice of polygamy and punished participants with a fine and imprisonment of up to five years. The act dissolved the corporation of the Church of Jesus Christ of Latter-day Saints and directed the confiscation by the federal government of various church properties and businesses, leaving President Wilford Woodruff to wonder whether or not the church would ever be able to pay its debts. In addition, there was the cost of legal fees as well as support for polygamous families whose husbands and fathers were in prison.[29] In the summer of 1891, Hafen returned home due to his family's dire financial circumstances. Church support was ongoing for the remaining art missionaries, and in the fall Cannon wrote to Pratt:

> We feel deeply interested in your success. We want you to become good artists, and to avail yourselves of all the advantages which the French government has so liberally put within the reach of students. . . . You have our prayers that you may be very successful in gaining a knowledge of art. We desire you to have favor in the eyes of the professors and your fellow students, and also to have favor with the Lord.[30]

Hafen maintained contact with his fellow artists in Paris, and in April 1892, he informed them that the temple was nearing completion and he would be making arrangements for the mural painting. That same month the artists heard directly from the First Presidency. A letter from Wilford Woodruff, George Q. Cannon, and Joseph F. Smith stated:

> We shall have the rooms selected that we wish to have artistically decorated and shall do all in our power to have the walls put in a suitable condition for the work. We shall probably give Brother Hafen some work to do, but shall reserve other important rooms until we hear from you concerning your intentions . . . we do not wish to suggest anything that will conflict with what you consider your progress in art. We would like you to get the full benefit of the teaching which Paris furnishes.[31]

While church leaders did not wish to pressure the artists to return before they felt ready, they needed the murals done in time for the temple dedication in April 1893. The letter continued:

> At the same time . . . we would be pleased to have you return home to spend the fall and winter months finishing the Temple. It may be that you would be pleased to have the size of the rooms given you that we wish artist work put upon, and also the character of the painting and then if you were furnished with these you might be able to get your designs to better advantage there. . . We would like to get the benefit of the best artistic skill now in the Church in the decoration of this grand building.[32]

The following month the remaining art missionaries received a letter from Hafen asking them to send in some sketches for two rooms in the temple, the garden room and the world room. They were informed that the artist who submitted the best sketch would be given the contract with the privilege of inviting others to assist. The church dispatched additional funds totaling $1,500 to the artists in the spring of 1892. However, in a letter of May 1892 to Pratt, Fairbanks, Haag, and Evans, the First Presidency expressed some disappointment at having not received a reply regarding what the artists might be envisioning for the mural decorations. Church leaders sent temple plans and dimensions to assist them, but there is no record that any preparatory drawings were done in France. During the early summer of 1892 Fairbanks and Pratt were again painting in Auvers-sur-Oise under the tutelage of Albert-Gabriel Rigolot (1862–1932), an instructor at Académie Julian who worked in the landscape tradition of the Barbizon School as well as in Impressionism. It would be their last excursion into the French countryside, as Pratt returned home that July and Fairbanks did so in August.

THE TEMPLE MURALS AND THE QUESTION OF PATRONAGE

There is nothing recorded in LDS history to explain why murals became part of temple interiors after the church settled in Utah.[33] The visual arts had been a part of Utah culture from the early decades of Mormon settlement. Artists found work painting portraiture and also stage curtains and scenery for the Salt Lake Theater, founded in 1862. Numerous artists were engaged in painting panoramas, large-scale paintings depicting historical events in Mormon or scriptural history. The canvases were sewn together and rolled on a pole so that the images could proceed from one to the next, accompanied by a written script.[34] The implementation of temple murals also coincided with an exceptional growth period in the United States of the art of mural painting. In the last decades of the nineteenth century, buildings grew larger and more classical in size and style, and churches and other major structures employed artists to embellish their interiors. In 1876–1877, a team of American artists led by John La Farge (1835–1910) painted murals covering 21,500 square feet of the interior of Trinity Church in Boston, initiating a new era of architectural decoration. Not long after the Trinity Church murals were completed, Utah artists were commissioned to paint murals on walls of the St. George temple, the first Mormon temple completed in Utah. Despite Utah's geographical isolation from urban cosmopolitanism, its citizenry was not ignorant of cultural trends in the Northeast, nor was the church hesitant to adopt these trends to enhance its religious architecture. In 1892, for example, the church commissioned three stained glass windows for the Salt Lake temple from the prestigious Tiffany Glass and Decorating in New York.

The earliest LDS Church precedent to temple murals occurred in 1855–1856, when William Ward (1827–1893), an early Utah architect, sculptor, and artist, was hired to paint trees, animals, and plants on the walls of the endowment house in Salt Lake City. This structure, on the northwest corner of the temple block, was used for marriages and other sacred ordinances prior to the completion of the temple.[35] Ward's paintings, along with real plants, were intended to evoke the Garden of Eden. The purpose of the murals in all LDS temples was to envelop the temple-goer within a ritual ceremony performed in a series of rooms that were decorated to depict various scenes from Genesis. Within these rooms, patrons received ordinances and instructions deemed necessary to be exalted in heaven.[36] Patrons proceeded from the creation room to the garden (of Eden) room and the world room, the last representing the land into which Adam and Eve were cast from the Garden of Eden. The murals were the stage set, the scenery, for the drama unfolding about the beginning of humankind as presented by live actors. The murals were an enhancement of the temple experience, the surfaces upon which the patrons' eyes would gaze while listening to and participating in the ceremonies. Finally, temple-goers reached the celestial room, symbolic of the highest degree of heaven, which was beautifully furnished and brightly lit but void of murals.

In October, two months after the last of the art missionaries returned to Utah, they, along with Weggeland, were informed by church architect Joseph Don Carlos Young that the First Presidency wished the artists to begin painting the garden and world rooms of the Salt Lake temple as rapidly as possible. The dedication of the building was planned for the following April. However, it wasn't until January 1893 that the walls were finally ready to receive artwork. Hafen and Evans worked on the garden room, assisted by Pratt, who helped paint foliage, and their former teacher Weggeland, who painted the animals. The world room was painted by Weggeland, Evans, and John B. Fairbanks. Their academic studies of the human figure would not be put to use, as Adam and Eve were not depicted in the murals, presumably because the temple-goers were to project themselves into those roles.

Several preparatory oil sketches have survived, including one of the Garden of Eden by Hafen. Brilliant light filters through the landscape; the sensitively rendered tiger, lion, and sheep, shown in peaceful coexistence, are backlit by the sun. There is a sophisticated handling of three-dimensional space filled with diffuse atmospheric effects, which reflects Impressionist influence, as do the pastel colors. Delicately painted plants and trees frame the bucolic interior. Another preliminary unsigned study of the Garden of Eden was possibly painted by Weggeland, who was assigned to paint the animals. The creatures are rendered in a rather primitive fashion, their faces cartoon-like, evoking the stylistic naiveté of the many paintings entitled *The Peaceable Kingdom* by American folk artist Edward Hicks (1770–1849). One would have hoped the finished mural would have been an improvement on these weaknesses, but a surviving photo of the finished mural shows a depiction very similar to this particular oil sketch. Numerous competently painted unsigned studies for the garden room, ranging in size from 24″ × 18″ to 30″ × 36″, have also survived that represent various sections of the wall—tall branches dotted with birds, swans in a lake surrounded by flowering plants, a stream flowing through a pastoral scene with a bear, camels, grazing giraffes, and herons, all painted with pastel hues.[37]

A series of delicately painted smaller-scale renderings of the garden room complete with numbered grids for transference to the walls also have survived. Their sophisticated brushwork and compositions indicate they were probably done by the more competent Pratt, Hafen, or Evans. Lush foliage fills the scene; rich colors abound, ranging from blues and lavenders to a wide range of greens. The brushwork is active, animating the trees and sky and suggestive of a vital, fertile land. Several of the oil sketches have animals blocked into the grids, their basic but well-rendered anatomy suggesting a hand other than Weggeland's. In one study, a waterfall cascades over rocky terrain; the form of a bear is depicted crossing the stream. There are deer among the trees on a mound of greenery, and bison in the distance. While conceived as a sketch, the painting is well thought through in terms of coloration and composition.

On April, 7, 1893, the Salt Lake temple was dedicated. Church president Wilford Woodruff blessed every part of the temple in his dedicatory prayer, from the curtains,

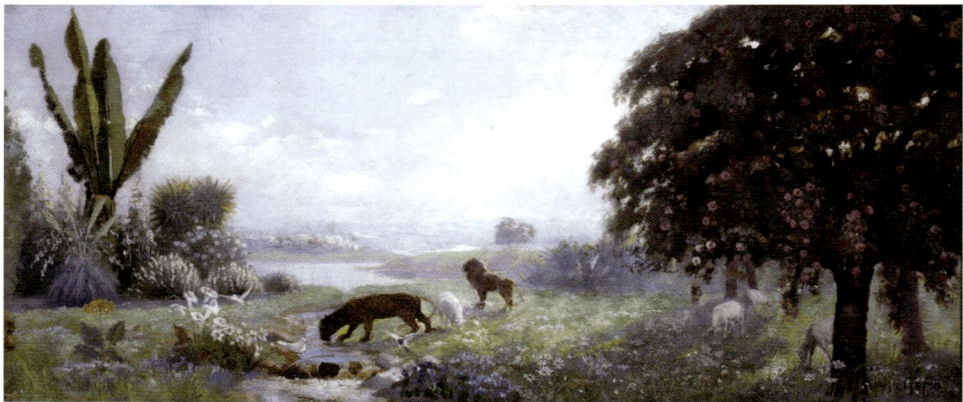

Fig. 12.4 John Hafen, *Garden of Eden Study*, oil on canvas, 16″ × 36″, Church of Jesus Christ of Latter-day Saints Church History Museum.

glass, china, and precious stones to the more mundane washbasins, pipes, and wires. Also consecrated were the pictures and statuary. A local journalist noted how the "genius of the artist" had transferred vividly realistic scenes to the walls and ceiling: "Forest scenery, streams, mountains and wild beasts are depicted with such marvelous skill and startling effect that the spectator is almost convinced that he is standing in the midst of the creation wilds." The author also remarked that "three young artists were sent to Paris to study frescoing and equip themselves for that branch of the work."[38] The artists were not given credit by name, nor were their studies in Paris correctly described, as they were not studying the art of fresco, but it was clear that their mission abroad was familiar.[39]

There was also a lengthy article about the finished temple for the church's youth magazine *The Contributor* in which there is scant mention of the murals and again no mention of the artists by name. The author writes that the walls and ceilings of the garden room "are luminous with warm and natural effects in landscape, beasts, and birds." The world room is described as "gorgeously frescoed and in its harmony of coloring and accuracy of drawing is as enchanting as a dream."[40]

The murals were further described by James E. Talmadge in his 1912 book *The House of the Lord*. He wrote of the tranquility of the garden room:

> There are sylvan grottoes and mossy dells, lakelets and brooks, waterfalls and rivulets, trees, vines and flowers, insects, birds and beasts, in short, the earth beautiful,—as it was before the fall . . . for in every part . . . it speaks of sweet content and blessed repose. There is no suggestion of disturbance, enmity or hostility; the beasts are at peace and the birds live in amity.[41]

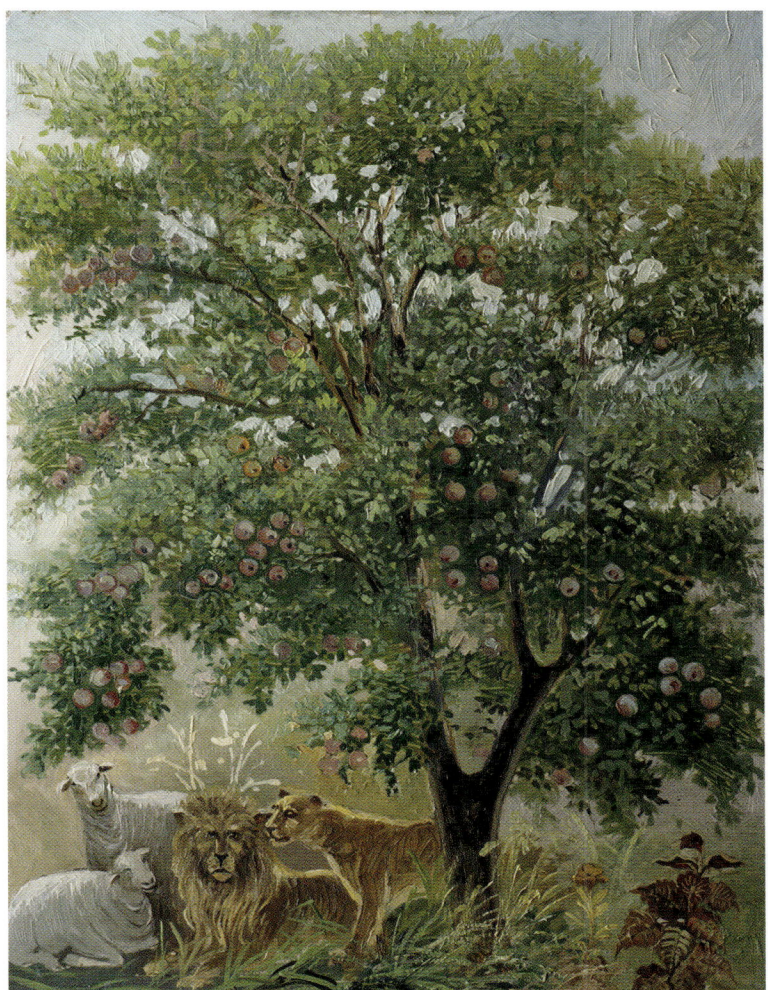

Fig. 12.5 Unsigned (attributed to Dan Weggeland), *Garden Room Study,* oil on board, 24″ × 18″, Church of Jesus Christ of Latter-day Saints Church History Museum.

Talmadge also contrasted the calm of the garden room with the contention depicted in the world room:

> Here the rocks are rent and riven, the earth-story is that of mountain uplift and seismic disruption. Beasts are contending in deadly strife. . . . The more timorous creatures are fleeing from their ravenous foes or cowering in half-concealed retreats . . . the trees are gnarled, misshapen, and blasted; shrubs maintain a precarious roothold in rocky clefts; thorns, thistles, cacti, and noxious weeds abound; and in one quarter a storm is raging.[42]

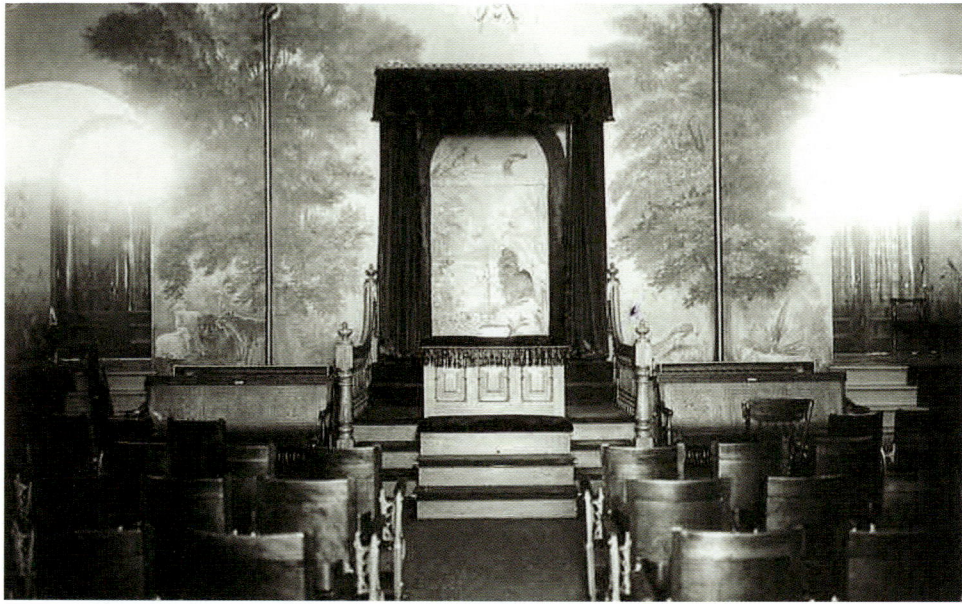

Fig. 12.6 Charles R. Savage, *Garden Room, Salt Lake Temple,* 1911, photograph, Church History Library, The Church of Jesus Christ of Latter-day Saints.

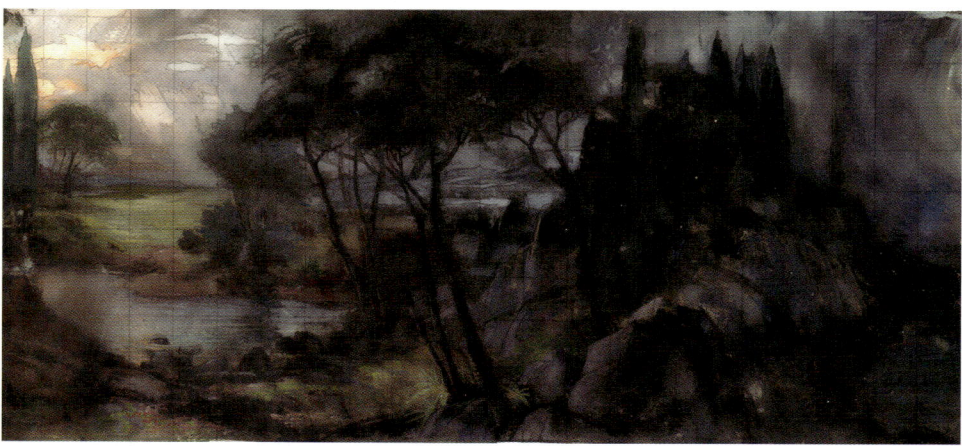

Fig. 12.7 Unsigned, *Garden Room Study, Salt Lake Temple,* c. 1892, oil on board, Church of Jesus Christ of Latter-day Saints Church History Museum.

While these descriptions are highly engaging, the few photographs that exist of the murals reveal wall paintings that are competent but underwhelming, a disappointment especially given the promising garden room studies. Granted, these photographs lack clarity and are in black and white, making it difficult to fully assess the murals' aesthetic

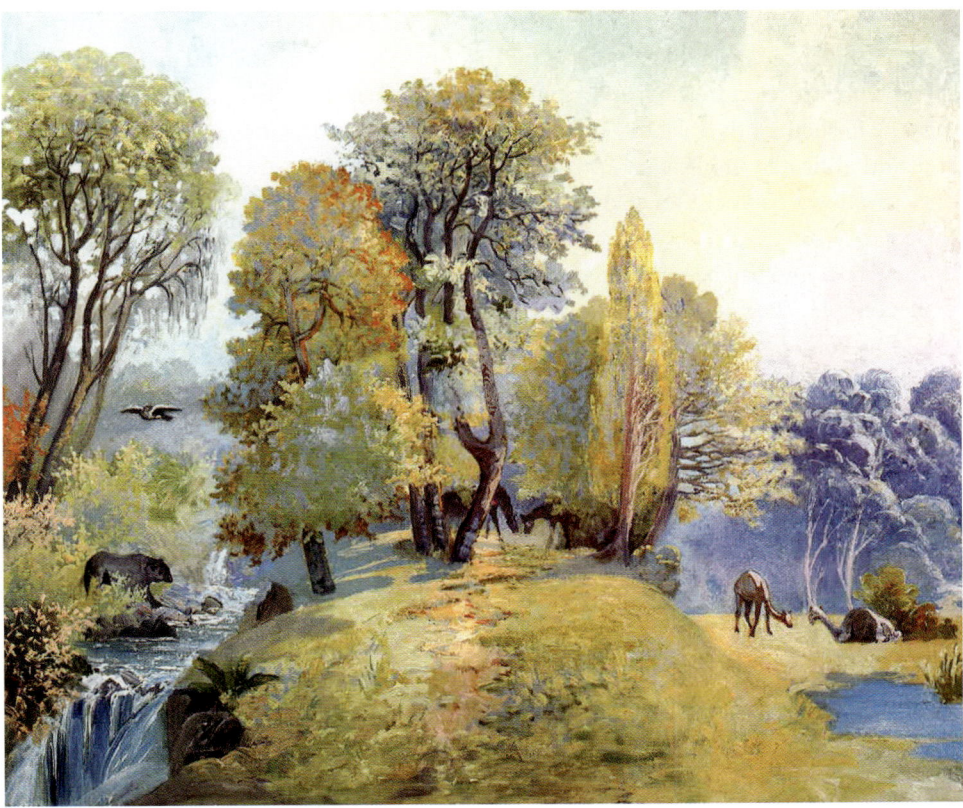

Fig. 12.8 Unsigned, *Study for the Garden Room, Salt Lake Temple*, c. 1892, oil on canvas, 30″ × 36″ Church of Jesus Christ of Latter-day Saints Church History Museum.

qualities. Photos of the world room show the craggy and partially decaying trees described by Talmadge and enmity between animals, such as a pair of rams whose horns are locked in battle and two lions ferociously fighting. However, the delineation of these animals is rudimentary. The murals' lack of complexity and finesse was likely due to the short time frame the artists had to execute the job, which amounted to little more than three months.[43] The academicism taught at the Académie Julian, such as tight drawing and careful building of form, are not present, but these attributes run counter to the typical broad style of mural painting. Judging by the quality of many of the preliminary studies, however, the art missionaries' skills certainly increased after Paris. Sadly, the high aesthetic aspirations on the part of both the artists and church leaders were subsumed by institutional needs and time constraints.

The Paris Art Mission has been referenced over the years as an enviable act of art patronage by the LDS Church, but such an appellation is debatable. John B. Fairbanks, in a letter to church president Joseph F. Smith, refers to the money they were given as a loan.

Indeed, on June 20, 1890, Hafen, Pratt, and Fairbanks all signed a statement attesting that they had been given by the Presiding Bishopric "a loan to assist me in going to Paris to obtain instruction in the fine arts which amount I promise to pay after my return to this city in such kinds of labor in my profession as may be required."[44] Apostle Anthon H. Lund indicated in his diary entry of January 13, 1893, that the money given the artists was a down payment for a commission and noted with sarcasm:

> The artists who had been in Paris and Bro. Weggeland gave us their bid for decorating the Temple. They only asked the small sum of 17000 dollars! Bro. Joseph F. Smith said he considered it unreasonable and outrageous. The artists expressed themselves as having only charged one third of what such work is generally rated at. The brethren generally thought it was unfair for them to ask such a price especially as the Church had advanced means to educate them. They were requested to amend their bid.[45]

The artists would receive far less than their request. Each was paid $300 a month for their work on the murals. The cost for the art mission itself totaled $3,660, a relatively minor outlay, representing only about one-tenth of 1 percent of the $3.5 million it cost to build the temple.

From an art historical standpoint, patronage of the arts typically offers a degree of long-term financial security; most often it took the form of either commissioning artworks on an ongoing basis or providing for day-to-day needs so that an artist was free to work without being concerned with living expenses. Perhaps a truer example of LDS Church art patronage than the art mission came in the form of a stipend paid in 1901 to Hafen, by then a father of ten, to assist him with his ongoing economic difficulties. Hafen contracted to receive $100 a month for two years, at the end of which time he would receive $1,000. He would ultimately receive a total of $4,000 in exchange for more than two hundred paintings.[46]

The church leaders provided not only financial support but also encouragement in their letters to the missionaries. One such communication from George Q. Cannon expressed a vision for a benefit broader than just the temple murals: "We want to see our young men qualified in every direction, so that the Lord's name may be glorified and his cause advanced through their labors and their proficiency in all the arts and sciences."[47] Although the Paris Art Mission was not exemplary of art patronage in the traditional sense, it was a pronounced demonstration of the church's desire to have its artists excel and thereby enrich not only the temple but also the Utah art community at large.

FROM THE INNER SANCTUM OF THE TEMPLE TO THE OUTER WORLD: UTAH LANDSCAPE AS ALLEGORY

The Paris Art Mission resulted in benefits for Utah art far beyond the completion of the original temple murals, which have long ceased to exist.[48] The artists' contributions to arts organizations and art education in Utah were widespread. Inspired by what they had seen in France, the artists held in 1893 what would become an annual exhibition under the auspices of Utah's first strong local artists association, the Society of Utah Artists, formally organized in 1895.[49] Many of the paintings they produced in France were on public view for the first time. An article from an 1897 periodical noted the success and influence of these annual exhibitions:

> Continuing usually about a month, with as many as forty of the best pictures sold, and the whole community awakened through the papers and personal interviews to the subject of art, no one could doubt, not only that the artists themselves are benefitted but that the public taste is educated and stimulated. So great was the interest aroused at the recent exhibition . . . that the schools, as a whole, were enabled to attend.[50]

These exhibitions gave everyone the opportunity to view paintings by the French-trained artists, as not all citizens had access to the temple interior once the dedication took place. Arts activist Alice Merrill Horne waxed nostalgic, recalling "the glory of those first annual exhibitions" when "the town invariably turned out to see. And in those days, people bought pictures."[51] Even if the initial excitement around the artists' journey waned, their influence continued. Hafen's donation of a painting in 1903 to Springville High School planted the seed for subsequent donations from other artists, and eventually the formation of the Springville Museum of Art. Edwin Evans established the Academy of Art in Salt Lake City along with Hafen and Harwood. Evans also served as the president of the Institute of Fine Arts at the University of Utah, where he taught for nearly twenty years. Evans, Fairbanks, and Hafen taught at Brigham Young Academy in Provo. Fairbanks was the first supervisor of art education in the Ogden city schools.

Perhaps the greatest legacy of the Paris Art Mission is the proliferation of paintings produced by the art missionaries after their return home. Their creative output after Paris constitutes some of the most stunning examples of late nineteenth- and early twentieth-century Utah art. The influence of the Barbizon School and Impressionism persisted in their work long after their return to Utah. In 1905, Hafen wrote a letter of introduction to a potential collector in Salt Lake City, touting his French credentials and experiences:

> I have enjoyed a very thorough training in the Julian Academy of Paris under the greatest of French masters; besides living and associating on the grounds and in the studios of the Barbizon painters Daubigny, Rousseau, Millet and others, thus imbibing the art influence and spirit of these great men in their native haunts.[52]

The influence of the Barbizon School is seen in Hafen's painting *Forest Solitude, Brighton* (1902), which depicts a serene and intimate woodland interior with limited color range, close values, and poetic atmosphere. A red dirt path cuts through fields dotted with wildflowers, bringing the viewer into a thicket of dark green trees. A long tree trunk lies

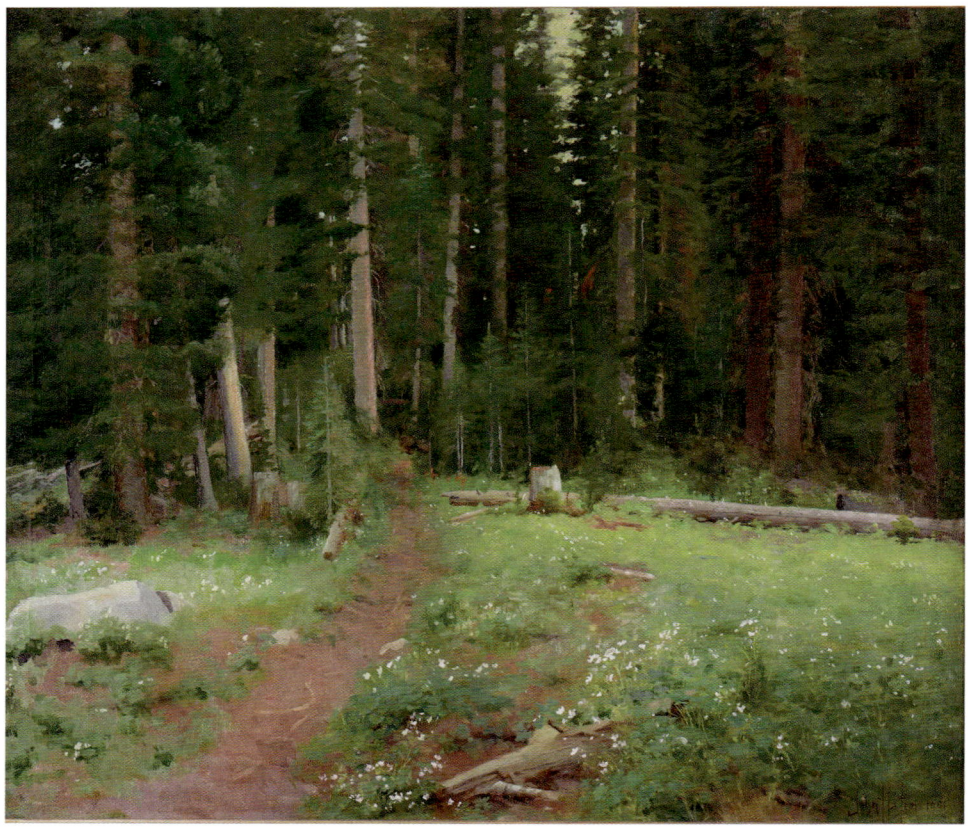

Fig. 12.9 John Hafen, *Forest Solitude*, 1902, 36″ × 42″, oil on canvas Church of Jesus Christ of Latter-day Saints Church History Museum.

at the edge of the timberland, creating a strong horizontal line to offset the dominance of verticality in the forest trees. There is only a hint of sky where the trees slightly part along the upper edge and thus no flood of sunlight to disturb the deep tonal harmony.

Hafen's *Girl Among the Hollyhocks* is, in contrast, a striking example of Impressionist influence both thematically and stylistically. Young women placed within floral gardens were a popular subject for both American and French Impressionists, with the potential to depict sunlight, dazzling color, and decorative exuberance. Hafen painted his daughter Delia admiring a tall stand of hollyhocks in their backyard. Delia is shown turned away from us, her identity unimportant, as is typical for Impressionism. The true subject is the light and atmosphere that envelop her. She does not dominate nature but is placed comfortably within it. The daubs of paint imitate the flickering nature of sunlight. Her figure and the forms of the flowers blend together in a mass of sunlight and shadow, the color of her white dress and pink hair bows echoing the color of the flowers.

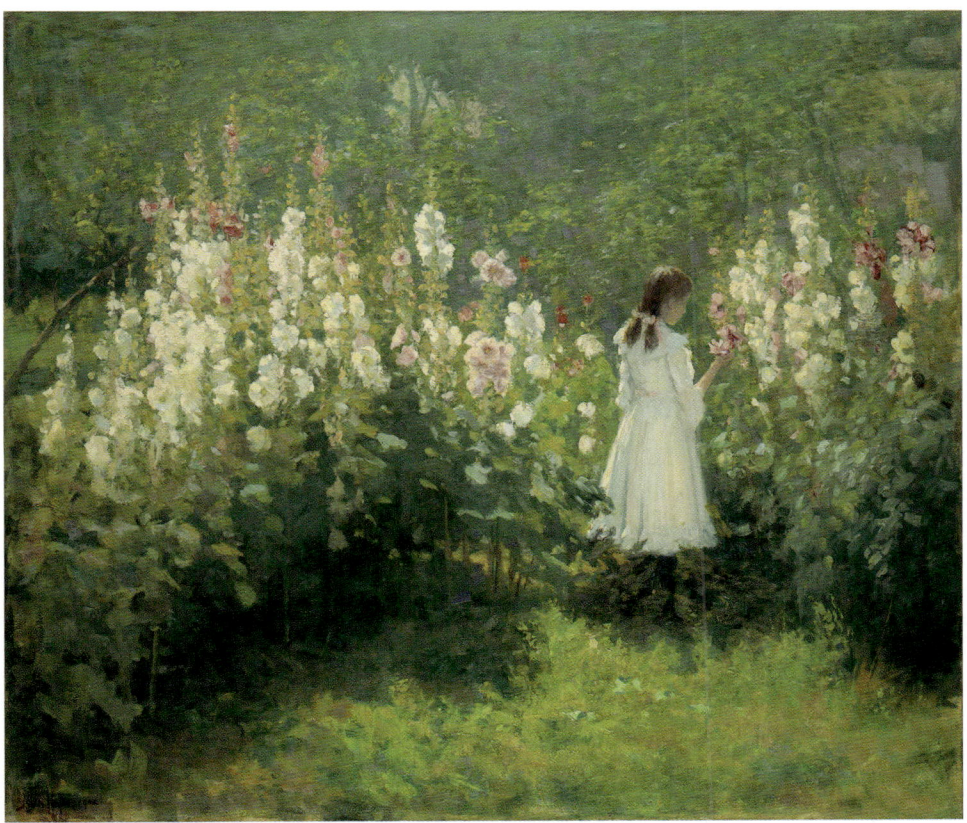

Fig. 12.10 John Hafen, *Girl Among the Hollyhocks*, 1902, 36″ × 41″, oil on canvas, Church of Jesus Christ of Latter-day Saints Church History Museum.

Hafen, Pratt, Evans, and Fairbanks all painted harvest scenes in France and continued to depict that theme once back home in Utah. The state was still largely agrarian and the images embody the ongoing pioneer ethic of hard work. Pratt's *The Harvest* (1896) is similar to Edwin Evans's French scene *Grain Fields* (see Figure 12.3).[53] Both works contain the sunlight effects and vigorous brushwork of Impressionism. The academic armature of one-point perspective seen in Evans's work persists in Pratt's depiction. The haystacks form directional lines that lead the viewer from the foreground to the farmers and horses involved in threshing the grain in the distance. Even the slope of the distant mountain range takes us to the focal point of activity.

Depictions of the Utah landscape, those purely scenic and those of farm labor, are not merely topographical or the sum of their aesthetic components. The images are embedded with theological implications. Just as the untouched wilderness of the Northeast was viewed as the new Eden by painters of the Hudson River School in the 1820s–1840s, Utah was symbolic of an Edenic place of refuge for a beleaguered

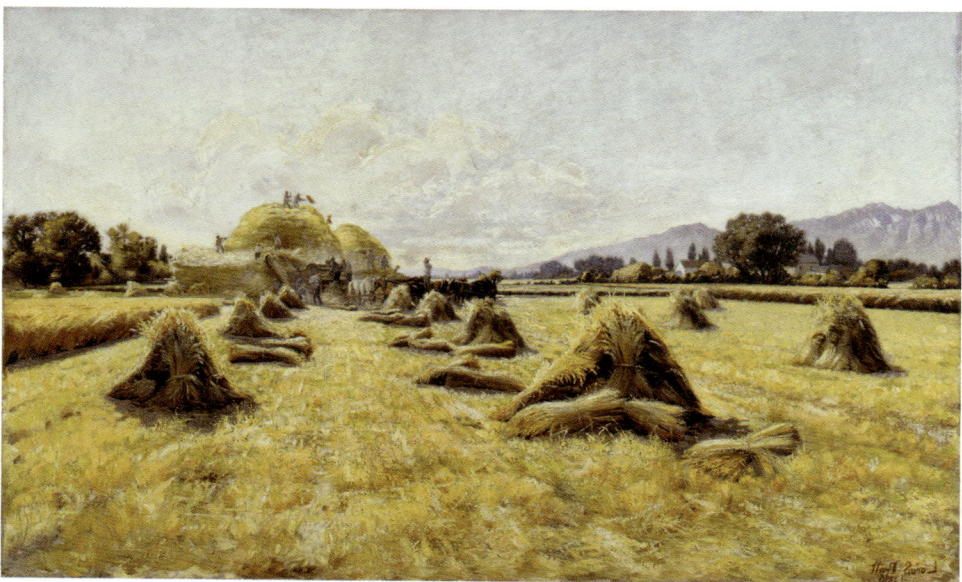

Fig. 12.11 Lorus Pratt, *The Harvest*, 1896, 30″ × 48″, oil on canvas, Church of Jesus Christ of Latter-day Saints Church History Museum.

religious body. However, the Utah Territory was a desert—not the fecund fields and forests that the Hudson River School artists celebrated. The depictions of grain stacks or of men harvesting in the fields are often cast against the region's dramatic mountain ranges, an intersection of the two realms depicted by the art missionaries in the temple. Through hard work, the Mormons were cultivating their own garden in the temporal world. While there is no visible enmity between humans or animals, there is certainly an allusion to the divine mandate given to Adam and Eve after they left the Garden of Eden: "In the sweat of thy face shalt thou eat bread."[54] Utah would become paradise regained and reclaimed through hard work, exemplary of Henry Nash Smith's reference to the American agrarian dream as "the Garden of the World."[55] The art missionaries' temple murals of the Garden of Eden and the world conceptually spilled over and onto their easel paintings.

In Hafen's *Bluffdale* (1902), a frieze of shimmering poplar trees on the left evokes Monet's series *Poplars on the Ept River*, which had been on view in Paris in 1891. A solitary man, a farmer perhaps, walks through an open field toward an expansive valley in the distance. This is not Adam alone in the garden; houses dot the distant valley. Neither is he Adam in the lone and dreary world, for the landscape that lies ahead is welcoming and bright. The man carries a shovel on his shoulder, indicative of some labor he has either left behind or is heading toward. The log fencing along the path is a more subtle indication of the presence of humans. The man is civilizing nature but does not diminish its glory. While the Salt Lake temple murals have ceased to exist, the landscape

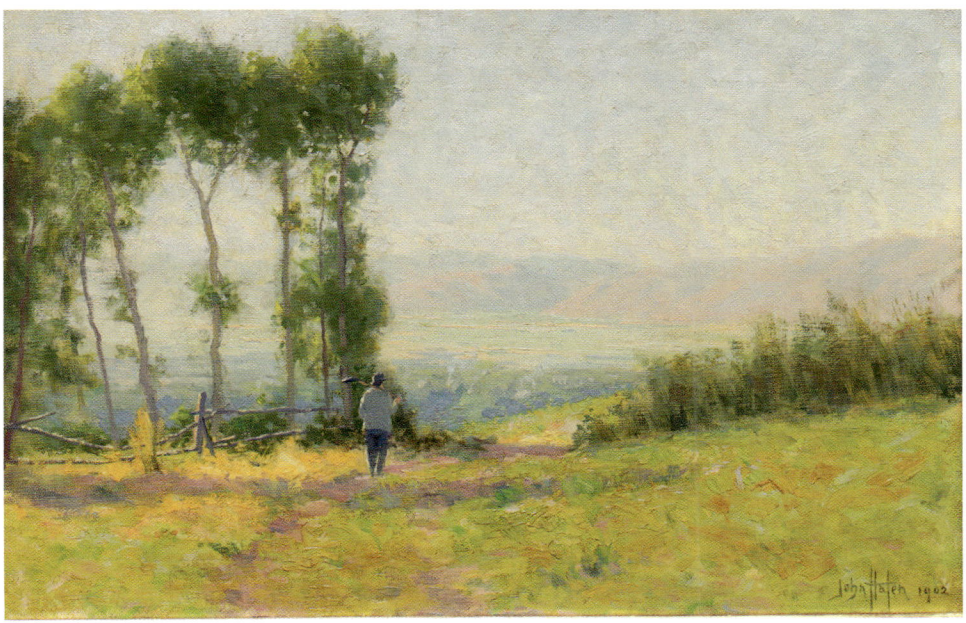

Fig. 12.12 John Hafen, *Bluffdale*, 1902, 16″ × 24″, oil on canvas, Church of Jesus Christ of Latter-day Saints Church History Museum.

paintings by the art missionaries with their inherent spiritual geography remain and continue to uplift and enrich the visual consumers of Utah art history.

NOTES

1 Brigham Young identified the site for the construction of a temple a mere four days after the Mormons arrived in the Salt Lake Valley, which was on July 24, 1847.

2 There were no murals in the first two Mormon temples, built in Kirtland, Ohio (dedicated in 1836), and Nauvoo, Illinois (dedicated in 1846). The St. George temple, completed in 1877, was the first temple to have murals, painted in 1881 by Dan (Danquart) Weggeland, Carl Christian Anton (C. C. A.) Christensen, and Samuel Jepperson (1855–1931). John B. Fairbanks painted the world room in 1917–1918. The Logan temple, dedicated in 1884, was the second to have murals, which were painted in 1883 by Dan Weggeland, William Armitage (1817–1890), and Reuben Kirkham (1845–1886), possibly with assistance from C. C. A. Christensen. The Manti temple, dedicated in 1888, had murals by Danquart Weggeland and C. C. A. Christensen.

3 Letter from John Hafen to George Q. Cannon, March 25, 1890, Harold B. Lee Library, Brigham Young University Special Collections, quoted in Linda Jones Gibbs, *Harvesting the Light: The Paris Art Mission and Beginnings of Utah Impressionism* (Salt Lake City: Church of Jesus Christ of Latter-Day Saints, 1987), 17.

4 The fact that Pratt was the son of Orson Pratt, a founding member of the church's Quorum of the Twelve Apostles, may have aided the petition. This chapter seeks to build upon and expand the author's earlier research on the topic of the Art Mission, which was the subject of an exhibition at the Museum of Church History and Art (now the Museum of Church History) and accompanying catalogue: Gibbs, *Harvesting the Light*. For more biographical information on individual artists, see Robert S. Olpin, *Dictionary of Utah Art* (Salt Lake City: Salt Lake City Art Center, 1980), Robert S. Olpin, Vern Swanson, and William Seifrit,

Utah Art (Layton, UT: Gibbs Smith, 1991): Robert S. Olpin, Vern G. Swanson, and William C. Seifrit, *Artists of Utah* (Layton, UT: Gibbs Smith, 1999).

[5] At this time, Hafen lived next door at the time to Charles R. Savage (1832–1909), Utah's acclaimed photographer, who had hired him as an assistant in the late 1870s. Hafen would soon leave Salt Lake, establishing his own photographic gallery first in American Fork and then in Springville, where he would permanently settle.

[6] The University of Deseret, founded in 1850, is Utah's oldest institution of higher education. It became the University of Utah in 1892, four years before Utah achieved statehood. Prior to the art mission, Pratt had studied in New York, during which time he visited the Centennial Exposition in Philadelphia, where he saw a range of American and European painting. This experience instilled in him a desire to go abroad, and in 1885 he traveled briefly with his wife and children to Paris.

[7] There was a precedent to the Paris Art Mission when Brigham Young sent temple architect Truman O. Angell (1810–1887) to Europe in 1856. Angell was set apart as a missionary and instructed to make sketches of major architectural structures to inspire him in his designs.

[8] The frontier line had been defined as a point beyond which the population density was less than 2 persons per square mile; in 1890 no such demarcation existed.

[9] John Hafen Papers, Box 2, Folder 16, p. 41. L. Tom Perry Special Collections, Harold B. Lee Library, Brigham Young University, Provo, UT (hereafter referred to as Special Collections, BYU).

[10] John Hafen, "An Art Student in Paris," *The Contributor* 15, no. 8 (June 1894): 485

[11] For a thorough history and review of the Académie Julian, see H. Barbara Weinberg, *The Lure of Paris: Nineteenth Century American Painters and Their French Teachers* (New York: Abbeville Press, 1991), 221–262.

[12] John Hafen Papers, Box 2, Folder 16, pp. 103–104, Special Collections, BYU. The first Julian studios were in Montmartre; the school expanded due to increased demand, and in 1890, Julian opened a branch in the Latin Quarter. This location, housing six to eight studios and administrative offices, soon became the Academy headquarters and was where the Utah artists attended. By the turn of the century, there were eighteen locations.

[13] John Hafen Papers, Box 2, Folder 16, p. 105, Special Collections, BYU.

[14] "Young Utah in Paris," *Deseret Semi-Weekly News,* December 26, 1890, 4.

[15] Unlike the École des Beaux Arts, which did not admit women, both male and female students were welcome at the Académie Julian, where they were segregated in different ateliers.

[16] John Hafen Papers, Box 2, Folder 16 p. 106, Special Collections, BYU

[17] The drawing is in the collection of the Church History Museum, Salt Lake City. Herman Haag's life was cut short by complications from a childhood illness, and he passed away at the age of twenty-four in 1894. He was unable to participate in the painting of the temple murals.

[18] The Société des Artistes Français was established in 1881 and took over the management of the formerly government-sponsored Paris salons, which had been in existence since 1667. The Salon des Indépendents, formed in 1884 in opposition to the rigid traditionalism of the dominant salons, did not have juried selections. In December 1890, the leader of the Société des Artistes Français, William Bouguereau, declared that this new salon should be an exhibition of young, not yet awarded artists. Ernest Meissonier, Puvis de Chavannes, Auguste Rodin and others rejected this proposal and made a secession. They created the Société Nationale des Beaux-Arts, immediately referred to in the press as the Salon du Champ de Mars or simply the Nationale.

[19] The Barbizon School was named for the village of Barbizon, on the edge of the Fontainebleau Forest, where many of the school's practitioners painted. The most notable members included Jean-Baptiste-Camille Corot, Charles-François Daubigny, Jules Dupré, and Jean François Millet.

[20] The painting later won an honorable mention in national competition at the 1893 World's Columbian Exposition.

[21] The group formally organized in 1898 and became known as the Ten or the Ten American Painters.

[22] Letter from John Hafen to Thora Hafen, October 19, 1890, quoted in Linda Jones Gibbs, *Harvesting the Light*, 25.

[23] Letter from John Hafen to George Q. Cannon, May 26, 1891, MSS 356, Box 2, Folder 3, Special Collections, BYU.

[24] Letter from John Hafen to Thora Hafen, undated, Box 2, Folder 2, #23, Special Collections, BYU.

[25] John Hafen Papers, undated notebook, Box 2, Folder 16, p. 33, Special Collections, BYU.

[26] John Hafen, "An Art Student in Paris II," *The Contributor*, July 1894, 346.

[27] John Hafen Papers, letter from George Q. Cannon to John Hafen, March 7, 1891. Box 2, Folder 3, Special Collections, BYU

[28] John Hafen Papers, letter from George Q. Cannon to John Hafen, March 7, 1891, Box 2, Folder 3, Special Collections, BYU.

[29] The Mormon church did not ban the practice of polygamy until September 24, 1890, in a document known as "The Manifesto." Nevertheless, plural marriages continued to be performed until 1904, when a second manifesto was issued.

[30] Letter from George Q. Cannon to Lorus Pratt, September 12, 1891, courtesy of Mr. and Mrs. David Glover. Quoted in Linda Jones Gibbs, *Harvesting the Light,* 31, 32.

[31] Letter from the First Presidency to John Clawson, Lorus Pratt, John B. Fairbanks, Edwin Evans, and Herman Haag, April 18, 1892, quoted in Linda Jones Gibbs, *Harvesting the Light,* 33.

[32] Letter from the First Presidency to John Clawson, Lorus Pratt, John B. Fairbanks, Edwin Evans, and Herman Haag, April 18, 1892, quoted in Linda Jones Gibbs, *Harvesting the Light,* 33.

[33] There had been no murals in the Nauvoo temple or Kirtland temple. The only art in the Nauvoo temple was portraiture of church leaders. As far as a basis in ancient times for the subject matter of Genesis in LDS temple murals, David M. Calabro has explored the idea of biblical texts, Genesis in particular, as scripts for the progression of ritual dramas that were enacted in the Israelite temple. See David M. Calabro, "Joseph Smith and the Architecture of Genesis," https.www.academia.edu/37488023.

[34] Randy Astle draws a corollary between the panoramas and temple murals in which the concept of large-scale narrative paintings was brought into the sacred spaces of the temple for instructional purposes. Randy Astle, *Mormon Cinema, Origins to 1952* (New York City: Mormon Arts Center, 2018), 45

[35] The endowment house was demolished in 1889 due to the fact that plural marriages had been solemnized there and the church was trying to deescalate conflict with the U.S. government over polygamy. Only members who are deemed worthy via personal interview processes with patriarchal leaders are granted permission to enter the temple. Within the temple, Mormons are instructed that the knowledge, tokens, and signs given to them will provide passage through the veil into the Kingdom of Heaven.

[36] Since the 1970s the use of film has increasingly taken the place of live drama, which negates the need to move from room to room prior to entering the celestial room.

[37] These temple mural studies are in the collection of the Museum of Church History, Salt Lake City.

[38] "Dedicated to the Lord," *Salt Lake Herald,* April 7, 1893, 6.

[39] Some of the murals were painted directly on plaster. Fresco painting, however, involves the mixing of paint into wet plaster so that the painting literally becomes part of the wall and is not simply applied on the surface.

[40] James A. Anderson, "The Salt Lake Temple," *The Contributor* 14, no. 6 (April 1893): 288, 289.

[41] James E. Talmage, *The House of the Lord* (Salt Lake City: Deseret News, 1912), 186.

[42] Talmage, *The House of the Lord,* 187–188.

[43] It is possible that Hafen had earlier access to the temple for preparatory work, since he came home a year before his fellow missionaries, but there is no record of any actual painting prior to early 1893.

[44] Archives, Historical Department, quoted in Linda Jones Gibbs, *Harvesting the Light,* 104n4.

[45] Anton H. Lund, *Danish Apostle: The Diaries of Anthon H. Lund,* edited by John P. Hatch (Salt Lake City: Signature Books, 2006) 10.

[46] Among those that came into church ownership were a few done in France. Unfortunately, such works as *River Oise, France* and *Old House in Auvers* have since disappeared from the collection.

[47] Letter from George Q. Cannon to Lorus Pratt, September 12, 1891, courtesy of Mr. and Mrs. David Glover. Quoted in Linda Jones Gibbs, *Harvesting the Light,* 31, 32.

[48] Most of the original world room murals had to be repainted as early as 1922 because of problems with peeling plaster. This was done by John B. Fairbanks and his son J. Leo Fairbanks using original sketches. In

1938 Mabel Frazer and one of her students, Lura Redd, repainted the garden room. This was necessitated by previous attempts at cleaning the murals, which caused the colors to fade, and also inadequate attempts to retouch parts of the murals when wall pipes were removed. In 1987 only one small part of the original murals remained. By 2021, all the murals had been removed and the endowment ceremonies completely converted to the use of film to portray the Genesis story.

[49] Edwin Evans was president, John Hafen vice president, Herman Haag secretary, and Lorus Pratt a charter member.

[50] Elsie Reasoner, "Art in Salt Lake City," *Great West*, January 1897, 354, quoted in Linda Jones Gibbs, *Harvesting the Light,* 40.

[51] Alice Merrill Horne, *Devotees and Their Shrines* (Salt Lake City: Deseret News, 1914), 111.

[52] John Hafen Papers, letter from John Hafen to Mrs. M. H. Walker, March 23, 1905, Special Collections, BYU.

[53] Lorus Pratt's *The Harvest* of 1896 is very similar in style and subject matter to a painting entitled *The Threshing Machine* done in 1893 by his French teacher in Auvers, Albert-Gabriel Rigolot (Museé des Beaux-Arts des Rouen).

[54] Genesis 3:16.

[55] Henry Nash Smith, *Virgin Land* (New York: Random House, 1950), Book 3, quoted in Barbara Novak, *Nature and Culture: American* Landscape *Painting 1825*–1875 (New York: Oxford University Press, 1980), 4.

13

LDS ARTISTS AND THE ART STUDENTS LEAGUE OF NEW YORK

GLEN NELSON

"And on Christmas morning (1907), the chimes of Chelsea . . . were ringing out a welcome," wrote Waldo Midgley, documenting his arrival in New York from Utah to study art making. "Out we went for a first look at the big city. The Ninth Avenue 'L' rumbled by overhead, fabulous Broadway, ablaze with light. Kind people . . . answering questions of two starry-eyed young fellows. The next morning we were off to see the wizard—The Art Students League."[1]

Midgley and his fellow Utahn Hal Burrows were following the lead of a friend from Salt Lake City, Mahonri Mackintosh Young, who had left home in the fall of 1899 to study at the Art Students League of New York. These budding artists, and dozens of others like them, came at considerable sacrifice. Young, for example, noted that he worked for two years at the *Salt Lake Tribune*, making roughly $5 a week as a general lackey, to afford himself just a few months' study at the league.[2]

These artists had limited options closer to home for study of cursory skills, and students of the visual arts in the Western European tradition were desperate to enlarge their education beyond parochial classes and to obtain exposure to the canon of the art of the world. For them, this training required a reverse migration to the urban centers of the East and West Coasts of the United States and to Europe.[3] The end of the U.S. Civil War had been the catalyst for American art students to study abroad, mostly in two cities: Paris and Munich. Artists from Utah continued that movement.

The journey of LDS artists of the generation before Young to urban centers for study started a bit later, but before the end of the century a notable and historic group of Utah artists studied in Paris at the École des Beaux-Arts, the Académie Julian, and elsewhere.[4] However, beginning at the turn of the twentieth century a much greater number of LDS artists decamped to New York City—nearly a hundred artists in all—and they studied at and then perpetuated the practices and ethos of what became an unsurpassed source of outside cultural influence on Mormon art: the Art Students League of New York.[5]

An understanding of this influence transcends issues of style and subject matter, although both are significant, identifiable, and heretofore underexamined. It was a unique social order, and returning "Leaguers" exported it into Mormon culture. The socialities of the league, its empowering attitudes toward women, its embrace of philosophical duality, its openness to modernism, the prominent role of teachers as mentors, and the expectation that students immerse themselves in and engage with the city itself all are visible in the works and lives of these LDS former league students as they became independent artists and university educators in the West. Furthermore, the legacies of their New York experiences differ from those of LDS artists studying in Europe. These novel factors continued in the artists' methodologies for their future students, providing those yet to venture forth a tantalizing look at fine art visual culture from a safe distance, but more importantly exposing them to the attitudes of progressive thinking about art and artists found in New York.

Today, we struggle to imagine how challenging it was a hundred years ago or more to become competent drawing the figure. A significant barrier was access to live models. For example, after Young returned from Paris in 1905, he started a life drawing class twice a week in Salt Lake. He had difficulty finding models to hire and even engaged sex workers, something that scandalized the locals.[6] Regardless, such training was of paramount concern. In New York and later in Paris, Young absorbed both technical skills in depicting the body and admiration for artists whose engagement with the working class he would seek to depict.

In 1900, at the league, Young completed a drawing in a sketch class, *Gentleman with Gloves* (1900). It portends what would become the artist's endless fascination with the figure—the male figure in particular. The model stands in formal attire. His textured topcoat is rendered carefully with the repeated verticality of stripes. The mustachioed man holds flaccid gloves in his left hand and an attenuated umbrella in his right, and he stands with the weight on his right leg, which gives the impression of movement to an otherwise static pose. Young projects the subject as something other than the solid masculinity that will be a hallmark of his later work.

Young makes no emotional connection with the subject, whose eyes do not meet the artist's gaze. The figure represents a social class with which Young does not sympathize. The man's body does not face forward, and the resulting impression is that he is a character who is less than forthright and open. He strikes a receding pose, and in that choice, Young suggests that the gentleman is posturing. The drawing is significant for what it does not contain and what Young will abandon as subject matter.

Young's tastes will go instead to the worker, and his long career in years to come will concentrate on figures that are nearly the opposite of this gentleman: stevedores, farmers, construction workers, washerwomen, workers outdoors, Native Americans,

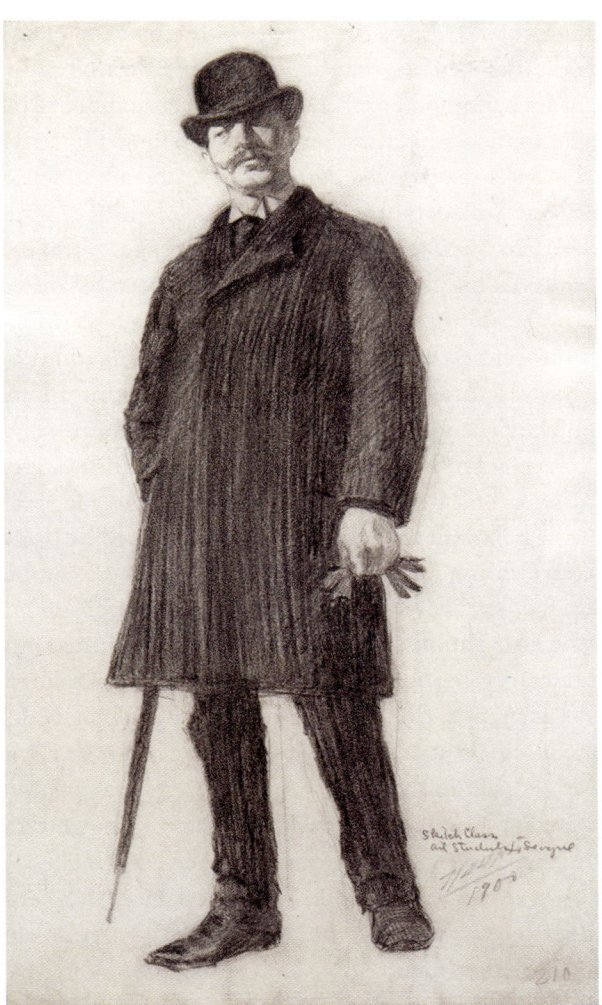

Fig. 13.1 Mahonri M. Young, *Gentleman with Gloves,* 1900, graphite, 14 9/16″ × 8 9/16″, Brigham Young University Museum of Art, purchase/gift of Mahonri M. Young Estate, 1959.

and others who embody the physicality of labor. One is reminded of the artist's grandfather Brigham Young, who sought to dominate the western desert through ameliorating work. Brigham wrote, "Instead of searching after what the Lord is going to do for us, let us inquire what we can do for ourselves."[7] Mahonri's life and body of work are about doing. His art embodies, represents, and ennobles effort—the more strenuous the better.

Young caught the attention of the public, even gaining celebrity, when he made art about the boxing craze of the mid-1920s. Although he also made drawings and painting of athletes in the boxing ring, his boxing paintings were never entirely successful—indeed, the same could be said generally about his works on canvas. Young's strengths were line rather than color. Despite his interest in the body, the human figures in his landscapes can appear like sketches, their faces often reduced to hazily executed roughs. Sculpture, on the other hand, and boxers in particular, brought out Young's gifts for dynamics and balance, emotion amid exertion, and storytelling. His series of sculptures on boxing, particularly works that show a dynamic ensemble of athletes and referees, are the opposite of the New York dandy posing.

Right to the Jaw (1926) epitomizes the artist's concerns regarding the materiality of the work, as he said, "To me the problem has always been to animate the inert and lifeless material, whether bronze, stone, or wood, and to make it function like one of nature's own creations." If he was relatively unsuccessful animating paint, the sculpture in this series displays everything he might have yearned for in an appeal to connect with the viewer through works brimming with natural life. As the viewer walks around the work, the light interacts with the surfaces cinematically, as if they are in constant motion. The viewer becomes like the referee in a ring who circles and stalks the perpetually moving pugilists in search of new angles to view the bout, to be part of the action but removed from it as an observer. If Young struggled to convey the complexities of the face as a painter and draftsman, his sculptural works give the opposite impression, of ease and spontaneity. The articulation of the musculature of exhausted athletes in the final minutes of a bout transfers emotion into ricocheting, off-balance, kinetic sensations.

Young's paintings align with the American Realist movement, which gained traction temporarily as a predominant style, particularly during the Great Depression, when interest in art for art's sake diminished and was replaced by a fascination with and admiration of the heartland and labor. In the 1940s, Young continued to mine this imagery and drew from his New York experience observing the construction of skyscrapers. In the painting *Riding the Girder* (circa 1940) and the medallion of the same image, *Riggers Riveters* (1943), the latter produced in New York for the Society of Medalists, the artist captures men high above the ground riding an I-beam as it is hoisted in the air. Like his best sculpture, the composition is a dance of balance. In this case, the placement of the figures must be exact in order to keep the beam aright. By extension, the elements of the image are ordered to feel natural and yet dangerous. The event's precariousness—these men are not in harnesses, protected from falling—is emphasized in the composition. There is a hook at the top center with a secure cable, but also a rope at the far end of the beam, where the tension of the vanishing point guides the eye to other human-made structures, factories, and bridges. The men are stylized in Young's manner of painting, with faces reduced in prominence or turned away entirely, which betrays no emotion of what the workers are thinking in the moment.

It is interesting to compare the figures in the painting to those in the medallion. In the relief coin, Young is precise and expressive. In the painting, the figures are vague, even generic, as if one laborer is like any other. The artist's admiration for European realist painters such as Jean-Baptiste-Camille Corot is translated to Young's native country in these images, which are the embodiment of American ambition. What is

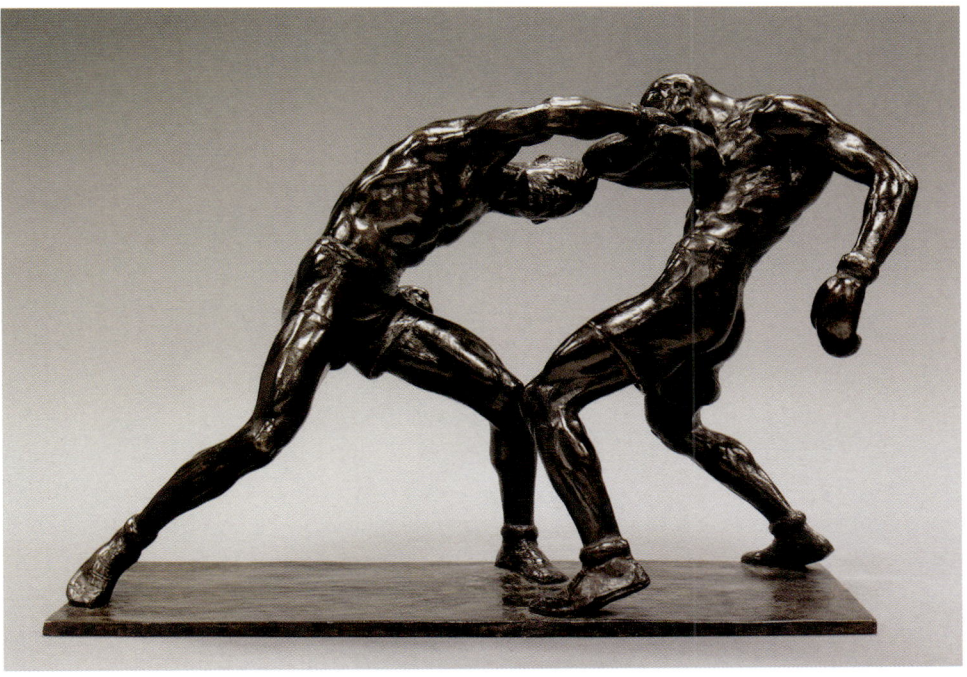

Fig. 13.2 Mahonri M. Young, *Right to the Jaw,* **1926, bronze, 14″ × 19 5/16″ × 9 1/2″, Brigham Young University Museum of Art, purchase/gift of Mahonri M. Young Estate, 1959.**

more singularly American (or New York) than a skyscraper? For example, the Empire State Building was begun in 1930, and the 102-story building was completed a mere one year and forty-five days later, making it one of the more iconic construction efforts in the world. These same fascinations appear over the course of Young's long career, including works connected to Mormonism directly: his sculptures of Joseph and Hyrum Smith (1907) in Temple Square (they originally sat in niches on the temple's east wall), his heroic marble sculpture of Brigham Young (1950) that sits in the U.S. Capitol Building in Washington, D.C., and his massive ode to his pioneer heritage, the This Is the Place Monument (dedicated in 1947), in Salt Lake City, Utah.

Imagine, then, what the career of Mahonri Young would have been without immersion into the technique of rendering the figure and the influence that the Art Students League had on him. Of course, the league's original reason for existence was to give students access to life drawing from a live model. Young studied at the league and later returned as an instructor, teaching there for forty years. Other young LDS artists must have sensed the same deficit of training and were determined to find instruction that could provide a pathway to a visual arts career. This speaks to the primacy of training in their development of skills as well as the liberation of mental constraints regarding

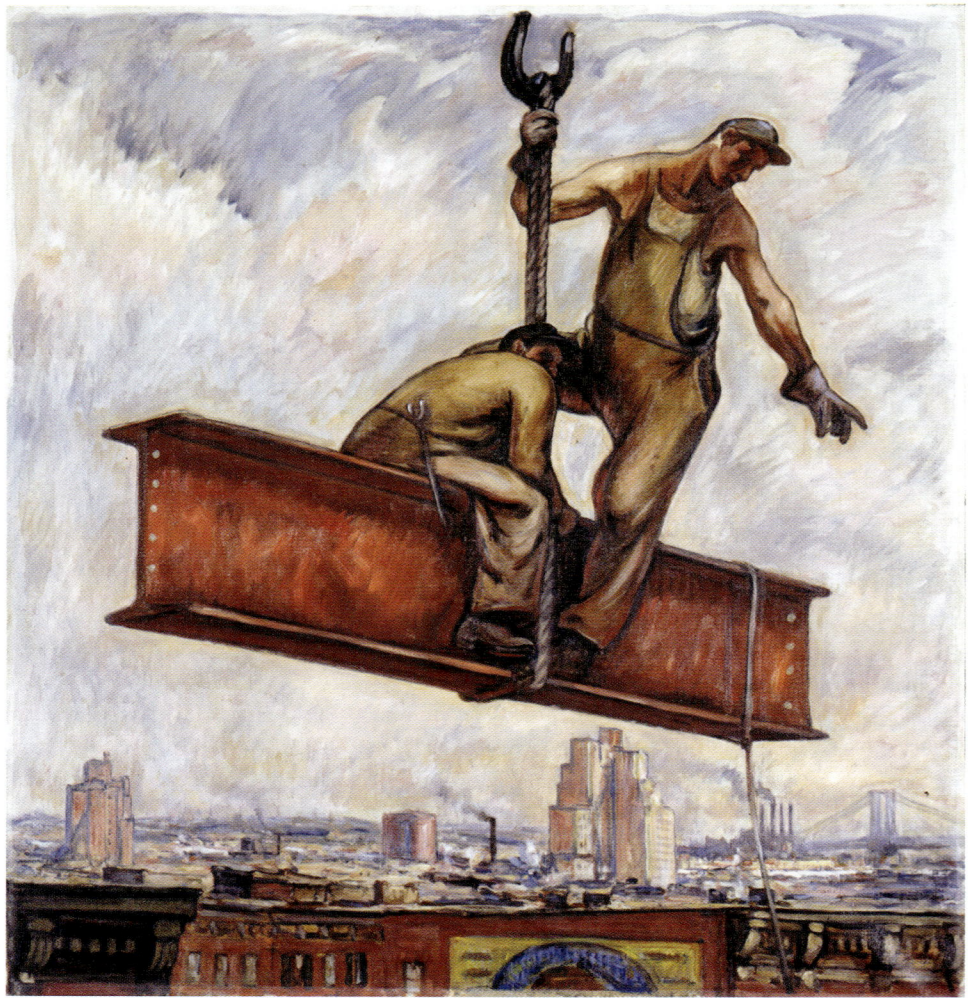

Fig. 13.3 Mahonri M. Young, *Riding the Girder*, c. 1940, oil on canvas, 42 3/8″ × 39″, Brigham Young University Museum of Art, purchase/gift of Mahonri M. Young Estate, 1959.

what is possible, which makes the influence of the Art Students League feel even more significant.

Stepping back for added context, some fifty years after the 1830 founding of the Church of Jesus Christ of Latter-day Saints, the body of its visual culture as presented by its publications and the works displayed in its public spaces had been built largely by accretion rather than by conscious design. In contrast to a recognizable aesthetic tied to a religious culture such as the Shakers produced, for example, there was no template regarding what Mormon art should look like nor where it should come from. Geographically, toward the end of the nineteenth century, the majority of the members

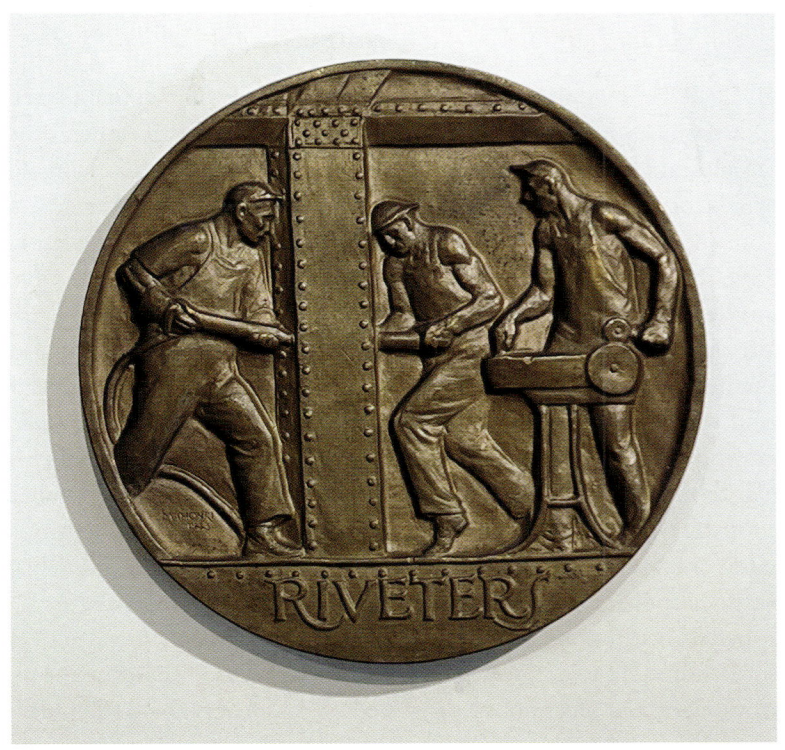

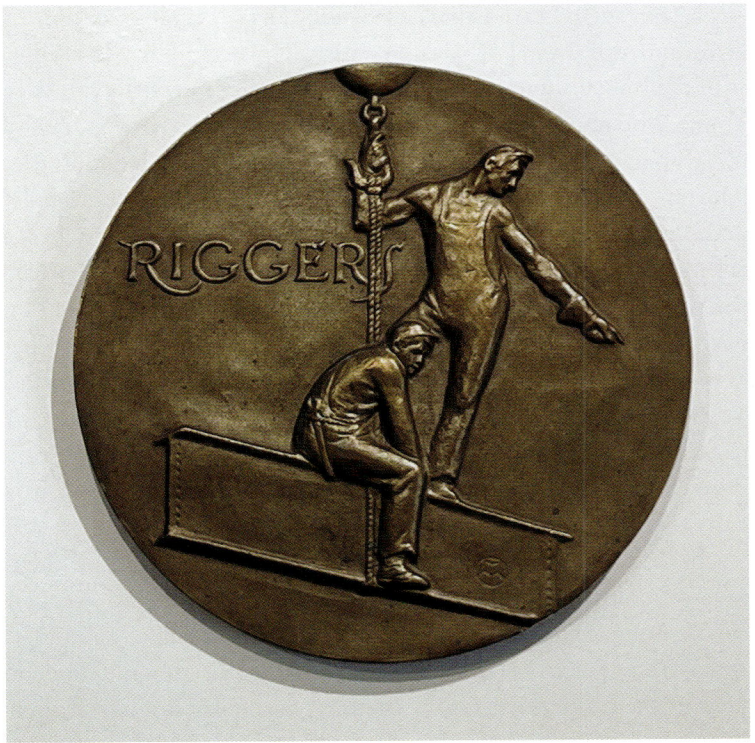

Fig. 13.4 Mahonri Macintosh Young, *Riggers/Riveters*, 1945, bronze, 2 7/8″ × 1/4″, collection of Kent Christensen. Photographs courtesy of Kent Christensen.

of the faith resided in a western American landscape. Many of its trained and untrained artists and artisans emigrated to remote geographic regions as if drawn by a magnet, and they acculturated from their disparate previous residences into a chain of relatively homogeneous colonies[8] in a longitudinal corridor from Alberta, Canada, to Juárez, Mexico,[9] but they congregated heavily in the middle of that band, in what would become in 1896 the state of Utah. Despite their linked communities, their art had no predominant style.

Regarding influence, the binding forces having to do with style might appear to be little differentiated from those of any group of people who live in a relatively tight geography and who have similar exposure to culture-making endeavors. And yet, here is a people who think of themselves as a body, who have a system of belief that reads as particular to themselves, who think of each other collectively as a "peculiar people," who have artistic traditions that yearn to express this unique, shared identity, including stories, music, literature, and an institution that serves as a patron, particularly when the arts were a proponent of its general messaging. Add to that, in visual art, a relatively small number of institutions of instruction that beget artists, critics, and professors, creating something akin to a genealogical lineage of influence. These are the makings of a school of thought and must not be dismissed out of anxiety that individual artists be seen as independent. It is simplistic to say that the Art Students League was that school in a literal sense, but such a statement is not wholly an exaggeration either.

The sheer number of these LDS-league artists lends credibility to the idea of influence. Many of the league alumni returned home to build careers; notable exceptions are Mahonri Young, who remained in the New York area after studying at the Art Students League, and Lynn Fausett, who served a three-year term as president of the league, from 1933 to 1936, ten years after his initial entry as a student.[10] More commonly, returning artists from the league developed careers as artists and/or influential teachers and critics. Notable examples include LeConte Stewart, Mabel Frazer, Avard T. Fairbanks, Louise Farnsworth, Minerva Teichert, George Dibble, Mary Teasdel, and Jessie Larson, many of whom became professors at universities in Utah and elsewhere, thereby perpetuating the league's somewhat unorthodox views about the alchemical making of the artist and how one artistic style relates to another.

The Art Students League of New York was the leading institution of its kind in the United States, and generations of the nation's most highly regarded artists studied and/or taught there.[11] A testament to the league's ability to nurture a variety of artistic approaches is found in the extraordinary range of its artists and their modes of expression—essentially, every ism of the twentieth century found acceptance at the league. It would be inaccurate to claim that its training aimed at anything specific or different for LDS student artists than for others, despite the aforementioned leadership at the league, but the LDS artists took something particular and new from it nonetheless. They found peers who were like-minded regarding personal artistic development and whose dedication to art contrasted with the accepted notions of art from agrarian frontier life.

Of further note was that their Mormonness was embraced. Beyond the technical training and mechanics of art making, Leaguers returning home brought with them a tacit outside acceptance—or at least an absence of outright rejection based on prejudice related to religious identity, which was a widespread legacy of anti-Mormon sentiment for much of the nineteenth and early twentieth centuries.[12] All of the above provided an indication that others in the culture huddling together in post-migration settlements might once again venture out freely into the world.

The league was an unlikely source of encouragement regarding the inclusion of LDS history and doctrinal narratives into these artists' works, but such became the case, and it led the way to a preponderance of Utah scriptural and religious themes and landscapes as subject matter, aspects of which pervade the culture even today. Further, the success of artists trained at the Art Students League fueled the ambition of younger generations throughout the Mormon West. Notable is the number of LDS women to emerge from the league and their later influence as educators and artists.

The church's origins in upstate New York with Joseph Smith and a small group of others responded to a perceived dearth of truth and led to a moment of clarity and the creation of an entirely new entity. In those respects, its path shares something with the league. The Art Students League of New York began in 1875 when students of the National Academy of Design protested the loss of their life drawing classes and a refusal of access to the academy's library, voiced a general dissatisfaction with their training as artists, and expressed fears that the unstable financial situation at the academy imperiled their technical progress. They sought to fill a void and be more complete as artists, even if that meant creating by themselves an institution from nothing. They didn't ask exactly, as Joseph Smith did, which church (or art school) was right, but they did come to the same conclusion he had: that the existing options were unacceptable.

They gathered in June, released an announcement of their intent in July, and began operations in September in a leased space with approximately seventy members who paid $5 a month. They called it "the first independent art school in this country, and the only one holding life classes in session every weekday."[13] At the time, more than a dozen art schools and artist associations functioned in New York City, but the league stood apart, even as a fledgling entity, because of its emphasis on drawing the figure, its governance, and its attempts at inclusive approaches to art itself.

Although it was forward-looking, the league reacted to the trends of its day. In the mid-1870s, a revival of American art began with the return of American students who had been abroad in Paris and Munich. In the United States, this coincided with an era of industrialization, dramatic immigration to the country from Europe, and rapid economic development for the socially advantaged (which Mark Twain and Charles Dudley Warner labeled the Gilded Age). Distrustful of earlier artists and the authority figures of the Academy and eager for fresh ideas to match the new age, they found in the student-controlled league progressive attitudes toward art and society. Gender parity was built into its constitution, for example. The governing board consisted of a president, two vice presidents (one male and one female), and four other members (two women and two men).[14] Such integration continued into the classroom studio. Sketches from 1877 of league classes show men and women behind easels (although for nude drawing classes, male and female students were separated).

Of paramount importance to students was the accessibility to life drawing classes. Other institutions taught the figure from sculpture; live models—nude and draped—and the analysis of how to depict them distinguished the league. Annual reports trumpeted the quality of its models, the number of poses given, and that the school had offered study from the nude "eight and one-half hours per day, or fifty-one hours per week."[15]

The fine art issuing forth from American artists in the era relied on understanding the figure. Certainly, landscape continued to be an important American theme, but being a painter implied being conversant with depicting the body. Of course, art technique was aimed at more than the aspirational fine artist. People considering work in the fields of journalism, illustration, cartooning, advertising, architecture, and others needed technical facility in order to gain employment too. Without that technical education, an artist's career—of whatever stratum—was imperiled.

For LDS artists without previous training, gaining a solid education and learning the craft of art was more than mere self-improvement. Art societies—and indeed, many of the art clubs in New York at the turn of the century are representative examples—catered to a bisected audience: those who sought professional training or those who viewed art making as a pleasant diversion. The LDS artists were firmly in the former camp, and they had more at stake than many of their classmates because they risked more. The league was far from home, and attending its classes required tremendous sacrifices.

These young LDS artists were often the first in their families to venture outside of their small communities again after decades in a sort of self-imposed exile precipitated by anti-Mormon violence and the murder of Joseph and Hyrum Smith in 1844 in Illinois, expulsion of the Saints from their homes in the Midwest, and a harrowing trek to a barren valley in the Rocky Mountains near the Great Salt Lake. If those issues suggest some emotional risks involved, consider the financial challenges of moving to New York as well.

After its initial founding and the immediate success in gaining students, the Art Students League of New York faced a dilemma: What should be its philosophy? Should it coalesce around a single notion of artistic practice? Should its program of training reflect the school of Paris or the school of Munich? Instructors at the league represented both possibilities. Generally speaking, the Paris school favored careful, academic depictions of the figure. Accuracy was seen to be the foundation of excellence. Even the diverging modes of Impressionism found a base in academic technique.

The German approach was different. In his 1940 history of the league, Marchal E. Landgren describes the tension:

> The Munich school was in revolt against the careful, absolute drawing which Mr. Waller and the Paris academies favored. It fostered the technic of direct drawing on canvas with heavily laden paint brushes, a method which hid many of the defects of the painter by giving an appearance of technical virtuosity. Munich echoed the dull tones of the old masters, and the work of its disciples was once called "smoked and rancid" imitations of the great. Its appeal to the students was no doubt the appeal of spontaneity and expression and, of course, the appeal of the radical movement.[16]

Robert Henri wrote that the Munich School taught drawing with slashing brushstrokes, and he himself adopted the Munich School's approach to rapid brushwork as a way to capture intense feeling. In its early years, the league favored the Munich School, but the two philosophies coexisted, and students could easily toggle between them. Instructors were hired and reengaged to maintain a balanced view of what art could be. A cursory glance at a selection of early instructors points to their aesthetic diversity: William Merritt Chase, Thomas Eakins, Frank Duvenck, J. Alden Weir, J. H. Twachtman, Kenyon Cox, Augustus Saint-Gaudens, Childe Hassam, Walter Shirlaw, and Lemuel E. Wimarth.[17] In fact, the ability to hold both approaches as viable gave students power to select their own path and to develop gradually. Moreover, the student-professor relationships were intimate and transcended the studio or classroom environment. League students socialized with their professors frequently in their homes and studios in casual as well as educational activities, which added a layer of mentorship that would have been unheard of (or even scandalous) in the storied academies of Europe.

One can see, therefore, how LDS students at the league would internalize the philosophy that the world of art was an open book of possibility and that they could seek out figures who would be best suited to their specific personalities and goals. Today, the concept of such a spectrum of justifiable options from a single institution is taken for granted, but at the league more than a century ago, young LDS artists from the West were molded by self-direction and supported without becoming copies of their teachers.

An illustrious example of league instructors in this regard was Robert Henri, who taught at the league in 1916–1917 and who often admonished students to paint "what is real to you." Among LDS artists, collectors, and scholars today, Henri's advice to artist Minerva Teichert that she return home and paint the Mormon story has grown to feel like a ringing endorsement of LDS culture and history generally, while more likely it was a typical identity-driven admonition from Henri to students.[18] Nevertheless, its legacy came to be seen as something like a stamp of approval of all of LDS art, including artists who imagine themselves being validated from the outside and told to express their religious sense of self and history.

The exchange between Henri and Teichert has grown to mythic stature in Mormon culture. Like many origin stories, there exist multiple versions of it, which are worth examining briefly. The recounting of the exhortation differs slightly when it is told by the official church, by academics, by commercial gallerists, and on social media. Each takes and emphasizes an element of it, and their distinguishing characteristics highlight how, in the culture's shared identity, Henri is speaking to more than a single artist from Idaho. It is read today nearly as a justification for an entire culture's visual production.

Teichert's own handwritten manuscript of the conversation is the following, as recorded in a master's thesis by the artist's granddaughter and champion, Marian Eastwood Wardle:

> Before I left Henri said, "Has anyone ever told your great Mormon story?" "Not to suit me," I answered. "Good Heavens girl, what a chance, you do it. You're the one; Oh to be a Mormon! . . . That's your birthright. You feel it. You'll do it well." I felt that I had been commissioned by this great friend.[19]

In 1989, an official church publication, *Ensign,* published an article that was part of a movement to rehabilitate Teichert's reputation after years of neglect. It coincided with an exhibition at the LDS Church Museum of History and Art, across the street from Temple Square. The magazine, in keeping with its general purpose of highlighting its members and projecting religious values to a larger public, described the relationship of Henri and Teichert grandiosely: "Robert Henri, a renowned teacher and prominent American realist, reportedly ranked her among his top three students—along with George Bellows and John Sloan, later recognized as foremost twentieth-century American artists."[20] Its version of the story highlights a missionary moment: "'Oh, to be a Mormon.' I said to him, 'You could be.' He paused almost reverently for a moment, then answered, 'That's your birthright. You feel it. You'll do it well.' I felt that I had been commissioned."[21]

An October 2008 *Ensign* article, this time coinciding with an exhibition of Teichert's work at the Museum of Art at Brigham Young University, the largest repository of her works, streamlined the anecdote, but in doing so reframed the admonition as a direct calling: "During Minerva's studies in New York, noted American realist painter Robert Henri challenged her to paint the 'great Mormon story.' With that goal she painted many theatrical depictions of Mormon pioneers, the West, and Book of Mormon scenes."[22] Small distinction, but this story has been told and retold so many times and with subtle variations, as if to give license to all young LDS artists to go and do likewise. The implication is that the "Mormon story" is worthy of fine art. In this aspect, it combines with admonitions from the 1970s church leadership calling on artists in the church to use their talents for the betterment of the Kingdom, and in the minds of artists this galvanized their ambitions to make great art—whatever that means to them—and to make art that serves a greater purpose.

For a 2018 gallery exhibition in Salt Lake City, art historian and gallerist Micah Christensen noted yet another side of the Teichert experience in quoting the artist—that of divine intervention. As a preamble to the anecdote, Teichert is quoted as saying, "It was as if the Lord intervened just so I could have him as an instructor. Mr. Henri gave me the clarity of purpose for my painting and vocalized an inner whisper as I struggled to find my art style."[23] These variations have all the hallmarks of mythmaking that continue to resound even if younger artists have no idea who Henri was and only a vague perception of Teichert's personal story.

There is no denying that it was an impactful moment for Teichert and informed the rest of her career. She had written to her mother to say that she considered Henri to be "the greatest modern portrait painter in the world."[24] Teichert named her second son Robert Henri Teichert, and she kept up a correspondence with her former teacher for many years. Still, the culture took something more from the conversation: validation.

Teichert's training at the league was somewhat brief, just as Young's initial introduction in New York had been. Her career ambition was to be a muralist. Already a competent artist, she sought additional instruction to refine her skills and trained at the Art Institute of Chicago for two terms in 1909–1910, after which she returned to Idaho broke and in debt before returning for another term in 1912. At that point, she saved money to study in New York by sketching cadavers and performing as a trick roper and Indian dancer. In New York, Teichert registered for painting and mural classes at the Art Students League in the spring and fall of 1915, just as Henri arrived to teach at the institution, and she remained at the league until the spring of 1916.

Even a short stay in New York at the league was transformative for these artists—not just because of the formal instruction the league provided but also because of the exposure to museums and galleries in the metropolis, which provided stimulation that could not be gathered otherwise in an era before mass color publication made works more accessible.

The 1915 drawings by Teichert in the permanent collection of the Brigham Young University Museum of Art were created during her stay at the Art Students League and show her confidence in anatomical depiction of the figure. Of them, one of the most finished is *Standing Indian Model* (1915). Teichert grew up near the Shoshone-Bannock Reservation in southeastern Idaho. She had a lifelong interest in Indigenous peoples, whom she frequently painted in two main bodies of works: Book of Mormon paintings and images of the frontier West. This drawing, created in New York City, is rendered sympathetically and vulnerably. It features a male figure wearing a loincloth and coverings on his feet. His long hair is pulled back and parted, and his right arm is raised to his temple.

One wonders what the student from Idaho might have thought when the league's Indigenous model appeared that day in 1915 and how she might have identified with him, maybe even recognized in him some kind of geographic connection. Here she was, sitting in the middle of the island of Manahatta, as the original inhabitants, the

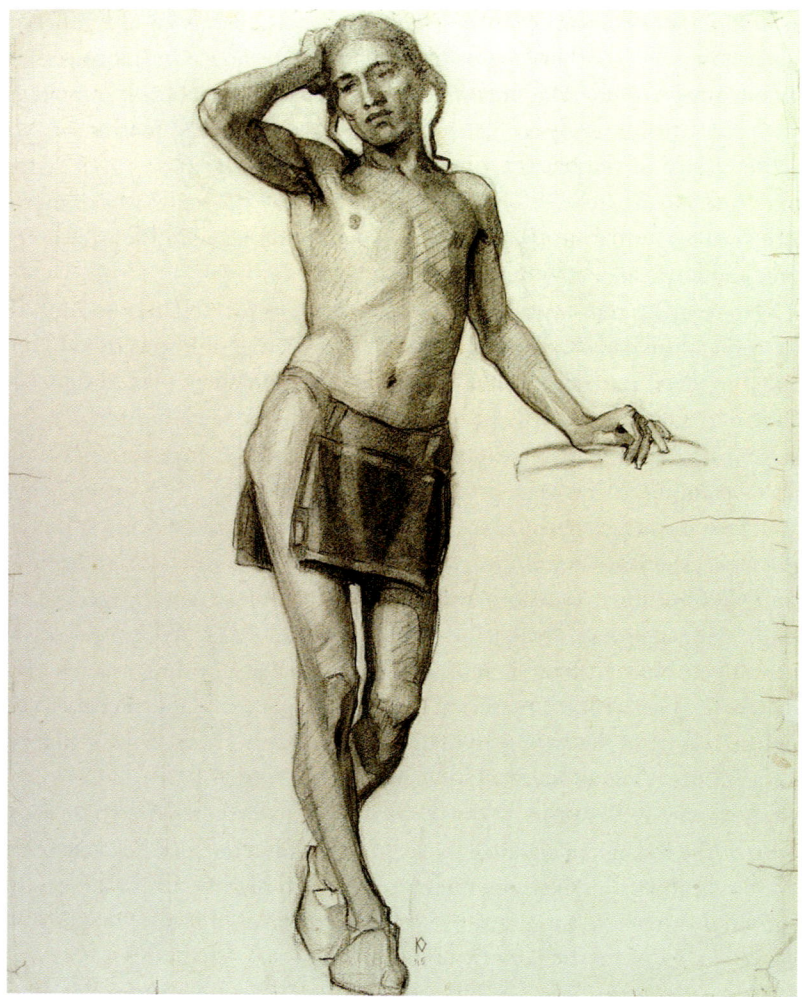

Fig. 13.5 Minerva Teichert, *Standing Indian Model,* 1937, charcoal, 19½″ × 24 3/16″, Brigham Young University Museum of Art, gift of Teichert Family Collection, 1997.

Lenape, called it, preparing for a career of painting the stories of the West, including many Native Americans. Anything more is conjecture, but the drawing itself is sensitive, free of the bluster of stereotypes that Hollywood films of the 1930s and later would ingrain in American culture. That sensitivity too, perhaps, was part of her New York training and its goals of inclusivity.

Teichert was the first woman commissioned to paint a mural for a sacred temple. Those images as well as religious paintings that illustrate the Book of Mormon and imagery of pioneers are her most recognizable artistic contributions. They are works that are nearly canonical to those of the faith. A departure in many respects is her painting

Immigrants to New York City (Jewish Refugees) (1938).[25] This painting, which was created as a wave of refugees fled Germany, takes the artist back to the days of her study in New York. The setting is the harbor in lower Manhattan, with the Statue of Liberty prominently featured in the space between the foreground, in which the passengers are seen approaching, and the background, with the skyscrapers of the city. She presents the figures vertically in concert with the buildings. The figures project weariness after a four-day journey from Europe, and the artist shows a family grouping hesitant and hopeful alongside a man carrying a musical instrument in awe at the approaching vista. Teichert has given the work a subtitle to indicate the passengers' identity, which is also conveyed by beards, forelocks, head coverings, and clothing of those shown in profile. A haze covers the piers, and the tall buildings emerge as a brilliant and warm backlit panorama, signaling a new beginning.

The painting reflects events of the time. In the period between 1933 and 1939, roughly ninety thousand German Jewish immigrants came to the United States. New York would have been their principal port of entry. The largest number arrived in 1938, the year Teichert painted *Immigrants*. The artist was attempting to effect change in society by drawing attention to a pressing issue of the day. To some degree, her awareness of the plight was heightened because of her son, Herman, who was serving as a full-time missionary in Germany at the time and sent letters home that described the persecution of Jews there. It must have resonated with her given that her ancestry was German—both her husband's grandparents and her own were born in Germany. Teichert had her own Jewish New York social connections. While studying at the Art Students League, she lived two blocks away from the apartment of LDS missionaries and attended church in Harlem. At the league, she befriended a classmate, Louise Waterman Wise, a woman from a prominent Jewish family and the founder of the Women's Division of the Jewish Congress. Her husband was a Zionist movement leader, Rabbi Stephen Samuel Wise, who would go on to found the American Jewish Congress. Teichert wrote to her mother about Louise, "She chose me as a friend last summer and we became fast friends before I knew who she was. Day before yesterday, she invited me to go to Carnegie Hall to hear her husband talk on woman's suffrage. I was of course invited into their box. . . . Of all the men I have heard Rabbi Wise far outdistanced them all. Oh I wish you could have heard him."[26]

The painting brings these personal connections and sensibilities together in a cityscape that had become her emotional portal to being an artist. A final aspect of the painting is its social progressivism. In 1938, 80 percent of Americans were against increasing the number of refugees permitted into the country. Here, Teichert humanizes the Jewish immigrants, acknowledging their despair and hope, by treating them sympathetically. This attempt to encourage empathy is supported visually by placing the viewer directly onto the vessel in an open space on deck, pulling through a shroud of fog.[27] Teichert's art dealer in Utah, a legendary figure, Alice Merrill Horne, wrote to Teichert to praise the painting: "Dear Minerva, this last [*Immigrants*] is a masterpiece.

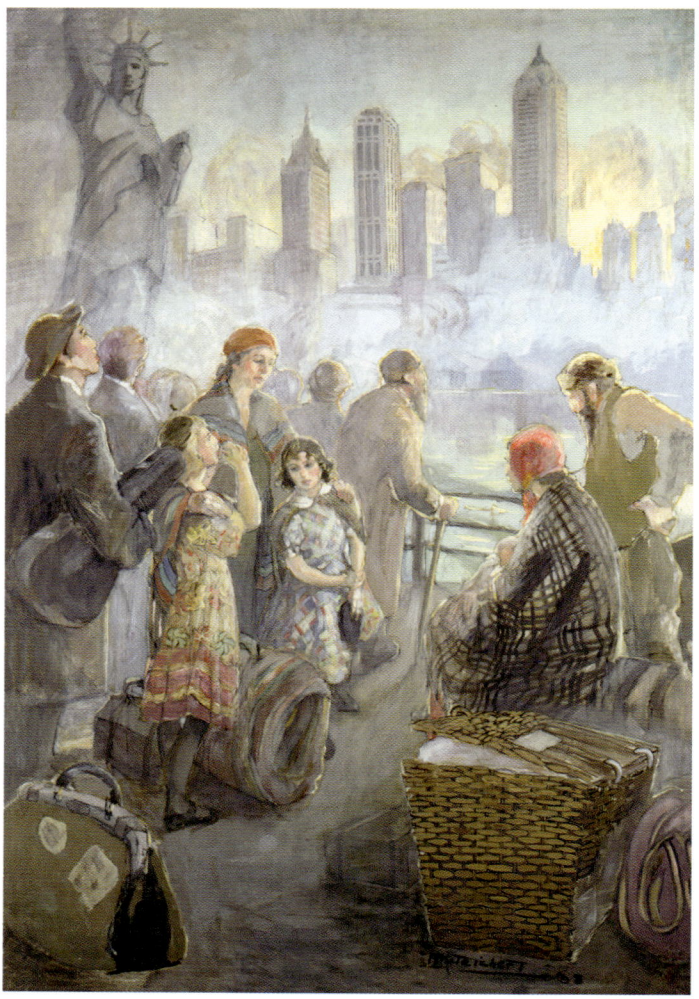

Fig. 13.6 Minerva Teichert, *Immigrants to New York City*, 1938, oil on canvas, 59 1/4″ × 37 1/4″, Brigham Young University Museum of Art.

. . . Congratulations. It has been direct—and nothing interfering with your passion, so chaste is the gift."[28] In 1948, Teichert wrote, "We must paint the great Mormon story of our pioneers in mural decorations so that 'he who runs may read.' This story thrills me, fills me, drives me on. . . . We'll tell our stories on the walls."[29]

A final example of Teichert's work is *Zion Ho (Handcart Pioneers),* a celebratory image of a pioneer family entering the Salt Lake Valley. This well-known work is one of many paintings by the artist that focus on a woman's experience. As a granddaughter of Mormon pioneers who made the trek from Winter Quarters as well as a niece of a soldier from the Mormon Battalion, Teichert noticed a disconnection between the stories she grew up hearing and the official record of the migration west. To her mind, the accepted history omitted the stories of ordinary believers, and women in particular.

Her creative approach to visual storytelling—and her work boils down to a driving, narrative urge—resisted strict biography. Rather, she sought universality in anonymity and generalization in her pioneer images. Although she had every right to depict her direct ancestors in paint, she chose instead to allow viewers to see themselves in the pioneer works. Often, as in this painting, which is in the collection of the Church History

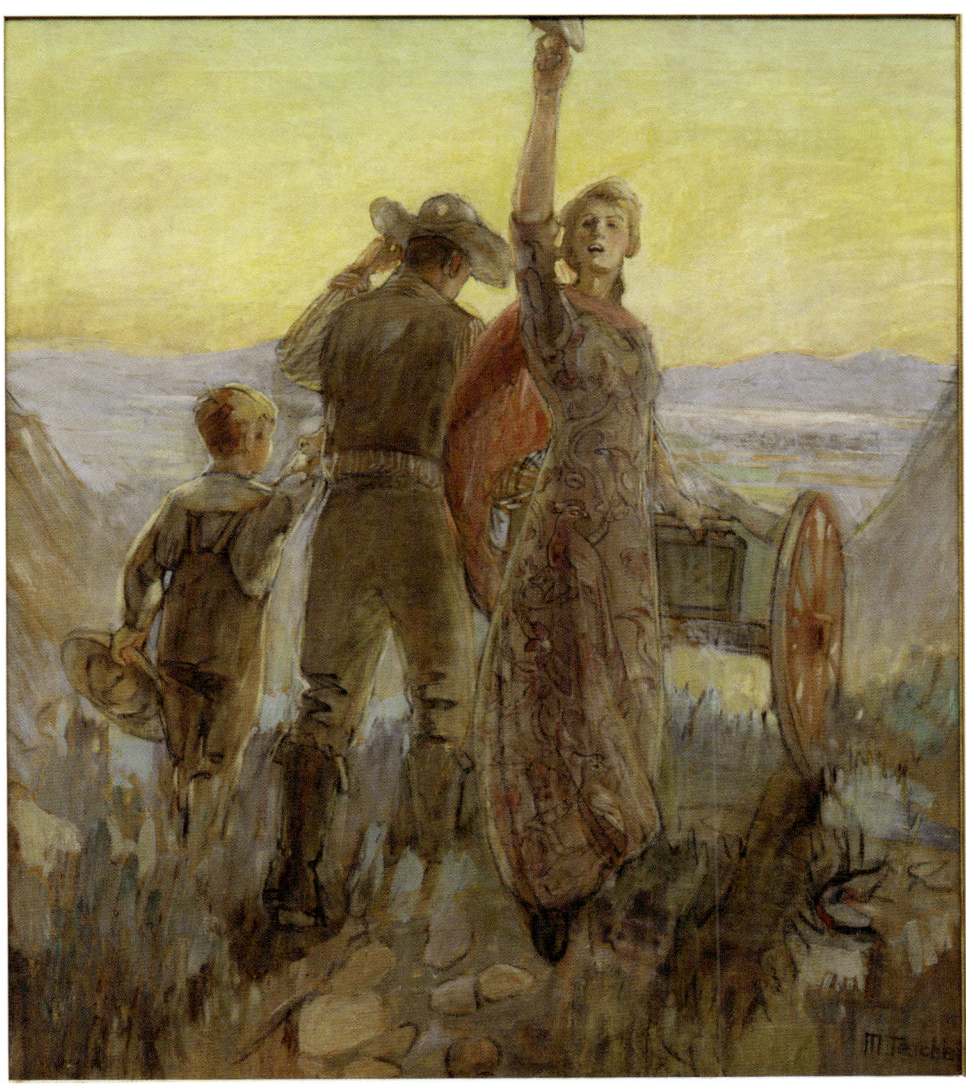

Fig. 13.7 Minerva Beretta Kohlhepp Teichert, *Zion Ho! (Handcart Pioneers),* oil on canvas, Church of Jesus Christ of Latter-day Saints Church History Museum.

Museum, characters are sketchily depicted, their faces turned away from the viewer entirely or gauzily softened to the point of indistinguishability. Still, they are not generic. Teichert embedded in them specifics that were resonant to her and her family.

One scholar of the artist noted that Teichert's aunt had given her a linen textile fragment taken from her great-grandmother's wedding dress, "one sky-blue but faded to old ivory, stamped with red birds." This patterned fabric is visible in *Zion Ho! (Handcart Pioneers):*

> In a valiant, confident, and triumphant posture, the woman wearing the dress patterned with birds-of-paradise in *Zion Ho!* takes her place, central to the composition and with certainty on the Western frontier. She, along with her husband and son, have reached the Salt Lake Valley. The meaningfulness of the bird-of-paradise design and the history of Teichert's maternal ancestors enable the exuberant figure to suggest that her accomplishment on the Western frontier is connected to the contributions of other women. She stands taller than her husband and son, and her jubilant, outstretched arm, her direct countenance, delineated description, and flowing, red Paisley shawl, serve to affirm her significance. This sharing of a family heirloom indicates an ongoing connection among Teichert's women family members, and Teichert herself becoming a keeper of family treasure. Teichert in turn shares this strong female connection with younger generations who witness this moment of celebration.[30]

Some contemporary scholars have referred to Teichert's technique as Impressionist, a term the artist disliked.[31] Perhaps the paintings correspond to Impressionist work in an entirely different sense, one that doesn't involve its color palette: as a pattern of commercial adoption. The nineteenth-century French artists displayed their work to the derision of the salon, but within a generation or two, the outcasts' art was collected widely by American industrialists as trophies of their gentility, and today these "pretty" pictures form the centerpiece of many a fine art museum in America.

Teichert's reputation traced a similar path, from rejection to acceptance to acclaim. Near the time of her death in 1976, her paintings were not well regarded. She had little commercial success, and though she offered the church her works, it routinely rejected them. She tried without luck to sell major series of paintings, and instead bartered them away. After her death her reputation shifted dramatically with a series of exhibitions, publications, and scholarship in Utah. Today, her work feels indispensable to the culture and the epitome of what can be achieved with determination and talent.

She was once asked about her painting style, and she replied with a statement that nearly feels like a manifesto based in the approval she received from Robert Henri at the Art Students League. She wrote, "[Latter-day Saint artists] shall develop an art as great as the Egyptians. Theirs is the art of a people, magnificent after millennia. So should our art, rich in story and backed by a great faith be so glorious that future generations may say, 'This is the art of a great race.'"[32]

A third example of LDS artists trained at the Art Students League who had a large impact on the culture is LeConte Stewart. Wallace Stegner, the much-decorated novelist and western writer, gave an appraisal of the Utah painter that aimed to situate his work in superlative terms: "It is probably the finest picture ever painted by a Utahn, or in Utah; and unlike most of its competition, it totally resists the temptation to sensationalize Utah scenery."[33] Stegner was referring to Stewart's *Private Car* (1937). In the painting, faceless men in Utah are seen riding the rails of the Union Pacific Railroad. Its title is a play on the notion of exclusivity, laid low by the brutality and deprivation of the Great Depression. All of this is set against a backdrop of a placid, if eerie, Utah landscape.

Utah suffered during the Depression. Its unemployment rate in 1933 was the fourth–highest in the country (at 35.8 percent), wages for employed workers plunged 45 percent, and by 1933 nearly one-third of all Utah residents were in some way on the government dole. All of the issues that buffeted the nation were present in Utah—homelessness, drops in income, protests, rising divorce rates, labor disputes, food insecurity, and gender discrimination in the workplace, for example—but a local difference was that the religious culture had considered itself to be impervious to such issues, to be independent of a government that it had fled, then fought, then tolerated, and to which it finally acquiesced in order to gain statehood. The state's population was resistant to the New Deal and its programs; however, it ultimately became at least as needy as any

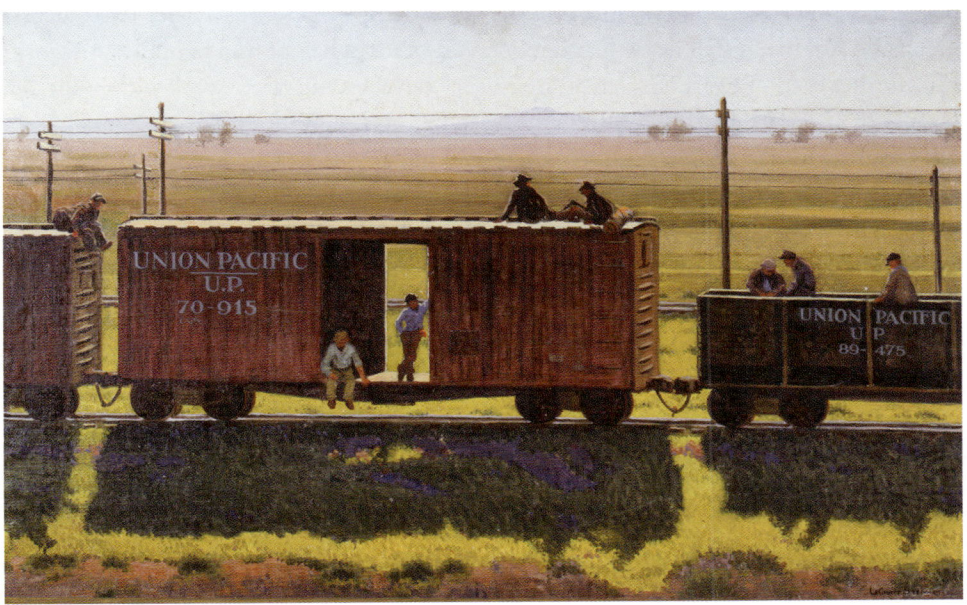

Fig. 13.8 LeConte Stewart, *Private Car*, 1937, oil on canvas, Church of Jesus Christ of Latter-day Saints Church History Museum, LDS 55-2490.

other state, if not more so. Utah ranked ninth among the states for per capita federal spending, far above the national average. Even after the church established its capstone project, the Church Welfare Plan, it was dwarfed by federal non-repayable expenditures in Utah, which were greater than church programs by a factor of ten. The state's character changed. The dominant party since its statehood (1896) was Republican, but the crucible of the Depression flipped the state to the Democrats from the early years of the Depression until the late 1940s.[34]

Certainly, residents of the state, including LDS members (the majority of its population), must have wondered what the state was becoming and perhaps, in a crisis of conscience, who they were becoming. With that turbulent history as a backdrop, Stewart's *Private Car* takes on a powerful tone of a painting completed in a decisive moment of the culture's dynamism. These men on the rails may have represented thousands just passing through looking for opportunities somewhere, anywhere, but in the history of the art of the LDS people, it reads as something more like a creative capitulation, when painting a colorful landscape was no longer artful enough without a social message attached to it.

After he saw a magazine advertisement for the Art Students League program, the teenage Stewart declared, "I made up my mind there and then that I was going."[35] To pay for it, he worked and saved, as Mahonri Young and Minerva Teichert and countless others had, independent of family financial support. In his case, Stewart labored in the fields of Idaho and did sign lettering for local businesses. His father voiced concern that the art business could not become a living, to which the young artist replied, "But I can have fun doing it."[36] There is subtext to the rejoinder. Stewart was accustomed to heartbreak and surely felt that he deserved relief. Why should he not find happiness in work? His mother died of heart failure when he was twelve, leaving a six-week-old infant. All four of his siblings died of childhood disease before LeConte turned sixteen. Then in 1911, during his last year in high school, he endured another loss when his father passed away, leaving him the sole survivor of his family. Undeterred, Stewart continued to work and save for New York by becoming a sixth-grade teacher in Murray, Utah.

Finally, in 1913, having saved $600, he attended a semester of the Art Students League's summer program before enrolling in the fall in its New York City home. He described his total dedication to the league: "I had to pay tuition, so I sacrificed everything else. I rented a top room with no windows, and there were bedbugs. I became quite sick, but I was determined to become certified, so I stuck it out." He returned to Utah in the spring on his last $5.[37]

Stewart served as a full-time LDS missionary in 1917, married while he was painting murals in the Hawaii temple, and then began teaching, but he always continued painting. At the University of Utah, he served as the department chair from 1938 to 1956. He had said after 1929 that he wanted to turn away from the peace and solitude of nature and instead represent the human cost of the crisis. About his austere subject matter, a recent curator wrote that the artworks "evoke images of abandonment and isolation that had roots in his childhood."[38]

Stegner wrote of the 1937 Stewart work, "This last painting . . . demonstrates how much power there still is in realism when realism is the expression of a passionate vision. All of Stewart's characteristic touches are there—the muted colors, the homely detail, the bleak, ambiguous message. The desert light that gilds those uprooted ones seems also to threaten them. They are silhouettes before flames."[39] Stewart makes the landscape a symbol and thereby elevates it from the decorative.

This distinction between Realism and realistic paintings is significant. The latter, which glorify the merely attractive landscape, had been the bread and butter of the region's artists since the first white people settled into the land. Stewart's love of the natural environment was as intense as that of any other Utah artist; however, in his Hopperesque paintings, lithographs, and drawings of the period, he tapped into the inherent loneliness of the unpopulated landscape, which he captured with moody intensity, or "bleak clarity," as Stegner would write. His approach to landscapes was informed by his experience away from it. They project, one could say, what someone who studied in a city, such as at the Art Students League, and was exposed to a broader view of art might have as a reaction to natural subject matter—namely, that it required additional layers of meaning to maximize its impact. Further, the effects achieved in works such as *Private Car* had the weight of authenticity and autobiography behind them.

These three examples—Young, Teichert, and Stewart—stand ably for the dozens of other LDS artists who studied at the Art Students League, each of them transformed by the New York experience and worthy of expansive academic study. This trio's influence on the art of the Mormon people is difficult to overestimate: Stewart taught hundreds of students during his years at the University of Utah and became one of the state's most cherished painters; Teichert's work and story have become so iconic in the global LDS community that when the Manti temple was threatened with demolition in 2021, her many champions decried the potential loss of her murals in the sacred building and convinced decision-makers to protect the storied space (as President Russell M. Nelson said, "As we have continued to seek the direction of the Lord on this matter, we have been impressed to modify our earlier plans for the Manti Utah Temple so that the pioneer craftsmanship, artwork and character will be preserved, including the painted murals loved by so many. We will leave those murals where they are located now—inside the Manti Utah Temple");[40] and Young's monuments to his ancestors and to the church founders' lives stand as timeless Salt Lake City landmarks. In each case, a direct line can be traced from their iconic works, philosophies, and reputations to their student origins at the league.

The Art Students League of New York remains at its historic location, 215 West 57th Street near Carnegie Hall, where it has resided since 1892. It recently sold its air rights overhead for $31.8 million,[41] which guarantees its financial future and ability to stay in its home while towering skyscrapers rise all around it. It is no longer the primary source of art education in America, of course. As colleges and universities developed studio programs to become art academies themselves—sometimes staffed by educators who studied at the league—the league's singular nature was dissipated but never extinguished. More important to the question of influence is the legacy of those former Leaguers as they became university professors and private instructors (something that happened frequently in Utah), thereby continuing the league's legacy by the proxy of its former students.

That is not to suggest that all of the art emerging from these artists shares a purpose or style. In that sense, the plurality reflects the sensibility of the league's broad approach to teaching. It is unsurprising that as LDS artists became professors themselves, they replicated the advice they had received and the general sense of comfort with a multiplicity of philosophies, frequently joining forces with peers whose approaches were dramatically different from their own. When Leaguers became Utah university professors, their departments largely resisted the narrow school-of-thought curricula that one might have anticipated in a regional setting in the mid-twentieth century and beyond.

Back in 1875, the league announced its new existence with lofty goals: "the attainment of a higher development in Art studies; the encouragement of a spirit of unselfishness among its members; the imparting of valuable information pertaining to Art as acquired by any of the members . . . ; mutual help in study, and sympathy and practical assistance (if need be) in time of sickness and trouble."[42] It was a letter of protest that began a movement, and like any movement, it grew and affected the lives of others far beyond its initial reach. This includes the art of the LDS people.

NOTES

[1] Robert S. Olpin, *Waldo Midgley: Birds, Animals, People, Things* (Salt Lake City: Utah Museum of Fine Arts, 1984), 12. Ultimately, Midgley chose to study at the Henri School on 80th Street, but this remembrance of his first impressions of the city with fellow Utah artist Hal Burrows is typical of the experience of young LDS artists searching an education in art making.

[2] Young arrived in New York in the fall of 1899 and ran out of money by early April. See Norma S. Davis, *A Song of Joys: The Biography of Mahonri Mackintosh Young, Sculptor, Painter, Etcher* (Provo, UT: M. Seth and Maurine D. Horne Center for the Study of Art, Brigham Young University Museum of Art, 1999), 36, 38–47.

[3] Bennard B. Perlman, *Painters of the Ashcan School: The Immortal Eight* (Cincinnati, OH: North Light, 1979), 108.

[4] See Linda Jones Gibbs, *Harvesting the Light: The Paris Art Mission and Beginnings of Utah Impressionism* (Salt Lake City: Corporation of the President of the Church of Jesus Christ of Latter-day Saints, 1987).

[5] The following list is complied by the author and based on research by him and additional scholarship generously shared by Vern Swanson, Donna Poulton, Angela Swanson Jones, and Micah Christensen from the *Dictionary of Utah Fine Artists, 2022.* From a list of eighty-one artists with Utah connections who studied at the league (and it can be assumed that the list is incomplete, given that LDS artists came to study from various states and others are simply unidentified), the following LDS students at the league are verified on the rolls of the church as members: Daniel "Dan" Bischoff Baxter (1948–1986), Verla Leone Birrell (1903–2001), Grace Elizabeth Cutler (1906–1998), Donna Day (1912–1996), George Smith Dibble (1904–1992), Maxine Stoddard Englund (b. 1928), John Henry Evans Jr. (1906–1988), Avard Tennyson Fairbanks (1897–1987), Gerald "Jerry" Dale Fairclough (1938–2017), Louise Taylor Richards Farnsworth

(1878–1969), Lynn Fausett (1894–1977), William Dean Fausett (1913–1998), Lorin George Folland Jr. (1920–2004), Mabel Frazer (1887–1982), Arlyn LaMoyne Garside (1932–2012), Mark Allen Graham (b. 1958), Jimmie Floyd Jones (1933–2009), Frank Ward Kent (1912–1977), Ranch Shipley Kimball (1894–1980), Torlief Severin Knaphus (1881–1965), Jessie Cowley Larson (1912–2001), Julia "Judy" Fransworth Lund (1911–1996), Wilson Jay Ong (b. 1958), George Herman Palmer (1894–1947), Caroline Keturah Parry Wooley (1885–1967), Oliver Horace Parson (1916–2013), Alex Rane (b. 1986), Gaylynn Lorene Pettersen Ribeira (b. 1981), Kenneth "Ken" Pauling Riley (1919–2015), Cornelius Salisbury (1882–1970), Mary Rose Sauer (b. 1986), John Septimus "Jack" Sears (1875–1969), Bruce Hixson Smith (b. 1936), S. (Sidney) Paul Smith (1904–1990), Mary Ruth Ballard Snow-Corr (1908–2004), Trevor Jack Thomas Southey (1940–2015), J. Kenneth "Ken" Spencer (b. 1968), Lawrence Squires (1887–1928), LeConte Stewart (1891–1990), Sandra Wilson Bickmore Summerhays (1942–2019), Justin Jay Taylor (b. 1976), Mary H. Teasdale (1863–1937), Minerva Bernetta Kohlhepp Teichert (1883–1976), Morton Wayne Thiebaud (1920–2021), Glen H. Turner (1918–1993), Theodore "Ted" Milton Wassmer (1910–2006), Harris Taylor Weberg (1898–1979), Mary Lois Sharp Wheatley (1926–2013), and Mahonri Macintosh Young (1877–1957).

6 Olpin, *Waldo Midgley,* 11.

7 Remarks made by President Brigham Young in the tabernacle, Great Salt Lake City, January 26, 1862. See *Journal of Discourses* online, https://www.josephsmithfoundation.org/journalofdiscourses/speakers/brigham-young/necessity-of-paying-due-attention-to-temporal-duties-c/.

8 The homogeneity of Mormonism is and was never as total as is commonly presumed. From its founding, missionaries traveled to nearly every continent, and their converts certainly included makers of art and objects of many kinds. Even if all of their work was uncovered and documented, it is inconceivable to imagine that all of these creative individuals might share a visual style so similar as to feel like a single school of thought. Adding to such issues are at least three notable facts: that multiple religious denominations have evolved separately from the original 1830 institution; that many people in the religion have come from other cultures and religions and have brought with them the art of their cultures to merge into a new artistic identity; and that the spectrum of Mormonism is as wide as that of any other religion and includes those who culturally identify as Mormon, others who are casual believers, and those who are connected devoutly to the Church of Jesus Christ of Latter-day Saints.

9 See Church of Jesus Christ of Latter-day Saints, "Colonies in Mexico," https://abn.churchofjesuschrist.org/study/history/topics/colonies-in-mexico?lang=eng&abVersion=V01&abName=GLOB88, accessed November 5, 2021.

10 Marchal E. Landgren, *Years of Art: The Story of the Art Students League of New York* (New York: Robert M. McBride, 1940), 111.

11 Even a partial listing of league artists reads like a who's who of greatness. A small sampling: Thomas Hart Benton, Helen Frankenthaler, Hans Hofmann, Roy Lichtenstein, Louise Nevelson, Louise Bourgeois, Lee Bontecou, George Grosz, Reginald Marsh, Georgina O'Keeffe, Robert Rauschenberg, Mark Rothko, Cy Twombly, Donald Judd, Jackson Pollock, Frederick Remington, Bernice Abbott, Ai Weiwei, Romare Bearden, Red Grooms, Eva Hesse, Yasuo Kuniyoshi, John Marin, Marison, David Smith, Robert Smithson, Joseph Stella, and Clyfford Still. Taken from "Prominent Former Students of the Art Students League of New York," https://theartstudentsleague.org/some-prominent-former-students-ofthe-art-students-league-of-new-york/, accessed January 28, 2022.

12 This acceptance occurred at roughly the same time that LDS businesspeople and scientists began to attain recognition in their fields.

13 Landgren, *Years of Art,* 21.

14 Landgren, *Years of Art,* 21.

15 Landgren, *Years of Art,* 29.

16 Landgren, *Years of Art,* 33.

17 For a full list of instructors from 1875 to 1940, see Landgren, Years of Art, 112–116.

18 See "M. Teichert: Artist of Dramatic Vision," *Ensign,* October 2007, https://www.churchofjesuschrist.org/study/ensign/2007/10/m-teichert-artist-of-dramatic-vision?lang=eng.

[19] Minerva Teichert, handwritten manuscript cited in Marian Eastwood Wardle, "Minerva Teichert's Murals: The Motivation for Her Large-scale Production" (master's thesis, Brigham Young University, 1988).

[20] Jan Underwood Pinborough, "*Minerva Kohlhep Teichert: With a Bold Brush,*" Ensign, April 1989, citing Teichert's unpublished 1947 manuscript, https://www.churchofjesuschrist.org/study/ensign/1989/04/minerva-kohlhepp-teichert-with-a-bold-brush?lang=eng.

[21] Pinborough, "Minerva Kohlhep Teichert."

[22] "M. Teichert: Artist of Dramatic Vision."

[23] Micah Christensen, "Minerva Teichert and Robert Henri," May 25, 2018, *Anthony's Fine Art and Antiques* (blog).

[24] Wardle, "Minerva Teichert's Murals," 12.

[25] Minerva Beretta Kohlhepp Teichert (American, 1888–1976), *Immigrants to New York City (Jewish Refugees)* (1938), oil on canvas, 59 1/4″ × 37 1/4″, Brigham Young University Museum of Art.

[26] Minerva Kohlhepp to Ella Kohlhepp, October 31, 1015, Minerva Kohlhepp Teichert (1888–1976) Collection, 1900–1998, Special Collections, BYU, as cited in Deirdre Mason Scharffs, "*Refiguring the Wild West: Minerva Teichert and Her Feminine Communities*" (master's thesis, Brigham Young University, 2016), 30–31, https://scholarsarchive.byu.edu/cgi/viewcontent.cgi?article=6846&context=etd.

[27] See Phillipp Malzl, "MOA Mini-Tour: Minerva Teichert's 'Immigrants to New York City,'" Brigham Young University Museum of Art, Facebook Live, June 21, 2019.

[28] Alice Merrill Horne to Minerva Teichert, April 30, 1932 (?), cited in Scharffs, "Refiguring the Wild West," 39.

[29] Amy L. Williamson, "*Storytelling Through Brushstrokes: Minerva Teichert's Visualization of the Mormon Pioneer Experience and Messages to Her Audience*" (master's thesis, Utah State University, 2009), https://digitalcommons.usu.edu/cgi/viewcontent.cgi?article=1393&context=etd.

[30] Scharffs, "Refiguring the Wild West," 25–26.

[31] John Teichert reported that Minerva never used the term to describe her work and disliked it. See Williamson, "Storytelling Through Brushstrokes."

[32] See Scharffs, "Refiguring the Wild West," citing Teichert correspondence.

[33] Wallace Stegner, "The Power of Homely Detail," *American Heritage Magazine,* August–September 1985. Stegner won the Pulitzer Prize in 1972 for *Angle of Repose* and the National Book Award in 1977 for *The Spectator Bird.* The Stegner Fellowship program at Stanford University is a creative writing fellowship, and the Wallace Stegner Prize in Environmental or American Western History is administered by the University of Utah Press in recognition of the best monograph on a Western topic received by the press. In 1992, Stegner refused a National Medal from the National Endowment for the Arts in protest that the NEA had become too politicized.

[34] For the effects of the Great Depression on Utah, see John S. McCormick's *Utah History Encyclopedia* (1994), cited in "The Great Depression," History to Go, Utah Deparment of Cultural and Community Engagment, May 10, 2016, https://historytogo.utah.gov/great-depression/.

[35] Robert O. Davis, "Desert, Brush, and Oil: A Portrait of LeConte Stewart," *Ensign,* February 1985.

[36] Davis, "Desert, Brush, and Oil."

[37] Davis, "Desert, Brush, and Oil."

[38] Carma Wadley, "UMFA, Church History Museum Collaborate on LeConte Stewart Exhibit," *Deseret News,* July 16, 2011, https://www.deseret.com/2011/7/16/20203999/umfa-church-history-museum-collaborate-on-leconte-stewart-exhibit.

[39] Stegner, "The Power of Homely Detail."

[40] Peggy Fletcher Stack, "'Leaders Listened'—Treasured Murals Will Stay in Manti Temple; Ephraim Will Get an LDS Temple, Too," *Salt Lake Tribune,* May 1, 2021, https://www.sltrib.com/religion/2021/05/01/breaking-treasured-manti/.

[41] Jesse Denno, "Suit Against Art Students League Board Decision to Sell Air Rights Fails on Appeal," *CityLand,* March 16, 2016, https://www.citylandnyc.org/suit-against-art-students-league-board-decision-to-sell-air-rights-fails-on-appeal/.

[42] Landgren, *Years of Art,* 18.

14

GEORGE DIBBLE AND MODERNISM IN UTAH

GLEN NELSON

Two and a half years before his death of cancer in 1992 at the age of eighty-eight, George Smith Dibble was given a retrospective of sixty years' worth of his paintings at the Utah Museum of Fine Arts on the campus of the University of Utah. The exhibition's subtitle, *Painter, Teacher, Critic*, refers to Dibble's lifetime of making art, his decades of teaching art at Utah State University, Brigham Young University, San Jose State University, the College of Southern Utah, Washington State University, and the University of Utah, his work as an author, and his nearly forty-year tenure as art critic for the *Salt Lake Tribune*. At the time of the retrospective, the museum's director, Frank Sanguinetti, wrote in the exhibition catalogue that it was "long overdue."[1] Given Dibble's struggle in his community for acceptance, which this chapter seeks to use as a case study to describe prejudice aimed at a twentieth-century creative arts movement, there was more to the understatement than that.

Dibble was a modernist painter—his preferred medium in maturity was watercolor—and a recounting of his struggle for acceptance in Utah despite his many platforms of influence serves to illuminate the failure of his regional and religious cultures to embrace artistic change. As an individual, he pressed forward nevertheless and found his voice inspired by the landscape of the West. However, the thinly veiled animosities he experienced had wider and debilitating consequences. While this distrust of the new was a pervasive sentiment throughout the twentieth century in many places, Utah's—and, to the extent that the state's culture overlapped with the religious culture of its largest demographic, the Church of Jesus Christ of Latter-day Saints, the church's—unwillingness to accept emerging philosophies of visual art had a reverberating impact on a people already sidelined geographically and socially and on its creative artists and art students. Further, it hobbled artists' professional aspirations and their ability to compete for critical attention and patronage outside of the region because works made in traditional modes of Realism that had been abandoned by progressive artists looked increasingly out of date and out of touch as the century proceeded. It created a schism for young artists still in the process of finding their voice, who considered new art worthy of exploration. In LDS culture specifically—although other religious cultures manifested parallel responses—modernism was sometimes equated with evil, Communism, and atheism, and these unfair and prejudiced attitudes forced LDS artists interested in pursuing modernism (which is a broad term that encompasses many movements of the twentieth century) into combative or defensive postures that undermined their status in the community, which in turn lent the culture, when viewed from outside, a further reputation for backwardness.

TRASH

A telling episode of this prejudice occurred regarding Dibble's painting *Cedar Breaks No. 2*.[2] The story is offered here as a representative tale, with the acknowledgment that innumerable modern artists could tell similar anecdotes regarding their own works of the period, including some in LDS culture, and including some even today. It is a narrative about Dibble's most famous work, which Robert S. Olpin eventually placed on the back cover of his influential survey of Utah art in 1991. It appeared on the back cover of Dibble's 1989 retrospective catalogue too, and the artist used it on the front cover of his textbook published by Holt and Rinehart (1967), *Watercolor: Materials and Techniques*. According to the artist's granddaughter, the story goes like this.

Cedar Breaks No. 2 was created in 1952 during a period when the artist spent his summers in southern Utah as a visiting professor at Branch Agricultural College (Southern Utah University today). Slightly to the east of the small college town is Cedar Breaks National Monument, a striking geologic amphitheater at the top of the Colorado Plateau that starts at ten thousand feet above sea level and drops two thousand feet within a span of some three miles, a space marked by eroded, variegated cliffs and canyons nearly barren of vegetation. The location sparked the artist's imagination, and he commented about trying to harness "a wild nightmare of colors," adding, "The whole landscape assails you, overpowers you. You don't know where to tackle it."[3] Dibble returned repeatedly to the dramatic, colorful, almost alien vista, a favorite site for artists and camera-wielding visitors, and he created a series of works on that landscape, which can be seen now as a breakthrough point in his evolving thought processes. He noted that after wrestling with the image, he created *Cedar Breaks No. 2* from memory. Dibble's son Jonathan remarked about the struggles and constraints, "He had to live off what paintings he could sell on top of what he could earn as a teacher. It wasn't until *Cedar Breaks No. 2* that he found himself."[4]

The 22″ × 29.5″ watercolor reads immediately as a landscape, if an atypical one. Particularly in the distance, two ranges of mountains appear as reductive but representational horizontal forms. The right side of the painting is populated with densely placed, abstracted trees and low brush, in contrast with the left side, which the artist leaves nearly blank, although the most recognizable form of the work is here: a lone pine. The primary visual feature of the work is the series of overlapping rectangular shapes in the

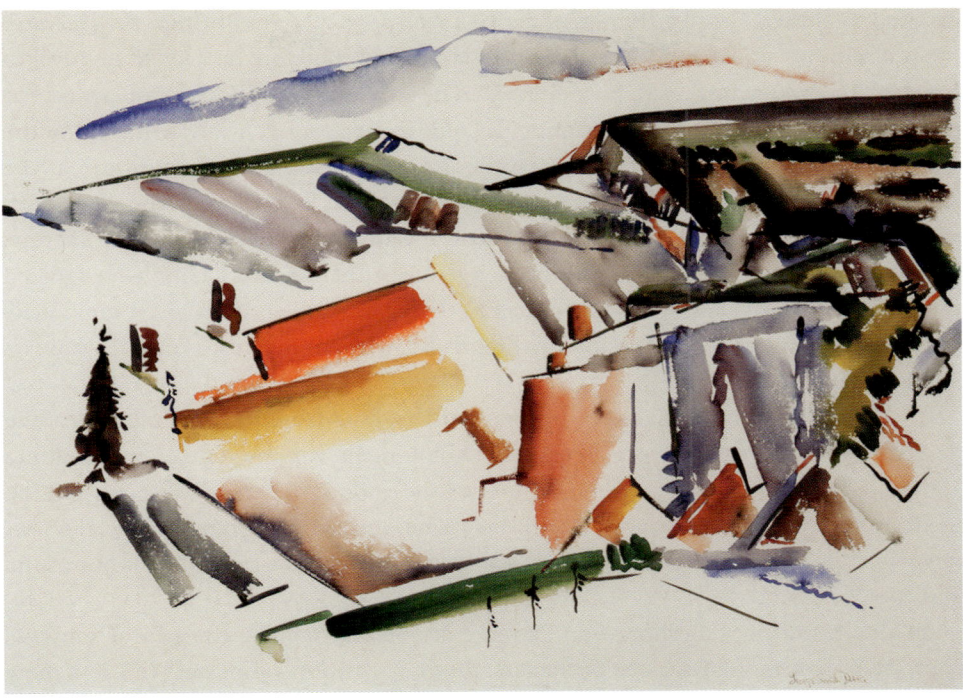

Fig. 14.1 George Smith Dibble, *Cedar Breaks No. 2*, 1952, watercolor, 22″ × 30″, private collection of Jonathan A. Dibble.

center delineated by thin black lines and brushed with planes of warm reds, yellows, and violets. Its balance is derived from the vivid red and yellow strokes, broadly applied to represent recurring formations that the artist has collapsed into bold forms. *Cedar Breaks No. 2* manages to feel both structured and spontaneous. This is a painting about restraint and reduction—highlighted further by the transparency of his medium—but the boldness of its color and the simplicity of its rhythmic geometries somehow seem inevitable for a geological landscape that itself feels grandly geometric.

In the body of Dibble's work to this point, this painting is a culmination of the artist's impulse to reduce to simplified gestures the most salient elements of a landscape, to feature vivid colors juxtaposed against each other, and to embrace the white space of the paper itself, almost as a visual palate cleanser and its own delineator of spatial volumes, in order to condense the effects of each stroke. In brief, these heightened effects, which are consistent with the experience of being in the landscape but diverge from the verisimilitude of its reproduction, are what make it modern.

Despite a general unease with modernism in Utah, *Cedar Breaks No. 2* won a statewide art show in the mid-1950s, and the Utah State Agricultural College (Utah State University today) acquired the painting. A few years later, as Dibble considered which of his works to feature on the cover of his textbook on watercolor techniques, which he planned to illustrate with examples of his own works, he thought of *Cedar Breaks No. 2.* He was without a quality photograph of the work, and therefore he needed to travel to Logan, Utah, where it resided. However, when he arrived at the school, he was informed that there was no record of the painting. It could not be found, nor was it listed in the school's art inventory. One can imagine the artist's devastation and confusion at the loss of *Cedar Breaks No. 2.* His artistic career to that point had not been showered with accolades. The loss of the painting was a loss of hard-fought recognition and approbation as well as of what he surely considered a treasured creation. Dibble recognized that for him, creative lightning had struck in the 1952 work and had given him a new direction: "I could feel good about anything I did, without regard to rules. That was a liberating experience."[5]

This story was retold in 2012 by the artist's granddaughter Sarah Dibble. She describes what happened next: "Puzzled, Dibble made his way out of the building and passed the janitor's office when he noticed the door of the office was open and the painting thumb tacked to the wall with no frame or mat. After inquiring of the janitor where he had found the painting, Dibble was told that he had taken it out of the garbage."[6]

In this disturbing anecdote—an extreme act of censorship—the janitor must be contrasted with more nefarious characters, those in positions of power who somehow determined that a work in a permanent collection and an object of university property would be not merely hidden from view or even deaccessioned but thrown away and its history expunged. The tale is even sadder given that Utah State University had been historically the state's leading academic institution for modern visual artists.

Dibble had faced such attitudes in Utah previously. They began even before the artist returned to Utah in 1940 after his studies in New York at the Art Students League (1929–1930) and at Columbia University (1935–1940). In an era when there were few venues to display fine art in the state, local artists looked to state fairs and similar invitational events as important professional showcases. In 1938, Dibble entered a work, *Pay Dirt,*[7] into the state art show. In the image, faceless, abstracted workers toil at an industrial site. The painting won a Purchase Award, and it subsequently entered into the state's collection. Dibble later discovered that while it was in the collection, an artist and teacher, Cornelius Salisbury, took the work to "clean" it. Again from Sarah Dibble's account: "Salisbury got a hold of the painting and scrubbed it with a wire brush in hopes to destroy it, as Dibble believed."[8] When the artist was offered the opportunity to replace the painting, Dibble declined. The Utah Division of Arts and Museums now notes the story of its vandalism online, as well as whenever the work is exhibited.[9]

In 1940, Dibble entered an even more abstract painting at the Utah State Fair, *Long Island Sound.*[10] This painting from 1939 had been previously exhibited and admired in New York at an intercollegiate show while the artist was finishing his master's degree at Columbia University. Its submission to the Utah fair was a risk, given that the painting challenged viewers to interpret how the overlapping shapes evoked a New York seascape

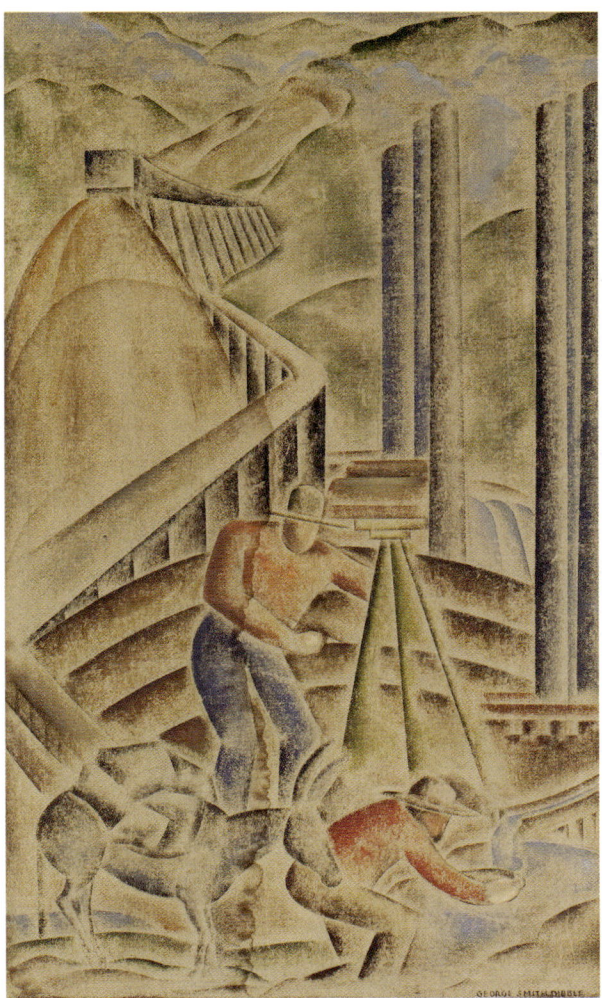

Fig. 14.2 George Smith Dibble, *Pay Dirt*, 1938, pastel on canvas, 45″ × 27″, State of Utah Alice Merrill Horne Art Collection. Courtesy Utah Arts & Museums.

at all. The artist said it referred to the sea "in the most extreme sense."[11] At the time, he was working at Utah State as a visiting professor under Calvin Fletcher, who defended modernism and sought to expose students to a more open field of opportunity.

Sarah Dibble relates, "After entering this painting in the Utah State fair, Dibble returned to see the exhibit. Upon viewing the show, he discovered that his work was accepted and won a cash prize. He also discovered that it had been moved to the amateur section of the exhibition. When he investigated the reason for what he viewed as a demotion, he was told by the jury that his highly modern style was not considered to be professional art."[12] The artist protested to the jury, who eventually put the painting back

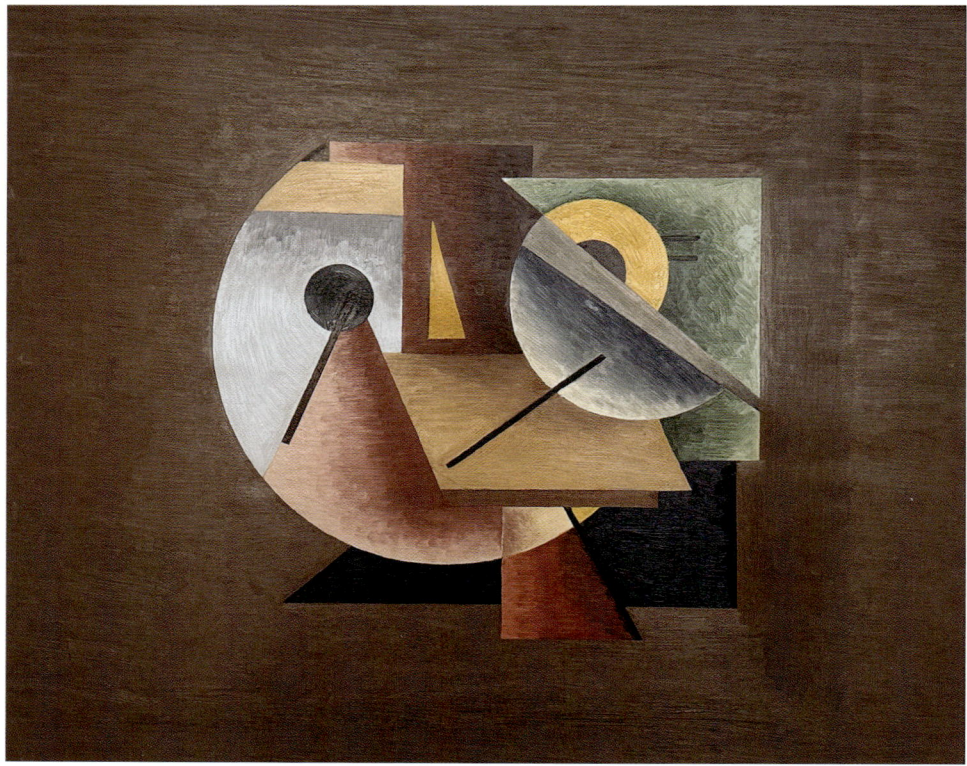

Fig. 14.3 George Smith Dibble, *Long Island Sound*, 1939, oil on paper, 20″ × 24.5″, private collection of Sarah Dibble.

into the professional category, although they stripped it of its cash prize. Subsequently, over the next two decades the fair handed out separate awards—for traditional painting and for modern painting.

DISDAIN AND DISTRUST

One can understand that an uninitiated viewer might fail to respond to new modes of painting, to be suspicious of them, and even to dislike them at first sight. It was an era in which relatively few people ventured very far from home and therefore had limited exposure to art made outside their region. There was no fine art museum anywhere near Utah that had works in its permanent collection to show consistently the recent trends in Paris, New York, and other metropolitan art centers or to follow the evolutions of modernism over the previous fifty years. This is not to say that the public was disinterested. As temporary exhibitions came through the state from time to time, they generated considerable attention. Locals were curious. The rejection of works by Dibble and his colleagues, on the other hand, is different. The actions of prejudice and censorship described above were acted out not by an uninformed public but by trained juries, personnel in charge of fine art collections, other artists, and academic institutions. These were petty, punitive actions meant to demean and marginalize. It must certainly have been hurtful to Dibble that these attacks often came from people of his own faith and from other artists.

Traditionalists, who were often artistic gatekeepers, felt threatened by modernism. Avard Fairbanks, whose many commissions of religious works for the LDS Church, including several historical public works and sculptures of the angel Moroni adorning temple spires, likely spoke for many when he derided modern art as "laboratory experiments" and claimed "that they destroyed and debased art."[13] The chair of the art department at Brigham Young University, B. F. Larsen, pulled Dibble, a lifelong member of the LDS Church, aside and said, "Now look, if you persist in following this modern trend, you will find yourself in the Communist camp. It'll do you no good!"[14]

At the end of his life, referring to this period, Dibble stated, "You see, this was the same general time when Fairbanks was preaching to the whole and sundry here that art was 'going to the dogs.'"[15] Art and Communism were linked, in the minds of some Utahns, after the 1936 exhibition of works by Diego Rivera and the 1937 exhibition by Frida Kahlo in Salt Lake City at the Art Barn, which incited local debate about Marxism and its relationship to painting. Likely, the 1934 controversy of the destruction of Rivera's mural in New York City's Rockefeller Center because of perceived leftist imagery hung over the Salt Lake City exhibitions too. The view that there was a direct connection between modern art and leftist thought was somewhat widely held across the nation. Scholar Karal Ann Marling noted, "Calling someone a modernist was tantamount to calling him a communist, un-American, or 'Red.'"[16] Add to that the reactions of a conservative, religious state, where many equated Communism with atheism, and one can see how personally and spiritually consequential these comments must have seemed to Dibble.

George Dibble's art did not aim at protest. His goal was not rebellion, nor, for that matter, social justice; rather, he had found in modernism a method that fit his voice and allowed him to reframe landscapes and still lifes to make them new. He said, "I found my style at the Art Studen[ts] League. School was drudgery until I got to New York and realized I had a point of view, that I could use it and get recognition for it."[17] He returned to Utah in 1930 and worked as a teacher; he went back to New York in 1935 and furthered his education at Columbia University, where he earned his bachelor of arts in 1938 and his master of arts two years later. In New York, his exposure to Cézanne, Cubism, and other ideas of modernism influenced him greatly. Regarding Cubism, he said, "I found it quite interesting to me because I found that it was strengthening to organize the canvas in spatial terms, in terms of concept. The multiple viewing[,] for example, understanding what's inside the cup as well as outside, was fascinating."[18] He embraced asymmetry, working with less in terms of palette and subject matter, and he referred to painting as choreography.[19]

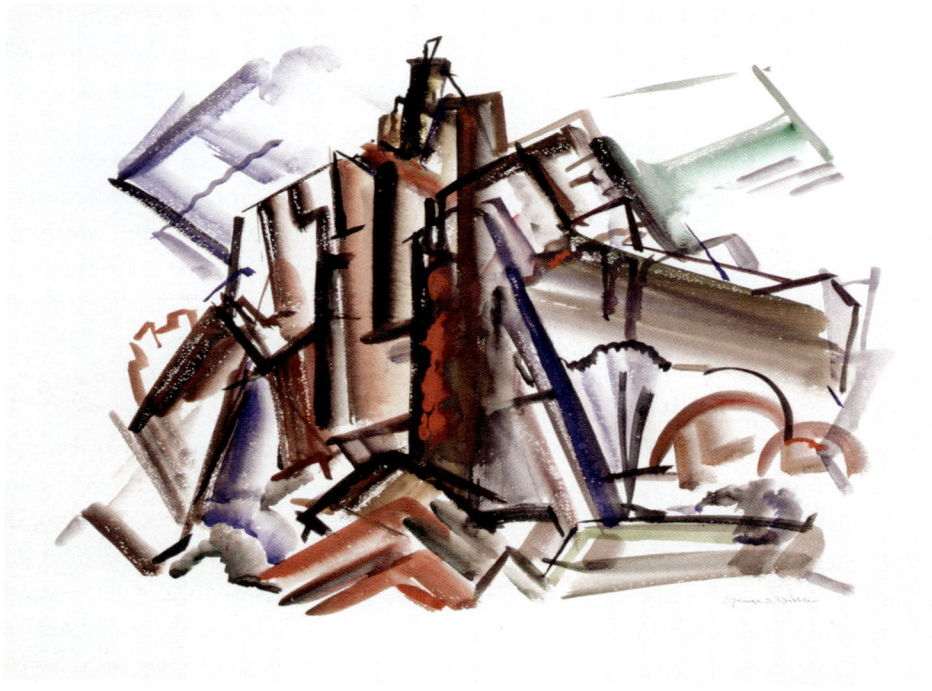

Fig. 14.4 George Smith Dibble, *Temple of Sinawava (Zion's Park)*, 1953, watercolor, 22 1/8″ × 30″, Brigham Young University Museum of Art, gift of the estate of George Smith Dibble, 1992.

Nonetheless, Dibble softened his approach to painting in the 1940s while teaching at the University of Utah alongside LeConte Stewart. Stewart too was a landscape painter and trained in New York, yet his views of contemporary art practices were completely opposed to Dibble's. Stewart had a strongly negative reaction to modernism, having witnessed the Armory Show of 1913 when he was studying at the Art Students League of New York. The exhibition introduced European modernists to the United States, and Stewart was swept up in the accompanying public furor. Decades later, Stewart continued to call modernism a "disease," and as Utah modernists began to gather in the early 1940s, he contested the legitimacy of modernism itself.[20]

By the time Dibble came to work at the University of Utah, Stewart was serving as the chair of the art department, and in order to gain tenure, Dibble felt he had to rein in his style to placate the conservative tastes of the faculty, Stewart in particular. An undated painting created in the 1940s is Dibble's *Mount Olympus*,[21] which is a work that merely hints at a Cézannesque approach to landscape painting. The work depicts the mountain, which is a prominent peak on the east side of the Salt Lake Valley and visible from locations throughout the city. In the painting, facets of the mountain and merging fields below are almost divided into geometric volumes—almost, but not quite. The artist pulls back, blends the shapes together, and stops short of confronting the viewer

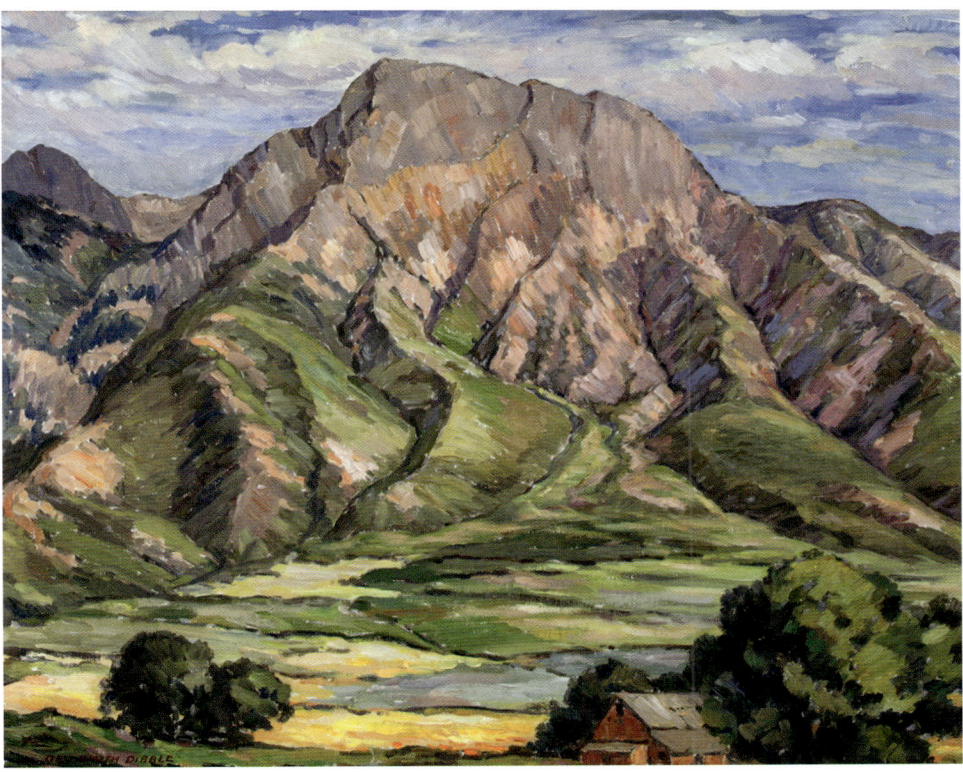

Fig. 14.5 George Smith Dibble, *Mount Olympus*, 1940s, oil on canvas, 24″ × 34″, private collection of Jonathan A. Dibble.

with the challenge to assemble the image from its fragmented elements. If the objective was to create a work that could pass as traditional with his peers, the experiment was successful. LeConte Stewart told Dibble condescendingly, "Now that is a damn good painting,"[22] with the clear insinuation that Dibble's more modernist works did not meet with same approval from him.

In 1949, Dibble became associate professor. In 1953, he was named the *Tribune* art critic. Then, in 1956, LeConte Stewart retired from the university. This freed Dibble at last to embark on a body of modernist works that he had begun making after *Cedar Breaks No. 2*. Further, other universities in the state began to hire modern artists on their faculties. Taken together, these events heralded the artist's mature style.

MANIFESTOS

Dibble was not the only artist to have experienced censorship for making modernist work. As Robert S. Olpin later wrote, the modern artists of Utah set out to prove that there were more than two kinds of art in Utah, either "good" or "modern."[23] Dibble had not abandoned modernism or fully repressed it before 1956. If his 1940s work showed

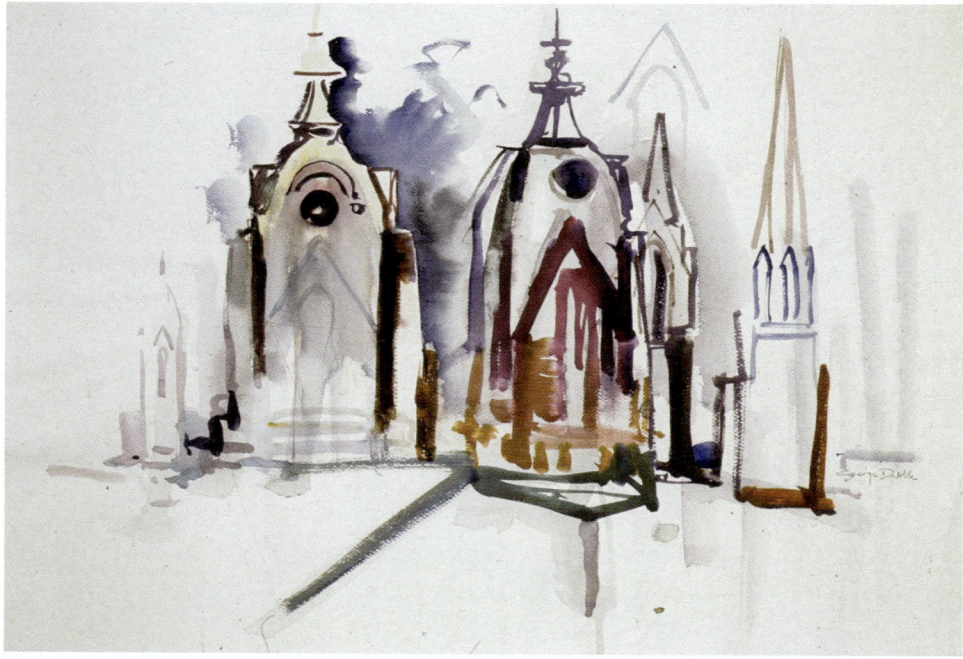

Fig. 14.6 George Smith Dibble, *Assembly Hall* (detail), watercolor, 22″ × 30″, Church of Jesus Christ of Latter-day Saints Church History Museum.

less of his progressive thinking, his work as an influencer and educator made up the difference. Around 1941, a group of Utah painters interested in modernism came together at the Art Barn at the invitation of Don Goddall, the director of the Utah State Art Center. The nine artists—Donald B. Goodall, Harry Reuben Reynolds, Leone Eitel,[24] George Dibble, Calvin Fletcher, Clara Irene Thompson Fletcher, Henry Neil Rasmussen, Millard Fillmore Malin Jr., and Alberta Johnson Kondratieff (all but the first two of whom were LDS Church members)[25]—became the "Modern Artists of Utah." Through casual conversations and formal seminars, together they drafted and issued the "Modern Art Manifesto." They sought to reduce hostility in the community toward modernism and familiarize the public with what they were trying to achieve. It was the first time that artists in Utah had attempted to draft a document in support of modern art—it is a historic document in the history of Mormon art as well—and it merits full reproduction here:

The Modern Artist does not attempt to reproduce the photographic or surface appearance of things but,

1. Uses individually conceived forms, the products of his experience, to express his aesthetic ideas and emotions, in terms of the particular medium employed.

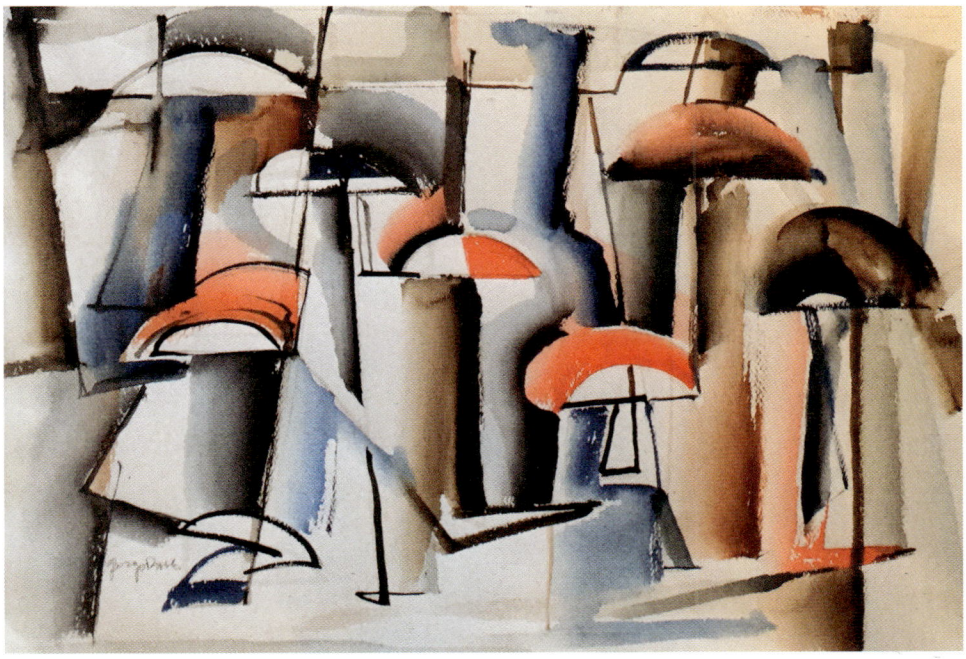

Fig. 14.7 George Smith Dibble, *Sketch for Cubist Breaks*, watercolor, 15.5" × 22", Church of Jesus Christ of Latter-day Saints Church History Museum.

2. Employs the design elements contained in plastic form, including relationships of line, tone, space, plans, texture, color and subject matter.
3. Uses emotional and intellectual freedom in organizing the subject into unified form.
4. The modern artist respects the validity of the picture field. This picture field is composed of front, back and side planes, determined by the artist.

It is the hope and desire of the persons listing the above aims that the Utah artists trying to achieve similar ideals will join with them in an exhibition of their work. No other qualification than a similarity in purpose is required for entrance. The exhibition will be held January 6 to 27, 1942 at the Utah State Art Center, Salt Lake City. If you are attempting similar objectives, you are cordially invited to join. Since complete realization of all these aims has as yet been reached by no one artist, it is stressed by the committee that purpose is more important, currently, than effectiveness of achievement in this first bringing together of Modern Artists in Utah.

In the same year in which their manifesto appeared, Dibble and another Utah modernist painter, Bill Parkinson, also LDS, participated in an exhibition at the Utah Art Center that showed its concepts in action.[26] Considered to be the first exhibition in

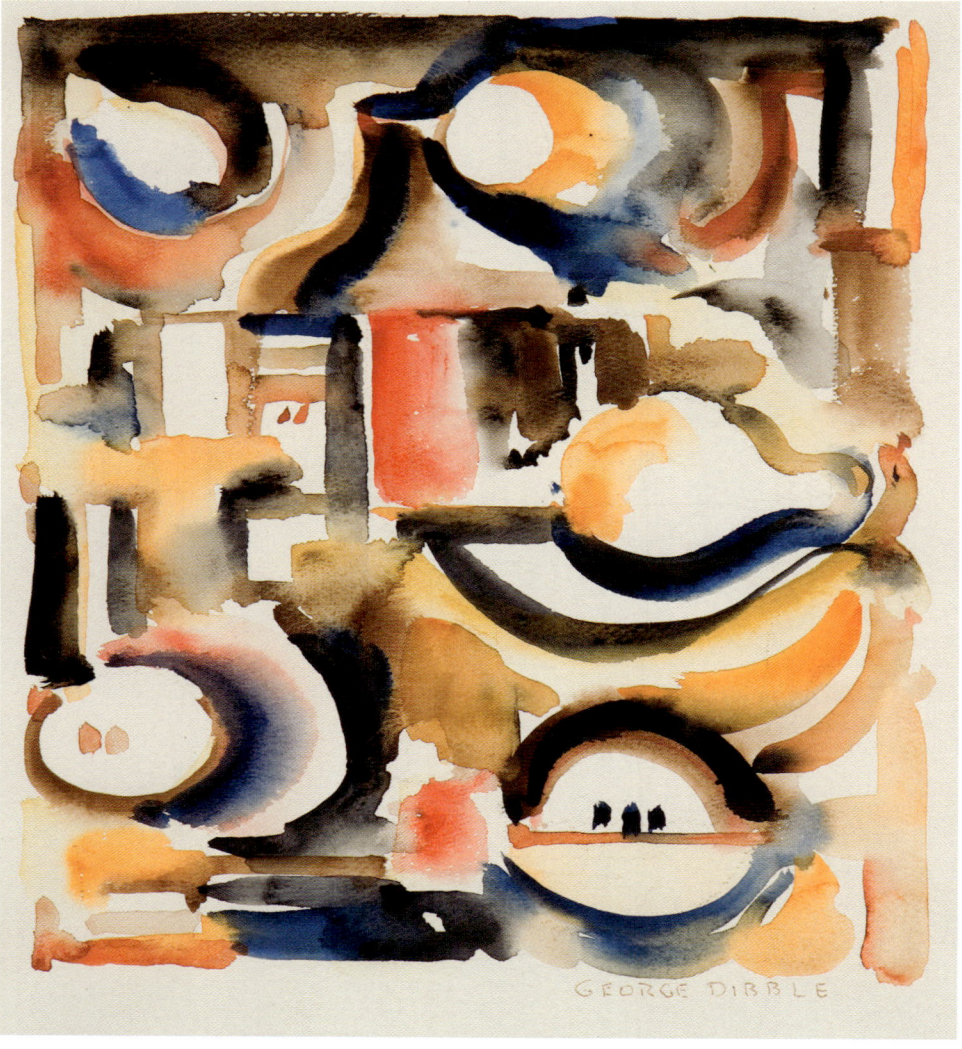

Fig. 14.8 George S. Dibble, *Cubist Still Life*, n.d., watercolor, Permanent Collection of the Utah Museum of Fine Arts, gift of Jonathan A. Dibble.

Utah with abstract art that featured local artists, it marked an opportunity for the public to see how the philosophical tenets of the manifesto were concretized into art, even if Dibble's contributions were stylistically tame relative to what was happening in the rest of the country.

However bold these works seemed to local viewers, they were practically old-fashioned when compared to newly emerging works on the East Coast and elsewhere. For context, consider another manifesto published in 1943 in New York, less than two years after the Utah document. In a letter to Edward Alden Jewell, art editor of the *New*

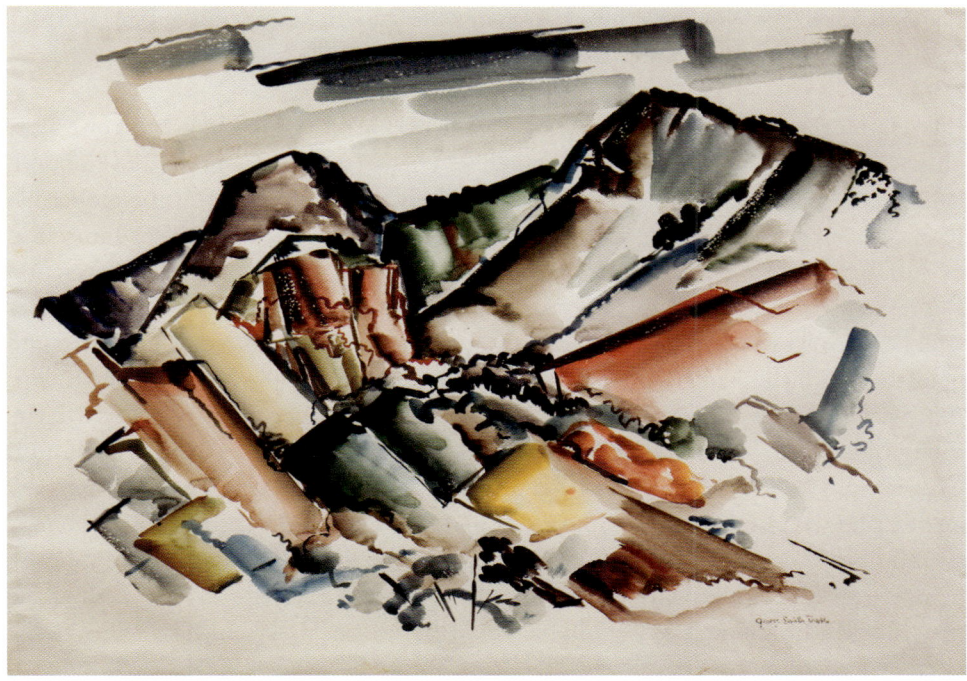

Fig. 14.9 George S. Dibble, *Cedar Canyon*, 1955, watercolor, Permanent Collection of the Utah Museum of Fine Arts, gift of Jonathan A. Dibble.

York Times, after a review of pictures at the Federation Show in which Jewell confessed his "befuddlement," Mark Rothko with Adolph Gottlieb and Barnett Newman wrote what became a manifesto of an emerging art movement, Abstract Expressionism. Akin to the Utah artists, the New York painters noted the difficulty that the public had with their works; as the eastern artists wrote, "We seem to have created a bedlam of hysteria."[27]

Note the tone of the letter, excerpted here:

3. It is our function as artists to make the spectator see the world our way—not his way. . . .

5. It is a widely accepted notion among painters that it does not matter what one paints as long as it is well painted. This is the essence of academicism. There is no such thing as good painting about nothing. We assert that the subject is crucial and only that subject matter is valid which is tragic and timeless. That is why we profess spiritual kinship with primitive and archaic art.

Consequently if our work embodies these beliefs, it must insult anyone who is spiritually attuned to interior decoration; pictures for the home; pictures for over the mantle; pictures of the American scene; social pictures; purity in art; prize-winning potboilers;

the National Academy, the Whitney Academy, the Corn Belt Academy; buckeyes, trite tripe; etc.[28]

It is a letter that probably would not have gone over very well in Utah. Still, one must put the Utah modernists—and their audiences—in perspective. Dibble's most modern landscapes, such as *Cedar Breaks No. 2,* came forty years or more after the modernist John Marin produced works with similar methods and made a name for himself as one of America's earliest modernists. They bear little resemblance to Abstraction Expressionists' breakthrough canvases, which took non-representational art further still. Dibble owes a considerable debt to Marin, whose work was widely exhibited and published and who had a retrospective exhibition in 1936 at the Museum of Modern Art, while Dibble was studying at Columbia. Dibble later acknowledged Marin, though he noted, "I wasn't consciously aware of being influenced by his work until later, in the 1940s."[29] In Dibble's 1966 textbook, *Watercolor: Materials and Techniques,* he describes Marin this way: he "pursued objectives beyond the confines of visual representation. Working on the urban scene and in the fields of his native New Jersey, he developed effective symbols for the tensions existing in nature." Other than the reference to the Garden State, Dibble could have been describing his own artistic approaches.[30]

DIBBLE, THE CRITIC AND THE MAN

One would imagine that Dibble the artist—dedicated to modernism—would inform the work of Dibble the critic. Somewhat surprisingly, it does not. Dibble's body of published art criticism is largely free of agenda-driven impulses other than the fact that he wanted to advocate for the artists and provide them a platform to be appreciated. In his obituary, his gallerist of twenty-five years, Bonnie Phillips, said, "George Dibble was never scared of art. He taught me there is this generosity of spirit that one artist can have toward other artists in not being too judgmental about their work but being open to it."[31] Olpin quoted Dibble from a 1978 *Tribune* interview as saying, "In my criticism, I try to encourage things growing and developing"—making the point that Dibble was a non-critical critic.[32] In 1988, Olpin noted of Dibble, "For the past 35 years he has, in the most articulate way, managed to tell the absolute truth about hundreds of local artists and hold on to his job at the same time. He has done so by writing different things to different people simultaneously. For those who have extensive background in art, what Dibble has to say is pertinent and thought provoking. For those whose artistic training is less sophisticated, enough is there to inform and challenge."[33]

Artist and scholar Will South described Dibble's published art criticism a bit differently:

Few people understood what George attempted to do with his column at *The Tribune.* It would have been easy for him to critically disassemble a good many of the shows he reviewed. Part of the reason he chose to emphasize the positive was that over his own long career he had seen local artists suffer the kind of lack of encouragement that made them seek careers elsewhere. George wanted to help create an environment where artists felt not only wanted but needed. Along the way, if the general public became more educated regarding the visual arts, so much the better.[34]

After the artist's passing in 1992, Olpin generously summarized his friend: "He was one of the progressive artists in our state early on, and pivotal to the modernist development in Utah. He was a magnificent educator, so open-minded, so liberal within a society that was and has remained closed in a lot of ways. He was one of the foremost people to say the best art is about ideas."[35]

SCANDAL AND ITS MYTHOLOGY

It is not particularly striking that a geographically remote culture would feel hesitant to embrace outside artistic ideas, but the most pivotal moment in the twentieth century's visual art history has a little-known LDS connection that hints at how it might have developed differently.

The mythology of the modern art scandal, the kind of event that shifts breathless media coverage from the back pages of fine art sections to above the fold, so to speak, follows a predictable trope: blaring headlines document the public's shock, disgust, outrage, and protest in reaction to the wildness of a brazen artist who is an affront to society.

One of the most notorious such exhibitions in the history of America was the Armory Show of 1913. Two aspects of the exhibition produced its lasting importance: the showcase of new, daring works from Europe, and the reaction of the public to the exhibition. In the case of the Armory Show, while the notoriety was not entirely baseless, the exaggerations have a greater staying power with the general public than eyewitness accounts of the events would support. The perceived shock lingers and affects people far removed from the original event. It is easy to imagine someone saying that they hate Stravinsky's *The Rite of Spring* without having heard a note of it, for example, or a young writer to think, without having read such novels, *I will not write fiction like James Joyce because it is scandalous*. In many cases, the initial critical and public reactions were not the *succès de scandale* that lingers in the minds of the public now, or were exaggerations of it. The fact is that none of these harbingers of the new provoked the riots that people want to associate with them, at least not the narratives that pro-modernists and anti-modernists cling to ferociously.

As Milton W. Brown, an expert on the Armory Show,[36] wrote about the waves of its criticism:

The early press reactions were mostly favorable and from an editorial point of view remained so to a very great extent. It was only after the largely conservative critical fraternity began to whip up an esthetic witch hunt and the know-nothing yellow press found in some of the exhibits a source of low humor that the tide began to turn and the public came to gape, snicker, and jeer. These jibes were sometimes good-humored, sometimes tinged with philistine nastiness, and frequently inept, but the critical attacks were hysterically vicious.[37]

"Mostly favorable" is a far cry from viciousness. What changed? After seismic events of this kind, what followed in terms of critical and public reaction was a riot of another sort: a battle not between the artist and the public but between the extremes of the audience itself, a calcified retrenchment into tribes, pro- and anti-, based on their comfort or discomfort with the new. The outsized emotionality accelerated and justified observers' decisions to side with one or the other edge of combatants, as if a spectrum of reaction to art had to be reduced to two simplified options: embrace it or reject it. This division overshadows an investigation into the historical accuracy of the "riot" narratives. It was easier to repeat the story of tumult than to reckon with the artwork itself. Cynics intone that everyone benefits from such tension and there is no such thing as bad publicity, as Mae West implied after her play *Sex* (1927) opened and she was hauled off to jail, saying, "I expect it will be the making of me."[38] However, regarding innovation in art, culture wars can also be a zero-sum game.

The argument is larger than art. Note in the following unsigned *Times* editorial printed on the day after the closing of the Armory Show how the issues of art are conflated with crises of society. Its breathless condemnation—as well as an opposing view, which follows—are worth reading in full:

> It should be borne in mind that this movement is surely a part of the general movement, discernible all over the world, to disrupt and degrade, if not to destroy, not only art, but literature and society, too. There is a kind of insanity extant which has its remote origin, it must be said, in the earlier developments of the democratic spirit. Its kinship to true democracy and to real freedom in thought, action, or expression, however, is slight and indefinite, but the cubists and futurists are [their] own cousins to the anarchists in politics, the poets who defy syntax and decency, and all would-be destroyers who with the pretense of trying to regenerate the world are really trying to block the wheels of progress in every direction.[39]

Unsurprisingly, there was an equally vigorous statement published earlier in the run of the exhibition that took the opposite view:

> The dry bones of a dead art are rattling as they never rattled before. The hopeful birth of a new art that is intensely alive is doing it. A score or more of painters and sculptors who decline to go on doing merely what the camera does better, have united in a demonstration of independence—an exhibition of what they see and dare express it in their

own way—that will wring shrieks of indignation from every ordained copyist of "old masters" on two continents and their adjacent islands.[40]

The layering of such spirited debates onto a backdrop of something as dramatic as a riot melds over decades into something monumental, if ahistorical. Furthermore, it moves almost to the territory of marking identity, the kind of reasoning that leads someone to more profound soul-searching: *Am I for this or against it? Am I this kind of person or that kind?* This manufactured uproar regarding modernism, which is a self-perpetuating, propagandistic story used by opposing sides to the benefit of one at the expense of the other, is accompanied by an unwillingness to study the events or works in detail and a failure to process a response to art in a nuanced fashion. It is art as ammunition.

MODERNISM AND MORMONISM

Unfortunately, related tendencies to label art stylistically and vilify or deify artists of dissent are a recurring theme of Mormon art informal discourse as well, beginning in the early twentieth century and continuing into the present. One sees in the reactions to the relatively tame modernism of George Dibble an overblown reaction that relates more to Armory Show–like shock than to the works that faced viewers in Utah in the 1940s, 1950s, and later. These caustic shots over the bow from both extremes have an outsized influence on LDS audiences and artists alike, who are culturally prone to see all things as spiritual and who often view complex issues as black or white, good or evil, uplifting or sullying. Moreover, in religious cultures the labels accompanying artists teem with rigid judgments of character, patriotism, and righteousness. For a host of reasons, then, which this chapter has sought to articulate with reference to Dibble and the reactions his works elicited from LDS people and from Utah as examples, much of the past century's art from LDS culture sits on the battlefield of modernism.

The twentieth century did not start that way. The Armory Show itself included a Mormon connection. Mahonri Young, the grandson of prophet Brigham Young and one of LDS culture's leading creative artists in his era, was on the small committee that organized the exhibition. Further, eight of the works in the show were by Young. These included sculpture and drawings.[41] That is not to suggest that Young was a modernist, although he certainly had access to the shapers of the movement in its earliest days. In Paris, Young befriended Leo Stein, the early collector of Picasso's work, and, by association, his sister Gertrude, who would become Picasso's champion. Young commented throughout his life that although he understood well the movements of Cubism and Fauvism, for example, they were not for him. Early on, he spoke dismissively of Picasso after Gertrude showed him her recent acquisitions. Young described the Blue Period artist as a "meteor which flamed so erratically and extravagantly across the sky of 20th century art."[42] Still, when he saw the Spaniard's *Frugal Repast* (1904), Young had a more appreciative response: "It is a very unpleasant performance, but it is a splendid work and it is beautifully and competently drawn. The . . . emaciation is so exaggerated as to leave the figures hardly human, mere corpses so dehydrated to be but skin over bones. Nevertheless, they do exist and they seem to be alive."[43]

Young is an interesting example of a reaction to modernism because although he was no modernist himself—he had no real use for it—neither did he condemn it. He might have said he digested it and found it not to his taste. Young's biographer wrote, "Neither style [Cubism nor Fauvism] was adequate nor relevant to Young's vision of struggling pioneers, mystic Hopi dancers, and stevedores. Because he had another story to tell, his choice of style had to lie somewhere within the realms of Realism."[44] That is possible. Another conclusion is that Young simply continued along the stylistic path on which he had begun.

There were financial consequences for artists of Young's style as modernism came to America. Some collectors began to tire of Old Masters and traditional expressions in art in favor of newer tastes, and dealers seized on the opportunity, both for them and for new clientele, presented by emerging and differing styles. Meanwhile, artists were left with decisions regarding style: to stay on the path or to explore.[45]

Young's reactions to modernism do not betray professional jealousy, however. Rather, his exposure to emerging art in Paris in the early twentieth century and his continued dialogue with modernist philosophies in New York led him to value the conversation as part of a spectrum of expression. The distinction is significant, and had Young been a voice in Utah to explain the Armory Show's impact on culture, and even on his LDS culture, one wonders what kind of difference he might have made. What might have evolved in the shadows of the church's headquarters in Salt Lake City if Young or someone with similar credibility to Utah audiences had energized galleries, collectors, critics, and even naysayers to take a closer and more open look at modernism?

Young did not have to embrace modernism in his own creative practice to bring it onto American shores nor to be conversant with it. Again, it is valuable to note that his reaction to modernism did not default to the emotional extremes of love or hate, even though others around him were polarized and likely expected stronger reactions from him, an artist firmly in the Realist sphere. LDS artists following him had less of that luxury and were often forced to pick sides, as were their audiences. They were not on-site, as it were, the way Mahonri Young was in Paris, when modernism was born, nor did most of them live in populations with extended exposure to such works over decades, which likely moderated extreme reactions to it.

The Armory Show's visitors' reactions to new works from Europe formed a template of what was to come for artists and audiences in LDS culture as they were exposed to modernism. For artists, a brush with new pictorial ideas sprang typically from their educations, largely in urban centers. There, in emerging galleries and forward-leaning museums, they found works that they likely never would have seen in their hometowns. The same can be said for the general LDS public. At some moment the average viewer encountered modernism, too, and depending on how it was presented and discussed, their relationships with it largely continued down the path on which they started: curiosity or derision.

THE POPE, CONTEMPORARY ART, AND LDS CULTURE

The Church of Jesus Christ of Latter-day Saints has never addressed contemporary art in the same direct fashion as Pope Paul VI did at the end of the Second Vatican Ecumenical Council in 1965, although two years later, Spencer W. Kimball, who would become the president of the LDS Church in 1973, gave a discourse aimed at artists and educators at Brigham Young University that was volcanic and epochal in its own way.[46] Pope Paul appealed to believing artists with these words:

> To all of you, the Church of the council declares to you through our voice: if you are friends of genuine art, you are our friends. The Church has long since joined in alliance with you. You have built and adorned her temples, celebrated her dogmas, enriched her liturgy. You have aided her in translating her divine message in the language of forms and figures, making the invisible world palpable. Today, as yesterday, the Church needs you and turns to you. She tells you through our voice: Do not allow an alliance as fruitful as this to be broken. Do not refuse to put your talents at the service of divine truth. Do not close your mind to the breath of the Holy Spirit.[47]

Immediately after this letter, written to engage contemporary artists and reinstate dialogue between its church and living artists, the Vatican established the Collection of Contemporary Religious Art, now one of the largest museums at the Vatican. At the museum's opening in 1973, Pope Paul described the capacity of modern art to marvelously express "beyond the genuinely human, also that which is religious, divine, Christian."[48] Today, that collection contains approximately eight thousand works by Bacon, Chagall, de Chirico, Dalí, Fontana, Kandinsky, Klee, Matisse, Picasso, and many other modernists. It goes without saying that Dibble, his modernist peers, and generations of progressive artists in LDS culture since have craved such an invitation and commitment to collecting and showcasing their work.

As a body that commissions art to adorn its own temples and to share its message with the broader public, the LDS Church has been solidly committed to Realism and illustration instead, the most familiar and easily digestible storytelling styles. Other faith traditions, meanwhile, have welcomed the ability of abstraction, for example, to speak to the unknowability of God. LDS reliance on Realism in its publications and worship spaces came gradually to be an evolving manifesto of its own. The incongruity was that fine artists who were not engaged in illustration bumped into cultural expectations that verisimilitude was the most appropriate depiction of something. Secondarily, the enshrinement of Realism and illustration has led the culture—always leaning toward obedience and even overcompliance—to accept that those kinds of artistic representations are, so to speak, just and true.

Unease with modernism in LDS culture is distinguishable from an aspect of artistic depiction that, for many members, is a non-starter: the nude figure. A full examination of this ongoing tension is beyond the scope of this chapter, but one story from 1934 is illuminating nonetheless. While not rising to a level as scandalous as the Armory Show in New York had been twenty years earlier, the Salt Lake City papers covered a local art exhibition scandal in 1934 with these headlines: "Art Barn No Prude; Says Nude Not Lewd: Lovely Lady (in Oils) Hangs in Gallery After Art Lovers Decide Petticoats Unnecessary" (*Salt Lake Telegram*)[49] and ". . . How Far Can Art Go in Utah" (*Deseret News*).[50] The occasion of the controversy was the exhibition of works by A. Franz Brasz, president of the California Watercolor Society, at a local institution, the Art Barn, a precursor to today's Utah Museum of Contemporary Art, in Salt Lake City. The exhibition included paintings of two nudes. It was not the first time that nudes were exhibited by the young institution, but these Brasz images were created in a modernist style and drew protests. The distinction is notable. A different nude by the same artist exhibited the previous year did not draw similar ire from the public. It was the combination of the figure and its modernism that ignited the issue with the Utah public.

Artist and historian Will South described the events and how the sponsoring art organization sought to placate the community:

> A public debate was scheduled, and all interested people invited, including Mr. Brasz. Prior to the event, Alta Rawlins Jensen, a spiritual as well as administrative leader for the Art Center, told the press: "I think that we should settle the question for all time. It is a time to find out if Utah is a bit of a backwash, remote from the main current in progress, or if culture here has grown to maturity, where truth and beauty can be seen in the nude as well as in the other art. We will never develop any art that is real or great in Utah until art can be anything it wants to be."[51]

Ultimately, the furor blew over, but Alta Rawlins Jensen's challenge to the state to deal with its sensitivities fizzled as well. Nothing changed. Her salvo "until art can be anything" proved prophetic, however, and one might reasonably ask whether the culture—now a global religion—has allowed its art and artists to be what they want to be, even now.

Today in visual art, modernism—however broadly it is defined—is largely fractured into a host of Postmodern movements or philosophies that defy grouped categorization altogether. Today, art tethered to identity, gender, social justice, and any number of pressing issues has transformed all areas of creative and performing arts discourse in such dramatic ways that it feels almost quaint to imagine that exhibiting a modernized, reductive cityscape or landscape from the 1950s or an abstracted nude descending a staircase in 1913 could be a radical act that would elicit public anger and even violence. And yet, the ability of LDS culture to embrace the newness of art remains an enduring challenge for that culture and—to the extent that art has the power to change society—a significant handicap that transcends art. To its believers, doctrinally the gospel is not closed nor closed off, but culturally it may be another matter. The question to ask now is not whether LDS culture embraces artistic styles created a century ago—is anyone scandalized by abstraction anymore?—but whether it encourages and advocates for works from its people that embody newness, the hallmark of the modernists of the twentieth century. The answer to that question is the most telling lens and significant indicator of where LDS culture and its art are headed next.

NOTES

1 Robert S. Olpin, *George Dibble: Painter, Teacher, Critic* (Salt Lake City: Utah Museum of Fine Arts, 1989), from "Director's Statement" by Frank Sanguinetti, 7.

2 George Smith Dibble (American, 1904–1992), *Cedar Breaks No. 2* (1952), watercolor, 22″ × 30″, private collection.

3 Nora Eccles Harrison Museum of Art, *In Memoriam: George Dibble* (1933) (exhibit catalogue), 25, https://digitalcommons.usu.edu/cgi/viewcontent.cgi?article=1018&context=artmuseum_cat.

4 Nora Eccles Harrison Museum of Art, *In Memoriam: George Dibble,* 25.

5 Nora Eccles Harrison Museum of Art, *In Memoriam: George Dibble,* 25.

6 Sarah Dibble, "George Dibble and the Struggle for Modern Art in Utah" (master's thesis, Brigham Young University, 2012), 43.

7 George Smith Dibble (American, 1904–1992), *Pay Dirt* (1938), pastel on canvas, 45″ × 27″, State of Utah Alice Merrill Horne Art Collection.

8 Dibble, "George Dibble and the Struggle for Modern Art," 27.

9 See *Pay Dirt,* State of Utah Alice Merrill Horne Art Collection, https://utahdcc.secure.force.com/public/PtlArtifactDetail?id=a0n70000001TuyuAAC&bcn=Artifacts&bcu=https%3A%2F%2Futahdcc.secure.force.com%2Fpublic%2FPtlArtifacts%3Ffield%3DartApp__Artist__c%26heading%3DGeorge%2BSmith%2BDibble%26ps%3D0%26value%3Da0j70000000BlbOAAS%26refURL%3Dhttp%253A%252F%252Futahdcc.secure.force.com%252Fpublic%252FPtlArtifacts&ps=0, accessed May 5, 2022.

10 George Smith Dibble (American, 1904–1992), *Long Island Sound* (1939), oil on paper, 20″ × 24 1/2″, private collection.

11 Dibble, "George Dibble and the Struggle for Modern Art," 27.

12 Dibble, "George Dibble and the Struggle for Modern Art," 28.

13 Avard Fairbanks, quoted in "George Dibble and the Struggle for Modern Art," 29.

14 Olpin, *George Dibble,* 14.

15 Olpin, *George Dibble,* 14.

16 Karal Ann Marling, *Wall to Wall America: A Cultural History of the Post Office Murals in the Great Depression* (Minneapolis: University of Minnesota Press, 1982), 24 cited in Dibble, "George Dibble and the Struggle for Modern Art," 30.

17 Utah Artists Project, "George S. Dibble," https://www.lib.utah.edu/collections/utah-artists/UAP-George-Dibble.php, accessed April 22, 2022.

18 Utah Artists Project, "George S. Dibble."

19 Additional works by George Smith Dibble (American, 1904–1992) illustrating this chapter are:

Temple of Sinawava (1953), watercolor, 22 1/8″ × 30″, BYU Museum of Art, gift of the estate of George Smith Dibble

Cedar Canyon (1955), watercolor on paper, 9 5/8″ × 27 1/4″, gift of Jonathan A. Dibble, Utah Museum of Fine Arts

Assembly Hall Detail (circa 1967), watercolor, 22″ × 30″, Church History Museum

Sketch for Cubist Breaks (undated), watercolor, Church History Museum

Cubist Still Life (undated), watercolor on paper, 13″ × 12″ (21 3/4″ × 21 1/2″ sheet size), gift of Jonathan A. Dibble, Utah Museum of Fine Arts

[20] Will South, "The Federal Art Project in Utah: Out of Oblivion or More of the Same?," *Utah Historical Quarterly* 58, no. 3 (1990), https://issuu.com/utah10/docs/uhq_volume58_1990_number3/s/161916.

[21] George Smith Dibble (American, 1904–1992), *Mount Olympus* (1940s), oil on canvas, 28″ × 34″, private collection.

[22] Dibble, "George Dibble and the Struggle for Modern Art," 36.

[23] Robert S. Olpin, *Utah Art, Utah Artists: 150 Year Survey* (Layton, UT: Gibbs Smith, 2001), 140, cited in Dibble, "George Dibble and the Struggle for Modern Art," 33.

[24] Leona Eitel Day (American, 1914–2005) has often been mislabeled in the group Modern Artists of Utah as "Leone Eitel."

[25] Their membership in the Church of Jesus Christ of Latter-day Saints is confirmed by baptismal and confirmation records found on familysearch.org, accessed May 3, 2022. Although Harry Reynolds was not LDS, his wife, Zina, was a member.

[26] William Jensen Parkinson (American, 1899–1933) was also a member of the LDS Church; https://www.familysearch.org/search/tree/results?q.anyPlace=utah&q.givenName=bill%20&q.surname=parkinson, accessed May 4, 2022.

[27] *New York Times,* June 13, 1943. The letter by Rothko, Gottlieb, and Newman was written June 7 and appeared in the paper one week later.

[28] "Brief Manifesto: Mark Rothko with Adolph Gottlieb, and Barnett Robinson" (reprinting letter to the editor, *New York Times,* June 19, 1943), *Medium,* posted by Pedroso-Roussado, November 7, 2017, https://proussado.medium.com/brief-manifesto-mark-rothko-with-adolph-gottlieb-and-barnett-newman-bf016 50381d1.

[29] Olpin, *George Dibble,* 12.

[30] George Dibble, *Watercolor: Materials and Techniques* (New York: Holt, Rinehart and Winston, 1966), 127.

[31] Ann Poore, "George Dibble: A Retrospective Recollection," *Salt Lake Tribune*, June 7, 1992.

[32] Catherine Fehr, "Art Is a Way of Living for Watercolorist George Dibble," *Salt Lake Tribune,* May 21, 1978, E5, cited in Olpin, *George Dibble,* 17.

[33] Olpin, *George Dibble,* 17.

[34] Poore, "George Dibble."

[35] "George Dibble, U. Professor, Tribune Art Critic, Dies at 88," *Salt Lake Tribune,* June 2, 1992, https://www.lib.utah.edu/collections/utah-artists/UAP-George-Dibble.php#collapseThree/.

[36] The official title of the exhibition was *The International Exhibition of Modern Art.* It was mounted by the Association of American Painters and Sculptors in New York from February 17 to March 15, 1913, and traveled subsequently to Chicago and then to Boston.

[37] Milton W. Brown, *The Story of the Armory Show* (New York: Abbeville Press, Joseph H. Hirshhorn Foundation, 1988), 45.

[38] Emily Wortis Leider, "Where Mae West Was Even Racier," *New York Times*, December 5, 1999.

[39] Brown, *The Story of the Armory Show,* 167, quoting an unsigned editorial in the *Times* on the day after the Armory Show closed, March 16, 1913.

[40] Brown, *The Story of the Armory Show,* 179, quoting an editorial in the *Sunday Times* by Alfred Stieglitz, January 26, 1913.

[41] For a catalogue raisonné of the Armory Show, see Brown, *The Story of the Armory Show,* 244–328. Young's works are found on 326–327.

[42] Norma S. Davis, *Song of Joys: The Biography of Mahonri Mackintosh Young, Sculptor, Painter, Etcher* (Provo, UT: Brigham Young University Press, 1999), 98.

[43] Mahonri M. Young, "Miscellaneous, Cont.," MSS 4.6.38, Brigham Young University, cited in Davis, *Song of Joys,* 89.

[44] Davis, *Song of Joys,* 132.

[45] See Brown, *The Story of the Armory Show,* 131. An unsung consequence of the Armory Show of 1913 was the repeal of the duty on contemporary art imports, which opened the market of European works to the American public further.

[46] Many LDS artists living after 1967, when Spencer W. Kimball gave a call to artistic arms in his "Education for Eternity" (published in 1977 as "The Gospel Vision of the Arts"), considered his invitation

to be transformative; however, his examples of artists to emulate, other than the makers of Hollywood epics, were traditional and pre-twentieth-century.

[47] Pope Paul VI, "Address of Pope Paul VI to Artists," December 8, 1965, at the closing of the Second Vatical Ecumenical Council, https://www.vatican.va/content/paul-vi/en/speeches/1965/documents/hf_p-vi_spe_19651208_epilogo-concilio-artisti.html, accessed May, 4, 2022.

[48] Paul Hofmann, "Pope Opens Vatical Gallery Modern Art Holding 600 Works," *New York Times,* June 24, 1973, https://www.nytimes.com/1973/06/24/archives/pope-opens-vatican-gallery-of-modern-art-holding-600-works-borgia.html.

[49] "Art Barn No Prude; Says Nude Not Lewd: Lovely Lady (in Oils) Hangs in Gallery After Art Lovers Decide Petticoats Unnecessary," *Salt Lake Telegram*, April 26, 1934.

[50] "...How Far Can Art Go in Utah," *Deseret News*, April 12, 1934.

[51] Will South, *Making and Breaking Tradition: A History of the Salt Lake Art Center* (Salt Lake City: Salt Lake City Art Center, 1991), 10.

15

"DRAW ALL MEN UNTO HIM"

The Mormon Art and Belief Movement

MENACHEM WECKER

In the early 2000s, a Brigham Young University staff member called Gary Ernest Smith's Highland, Utah, home: "Are you Gary Smith the artist?" After confirming it was he, Smith learned that university staff had discovered one of his paintings beneath a bucket on a Wilkinson Student Center broom closet floor. Did he want it back? Smith said he would rather repossess the canvas than have it remain beneath a bucket, but was BYU sure it wanted to yield a picture that the student body had purchased in the 1960s? Then Smith learned his picture's unlikely story.

More than two decades prior, BYU president Ernest L. Wilkinson saw the picture—titled *Eternal Plan*—hanging on a wall in the student center and insisted, "Take that painting down!"[1] That was how it wound up in the closet. All along, Smith had assumed that his picture, which the student body had bought for about $150,[2] was hanging somewhere in the student center without incident. "It was nothing obtrusive at all," he told me. "It just happened to have a couple of floating nude figures in it."[3]

Therein lay the rub. Brigham Young University is one of several schools associated with orthodox religious traditions where art students do not work from nude models[4] and where the administration eschews distinctions like Sir Kenneth Clark's between "nude" and "naked." Brigham Young University does not have a medical school, but at Yeshiva University, which is associated on the undergraduate level with Orthodox Judaism, art classes exclude nude models, while future physicians study the nude human body without incident.[5] This suggests, contradictorily, that the nude body is deemed alluring and tempting for art students, while it is a professional concern and desexualized anatomy for medical students.[6] Over the centuries, tensions like these have led to fig leaves and other obstructions strategically masking painted and sculpted figures.

BYU professor Dale Thompson Fletcher reproduced *Eternal Plan* in black-and-white in a 1967 article in the independent quarterly *Dialogue: A Journal of Mormon*

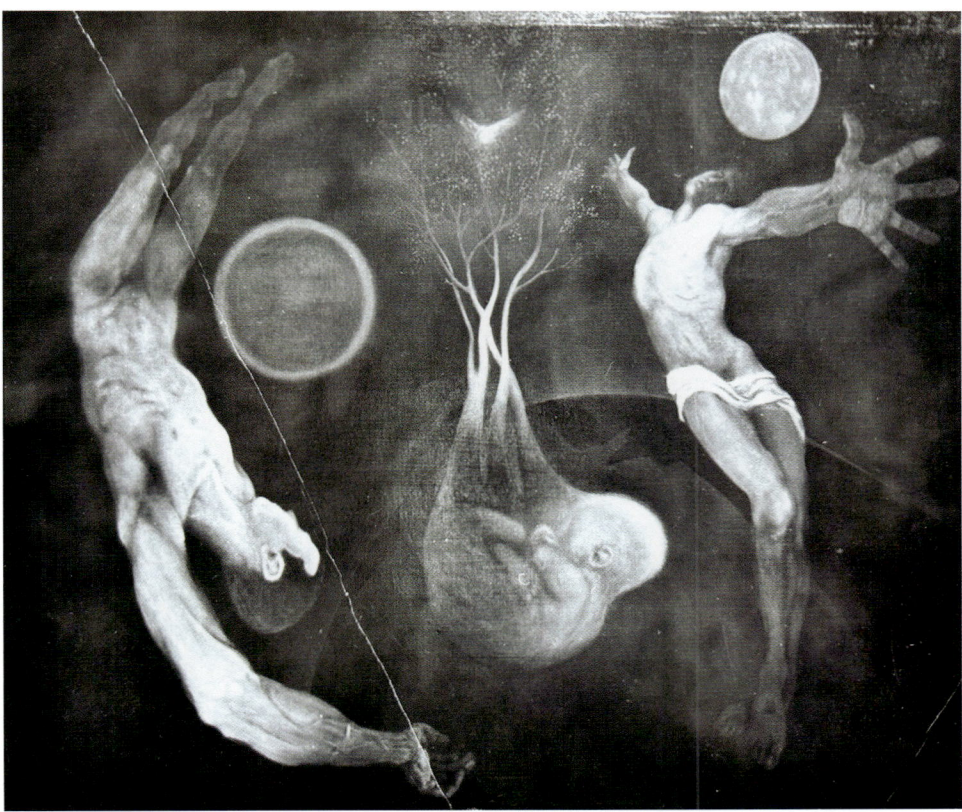

Fig. 15.1 Scan of Gary Ernest Smith's Eternal Plan from Dialogue journal. The original piece was acrylic on canvas, dated 1966. "We have permission from *Dialogue* to publish the image. So we could say something like "Printed with permission," if that's our style.

Thought, then in its second year of publication.[7] The article addressed an art exhibit at the Salt Lake Public Library from December 10, 1966, until January 1, 1967, which, along with the preparations leading up to it, is widely viewed as the onset of the Art and Belief movement. Almost called *A Light for the Kingdom,* the exhibition had its name changed to *Art and Belief* after discussion that spanned two meetings.[8] "We just finally realized that what we were struggling with is art and belief," artist Dennis Smith said.

The blurry image Fletcher reproduced features a dove—reminiscent of medieval Catholic portrayals of the Holy Spirit—hovering above a tree, whose umbilical-cord roots nourish a fetus. Two nude men bookend the baby; an upside-down figure to the right reaches his right hand beneath the infant, and the other figure spreads cruciform. A loincloth barely covers the latter's genitals, and his foreshortened right hand poises to grab the viewer. An orb, which Gary calls a red moon,[9] appears above the figure, and Smith suspended another circle ("the Earth losing its light") between the other man and the baby. Gary rendered the musculature carefully, but the figures, with their exaggerated, stretched bodies, suggest a dream or prophecy.

Gary had just two weeks to enjoy the reunion with his prodigal work before BYU asked for it back. He agreed, and possession of the work seesawed again between creator and collecting institution. "It's probably in a closet somewhere," he deadpanned. "But probably without a bucket in it."[10]

The painting's fate serves as a microcosm of the story of the Mormon Art and Belief movement, of which Dennis, Fletcher, and Gary were three-quarters of the founding quartet, with Trevor Southey as the fourth member. Gary's deeply personal work touching on his faith and life's fundamental questions found few cheerleaders within his own religious community, not to mention at his alma mater.

The questions that Gary's painting and its circumstances raise, which mirror those that continue to swirl around Art and Belief,[11] are as compelling as those surrounding art history's great movements. Just like the Impressionists or the Pre-Raphaelites—whom the Art and Belief artists cite as direct inspiration—these four artists sought to swim against the aesthetic tide to chart new territory. They did so often against intense opposition, from which they drew strength, but which also was draining and confounding to them.

Because little of this movement is known,[12] this chapter will tackle Art and Belief via the "five W's," albeit in unconventional order.

1. *Who* was this initial group of artists, which wanted so much to create serious work that would appeal to both their church community and the mainstream art world, but which found few takers? In what ways were the four similar, and how did they approach their work and their faith divergently? And what place, if any, do their followers have in Art and Belief?

There is some controversy about the next questions, which I will group:`

2. *When* did Art and Belief occur? The start date is generally accepted as 1966 with the library exhibit, but delineating the movement's chronological boundaries encounters major forks in the road, at which points experts have chosen differently.

3. The same goes for *where* Art and Belief was set. The movement's geographical contours, like its chronological ones, raise another question: what *was not* Art and Belief?

4. *What* precisely was the movement after? From what undesirable (to the artists) prior artistic approaches did the four try to distance themselves, and what did they believe they were pioneering?

5. *Why* was the movement important in the 1960s, and given that it was evidently too edgy for the church and too religious (too Mormon?) for the secular art world,

why should we continue to pay attention to it today? Scholars are divided here too. Some see it as a failure, and others judge its impact to have been quite the opposite.

Using these questions as guideposts, this chapter contends that the movement remains significant more than fifty-five years after its inception and speaks to contemporary concerns in important ways. The Art and Belief artists sought—with measured success—to maintain their individuality and personal connections with their faith while also working within a tradition and close-knit community. They explored texts and symbols they held sacred; many found their manner unorthodox, but they felt they treated those texts and symbols with the utmost maturity. And at their core, they believed that art could be infused with faith and maintain the highest aesthetic standards while it preached a holy message. "So attention must be paid," it instructs, channeling Linda Loman, the wife and mother in Arthur Miller's *Death of a Salesman,* who makes one of literature's great and beautiful pleas in favor of the heroism of regular people. "It's not to be allowed to fall into its grave like an old dog. Attention, attention must be finally paid to such an Art and Belief movement."

WHO WAS ART AND BELIEF?

When I asked scholars and artists about Art and Belief, I almost invariably heard the metaphor of a stone cast into the water, producing ripples upon ripples. Depending upon how one counts, there could be three or four Art and Belief "waves" already, but deciding who was part of the movement remains controversial.

The son of painter and professor Calvin Fletcher, Dale Fletcher (1929–1990) worked as a janitor at BYU in 1965, later joining the university's art faculty, and in the late 1970s he directed BYU's art gallery. His theories, which arose within the context of the Vietnam War and pushed against the New York–centric art world of the 1960s, inspired three students, Dennis, Gary, and Southey. According to Fletcher, the four formed the core of the Art and Belief movement.[13]

Fletcher's works in the 1950s—such as *Design No. 7: Intruder* (c. 1955), *Abstract* (1956), and *Lifting by Leverage* (1956), all part of the Springville Museum of Art collection—are thickly rendered and non-figurative, offering little hint of what would soon follow. Vern Swanson, former director of the Springville Museum, attributes Fletcher's artistic conversion to his narrowly surviving a car accident that killed a deer.[14] Afterward, to Swanson, Fletcher appeared to dedicate himself with vigor to using his artistic talent to build up the Kingdom of God.[15] Fletcher "unexpectedly resigned [from BYU] to pursue a cult of pyramidology," per the Springville Museum.[16] He also remarried without divorcing his wife, and as of 1972, according to Swanson, became an apostate privately while outwardly remaining within the church.[17]

Born in Alpine, Utah, in 1942, Dennis Smith was inspired from a young age by Norman Rockwell's *Saturday Evening Post* paintings. Alpine was then a community of just six hundred, with only fourteen kids his age (nine boys and five girls), and Dennis was bused six miles a day to school in American Fork. His lower-middle-class family owned a forty-nine-acre farm, which was of insufficient size to sustain them, so his father worked at a local steel plant. By twelfth grade—encouraged by "eccentric" teacher J. Niles Washburn, who exposed Dennis to great literature and William Blake's religious paintings and "lit a spark"—he knew that somehow and someday he would be a great artist.

After more than a year (1960–1961) studying at BYU, Dennis left for a two-and-a-half-year mission in Denmark—whence most of his ancestors hailed—which was his first time out of Utah. He left behind a young woman (later his wife) who promised to wait for him. Grappling with his faith, he described "questioning the very words I would say as a missionary."[18] In his free time, he absorbed Danish museum collections, which continued to impact him long after he returned to Utah for his BYU degree, receiving it in 1966. After a year of graduate school, he studied at the Danish Royal Academy of Art and then returned to Utah for good.

His broad artistic repertoire came to include figurative sculptures (particularly children), paintings, sculptures of flying machines, drawings, and prints. Contemporaneous paintings embrace autobiography,[19] and on a tour of hundreds of his works in Alpine, Dennis pointed out trucks on roads heading out of town that stood in for him, and conspicuous angels hovering (à la Marc Chagall's shtetls) over Utah landscapes, many with depictions of his family homes. Stylistically, Dennis's impasto paint application recalls works of Georges Rouault, Marsden Hartley, Chaim Soutine, and others. The canvas *January Sledders* (2019) was one of dozens I saw in Alpine, Utah, that illustrated this.[20] The work is a symphony of thickly applied paint that spans the rainbow, its composition so alive with movement that it takes the viewer a moment to locate the silhouetted figure dragging a sled through the snow, illuminated by sunrise or sunset; trees, houses, and mountains alike appear to dance, or at least to sway.

Gary Smith (born 1942) grew up in rural Oregon, and although his father was a baptized member of the LDS Church, his family had drifted away from the church. Gary's parents encouraged him to make art, including sending him for watercolor lessons in Baker City with a Catholic nun. After a few lessons, in which they worked on the same subject, Sister Rigoberta saw Gary's painting and told him it was better than hers, and he did not need her.

Gary went to BYU from 1966 to 1967, and he later earned an MFA there. A convert to the church, Gary left BYU in 1968 to serve in the U.S. Army as an illustrator in Korea, returning to Utah in 1970 to teach art at BYU and, in 1971, to direct its gallery. In an interview in his home and studio, Gary shared not only his work—spanning drawing, painting, cartooning, and sculpture—but also a language he created during his studies at BYU, which he incorporated into Egyptian-influenced paintings.[21] After leaving BYU, he became well known for large landscapes and figurative paintings, often of cowboys with obscured faces—a tactic to invite viewers to project their own imagery. Gary cites as inspiration the spiritual connection to the land, where life begins and ends; returning to the farm on which he grew up; and roaming fields. "I was old enough to have been in that transitional stage from animals to mechanism," he told me. "I did a whole series in homage to those working people."[22]

Two self-portraits at the Springville Museum seem to capture Gary's frame of mind during his time at BYU. In the double self-portrait *Decision*,[23] the artist, clad in dark pants and a white button-down shirt, looks directly at the viewer from the center of

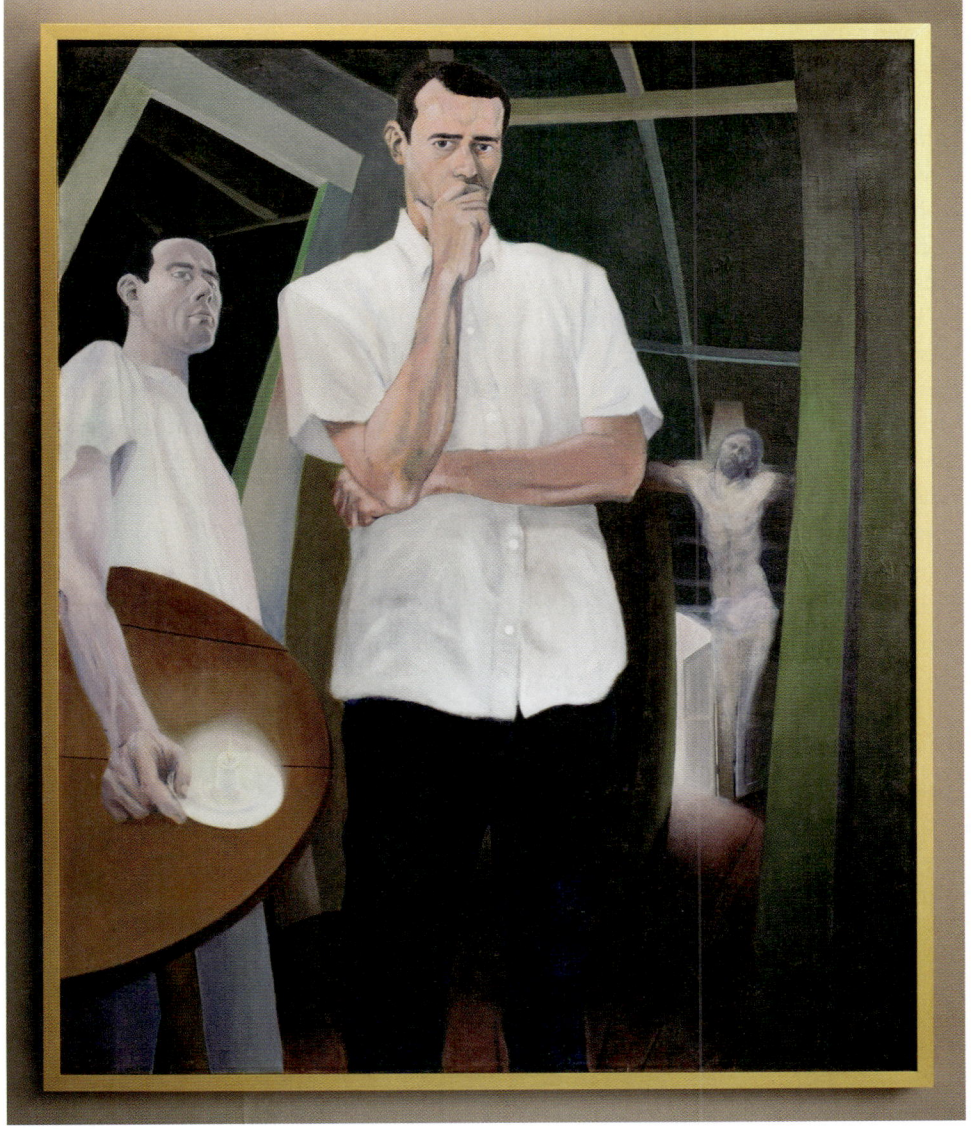

Fig. 15.2 Gary Ernest Smith, *Decision*, 1968, acrylic on canvas, 60″ × 52″, Springville Museum of Art.

the composition. He holds his right hand up to his face, covering his mouth and with his index finger resting just below his nose—lost in thought. To his right, another, less formally attired version of the artist holds a candle over a table and looks at his mirror image. In the background, Christ appears on the cross, set in a window-filled interior, but one that is darkened (save for the candle) by the blackness of night. There is tension between confident brushstrokes and the composition's sophistication, on the one hand, and the irresolution and self-consciousness of the figures, on the other.

Two years later, in 1970, Gary painted *Self Portrait: Divine Symmetry and Sacred Geometry*, in which the artist again meets the viewer's gaze, this time as he is at work on a canvas. As in Rembrandt's famous *Artist in His Studio* (c. 1628, at Museum of Fine Arts, Boston), where the Dutch painter teases the viewer by offering only the back of the canvas, Gary too hides the painting-within-a-painting from the viewer. The canvas within the work is propped up against what might be the back of a chair, and two cropped works hanging on the wall behind Gary—one figurative and the other linear—evidently allude (per the painting title) to sacred geometry and divine symmetry. The artist's face, half submerged in shadow, is pained or resolute.

The Rhodesia-born Trevor Jack Thomas Southey (1940–2015) devoted himself to making art at a young age, as an often bedridden child with rheumatic fever. He grew up lower-middle-class, and after studying in England and in South Africa, he set off for BYU—where he earned two degrees, including his master's in 1969—via the 1964 New York World's Fair. There he took particular interest in the Vatican pavilion, home to Michelangelo's *Pietà* (1498–1499), which made him cry, and in the LDS Church's display, which he found uninspiring.[24] In a letter to Elder Mark E. Petersen dated November 16, 1967, Southey wrote that after experiencing his first real contact with official LDS Church art at the World's Fair, "I must frankly say that I was disappointed and even a little ashamed." He noted that many people came to see it and were impressed, but

> I felt that there was an attempt at pretending that the art work had great merit which it did not . . . great deficiency in the organization of the figures, the sickly sweetness of the color, anatomical and proportional problems with the figures and a tendency to permit superficial details such as flowers and the folds in the robes to destroy the basic beautiful forms and shapes.[25]

As a convert to the church (like Gary),[26] Southey arrived in Utah in 1965 with notions of creating a kind of Mormon Sistine Chapel, and his large paintings (often diptychs and triptychs) owe a good deal to Michelangelo—or, as Southey referred to himself, as a "hiccough (hiccup) of the Renaissance."[27] He taught at BYU for a time, resigning from the faculty in 1977 and moving to San Francisco to live openly as a gay man.

Spending even a moment with Southey's art and Baroque poetic writings, one immediately registers his romantic nature. And the man who dreamed enormously often found that life disappointed, as with his expectations of the Mormon pavilion in New York, with his arrival in Salt Lake—a Zion that proved more industrial and commercialized than he imagined—and of the "Edenic" commune he helped found in Alpine, where tight funds meant snug accommodations and cows actually had to be milked and manure laid.

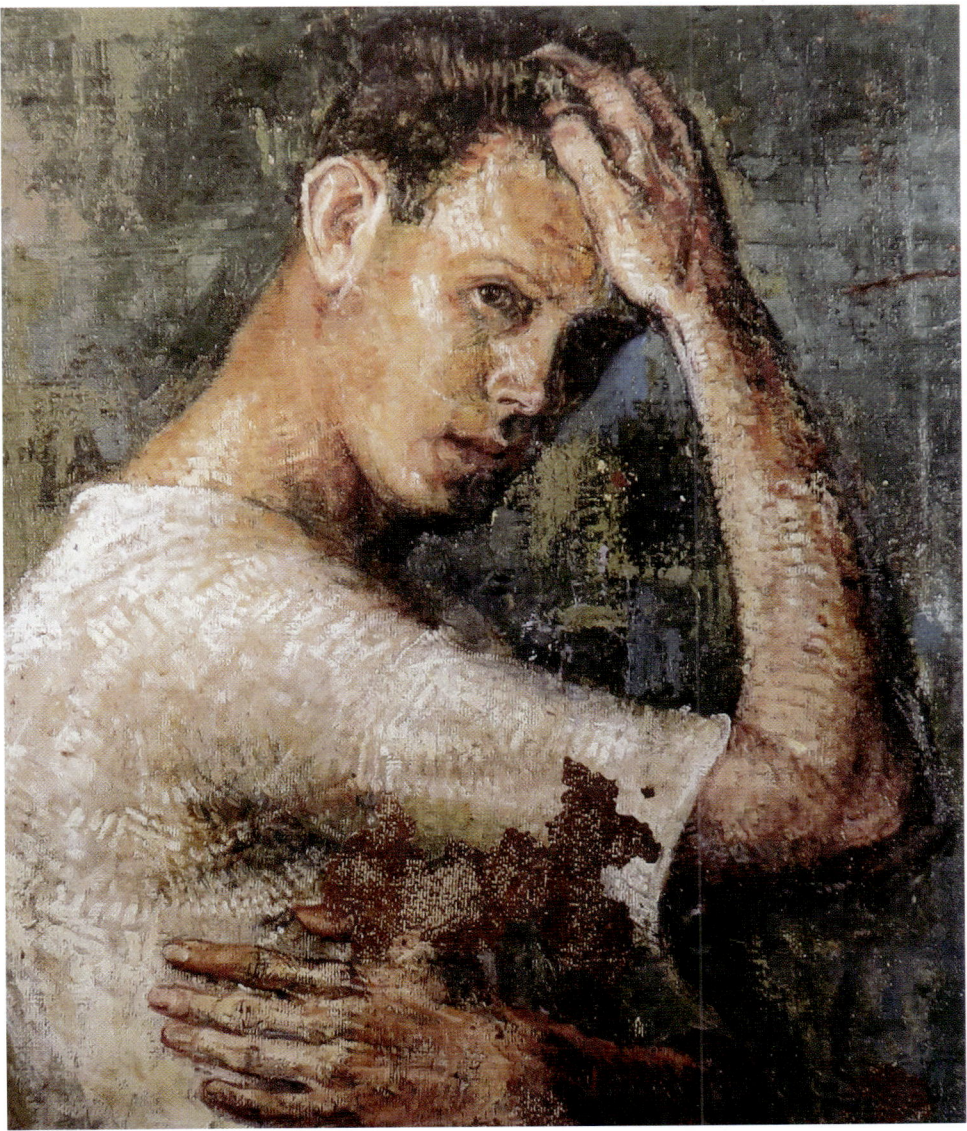

Fig. 15.3 Trevor Southey, *Self Portrait*, 1959, oil on panel, 25″ × 22″. Courtesy of the Southey family.

In a self-portrait that Southey created in 1959, before he came to Utah, the artist cropped himself out from the chest down. His right hand rests on his forehead as he eyes the viewer in three-quarter view, and his left hand rests on his chest below his right armpit. White brushstrokes, like tire tracks, cover much of the shirt, the arms, and the face, and throughout the picture Southey juxtaposed heavy impasto with thinly painted portions, where raw canvas shows through. As with Gary's self-portraits a few years later, this is a picture of a man who is finding his way, and who is literally emerging boldly from the background in some ways and elsewhere fading back into it. These and other self-portraits of the Art and Belief founders depict men who were ripe for change and who had a lot of questions that they were ready to work hard to answer.

So the four Art and Belief principals arrived at BYU at different times, coming from vastly different places, but the library exhibit in 1966 and the First Festival of Mormon Arts at BYU in 1969 are key markers of the Art and Belief movement. By 1978, Fletcher had departed from BYU and Southey had resigned, and Southey, Dennis, and Gary had set up their own "Eden" in Alpine, Utah, where Dennis grew up.

With their geographical differences, wide-ranging approaches to art-making and media, and varied life and religious journeys, this odd quartet agreed on a lot but also disagreed on quite a lot. "You could hardly have asked for more different people as far as backgrounds were concerned. The draw toward one another had to be very strong to make a bonding occur," said Dennis.[28] "We just were so totally diverse. We had nothing in common other than our art."

Swanson, who was part of the Art and Belief meetings from the start, describes himself alternatively as "fly on the wall," "hanger-on," and "total groupie." To Swanson, the four principal artists were the Art and Belief *group;* he and others were part of the *movement.*

Wulf Barsch led a second "wave," per *Deseret News* reporting quoting Swanson. That wave included Doug Himes, Alex Bigney, and Lee Udal Bennion.[29] A third wave of students who graduated from BYU between 1987 and 1989 began with a trip to Europe in 1998. The trip was organized by Todd Stilson and Christopher Young for themselves and seven others—Steve Adams, Brad Aldridge, Bruce Brainard, Doug Fryer, Brian Kershisnik, Ron Richmond, and Michael Workman. All nine studied at BYU with Barsch and Himes (of the second wave) and with Jim Christensen, Hagen Haltern, Wayne Kimball, Robert Marshall, and Bruce Smith. David Linn, Rebecca Wagstaff, and Clay Wagstaff also belong to the third wave, according to the newspaper.[30]

Dennis, meanwhile, believes that his current work is still part of Art and Belief, which would almost make it a movement, like the British Empire, upon which the sun never sets. Engaging each wave in depth is beyond the scope of this essay, and Swanson's forthcoming vast, multi-hundred-page volume on the Art and Belief movement promises to cover that and more with great erudition. For our purposes, the four founders are the focus, with the understanding that they inspired many, who rode under their banner to varying degrees and whose work the founders would appreciate and claim happily to varying degrees.

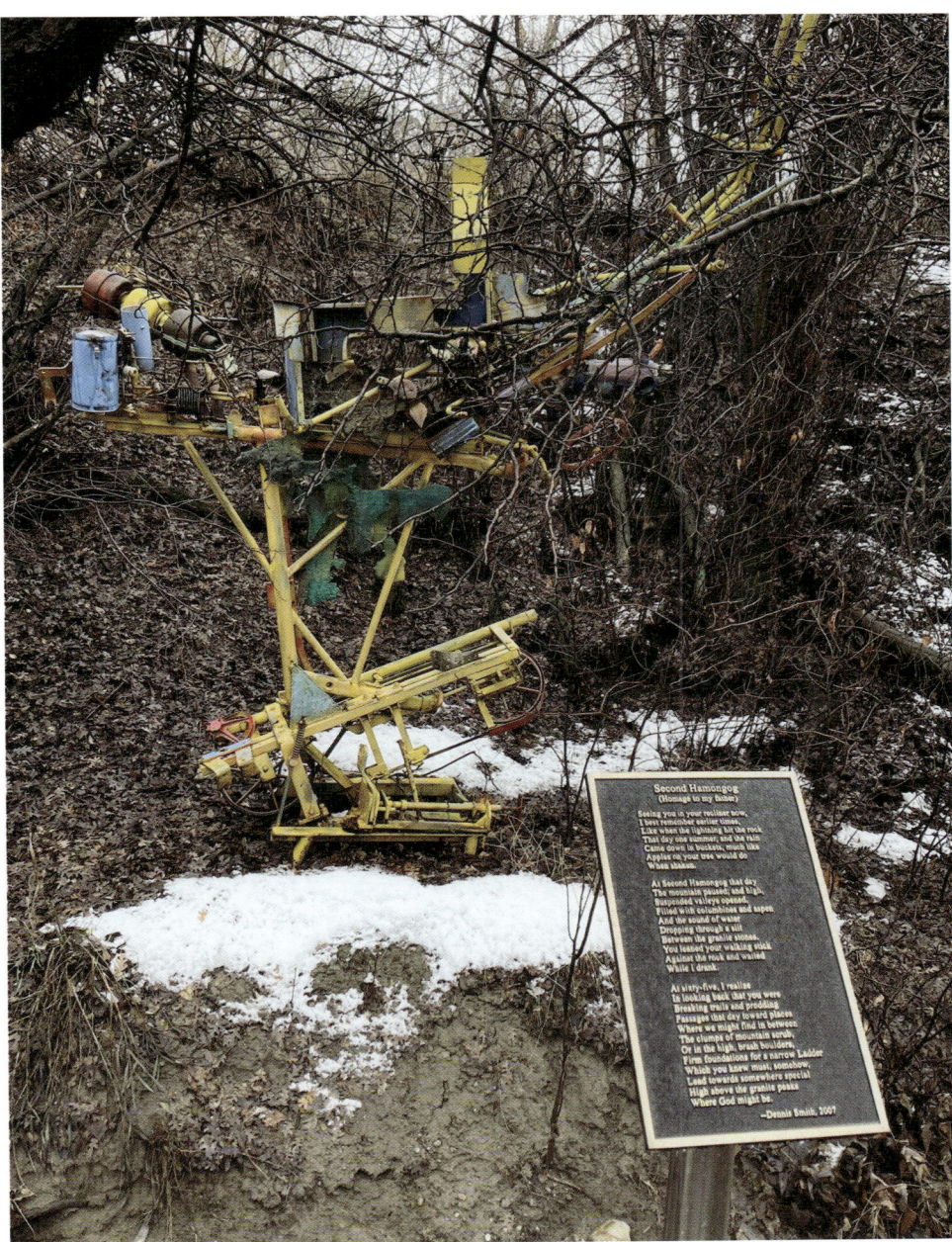

Fig. 15.4 Dennis Smith, *Second Hamongog (Homage to My Father)*, 2007, assemblage, welded steel and found objects. Photo taken by the author.

WHEN AND WHERE WERE ART AND BELIEF?

In a poem reproduced on a plaque beside his 2007 sculpture *Second Hamongog (Homage to My Father)*, Dennis, then sixty-five, wrote lovingly of his dad breaking trails and prodding passages:

> Where we might find in between
> The clumps of mountain scrub,
> Or in the high, brash boulders,
> Firm foundations for a narrow Ladder
> Which you knew must, somehow,
> Lead towards somewhere special
> High above the granite peaks
> Where God might be.

The sculpture, which Dennis made long after he left BYU, consists largely of a yellow metal frame of found objects that looks like an ironing board or a hospital bed, with "arms" going in a variety of directions. A variety of other objects, some conical and others spheroid, round out the abstract ensemble. Hawthorn bushes around the sculpture are beginning to claim the work, much to the artist's joy.

His father was much more orthodox religiously than he, explained Dennis. "I'm more of an agnostic. I keep my fingers crossed."[31] When I asked if he sees his recent work as connected to that of his time at BYU, I expected him to say there was some connection but that he had moved on long ago. Instead, Dennis told me that what he makes today is still part of Art and Belief. "I see them all as a continuum," he said.[32]

This view of an Art and Belief movement upon which the sun still has not set is not standard. There appears to be nearly unanimous agreement that the movement began amid 1966 preparations for the first exhibit,[33] and to Swanson, the former Springville Museum director, the movement ended in 1972 with Fletcher's apostasy and when the other three founders moved to Alpine from BYU. "Because where is the belief?" he said.[34] The group grew to include artists Frank Riggs, Neil Hadlock, and others. "My friend Neil, whom I dearly love, couldn't stand the Art and Belief movement," said Swanson, who does not remember ever seeing Hadlock at an Art and Belief meeting. "He was critical every time they talked."[35] Gary told me that Hadlock was a valuable colleague in Alpine from whom he and others sought feedback on their ideas and artworks because of his opposing perspective.[36]

The Springville Museum appears to have produced the only major show about the movement, the 2018–2019 exhibit *Beginnings: The Mormon Art and Belief Movement*. The museum's recently retired director, Rita Wright, sees Art and Belief as a "very culture-specific movement," which historians have neglected due to its regional nature[37] and because it took place at BYU, which represents a blind spot for many scholars. "It was nurtured in a private university, with artists doing something that was definitely different from the company line," Wright said. "Mormon art at that time was not as conceptual, and BYU was taking a little bit longer in arts to develop."[38]

In his 1976 painting of Alpine, titled *Eden Farm,* Southey depicts a nude man and woman standing to the left of the frame. An ear of corn, loaf of bread, and fallen flower float between them—all things (with an egg and some peas) needed to sustain an Edenic commune. Another nude man to the right pours milk into a bowl that a nude young boy holds as a cow looks on from behind. The whole scene is set in an abstracted landscape, which Southey rendered in earth tones but which offers no details that help the viewer identify a particular location.

Southey said he gained the courage to admit the picture portrayed his ideal family: "My wife. My partner," he said. "This is my ideal of a family, because my beloved wife and I never had a natural marriage by my standard, and eventually it broke down. Eden Farm died in a way, because I'd get up every morning, and going through my mind would be, 'And shot himself through the head,'"[39] Southey elaborated in an interview for the PBS documentary *The Mormons.* "It made no sense, but it made every sense. And there was no running away from it. I was committing a kind of spiritual suicide," he explained.[40]

There was also no running away from the idea that all sorts of would-be Edens turn out to be more complicated than the utopias they had been imagined to be. Yet the

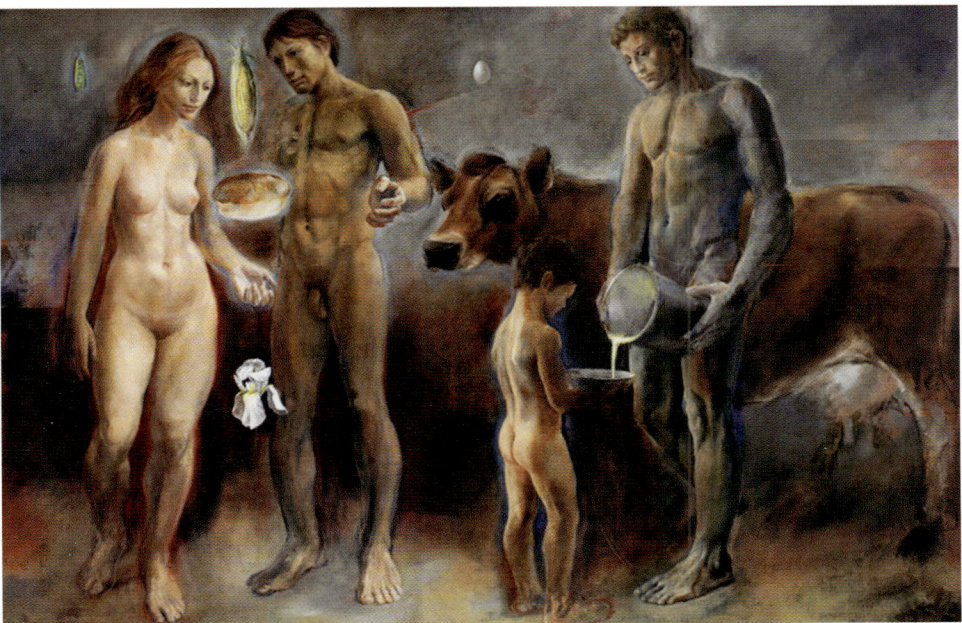

Fig. 15.5 Trevor Southey, *Eden Farm,* 1976, oil on board, 48″ × 72″. Springville Museum of Art. Courtesy of the Southey family.

connection between the Art and Belief artist and the land—and concept—of Eden demonstrated the significance of place and geography.[41]

Geography was also very important to Dennis. He notes that most local artists felt Utah was too insular, causing them to leave for San Francisco or New York. "We were some of the first ones that, because we really delved into it deep, we began to realize that we didn't have to leave the church in order to be ourselves, and that even though the church might not feel strongly about what we were doing that we damn well were going to go ahead and do it," he said.[42]

WHAT WAS ART AND BELIEF?

Fletcher's 1959 painting *An Artist Called of God (Big Black)*, purchased by the Springville Museum in 1994, recalls Robert Rauschenberg's black paintings of the early 1950s. Fletcher's picture contains an inscription on the top margin: "Aholiab," with an ocher-gold seven-branched candelabrum, like the menorah in the Jewish Tabernacle and Temples. The term refers to artist Ohaliav,[43] son of Achisamach, described in Exodus 31:6 and elsewhere as assisting Betzalel, son of Uri, son of Chur, in designing the Tabernacle,[44] which the Jews transported in the desert between Egypt and the Holy Land; after their arrival in Canaan, the First Temple would eventually replace the Tabernacle. The work, according to a label in the Springville Museum exhibit, "has an almost mythic history and importance to the Mormon Art and Belief Movement and its philosophies."

The story of how Fletcher created the picture, initially titled *Black to Bury By,* is described this way by the Springfield Museum:

> A dark spot on the canvas riveted his attention and finally the painting was almost entirely black except for a thin white horizon at the top with a golden menorah. He intuitively glued on a plastic sheep[45] and wrote upon it at the margin "Aholiab" and titled the picture *Artist Called of God* after the old testament artisan. After this eerie experience, which frightened him, he never again painted another non-objective work.[46]

The museum's description quotes both Fletcher's and a Marvin Payne's recollection that Fletcher haphazardly opened a Bible, which revealed Exodus 31:1–6, and his finger pointed to the verse about God directing Moses to instruct Betzalel and Ohaliav to construct the Tabernacle—in other words, to make sacred art. As Fletcher described it, he had gone to bed the prior night thinking he would give up painting altogether, but after the Bible directed him to Exodus, he was struck "so forcibly that I have never gotten over it. I'm still trying to comprehend it, but somehow it was a catalyst."[47]

Fletcher's work, which scared him, set a certain weighty tone for the movement's future. He would eventually pen an Art and Belief manifesto[48] in which "purity" was an essential component, recalls Wright, who took classes at BYU with many of those in the movement's orbit. According to Wright, purity referred to the high modernist idea of

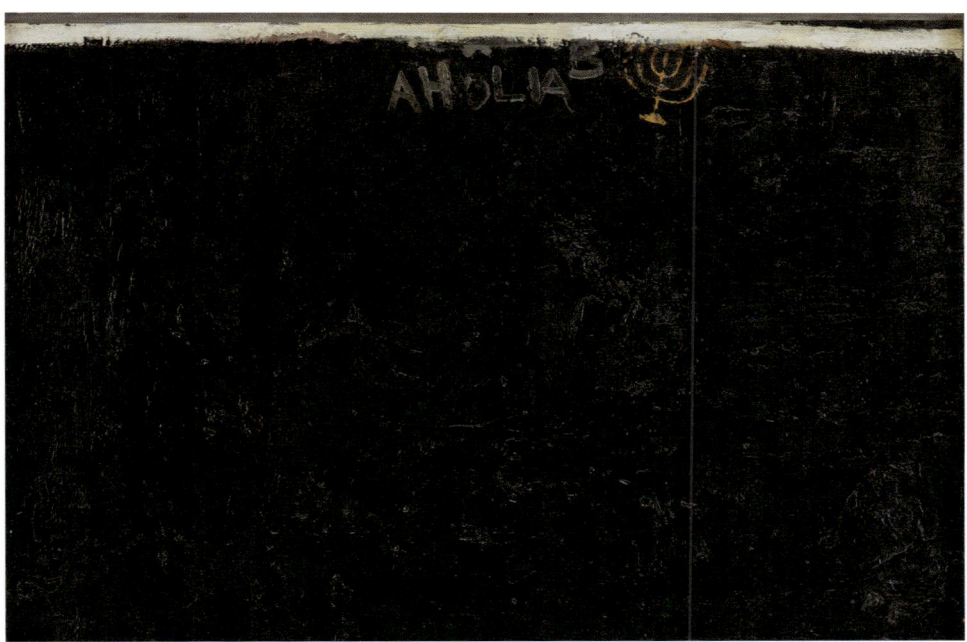

Fig. 15.6 Dale Thompson Fletcher, *An Artist Called of God (Big Black)*, 1959, oil on canvas, 24″ × 36″. Courtesy of the Springville Museum of Art.

working with the object itself (say, the paint) rather than something representational.[49] But unlike their allegedly secular modernist peers, these artists had spiritual purity in mind—or, in her words, "their own little refining spiritual fire."[50]

Swanson presented Fletcher's Art and Belief manifesto almost in full in a Sunstone Salt Lake Symposium on January 1, 1991. (He later clarified two errors in an interview with me in 2022.)[51] The manifesto declared the purpose of the movement ("upbuilding the kingdom of God on earth"), intended to integrate nature, define beauty, and temper emotions without losing its expressiveness. The manifesto also called for Mormon artists to emerge from the shadow of the Old Masters (Henri Matisse, Pablo Picasso, and Rembrandt) and to "dare to go on and produce new kinds of art that would thrill mankind and establish faith." And, somewhat optimistically, "the people would begin to open their eyes, and the critics would at last close their mouths."[52]

Swanson recalls that Fletcher penned the manifesto, which was presented and appears in the minutes of an Art and Belief meeting on June 25, 1966. At the meeting, according to Swanson, the proposed manifesto was accepted.

In Appendix C of his 1969 thesis at BYU, Southey recorded, under the heading "The Art and Belief Group," the following, dated February 1969:

"Art and Belief" is a group of LDS artists and other interested people with no official organization, who have been meeting periodically since the spring of 1966 to pursue the following objectives:

(1) To use their talents for the upbuilding of the kingdom of God.

(2) To promote the evolvement of a significant Mormon culture through the convergence of art and the Mormon philosophy.

(3) To share the results of their work with interested people.

(4) To provide for the free exchange of views to stimulate their individual creative efforts.[53]

Fletcher wanted to create a Mormon art that was worthy of being both "Mormon" and "art," according to the Springfield Museum's Emily Larsen.[54] Writing in *Dialogue* reviewing poetry by Carol Lynn Pearson that was illustrated by Trevor Southey, Fletcher predicted that the Pearson-Southey book would soon be in most Mormon homes as "a classic example of something we are going to see more of, Mormon Art." He added that he had some misgivings about "Mormon art" as a term, "because it invites misunderstanding, but for me it has a particular and serious meaning."

Mormon art's "essential ingredients, Fletcher wrote, "are the light of the key of knowledge and the application of the law of consecration of talents. Of course, to be art at all presupposes a sensitivity to artistic form."[55] The poetry is Mormon art and is so imperative, he continued,

> because the key of knowledge is not just a truth, nor just another truth, but the critical truth for us and the answer to the philosophical, political, social, and personal dilemma of our times, and it is the inner light and warm glow at the heart of Mormonism which illuminates all the other facets of the Gospel without which light these other facets, all those beliefs which have counterparts in other churches, become dead forms without power to save man because the Spirit is missing, and without this light factions appear in the Church, but with it we will have monolithic solidarity until it rolls forth to fill the whole earth.

Southey further summed up the Art and Belief theory when he talked sadly about creating a Mormon Vatican, a place saturated in beauty, with like-minded artists. "For a young church, the church had no idea what to do with that. It was a foreign concept to most members, and certainly to the leaders, who are mostly gleaned from the businessmen of the church," said Nathan Florence, who co-directed a documentary about the artists of the Art and Belief movement in 2022, titled *Bright Spark*. "For them, it's like, 'I don't know. You guys are weird. Stand over there.'"[56]

Those tensions between institutional narrative and personal interpretation came to the fore early and often. In the documentary, Southey recalled that when he first approached the church upon arriving in Salt Lake, he was asked to create an artwork of the First Vision. When he did so, he was told to go back and research the number of buttons that, historically, Joseph Smith would have had on his clothes and to bring the artwork into alignment with that historical research. "We don't want this country boy. We want Joseph Smith as potential leader," Southey said in the film, repeating what the church patrons told him.[57] "It was so soul-destroying to ignore the spirit of the whole thing, of the fourteen-year-old boy struggling with this conflict, to count the buttons on his jacket. That didn't matter. . . . I knew I was in trouble then."[58]

Speaking in the film, Hadlock submitted that the church wanted "illustration," which he defined as answering questions, while the Art and Belief artists wanted "art," which he saw as posing questions. Southey disagreed, saying that art both asks and answers questions. Gary weighed in with "We were all interested in excellence." Dennis added:

Abstract Expressionism was melting away, and all the new isms were coming to the fore. New York was the new world capital of art, and we all aspired toward contemporary significance. That is a thing that we struggled with, through the early part of our careers, was, "How do I get my stuff accepted by the General Authorities in the Church, and at the same time, in the Museum of Modern Art?" I mean that's a broad bridge to try to stretch across.[59]

In an interview, Gary told me the group wanted to "take art beyond the illustrative quality into what we call a higher art." Further, the aim was "to take it beyond just the narrative—even talking about doctrinal concepts and trying to bring some kind of visual understanding to things like doctrine, which is much more difficult. Because it has a much more symbolic quality to it."[60]

Perhaps a work that embodies the ambitions of the movement to treat religious subjects with both theological and aesthetic sophistication is Southey's 1975 triptych *Jesus and Mary: The Moment After*. The resurrected Jesus, flanked by a white rose in the center, looks to his left at Mary Magdalene, who faces a crimson rose. On the left panel, a shrouded figure, surely Jesus entombed, hovers within an abstracted setting of deep blues, greens, and reds. Southey rendered his Jesus with visible stigmata on the hands and legs, positioning the hands in sacred gestures allegedly used in Mormon worship.[61]

According to Ashlee Whitaker, curator of religious art at the BYU Museum of Art, Southey was playing with drapery in this and other works "specifically because of the tension at BYU with the nude form, and to him, as a student of the Renaissance artists, the nude form was everything. There's nothing more divine and godlike in its aspiration than that." To Whitaker, Southey's use of geometric shapes, such as the rectangle on Jesus's chest, reflects the influence of Fletcher, who often broke figures down into sacred symbols and shapes, and she added that the broader triptych is mysterious in its narrative. Mary looks rather pale, "almost icy," while Jesus looks more like a "very wiry" carpenter than stereotypical fair-faced European depictions, with noted "prominent coloring" in his veins. "It's almost like it's coursing with life," she said.[62] The hands,

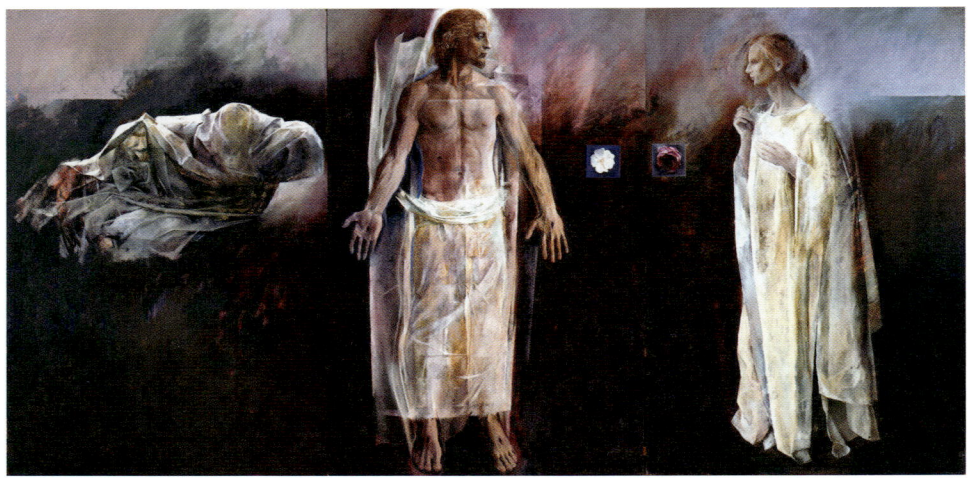

Fig. 15.7 Trevor Southey, *Jesus and Mary: The Moment After*, 1975, oil on masonite board, 72″ × 48″, Brigham Young University Museum of Art.

·one turned up and the other down, may gesture heavenward and earthward respectively, according to Whitaker, with Jesus bridging the two via grace.

"Unlike the impassive, prettified Christs who dominate official Mormon illustration, Southey's Savior was undoubtedly the son of a carpenter," K. Mitchell Snow wrote. "He is a Semitic man, wiry and plain, the personification of Isaiah's prophecy that 'when we shall see him, there is no beauty that we should desire him.'"[63] How one is to know that this is a Semitic Jesus is debatable. It certainly looks different from Rembrandt's paintings of Jesus, for which he used his Jewish neighbors as models.[64] But Snow and Whitaker are correct that Southey has presented a more vulnerable Jesus than many other greatly stylized depictions, in which he looks more like a type of person than a specific person one might meet on the street.[65]

This "broad bridge" of which Dennis spoke and the artists' very grand ambitions are at the core of one of the main, opera-worthy tragedies of the Mormon Art and Belief movement—that it ought to have been a match made in heaven between the artists, the church, and Brigham Young University. Sadly, the parties ended up talking past each other in many ways.

Despite their efforts to craft a Mormon art movement, in a September 12, 1967, address to Brigham Young University faculty and staff, Spencer W. Kimball laid out his idea of "education for eternity,"[66] by which he meant that BYU ought to educate not only the "whole man"[67] (a concept of education perhaps akin to the ancient Greek *paideia*) but also the "eternal man." Throughout the talk, Kimball focused on the arts in a bold and dramatic way, beginning with John Taylor, the church's third president, who predicted that one day Zion would be a pilgrimage destination for even kings of the world, who would trek to gaze upon its beauty. Surely BYU could produce artistic genius surpassing Richard Wagner, Kimball submitted, "but less eccentric, more spiritual." The same, he said, went for Verdi and Bach.

Not only ought Mormon creatives exceed the skill and accomplishment of history's greatest artists, but there should have been an "ever widening gap" between BYU and other universities. That is because, essentially, the best art cannot happen to bad people, or to those who are not imbued with the Holy Spirit. "In the field of both composition and performance, why cannot the students from here write a greater oratorio than Handel's *Messiah*?" Kimball asked, adding:

> They can use the coming of Christ to the Nephites as the material for a greater masterpiece. Our BYU artists tomorrow may write and sing of Christ's spectacular return to the American earth in power and great glory, and his establishment of the kingdom of God on the earth in our own dispensation. No Handel nor other composer of the past or present or future could ever do justice to this great event. How could one ever portray in words and music the glories of the coming of the Father and the Son and the restoration of the doctrines and the priesthood and the keys unless he were an inspired Latter-day Saint, schooled in the history and doctrines and revelations and with rich musical ability and background and training?

The same was true for Leonardo, Raphael, and Michelangelo,[68] whom Kimball name-checked as well, and he referred to the "controversies which arose" with Pope Julius II's commission of Michelangelo to create his tomb—controversies that "embittered a large part of the great artist's life."[69] Art and Belief artists too described embittering interactions with the LDS Church as patron, but in this talk Kimball again saw fault not with the Catholic Church but with the artist (Michelangelo), whose soul he diagnosed as full of "immorality and sensuality and intolerance." In addition, he questioned Rembrandt, whose "morals also have been subject to criticism," although he allowed that the seventeenth-century Dutch painter had an original style that was "founded on the work of no other artist."[70] Raphael too suffered as a man in Kimball's estimation:

> It has been said that many of the great artists were perverts or moral degenerates. In spite of their immorality, they became great and celebrated artists. What could be the result if discovery were made of equal talent in men who were clean and free from the vices, and thus entitled to revelations?

Kimball's talk, which came nine months after that first Art and Belief exhibit opened at the Salt Lake library, announced that for years he had been awaiting a Mormon artist doing proper justice, in whatever medium, to central Mormon theology and biblical narratives. "The story of Mormonism has never yet been written nor painted nor sculptured nor spoken. It remains for inspired hearts and talented fingers yet to reveal themselves," he said. "They must be faithful, inspired, active Church members to give life and feeling and true perspective to a subject so worthy. Such masterpieces should run for months in every movie center, cover every part of the globe in the tongue of the people, written by great artists, purified by the best critics."

Whether Kimball had seen or was aware of the Art and Belief exhibit at the library a few months prior is not clear,[71] but Southey's writings suggest that the two spoke. At the very least, some of the ways Kimball talked about high Mormon art line up almost exactly with the ways the Art and Belief artists envisioned their own mission statements. Southey, for example, wrote that after seeing the great Catholic masters in Europe for the first time, "I knew that greater art was possible in the spirit of the restored church. Perhaps I was to be the one vehicle for that new Renaissance."[72] Over the next decade, artists continued to be a focus for church leaders, including Boyd K. Packer, then of the Quorum of the Twelve Apostles and a future president of the quorum, who delivered the talk "The Arts and the Spirit of the Lord" at BYU on February 1, 1976,[73] when Art and Belief was winding down at BYU and had been around long enough to reach the age of accountability (and to be baptized if necessary). Packer's talk, which instantly became infamous among artists, echoed many of Kimball's points.

It is also unclear whether Packer was aware that his concern about the church going outside its member rolls to commission art also plagued the Art and Belief artists, primarily Southey, who felt passed over.[74] Without mentioning Art and Belief, Packer offered his diagnosis. It was not that Mormon artists were incapable technically of producing artistic masterpieces. "I am reminded of the statement 'There are many who struggle and climb and finally reach the top of the ladder, only to find that it is leaning against the wrong wall,'" he said. Packer would reiterate that metaphor two more times in the talk.[75]

The notion of that disoriented ladder, which took a wrong turn and evidently misread its map, came up often in conversations with both Dennis and Gary and with scholars and curators, most ridiculing the metaphor and viewing it as an example of the establishment church misunderstanding art and its artist members. "When he said that, all of us who were in Art and Belief said, 'Well, son of a bitch,'" Dennis said. "Here I have been trying to figure out how to use my work to express where the deepest feelings I have are, and now he's saying that unless it fits within their expectations of what it should be, I've got it leaning against the wrong wall."[76]

In the talk, Packer added remorsefully that the church president and other leaders must pay careful and anxious attention to music at meetings and during worship, for "if the musicians are left to do what they want to do, the result will not invite the Spirit of the Lord."

This view of "appropriate" settings for music, wherein certain classical music is quiet and contemplative, and therefore a good fit for religious worship, while rock music is loud and not a proper fit for a situation where "anything spiritual [can] happen," is presented not as the taste or preference of a man of a certain age but as truth revealed by one whose credentials "relate to spiritual things."[77] From that perspective, Packer departed, perhaps, from Kimball's view that Mormon artists must succeed on the secular art stage *and* achieve their special extra calling. To Packer, Mormon artists at the highest levels tend to try to attract attention to themselves and to their skill rather than creating truly inspiring art. Packer's belief seemed to be that artists are completely free—from tyranny of the market, for one thing—insofar as they work for the church, whose patronage allows them to create what they most desire.

To Matt Black and Nathan Florence, the co-directors of the *Bright Spark* documentary, Packer's talk is all about the ways that the church sought to control artists. Black noted that everyone from Shakespeare to Willa Cather was cited, but "there's such a difficulty and a lack among the leadership of the Church, and what I've referred to a lot as the 'institutional Church,' to really open itself up to that sort of inquiry that great art requires," he told me. Florence added that some artists are seen as more equal than others. "They never trot out 'Why don't we have any religious artists like Hieronymus Bosch?'" he said.[78]

In Florence's experience, artists do not recall Kimball's talk but absolutely remember Packer's. "Because that's the one that calls them out," he said. Black noted that the church's hope to surpass the patronage of the Catholic Church necessarily hit some snags. "That's the real difference between Rome and Salt Lake City; we just didn't have the kind of financial traction that they did," he said.[79]

One of the most fascinating symbols that the Art and Belief artists pioneered is the tree house, which both Dennis and Fletcher drew upon extensively. Wright, who took a Renaissance history class with Fletcher, had Fletcher's *Another Tree House* (c. 1976) hanging in her former office, and she connected the phases of the moon in the work—which depicts a man with four arms, semi-evocative of Leonardo da Vinci's *Vitruvian Man* (c. 1490)—with the images of the moon that had been taken by early astronauts coming back from space. She also notes the complex symbolism in the work, including the central rainbow, a variety of stars, a red thumb, and gestures similar to sacred gestures in the Mormon church. "Dale Fletcher was a nut about sacred geometry," she said. "It's very cosmic to me, and I think that was the thing about Art and Belief that it was touching more than just this earth. They were trying to get out into the expansive universe in a mid-twentieth-century way to see how these patterns, these ideas, were much more universal than what we were getting generally."[80]

If Packer thought that too many Mormon artists had their ladders propped up against the wrong wall, Fletcher's personified treehouse had its head in space, contemplating lunar cycles. Dennis, meanwhile, depicted tree houses as places where children become like God.[81] Growing up in an apple orchard, Dennis and his brother had more than half a dozen tree houses, and he found that climbing into the tree house separated him from the earth. "You can see the world underneath you, and the world can't see you," he told me. "So you kind of become God."[82]

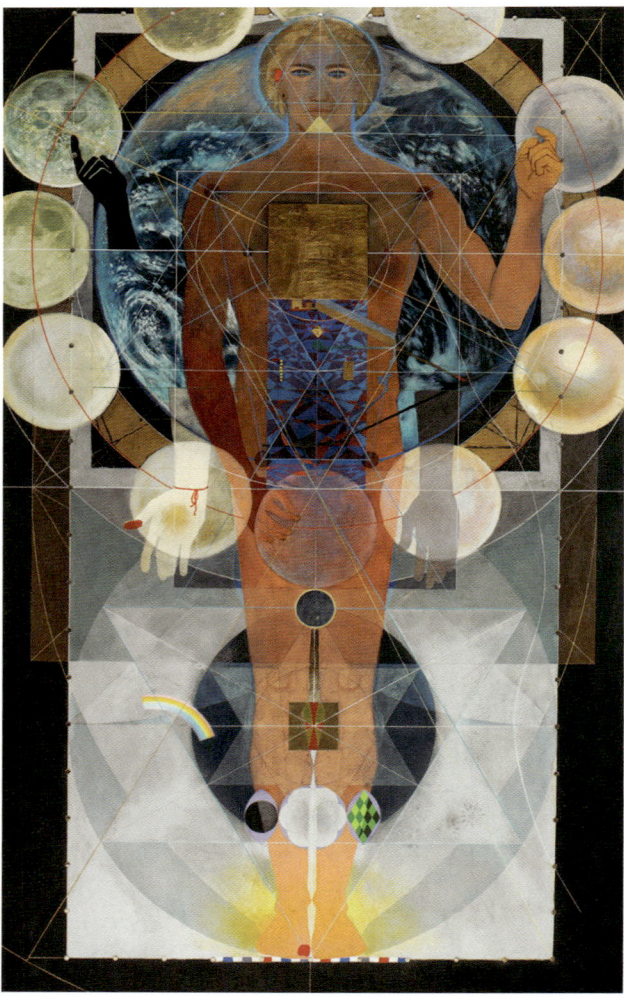

Fig. 15.8 Dale Thompson Fletcher, *Another Tree House*, ca. 1976, mixed media, 80″ × 50″, Springville Museum of Art.

WHY IS ART AND BELIEF STILL RELEVANT?

The long-standing effect of Art and Belief is in conveying the idea that there is a unique, Mormon art, Wright told me—"to feel empowered by these artists, who were talking about their personal experience, doing it in whatever style," she said. "Their styles really diverge. There's not a consistent style, but I think what is consistent is the next generation of artists, or some of their students, caught on to that idea that this was unique to this people and this time."[83]

Swanson believes Art and Belief is a major achievement in the state's history. "It is the most consequential art movement that has happened in the history of Utah art," he

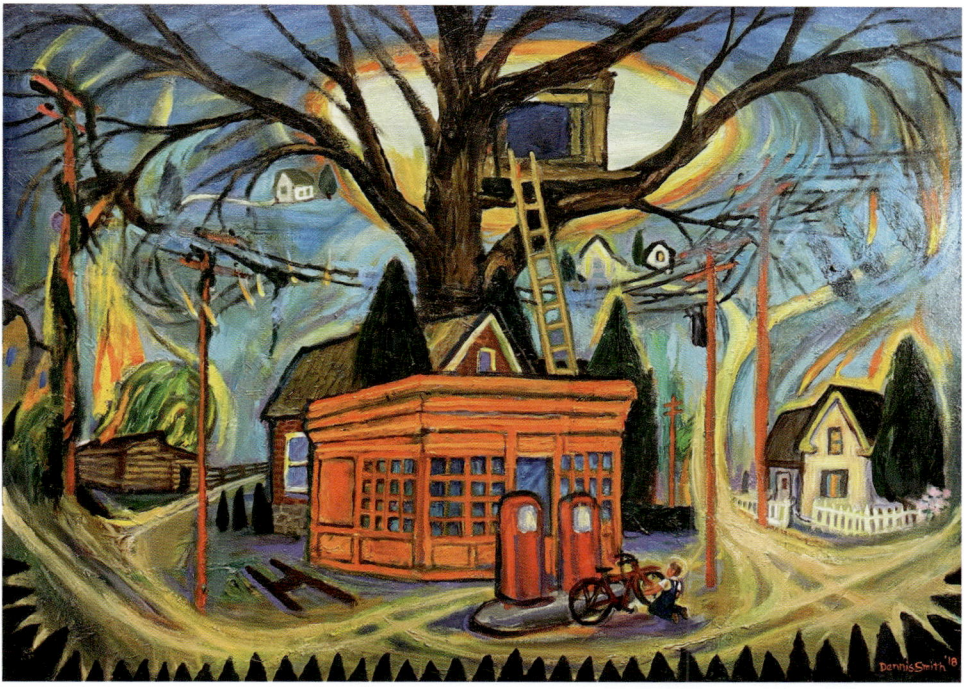

Fig. 15.9 Dennis Smith, *Where Do We Go,* 2018, oil on canvas, 30″ × 40″. Courtesy of the artist.

said.[84] I ran that by Gary, who laughed. "Having been a part of it, I just remember the commitment," he said. "We did include a lot of people in it. It wasn't even like we have an organization here."[85] To this day, Gary continues to hear from artists who say that Art and Belief inspired them. That was particularly the case after Black and Florence's film *Bright Spark* came out in 2022.

"Like the Pre-Raphaelite Movement in England, it made up in height what it lacked in length. It didn't really last that long. The Pre-Raphaelite movement, about four years. Art and Belief lasted a bit longer, about 1965–1966 to 1972–1975," Swanson said. Swanson believes that the Art and Belief artists achieved their initial aim when the Mormon Arts Festival launched. "That was exactly what they wanted," he said, but he noted none of them trusted BYU dean Lorin F. Wheelwright, who oversaw the launch of the Mormon Arts Festival in 1969. The festival took off in a big way, but it escaped the Art and Belief founders' control. "Watch out what you pray for. You might get it," Swanson said. "The Mormon Arts Festival was exactly what they wanted."[86]

Asked to assess the movement's success, Swanson said it is difficult to evaluate movements even more than fifty years later. "The Mormon Art and Belief movement is getting more successful by the day," he said. "It changed Utah. It changed the church. And it changed members of the church. . . . The rock has been thrown into the water,

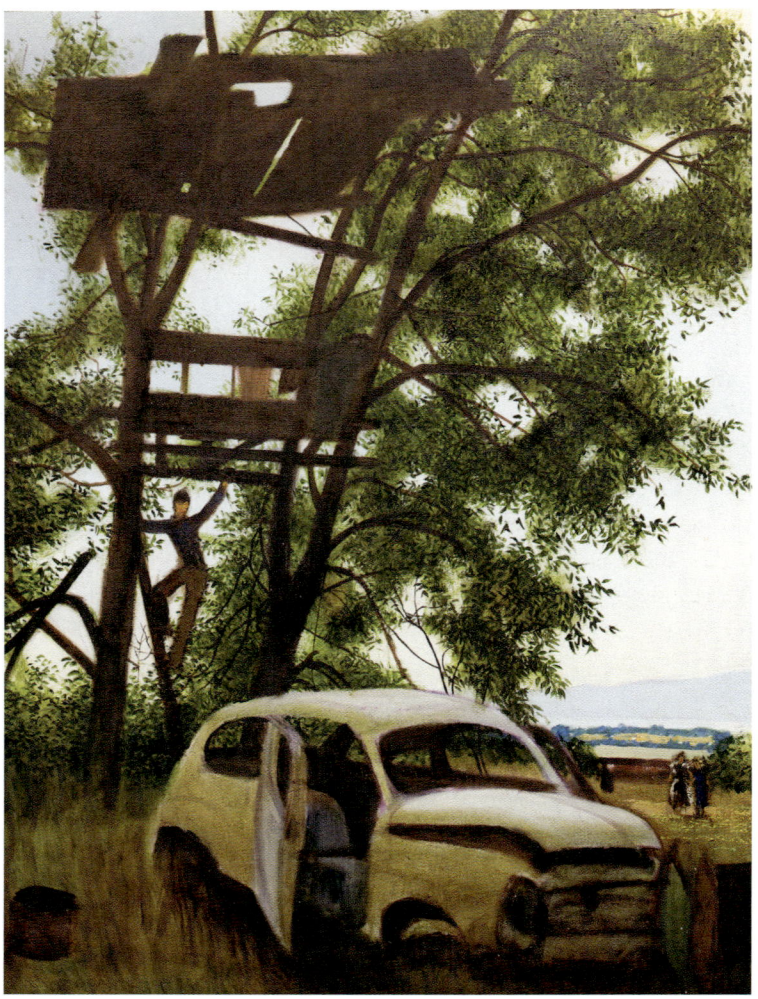

Fig. 15.10 Dale Thompson Fletcher, *Treehouse and Old Car*, c. 1974, oil on canvas, 40″ × 29.75″, Springville Museum of Art.

and the ripples keep coming and coming."[87] Swanson cited Franz M. Johansen as "the proto–Art and Belief artist," and said that before Art and Belief, isolated Mormon artists tackled serious Mormon subject matter. "The amount was not very much, and there was no buzz around it," he said. "It was here and there." With Art and Belief, "it was red hot." He added, "For two years, I was on my tiptoes, because I had dancing shoes on. I was just gliding through."

    "Measured against almost all metrics, the Art and Belief group and the movement were a success," Swanson said at one point in our conversation. "Individually, it put the three young artists on the map, and it definitely inspired succeeding generations of LDS artists to work 'sacramentally.' Worldwide, LDS religious art now dominates the genre to a great extent." The artists had their fingers on the pulse of their time within the Mormon church, and, according to Swanson, they launched a religious art renaissance. "We haven't seen the end of this," Swanson said. "As this secular world descends into greater darkness, the candle that contemporary LDS religious artists hold is shining that much brighter."[88]

Terryl Givens sees the movement differently. Art and Belief, to him, was "one case where the conflict between authority and freedom, the sacred and the secular, certainty and searching, finds no happy resolution."[89] Southey eventually moved to San Francisco, Fletcher pursued other interests, "and the effort dissipated," Givens writes. "A measure of the movement's failure is evident in the decision, in 1985, to excise the word 'Mormon' from the name of the group's festival." It was ironic that the arts festival was stripped of its Mormon title the year after the church dedicated the Museum of Church History and Art near Temple Square. "Together, these two events suggested that the past of Mormon art looked brighter than its future," Givens wrote.

"As the Art and Belief movement lost steam, BYU—the church's best hope for fostering Mormon art—continued in the direction of other university art departments, toward nonobjective, nonfigurative art, 'soft postmodernism' in Vern Swanson's words," Givens added.[90]

In 1972, BYU published a coffee-table volume, *Mormon Arts: Volume One,* edited by Wheelwright and drawing inspiration from the Art and Belief movement and from the Mormon Festival of Arts. In his introduction, the BYU dean wrote, "The subtitle, *Volume I,* embodies the spirit of the work. Other volumes must follow until a comprehensive body of art works, literature, and aesthetics infuse our Mormon culture."[91] Alas, no other volumes followed.[92] If one were inclined, one could chalk that up to a failure of the movement and its intellectual children.

But from another perspective, Art and Belief is like that painting of Gary Smith's that wound up in the closet and almost miraculously survived intact, phoenix-like, despite being under a bucket, perhaps for decades. Both in Utah and certainly outside of Utah, it is often hiding just out of plain sight, and it has much of the recipe for compelling storytelling in spades: colorful characters; well-developed scenes; tension within families, friend groups, and church; and very arresting visuals. And with documentaries about people leaving orthodox faith traditions abounding on many streaming platforms, the story of Art and Belief is far more engrossing and edifying. The Salt Lake City gallerist David Ericson, who was an early champion and financial backer of the Art and Belief artists, told me that the Mormon church was then, and to an extent remains, *persona non grata* (or perhaps better, *ecclesia non grata*) in the United States outside its core areas. "You can make fun of them all you want," he said. "The Mormons are *personae non gratae* to most of the country."[93]

Trying to sell artwork in Provo to students and professors in the community, who barely made more than high school teachers, was a losing proposition, according to

Ericson. "There wasn't enough market for them [the artists] to sustain what was going on," he said. "They were painting these things, and they couldn't get enough market, enough people to understand what they were doing." From 1930 to 1970, no one in Utah was making a living just as an artist, according to Ericson. The best one could hope for was a tenured job, teaching art and painting on the side.

"Essentially, the Utah universities' art programs were training people to become high school art teachers," he said. The reason the Art and Belief movement became important is that this group of students and Dale Fletcher came together and said, "If Mormonism is real and we're going to make a difference, let's figure out how we can paint our culture and our society and our beliefs. And that's the whole basis of it."[94]

So why didn't it spread, like the Pre-Raphaelites? "Our guys never moved out of Utah. They couldn't afford to travel to New York to find a dealer. It was an economic thing," Ericson told me. So why haven't major museums "discovered" them since, as they look for neglected works and artists? Ericson thinks it's hard because of the overt religious aspect. "You go look and see what religion is doing in the world today. I mean, in Europe they're decommissioning a church every day," Ericson said. "It's a broad aversion to religion, and then it's a specific aversion to Mormonism."[95]

In one of our conversations, Dennis told me, "We don't talk about Art and Belief anymore, because we've all gone our separate ways."[96] That may have been the case for the core group, but that does not mean that the rest of us cannot and should not.

NOTES

[1] In a 2017 interview with Micah Christensen, of the Zion Art Society, Smith recalled it as "Take that ugly painting down!" To me he recalled it as "Take that painting down!" in a January 26, 2022, phone interview.

[2] Per the U.S. Bureau of Labor Statistics inflation calculator, the $150 for which Smith sold the work in May 1967 corresponds to $1,363.72 in March 2023 dollars. Smith provided a copy of the May 11, 1967, letter from Steve Nadauld and Russ Booth, co-vice presidents of culture at Associated Students Brigham Young University, in which the two offer $150 for *Eternal Plan*. "We would like very much to have this work for the Wilkinson Center collection," they wrote.

[3] Phone interview with the artist, January 27, 2022. The picture technically depicts nudes, but might be interpreted as more or less tame, depending upon one's perspective and beliefs.

[4] Email correspondence with Tyler Stahle, media relations manager at BYU, December 20, 2022.

[5] In February 2015, the university transferred the ownership of its medical school, Einstein, to Montefiore Health System. See "Yeshiva U Sheds Half of $1B Endowment Along with Medical School Liabilities," Jewish Telegraphic Agency, February 19, 2016.

[6] Depending on the institution, models may wear bathing suits or be fully clothed.

[7] Dale Fletcher, "Art and Belief: A Group Exhibition," *Dialogue: A Journal of Mormon Thought* 2, no. 1 (1967): 48–52.

[8] Phone interview with the artist, January 26, 2022. The artist is sometimes referred to as Dennis von Smith, or Dennis V. Smith. From here on, this chapter will refer to Dennis Smith and Gary Ernest Smith by their first names.

[9] Interview in person with the artist in his studio, March 2, 2022. In a January 2023 email, Gary wrote that *Eternal Plan* and *Decision* (which is addressed below) are "two early paintings [that] were my very first attempts to take some complex scripture and doctrine and portray it in symbols." He further shared a 1966

entry from his journal in which he described the work: "It is a painting of the last days with the embryo of the fetus representing the birth of mankind and roots that nourish the tree of life that represents all of humanity. There is a subtle, pictorial, reference to the Earth," he wrote. "The dove is a symbol which testifies of truth. The Christ symbol is in a crucifix position representing the Savior of mankind extending his hand. The red moon (moon turns to blood), a scriptural last days reference. The figure on the left is in a floating, spiritual state awaiting resurrection. The large circle is the sun losing its light."

[10] Phone interview with the artist, January 27, 2022. During a visit to the BYU campus, I tried extensively to track down the work's current location. I did not see it on a walk-through of the student center, and several experts in the know indicated that the work—given the nudity—would not be likely to hang today for the same reason it was removed decades ago. Several people with deep knowledge of the university's art collection are unaware of the work's location, and it remains a mystery why a BYU employee would have contacted the artist rather than curators at the BYU Museum of Art, mere steps from the student center. (I note here that I am not, nor have I ever been, a member of the Church of Jesus Christ of Latter-day Saints. My name may reveal that I was raised Orthodox Jewish. I have reported somewhat extensively on art associated with the church as a journalist, but I am very grateful to all those who explained things to me along the way.)

[11] Many books and articles have been published on "art and belief," but the movement's name is so broad that it is difficult for researchers to disentangle it from general references to religious culture that have nothing to do with the movement that began at BYU. One way to narrow searches is by referring to it as the "Mormon Art and Belief movement," but that too has its limitations.

[12] I was shocked in the research process to find it virtually invisible at many of the nation's most renowned art museums, including those that purport to tell the story of American art in a comprehensive fashion, including across the Smithsonian Institution. I was also surprised to find that the most important books on the Art and Belief movement could not be found even at major Washington, D.C., libraries and that it was necessary to go to Salt Lake City to obtain many of the relevant materials. I am very much in debt to the curatorial and library staffs at BYU and at Springville Museum of Art.

[13] In the documentary *Bright Spark: The Reconciliation of Trevor Southey,* dir. Nathan Florence and Matt Black (Purdie Distribution, 2022), Southey noted that BYU appointed Fletcher the group's academic chaperone, but from the university administration's perspective, it could not have found a worse person to be the students' watcher.

[14] Phone interview with the former museum director, April 11, 2022.

[15] Sunstone Salt Lake Symposium, January 1, 1991.

[16] Utah Artists Project, https://lib.utah.edu/collections/utah-artists/UAP-Dale-Fletcher.php.

[17] Phone interview with the former museum director, April 11, 2022.

[18] Phone interview with the artist, January 26, 2022.

[19] He uses a term that a colleague at the Alpine Art Center coined: "memory collages." Interview in person with the artist, March 2, 2022.

[20] An image of the work in question appears on the website of David Ericson Fine Art: https://www.david ericson-fineart.com/wp-content/uploads/2022/03/january-sledders_-16x20-2340-min.jpg.

[21] Interview in person with the artist, March 2, 2022. Of the language he created, Gary told me: "I said if the Egyptians can do it, I can." Indeed, he could and did. I used a key he provided to translate one of his inscriptions, and it worked perfectly.

[22] Interview in person with the artist, March 2, 2022.

[23] When he sent me the image via text message, Gary titled it *Self Portrait Contemplating Eternity.*

[24] As K. Mitchell Snow puts it in Trevor Southey, *Trevor Southy: Reconciliation* (Salt Lake City: Signature Books, 1998), 14, "He was humbled by the power of Michelangelo's *Pietà* on display in the Roman Catholic pavilion and humiliated by the pedestrian paintings that decorate the Mormon presentation. When he learned that the work was the product of a Seventh-day Adventist illustrator, Southey was even more determined to make a difference in Mormonism's aesthetic presentation." See also *Bright Spark,* dir. Florence and Black.

[25] Trevor Southey, letter to Elder Mark E. Petersen, 1967. Ironically, Bertel Thorvaldsen's sculpture *Christus,* a replica of which was part of the LDS church's pavilion at the World's Fair, forms the church's new logo, as Ashlee Whitaker Evans, of the BYU Museum, alerted me. See Church of Jesus Christ of Latter-day Saints, "The Church's New Symbol Emphasizes the Centrality of the Savior," April 4, 2020, https://newsroom.churchofjesuschrist.org/article/new-symbol-church-of-jesus-christ.

[26] In Southey, *Trevor Southy: Reconciliation,* 55, Southey added that even at a young age, as he was observing apartheid in South Africa, he was "aghast" that the church excluded Black people from the priesthood.

[27] Southey, *Trevor Southy: Reconciliation,* 4.

[28] Sunstone Salt Lake Symposium, 1991.

[29] Dave Gagnon, "The Third Wave," *Deseret News,* October 20, 2002, https://www.deseret.com/2002/10/20/19684031/the-third-wave.

[30] Gagnon, "The Third Wave."

[31] Phone interview with the artist, January 26, 2022.

[32] Interview in person with the artist, March 2, 2022.

[33] One noted exception is Laura Allred Hurtado, who dates the beginning of the movement to 1964. Laura Allred Hurtado et al., *Immediate Present* (New York: Mormon Arts Center, 2017), 4.

[34] Phone interview with the former museum director, April 11, 2022.

[35] Phone interview with the former museum director, April 11, 2022.

[36] Phone interview with the artist, January 27, 2022.

[37] Matt Black, co-director of the documentary *Bright Spark,* thinks things are changing and regional art movements are gaining more respect. "I think we're just getting to a place where hopefully people are stepping away from the sort of monolithic, everything that happened in the art world happened in New York or L.A., and then the rest of the world just sort of falls off," he said. Video-chat interview with the film director, August 13, 2021.

[38] Video-chat interview with the museum director, April 17, 2021; in-person interview with the museum director, March 3, 2022.

[39] *Bright Spark,* dir. Florence and Black.

[40] *The Mormons* (aired April 30, 2007), *American Experience* and *Frontline*, Transcript available at https://www.pbs.org/mormons/etc/script2.html.

[41] In a video-chat interview on April 17, 2021, Emily Larsen, then head of exhibitions and programs at Springville Museum of Art (now director), noted that some see *only* the communal living in Alpine (Eden) as the real Art and Belief movement, while others see it as a different movement altogether: the North Mountain Artists Cooperative. Others still see Art and Belief as a Provo/BYU movement and not one that continued to Alpine. For her part, Larsen thinks Art and Belief unfolded in both Provo and Alpine. "Geography and place are really important to the kind of mythology of the story," she told me. She added that when Southey found Salt Lake and BYU were not the Mormon art Mecca he had expected, "He was really disappointed with what he found in the art world, and so he wanted to create that himself."

[42] Phone interview with the artist, January 26, 2022.

[43] My transliteration, which I believe to be closer to the original biblical Hebrew name, אהליאב.

[44] The Hebrew term is משכן, which means "dwelling place."

[45] When I saw the painting in storage at the Springville Museum, no plastic sheep was to be seen.

[46] Marvin Payne, "Dale Thompson Fletcher," Springville Museum website, http://webkiosk.springville.org/artist-maker/info/203.

[47] Payne, "Dale Thompson Fletcher."

[48] Research and interviews for this chapter turned up no definitive proof whether Fletcher penned the manifesto shortly after the beginning of the movement or prior to it.

[49] For more on purity in modern art, see, for example, T. J. Clark, "Clement Greenberg's Theory of Art," *Critical Inquiry* 9, no. 1 (September 1982), 139–156.

[50] In-person (March 3, 2022) and video-chat (April 17, 2021) interviews with the former museum director.

[51] Phone interview with the former museum director, April 11, 2022.

[52] Sunstone Salt Lake Symposium, 1991; phone interview with the former museum director, April 11, 2022.

[53] Trevor Southey, "A Survey to Determine the Public Responses and Attitudes Toward the First Festival of Mormon Art at Brigham Young University" (master's thesis, Brigham Young University, 1969).

[54] Video-chat (April 17, 2021) and in-person (March 3, 2022) interviews with the curator. For a very erudite examination of the meaning of "Mormon art," see Hurtado et al., *Immediate Present,* 7–13.

[55] Dale Fletcher, "God, Man, and Art," *Dialogue: A Journal of Mormon Thought* 2, no. 4 (1967): 123–126.

[56] Video-chat interview with the filmmaker, August 13, 2021.

[57] Quoted in *Bright Spark,* dir. Florence and Black.

[58] In a more humorous example, in the film Dennis recounted working on eleven large sculptures in Nauvoo about the role of women in the church. Two apostles were whispering, and finally someone else asked him, "Do you think you could make the breasts any larger?" As Hadlock told it, Smith held some clay in his hands and kneaded it before asking the others, "Show me?" They said it was okay, good enough, Hadlock concluded.

[59] *Bright Spark,* dir. Florence and Black.

[60] Phone interview with the artist, January 27, 2022.

[61] Cited in an interview with an expert who asked to remain anonymous.

[62] In-person interview with the curator, March 3, 2022.

[63] K. Mitchell Snow, in Southey, *Trevor Southy: Reconciliation,* 18.

[64] See Lloyd DeWitt, ed., *Rembrandt and the Face of Jesus* (New Haven, CT: Yale University Press, 2011).

[65] Of course, Jesus—to believers—was not just anyone whom one might meet on the street, so this is a more complicated discussion than just realism versus stylization.

[66] Spencer W. Kimball, "Education for Eternity," address to BYU faculty and staff, September 12, 1967, https://educationforeternity.byu.edu/w_swk67.htm.

[67] Throughout Kimball's talk, he referred exclusively to male artists and imagined just a young Mormon boy who might be inspired to greatness—gender assumptions that "are typical of the period in which he was speaking. However, the idea that greatness does not reside only in the past has echoes of two long-standing Mormon beliefs: first, the belief in continued revelation, and, second, the belief that among the Latter-day Saints is the potential for profound expression, lying in wait until the day it comes out of obscurity." Hurtado et al., *Immediate Present,* 2.

[68] For a very thoughtful response to this charge for Mormon art superior to the established canon, see John M. Rector and Kristen N. Rector, "What Is the Challenge for LDS Scholars and Artists?," *Dialogue: a Journal of Mormon Thought,* 36, no. 2 (2003), 33-46.

[69] This is ironic, given that the Art and Belief artists would later bemoan the church's insistence that their depictions of the prophet Joseph Smith, which they felt were deeply felt and psychologically significant, have the requisite, historically accurate number of buttons on the garments.

[70] Pieter Lastman (1583–1633) was obviously unavailable for interview, or perhaps Kimball was unaware of Lastman's work and influence as a teacher of the young Rembrandt.

[71] Hurtado takes him to task for appearing to be oblivious to Minerva Teichert's work decades prior. Hurtado et al., *Immediate Present,* 2.

[72] Southey, *Trevor Southy: Reconciliation,* 59.

[73] Boyd K. Packer, "The Arts and the Spirit of the Lord," speech, February 1, 1976, https://speeches.byu.edu/talks/boyd-k-packer/arts-spirit-lord/.

[74] See, for example, Trevor Southey, letter to Elder Mark E. Petersen, November 16, 1967, 2, where Southey writes: "I do hope you will understand that my comments are made merely because I believe that thousands of people are distracted from the power and beauty and truth of our message by the poor quality of some of our visual aids. I believe that this could be avoided if more of this work was done by members of the Church—that is those who are qualified to do it both academically and spiritually. Of course if such people are not available then naturally non-member artists would have to be used." Southey goes on to recommend, in part, that "artists in the Church should be made aware well in advance of all major art projects which the Church proposes to have done. This could be done with a small insert in official Church publications."

[75] Lecture delivered at YMMIA conference, June 3, 1888, in Brian H. Stuy, comp. and ed., *Collected Discourses* (Burbank, CA: BHS Publishing, 1987), 1:154.

[76] Phone interview with the artist, January 26, 2022.

[77] Fascinatingly, Packer cites as proof of this notion of "appropriateness" a highly personal anecdote, which he evidently views as universal. When he feels self-conscious at the pulpit, Dr. Packer has found that the sacred music that he considers "appropriate" inspires him and helps him overcome his anxiety, after which the words flow. That ease is not replicated when he has heard "inappropriate" sacred music prior to his talk. This evidently deeply felt set of experiences that motivates and concretizes Packer's aesthetic views could be the subject of its own chapter, as could his assessment of artist C. C. A. Christensen, whom "some would say [is] not even a good one [painter]." To Packer, the artist's works are masterly because of his reverence for spiritual heritage: "I do not think it strange that the world would honor a man who could not paint very well," he said.

[78] Video-chat interview with the filmmaker, August 13, 2021. Florence did not make this point, but he may have meant in part that the Dutch artist Bosch (c. 1450–1516) was known for his portrayals of, among other things, misbehaving priests, including those being tormented in hell. In some ways, Bosch was an institutionalist, part of a prominent Catholic order that granted him privileges to a chapel in Den Bosch's main cathedral, but in other ways, his brush spared no one, no matter how powerful. See, for example, Menachem Wecker, "Largest-Ever Retrospective Underscores Hieronymus Bosch's Catholic Faith," *National Catholic Reporter,* April 23, 2016, https://www.ncronline.org/largest-ever-retrospective-undersco res-hieronymus-boschs-catholic-faith.

[79] Wecker, "Largest-Ever Retrospective."

[80] In-person interview with the museum director, March 3, 2022.

[81] Dennis told me that he believes neither he nor Fletcher ever brought up which one first painted tree houses, because neither wanted to know who copied from whom. Phone interview with the artist, January 26, 2022.

[82] In-person interview with the artist, March 2, 2022.

[83] In-person (March 3, 2022) and video-chat (April 17, 2021) interviews with the museum director.

[84] He said something similar at the Sunstone Salt Lake Symposium on January 1, 1991. But he amended the quote in an email correspondence in February 2023.

[85] In-person interview with the artist, March 2, 2022.

[86] Phone interview with the scholar, April 11, 2022.

[87] Phone interview with the former museum director, April 11, 2022.

[88] Phone interview with the former museum director, April 11, 2022.

[89] Terryl L. Givens, *People of Paradox: A History of Mormon Culture* (Oxford: Oxford University Press, 2007), 335.

[90] Givens, *People of Paradox,* 335.

[91] Lorin F. Wheelwright, ed., *Mormon Arts: Volume One* (Provo, UT: Brigham Young University Press, 1972), v.

[92] "Certainly labeling the catalog a first volume released the authors from the responsibility to be comprehensive and allowed for an open canon." Hurtado et al., *Immediate Present,* 6.

[93] Phone interview with the gallerist, January 13, 2022.

[94] Phone interview with the gallerist, January 13, 2022.

[95] Phone interview with the gallerist, January 13, 2022.

[96] Phone interview with the artist, January 26, 2022.

16

RACE AND LATTER-DAY SAINT ART

W. PAUL REEVE

When Janan Graham-Russell, an African American convert to the Church of Jesus Christ of Latter-day Saints, entered the Chicago temple for the first time, she was struck by the art that she encountered, but not in a positive way. One painting in particular captured her attention. "I was looking at the artwork, walking to the baptismal font," she recalled, when she stopped at a portrait and absorbed its implications. "It was this beautiful portrait of Jesus," she remembered, and he was "surrounded by angels in full glory and they were celebrating his presence in heaven and I looked closer and all of the angels were white."[1]

A question struck Graham-Russell: Was this how her fellow Saints saw the eternities? Did only white people belong there? "If they see the eternities this way, how do they see me?" she wondered. "Do they look at my face, do they look at my experiences," she pondered. "I felt that in the temple my brothers and sisters didn't see me, not only on a cultural level, but on a theological level."[2] It was an unsettling introduction to the problem of whiteness in Latter-day Saint theology and history, and Graham-Russell's encounter with it came through art.

As Graham-Russell learned, in order to understand race and Latter-day Saint art, one must first understand the power of whiteness in Latter-day Saint history, theology, and culture. Whiteness has informed the Latter-day Saint worldview and is thereby reflected in its art. This chapter explores the complex history of race and the Church of Jesus Christ of Latter-day Saints using whiteness as an interpretive lens.

In Latter-day Saint history, whiteness became a fulcrum between negative racial perceptions from the outside and a corresponding desire on the inside for respectability and acceptance. Art was one way that outsiders attempted to ascribe a degraded racial identity to Latter-day Saints in the nineteenth century, especially through political cartoons and dime novel illustrations. Latter-day Saint artists, meanwhile, aspired toward whiteness from the inside. Such a dynamic helps to explain the near absence of Black Latter-day Saints in nineteenth-century Latter-day Saint art and a proclivity to imagine Native American redemption as a part of the faith's journey toward whiteness. Latter-day Saint art also tended to filter other ethnic groups through a white lens, which implied that white was normal and anything not white was seen as a deterioration away from whiteness or even a curse.

In the second half of the twentieth century, things began to change. Latter-day Saint artists from around the globe began to decenter whiteness and thereby reshape the faith's visual culture in important new ways. "All flesh is mine," Jesus Christ declared in 1831 to the faith's founding prophet, "and I am no respecter of persons" (D&C 38:16). It was a scriptural ideal that Latter-day Saint artists have only begun to reclaim. In the twenty-first century their art continues to shape a more inclusive sense of the faith's history as well as the untapped strength of its current global diversity. Artists have also begun to imagine what an inclusive theological vision might look like, one in which the God of "all flesh" leaves no one out—not in this life or in the next.

WHITENESS AND LATTER-DAY SAINT HISTORY

Joseph Smith claimed at least five revelations in the 1830s stipulating that the Latter-day Saint gospel message was to be preached "unto every creature," a universal vision that some early Latter-day Saints took seriously.[3] From the 1830s through the 1850s missionaries scoured the globe in search of converts. They preached to Native Americans and African Americans (both free and enslaved) and proselytized in Europe, South Africa, China, Jamaica, India, Siam, and other locations. The Latter-day Saint notion of "gathering" people into the gospel fold was expansive.[4]

Even so, the Book of Mormon, the signature scripture of Joseph Smith's new religion, deployed racialized language to equate whiteness with purity and righteousness, and blackness with sin, filthiness, and depravity. White was "delightsome" in Book of Mormon parlance, whereas blackness was "loathsome." Nineteenth-century Latter-day Saints believed that Native Americans were fallen descendants of Book of Mormon peoples, particularly a dark-skinned group called the Lamanites who eventually destroyed their lighter-skinned kinship group, the Nephites.[5]

In a fraught nineteenth-century American racial culture, the ways in which such racial understandings played out varied according to prevailing U.S. racial hierarchies and the faith's unfolding racial theology. As white Latter-day Saint leaders articulated it, the racialized language of the Book of Mormon applied to Native Americans, not to people of Black African descent. Latter-day Saints viewed Native Americans as people in need of redemption. Brigham Young, in contrast, claimed that Black people were cursed descendants of Cain, a condition he said made them ineligible for the faith's lay priesthood and its highest temple rituals. Latin Americans, Asians, and especially Pacific Islanders escaped such exclusions but were still situated within a hierarchy of whiteness.[6]

NATIVE AMERICANS

The earliest artistic representations of racial diversity from an outside perspective depicted Joseph Smith preaching to Native Americans. Henry R. Robinson and Edward Williams Clay's 1844 lithograph *Joseph the Prophet Addressing the Lamanites* is an early example. It is a relatively benign depiction of an imagined relationship between Native Americans and Latter-day Saints. By the time the lithograph appeared in print, accusations about Latter-day Saints and their interactions with Native Americans had already coalesced around three main themes: that Latter-day Saints preached to Native Americans in order to conspire against white Americans, that Latter-day Saints intermarried with Native Americans, and that Latter-day Saints in their behavior and actions sometimes descended below the level of Indigenous people to become more savage than the "savages."[7]

The Robinson and Clay lithograph, however, avoided those themes to suggest a more peaceful intent. Joseph Smith is certainly depicted in a culturally superior position, but his aim is racial redemption, not violence. Smith stands with one hand outstretched and the other holding the Book of Mormon. His message from that book was meant to convey a chosen identity for Native Americans. At the same time, however, Smith preached that message from a place of civilized refinement to a "primitive" people. Smith is dressed in a formal suit, vest, and coat with tails. His black shoes are polished and fashionable. He stands to preach in an assertion of authority, while his Native American audience sits to listen, a docile group wrapped in blankets and adorned with feathers and Indigenous jewelry. Their faces are passive if not kind, and no weapons of war are included in the scene. The setting is a forest with trees and shrubbery into which the Native Americans blend, a symbol of their society and a way to signal their status in Euro-American eyes as children of nature. In the artists' view, Smith has brought Indigenous people not merely a gospel message but also civilization, refinement, a chance for redemption, and a new way of life. In short, Smith represented the whiteness that Latter-day Saints were about to lose as they fled west.

By the 1850s, outsiders imagined more sinister intent. Latter-day Saints forsook the United States in 1846 and arrived in northern Mexico in the summer of 1847. When they moved west, some outsiders imagined that Latter-day Saints had purposely left civilization behind in order to join the Indians. In the process, they descended the American racial ladder, a fearful deterioration backward into barbarism and even savagery. Latter-day Saints became "white Indians," people who had betrayed their racial identity to degenerate beyond the limits of depravity of which even Native Americans were capable.[8]

An 1855 dime novel made this point explicit even as it popularized the idea that Latter-day Saints disguised themselves as Indians and murdered people on the overland trail. It was a stereotype that emerged as early as 1850, at least seven years before Latter-day Saints did in fact kill 120 innocent members of the Baker-Fancher

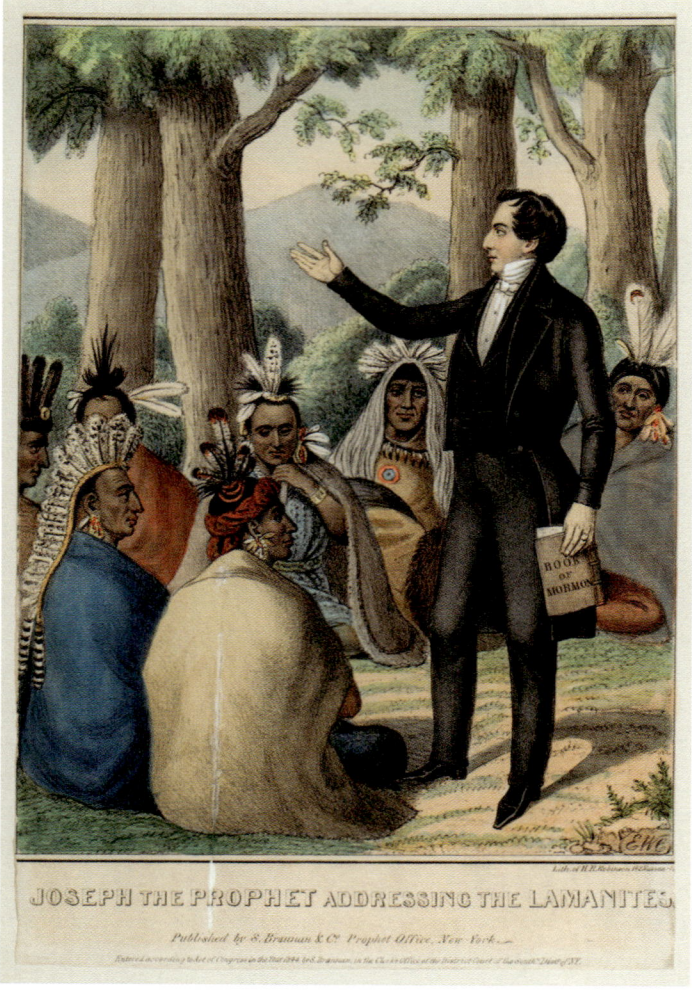

Fig. 16.1 Eward Williams Clay and Henry R. Robinson, *Joseph the Prophet Addressing the Lamanites*, 1844, lithograph, 10″ × 8″, National Museum of American History.

party in what became known as the Mountain Meadows Massacre.[9] Alfreda Eva Bell's sensationalized dime novel *Boadicea, the Mormon Wife*, picked up on this theme and gave it literary and pictorial expression. In explaining the disappearance of one male character in her novel, Bell indicated that "one of the peccadilloes of the Mormons consists in disguising themselves in Indian costume, and waylaying such persons as are obnoxious to them, and putting them to death." The blame for such atrocities fell on the Indians, but "even those poor savages were incapable of committing deeds so infamous, so bloodthirsty, and so cruel, as were common practices of the Mormon Elders, under the name of religion."[10]

The accompanying illustration offered visual "evidence" of such allegations. Simply captioned "Mormons Disguised as Indian Spies," the sketch featured two allegedly white Latter-day Saints in the foreground, both shirtless, dark-skinned, and skulking with violent intent. An unsuspecting traveler on horseback enters the scene as the obvious target of the malicious resolve of these "Indian spies." The illustration was the near polar opposite of the Clay and Robinson lithograph from the previous decade. The Mormons no longer represented civilization but now stood in its way.

The setting was again the wilderness, but this time the Latter-day Saints blended into their environment. In moving west Mormons had gone native and were far from

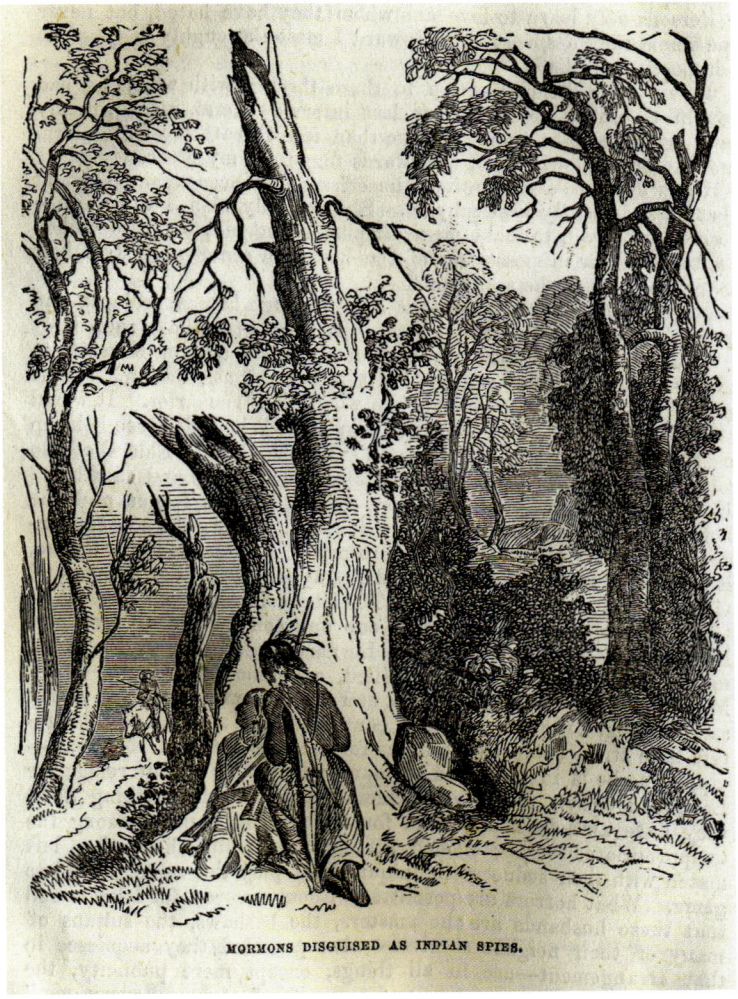

MORMONS DISGUISED AS INDIAN SPIES.

Fig. 16.2 *Mormons Disguised as Indian Spies,* 1855. Reprinted from Alfreda Eva Bell, *Boadicea: The Mormon Wife. Life-Scenes in Utah* (Baltimore: Arthur R. Orton, 1855), p. 81, Special Collections, Rare Books Division, J. Willard Marriott Library, University of Utah.

peaceful. They were armed with guns and now represented a barrier to the white traveler, and by extension to national progress.[11] In fact, in a blend of pictorial imagination and actual politics, just two years later, U.S. president James Buchanan justified a military expedition against the Latter-day Saints in what came to be called the Utah War with the accusation that "they stand a lion in the path." Latter-day Saints, he claimed, were guilty of "encouraging, if not exciting, the nomad savages who roam over the vast unoccupied regions of the continent to the pillage and massacre of peaceful and helpless emigrant families traversing the solitudes of the wilderness."[12] Such accusations continued for the rest of the nineteenth century, spurred on by the fact that Latter-day Saints did murder innocent migrants on the overland trail in 1857. Especially when Latter-day Saints entered the national imagination, fears of Mormon-Indian conspiracies were never far behind.[13]

Even as depictions from the outside called into question Mormon whiteness, Latter-day Saint artists chose to emphasize gospel uplift in depicting their interactions with Indigenous people. In many regards such paintings followed the lead of the 1844 Clay and Robinson lithograph. Rather than the nefarious resolve of the political cartoons and dime novels, Latter-day Saint artists imagined peaceful progress as the result of Mormon interactions with Native peoples.

A representative example is Carl Christian Anton Christensen's *Joseph Preaching to the Indians*. It constituted one scene in a twenty-three-piece Mormon panorama series, which the Danish-born artist stitched together and used in speaking engagements to Latter-day Saint audiences. The series focused on early events in Latter-day Saint history and was designed to educate the rising generation of Latter-day Saints on significant moments in the young faith's founding decades. It emphasized scenes of persecution, trial, and sacrifice and was meant to instill faith in the next generation of Latter-day Saints, who were then growing up without the same kind of violent opposition that the founding generation had faced.[14]

Christensen's painting features what became a repeated scene in Latter-day Saint art: Joseph Smith preaching to Native peoples. Smith stands with one arm outstretched and the other clutching a book, no doubt meant to be the Book of Mormon.[15] As Christensen depicts it, light, refinement, domesticity, and civility emanate from the right third of the painting, with Smith and his followers the focal point. A child, well-dressed men, and a woman seated in a chair holding an umbrella and with a pet dog next to her all signal a sense of peace and order—the fruits of the gospel message that Smith preached. Smith and his group are noticeably white and bear the markings of culture and refinement. The chair is the only piece of furniture depicted in the scene and a woman occupies it, a signal of sophistication, civility, and gender distinction, all of which are absent among the Native Americans. Some Native Americans even blend into the foliage at one end of the circle they form around Smith, with the wilderness subsuming them. Their teepees in the background stand in contrast to the white Latter-day Saint woman's chair and umbrella, a difference in levels of cultural advancement

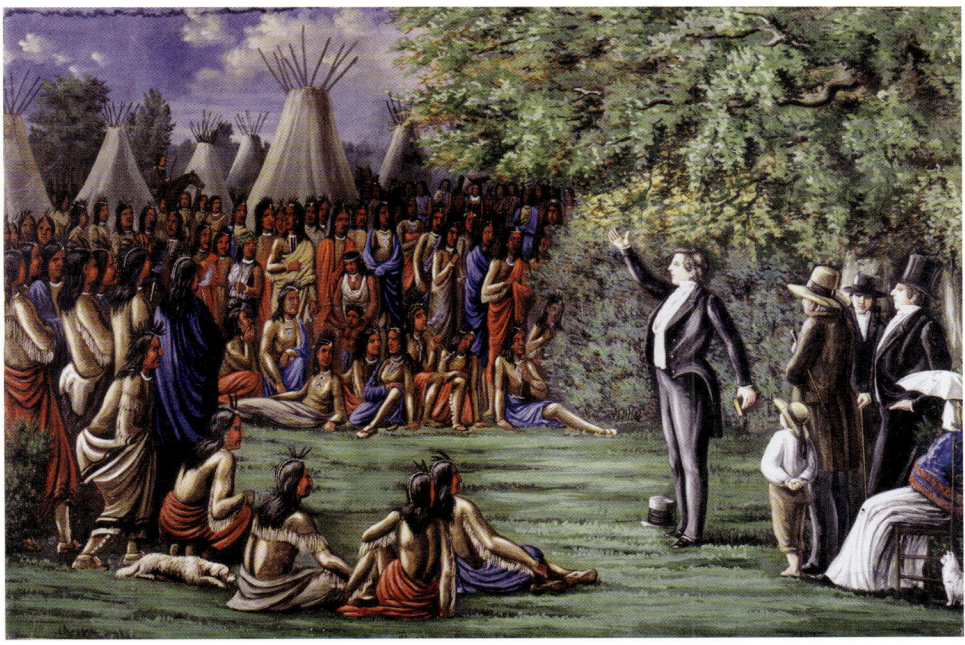

Fig. 16.3 C. C. A. Christensen, *Joseph Preaching to the Indians*, c. 1878, tempera on muslin, 76 1/2″ × 112 3/4″, Brigham Young University Museum of Art, gift of the grandchildren of C. C. A. Christensen, 1970.

and an indication of Indigenous primitiveness. The red clothing of some of the Native Americans matches the red faces of all the Native Americans and marks the key distinction between the two groups.[16]

Christensen's depiction thus symbolizes the power of whiteness in the gospel message Smith preaches. As Smith believed, the Book of Mormon described the ancestors of Indigenous people who had fallen from grace. As a result, "they did become an idle people, full of mischief and subtlety, and did seek in the wilderness for beasts of prey" (2 Nephi 5:24). But if they would repent, the Book of Mormon promised, the "scales of darkness" would fall from their eyes and they could become "a white and delightsome people" (2 Nephi 30:6). Smith eventually changed the word "white" to "pure" in the Book of Mormon, an indication of its intended metaphorical meaning. Yet his own correction became lost in the book's publication history until it was eventually restored, though not until the 1981 edition. In the interim, some Latter-day Saints believed that gospel uplift quite literally meant racial uplift and that a lightening of skin color accompanied repentance.[17]

From the Latter-day Saint perspective, Smith preached a message of purity to an impure people, something Christensen's depiction captures well. Smith brought redemption to Native peoples, not the other way around. Smith promised them a future role in the ultimate Christian triumph over wickedness. Christensen's image depicts Native Americans as "children of nature," racialized versions of Native peoples that allowed Latter-day Saints to play up their theological vision of gospel uplift and to emphasize a promised role for Native Americans in the building of a Latter-day Zion.[18]

Latter-day Saints did convert Native Americans, sometimes in mass baptisms, but the hoped-for widespread redemption did not materialize to the degree that Latter-day Saints initially imagined. Especially after Latter-day Saints arrived in the Great Basin and built settlements among Native Americans, the practicality of colonization often won out over theological ideals. Latter-day Saint scripture referred to those who would be redeemed in the last days as a "remnant" of the biblical Jacob, but when the anticipated conversions did not happen Brigham Young began to wonder how small the "remnant" might be. He questioned if the existing generation would have to die off before a Lamanite redemption could be realized. In the meantime, Young said, existing Native Americans might just as well "die and be damned."[19]

Especially in the twentieth century, Latter-day Saints shifted their view southward beyond the boundaries of the United States to imagine church growth in Latin America as the fulfillment of the promised redemption that Indigenous people in the United States had left wanting. They applied the term "Lamanite" from the Book of Mormon to Latin American peoples (as well as Pacific Islanders) and saw their conversions as a realization of the book's promises.[20] Even so, whiteness informed this shift and its corresponding art.

LATIN AMERICANS

As Latter-day Saint missionaries looked south of the U.S. border they drew on the Book of Mormon to inform their understanding of peoples in North, Central, and South America. In 1852, Latter-day Saint apostle Parley P. Pratt, for example, concluded that Lehi's descendants (Nephites and Lamanites) had "peopled the entire continent of North and South America." Pratt included "Peruvians, Mexicans, Guatemalans," as well as "descendants of every tribe and tongue of this mysterious race" in his description.[21] He believed that "perhaps nine-tenths of the vast population of Peru, as well as of most other countries of Spanish America, are of the *blood of Lehi*."[22]

As Latter-day Saint artists began to imagine what the "blood of Lehi" might have looked like in their art, they tended to depict white European Christians. The art focused on the generally more righteous Nephites, who avoided the "sore cursing" or the "skin of blackness" that came upon the Lamanites, but Lehi and his family originated in the Middle East, not Scandinavia.

C. C. A. Christensen, who had earlier imagined Joseph Smith preaching to the Native Americans, turned his artistic attention toward the Book of Mormon in the 1870s to paint a twenty-two-foot panorama. Christensen designed his eleven-panel scroll to depict the Christian history of the world, from the creation of Adam and Eve down to Joseph Smith receiving gold plates from a resurrected Book of Mormon prophet, the angel Moroni. Latter-day Saint missionaries George Washington Hill and Dimick Huntington then used the panorama as a preaching tool as they spread the Latter-day Saint gospel among Goshute, Ute, Paiute, and Shoshone peoples.[23]

Christensen's panels depict white as the default and normal skin color for humanity. Adam and Eve are white, Cain and Abel are white, Lehi and his family fleeing Jerusalem are white, Jesus and John the Baptist are white. New World peoples, even after the "skin of blackness" came upon some of them, are nonetheless depicted as white. In the penultimate panel, Christensen depicts the Book of Mormon prophet Moroni around 400 CE, hiding the golden plates on which he and other leaders had engraved the record of his people—the same record that Joseph Smith would claim to translate centuries later into the Book of Mormon. In this scene Christensen depicts Moroni in a European-style helmet and body armor, with the remnant of his people in the background also outfitted with European-style armaments, fighting a final battle in which the Nephites, who have fallen to a level of depravity worse than the Lamanites, will be annihilated. In the final panel Christensen depicts a white, angelic, and resurrected Moroni delivering those same plates to Joseph Smith, the founding prophet of the Latter-day Saint movement.[24]

It is not certain how Dimick Huntington and George Washington Hill used these panels in practice or what messages they shared to coordinate with each scene. The visual lesson was nonetheless clear—white is normal. Unlike Christensen's earlier painting of Smith preaching to Native peoples, there is no racial diversity depicted across the span of his eleven panels. White and European were the default lenses through which he viewed Latter-day Saint cosmology. It was an ironic message given that whiteness was simultaneously aspirational for Euro-American Latter-day Saints simply because their own racial status was under attack from the outside.[25]

An early quasi-official effort to depict the Book of Mormon in film, the 1913 *Life of Nephi*, did move beyond European style dress to imagine Middle Eastern clothing and culture for the white actors.[26] Even still the most influential imagination of what Book of Mormon people might have looked like did not come until the 1950s. Arnold Friberg, a Latter-day Saint artist, crafted twelve artistic scenes that were eventually included in paperback missionary versions of the Book of Mormon. In the twentieth century Friberg's images became the most iconic artistic depictions of the Latter-day Saints' signature scripture. Adele Cannon Howells, the faith's general Primary president, charged with the religious education of the church's children, commissioned Friberg's paintings in an effort to bring the scriptures to life for her young audience. An entire generation of Latter-day Saints was thus raised on Friberg's renditions, and he became the faith's most well-known "painter of scripture."[27]

While Friberg does depict some variations in skin tone in his Book of Mormon paintings, white and European are nonetheless dominant. Like Christensen before him, Friberg imagines Scandinavian-looking people, as the Book of Mormon's protagonists. In fact, one criticism of Friberg's paintings is the white hypermasculinity they exude. As one scholar noted, Friberg's Book of Mormon art suggests "a surreal, mythic civilization borne by heroic European-style men in ancient America not at all in keeping with the usual notions about the pre-Columbian peoples."[28]

Friberg's *Alma Baptizes in the Waters of Mormon* is an illustrative example, especially when compared with a twenty-first-century depiction of the same scene, this one by Jorge Cocco Santángelo, a Latter-day Saint artist from Argentina.[29] The Book of Mormon describes a prophetic leader named Alma performing baptisms at a secret wilderness location called the waters of Mormon. Alma's teachings at the waters of Mormon stood in contrast to those of a wicked political leader of his day and defied that leader's authority. Alma nonetheless converted more than two hundred followers who were willing to seek "the redemption of Christ" and accept baptism by immersion at his hands as a symbol of their rebirth (Mosiah 18:13). In Friberg's rendition a bare-chested Alma baptizes a blond-haired woman dressed in a flowing white gown as light floods them and makes them the focal point of the scene even though they are distant figures. Other blond- and brown-haired people frame the picture, set against a lush tropical locale with mountains in the background. The physical setting was no doubt meant to conjure Central or South America, but the people do not.

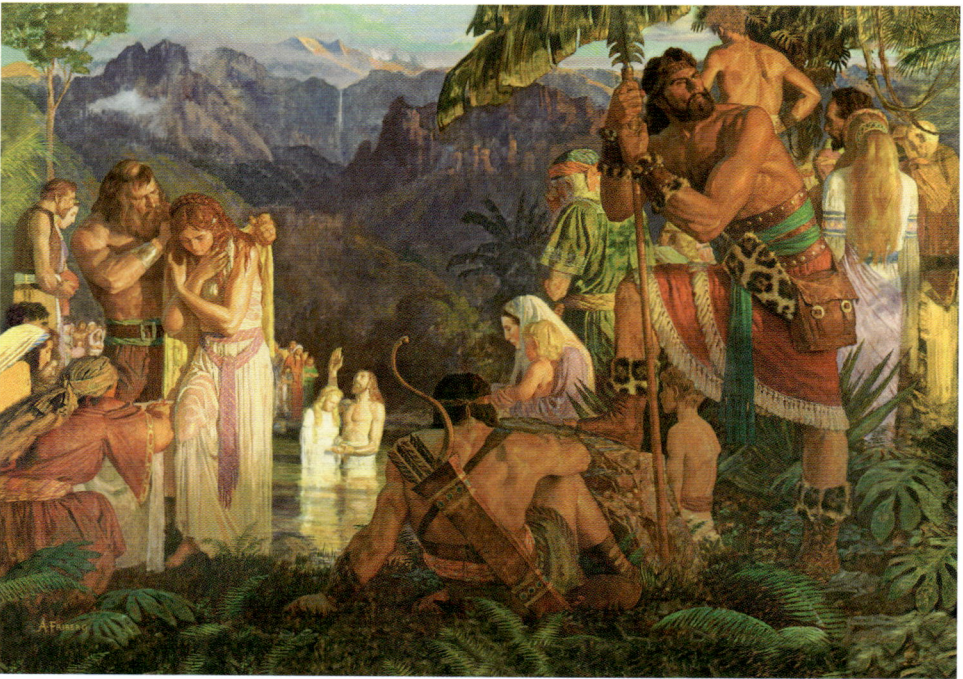

Fig. 16.4 Arnold Friberg, *Alma Baptizes in the Waters of Mormon*, 1950–1954, Church of Jesus Christ of Latter-day Saints Church History Museum.

In Santángelo's *The Waters of Mormon*, in contrast, there are no blond-haired people. The setting is again easily imagined as Latin America, but this time the people are too. Alma and his proselytes are brown-skinned and wrapped in blankets and clothing meant to suggest a pre-Columbian civilization. The hairstyles of the men, the facial features of those depicted, and the jewelry also signal the pre-Columbian era. Alma raises his right hand to the square at the center of the scene, the same pose and focal point as in Friberg's depiction. The rituals, in other words, are imagined identically, but the people engaged in those rituals are distinct. Friberg envisions a white European redemption, even in Latin America, while Santángelo sees an Indigenous redemption, an important shift in perspective. Santángelo paints Alma as a pre-Columbian prophet, a person with authority, and an early Christian leader in the Americas. He established a church, ordained priests, baptized with authority, and taught principles of empathy and selflessness, and in Santángelo's version he was brown-skinned when he did so.

The transition from Friberg's *Waters of Mormon* to Santángelo's is important. It marks the late twentieth-century transition that took place as the faith grew in global locations, especially Central and South America. It marked through art the demographic shift that occurred in 1996 when for the first time there were more Latter-day Saints who

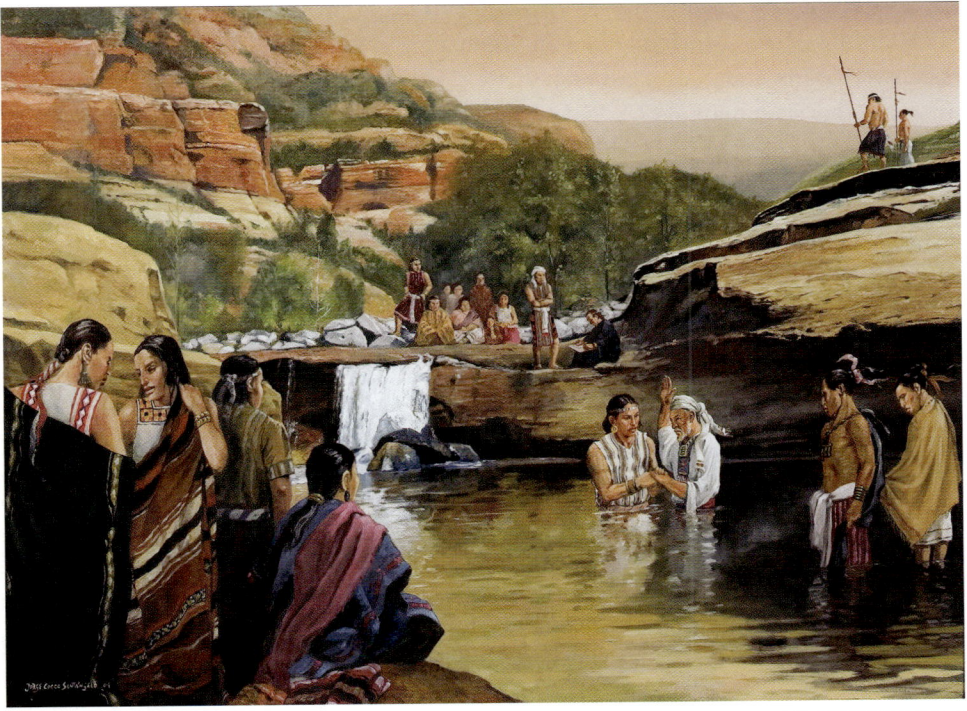

Fig. 16.5 Jorge Cocco Santángelo, *The Waters of Mormon*, 2005, oil on canvas, Church of Jesus Christ of Latter-day Saints Church History Museum.

lived outside of the United States than within.[30] That transition opened the possibility for a global group of Latter-day Saint artists to begin to imagine themselves in Latter-day Saint scripture, and by extension as prophets and leaders. At the same time, such artists began to decenter the white European art that dominated depictions in the prior two centuries.

LATTER-DAY SAINTS OF BLACK AFRICAN DESCENT

Whiteness dominated the nexus between Black and white in Latter-day Saint art even more so than in the Native American and Latin American examples. From the outside looking in, political cartoons and illustrations projected fears of race mixing onto the Latter-day Saints. This was a persistent theme in the nineteenth century that played on fears of polygamy to suggest that if left unchecked it would do more than destroy the traditional family; it would destroy the white race.[31]

Especially after Latter-day Saints openly announced the practice of polygamy in 1852, anxiety over race mixing escalated among outsiders. Political cartoons across the course of the nineteenth century imagined polygamy as a Latter-day Saint system of racial corruption with the survival of American democracy at stake. As Senator John C. Calhoun argued in 1848, democracy was the "government of a white race"; in his estimation non-white peoples were racially incapable of participating in self-government, and as a result race mixing threatened America's experiment in self-rule.[32] Thus, when outsiders imagined Mormon men intermarrying with a variety of racial groups—Asians, Africans, and Native Americans, most prominently—they feared the degraded offspring that such marriages would produce and what that meant for democracy.[33]

Outsiders projected such fears onto Brigham Young's own family in one political cartoon. In the fall of 1871, Young was arrested on charges of "lascivious cohabitation" stemming from his polygamous marriages. The case dragged on through the spring of 1872 before it was eventually dismissed, but not before the national press made light of the situation.[34] *Frank Leslie's Budget of Fun,* a pictorial magazine published in New York City, ran a political cartoon designed to imagine what the scene must have looked like when federal marshals hauled Brigham Young off to court.[35]

The picture, simply titled *Affecting Parting of Brigham Young from His Interesting Little Family,* was meant to depict Brigham Young's own family as an example of racial deterioration. The first wife to reach out to Young was a Black woman meant to conjure the "black mammy" stereotype from the plantation South. The cartoon suggested that the leader of the Latter-day Saints engaged in interracial marriage and produced tarnished offspring.[36]

Beyond that, the white wives and children were also meant to portray the degrading effects of polygamy. The heavy brow and forehead, the flat nose, and the angle of the upper face were all key elements designed to evoke primitive, beastly, and apelike features. Brigham Young himself was depicted with bent legs and long arms hanging down in gorilla fashion. He appears disheveled, with his back to the viewer to further

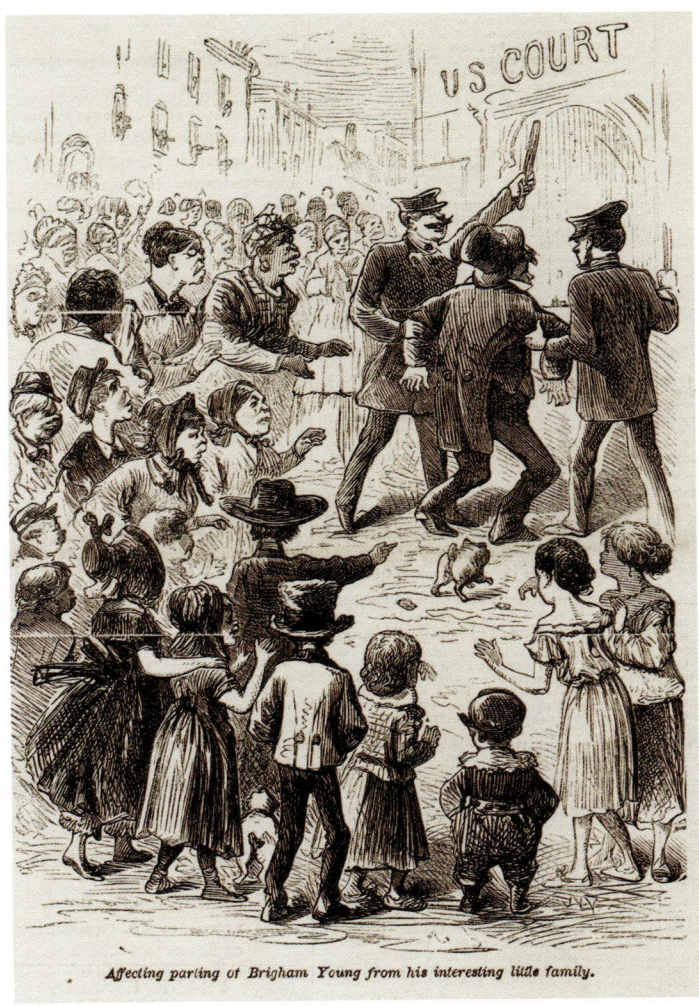

Affecting parting of Brigham Young from his interesting little family.

Fig. 16.6 **Affecting Parting of Brigham Young from His Interesting Little Family,"** *Frank Leslie's Budget of Fun*, January 1872, Library of Congress.

dehumanize him—more animal or object than human. The intended message was clear: Brigham Young presided over a backward evolutionary descent in his own family, and by implication, Latter-day Saints as a whole threatened Western civilization with racial decline.[37]

The most significant way to claim whiteness in a fraught nineteenth-century racial culture was in distance from blackness, and Latter-day Saint leaders did just that—they moved away from their own Black converts across the course of the nineteenth century.[38] Beginning in 1852 Brigham Young publicly defined people of Black African descent as theologically cursed and barred them from priesthood ordination and temple worship. By the first decade of the twentieth century, they were erased from collective Latter-day Saint memory altogether—this despite the fact that the first documented African American Mormon, a formerly enslaved man known as Peter, joined the faith in its founding year and there have been Black Latter-day Saints ever since.[39] Their erasure from Latter-day Saint history explains their near absence from Latter-day Saint art.

The singular exception tended to be Black 1847 pioneers who remained practicing Latter-day Saints and therefore enjoyed a place of prominence in the faith by the end of the nineteenth century. Three Black enslaved men, Green Flake, Oscar Smith, and Hark Wales, arrived in the Salt Lake Valley on July 22, 1847, two days ahead of Brigham Young. They were a part of Young's vanguard party, which set out that spring to establish a new settlement in the Salt Lake Valley. In mid-July, the three enslaved men, along with thirty-nine other men and twenty-three wagons, separated from Young's group and forged ahead to improve the trail and chart a course into the valley.[40] Later that year, Jane Elizabeth Manning and Isaac James, along with their son Silas and Jane's son Sylvester, arrived in the valley as free Black Latter-day Saints. Jane, a convert from Connecticut, and Isaac, from New Jersey, were both pioneering Black Saints, as much a part of the Latter-day Saint movement across the continent as their white counterparts. Other free and enslaved men and women followed.[41]

The Black 1847 pioneers received significant attention in the nineteenth century, at least at the territory's annual Pioneer Day celebrations, a tradition that became an official state holiday by the twentieth century. Pioneer Day celebrations were designed to mark the entrance of the Latter-day Saints into the Salt Lake valley, and those who arrived in 1847, both white and Black, were particularly revered. Green Flake was a notable example. He was frequently featured in Pioneer Day celebrations and sometimes gave talks or was otherwise remembered at the annual commemorations. In 1888, for example, the rural community of Union, at the southern end of the Salt Lake valley, held an "interesting programme of speeches, songs, recitations, [and] music by the Central Silver Band." Among the speakers that day was "Mr. Green Flake, one of [the] Pioneers, who gave a short account of the travels of the Pioneers across the plains."[42] Flake again spoke at an event in 1893 and was regularly honored as an 1847 migrant.[43]

In 1897, at the fiftieth anniversary of the Saints' arrival in the valley, the *Salt Lake Tribune* ran a series of articles that marked different milestones along the overland journey. One of those articles featured a line drawing of Flake, a portrait based on a photograph. It features Flake in a suit and tie with a dignified look on his face. He stares into the distance, perhaps meant to convey a sense of the atypical path his life had taken over the years, from the plantation South to mining and farming in the Intermountain West and from enslavement to freedom as a Black Latter-day Saint. The accompanying article noted that he was "one of the original pioneers of Utah" and that "he is a colored man," an intersection of identities that the *Tribune's* readers in 1897 may have found atypical but which had not yet been erased. The *Tribune* reminded its readers that Flake was born into slavery and that he was also baptized a Latter-day Saint. He "became a valued man in the pioneer company," the newspaper reported, and "is very well known in Salt Lake." The paper tried to track down photographs of Oscar Smith and Hark Wales, Flake's two enslaved companions from 1847, in order to include drawings of them alongside Flake, but "all efforts to secure their photographs have been fruitless," it noted.[44]

The fact that Flake had entered the Salt Lake Valley as an enslaved Latter-day Saint who then remained devout for the rest of his life perhaps accounted for the *Tribune* drawing a picture of him in the first place. The intersection of Flake's various identities was certainly atypical when juxtaposed against the rest of the 1847 pioneers. The *Tribune's* fiftieth-anniversary series listed the names of those pioneers, but few of them were also singled out for artistic renderings. The newspaper's reports did not shy away from slavery or racial diversity, evidence that at least in the nineteenth century Black Latter-day Saints were included in the pioneer story.[45]

Jane Elizabeth Manning James, another 1847 Black pioneer, also garnered attention, the only one of her family to do so.[46] Jane divorced her husband, Isaac James, in 1870, after which Isaac moved away; their son Silas died in 1872 and the LDS Church excommunicated Sylvester in 1885, leaving Jane as the lone representative of the family in late nineteenth-century Pioneer Day celebrations.[47] In 1892, however, her brother Isaac Manning joined her in Salt Lake City and became her partner at such outings. Isaac Manning was also an early convert to the faith but had stayed in the Midwest following the murder of Joseph Smith. In 1876, he joined the Reorganized Church of Jesus Christ of Latter Day Saints but then was rebaptized into the Church of Jesus Christ of Latter-day Saints after his move to Salt Lake City. He and Jane had worked in the Nauvoo Mansion House for Joseph and Emma Smith in the 1840s, a personal connection to the founding prophet, which made them pioneer celebrities of sorts by the end of the century, when the generation of Latter-day Saints who could claim a personal connection to Smith grew increasingly small. Newspaper reporters frequently tracked down the siblings to interview them and listen to them reminisce about their interactions with Joseph Smith.[48]

Such was the case in 1899 when the *Salt Lake Herald* ran a story erroneously titled "First Negroes to Join the Mormon Church." Jane and Isaac were not the first, but they were early Black converts. In any case, the point of the story was to highlight their connection to Joseph Smith: "Aunty Jane and Uncle Isaac are two delightfully typical old colored people who enjoyed the privilege of living in the family of the Prophet Joseph Smith, and who glory in telling all about it," the *Herald* claimed. Readers learned that "Uncle Isaac presided over the culinary department of the prophet's establishment while Aunt Jane did the washing." Like with Green Flake, the story featured line drawings of the siblings, which were labeled "Uncle Isaac" and "Aunt Jane," "TWO CITIZENS WHO LIVED WITH THE PROPHET JOSEPH."[49] The artistic renderings depict the couple in profile and were drawn to convey a sense of dignity and even stature as

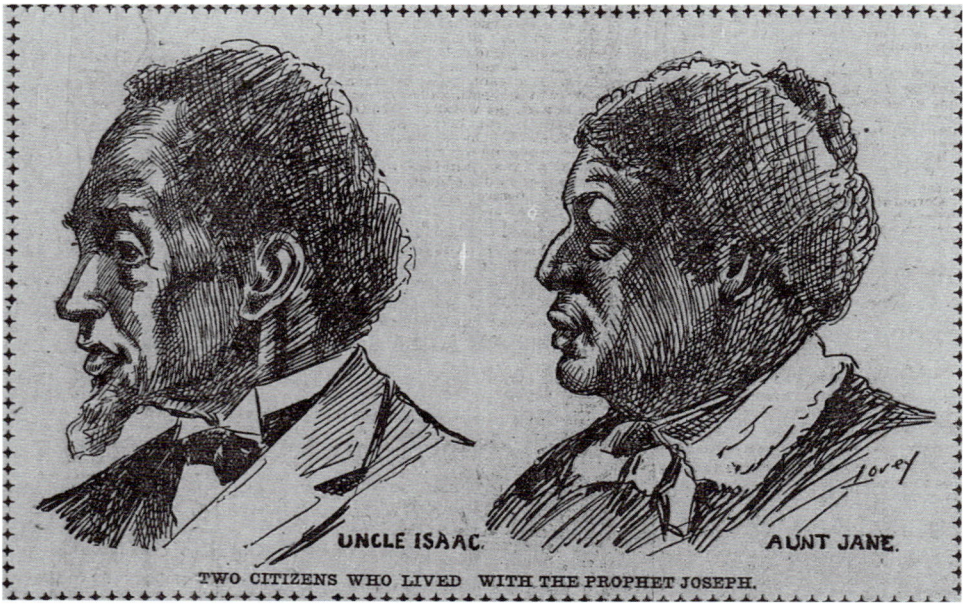

UNCLE ISAAC.   AUNT JANE.

TWO CITIZENS WHO LIVED WITH THE PROPHET JOSEPH.

Fig. 16.7 "First Negroes to Join the Mormon Church", Salt Lake Herald, October 2, 1899, p. 5.

seasoned Latter-day Saints who were honored pioneers because of their connections to the faith's revered founder.

The titles "Aunt Jane" and "Uncle Isaac" indicated a sense of inclusion and respect even as it signaled racial distance. They were members of a broader Latter-day Saint family, but always extended members. The *Herald*'s art honored them as "citizens who lived with the prophet Joseph," but their theological citizenship had its limits by that point. Latter-day Saint leaders had barred them from the faith's highest rituals despite James's repeated pleadings otherwise, a fact that newspaper line drawings could not convey.[50]

Over time, however, especially as Latter-day Saint leaders hardened the faith's racial restrictions in place at the beginning of the twentieth century and the prominent Black pioneers passed away, Black people in Latter-day Saint publications came to be objects of pity or paternalism, or something to laugh at but certainly not revere. Enslaved and free 1847 pioneers faded from collective memory and with them so too did the newspaper line drawings of Flake, James, and the Mannings. Latter-day Saint art that depicted the faith's westward migration failed to include Black Latter-day Saints at all. As the faith became secure in its whiteness, it participated unabashedly in racism aimed at blackness.[51]

In 1920, the *Juvenile Instructor*, the church magazine intended for its children and youth, featured a photograph of an African American baby and young boy over a poem titled "Little N—— Baby." The unlabeled photograph serves no purpose other than to

offer readers a visual example of such a baby, which the poem then describes in pater-
nalistic and condescending tones. It repeats the n-word at the beginning of each of the
poem's four stanzas: "Little n—— baby, just arrived from heaven above / My heart is
full of tenderness for you / Beneath that dusky skin a guileless heart I see / Alovin' just
like white folks' babies do." "Little n—— baby, rest on your mammy's breast," the poem
continues, "and angels will watch over while you sleep." Black Latter-day Saint pioneers
were gone and nondescript children took their place, infants who were meant to stand
in for all members of their race. Black babies were non-threatening and even endearing,
according to the poem; after all, they gave love "just like white folks' babies do." They
were something to be pitied, not feared; the black baby's "dusky skin" hid only "a guileless heart," the poem declared. However, in infantilizing Black people the poem made
them into perpetual children, people who could never be equal to white Latter-day
Saints and who were always in need of a "mammy's breast."[52]

In the 1950s, after *Brown v. Board of Education* set the nation on a path toward integration, some church magazines did attempt a more inclusive vision, short-lived though
it was. In March 1959, *The Improvement Era* ran a report on the faith's mission efforts
in South Africa that featured a picture of a white child standing next to an African
child.[53] In September of that same year, the *Instructor* magazine published an article
on tolerance that highlighted an interracial group of young adults in a social setting.[54]
The following month the *Relief Society Magazine* included an article that decried any
person who "expresses pride in the American Bill of Rights and then seeks to protect his
own real estate by restrictive covenants."[55] All three stories and their visual depictions
seemed to suggest inclusivity, albeit in subtle ways.

The string of visual and written messages was too much for at least one anonymous
reader to stomach, however. The unnamed subscriber penned a letter in opposition to
the implied messages in these church publications. "We expect to be bombarded from
every side with the man-made philosophies of all races intermingling indiscriminately,"
the writer explained, but "to see the innocent introduction of these things presented
in our own literature under the guise of righteousness seems something else again."

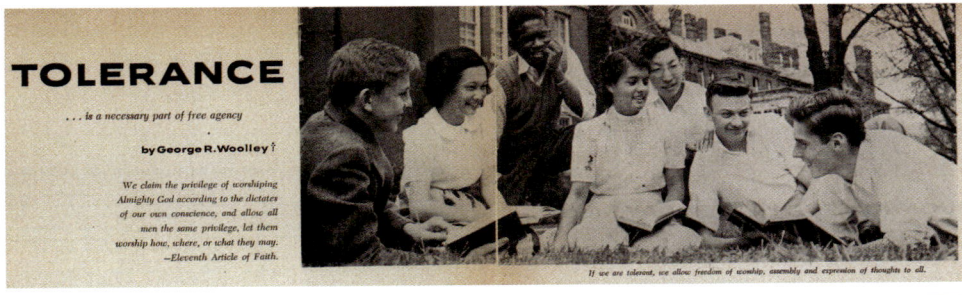

Fig. 16.8 George R. Woolley, "Tolerance is a necessary part of free agency," *The Instructor*,
September 1959, 286–287.

The writer pointed specifically to the image in the *Instructor* as a matter of concern: "a photograph of a group of young people lounging picnic fashion on the grass, a Negro among them," simply went too far. "When the Lord sees fit to send missionaries to [Negros] I shall rejoice for the race," the writer explained. "However, I do not think that this particular race should have picnics with our youngsters of marriageable age with all barriers removed. Nor do I think such things should be presented in our magazines for consumption of our uneducated youth."[56]

Latter-day Saint leaders responded to the letter writer's concerns with support, not correction. In fact, they instructed those responsible for church magazines not to forget "that the negro may not have the priesthood no matter what the degree of negro blood may be" and that "we cannot support social contacts between the races but must discourage it." Such contacts "may result in mixed marriages, the offspring of which will not have the right of priesthood," leaders warned.[57]

It was an exchange over visual art that illustrated the ways in which the fear of race mixing, once projected onto the Latter-day Saints in the nineteenth century, had become thoroughly internalized by the twentieth century. It also accounts for the lack of Black people represented in Latter-day Saint visual culture for much of its history. Undefiled whiteness was the racial ideal, measured in distance from blackness.

In June 1978, the leader of the faith, Spencer W. Kimball, ushered in a slow reversal process when he announced a revelation that returned the church to its universal roots and reintegrated its priesthood and temples. It was the dawning of a new day for the faith and ushered in a reimagination of its racial representation in art. Quilts and paintings soon included scenes of seated black men surrounded by standing white men, hands laid on the black men's heads in the Latter-day Saint ritual of priesthood ordination.[58] Black pioneers in Africa and in America were sometimes featured in the paintings of the post-1978 era, as were twentieth-century African American Saints.[59]

A significant transition, however, came when Black Latter-day Saint artists began to paint themselves as Latter-day Saints. In 1992, for example, the Church History Museum commissioned a series of batiks (a textile technique that uses wax and dye to color fabric) from Sierra Leonean artist Emile Wilson. The series features images of Latter-day Saints in Sierra Leone living their religion in day-to-day practice. A Black man baptizes another Black man in one scene, while Black missionaries are featured in another. *Blessing and Naming of a Baby* and *Latter-day Saints Attending Church in Sierra Leone* are self-explanatory titles of two additional pieces in the collection. Other scenes depict Latter-day Saints blessing the sick and confirming a new member of the church, rituals that Latter-day Saints around the globe would readily recognize in Wilson's portrayals, except for the fact that they feature only Black people, something atypical in congregations outside of Africa.

Most arresting, however, are Wilson's depictions of Joseph, Mary, and the baby Jesus in one scene and the Last Supper in another. All of the people portrayed in these iconic settings are Black, a visual reclamation of blackness from its cursed Latter-day Saint past and a dramatic reimaging of it as holy and even divine. Wilson did not stop there, however, but included an image of a Black Christ nailed to a cross. It is juxtaposed against a white and blue background scarred with lines and creases, almost chaotic in its composition. Black Jesus however, hangs solemnly in the foreground, detached from any earthly mooring except for the cross that stretches his arms in peaceful triumph. The chaotic white background almost transforms into angel wings ready to bear him away. Wilson's Black Jesus has risen above earthly chaos and sorrow and offers all believers healing in his wings. It is a powerful image that places blackness at the center of Latter-day Saint salvation rather than at its margins, to which it had been relegated for much of Latter-day Saint history.

ASIA, THE MIDDLE EAST, AND THE PACIFIC ISLANDS

As outsiders attempted to situate the newly born Church of Jesus Christ of Latter-day Saints within a nineteenth-century religious context, they sometimes sidestepped Native Americans and people of African descent altogether. Some observers suggested that Mormonism was more akin to Eastern religions than to Western ones, despite the fact that it was an American-born faith. As some outsiders articulated it, the "Mormon Problem" was really a contest between Eastern and Western civilizations with Mormonism more Eastern than Western, an exotic Other that did not fit into Christian categories.[60] In 1854, for example, Congressman Caleb Lyon placed Mormons alongside "Persians, Hindoos, and Musselmen" in his religious categorization, while a Protestant minister similarly situated Mormons with "Mohammedans, Hindoos, Fugians, Caribs and Hottentots."[61]

In 1879, the Supreme Court of the United States pushed such conflations forward when it first ruled on the constitutionality of polygamy. In a unanimous decision, the Supreme Court rejected Latter-day Saint claims to polygamy as a religious principle protected by the First Amendment. The court ruled that the Constitution protected religious belief but not action. Latter-day Saints could believe in polygamy all they wanted, but they could not practice it. Writing for the Court, Chief Justice Morrison Waite justified his decision in part by using a racial argument. "Polygamy has always been odious among the northern and western nations of Europe," he argued, "and, until the establishment of the Mormon Church, was almost exclusively a feature of the life of Asiatic and of African people."[62] In practicing polygamy, in other words, Latter-day Saints violated the standards of what it meant to be white and European.[63]

Especially as Congress debated solutions to the "Mormon Problem" and "China Problem" in 1882, newspapers across the nation exaggerated the conflation. Congress, in fact, passed the Chinese Exclusion Act and the Edmunds Act (a law aimed at polygamy that made "unlawful cohabitation" a crime) within two months of each other.[64] It was a comparison that the nineteenth-century press could not resist. Newspapers variously labeled the two issues "the vexed Chinese and Mormon questions," "the Mormon and Chinese curses," and "the Chinese and Mormon problems."[65] One California

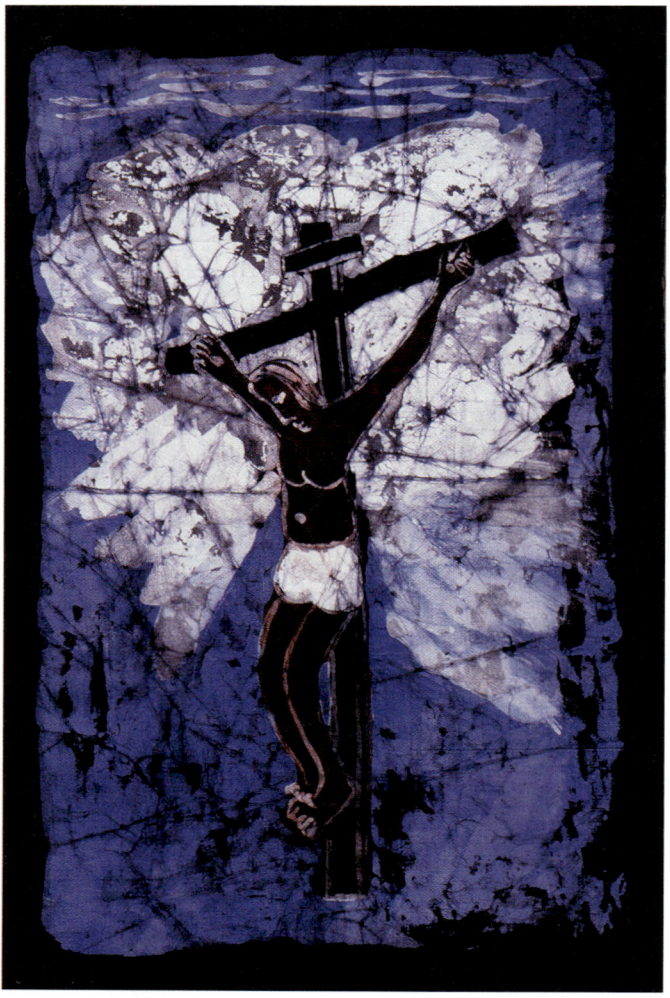

Fig. 16.9 Emile Wilson, *Christ on the Cross*, 1992, batik, Church of Jesus Christ of Latter-day Saints Church History Museum.

newspaper even ran a headline that declared, "Chinese and Mormons. Two Classes of People Who Must Be Made to Go."[66]

Ironically, by the 1890s, as Latter-day Saints began a slow transition out of polygamy, they started to participate in the same kind of racial Othering that had been deployed against them. In 1893 and 1894, for example, *The Contributor*, a publication for the young men of the church, ran a sixteen-part series titled "Ramblings Around the World." The series featured reports from Latter-day Saint G. H. Snell, who took a journey to the Near and Far East and filed regular descriptions of his travels. The first twelve accounts chronicled Snell's journeys across Asia and were peppered with racialized descriptions.

In Snell's estimation, Chinese travelers were "mongrel," "motley," and "villainous," and their religious practices were marred by idol worship. He found China to be a "filthy empire" filled with the "oder [*sic*] of nationality." When his stay ended, Snell expressed relief at finally leaving. By that point he was "tired out and disenchanted with the whole Chinese Empire and its almond-eyed race."[67]

Snell's impressions of Egypt were equally disparaging. He described a "burnt umbered Arab," "beggars and thieves and loafers asleep on the curbstones," and "naked children of a blue-black color" who made "modern mud pies." These children, Snell reported, "always have a legion of flies swarming about their faces and rimming their eyes,"

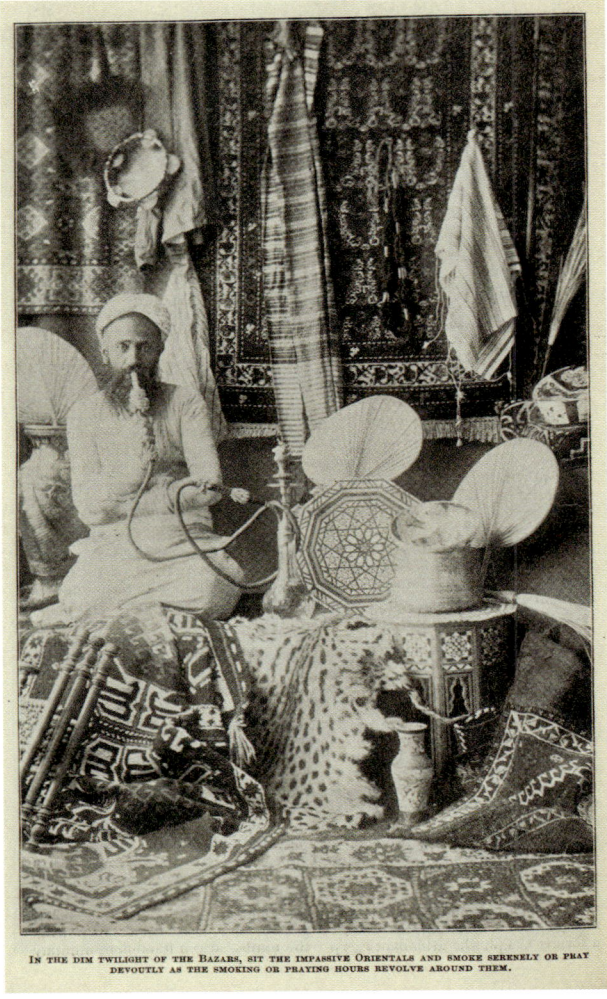

IN THE DIM TWILIGHT OF THE BAZARS, SIT THE IMPASSIVE ORIENTALS AND SMOKE SERENELY OR PRAY
DEVOUTLY AS THE SMOKING OR PRAYING HOURS REVOLVE AROUND THEM.

Fig. 16.10 G. H. Snell, "Ramblings Around the World," *The Contributor* 15, no. 4 (February 1894), 208.

but they did not bother to brush the insects aside. According to Snell, some travelers wondered how the children could stand such constant annoyance, but Snell responded that his "sympathies are with the flies."[68]

A picture of a man in one of the bazaars Snell visited accompanied his report. It featured a man sucking on a hookah tube surrounded by a variety of Eastern rugs, the man seemingly desensitized to the world around him. As Snell described it, "in the dim twilight" the "impassive, unspeakable Oriental" sits, "as in a trance, and smokes serenely or prays devoutly as the smoking or praying hours revolve around him."[69]

In sum, Snell's reports were little more sympathetic to the people he met than were visitors to Salt Lake City who imagined vile sultanates dominating Latter-day Saint harems in the Great Basin, an "Oriental" problem on American soil.[70] The visual depictions that accompanied Snell's reports only served to emphasize a degraded and foreign identity for the people of Asian and Middle Eastern descent. Latter-day Saint readers of *The Contributor* thus consumed visual images meant to affirm their passage to whiteness, marked in distance from "Oriental" Others.

Latter-day Saints had much more success winning converts in Pacific Island locations such as Samoa and Tonga than in Asian countries, even though they did expand their presence in Asia in the twentieth century.[71] From among the Polynesian converts Latter-day Saint artists began to claim their own religious space in the late twentieth century. Fanga Lavulavu, a Tongan artist, is one such example. In 1989, he created a tapa cloth scene titled *Even to the Isles of the Sea,* a visually striking depiction of Latter-day Saint missionaries preaching in Tonga. In doing so, Lavulavu used a traditional Pacific Island art form, the tapa cloth, which was made from the bark of paper mulberry trees and more typically colored with vegetable-derived dyes in elaborate earthtone designs.[72] In Lavulavu's depiction, however, he uses paint and tapa cloth to illustrate a deeply textured scene, the spreading of the Latter-day Saint gospel "even to the isles of the sea." Lavulavu's title invokes passages from the Book of Mormon promising that God will "remember the isles of the sea" in the last days and gather the "house of Israel" there (1 Nephi 19:16).

The iconic white shirts, ties, and name tags of the two missionaries are the focal point of the scene, especially as they draw the eye's gaze and stand in contrast to the darker island foliage. It is an inviting setting, friendly and warm. There is nothing threatening about the missionaries or seemingly intrusive about their presence. The color scheme of the missionaries is even recycled throughout the image, making the missionaries blend with their environment. They are not knocking on someone's door unannounced but have met another Tongan on the road and engaged him in conversation. Their American-centric white shirts and ties, the missionary "uniform," are paired with Tongan lava-lava wraps and sandals to signal cultural blending and even suggest Pacific Islander ownership of the Latter-day Saint message. Lavulavu does not depict white missionaries from Utah as a colonizing force; he portrays Tongan missionaries from Tonga at home in their surroundings. The tropical leaves in the lower right-hand

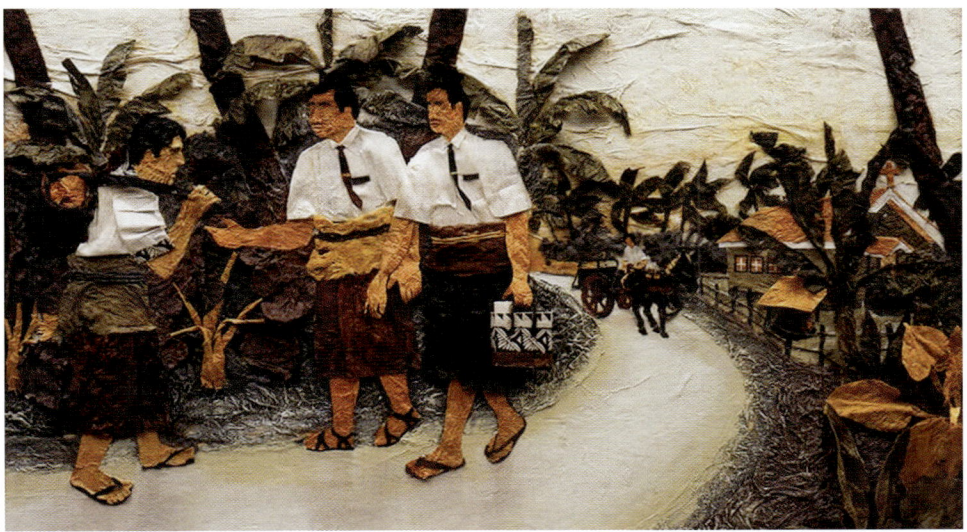

Fig. 16.11 Fanga Lavulavu, *Even to the Isles of the Sea*, 1989, tapa cloth and paint, Church of Jesus Christ of Latter-day Saints Church History Museum.

corner of the scene even reach outside the bounds of the setting to convey an inability to contain the local culture within a Western frame. With Tonga at its center, the Latter-day Saint message will inevitably spread.

In 2015, Cambodian artist Sopheap Nhem went even further than Lavulavu in centering her understanding of Latter-day Saint cosmology in Asia. Nhem's painting envisions an Asian Savior surrounded by Cambodian children who are drawn to him and welcomed by his warm embrace. Nhem chose pink and orange for her dominant colors because in her mind they symbolize peace and regality, ideas she associates with Jesus and his entreaty to "suffer little children to come unto me" (Luke 18:16).[73]

Her vision of Jesus evokes images of Eastern spiritual leaders and their teachings of transcendent holiness and peace. Lotus flowers, symbols of purity and rebirth, surround Jesus and the children, while doves encircle the Savior in concert with the children—a beautiful blending of the human and natural worlds that offers a sense of tranquility. The children themselves are almost universally fixated in gentle awe on Jesus and are pulled toward him in the hope of the renewal he exudes. It is not a traditional depiction of a Latter-day Saint Jesus. In Nhem's brush, the Latter-day Saint gospel has become Eastern instead of Western, and—unlike the nineteenth-century marginalization such accusations were meant to produce—Nhem's vision centers Asia as something to be embraced rather than feared.

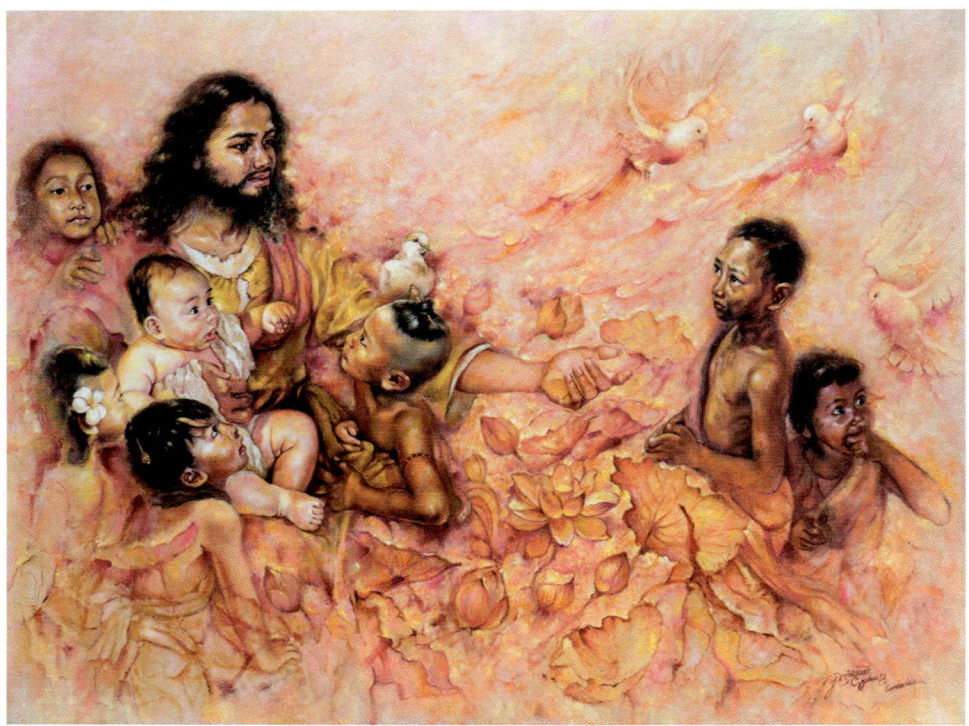

Fig. 16.12 Sopheap Nhem, *Early Morning with the Savior*, 2015, oil on canvas, Church of Jesus Christ of Latter-day Saints Church History Museum.

CONCLUSION

Whiteness has dominated Latter-day Saint history and theology and therefore its art for much of the faith's nearly two-hundred-year history. In the nineteenth century outsiders imagined racial decline bound up in Latter-day Saint polygamy and created political cartoons to reflect those fears. Latter-day Saints, in contrast, imagined racial uplift as integral to their gospel message. Their art centered white Latter-day Saints, sometimes to the near exclusion of other groups. Euro-American Latter-day Saints hoped to bring Native Americans, Latin Americans, Pacific Islanders, and Asians with them on the journey toward whiteness while they left people of Black African descent behind.

In the twentieth- and twenty-first centuries, however, Latter-day Saint artists around the globe have pushed the faith's racial art in new directions. They have begun to imagine themselves in Jesus. In doing so, they have placed various ethnic identities at the center of Latter-day Saint theological representations rather than allow themselves to be relegated to its margins. They have also begun to imagine racial diversity in their visions of heaven and the afterlife and to otherwise decenter whiteness.[74] Rather than stand in the way of such artists, the Latter-day Saint Church History Museum, with its International Art Competition, seems intent on pushing them forward.[75]

If the art for the renovated Washington, D.C., temple is any indication, the church as an institution is too.[76] When Latter-day Saint leaders rededicated the iconic temple in 2022, the art that longtime temple patrons found inside was different from what had been there before—and deliberately so. Leaders selected art to reflect the diverse membership of the local community as well as that of the global church. In fact, when Nowah Afangbedji, a convert to the faith from the African nation of Togo, first entered the newly refurbished temple, he encountered art significantly different from what Janan Graham-Russell experienced at the Chicago temple decades earlier. While Graham-Russell only saw white angels in the painting she encountered and wondered if her new faith imagined her in the afterlife, the art in the rededicated D.C. temple offers a belated answer.[77] Latter-day Saint leaders commissioned artist Dan Wilson to paint a new version of Jesus Christ's anticipated reappearance. The resulting painting, *His Return,* now has a prominent place in the temple entrance. Among the more than three hundred angels who announce the Second Coming of Jesus Christ are people "of all colors"—a particular thrill for Afangbedji to witness. "This is a new temple in a way," he said, in part because "the artwork is different."[78] Certainly, if the Church of Jesus Christ of Latter-day Saints is to reckon with the power that whiteness has played in its history and theology, then the way that it represents that history and theology in art must be at the heart of that reconciliation.

NOTES

[1] Janan Graham-Russell, "Race and Mormon Women," Black, White, and Mormon I, conference, University of Utah, 2015, https://www.youtube.com/watch?v=zrYvOLK2B-I&t=3562s.

[2] Graham-Russell, "Race and Mormon Women."

[3] D&C 58:64; 68:8; 80:1; 84:62; 112:28.

[4] Christopher C. Jones, "'A Very Poor Place for Our Doctrine': Religion and Race in the 1853 Mormon Mission to Jamaica," *Religion and American Culture: A Journal of Interpretation* 31 (Summer 2021): 262–295; Reid L. Neilson, *Early Mormon Missionary Activities in Japan, 1901–1924* (Salt Lake City: University of Utah Press, 2010); Laure F. Maffly-Kipp and Reid L. Neilson, *Proclamation to the People: Nineteenth-C entury Mormonism and the Pacific Basin Frontier* (Salt Lake City: University of Utah Press, 2008); Amanda Hendrix-Komoto, *Imperial Zions: Religion, Race, and Family in the American West and the Pacific* (Lincoln: University of Nebraska Press, 2022); Marjorie Newton, *Tiki and Temple: The Mormon Mission in New Zealand, 1854–1958* (Salt Lake City: Greg Kofford Books, 2012); Marjorie Newton, *Mormon and Māori* (Salt Lake City: Greg Kofford Books, 2014).

[5] W. Paul Reeve, *Religion of a Different Color: Race and the Mormon Struggle for Whiteness* (New York: Oxford University Press, 2015), chap. 2; Jared Hickman, "The Book of Mormon as Amerindian Apocalypse," *American Literature* 86, no. 3 (September 2014): 429–461; Armand L. Mauss, *All Abraham's Children: Changing Mormon Conceptions of Race and Lineage* (Urbana: University of Illinois Press, 2003), chap. 3; Max Perry Mueller, *Race and the Making of the Mormon People* (Chapel Hill: University of North Carolina Press, 2017), chap. 1.

[6] Reeve, *Religion of a Different Color;* Matthew Kester, *Remembering Iosepa: History, Place, and Religion in the American West* (New York: Oxford University Press, 2013); Hokulani K. Aikau, *A Chosen People, a Promised Land: Mormonism and Race in Hawaii* (Minneapolis: University of Minnesota Press, 2012).

7 Reeve, *Religion of a Different Color,* 59–64.

8 Reeve, *Religion of a Different Color,* chaps. 2–3.

9 Reeve, *Religion of a Different Color,* 87–100; Ronald W. Walker, Richard E. Turley Jr., and Glen M. Leonard, *Massacre at Mountain Meadows: An American Tragedy* (New York: Oxford University Press, 2008).

10 Alfreda Eva Bell, *Boadicea; The Mormon Wife: Life-Scenes in Utah* (New York: Arthur R. Orton, 1855), 81.

11 Bell, *Boadicea,* 81.

12 *Message from the President of the United States, to the Two Houses of Congress at the Commencement of the First Session of the Thirty-Fifth Congress,* House of Representatives, Ex. Doc. No. 2, 35th Cong., 1st Sess. (Washington, DC: Cornelius Wendell, 1857), 7–8.

13 See, for example, Thomas Nast, "When the Spring-Time Comes, Gentle'—Indian! Polygamous Barbarian, 'Much Guns, Much Ammunition, Much Whiskey, and Much Kill Pale Face,'" *Harper's Weekly,* February 18, 1882, 109; Reeve, *Religion of a Different Color,* chap. 3.

14 Shawn Rossiter, "Persecution Paradigm: C. C. A. Christensen's Mormon Panorama at the BYU Museum of Art," *15 Bytes,* September 3, 2015, http://artistsofutah.org/15Bytes/index.php/persecution-paradigm-c-c-a-christensens-mormon-panorama-at-the-byu-museum-of-art/#comments.

15 Laura Allred Hurtado, "Other Works by C. C. A. Christensen," *Pioneer* 66, no. 1 (2019): 62–64; Laura Allred Hurtado and David Grua, "Painting the Mythical and the Heroic: *Joseph Preaches to the American Indians," Juvenile Instructor,* November 19, 2013, https://juvenileinstructor.org/painting-the-mythical-and-the-heroic-joseph-smith-preaches-to-the-american-indians/.

16 Nathan Rees, "C. C. A. Christensen, Joseph Preaching to the Indians," object narrative, in *Conversations: An Online Journal of the Center for the Study of Material and Visual Cultures of Religion,* 2014, doi:10.223322/con.obj.2014.48.

17 Mauss, *All Abraham's Children,* 116–121; Royal Skousen, ed., *The Book of Mormon: The Earliest Text* (New Haven, CT: Yale University Press, 2009), 148, 754.

18 Reeve, *Religion of a Different Color,* 55–59; Mauss, *All of Abraham's Children,* chap. 3.

19 John D. Lee, *A Mormon Chronicle: The Diaries of John D. Lee, 1848–1876,* ed. Robert Glass Cleland and Juanita Brooks (San Marino, CA: Huntington Library, 1955; repr., Salt Lake City: University of Utah Press, 1983), 108. For broader context, see Reeve, *Religion of a Different Color,* chap. 3.

20 Mauss, *All of Abraham's Children,* chap. 5; John-Charles Duffy, "The Use of 'Lamanite' in Official LDS Discourse," *Journal of Mormon History* 34, no. 1 (Winter 2008): 118–167.

21 Parley P. Pratt, "Proclamation! To the People of the Coasts and Islands of the Pacific (Ocean), of Every Nation, Kindred, and Tongue," *Millennial Star* 14 (September 18, 1852), 469.

22 Parley P. Pratt, *The Autobiography of Parley Parker Pratt* (Salt Lake City: Deseret Book, 1985), 368, emphasis in original. For an indication of the ways that early Latter-day Saint missionaries to Mexico racialized the people they encountered there, see Jared Tamez, "'Out of This Part of Babylon': Colonizing Mexican Mormons and the Decline of the Mexican Mission of the Church of Jesus Christ of Latter-day Saints, 1879–1889" (master's thesis, University of Utah, 2012).

23 Laura Allred Hurtado, "'It Is Priceless': C. C. A. Christensen's Untitled [Huntington/Lamanite Panorama]," *Pioneer* 66, no. 1 (2019): 8–37; R. Devan Jensen, Scott R. Christensen, and Darren Parry, "'Like Fire in the Dry Grass': Shoshone Conversions and the Christensen Teaching Scroll," *Pioneer* 66, no. 1 (2019): 38–47.

24 Hurtado, "It Is Priceless," 16–37; see 34–35 for *Moroni Hiding the Plates* and 36–37 for *Moroni Giving the Plates to Joseph Smith.*

25 For a history of the missionaries' use of the panels in the 1870s see Jensen, Christensen, and Parry, "Like Fire in the Dry Grass," 41–45.

26 Ardis E. Parshall, "Mormon Movies: *Life of Nephi,* 1915," Keepapitchinin.org, February 6, 2018, http://www.keepapitchinin.org/2018/02/06/mormon-movies-life-of-nephi-1915/.

27 Vern Swanson, "The Book of Mormon Art of Arnold Friberg: Painter of Scripture," *Journal of Book of Mormon Studies* 10, no. 1 (2001): 29–30.

28 Swanson, "The Book of Mormon Art of Arnold Friberg," 30.

29 On Santángelo, see Herman du Toit, "By Simple Yet Propitious Means: The Art of Jorge Cocco Santángelo," *BYU Studies* 55, no. 2 (2016): 99–106.

30 David Knowlton, "Mormonism as a World Religion," in *Mormonism: A Historical Encyclopedia,* ed. W. Paul Reeve and Ardis E. Parshall (Santa Barbara, CA: ABC-Clio, 2010), 359–364.

31 Reeve, *Religion of a Different Color,* chaps. 4–7.

32 *Congressional Globe,* 30th Cong., 1st Sess. (Washington, DC: Blair and Rives, 1848), 98.

33 Reeve, *Religion of a Different Color,* chaps. 4, 6, and 7.

34 Reeve, *Religion of a Different Color,* 174–176.

35 *Frank Leslie's Budget of Fun,* January 1872, 16.

36 Reeve, *Religion of a Different Color,* 174–176.

37 Reeve, *Religion of a Different Color,* 174–176.

38 Reeve, *Religion of a Different Color,* chaps. 5–7; Ariela J. Gross, *What Blood Won't Tell: A History of Race on Trial in America* (Cambridge, MA: Harvard University Press, 2008), 138–139.

39 Reeve, *Religion of a Different Color,* chaps. 5 and 7; Matt McBride, "Peter," *Century of Black Mormons,* https://exhibits.lib.utah.edu/s/century-of-black-mormons/page/peter.

40 *Council of Fifty, Minutes,* ed. Matthew J. Grow, Ronald K. Esplin, Mark Ashurst-McGee, Jeffrey D. Mahas, Matthew C. Godfrey, and Gerrit J. Dirkmaat (Salt Lake City: Church Historian's Press, 2016), 472; "Transcript for *Pioneering the West, 1846 to 1878: Major Howard Egan's Diary,* edited and compiled by William M. Egan (1917)," entry for July 13, 1847, https://history.churchofjesuschrist.org/chd/transcr ipt?lang=eng&name=transcript-for-pioneering-the-west-1846-to-1878-major-howard-egans-diary-edi ted; John Brown, Reminiscences and Journal, vol. 1, 1843 May–1860 April, MS 1636, 54–55, Church History Library, Church of Jesus Christ of Latter-day Saints, Salt Lake City, Utah; Megan Weiss, "Hark Wales," *Century of Black Mormons,* https://exhibits.lib.utah.edu/s/century-of-black-mormons/page/wales-hark; Benjamin Kiser, "Green Flake," *Century of Black Mormons,* https://exhibits.lib.utah.edu/s/century-of-black-mormons/page/flake-green; W. Randall Dixon, "From Emigration Canyon to City Creek: Pioneer Trail and Campsites in the Salt Lake Valley in 1847," *Utah Historical Quarterly* 65, no. 2 (Spring 1997): 155–164.

41 Quincy D. Newell, *Your Sister in the Gospel: The Life of Jane Manning James, a Nineteenth-Century Black Mormon* (New York: Oxford University Press, 2019), chap. 5.

42 "The Twenty-Fourth at Union," *Deseret News,* August 1, 1888.

43 "Echoes of the 24th," *Salt Lake Herald,* July 26, 1893. For other examples, see "The Pioneer Company," *Utah Enquirer,* August 3, 1888; "The Pioneers of 1847," *Deseret News Weekly,* August 25, 1894; "Salt Lake News," *Ogden Standard,* August 21, 1894; "The Days of Forty-Seven," *Salt Lake Tribune,* August 21, 1894.

44 "Fifty Years Ago Today," *Salt Lake Tribune,* May 31, 1897.

45 "Fifty Years Ago Today," *Salt Lake Tribune,* May 31, 1897.

46 Newell, *Your Sister in the Gospel,* chap. 5.

47 Newell, *Your Sister in the Gospel,* 89–93, 95, 107.

48 W. Paul Reeve, "'I Dug the Graves': Isaac Lewis Manning, Joseph Smith, and Racial Connections in Two Latter-day Saint Traditions," *Journal of Mormon History* 47 (January 2021): 59–63.

49 "First Negroes to Join Mormon Church," *Salt Lake Herald,* October 2, 1899, 5.

50 Reeve, "I Dug the Graves," 62–63; Newell, *Your Sister in the Gospel,* 128–130.

51 Reeve, *Religion of a Different Color,* chap. 7; Ardis E. Parshall, "The Ugliest Post Keepa Has Ever Published," Keepapitchinin, June 2, 2009, http://www.keepapitchinin.org/2009/06/02/the-ugliest-post-keepa-has-ever-published/; Ardis E. Parshall, "Ads You're Not Going to See Again Anytime Soon—Chapter 3," Keepapitchinin, August 2, 2008, http://www.keepapitchinin.org/2008/08/02/ads-youre-not-going-to-see-again-anytime-soon-chapter-3/.

52 Frank Steele, "Little Nigger Baby," *Juvenile Instructor* 55, no. 1 (January 1920): 44; Parshall, "The Ugliest Post Keepa Has Ever Published."

53 John G. Kinnear, "South African Mission," *The Improvement Era,* March 1959, 149.

54 George R. Woolley, "Tolerance . . . Is a Necessary Part of Free Agency," *The Instructor*, September 1959, 286.

55 Elder Blaine M. Porter, "Social Science—Spiritual Living in the Nuclear Age," *Relief Society Magazine*, October 1959, 702.

56 Memo from Thomas G. Truitt, Historian's Office, January 19, 1970, enclosure, anonymous to David O. McKay, October 6, 1959, Church History Library, Church of Jesus Christ of Latter-day Saints, Salt Lake City, Utah.

57 Memo from Thomas G. Truitt, Historian's Office.

58 See, for example, William Bernard McCarl, *Joseph Freeman Receives the Priesthood*, 1978; Tamara Howell, *Blacks Receive Priesthood*, 1980; Oakland California Stake Relief Society, *Sesquicentennial Quilt*, 1980; and Emma Allebes, *To All Worthy Male Members*, quilt, 1990.

59 See, for example, Doug Martin, *Portrait of Joseph Freeman, Jr. with Wife Isapella Freeman and Daughter*, 1979; Emmalee Powell, *Joseph William Billy Johnson: Holiness to the Lord*, 2007; and Anthony Sweat, *The Ordination of Q. Walker Lewis*, 2017.

60 Reeve, *Religion of a Different Color*, chap. 8.

61 Caleb Lyon, *Congressional Globe*, 33rd Cong., 1st Sess., May 4, 1854, 1100–1101; *Mormonism: An Address, by Hon. D. C. Haskell, M.C. of Kansas, at the National Anniversary of the American Home Missionary Society, in Chicago, June 8, 1881* (New York: American Home Missionary Society, 1881), 14.

62 *Reynolds v. United States* (1879), 98 US 153, 161–168.

63 W. Paul Reeve, *Let's Talk About Race and Priesthood* (Salt Lake City: Deseret Book, 2023), 33; Reeve, *Religion of a Different Color*, 239–240.

64 Reeve, *Religion of a Different Color*, 240–242.

65 *Milwaukee Daily Sentinel*, November 6, 1880; "The Indian Policy," *Idaho Avalanche*, April 29, 1882; "The Chinese and Mormon Problems," *Independent Statesman* (Concord, NH), March 23, 1882; "Missionary Work," *Daily Inter Ocean*, December 3, 1880.

66 "Chinese and Mormons," *Daily Alta California*, March 15, 1882.

67 G. H. Snell, "Ramblings Around the World," *The Contributor* 14, no. 7 (May 1893): 336, 338; 14, no. 10 (August 1893): 485, 489; 14, no. 11 (September 1893): 513; Reeve, *Religion of a Different Color*, 244–245.

68 G. H. Snell, "Ramblings Around the World," *The Contributor* 15, no. 4 (February 1894): 209.

69 G. H. Snell, "Ramblings Around the World," *The Contributor* 15, no. 4 (February 1894): 210.

70 Reeve, *Religion of a Different Color*, chap. 8.

71 Maffly-Kipp and Neilson, *Proclamation to the People*; Neilson, *Early Mormon Missionary Activities in Japan*; Newton, *Tiki and Temple*; Newton, *Mormon and Maori*; Hendrix-Komoto, *Imperial Zions*; Kester, *Remembering Iosepa*; Aikau, *A Chosen People*.

72 *Pacific Island Tapa Cloth*, RISD Museum, July 17–October 18, 1992, https://risdmuseum.org/exhibiti ons-events/exhibitions/pacific-islands-tapa-cloth.

73 Peggy Fletcher Stack, "Art Competition Features an Uncommon Mormon Savior: A Brown Jesus," *Salt Lake Tribune*, July 22, 2016, https://archive.sltrib.com/article.php?id=4112042&itype=CMSID.

74 See, for example, Stephanie Billings, *The Heavenly Host Praising God*, 2019, United States, digital print; Julie Yuen Yim, *Partake of His Goodness*, 2022, Hong Kong, Chinese ink and colors; Caylee Murdock, *One by One*, 2022, Canada, oil; Ima Naranjo Hale, *The Great Spirit Created All*, 2022, Utah, acrylic on board; David Ade Blarinwa, *Lehi's Vision*, 2022, Nigeria, wood.

75 See Laura Paulsen Howe's chapter in this volume.

76 See Colleen McDannell's chapter in this volume.

77 Graham-Russell, "Race and Mormon Women"; Tad Walch, "Local Latter-day Saints Say Washington D.C. Temple Artwork Now Reflects Them, Their City and Church," *Deseret News*, April 29, 2022, https://www.deseret.com/2022/4/29/23034234/washington-d-c-temple-lds-mormon-church-local-latter-day-saint-artwork-reflects-city-church.

78 Howard M. Collett, "Get to Know the Artist Who Made the Second Coming Painting in the Washington D.C. Temple," *Church News*, August 9, 2022, https://www.thechurchnews.com/members/2022/8/9/23278596/artist-dan-wilson-painting-washington-dc-temple-rotunda-second-coming-jesus-christ-angels; Walch, "Local Latter-day Saints."

17

NATIVE AMERICANS, MORMONISM, AND ART

CARLYLE CONSTANTINO

I had people reach out to me and say, "She was never real to me until I saw your piece [*Heavenly Mother*] because she looked like me now." Or "My child loves this piece, I put it in their room, and they say, 'She looks like Grandma.'" I create these pieces of art and the goal is to sell the painting. Then, suddenly, it has this wider reach than I ever thought would be possible.

— Kwani Povi Winder, Santa Clara Pueblo Tewa
(interview with author, November 2022)

The implications of Winder's sentiments are profound. Throughout the nineteenth century and the better part of the twentieth, Native American relations with Mormonism—and, by extension, the Church of Jesus Christ of Latter-day Saints—were complicated and, oftentimes, problematic. With the Latter-day Saint pioneers' movement westward in the mid-nineteenth century and the subsequent growth of the church, encounters with Indigenous peoples were inevitable. Artists embraced opportunities to depict these new encounters. Yet, as is often the case, there is more to this story.

In a telling comparison of two works by renowned Latter-day Saint artist (and early convert to the church) C. C. A. Christensen, shifting attitudes toward Native Americans are evident. The first piece, titled *Indian Encampment at Manti*, portrays a vivid and lush landscape. Situated prominently in the foreground is an encampment of Native Americans. Considering the location of Manti, the group is likely part of the Ute tribe. Figures can be seen standing near open tepees, and others are warming themselves by fires; one figure near the front can be seen carrying a baby on her back. It is lively and exudes a warm, peaceful feeling. Upon closer inspection, however, it becomes apparent that the Native Americans are not alone. Several white-topped wagons are huddled in a circular formation along the background. Though not particularly threatening, the appearance of wagons is curious and a bit unsettling. Why are they stopped? Where are

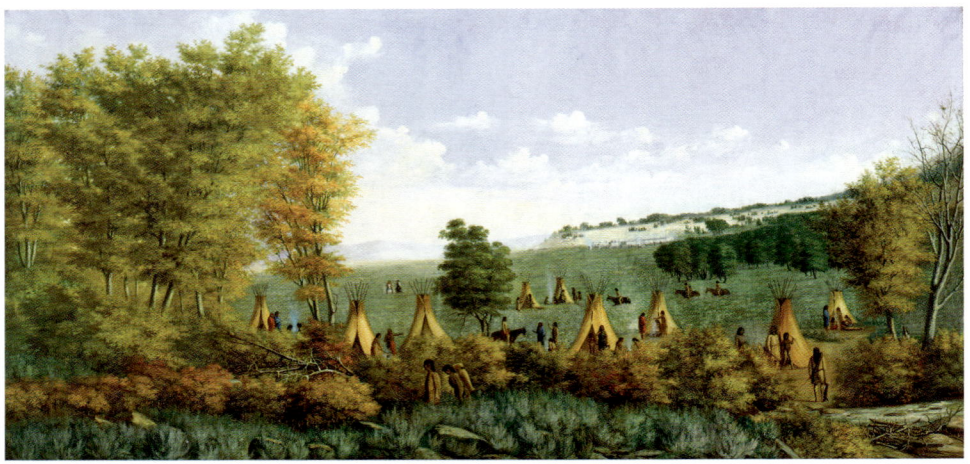

Fig. 17.1 C. C. A. Christensen, *Indian Encampment at Manti,* 1880, oil on canvas, 35″ × 72″, Church of Jesus Christ of Latter-day Saints Church History Museum.

they heading? One cannot help but wonder how the scene will unfold in the impending moments.

Compare this work, painted in 1880, with a piece Christensen completed twenty years later. *Handcart Pioneers* features Latter-day Saint pioneers wading through a narrow river. An initial glance lands upon the family unit central to the image: a man pulling his family's wagon with the aid of a boy. Younger children appear inside the wagon, while another is carried atop a figure's shoulders. Others follow close behind, pulling their respective wagons. Those who have already reached dry ground are settling in for a moment, likely grateful for some much-needed rest. One woman is breastfeeding her baby. The familial interactions are sweet. Yet, in stark contrast to the previous painting, *Handcart Pioneers* contains a palpable sense of urgency. Six faceless figures ride out from the background toward the pioneers. The leader appears to be shirtless. His hair is dark and long. And while those following him are blurred, one can guess that they too are Native Americans. A few pioneer figures are pointing toward the oncoming figures. They might be wondering who the riders are or how to approach the situation. With the white pioneers shown now as the main characters—contrasted to *Indian Encampment at Manti*—the overall tone has shifted from welcoming to worrisome. This brief but pivotal comparison elucidates just some of the complexities inherent in Native American relations with Latter-day Saints, and vice versa.

Circling back to Winder's words, this chapter intends to survey the evolution of representations of Native Americans by Latter-day Saint artists as well as self-representation among Native American Latter-day Saint artists from the nineteenth

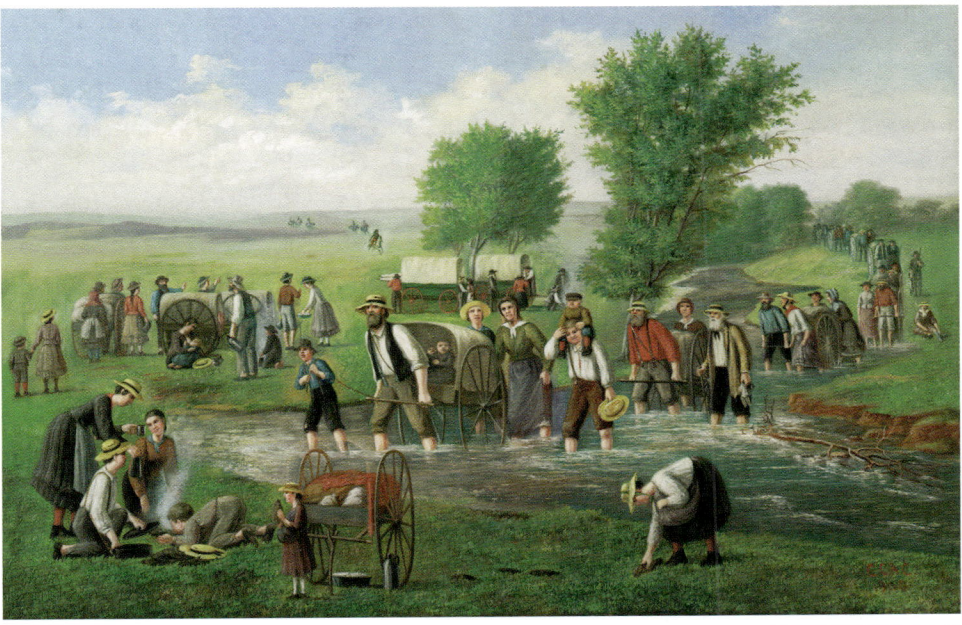

Fig. 17.2 C. C. A. Christensen, *Handcart Pioneers*, 1900, oil on canvas, 24″ × 37″, Church of Jesus Christ of Latter-day Saints Church History Museum.

century to the present, with an effort to emphasize the many intricacies and sensitivities that come with such an examination. It will attempt to accomplish this by illustrating how Native Americans shifted from being the "viewed/object" to becoming the "viewer/creator." This is by no means an exhaustive investigation; yet this chapter will, hopefully, foster understanding and a renewed appreciation for art production as it intersects with subjectivity, identity, and Indegeneity.

TWO PEOPLES

Following the founding of Mormonism and Joseph Smith's rise to prominence in the early nineteenth century, Latter-day Saints experienced everything from mild suspicion to blatant aversion regarding their "peculiar ways." Non-members, leaders of other faith congregations, local government leaders, and national politicians expressed, in varying degrees, opposition to practicing members of the Church of Jesus Christ of Latter-day Saints. It is against this backdrop of persecution and exclusion that the Saints, under the direction of Brigham Young, fled to the West, specifically to Utah and parts beyond. Terryl L. Givens asserts: "The quest for Zion was for the Saints a search for Eden—but it was always an Eden in exile."[1] Early members of the church thus traversed physical *and* psychological winters. They were outcasts in the truest sense of the word.

Similarly, Native Americans were at times ignored, misunderstood, despised, and killed. However, their hardships began much earlier than the advent of Mormonism. Native Americans had been displaced from their homelands for centuries prior to the arrival of pioneers in the Great Salt Lake Valley. In turn, Native Americans have been viewed as "savages" needing to be exterminated, romantic warriors who were part of a vanishing race, lost souls needing to be saved and assimilated into white culture, and now, hopefully, as individuals with tribal sovereignty and empowerment. And as enacted by Christensen's paintings, the meeting of Native Americans and Latter-day Saints in Utah resulted in the eventual displacement of the Native American tribes within the region, including Ute, Goshute, Paiute, Navajo, and Shoshone. Making sense of this difficult past brings an added layer of significance to artworks by or depicting Native peoples, especially whether the art displaces them or seeks to re-place them in the fore-ground. Historian Jared Farmer suggests (using a term familiar to art historians) that "in high relief, Utah history exposes an unsettling incongruity of U.S. history: the senses of place that make present-day Americans feel at home would not exist without past displacements."[2]

Such displacements and power differentials have haunted artistic creations. Thus in turning to the art itself, it is crucial to remember the positionality of the artist. Latter-day Saint artists, particularly in the nineteenth century, were mainly white men. Though initially from different backgrounds and countries, the majority of Latter-day Saint artists who lived in Utah experienced relative comfort compared to the Native Americans living on nearby lands. Rather than dismiss all art by white Latter-day Saints as inaccurate, it is more enlightening to examine their work as telling modes of representation. I am interested here in the ways Latter-day Saint artistic depictions of Native peoples reveal and perform Latter-day Saint identity and culture. These works "exteriorize" or circulate and make visible Mormon culture through representations of Native bodies. As Edward Said wrote: "Another reason for insisting upon exteriority is that I believe it needs to be made clear about cultural discourse and exchange within a culture that what is commonly circulated by it is not 'truth' but representations."[3] Said's comments are especially enlightening here. Acknowledging the artists' biases and places of privilege is a first but crucial step toward appreciating their technical skill and sincerity regarding the craft.

The works and artists examined portray their own personal visions of Native American subject matter. Furthermore, one would do well to consider this bold assertion by art historian and theorist bell hooks:

Within complex and ever shifting realms of power relations, do we position ourselves on the side of the colonizing mentality? Or do we continue to stand in political resistance with the oppressed, ready to offer our ways of seeing and theorizing, of making culture, towards that revolutionary effort which seeks to create space where there is unlimited access to the pleasure and power of knowing, where transformation is possible?

The choice is crucial. It shapes and determines our response to existing cultural practice and our capacity to envision new, alternative, oppositional aesthetic acts.[4]

To modify hooks's words slightly, there must also be space for acts of healing. As works are examined and artists discussed, the dialogue will naturally transition from nineteenth-century white artists (who depicted Native American subject matter) to early- to mid-twentieth-century Native American artists (who produced art pieces to trade or sell) to, finally, twentieth- and twenty-first-century Native American Latter-day Saint artists (who seek to navigate their cultural heritage alongside their faith).

NINETEENTH CENTURY

Danquart Weggeland

Like C. C. A. Christensen, Danquart Weggeland immigrated to the United States following his conversion to the faith. Born in Norway, Weggeland traveled around Norway and Denmark taking painting classes and honing his craft. The two artists met in Norway while Christensen was serving a mission for the church, and they maintained their friendship after arriving in Utah, separately, in the 1860s. Though they worked together often on art commissions, their styles are distinct. In particular, Weggeland's work *Sara Maraboots Dyson Hatch* is compelling both for the medium used and for the story behind the figure represented. The work is oil on leather, a noticeable departure from canvas. It is possible Weggeland chose leather for this piece so that it would seem more identifiably Native American. The content is a three-quarter-length portrait of a Native American woman with a child strapped to her back. Though her body is turned away from the viewer, her head is turned so that she is looking directly straight ahead. Her features are smooth and details are kept to a minimum, with the exception of the richly pigmented red pattern covering her clothing. Without any context, the woman might seem inconsequential, perhaps even unremarkable. Knowing the woman's identity and her background, however, is pivotal to appreciating the narrative.

Sara Maraboots was the daughter of Spaneshanks, a Navajo chieftain, and a Paiute mother. Orphaned at seven years old, Maraboots was placed with the family of Ira Hatch, a white Latter-day Saint who had served a mission in the Four Corners region of the United States in his early twenties. It was Hatch's family who gave Maraboots her new name. Maraboots became Ira's second wife and gave birth to four of his children (one being the child depicted on her back in Weggeland's work). Hatch spent most of his life as a missionary to nearby tribes, in turn visiting the Navajo, Hopi, and the Mojave. It is important to note that Weggeland painted Maraboots not from life but rather from a photograph. Further complicating this piece are the appropriation of the leather hide as a medium (leather that was purchased in the state fair) and portraying Maraboots and her child from a photograph *after* she had died.[5] This means despite the relative polish and impressive portrayal Weggeland achieved, it was all done without consent from

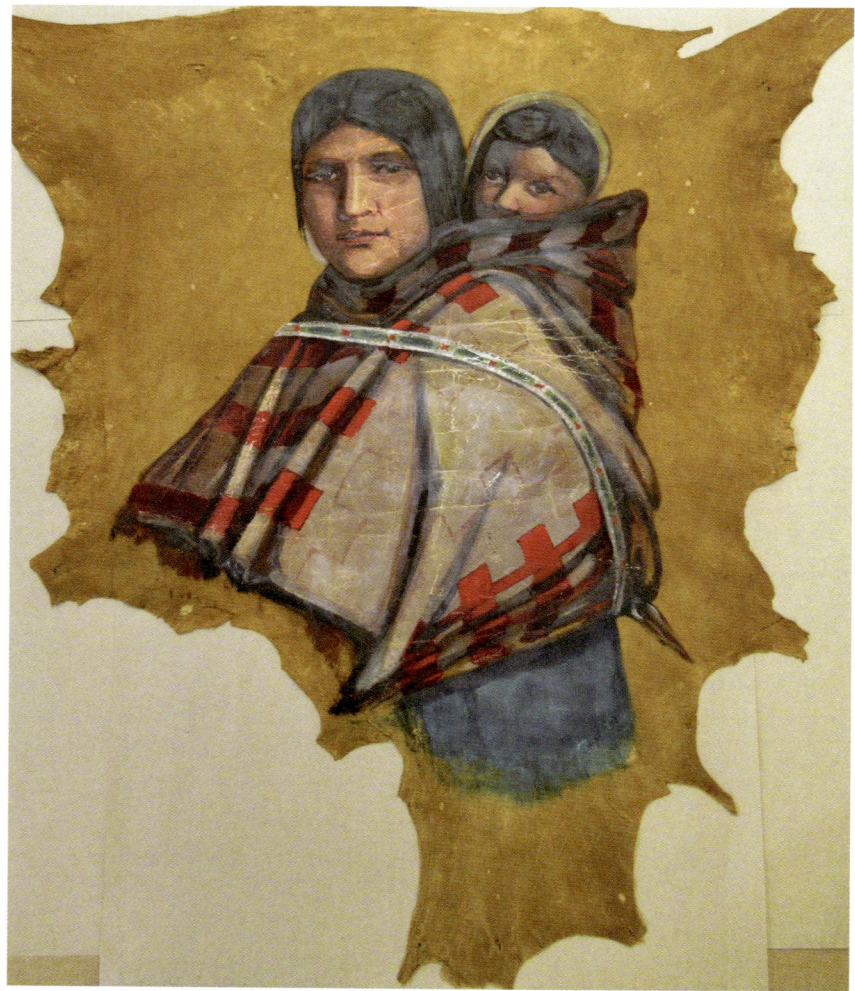

Fig. 17.3 Danquart Weggeland, *Sara Maraboots Dyson Hatch*, after 1870, oil on leather, 40″ × 40″, Church of Jesus Christ of Latter-day Saints Church History Museum.

the subject. It could even be seen as the initial inklings of what Elizabeth Hutchinson has termed "the Indian craze," a fascination with all things Native American, such as blankets, crafts, leather, tribal clothing, and so on.[6] Weggeland was certainly not the only artist to succumb to the craze.

Cyrus Dallin

Though he was not a practicing Latter-day Saint for most of his life, Cyrus Dallin was one of the most influential sculptors to work among the Latter-day Saint community in Utah.[7] Dallin was born in Springville, Utah, in 1861, but he spent much of his life on the East Coast, primarily in Boston. His talent was constantly praised by classmates and teachers, and he spent the better part of his adult years teaching art classes. He was a prolific sculptor. Dallin was commissioned by the church to sculpt the angel Moroni statue for the Latter-day Saint temple in Salt Lake City, a statue that has been replicated by various sculptors since. However, perhaps more than any other single subject, Dallin rendered models of Native Americans in his work. Referencing his childhood, Dallin reminisced how he "found the Indian to be neither an uncivilized savage nor a belligerent foe. The friendly Ute Indians who came each spring and fall to pitch their colorful tepees near Springville traded their game and pelts for goods produced by the villagers."[8] Dallin sculpted many Native American figures. Perhaps owing to his good feelings from when he was a youth, Dallin evidently enjoyed creating Native American statuary and figurines. The Utah native turned Bostonian sympathized with the plight of Native Americans more than most, reiterating throughout this career the "unfairness of the white man's treatment of the Indians."[9] He may have been more sensitive than others on the subject.

Mahonri Young

Born into the most prominent Latter-day Saint family at the time, Mahonri Young—a grandson of Brigham Young—is arguably the most prominent Latter-day Saint artist born prior to 1900.[10] The monuments he created reside in public spaces, museum settings, and the United States Capitol, to name a few. He, like Dallin, stopped attending church at a young age, yet he likewise sought commissions from the church. Like his predecessors, Young composed works that featured Native American figures. These particular works were typically paintings (oil on canvas), etchings, and drawings—not his oft-used medium of sculpture. His work formerly titled *Indian Woman and Sheep* technically appears to be in the Post-Impressionist style that was popularized in France during the latter half of the nineteenth century. Young studied in Paris at the turn of the twentieth century, so he was likely heavily influenced by the artistic styles of the period.[11] *Indian Woman and Sheep* is characterized by a warm, muted tone. Thick brushstrokes form the different elements in the scene: the dirt ground (or possibly dried grass); a single, unyielding tree in the foreground with others farther back; fluffy white clouds amid a light blue sky; a resolute goat standing erect; and, most noticeably, a figure standing near the tree, shaded by its dark green leaves. Her face remains hidden. It is only from the title that one knows she is Native American. However, the title is problematic. A former curator at the Church History Museum allotted the title to the painting—it was not given by the artist.

Taking a broad guess, the woman is most likely Navajo. Several of Yong's etchings are housed at the Philadelphia Museum of Art (another testament to Young's prominence). Two works, respectively titled *Navajo Shepherdess* (c. 1915) and *Navajo Watering Place* (c. 1932), contain striking similarities to *Indian Woman*. The same stubborn tree, a gaggle of goats, and at least one female figure stands to the side. Her profile is always displayed in side view, never straight on. Considering this, it seems logical to bridge the gap between the etchings and the oil painting housed at the Church History Museum. So, perhaps a better title for the painting is *Sheep and Navajo Woman*. Furthermore, this is not to ignore the outside gaze being imposed upon the viewer by the artist.[12]

To reiterate Said's earlier points, Young portrayed Navajos and other Native Americans according to his beliefs and attitudes about Native Americans. Mick Gidley, a historian of photography, asserts that "to visitors in a new land—certainly to settlers—the original inhabitants were profoundly *Other:* The settlers may have had to struggle physically with the indigenous people for possession of the land, and in the process the original inhabitants became that which the settlers defined themselves against."[13] Young's inclusion of the Navajo woman as somewhat of a footnote suggests that her presence is important only in that she represents a type: the Navajo woman. Young was not unique in his approach. Artists in and outside the church, including photographers, romanticized Native Americans in their work well into the twentieth century.

Photography

The Church History Library contains an extensive collection of photographs by Charles William Carter, known professionally as C. W. Carter. One of these photographs in the carte de visite style—an image that could be passed along as a calling card or other type of gift—depicts two Native American men sitting in chairs

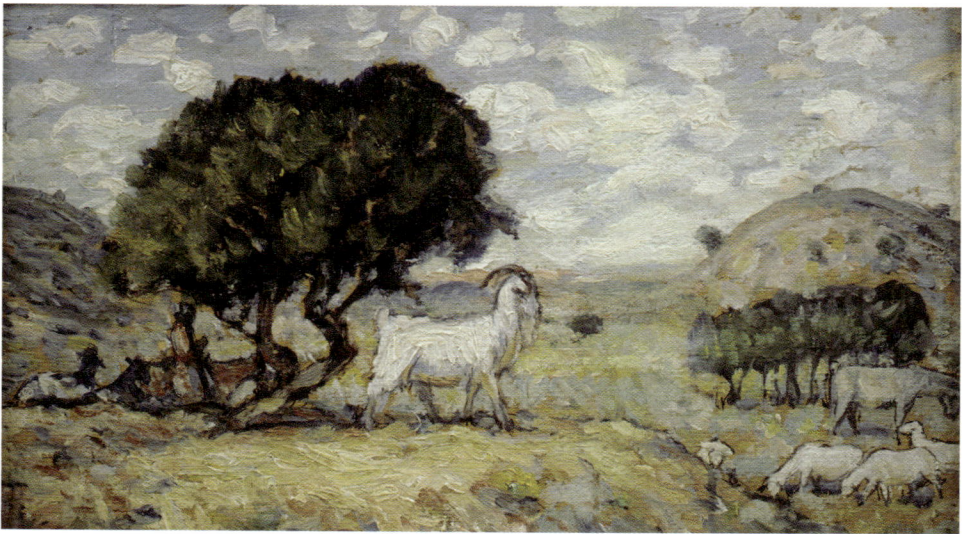

Fig. 17.4 Mahonri Young, *Navajo Woman and Sheep* (previously titled *Indian Woman and Sheep*), date unknown, oil on canvas, 13.5″ × 8″, Church of Jesus Christ of Latter-day Saints Church History Museum.

that have been placed back to back. They are outfitted in tribal clothing. Like the woman in Young's painting, the figures in Carter's photograph are situated so that the viewer can see only their profiles. The date (1882) is written on the back of the card. An address is stamped alongside the date, reiterating its function as a business card.[14] Carter, along with Charles Roscoe (C. R.) Savage and other lesser-known Latter-day Saint photographers, photographed their environment, the American West, including the peoples in it. Carter was dedicated to the craft, evidenced by his skillfully composed scenes. Yet one must assess his positionality. Undoubtedly influenced by rumors of a "vanishing Indian," Carter likely photographed peoples he thought would one day become extinct. In so doing, he reiterates—perhaps unintentionally—the common tropes of stoic figures stuck in a romantic past. In a volume on women photographers of the nineteenth and twentieth centuries, the authors define this phenomenon: "Created and circulated in the service of a range of often conflicting agendas . . . such images attest to photography's role in consolidating Indians as visual territory."[15] Carter was certainly not the only photographer to employ these attitudes.

Perhaps the most famous individual to work among Native Americans was Edward S. Curtis. Curtis was not a Latter-day Saint nor was he affiliated with the church. However, his vast collection of photographs of Native Americans should be considered within this dialogue. As I've written elsewhere, "The majority of Curtis's images present a type, intentional or not." Instead of engaging in a dialogue with his models, he tried to efficiently signify authenticity by outfitting his "his sitters in traditional clothing or ceremonial garb that belonged to disparate tribes." The cumulative effect yields a comprehensive but flawed representation of Native peoples. Dressed according to heritage but with their individuality muted, they appear as "stoic faces and detached figures."[16]

A litany of other photographers could be discussed in this context, but the conversation ultimately revolves around the same issue. Artists and photographers sought to capture Native individuals in problematic and inaccurate ways. While it was never merely documentation, how can the camera (and paintbrush, etc.) be used as a tool of understanding and sensitivity rather than for capturing and controlling? Moving into the twentieth century, the conversation shifts to trading posts, Book of Mormon art, arts production in Utah, and self-representation.

TWENTIETH CENTURY

A new, direct connection between Latter-day Saints and Native Americans developed in the early twentieth century. In the southwestern region of the United States—specifically among the Navajo in parts of New Mexico—trading posts were established to facilitate exchange between the local community and Navajos (Diné). Though numerous posts popped up in the region, this chapter focuses solely on one because of its distinct connection with the Latter-day Saint community. The Toadlena Trading Post, located several miles west of Newcomb, New Mexico, was particularly influential on the art production of the area. George and Lucy Bloomfield were devout Latter-day Saints who managed the Toadlena Trading Post from 1911 to 1942. Because of their positionality as practicing Latter-day Saints *and* traders, the Bloomfields often acted as missionaries to visitors and passers-by.[17] To this day, a Latter-day Saint chapel sits just up the road from the trading post in the tiny town of Toadlena. The Bloomfields, like other Latter-day Saint traders, promoted the production of weavings made from wool that had not been dyed. This style, featuring neutral colors such as tan, white, brown, and black, came to be known as the Two Grey Hills style. Arguably the most recognized Navajo weaver who worked in the Two Grey Hills style was Daisy Taugelchee.[18]

Daisy Taugelchee

Despite the need to produce in the Two Grey Hills style, Taugelchee flourished as a weaver. She crafted her weavings with such skill and mastery that she was given the label of Legendary Master Weaver, a title bestowed upon very few.[19] Taugelchee enjoyed the weaving process. Due to a supportive spouse who helped with much of the housework, she was able to dedicate significant time during the day to work on her weavings.[20] Taugelchee's weaving titled *Two Grey Hills* exemplifies the namesake style. Two diamond shapes occupy the center of the weaving. Stark geometric patterns surround the diamonds. Only neutral colors have been utilized in the production of the weaving, another trait of the style. A bold, dark border encloses the interior pattern. The contrast between the deeper shades and bright whites is visually stimulating. It is a masterpiece. Additionally, there is an interesting story about how the Church History Museum acquired Taugelchee's weaving. Quoting a former curator from the museum:

> Daisy spent twenty-three months weaving this rug. Fern Smouse [George and Lucy Bloomfield's daughter] received this masterpiece of Two Grey Hills Navajo weaving from her husband who had commissioned it from the finest Navajo weaver in this style in her day. Fern was so attached to this rug that she told her family that she wanted to be buried in it. When Fern died, the family dutifully wrapped her body in the rug. But before burying her, they removed the rug because they couldn't bear to bury this Navajo masterpiece. The Smouse family then donated the rug to the Museum of Church History and Art [Church History Museum] because they felt that the Church was a good place to not only preserve the rug, but also because the Church was a good custodian.[21]

The curator's last line is key. For over a century, the Church of Jesus Christ of Latter-day Saints acted as custodian (controller) of images of Native Americans in church

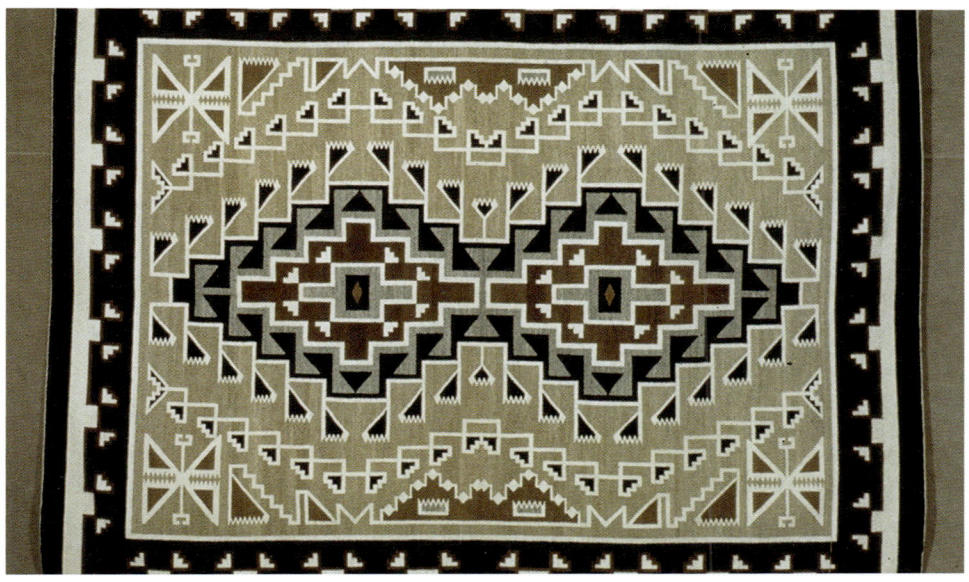

Fig. 17.5 Daisy Taugelchee, *Two Grey Hills*, 1940, wool, 59.5" × 71.25", Church of Jesus Christ of Latter-day Saints Church History Museum.

spaces and printed materials. There is a reason for this, found within discourses on the "Lamanite" people.

The "Lamanite" People

In his chapter in this volume, W. Paul Reeve summarizes the Lamanite connection. He explains that "nineteenth century Latter-day Saints believed that Native Americans were fallen descendants of Book of Mormon peoples, particularly a dark-skinned group called the Lamanites, who eventually destroyed their lighter-skinned kinship group, the Nephites."[22] Reeve delineates his thoughts on Native American relations with Latter-day Saints by examining how whiteness was favored in artistic representations of the early Saints and Native Americans.[23] For a long time, Latter-day Saints adhered to the notion that they needed to redeem their Lamanite sisters and brothers from their ancient sins. But it went further than that. Latter-day Saints used the scriptural term "Lamanite" in day-to-day conversation to refer to living Native Americans.

Included in a family's personal photo album is a photograph of two Native American men. Each man is sitting atop a horse. They are outfitted in full regalia, complete with feathered headdresses. The photograph appears out of place within the photo album, which contains intimate images of (white) women lounging on grassy lawns and relaxing in hammocks. The title given to the image is perhaps even more startling: *"Lamanites" (Mormon for Indians) Pioneers Parade July 24, 1899.* Note the parentheses: "(Mormon for Indians)." This wording seems to suggest that Latter-day Saints

(Mormons) speak an entirely different language. This hearkens back to Givens's asser-tion that Latter-day Saints are a peculiar people.[24] The period of Lamanite references and connections is problematic. The church commissioned white artists to create images of Native Americans because, for many Latter-day Saints (and to be fair, much of American society outside the church), white equaled civilized and Native American (Lamanite) equaled primitive.[25] "Lamanite" was used as a representation (back to Said's point) to create difference between an imagined savage state and a white, delightsome state of being. This is probably no more apparent than in the Book of Mormon paintings produced in the mid-twentieth century.

Book of Mormon Art

Book of Mormon art has long been synonymous with one name: Arnold Friberg.[26] An illustrator by trade, Friberg's technique and skill were "aided by his traditional method: from his sketches and use of live models he made photographs, drawings, and oil studies before painting his canvases."[27] Copies of his paintings can be found in Latter-day Saint chapels around the world. His original Book of Mormon paintings are currently on view inside the Conference Center in Salt Lake City. Friberg's Book of Mormon characters have been lauded and chastised both within and outside the Latter-day Saint community. While some appreciate his overtly muscular, heroic-type men and beautiful (fair-skinned) women, others do not. Friberg has received specific criticism for basing his figures on Euro-American (white) models.

One such figure can be seen in *Ammon Defends the Flocks of King Lamoni.* The cen-tral, imposing figure is a white man, supposedly Ammon. His almost-glistening body is positioned outward, perhaps so that the viewer can appreciate his obvious strength. Ammon's head is turned back over his right shoulder. He is also noticeably clean-shaven, as opposed to the bearded figures moving forward from the background. Like in Christensen's *Handcart Pioneers,* several figures—representing Lamanites—can be seen rushing toward Ammon (a Nephite), despite his gleaming, outstretched sword. Those among the charging individuals have noticeably darker skin tones than Ammon, but only by a few shades. Otherwise, they could be white. One figure, however, is markedly different. Friberg included one figure coded as Native American in the group of tanned men. His features are strikingly like the stone-faced images of Native Americans that were circulated throughout the art world during the nineteenth and twentieth centuries. Friberg likely saw and possibly studied some of these photographs—think images by Curtis, William Henry Jackson, C. R. Savage, Laura Gilpin—prior to or during pro-duction of his Book of Mormon series. With the inclusion of the recognizable Native American figure, Friberg reinforces the Lamanite–Native American connection. But it also raises a question: why has Friberg included only one Native American in the painting?

Friberg was not the only Latter-day Saint artist to paint Book of Mormon scenes. Minerva Teichert, beloved in the Latter-day Saint community, was heavily inspired

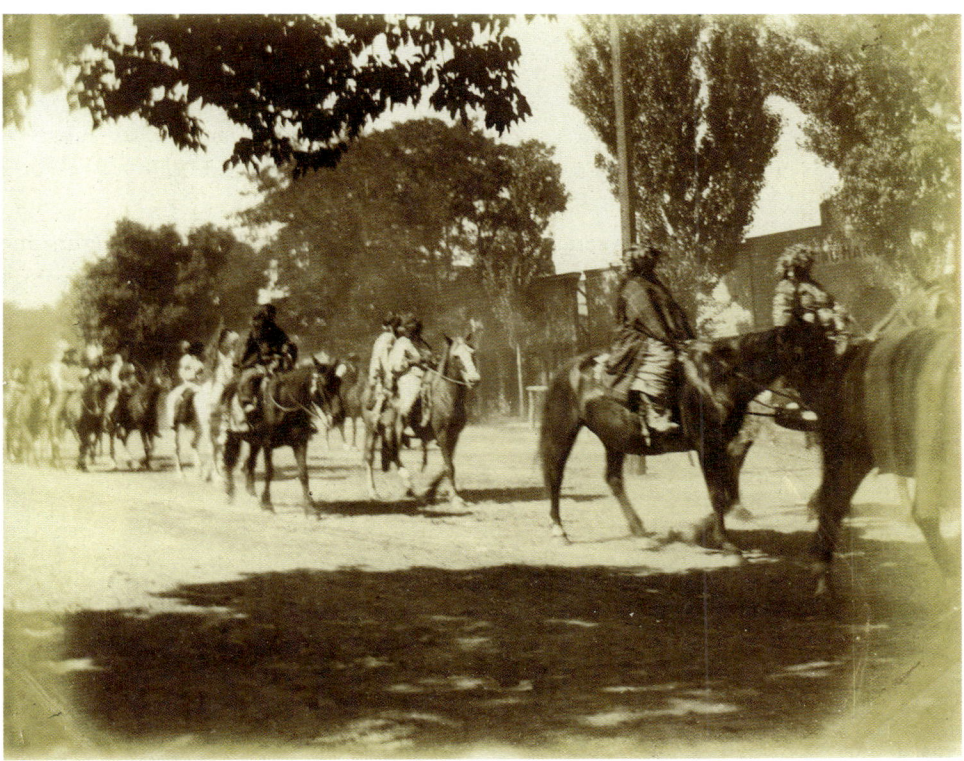

Fig. 17.6 *"Lamanites" (Mormon for Indians) Pioneers Parade July 24, 1899,* from untitled album, 1899, Church of Jesus Christ of Latter-day Saints Church History Library.

by biblical and Book of Mormon narratives. Teichert's paintings are known for their pastel shades, softened edges, and general ethereal qualities. Her pieces are stunning. During much of her career, Teichert worked closely with Alice Merrill Horne, the "high priestess of the Utah Mormon art scene."[28] Horne was a fierce advocate for the arts and especially women artists. She fostered connections between artists and potential commissions.[29] Because of sustained interest in Native American subject matter, Horne encouraged Teichert to paint Native Americans in her work. This carried over into Teichert's Book of Mormon paintings.

Last Battle Between the Nephites and the Lamanites illustrates the dramatic final meeting between the Nephites and the Lamanites described in the Book of Mormon. The Lamanites trample over the Nephite bodies. A few of the Lamanites are pointing their spears downward for protection and to kill anyone who might still be showing signs of life. The reddish background heightens the sense of conflict and death. One figure aims his bow and arrow at an unclear target. Contrary to Friberg, Teichert has painted all of the Lamanites to resemble Native Americans. Three figures wear full feathered headdresses. They have long, dark hair. Most of them are bare-chested. The individuals

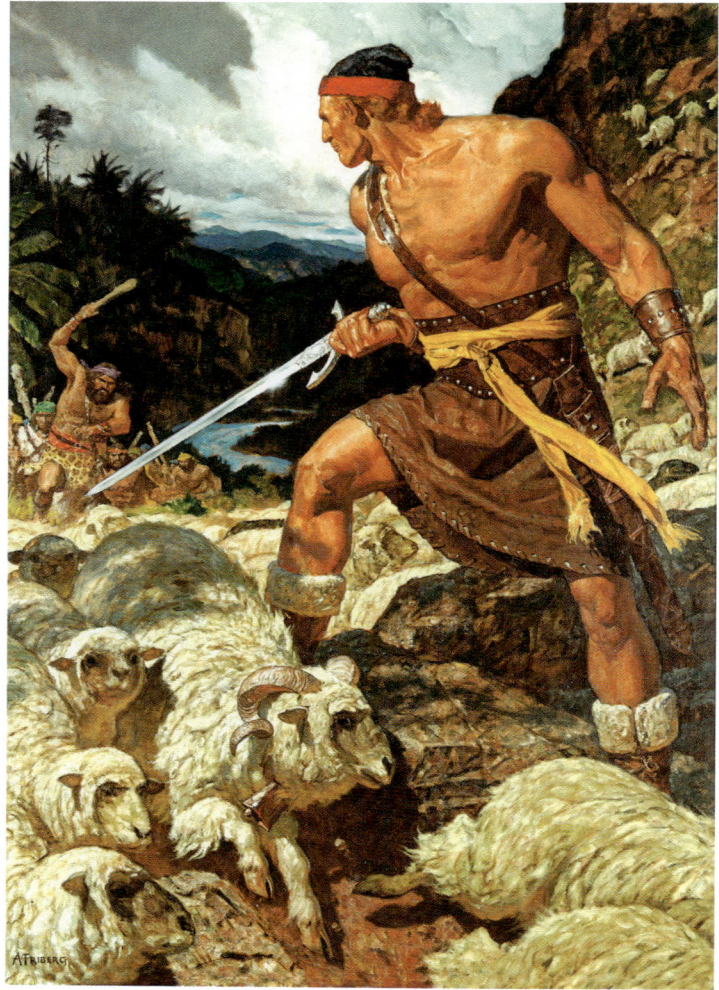

Fig. 17.7 Arnold Friberg, *Ammon Defends the Flocks of King Lamoni*, 1954, oil on canvas, 44″ × 32″, Church of Jesus Christ of Latter-day Saints Church History Museum.

are a stark departure from Friberg's tanned models. However, Teichert's painting is not exactly as it appears. *Last Battle Between the Nephites and the Lamanites* was not initially a Book of Mormon painting. Teichert had already painted the piece, and when she chose it for her Book of Mormon series, she swapped out the title.[30] Knowing this helps elucidate the reasons Teichert's painting prominently features Native Americans, and the change in title illustrates the problematic interchangeability of the cultural titles Lamanite and Native American.

The Book of Mormon paintings produced by Friberg, Teichert, and others in the mid-twentieth century are beautiful testaments to individual and collective faith. Yet they were created by white men and women. Just as Friberg's final images were filtered through European-looking models, Native American (Lamanite) experiences were filtered through Euro-American artists, members, and leaders within the Latter-day Saint community.

The Utah Scene

Because the church headquarters was established in the heart of downtown Salt Lake, the base for Latter-day Saint art and education naturally formed in Utah. Additionally, several Native American tribes lived in the region. In the 1950s, owing to the large number of Native Americans throughout Utah and the greater Southwest, the church organized the Indian Student Placement Service. Essentially, Native American children left their homes on their respective reservations and were housed with well-to-do "foster" families throughout Utah. Spencer W. Kimball, then a member of the Quorum of the Twelve Apostles, advocated for the creation and expansion of the program. Earlier in his career with the church, Kimball had been the chairman of the Committee of Indian Relationships. In his various capacities, Kimball forged ties with the local

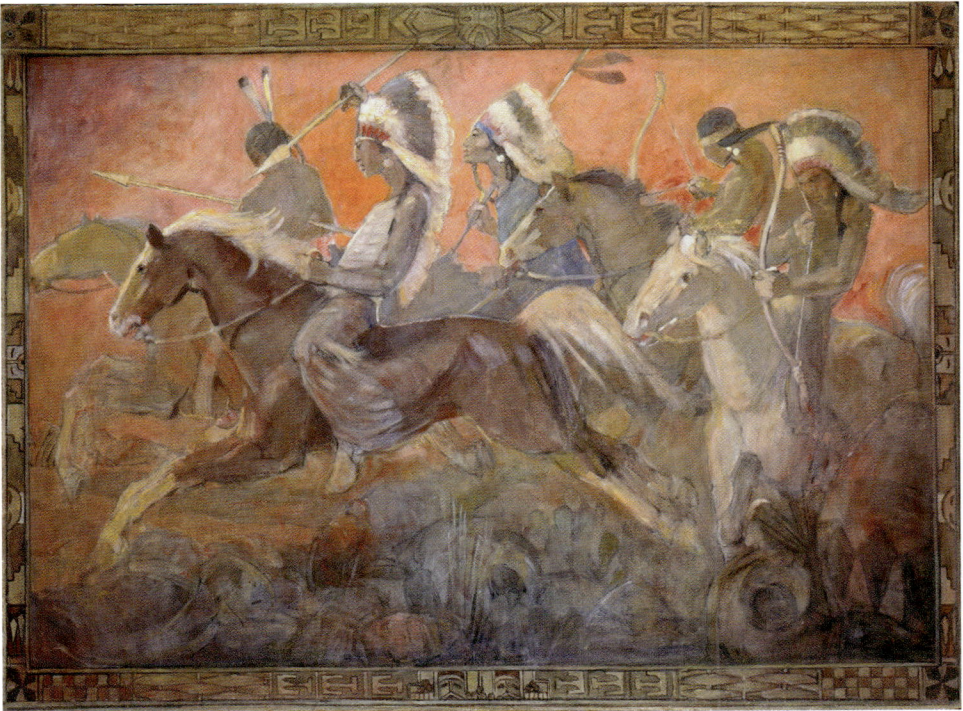

Fig. 17.8 Minerva Teichart, *Last Battle Between the Lamanites and the Nephites*, 1949–1951, oil on masonite, 36″ × 48″, Brigham Young University Museum of Art.

tribal communities. In return, the tribes gifted Kimball with pottery, beading, figurines, weavings, and other traditional pieces.

In an undated photograph, Kimball holds a portrait of himself. Within the portrait, a feather sits in his hair. A Native American man, naked from the waist up, seems to be floating in the clouds just over Kimball's right shoulder. In this painting, Kimball seems to be visited (and blessed) by a higher Native American power. Outside the portrait, Kimball wears a headband with the words "CHEIF [*sic*] KIMBALL" glaring across the front. A single feather has been placed at the back of the headband. The painting of Kimball (and additional accessories) undoubtedly served to strengthen the Latter-day Saint connection to Native Americans, or at least to justify them. Connections were also bolstered with the Native American community on Brigham Young University's campus in Provo. In the late 1960s, Kimball spearheaded the Miss Indian BYU pageant. The winner was the individual who would best represent her tribe while simultaneously advocating for other Native American students on campus. During the pageant, the candidates—dressed in traditional regalia—displayed artistic practices native to their tribes.[31]

It is important to note that the increase in Indigenous students at BYU in the early 1970s can be directly linked to the development of the Indian Student Placement Service. Kimball and others claimed that the ISPS provided an educational opportunity for Native American children—the majority of whom were Navajos—to learn alongside Latter-day Saint peers. In a statement about the ISPS from the church's website, President Kimball proclaims that the program "was inspired of the Lord."[32] However, the program received significant criticism. Many argued that the program provided a convenient opportunity for the church to convert Native American youth. Furthermore, others suggested that Native American children should not be assimilated into white Mormon culture but instead should empower tribal unity and traditions by remaining with their families on the reservation.[33]

Similar criticisms surfaced with the opening of the Intermountain Indian School in Brigham City, about fifteen minutes north of Salt Lake City along 1-15. Also built in the 1950s, Intermountain was a boarding school that housed Navajo children until its closure in the mid-1980s. Though the school did not have direct connections to the church, several students who lived there had experienced the ISPS beforehand. Henry Tinhorn was a Navajo youth who, before entering Intermountain, spent time in boarding schools and with foster families as part of the ISPS. Tinhorn immersed himself in poetry as a way to make sense of the complicated and often cruel world around him.[34]

For the Navajo youth in the Intermountain Indian School, art provided a bridge to cope. Art fostered healing. Considering the tough and, frankly, traumatic history between the Latter-day Saint community and Native Americans, it is more important than ever to create space for Indigenous artists to share their work. In 1994, Church History Museum curators Richard Oman and Mark Staker put on an exhibit titled *Sacred Connections: Art and Native American Latter-day Saints in the Southwest*. Oman

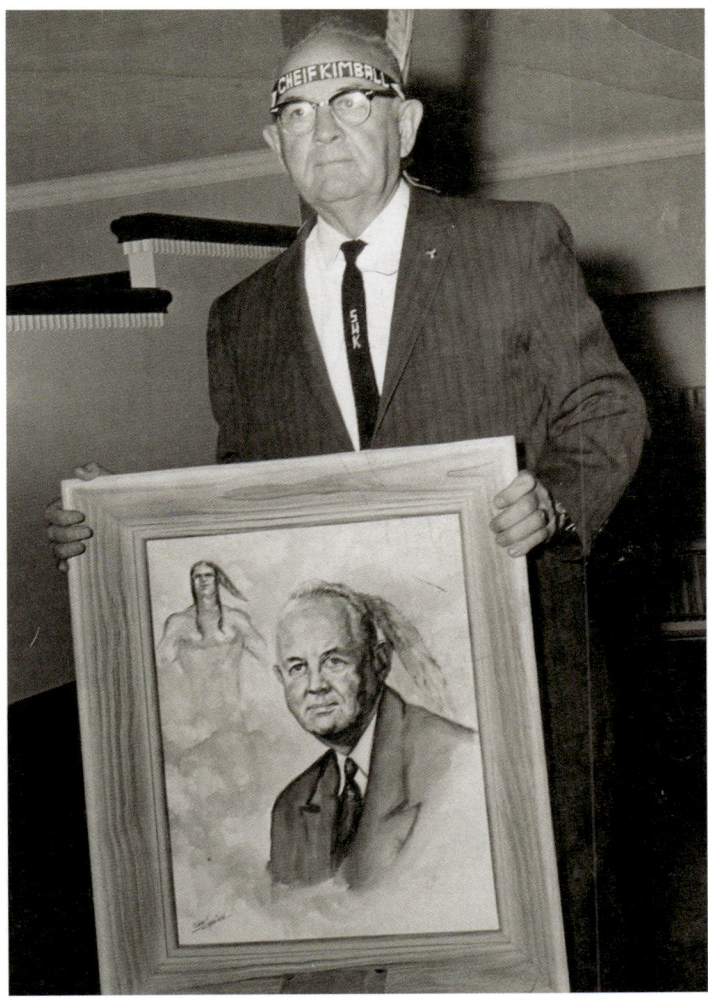

Fig. 17.9 Photograph of Spencer W. Kimball holding framed portrait of himself with feather in hair, *Deseret News* Photograph Collection (MS 22200), Church History Library, The Church of Jesus Christ of Latter-day Saints.

and Staker were the first persons to curate an exhibit focused on the artistic relations between Latter-day Saints and Native Americans. The exhibit included weavings, kachina dolls, pottery, baskets, interviews with artists, and other elements.[35] When asked why he wanted to design this specific exhibit, Oman shared that he "wanted to help people understand the spiritual quality of their [Native American] art. It's all wonderfully connected and beautifully crafted. The quality of the craftsmanship—give these artists their due space."[36] To underscore Oman's point, Native American artists need to be given their due space. The next section centers around self-representation because that is the first step toward healing and empowerment.

TWENTY-FIRST CENTURY: SELF-REPRESENTATION

Self-Representation

This section focuses on Native American Latter-day Saint artists. But before examining the work, we need to know what is at stake. Up until this point, this chapter has largely focused on representations of Native Americans by white Latter-day Saint artists. This dynamic dominated the Latter-day Saint art world throughout the nineteenth century and much of the twentieth. In her seminal work, *Decolonizing Museums: Representing Native America in National and Tribal Museums,* historian Amy Lonetree suggests a first step in acknowledging Native self-representation. Even though she specifically centers her argument on Indigenous representation in museum spaces, her words enrich and complicate the dialogue here. Lonetree asks, "What happens when museums do the decolonizing work? Museums become places for building momentum for healing, for community, and for restoring dignity and respect. . . . In other words, museums become a means for repairing colonization's harm."[37]

The International Art Competition, held every three years by the Church History Museum, is one way Native American artists can be seen and heard in the Latter-day Saint community. The works shown in the competition have increasingly been global in nature. This is a concerted effort by the current curators.

Les Namingha

Another way to empower Native American representation is to honor familial spiritual and artistic heritage. One exceptional piece of art in the museum's collection is a pot created by Hopi potter Les Namingha. Namingha's technical mastery is evident. The contrasting colors and geometric shapes combine in a compelling and beautiful composition. However, it goes deeper than that. As indicated by the title, *Three Degrees of Glory,* Namingha has displayed the three degrees of glory specific to LDS cosmology: telestial, terrestrial, and celestial.[38] Or, rather, he has represented *his* version of them. It is deeply personal. It is faith-filled.

Namingha is a great-great-grandson of Nampeyo, who is credited with reviving the ancient Hopi practice of pottery-making. Though Nampeyo was not a member of the church, her daughter Fannie Nampeyo—a celebrated potter in her own right—joined the church in the early twentieth century along with her husband, Vinton Polacca. All of their living children learned to make pottery and excelled. The artistic tradition started with Nampeyo has continued to the present day and perhaps will extend beyond that.

Kwani Povi Winder

This chapter began with a quote by Kwani Povi Winder, a working Santa Clara Pueblo Tewa artist. Winder is also a wife and mother. Like Namingha, Winder has an artistic ancestry. Her maternal grandparents were artists, as is her mother. Ironically, Winder's mom, Ima Naranjo Hale, participated in the Miss Indian BYU pageant during her time at school. A charming piece, titled *Noah and Ark*, was a collaboration between Winder's grandparents, her mom, and another relative. While the figures and ark appear to be relatively simple in nature, the smooth black figurines are reminiscent of Santa Clara Pueblo pottery. Pottery in that particular pueblo is known for its incredibly smooth and shiny black appearance. *Noah and Ark* is a sweet, subtle example of combining cultural heritage with spiritual beliefs. The piece is rich with meaning.

Winder furthers the cultural connection in her painting *My Prayer*. The piece is a three-quarter-length portrait of Winder's mom, Ima. She is wearing traditional Native clothing and jewelry. Her dark, long hair emphasizes her strong, thoughtful gaze. Winder has placed silver leaf in a halo motif around her mother's head, deepening the inherent spirituality. This woman is friendly and knowable. She is not stuck in a romantic past. We too hope not only to understand her but also to understand ourselves better. Winder, one of the most well-known Native American Latter-day Saint artists working today, recently shared her thoughts with me about her work. Both the art and the voice of individuals like Winder need to be acknowledged. Because her words are

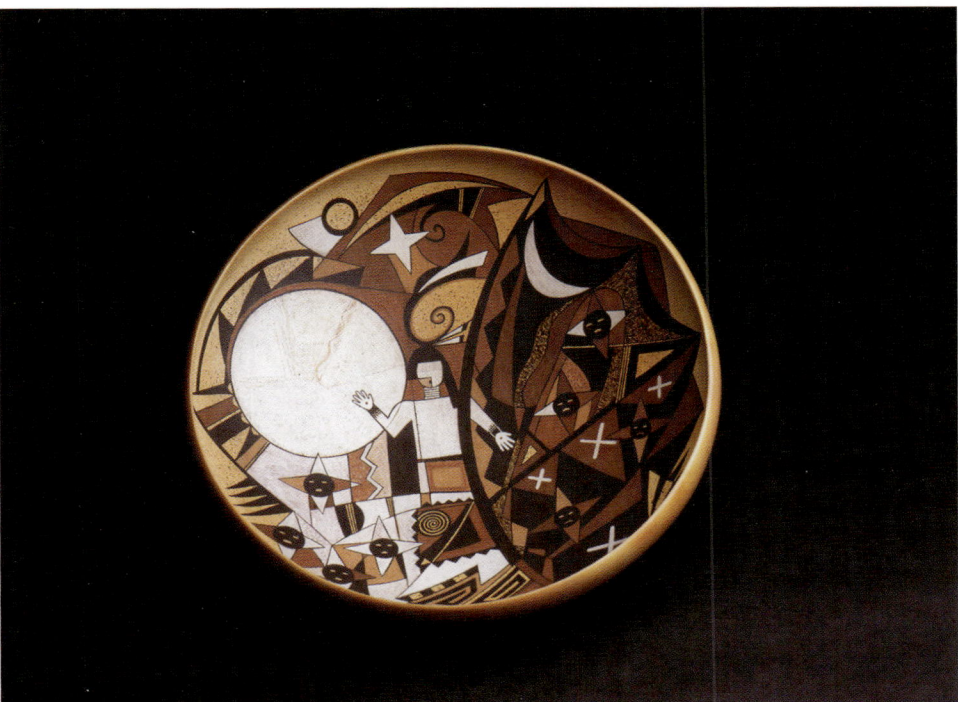

Fig. 17.10 Les Namingha, *Three Degrees of Glory*, 1994, ceramic, 13.5″ × 3.75″, Church of Jesus Christ of Latter-day Saints Church History Museum.

poignant and help foster spaces of healing, empowerment, and understanding, I am including a selection below.

Kwani Povi Winder, Interview with Author, November 21, 2022

Constantino: Do you ever feel a sense of pressure? Like, I am an indigenous artist, I am a Latter-day Saint, there's not many of us, so I want to do good work. Do you ever feel any kind of pressure on you because of that?

Winder: No, I definitely, I get anxious about it at different points of being in the spotlight, or knowing that people are going to be looking at what I do. Wanting to represent my culture the right way and not misrepresent anything. I didn't grow up on the reservation, so there's this hesitancy with me of feeling a little bit of an imposter even though I definitely embrace and am intentional about connecting with my culture. There's always this little bit of, I don't know if this is right. But I also have learned that it's my experience, and I can share my experience and I can share how I feel about these things and I'm not thinking for someone else. So, it's okay. I'm still learning how to be more comfortable with that and not caring so much what other

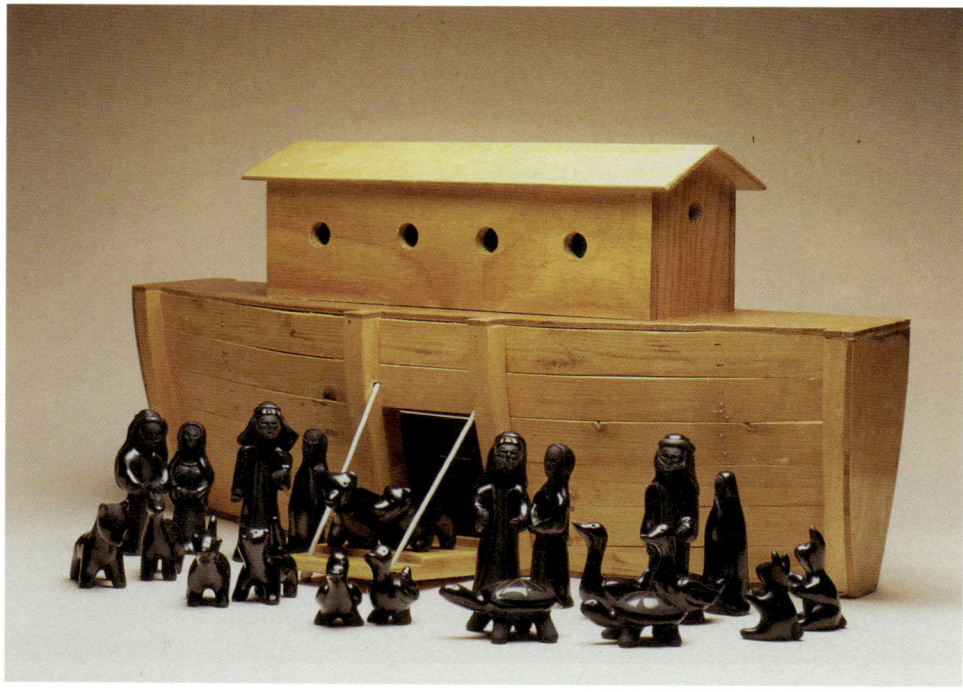

Fig. 17.11 Jose Eugene Naranjo, Mary Isabel Naranjo, JoeAnn Naranjo Montoya, Ima Naranjo Hale, *Noah and Ark*, 1990, ceramic and wood, 19.5″ × 16.5″, Church of Jesus Christ of Latter-day Saints Church History Museum.

people think in my community. I care about connecting with them and being intentional and being correctly represented.

For Winder, representing her Santa Clara Pueblo Tewa culture is clearly complicated. Acknowledging that she did not grow up on the reservation, she says she makes a concerted effort to be authentic to her Native American culture while reconciling that with her own personal religion. This reveals the difficulty with simplistic ideas about race or representation. As evidenced by Winder's work, Latter-day Saint Native American artists are not monolithic but rather exist in an evolving, complex dynamic

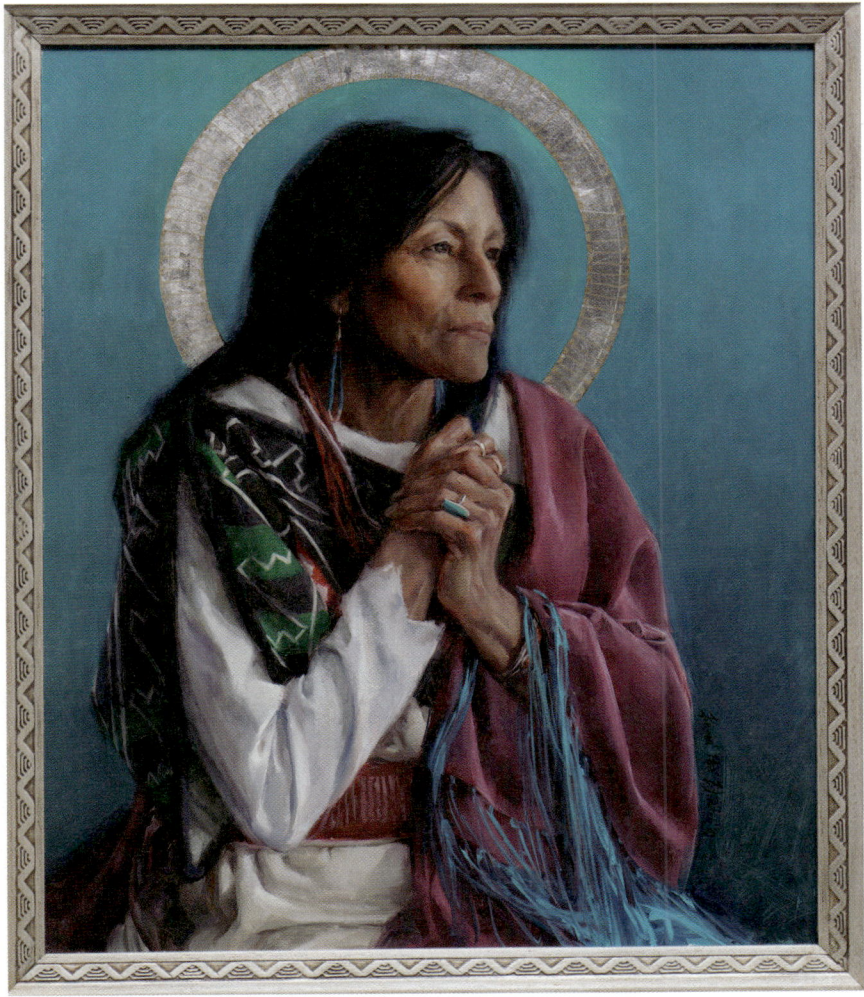

Fig. 17.12 Kwani Povi Winder, *My Prayer*, 2018, oil on canvas, 24″ × 20.25″, Church of Jesus Christ of Latter-day Saints Church History Museum.

between spirituality, cultural identity, and self-representation. Winder's work is especially enriched by her artistic heritage.

Constantino: Your mom is an artist?

Winder: Yeah, she is. I don't know if she'll admit it or not. I grew up in an art household and she was always doing art with me and she taught elementary school for a long time. And now that she's been retired, I've kind of pushed her, like, "Spend a little bit of time on your art. This is something you enjoy. You're an artist." Both of us have paintings at the Church History Museum for the International Art Competition. I'm like, "Mom, that's hard to do and you're still doubting if you're an artist?" She's really been quite inspiring to me.

Constantino: And I understand that your grandparents were artists?

Winder: I come from a line of potters. That's how my grandparents made a lot of their money. They would go around to shows when my mom was younger and set up a table.

Constantino: Are you inspired by their work? Your grandparents' and your mom's?

Winder: Yes, a lot more of my recent Native paintings have been trying to incorporate, especially with the metal leafing, trying to incorporate the pottery design that would be used in our village, using that as symbolism for some of the spiritual things that I'm trying to convey. But trying to marry the two: that heritage of pottery making that also go with the representational style that was kind of interesting to see the progression of that. I would say the most culminating piece so far has been the piece I have in the Church History Museum, which is a lot of symbolism and pottery shapes and figures and things that you would see on regular pottery.

Winder is simultaneously inspired and empowered by her heritages: her family and her Native American culture. By incorporating pottery symbols from her tribe into her work, Winder shows that it is possible to marry tribal identity with religious beliefs. In discussing the religiosity of her work, Winder underscores the importance of her process and purpose.

Constantino: Do you know beforehand what you are going to paint? Or is it kind of a journey as you start to figure out, this is going to be this person, or …

Winder: There is usually a story or an emotion I want to convey. With the Eve painting, this is how it often goes, I have an idea in my head, a shape or a figure. I have the shape of her hand outstretched and her wearing this robe. I wish I could show you the sketch. It was kind of a little bit like Christ, the *Christus* with his hand outstretched. But wanting to take, honor the feminine and honor the creative side of women that you don't see mentioned or acknowledged other than in the temple. And then I knew I wanted Native designs at the bottom and the top. A lot of time it comes as an idea or an image that comes into my head. And usually there's an emotion tied to it and sometimes a scripture. It's scriptural in the sense that there's hope or joy or pain or suffering. There's something that you get from the scriptures that I'm trying to convey.

Constantino: I think even just looking at the title conveys something as well. I love that. One last question: what would you hope that people would get out of looking at your art?

Winder: I think foremost is, honestly, a love from God. Light. That people cry looking at my paintings and they may or may not recognize, but sharing that spirit and putting the spirit into the paint. People respond to that. They can tell it's different, and even if they're not my same religion and don't believe anything that I do, if they feel light or joy or are uplifted, that is my primary goal. To share light and goodness. So that is what I always try to share, and there's layers to it. That is my main goal, to help someone feel the spirit in a way or be touched or feel lighter or feel brighter or enrich their lives. Or make them a better person because they saw something that made them feel a bit deeper or just try to connect with them. That's why a lot of my figures have pretty strong emotions quite often. It's part of the posing, but it's also what I'm thinking about when I'm painting. And hoping that will happen to those that view it. I always tell people, that my painting is not finished even though I'm finished. It takes someone viewing it and that connection with them and their experiences is what finishes the painting and that looks different for a lot of people.

Constantino: It's so true.

Winder: I'm always fascinated when I go to art shows and I have this wide array of different types of paintings, different colors, and I've connected with each one of them, there's a reason why I painted each one. But it's interesting the one that there's different people that hone in on different ones. And I've learned it's just because of their experience or their life or something in their past in their history. And then there's this connection between me and them because of that. And it's always different for each person.

Creating connections, as Winder discusses, is foundational to her artistic journey. Nurturing her own connections to family, building a connection to God, and finding connections through her art with other people. This is particularly true as she navigates her position as a Native American woman in the church.

Constantino: There's a hard history between Indigenous people and the church. How do you reconcile that? Do you have any issues with anything in history—how do you navigate that?

Winder: Part of it is, I don't know all of it. I may change once I find out more. [Laughs] But I take the viewpoint that we learn from our past. There's always things that could have been done differently or shouldn't have happened, really. I also know that there are mixed experiences. You think about the Indian Placement Program. My family had an incredible experience with it and are very close to the families that they were placed with, and see them all the time. But I know other people that it was detrimental to them. So I recognize that everyone has different connections and experiences. I think the other part that makes a difference for me is my grandparents were converts to the church and the first ones in their village to join the church. Knowing how hard it was to give up their Indian way, leaving their way of life, they made sacrifices. Knowing the type of people my grandparents were and how strong they were in themselves, they wouldn't have done that if there wasn't something here. That heritage and foundation has made it easier for me to trust a little bit when I feel disoriented. They came here for a reason and I still feel encouraged to stay and figure out why I need to stay, because they saw something. When I start doubting myself I just think through things. They laid out this foundation that I'm building on. I don't know all the answers and I'm okay with that. Some people aren't. Some people need to know. I think it's because I am an artist—that's part of it. I'm okay with sitting in uncomfortable growth. As an artist, you always see what's wrong before you can change it. I'm okay feeling a little fluid in the church. Sometimes I'm closer, sometimes I'm further out. As I've grown up I've realized there's a different level people are at all the time, and it's not as black and white as I thought it was when I was a kid.

Constantino: Your family were pioneers.

CONCLUSION

In many ways, acknowledging the past is the only way forward. The relationship between the Church of Jesus Christ of Latter-day Saints and Native Americans should not be simplified. It is complex and problematic, but it is also nuanced and hopeful. The evolution of art throughout the nineteenth century up to the present day within the church is evidence of a growing—and needed—inclusion of marginalized voices. This includes Native Americans. As articulated by Winder, the notions of representation and identity go beyond the dichotomy of "subject/object" and "background/foreground." The artistic process involves, in turn, reflection, struggle, pain, acceptance, and joy—a process akin to reconciling with a tough history.

Referencing Winder's quote at the beginning of the chapter, this process is about helping others to be seen. It is about giving a voice to those who think they have none. This includes not just Winder but also a host of other Latter-day Saint Native American artists throughout the years: Harrison Begay (Navajo), Fannie Nampeyo (Hopi), Tammy Garcia (Santa Clara Pueblo), Leta Kieth (Navajo), Lucy Lueppe McKelvey (Navajo), Thomas Polacca (Hopi), Shirley Benn (Paiute), Robert Yellowhair (Navajo), and Phillip Sekaquaptewa (Hopi), to name a few. Though this chapter is one space to think about healing and empowerment, another important space, to reiterate the point made by Amy Lonetree, is the museum. Building community and respect can happen only if Native American artists are included in planning exhibitions, museum education, and arts programs. It is, then, among a wider audience that Native Americans—and other non-white members of the church—will become empowered in their own right. That is true healing.

NOTES

[1] Terryl L. Givens, *People of Paradox: A History of Mormon Culture* (Oxford: Oxford University Press, 2007), xiv–xv.

[2] Jared Farmer, *On Zion's Mount: Mormons, Indians, and the American Landscape* (Cambridge, MA: Harvard University Press, 2008), 16.

[3] Edward W. Said, *Orientalism* (New York: Pantheon Books, 1978), 21.

[4] bell hooks, *Yearning: Race, Gender, and Cultural Politics* (Boston: South End Press, 1990), 145.

[5] Laura Paulsen Howe, curator at the Church History Museum, conversation with the author, November 18, 2022.

[6] Elizabeth Hutchinson, *The Indian Craze: Primitivism, Modernism, and Transculturation in American Art, 1890–1915* (Durham, NC: Duke University Press, 2009).

[7] Rell G. Francis, *Cyrus E. Dallin: Let Justice Be Done* (Springville, UT: Springville Museum of Art, 1976), 4.

[8] Francis, *Cyrus E. Dallin*, 36.

[9] Francis, *Cyrus E. Dallin*, 44.

[10] Thomas E. Toone, *Mahonri Young: His Life and Art* (Salt Lake City: Signature Books, 1997), ix.

[11] Toone, *Mahonri Young*, 26–40.

[12] After the initial conversations about this piece with the curator, we decided to change the title in the Church History Museum database. The new title, which is used for the image in this chapter, is *Navajo Woman and Sheep*.

[13] Mick Gidley, *Edward S. Curtis and the North American Indian, Incorporated* (Cambridge: Cambridge University Press, 1998), 5.

[14] Photograph of Native Americans, PH 10373, Kathryn P. Fong Photograph Collection, circa 1882, Church History Library, Salt Lake City, UT. The address stamped on the back of the photograph reads: "C. W. Carter's Photograph Gallery and View Emporium, Nos. 2 and 4 Third South St. Cor. Main, Salt Lake City, Utah, Tin Types Taken."

[15] Susan Bernardin et al., *Trading Gazes: Euro-American Women Photographers and Native North Americans, 1880–1940* (New Brunswick, NJ: Rutgers University Press, 2003), 13.

[16] Carlyle Constantino, "Emerging from the Archive: Helen M. Post's Photographs of Twentieth-Century Navajos," *Utah Historical Quarterly* 87, no. 4 (2019): 322.

[17] Mark Winter, *The Master Weavers: Celebrating One Hundred Years of Navajo Textile Artists from the Toadlena/Two Grey Hills Weaving Region* (Newcomb, NM: Historic Toadlena Trading Post, 2011), 80.

[18] Winter, *The Master Weavers*, 80–81.

[19] Winter, *The Master Weavers*, 80.

[20] Winter, *The Master Weavers*, 82. Taugelchee's first husband, Chee, enjoyed cooking and prepared meals for the family.

[21] Former curator at the Church History Museum, email message to author, November 29, 2022.

[22] W. Paul Reeve's chapter in this volume.

[23] W. Paul Reeve's chapter in this volume.

[24] Givens, *People of Paradox*, xv.

[25] Givens, *People of Paradox*, xv.

[26] Vern Swanson, "The Book of Mormon Art of Arnold Friberg: Painter of Scripture," *Journal of Book of Mormon Studies* 10, no. 1 (2001): 28. Friberg created his first work featuring a religious theme in 1950. He began working on the Book of Mormon series shortly thereafter.

[27] Swanson, "The Book of Mormon Art of Arnold Friberg," 29.

[28] Heather Belnap's chapter in this volume.

[29] Heather Belnap's chapter in this volume.

[30] Laura Paulsen Howe, curator at the Church History Museum, conversation with author, November 18, 2022.

[31] TMF Department Yearbook, 1971–1972, UA 1225, Box 21–22, Multicultural Education Department Records, L. Tom Perry Special Collections, Brigham Young University, Provo, UT.

[32] Church of Jesus Christ of Latter-day Saints, "A Conversation About Changes in the Indian Student Placement Service," October 1985.

[33] Elise Boxer, "'The Lamanites Shall Blossom as the Rose': The Indian Student Placement Program, Mormon Whiteness, and Indigenous Identity," *Journal of Mormon History* 41, no. 4 (2015): 132.

[34] Farina King, Michael P. Taylor, and James R. Swensen, *Returning Home: Diné Creative Works from the Intermountain Indian School* (Tucson: University of Arizona Press, 2021), 35.

[35] Exhibit catalogue for "Sacred Connections: Art and Native American Latter-day Saints in the Southwest, 1994 October 22," CR 100 303, Folder 1, Gallery Guides for Museum Exhibits, Church History Library, Salt Lake City, UT.

[36] Richard Oman, phone interview by author, January 5, 2023.

[37] Amy Lonetree, *Decolonizing Museums: Representing Native America in National and Tribal Museums* (Chapel Hill: University of North Carolina Press, 2012), 171.

[38] Church of Jesus Christ of Latter-day Saints, "Kingdoms of Glory," June 2023. https://www.churchofjesu schrist.org/study/manual/gospel-topics/kingdoms-of-glory?lang=eng.

18

THE PIETY OF PERSPECTIVE

Bodies, Media, and Cinematic Experience in Latter-day Saint Film, 1970–2020

MASON KAMANA ALLRED

The year 1974 could have signaled the birth of Mormon cinema. Just a few years after Ragnar Lasse-Henriksen won the Silver Bear at the Berlin film festival for his debut Norwegian film, *Love Is War*, 1974 saw the arrival of Jose Oliveira's *The Dead, the Devil, and the Flesh* (*Los Muertos, la Carne, y el Diablo*) in Madrid and Lino Brocka's *Weighed but Found Wanting* (*Tinimbang Ka Ngunit Kulang*) in Manila. All three directors were Latter-day Saints, and all three films were influenced by the directors' experience with Mormonism. Unfortunately, the coincidence and its possible relevance for global Latter-day Saint culture went unnoticed.

Instead, most scholars locate the emergence of a Mormon film tradition in the year 2000. Even though Latter-day Saints have made feature films since the early twentieth century, 2000 marked the premiere of Richard Dutcher's film *God's Army*, which prompted a new wave of homemade cinema, including historical films, documentaries, missionary films, and a slew of comedies.[1] Many of these were quite successful among audiences in the "Mormon corridor" of the western United States, and some deliberately explored the medium's religious potential.[2] But it is important to recognize that this body of work represented a narrow perspective that was not only white, male, and middle-class but also exclusively American. I argue that turning to the earlier moment of the 1970s reveals a vibrant, global, and ambitious model for Latter-day Saint cinema that might inspire new, diverse futures.

Of course, independent feature films offer a personal perspective of their creator, yet Mormon film—limited here to work created by Latter-day Saints that bears some influence from the Latter-day Saint experience or doctrine—reveals some thematic patterns. For instance, Oliveira's film considered a Latter-day Saint understanding of the role of sex and embodiment through the relationship of a married couple, even beyond the grave, in a Spanish mixture of religious fantasy and horror. And Brocka's film used harsh lighting and sound to depict inequality and misogyny, with an ultimate message of re-birth inspired by the director's experiences as a Latter-day Saint missionary in Hawaii. Despite these differences in narrative and cinematic styles, both films centered on a core element of Mormon cinema: the materiality of the human body.

Revealing and concealing the cinematic human body while appropriately appealing to the material bodies of audiences has been a consistently fraught prospect for Latter-day Saints. Even a cursory engagement with Mormon cinema reveals an aversion to the "body genres" of horror and eroticism.[3] Instead of gore or sensuality, much Latter-day Saint cinematic fare has focused on sentimentalism and humor, because in the LDS re-ligious worldview laughing and crying have been seen as appropriate physical responses to entertainment.[4] However, as evidenced in Oliveira's and Brocka's films, among others discussed in this chapter, some Mormon films engage the body in more complex and creative ways.

These international films from the 1970s eschew graphic depictions of sex and vio-lence, but the body, used as a conduit to structure the characters' interactions and power relations, remains a central theme. Whether along the lines of sex, life and death, gender, (dis)ability, or appearance, this focus on the body reveals a positive theology of em-bodiment even in worlds riddled with corporeal misuse and abuse. Appreciating these earlier films centers the experimental efforts of later cinema to work through Mormon anxieties around media in the twenty-first century, after decades of official rhetoric stressing the danger of "worldly" movies, music, and literature. Put simply, whereas 1970s Mormon cinema evinces a radical coming to terms with living in a body, at least in the films discussed in this chapter, the new Mormon cinema of the 2000s often explores the promise and threat of interacting with media.

In a phenomenological sense, each approach analyzed here uniquely balances the possibilities of locating experience somewhere between the body of the viewer and the body of film.[5] This often entails more than merely identifying with characters onscreen or filmmakers behind cameras. As Jennifer Barker writes, this focus on the embodied reception of films reveals how "we are embedded in a constantly mutual experience with the film, so that the cinematic experience is the experience of being both 'in' our bodies and 'in' the liminal space created by that contact."[6] Viewers know they are outside the film, but enter its sensuous world via their own senses. Films appeal to the bodies of their audiences in sophisticated ways that underscore the materiality of flesh as the ground of cinematic experience. With a similar attention to affect and embodiment, I am interested in the ways Latter-day Saint cinema seeks to explore the body in content and form, in order to touch the audience in particular ways.

Rather than offer a broad overview of genres and titles from Latter-day Saints or the church itself, as has been done elsewhere, I approach several titles between 1970 and 2020 thematically.[7] The films treated here shape a duality in experience based on a cosmology of eternal bodies but duplicitous mortal media. By attending to the materiality of the body, they also unleash the potential of film to expand the viewer's consciousness through diverse media experiences.

GLOBAL BODIES

While all were men, the three filmmakers in the 1970s offered global perspectives in addition to showcasing the Mormon fascination with the body. The opportunity to see the world in diverse ways shined through each film's ability to embed Mormon experience and thoughts around embodiment in various local contexts. Ragnar Lasse-Henriksen's 1970 Berlinale entry, *Love Is War*, paved the way. Written and directed shortly after the filmmaker participated in the endowment ceremony of the Latter-day Saint temple, the film seems to reference the biblical story of creation and the Garden of Eden, which is central to the temple ceremony.[8] Without any explicit Mormon motifs (at least at first glance), Lasse-Henriksen's film follows the relationship of the woman Gro and the man Espen, who meet—as it so happens—in a botanical garden.

Oversaturated images of swimming, running, and snippets of everyday life with voice-over ruminations on love, birth, death, and belief run in sequence but often defy chronology or logic beyond additive associations. Formally experimental in its play with space and time, the film was ambitious in its adaptation of a European art-house mode not previously seen in the work of Latter-day Saint filmmakers. It also broke with the ready answers and omniscient voice-of-God style of institutional films, such as *Man's Search for Happiness* (1964), created by Judge Whitaker after he left Disney and founded the motion picture studio at Brigham Young University in 1952. *Love Is War* was a completely different type of creation. Instead of providing answers, it was more exploratory in form and content. And while it continued the innovations of the Scandinavian and European waves of new cinema, the film also offered a means of subtly exploring Latter-day Saint theology without alienating the viewer.

An evocative scene, for instance, shows Gro lying in a hospital bed as she hauntingly asks in voice-over, ostensibly about an abortion: "This isn't the same as murder, is it?" Latter-day Saints engaging reproductive rights in cinema was unprecedented and paved the way for more conversations and visual exploration broadly. At one point Espen fashions a divining rod, a significant instrument in Mormon and American folk history, and continues to seek for answers. In many ways, the work with the divining rod and sonic questioning in voice-overs from multiple subjectivities parallel the film's inquisitive gaze. As his son once told me in conversation, Lasse-Henriksen was convinced cinema was a unique type of applied theology, an artistic means of exploring celestial truth.

Bodies also galvanize the connection between the characters and the audience in *Love is War*. At one point, Gro and Espen bite into lemons together. In extreme close-up, their faces instantly pucker in response. This scene echoes the forbidden fruit of the Eden story, but it also transforms it into what is inevitably (and deliberately) a visceral experience for the viewer by trading the more common sweet apple of Edenic depictions for a bitter lemon. Because bodies are celebrated as means to connect with others and become like the embodied God in heaven, framing the consumption of lemons in close-up rendered the Latter-day Saint telling of that biblical bittersweet moment of "falling" from paradise as progress—viscerally sweet to bitter, but theologically bitter to sweet. By rooting this in bodies eating, the film compels audiences to feel, almost taste, the effect through their eyes. Watching the Fall was now a cinematic sensation.

In 1973, just a few years later, Jose Maria Oliveira, a Latter-day Saint convert and Spain's first stake president, released his debut film, *Beware of Darkness* (*Las Flores del Miedo*) in Madrid. But Oliveira immediately turned to his next and more ambitious project, *The Dead, the Devil, and the Flesh*, released the following year, 1974.[9] The creativity of *The Dead* starts with the opening sequence, as the protagonist, Juan, begins the film—like Joe in *Sunset Boulevard* (1950)—already dead. The film then plays as an extended flashback initiated by Juan's brother reading a book about the afterlife Juan had

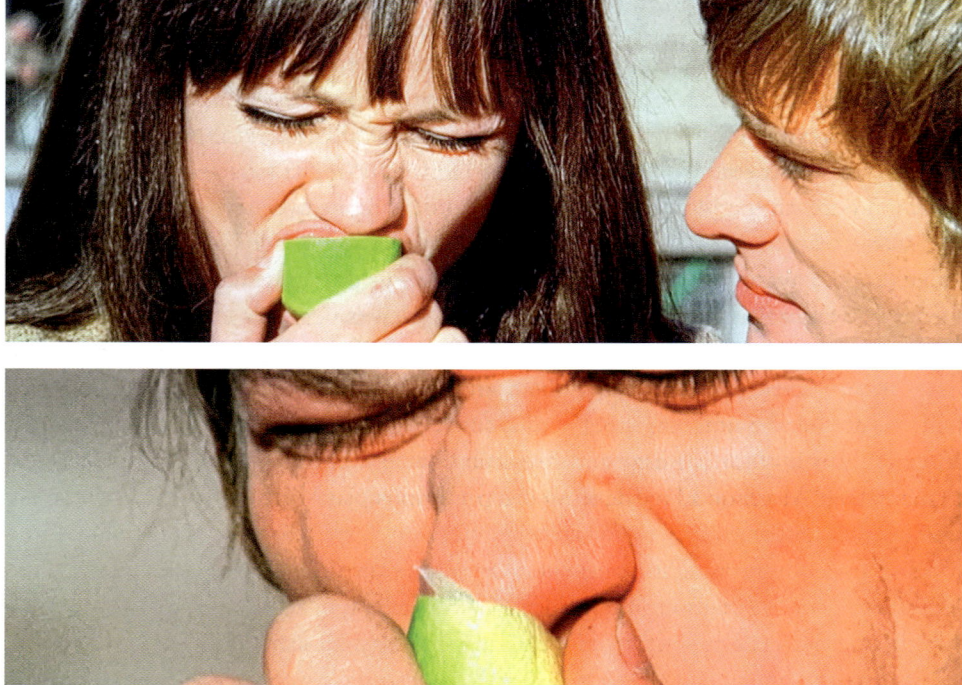

Fig. 18.1 *a* and *b*. Espen and Gro partake of bitter lemons in *Love Is War*, dir. Ragnar Lasse-Henriksen, 1970. Courtesy of Magnus Henriksen.

been writing shortly before his demise. The bulk of the film follows Juan as he lectures on the afterlife and strives to follow a Latter-day Saint understanding of the gospel of Jesus Christ, even as his wife mocks him and cheats incessantly behind his back with numerous men. When a roadblock prevents his return home one evening, Juan finds shelter at the local Catholic church. That night Juan crosses the threshold of the church's cemetery and mysteriously ends up in the spirit world only to find the spirit of his dead wife, who was just murdered by one of her lovers.

Abounding with symbolism, Oliveira's film is interested in the connections and especially the continuities between the living and the dead and the role of the body (or lack thereof) in both states. This fascination with the metaphysical is fantastically captured in the film's only and sudden choreographed dance scene, where a dance with death becomes a dance without sex. Addressing the seated spirits before him, the evil spirit Korijor calls out, "Now let's dance, and rhythm will bring back memories of the body you used to have." Just then the disembodied spirits arise to execute an erotic (read: hip gyrations)—yet hollow—dance number, mixing popular disco and postmodern movements as they sway to the command of Korijor, their puppet master. With faces drained of all emotion, the dancers move—sometimes in unison—but are unable to truly connect with each other.

The scene is first shot from a low angle to frame the bottom half of the swaying bodies and then cycles between long shots of the group to close-ups of hips gyrating and bodies embracing in the hope of feeling what they once felt. As Juan's more trustworthy guide, Alma, explains, "Sex here is pure imagination." Accordingly, the dancers move in mysterious ways meant to emulate a residue of frenetic bodily passion. The kinetic dissonance comes through their odd utilization of the distal edges of their bodies without engaging their core, seemingly pulled by urges they don't control and can never fully satisfy.[10] Their anatomy doesn't flow or seem to fit—as if they are dancing in a body not their own, or none altogether. In this way *The Dead* provocatively emphasizes the fundamental Mormon doctrine of embodiment as a blessing, by imagining its devastating loss. For, in Latter-day Saint belief, the body not only enables agency but also, thankfully, constrains the limitless mind.[11] This scene encapsulates the double-edged sword of sexuality as both divine urge and demonic drive full of deceptions. As it happens in so many later Mormon films, dancing is a precarious play with expression and control (more on this later).

The Dead came in the wake of the New Spanish Cinema movement, even within the long tradition of promoting the ideals of nation, family, and religion with strict censorship. This cultural promotion of cinema also marked the end of Francisco Franco's dictatorship, at which point censorship of explicit sexuality in films and movie posters would give way to repressed desires and erotic cinema would experience a flashpoint with lasting effects.[12] Although censorship did not officially end until 1977, an emergent interest in horror made up more than a third of all Spain's domestic films from 1968 to 1975.[13] Audiences found delight in their own versions of gothic figures and

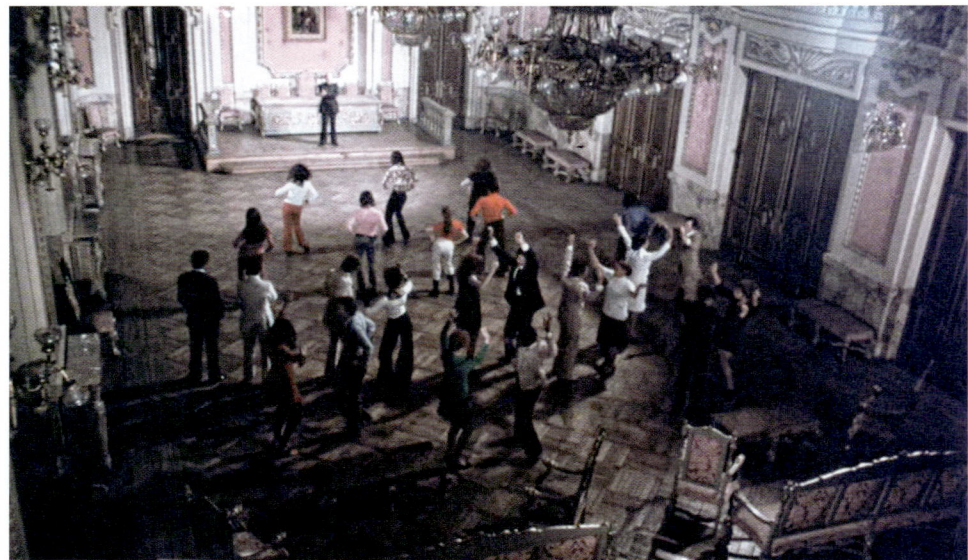

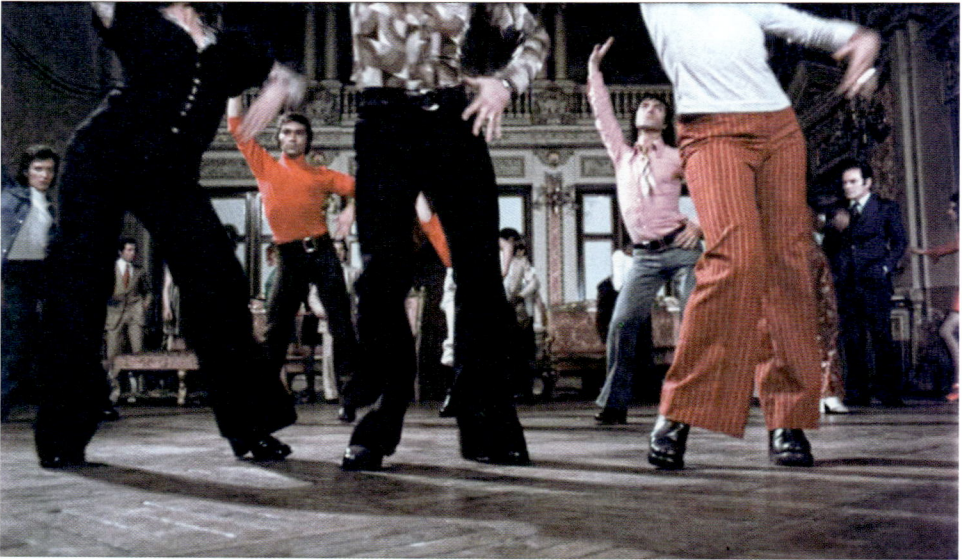

Fig. 18.2 *a* and *b*. The spirits of the dead dance at Korijor's command in *The Dead, the Devil, and the Flesh*, dir. Jose Maria Oliveira, 1974. Courtesy of Brigham Young University.

B-movie horror.[14] Spanish critics connected this fascination with their unique national context. They were convinced "the (dis)pleasures associated with the commercial exploitation of eroticism and sexuality in horror films were symptomatic of the repressive socio-cultural situation in Spain."[15] As Franco's repressive control started to wane, latent sexual tensions under the celluloid skin of cinema began to manifest themselves in increasingly explicit and exploitative images.

Oliveira's films toyed with these emerging demands for horror and sexuality onscreen; however, his interweaving of Mormon doctrine made his work conjure more than pure "manifestations of Spanish national identity" and diverge from the general exploitation and more graphic horror of the period.[16] His work should also be understood against the backdrop of the less sensational religious cinema that continued to fill a niche market.[17] The result was a hybrid religious fantasy film boldly grounded in Latter-day Saint doctrine but squarely set within a local Spanish and Catholic context.

While praising the hallucinatory tone of the film, one reviewer felt this was at odds with its religious sincerity, writing, "From the images, from the dialogue—both somewhat pretentious—we discover that the producer believes wholeheartedly in what he is doing."[18] Oliveira's use of horror conventions was less about getting people into the theater and more about exploring and sharing Latter-day Saints' imaginative theology of embodiment and the coterminous world of the spirits. For *The Dead* was from the outset a "film that could easily irritate, enthuse with difficulty but never leave audiences indifferent," as the same critic noted.[19] This heady approach to communion between the dead and the living marks Oliveira's attempt to treat embodiment and sexuality without visual sensationalism. Instead, Oliveira displaced the themes in symbolism or visual suggestion. His method deviated from the trend in both religious and horror cinema in Spain at the time. Where contemporary audiences connected Oliveira's cinematic foray into the dead to Emeric Pressburger and Michael Powell's 1946 film *A Matter of Life and Death* and André Delvaux's *Rendez-vous à Bray* (*Appointment in Bray*, 1971)—no doubt because of the dream-like tone—the film had equal affinities with Bergman's *Seventh Seal* and Antonioni's work on alienation. These existential themes helped universalize the film's Mormon infusions.

At one point in the film, Juan answers a ringing telephone in the spirit realm. On the other end, Korijor summons Juan, informing him he has been "invited to the theater." Just then the camera zooms in on Jusepe de Ribera's 1631 painting *Magdalena Ventura with Her Husband and Son,* of a bearded woman nursing her child. This sly editing choice underscores the circus-like preoccupation with appearances and bodily signifiers at Korijor's disposal, not by reaching back into Utah Mormon customs or motifs but rather by citing a canonical Spanish painting. In Mormon life as in film, surface matters. Bodies and appearances can lead to ultimate happiness or damning self-deception.

Korijor has much to teach Juan. And like in *The Exorcist* (1973), a film that left a great impression on Oliveira during his work on *The Dead,* the dark side speaks in twisted half-truths.[20] "Watch," Korijor yells at Juan with impatience as a curtain rises on the stage before them to reveal a solitary spinning wheel. Placing Juan in a theater viewing and discussing representation on a screen, like Oliveira's film itself, implies enlightenment through engaging with art. "The wheel represents man. He has always existed and has no end. That is why he is free forever in life and in death," continues Korijor, now directly into Juan's ear. But Juan counters by emphasizing the need for order and the desire to improve as important additions to Korijor's oversimplification that would otherwise turn eternal existence into futile spinning of wheels: hollow eternal recurrence instead of steps toward becoming like God.

All the theatricality and discussion focus on the fundamental role of the body in Latter-day Saint notions of progress—moving beyond the spinning wheel. Agency with a body enables an individual to grow and develop through godly actions, including sexual intercourse. Sexual purity in Mormonism is ultimately not abstinence.[21] But without a body, sex becomes only an exercise in imagination. This helps foreground the productive displacement of sex into spirit dancing. As it happens in so many Mormon films, dancing—letting go through bodily movements—is both losing oneself and potentially finding oneself for the first time.

TRAUMA AND THE BODY

While the body enables progress, it can also facilitate devastating deeds, as seen in Lino Brocka's film *Weighed but Found Wanting*, which also premiered in 1974, some seven thousand miles away in Manila. Brocka's film equally visualizes the power of the body, but here within the localized tyranny of gender norms, appearances, and tradition in a small town in the Philippines. The film follows Junior, a teenage boy who comes to realize his father is a serial adulterer and is responsible for turning one of his former lovers, Kuala, into the "village idiot." Kuala's current mental state is revealed to have been the result of the trauma from an unwanted abortion Junior's father had forced her to undergo. Junior only realizes this later in the film after befriending Kuala and the kind leprous outcast Berto, who has taken Kuala under his care.

Part of the film was inspired by Brocka's missionary experiences in Hawaii. As a young college student, Brocka met with missionaries and soon joined the Church of Jesus Christ of Latter-day Saints. He decided to become a missionary himself in 1965, and his time serving in the Hawaiian Islands proved life-changing, especially his service with the leper colony of Kalaupapa on Molokai.[22] In interviews, Brocka would light up when he discussed how he taught the locals to dance and put on plays, and how much he cherished his time spent providing care to them. In fact, as Brocka put it, his mission years "turned out to be the most wonderful two years of my life. It changed everything about me, working with those lepers."[23] Although this time was transformative for Brocka, the openly gay filmmaker felt increasingly at odds with the organization and rigidity of the Latter-day Saint church. Even as he distanced himself from the institution after coming out, Brocka's experiences with Mormonism continued to influence his work.

In his attempt to find goodness among suffering, Brocka patterned *Weighed but Found Wanting*'s compassionate character Berto after one of the residents of the Kalaupapa colony.[24] Witnessing Berto's unexpected love throughout the film teaches Junior and the viewer to look beyond the unsettling suffering written on Berto's and Kuala's socially undesirable bodies. Junior learns to appreciate Berto and Kuala, despite the village's mocking and ostracizing. But leaving the story at that would be too easy on the viewer. For the narrative to be transformative, emotional and physical pain had to be viscerally felt.

The opening scene is harsh and should come with its own trigger warning. The scene shows Cesar, Junior's father, restraining Kuala's struggling body as an elderly woman performs an abortion. Filmed in high contrast, fully desaturated in an almost sepia tone, the scene is formally arresting, signifying an earlier temporality and severe trauma. After Kuala buries the fetus under a large barren tree in the fields, the audio rises to an almost shrill cacophony of moans, shrieks, and odd noises, reflecting a shattered and incoherent inner monologue. The camera shows Kuala staring at the unbearably bright sun in rapid close-ups from different angles, until she walks right into the camera. The editing and cinematography amplify the power of bodies, both onscreen and in the theater. Accordingly, the film invites the viewer to vicariously feel some of this pain through disruptive formal techniques alongside painstaking imagery, as it attempts to transfer the discord to the viewer's body. This is hard to watch and uncomfortable to listen to.

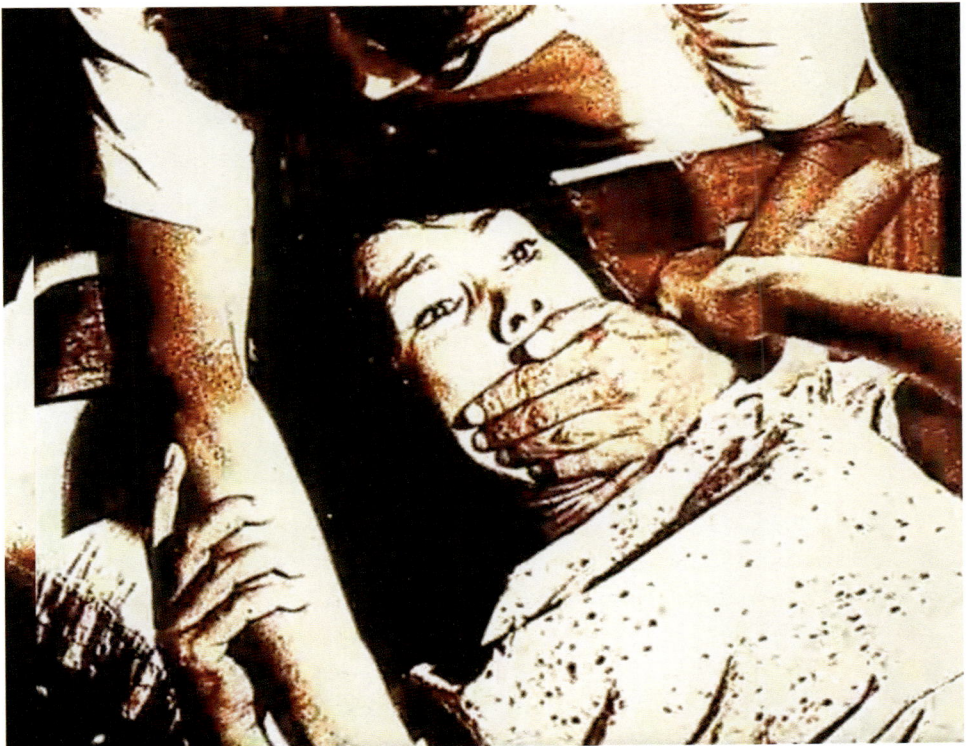

Fig. 18.3a *a.* Kuala is violently restrained in *Weighed but Found Wanting*, dir. Lino Brocka, 1974, Unico Entertainment.

There is not even enough time to fully register the visuals or decipher the audio, as chaotic stimuli permeate the scene.

The cut to the present in the next scene, fully colored and in the town, provides an abrupt low-angle shot of a large red truck just as it drives *over* the camera. As if to perfectly capture an experience of being formally aligned with Kuala's suffering, the audience is run over, or "hit by a truck." In fact, as Kuala in the background comes into focus, another red truck streams across the screen and displaces her. Visually, she too is run over. This quick sequence is only a pithy visual metaphor for Kuala's intense suffering, witnessed by the viewer, but it underscores what the film is achieving. By focusing on bodily experience, the film seeps out beyond the screen and into the viewer—to get under their skin. The audience is uncomfortably put into her experience and traumatized to better empathize with Kuala, as Berto will do later.

Instead of comforting a passive audience or slipping into familiar sentimentality, as in more popular films from Latter-day Saint creators, the film realizes the way film touches audiences.[25] As Vivian Sobchack describes this affective power of cinema, "We are in some carnal modality able to touch and be touched by the substance and texture

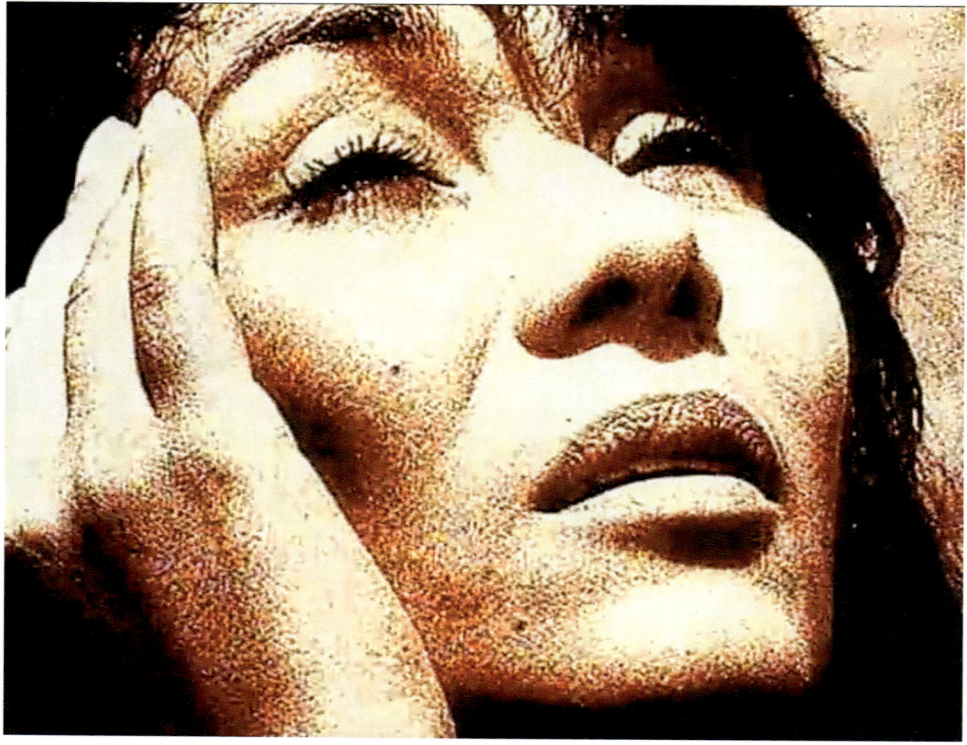

Fig. 18.3b *b*. A traumatized Kuala stares at the sun in *Weighed but Found Wanting*, dir. Lino Brocka, 1974, Unico Entertainment. All rights reserved.

of images; to feel a visual atmosphere envelop us; to take flight in kinetic exhilaration and freedom even as we are relatively bound to our theater seats."[26] If bodies are truly central to Latter-day Saint theology, the bodies of audiences should matter *as matter* just as much as the bodies, choices, and movements of the characters onscreen.

The unfair treatment of gendered bodies bears weight in both Oliveira's film and Brocka's. Both directors denounce with meticulous detail the choices of characters in committed heterosexual relationships to cheat on their loved ones. While adultery is a major theme in both films, *Weighed* (unlike *The Dead*) demonstrates that it is clearly the men in the town who perpetrate so much of the sexual oppression and violence. Certain bodies exercise abusive power over other bodies, as the opening scene foregrounds. Where women in Oliveira's film had either no redeeming qualities or no dimensions to their character except to seduce men, in Brocka's film they are clearly the survivors that bear the traumatic scars of un-Christian conduct on their bodies and psyches at the hands of unscrupulous men.

In *Weighed,* no one understands or appreciates Kuala's trauma, except perhaps the audience, by virtue of that vicious opening scene of vicariously feeling her suffering on the level of form. But at a key turning point in the film, Berto uses a baby rattle to attract Kuala. She smiles and edges closer to him as he repeatedly shakes the toy. Shot with a shaky handheld camera from both POVs, the scene is as haunting as it is hopeful. Ultimately Berto combats stereotypical narratives of male lust in a demonstration of nurturing love as he brings Kuala into his care through the very toy that might remind her of shattered hopes. Importantly, the scene dissolves over the landscape and rising sun into the following scene, where children take Kuala's rattle and tease her, while Junior's father, Cesar, looks on and warns his son to stay away from Kuala. In direct contrast to Cesar, Berto is the only one who cares for, feeds, and shelters Kuala. "No one will make fun of you here," he assures her. Berto provides an alternative fulfillment of the knight in shining armor cliché, and it is initially unclear how selfless his intentions really are.

After living with Berto for several months, Kuala becomes pregnant. Once the meddling women's Christian society gets wind of this, they take her from Berto and keep watch over her in the church. But in a heart-wrenching final scene, both Kuala and Berto die while trying to convince a doctor to deliver the baby—Berto from a trigger-happy cop and Kuala from blood loss during the birth—offering a sobering take on the biases embedded in law enforcement and healthcare. Fortunately, their baby survives. Junior carries the newborn infant—a substitute for Kuala's violent loss in the opening of the film—across the cemetery and holds it in front of the stunned and hopefully enlightened townspeople. Like the many sunrises and sunsets throughout the film, martyred and marginalized bodies might provide the love necessary to enact rebirth among vicious cycles of injustice.

It was precisely its portrayals of "the 'other' in Filipino society, such as the leper and village idiot," that made the film groundbreaking, according to film scholar Arminda Santiago.[27] The social outcasts that cinema generally rendered invisible were the heart of Brocka's films. In fact, it was during his time as a Latter-day Saint missionary, contemplating the "contradictions of life"—especially the "complaints of his able-bodied friends," which he compared "with the positive attitudes of the lepers"—that Brocka further developed his empathy for the downtrodden that would shape his cinematic style.[28] To work through gender-based violence and oppression against people with disabilities, Brocka first had turned to writing and directing plays within the colony, resulting in later commentary in the form of film.

In equal measure with his empathy, Brocka's critical consciousness and resistance to authority were also cultivated during his missionary experiences, as he felt caught between a hierarchical and rigid structure and the extreme suffering and isolation of those he served.[29] These hard lessons forged Brocka and his larger portfolio. In his own estimation, it was his relentless questioning that ruffled feathers and pushed Brocka to distance himself from the church. That kind of inquiry could be contagious. As Brocka reported, "I asked a lot of questions and they didn't like that because some of the missionaries started asking questions also, and it was felt that I was trying to provoke a mutiny and dissatisfaction."[30] His probing and "rebellious" cinema, however, might still inspire a type of ethical, even moral questioning—one that seeks truth without drowning in only cynicism. It might teach the piety of taking on the perspective of others. It's not enough, for Brocka, to simply show poverty or injustice. Rather than remaining comfortable in dominant perspectives, film needs to change people and investigate why things are the way they are through a diversity of viewpoints and experiences.

Because of his "third world" outside position, Brocka was able to not only sidestep but actually resist the "martial law" of Hollywood productions of the time, which he felt held to the maxim "If you want to entertain people, don't disturb them."[31] Brocka rejected this Hollywood mentality, which only glorified the winners and always provided a manufactured happy ending, though some Latter-day Saint audiences expected and preferred it. For Brocka, this kind of Hollywood filmmaking didn't translate to the everyday reality of life in the Philippines. Deep within his bones he was convinced the "role of cinema" was "not just to reflect but to confront you with certain realities."[32] Although this kind of confrontation could be uncomfortable, it meant Brocka made movies that had something to say.

Weighed but Found Wanting has been described as "Brocka's social epic, a tapestry of caricatures lampooning small-town life that at the same time reserves its pity for the community's outcasts."[33] His redemptive lens not only offered a new perspective but also took seriously and kindly the subjectivity of outcasts, putting the viewer in their shoes and compassionately narrating their plight. The unique ways films such as his frame and narrate bodily suffering might serve to render a positive theology of embodiment visible and an experience for the audience. Like Oliveira, and Lasse-Henriksen before him, Brocka offered a cinema that investigated sex, death, and embodiment in form and content, rather than flee from these fleshy knots.

MEDIA AMBIVALENCE

Presumably unaware of these earlier diverse perspectives, twenty-first-century Mormon cinema more readily bears the charged attitude toward media inculcated in Latter-day Saint youth throughout the 1980s and 1990s. While embodiment continues as a red thread, many of these films directly and visually engage the fraught interaction with music, dance, images, and books grappled with in discourse of the preceding decades. Even though media have helped galvanize understanding of Latter-day Saint theology, they can be unpredictable and require strict policing.[34] Whether threatening or liberating, media are channels of connection. This means that media onscreen can evoke suspicion precisely because they can provide characters with new opportunities to at once express themselves and connect with others.

For Latter-day Saint audiences, media are metafilmic portals to other worlds, or even *the* world. Because of this, Saints are perhaps torn in their artistic expressions. As Terryl Givens writes, "A field of tension seems a particularly apt way to characterize Mormon thought," which in turn shapes cultural expressions.[35] In cinema especially, the paradox of a body-positive theology and the aversion toward displaying an "immodest" body onscreen to arouse or shock the body of the audience becomes an unspoken tension and aesthetic regime. Generally, laughing or crying have been the only acceptable modes of corporeal expression in Mormon film.[36] Thus, a thrilling angst emanates from the framing of media consumption as a transitional medium in Mormon cinema—as a conduit to or even proxy/heuristic for alternative bodily experiences.

With this kind of cultural specificity, it is perhaps understandable that so few Latter-day Saint titles of note transcended their provincial market in Utah during the 1980s and 1990s. To be clear, Latter-day Saints produced many films and videos, but they were often documentaries or based on church history, as these were safer genres.[37] Idiosyncratic or fictional feature films were much rarer. During this time church leaders and manuals also condemned media content with new urgency, as VHS and cable TV expanded viewing options in the home.

In 1986 church president Ezra Taft Benson taught, "Consider carefully the words of the prophet Alma to his errant son, Corianton, 'Forsake your sins, and go no more after the lusts of your eyes.'" For his own day, Benson interpreted this phrase to mean "movies, television programs, and video recordings that are both suggestive and lewd. Magazines and books that are obscene and pornographic." Against these media influences, Benson counseled the youth specifically "not to pollute your minds with such degrading matter, for the mind through which this filth passes is never the same afterward. Don't see R-rated movies or vulgar videos or participate in any entertainment that is immoral, suggestive, or pornographic."[38] Whatever Benson might have meant about irredeemable minds and damaged goods was often reduced to outsourcing media literacy and consumer decisions as a ban on R-rated movies in the United States.

Even though some have recently sought to reevaluate this counsel and parse the intent and audience, many Latter-day Saints found comfort in the simplicity of following the concrete counsel. As church leader Elder Cree L. Kofford taught in 1998, "What difference does it make why it is rated R? The fact is, a prophet of God has said not to go to R-rated movies. That ought to be enough."[39] Other leaders sought to clarify or expand on the directive. As president of the Seventy, Elder J. Richard Clarke taught, "Any film, television show, music, or printed material unfit for youth is also unfit for parents. Those who rationalize acceptance of immoral material on grounds of maturity or sophistication are deceived."[40] Elder H. Burke Peterson acknowledged, "I know it is hard counsel we give when we say movies that are R-rated, and many with PG-13 ratings, are produced by satanic influences." But he also stood firm in his conviction that Latter-day Saint "standards should not be dictated by the rating system. I repeat, because of what they really represent, these types of movies, music, tapes, etc. serve the purposes of the author of all darkness."[41]

This sense of media's pernicious power was captured in the "Mormon ad" full-page graphics geared toward youth and included in church magazines. One such ad from 1992, titled "You Are What You Watch," visualized the logic of media with direct and permanent effects. The image shows a TV-headed youth somewhere between Mike Teavee of Willy Wonka fare and the Garbage Pail Kid Tee-Vee Stevie (1985). But where Mike Teavee entered the technology in the book (1964) and film (1971), Tee-Vee Stevie sits with—just like the Mormon ad—a TV set for a head and is surrounded by six CRT televisions with a camera pointed at him. The message to Mormon youth was clear and almost horrific: you become what you consume.

Media consumption was also pictured as a fatal cliff, or "living on the edge," in a 1999 Mormon ad with a young girl watching television. And another Mormon ad from 2002 shows an ice cream cone with whipped cream, a cherry on top, and a cockroach embedded within the top scoop. "It's Great Except for . . . except for the bad parts," reads the text. As the church's *For the Strength of Youth* pamphlets and articles put it in 1990, "If you have any question about whether a particular movie, book, or other form of entertainment is appropriate, don't see it, don't read it, don't participate."[42] The head of the church's audio-video division clarified, "Some will argue that a particular movie is rated PG-13 or R because of violence or 'just one scene,' but that otherwise the film is excellent. What that means is that some excellent movies should not be viewed by those who are striving to live the standards outlined in *For the Strength of Youth*."[43] The difficult tension between safe and familiar entertainment, on the one hand, and challenging (at times uncomfortable, even disturbing) art, on the other, has persisted as a stumbling block for Latter-day Saint expression and criticism. The emphasis on safe entertainment has certainly shaped film production around the turn of the twenty-first century. Against this backdrop, a charged ambivalence around myriad types of media in Mormon film seems not only understandable but also therapeutic. Film doubles as a

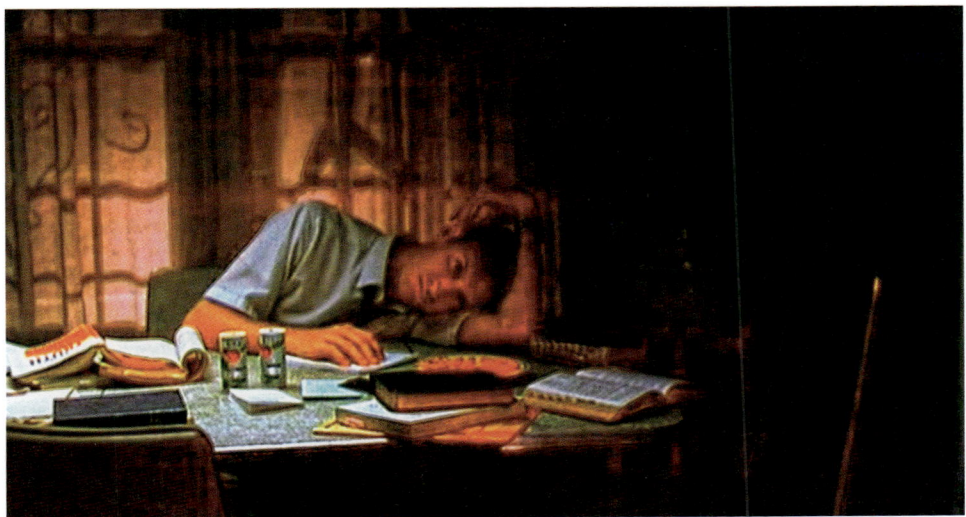

Fig. 18.4a *a.* Elder Kinegar wallows over "anti-Mormon" literature in *God's Army*, dir. Richard Dutcher, 2000, Zion Films.

cultural coping mechanism, an experiential working-through of the power and appeal of media.

In *God's Army*, for instance, anti-Mormon literature clearly denotes dangerous media to be avoided. It might have opened the character Elder Kinegar's mind or challenged his views, but it ultimately leads to his loss of faith, depression, and abandonment of his mission. Yet, in a humorous tone, Jared and Jerusha Hess's Sundance darling *Napoleon Dynamite* (2004) reveals the film's and the protagonist's turning point, when Napoleon finds his confidence after discovering a VHS tape of *D-qwon's Dance Grooves* on a disorganized shelf at a secondhand store. By watching the video of a Black man teaching viewers how to dance, Napoleon finds entrance into another world and provides the comedic release for the audience when he unabashedly rocks out on stage to Jamiroquai's "Canned Heat" from another tape, a cassette handed to him by his brother Kip's online (now present and very real) Black girlfriend Lafawndah. It is precisely Kip's online "chatting with babes" and now Napoleon's music that provide connection out of the insular racial culture of Idaho to the wider world. Napoleon applies the moves from D-qwon to help his friend Pedro win the election for student body president. Here, unlike the dangerous media and seductive dancing of other films, Napoleon's interaction with tapes is a positive metafilmic force—the tapes here serve as a metaphor for cinema itself, and thus the film is in some measure a film about the power of film. Narratively, the tapes offer our protagonist (and the audience) entrance into another perspective, understanding, and experience.

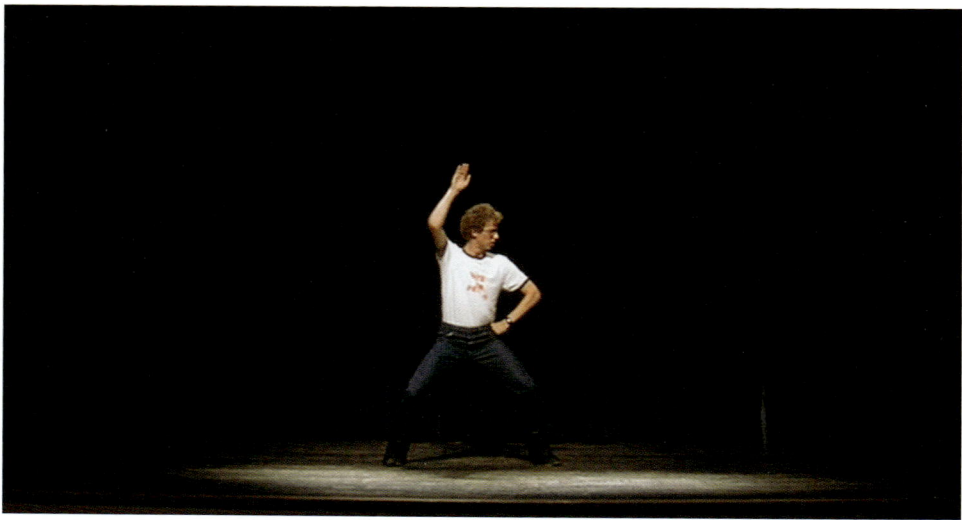

Fig. 18.4b *b*. Napoleon breaks into dance in *Napoleon Dynamite*, dir. Jared Hess, 2004, Twentieth Century Fox Home Entertainment.

But media like this that open up another world would often be framed with a certain hesitation, perhaps by warily suggesting their pitfalls. These portrayals fall somewhere between the cautionary warning of *God's Army* and the playful abandon of *Napoleon Dynamite*. For instance, dancing to an electro-synth version of the hymn "Hie to Kolob," in Trent Harris's *Plan 10 from Outer Space* (1995), is full of synchronized Masonic gestures, as entrance into a secret alien plot and reversal of gendered power in Mormon Salt Lake City. And in Jerusha Hess's *Austenland* (2013), the entire narrative details a woman too enveloped by the world of Jane Austen novels and movies, which shape and distort her views, ultimately leading her away from immediate reality rather than toward a more profound engagement with it.

Nandan Rao's film *Hawaiian Punch* (2013) weaves this ambivalence around media right into the flow of the film. The film follows a group of young men in Laie, Hawaii, who have recently returned from full-time missionary service and are working through their post-mission crises of faith, even as they play, swim, date, and converse. At several points, the film allows entire songs to play as diegetic sound, forcing the viewer to experience the music in real time with the characters. Sitting alone on a couch, Nick, one of the main characters, plays a French rap song with the lyrics "We just go out to forget all our problems . . . so we just dance. So we just dance." But later, in a particularly Latter-day Saint engagement with media, a static close-up shows him sitting at his laptop rapping aloud to Notorious B.I.G. but omitting the profanities as he awkwardly tries to follow along. This song streaming from his computer represents a world not his own, both appealing and punctuated words with unmentionables by a Mormon mouth.

In the follow-up short film *Greek Yogurt* (2017) Nandan returns to his mission area in Athens, Greece, but is alone and disconnected, scrolling through social media by day and losing himself in music by night. Only in the club does the film's editing fragment enough to sync up with Rao's erratic dance movements, just enough to defer his apparent listlessness.

Media appear as dangerous distractions, because they often provoke bodily reactions, such as arousal, anger, or abandonment of inhibitions, missions, and norms. But they might also open up portals and expand consciousness. If users are open to their challenges and effects, media might even open their hearts and minds to help make powerful connections between self and community. As Latter-day Saint literary critic Wayne Booth suggested, media (and for him books specifically) are like different types of friends, or "the company we keep." But to find mutual benefit from these interactions, one must first "surrender" to "discover their power."[44]

That power of surrendering can be thrilling and at times uncomfortable as it leads to foreign experiences and new understanding. Encounters with media can confront audiences to catalyze deep understanding, much as photographs do in first-time director Tshoper Kabambi's film *Heart of Africa* (2020). The film recounts the true story of a revolutionary soldier turned Latter-day Saint missionary in the Congo. While the conventional love story between Elder Ngandu and a local Latter-day Saint woman he meets shortly before his baptism frames his motivation and the reward of conversion, there are many unique and sophisticated elements to *Heart of Africa*'s version of the Mormon missionary genre.

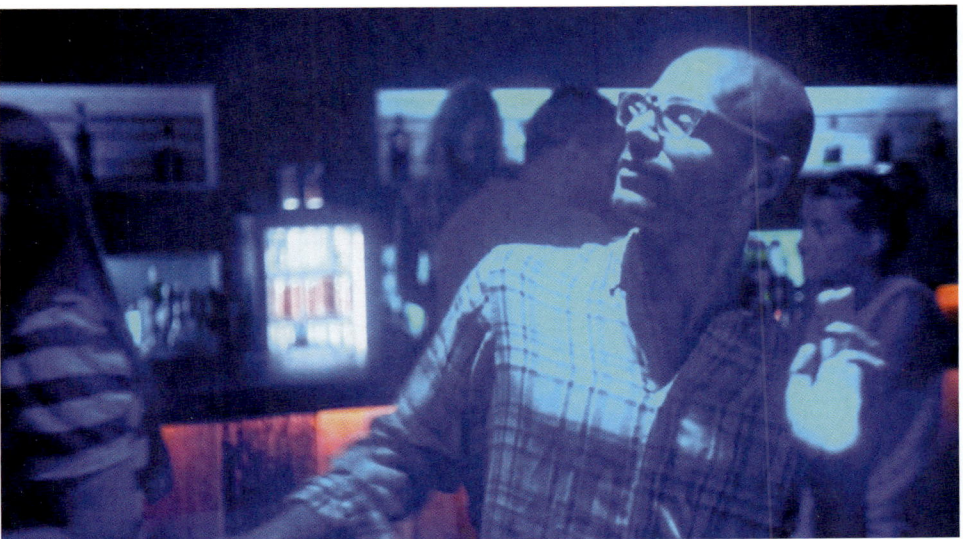

Fig. 18.5 Nandan goes clubbing in *Greek Yogurt*, dir. Tor Kristian Anestad and Nicholas Boissonneault, 2016, Newhard Entertainment.

At a crucial turning point in the narrative, an exterior long shot of an elevated structure above the water cuts to an interior close-up of a photograph showing dismembered Black bodies, forcing the viewer into what feels like a darkroom with only red light, as if the photos have just been freshly developed. The proximity of the shot puts the viewer right up against the harsh reality of the images. "They were all murdered," states Mwabila, the revolutionary leader who took Ngandu in after his parents were killed. "The white man ate their babies," Mwabila adds. But these are different white people in the present, Ngandu counters. Just then Ngandu catches a glimpse of another photograph and remarks how the mustached figure resembles his white companion from Idaho.

The use of photography and instructional dialogue layers past violence and racism of Belgian colonialism and enslavement over current white presence, highlighting another power of media. These photographs serve as media witnesses. Rather than please, these media provoke and prod in uncomfortable ways. Instead of showing bodies to be sensual, they are uncomfortably indicting. They are reminders of a brutal racist past, as Elder Ngandu is told, and bring the protagonist and the audience into the thorny issue of Mormon identity and history within this particular context.

Mwabila's history lesson suggests the complicity of the hierarchical and largely white missionary program Ngandu has joined, which is headquartered in Utah. Mwabila wants Ngandu to recognize how this past informs the present. Waving his stick, he speaks directly at the camera, removing the fourth wall and implicating the viewer. "You are our hope," he says, reminding Ngandu of his potential among his tribe. Torn between two worlds, Ngandu must acknowledge the violence of the past depicted in the photographs,

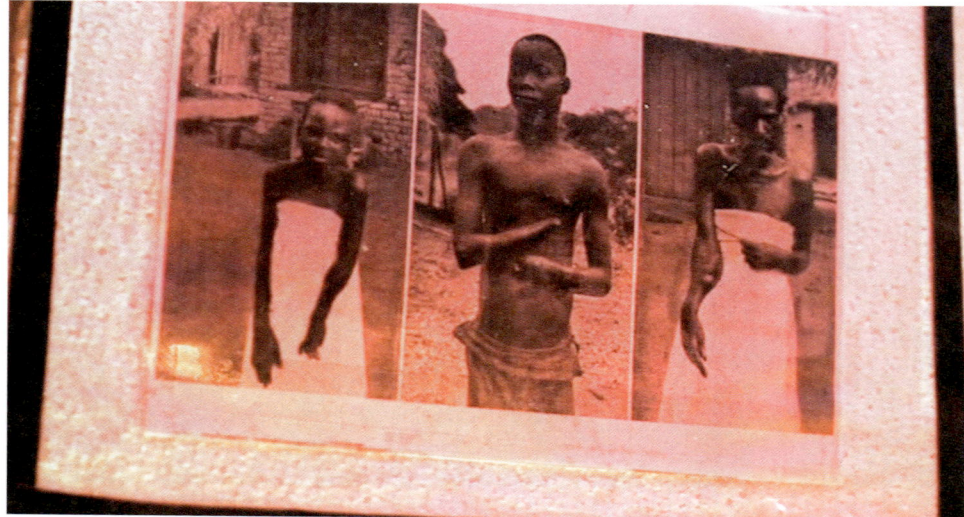

Fig. 18.6 POV of Elder Ngandu confronting colonial history through photos in *Heart of Africa*, dir. Tshoper Kabambi, 2020, Excel. All rights reserved.

while also fighting for his future among the Mormons. That ambivalence—that very much "in the world, but not *of* the world," or even community—permeates Ngandu's and the general Latter-day Saint psyche.

A similar tension suffuses Rebecca Thomas's debut feature, *Electrick Children* (2012), which captures the Mormon cinematic body as a site of bridled passion in perhaps the most visually concise and narratively provocative way. The film is initially set in an oppressive version of Utah, as if to parallel how the film itself breaks free from the environment and perspective of Utah-based Mormon cinema that came just before. Within the narrative of *Electrick Children,* pop music from mainstream American culture animates the body of the film's protagonist, Rachel, and even provokes her to escape her insular fundamentalist Mormon family.

After discovering a cassette tape and player, the fifteen-year-old Rachel, played by Julia Garner, listens at first with fearful curiosity until she sways in step with the beat, mesmerized by the tinny 1980s pop song "Hanging on the Telephone" emanating from the plastic player held against her ear. A close-up from behind slowly moves up Rachel's body from boots to bare legs, exposed by a borrowed nightgown that is too small for her frame, making her appear extra childlike. But this is a subversion of the classic tilt shot or body pan that so often sexualizes the female body in cinema.[45]

The film's focus on Rachel's emotions and perspective supersedes any potentially objectifying fragmentation of her body. Instead of making the female body into a spectacle, this technique enables Rachel's body to advance and determine the narrative. Just as the camera reaches her knees, the diegetic audio of the song transitions into full stereo sound with non-diegetic quality. Even as the camera brings the audience closer

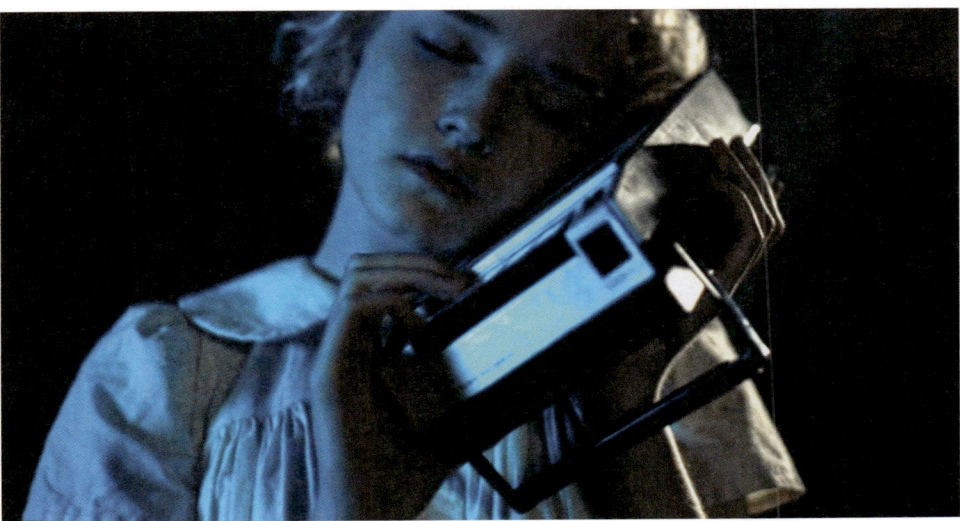

Fig. 18.7a *a.* Rachel listens to forbidden pop music in *Electrick Children,* dir. Rebecca Thomas, 2012, Revolver Entertainment.

and focuses on Rachel's legs beginning to dance, this technique functions as a sonic invitation into her headspace and experience. The viewer is no longer a distant observer. Their ears adjust. They now hear as she hears and feel her feeling the beat.

After this transformative experience, Rachel comes to the realization that she is pregnant, and she believes the music is the cause. As she puts it, the tape deck is "God's vessel." This scene beautifully heightens and refracts a Mormon ambivalence toward the power of media and weaves the entire plot around it. Cutting to close-ups of Rachel's body might not just signify a loss of innocence or a violent objectification of her body, as Linda Nochlin has described of modern representationalism. As Nochlin acknowledges, the impulse of cropping is also a technique to pulverize and move beyond the past and "its repressive traditions."[46] Instead of cropping to sexualize the female body, Thomas edits it and focuses it in parts to invite the viewer into Rachel's interiority as she unexpectedly changes. As Rachel dances into a new identity, the film cuts up her body with close-ups to signal a personal awakening. The viewer joins Rachel as she dances herself into a new perspective.

In many films, dancing provides a cinematic site for the body of the viewer to feel the movement of film and characters onscreen. Dancing in Mormon cinema, then, offers a particularly expressive mode of articulating the borders of expression and containment. Of course, northern Utah was the site of the film *Footloose* (1984), where a Christian minister had outlawed dancing. And as Trey Parker and Matt Stone have said in interviews regarding the inception of the musical *Book of Mormon,* Mormons seem like they could break into song and dance at any moment. In the spirit of Brigham Young's 1847 revelatory admonition "If thou art merry, praise the Lord with singing, with music, with dancing, and with a prayer of praise and thanksgiving," the Saints are even dancing in the opening scene of the Hollywood film *Brigham Young* (1940).[47]

Similar to their stance toward media, Latter-day Saints perceive dancing as full of positive opportunities. Unlike Shakers, who wanted to essentially dance the body away to provoke visions or possessions by Native spirits, dancing for Latter-day Saints could reflect the ultimate and day-to-day entanglement of body and spirit.[48] The earliest Mormon inclinations were largely free and expressive, reflecting the "trend in American social dancing towards socializing and recreation and away from etiquette and formality."[49] Dancing might even express the glory of embodiment beyond its articulation in language. On this model, the disembodied dance of spirits in *The Dead, the Devil, and the Flesh* preaches gratitude for the body. The dancing of Napoleon Dynamite brings laughter as a joyful social act of unrestrained abandon and selflessness. Nandan Rao's fractured dancing in *Greek Yogurt* reflects his own aimless and lonely wandering. But Rachel's dance brings a media interaction onscreen into the realm of the definitive Mormon mediation of childbirth. Dance here is perhaps a dance with the Lord, but it is also a "(pro)creative" dance with destiny.

Leading up to Rachel's musical moment, her mother recounts a bedtime story to Rachel and her siblings of how she "found" her daughter. The mother narrates the

Disney fairytale opening, "Once upon a time there was a princess," but Rachel cuts her off and convinces her to tell them a *real* story, specifically "the one about the red Mustang." Shifting from the fantasy world to lived memory, the mother makes each child swear to never repeat the "top secret" story by making covenant gestures: peace signs with their hands while they bow their heads. Then she begins the story, again with "once upon a time," but immediately she shifts to nearby reality: "Just on the other side of the red bluffs of southern Utah, a princess . . ." Fairytale flourishes punctuate her memory. As a princess, she was, indeed, "looking" for Rachel. After the mother "felt something, that special kind of feeling that leads you in a specific direction," she says she found "it." A close-up of Rachel closing her eyes provides entry to her imagination, which cuts to legs, touching, and a red car—indexes to sexuality and the sensory world outside Rachel's experience. This is the narrative primer to Rachel's own impending sexual experience.

In Rachel's headspace, the film utilizes a totally different color palette, saturated and darkened with golden-hour sunset hues. Appropriately, the camera never settles on a single perspective as it wanders around, both framing the silhouetted figure of the mother and sneaking glances of a red Mustang and a tattooed man sitting in the driver's seat. The man and woman kiss. Images of the man's hand caressing the woman's thigh fill the frame. As Rachel continues to imagine her mother's encounter, the images blur in slow motion. This mode of filmmaking nicely shoehorns a fundamentalist Mormon minority culture into the language of cinema. Seemingly "slight and 'meaningless,'" the shots "call up volumes of images that are not or cannot be represented."[50] As she does throughout the entire film, Thomas exaggerates and explores Mormon embodiment in general, channeling it through Rachel's body and subjectivity.

Days later, when Rachel ends up pregnant, the mother blames herself, stating, "I shouldn't have been filling your head up with all those stories." For in Rachel's life, her mother was originally the only medium from outside, the only source of foreign stories and mental images before she encountered the cassette. This significant shift from mother's mouth to cassette as primary conduit of information transfer is also suggestive of Friedrich Kittler's contention that "hallucinatory sensuousness" historically shifted from oral/written culture to recording devices.[51] Stories might lead to mimicry and fantasy, but here Rachel is convinced something miraculous happened through "God's vessel, the tape deck." A magical medium has enlightened her, opened her eyes, and her interaction has created new life.

The film vacillates between trusting the words of the female character and entertaining more sinister but plausible explanations. It is possible that Rachel, much like the protagonist of Roberto Rossellini's controversial short film *The Miracle* (1948, released in 1950 in the United States), has perhaps been taken advantage of by her father or brother, but her faith and courage remain intact.[52] Rachel's faith in media also remains intact. Early on, Rachel prays in front of her prophet stepfather, thanking her heavenly father for tape recorders and telephones. Rachel even records her own narration on the tape, which plays as a kind of cassette-quality voice-over throughout the film.

The song that she believes caused her immaculate conception also later inspires Rachel to flee to "sin city" to find the singer. Her time in Las Vegas is the visualization of a sort of Alice in Wonderland entering the foreign and thrilling world of the cassette tape. Thomas again explores this scary liberation from the experience of Rachel's body from the heartfelt and powerful perspective of her optimistic, humble, yet naive protagonist. Rachel is perhaps a somewhat unreliable protagonist in her inexperience, but she is a sincere one, who not only hears pop music for the first time but also urinates, misses her period, and vomits onscreen. The unknown and even unknowable outcome that directly affects Rachel's body complicates "the intertwined pleasures of glances and dances" often associated with the female body.[53] Experienced solely through her body, perspective, and recorded testimony on tape, her performance constrains any possible interpretation of the film.

Like Oliveira and Brocka, Thomas blatantly eschews nudity or objectification, opting instead to signify sexual awakening through a curious young woman's perspective. Scenes depicting storytelling, imagination, and a scattered montage of embraces powerfully approximate the experience of catching mentions, images, or other small pieces of the enigmatic puzzle that is sexuality, especially for youth. Returning again to the—at once haunting and healing—scene of Rachel dancing with the cassette player, the film effectively ventures beyond what is known to Rachel. It portrays seeing outside oneself to break free from parochialism and traditions that might hold one back. In fact, the tape becomes a powerful vessel, both as provoking awakening and as a material device

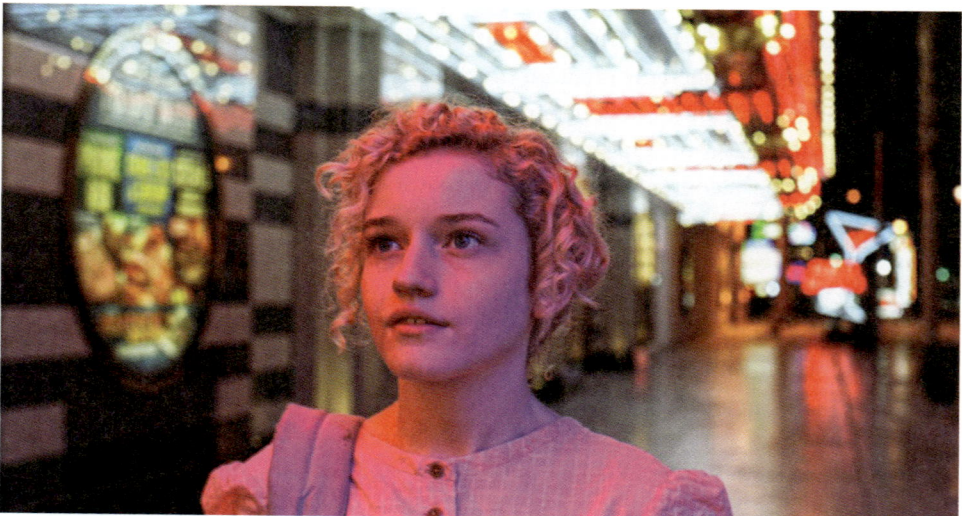

Fig. 18.7b *b.* Rachel flees to Las Vegas in *Electrick Children,* dir. Rebecca Thomas, 2012, Revolver Entertainment.

containing Rachel's testimony. The tape witnesses Rachel's own truth in medium-specific ways, but—as the film should do with its viewers—the tape also gets her out of her own world.

CONCLUSION

Media interactions on the Latter-day Saint screen crystallize the paradox of a body-positive (even sex-positive) theology and the aversion toward displaying too much of the character's body to arouse or shock the audience's body. This unspoken aesthetic regime shouldn't be too easily dismissed or oversimplified. For living in a body is the ultimate and fundamental media interaction both in the Latter-day Saint faith and in its cinema.

Based on this unique Latter-day Saint doctrine, dancing is perhaps a powerful visual means of targeting the immersive appeal and danger of cinema. Dancing from early church history on has been a way to cope with collective trauma, connect diverse cultures, and most importantly lean into the entanglement of the physical and the spiritual.[54] Expanding the cinematic interrogations of such bodily urges, expression, and thrills allows for diverse explorations of embodiment and media. Scenes of dancing and interacting with media onscreen also capture the effect and potential of cinema to open the viewer's mind and expand their worldview, literally through the perspective of the camera. Consuming these kinds of films should be a transformative dance with art.

Because cinema functions like media and pop culture in many of these scenes, it provides Latter-day Saints with opportunities to both express themselves and learn from and understand others. Films are connection points between audiences, creators, and characters. In line with Latter-day Saint thought, media are metafilmic portals to other worlds, or even *the* world. They are fodder for cautionary tales and the hope of progress. Film, figured as interactions with media onscreen, might offer Saints opportunities to uniquely realize the scriptural promise that finding oneself requires a certain letting go.[55] Losing oneself in experiences that come from others also entails temporary entanglement with other lives and perspectives to try on and feel out. Media are powerful sparks within Mormon cinema precisely because they mark the edges of the map, where one might venture to expand their subjectivity and—for better or worse—lose themselves.

NOTES

[1] Randy Astle. *Mormon Cinema: Origins to 1952* (New York: Mormon Arts Center, 2018). On the first feature-length film sponsored by the church, see Mason Kamana Allred, *Seeing Things: Technologies of Vision and the Making of Mormonism* (Chapel Hill: University of North Carolina Press, 2023), 103–132.

[2] Terryl Givens, *People of Paradox: A History of Mormon Culture* (New York: Oxford University Press, 2007), 265–283.

[3] See Linda Williams, "Film Bodies: Gender, Genre, and Excess," *Film Quarterly* 44 (Summer 1991): 2–13; Carol Clover, "Her Body Himself: Gender in the Slasher Film," *Representations*, Autumn 1987, 187–228.

4 Scott Parker, "Watching Bodies: An LDS Ethic of Spectatorship," in *Mormonism and the Movies*, ed. Chris Wei (Newburgh, IN: Common Consent Press, 2021), 178–179.

5 Often inspired by the philosophy of Maurice Merleau-Ponty, film phenomenology focuses on the affective, sensuous, and embodied experience of cinema. For prominent examples, see Vivian Sobchack, *Address of the Eye: A Phenomenology of Film Experience* (Princeton, NJ: Princeton University Press, 1992); Vivian Sobchack, *Carnal Thoughts: Embodiment and Moving Image Culture* (Berkeley: University of California Press, 2004); and Laura Marks, *The Skin of the Film: Intercultural Cinema, Embodiment, and the Senses* (Durham, NC: Duke University Press, 2000).

6 Jennifer Barker, *The Tactile Eye: Touch and the Cinematic Experience* (Berkeley: University of California Press, 2009), 19.

7 For an overview of the historical waves of Mormon cinema, see Randy Astle, "A History of Mormon Cinema," *BYU Studies Quarterly* 46, no. 2 (2007): 18–20.

8 For an overview of the ceremony's purpose and content, see Church of Jesus Christ of Latter-day Saints, "About the Temple Endowment," https://www.churchofjesuschrist.org/temples/what-is-temple-endowment?lang=eng.

9 I am grateful for Jonathan Martin's assistance in locating a copy of this film and getting me in touch with the director.

10 I am indebted to Roxanne Gray's helpful insights into this choreography.

11 John Durham Peters, "Reflections on Mormon Materialism." *Sunstone* 16 (March 1993): 17–21.

12 Antonio Lázaro-Reboll, "Sexual Horror Stories: The Eroticisation of Spanish Horror Film (1969–75)," in *Spanish Erotic Cinema,* ed. Santiago Fouz-Hernández (Edinburgh: Edinburgh University Press, 2018), 74–91.

13 Antonio Lázaro-Reboll, *Spanish Horror Film* (Edinburgh: Edinburgh University Press, 2012), 11.

14 Xavier Aldana Reyes, "Fantaterror: Gothic Monsters in the Golden Age of Spanish B-Movie Horror, 1968–80," in *B-Movie Gothic: International Perspectives*, edited by Justin D. Edwards and Johan Höglund (Edinburgh: Edinburgh University Press, 2018), 96.

15 Lázaro-Reboll, "Sexual Horror Stories," 76.

16 Nicholas Schlegel, *Sex, Sadism, Spain, and Cinema: The Spanish Horror Film* (Lanham, MD: Rowman & Littlefield, 2015), xv.

17 Jorge Perez, *Confessional Cinema: Religion, Film, and Modernity in Spain's Development Years, 1960–1975* (Toronto: University of Toronto Press, 2017), 32–37.

18 Review from local Madrid newspaper *Espectaculos*, [August?] 22, [1974]. In possession of Jose Maria Oliveira, translated by James Tueller.

19 Review from local Madrid newspaper *Espectaculos*, [August?] 22, [1974]. In possession of Jose Maria Oliveira, translated by James Tueller.

20 The director shared this in conversation with the author, October 15, 2020.

21 Samuel Morris Brown and Kate Holbrook, "Embodiment and Sexuality in Mormon Thought," in *The Oxford Handbook of Mormonism*, ed. Terryl L. Givens and Philip L. Barlow (New York: Oxford University Press, 2015), 296.

22 Mario Hernando, *Lino Brocka: The Artist and His Times* (Manila: Sentrong Pangkultura Ng Pilipinas, Cultural Center of the Philippines, 1993), 220.

23 Latika Padgaonkar and Rashmi Doraiswamy, eds., *Asian Film Journeys: Selections from Cinemaya* (New Delhi: Wisdom Tree, 2011), 323.

24 Jose B. Capino, *Martial Law Melodrama: Lino Brocka's Cinema Politics* (Berkeley: University of California Press, 2020), 7.

25 Astle, "A History of Mormon Cinema," 144.

26 Sobchack, *Carnal Thoughts,* 65.

27 Arminda V. Santiago, "The Struggle of the Oppressed: Lino Brocka and the New Cinema of the Philippines" (master's thesis, University of North Texas, 1993), 13.

28 Padgaonkar and Doraiswamy, eds., *Asian Film Journeys,* 323.

29 Santiago, "The Struggle of the Oppressed," 110.

30 Padgaonkar and Doraiswamy, eds., *Asian Film Journeys,* 323.

31 Hamid Naficy, "The Americanization and Indigenization of Lino Brocka Through Cinema," *Framework*, 1992, 146.

32 Naficy, "The Americanization and Indigenization," 146.

33 Noel Vera, "Lino Brocka: The Heart of Philippine Cinema," Center for Asian American Media, March 7, 2010, https://caamedia.org/blog/2010/03/07/essay-lino-brocka-the-heart-of-philippine-cinema/.

34 Gavin Feller, "Media as Compromise" (PhD diss., University of Iowa, 2017), 12–13; Mason Kamana Allred, "Developing the Dead: Spirit Photography, Mormonism, and Noise," *Journal of Mormon History* 48 (2022): 108.

35 Givens, *People of Paradox*, xiv.

36 David Walker, "Mormon Melodrama and the Syndication of Satire: From *Brigham Young* (1940) to *South Park* (2003)," *Journal of American Culture* 40, no. 3 (2017): 259–275; Airen Hall, "Melodrama on a Mission: Latter-day Saint Film and the Melodramatic Mode," *Journal of Religion and Film* 16 (October 2012): art. 5.

37 Randy Astle and Gideon O. Burton, "The Fourth Wave: The Mass Media Era (1974–2000)," *BYU Studies Quarterly* 46, no. 2 (2007): 114–121.

38 Ezra Taft Benson, "To the 'Youth of the Noble Birthright,'" *Ensign*, April 1986.

39 Cree L. Kofford, "Marriage in the Lord's Way," *Ensign*, July 1998, 16.

40 J. Richard Clarke, "To Honor the Priesthood," *Ensign*, May 1991, 42.

41 H. Burke Peterson, "Touch Not the Evil Gift, nor the Unclean Thing," *Ensign,* November 1993, 43.

42 *For Strength of Youth* (Salt Lake City: Church of Jesus Christ of Latter-day Saints, 1990), 12.

43 William A. Schaefermeyer, "Can I Watch a Movie?," *Ensign,* December 1991.

44 Wayne C. Booth, *The Company We Keep: An Ethics of Fiction* (Berkeley: University of California Press, 1988), 32.

45 For an example of Laura Mulvey's theory of the male gaze in cinematography, see Anjeana K. Hans, "'Schatten: Eine nächtliche Halluzination': Staging the Punishment for Women's Emancipation," *New German Critique* 120 (2013): 59. For wider application of these techniques in marketing, see Matthew P. McCallister and Lauren J. Carvalho, "Sexualized Branded Entertainment and the Male Consumer Gaze," *Triple C: Communism, Capitalism, and Critique* 12 (2014): 299–314.

46 Linda Nochlin, *Body in Pieces: The Fragment as a Metaphor of Modernity* (London: Thames and Hudson, 1994), 38, 1.

47 D&C 136:28.

48 Christopher Smith, *Dancing Revolution: Bodies, Space, and Sound in American Cultural History* (Urbana: University of Illinois Press, 2019), 70; Lindsay Stewart Cieslewicz, "Dance and Doctrine: Shaker and Mormon Dancing as a Manifestation of Doctrinal Views of the Physical Body" (master's thesis, Brigham Young University, 2000), 28–29.

49 Cieslewicz, "Dance and Doctrine," 65.

50 Laura Marks, *The Skin of Film: Intercultural Cinema, Embodiment, and the Senses* (Durham, NC: Duke University Press, 2000), 43.

51 Friedrich Kittler, *Discourse Networks, 1800/1900* (Stanford, CA: Stanford University Press, 1990), 28, 117.

52 Stephen Tropiano, "Il miracolo (The Miracle)," *Quarterly Review of Film and Video* 27 (2010): 441.

53 Lori Landay, "The Mirror of Performance: Kinaesthetics, Subjectivity, and the Body in Film," *Cinema Journal* 51 (2012): 131.

54 Leona Holbrook, "Dancing as an Aspect of Early Mormon and Utah Culture," *BYU Studies Quarterly* 16, no. 1 (1976): 121.

55 Matthew 10:39.

19

LATTER-DAY SAINT
FEMINISM AND ART

AMANDA K. BEARDSLEY

Triangular butterflies of white rice paper connected by copper wire lightly cascade from the ceiling of a gallery in a single, unwieldy column. As the sculpture turns with the breeze of movement within the Dumbo gallery space, inky names appear and disappear with the shift of time and atmosphere. Each name represents an ancestral inscription in Latter-day Saint artist Valerie Atkisson's family tree. The 2014 work, titled *Hanging Family History (Matriarchically Oriented),* is described as a "three-dimensional map" or "portrait of all the known individuals that are part of her genetic make-up."[1] Atkisson's name and birthdate sit at the apex of the structure, while wire loops at each corner of the angular forms attach her to the lineage, starting with her mother and father, who expand the form out to her maternal and paternal grandparents, and so on for seventy-two generations.

Atkisson has created several family history pieces, including murals and drawings that spotlight the centrality of the genealogical archive within her faith in the Church of Jesus Christ of Latter-day Saints, alongside the gendered nature of those histories. The strong allusion and counter to paternalism in creating several maternal lineages evokes practices of recuperating "her-stories" within a matrix of male-dominated history. The material process of the work—the labor of cutting paper, piecing the paper together in a rich textile, and knitting together copper wire—further alludes to traditions of women's work in a way that transforms the industrial inflections of the materials. Moreover, the conceptual pastime of genealogical work presents another facet of gender-based practices in the Latter-day Saint faith, where women have been the primary agents of autobiographical and family history to make a place for themselves in a patriarchal religion and world.[2]

Atkisson is one of many artists building on feminist thought in both art history and Latter-day Saint discourse. Artists working on themes specific to LDS feminism have played a significant role in shaping both Latter-day Saint culture and feminist

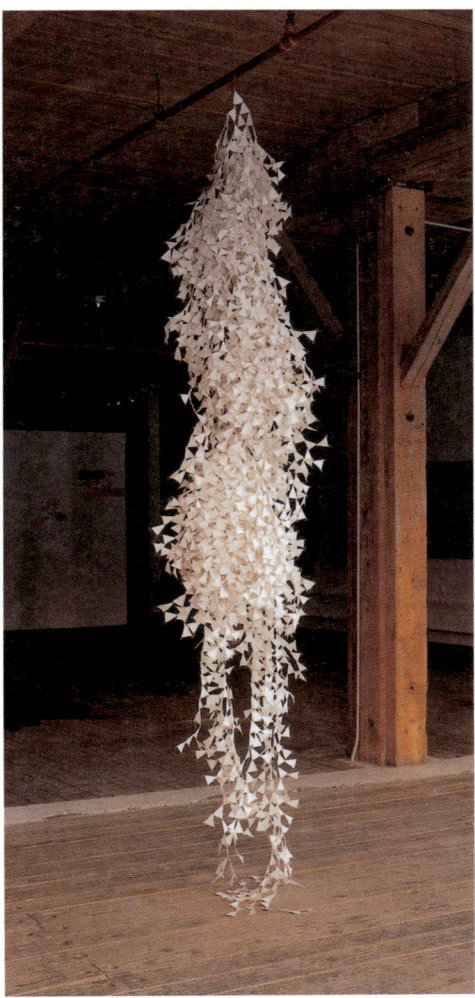

Fig. 19.1 Valerie Atkisson, *Hanging Family History (Matriarchally Oriented)*, 2002, ink, rice paper, copper wire, 14′ × 2′ × 2′, Church of Jesus Christ of Latter-day Saints Church History Museum. Image courtesy of the artist.

movement. Many have looked toward liturgical practices as inspiration while also making a forthright effort to recover lost histories and women in the fabric of time. In these efforts, their work reimagines what is arguably one of the most central institutions associated with the LDS faith: the genealogical archive.

Genealogy is a practice within Mormonism that gestures toward a scrupulous practice of recordkeeping that characterizes the faith.[3] Its importance to this chapter is in its pervasive influence in the liturgical and artistic gestures discussed herein, especially as artists leverage it as a means to effect change. Existing as both a physical building and an online database, the LDS genealogical archive contains names of those who have passed away and supplies them to the ritualistic space of the temple, where they are later embodied in proxy ordinances. It is a space that traces the histories of these names, linking them to past generations, and houses the textual traces as material objects of those who no longer exist. The genealogical archive is also considered part of a machinery that includes the self-referential scriptural histories of the religion's founding text, the Book of Mormon, and the massive stronghold of genealogical databases that aspire to contain the records of all humankind, past and present.[4] In one sense, the genealogical archive reflects an act of collecting and constituting a connected history of humankind—it comprises the tiny mundane tasks, the accounting measures, the collections, the things humans deem worthy of putting on a shelf—to construct a sphere of knowledge or story about the world. In another, it constitutes a dominant paradigm of cultural memory where the collectors and systems used to collect often skew toward the biases and selective processes of those in power.[5] In its reliance on systems of classification and measurement, it can generally exclude or condense the time-reliant techniques that similarly authenticate lineage and personhood. This makes the archive a powerful and expansive productive tool of history, reality, truth, understanding, behavior, artistic standards, careers, theory, and even memory.

With such a strong presence within the LDS faith, the genealogical archive presents a central node within which to mine artistic content specific to religious praxis and feminist strategies. Counterarchiving measures have become popular as alternative modes of bookkeeping, measurement, and recording as a resistance tactic within feminist movement. Giovanna Zapperi talks about "feminist time . . . a notion of temporality that comprises returns, accelerations and discontinuities," making apparent the subjective nature of knowledge production. Feminist time interrogates how perceptions of historical time, constructed by institutional powers like the genealogical archive, are inextricably bound to gender.[6] The turn toward archival critique characterized by feminist time offers a compelling parallel to what has been defined by art historian Hal Foster as an "archival impulse" in contemporary art, which includes practices from the perspective of "artist as historian," the role that media play in authenticating experience, and epistemological questions in the production of historical narratives.[7] Comparing these countertactics to Mormon artistic output recuperates a rich array of work that deepens understandings of feminism.

Using the genealogical archive as its framework, this chapter offers a survey of artists whose work comments on, is influenced by, or contributes to feminist discourse within the LDS faith. This chapter will focus on the efforts of LDS feminist artists since the 1970s to demonstrate the role artists have played in shifting the dialogue surrounding women and their rights as they relate to LDS material culture. While this survey includes art made by predominantly women artists, it rejects any forthright essentializing of their practices as decidedly "feminine." To characterize the work of women in this way overlooks the varied and nuanced contributions of individual artists.

However, to ignore the personal and political significance of gender in the artistic process is itself problematic.[8] The goal here is not to pigeonhole the work of these artists as "Mormon feminist art." Rather, discursive roots in feminism *and* the LDS faith inevitably find expression in the works created.

By analyzing the interplay between feminism and Mormonism in case studies, this chapter highlights several emergent themes, from artists working loosely within topics specific to feminist art-making, including questioning the place of their rights and labor in various sociohistorical conditions, to constructs and performances of masculinity and femininity, domestication, power and oppression, the marginalization of women, subject-object relations, intersectionality, and blood and menstruation.[9] Building on these themes, then, perhaps a Latter-day Saint feminist art deals with similar subjects unique to gendered Mormon experiences and spaces—polygamy, a Heavenly Mother, gendered labor specific to LDS praxis, the Relief Society, celestial marriage, genealogy, and temple rituals. Artists taking up these themes create the potential to reconcile, reexamine, and reconstruct traditions, placing the religion in a critical yet constructive light.

ARCHIVE AS GENEALOGICAL "HER-STORY"

Though rich histories of LDS feminism have emerged in the past few decades, there have also been noteworthy parallel actions within visual and material culture that merit similar attention. Wheelwright, Steenblick, and Brooks's *Mormon Feminism,* for example, draws a vivid history of what the feminist movement has looked like throughout Latter-day Saint history, including a rich archive of primary documents beginning with the origin of the faith. As the authors point out, Mormon women have actively advocated for women's rights, setting the stage for voting, equal rights, consciousness-raising, and collective action.[10] This brand of feminist labor is slowly gaining notoriety as names such as Emmeline B. Wells, Seraphina Young Ford, and so on show up in the canons of feminist history. At the same time, Mormon "mommy blogs" on the internet have opened avenues of cyberfeminist activism that serve as primary documents of the 1990s and early 2000s while also operating as engines of change.[11] These early blogs constitute a powerful counterarchive of feminist communication that brings attention to the often cursory nature of labor that is gendered female, including that of the housewife and mother—though the absorption of these early blogs into the media campaigns of the LDS Church arguably reinforces hegemonic and capitalist notions of motherhood.[12]

This strong pool of literature, images, and media complicates conventional definitions of feminism, but it also demonstrates the religious contributions that made the movement what it is. While Wheelwright, Steenblick, and Brooks make popular these histories, they also posit their own definition of Mormon feminism, which attempts to reconcile the seemingly irreconcilable tenets of a feminist movement predicated on equality and a religion that upholds a rigid hierarchy of male patriarchy.[13] In other words, they attempt to rebuke the claim that Mormon feminism is an oxymoron. From this, the authors argue that the LDS faith allows for its own brand of feminism insofar as its history includes women who initially fought for women's rights successfully and contributed to the feminist movement, while also upholding a theology that allows for equality among the sexes in some doctrinal senses and not in others (priesthood offices denied to women being one example).

The upsurge of literature addressing the lack of writing about LDS feminist thought/ practice provides ample opportunity for the arts to undertake similar tasks. The 1992–1993 exhibition *Out of the Land: Utah Women,* which traveled to the National Museum for Women in the Arts in Washington, D.C., highlighted rich artistic output alongside didactic commentary telling the stories of women who created "female imagery" inspired by "the land." Themes mentioned in the catalogue include "a remarkable and, at times, profound shift from exterior and surface toward psychological depth, introspection and self exploration." Shauna Clinger's *Rebirth* represented a "sense of the artist's psychological [and] physical presence." Meanwhile, many of the other works in the exhibition suggested "entrapment" or being "bound" within the confines of a gendered order. Trent Alvey's *Toaster Worship* commented on the domestic labor associated with "women's spaces" such as the kitchen, elevating everyday appliances with a neon halo. Rebecca Clark Knudsen's *Eternal Maternal* provided a handmade quilted statement akin to Atkisson's maternal pedigree.[14] These pieces find subversive significance in plumbing the depths of spaces and practices traditionally associated with women, especially as they relate to maternal themes.

Later exhibitions similarly grouped Utah women artists together without mention of religious influence. In 2013, Jeff Lambson curated *Work to Do* at the Brigham Young University Museum of Art. This exhibition focused on "questions surrounding women's work, the complex roles in which women engage on a daily basis and the unique ways each artist navigates the gender politics of the Beehive State [Utah]."[15] Though the exhibition provides a multiplicity of perspectives that depart from the maternal, and despite its location at a Latter-day Saint institution, religious identity sits on the periphery. Instead, the show, which features many artists who self-identify as Mormon or whose work takes up explicitly Mormon subject matter, seems to seek acceptance from mainstream feminism by downplaying religious nuance.

Similarly, the 2021 exhibition *To the Front: Perspectives on Equality, Gender, and Activism,* which took place at the Rio Gallery in Salt Lake City, was careful to leave the influence of the LDS faith on the side. The foreword in the show's catalogue omits any reference to religious influence by tracing a largely secular history regarding the fight for women's rights. It is hard to ignore the profound cultural context of Mormonism that inevitably marked much of the work on display. Installation artist Stephanie Leitch's work, which often comments on the artist's personal relationship with the LDS faith, was "about hand processes and materials, referencing feminine craft through dexterous repetition, along with encoded mysticism." In her statement, Leitch

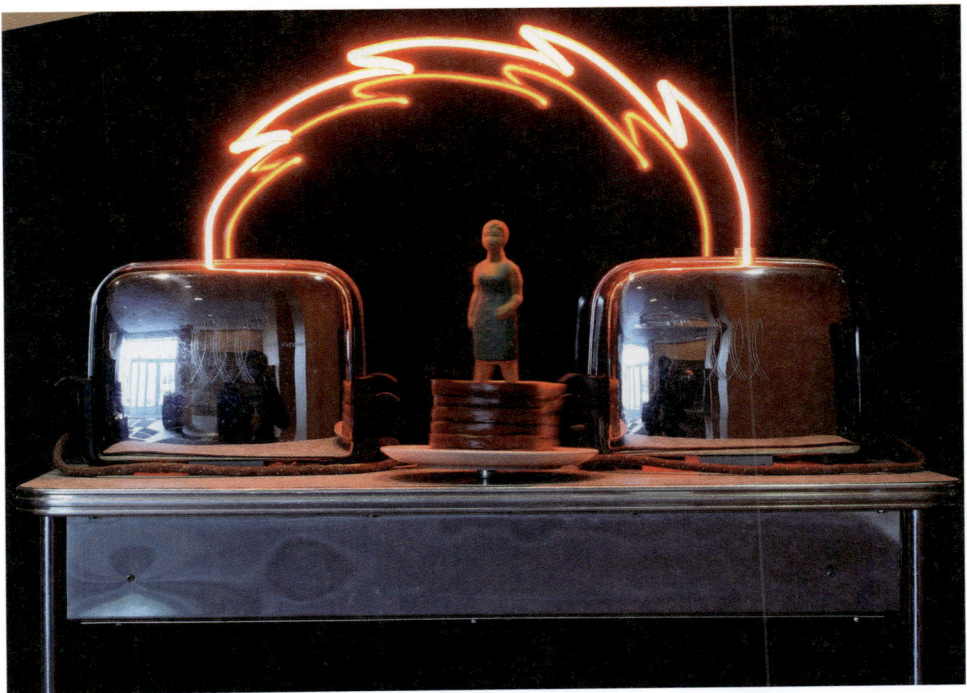

Fig. 19.2 Trent Alvey, *Toaster Worship*, 1990, mixed media, Permanent Collection of the Utah Museum of Fine Arts, gift of the artist.

relays, "In reappropriating visual relics from my upbringing and surroundings I am re-contextualizing them as abstraction—making them accessible to anyone."[16] The language skirts the deep relationship such work inevitably has with Leitch's "upbringing and surroundings" in Utah Mormonism.

These exhibitions offer insight into the issue many artists might have with being labeled a "Mormon" or "feminist" artist, which could be seen as reductionist and potentially polarizing for their brand.[17] Notwithstanding the fact that religious art has not fared well in contemporary art history from a critical standpoint (one might think about the many forms of iconoclasm and subversive commentary on religion in Andreas Serrano's or Maurizio Cattelan's work),[18] adding "feminist" to the mix might compound the stigmatization of such labels. At the same time, religious identity is noteworthy and an intrinsic part of many of these artists' processes and inspiration, warranting its recognition these past few decades.[19] Acknowledging Latter-day Saint presence in their work is fundamental to understanding the cultural contexts that allow their art to operate as historical documents that inform the ways in which art both shapes and is shaped by environment. Indeed, emerging accounts of women's labor as it relates to both Utah identity and Mormonism—for example, in the work of scholars such as Heather Belnap, who traces the histories of nineteenth-century LDS women artists to demonstrate their role in building social capital within a global framework, and Jenny Reeder, who examines nineteenth-century female quilt-making and hair art as a form of community-building and documentation—have gone a long way in shifting common misconceptions about any passive role that women played in instituting Mormonism.[20]

Allusions to Latter-day Saint identity are perhaps most forthrightly explored in the 2022 exhibition *The Sacred Feminine in LDS Art and Theology,* a project of the Center for Latter-day Saint Arts in New York City. Within the exhibit, LDS artists take up the

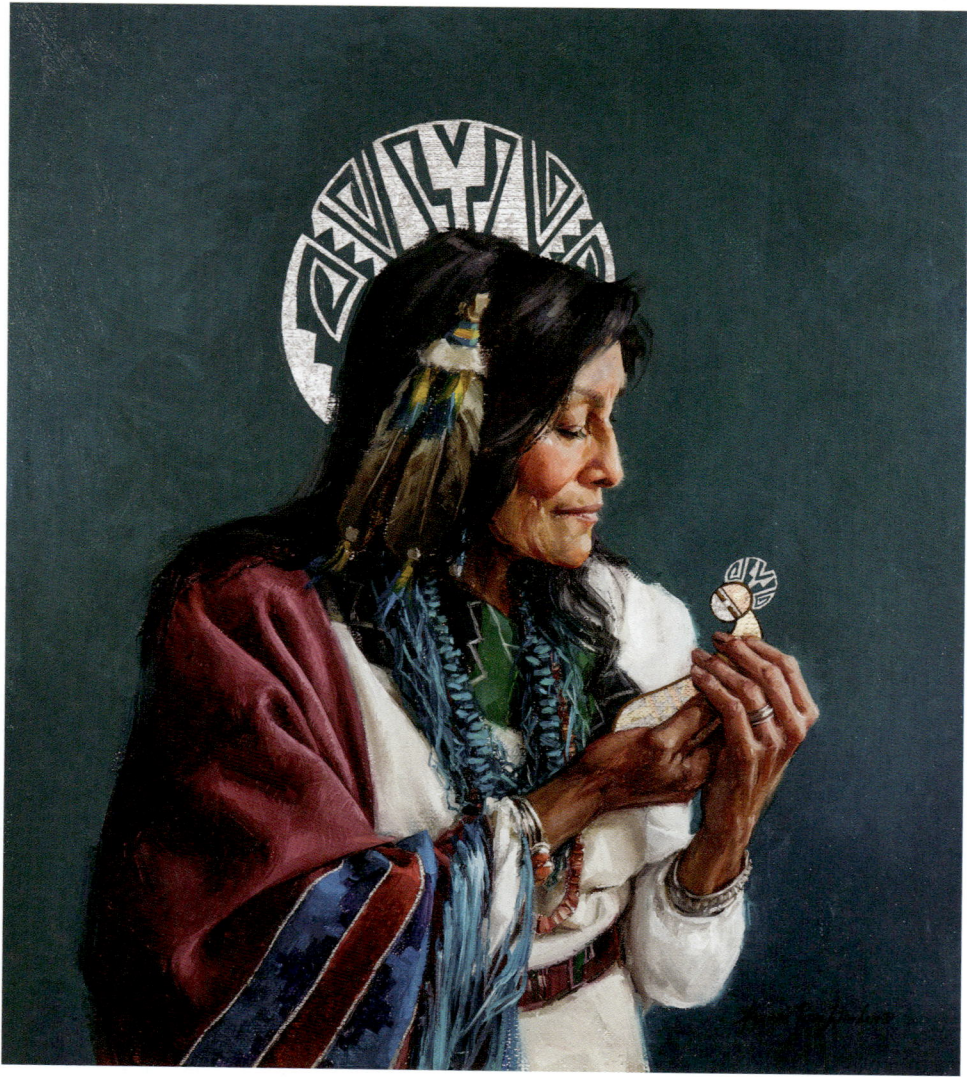

Fig. 19.3 Kwani Povi Winder, *Welcome Home,* 2019, oil and metal leaf on linen panel, 16″ × 14″, collection of the artist.

theme of a Heavenly Mother, "engag[ing] with the concept of a feminine presence to which our spirits yearn, which is simultaneously more vast and unfathomable than the mortal experience can comprehend."[21] Though the focus of the exhibit centers on an essentialist notion of womanhood that aligns with the second-wave feminist embrace of the divine goddess (more on this later), viewers are presented with a progressive version of LDS faith that attempts to rebuke patriarchy in religion through the work of a diverse set of self-identifying Latter-day Saint artists. Kwani Povi Winder's *Welcome Home* (2019), an oil-on-linen painting from the exhibition, for instance, depicts a deity that blends the artist's Pueblo Indian heritage with LDS symbolism.[22] In the painting, a Native American woman stands against a dark turquoise background with feathers in her dark hair and silver leaf crowning her head while she cradles a small figure in her hands. As Winder explains, she "intended the metal leaf design behind [the main figure's] head to be a crown of glory and her godhood status, and the small figure she

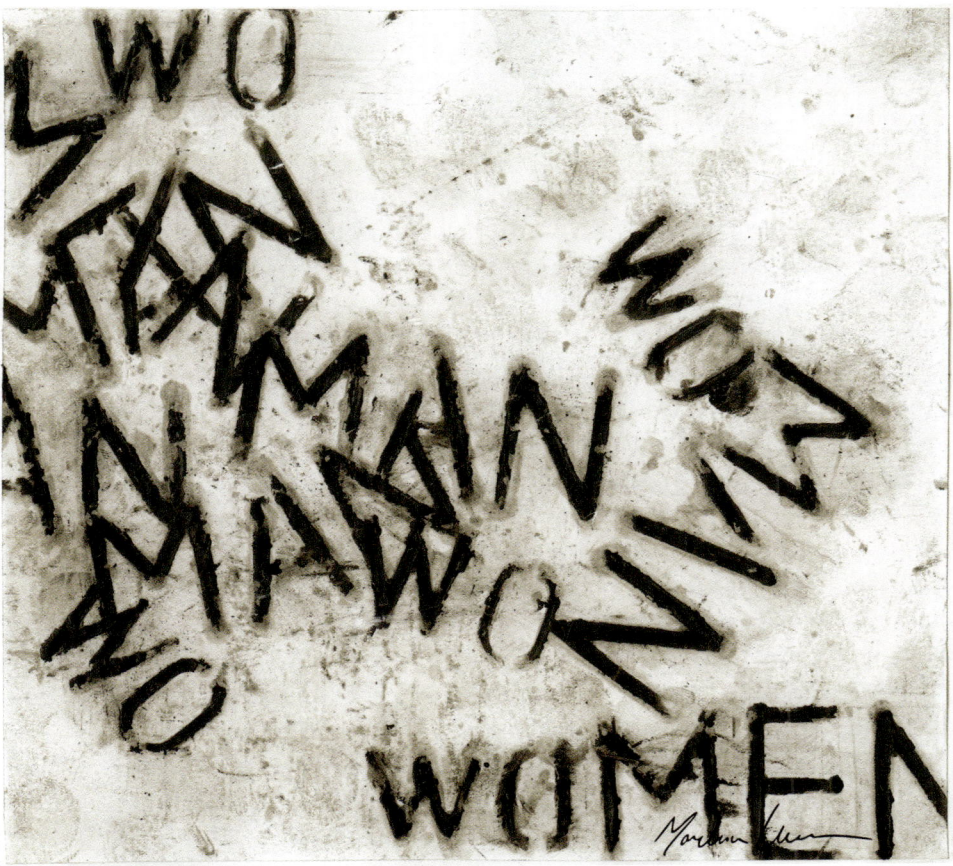

Fig. 19.4 Marlena Wilding, *WO MEN*, 2014, oil pastel, 9″ × 7″. Courtesy of the artist.

holds has a similar glory that is a type and shadow of their Heavenly Mother to show that they themselves are on the same path."[23] This image works against the primacy of a religious canon of art that generally displays white masculinity in the form of a God. While these iterations of the divine feminine align with the feminist ideals of the 1970s in some ways, they are a relatively recent phenomenon within Mormonism, with almost no images of a Heavenly Mother appearing before 2012.[24]

The seeming disconnect between the mainstream feminist movement's embrace of the divine feminine of the 1960s and 1970s and the more recent upsurge of that concept in LDS iconography is significant. *Sacred Feminine* presents a Mormon feminist iconography that appears decades later and continues to showcase techniques and mundane tasks, sometimes even elevating them to explorations of the divine feminine. In so doing, perhaps these works move the needle on thinking about work and techniques that would not generally belong in the canon of high art, even while enforcing a belated essentialism regarding femininity that feminists of the 1990s and 2000s have attempted to undo.

INTERSECTIONAL EXCAVATIONS

Second-wave feminist output poses an essentializing and exclusive brand of feminism, as many artists and theorists have pointed out.[25] To attempt to identify and place on a pedestal all the characteristics that make a person female is to limit the experience of womanhood to an anatomy, reinforcing an unbalanced power dynamic. The idea of a Heavenly Mother, for example, might recall critiques of the divine feminine, of reducing women to the role of motherhood or that of the beautiful caretaker who is innately nurturing and maternal. While many women have rightly found solace in such a characterization, the focus on fertility reinforces a narrative that anyone without a uterus, breasts, or the capacity for childbirth is not a real woman, a line of thought that is self-evidently alienating to trans, non-binary, and intersex folks, as well as infertile, post-menopausal, and voluntarily childless cis women (women who identify with the gender assigned to them at birth).[26] In commenting on the often exclusionary terrain of feminist movement within the faith, LDS writer Janan Graham-Russell points out, "'Woman' is not a universal experience and should never be regarded as such, whether in the Church or outside of it."[27] Graham-Russell distinguishes the pitfalls of reducing womanhood to what Kimberlé Crenshaw has referred to as a "single-axis" identity,[28] meaning that the experiences of Black people, Indigenous people, people of color (BIPOC individuals), and other marginalized groups often are relegated to a position of less importance within a structure in which the default is cis-gendered whiteness. Indeed, out of the exhibitions listed above, it is not until 2021 that exhibitions begin showcasing artists of color, demonstrating systemic forms of exclusion that cast feminist art history as predominantly white and heteronormative.

Artists such as Marlena Wilding have made explicit the complicated relationship race has to the LDS faith as she has expressed her struggle to relate to dominant feminist and white narratives. In her work *WO Man* (2014), Wilding uses mixed media and heavy encaustic acrylic to repeat variations of the word "woman" on the canvas. The lettering appears to be stamped in black paint over thick shades of white and gray paint. The title similarly references a linguistic addendum to the word "man," as if female identity were simply an afterthought—made from a rib taken from Adam's body. The use of only black and white offers symbolic inflections regarding race and gender as binaries—a refusal to offer any images or concepts of gender beyond the simple symbolic nature of letters and words, which, in C. S. Peirce's taxonomy, are the most artificial of signs.[29] The repetition and arbitrary assignment of color field to word debunks any assumed natural or inherent ties between color, sign, and meaning.

In her *Untitled* (2014) acrylic collage, Wilding addresses a reality informed by systemic racism/sexism and its influence on policing. The image depicts a pixilated portrait of a man with mugshot-letterboard-style font stenciled across his chest. A large white brushstroke hastily obscures more than half his face, muffling his mouth, separating head from torso in a violent gesture that plays with positive and negative space. Black swaths of background peek through the overwhelming mass of snowy acrylic that silhouettes and harshly frames the figure, hinting at a more substantial image that continues beneath the heavy whiteness. A red printed arc punctuates the lower quadrant of the image and seems to delineate the parameters of the portrait placed before the literal whitewashed effect of Wilding's brushstrokes. Wilding seems to ask a question regarding processual order, as the viewer must decipher which element came first: black or white. At the same time, the symbolically loaded use of color and weighty application of paint over print relays a powerful image of violent silencing and the cheap reproduction of a flattened Blackness overtaken by a world that grants expressiveness and gestural freedom to whiteness.

When discussing *Untitled*, Wilding referenced her family's experience, specifically those who she states have been "in the system." In a talk, she said:

> I have brothers that had a different experience than mine, you know being a Black woman in Utah ... but my brothers all had interesting experiences where they had to learn how to not to be a threat....When there's so much generational trauma—I think of it like this, it's like the flies in the jar experiment. After three days in a sealed jar, the flies no longer are motivated to fly or jump higher than the jar. And after the fourth day, the lid is taken off and the flies have no desire to leave the jar. They have been conditioned to have limits on their flight/high jump. And because of this, even their offspring will also follow the condition programmed behavior and they too limit their potential ... [T]he system that we live under doesn't always allow for people to continue their lives; it doesn't always favor evolution.[30]

Wilding references the gendered treatment of race in a predominantly LDS community and more broadly within the United States. While it might seem like the illusion

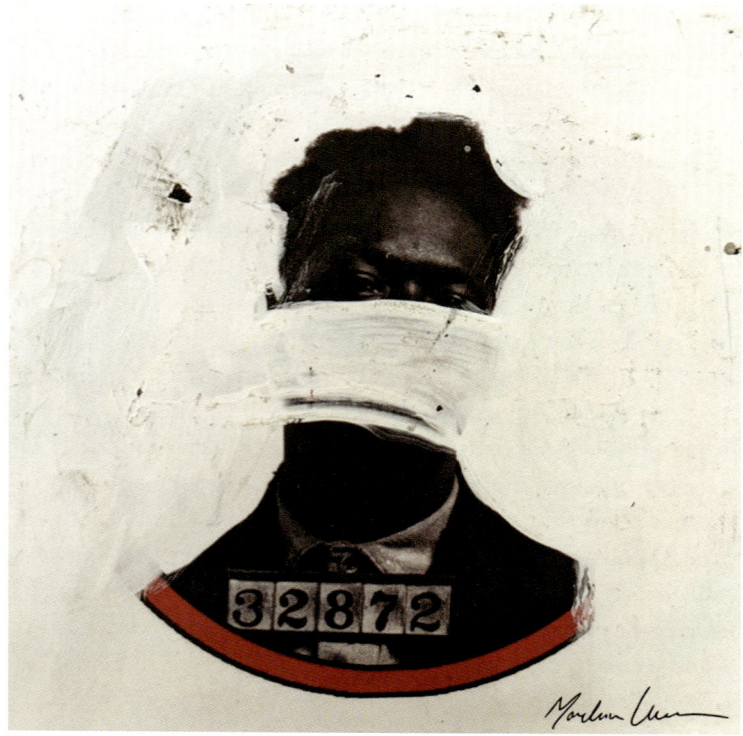

Fig. 19.5 Marlena Wilding, *Untitled*, 2014, mixed media acrylic collage, 9.5″ × 7.5″ with border. Courtesy of the artist.

of freedom exists, there are traumatic strongholds, the residue and realities of which contain Black identity and shape behavior and responsiveness. Importantly, she brings attention to the construction of Black masculinity as it operates as a projection onto racialized bodies while also systemically shaping them into the mold of "criminal."[31]

In many ways, *Untitled* reflects a cruel irony experienced by the artist as a result of its creation when Wilding was a student at Brigham Young University. In a standard class-room critique, Wilding explains the horror and shame she felt when her art professor reduced her work to "shock art," causing her to hide it away, drop her career as a serious artist, and move toward other pursuits for the next six years.[32] While this was likely only one of numerous microaggressions experienced by Wilding within the church, the lack of affirmation and absence of constructive critique points toward why many Black LDS members have in common the experience of "putting on a mask" to avoid such treatment. Darren T. Smith writes that the "mask that Black LDS members wear forces them in one of two directions—either capitulate to the racist ideology in the Church or fight with half-hearted activism in a sea of Republican-style opposition."[33] To Smith, *Untitled* "symbolizes the exhaustion of emotion work performed by Black people who

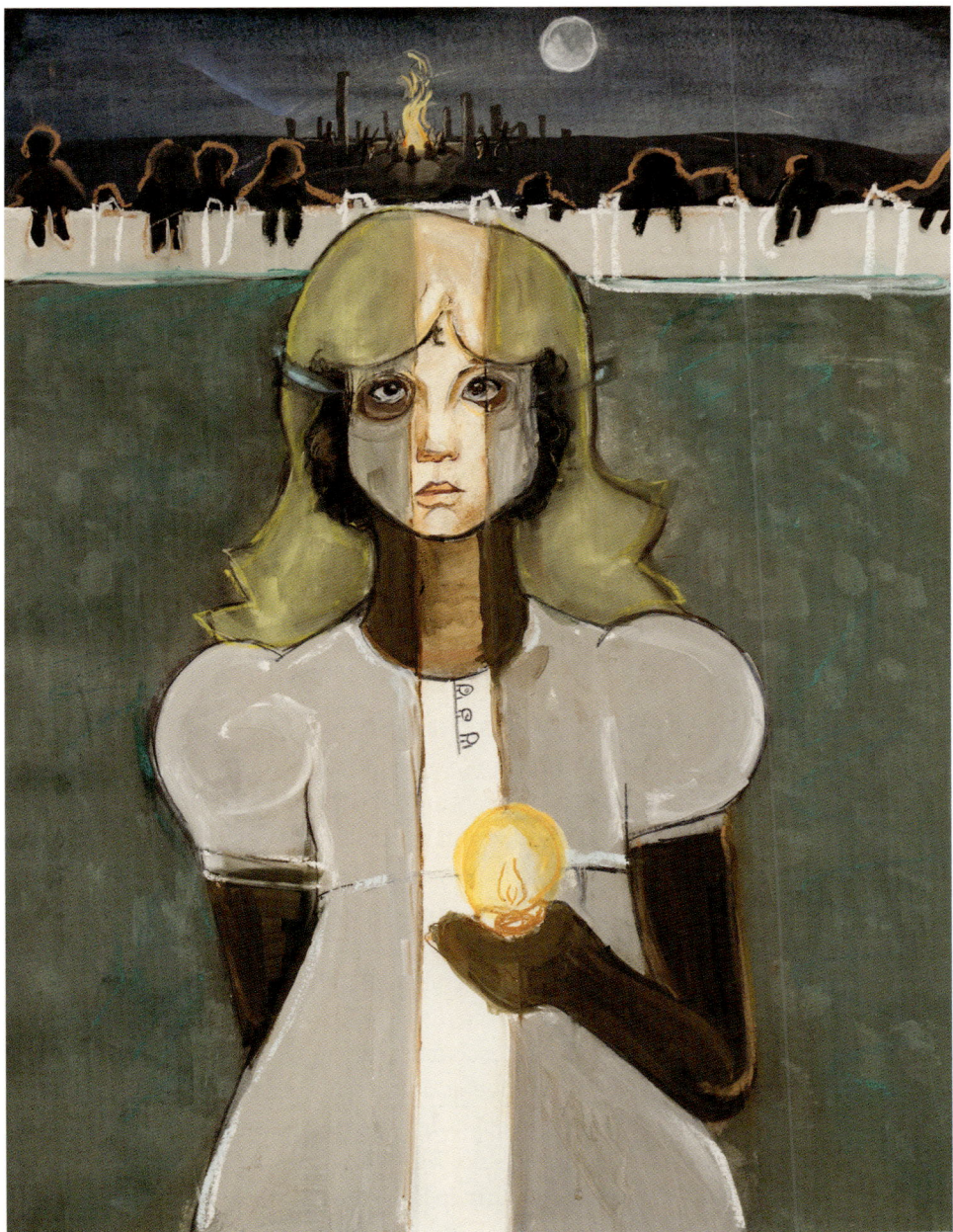

Fig. 19.6 Marlena Wilding, *Off the Fence*, 2022, watercolor, acrylic and chalk pastel, 18″ × 24″. Courtesy of the artist.

live, work, or worship in segregated white spaces . . . In a community that is supposed to affirm you, Black members of the LDS Church often find themselves apologizing or making excuses for blatant racist folklore perpetuated by white men who are enabled by white women."[34]

Indeed, Wilding further explores a more forthright masking in her self-portrait *Off the Fence* (2021). This painting of her younger self depicts a young Black girl with a white face and blond wig. Details such as curly hair and brown skin peek through eye holes and at the nape of her neck. As Wilding has stated, "I felt like I always had to put a mask on to fit into the group and society. . . . I knew how to codeswitch or act a certain way around people to make them feel more comfortable."[35] When she removed her mask in a predominantly white space and offered a poignant and timely critique of race within the LDS faith and America, Wilding was punished, her art and identity dismissed as a cheap ploy. *Untitled* and *Off the Fence* depict the toll such a masking might enact in a sea of constricting whiteness, while also blatantly revealing a lack of nuance in pedagogical response and viewership toward race and gender that has been evident in a largely homogeneous feminist movement. This instance also seems to say something about the cultural conceptualizations of (Utah) Mormon art. Some might say art should provoke, challenge, and even make us uncomfortable; some BYU art professors (and many church members) might disagree.

REIMAGINING THE ARCHIVE

The recovery and reappropriation of the image of a Black man in *Untitled* represents a counternarrative strategy used by artists to recontextualize and reframe how we generally understand images. Within the Mormon context, Wilding's work offers a visual genealogy of unnamed bodies and souls that have received little attention until relatively recently. Indeed, though Wilding turned away from showing her work, she later brought it out of hiding to show to an eager audience hungry for diverse expression in the wake of the 2020 George Floyd murder and the resultant heightened awareness of systemic racism in America. Since then, she has created a repository of imagery that challenges the dominance of white narratives. For example, her watercolor collage *Eve* (2018) depicts a presumed matriarch of civilization as a breastfeeding Black woman. The biblical figure nurses a more ethnically ambiguous infant, referencing the "outsourcing [of] breastfeeding . . . as it had been occurring since the biblical times."[36] Across the woman's clavicle, Wilding included the word "eve" written in Hebrew. Rather than adhering to traditional Hebrew spellings of the name Eve, Wilding used the word for "eve" or "evening," a symbolic reference to what she calls the yin/yang of light and dark, or an embrace and revision of the coding of dark = evil and white = good to show their symbiotic interdependence. To Wilding, darkness was part of her identity, even before she knew it was, so she spotlights its necessity and destigmatizes its negative connotations.[37] In so doing, she crafts an alternative genealogical understanding of the biblical origin story of humankind.

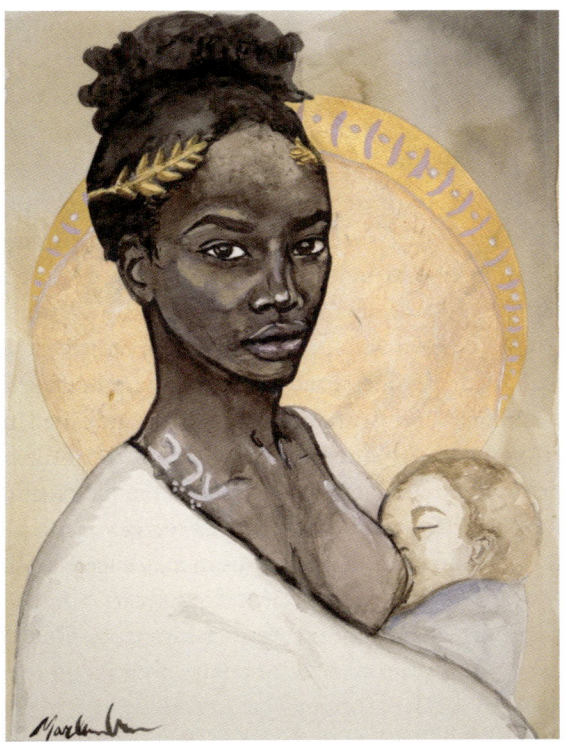

Fig. 19.7 Marlena Wilding, *Eve*, 2018, watercolor and acrylic collage, 9″ × 12″. Courtesy of the artist.

Shifting the linguistic narrative is one strategy for Wilding; meanwhile, she attempts to tell a fuller history—to fill in the gaps of time where contributions were made but not recognized—to archive the stories that are not contained in LDS lore or narratives. In another mixed media collage, a commission titled *All Are Alike unto God* (2021), Wilding painted a portrait of Isaac Lewis Manning, an early Black convert to the LDS Church. Such images create a collection of bodily presences not generally shown in LDS spaces, deepening understanding of a more diverse community and history.[38] They also offer a deeper sense of human connectivity than the genealogical archive attempts to achieve insofar as it tells the history of the "family of man" through an individual who fits neatly into the stories of Mormon becoming. *Untitled* similarly integrates forms of indexing in the use of photography and the categorical numbering of a human through the carceral system. In Wilding's work, however, the point is not just to add names to an already constituted history, nor to propose alternative views of it, but to uncover genealogies that suddenly become visible in a given historical time and context. The invisibility of women or Black members of the LDS Church from the past can be counteracted, those individuals made visible, under specific historical, cultural, and subjective conditions.

Artists Amy Jorgensen and Georgina Bringas similarly comment on the indexing systems often wielded to define human nature and experience. In a series of pigment prints, titled *Body Archive* (2003–present), Jorgensen attempts to find an alternative to institutional archival practices through an ongoing and painstaking experimental process. Each print in the series features a piece of Jorgensen's body recorded by placing light-sensitive emulsion on its surface to capture a reactive recording of movement and contour that is transferred to 4″ × 5″ slide film. Because the materials react to heat and light, they work outside of the bounds of traditional photography through a camera-less process that similarly records an abstraction of time and space. The images themselves are a series of glossy and impenetrable case studies, many resembling the scopic formulations of bodily debris found through the lens of a microscope or overexposed film, a view of the body that refuses unmediated human vision. In one image, small hair-like filaments emerge from a dark form that covers over half of the composition. The faint light of a presumed background silhouettes the fibers, offering something of an illusion of space and overlapping form. Shades of crimson, pink, and blue overwhelm the image, creating a colorful array of documentation while offering very little insight into what or where we are witnessing of Jorgensen's body.

As "an investigation of personal and cultural assumptions linked to notions of the body, science, narrative, authorship and documentary photographic practice," Jorgensen views her body as a site of "visual testimony . . . an archive, my skin the surface through which I experience the world."[39] Though Jorgensen does not claim the Latter-day Saint faith, this focus seems a pointed reference to the power of testimony, a ritual with which she grew up and is familiar.[40] Latter-day Saint testimony marks a practice of conversion and community-building and "remains the keystone of the restored gospel."[41] Missionaries often bear their testimonies as a means of faith-building, while members are often invited to speak up in testimony meetings that generally occur once a month. As church leader Spencer W. Kimball stated, "A testimony is not an exhortation; a testimony is not a sermon; it is not a travelogue. You are there to bear your own witness . . . every time you bear your testimony it becomes strengthened."[42] Oftentimes members bear testimony of their knowledge that the LDS Church is true and that Jesus Christ is the redeemer of this world.[43]

In a way, a testimony is an aural reassertion of the archive. In its utterance, it catalogues a moment of conversion and bears witnesses to a piece of knowledge taken as truth. The more people who bear testimony—the more testimony is repeated—the stronger a knowledge base becomes. In her allusion to testimony, Jorgensen's work comments on the systems that form knowledge, the technological forms of memory[44] (like a photograph) that serve as testimony, or archives compiling visual and aural collections that constitute a narrative of the self. In sharing a testimony of her body in a site like Utah, she also comments on a practice that binds individuals into a body of Christ, a community. Such a practice presumably bears and shares diverse, unique, and authentic testimony, but that testimony resonates communally, becoming one.

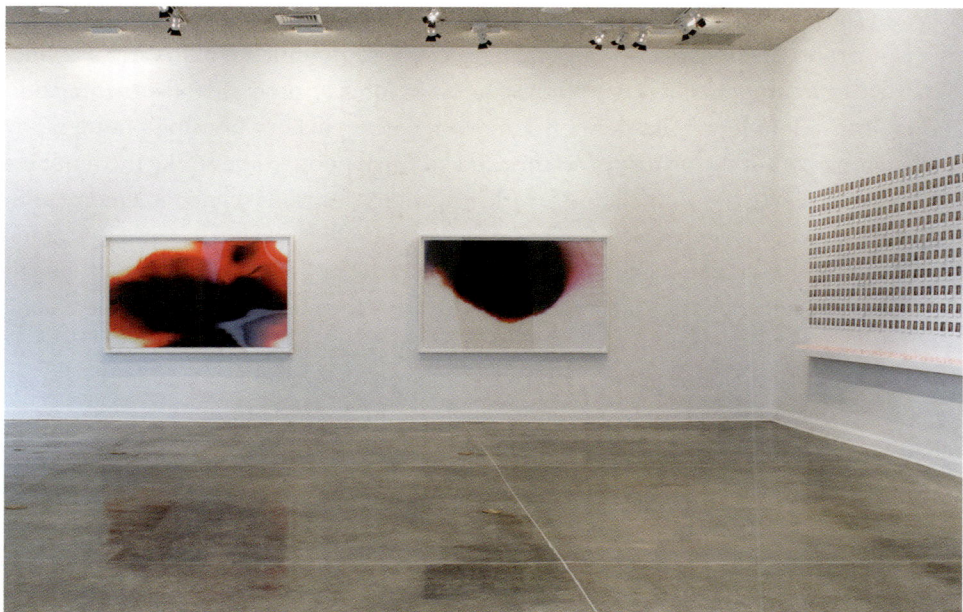

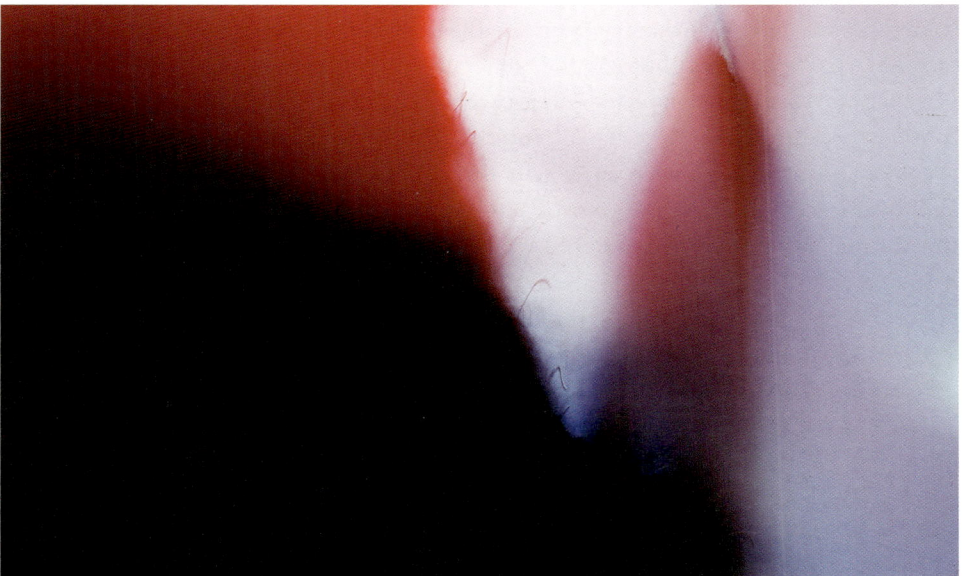

Fig. 19.8 *a.* Amy Jorgensen, installation view of *Body Archive* at the Utah Museum of Contemporary Art, Salt Lake City, in 2014. Courtesy of the artist.
b. Amy Jorgensen, *Body Archive, 2-24-13*, 2003–present, archival pigment print, 12″ × 12″. Courtesy of the artist.

With the female body as the main subject under investigation, Jorgensen's work further constitutes a feminist perspective that questions the dominance of the archive while constructing a counterarchive within the context of forensic processes of authentication and identification. Jorgensen draws from a very specific history of using photography to document within the history of science and criminal photography. Like the numbers used beneath a mug shot in Wilding's work, Jorgensen's imprints reference a moment in time and purport to identify a bodily location. Such numbers recall Alphonse Bertillon's Signaletic Anthropometrics, a measurement system applied to human bodies, which was adopted by police forces across the Western world beginning in 1888.[45] Bertillon's system established a technical means of identification and classification through measurement and "mathematical rules" that fixed images of both criminality and insanity long associated with histories of scientific racism and sexism. His work compiled and relied on an archive that allowed institutions to track, identify, and surveil individuals using observation and visuality as empirical evidence. In turn, it signaled a truth believed to be inherent in a photograph.

As Georges Didi-Huberman states, Bertillon relied on the connotative capacity of photography, which "is always supposed to authenticate the existence of its referent, and in this way it always grants us some knowledge, and is always justified in pointing to something in itself like a 'that has been.'"[46] The exactitude implied in photography—the fact that what we see in a photograph is generally believed to match the moment and experience of what is being depicted—was particularly fitting in the monitoring of women in mental institutions, where female subjects, similar to criminals, underwent photographic scrutiny to establish pseudo-scientific conditions like hysteria, a pathology that kept women captive under the guise of "emotional instability" for centuries.[47] Moreover, it instituted a male clinical gaze that solidified a social hierarchy and narrative of humankind reliant on photography and archival processes.

Returning to Jorgensen, then, the utilization of photography and archive reference a particular moment and use that established patriarchal dominance over women and other marginalized bodies, on the one hand, and religious specificity, on the other. As Zapperi states, "Woman's reappearance across documentary reconstructions reminds us of the constitutive relationship between time and the image: it is when it is visualized that the past becomes tangible and recognizable."[48] In photographing her own anatomy through the emulsion process, Jorgensen closes the gap between representation or documentation (what is generally seen in the photograph) and the "real" moment that photography purports to index truthfully. While photography generally requires a camera, *Body Archive* removes the apparatus of production that generally mediates the gaze, allowing her body and the alchemical mix of materials to document her existence. In a sense, her body is the camera, the apparatus of production—she embodies the recording process, making her the authority on her physical condition. To document one's existence in this way is a powerful statement in asserting presence, perhaps in a world that often undermines, ignores, or mediates that presence. After all, to be the surveiller or the one who takes the photograph is to be in control of the image itself. To be the camera is to assume an authority granted to mechanical objectivity and not generally granted to humans, let alone women who have been scientifically maligned with madness.

Within the context of Utah, *Body Archive* inevitably intersects with site-specific forms of indexing that participate in identifying the self within a genealogical history of humankind. To look at a genealogical chart is to understand a condensed testament of individual units that measure presence—a birth, marriage, or death certificate; a medical chart documenting weight, height, eye color; family photographs with inscribed names; newspaper clippings; DNA evidence. In many ways, the genealogical archive relies on such fragments of documentation to construct an individual. As scholar Kit Hermanson recalls regarding the process of using genealogy to understand their sense of belonging in the Latter-day Saint faith: "We were Mormon by blood. Our blood was transposed into a text on my computer monitor and the words there told me I belonged."[49] Each triangle on Atkisson's family history installation serves as additional testament to the blood, flesh, and bodily measurements that have come to instantiate human presence and family appendages that make a lineage; each microscopic filament of hair and cellular landscape of skin emulsified in Jorgensen's prints likewise crafts a chart of her presence and fragmented genealogical archive of the self.

Mexico City–based LDS artist Georgina Bringas (1975) utilizes sculpture and installation to articulate similar gendered, religious, and scientific themes attached to the archive. Bringas's work relies on systems of calculating time and space through established units and comparing those through alternative forms of quantification, including experiential methods. In her 2010 work *Enciclopedia: Todos los minutos de hoy (Encyclopedia: All Today's Minutes)*, the artist filled twenty-four black leather notebooks with sixty pencil drawings per notebook, an explicit form of recording and thereby archiving time in a way that is almost secretarial in its tedium. Each drawing resembles the hands of a clock in different positions. Metal bookends like those found on a public library shelf contain the notebooks. The work is unassuming and smacks of everyday bureaucratic environments, stripped of identifying details, such as words or title frontispiece. Each book cover includes the hour. For example, one notebook includes "5pm–6pm" in recessed debossed print on one of the covers to indicate the hour, while other covers did the same for different hours. The work revels in serial repetition in several ways: in the inclusion of multiple books, which align with the twenty-four hours of the day; in the repeated image of the same clock with slightly different times on each page; and through a monochromatic palette of black, gray, and white. Viewing the work as a whole reduces it to straight lines and geometry, as each notebook set against another blends into a dry statement on redundancy and boredom.

Bringas's choice of title alludes to a human reference system: the encyclopedia, an authoritative tome that identifies facts and offers information on many subjects, a form of standardized information. Encyclopedic knowledge is the authority of assumed universality, somewhat akin to measurement itself—something one might go to whenever one

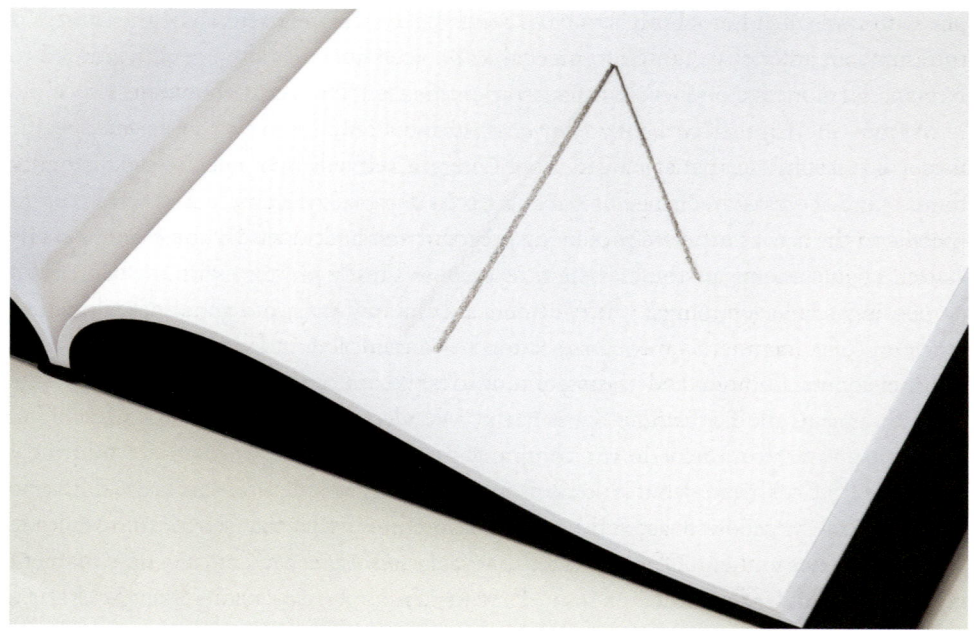

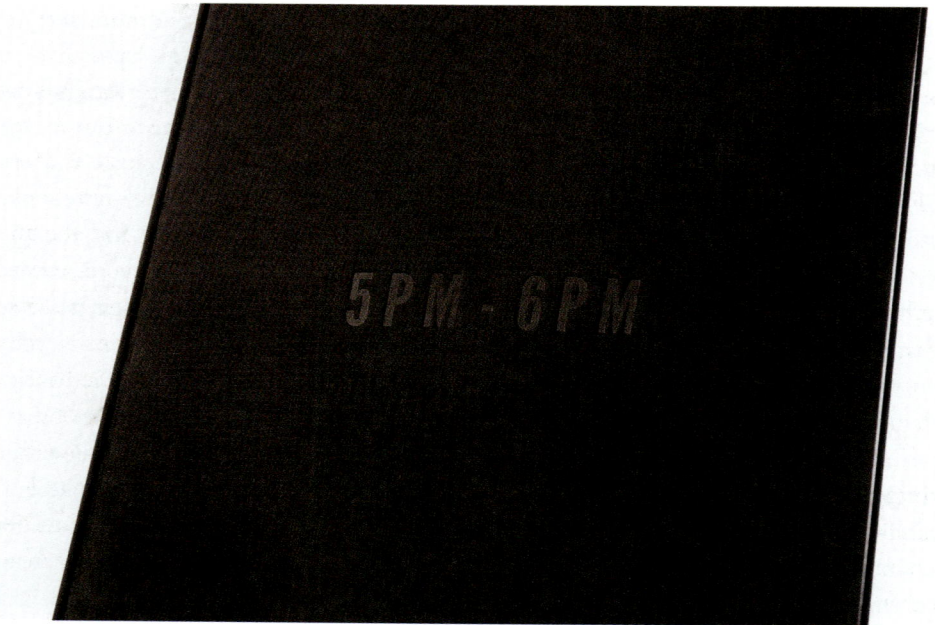

Fig. 19.9 *a* and *b*. Georgina Bringas, *Enciclopedia todos los minutos de hoy (Encyclopedia. Today's every minute)*, 2010, 24 books, 21 cm × 28 cm each, hardcover, 1,440 pencil drawings. Courtesy of the artist.

needs to understand anything about the world at a certain moment in time, a unit of summary, a marker of the abstract things that are accessible only through representation. Revisiting an archive of encyclopedias from across time tells of how humans conceived of their world. Brigas's *Enciclopedia,* however, flips the function from the universal to the personal and spiritual, in that she literalizes time as a marker of her own experience within the pages. According to Bringas, the clock on each page represents a different moment specific to the artist's experience of being pregnant and bedridden for three months. She states, "I could not do anything at the time because I had a problem with my baby, but it was boring, so I began to make every minute about a way to try to feel calm, to feel comfortable ... for me it was a way to understand that condition."[50] It was this attentiveness to the everyday condition and passing of time in bed that allowed her to also find the spiritual. To her, a work like *Enciclopedia* is "a way to understand the world, to measure it because it is a way to capture it, to put it inside of something (like a clock, which can tell me this is the time of this day), but it's something that also makes me feel safe ... Our time on this earth is very speedy, so fast, just a minute, but I try to extend that as a means to enjoy it. I feel this relates to the [LDS] Church, the gospel, because we are here just for a moment trying to understand our life."[51] In an effort to calm and cosmologically situate herself, Bringas created a therapeutic, deliberately tedious artwork that attempted to access the maternal and spiritual through being present and mindful and recording duration itself.

Enciclopedia recalls similar work in the history of minimalist and conceptual art. On Kawara's *Today* series, or date paintings, for instance, was a nearly five-decade-long project started in 1966 that included a meticulous and unitary documentation of his labor by painting a date monochrome of blue, gray, or red. While the artist did not follow any overarching principle regarding choice of dates, the work acts as a commentary on the regularized passage of time—that the calendar is a human construct, and that cultural context and personal experience shape quantifications of time. Kawara's work suggests that people do not experience time in the same way, that culture, point of view, and other contexts affect the way humans experience the world. The painstakingly handmade quality of the painting to look like printed materials reinforces the human role in constructing time, working against the assumed universality that such markers of time and space hold. In contrast, Bringas frames her personal markers of time with a printed, standardized text on the outside of her books, alluding to the universal standard that likewise frames experience. The hand-drawn clocks within, however, demarcate her human experience within assumed universality, offering a stronghold of certainty in an uncertain time.

Indeed, rather than creating individual subjectivities of experience, Bringas discusses the hope that her art will connect people, that it will provide a space where the abstract concepts that lie at the periphery of language and understanding—things like faith and space—might be bridged in common understanding. In personal statements about her art Bringas has often quoted Scottish scientist Lord Kelvin, who wrote, "When you can measure that of what you're talking about, and express it with numbers, you know something about it; but when you cannot measure it, when you cannot express it with numbers, your knowledge is scarce and unsatisfactory. Measuring can be the beginning of knowledge."[52] To Bringas, measurement is learning and has deep ties to classification systems such as the encyclopedia. She states, "I found that in my work I was trying to assign values to experiences and objects as a way of evidencing the unobservable, making personal interpretations of these situations by perceiving and quantifying their evidence, evidence that they are for me the results of my work."[53] To her, art is a "proposal about the world and its operation," the instruments of measurement that she utilizes to document her personal experience while containing the possibility of expanding common understanding.[54]

In a feminist twist on this conceptual form of time-keeping that has an intimate connection with Bringas's maternity theme, Mary Kelly's *Post-Partum Document* (1973–1979) consists of six cases of documentation following the development of the artist's son, including feeding charts and liners from the inside of a baby's cloth diapers, alongside specific time intervals. Each artist offers a time stamp of their personal experience, a meditation on and physical incarnation of the minutes and hours of existence that brought significance to life and the passing of time. Each artist articulates a relationship between memory and temporality such that the often cursory labor of motherhood (even expectant motherhood) emerges as a significant moment worthy of classification. For Bringas, labor takes on a different connotation in the expectations—the excitement and tangible fears of motherhood, and the quite literal physical experience of laboring that brings an individual into the world. In a way, her work tallies and quantifies the hours of banal work that often goes unacknowledged. Meanwhile, Kelly explores the effacement of parenting work once the tiny human enters the world by collecting the markers of doing, whether it is in the thankless task of changing a diaper or having one's efforts overwritten by a toddler's scribbles. Nevertheless, their efforts position the construction of historical time as being inextricably bound to the construction of gender.

Jorgensen and Bringas both draw from science and technology to comment on the role classification plays in knowledge production, especially as it pertains to genealogical systems. Jorgensen quantifies her body through alchemical process and technological rendering. With Bringas, genealogy exists in the mathematical and unitary forms of measurement that likewise substantiate presence, self, and progeny. In their deferral to scientific observation and processes, both allude to the male-dominated field of science, where women have always been but where they have rarely been acknowledged as expert.[55] Science as a discipline is tinged by a patriarchy that influences everything, from the instruments we use to the facts we produce. Indeed, to assume that science is value-free or without biases is naive at best, but this assumption of neutrality or objectivity nevertheless largely props up the masculine hegemony of science.[56] Perhaps the patriarchal biases surrounding technoscientific method become even more evident in Bringas's other works, canvases that include the layering of colorful measuring tape (a reference to the tools her mother used to keep her clothed) in abstract geometries. To place this tool of measure-ment within the male-dominated canons of abstraction and science shifts the paradigm to make visible those forms, individuals, and techniques that are generally excluded.

PERFORMING THE ARCHIVE

While Jorgensen, Wilding, and Bringas include themes of documentation in their work, they allude to a performative process of moving through a gendered world. Their gestures constitute archives of the self—a genealogy of human activity that attests to their presence and experiences. In a more literal telling of this performativity, the work of Angela Ellsworth examines queer identity as it relates to her family and Mormon up-bringing. She has staged several performance pieces that question the complex network of sexuality built into the history of the church and throws into stark relief subversive relationships that might parallel taboos associated with homosexuality. In her investiga-tion of her family lineage and her ties to polygamy she offers an expansive genealogical undertaking that reveals the threads and seams that make up cultural normativity.

In her *Plural Wife Project* (2009–2014), Ellsworth focuses on sister-wives as a "point of departure for discussing contemporary issues around nonheteronormative relationships [by] reimagining a community of women with their own visionary and revelatory powers as they pioneer new personal histories."[57] The project consists of per-formance and sculptures, including *Seer Bonnets: A Continuing Offense* (2009–2010), a series of pioneer bonnets made from pearl-tipped corsage pins and fabric set at different heights on steel and wood pedestals. Each prairie-style bonnet is meant to represent each wife of nineteenth-century LDS leader Lorenzo Snow, who faced federal charges for polygamy.[58] The exterior of each bonnet includes exquisite patterning by thousands of pins, creating a mosaic of swirling shapes and textures. The pearly white designs and the alternating heights grant each bonnet a subtle individuality. In contrast to the beau-tifully decorated exteriors are violent underbellies of needles on the bonnet's interior. The ribbons to tie the headdress showcase this juxtaposition more clearly, as they wind their way down to the pedestal, their twisting sides revealing either pointy steel or soft pearl. To wear one of these bonnets would likely cause unbelievable pain and injury, drawing a clear metaphor of interior suffering alongside a shiny veneer of exterior self-fashioning. The duality of interior/exterior is mirrored by absence and presence, where the bonnet signifies the absence of the body that would generally wear such clothing.

Clothing is important in Ellsworth's work, likely because clothing has long signi-fied gender expression and performativity, according to queer theorists.[59] *Seer Bonnets* exhibits pieces that represent more than what is on display, including the struggle of a generation of women that helped settle a religion yet received very little credit.[60] In the title's reference to founder Joseph Smith's seer stone, which helped him translate the Book of Mormon, the works invert the gendered notion of male prophecy by using the objects that authenticated scripture. As Marie Dallam states, "The bonnets are tools that give women heightened understanding as well as the potential to envision entirely

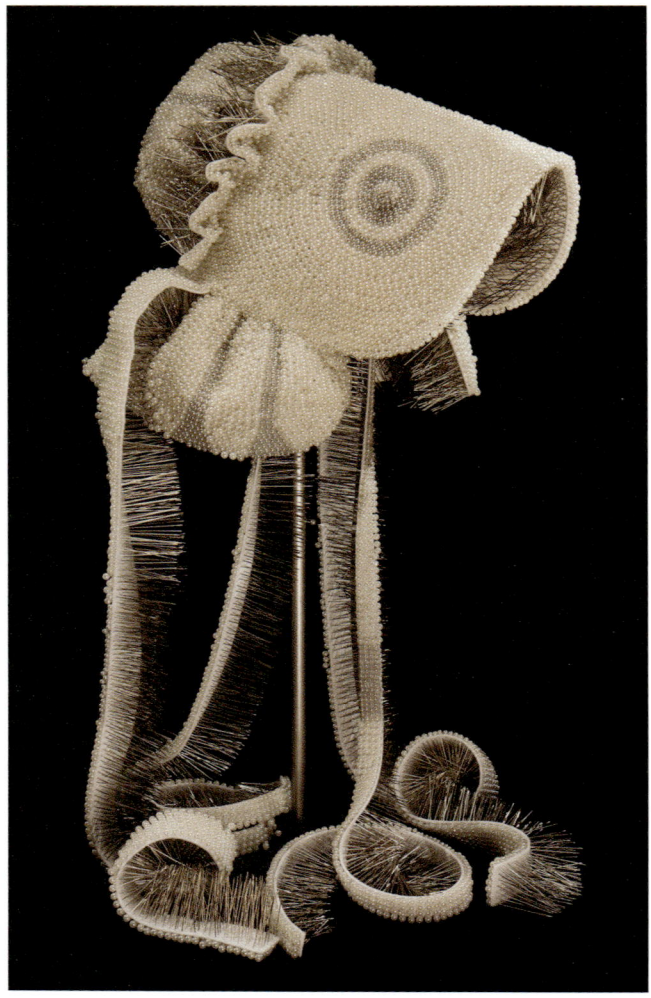

Fig. 19.10 Angela Ellsworth, *Seer Bonnet XII*, 2009–2010, corsage pin, fabric, Permanent Collection of the Utah Museum of Fine Arts, purchased with funds from the UMFA Young Benefactors and the Phyllis Cannon Wattis Endowment for Modern and Contemporary Art.

new possibilities."[61] This is not an essentialist argument that women have special forms of insight and intuition separate from men, but instead is a recognition that women in Latter-day Saint history were equally suited and undertook many of the same faith-building and visionary practices credited to men.

On the other hand, *Bonnets* also offers insight into the struggle of needing to adhere to a heteronormative monogamy, a state-enforced relationship configuration that ran contrary to the choices made by (mostly) grown adults in early Mormonism. Indeed, while Snow navigated the prohibition of polygamy, many of his wives had to retreat into a different relationship orientation, living with family members or as "single"; thus, much of the burden of maintaining the facade of monogamy fell on them.[62] In this reading of Ellsworth's work, polygamy could be seen as paralleling restrictions surrounding queer love, insofar as same-sex companionship has historically been prohibited. Perhaps for Ellsworth, spotlighting polygamy in this way—as less of a repressive force for women and more of a mature adult relationship configuration—presents an option for coalition-building while also outlining a rhetorical understanding of homosexuality in the Latter-day Saint faith, which notoriously has been against queer freedom.[63]

In pairing the bonnets with the theme of polygamy, Ellsworth also comments on same-sex companionship. As Dallam argues, Ellsworth "presents polygamy as a radical reconstruction of domestic life: a social setting with intrinsic positive potential for women to demonstrate both mutual support and personal strength, without reference to husbands." In Ellsworth's performance piece *Meanwhile, Back at the Ranch* (2010), another part of the *Plural Wife Project,* multiple performers dressed in pastel prairie dresses generally used by fundamentalist polygamist sects dance in a Sydney Museum of Contemporary Art gallery. The title is an idiom from old western cinema referring to a simultaneous happening, signaling a cut between two different storylines and locations. The use of this cliché signals a dual reality between a main narrative of the central protagonist and another reality to which only viewers are privy. The implied humor of the saying is that the characters in one scene are oblivious to what is happening "back at the ranch."

This dual storytelling is evident as the performers move in prescribed sequences punctuated by signs of what could be interpreted as queer cruising or moments of romantic signaling—prolonged eye contact with the slight arch of an eyebrow, the lingering touch of fingers in parting, intimate conversations in corners interrupted by intrusive presences. As the work progresses, performers dance with each other, winding arms reach around bodies to hold one another in prescribed movement, and wandering hands grasp a waist or softly brush a cheek as they follow the steps generally reserved for heterosexual dancing configurations. In these stolen moments outside the watchful eyes of the cinematic protagonist or learned motions of the dance (perhaps, in this context, the patriarch of the family, who is meanwhile off elsewhere), sexual fantasy, expression, drama, and merrymaking abound. The facade of the dominant narrative—the regimented steps and movement—crumbles if one closely observes the coded gestures of the performers.

Ellsworth describes *Meanwhile* as a performance that explores "ideas of membership, rituals of endurance, and non-heteronormativity."[64] To the artist, the work is an intimate self-exploration of lineage and how that lineage constitutes relationships to the faith and socially choreographed movement. Both Ellsworth's performances and sculptures embody genealogy, and, in much the same way as many Latter-day Saint rituals, act quite literally as proxy for the names listed on family history charts that reside within the databases of the Mormon genealogical archive. The elements of *Seer Bonnets*, for instance, are proxies for Snow's wives, while the performers in *Meanwhile* stand in for the women who are not often seen, known, or documented. Repeating and revealing their presence in her work places them in a different genealogy—one that, while in some ways ancillary to bloodlines, constitutes a shared lineage of labor, orientation, collaboration, vision, and chosen family. As a system of signification—of clothing, items, and symbols that demarcate that *this* is who *you* are—the genealogical archive contributes to a systematized community.[65] While the performative enactment of the genealogical archive in the traditional (patriarchal) Latter-day Saint sense relays a sense of identification with a larger collective family as a means to call into action its participants in a powerful way, Ellsworth's work reenacts that process to deconstruct and interrogate the normative movements crafted by such systems.

Within LDS discourse and feminist movement, many artists have taken up a call to excavate the male-dominated sites of history to find individuals who were essential to building a culture and religion. Indeed, one of the threads that ties many of these artists together is a personal interest in lineage and gendered labor. Where Atkisson had to undertake an extensive research agenda to compile a history that could be a sculptural instantiation of her genealogy, and Ellsworth enacts the lines that connect her to the heteronormative practices made solid by such a genealogy, Wilding and Bringas look to their family and religious histories to craft intricate narratives that institute counterarchives. The power in this strategy allows all artists to reimagine family, race, gender, and sexuality in a way that decentralizes patriarchy. Intrinsic in their acknowledgment of women's needed-but-silenced role is a recuperation of significant efforts, not only as mothers but also as practitioners and skilled laborers. It isn't just about collecting and resuscitating the forgotten, then—it is about working, instituting, and enacting an alternative archive to affect change.

NOTES

[1] Valerie Atkisson's artist's webpage, https://www.valerieatkisson.com/work/horizon-dd9yx.

[2] Katherine Sarah Massoth, "Writing an Honorable Remembrance: Nineteenth-Century LDS Women;s Autobiography," *Journal of Mormon History* (2013): 108. See also Jenny Reeder's chapter in this volume on the significant role women played in recordkeeping in the nineteenth century.

[3] As media scholar John Durham Peters suggests, because Latter-day Saints "envisioned recording practices that could bind earth and heaven and the living and the dead into a single archive," they offer a rich avenue for exploring the media possibilities of the "techniques of bookkeeping, paperwork, and recording." John Durham Peters, "Recording Beyond the Grave: Joseph Smith's Celestial Bookkeeping," *Critical Inquiry* 42 (2016): 843. See also Gavin Feller, "Sacralizing Signals for the Institution and the Individual: KZN and the LDS Church's Discursive Approach to Radio as a New Medium, 1922–1927," *Culture and Religion* 16 (2015): 327–343; Mason Kamana Allred, "Circulating Specters: Mormon Reading Networks, Vision, and Optical Media," *Journal of the American Academy of Religion* (2016): 1–23. Peter McMurray, "A Voice Crying from the Dust: The Book of Mormon as Sound," *Dialogue: A Journal of Mormon Thought* 48 (2015): 3–5.

[4] Familysearch.org, ldsgenealogy.com, ancestry.com (though not owned by the LDS Church, it has a partnership with the organization and offers free access to members), and the older Ancestral File

(used by Atkisson to create *Hanging Family History*) have all been largely owned by or associated with the Latter-day Saint faith.

5 Wolfgang Ernst, "Archive, Storage, Entropy. Tempor(e)alities of Photography," in *Poetics and Politics of the (Photo) Archive*, ed. Krzysztof Pijarski (Warsaw: Fundacja Archeologia Fotografii, 2011), 57; J. J. Long, "Introduction," in *W. G. Sebald—Image, Archive, Modernity* (New York: Columbia University Press, 2010), 12–13; Michel Foucault, "The Historical A Priori and the Archive," in *The Archaeology of Knowledge* (New York: Pantheon Books, 1972), 126–131.

6 Giovanna Zapperi, "Woman's Reappearance: Rethinking the Archive in Contemporary Art—Feminist Perspectives," *Feminist Review* 105, no. 1 (2013): 21–47.

7 Hal Foster, "An Archival Impulse," *October* 110 (2004): 3–22. See also Okwui Enwezor, *Archive Fever: Uses of the Document in Contemporary Art* (New York: International Center of Photography, 2008).

8 Nancy Rivera and Scotti Hill, *Women to the Front: Perspectives on Equality, Gender, and Activism* (Salt Lake City: Utah Division of Arts and Museums, 2020): 2.

9 Griselda Pollock, "Feminist Interventions in the Histories of Art," in *Art History and Its Methods,* ed. Eric Fernie (London: Phaidon Press, 1995), 296–313; Peggy Phelan, *Unmarked: The Politics of Performance* (London: Routledge, 1993); Amelia Jones, *Body Art: Performing the Subject* (Minneapolis: University of Minnesota Press, 1998); Connie Butler, *WACK! Art and the Feminist Revolut*ion (Cambridge, MA: MIT Press, 2007).

10 Johanna Brooks, Rachel Hunt Steenblick, and Hannah Wheelwright, *Mormon Feminism: Essential Writings* (Oxford: Oxford University Press, 2016). See also Maxine Hanks, *Women and Authority: Re-emerging Mormon Feminism* (Salt Lake City: Signature Books, 1992).

11 Gavin Feller, "A Moderate Manifesto: Mormon Feminism, Agency, and Internet Blogging," *Journal of Media and Religion* 15, no. 3 (2016): 156–166. See also Brooks, Steenblick, and Wheelwright, *Mormon Feminism,* 19; Jessica Finnegan and Nancy Ross, "I'm a Mormon Feminist: How Social Media Revitalized and Enlarged a Movement," *Interdisciplinary Journal of Research on Religion* 9, no. 12 (2013).

12 Chiung Hwang Chen, "Diverse Yet Hegemonic: Expressions of Motherhood in 'I'm a Mormon' Ads," *Journal of Media and Religion* 13, no. 1 (2014): 31–47.

13 Brooks, Steenblick, and Wheelwright, *Mormon Feminism,* 2–9.

14 Linda Jones Gibbs, "Out of the Land—Then and Now," in *Out of the Land: Utah Women* (Salt Lake City: Paragon Press, 1992), 3–4.

15 "New Contemporary Exhibition at BYU MOA Explores Utah's Unique Gender Politics," BYU University Communications, April 30, 2013, https://news.byu.edu/news/new-contemporary-exhibition-byu-moa-explores-utahs-unique-gender-politics.

16 Rivera and Hill, *Women to the Front,* 7.

17 Kristin Rowe-Finkbeiner, *The F-Word: Feminism in Jeopardy—Women, Politics and the Future* (Emeryville, CA: Seal Press, 2004). Anthea Butler points out, "For many Mormon women, the idea of being a Mormon as well as a feminist is unthinkable and incompatible with the faith." Anthea Butler, "Review Panel," *Mormon Studies Review* 4 (2017): 95.

18 James Elkins, *On the Strange Place of Religion in Contemporary Art* (New York: Routledge, 2004).

19 See Eleanor Heartney, *Postmodern Heretics: The Catholic Imagination in Contemporary Art* (New York: Midmarch Arts Press, 2004); Jennie Klein, "Goddess: Feminist Art and Spirituality in the 1970s," *Feminist Studies* 35, no. 3 (2009): 575–602.

20 Heather Belnap, *Marianne Meets the Mormons: Representations of Mormonism in Nineteenth-Century France* (Urbana: University of Illinois Press, 2022); see also Jenny Reeder and Ashlee Whitaker Evans's chapters in this volume. Marie W. Dallam also begins to trace a feminist history of Mormon art in her article "Art, Religious Memory, and Mormon Polygamy," *MAVCOR Journal* 5, no. 1 (2016). In addition, Laura Allred Hurtado, Scotti Hill, Lindsay Hansen-Park, Sonja Farnsworth, and others have contributed exceptional discourse around Mormon women artists.

21 Margaret Olsen Hemming, "The Sacred Feminine in LDS Art and Theology," Center Gallery, January 5, 2022, https://www.centergallerynyc.org/exhibitions/the-sacred-feminine-in-lds-art-theology.

22 Hemming, "The Sacred Feminine in LDS Art and Theology," 13.

23 Kwani Povi Winder, email message to the author, January 3, 2023.

[24] Hemming, "The Sacred Feminine in LDS Art and Theology," 2.

[25] Judith Butler, *Gender Trouble* (New York: Routledge, 1990); Diana Fuss, *Essentially Speaking: Feminism, Nature, and Difference* (New York: Routledge, 1989); Audre Lorde, *Sister Outsider* (Freedom, CA: Crossing Press, 1984).

[26] Catherine Clune-Taylor, "Securing a Cisgendered Futures: Intersex Management Under the 'Disorders of Sex Development' Treatment Model," *Hypatia* 34, no. 4 (2019): 690–712. Taylor G. Petrey, "Rethinking Mormonism's Heavenly Mother," *Harvard Theological Review* 109 (2016): 316.

[27] Janan Graham-Russell, "On Black Bodies in White Spaces: Conversations of Women's Ordination and Women of African Descent in the Church of Jesus Christ of Latter-day Saints," *A Life Diasporatic* (blog), September 23, 2013, https://alifediasporatic.wordpress.com/2013/09/23/on-black-bodies-in-white-space-conversations-of-womens-ordination-and-women-of-african-descent-in-the-church-of-jesus-christ-of-latter-day-saints/.

[28] Kimberlé Crenshaw, "Demarginalizing the Intersection of Race and Sex: A Black Feminist Critique of Antidiscrimination Doctrine, Feminist Theory and Antiracist Politics," *University of Chicago Legal Forum* 1, no. 8 (1989): 139.

[29] C. S. Peirce, *Collected Writings,* ed. Charles Hartshorne, Paul Weiss, and Arthur W. Burks (Cambridge, MA: Harvard University Press, 1931–1958).

[30] Marlena Wilding, "Dialogue Fireside with Marlena Marie Wilding: Art: The Spiritual Language of the Soul," YouTube, posted by Dialogue Journal of Mormon Thought, May 19, 2021, https://www.youtube.com/watch?v=EqrsmgT-bRk.

[31] Within bell hooks's theory of feminism, the construction of masculinity contributes to the oppressive nature of patriarchy, making feminism applicable to all genders. bell hooks, "Understanding Patriarchy," in *The Will to Change: Men, Masculinity, and Love* (New York: Atria Books, 2004), 17–34.

[32] Marlena Marie Wilding, in discussion with the author, March 16, 2022.

[33] Darron T. Smith, "The Mask We Must Wear in a Racist Society: Reflections of Black Suffering in the LDS Church Through Art," *Dialogue: A Journal of Mormon Thought* 54, no. 1 (2021): 153.

[34] Wilding, in discussion with the author, March 16, 2022.

[35] Wilding, in discussion with the author, March 16, 2022.

[36] Marlena Wilding, "Eve," 2018, watercolor collage, Instagram post July 5, 2020, https://www.instagram.com/p/CCSgFvBBysY/.

[37] Wilding, in discussion with the author, March 16, 2022.

[38] Concerted efforts to recover histories of Black members have also been made by Paul Reeve's public history project, "Century of Black Mormons." W. Paul Reeve, "Century of Black Mormons: A Preliminary Interpretation of the Data," *Current Research in Digital History* 2 (2019), https://doi.org/10.31835/crdh.2019.03.

[39] Amy Jorgensen, "Body Archive Statement," artist's personal website, accessed June 19, 2021, http://www.amyjorgensen.com/uploads/2/0/7/1/20711900/body_archive_statement_jorgensen.pdf.

[40] Amy Jorgensen, in discussion with the author, October 20, 2022.

[41] Jason Swensen, "Seventy Says Personal Testimony of Book of Mormon 'Essential' to Missionary Work," *Church News,* January 23, 2018, https://www.churchofjesuschrist.org/church/news/seventy-says-personal-testimony-of-book-of-mormon-essential-to-missionary-work?lang=eng.

[42] Spencer W. Kimball, "The What and Why and How of Bearing a Testimony," *New Era,* August 1981, 4–7.

[43] Kimball, "The What and Why and How," 4.

[44] Wolfgang Ernst, "Archive, Storage, Entropy. Tempor(e)alities of Photography," in *The Archive as Project—The Poetics and Politics of the (Photo) Archive,* ed. Krzysztof Pijarski (Warsaw: Fundacja Archeologia Fotografii, 2011), 56–66.

[45] Georges Didi-Huberman, *The Invention of Hysteria: Charcot and the Photographic Iconography of the Salpêtrière* (Cambridge, MA: MIT Press, 2004), 54–55.

[46] Didi-Huberman, *The Invention of Hysteria,* 60–61.

[47] Cecily Devereux, "Hysteria, Feminism, and Gender Revisited: The Case of the Second Wave," *ESC: English Studies in Canada* 40 (2014): 19–45.

[48] Zapperi, "Woman's Reappearance," 25.

[49] Kit Hermanson, "Archive of the Covenant: Reflections on Mormon Interactions with State and Body," *Dialogue: A Journal of Mormon Thought* 53 (2020): 80.

[50] Georgina Bringas, in conversation with the author, March 10, 2022.

[51] Georgina Bringas, in conversation with the author, March 10, 2022.

[52] Georgina Bringas, "To Measure Is to Learn," artist's personal website, http://www.georginabringas.com/textos/manualesp.pdf, accessed March 8, 2022.

[53] Bringas, "To Measure Is to Learn."

[54] Georgina Bringas, "Artist Statement," Abstract in Action, http://abstractioninaction.com/artists/georgina-bringas/#, accessed March 8, 2022.

[55] See Banu Subramaniam, "Moored Metamorphoses: A Retrospective Essay on Feminist Science Studies," *Signs* 34 (2009): 951–980.

[56] Subramaniam, "Moored Metamorphoses," 951–980; Heather Douglas, *Science, Policy, and the Value-Free Ideal* (Pittsburgh: University of Pittsburgh Press, 2009).

[57] Angela Ellsworth, "Artist's Statement: The Plural Wife Project," *Frontiers: A Journal of Women Studies* 33:1 (2012): 48.

[58] Dallam, "Art, Religious Memory, and Mormon Polygamy," 15.

[59] Butler, *Gender Trouble*.

[60] Amanda Beardsley, "The Female Absorption Coefficient: The Miniskirt Study, Gender, and Mormon Architectural Acoustics," *Technology and Culture* 62 (2021): 659–684; Mary Campbell, *Charles Ellis Johnson and the Erotic Mormon Image* (Chicago: University of Chicago Press, 2016).

[61] Dallam, "Art, Religious Memory, and Mormon Polygamy," 15.

[62] Campbell, *Charles Ellis Johnson and the Erotic Mormon Image*, 115–144.

[63] Though the Latter-day Saint faith has become more lenient in its attitudes toward same-sex attraction, it has historically taken a strict stance against homosexuality. Gregory A. Prince, *Gay Rights and the Mormons: Intended Actions, Unintended Consequences* (Salt Lake City: University of Utah Press, 2019).

[64] Angela Ellsworth, "Sister-Wives," Angela Ellsworth personal website, http://www.aellsworth.com/sister-wives, accessed January 6, 2023.

[65] Long, "Introduction," 12–13; John Tagg, "The One-Eyed Man and the One-Armed Man," in *The Disciplinary Frame: Photographic Truths and the Capture of Meaning* (Minneapolis: University of Minnesota Press, 2009), 12.

20

"WHO DID I LEAVE OUT AND SHOULD HAVE INCLUDED?"

The History and Influence of the International Art Competitions at the Church History Museum

LAURA PAULSEN HOWE

A quilt by Carol Johnson hung in the twelfth International Art Competition exhibition (2022) at the Church History Museum in Salt Lake City. Titled *Pew Shoes,* this piece is the artist's response to the competition's theme, "All Are Alike unto God."[1] To create this work, Johnson sketched the feet of those sitting in pews in front of her in Latter-day Saint church meetings.[2] Johnson's quilt depicts shoes that symbolize different members of her congregation, including sandals, work boots, and high heels. Some shoes have been removed. One pair adorns feet pushing organ pedals. A barefoot baby sleeps among the shoes, and a small pink pair rests next to a discarded face mask, referencing the 2020–2021 mask mandates in Latter-day Saint meetinghouses during the worldwide pandemic. "I wanted the finished piece to reflect the wonderful diversity of members of the Church of Jesus Christ of Latter-day Saints I have met around the world and God's love for all of them," Johnson mused.[3] Her reflections caused her to ask several questions: "Who has two left feet? No shoes? Do you see the deacons?"[4] And finally, "Who did I leave out and should have included?"[5]

That final question—"Who did I leave out and should have included?"—is analogous to the questions that drive museum curators. A curator acquires objects that fill gaps in an institution's collection based on that institution's collecting priorities. The Church History Museum has been part of the Church of Jesus Christ of Latter-day Saints'

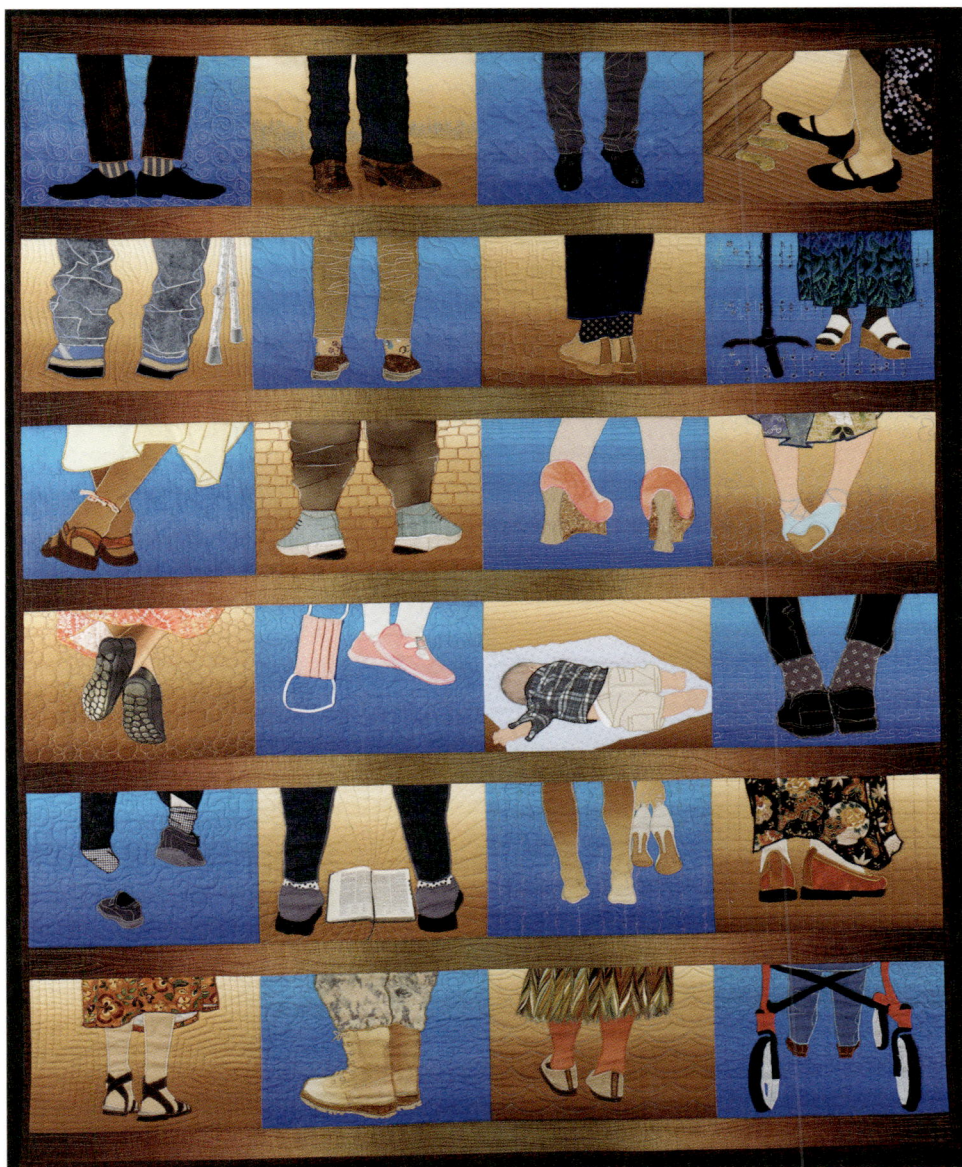

Fig. 20.1 Carol Johnson, *Pew Shoes*, 2021, fabric and thread, 51.25″ × 40.25″. Courtesy of the artist.

Church History Department since it opened in 1984.[6] Therefore, its collection has always existed to help fulfill the divine mandate to the church historian and recorder—to "let there be a record kept among you."[7] In this context, the Church History Museum art collection serves as an archive of objects of "enduring historical value [that] document the history of the Church."[8] It is therefore important that the art curator of the

Church History Museum, when looking at the existing collection of objects that document the history of the church, ask what has been left out and what should be included.

The history of the triennial International Art Competition traces the attempts of curators to acquire art that more completely documents the history of the church—including the lived history of its current members. In many ways, the Church History Museum has accomplished its goals. The art collection maintained by the Church of Jesus Christ of Latter-day Saints is certainly more representative of its worldwide membership than it was in 1984. But as the current art curator at the Church History Museum, I am often asked how influential the competitions are on Latter-day Saint visual culture. As an art professional myself, I often think about who has been left out of that visual culture and who could be included to better accomplish the purpose of the institution—to bring individuals to Christ. Some artists who entered these competitions have had a great impact; their works have been used in church products with a greater reach than the Church History Museum—magazines, visitor's centers, temples, meetinghouses, and so on. But the fact that art is used by many departments within the Church of Jesus Christ of Latter-day Saints institution and used differently by each department dictates that the art competitions' impact is necessarily limited.

WHO WAS LEFT OUT? MOTIVATION FOR AN INTERNATIONAL ART COMPETITION

While the church accrued art and artifacts throughout its history, the late 1970s were the first time art professionals were hired to catalogue those works and begin thinking about how the items collected reflected the current makeup of the church. They discovered that the church's collection largely represented the beginnings of the modern church and the history of church members living in the Intermountain West—the "Mormon corridor." This insular collecting practice revealed a penchant for European naturalism and resulted in an unfortunate cultural homogeneity. Members living outside the Intermountain West, especially art from these members, had been left out.

The establishment of the Museum of Church History and Art in Salt Lake City, Utah, in 1984 coincided with an institutional focus on Latter-day Saints living outside of the United States. While Latter-day Saints had been invited to gather to Zion—defined post-1847 as the Intermountain West—in 1973 Latter-day Saint apostle Bruce R. McConkie gave a discourse at the Mexico City Area Conference, saying:

> The place of gathering for the Mexican Saints is in Mexico; the place of gathering for the Guatemalan Saints is in Guatemala; the place of gathering for the Brazilian Saints is in Brazil; and so it goes throughout the length and breadth of the whole earth. . . . [Every] nation is the gathering place for its own people.[9]

In 1984, despite a tradition of art that was created by members of the church living in the Intermountain West or approved by leadership living in the Intermountain

West, 3,044,755 members of the church lived outside Utah, Idaho, and Arizona, with 1,525,184 members of the church living in those states.[10] The artistic tradition that was correlated in the 1970s and exported around the world was purchased, created, and approved by a culture reflecting a minority of its members.

The Museum of Church History and Art was dedicated that same year. In an article written for *Ensign,* the church's monthly publication to the English-speaking world, Homer G. Durham, then church historian and recorder with stewardship over the new museum, declared the museum's mission:

> Church history is being made in many lands. Just as families everywhere treasure items to pass on, the museum preserves the important and the durable. . . . All should be grateful to the First Presidency for having the vision to have this structure built, a place where pioneering work of the Church all over the world can be displayed.[11]

Durham emphasized the global church as he stated the collecting focus: "The museum is continually looking for artifacts and art that tell the history of the Church from 1820 to the present, which includes history that has been and is now being made in the many countries of the world where the gospel has been preached and has taken root."[12]

However, the ability to gather items reflecting non-Eurocentric art traditions was limited, and support was scant for curators traveling to collect global works.[13] So when Jack and Mary Lois Wheatley approached the museum in 1986 with a plan for an art competition to encourage the creation of Latter-day Saint art, museum personnel proposed the competition be church-wide.[14] Curator of Acquisitions Richard Oman saw this Fine Arts Competition as a chance to bring "fieldwork" to Salt Lake City.[15]

WHO SHOULD BE INCLUDED? MOUNTING AN INTERNATIONAL ART COMPETITION

Informing artists of a church-wide competition was a herculean effort. Museum staff sent entry forms to all 2,500 known Latter-day Saint artists. Forms were also mailed to all stake presidents in the English-speaking world and all LDS Institutes of Religion. The museum personnel also invited faculty and students at college art departments where they suspected there would be many members of the church (in Utah, Idaho, and Arizona) and local art galleries. All together, these efforts resulted in five thousand invitations to participate. The effort to inform the non-English-speaking world was limited to advertising in the international magazines of the church.[16]

Curators desired to showcase global styles. The docent guide introduced the show:

> A great effort was made to include pieces from a very broad stylistic background. Some of the art selected may seem unfamiliar in style to what you are accustomed to seeing in the Museum's previous exhibitions. Sometimes the art is very different because it

is following a national or regional style that is very different from what we are accustomed to here in Utah.[17]

The guide then queried readers, "If you traveled to a distant part of the world and it looked just like Bountiful [Utah] wouldn't you feel cheated?"[18] However, the breadth of style was necessarily limited by the media accepted: only paintings (defined as watercolor, oil, acrylic, and mixed media), drawings (including pastels, it was noted), prints, and sculpture—all media privileging Eurocentric art traditions—were accepted.[19]

The resulting 1987 Fine Arts Competition had 1,031 entries from over 600 artists.[20] Artists submitted slides and photographs of their work, and 250 works were sent to the museum to be juried. Those 250 works were narrowed down to 175 for the final show by Mary Lois Wheatley and four church employees.[21]

From that first show, the nature of the competition would evolve. Richard Oman recalls a conversation he had with a translator from Tonga who was translating the call for art in the church's international magazine. Oman remembers the translator saying, "I don't know how to translate the word 'fine arts,' it doesn't have any meaning in Tonga." Oman tried to explain the Western paradigm of fine art versus folk art and the media accepted for the 1987 Fine Arts Competition—sculpture, paintings, drawings, and original prints. The translator asked, "Does that include basketry? Does that include finely woven mats? Does that include *tapa* cloths?"—referencing the art forms Tongans have historically used to express themselves. Oman had to inform him that those media weren't accepted as part of the show. "Oh," responded the Tongan translator. "I guess we're not invited to this one."[22]

The second art competition, in 1990, still funded by Jack and Mary Lois Wheatley, was open to all media, including "textiles, quilts, embroidery, pottery, ceramics, jewelry, wood carving, sculpture, photography, stained glass, drawing, prints, paintings, needlework, leatherwork, metalwork, basketry, watercolor, and mixed media."[23] By the fourth competition in 1996, the competition was funded internally, and a competition held every three years was established. The twelfth competition—the most recent—had entries from 859 artists and resulted in a show of 148 works.

Besides broadening the media, the museum continues its efforts to encourage global artists. Artists make use of the church's worldwide distribution centers to ship works to Salt Lake City. Scholarships are available to those for whom the cost of shipping is prohibitive. Recent competitions have been advertised on some of the church's global area pages. And the competition is still advertised in *Liahona*, the church's global publication.

For the first nine competitions, the jury consisted primarily of church employees with an occasional invited outside expert.[24] Richard Oman, who sometimes invited those outside experts, explained his intent in inviting outside jurors: "I had a goal of what I wanted this to do. I wanted it to do field work outside of our immediate area. I wanted it to enfranchise the members of the church. . . . I wanted to get it international.

I wanted to beef up the jury with people who would have the broader mission. . . . The nitty gritty was I wanted to have two votes."[25]

Glen Leonard, director of the Museum of Church History and Art between 1979 and 2007, commented on styles both within and without the United States when asked what he saw as the art competition's value: "By including art from other countries, [whose styles] are different than art here, we were showing [the artists] that they mattered. And we were showing us that they mattered." Leonard then went on to reference the style that tended to be preferred in Salt Lake City and the bias revealed in that preference: "We are a global church. But there were older people than us who were so locked into classical art. It was harder for them to see all of the 'strange stuff.' [They asked questions like,] 'Is that art?' For some people, that is a hard question, because they live in that Euro-American view of art."[26]

WHO SHOULD BE INCLUDED? ART OUTSIDE THE LATTER-DAY SAINT CORRIDOR

Even though each art competition has had on average only 19.6 percent of its makeup from artists who live outside the United States, some truly wonderful works expressing Latter-day Saint faith outside of a Eurocentric tradition have been collected out of the international art competitions.[27] The increasing number of artworks from outside the United States reveals the ways Latter-day Saints often adapt existing styles, symbols, and forms from their respective cultures by infusing them with distinct Latter-day Saint content. In these cases, the work becomes Latter-day Saint because the art form is consecrated toward expressing what are powerful religious truths for the creators.

Aoba Taiichi's earthenware work that he created for the third competition, in 1994, *Become Familiar with the Scriptures,* is one example of this translation of existing forms into Latter-day Saint expressions. Aoba was trained by his father, renowned Japanese artist Aoba Taiyo. Aoba Taiichi notes, "I started this [ceramics] work in 1975 with my father, a ceramicist. In the same year, I learned the gospel from a missionary and was baptized, so my ceramic art history and religious history are the same."[28]

Japanese porcelain is a tradition that dates to the Neolithic period. At the end of the fifteenth century, under the stewardship of Murata Jukō, drinking tea was formalized into a ritual, *cha no yu*. Within the context of the tea ceremony, aesthetic and spiritual ideals developed—ideals that would influence Japanese clothing, architecture, meals, and art in the form of scrolls and ceramics. For Aoba, working in his father's workshop, the ritualized tea ceremony was the primary driver of the ceramics market, and as Aoba chose to adopt the Latter-day Saint Word of Wisdom—a commandment that prohibited, among other things, the drinking of tea—abandoning the tea ceremony had serious familial and financial implications.[29]

Aoba found new ways to maintain his cultural expression. His unique ceramic work evinces a personal translation of a Japanese cultural art into a Latter-day Saint–inflected version. Although he didn't inherit his father's workshop, Aoba founded his

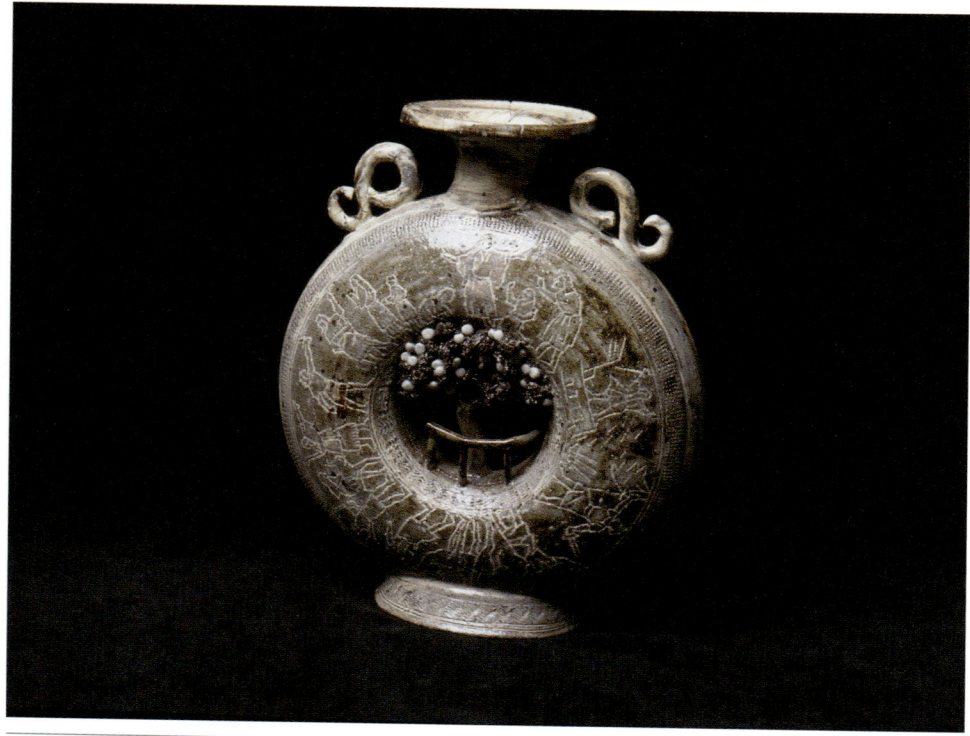

Fig. 20.2 Aoba Taiichi, *Become Familiar with the Scriptures*, 1993, ceramic, 14″ × 11″ × 4.5″, Church of Jesus Christ of Latter-day Saints Church History Museum.

own, and his works have proven popular. *Become Familiar with the Scriptures* uses traditional Japanese methods. He fires his works for seventy-two consecutive hours in kilns built from salvaged brick and fueled by wood.[30] Aoba comments, "It is difficult to keep burning wood for 70 hours, but the flame of firewood brings a unique change and expression to the work."[31] Aoba creates his own glazes by burning plants and crushing stones into powder.

The form of the work supports the meaning Aoba was striving to convey. "In making this work," Aoba explains, "I wanted to make the theme of God's love. I wanted to express how faith in Jesus Christ leads people to happiness through repeated guides, peace and war, prosperity and pride in the history of the Nephites."[32] Although it was a challenge to make a ring with a central cavity on a potter's wheel, the ring allowed the rest of the ceramic to serve as a frame for the tree of life, the Book of Mormon symbol of the love of God in the center of the piece. Aoba uses the traditional technique of *zougan* (象嵌), or inlay, by carving patterns and scenes on the surface of the clay before it has completely dried, filling that engraving with a different color of mud, and scraping it smooth before firing.

Aoba has inlaid various scenes from the Book of Mormon around the ring. At the top of the vase stands Jesus Christ and his visit to the Americas as described in the Book of Mormon.[33] He stands solidly, his hands stretched toward the worshipers who bow before him. Moving clockwise around the ring, Aoba has included Samuel the Lamanite, a prophet who stood on a wall to proclaim the coming of Jesus Christ.[34] The scriptural account states that listeners threw stones and shot arrows at Samuel in anger, but that none of these stones and arrows hit Samuel. In Aoba's depiction, the engraved lines from the right appear headed directly toward Samuel; the viewer is left to assume that divine intervention must protect Samuel from the onslaught.[35] Next stands Captain Moroni, the military commander who creates a banner to rally people to join him in resisting a group of political dissenters.[36] The figure to the right of Moroni represents those who elected to support him.[37] Around the bottom of the ring Aoba included the family of Lehi departing into the desert, and the adjacent horse and sword indicates the eventual separation of the Nephites and Lamanites.[38] The figure threatening with a sword represents those who deny the birth of Christ, while those who kneel acknowledge the presence of the Savior. Each story represents a key moment in the pattern in the story from humility to pride, from prosperity and destruction, a repeated cycle that's alluded to in the figure-eight handles that adorn the vase.[39] On the vase's stand, Aoba engraved wavy lines, indicating that the stories above happened across the waters both from biblical lands and from Japan, Aoba's homeland. Aoba's art highlights scriptural moments of faith and sacrifice that reflect his own faith journey.

For the seventh International Art Competition, hung in 2006, Jeronimo Lozano created *Our Heritage of Faith*. Lozano was raised in Huamanga, Ayacucho, Peru, a mountain city and cultural destination. Lozano attended various *colegios* for specialized art training and attended the School of Fine Arts at the University of Lima. There, he was encouraged to study the artistic traditions of Peru and spent twelve years (between 1967 and 1979) traveling Peru to learn art forms from artists living throughout the Andes. He returned to Ayacucho, where he founded the Artists Workshop Guamangensis and sought to perfect the art forms he had learned in his travels.[40]

One of the art forms Lozano studied was Peruvian *retablos*. These portable altarpieces with doors that open and shut reflect the cross-cultural traditions of Peru. Before European settlers arrived, Indigenous peoples of the Andes used portable objects (religious plaques, stone figures, or metal figurines that were sometimes dressed in colorful textiles) in religious worship and burials. When Christianity arrived in the Andes during the sixteenth century, this tendency to carry portable religious items meshed well with portable saints and altarpieces carried by Spanish missionaries.[41] By the early part of the twentieth century, artists created wooden boxes containing flour-paste figures on internal shelves and decorated with bright colors and floral arabesques.[42] In the 1940s, anthropologist Alicia Bustamante influenced the form through her work with artist Joaquín López Antay, who made *cajones de San Marcos,* or *retablos* featuring Saint Mark. Bustamante labeled the work of López Antay as "classic" *retablos* and dictated that this

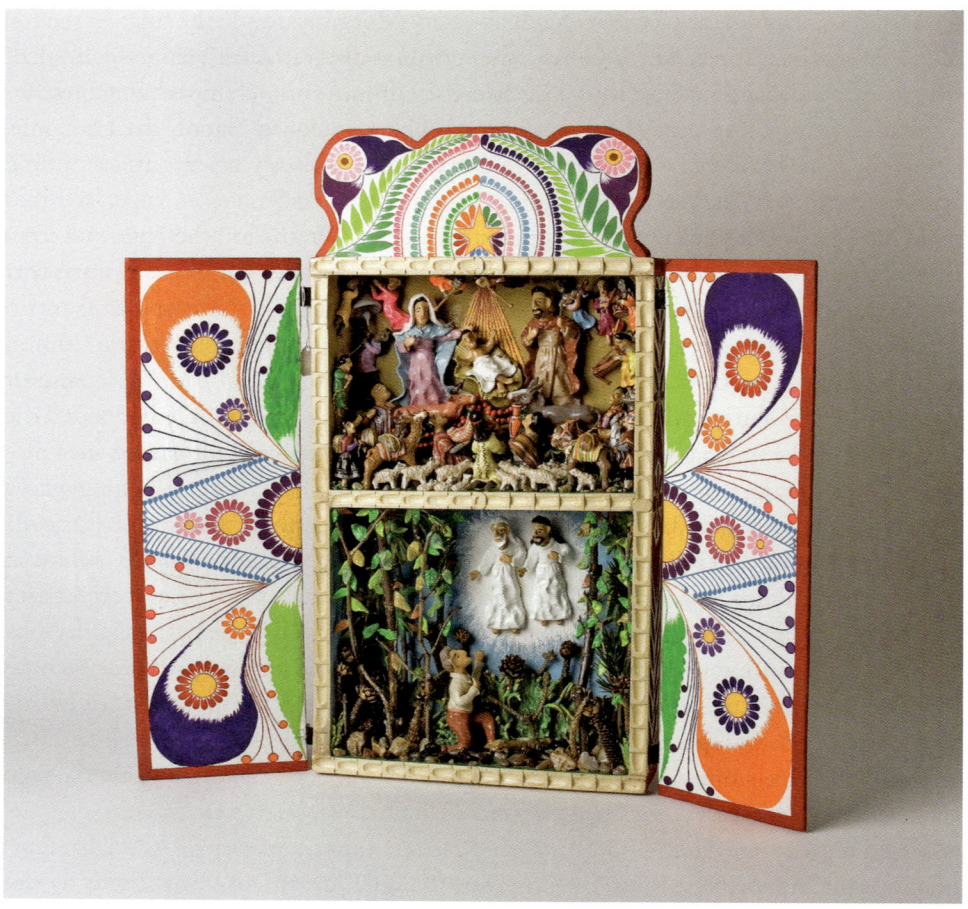

Fig. 20.3 Jeronimo Lozano, *Our Heritage of Faith*, 2005, wood and painted clay, 28″ × 28″ × 4″,
Church of Jesus Christ of Latter-day Saints Church History Museum.

standard form had one shelf to create two compartments.[43] The top shelf was set aside
for images of saints. The bottom shelf was reserved for *costumbrista,* or local scenes of
everyday life.[44] Lozano was trained by López Antay.[45]

Political circumstances led Lozano to leave Peru in 1994. Due to the rise of the
Partido Comunista del Perú–Sendero Luminoso, terrorist activities threatened Lozano
and his work in both Ayacucho and Lima.[46] He came to the United States as part of a
performing arts group and found himself in Salt Lake City. While living with a Latter-
day Saint family, he was offered a Book of Mormon and decided to join the Church of
Jesus Christ of Latter-day Saints. Lozano stayed in Salt Lake City for the rest of his life,
viewing himself as an ambassador for Peruvian culture.[47] In 2008, Lozano received an
NEA National Heritage Fellowship.[48]

Our Heritage of Faith is a classic *retablo* after the format described for the work of Lozano's teacher, López Antay. Closed, the retablo is decorated with a purple butterfly. The two doors swing out to reveal a lively scene within. Rimmed in red, the doors are painted in dark purple, orange, yellow, green, and blue, colors commonly used by *retablo* makers that match the flowers above. The flowers resemble *margaritas* (daisies), flowers common in the Andes Mountains.

Inside we see one shelf creating room for two scenes. On the top shelf we see a scene typical in Peruvian *retablos*. Mary, dressed in purple and blue, welcomes the newborn baby Jesus with her espoused, Joseph. As is common in San Marcos boxes, the scene is filled with animals—sheep, an alpaca, a cow, a horse, and a donkey. All visit the Christ child, accompanied by shepherds wearing clothes that resemble traditional Andean clothing—wide skirts called *polleras*, alpaca ponchos, and brightly colored *llicllas,* or capes. Below the tiny Savior, a trio of kingly worshipers offer gifts of Andean ceramics. The heavenly realm is reserved for the most joyful depictions. Against an otherworldly gold background, angels dressed in brightly colored garments play musical instruments. In the center, two angels blow trumpets. On the right, angels play a *charango* (similar to a ukulele), a violin, a *tinya* or *kirki* (a handheld percussion instrument), and an Andean harp, while several angels work together to ring a massive bell on the left.

While saints occupy the top shelf of the classic *retablo* form, the bottom shelf is reserved for *costumbrista,* or scenes of everyday life. True to form, the scene below does not take place against a supernatural gold background but is decidedly earthly. Leafy trees reach high, while stones and pine cones fill the ground beneath. It is in this everyday realm that Lozano places the figure of Joseph Smith, kneeling in prayer, but with one hand up to acknowledge the sudden and miraculous appearance of divinity. Against a blue sky, two figures representing God the Father and Jesus Christ have come to visit the boy prophet. Lozano has reinforced their corporality by giving them different hair colors; God the Father has flowing white hair, while his son Jesus Christ has black hair. Christ's resurrected body is also made more real by the stigmata on his hands and feet, an identifying witness to his perfected physical form.

For the eighth International Art Competition, in 2008, artist Colleen Wallace Nungari created a work titled *Coming of Christ*.[49] Nungari creates acrylic dot paintings, an art style employed by First Nations peoples in central Australia. The art form has its roots in Aboriginal spirituality but is expressed in European media.

Aboriginal spirituality is expressed through Dreaming stories. The Dreamings are a series of sagas about ancestral beings whose wandering marks world history. These spirits move over the land and create life and the landscape's physical characteristics. More than a creation myth, the Dreamings have practical realities in Aboriginal life. An individual Dreaming gives identity to individuals. The Dreamings also identify the land's association with First Nations people. For example, the Dreaming path taken by Honey Ant belongs to those who live in Ngkwarlerlanem and Arnkawenyerr and identifies the borders of those places. This implies a responsibility to the environment

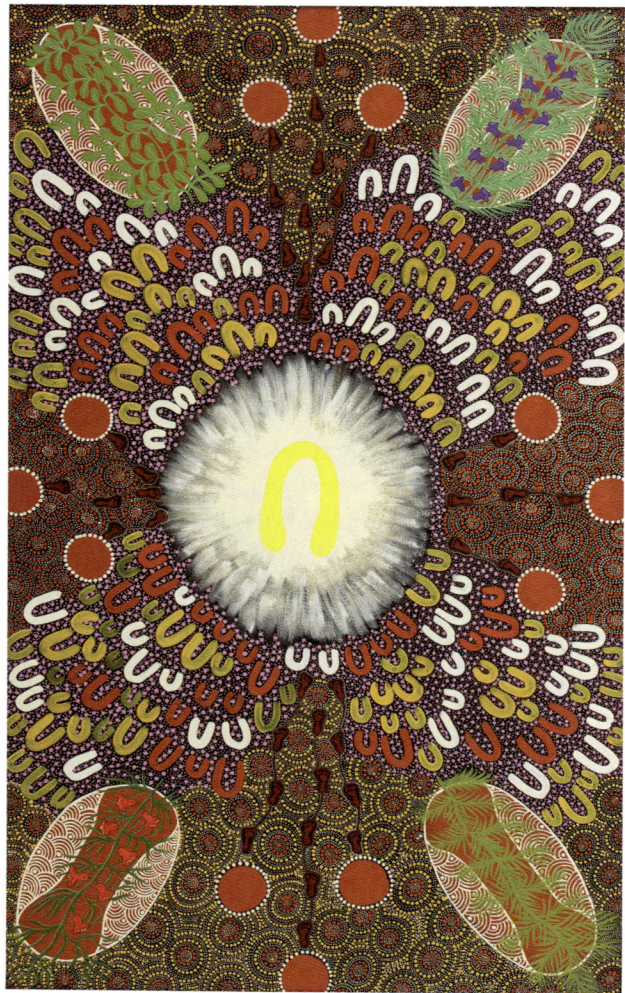

Fig. 20.4 Colleen Wallace Nungari, *Coming of Christ*, 2008, acrylic, 59.25″ × 36.25″, Church of Jesus Christ of Latter-day Saints Church History Museum.

in which a cultural group lives. The Dreaming also indicates kinship relationships and social organization. Those individuals with shared totemic Dreamings have obligations toward each other. The totems determine how people are related, whether one can marry, and who supports whom. Because a Dreaming is individual to each nation, clan, family, or individual, the language word "Dreaming" is incomplete. It is more accurate to refer to the spirituality of each nation by the word identified in each nation's language. For those who speak Arrente, the language Nungari speaks, the term is *altyerre*.

Altyerre sagas are performed. Historically, they are not written down, but sung and danced. In the performance, props are used, including body and ground painting, decorative shields, spears, and other objects.[50] On these props, performers paint the pathways taken by the ancestral beings. Therefore, the land itself is a record of the *altyerre* beings' pathways, and the marks made on bodies, on the ground, and on shields and spears are a record of the record.[51]

A new art form was born in 1971 at Papunya near Alice Springs. Geoffrey Bardon, a white teacher from Sydney, arrived to teach the art to the children of displaced First Nations people in 1971.[52] Bardon established a relationship with several important older men in the community, including Kaapa Tjampitjinpa, Billy Stockman Tjapaltjarri, Long Jack Phillipus Jakamarra, Old Mick Jakamarra, and Uta Jangala. Using European acrylics and canvases provided by Bardon, these artists painted their Dreaming stories, the same forms traditionally depicted on the ground, bodies, and other props used when performing Dreamings.[53]

Nungari, the creator of *Coming of Christ*, was raised by the highly respected artist Kathleen Wallace Kemarre. Kemarre spent her adolescence at a Catholic mission school, where she incorporated Christian beliefs into her worldview. Kemarre states, "I paint on canvas because it is a modern way to keep the [*altyerre*] stories alive and offer this knowledge to other people."[54] Nungari was born in 1974 and raised by Kemarre, who bridged these different mindsets—Christianity with *altyerre,* and *altyerre* performative worship with European media. Nungari recalls, "I remember watching [Kemarre] paint when I was only three years old. She would sing Aboriginal songs and tell me the stories of the Dreamtime ancestors and the land."[55] Kemarre also taught Nungari to paint.[56]

In 2008, Nungari earned a Purchase Award for her painting *Coming of Christ* in the eighth International Art Competition. She currently lives in Mulga Bore, a community of about two hundred Eastern Arrente individuals. Nungari referred to Mulga Bore in 2008 as "the only Aboriginal community of Latter-day Saints in Australia."[57] Her mother-in-law met missionaries from the Church of Jesus Christ of Latter-day Saints in Alice Springs, and she and her family joined. Nungari was baptized around 1998. In her artist statement, Nungari notes that Latter-day Saint missionaries read the Book of Mormon to her each week. She comments, "The Church has transformed my life. My favorite things are my family, the Book of Mormon, and painting stories."[58] Nungari's art continues to record that which is sacred to her and strives to pass on her spiritual and artistic heritage to her children. She comments, "Now I illustrate the Dreamtime stories and the scripture stories when I paint. [My husband] Collin and I have five children we are raising in the Church. Now, I am teaching my daughter Ayara about the Book of Mormon and the stories of the Dreamtime as we paint together."[59]

Nungari uses the artistic language familiar to her to tell of Christ's coming to the Americas as explained in the Book of Mormon.[60] Because acrylic paintings done by First Nations people in central Australia recorded the wanderings of *altyerre* beings through landscape, they are done from an aerial viewpoint, as if the viewer were looking at a map of the path an *altyerre* being or ancestral spirit might take. In *Coming of Christ,* Nungari employs the same viewpoint; the viewer has a bird's-eye view of the scene below.

While iconography is individual to each site and *altyerre* being, some symbols are standard. Nungari paints several U-shapes in the painting—one large U in the center of the piece with many smaller U's oriented around the central U. In acrylic paintings from central Australia, the U-shaped figures represent people sitting.[61] Typical of acrylic art from this region, the viewer sees human tracks painted just as they might appear on the ground.[62] These tracks approach the central U from four directions, indicating the gathering of all peoples to Christ. Plant species and other objects often show up in a stylized but figurative manner in the work of Western Desert artists.[63] Nungari has included an *urtne* in each of the four corners of the painting.[64] These shallow wooden vessels are made for carrying items and are often placed on the head if one is traveling a great distance. A different sprig of medicinal plant, or "bush medicine," is inside each *urtne:* red river gum, a skin cleanser; rock fuchsia bush, used to ease cold and flu symptoms; a branch of a tea tree, a shrub that could be used to treat infection; and a flowering emu bush, an antiseptic.[65] Thus, Christ's healing is carried and made available to all, made real in the tangible symbols of the *urtne* and the medicinal plants.

Joseph Lajabu Banda, an artist from Malawi, participated in the eleventh and twelfth art competitions. Based on his submissions, the Church History Museum purchased *Hold to the Rod*. Wood carving is a traditional form of art in Malawi. Masks influenced by abstract forms are common, but wooden pieces can also be decorated furniture or plaques featuring scenes of everyday life. Wood carving is an art passed through the patriarchal line from father to son. Indeed, Banda's grandfather and uncles were artists who sold primarily to tourists visiting the country.[66] While living in his grandparents' home, Banda learned to carve from his grandfather.[67] Acrylic painting arrived in Malawi more recently. Banda remembers that his mother always provided pencils and

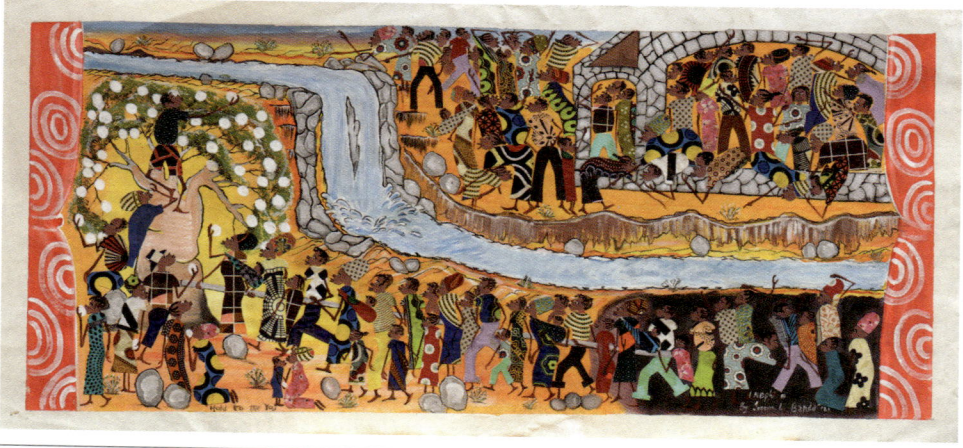

Fig. 20.5 Joseph Lajabu Banda, *Hold to the Rod,* **2019, wood, acrylic, and chitenge cloth on canvas, Church of Jesus Christ of Latter-day Saints Church History Museum.**

crayons for him, even when it was financially difficult.[68] Banda both carves wood and works in mixed media.

In the early 2000s, Banda felt a bit like church prophet Joseph Smith. "I grew up in a community where there were many churches," Banda recalled. His mother was Catholic and his grandparents were Pentecostal. "Just like Joseph Smith, I had a lot of religious questions within my soul."[69] Banda attended one church when he was hired as a musician. While practicing, he noticed the pastor reading a book, which he promptly hid when Banda questioned him about it. When Banda later met missionaries from the Church of Jesus Christ of Latter-day Saints (one from Utah, one from South Africa), he recognized the cover of the Book of Mormon as the same as the cover of the book hidden by the pastor, and Banda began reading. Three months later he chose to be baptized.[70]

After accepting a challenge by Latter-day Saint missionaries to read the Book of Mormon in one hundred days, Banda decided to paint his first gospel scene in 2011. "When I think of painting something," Banda recalled, "the first thing to come to mind was Lehi's dream."[71] He emphasized his desire to express the story in his own cultural language: "I did it in an African way, not the way the other artists have done."[72] The missionaries, seeking a gift for visiting church leader Elder Russell M. Nelson, purchased the painting, paying in shoes, white shirts, and ties. After this first sale, Banda has returned to the theme of Lehi's dream several times.

In his work *Hold to the Rod*, Banda painted the story of Lehi's dream described in the Book of Mormon.[73] It has the elements mentioned in Latter-day Saint scripture: a tree with white fruit; a group of people moving toward the tree, hanging on to an iron rod; a river; and a large building occupied by another group of people laughing and jeering at the other group. But Banda has personalized the story. Banda has painted Lehi's tree of life as a baobab, a tree native to Malawi that truly has been a nutritional tree of life. The baobab stores water in its trunk during Malawi's rainy season and provides a nutrient-dense fruit even when the land is arid.[74] The fruit of the tree, like the fruit in Banda's painting, is long and oblong. The baobab fruit's meat is particularly sweet, seeming to resemble the fruit in Lehi's dream described as "the most sweet, above all that I ever before tasted."[75] The baobab fruit is traditionally harvested by climbing the tree, and in Banda's image Lehi is in the branches, sharing the fruit with his family and friends by throwing it to the men, women, and children waiting beneath. Each figure is dressed in *chitenge* cloth, a batik fabric originally introduced to Africa by Dutch colonists in the nineteenth century but worn today in Malawi by women and more recently men. The river of water mentioned in Latter-day Saint scripture resembles one of the many rivers that flow from Lake Malawi, a body of water that spans the entire eastern border of the country, and includes a waterfall similar to one of several in the country. The figures in the building across the river gesture wildly, their exuberant jeering reflected in their pointed arms and accusatory stances. Banda seems to indicate that the story is a vision unfolding for an audience; curtains of patterned *chitenge* material appear pulled back to reveal the scene. While the piece is mixed-media, using acrylic paints, *chitenge* fabric, and banana fiber, the frame is more traditional, carved in *malaina* wood using the same technique Banda learned from his grandfather. "I strive to carve my art with an African feel," states Banda, "although I know that all these were not African but I always want them to be unique and original."[76]

WHO SHOULD BE INCLUDED? CONTEMPORARY ART

Changes came to the International Art Competition in 2015. Laura Allred Hurtado was hired as a curator for the Church History Museum in 2013. She noticed the value of the show: "[The International Art Competition] set up an openness and commitment dating back to the 80s that different voices matter."[77] As a new curator, she also had an obligation to look at the existing collection and note where there were gaps. Hurtado observed that contemporary art hadn't been previously prioritized and sought to include contemporary art to "expand the visual and cultural narrative of the Church by representing the full spectrum of the cultural and artistic practices of its people."[78]

In addition, the decision was made that while the ninth art competition (2012) had only three jurors, the tenth (2015) should have five. Alan Johnson, director of the Church History Museum from 2013 to 2022, explains the motivations for this change: "The move from three to five jurors was to get a broader mix of expertise and perspectives in order to include, showcase, and acquire different types of media and artistic styles."[79] Later, that diversity of perspectives would include artists and art critics, sculptors, painters, folklorists, and people of color. The decision was also made that the jurors would be professionals from outside the institution; Hurtado served as the jury foreperson but did not have a vote.[80]

One such work is *Fitting Fragments* by Paige Crosland Anderson. Anderson grew up in Provo, Utah, and graduated with a BFA in fine arts from Brigham Young University. Anderson paints layers of acrylic paint until there are innumerable indistinguishable layers. She uses a ruler and masking tape to block some areas of paint as she creates geometric shapes, choosing to sometimes sand away layers, leaving some shapes multicolored and rough. The resulting pattern reminds viewers of quilt patterns, a conscious reference to an art form with a long heritage in Latter-day Saint women's arts. Anderson's first paintings were based on patterns she had seen in her grandmother's quilts.[81] "It's not just the patterns of quilts that inspire me," comments Anderson. "It's their ties to women, to women's work, to meditation and focus. It's their association with warmth, with family, with creating something to give to another."[82]

For her piece *Fitting Fragments,* which hung in the eleventh International Art Competition, Anderson ponders what belief means. She notes, "[This work] is a visual diary of my meditations and incongruities and paradoxes I have encountered as a faithful Latter-day Saint."[83] While painting, she sometimes puts down her brush to write down thoughts or questions. "All things point to the nature of God," she muses. "He created lions and tornadoes and unwieldy jungles and desolate spaces. What does that mean about Him? Is He wild? Is he desolate?"[84] These spaces to ponder are where she feels

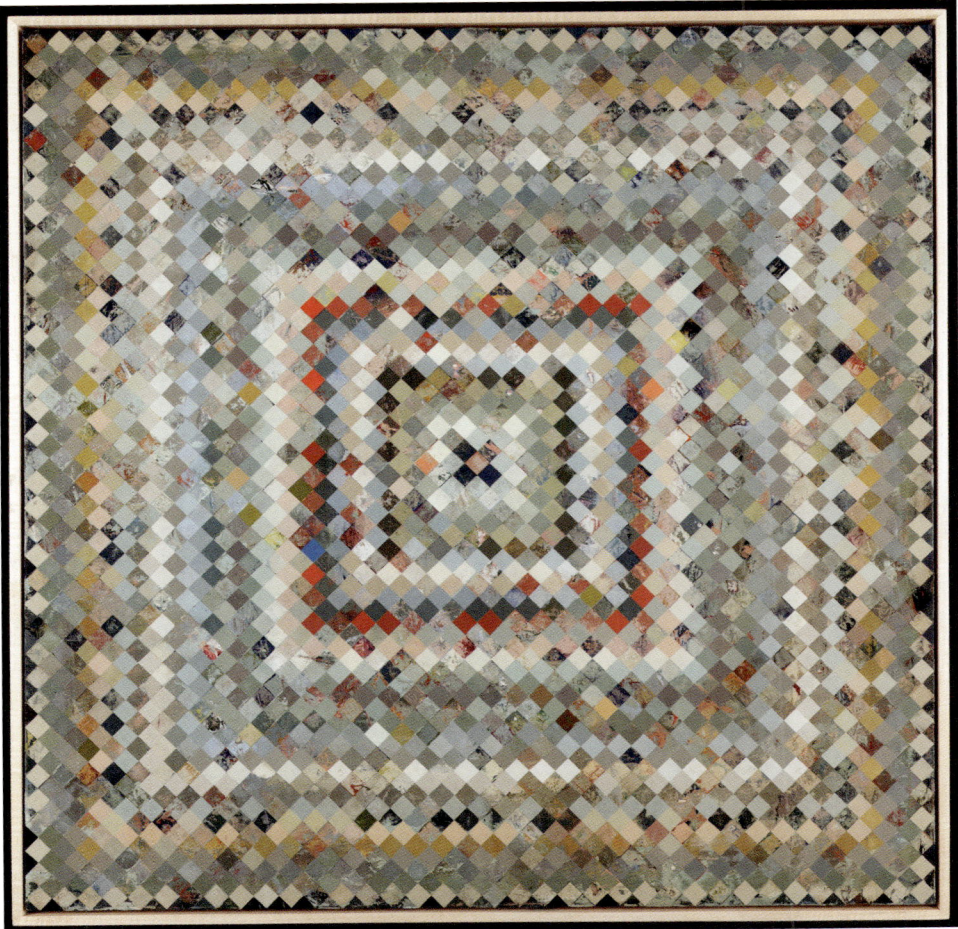

Fig. 20.6 Paige Crosland Anderson, *Fitting Fragments*, 2018, oil on panel, 36″ × 36″. Courtesy of the artist.

the most growth as a disciple.[85] "[My] working meditations have focused on how one truth leads to a dozen questions, how pulling one theological strand sometimes unravels another, and just how vast our doctrine is."[86] The work supports this interpretation. Next to squares confidently filled in with saturated color sit squares that seem fuzzy and undefined. But the beauty of the painting results from the contrast, symbolizing the faithful effort to believe.

Another work from the eleventh International Art Competition acquired to help fill the gap of contemporary art is Danielle Hatch's *And I Am Here,* created in 2018. An artist with a BA in architecture from Wellesley College and an MFA in spatial studies from the University of California at Santa Barbara, Hatch creates performance, installation, and sculptural pieces.[87]

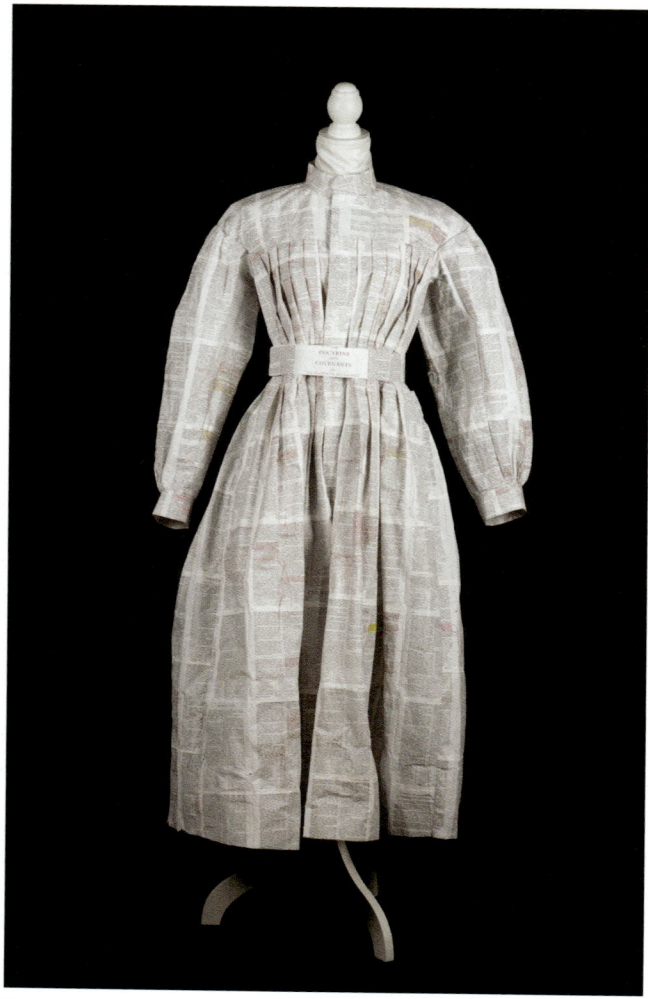

Fig. 20.7 Danielle Hatch, *And I Am Here,* 2018, paper and thread, 60″ × 30″ × 12″, Church of Jesus Christ of Latter-day Saints Church History Museum, LDS 2019-36.

In creating this work, Hatch was inspired by the Church of Jesus Christ of Latter-day Saint's "I Was a Stranger" initiative. This program, introduced in 2016, invited women of all ages to assist refugees in their local communities. Hatch chose to volunteer with the refugee community in Dallas, Texas. This experience inspired her to research Latter-day Saint refugees who went to Mexico in the 1880s, and she spent time reading the accounts of nineteenth-century Latter-day Saint women. She felt pushed to create a work that explored "how spiritual belief and impressions are converted into day-to-day temporal life."[88]

Hatch looked to a symbol of her belief—her childhood set of scriptures. Worn from twenty years of use, the scriptures were beginning to fall apart. Thinking of the lived experience of nineteenth-century women, Hatch created a fabric of scripture paper from the pages of her Book of Mormon and Doctrine and Covenants, complete with hand-stitched highlights over her marked verses. Hatch cut the paper to create pattern pieces and sewed these pieces into an 1860s work dress. Her faith mirrored the faith of the refugees she served. The nineteenth-century Latter-day Saint refugees had become imprinted into the fabric of her life. Rich borrowed her title from a poem by Adrienne Rich: "This is the place. And I am here."[89]

WHO IS LEFT OUT? THE ART COMPETITION'S INFLUENCE ON LATTER-DAY SAINT VISUAL CULTURE

In the construction of Latter-day Saint visual culture, how influential have the International Art Competitions been? In some ways, quite significant. Walter Rane is an artist who has become well-known to Latter-day Saints and whose introduction to the Latter-day Saint art world came via the International Art Competitions. Rane grew up in California and was working as an illustrator in Connecticut and New York when he heard about the 1987 Fine Arts Competition, now considered the first International Art Competition. Rane decided to enter his painting *Mother and Child*, and it won a Merit Award. Three years later, the museum held a second International Art Competition (1990), and he decided to enter *And the Child Grew and Waxed Strong in Spirit*, an image of the boy Jesus in the carpenter shop of his father, Joseph. The museum would purchase that painting, and within a couple of years it seemed to have a use for nearly everything Rane could create. The timing worked out well for Rane, too, as computer illustration was becoming the fashion in illustration: "As soon as I started doing paintings with a scriptural subject matter, all my childhood of studying Rembrandt books just kind of lit fire, and I just loved it."[90] Rane's works were quickly acquired and reproduced for use in magazines and publications, for meetinghouses, for temples, and for visitors' centers. Today, fourteen original Walter Rane paintings hang in Latter-day Saint temples, ten paintings hang in the Conference Center in Salt Lake City, and the Church History Museum counts seventy-two works by Walter Rane in its catalog.

Rose Datoc Dall is another artist who credits the International Art Competition with opening the world of Latter-day Saint art. Dall was trained in art history and fine art at Virginia Commonwealth University of the Arts and earned her BFA in 1990. While she was at school, she joined the church after having been fellowshipped by a childhood friend. Dall got married near the end of her schooling and had several children soon after that. While she found success and was in a few shows, she discovered that maintaining a full-time art career was unmanageable with small children around. It was when she discovered the International Art Competitions that she decided it was time to begin painting in earnest, and to begin painting spiritual themes.

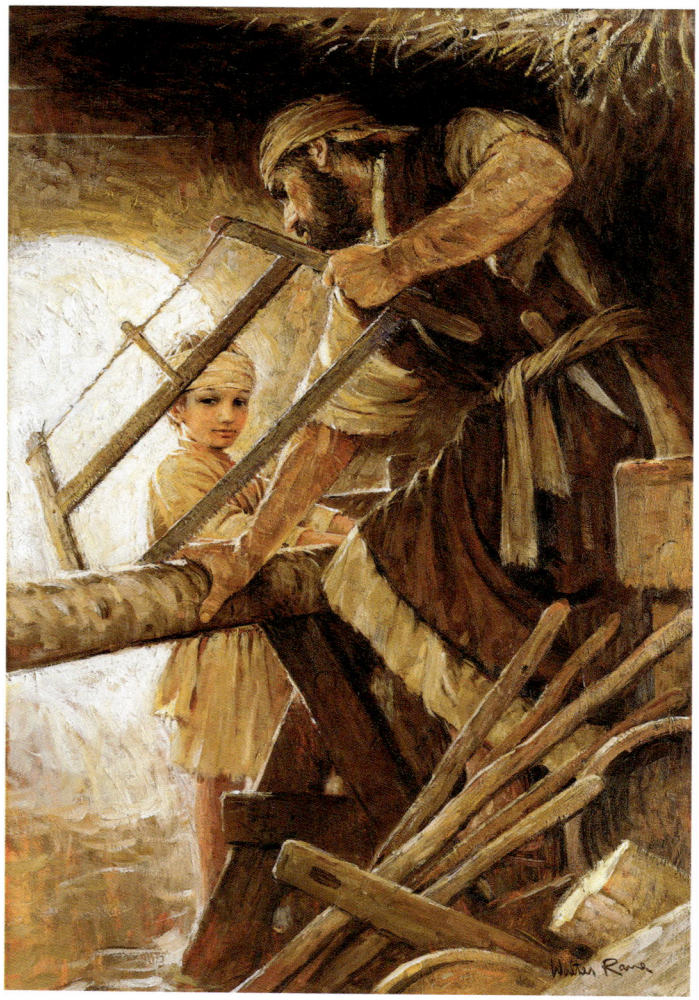

Fig. 20.8 Walter Rane, *And the Child Grew and Waxed Strong in Spirit,* 1990, oil on canvas, 41.25″ × 31.25″, Church of Jesus Christ of Latter-day Saints Church History Museum.

Dall's work was featured in the fifth, sixth, and seventh international art competitions, and she won her first Purchase Award in 2005 from the eighth competition for her painting *Flight.*

Dall would earn Purchase Awards from the next three competitions—for *First News of the Resurrection,* from the ninth International Art Competition (2012), for *Loaves and Fishes,* from the tenth (2015), and for *Living Waters,* from the eleventh (2019).[91] *Loaves and Fishes* currently hangs in the Conference Center, and the new temple visitors' centers in Mesa, Arizona, and Tokyo, Japan, have large reproductions of her works. When asked what the influence of the International Art Competition was on her career,

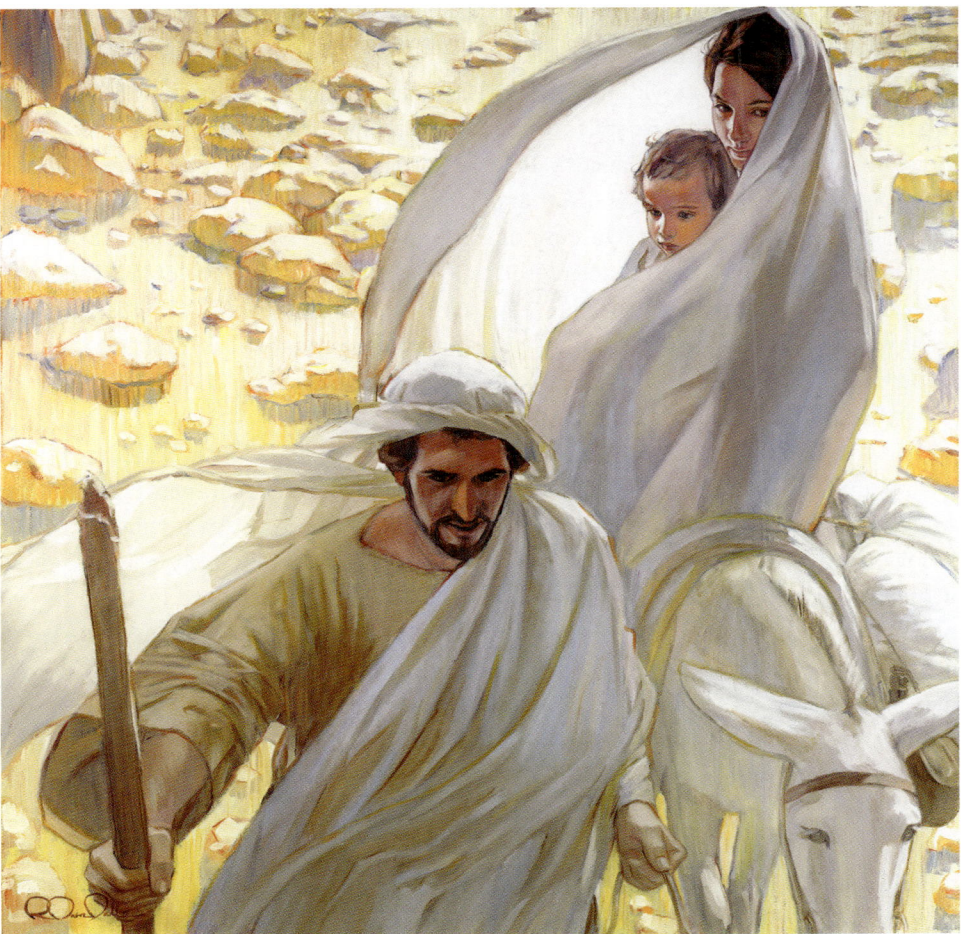

Fig. 20.9 Rose Datoc Dall, *Flight*, 2008, oil on canvas, 54″ × 54″. Courtesy of the artist.

Dall responded, "I think it's huge, because I don't think I ever would have gone down this path. I never saw myself creating religious art. . . . I think [the competitions] are how I got identified as an artist. That's the thing that launched my career."[92]

Recently, the Latter-day Saint art world has become aware of Jorge Cocco Santangelo, an artist from Argentina who was known to museum staff as early as 1986, and who earned a Purchase Award for his work *The Waters of Mormon* in the seventh International Art Competition in 2005, and showed *Jesus Christ Heals the Sick in America* in the eighth International Art Competition (2008). Cocco Santangelo has served on several university faculties, including the University of the Americas in Puebla, Mexico.

Cocco Santangelo first discovered the information about the art competitions in the *Liahona*, but, he said, "The Competition was unknown to us and since there was no internet yet, there was no place to find out more about it, or what the rules were or how often it took place. So, I think I could not participate until years later when information was more readily available."[93] When he did start participating in the art competitions, he employed a different style than he used elsewhere. He noted that in the 1960s, he began to experiment with art styles of the twentieth century, including Surrealism, abstraction, and Cubism. He visited Salt Lake and showed his work to curators at the Museum of Church History and Art and other art institutions in the area, including Brigham Young University's Museum of Art and Deseret Book.[94] "However," Cocco Santangelo commented, "considering the type of art published by the church, I had to go back to painting realistic and figurative art to conform with the unspoken rules of what was the Church looking for in religious art. . . . It was very frustrating, but I understood that for the time being, to succeed as a Mormon artist, I needed to paint more in the style of illustration and classical art."[95]

For the tenth International Art Competition, in 2015, Cocco Santangelo was encouraged by his son Amiel to paint in a Cubist style he was experimenting with. The resulting painting was *El Llamado,* and it earned both a Purchase Award and a Visitors' Choice Award. In the image, the Savior stretches forth his arm to Simon and Andrew fishing on the Sea of Galilee. "Come ye after me," the Savior says, "and I will make you fishers of men."[96] Cocco Santangelo has fractured the images and made negative space positive, as the Cubists did before him. But the resulting lines help reinforce the Savior's message. Lines run horizontally, echoing the Savior's outstretched arm, to indicate the call he is issuing to the fishermen on the boat. The lines that run vertically pull attention up, as if reminding the fishermen that he is here to elevate them to a higher purpose. Finally, lines that run diagonally from left to right draw together the disciples and the Savior, reminding the viewer that it is by a connection to the Savior that they are able to be lifted. The blues and greens of the piece recede behind the white sail of the boat, moving into the light atmosphere that emanates from the Savior; indeed, it looks as though Christ stands in a pillar of symbolic light.

Cocco Santangelo's gamble paid off. "Winning the Purchase Award at the 10th International Art Competition in 2015 changed the course of my artistic path," he remembered.[97] Amiel proposed that instead of just purchasing the one painting that had earned the Purchase Award, perhaps the museum would like to purchase sixteen. Indeed, the museum did, and, combined with an exhibition, the acquisition opened doors for Cocco Santangelo, who now has a deal with Deseret Book. Cocco Santangelo comments, "[The International Art Competition] opened the doors to a very closed market that seemed monopolized by a handful of established Utah artists."[98]

Clearly, the International Art Competitions have influenced Latter-day Saint visual culture in substantive ways. But Cocco Santangelo's experience highlights the ways in which that influence is limited. The Church History Museum is a division within the Church History Department, whose goal, as mentioned earlier, is to help the church historian and recorder fulfill the scriptural mandate "Let there be a record kept among you."[99] Within that context, acquiring art serves a unique purpose. Art (in all its stylistic

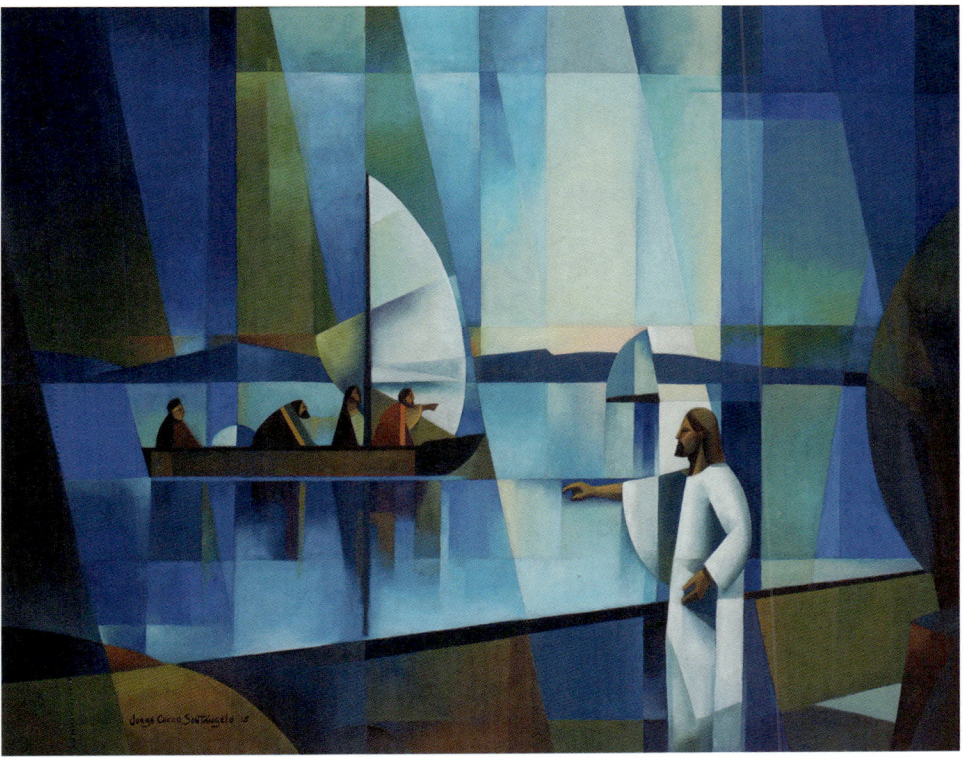

Fig. 20.10 Jorge Cocco Santangelo, *El Llamado*, 2015, oil on canvas, 34.25″ × 41.75″. Courtesy of the artist.

variety) serves as primary source documents for the lived experience of Latter-day Saints. Currently, the Church History Department has a goal to collect art "that captures the contemporary Latter-day Saint experience from artists worldwide who use a variety of materials and artistic styles. In doing so, [it seeks] to expand the visual and cultural narrative of the Church by representing the full spectrum of the cultural and artistic practices of its people."[100] In order to fulfill that mandate, the art curator for the Church History Museum must seek to fill gaps in that visual and cultural narrative. Certainly, a curator acquiring art for a museum considers use-case as one of the justifications for the acquisition, and perhaps acquiring art that might be used by other church departments could be one possible use. But there are many other ways a work of art could be used, including a display in a museum context, a decidedly different context than its display in a temple, a magazine, or a meetinghouse. The museum collection might also be viewed as a visual archive—a place where objects are preserved that might be helpful to historians wondering who the Latter-day Saints are and what they thought about. The international art competitions help fill these gaps.

But even though the Church History Museum is the institutional entity acquiring art as an archive, it is not the only entity at the Church of Jesus Christ of Latter-day Saints that has a role in creating a Latter-day Saint visual culture. Art is also used in meetinghouses, temples, church magazines, and visitors' centers, and on social media. It is used in curriculum manuals and as teaching aids. Historically, these efforts have not been coordinated. Each of these uses is overseen by a different department within the organization of the church. And practically, while all departments share the goal to help individuals come to Christ, the way they do that and the role art plays in that process differs depending on the nature of the venue or context in which the art is seen. For the Meetinghouse Facilities Department, the stated purpose of art is to create a reverent atmosphere and to make clear the centrality of Jesus Christ in Latter-day Saint worship.[101] The Temple Department feels strongly that the temple must not become an art gallery or museum. However, they note that art in the temple should be more than a decorative element. It should "enrich the spiritual experiences that are distinctive to the temple."[102] The Priesthood and Family Department oversees the production of magazines and manuals and uses art to depict a story or a principle. As a result, the art they use tends to be didactic and illustrative. In many of these contexts, academic painting has been seen as most useful in accomplishing these different roles. This is likely why the artists found through the art competitions whose works have had the most significant impact—like Walter Rane, Rose Datoc Dall, and Jorge Cocco Santangelo—have worked in a figurative style.

For several of these departments, and especially if the artwork portrays the Savior, use of a certain work of art is contingent on the approval of the General Authorities who are assigned stewardship of that department. And the stylistic preferences of those with administrative authority play into whether they find a work reverent, instructive, or not distracting. Most associations with a certain art style are culturally driven, and most of the General Authorities are white men who were raised in the United States.

The fact remains that figurative paintings, especially figurative academic paintings, are overwhelmingly created by Eurocentric white male artists. There are several reasons for this. First, Eurocentric art privileges three-dimensional illusionism in a way that isn't a priority in many other artistic traditions. For example, Japanese artists were not interested in replicating an exact depiction of nature. The artistic language that developed in Japan and other Asian countries had landscape as a dominant element (in which the landscape was seen from a high vantage point) and contained little to no modeling of figures. When art that did prioritize three-dimensional illusionism arrived in Japan at the hands of Portuguese in the sixteenth century and later with other European traders, the Japanese pejoratively called it *nanban* art (南蛮美術), or the art of the "southern barbarians." While it is more common today to see art that combines three-dimensional illusionism with more traditional Japanese scenes, naturalistic depictions still proclaim a Eurocentric mindset in Japan, and the creators are overwhelmingly Eurocentric themselves.

It is also true that most artists working in an academic style are white. To be able to paint successfully in this style requires a high degree of training, access to art supplies, and often study in Europe. Michelle Franzoni Thorley is a Mexican American artist who received a Purchase Award from the twelfth International Art Competition (2022) for her work *Making Space for Us*. In an interview on the *First Name Basis* podcast in 2020, Thorley explained her perspective on the challenges facing artists of color desiring to work in a classic naturalistic style: "Being an oil painter, a visual artist, is a privilege, and it has been for centuries. Most artists had to have some wealthy sponsor to pay for the paints and the materials and the solvents and the frames. It's no different with education. There are not a lot of opportunities for people of color—people like me—to have a higher education to be able to paint very finely in the European style."[103] Thorley goes on to explain some social barriers for people of color desiring to be artists: "In most families, especially recent immigrants, if they're going to pay for [their children] to go to school, they're not going to pay for them to be artists."[104]

Finally, most artists working in this preferred style are men. As a matter of doctrine, Latter-day Saint women are encouraged to be mothers. In the United States, this has translated to Latter-day Saint women choosing to remove themselves from

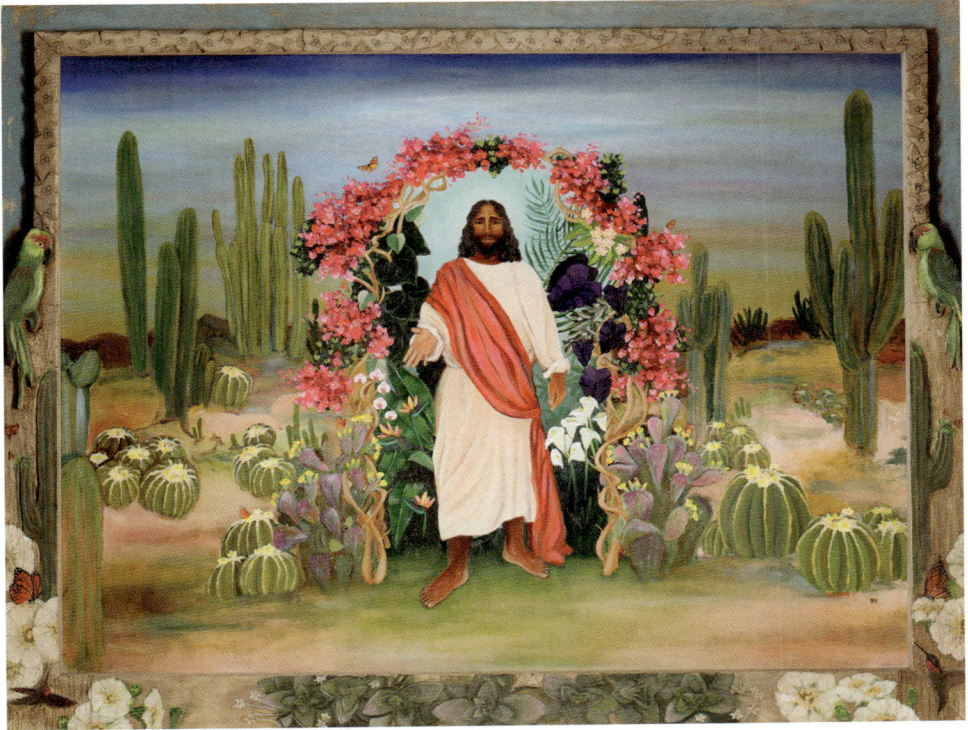

Fig. 20.11 Michelle Franzoni Thorley, *Making Space for Us*, 2021, oil on canvas, 42″ × 56″. Courtesy of the artist.

the workforce. Using the data found in the American Religious Identification Survey in 2008, sociologists Rick Phillips and Ryan T. Cragun found that between 1990 and 2008, while Latter-day Saint women are college educated at the same rates as women outside of the Latter-day Saint faith, Latter-day Saint women are more than twice as likely to report that they are housewives than women who were not of the Latter-day Saint faith (26 percent versus 13 percent). Additionally, Latter-day Saint women are less likely to report that they work full-time (25 percent versus 39 percent).[105] It's safe to assume female Latter-day Saint artists are subject to the same trends.

For Latter-day Saint mothers who do choose to create as they raise their children, managing an art career takes some finagling. Rose Datoc Dall recalls trying to establish an art career with a young family:

> I was trying to really get things going. . . . I had every intention of working full time, but that was pretty unrealistic with these young kids. . . . I was kind of in a crisis mode because I wanted to produce all this art, I wasn't really able to make the time for it. My bandwidth was spent—most of the time I was mentally exhausted, and how can you then tap? You know, there's not much to tap into when you're just spiritually exhausted.[106]

These issues take time away from efforts of artists who are mothers to refine their craft, and training to be a masterly academic painter takes time.

The perspectives of women and BIPOC artists should layer onto the work that they do in meaningful ways. Those perspectives have the potential to add value to their work, not to be a liability. And they're not a liability—unless an artist wants to work in the style that is considered most useful in many church departments.

The Church of Jesus Christ of Latter-day Saints is aware at all levels that it needs to do more to reflect the diverse makeup of their membership in their products. For example, in a 2021 Leadership Enrichment Series presentation made available to church employees, Gerrit W. Gong, apostle for the Church of Jesus Christ of Latter-day Saints, pointed out:

> In 1980—and if you're just visualizing, if you took the Church and you said, "Here's a congregation of 100 people. What does our average Church congregation look like?" Seventy-two of our members are in the United States and Canada, 17 in Latin America, 7 in the Asia/Pacific areas, 4 in Europe. We have a few members by 1980, but not very many in Africa, so it's less than 1 percent.[107]

He continued to extend that metaphor to 2020 and projected it to 2050:

> Jump to today. So, if we're looking at today in 2020, 42 in U.S. and Canada members, 40 in Latin America, . . . 11 in the Asia/Pacific, 4 in Africa—4 in Africa already—3 in

Europe. Here's 2050. Just the same slope for one more generation. Thirty-six in the United States and Canada, 42 in Latin America, 11 in Asia/Pacific, 8 in Africa, 3 in Europe. Think about the implications of this for the work that each of us does.[108]

In that same training, Gong introduced Jonathan Wing, product manager for RootsTech in the Family History Department. Wing was asked to respond to the statistics shared by Gong, and he reflected, "[Thinking] about the global Church—just knowing and recognizing that there are differences is just the surface. Knowing how they're different and how that informs or adjusts the way that we create products or messages to touch the hearts and minds of members around the world—that's where the real work needs to happen and can continue to happen."[109] The visual culture of the Latter-day Saints, viewed as a message-carrying product, requires that same examination.

Tanner Kay, senior product manager of Visitors' Centers and Guest Experiences, has looked at research in this area, as he's been involved in the recent Temple Square construction, and noted:

Seeing art is one of the most preferred methods among our guests who visit Temple Square to learn about our faith. Guests appreciate seeing a variety of art in different mediums and by different artists and styles that are representative of the global Church. As the Church grows in different areas of the world, it is more and more appreciated by guests to have a collection of art that represents that ongoing growth. Guests want to see or to easily imagine themselves in the artwork, wherever they may be from, or whoever they may be.[110]

Certainly, the message to be more inclusive in the message of Latter-day Saint art is a conversation happening in several departments.

The argument could be made that the International Art Competitions, in their efforts to reflect the breadth of cultural and visual production of worldwide Latter-day Saints by bringing the art to be shown in Salt Lake City, is colonial. Indeed, if art reflecting a diversity of perspectives only comes into church headquarters and the only art going out from church headquarters reflects a Eurocentric academic style from creators who are mostly white males, it is colonial. Since 1987, curators at the church's museum have made efforts to share the work of worldwide Latter-day Saints beyond the physical walls of the Church History Museum. Richard Oman sought to get works from the Church History Museum in the journal *BYU Studies,* in church magazines, and in *Church News* during his tenure.[111] Under the direction of church historian and recorder Marlin K. Jensen (2004–2012), the Church History Department sought ways to decentralize its approach to collecting, preserving, and sharing the history of the church.[112] This included an offer to assist church-defined areas throughout the world with exhibitions that celebrated their local history. While Laura Hurtado was art curator over global acquisitions, this included a hope for area-based art competitions; so far, global areas have not taken up the idea.[113] But technology has made it possible to expand the art competition's accessibility worldwide more than ever before. Alan Johnson, Church History Museum director from 2013 to 2022, commented on how he's seen the art competition extend its reach during his tenure.[114] When asked what he attributed that extended reach to, Johnson cited "changes in technology, and the embracing of those technologies by the church at large, which provided access to established channels [including online exhibitions and social media] resulting in increased awareness and exposure."[115]

In reflecting on the International Art Competition, Hurtado commented, "I think there's something meaningful about really trying to cast a wide net of voices and experiences, and media, and styles, and perspectives. And I think it does help shift the culture in meaningful ways. It keeps us from looking at things that are familiar to us only and allows us some new lenses and new experiences. And I think there's something really powerful in that."[116] Oman compared the art competitions to an "international churchwide fast and testimony meeting."[117] And maybe that is enough to accomplish the purposes of the Church History Museum mission statement, which is "To provide opportunities for our patrons to connect to the history of the Church and the growing spiritual, artistic, and cultural legacies of the Latter-day Saints, so that they may reflect on the faith and sacrifices made by members of the church, increase their own faith in Jesus Christ and gain a greater understanding of God's dealings with men and women on this earth, and desire to know Him from what they experience here."[118] But if the expectation is to have a big impact on Latter-day Saint visual culture, under the current operations of the institution, its effects are necessarily limited.

CONCLUSION

So, who has the church left out and should have included? What unique pairs of "shoes" have been ignored or gone unnoticed? Indeed, even as the Church History Department seeks to broadly "keep and share a record of [God's] Church and its people," there are still gaps in the Church History Museum collection.[119] For example, the Church History Museum has not sufficiently captured the Latter-day Saint experience of African Americans, women, and LGBTQ+-identifying members of the church. The art in the Church History Museum, although quite diverse in many ways based on its 1987 goal to collect art globally, still largely tells the story of what it means to be a white cisgender male Latter-day Saint in the Intermountain West. To this end, the International Art Competitions remain the most effective way to identify art that helps fill these gaps. And while there are many departments that use art to accomplish their purposes, most with a greater reach than the Church History Museum, recent conversations between departments hint at greater future collaboration. So the question posed by Carol

Johnson's artwork remains relevant and should continue to drive the work of those responsible for acquiring art for the Church of Jesus Christ of Latter-day Saints.

NOTES

[1] Church of Jesus Christ of Latter-day Saints, "Pew Shoes," https://history.churchofjesuschrist.org/museum/artcompetition/2022/entries/98?from=home, accessed May 6, 2022.

[2] Carol Johnson, artist statement submitted for the twelfth International Art Competition at the Church History Museum. Full statement in possession of the author.

[3] Carol Johnson, artist statement.

[4] Carol Johnson, artist statement.

[5] Carol Johnson, artist statement.

[6] In 1984, the department was called the Historical Department. In 2000, this department merged with the Family History Department and was redubbed the Family and Church History Department. The Family History Department and Church History Department separated again in 2008. The museum was originally called the Museum of Church History and Art but was christened the Church History Museum in 2008.

[7] Doctrine and Covenants 21:1.

[8] Church History Department, "Collection Development Policy of the Church History Department of the Church of Jesus Christ of Latter-day Saints, Version 1.2," November 26, 2019.

[9] Bruce R. McConkie, in *The First Mexico and Central America Area General Conference of the Church of Jesus Christ of Latter-day Saints Held in Mexico City, Mexico August 25, 26, 27, 1972 with Report of Discourses* (Salt Lake City: Church of Jesus Christ of Latter-day Saints, 1973), 45. The idea was repeated in the 1972 October General Conference by church president Harold B. Lee.

[10] William B. Smart, ed., *The Deseret News 1985 Church Almanac* (Salt Lake City: Deseret News, 1985).

[11] Homer G. Durham, quoted in Kerril Sue Rollins, "The New Church Museum: LDS Artifacts and Art Portray Church History," *Ensign*, April 1984, 53.

[12] Rollins, "The New Church Museum," 50.

[13] When curator of acquisitions Richard Oman sought works outside of a Western aesthetic, he first collected works in the Mormon corridor and accessible art from southwestern Native American Latter-day Saints. Oman noted that the most highly collectible art by Latter-day Saints was created by Hopi-Tewa and Navajo members of the church, including by the descendants of famed Hopi-Tewa potter Fannie Nampeyo. Nampeyo and her husband, Vinton Polacca, joined the Church of Jesus Christ of Latter-day Saints in 1937. Oman's efforts would later include harnessing the efforts of mission presidents and their wives, whose work often brought them in contact with artists worldwide.

[14] Glen M. Leonard and Richard Oman, "Fine Arts Competition Gallery Guide," October 28, 1987.

[15] Richard Oman, interview by author, Salt Lake City, November 2, 2021.

[16] Leonard and Oman, "Fine Arts Competition Gallery Guide."

[17] Leonard and Oman, "Fine Arts Competition Gallery Guide."

[18] Leonard and Oman, "Fine Arts Competition Gallery Guide."

[19] Museum of Church History and Art, "Artist Entry Form."

[20] Artists were allowed to submit up to two works.

[21] Leonard and Oman, "Fine Arts Competition Gallery Guide."

[22] Richard Oman, interview by author, Salt Lake City, November 2, 2021.

[23] Third Gallery Guide.

[24] Jurors from the art competitions generally included church employees Glen M. Leonard, Richard G. Oman, Robert O. Davis, Warren F. Luch, Paul Anderson, Michael Kawasaki, Marjorie Condor, Ralph Clark, Kevin Nielson, and Cecile Nugent. Outside jurors included Mary Lois Wheatley, David Ericson, Carol Edison, Steven Epperson (who had been a church employee but was working for BYU when he served as a juror), Deirdre Paulsen, and Ellie Sonntag. Records from the seventh, eighth, and ninth competitions do not include juror information.

[25] Richard Oman, interview by author, Salt Lake City, November 2, 2021.

26 Glen M. Leonard, interview by author, March 11, 2022.

27 Percentage of works from outside the United States for the first through the twelfth competitions is as follows: Fine Arts Competition: first, 11 percent; second, 29 percent; third, 21 percent; fourth, 20 percent; fifth, 23 percent; sixth, 24 percent; seventh, 25 percent; eighth, 31 percent; ninth, 20 percent; tenth, 11 percent; eleventh, 22.5 percent; twelfth, 20 percent.

28 Aoba Taiichi, email message to the author, March 3, 2022.

29 "Gospel, Art Enrich Life of Japanese Craftsman," *Deseret News*, September 11, 2000, https://www.dese ret.com/2000/9/11/20777437/gospel-art-enrich-life-of-japanese-craftsman.

30 Deseret News, "Gospel, Art Enrich Life of Japanese Craftsman."

31 Aoba Taiichi, email message to the author, March 3, 2022.

32 Aoba Taiichi, email message to the author, March 3, 2022.

33 3 Nephi 11:9–12.

34 Helaman 12:2–4.

35 The direct arrows and Samuel's flowing capes remind Latter-day Saint audiences of Arnold Friberg's painting *Samuel the Lamanite Prophesies of Christ*. Certainly, Friberg's paintings of the Book of Mormon and other works by Del Parson and John Scott that were included in the first pages of the 1981 Book of Mormon influenced works created by worldwide Latter-day Saints after that date.

36 Alma 46:11–12, 19–20.

37 Aoba Taiichi, email message to the author, April 26, 2022.

38 2 Nephi 5.

39 Aoba Taiichi, email message to the author, April 26, 2022.

40 Jeronimo Lozano, "Jeronimo Lozano," interview by Valen Hunter, *Mormon Artist*, October/November 2010, 21.

41 Mary Strong, *Art, Nature, and Religion in the Central Andes* (Austin: University of Texas Press, 2012), 196.

42 Strong, *Art, Nature, and Religion*, 206.

43 Strong, *Art, Nature, and Religion*, 151.

44 Strong, *Art, Nature, and Religion*, 209.

45 "Jeronimo E. Lozano," National Endowment for the Arts, https://www.arts.gov/honors/heritage/jeron imo-e-lozano, accessed April 25, 2022.

46 "Jeronimo E. Lozano," National Endowment for the Arts.

47 Jeronimo Lozano, "Jeronimo Lozano," interview by Valen Hunter, 25.

48 "Jeronimo E. Lozano," National Endowment for the Arts.

49 People from Aboriginal nations often have multiple names. They may have a European first name and/ or surname. Sometimes the surname refers to the pastoral station where they or their parents worked. They also have a skin name, which indicates a person's bloodline and conveys information about how generations are linked and how they should interact. The skin name also indicates rights over certain Dreamings. For Colleen Wallace Nungari, Wallace is her European surname. Nungari is her skin name.

50 For an account of how the *altyerre* is performed, see Kathleen Wallace Kemarre and Judy Lovell, *Listen Deeply, Let These Stories In* (Alice Springs: IAD Press, 2009), 10–14.

51 Ian McLean, *Rattling Spears: A History of Indigenous Australian Art* (London: Reaktion Books, 2016), 18–19.

52 The peoples present were primarily Pintuipi, although there were also Luritja, Arrente, Anmatyerre, and Walpiri.

53 Portraying these Dreamings for the public has required a negotiation of sacred symbols. While early artists at Papunya were freer in the images they painted, including figural representations of the ancestral beings, current Dreamings painted in acrylic are carefully monitored by those in communities responsible for keeping the stories sacred, sometimes removing some symbols.

54 Wallace Kemmare and Lovell, *Listen Deeply*, 4.

55 Colleen Wallace Nungari, artist statement submitted for the eighth International Art Competition at the Church History Museum. Full statement in possession of the author.

56 Nungari, artist statement.

57 Nungari, artist statement.

58 Nungari, artist statement.

59 Nungari, artist statement.

60 3 Nephi 11.

61 Christopher Anderson and Françoise Dussart, "Dreamings in Acrylic: Western Desert Art," in *Dreamings: The Art of Aboriginal Australia*, ed. Peter Sutton (New York: Asia Society Galleries and George Braziller, Inc., 1988), 89.

62 Anderson and Dussart, "Dreamings in Acrylic," 89.

63 Anderson and Dussart, "Dreamings in Acrylic," 89.

64 The Anglicized word for an *urtne* is *coolamon*.

65 Colleen Wallace Nungari, Facebook message to the author, December 28, 2022.

66 Joseph Lajabu Banda, interview by Kathleen Irving and David Irving, Blantyre, Malawi, January 20, 2022.

67 Joseph Lajabu Banda, interview by author, Salt Lake City, February 1, 2021.

68 Joseph Lajabu Banda, interview by Kathleen Irving and David Irving, Blantyre, Malawi, January 20, 2022.

69 Joseph Lajabu Banda, email message to the author, February 17, 2022.

70 Joseph Lajabu Banda, email message to the author, February 17, 2022.

71 Joseph Lajabu Banda, interview by Kathleen Irving and David Irving, Blantyre, Malawi, January 20, 2022.

72 Joseph Lajabu Banda, interview by Kathleen Irving and David Irving, Blantyre, Malawi, January 20, 2022.

73 1 Nephi 8.

74 Baobab fruit provides high levels of calcium, iron, potassium, and vitamin C.

75 1 Nephi 8:11.

76 Joseph Lajabu Banda, email message to the author, January 16, 2021.

77 Laura Allred Hurtado, March 22, 2022.

78 Church History Department.

79 Alan Johnson, interview by author, Salt Lake City, April 30, 2022.

80 Jurors for the tenth, eleventh, and twelfth art competitions included Glen Nelson, Rita Wright, Campbell Gray, Shu Chih Murray, Laura Durham, Herman Du Toit, J. Kirk Richards, Jean Richardson, Analisa Coats Sato, Elaine Thatcher, Fidalis Buehler, Rose Datoc Dall, Amy Maxwell Howard, Heather Belnap, and Nnamdi Okonkwo.

81 Paige Crosland Anderson, interview by Leslie Graff, Segullah, September 10, 2014, https://segullah.org/introducing-featured-artist-paige-crosland-anderson.

82 Paige Crosland Anderson, interview by Leslie Graff.

83 Paige Crosland Anderson, artist statement submitted for the eleventh International Art Competition at the Church History Museum. Full statement in possession of the author.

84 *Artful*, season 1, episode 1, "Brian Kershisnik and Paige Anderson," BYUtv, https://www.byutv.org/player/b5a3af8f-cb9f-4e8e-85eb-2a2de8761c84/artful-brian-kershisnik-and-paige-anderson, accessed April 29, 2022.

85 Paige Crosland Anderson, artist statement.

86 Paige Crosland Anderson, artist statement.

87 Danielle Hatch, "Bio," https://www.daniellehatch.com/about, last accessed April 29, 2022.

88 Danielle Hatch, artist statement submitted for the eleventh International Art Competition at the Church History Museum. Full statement in possession of the author.

89 Danielle Hatch, artist statement.

90 Walter Rane, interview by author, Salt Lake City, April 21, 2021.

91 Rose Datoc Dall would serve as a juror for the twelfth International Art Competition. Several docents at the Church History Museum lamented this juror choice, for it meant there would not be a Dall piece hanging in the exhibition.

92 Rose Datoc Dall, interview by author.

93 Jorge Cocco Santangelo, email communication with author, April 29, 2022.

94 In fact, the Church History Museum has two works that Jorge Cocco Santangelo donated to the museum in 1986. They are titled *The Voice That Cries from the Dust* and *The Covenant,* and they are markedly Surrealistic.

95 Jorge Cocco Santangelo, email communication with author, April 29, 2022.

96 Mark 1:16–17.

97 Jorge Cocco Santangelo, email communication with author, April 29, 2022.

98 Jorge Cocco Santangelo, email communication with author, April 29, 2022.

99 D&C 21:1.

100 Church History Department, "Collection Development Policy."

101 The Church of Jesus Christ of Latter-Day Saints, *General Handbook: Serving in the Church of Jesus Christ of Latter-day Saints,* 35.5.1.

102 Temple Department, The Church of Jesus Christ of Latter-day Saints, "Temple Art Standards and Guidelines."

103 "Diversity and Inclusion in LDS Art," *First Name Basis* (podcast), directed by Jasmine Bradshaw, featuring Michelle Franzoni Thorley, May 20, 2020, 37:19, https://firstnamebasis.libsyn.com/215-diversity-and-inclusion-in-lds-art.

104 "Diversity and Inclusion in LDS Art."

105 Rick Phillips and Ryan T. Cragun, *Mormons in the United States 1990–2008: Socio-Demographic Trends and Regional Differences* (Hartford: Trinity College, 2011), http://commons.trincoll.edu/aris/files/2011/12/Mormons2008.pdf.

106 Rose Datoc Dall, interview by author, Salt Lake City, April 26, 2022.

107 Gerrit W. Gong, "Alignment in a Time of All Nations, Kindreds, Tongues, and People: Working to Build the Global Church," Leadership Enrichment Series, September 15, 2021.

108 Gerrit W. Gong, "Alignment in a Time."

109 Jonathan Wing, quoted in Gong, "Alignment in a Time."

110 Tanner Kay, email message to the author, May 3, 2022.

111 Richard Oman, interview by author, Salt Lake City, November 2, 2021

112 Marlin K. Jensen, "Minding the House of Church History," *Journal of Mormon History* 39, no. 2 (Spring 2013): 86.

113 Laura Allred Hurtado, interview by author, Salt Lake City, March 22, 2022.

114 Alan Johnson, interview by author, Salt Lake City, April 30, 2022.

115 Alan Johnson, interview by author, Salt Lake City, April 30, 2022.

116 Laura Allred Hurtado, interview by author, Salt Lake City, March 22, 2022.

117 Richard Oman, interview by author, Salt Lake City, November 2, 2021.

118 "Church History Museum Mission Statement," in possession of the author.

119 Jensen, "Minding the House," 83.

21

BEING RELEVANT

On the BYU Department of Art in the Twenty-First Century

ANALISA COATS SATO

For Gi (Ginny) Huo's BFA thesis exhibition at Brigham Young University in the spring of 2008, the college senior presented an ambitious performance titled *365 Hygienic Collections*. Amid tidy accumulations of used paper towels (the "collections" referred to in the title) and for hours at a time, Huo, dressed in white, stoically carried out an obsessive ritual of handwashing at a small basin: lather, rinse, dry; carefully discard paper towel; repeat. Twelve neat rows of these crumpled towels lined the gallery's floors, each roughly equidistant from the others, while twelve clusters of clear plastic bins populated the forty-foot wall, these too filled with wadded paper. An audio track of paper towels being pulled from a dispenser played on loop, over which was layered the sound of the artist periodically pulling towels from an actual wall dispenser as needed.

This performance could only be glimpsed from a distance. Rather than passing into the exhibition space proper, viewers would enter a darkened gallery and encounter a false wall that had been drilled with a constellation of small round holes at varying heights. The light filtering through the holes would guide viewers to peep through them, each an aperture revealing the performance and installation (the arrangement of paper towels, wall bins, and so on) on the other side.[1] Huo's tableau invited its viewers to be voyeurs, implicitly drawing attention to the awkwardness of their position as such by requiring some of them to crane or stoop in order to see. Yet what was peeped did not titillate so much as it puzzled. Should the artist's actions be understood as a kind of distress signal?

A conventional gallery space with wood floors, neutral walls, and track lighting served as backdrop for the project, though the space was deemphasized by the viewers' not being able to enter it—perhaps another demonstration of the control being channeled upon the artist's chapped hands and the discarded paper towels. Why were these towels

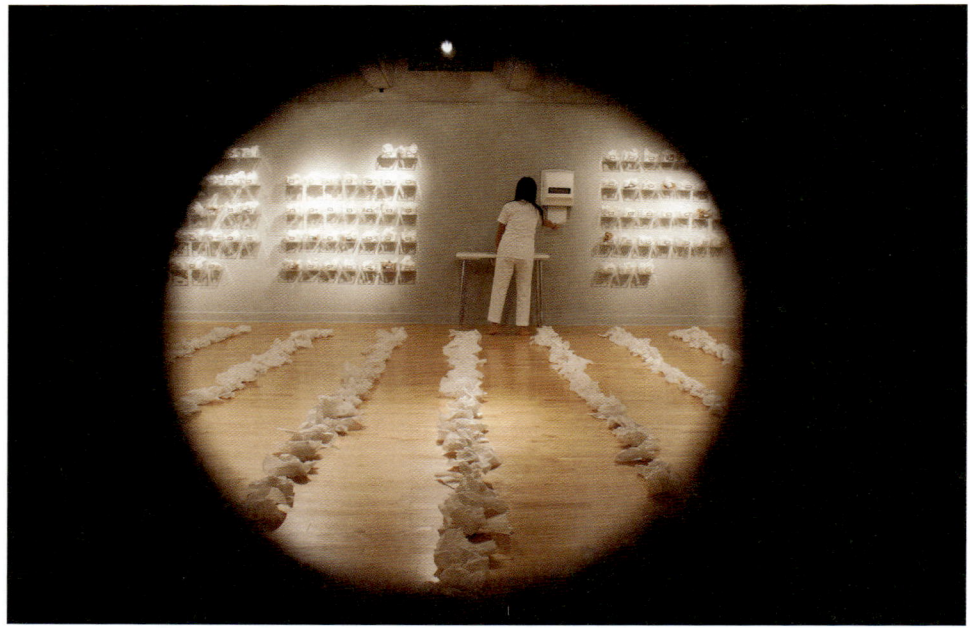

Fig. 21.1 Gi (Ginny) Huo, *365 Hygienic Collections* (detail), 2008, performance with installation. Courtesy of the artist.

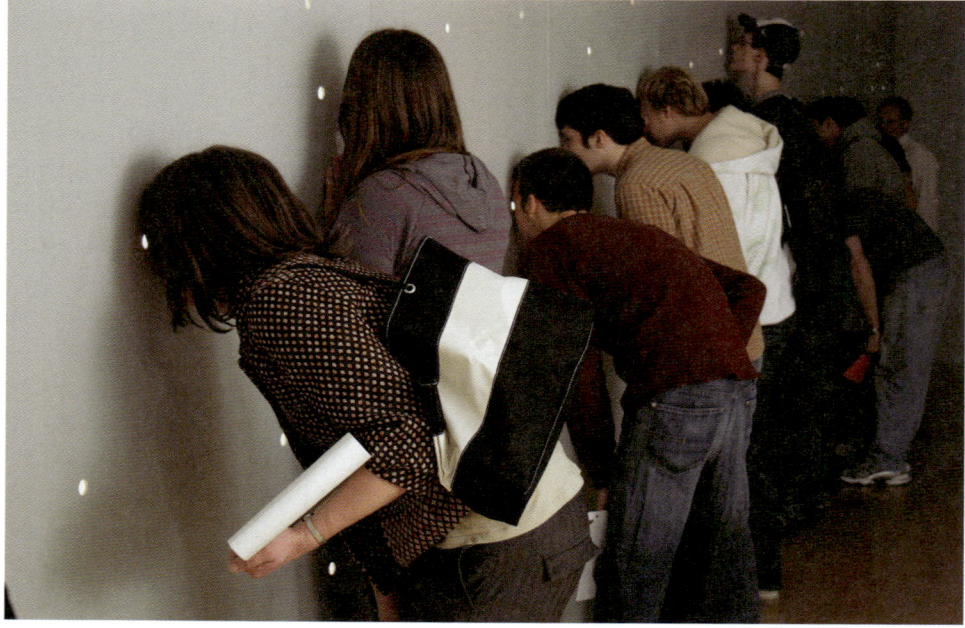

Fig. 21.2 Gi (Ginny) Huo, *365 Hygienic Collections* (detail), 2008, performance with installation. Courtesy of the artist.

kept, catalogued even, after fulfilling their usefulness? After each round of handwashing, drying, and discarding the towel at the end of one of the twelve rows, Huo would then take a dried towel from the opposite end of the same row and place it in one of the 365 (365!) plastic wall bins. This large quantity of bins, as installed on the gallery wall parallel to the screen, effectively formed an oversized calendar, holding evidence of a simulated year's worth of handwashing. Indeed, it seems that in *365 Hygienic Collections* much emphasis was placed on evidence. Huo appeared to assert that it was not enough to have clean hands; one must be able to prove that the cleansing occurred by showing its tangible aftermath. Furthermore, there must be witnesses to the cleansing, roles unwittingly filled by the viewers watching through the peepholes.

* * *

As an institution of higher education, Brigham Young University is undeniably distinct. Of the three campuses owned and operated by the Church of Jesus Christ of Latter-day Saints, this is the flagship. It differs from many private universities with theological affiliations in the United States for its high rate of religiosity among students and faculty.[2] That is to say, BYU is a religious university not only in name but also in the ongoing practices of its community members. It is worthwhile to consider the implications of a shared faith for the university's Department of Art, because university art departments are often a step along a career path into the art world—the many-tentacled system of

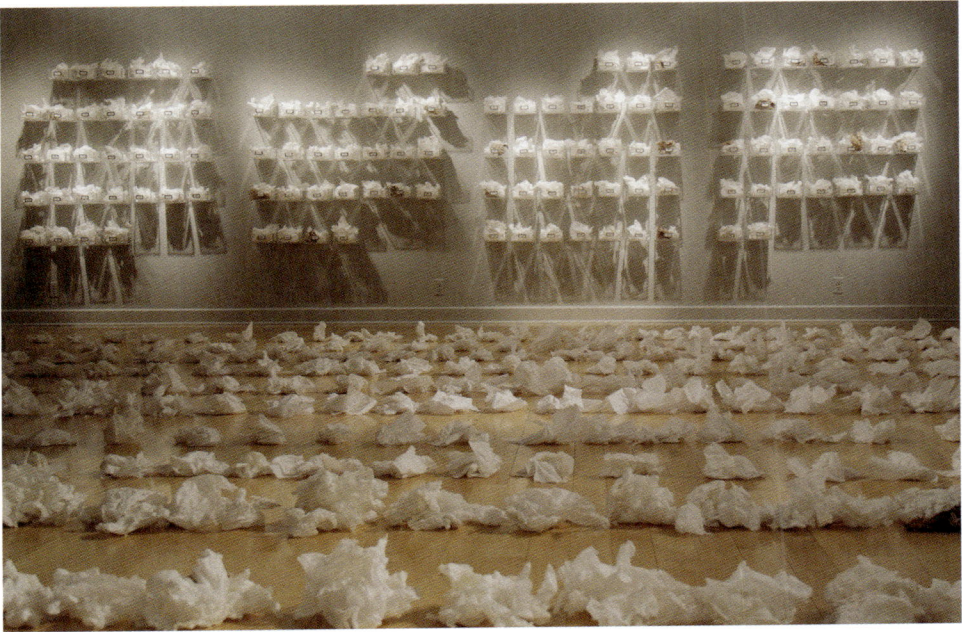

Fig. 21.3 Gi (Ginny) Huo, *365 Hygienic Collections* (detail), 2008, performance with installation. Courtesy of the artist.

institutions, publications, and professionals that can be wary of engaging with organized religion generally and contemporary Christianity specifically.[3] For their part, artists at BYU might be wary of what can seem like an anything-goes ethos in the contemporary art world; conversely, they might feel they cannot address the subjects they want to address at BYU, which is decidedly not anything goes. Thus, frictions surface: artists find themselves simultaneously aspiring to participate in this wider network, navigating the unique environs of the university, and attending to the fundamental concerns of what form their work will take and what it might say.

Art students at BYU can be keenly aware of the line they walk. "We are trying to be relevant," explains Dalila Sanabria, recalling how she felt as an undergraduate in the department before graduating with a BFA in 2019.[4] She describes an unspoken understanding among her peers that overtly religious work could come off as didactic at a school like BYU, even among peers who share the faith. While students do want to explore meaningful experiences and ideas, they might well choose to do so through means and subjects that are not so easy to read. Their belief is already a common thread, as Sanabria notes; making work that explores this shared experience in a pedestrian way, regardless of technical skill, would not distinguish one within the studio art classes, nor would it serve future art world ambitions.[5] The contemporary art world rewards a point of view, and the art department is striving to engage with that world, despite the potential frictions.

Peter Everett, a professor of painting and drawing who joined the department in 2000, identifies a shift in faculty purview during his time at BYU: from regional to national and international, particularly in terms of the opportunities sought for students. "Over the years with retirements and new hires we have built a faculty with extensive connections and experience with a broader art world," he observes. "These new hires have graduated from major art programs and exhibit nationally and internationally and push students to do the same."[6] This shift in purview is reflected in other changes as well, such as the expansion of the visiting artist program, but it is the department's ongoing support of undergraduates in their graduate school applications that is perhaps most consequential when it comes to fostering connections between the department and the art world at large.

Huo and Sanabria represent a contingent of BYU fine arts graduates from the last fifteen to twenty years who have benefited from the more ambitious purview. The work they made at BYU, especially their thesis exhibitions, reflects the formal and conceptual sophistication they were developing in the BFA program, and the work's themes and materials are indicative of both artists' desire to "be relevant," in Sanabria's words—to participate fully in the art world structures outside the university. This chapter will look closely at Huo's and Sanabria's thesis exhibitions as a way of making specific the experience of studying art at BYU in the twenty-first century. The exhibitions raised thought-provoking considerations for Mormon viewers, and given that both projects accounted for the viewer, and even required the viewer for their full realization, it seems pertinent to think about how the work might have read for these viewers. While the two student projects and the issues they raise will be the focus of the examination to follow, the art department is repeatedly crowding in around the edges; its vision of what contemporary art education at BYU should look like has shaped the production of the work discussed in this chapter, and to an extent the department's values will be addressed here, particularly the way it has valued the exhibition format as a pedagogical tool. The chapter will also consider how these exhibitions might relate to contemporary art history beyond a Mormon context, as contributing to those discourses has mattered both to the artists and to the department.

"All art is generated by a specific people in a specific place," artist Ernesto Pujol has argued; accordingly, "art schools need to act as site-specific entities."[7] Pujol means this in the sense that art schools should be responsive to the educational needs of their students instead of adhering to orthodoxies, but the sentiment might be construed another way, as an appeal to art schools (or departments) to be critically aware of the specific sites they occupy—occupy physically, yes, but also historically, culturally, and ideologically. This awareness of the multilayered nature of the site of production would then ideally seep into the teaching and art-making happening there, transferring this concept of site-specificity onto those actions. In examining these examples of student work, their potential for site-specificity is something to evaluate: to what extent is each project commenting on, or showing awareness of, the site in which it has been produced? Or perhaps it goes further; as a concept, site-specificity can be governed by opposing impulses—to integrate with, or to interrupt.[8] Which of these impulses each project demonstrates is also a matter for debate.

* * *

There was a clinical quality to Huo's *365 Hygienic Collections*, with its neatly labeled bins glossy under the track lighting, the white plastic tabletop with stainless steel legs and basin, even the automatic paper towel dispenser attached to the wall. This quality carried over to Huo's white shirt and trousers, which at a distance call up medical scrubs. But within this specific site, the artist's uniform had the potential to function as an esoteric reference point: it resembled the boxy white cotton-polyester jumpsuits often worn for baptism, the sacred rite that initiates official membership in the Church of Jesus Christ of Latter-day Saints.[9] In wearing a uniform that evokes baptism while performing a ritual of repetitive handwashing, Huo's performance could be read as merging notions of "clean"—which the baptismal rite also does, by using a literal immersion to symbolize a spiritual cleansing or renewal. The performance might further be read as a reenacting of religious scrupulosity.

Huo clarifies that they were not thinking about baptism or any aspect of their faith when creating the senior thesis project.[10] Rather, the artist was thinking about a period of struggling with compulsive handwashing during childhood. Revisiting that compulsion, performing it for viewers, was a means to share the story and find relief. As

Huo explains, "It was in a way cathartic to talk about my past. When performing the performance it felt soothing to organize the paper towels and wash my hands."[11] The performance may have soothed the artist psychologically, but physically it was painful; their hands became cracked and raw, an unintentional byproduct of repeated exposure to soap and water and rough paper. As for the white uniform, this appealed to Huo because it matched the bleached paper towels.

Yet the connection with baptism is warranted, given the artist's concern with becoming clean and the fixation on proof, as well as the specificity of the context and place. Though Huo had decided to carry out the performance at set times in the BYU gallery with or without viewers, they also saw the performance as centered on this action of letting the viewers in on a private ritual—hence the need for the peephole wall.[12] The work's meaning was fully realized only when viewers were present, just as the Mormon baptismal rite requires witnesses to be considered legitimate.[13] More broadly, *365 Hygienic Collections* could be said to recognize the importance placed on witnesses from the initial establishment of the Mormon faith in the nineteenth century. In the Doctrine and Covenants, a canonized book of scripture that codified many doctrines of the church between 1823 and 1844, it is proclaimed that "in the mouth of two or three witnesses shall every word be established."[14] Huo may not have intended for this ingrained prioritization of witnesses to seep into the project, but regardless, the association is there to be made. That the artist performed this work at BYU makes it more important to consider these associations. In another context, the work would not as effectively raise the specific ideas it raised here.

This is not to suggest that the project makes a critique of the baptism ritual. Huo's intentions acknowledge that they were not addressing their religious life. But the site inescapably factors into the meaning. In washing and drying their hands in front of a BYU audience for hours at a time, Huo ruminates on the futility of trying to become clean, regardless of physical evidence to the contrary (the discarded paper towels, the artist's chapped hands) and despite the presence of witnesses. In a space occupied by viewers who would be familiar with the concept of spiritual cleanliness and the symbolism of renewal implicit in the baptism rite, a work that presents the artist's challenges to accept themselves as clean could initiate thoughtful conversations about the viability of faith and the Christian enterprise.

Did *365 Hygienic Collections* integrate into its site or interrupt it? Huo's clinical aesthetic, pared down in terms of material and color, was calming; even though the floor was crowded with discarded paper towels, the orderliness of the installation seamlessly layered over the white-cube competence of the gallery space. The dividing wall was a surprise, a rupture in expectations, but still, the visual qualities of the installation and the artist's measured actions would have suited the site. But one could also argue that the clinical aesthetic functions as a decoy, quietly slipping potentially interruptive ideas through the peepholes in the wall. If viewers were to catch a glimpse of the artist's hands, it might puncture any sense of calm and provoke dismay. In recalling reactions to the project, Huo notes the positive feedback from friends and professors along with this: "Someone also wrote in my reflection book something along the lines of *Is this art?* In that case, I'm glad that my work was raising that question for someone."[15] Yet it is a question that only scratches the surface, for there are these knottier issues to consider.

Huo had the rare experience of overlapping at BYU with their mother, Heysook Cho, who was an MFA student in ceramics. Born in Seoul and having been introduced to ceramics as an undergraduate there in a large course with limited access to a mechanical wheel only, Cho would complete her degree twenty years later in Chicago, where the hand-building experience that had not been a part of the curriculum earlier in her education was finally on offer.[16] The hand-building continued at BYU, and for *Gong Ki Noi Yi,* her MFA thesis exhibition in 2006, Cho presented a sculptural take on a game of jacks, the Korean five-stone version that she had played as a child. The exhibition included two oversized hands, positioned palms up on a plinth, and a collection of ceramic orbs—some small and positioned on and around the hands, others perforated and large and suspended from the ceiling, like jacks tossed into the sky, as the artist describes them. Cho frames her childhood experience with the game through materials; after scavenging playing stones from the sand pile of a local construction site, she recalls, "I would grind them with a soft sandpaper to make them round and smooth and shiny."[17]

Huo credits Cho with being their first entry into art, a model of how to pursue a lifelong creative practice, but there is also this materialist sensibility, or Cho's experiencing the world through materials, that appears to have been passed on as well. Prior to developing their thesis exhibition, Huo had become interested in materiality, experimenting with both paper pulp and steel. The artist was drawn to the contrasts between these dissimilar materials, particularly the slow process of molding paper pulp in contrast with the rapid process of welding steel.[18] Because *365 Hygienic Collections* incorporated performance, and because viewers were limited in what they could see by the dividing wall, the material impact of the project may have been understated. But we might see the artist's repeated crumpling of paper towels as an investigation into the properties of the material in real time, as well as a kind of sculptural act. In a department that historically had been dominated by painting, Huo's direct exploration of this common, inexpensive material can be seen as an interruptive act as well.

It is unusual for an undergraduate exhibition to demonstrate the potency of *365 Hygienic Collections.* Huo had been introduced to installation in a course taught by Valerie Atkisson a few semesters earlier, and Atkisson found Huo to be a "standout student" in that medium.[19] Adding performance to an installation at BYU circa 2008 was a bold choice, and an unexpected one as well, given that the artist's medium of specialization during the BFA was sculpture. This mixed-media approach was emblematic of the direction in which the department wanted to move, however. Starting around the period that Huo attended BYU, a number of esteemed art professors had retired or would soon retire: painters Bruce Smith in 2006 and Robert Marshall in 2008, master lithographer Wayne Kimball in 2009, and painter Wulf Barsch in 2010.[20] This cohort favored representational images and somewhat narrative content in their own work. With their departures and the subsequent hiring of a new generation of professors, as Everett noted, the department would gradually take on an altered character, one more conceptually inclined and tilted toward the art world outside the university.

* * *

We might take a moment to consider the tasks of the university art department in the twenty-first century. Beyond Pujol's recommendation that it act as a "site-specific entity," what is the art department meant to do? There is no doubt that art education can play a significant role in shaping artists, as a rich and deep-rooted body of literatures attests.[21] Art schools and departments function in a number of capacities: they pass on technical skills, enabling students to handle the tools and materials of a given medium; they cultivate intellectual rigor, training students to recognize how meaning is created in art and to approach their own work armed with this knowledge; they professionalize, preparing students to operate within existing art world systems and to support themselves as artists. Traditionally art schools have done all of this, but the degree to which one task is valued above others changes over time, and not uniformly. Writing about the state of global art education in the aughts, museum director Charles Esche has observed that some art schools "are still locked into nineteenth century models of life drawing and hand-eye control, while others are still exploring the legacies of 1960s free expression."[22] This unevenness persists today.

BYU might have retained elements of older models of art education into the twenty-first century because of the unique conditions of the university.[23] The concept of talent, historically prized by the European fine arts academies, is viewed as a divine gift within Mormon theology, and adherent Mormons might see it as a responsibility to exercise artistic talent to the benefit of their communities.[24] Invention, the fostering of which was a goal of the modernist art education at the Bauhaus in the early twentieth century, is also upheld in Mormon theology as divinely cultivated.[25] But a poststructuralist approach, born of 1960s social upheavals and valuing interdisciplinarity and a critical stance, has increasingly, if belatedly, come to the department. Everett singles out hybridity as an organizing principle in recent years, observing, "I think more than anything the art department has a strong sense of hybridity in the work produced. I think this is largely because of how the faculty are very open to a range of approaches and have created an open department structure where students can move fluidly between disciplines."[26] When Sanabria graduated from the department in 2019, it was with the impression of a department in which painting remained central, which suggests that institutional change happens incrementally.[27]

On the topic of historical models of art education, the issue of artistic influence must also be addressed. As theorist Thierry de Duve has argued, the passing down of aesthetic concerns or styles from one artist to another, or in this case from professor to student, is no longer happening in art schools, or at least not so directly. Instead, "art culture" is being transmitted by the institutions that exhibit art—museums, galleries, and foundations—and also, to a significant degree, by specialized publications and other media.[28] Huo's experience as an undergraduate supported this; the artist speaks highly of the BYU sculpture professors and their thoroughness in teaching technical skill, but Huo felt more influenced aesthetically and conceptually by the well-known PBS series *Art in the Twenty-First Century,* especially episodes featuring Ann Hamilton and Paul Pfeiffer.[29] Were de Duve making this argument today, rather than in 2009, it is certain that social media would also find a place in his account. Given students' access to images and information via these channels, it would be inaccurate to suggest that the BYU art faculty are dominant sources for what gets transmitted in the work of their students. Influence still matters, generally, but isolating specific influences in an image- and information-saturated world might not be particularly useful.

This is not to say that we cannot suss out distinct cadences that have emerged from BYU in the twenty-first century. There is a sizable cohort of painters who have practiced varieties of abstraction, for example, including Todd Chilton (BFA 2002) and Jason Metcalf (BFA 2011) as well as Everett. The Bonneville Salt Flats have featured as the setting for a number of works, including that of Jean Richardson (MFA 2007), Levi Jackson (BFA 2011), and professor Christopher Lynn.[30] The use of scrolls, an evocatively scriptural format, has been employed by Betsy Brown (BFA 2011) and Aloe Corry (BFA 2016).[31] In an essay on twenty-first-century BYU alumni of the art department, museum director Laura Hurtado further identifies mysticism and the use of craft materials as important threads, with the former represented by the drawings of Casey Jex Smith (BFA 2003) and sculpture of Mary Baum (BFA 2014) and the latter by fiber and cloth work by Kathryn Knudsen (MFA 2007) and Rachel Stallings Thomander (BFA 2013).[32] Everett recalls that a widespread collage aesthetic became noticeable during his first years in the department, in another example.[33] These recurrent motifs suggest some level of sharing between professors and students or among peers. Nevertheless, de Duve's case for the art school's reduced role in spreading aesthetic influence is convincing.

Influence is less of a value in the twenty-first-century art department, then. But other values have carried over from preceding generations, including the department's emphasis on student exhibitions.[34] As the culminating experience of the undergraduate and master's degree programs, the thesis exhibition would be seen as consequential at any university, but this department seems to devote remarkable energies to helping students not only produce thesis-level bodies of work but also actively shape how their work will be presented. Gary Barton, a longtime printmaking professor in the department, describes the thesis exhibition as an extended mentoring process. He meets with his advisees regularly in the lead-up to their proposal submission as they formulate their ideas and then more frequently throughout the planning and execution stages. The student's entire committee convenes a few times as well, to offer feedback on the proposal and drafted project report and ultimately to evaluate the installed exhibition on a walk-through with the student. Occasionally further work would be required of the student, which Barton oversees to approval.[35] Barton's advising process is just one example, but it speaks of a departmental culture that values these exhibitions and offers abundant opportunities for dialogue among students and professors.

There has also been an investment in displaying student work with visual coherence and spatial awareness—as though each exhibition were an installation, former campus gallery director Jason Lanegan observes.[36] The Harris Fine Arts Center, in which the Department of Art was housed for nearly six decades until the building's demolition in 2022, featured a large amount of exhibition space; most favorable for thesis exhibitions was Gallery 303, the roughly forty-foot-square space where Huo presented, but there was also the B. F. Larsen Gallery in the atrium plus various foyers, walls, and inset balconies throughout the building.[37] As director of the campus galleries from 2007 to 2019, Lanegan established a process for collaborating with students on their thesis exhibitions, working through the logistics of the installation with them to make sure their installation choices were in sync with the concept of the work. The student would vet these choices with their advisor; then Lanegan and his team of student assistants would collaborate at the direction of the exhibiting student to construct the necessary non-art components (plinths, mounts, and so on) and install the exhibition.[38] Throughout the process, then, the student would act as artist, curator, and exhibition designer, with the support of their advisor and the gallery director's team. This sustained back-and-forth between the student, their advisor, and the gallery has undoubtedly led to more robust student exhibitions, and it shows how the department has used the exhibition format as a fundamental pedagogical tool.

The exhibitions' usefulness goes beyond pedagogy, however. "One of the ways [the department faculty] rate success is students getting into MFA programs," Lanegan ventures, and high-caliber MFA programs at that.[39] Everett's observation about the department's new hires coming from major graduate programs and encouraging their students to apply to those same programs seems to confirm this.[40] A promising (and well-photographed) senior thesis exhibition would be an important component of students' applications to those programs. Huo's successful application to the MFA program at Maryland Institute College of Art (MICA) was doubtless strengthened by the documentation of an intriguing thesis exhibition. As de Duve asserts, "The art schools best suited to the current world—and, no doubt, the best schools—are those that deliberately underscore that they consider themselves part of the *artworld* establishment."[41] The emphasis on polished thesis exhibitions at BYU is both an acknowledgment of the significance of that art world establishment—which arguably values the exhibition more than any other form of culture transmission—and an attempt to thrive within its confines.

* * *

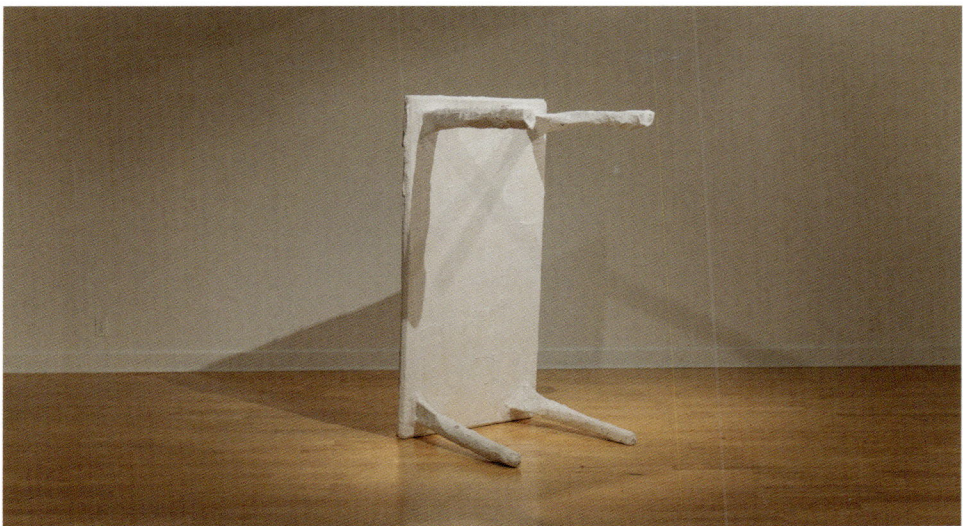

Fig. 21.4 Dalila Sanabria, *Legs* (from *Remnants*), 2019, cardboard, bandage wraps, and joint compound on found table, 61″ × 42″ × 30″. Courtesy of the artist.

The six large objects on view in Gallery 303 in the fall of 2019 spoke plainly of upheaval. Restricted to an austere palette of paper-pulp brown and plaster white, these objects—including an upended dining table and bookcase, a sofa missing its cushions, a tidy but towering stack of packing boxes—would easily invite associations with moving house and more broadly with transition. The surfaces of the objects were exaggeratedly tactile: the lines of the dining table were distorted by a buildup of cardboard, bandage wraps, and joint compound, and the visible panels of the boxes alternated between puckered, moisture-damaged cardboard and slatherings of more joint compound.[42] They were uncanny objects, the familiar made subtly strange, with the haptic qualities of their surfaces both inviting and discouraging touch. In addition to the furniture and wall of boxes, there were two large canvases leaning against the gallery walls, encrusted with the same materials that had been applied to the other objects: torn sections of cardboard and bandage wraps, plastered over with thick swipes of joint compound. One of the canvases simultaneously resembled a topographical map, an architectural model, and a roughly hewn section of drywall. It is as though those leaving had attempted to take with them a tangible reminder of the structure itself, as if to re-create that sense of place somewhere else.

Together these six objects made up *Remnants*, Sanabria's BFA thesis exhibition. This was the first time that the artist had utilized cardboard, which she was drawn to for what it could convey: disposability, impermanence, associations with transit, and its overall function as "a container of things."[43] Over time, the cardboard elements of the exhibition would age poorly, attracting dirt and sagging under the weight of gravity. Adding

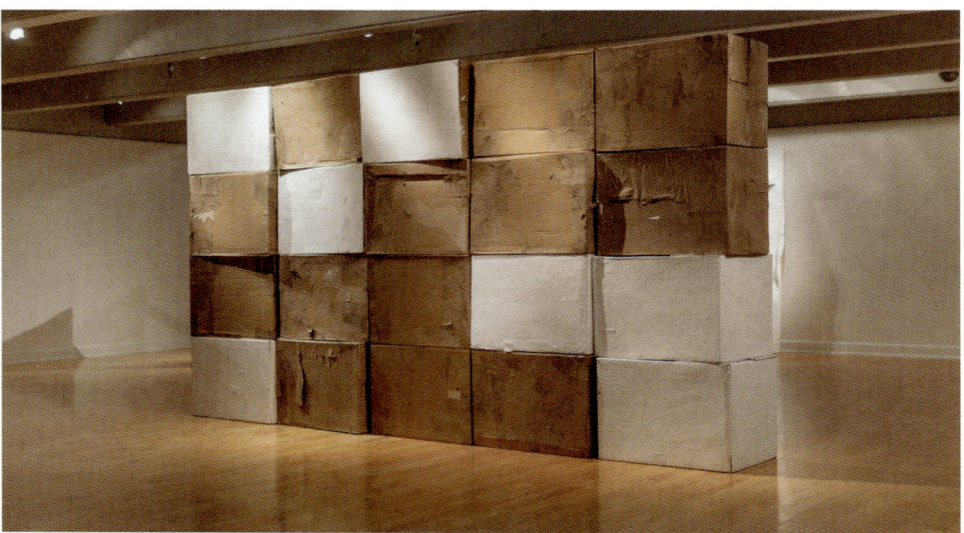

Fig. 21.5   Dalila Sanabria, *Wall* (from *Remnants*), 2019, cardboard strips and joint compound on cardboard boxes, 108 × 144 × 24″. Courtesy of the artist.

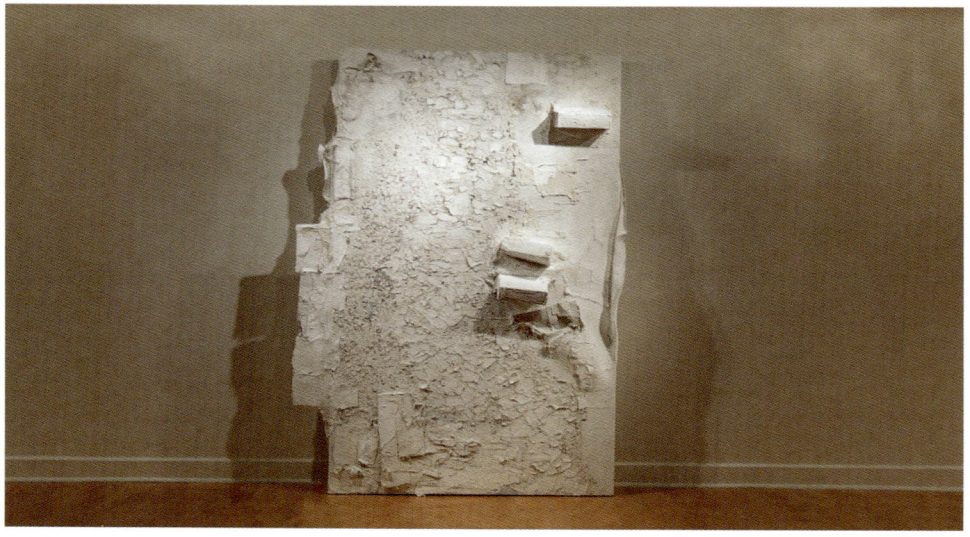

Fig. 21.6   Dalila Sanabria, *Packed* (from *Remnants*), 2019, cardboard, bandage wraps and joint compound on canvas, 84 × 67 × 12″. Courtesy of the artist.

the joint compound was another way to convey impermanence materially, because it would become "flaky" as it settled and aged, and metaphorically, because it signifies the acts of construction or repair—acts that are vehicles of change. Joint compound is used to cover drywall seams during construction, but it can also be used to repair nail holes and other wall damage before a move. Both materials are fragile, though not precious; they are inexpensive, accessible, and handled or discarded regularly.

For Sanabria, this concern with impermanence was connected to a particular childhood event. In a blog post for the Humanities Center at BYU, where the artist held a fellowship in 2018, she described her father's deportation to Colombia from Florida when she was twelve. This event necessitated her family's rushed move to Colombia, a country she had never visited, with a language she did not speak.[44] One can imagine the disarray of furniture shifted from its familiar places, packing boxes cluttering surfaces, and joint compound scraped over nail holes in preparation for their home's new owners. Sanabria's sense of stability and permanence would have been dismantled along with the contents of the house, and those mundane materials would come to stand in for the experience. In her account, the artist mentions she was sitting at the dining table and gluing together cardboard and paper for a school project on the evening the immigration agents knocked at the door to tell her mother that her father had been deported earlier that day, adding another layer of meaning onto the choices of materials.[45] Like Huo's *365 Hygienic Collections*, Sanabria's *Remnants* was deeply personal, but it raised topics with potential to resonate at BYU.

In terms of demographics, the BYU student body shows a high level of similarity not only in terms of religious beliefs but also in terms of student race and ethnicity (81 percent white as of 2022).[46] There is the demographic quirk of the mission factor, which means that most BYU students are Mormon, are white, and have lived abroad.[47] This quirk might lead some at BYU to overestimate how welcoming the university community is toward diversity. In 2021 the university published a report on race, equity, and belonging on campus, as commissioned by the university's president in response to global protests over the killing of George Floyd. One key finding highlighted in the report was that "many BIPOC students at BYU feel isolated and unsafe as a result of their experiences with racism at BYU."[48] During her time at the university Sanabria had experienced this painful dynamic, and it spurred in the artist a heightened awareness of what her work could convey to predominantly white viewers.

Still, when asked about the potential audience for *Remnants*, Sanabria said she had not really considered it. She said she had assumed the exhibition would be seen by her peers, the faculty, and the community at large, primarily a demographic of "white people of a certain religious background."[49] One can understand why, at the time, the artist might not think overly much about the viewers' response to her exhibition. The project was a way to work through her personal history, which continued to feel raw; her parents remained in Colombia, unable to visit the United States while waiting out the ten-year penalty for the deportation. Yet Sanabria had taken care to make the exhibition's message elusive, which suggests that, even without overthinking it, art students at BYU develop a sense of what might be objectionable to potential viewers of their work. It suggests that the artist was thinking about the viewers more than she had consciously acknowledged, in terms of both what she wanted to say to them and what they might be willing to accept. In retrospect, Sanabria would recognize that with *Remnants,* she sought to make "work that could be acceptable to this community but also something that was still generative for me, and honest and sincere."[50] It would be a delicate balance to strike.

Potential viewers of visual art at BYU do not form a monolith in all attributes. It is well established that Mormons lean conservative in terms of political ideology and Republican in terms of political party affiliation, but at BYU this might be changing due to its younger population.[51] And certain conservative platforms divide Mormons more than unite them—including views on immigration. On the question of whether immigration strengthens or burdens the U.S. economy, respondents to a major 2012 Pew study of Mormons in the United States were evenly split, nearly aligning with the responses of the general public (rather than other conservative groups). Among younger Mormons in the study, there was a modestly higher number of respondents seeing immigration as strengthening.[52] Effectively the data depict an issue on which Mormons are less conservative than might be expected, an anomaly that likely results from official positions the church has taken in recent years.[53] Even so, Sanabria's *Remnants* might have found some viewers at BYU who considered her father's deportation just.

The word "remnant" has had a particular resonance within Mormon doctrine. In a broad sense it describes any descendants of the biblical Jacob, or Israel, but early in the church's history the term came to be applied to Indigenous Americans—first to American Indians in the United States, then to Indigenous peoples of South America as well.[54] A related doctrine asserted that the remnant would be "gathered" through missionary efforts and united with white Mormons, who were believed also to be among Israel's descendants.[55] But the second half of the nineteenth century and much of the twentieth would bring a succession of problematic developments to the relationship between white Mormons and Indigenous Americans, and by the end of the twentieth century, church leadership would begin to move away from the idea of physically gathering the scattered remnant.[56] With the title of her project, however, Sanabria recalls these (still deep-seated) doctrines about the remnant and elegantly links them to twenty-first-century debates about immigration, especially immigration to the United States from South America.

Remnants reckoned with the scattering of Sanabria's family in 2009. After her father's deportation to Colombia, her mother was forced to quickly pack up the family's possessions and sell their house before moving with Sanabria and her three siblings to Colombia, where they reunited with their father. The family was abruptly compelled to leave the communities they had belonged to in Florida, including the ward (or congregation) in which her father had previously been a bishop.[57] If her parents' earlier lives could have been read as outcomes of remnant-gathering, these two converts uniting with other literal or spiritual descendants of Israel in the United States, the deportation—the re-scattering—would have been a crisis on a number of levels, not least a crisis of faith. When Sanabria speaks of confronting the inevitability of impermanence through the bare sofa frame or the flaking layers of joint compound, there is a distinct, culture-bound experience at play, and the religious dimension of that is profound. *Remnants* is not a meandering riff on universal impermanence. It opens a specific conversation about the South American immigrant experience, about U.S. policy and political rhetoric in the early twenty-first century, and about Mormonism's intersections with all of it. It is a conversation perfectly suited to play out—potentially to interrupt—at the site of BYU.

Like Huo's exhibition, Sanabria's *Remnants* emphasized the abundance of exhibition space on campus, and as Huo also had done, she occupied it with spatial cohesion. Sanabria has described the objects in her exhibition as "not specific in their places," yet the installation was conscious of how it inhabited the gallery.[58] The looming wall of cardboard boxes determined how viewers would move through the space, acting as a boundary that blocked their bodies as well as their sight lines. Sanabria herself points out the echoes of Minimalism in her installation, most evident in this wall of uniformly sized, rationally arranged boxes and in the other objects' deliberate positioning in relation to floor and walls.[59] These boxes can refer to other things as well, though, if we allow them to. Reading onto *Remnants* the explicit politicization of immigration in the United States that has intensified during Sanabria's lifetime is inevitable. By forcing viewers to circumvent the packing boxes, the artist knowingly recalls the most contentious symbol of that politicization unfolding nationally during her undergraduate years: the wall on the U.S.-Mexican border.

* * *

Sanabria's engagement with a legacy of Minimalist objects in *Remnants* is surprising, given that Minimalism peaked in the 1960s, but also not surprising. The enduring lessons passed on from that art historical moment, with its commitment to unorthodox materials, cleanly articulated forms, and carefully calibrated relationships between viewer and object, would suit in an environment in which one wanted or needed to be vaguely allusive about challenging content. There can be a kind of defensiveness built into this visual language; one can guide the conversation toward materials, form, and space, and for some viewers that will be enough.[60] But as Sanabria's boxes poignantly demonstrated, these elements always mean something. Sculptor Felix Gonzalez-Torres, whose late 1980s and early 1990s work was often likened to Minimalist objects, pushed back against understanding Minimalism as being purely formal: "Minimalist sculptures were never really primary structures, they were structures that were embedded with a multiplicity of meaning. Every time a viewer came into the room these objects became something else."[61] This revised understanding is the legacy that Sanabria continued, as does Huo, to a lesser extent, the latter with their use of industrially fabricated non-art materials (bleached paper towels, plastic wall bins) and the deliberate placement of those materials.[62] The viewer "coming into the room" and bearing witness at this site of BYU ends up being central to the realization of both projects; Huo calls to their bodily imagination, while Sanabria calls to their humanity.

The exhibitions showed an awareness of other established concerns in contemporary art. In the case of *Remnants,* experiences of migration or asylum-seeking and the ruptures caused by these transitions are well-trod ground in a global art world. The upended table in Sanabria's exhibition particularly recalls Doris Salcedo's *Unland* (1995–1998): a group of three sculptures, each a composite of found tables that have been bisected and reattached to a mismatched half. In a surreal turn, the tables have patches of human hair and silk fibers that appear to be sprouting from their surfaces, embedded into innumerable tiny holes drilled into the wood. Though difficult to see from a distance, the tactility of the hair and silk against the worn surfaces of the wood suggests something flesh-like, as though the tables are becoming animate. Salcedo, as a Colombian artist, had in mind the long-entrenched Colombian civil war and specifically children who had seen their parents killed in the conflict.[63] Upon learning this, it is a short jump to then see these composites as stand-ins for those left behind and indelibly altered by the destruction of their family unit.

Sanabria's *Remnants* also addressed things lost; although she did not lose any family members as permanently, precious intangibles—a sense of security, trust, perhaps faith—had gone missing, and the artist evoked these in their absence using domestic objects. While it might be tempting to linger over typological similarities in this comparison (Salcedo's tables, Sanabria's table), it is the surfaces of Sanabria's objects, the vulnerability of the flaking joint compound and warped cardboard, that most poignantly link her work to Salcedo's and carry the weight of *Remnants*'s pathos.[64] At BYU, "mark-making has always been really important," Sanabria observes.[65] This was usually the case in painting, but in sculpture it could translate into a concern with surface quality, which the artist manipulated not only to anthropomorphize her objects, as Salcedo had done, but at the same time to emphasize their inanimateness. In the absence of human presence, these surfaces begin to disintegrate.

In addition to sculptural precedents, Huo's project built upon a history of performance art. *365 Hygienic Collections* recalled an influential feminist performance titled *Ablutions* (1972), a collaboration among artists Suzanne Lacy, Judy Chicago, Aviva Rahmani, and Sandra Orgel, which presented bathing as a response to and reenactment of trauma, in that case the trauma of rape. The artists filled a friend's studio space with metal tubs containing viscerally repulsive substances—raw eggs, cow's blood, and liquid clay—that two performers took turns bathing in, while a third was bound up in full-body gauze bandages by a fourth performer. Broken eggshells, rope, and bovine kidneys littered the studio floor, set to the soundtrack of an audio tape of women recounting their assaults.[66] This sensory chaos and the horror it raised in its viewers mocked the idea of performing ablutions and the rituals of washing up—which gets at the heart of the performance, the difficulty in coming to terms with trauma and the seeming impossibility of repairing it.

The deliberate repulsiveness of the *Ablutions* space and its performers' counterproductive attempts at cleansing themselves make for a striking contrast with the near-antiseptic *365 Hygienic Collections*. The more quotidian detritus of Huo's ritual is markedly ordered, the space sanitized, the actions reasonable, even laudable, to a point—washing one's hands is healthy, is it not? If the excesses of *Ablutions* speak of a scrambling for comprehension in the aftermath of a terrible event, the controlled abundance of *365 Hygienic Collections* speaks of a numbing sameness—we wash our hands every day, every day, every day. Yet despite their obvious differences, both *Ablutions* and *365 Hygienic Collections* testify to futility. Both performances say something about the difficulties of believing oneself clean. For Huo, performing within the site of BYU, this dilemma initiates complicated discussions not only about the artist's personal experiences but also about the broader implications it raised for the viewers.

Looking back at *Ablutions* a decade on, art historian Moira Roth would ask of it, "What is the audience's stake in personal performances which seem created exclusively to satisfy the therapeutic needs of the artist?"[67] Huo's performance of *365 Hygienic Collections* might indeed satisfy the artist's own therapeutic needs, but this does not preclude the viewer from forming an authentic connection with it. In trying to articulate for viewers at BYU the nature of compulsion, Huo presents an experience that is either known or unknown to them. But viewers can certainly feel something regardless—this is what art does. It is important to read Huo's performance in terms of what it meant to the artist, but it is also important to examine what it might bring up for its specific audience. This allows the work to move beyond catharsis. The same could be said of Sanabria's *Remnants:* most viewers were unlikely to have shared her experience of deportation and displacement, but perhaps they could feel and think and question as a direct result of seeing the work at BYU and all that entails. Whatever catharsis resulted for the artists from the process, viewers can still have a stake in the work.

***

Work produced at BYU would be foundational for both artists' subsequent practices. While in the MFA program at MICA, Huo was drawn toward exploring the Korean folk wisdom that had been passed down in their childhood, such as the admonition not to sleep in a room with an electric fan running. "What was fascinating for me at the time," Huo explains, "was beginning to understand belief systems: why and how someone believed something, which had no proof of evidence."[68] A concern with proof, that unavoidable subtext of *365 Hygienic Collections,* grew more pronounced in the artist's graduate work. The interactive installation *Whisper Down the Lane* of 2009 explores this concern. Continuing the large scale that Huo had first explored in the thesis exhibition, the maze of metal ductwork played host to games of telephone among viewers. Participants would be given a card with some piece of folk wisdom on it and then duck into the gaps in the suspended structure and try to pass it on. The ducts would become an echo chamber of competing whispers, decreasing the odds that any one message would make it through the process intact. The playfulness of the interaction, combined with the absurdity of seeing the viewers' bodies half engulfed by the cheery yellow structure, might have obscured the seriousness of the artist's inquiry: how do we accept knowledge that has reached us through a process that seems precarious? Huo might be asking this question about belief as much as about cultural heritage.

Near the end of her first year of the MFA program at Cranbrook Academy of Art, Sanabria made *The Red Front Door* (2022), a video that incorporated footage of actors she directed in a set that she built (which also functioned as an installation in which the video would be screened).[69] For the first two and a half minutes of the video, the camera focuses on a freestanding red door positioned in a marshy, riverside landscape. A tall figure in dark clothing, discernible only in silhouette because of the obscuring pane of privacy glass, knocks repeatedly at the door, eventually progressing to mild kicking and pounding. The figure does not seem particularly angry, just officious, and the scene is deliberately preposterous; why does the figure bother with pounding at the door when there are no walls to keep them out? There is not even a doorknob, only a circular hole where a doorknob should be. Yet in its persistence, the knocking becomes disquieting, even menacing. The voice-over only increases this quality: interspersed with the sound

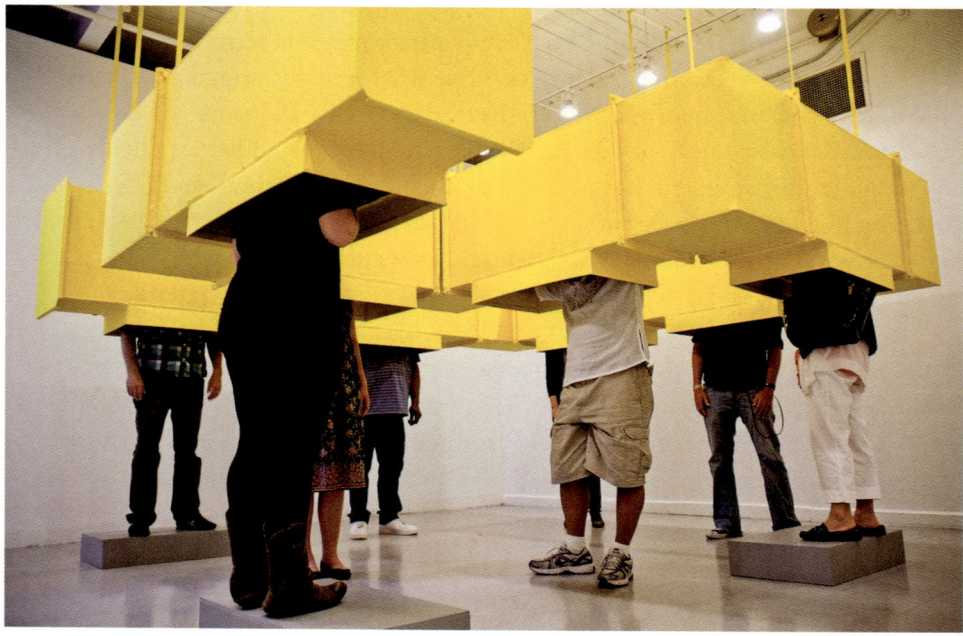

Fig. 21.7 Gi (Ginny) Huo, *Whisper Down the Lane*, 2011, painted air ducts, cards, and wood, 12′ × 11′ × 12′. Courtesy of the artist.

of knocking is a recitation of Bible verses from the book of Matthew, chapter 7—"Ask, and it shall be given you; seek, and ye shall find; knock, and it shall be opened unto you."[70] This is an evocation of Sanabria's *ur*-trauma, the immigration officials knocking at the door to tell her family that her father had been deported. But it also brings to mind the cliched image of Mormon missionaries "tracting," knocking on doors in search of potential converts, which her parents had been. Sanabria conflates the two in a more emphatic way than her earlier allusion to the border wall. "I've gotten a lot bolder since BYU," the artist acknowledges. "There are things that didn't come to the surface then that are coming to the surface now."[71]

Huo's *365 Hygienic Collections* and Sanabria's *Remnants* pair well for several reasons: they share a Minimalist-inflected sensibility, they embrace fragility in form and content, and they demonstrate that viewers could become a key element in the realization of the work. They tell intimate stories that can be extrapolated to discussions about religious faith, specifically Mormon takes on faith. Furthermore, both exhibitions demonstrate that student-artists could address their experiences and forms of knowledge with sophistication for a specific audience in a specific place, and they affirm the importance of the departmental framework that supported them. Still, as case studies, the thesis exhibitions of Huo and Sanabria can offer only glimpses into studying art at BYU in the twenty-first century. If this history continues to be examined, other compelling manifestations of it will surely emerge.

To be a Mormon in the world is to share a set of specific experiences and understandings. For student-artists, is there a better place for serious exchanges

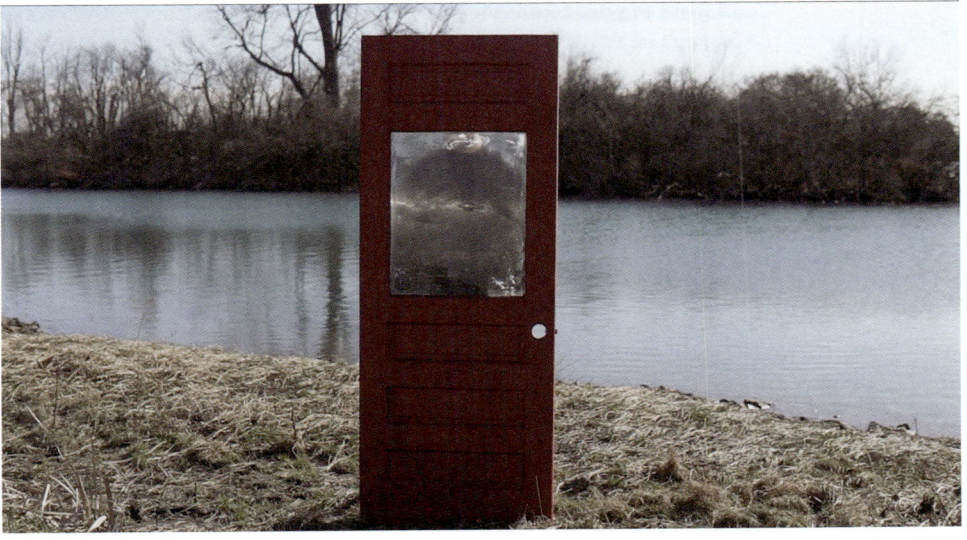

Fig. 21.8 Dalila Sanabria, still from *The Red Front Door*, 2022, video, 21:35. Courtesy of the artist.

centered on those shared experiences to play out than at BYU? The specificity of the site entails responsibility to examine challenging subjects, but it also allows students to broach religious content that could be harder to read or even unwelcome elsewhere. In the essay discussed above, Pujol further calls upon art schools to "stop dismissing religion as an anti-intellectual subject and conversation," lest they contribute to "decontextualizing and ultimately castrating global art, robbing it of its power by regarding it only through its formal qualities."[72] There is little danger of the BYU art department dismissing religion; it is too integral to the student-artists' lives. Yet there is perhaps a risk of sublimating the challenging, specific conversations that might be had about Mormonism or other terrains that ground art-making at BYU, turning them into ambiguous formalisms. More specific conversations might strengthen, rather than impede, students' ability to "be relevant," to access the art world beyond the university.

NOTES

[1] The installation could be viewed through the peepholes even when Huo was not present or performing. Gi (Ginny) Huo, email to author, August 29, 2022.

[2] In the 2021 edition of the Princeton Review's annual college survey, BYU was rated second for "Most Religious Students" (after the University of Dallas). See Robert Franek et al., *The Best 386 Colleges: 2021 Edition* (New York: Penguin Random House, 2020), 42.

[3] There is not a consensus as to whether the contemporary art world is fundamentally unwelcoming toward religious art. For more recent inquiries into the subject, see *Re-Enchantment*, eds. James Elkins and David Morgan (New York: Routledge, 2009) and Thomas Crow, *No Idols: The Missing Theology of Art* (Sydney: Power Publications, 2017).

[4] Dalila Sanabria, phone conversation with author, January 13, 2023.

[5] Sanabria, phone conversation with author, January 13, 2023; also Dalila Sanabria, Zoom conversation with author, May 24, 2022.

[6] Peter Everett, email to author, May 31, 2022.

[7] Ernesto Pujol, "On the Ground: Practical Observations for Regenerating Art Education," in *Art School (Propositions for the 21st Century)*, ed. Steven Henry Madoff (Cambridge, MA: MIT Press, 2009), 4, 10.

[8] In her authoritative essay on the topic, art historian Miwon Kwon differentiated between integrative and interruptive types of site-specificity, a distinction first articulated by Rosalyn Deutsche. See Miwon Kwon, "One Place After Another: Notes on Site-Specificity," *October* 80 (Spring 1997): 85–86n3.

[9] For church policies about the ordinance, see *General Handbook: Serving in the Church of Jesus Christ of Latter-day Saints*, sec.18.7, https://www.churchofjesuschrist.org/study/manual/general-handbook/18-priesthood-ordinances-and-blessings?lang=eng#title_number12, accessed May 28, 2022.

[10] Gi (Ginny) Huo, conversation with author, April 23, 2022. The artist uses they/them pronouns.

[11] Huo, email to author, August 29, 2022.

[12] Gi (Ginny) Huo, conversation with author, January 15, 2023.

[13] Historically the two requisite witnesses had to be adherent male church members, though this policy changed in 2019 to allow for adherent women and children to serve as baptismal witnesses as well. Sarah Jane Weaver, "Women Can Serve as Witnesses for Baptisms, Temple Sealings, First Presidency Announces," press release, October 2, 2019, https://www.churchofjesuschrist.org/church/news/women-can-serve-as-witnesses-for-baptisms-temple-sealings-first-presidency-announces?lang=eng.

[14] See D&C 6:28. Before its formal codification, however, this principle was evidenced by the first edition of the Book of Mormon in 1830, which included two witness statements offered by a combined eleven witnesses attesting to Joseph Smith's possession of engraved plates.

[15] Huo, email to author, August 29, 2022.

16 Heysook Cho, email to author, January 12, 2023. Cho earned her bachelor's degree at Roosevelt University, outside Chicago, but she was also taking ceramics classes at the Art Institute of Chicago.

17 Heysook Cho, email to author, November 10, 2022.

18 Huo, conversation with author, January 15, 2023.

19 Valerie Atkisson, email to author, December 30, 2022. Huo found Atkisson's installation class especially influential—"it really opened things up for me." Huo, conversation with author, January 15, 2023.

20 I am grateful to Jason Lanegan for first bringing this series of retirements to my attention. Jason Lanegan, Zoom conversation with author, May 23, 2022.

21 For example, some notable studies of art education in the twentieth century include Magdalena Droste, *Bauhaus 1919–1933* (Cologne: B. Taschen, 1990); Howard Singerman, *Art Subjects: Making Artists in the American University* (Berkeley: University of California Press, 1999); Mary Emma Harris, *The Arts at Black Mountain College* (Cambridge, MA: MIT Press, 2002); and Philip Kaiser and Christina Végh, eds., *Where Art Might Happen: The Early Years of CalArts* (Hannover: Kestner Gesellschaft, 2020).

22 Charles Esche, "Include Me Out: Helping Artists to Undo the Art World," in *Art School (Propositions for the 21st Century),* ed. Steven Henry Madoff (Cambridge, MA: MIT Press, 2009), 103. As Esche argues (103–104), although contemporary art production was "radically globalized" in the aftermath of the collapse of Communism in 1989, global contemporary art "has continued to build on Western traditions" of art education.

23 A classic essay on art education that articulates the differences among Western models is Thierry de Duve's "When Form Has Become Attitude—and Beyond," in *The Artist and the Academy: Issues in Fine Art Education and The Wider Cultural Context,* ed. Stephen Foster and Nicholas de Ville (Southampton, UK: John Hansard Gallery, 1994), 27–36.

24 For doctrinal clarification one might look at D&C 82:18, which dates to 1832: "And all this for the benefit of the church of the living God, that every man may improve upon his talent, that every man may gain other talents, yea, even an hundred fold, to be cast into the Lord's storehouse, to become the common property of the whole church."

25 As one doctrinal example, there is an exchange in the Book of Mormon in which God prods a man identified only as the brother of Jared to help invent a creative solution to his problem of darkened sea vessels: "What will ye that I should do that ye may have light in your vessels?" See Ether 2:3.

26 Everett, email to author, May 31, 2022. See also de Duve, "When Form Has Become Attitude," 36.

27 Sanabria, phone conversation with author, January 13, 2023.

28 Thierry de Duve, "An Ethics: Putting Aesthetic Transmission in Its Proper Place in the Art World," in *Art School (Propositions for the 21st Century),* ed. Steven Henry Madoff (Cambridge, MA: MIT Press, 2009), 16–17.

29 Huo, conversation with author, April 23, 2022. Hamilton is featured in Season 1, in the "Spirituality" episode (2001) and Pfeiffer in the "Time" episode of Season 2 (2003).

30 These examples include Richardson's *Brolly Ball* (2014), a series of photographs of a large weather balloon covered over with a patchwork of umbrella fabric; Jackson's *Esterbend* (2013), a video of a coyote pelt gamboling in an artificial breeze; and Lynn's photograph *Misplaced Wall (Desert Cascade)* (2017), a video of an abstracted cityscape of cardboard boxes falling. All use the Flats as the backdrop.

31 Brown's *Some Proof* (2011) and Curry's *Any Sound Not About Love Must Be Silent* (2019–) both utilize the scroll format.

32 Laura Hurtado, "Rippling Aesthetics," in *A 15-Year Expanse: Volume 1* (Provo, UT: Brigham Young University Department of Art, 2020), 12–14.

33 Everett, email to author, May 31, 2022.

34 According to Everett, student exhibitions have been an essential part of the art programs at BYU since the 1980s at least, but their twenty-first-century manifestations are especially accomplished. Everett, email to author, May 31, 2022.

35 Gary Barton, response to author's questionnaire on the BYU Department of Art, July 29, 2022.

36 Lanegan, Zoom conversation with author, May 23, 2022.

37 The quantity of exhibition spaces makes sense because the building had previously accommodated the university's permanent art collection until 1993, when construction was completed on the new BYU

Museum of Art. Rebecca Sumsion, "Harris Fine Arts Center Galleries Provide Student-Oriented Experiences," *Daily Universe*, May 30, 2017, https://universe.byu.edu/2017/05/30/harris-fine-arts-center-galleries-provide-student-oriented-experiences/.

[38] Lanegan, Zoom conversation with author, May 23, 2022. A dedicated workshop was added for the construction of installation needs.

[39] Lanegan, Zoom conversation with author, May 23, 2022.

[40] Everett, email to author, May 31, 2022.

[41] De Duve, "An Ethics," 17.

[42] To achieve these battered, water-damaged surfaces on the boxes, Sanabria soaked pieces of cardboard in water until she could deconstruct them by peeling off a layer of linerboard. The artist then glued these fragments onto the cardboard boxes like papier-mâché, as she describes it. Sanabria, Zoom conversation with author, May 24, 2022.

[43] Sanabria, Zoom conversation with author, May 24, 2022.

[44] Dalila Sanabria, "Aliens, Anchors, and How Words Still Matter," Humanities Center blog, December 3, 2018, https://humanitiescenter.byu.edu/aliens-anchors-and-how-words-still-matter/.

[45] Sanabria, "Aliens."

[46] Brigham Young University, "Facts and Figures," https://www.byu.edu/facts-figures, accessed April 30, 2022. Two-thirds of students come from outside the state (though not necessarily from outside the region), and a small sliver—about 5 percent—arrive from abroad.

[47] In 2016, the number of former missionaries (both domestic and international assignments) was reported as making up 63 percent of all students on the BYU campus. See Tad Walch, "BYU Sees Dramatic Jump in Number of Returned Missionaries," *Deseret News*, April 4, 2016, https://www.deseret.com/2016/4/4/20585929/byu-sees-dramatic-jump-in-number-of-returned-missionaries. BYU's study abroad programs, which serve 17 percent of students (as of the fall of 2021), also offer international experiences. See "Facts & Figures."

[48] BYU Committee on Race, Equity, and Belonging, "Report and Recommendations of the BYU Committee on Race, Equity, and Belonging," February 25, 2021, https://race.byu.edu/report, 4.

[49] Sanabria, Zoom conversation with author, May 24, 2022.

[50] Sanabria, phone conversation with author, January 13, 2023.

[51] See Michael Lipka, "U.S. Religious Groups and Their Political Leanings," Pew Research Center, February 23, 2016, https://www.pewresearch.org/fact-tank/2016/02/23/u-s-religious-groups-and-their-political-leanings/. For anecdotal evidence from well-placed sources on BYU's shifting political views, see Kate Blood Ferguson, "BYU Students Not as Conservative as Some Think," *Daily Universe*, July 7, 2017, https://universe.byu.edu/2017/07/07/byu-students-inches-away-from-political-conservatism1/.

[52] Gregory Smith et al., "Mormons in America: Certain in Their Beliefs, Uncertain of Their Place in Society," Pew Research Center, 2012, 63. The breakdown for Mormons of all ages was 45 percent "strengthen," 41 percent "burden," while for Mormons under fifty the breakdown was 49 precent "strengthen," 39 percent "burden."

[53] See Church of Jesus Christ of Latter-day Saints, "Immigration: Church Issues New Statement," official statement, June 10, 2011, https://newsroom.churchofjesuschrist.org/article/immigration-church-issues-new-statement; see also "Church Statement on Separation of Families at the US-Mexico Border," official statement, June 18, 2018, https://newsroom.churchofjesuschrist.org/article/church-statement-separation-of-families-at-us-mexico-border.

[54] In 1845, the Twelve Apostles officially proclaimed that "that the 'Indians' (so called) of North and South America are a remnant of the tribes of Israel; as is now made manifest by the discovery and revelation of their ancient oracles and records." As cited in John-Charles Duffy, "The Use of 'Lamanite' in Official LDS Church Discourse," *Journal of Mormon History* 34, no. 1 (Winter 2008): 126.

[55] Duffy, "The Use of 'Lamanite,'" 128.

[56] Duffy, "The Use of 'Lamanite,'" 152. Duffy's article succinctly traces the complicated history of these developments.

[57] Sanabria, phone conversation with author, January 13, 2023; see also Sanabria, "Aliens."

[58] Sanabria, Zoom conversation with author, May 24, 2022.

[59] Sanabria, Zoom conversation with author, May 24, 2022.

[60] Anna Chave has written about the contradictions inherent to Minimalist objects, which seemed to refuse to depict anything but actually succeeded at conveying a "rhetoric of power," in part by not adhering to sculptural conventions. See Anna Chave, "Minimalism and the Rhetoric of Power," *Arts Magazine* 64, no. 5 (January 1990): 44–63.

[61] Felix Gonzalez-Torres, interview with Tim Rollins, in *Felix Gonzalez-Torres*, ed. William S. Bartman (Los Angeles: Art Resources Transfer Press, 1993), 74. Gonzalez-Torres was responding to a particular quote by Minimalist Carl Andre, who claimed, "My sculptures are masses and their subject is matter."

[62] Huo describes the aesthetic of *365 Hygienic Collections* more generally as formalist. Huo, conversation with author, January 15, 2023.

[63] For a helpful overview of how *Unland* was made and the conflict it responded to, see Tanya Barson, "Unland: The Place of Testimony," in *Tate Papers* 1 (Spring 2004), https://www.tate.org.uk/research/tate-papers/01/unland-the-place-of-testimony.

[64] In reviewing *Unland* when it was first exhibited in 1998, critic Barry Schwabsky recognized in Salcedo's objects an "urge to endow Minimalist form with the pathos of the everyday." This is a useful description for what Sanabria is doing as well. See Schwabsky, review of Doris Salcedo at New Museum of Contemporary Art, in *Artforum* 37, no. 1 (September 1998): 153.

[65] Sanabria, Zoom conversation with author, May 24, 2022.

[66] The components of *Ablutions* are identified by Nancy Princenthal in *Unspeakable Acts: Women, Art, and Sexual Violence in the 1970s* (New York: Thames and Hudson, 2019), 75–81.

[67] Moira Roth writing in 1983, as cited in Princenthal, *Unspeakable Acts,* 81.

[68] Huo, email to author, August 29, 2022.

[69] Sanabria's video can be viewed online: *The Red Front Door*, Vimeo, https://player.vimeo.com/video/705128633, accessed May 25, 2022. The knocking figure returns later in the video to thoroughly crush and smear a tomato against the glass, to the soundtrack of a beating heart.

[70] Sanabria pulled this audio from the website of the Church of Jesus Christ of Latter-day Saints, so viewers who had used the site or its app to study would be familiar with the voice. Sanabria, Zoom conversation with author, May 24, 2022.

[71] Sanabria, phone conversation with author, January 13, 2023.

[72] Pujol, "On the Ground," 11. The second statement, about decontextualizing and castrating global art, paraphrases an argument articulated by critic Michael Brenson about museums, which Pujol extends to art schools.

22

TOWARD A LATTER-DAY SAINT CONTEMPORARY ART

CHASE WESTFALL

PRESENT CHALLENGES

In 2017, I had the opportunity to participate in the first Mormon Arts Center Festival, held at Riverside Church in New York.[1] Set within Riverside's time-worn Gothic Revival grandeur, the festival was a congress of Latter-day Saint scholars and creatives gathered for lectures, discussion panels, and a showcase of LDS achievement in the arts.

I was there in multiple, overlapping roles: as an interested member of the festival's target audience, as an exhibiting artist, and as hired staff. While in my personal practice I had spent innumerable hours hashing and rehashing the question of what it meant to be an LDS person making contemporary art, the festival was my first meaningful opportunity to confront that question in broader terms. It was a chance to reframe personal concerns in relation to the needs of a community of practitioners, to ask what an LDS contemporary art might properly be about and look like, and to encounter the consequences and implications of that inquiry from the other side, as a curator and audience member.

The festival featured the exhibition *Immediate Present,* a survey of contemporary LDS visual art organized by Laura Allred Hurtado in her post as global acquisitions art curator at the Church of Jesus Christ of Latter-day Saints History Museum in Salt Lake City, Utah.[2] Installed on temporary walls in the center of the festival's main hall, the exhibition sat symbolically at the heart of the weekend's events. It was the fixed inlet through which the tides of the three-day festival's activities and audiences ebbed and flowed.

Like the festival itself, *Immediate Present* was ambitious and thoughtfully organized. Consistent with its aims—and to Hurtado's immense credit—it offered something like a comprehensive survey, reflecting the breadth of contemporary practices by LDS artists. Alongside painting, printmaking, photography, and sculpture, it included video, animation, fiber and textile works, mixed media, new media, hybrid forms, installation-based practices, and objects and documentation from performance. Jeff Decker's sculpture *Low and B. Hold Mammon . . .* (2017), actual black rhino and ostrich taxidermies adorned as fantastical parade characters (complete with gilded baby jockeys), represented one outlandish extreme. Ben Howell's *Transcription II* (2016), a thirty-foot-long handwritten scroll of text from the Book of Mormon, offered a more subdued form of processional.

The exhibition, however, also evidenced some of the challenges facing LDS artists as they navigate a generally conservative social and ecclesiastical culture in a faith community without robust systems of patronage or a clear legacy in the visual arts. These challenges were expressed variously in some of the exhibition's distinguishing traits, including the conspicuous absence of a unifying style, shared material, formal or conceptual strategies; a preponderance of religious imagery, narratives, themes, and allegory; and a propensity for representational imagery and the human form—depicted either naturalistically or in a variety of friendly, illustrative styles.

Despite the recency of the works' creation (all made between 2010 and 2017) and the implications of the exhibition's title, there was also a strange anachronism. Many of the works seemed to be speaking from (or to) other times; though chronologically contemporary, they were not meaningfully engaged with then-current tastes and practices in contemporary art, or the social and political concerns of their moment. Similarly (or symptomatically), there was a tendency toward formality and politeness in the demeanor of the works, which assumed a generally passive and deferential disposition toward their audiences and subject matter.

Emerging almost in the same moment, the 2017 Whitney Biennial offers an instructional contrast to *Immediate Present* in this regard.[3] Itself a staggeringly diverse survey of contemporary practices, the 2017 biennial's artists and artworks were fully attuned to the urgent questions and moods of the day. Rather than a deferential posture, they demonstrated an activist disposition toward aesthetic and political discourse, their audiences and communities, and even the Whitney itself, as their host institution. Like *Immediate Present,* the biennial was conceived in the tumultuous days surrounding the 2016 U.S. presidential election—days emblematized by the terrible conflict between community members and police in Ferguson, Missouri.[4] Looming was the spectacle of Trump versus Clinton, an ugly pantomime of a national ideological schism. These and other events had freshly opened old wounds in American society. Fittingly, one frequent observation from biennial commentators was its recurring turn to violence.[5] And several of the exhibition's most confrontational depictions of violence, including those by Jordan Wolfson, Dana Schutz, and Henry Taylor, became lightning rods for weighty and contentious public conversation—the reverberations of which are still felt today.

I am deeply sympathetic to the way LDS artists express their values through conscientious avoidance of graphic content (including graphic violence) and confrontational posturing, as well as their inclination toward a tenseless and allegorical transposition of questions of human moral action. These tendencies reflect important ethical commitments and offer certain rhetorical advantages and strengths. But this avoidance and transposition are also symptomatic of a general unwillingness among LDS artists to ask difficult questions of themselves and their audiences—even when such questions, and the discomfort they sometimes produce, can be purposeful or instructive. While it may be culturally understandable, this unwillingness must be overcome if the arts are ever to achieve the same spiritual and social utility for the Latter-day Saints as they have achieved within the broader cultural sphere. There is more than enough historical and doctrinal precedent in Christian and Latter-day Saint traditions to justify a disposition of productive questioning. As a corollary of art's activism, Mormon artists can look to their own heritage of prophetic disruption and intervention.

If reluctance is the rule, some of the works from *Immediate Present* were perfectly weighted exceptions, showing themselves capable and willing to ask complex questions and to challenge the tastes and assumptions of the festival's largely LDS audience without resorting to gratuitous content or open hostility. In Levi Jackson's haunting video work *Esterbend* (2015), a coyote pelt pulses, rising and falling mysteriously in a dramatic Utah desertscape. Set to Mahler's "Resurrection" Symphony No. 2, from which the piece derives its title, the gray and brown hide dances between ascension and burial, an abject spirit in a cinematic salt flat purgatory—whether under its own volition or at the bidding of some other power. Given the theme of the symphony, the pelt enacts a sputtering reanimation, like the bodily resurrection promised by LDS doctrines, only awkward and vulnerable. Despite that awkwardness, lifted by the ethereal soundtrack, the formal and scenic beauty, and the inexplicable nature of the pelt's movements, *Esterbend* retains something achingly transcendent. With the particularity of its landscape and symbology, the piece offers a complex metaphor for histories of migration, land use, and the displacement of Indigenous peoples and wildlife in the Mormons' westward expansion.[6] The use of digital video, the sharpness and clarity of the image, the tightly controlled cinematography, the tire tracks marking the cracked earth—along with its nuanced engagement of specific histories of pioneering—mark the work as contemporary, while offering a pointed, localized criticality like that seen at the Biennial.

Casey Jex Smith's *Seer Stone* (2015), a hyperrealistic drawing of a stone used by Joseph Smith as a prophetic aid in his translation of the Book of Mormon, provides another example of critical engagement. Jex Smith's drawing is based on images of the stone released by the LDS Church to the public in August 2015, after years of speculation and controversy.[7] Depicted against a graph-paper-like grid of intersecting red lines, the implied perspective of the rendered stone misaligns with the vertical, modernist plane of the background, lending the stone a slightly ominous hovering effect. This spatial malignment becomes a visual metaphor for the tension between systems of secular and spiritual knowledge, well known to communities of faith of all kinds, but acutely felt by Latter-day Saints reconciling their esoterica with a twenty-first-century

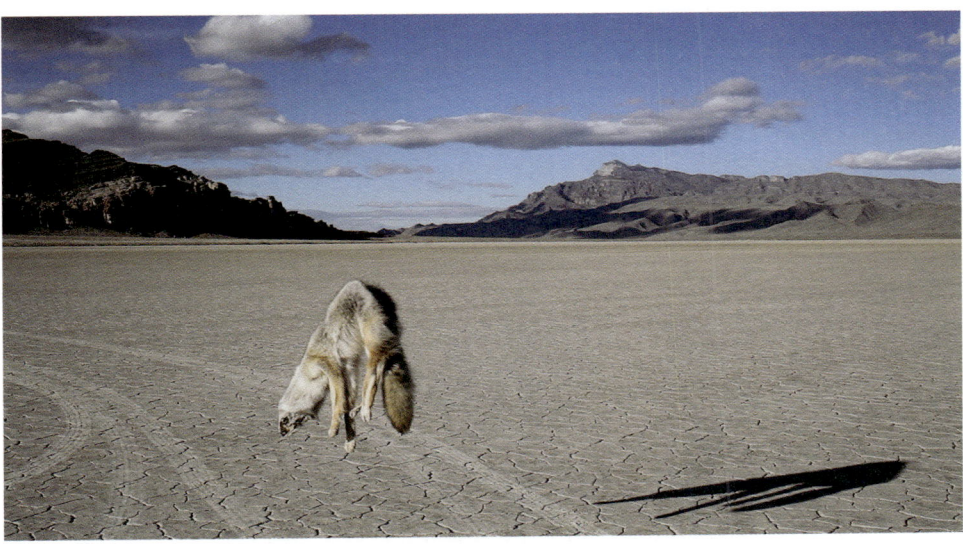

Fig. 22.1 Levi Jackson, *Esterbend* (2015), single-channel video, 3:30. Courtesy of the artist.

world. This juxtaposition further recalls the uneasy relationship between the actual history of Smith's use of this arcane prophetic instrument and the more palatable version of the Book of Mormon translation narrative foregrounded in church discourse, in which Smith's translation act in presented in more conventional terms.[8] A distortion in the red grid and umbral discoloration directly above the stone, like the shimmer of rising heat, suggests that the stone has an uncanny physical or spatial influence on its setting. As poet Tyler Chadwick expresses it in a poem commissioned in response to the work, this shimmer suggests the stone's power to introduce "a ripple in history's grid."[9] Such details amplify the effect of charismatic media—in a stone that, for many inside and outside the faith, signifies occult eccentricity. The swirled patterning of the stone's striated surface suggests a cosmos, heightening the gravity of the image.

Beyond the exhibition, the Mormon Arts Center Festival's other programs offered rich experiences as control points and landmarks for orienteering the terrain of LDS creative culture: the shock and thrill of a performance by Spanish avant-garde composer Francisco "Paco" Estévez; incisive papers delivered by LDS intellectuals such as Adam Miller and Jared Hickman, who offered relatable perspectives on the travails of Mormon creativity, its perils, rewards, and aspirations; the provocative strangeness of the fiction of Steven L. Peck (in a discussion of his then forthcoming novel *Gilda Trillim: Shepherdess of Rats* [2017]); and many other personally meaningful experiences.[10] As with *Immediate Present,* each of these experiences also raised questions, hinted at gaps and deficits, or brought challenges into focus. But the summative impression was decidedly positive. And the cumulative credibility of the festival's organizers, artists, performers, and speakers suggested that a critical mass might be reached, and that these

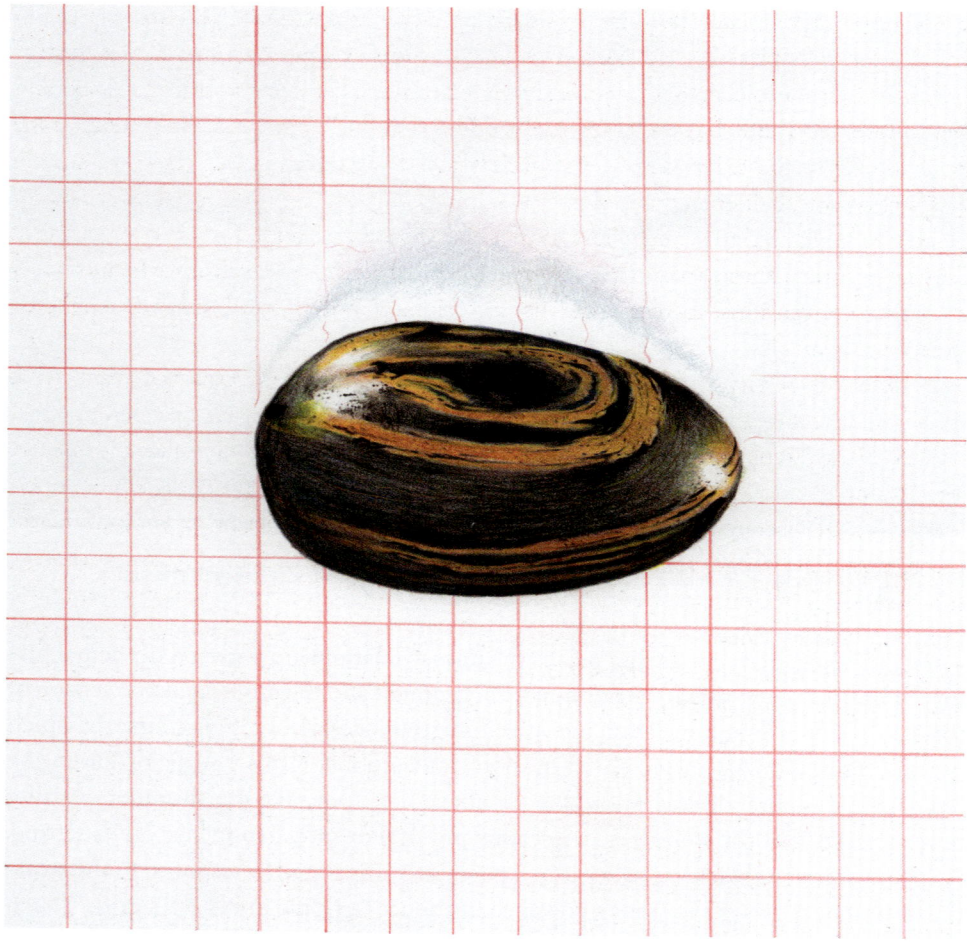

Fig. 22.2 Casey Jex Smith, *Seer Stone* (2016), colored pencil on paper, 7.5″ × 7.5, Church of Jesus Christ of Latter-day Saints Church History Museum.

voices might be coalesced into a lively discourse. Building from these observations, my intuitions as a working Latter-day Saint artist, and the sensitivities and understandings I've developed as a curator in the field, I am optimistic about the future of LDS contemporary art.

FAITH IN ART

Among many reasons to be encouraged about LDS contemporary art futures, let me offer four.

First is a rising generation of LDS artists who are more diverse in their personal and political identities, more sensitive and informed in their knowledge of contemporary art, and less encumbered by the problematic narratives that often burdened their predecessors. Specifically, they are disinheriting modernist narratives of Art (capital A) and Progress (capital P) and narratives of Mormon exceptionalism—two symmetrical ideological projects that became entangled in the LDS cultural consciousness and were preserved there, beyond their useful life spans.[11] Where preceding generations were subject to the exigencies of Art undertaken as a "sacred quest" (i.e., as a means of enacting and evidencing the divine destiny of the church), young LDS artists no longer feel obligated to advance idealized and exclusionary models of art or their faith. On the contrary, these artists demonstrate a willingness to break from Mormonism's totalizing conventions, to reexamine its exclusionary systems and expand its single-story narratives.

Next is the reality that the church is in a time of general transformation, with accelerating changes in its membership and demographics, increased transparency and critical self-awareness about its history (the release of the seer stone images is one salient example), and a governing organization that is thoughtfully pursuing a more open framework of discourse and identity. This includes the introduction of programmatic and operational changes that multiply and distribute the voices of instruction, authority, and orthodoxy.[12] Consistent with the church's stated mission, historical development, and foundational values, these changes put positive pressure on individual members to do more as creative, local agents within the divine program. They help set the stage for a more dynamic, inventive, and culturally impactful art within the church.

Third are LDS doctrines, cosmology, and principles of community engagement, which continue to offer radical models of—and technologies for—religious thought and communal action. Where artists and others can recenter the church's divergent theology, its value as a novel and exploratory religious model will speak for itself.

And fourth, as the discourse of art continues to evolve there are, increasingly, operational, and value alignments—what could be called affinities, structural symmetries or formal similarities—between the faith practices of the Latter-day Saints and the various practices of faith found in contemporary art. Ritual and ceremony, community formation, conscientious action and grassroots activism, practices of witnessing, evangelism and self-education, peer-to-peer networks of mutual care, and investment in anti-capitalist and anti-materialist economies of meaning and value, to name a few. Value alignments include empathy, inclusion, compassion, historical and genealogical awareness, solidarity, non-violence, accountability, individual agency, an insistence on the dignity of all human life—especially those lives to which dignity is most forcibly denied—and a belief that the world can and should be made new. These commonalities unite LDS faith and contemporary art in their mutual emphasis on *relationship*—on communal, familial, ecological, and historical ligature—and as activist and prophetic ways of *relating to* the world.[13] While certain antagonisms and sibling rivalries are inevitable, as LDS faith and contemporary art earnestly enact their programs, the best of their mutually redemptive impulses will find increased accommodation for—and affiliation with—each other.[14]

That art can be understood as a communal practice of faith is not a new concept. Art critic and commentator Julian Bell observes, "The painter, making a mark with the brush, believes in its meaningfulness: that is enough, for him and for those who believe too; this shared belief is a moment of representation."[15] More recently, the sculptor Vincent Fecteau expressed the faith practice of contemporary art in a decidedly meta-modernist way:[16]

> The creative process [is a] process that, I think, requires a substantial amount of faith: faith that materials can transcend their representational limitations and locate new meaning. For this transmutation to work, the viewer must also have faith in its possibility. That's one of the most beautiful things about art, the faith or will that can make a rubber band or a pushpin the location of all this meaning.[17]

Fellow sculptor Tony Cragg is more direct, laying the prophetic and meaning-making power of the artist bare when he asserts: "As an artist, one is taking the material of the world, imposing a set of forms on it in a very concentrated way, to actually reinvest our existence with meaning."[18] Meaning, of course, is an open value, and the artist must choose the kind(s) of meaning they want existence to take on. It is in the varieties of meaning, and the subject matter through which it is expressed, that LDS artists may still sometimes feel out of sync with their artist peers, or that their particular subjects and kinds of meanings are not shared or welcome. Ultimately, however, LDS artists must learn to look past these surface differences to understand that, in their own work and that of their fellow artists, it is not the ostensible content (the veneer of subjects and meaning) but the prophetic character of art that determines its value and cultural impact.

INTO THE EXPANSE

In 2020 the Brigham Young University Department of Art published *A 15-Year Expanse, Volume 1*.[19] For *A 15-Year Expanse*, Laura Hurtado (now in her current post as executive director of the Utah Museum of Contemporary Art) worked with Department of Art faculty and leadership to identify ten outstanding BYU alumni from the years 2000 to 2015. As with *Immediate Present,* Hurtado was tasked with producing a representative survey of current practices from a group of LDS artists. Though they share a curator and represent a roughly equivalent time span (the works in *Immediate Present* date between 2010 and 2017, those in *15-Year Expanse* between 2010 and 2019), significant differences in the scope, motivations, and circumstances of production for the two projects resulted in markedly different outcomes. Acknowledging those differences—because of them, in fact—*Immediate Present* and *A 15-Year Expanse* offer some productive points of comparison.

While *Immediate Present* stretches itself in an effort to faithfully capture the full breadth of its moment, *15-Year Expanse* is more focused and editorial in its framing. By means of that framing it is able—in contrast to the anachronism of *Immediate Present,* lamented above—to recommend itself convincingly as contemporary, that is, as relevant and timely. Traits and features that earmark its contemporaneity include the comparative lack of overtly religious narratives and imagery; a general deemphasis of representational imagery (and corresponding embrace of the nonrepresentational); a more current and art-historically self-aware approach to figuration when it is present; a rejection of legacies and formal vocabularies of "mastery," in favor of the idiosyncratic and provisional; and, in what I've previously referred to as the disposition of the work, a move away from deferential reserve toward intimacy, immediacy, candor, active engagement, and vulnerability. Hurtado's sharp essay and the book's very hip design work (by Provo-based publisher and design firm Actual Source, which boasts MoMA, LACMA, and film studio A24 as clients) further certify *A 15-Year Expanse*'s timeliness and stylishness.

There is more strangeness, playfulness, and uncertainty—and a lot more color. The blasé shoppers in Madeline Rupard's twenty-first-century genre painting *Drew and Michele in Costco* (2017) are just as denatured by the queasy, box-store lighting as the bins of flowers and commercial goods they drift past and meld with. In the funky, mitochondrial textile works of Katheryn Knudson and tweaked-out geometries of Todd Chilton's paintings, accumulated effort doesn't lead to refinement but is legible as labor: repetitive, imperfect, anxious, revisional, and without self-importance. The marks, gestures, seams, and boundaries in the craggy wood and pieced-glass sculptures of Mary Baum are similarly searching, uncertain, modest, responsive, and exploratory. In their spare and mournful elegance, Makia Sharp's photographic and sculptural memento mori are unpretentious. Self-effacing and self-conscious, these slyly playful works are aware of their pictorial, temporal, and semiotic limits. They quote and complicate the iconography of LDS rituals such as the sacrament, testing cultural norms of reverence and representation without undermining them.

In *A 15-Year Expanse* Hurtado's sensitivity as a curator of contemporary art is on full display as she selects and amplifies those artists and artworks that are best aligned with, and most conducive toward, the kind of critical conversations and futures for which many (like Hurtado and myself) have been anxiously waiting: one in which LDS visual artists may be meaningfully positioned in cultural matters at home and abroad.[20] In a gesture of prophetic self-actualization, *A 15-Year Expanse* simultaneously demarcates and steps into that future. More than simply sampling or reporting, it provides a statement of intent, as underscored by its designation as Volume 1.

That BYU Department of Art is the publisher and underwriter of this maneuver is symbolically important—and to the credit of that institution, its excellent faculty, and the foresight of departmental leadership. Within LDS circles, few institutions have more clout than BYU. Its sanctioning of this text automatically positions these artists and this work within the circle of trust for many Latter-day Saints. In challenging the expectations of LDS audiences, these artists may be extended the benefit of the doubt and encounter a few more open minds.

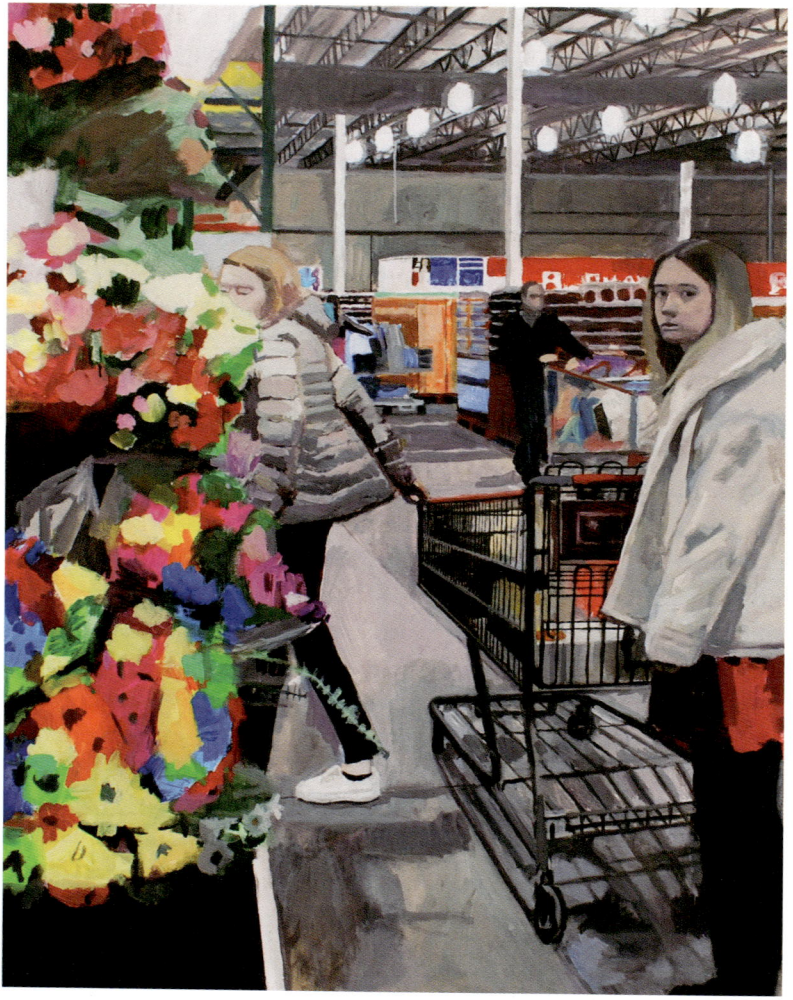

Fig. 22.3 Madeline Rupard, *Drew and Michele in Costco* (2017), acrylic on canvas, 40″ × 30″. Courtesy of the artist.

FROM LAW TO PARABLE

In comparing *Immediate Present* and *A 15-Year Expanse* we also see a shift from a depictive paradigm of making to an interrogative one, or what we might categorize as a move from a didactic to a parabolic mode. This shift parallels, subsumes, and correlates some of the more particular differences already noted. Significantly, it also demonstrates how an activist art might be productively deployed in a religious context.

Consistent with its propensity for—and privileging of—representational imagery, the artworks in *Immediate Present* generally model an illustrative relationship to their subjects. Compositionally dynamic and inventive works such as Walter Rane's *Tell Me*

Thy Name (2017), which reanimates the oft-depicted scene of Jacob's wrestling with the angel, or Jorge Coco Santangelo's *The Tempest—Peace Be Still* (2016), a unique take on Christ calming the troubled sea, remain, despite their pictorial inventiveness, largely traditional in what they communicate about these well-known stories.[21] Borrowing from Jewish thought (like any proper Mormon undertaking), we might categorize such depictions as part of a structure of *halakha:* a codex of conventionalized portrayals, interpretations, and orthodoxy that provides a framework for maintaining cultural continuity—that is, the law. In contrast, rather than repeat or validate its established forms and claims, the artists in *A 15-Year Expanse* explore the gospel's active value, testing and interrogating the redemptive temper of its precepts through extended reflection, material, pictorial, and symbolic experimentation in a practice we might call *aggadah:* the practical, anecdotal, folkloric application and lived exegesis of the law— that is, parable. In this turn to the parabolic and interrogative, the strongest of *A 15-Year Expanse*'s works retain an undeniable spiritual character—one that enacts, rather than illustrates, the interests and hopes of spiritually conscientious beings navigating a complex, fallen world. Where they do not lead with their religiosity, the works in *A 15-Year Expanse* are powered by their expression of LDS doctrines, histories, and sensibilities, even as these are expressed in surprising ways.

For example, Tiana Birrell's interdisciplinary and "rippling" aesthetic apparatus blurs boundaries between information and infrastructure, echoing the radical physicalism of LDS metaphysics, in which "there is no such thing as immaterial matter."[22] Consistent with a theology in which even the "spirit is matter, but it is more fine or pure," Birrell insists on the materiality of data, image, even ideology—and on their spatial and ecological implications. In light of Joseph Smith's teachings on the eternal nature of matter and the perpetual, episodic program of divine creation, Birrell's iterative structures, fractal logics, glitches, and copy/paste maneuvers enact the churning of finite quantities of material through infinite cycles of order and states of refinement. While Birrell does not assert or impose such theological meanings on her work, it offers rich interpretive possibilities through an LDS lens.

Rather than fetishize or mythologize a pioneer past, artists such as Jean Richardson apply a pioneer logic as they grapple with history, hold space, occupy self and landscape, encounter mystery and loss, invent, mend, stitch, improvise, and bushwhack their way through the frontiers and borders of LDS visual and material culture. The rolled and folded patchwork forms and evocative titles of Richardson's paper envelope works are apropos here: *Roaming, Wandering, Whereabouts,* and *Traversed* (all 2017) as well as the excursive, free-ranging energies of her *Brolly Ball* (a giant-size, kinetic "soccer ball" sculpture, pieced from hexagonal umbrella tops) and her tumbleweed works.[23]

LDS themes and gestures of material redemption, world-building, community, prophecy, history, opposition, creation, and care abound. Hurtado insightfully aligns these with the broader concerns of contemporary art, pointing to "efforts to unfix the

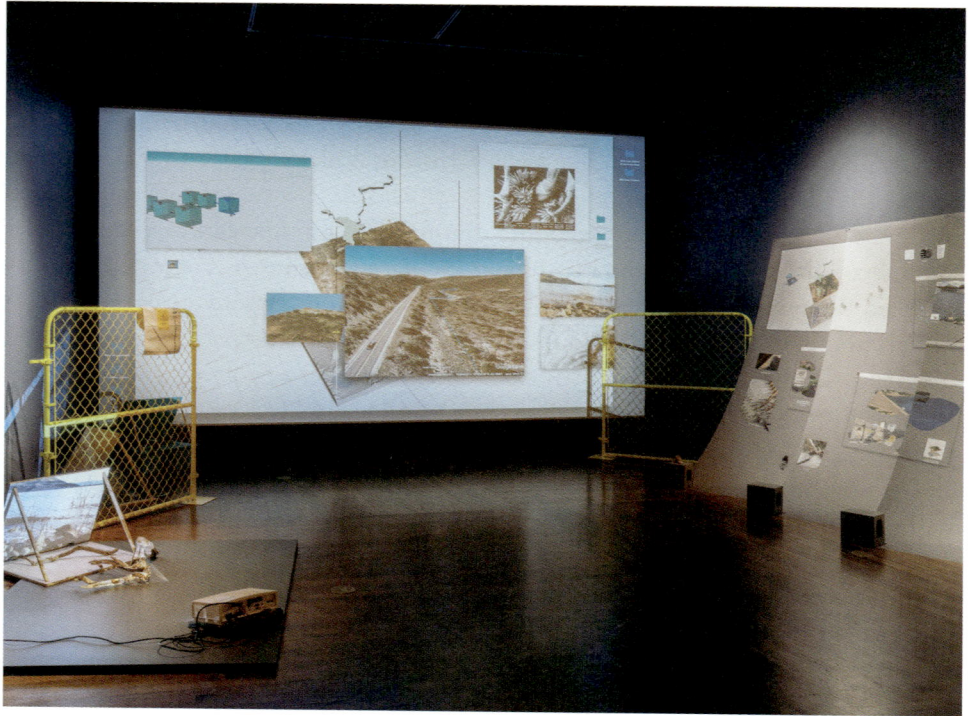

Fig. 22.4 Tiana Birrell, *The Weight of a Cloud* (2021), mixed media installation, dimensions variable. Courtesy of the artist.

clean binary between high and low and to engage the meaning of our times in regard to identity, diaspora, gender, materiality, capitalism, climate change and technology."[24]

Employing this parabolic mode, the artists in *A 15-Year Expanse* create works that are open, personal, relevant, and relatable. In their embrace of the unorthodox, the impoverished, and the misfit, the artists in *A 15-Year Expanse* become intimate partners to the quotidian anxieties, hopes, and fears of contemporary life. Rather than the formality that kept many of *Immediate Present*'s works at a distance—in a space of contemplation, removed from the lived conditions of their audience—the artworks in *A 15-Year Expanse* ask to be met and touched, offer copiously the touch of the artist, sputter and spill, resist framing, spurn plinths, drip, roll up, tumble, rupture, cake, crack, weep, clump, and play in the dirt. These are the unceremonious attitudes and engagements that increasingly characterize contemporary artistic practice, and which are at the heart of lived LDS discipleship—a discipleship epitomized by voluntary childcare and chapel cleaning, helping a neighbor during a move or at times of illness, birth, or death. As today's artists resist values and vocabularies of privilege and exclusivity, they seek alternative vocabularies that can align concerted and purposeful action with accommodation, care, and inclusion. LDS artists are positioned to offer discipleship as one of those vocabularies. Art, in turn, offers its strategies, forms, and language as a means of reinvigorating a creatively stagnant Christian cultural discourse.

CHANGING OUR THINKING

The definitive articulation of aspirational "greatness" for LDS art comes from Spencer W. Kimball's *Education for Eternity* (1967), which calls for superlative achievement in the arts as a proof and creative apotheosis of the divine truth of the Restoration.[25] A more nuanced and, for arts practitioners, perhaps more instructive expression can be found in Steven Sondrup's thoughtful preface to the book *Arts and Inspiration: Mormon Perspectives* (1980) and in the provocative and insightful collection of essays that follows, including contributions from church leaders such as Boyd K. Packer and major Mormon cultural figures including composer Merrill Bradshaw, artist Trevor Southey, and literary critic Wayne C. Booth.[26] Kimball's call to achievement, colloquially known as the "Kimball Challenge," has already been the subject of much commentary—including an excellent collection of essays published on the occasion of the first Center for Latter-day Saint Arts Festival (referenced previously), a thoughtful analysis offered by Hurtado in the catalogue essay for *Immediate Present*, and in other places here in this volume.

Following from Kimball's "challenge," the working conundrum for LDS artists has been the simultaneous satisfaction of two separate but equally demanding standards: the standard of the world (the external critical standard) and the gospel standard (the internal spiritual—and, too often, cultural—standard). While this serving-two-masters schema has predictably proven problematic, the ideal that it signals—of a mutually satisfactory result—is, for my purposes here, upheld. It must also, however, be clarified and qualified. First, I do not believe in an art that would appeal equally to the tastes and predilections of art theorist Rosalind Krauss and LDS Church president Russell M. Nelson.[27] There is almost certainly too great a disparity in their training, personalities, politics, and so forth. But I do believe in an art that can make an earnest and equal appeal to the best of their shared humanity, principles, and values: an art that is oriented toward and motivated by a transformative vision that both would honor and even endorse. And so, one of the paradigmatic correctives that emerging LDS artists are tasked with (are, in fact, achieving) is the disruption of a pattern of dualistic thinking that presumes divergence in the fundamental demands and standards of art and faith. Left unchallenged, this dualistic thinking puts the LDS artist in the precarious, false position of feeling that in order to do meaningful work they must be stretched across an intervening chasm; that their work must constitute a site of reconciliation; or, most tragically, that they must ultimately choose between the two sides—holding to the one and despising the other.[28]

For some, lived experience has, unfortunately, reinforced this binary. LDS artists who passed through the gauntlet of postmodernism, the "culture wars" of the late twentieth century, and even the anti-Mormon murmurings surrounding Mitt Romney's 2012 presidential run are still a little shell-shocked and keep a nervous watch over the battle lines drawn in those times.[29]

Further contributing to this history of dualistic thinking is the previously invoked Mormon exceptionalism. Along with the standard pressures artists face, Mormon artists have often felt that they must excel because—apropos of the Kimball Challenge—their achievement in the arts has been foreordained as one authenticating expression of LDS specialness. Mormon arts and artists are implicated in a very simple, logical proof: If the church is true, its art will be great. If its art is great, then the church is true.

This conditional assertion—solipsistic as it is—may someday be validated. But as a preconditioner, flavoring both efforts and receptions, it has proven souring and stultifying. Artistic efforts that are rooted in it have found themselves rooted in shallow ground: forthwith they spring up, but when the sun rises, they get scorched.[30] Everything other than success becomes an indictment of the artist or the cause, neither of which is best served by the equation. Here we must not confuse a critique of Mormon exceptionalism with a rejection of the claim that there is something truly exceptional in what the Latter-day Saints offer as a history, a people, and an astounding theology. Exceptionalism is a failure of relationship and a clumsy interpolation of what may, in fact, be exceptional.

LATE MODELS

In 2020 and again in March 2022, I had the wonderful opportunity to do studio visits with graduating BFA and MFA students at BYU. Among the many insights gained through those interactions, these artists made their refusal of the old, oppositional, and exceptionalist thinking very clear. Graduating senior Caitlin Garcia voiced a common sentiment: "I never really felt there was a conflict—art and faith are the same thing to me in so many ways. . . . [Studying] art has introduced more room and nuance in my faith . . . it helps me to connect and think differently . . . it teaches [me] how to make room for uncertainty and discomfort, which are important experiences of faith."[31] This mindset was reflected time and again in students who, as soon-to-be graduates, betrayed no special Mormon anxiety or feelings of conflict in their pending engagement with the art world. In fact, they did not perceive the art world as something alien to and other than where they already were.

As LDS artists see types and likenesses of their own ethical and theological concerns in the empathy-driven, socially awakened practices of contemporary art, they will feel that they have voices and energies to lend to the cause. As they see echoes of the church's historical, operational, and doctrinal features in contemporary art's exploratory actions, strategies, and forms, they will recognize models for their own emerging critical engagement.

Two interconnected projects, AA Bronson's performance and text work *A Public Apology to Siksika Nation* and Adrian Stimson's installation *Iini Sookumapii: Guess Who's Coming to Dinner?* beautifully illustrate this potentiality.[32] Neither Bronson nor

Stimson is LDS. And the projects have no explicit connection to Mormondom, but they are replete with types, likenesses, and echoes that will carry significance for LDS artists and audiences.

Having been developed in close dialogue, *Public Apology* and *Iini Sookumapii* were presented together as part of the 2019 Toronto Biennial. For the biennial, Bronson made free published copies of his text available to visitors and addressed two public readings of the text to the Siksika people, represented at the biennial by Stimson (a member of the Siksika Nation) and a council of Siksika elders. Modeled after the New Testament Book of Galatians, Bronson composed and offered his public apology on behalf of one of his great-grandfathers, the Reverend John William Tims.[33] Tims was an Anglican missionary from England who in the 1880s worked to convert and colonize the Siksika Nation, a Blackfoot people and territory in western Canada. In that effort, Tims founded the Old Sun Boarding School for Boys, a residential school for Siksika youth that was named after Stimson's great-grandfather Old Sun, a Siksika Nation chief. Triggered by the death of several of the school's young residents, the Old Sun school became the site of an early, violent uprising against colonial authority, which forced Rev. Tims to flee the Siksika lands with his family in 1895. The school was reopened shortly thereafter and would go on to operate as a residual fixture of British colonialism until 1971.

Stimson's contribution to the biennial, *Iini Sookumapii: Guess Who's Coming to Dinner?* uses the form and ceremony of a communal meal to explore the legacies of the Old Sun school, both for Stimson's immediate family (his grandfather and father attended the school, and both his mother and father were employed there) and in its devastating cultural impact on the Siksika community. The work was also representative of an actual meal at which Bronson was first introduced to the Siksika elders and his and Stimson's intentions discussed. The symbolic "breaking of bread" of that introductory dinner became, for both artists, the first gesture in a deeply personal process of atonement. At the biennial, *Iini Sookumapii* served as the literal and figurative site of reception for Bronson's apology, which Stimson and the elders publicly accepted on behalf of their deceased.

In their joint effort toward reconciliation, these two projects encompass family history, Indigenous American history, narratives of western expansion, Protestantism and Reformation legacies in the "New World," missionary work, programs of Indigenous assimilation, sacrament, ceremony, councils of elders, patterns of sacred and biblical text, vicarious action on behalf of deceased ancestors, invocation, atonement, love, and, ultimately, forgiveness—all of which are deeply resonant, historically and doctrinally saturated concerns within an LDS context. Together, these projects confess and acknowledge a wounded history as a symbolic first step toward healing and restoration—a healing toward which both Bronson and Stimson expressed that they felt guided by higher spiritual forces. As Stimson commented, "The Blackfoot believe in a higher power. It does give you the feeling that larger forces are at work."[34] Stéphane Aquin, chief curator at the Hirshhorn Museum, called the collaboration "one of the most compelling and powerful I have seen in years."[35] LDS artists can only be encouraged when encountering contemporary works of this kind.

"REVOLUTIONARY" MORMONISM

Recent conversations with emerging artists of other (i.e., non-Mormon) Christian strains reveal attitudes similar to those expressed at BYU. These artists feel that their personal explorations of Christian spirituality are welcome as natural and valuable nodes within the rhizome of contemporary metaphysics. Artists such as Chino Amobi, John Chae, and Hunter Foster, with whom I've had the privilege of being in conversation, bring their personal and familial devotional experience—with its mysteries, contradictions, highs, and lows—into the center of their creative practice, where it serves and is received as a source of profound meaning, reflection, and invention.

In the cases of Amobi, Chae, and Hunter, one condition of that welcoming reception may be that in these artists' biographical particulars and in their work the Christian project is uncoupled from establishment authority. This rupture is evident in other significant cultural figures whose Christianity and/or explorations of Christian themes have been embraced even by a secular public because, in them, it takes on guises other than conservative white patriarchy—for example, musician Sufjan Stevens, author Marilynne Robinson, and academic and social activist bell hooks.

Though in recent decades the LDS Church has become synonymous with populist Republicanism, throughout its history the church and its people have as often played the role of renegade and outlaw. Mormonism's theologically and politically deviant brand of Christianity regularly put the early church at (sometimes violent) odds with neighbors and with municipal, state, and federal government. That Mormons are now found in the conservative establishment and perceived to be in cahoots with it is, from a historical perspective, a significant plot twist—which some, both within and without the church, have categorized as a failure to carry forward the prophetic, disruptive intent of the church's founding and founders. Historian Jan Shipps states: "As the history of Mormonism reveals, this movement was not conservative but virtually revolutionary. . . . Its members experimented with radical social and economic systems."[36]

In a comment directed at his historian peers but which begs for a more general application, Reorganized Church of Jesus Christ of Latter-day Saints (RLDS) historian Paul M. Edwards laments: "We have not allowed . . . the revolutionary nature of the movement from which we have sprung to make us revolutionaries."[37] Mormonism, then, offers revolutionary histories and theologies as shears and levers for its own project of uncoupling from authoritarian forces both external and internal. As they work creatively to extend the gospel message beyond the conformist and bureaucratic strictures of the modern church, LDS artists can help to reinvigorate and reanimate their own discourse, as well as a broader Christian discourse within contemporary art. By deviating from normative portrayals and recentering the church's "revolutionary" sociality and theology, a radically open space is created into which marginal and divergent life experiences can be gathered, audiences served, and social and emotional needs fulfilled. In just this way, Christ sought out those alienated by the theocrats of his day, and Joseph Smith went about gathering up the strangelings of his time.

TWO GOOD EXAMPLES

Following from this "revolutionary" thesis, and in support of the various claims and assertions made up to this point (my reasons for optimism, etc.), I would like to offer here two case studies of exemplary LDS contemporary art that pave the way for future gestures. The first is the exhibition *Hie to Kolob* by the artist Jason Metcalf, which took place at Martos Gallery in New York in 2015. The second is the broader oeuvre of the artist Rachel Thomander.

Example One

Jason Metcalf's *Hie to Kolob* is among the most discursively useful individual examples of LDS contemporary art.[38] Its unabashed legibility as an exploration of uniquely LDS theological tenets is key to this claim. It is a walk-in diorama of Latter-day Saint cosmography. Coming into the long, narrow gallery, the viewer enters at the dark end of a gradient of light, which brightens over the length of the room until it reaches its fullness at the far end of the space. On the wall to the viewer's left is hung a sequence of four large paintings that step out the increasing light levels. The first painting is almost entirely dark, the second has a nebulous purple glow, the third an orbed mass of emerging light, and the fourth a full nova, edge to edge, of bright white light. Sharing the farthest, brightest end of the gallery is an unusual sculptural work, a 12″ × 12″ square gold plate, displayed directly on the gallery floor in the corner opposite the bright white painting. The gold plate, titled *A Paved Work of Pure Gold* (2015), is illuminated by a spotlight of its own, producing a dramatic plume of golden-hued light. The title of the exhibition, taken from the LDS hymn "If You Could Hie to Kolob," is a key for decoding this immersive experience.[39] The hymn asks its singers to imagine traveling across time and space to reach Kolob, the star that, in LDS teachings, is closest to the planet on which God lives. The interstellar journey to Kolob then becomes a rhetorical foil for contemplating the endlessness of God's creation.

The four paintings are titled with astronomical coordinates, correlating them to real galactic positions. The brightest painting, *(α 8.5h 22.5m 20.02045s / δ −14.5° 0′ 14.059″)*, corresponds with Sagittarius A*, the cluster of celestial bodies at the orbital center of the Milky Way, which has been posited by different persons throughout the church's history as the actual location of Kolob. (And which, thickening this lore, was confirmed on May 12, 2022, to be the site of a supermassive black hole.)[40] For the title of the darkest painting, *( )*, hung at the dark end of the gallery, the parentheses that would bracket coordinates are left empty. As the thing furthest removed from the light of God's implied presence, this painting stands in for what the LDS call Outer Darkness, a condition of quasi existence reserved for a very few sinister ones who will be cast out and functionally

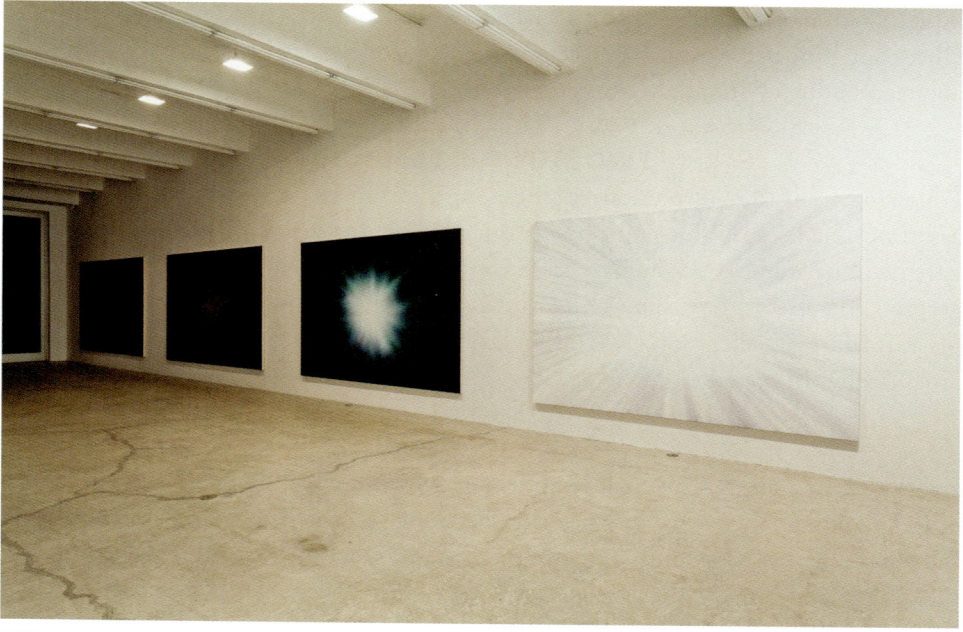

Fig. 22.5 Jason Metcalf, *Hie to Kolob* (2015), installation view. Courtesy of the artist.

forgotten at the end of time—outside of God's reckoning. The four paintings thus stand in for the four categories (or Kingdoms) of the LDS afterlife, represented in ascending order by quantity of light and proximity to God: Outer Darkness, Telestial Kingdom, Terrestrial Kingdom, Celestial Kingdom—the highest of these being the Celestial Kingdom, where the blessed will dwell in God's literal presence.

In its didactic consolidation of spatial and temporal dimensions beyond the mortal scale, the installation echoes distinctive patterns of Restoration revelation and apocalyptic literature.[41] In LDS scripture, prophets such as Nephi, Moses, and Joseph Smith—among others—relate being transported across time and space in visions that help them grasp the absolute scale and ontological endgame of God's work, a journey of light-years in the twinkling of an eye. This is an experience that, while it necessitates a softening of its strictures, ultimately underscores the spatiotemporal concreteness of God's universe. In a manner not inconsistent with relativity and quantum mechanics, the prophet is wafted outside their usual relationship to the timeline—transported not to an atemporal dimension but to a place of event horizon, like Kolob, where time is bent by unearthly forces and scales of gravity. Pulled outside the main stream of terrestrial time, the prophet sees what has been, what is now, and where it's all flowing away to. By enacting this prophetic translocation for all who visit the gallery, *Hie to Kolob* assumes the shape of prophecy, shifting the viewer's experience of space and time.

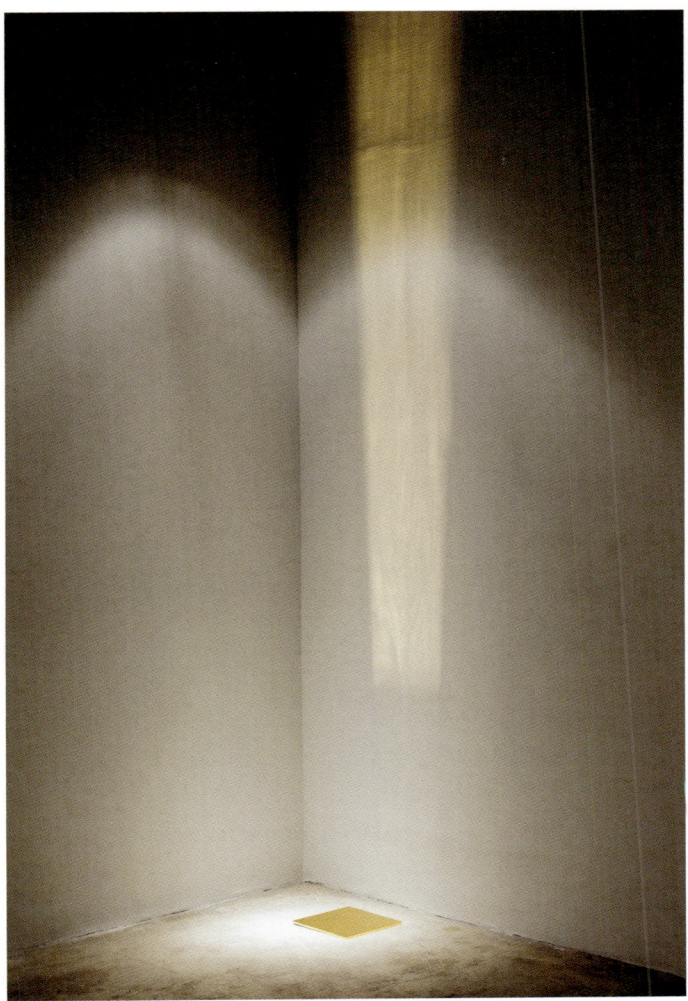

Fig. 22.6 Jason Metcalf, *A Paved Work of Pure Gold* (2015), 99.999999% pure gold-plated aerospace-grade aluminum, 12″ × 12″ × .5″, installation view. Courtesy of the artist.

This suggests a shocking but doctrinally justified question: What if God and the *más allá* are kept from our view not by some mystical obfuscation but by light-years of real distance? If we had a telescope strong enough, could we see God in his divine realm? Perhaps his supervision of us, from his dwelling place at the center of the galaxy, is an inversion of just such a technological gaze, his omniscience quite literally an omni-*science:* not a supernatural entitlement but a perfect knowledge that is the reasonable augmentation of parental observation under different conditions of time. In such a universe we can understand the LDS claim that "the glory of God is intelligence."[42] Within such a concrete cosmology, Psalms 147:3 takes on a deepened meaning, expressing not only

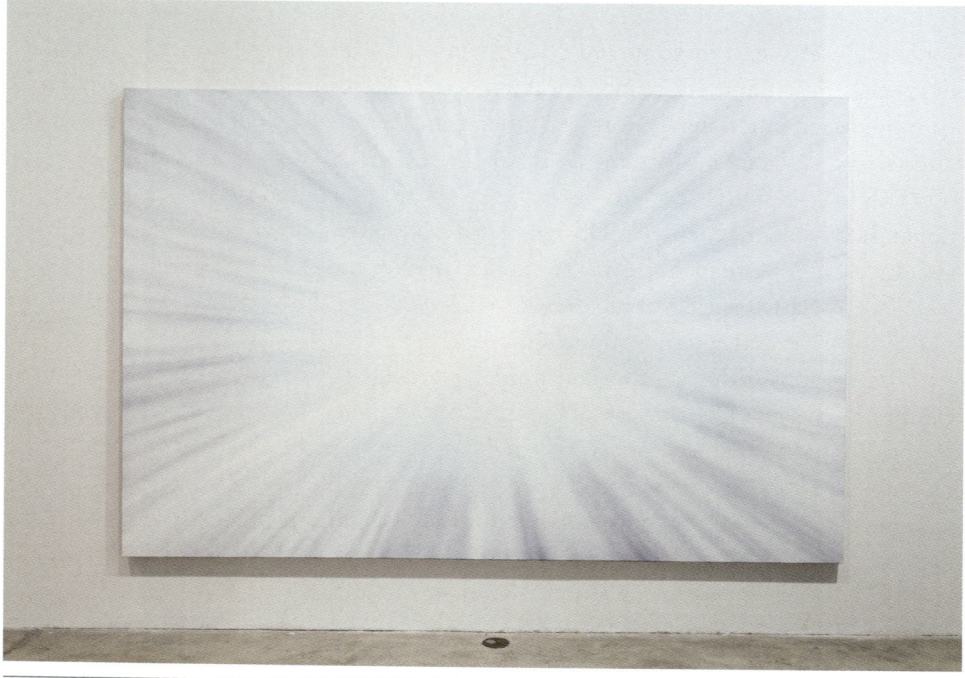

Fig. 22.7 Jason Metcalf, *(α 8.5h 22.5m 20.02045s / δ -14.5° 0′ 14.059″)*, 2015, airbrushed acrylic on canvas, 74″ × 111″. Courtesy of the artist.

lordly care and concern but also a literal and comprehensive astronomical accounting: *He telleth the number of the stars; he calleth them all by their names.*[43]

In articulating some of the most profound and extraordinary theological assertions of the LDS universe, *Hie to Kolob*'s compactness, scientific-illustration pictorial style, and matter-of-fact delivery imbue it with the guileless authority of a science museum exhibit. It is framed as simply presenting incredible facts. Its rich, theatrical staging of those facts is proportionate to their colossal and cosmic implications. Think planetarium. There is no cynicism or irony. Every artful element is consistent with the educative effort and, as he has expressed them to me, Metcalf's own feelings of curiosity, reverence, and wonder.[44] Rather than offering apologetics or making a romance, spectacle, or comedy of LDS theological oddities—proven paths of least resistance and greatest reward—Metcalf makes the bold choice to put the doctrines on display and let them make their own compelling case.

Not every commentary on the exhibition has framed it in exclusively sincere terms. An *Artforum* review expressed the following: "Titled after a Mormon hymn that incants aspirations to reach Kolob . . . [the exhibition] is a winking homage to the massive Christus installation at Salt Lake's Temple Square, colloquially known as Space Jesus."[45] While generally maintaining this "winking" categorization of the exhibition (from the perspective of being in on the joke), the author ultimately makes an important concession: "At heart these are not cynical works. . . . The experience may be dominated by special effect, but there is sincerity at its core."[46] Metcalf relates that one devout LDS collector commented that the project "belongs in a temple"—high praise, which further attests that the artist's gesture may be taken quite in earnest.[47] For temple-attending members of the church, the progressive, instructional theater of *Hie to Kolob* will be familiar. It is in the likeness of LDS temple rituals that articulate the same metaphysics and direct their participants toward a similar conclusion.

While the artist speaks of its "didactic consolidation" and insists on its sincerity, it is not simply a depictive or devotional gesture. Metcalf's reverence is not the facile kind. And expressions of his shrewd and probing intelligence emerge in the details of the exhibition. Details like the use of incandescent halogen lights, which, in the artist's words, "share the characteristics of starlight, getting hotter and whiter as their brightness increases."[48] Or the staggering constellation of historical, theological, metaphysical, and astrophysical concerns gathered into the exhibition's parousia, the gold-plated kaporet *A Paved Work of Pure Gold* (2015). Manufactured from 99.9999999 percent pure gold by NASA contractors, *A Paved Work* does more than symbolize the divine presence; it offers a literal station (read: standing place) for celestial beings.[49] The "facts," as I deemed them earlier, that the exhibition stages are being turned and examined by Metcalf's active mind. As the cultural experience and self-identity of the LDS Church have shifted in recent decades—from an emphasis on sacred initiation, esoteric knowledge, and priestly authority to a sociability of more conventional Christian feelings and observances—there seem to be fewer among the ranks of the church who are familiar with, or even interested in, Mormonism's absolutely radical gnostic astronomies. This gives *Hie to Kolob* a disruptive, revelatory power for both LDS and non-LDS alike.

Discussing the critical response to the exhibition, Metcalf concedes that his gesture was perhaps "slightly ahead of its time"—anticipating the art world's late, resurgent interest in spiritual systems.[50] The rapturous reception of the Hilma af Klint exhibition at the Guggenheim (2018–2019)—another exploration of obscure and idiosyncratic cosmologies—suggests that if the artgoing public wasn't quite ready for *Hie to Kolob* in 2015, they would be now.[51]

Example Two

While Mormon themes are less conspicuous in Rachel Thomander's work than in Metcalf's or some of their peers', there are no artists in whose practice the implications, meanings, and dispositions of LDS faith reverberate more deeply, or are more naturally and seamlessly integrated within a truly contemporary manner of making.

Thomander's 2017 work *I Love People* is a touchstone for many of the tendencies in her work that deserve our attention. It features the artist's mother as a single, standing figure, draped in a simple but vibrant cadmium red tunic, against an equally red back-drop. The mother's eyes are closed, but painted over with the open eyes of second sight—eyes that double suggestively as the patterned wings of a white butterfly painted across her face and forehead. Her tunic is emblazoned with an incredible collage of brightly colored fabrics and embroidery. Spiky, clunky, squared, and swooping shapes in primary and secondary colors suggest a child's construction paper jungle. But the arrangement of shapes, values, and colors betrays real formal sophistication and sensitivity. Centered on the tunic, in a large, lumbering type, perfectly attuned to its surroundings, the words "I LOVE PEOPLE" are embroidered in red stitching over pieced black fabric. The words and design are visible in their entirety thanks to the mother's hands, which, extended down, grasp the tunic on either side and hold it taut and flat, presenting it to the viewer.

Prophetic matriarchs and matriarchy are an important feature in Thomander's work, representing intergenerational lines of authority empowered by love and consolidated through acts of teaching and rituals of care. Sometimes, as in *I Love People,* these matriarchs are shown directly, properly regaled as prophetesses and priestesses. More often, their presence is implied via legacies of domestic and material labor, as in the punch rugs, vestments, ceramic vessels, rudimentary furnishings, and symbolic and educational objects that make up Thomander's varied practice. In that sense, the authorship of these objects, though they are produced by Thomander, is diffuse. They are understood to be contemporary emergences from within a vast continuity of traditions and authorship—traditions that include the craftwork of rural Colombia, where Thomander's maternal line originated. Works such as *Rabanadas de Zanahoria* (2018) amalgamate these ex-panded fields of authorship, varied traditions, and practices of making within a cere-monial ensemble. Brightly colored altars double as low tables (or perhaps it's the other way around), set with lumpy earthenware utensils, dishes, and animal-shaped vessels. A plump green candelabra holds long-handled spoons instead of candles. Fabric floor and wall coverings demarcate spaces of heightened significance and awareness—and possibly sites of sacrifice—but they are not rigid containers of their ceremonies, and the ritual accouterments spill over onto the surrounding walls and floors. Special garments, appliquéd tunics, and colorful knit ponchos stand by as ceremonial robes, ready to invest and endow their wearers. If ancient Israelites became ancient Americans, as the Book of Mormon narrates, *Rabanadas de Zanahoria* might well be the deconstructed tabernacle of their vegetarian descendants.

Significantly, Thomander's ceremonial tableaux are symbolic and not literal. They are meant not to be actualized but to evoke; meant not to be enacted but to be inferred, felt, and interpreted. They are material parables. In this way they offer a critical supplement to, rather than surrogate for, extant ceremonial observances within LDS faith. Similarly, Thomander's matriarchs are not postured in opposition to the church's frequently discussed patriarchal order but presented as a supplemental and complementary pro-phetic structure. They further the church's general program of prophetic empowerment, in which revelation and priesthood are operational at the familial level.

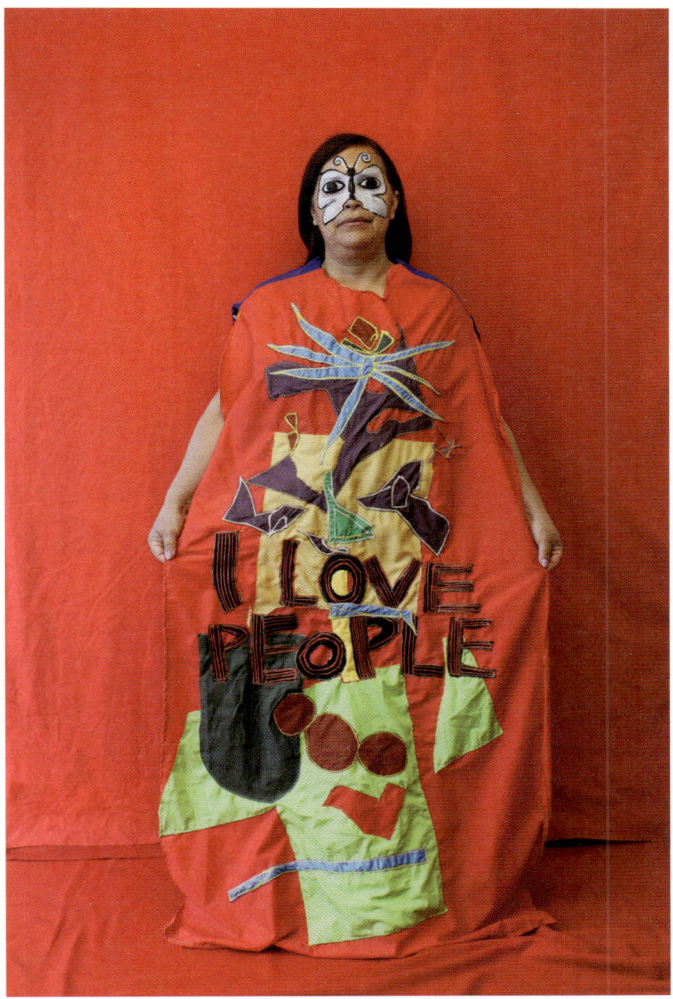

Fig. 22.8 Rachel Thomander, *I Love People* (2017), inkjet print, 11″ × 8.5″. Courtesy of the artist.

In offering symbolic rituals (or symbols of ritual), Thomander maps the relationship between the effectual and the symbolic—sharpening that difference where it matters, and flattening it where such perceptions of difference are harmful or distracting. In other words, Thomander's familial and domestic demi-sacraments (the implied performances of her works) underscore what is essential in LDS rituals, enlivening our appreciation of their symbolic and effectual aspects simultaneously.

Consistent with the temporal collapse of *Hie to Kolob*, Thomander is not interested in a linear presentation or experience of time—nor in a siloed expression of her own consciousness. Ceremonial time and parametric, ritual consciousness look backward and forward simultaneously. Across her body of work, Thomander's grandmother, mother,

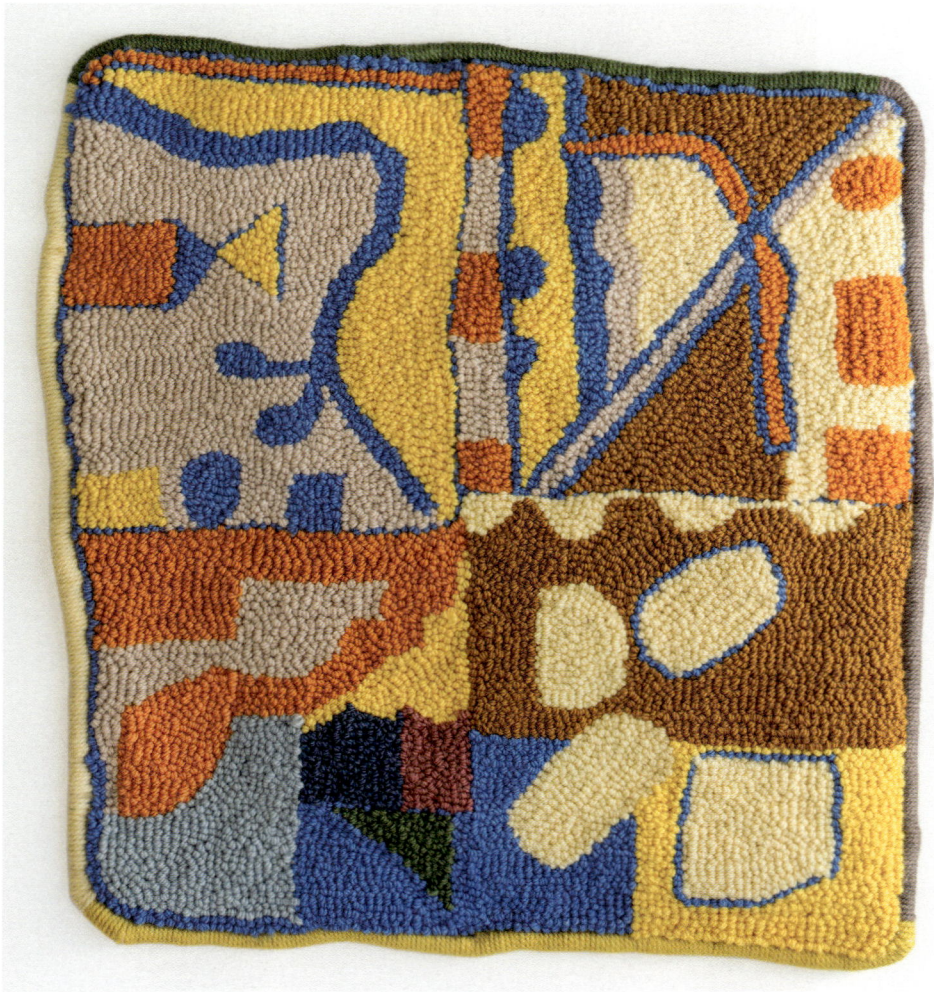

Fig. 22.9   Rachel Thomander, *Rug 7* (2020), hand-punched wool rug, 23″ × 22″. Courtesy of the artist.

self, and children are all synchronous equivalent features within a transgenerational landscape. In keeping with the latter-day logic of the church, Thomander's work thus fulfills, in aesthetic terms at least, the prophecy of Acts 2:17: *And it shall come to pass in the last days, saith God, I will pour out of my Spirit upon all flesh: and your sons and your daughters shall prophesy, and your young men shall see visions, and your old [wo]men shall dream dreams.*[52]

In this synchrony, Thomander's deskilled hand and marks become inscribed as both pre- and post-dexterous—marks that are the purview of the body at almost any point in its arc of capability, marks that honor the body as more than a site of strength and skill,

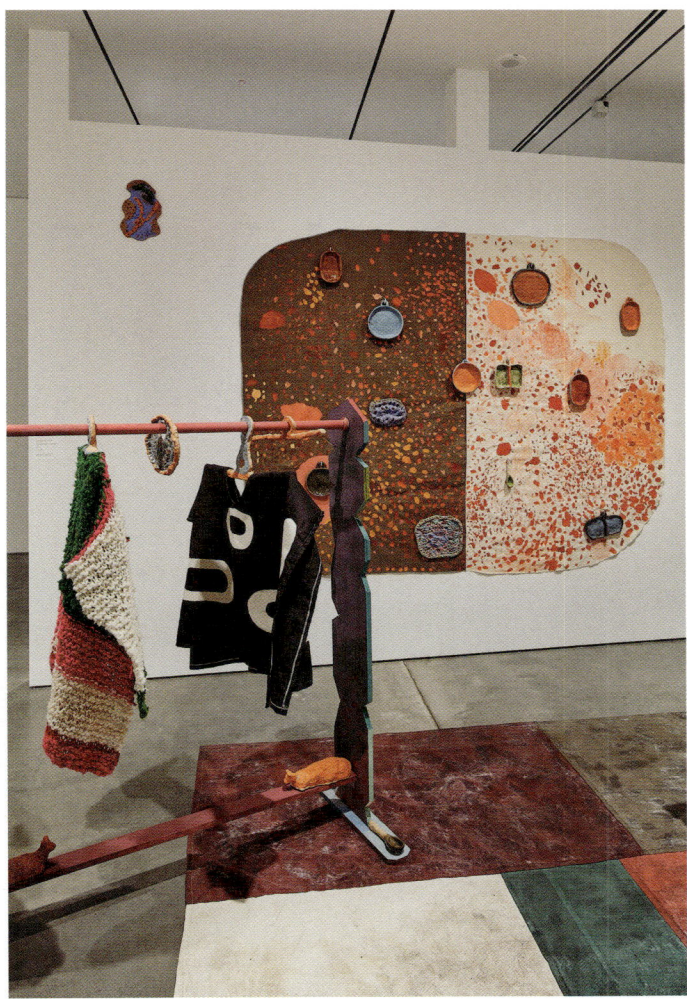

Fig. 22.10 Rachel Thomander, *Rabanadas de Zanahoria* (2018), ceramic, wood, fabric, wool, yarn, canvas and waxed canvas, acrylic paint, dimensions variable, installation view. Courtesy of the artist.

as a vessel of experience, care, and learning. Here Thomander lends a resounding prophetic harmony to the advocacies and alternative valuations put forward by emerging disciplines such as critical disability theory and in the practices of contemporary artists like Park McArthur who challenge capitalist and neoliberal economies that privilege ability and efficiency over equitability and accommodation. Properly aimed and attuned, as it is in Thomander's practice, LDS theology echoes and achieves this critical cultural function: first, by insisting on the absolute value of persons outside the capitalist zone of bodily and economic efficiency, and second—borrowing language from an essay by Colby Chamberlain on the work of McArthur—by "dispelling the myth of

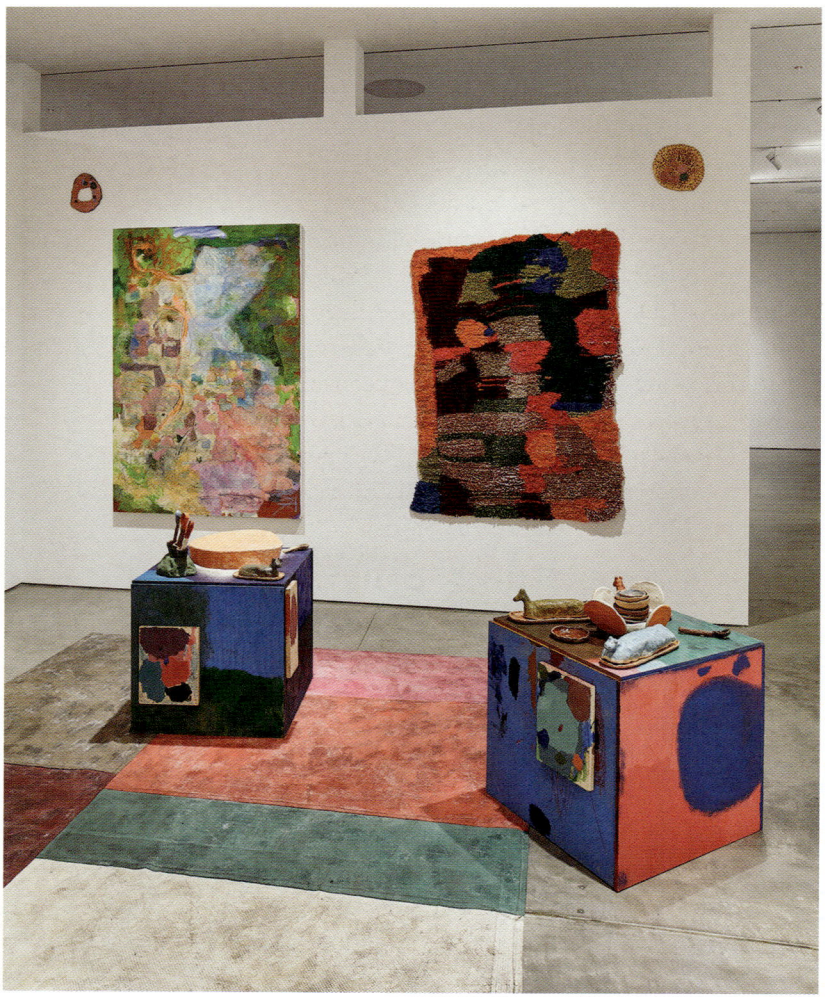

Fig. 22.11 Rachel Thomander, *Rabanadas de Zanahoria* (2018), ceramic, wood, fabric, wool, yarn, canvas and waxed canvas, acrylic paint, dimensions variable, installation view. Courtesy of the artist.

autonomy" and "undo[ing] the illusion of a stable, coherent and self-sufficient self."[53] In place of that myth and illusion, Thomander posits a radical and gracious model of interconnected and interdependent personhood. A kind of personhood consistent with Christ's repeated calls for oneness, and the LDS doctrine that redemption is to be found exclusively in community: *For their salvation is necessary and essential to our salvation . . . that they without us cannot be made perfect—neither can we without [them].*[54]

As a counterpoint to much of the non-denominational spiritualism of contemporary art, open-ended practices of mysticism, occultism, ancestor worship, Wicca, and animism, in which the invoked spiritual agents and their powers and operations remain largely unnamed and unknowable, Thomander situates her agents and their operations within a personal and knowable family tree and a specific LDS doctrinal framework.

Thomander was raised LDS by an American father and Colombian mother, and the multiple perspectives of her culturally blended upbringing afforded her a dimensional view of the dominant cultural scene. Thomander is open about a period of time she spent "away from the church" and notes that her decision to return was motivated by a series of deeply personal experiences.[55] These are relevant circumstances in accounting for the difference in the quality of her creative vision, which seems to be spun more directly from the threads of LDS doctrine than from the fibers of its mainstream visual culture—and to be committed to its values more than its assorted conventions. Thomander's relationship to the church has never been one of convenience or inertia. It is a devotional relationship that expresses itself in the authentic devotions of her practice. In ways that go beyond or feel cheapened by description, Thomander's way of being—the integrity (used here in its full, etymological sense) of her life as a unified undertaking—represents much of what might be aspired to by LDS artists.

THE PROPHETIC

As I have worked through this subject, notions of the prophetic have been a generative way of categorizing the critical, historically aware cultural work that I am calling for—work that I have alternatively described as activist. Where prophecy foretells, articulating and proliferating tomorrows, the prophetic manifests, acting on behalf of those tomorrows today. The prophetic explodes a localized experience of time, gathering the past into the present and accelerating these toward the future.[56] Simultaneously, it draws and infuses futurity and history into the present to attend to its needs now—offering visions, protest, remembrances, understanding, and—perhaps most needed—healing. In this way, the prophetic does not simply portend but exhorts toward specific behaviors and actions that can redeem the present, even as they are constitutive toward the messianic end.

Philosopher Cornel West employs the term "prophetic" in a similar way, using it to categorize an activist tradition within Black American culture that takes up cultural transformation as a sacred duty—as Christians like West take up the cross.[57] West also uses "prophetic" to qualify, and differentiate between, the radical, soteriological, future-enacting strains of any ideology—religious or secular—and those strains of the ideology that are complicit with the status quo. He speaks of revolutionary traditions of "Prophetic Judaism . . . Prophetic Christianity . . . Prophetic Islam," contrasting these with institutionalized forms of faith that have allied themselves to (and alloyed themselves with) structures of inequity and forces of empire.[58] Using it in reference to monumental figures such as Martin Luther King Jr., Rosa Parks, and Malcolm X, West also applies the term to creative giants including John Coltrane and Anton Chekhov. The prophetic, then, must also describe a kind of contemporary art that is focused on productive intervention into the aesthetic, social, or spiritual order.

The artist Theaster Gates provides one example of this kind of prophetic artistic prac-tice, in his stewardship of archives of Black cultural history, his struggles against legacies of divestment in Chicago's historically black South Side, his symbolic use of ceramics as a site for restorative fictions, and his "speaking in tongues," making himself a ritual, mu-sical vessel of prophetic voice in his work with the Black Monks of Mississippi.[59]

The prophetic is also powerfully modeled by artists such as Guadalupe Maravilla, whose healing objects and cleansing ritual "sound baths" were recently lauded by the *New York Times*.[60] Gestures of healing, like Maravilla's, are a believing investment in the future, and an implicit refusal to accept the painful or compromised conditions of the moment as the definitive assessment of value or fixed state of affairs. As an expression of the prophetic, healing sits at the nexus of past and future wellness, drawing on memory and futurity to renew and repair. In another healing effort, Maravilla worked closely with Brooklyn pastor Juan Carlos Ruiz to raise and distribute donations of food and cash to undocumented workers throughout the darkest days of the COVID-19 pan-demic, when these workers and their families faced incredible hardship resulting from New York's city-wide shutdown.[61]

While neither Gates nor Maravilla is LDS, LDS artists will recognize in them semblances of their own and the church's programmatic efforts to steward and restore.

Where prophecy is already a central feature and concern of LDS faith, using the term "prophetic" in this way provides a bridging vocabulary for correlating sacred and profane (i.e., secular) expressions of the activist impulse. It can also provide a litmus test to assess where and how LDS culture and art retain their prophetic, redemptive vitality—or, on the other hand, have yielded to the natural inertia of all human endeavors toward man-agement, consensus, and convenience: *Which say to the seers, See not; and to the prophets, Prophesy not unto us right things, speak unto us smooth things, prophesy deceits.*[62]

Not surprisingly, in contemporary art's recapture of the prophetic it is those artists and communities that have been most dispossessed by history who have led in the ef-fort: communities of color, queer communities, Indigenous, disabled, and neurodiverse. To recapture the prophetic for themselves, dislocation, both private and collective. They must embrace and enact their own peculiarity—and Mormonism's extravagant and heterodox theology.

The urgent need for prophetic energies and voices will be understood intuitively by practitioners of a faith founded on the prerogative of continuing revelation. Just as members would find it strange for the prophetic voices of today's church to speak to them only with the antiquated "thee" and "thou," they cannot be content with an art that speaks to them uncritically in voicings of the past. A revelatory art must constantly be seeking the language of its times.

Rather than seeing the church as a site of conformity, patronage, and largesse, LDS artists must engage their own LDS communities as sites of applied discipleship, conse-cration, and stewardship, where they are called to essential tasks of transformative and restorative cultural labor. If scriptural narratives confirm any sociological truth, it is that this kind of prophetic cultural work has always been, and will always be necessary.

NEW CANONS AND NEW KINGDOMS

LDS visual artists looking to do this work may be aided greatly by the formation of new canons. While we have worthy modernist forebearers including Mahonri Young and Minerva Teichert, the mixed legacies of the Art and Belief movement, and so on, we are wanting for arguments and histories that offer the foundations of a specifically contemporary art canon—a canon that expands the pantheon of foundational figures and begins to coalesce the important movements and voices of recent decades and today. Glen Nelson's recuperation of forgotten LDS artists such as Joseph Paul Vorst, whose Depression-era Social Realist art is a profound and prophetic expression of living Mormon faith, is an invaluable contribution to such canon formation.[63] Organizations such as the Center for Latter-day Saint Arts are providing financial resources, platforms, programming, publishing, and academic credibility for Mormon arts broadly—perhaps most crucially for LDS contemporary visual art, as exemplified by its sponsorship of *Immediate Present* (both the exhibition and the catalogue) and my own 2020 curatorial effort, *Great Awakening: Vision and Synthesis in Latter-day Saint Contemporary Art*, and its companion text.[64] My view of the canonical value of *A 15-Year Expanse,* as a gesture of cultural self-actualization, duly endorsed by BYU, will be understood. In these and other efforts—and in this essay, which I adjoin to the cause—we may have enough to set the stone rolling.

In referring to "the church" and "contemporary art" as I have, monolithically, I have worked somewhat against my own purposes. While the church projects continuity, in practice it is legion. Just so, there is no one, irreducible contemporary art. But there are trends and movements that give our moment its distinctive character, and I have tried to draw out some of these. Contrary to my monolithic treatment, it is the church's recent efforts to embrace its own plurality and to acknowledge the anxiety and uncertainty of the individual experience of faith that provide the most essential context and impetus for the hopes I have expressed—efforts that are being taken up and given form and force by the artists of the church. While the LDS Restoration saga insists on certain key events and preordained ends, the particular drama of each individual's journey is an open question. In harmony with the gospel's metanarrative, and in a profound application of its virtues, LDS artists can further the salvatory work of the church by keeping the collective culture radically open, accommodating, and welcoming of individual permutations. For artists such as Rachel Thomander, such efforts are not casual but deeply personal, working, as she expresses it, "to ensure a place for my own children in the future of the church."[65]

In Cauleen Smith's 2018 film *Sojourner,* twelve prophetic figures travel through the deserts of the American West. Fleeing conflict, they are guided by revelatory voices from a sacred past (broadcasts received through their crystal-powered transistor radio) as they seek their utopia and a new order of community.[66] Beyond the layered parallels between the film's narrative and Mormon history, Smith (who is not LDS) provides commentary for *Sojourner* that reinforces its surprising affinity to the LDS project: "We're generally cynical about ideas of utopia . . . but there *have* been instances [in the United States' history] where people managed to build intentional communities that were really successful."[67] Speaking to her motivations in making the film, Smith articulates a sentiment that is quintessential of the faith of contemporary art and utopist pragmatism of Latter-day Saint praxis: "I wanted to *build* a film that meditated on this idea [of radical community making] . . . connecting all these different historical points . . . to signify possibility." "It *is possible* to make a better world," she affirms, "people do it all the time."[68]

Truly, in museums, galleries, and studios, temples, chapels, and Sunday schools, the kingdom is at hand.[69]

NOTES

[1] Founded as the Mormon Arts Center, the organization changed its name to the Center for Latter-day Saint Arts in 2018, in alignment with guidance from church leadership to refer to the church by its full name: the Church of Jesus Christ of Latter-day Saints. Mormon Arts Center Festival, Riverside Church, New York, June 29–July 1, 2017.

[2] *Immediate Present,* Mormon Arts Center Festival, Riverside Church, New York, June 29–July 1, 2017, curated by Laura Allred Hurtado.

[3] The two exhibitions missed each other by only eighteen days—the biennial closed on June 11, 2017, and *Immediate Present* opened June 29, 2017. *2017 Whitney Biennial*, Whitney Museum of American Art, New York, March 17–June 11, 2017.

[4] "Ferguson Unrest: What You Need to Know," *Los Angeles Times*, March 13, 2015, https://www.latimes.com/nation/nationnow/la-na-nn-ferguson-unrest-what-you-need-to-know-20150312-htmlstory.html.

[5] Hrag Vartanian, "The Violence of the 2017 Whitney Biennial," *Hyperallergic*, March 21, 2017, http://hyperallergic.com/366688/the-violence-of-the-2017-whitney-biennial/.

[6] Paul Washburn, "The Coyote Dilemma," in Laura Allred Hurtado et al., *Immediate Present* (New York: Mormon Arts Center, 2017), 85.

[7] Peggy Fletcher Stack, "Mormon Church Releases Photos of 'Seer Stone' Used by Founder Joseph Smith," *Salt Lake Tribune*, August 21, 2015, https://www.sltrib.com/news/nation-world/2015/08/21/mormon-church-releases-photos-of-seer-stone-used-by-founder-joseph-smith/.

[8] Mason Allred and Mark Ashurst-McGee, "Seer Stones and the Translation of the Book of Mormon," Church of Jesus Christ of Latter-day Saints, https://www.churchofjesuschrist.org/study/eng/video/answers-to-church-history-questions/2017-11-0120-seer-stones-and-the-translation-of-the-book-of-mormon, accessed June 24, 2023.

[9] Tyler Chadwick, "This Poem Is Not the Seer Stone—," in Laura Allred Hurtado et al., *Immediate Present* (New York: Mormon Arts Center, 2017), 97.

[10] Adam S. Miller, "Why Jesus Loves Novels," in *The Kimball Challenge at Fifty: Mormon Arts Center Essays* (New York: Mormon Arts Center, 2017), 72–79; Jared Hickman, "Mormonism; Or, Art All the Way Down," in *The Kimball Challenge at Fifty: Mormon Arts Center Essays* (New York: Mormon Arts Center, 2017), 45–51; Steven L. Peck, *Gilda Trillim, Shepherdess of Rats* (Winchester, UK: Roundfire Books, 2017).

[11] The suggestion of any symmetry (read: compatibility) between modernism and Mormonism may seem strange given their ostensible dissimilarity, and claims made elsewhere in this volume of their incompatibility on aesthetic and other grounds. To clarify, I am not invoking modernism strictly as a twentieth-century movement of aesthetic/stylistic innovation, or as a general cultural trend toward secularization. I am thinking of modernism in more historical terms—that is, as a historicizing conception of progress

within human civilization and of human activity as building toward a grand conclusion. Insofar as modernism entails a kind of universalizing secular eschatology, it is dispositionally and operationally compatible with similar, eschatological and universalizing impulses in Mormonism.

12 Among others, these changes include increased emphasis on "home-centered, church-supported" faith; the 2018 change from a three-hour to a two-hour Sunday meeting schedule, with the intention that members spend this third hour in self- and family-directed study at home; and the decision to replace the long-established Home and Visiting Teaching programs with a "Ministering" model of member-to-member instruction and support.

13 Philip L. Barlow, "To Mend A Fractured Reality: Joseph Smith's Project," *Journal of Mormon History* 38, no. 3 (2012): 28–50.

14 A negative (and perhaps more realistic) formulation of this claim might be as follows: As art and faith continue to be opposed and devalued by the same authoritarian social forces, they will increasingly find themselves occupying and operating from the same marginal spaces—that is, as neighbors in the same cultural ghetto.

15 Julian Bell, *What Is Painting? Representation and Modern Art* (New York: Thames and Hudson, 1999), 37.

16 The term "metamodernism" has been used to categorize cultural developments since the postmodern. Its use here is vestigial of an earlier version of this chapter, which argued that metamodernism has supported, through the condition of metaxy (which gives it its name), the productive interplay between the cultural poles of art and faith that we see in our moment. See Gregg Henriques, "What Is Metamodernism?," *Psychology Today,* April 17, 2020, https://www.psychologytoday.com/us/blog/theory-knowledge/202004/what-is-metamodernism.

17 "Artists on Writers | Writers on Artists," *Artforum*, February 23, 2022, https://www.artforum.com/video/vincent-fecteau-and-derek-mccormack-87927.

18 Tony Cragg, *In Celebration of Sculpture* (New York: Infobase, 2011).

19 Laura Hurtado, *A 15-Year Expanse, Volume 1* (Provo, UT: Brigham Young University, 2020).

20 It is worth noting that the majority of the artists featured in *A 15-Year Expanse* received their undergraduate degrees at BYU, followed by graduate studies elsewhere—many at prestigious programs like SAIC, Pratt, RISD, MICA, and VCU. Here we may infer an effective template for future LDS artists: rigorous foundational training in a challenging but familiar setting, preparatory to a more expansive, cosmopolitan engagement.

21 Walter Rayne, *Tell Me Thy Name* (2017), etching, 16″ × 17″; Jorge Cocco Santangelo, *The Tempest—Peace Be Still* (2016), oil on canvas, 30″ × 40″.

22 "Rippling Aesthetics," in Hurtado, *A 15-Year Expanse,* 10–16; D&C 131:7–8.

23 Jean Richardson, *Brolly Ball* (2014), umbrella fabric, weather balloon, 87″ diameter.

24 "Rippling Aesthetics," 16.

25 Spencer W. Kimball, *Education for Eternity* (Provo, UT: Brigham Young University, 1967)

26 Steven P. Sondrup, ed., *Arts and Inspiration: Mormon Perspectives* (Provo, UT: Brigham Young University Press, 1980).

27 Rosalind E. Krauss is a preeminent American scholar, critic and theorist of modern and contemporary art. Russel M. Nelson is a retired heart surgeon and the current president of the Church of Jesus Christ of Latter-day Saints.

28 Matthew 6:24, KJV.

29 Brienne Walsh, "Casey Jex Smith: Fiend in the Void | Allegra LaViola Gallery," *Art Review*, December 2012; Casey Jex Smith, *Fiend in the Void,* Allegra LaViola Gallery, New York, October 10–November 10, 2012.

30 Matthew 13:3–9, KJV.

31 Caitlin Garcia in discussion with the author, March 3, 2022.

32 AA Bronson, *A Public Apology to Siksika Nation* (New York: Mitchell-Innes & Nash, 2020); Adrian Stimson, *Iini Sookumapii: Guess Who's Coming to Dinner?* (2019), mixed-media installation, dimensions variable, commissioned by the Toronto Biennial of Art.

33 "(AT HOME): On Art and Healing: Artist Talk with AA Bronson and Adrian Stimson," YouTube, posted by Hirshhorn, February 2, 2021, https://www.youtube.com/watch?v=KH2O4YjoSYw.

34 Rosemary Heather, "Beyond Apologies: Two Artists Set a Table for Reconciliation," *NOW Toronto* (blog), September 25, 2019, https://nowtoronto.com/culture/art-and-design/aa-bronson-adrian-stimson-reconciliation/.

35 "(AT HOME)."

36 Jan Shipps, Conference on Mormonism and American Politics (Part 3), YouTube, posted by Columbia University, February 21, 2012, https://www.youtube.com/watch?v=0Ggf5cqzSog, 03:40.

37 Lance S. Owens, "Joseph Smith and Kabbalah: The Occult Connection." *Dialogue: A Journal of Mormon Thought* 27, no. 3 (1994): 117–194.

38 Jason Metcalf, *Hie to Kolob*, Martos Gallery, New York, April 2–May 2, 2015.

39 "If You Could Hie to Kolob," for mixed chorus and organ; text by William W. Phelps, based on an English melody; arranged by Kenneth Plain (Orem, UT: Sonos, 2002), https://catalog.churchofjesuschrist.org/record/9a86db84-9861-4bb0-b816-6a4b4808d3f6/0?view=summary&lang=eng.

40 "Astronomers Snap First-Ever Image of Supermassive Black Hole Sagittarius A*," Massachusetts Institute of Technology, May 12, 2022, https://news.mit.edu/2022/first-supermassive-black-hole-sagitarrius-0512.

41 "Apocalyptic Literature," Oxford Bibliographies, last modified July 27, 2011, https://www.oxfordbibliographies.com/display/document/obo-9780195393361/obo-9780195393361-0005.xml.

42 D&C 93:36.

43 Psalms 147:3, KJV.

44 Jason Metcalf, conversation with the author, April 7, 2022.

45 Anne Prentnieks, "Jason Metcalf | Martos Gallery | New York," *Artforum,* https://www.artforum.com/picks/jason-metcalf-51540, accessed June 26, 2023.

46 Prentnieks, "Jason Metcalf."

47 Jason Metcalf, conversation with the author, April 7, 2022.

48 Jason Metcalf, conversation with the author, April 7, 2022.

49 "Station" is used here in its etymological sense, derived from Latin *stare,* "to stand."

50 Jason Metcalf, conversation with the author, April 7, 2022.

51 Hakim Bishara, "Hilma af Klint Breaks Records at the Guggenheim Museum," Hyperallergic, April 22, 2019, http://hyperallergic.com/496326/hilma-af-klint-breaks-records-at-the-guggenheim-museum/.

52 Acts 2:17, KJV.

53 Colby Chamberlain, "Critical care: Colby Chamberlain on the Art of Park McArthur." *Artforum International* 59, no. 2 (2020).

54 D&C 128:15.

55 Rachel Thomander, conversation with the author, September 21, 2020.

56 This function of the prophetic is amply expressed in many of the artworks discussed in this chapter, especially in Bronson and Stimson's projects for the 2019 Toronto Biennial, in Thomander's works, and in Metcalf's *Hie to Kolob*.

57 Cornel West, *Black Prophetic Fire: In Dialogue with and Edited by Christa Buschendorf* (Boston: Beacon Press, 2014), 2.

58 West states: "The dominant forms of religions are well-adjusted to greed and fear and bigotry. Hence well-adjusted to the indifference of the status quo toward poor and working people. Prophetic religion is an individual and collective performative praxis of maladjustment to greed, fear, and bigotry. For prophetic religion the condition of truth is to allow suffering to speak." Cornel West, "Prophetic Religion and the Future of Capitalist Civilization," in *The Power of Religion in the Public Sphere* (New York: Columbia University Press, 2011), 92–100; "Cornel West | On Being a Chekovian Christian and a Blues Man: Christianity, Pragmatism and Democracy," YouTube, posted by wheatoncollege, February 25, 2014, https://www.youtube.com/watch?v=EwPCJ9WpH7E.

59 Laura Robertson, "The Black Charismatic," Frieze, April 24, 2017, https://www.frieze.com/article/black-charismatic.

60 Patricia Leigh Brown, "The Artist as Healer," *New York Times*, April 7, 2022.

61 See @guadalupe__maravilla Instagram posts from April to September 2020; Danilo Machado, "Artist Guadalupe Maravilla Is Centering Mutual Aid and Indigenous Medicinal Practices," *Hyperallergic,* May 29, 2020, http://hyperallergic.com/567379/guadalupe-maravilla-is-centering-mutual-aid/; Jonathan Blitzer, "The Renegade Priest Helping Undocumented People Survive the Pandemic," *New Yorker*, August 17, 2020, https://www.newyorker.com/magazine/2020/08/24/the-renegade-priest-helping-undocumented-people-survive-the-pandemic.

62 Isaiah 30:10, KJV.

63 Glen Nelson, *Joseph Paul Vorst* (New York: Mormon Artists Group, 2017).

64 *Great Awakening: Vision and Synthesis in Latter-Day Saint Contemporary Art,* Center Gallery, New York, June 18–August 7, 2021, curated by Chase Westfall; Chase Westfall, *Great Awakening: Vision and Synthesis in Latter-Day Saint Contemporary Art* (New York: Center for Latter-day Saint Arts, 2021).

65 Rachel Thomander, conversation with the author, September 21, 2020.

66 Cauleen Smith, *Sojourner* (2018), digital video, 20:41.

67 "Cauleen Smith Imagines a Black, Feminist Utopia," SFMOMA, accessed June 27, 2023, https://www.sfmoma.org/watch/cauleen-smith-imagines-a-black-feminist-utopia-2/.

68 "Cauleen Smith Imagines a Black, Feminist Utopia."

69 Mark 1:15, KJV.

AN AFTERWORD

A Culture (and its Artifacts) in Search of Self

LAURA ALLRED HURTADO

In the shortest summary, this book creates a picture of collective identity—with all its contradictions, paradoxes, and connotations. It is an exploration of objects and, by extension, the makers whose experience—inside Mormonism, outside Mormonism, and in between—functions uniquely to hold up a mirror to the community at large and to ask questions regarding meaning, cultural integration, change, expression, belonging, public image, censorship, assimilation, and historical legacies, as well as community- and self-fashioned identities.

Within these reflections are a myriad of contradictions and intersections that I myself share. In my professional life, I have served on the Temple Art Committee, as the global acquisition curator at the Church History Museum, and as an independent curator of exhibitions and publications that included LDS artists, and have led a contemporary art museum that sits half a block away from Temple Square. I have written about culture from a position of belief and from a position of questioning. I have managed commissions on behalf of the church—serving as the very patron who establishes aesthetic standards and preferences and drafts acquisition policies—and I have sat outside of the role, wondering why, how, and who was making choices that at times felt reductive, colonial, and simplistic. If I were asked to define Mormon art—a philosophical question I've grown tired of and that has taken up so much of the discourse as to become distracting—not only would I struggle to answer, but I would likely wonder whether the question itself is worth asking, because of the circular and limiting nature of the inquiry itself.

That is to say that a big, ambitious volume like this is inherently studded with tensions because the people, art, and culture are likewise filled with them. So the portrait that it creates from the mirrored image is, a fractured and multiple one, of a people who, like many other groups, have sought, desperately at times, two opposing goals—both to embrace their unique otherness and to seek assimilation and wider cultural acceptance. The decades of cultural and visual material production this text covers reflect this binary pull.

This dance, of course, is not Mormonism alone. In Maria Stepanova's book *In Memory of Memory,* she writes of the Jewish experience in Europe and describes this push/pull of extreme polarities: "all those who hid their Jewishness like an embarrassing defect, or paraded it like a cockade in full view of everyone."[1] While each societal group has its own risks and meanings at stake when tackling the pull of assimilation and celebration of the particular (the Jewish experience unique with the pervasive shadow of antisemitism), there is something familiar in her writing and something human and universal in the tension—the desire to be part of a singular group as well as the longing to be accepted, to be seen as worthy, and to belong within a larger context of public discourse and art circles.

This tension is the core of the publication.

Terryl Givens writes extensively on the theological and theoretical issues at stake with Mormon cultural production in his influential book *People of Paradox,* as well as his essay included here. Writing about the "solar system of Mormon art," with its dichotomous relationship between the sacred and profane, between Eden and exile, his scholarship is a powerful exploration of the binary pull that exists not only in Mormonism but also, in fact, in so many communities where boundaries of otherness determine belonging.

But this argument and observation is not Givens's alone. It is a running theme throughout the entire volume—and in the artwork itself—as makers seek to define themselves through their objects through various shades. The writers do the same through their interpretations. To investigate this pull is to consider closely the lived experience of Mormon people, summarized even in the tenuous and at times divisive use of the now preferred term "member of the Church of Jesus Christ of Latter-day Saints" instead of the historic and once derogatory term "Mormon," throughout the last two hundred years.[2] But those labels are not the only two binaries. We live in a world of various terms—members, Latter-day Saints, PM (post-Mormon), TBM (true believing Mormon), inactive Mormon, ex-Mormon, MIPO (mentally out, physically in), Peter Priesthood, LDS, Molly Mormon, Mormons 2.0, ABM (active believing Mormon), middle-way Mormons, non-believer, non-member, part-member family, non-practicing, disfellowshipped, disengaged, Orthodox, excommunicated, progressive Mormon, X-ed, practicing—and so on and so forth. These labels alone reflect so many of the attempts at classifications for (and creating definitions of) complex faith paradigms, nuanced cultural priorities, boundaries of inclusion, Othering, political distinctions, and the various values at stake on an individual and personal level.

While this tension of belonging is articulated and lived by others (as captured by Stepanova), its particular Mormon manifestation lies in the historical experience of a people, first as isolated and insular exiles who left their home country and whose religious adherence was marked by several non-normative practices (martial, governmental, and economic, to name a few) that branded them as distinctly different from others of their era. Embracing this difference, Mormons were at one point seen, at least by some, as a distinctly American "ethnic group."[3] Out of this period of internality arises an epitome of isolationism, the Mormon Creed, which states, "Mind your own business. Saints will observe this. All others ought to."[4]

Coupled with (or born out of) this isolation comes a real human desire to be understood by others, as well as a broader campaign toward assimilation that seeks to revise branded and biased public images toward a picture of normalcy, Christianity, and new American conservatism, on one hand, or seeks acceptance into the larger postmodern, late-capitalist conversation and aesthetic preferences of the international art world, on the other, and everywhere in between. These tenuous pulls are also made manifest in the "I Am a Mormon" campaign, started in 2010, which sought to destabilize stereotypes, such as the exotic polygamist or the clean-shaven missionary, by providing images of Mormons as diverse and varied—from a Harley-Davidson sculptor to an Iranian human rights lawyer. These are *cool* people, with a multiplicity of identities, meaning, and markers, just like you, and *Mormon*! The images are designed specifically to communicate (or create) messages of gender and racial inclusivity. In both cases, from the creed to the PR campaign, these self-fashioned messages are artifacts of a particular time within a particular frame.

Such efforts play out through everyday markers and on deeply individualized fronts: those from whom their upbringing is shed like old skin, becoming merely a biographical footnote; those who loudly wear the badge of Mormonism; those who convert into the faith and blend their own traditions, nationalities, and communities with their new foundation; those who want simply to be seen as complex, whole people rather than filtered through a narrow and prejudiced lens of simplistic stereotype.

Throughout the chapters, these tensions manifest in various thematic ways. There's the trend in some of the scholarship to provide a lens on the cultural significance of outside art worlds on inside aesthetics (see the chapters by Jones Gibb, Belnap, Nelson, and Coats Sato), and there are a good number of essays that explore the struggle and tension of overly simplistic stereotypes, propaganda, public image, and popular perception (see the chapters by Astle and Rees). There are chapters that explore race, class, nationality, and colonialism and that seek to provide a more expansive visual history (see the chapters by Reeve, Allred, Constantino, and Howe); chapters that emphasize collective memory, the archive, gendered experience, and identity (see the chapters by Evans, Beardsley, and Campbell); those whose focus is on the impact of a single patron and the aesthetic bias, risks, goals, and priorities within (see the chapters by McDannell, Nelson and Dibble, Probert, and Wecker), and chapters dense with philosophical theory that speak to the overall cultural experience or spell out an ambitious path for the future (see the chapters by Givens and Westfall). Much more could be said of the quality and rigor of all of these strong and original contributions to the field, but specific references to Givens and Westfall are included here because of their efforts to summarize an overall

Mormon aesthetic theory. As the authors and the works they analyze demonstrate, context matters in defining and acknowledging the different parameters, goals, and objectives at stake.

Throughout the ages, art has always been shaped by patronage, and Mormon artists have long worked within a complex structure of church-led commissions. Such legacies drive aesthetic choices, cultivate artistic preferences, shape devotional imagery, and for some (as is the case with all art movements) serve as a counterpoint to push against. This publication shows, through a myriad of examples and complex manifestations, that within LDS cultural history the image has a complicated and nuanced role. Used in missionary work, as a public relations method, as a devotional object, as a didactic teaching tool, and more, artworks have been commissioned and harnessed by the church for a variety of reasons, uses, and purposes.

Within houses of worship arising from Protestant origins, the church itself has a kind of institutionalized iconoclastic anxiety about images. LDS chapels are generally bare save a very select few works on an approved list of beloved gospel art. The limited scope of approved images and their ubiquity throughout the world haven't always been such, but the aesthetic simplicity of current chapels captures colonial effects of the correlation practices designed to make a unified worship experience. Iconoclasm is even more the case now with the removal of all original art from ward buildings—an action born out of the desire to preserve cultural artifacts of historical significance[5]—and replacing them with quickly reproducible giclées, as if the poster has the same power of transcendence as the original. Within this debate, there exists a manifest tension between doctrinal self-reliance and economic modesty and frugality. But it also communicates a collective cultural anxiety and mistrust of the images, simultaneously communicating, in their absence, the power of art to create feelings, to set a tone, to send messages, and to ask questions. Images are messy. Basketball courts, burlap wallcoverings, and metal chairs are not. That is not to say that there isn't something comforting, powerful, and familiar in the uniformity and simplicity of such consistent material culture and objects that stand, much like a simple Shaker chair, as a symbol of a larger system of belief. For the limited scope of approved images, in their continuous repetition, becomes part of one's "visual piety," serving to create "the visual formation and practice of religious belief,"[6] as explained by art historian David Morgan, where "the act of looking itself contributes to religious formation, and indeed, constitutes a powerful practice of belief."[7] The mass production itself creates a loop of familiarity and sameness that helps make meaning through repetition and uniformity, creating a sense of reassurance, comfort, reaffirmation of belief, and consistency. And it is this very link among a "believing gaze," mass-produced and repeated images, and devotion that makes religious images all the more complicated and leaders all the more careful in their selection.

Working at the church made me intimately familiar with just how much is at stake with an organization that large. Like many large international operating bodies, leaders are careful, deliberate, and risk-averse. Those with positional authority seek not to offend, not to ruffle, not to upset, aiming to keep things consistent from country to country, sometimes without understanding the risk inherent in the aversion itself—the lack of originality and the tyranny of sameness that grow when ubiquity rules. That distrust or visual anxiety extends to temple art, which has, depending on the priorities of current leadership, vacillated between an art-heavy temple experience (where the murals help to support the doctrinal experience) and one in which the art functions solely as wallpaper (there to be seen as decorative and pretty but not studied, not looked at, not drawing attention to itself, and certainly not there to incite questioning). There is something beautiful in the primacy of the ordinance and in the singularity of the vision in LDS temple worship. LDS art in places of worship, nearly always plays a supportive role and often is relegated to the same status as lamps and carpet choices, functioning as decor, adding to a calm and devotional space, creating a "sensory template" for reflection on larger topics such as the ordinance itself.[8] It is positioned at the sidelines, on the periphery, where it belongs, where it can be controlled—where the messiness of interpretation or distraction can be contained.

When I served on the Temple Art Committee (from 2013 to 2020), many expressed feelings that the BYU art department had "forsaken" the church because of its output of artists working within a contemporary aesthetic practice. Wielding historic positional (and patriarchal) authority, and strongly asserted as an indisputable fact, modernism, for these longtime temple aesthetic influencers, was framed as godless, vacant, and immoral. There existed a clear boundary of acceptability that was policed aesthetically. With the expansion of temple buildings throughout the world, there is an increased need for a fresh inventory of landscapes and contemporary realism that young Mormon artists emerging from BYU do not, cannot, provide. Those artists are creating work designed to be looked at, engaged with, but their very practice and premise would be a disruption, a spectacle, within a space of controlled and carefully created serenity. The objectives of the two organizations capture the vastly different goals and objectives of and the ultimate tension between insular belonging and the needs of a specific function, on the one hand, and a specific place and the steps taken toward larger cultural assimilation and acceptance, on the other. They aren't in opposition; rather, such polarities speak of one body reaching toward opposite goals and needs.

Such extreme positional opinions regarding what images should be and what they should look like are, of course, not collectively felt, nor did they inform collecting practices in the Church History Department, which, to its credit, looks at art as a primary source material and seeks to gather a whole and complete document of the Mormon people and their cultural production broadly. The edict of the department is taken from D&C 21:1, which states, "Behold, there shall be a record kept among you." Doctrinally based, the mission of the department reflects the very LDS compulsion to collect, archive, and build a shared history by amassing a comprehensive record. The collective memory of the Mormon/LDS experience built through acquisitions and object-keeping tells a story of religious and social life as it has been uniquely manifested throughout the decades. This broad goal allows the Church History Museum (Church History Department) more leeway to engage with art beyond the assigned function of decoration, instruction, and devotion. Images are free from the heavy weight of standing as symbols between the natural world and a high doctrinal one and can function more loosely, standing in as larger symbols of the people, the individualized belief of the maker, and the expression of the culture of the time of the image's creation.

These multiple roles, however, have dizzying and confusing effects on makers. A tension overall remains for artists who are caught in these complicated and multivalent roles, who struggle to manage a demand for works that simply serve to illustrate doctrinal principles (supporting an article, manifesting an idea, illustrating a historical moment); the pervasiveness of temple aesthetic bias (pretty, uplifting, realistic, landscape); the collection of objects that dare to be looked at, to be engaged with, to ask questions, to be expansive, and to be unfixed; and their own personal output.

And yet.

Such parameters are only one fragment of aesthetic definitions of self and of communal legacy and belonging. How images function within the operating body of the corporate church headquarters—whose relation to images can be summarized and categorized—is just one fragment of the Mormon visual experience, as this beautiful volume so well articulates. Outside of church-led commissions and acquisitions, there remain the larger cultural experience and expression that are the byproducts of a people whose vantage point is informed by so many, many elements—of religion, aesthetics, personal expression, experimentation, legacy, and their own self-identity. There are the makers and the markets influenced by, participating within, running parallel to, or completely rejecting their religious origins. Art in this frame goes beyond the confines of church-led patronage and lands in the un-authorial multiple-lens unfixed-narrative vastness of self-expression.

Some artists have found success boldly identifying themselves as Mormon artists. These makers have found not only community but also (in some cases) a similar aesthetic practice (with an interest in landscape, realism, the figure when abstracted to primary form, metaphor, and scriptural or pioneer reference, as select examples), a shared vocabulary, and common lived experience. Many have also reaped financial rewards from harvesting Mormon economic markets, finding buyers who either align their stylistic choices with the church's preferences or are invested in the progression of Mormon culture and seek a richer, more diverse, Mormon artistic heritage. Either way, these patrons seek to support their own.[9]

There are just as many artists who aren't interested in the category or classification of "Mormon art," nor do they see their art as particularly LDS. There is a resistance to being pigeonholed into a singular identity because no one exists on a single-axis definition of self. In many ways the category feels, at best, made up. Artwork and culture are informed by, and about, so many other things, and there is a variety of lenses to use to analyze a work of art, be it through feminist, Marxist, formalist, iconographic, or postcolonial readings, with only one approach being biographical. Further, an artist's faith—whether integral to their lived and present experience or a shell discarded long ago—is one small thing of their entire identity, biography, and practice. This is especially the case with the artists whose work resists or ignores Mormon subject matter. There are some artists who so desperately prefer not to talk about it. They want their faith discussed not at all, or as a footnote. They want distance. They seek *relevancy*. They use words like "meditation," "magic," or "spirituality" as code for their private investment and scared beliefs. They want to speak to a wide audience and not just Mormon buyers.

While there has been some softening in recent years toward spirituality, religion still feels firmly vilified and taboo in art markets in the twenty-first century, especially when, in the very left-leaning circles of the global art world, religion can be quickly dismissed as code for American conservativism. I have attended a multitude of art fairs throughout the world, walked through hundreds and hundreds of galleries, auctions, studios, and museums—from New York to Mexico City, from Venice to Los Angeles, and beyond—and what I have witnessed aligns much more with the observations of Sarah Thornton, author of *Seven Days in the Art World*, that "contemporary art has become a kind of alternative religion for atheists."[10] At best, on a national and international curatorial and museology level, religion is tolerated in contemporary art practices only when approached obliquely, sideways, in code, or subversively, or when found or framed as a unique and singular cultural expression of Otherness or outsiderness that the institution bears witness to from the vantage point of spectator of the strange.

Some capitalize on this trend by using Mormonism's unique cultural legacy as material, emphasizing the curiosity of the experience, the magicalness of the theology, exploiting and exoticizing it. Indeed, the most well-known and critically accepted artworks produced in the twenty-first century that address Mormonism as a topic do so through the lens of the strange.

Take, for example, the work of artist and excessive provocateur Paul McCarthy, whose Mormon upbringing is mentioned often in relationship to the perceived incongruency to his investment in the abject and grotesque.[11] Mathew Barney's *Cremaster 2* (1999), a type of circular gothic western, uses Mormon and Masonic symbolism throughout, including bees, beehives, and swarms. Loosely recounting the real-life story of Gary Gilmore, who senselessly killed two people in Orem, Utah, in the 1970s, Barney uses choir voices emanating from the Mormon Tabernacle to stand as the jury who condemn Gilmore and sentence him to be executed by firing squad. Consider also Angela Ellsworth's *Sister Wives* performances, which borrow a Mormon fundamentalist aesthetic to explore her own pioneer heritage and queer experience, and her *Seer Bonnets* (2008–), which stand "in for the estimated thirty-five wives of Smith" and are considered by Ellsworth as "tools of translation,"[12] to name just a few.[13] But so many makers, even those stated above, fall somewhere in between those points, in the vast gray tension between assimilation, reference, distance, ignoring, and a tight embrace of the peculiar.

Falling within this "in between" is the lovely and haunting 2022 installation at the Bass Museum of artist Cara Despain's exhibition *Specter*—an exploration of the effects of nuclear weapons on the American West, especially for those like her mother and grandmother, who are "downwinders." One video installation, called *Test of Faith,* pairs declassified and digitalized footage of atomic clouds that are green, menacing, ghostly, dangerous, beautiful, and mesmerizing with the eerie soundtrack of the hymn and primary song "Love One Another." The multivalent title, and work, allude in part to what curator Leilani Lynch describes as "the appeal made by the military to many Mormon settlers in the fallout region, as well as to the county, to support the testing under the guise of an united patriotism."[14] Here, Despain walks a rare fine line of referencing her Mormon roots and theology without landing on a de facto polarizing place of proselytizing or exoticizing. There is simply the haunting pairing of the reality of atomic weaponry in Utah and the universality of the golden rule, which is more of a critique of the U.S. government and humankind's trend toward hypocrisy and harm than a direct and targeted comment on a uniquely Mormon experience.

This book succeeds in its navigation of such a complex and contested landscape of identities as they relate to Mormonism in part because the authors seek so often to stay within the realm of gray—reading artworks in a way that resists clean and simplistic classifications and categories. In sum, it amplifies art historical methodology by centering the art object as a primary source document, while using a myriad of lenses to read and interpret the work and the context and larger ecology in which it was produced and in which it was received. Within this frame, the volume seeks to show how each communicates meaning and identity to a larger cultural experience and body of people for whom the Mormon experience has come to be part of their life narrative, to whatever extent.

And in this way, insofar as the content is contained between the book covers, the volume tells a comprehensive story—however incomplete—from an anthropological and art historical lens of a doctrinal worldview, a particular people, their seemingly insular voices, their public personas, their aesthetic standards, their internal revisions, their investment in archived and collective memories, their efforts toward both singularity and assimilation, and more. The through line of the volume is nearly always an art historical story about community and belonging and the role that the image plays in creating, forming, defining, and setting boundaries around itself. Throughout the book, authors and artists sit in that place of tension between two conflicting communal goals—one that includes belonging, boundaries, and a clear definition of self, and the other that features a longing for integration into wider society.

Over more than two hundred years of cultural expression, there are also the messy yearnings and vulnerable voices of the multitudes affected by or loosely linked to Mormonism, who have through their objects made meaning of their experience—by either resistance or embrace, through assimilation or rejection, who see and speak and create nuanced, multivalent images with a lot at stake. These voices are just as relevant as those produced by headquarters. They are messy works, unable to be pinned down with a single reading. Where this book succeeds is in its exploration of identity—for those for whom the Mormon experience has significantly shaped their worldview, their artistic lens, their cultural experience, for better or for worse.

Imagining the future of Mormon art, Westfall echoes the through-line tension of the book when he writes poetically of the insularity that exists with Mormon communities. His is a clarion call for what he describes as radicalism, revolutionary actions, and change. Visioning toward the future, Westfall calls on Mormon artists and curators, including myself (and rightly so), to be less "deferential, formal, or polite," to establish new practices. And he seeks to deconstruct the populist aesthetic safety found in works made by and marketed to Mormons' commercial preferences. Asking for something entirely new, he challenges the Latter-day Saint art world to take up more politically rich and powerful stances—not only in aesthetic choices but also in subject matter. Idealistic and grandiose, Westfall draws on terms such as "prophetic" and the inherited roots of the religion as radical and revolutionary rather than looking to a faith that has settled into a place of visual, social, and political orthodoxy within a large authorial system of deference to select decision makers. He calls for change. He calls for action. He calls for aesthetic disobedience.

It is bold, idyllic, and optimistic. Is there a place where one can live a connected and deeply invested communal life without full subscription, with fluid boundaries, floating between, moving in and out of a community on one's own terms? A belief that is porous, open? With artwork that is radical, revolutionary, and unfixed?

Perhaps.

I don't know.

Yes/No.

I'm not sure.

Mormonism—by comparison to many other faith traditions—is still in its infancy, or at the very least in early puberty, and is awkward, naive, and still very much obsessed with policing its boundaries. These efforts are not wholly unique to Mormonism, either. Said scholar Eileen Barker, "New religions often make much sharper distinctions than older religions do between right and wrong, good and bad, as well as between 'us' and 'them.'"[15]

Binaries and boundaries are one thing. But what of the messiness of labels and the unfixedness of identities? And how should one exact those measurements in terms of cultural affiliation, collective memory, group concept of self, and narrative drafting? The relative newness of the religion is what makes such an inquiry all the more relevant and timely. What is a Mormon within this context? What is the difference between LDS, Saints, Mormons, and everything else, exactly? I ask these questions—and so does this publication—not to offer trite and clear answers but to leave such inquiries standing boldly with their unanswered question marks.

Cornel West, in a beautiful essay called "A Matter of Life or Death," defines identity first as "elusive," then as "vaporous," and then this way:

It's the longing to belong, a deep, visceral need that most linguistically conscious animals who transact with an environment (that's us) participate in. And then there is a profound desire for protection, for security, for safety, for surety. And so, in talking about identity we have to begin to look at the various ways in which human beings have constructed their desire for recognition, association, and protection over time and in space and always under circumstances not of their own choosing.[16]

As West articulates, identity is not just a simplistic label but a plurality of selves, linked to a visceral human need to have a sense of belonging, security, safety, and surety. And such assignments are not always of our own choosing or self-authored. We are all multiple, and there is not a term that fundamentally and nicely summarizes the lived experience of a broad collective people. Identity, while wrapped and formed around a communal experience, is deeply personal and complicated. Identity, in sum, is no simple thing, but all-encompassing.

What this very important book puts forth is an opportunity for a peculiar people (and those on the outside interested in them) to learn about and see themselves from a myriad of angles, using a variety of mirrors, filters, and identities, many of which will be unfamiliar and new—and, in seeing such multitudes of self, to have an opportunity to continue to draft and shape and form a more complex sense of community and a more porous definition of culture. This scope goes so far beyond *Ensign,* Deseret Book, the gospel art kit—in ways that are expansive, inclusive, broad, and at times uncomfortable, depending on your vantage point. It looks closely at the extent of Mormon visual and material culture and its paradoxes, its conflicts, its promises, its legacies, its troubles, its public image, its peculiarities, its self-fashioning, its identities, its boundaries, its biases, its beautiful visuality, its failures, its redefinition, its acculturations, its censorship, its people, its prophetic promise, its judgments, its redemption, its mother tongue, its belief, its hope.

NOTES

[1] Maria Stepanova, *In Memory of Memory* (New York: New Directions, 2021), 45.

[2] Lyman Kirkland, "Using the Term 'Mormon,'" Church of Jesus Christ of Latter-day Saints, April 19, 2010, https://newsroom.churchofjesuschrist.org/blog/using-the-term-mormon-; Julia Jacobs, "Stop Saying 'Mormon,' Church Leader Says. But Is the Real Name Too Long?," *New York Times,* August 18, 2018.

[3] Terryl L. Givens, *People of Paradox: A History of Mormon Culture* (New York: Oxford University Press, 2007).

[4] For more reading on the topic, see Michael Hicks, "Minding Business: A Note on 'The Mormon Creed,'" *Brigham Young University Studies* 26, no. 4 (Fall 1986): 125–132. A painted mirror with the Creed that once hung in the Logan temple until the late 1970s found way into my office at the Church History Museum in the early 2010s. While the mirror is a historical artifact, its continued presence in the temple carries its message of internal community and exclusion well into the late twentieth century.

[5] Peggy Fletcher Stack, "The LDS Church Is Removing Minerva Teichert Paintings from Its Own Chapels, Prompting a Question: Where Does the Art Belong?," *Salt Lake Tribune,* August 16, 2020.

[6] David Morgan, *Visual Piety: A History and Theory of Popular Religious Images* (Berkeley: University of California Press, 1998).

[7] Morgan, *Visual Piety,* 3.

[8] Morgan, *Visual Piety,* 5.

[9] For an in-depth discussion of the relationship between spiritual aura, authenticity, and economic capital as rooted in the original relationship between art and religion, see Jennifer Ford, "Spiritual Capital: The Economic Core of the Global Art Market and Its Origin in Church Financial Structures" (PhD diss., Institute for Doctoral Studies in the Visual Arts, 2018).

[10] Ford, "Spiritual Capital," 182.

[11] There is a myriad of well-documented articles that position McCarthey's Mormon upbringing as counterpoint to his art practice. See Stefanie Graf, "The Bizarre Art of Paul McCarthy: Fascinating or Nauseating?," *The Collector,* May 31, 2023, https://www.thecollector.com/paul-mccarthy-fascinating-bizarre-art/, for one one of the more recent examples. Graf says, "McCarthy grew up in a conservative and religious environment where people wouldn't talk about sex. This obviously influenced his work." McCarthy, for his own part, often seems to distance himself these clean and quick cause-and-effect readings.

[12] Angela Ellsworth, "Seer Bonnets 2008–Present," artist's website, http://www.aellsworth.com/seer-bonnets.

[13] The original proposal for this book included a chapter titled "Exocitized, Exploited, Ignored, or Made Strange: The Art World's Reception of Mormonism in the late Twentieth and early Twenty-First Century," which wasn't completed. But the scope of the proposed chapter mirrors those of Gibb, Belnap, and Nelson in its exploration of what Mormon artists (or Mormon subject matter) were received elsewhere.

[14] Leilani Lynch, *Cara Despain: Specter* (Miami: Bass Museum, 2022), 4.

[15] Eileen Barker, "One Person's Cult Is Another's True Religion," *The Guardian,* May 29, 2009.

[16] Cornel West, "A Matter of Life and Death," *October* 61 (1992): 20.

INDEX

For the benefit of digital users, indexed terms that span two pages (e.g., 52–53) may, on occasion, appear on only one of those pages.